ANNUAL REVIEW OF PSYCHOLOGY

ANNUAL REVIEW OF PSYCHOLOGY

VOLUME 50, 1999

JANET T. SPENCE, *Editor*
University of Texas, Austin

JOHN M. DARLEY, *Associate Editor*
Princeton University

DONALD J. FOSS, *Associate Editor*
Florida State University

http://www.AnnualReviews.org   science@annurev.org   650-493-4400
ANNUAL REVIEWS   4139 EL CAMINO WAY   P.O. BOX 10139   PALO ALTO, CALIFORNIA 94303-0139

ANNUAL REVIEWS
Palo Alto, California, USA

International Standard Serial Number: 0066-4308
International Standard Book Number: 0-8243-0250-8
Library of Congress Catalog Card Number: 50-13143

Annual Review and publication titles are registered trademarks of Annual Reviews.

The paper used in this publication meets the minimum requirements of American National Standards for Information Sciences—Permanence of Paper for Printed Library Materials, ANSI Z39.48-1992.

Annual Reviews and the Editors of its publications assume no responsibility for the statements expressed by the contributors to this *Review.*

TYPESETTING BY RUTH MCCUE SAAVEDRA AND THE ANNUAL REVIEWS EDITORIAL STAFF

PRINTED AND BOUND IN THE UNITED STATES OF AMERICA

PREFACE

With the publication of Volume 50 of the *Annual Review of Psychology*, our term as Editors comes to a close. That the series has appeared continuously for half a century is testimony to its contribution to the field and, coincidence though it is, we are honored to have our names associated with this landmark volume.

As readers are aware, the title of the series is accurate in the sense that a volume appears annually but not in the sense that the intent is to review the literature of the past year on a standard set of topics. Chapters in each volume cover a broad array of subjects that vary from one volume to the next. To the uninformed, the selection of topics for individual volumes (aside from the Prefatory chapters, each written by an eminent psychologist) may seem to constitute a broad but haphazard array. They are, however, selected according to a Master Plan composed of close to 20 major topic areas, each of which has two or more subheadings. The Master Plan also specifies the approximate frequency with which chapters devoted to the various subareas should appear, according to their prominence in the field and the amount of research attention they attract.

Psychology, of course, is not a static discipline, which necessitates periodic review and revision of the Master Plan. Over time, some once-dominant approaches lose their prominence whereas others gain ascendance; some areas of inquiry fade away and others emerge. In recent years, for example, chapters that fall under the rubric of neuroscience have increased in numbers, and even more recently, new topic areas have been added to the Master Plan, most notably evolutionary, health, and cross-cultural psychology. The tables of contents of the 50 volumes of the *Annual Review of Psychology* thus provide a kind of brief history of psychology post World War II.

Chapter authors for each volume are nominated by members of the *Review's* Editorial Committee. The excellence of the nominations and the willingness of authors to accept our invitation are the factors responsible for the enviable reputation the series enjoys. Although our invitations indicate the general topic they are asked to cover, authors have considerable freedom in shaping their chapters. Some provide a conceptual framework that not only pulls the available evidence together but points in new directions; others provide a synthesis or at least an overview of the current literature. Some chapters are balanced in presenting different approaches or interpretations of the data; other focus on a particular point of view while acknowledging alternatives.

Although the chapters are heterogeneous in many respects, they have in common a tremendous investment in time and effort that their preparation demands. (Based on personal experience, one of us estimated that if productive faculty members ordinarily devote one fourth of their scholarly time for a year to produce the chapter, then the five volumes that we edited represent at least a quarter century of work!) Anticipation of what is involved doubtless accounts for the number of graduate students and colleagues invited to serve as second authors.

Who should read the *Annual Review*? Although addressed to the expert, most chapters are comprehensible to peers outside of the authors' field and even to beginning graduate students. At one time, many of us expected students to read large portions of each *Annual Review* or to at least peruse a number of chapters to inform themselves about developments outside their own specialty. It is our impression, however, that students are now less likely to read the *Annual Review* unless they are assigned chapters germane to a particular course. When one considers the proliferation of books and journals, the fractionation of psychology into a variety of subdisciplines, and the growth of alliances with neighboring fields, this trend is understandable. The expense of buying still another book is an additional factor.

By the same token, the need for publications that make us aware of what is going on outside our own parochial interests is greater than ever. *Annual Review* chapters are now available on the Web; increased accessibility should help to increase readership, particularly among students.

Finally, we acknowledge with special gratitude the members of the Editorial Committee who served during our tenure and the authors of the more than 100 chapters that have appeared under our editorial aegis. We also thank for their invaluable assistance the several Production Editors who served during our editorial term: Amy Marks, Peter Orne, Noelle Thomas, and currently, Lisa Dean.

Responsibility for guiding the *Annual Review* into its second fifty years—and into the next millennium—is being assumed by Susan Fiske as Editor, and Carolyn Zahn-Waxler and Daniel Schacter as Associate Editors. We wish them well.

October, 1998

Janet T. Spence
John M. Darley
Donald J. Foss

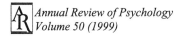*Annual Review of Psychology*
Volume 50 (1999)

CONTENTS

SOME RELATED ARTICLES IN OTHER *ANNUAL REVIEWS*

From the *Annual Review of Anthropology,* Volume 27, 1998:

Genetics of Modern Human Origins and Diversity, John H. Relethford
Current Issues in Linguistic Taxonomy, Peter A. Michalove,
   Stefan Georg, and Alexis Manaster Ramer

From the *Annual Review of Neuroscience,* Volume 21, 1998:

CREB and Memory, Alcino J. Silva, Jeffrey H. Kogan,
   Paul W. Frankland, and Satoshi Kida
Sense and the Single Neuron: Probing the Physiology of Perception,
   A. J. Parker and W. T. Newsome

From the *Annual Review of Public Health,* Volume 19, 1998:

Preventing Youth Violence: What Works?, Arthur L. Kellermann,
   Dawna S. Fuqua-Whitley, Frederick P. Rivara, and James Mercy
Strategies to Reduce Driving Under the Influence of Alcohol,
   William DeJong and Ralph Hingson
Mental Health and Managed Care, Mary L. Durham

From the *Annual Review of Sociology,* Volume 24, 1998:

*Warmer and More Social: Recent Developments in Cognitive Social
   Psychology,* Norbert Schwarz
*Was It Worth the Effort? The Outcomes and Consequences of Social
   Movements,* Marco G. Giugni

Annu. Rev. Psychol. 1999. 50:1–19

ON KNOWING A WORD

George A. Miller

Psychology Department, Princeton University, Princeton, New Jersey 08544;
e-mail: geo@clarity.princeton.edu

KEY WORDS: context, lexical semantics, polysemy, sense identification, WordNet

ABSTRACT

A person who knows a word knows much more than its meaning and pronunciation. The contexts in which a word can be used to express a particular
meaning are a critical component of word knowledge. The ability to exploit
context in order to determine meaning and resolve potential ambiguities is
not a uniquely linguistic ability, but it is dramatically illustrated in the ease
with which native speakers are able to identify the intended meanings of
common polysemous words.

CONTENTS

INTRODUCTION

The question of what it means to know a word has fascinated many psychologists, sometimes with consequences of considerable practical value to the science. Among historically more important examples one thinks of Galton
(1879) experimenting with word associations, Binet (1911) using word tasks

1

0084-6570/99/0201-0001$08.00

to test mental age, Thorndike (1921) trying to determine what words every high school graduate should know, Ogden (1934) selecting 850 words to define Basic English, or Bühler (1934) analyzing deictic words that acquire referential value from the contexts in which they are used. Clearly, word knowledge has provided fertile ground for psychological studies; the reason may be that it raises fundamental questions. That is to say, knowing a word is generally considered to be a matter of knowing the word's meaning, and meaning is one of those concepts of great importance for understanding the nature and limits of psychology.

My own interest in word knowledge grew out of an abiding curiosity about communication in general and linguistic communication in particular. Initially, my interest in words was part of a dislike for the behavioristic emphasis on their ostensive or referential function, an emphasis that seemed to ignore their relational or inferential aspects. It seemed obvious to me that words are interrelated in diverse and complex ways, and I explored several lines of evidence that testified to the psychological reality of those lexical interrelations.

As I have learned more about the lexical component of language, however, my reasons for continuing to study it have changed. Today I am fascinated by the human ability to contextualize, the ability to use context to determine meanings and to resolve potential ambiguities (Miller 1996). Whenever experience is meaningful, contextualizing is involved. People object to being quoted out of context, but nothing can be out of context; the objection is to being quoted in the wrong context. Contextualization is not exclusively linguistic, of course; using context to determine linguistic meaning is simply a special case of a general cognitive ability. But the easiest place to study contextualization is surely in the relation between words and their contexts of use.

Knowing a word involves knowing its meaning and therefore, in my view, knowing a word involves knowing its contexts of use. So my present concern is how to characterize that contextual knowledge; this chapter develops the question and reports how far I have come.

CRITERIA FOR WORD KNOWLEDGE

What is involved in knowing a word? One interpretation of this question is performative. It becomes: What tasks does knowing a word enable a person to perform? The answer gives a set of tasks that can provide evidence that a person really knows a word. This interpretation of the question has received much attention.

Psychologists have used various methods to determine whether a person knows a word (Beck & McKeown 1991). The simplest is to ask yes-or-no questions: "Do you know the meaning of x?" (Seashore & Eckerson 1940). Binet & Simon (1911) asked younger children to name objects or describe pictures; older children were asked to give definitions or to use the words in sentences. It is not clear who should be credited with inventing multiple-choice questions, but recognition of an associated phrase has become the most frequently used method to test word knowledge. And since none of these methods is infallible, they are sometimes used in combination. For example, Anglin (1993) first asked children for a definition; failing that, he asked for a sentence using the word, plus an explanation of what the word meant in that sentence; failing that, he used a multiple-choice question. Subjects were given credit for knowing the word if they succeeded at any of these tasks.

There are, of course, different levels of word knowledge between complete innocence and complete competence. The recognition vocabulary is much larger than the speaking vocabulary, for example. Cronbach (1942) described different kinds of knowledge of a word as the ability to define it, the ability to recognize situations for using it, knowledge of its alternative meanings, the ability to recognize inappropriate uses of the word, and the availability of the word for use in everyday life.

All of which is both true and useful. Yet, leaving aside various marginal states of knowledge, to say that a person who knows a word can use it correctly does not really describe what is involved in knowing a word. It is hard to avoid a feeling that problem and method have passed one another by.

What is involved in knowing a word? Another interpretation of that question is substantive. Then it becomes: What does a person who knows a word know? A ready answer is that a person who knows a word must know its meaning(s).

SEMANTICS

The study of meanings is semantics. The kinds of semantics are so diverse, however, that some rough distinctions are needed to render the topic manageable.

One important distinction is between logical and linguistic semantics. Logical semantics attempts to formulate a general theory of the set of meanings that a language can express, an axiomatized theory (usually for some logical or mathematical language) that can be shown to be consistent and complete. The semantics of Montague (1974) is a notable example of the application of those methods to a natural language. Linguistic semantics, on the other hand, is descriptive, a characterization of the meanings that have been expressed in natural languages; the semantics of Jackendoff (1972) and of Lyons (1977) are notable examples, although Lyons borrows more from logical semantics than Jackendoff does.

A second important distinction is between sentential and lexical semantics. Sentential semantics is concerned with the meaning of statements; because first-order logic can be applied to statements, this approach is sometimes favored by logicians. An example would be a verification theory of semantics. A verification theory might assume that the meaning of any sentence is the set of individually necessary and jointly sufficient conditions for the sentence to be true; then it might be further assumed that anyone who knew those conditions would understand the meaning of the sentence. Considering that isolated words are not generally true or false, they are, as far as sentential semantics is concerned, meaningless. Lexical semantics, on the other hand, assumes that words in isolation do have meaning; a sentence acquires its meaning by virtue of the words that compose it and the manner of their combination. This approach is generally favored by linguists; the lexical semantics of Cruse (1986) is a notable example.

The assumption that words have meanings presupposes an assumption, familiar since de Saussure's (1916) distinction between *signifie* and *signifiant*, that words are doubly entered in lexical memory, once phonologically and once semantically, with associations between them. Both the phonological (or orthographic) form and the concept that the form can be used to express must be learned. The word form is learned by hearing (or reading) it and by uttering (or writing) it; the word meaning may be ostensively grounded in immediate perceptual experience (as the concepts expressed by such words as *dog, green, fire, moon, rain,* and the like), or in some more complex manner (as the concepts expressed by such words as *democracy, mendacity, God, psychology,* or *climate*); whether all abstract words can be reduced to (or "grounded in") empirical experience is a question that long books have been written about (Miller & Johnson-Laird 1976). But it is generally assumed that words that can be used referentially (nouns, verbs, adjectives, adverbs) acquire their referential value by virtue of the concepts that they can express, and that this referential value is an important part of a language user's lexical knowledge.

Word form and word meaning are normally learned together. Indeed, one might define a word as an association between a word meaning and a word form that plays a syntactic role. The lexicon, on this view, is simply a list of all the form-meaning associations in the language—what Pustejovsky (1995) has called a "sense enumeration lexicon." When a word form is associated with more than one word meaning, it is said to be polysemous; when a word meaning can be expressed by more than one word form, those word forms are said to be synonymous.

The assumption that knowing a word entails knowing what the word means places the present topic squarely in the area of lexical semantics. But a caveat: To assume that word forms are associated with word meanings does not entail that everyone who uses the language will be able to explain those meanings. People communicate via sentences, seldom via isolated words. Consequently, people's understanding of the meaning of sentences is far more reliable than their understanding of the meaning of words. Their intuitions about the definitions of the words they utter and understand are fragmentary at best. Lexical semanticists try to tap semantic intuitions of native speakers by embedding questions about the meaning of a word in sentential contexts. But it is delicate work, often involving the recognition not of a word's meaning, but of a semantic anomaly. What people know when they know the meaning of a word is more a skill than a fact, the skill of incorporating that word appropriately into meaningful linguistic contexts.

Finally, a distinction should be noted between lexical semantics and lexicography. It is a lexicographer's task to compile associations between word forms and word meanings and to publish them in a convenient alphabetical list. Although lexical theory and lexicographic practice are ordinarily close, in addition to deciding what should be included in a lexical entry and how definitions should be written, lexicographers must actually write the definitions and at the same time worry about such practical matters as how to keep their dictionary down to a manageable size (Landau 1984). Commercial considerations aside, however, most lexicographers would argue that a good dictionary is the ultimate test of any theory of lexical semantics; they sometimes become impatient with criticisms from theorists who have never worked as lexicographers. As one lexicographer has put it, "most of the words one has to deal with when working through the alphabet turn out to be more recalcitrant than those chosen as examples in works on semantic theory" (Atkins 1992/1993:19).

Nevertheless, there is a consensus that the sense enumeration found in a standard dictionary is not the kind of lexicon required for linguistic or psycholinguistic theory. In particular, the domains that words refer to are themselves highly structured in ways that a simple alphabetical listing cannot reveal. Theories of lexical semantics try to take account of these multiple interrelations between and among lexicalized concepts.

Lexical Semantics

The English lexicon can be divided into closed-class words and open-class words. Closed-class words include all the little words—articles, prepositions, pronouns, conjunctions, and the like; membership in these classes changes slowly. Closed-class words generally play a grammatical role. Lexical semantics is concerned primarily with open-class words—the nouns, verbs, adjectives, and adverbs; these words can play a referential role and are always open to new members. So there is a creative aspect to the lexicon. Not only can new open-class words be coined to express new concepts, but familiar open-class words can also be used to express new concepts.

Two facts about open-class words are immediately apparent: There are a great many of them and their meanings are intricately interrelated. These two facts could hardly be unrelated. People would not be able to master so many different words if they were all totally independent of one another. But one of the central problems of lexical semantics is to make explicit the relations between lexicalized concepts.

Essentially, two ways of analyzing word meanings have been proposed, relational and compositional. Relational lexical semantics was first introduced by Carnap (1956) in the form of meaning postulates, where each postulate stated a semantic relation between words. A meaning postulate might look something like dog → animal (if x is a dog then x is an animal) or, adding logical constants, bachelor → man and never married [if x is a bachelor then x is a man and not(x has married)] or tall → not short [if x is tall then not(x is short)]. The meaning of a word was given, roughly, by the set of all meaning postulates in which it occurs.

Compositional lexical semantics, introduced by Katz & Fodor (1963), analyzes the meaning of a word in much the same way a sentence is analyzed into semantic components. The semantic components of a word are not themselves considered to be words, but are abstract elements (semantic atoms) postulated in order to describe word meanings (semantic molecules) and to explain the semantic relations between words. For example, the representation of "bachelor" might be ANIMATE and HUMAN and MALE and ADULT and NEVER MARRIED. The representation of "man" might be ANIMATE and HUMAN and MALE and ADULT; because all the semantic components of "man" are included in the semantic components of "bachelor," it can be inferred that bachelor → man. In addition, there are implicational rules between semantic components, e.g. HUMAN → ANIMATE, which also look very much like meaning postulates.

These two ways of analyzing entailments between words appear different at first, but the semantic relations they deal with turn out to be similar. It may even be the case that any analysis formulated in one theory can be translated into the other. In either case, the interrelations between words take the form of inferences: if something is, say, a bachelor, one can infer that it is also animate and human and male and adult and unmarried. For that reason, mastery of these interrelations between words has been called inferential competence, in contrast to referential competence (Marconi 1997).

What is important is the semantic relations between words, not the notation in which those relations are represented. Consider a few of the more important semantic relations (Cruse 1986, Lyons 1977, Fellbaum 1998).

A basic semantic relation between open-class words is *synonymy*. The traditional way to define synonymy is in terms of substitution: Two words are synonyms (relative to a context) if there is a statement (or class of statements) in which they can be interchanged without affecting truth value. In natural languages there are few instances of synonyms that can be exchanged in every context. For example, "snake" and "serpent" can be interchanged in many contexts without altering truth values, but not in the statement, "The plumber used a snake to unclog the drain." Another way to look at synonymy is as the extreme on a scale of semantic similarity.

Parallel to synonymy is the semantic relation of *antonymy*. Antonymy is sometimes used as a cover term for all kinds of lexical opposites, and sometimes used in a narrower sense to describe only the gradable oppositions where there is a neutral area between them. For example, "It is hot" implies that it is not cold, but "It is not cold" does not imply that it is hot, since there is a tepid range separating the antonyms "hot" and "cold."

Hyponymy is a semantic relation describing the inclusion of one class in another. Semantic intuitions about hyponymy can be tested by sentences like *x is a y* or *x is a kind of y*; it is sometimes called the ISA relation (pronounced "is a"). For example, the acceptability of "A dog is a kind of animal" is interpreted to mean that "dog" is a hyponym of "animal." Or in terms of class inclusion, considering that the class of animals includes the subclass of dogs, "dog" is a hyponym of "animal" [and "animal" is a hypernym (or superordinate) of "dog"]. Hyponymy generates hierarchies (sometimes called trees, taxonomies, or ontologies), thus dog → canine → carnivore → placental mammal → mammal → vertebrate → chordate → animal → organism → entity (where → is read "is a kind of").

A similar semantic relation between verbs, *troponymy*, can be tested by sentences like *x-ing is a manner of y-ing*. For example, if "marching is a manner of walking" is acceptable, then the verb "march" is a troponym of the verb "walk."

The semantic relation between words denoting parts and wholes is *meronymy*, which can be tested with such sentences as "The wrist is a part of the arm" or "An arm has a wrist," indicating that "wrist" is a meronym of "arm" (and "arm" is a holonym of "wrist"). Sometimes meronyms can be arranged in a hierarchy, as in the case of body parts. But there are also meronyms like "handle," which is a part of many things—hammers, umbrellas, briefcases, teacups, saucepans, and so on—so the hierarchy will usually be tangled.

Many other semantic relations can be described (Mel'cuk & Zholkovsky 1988), but the ones listed here are the relations that occur most broadly throughout the lexicon and are the most familiar. Even with this limited list, however, it is apparent that there is an interaction between syntactic categories and semantic relations. Every open-class syntactic category—nouns, verbs, adjectives, adverbs—has synonyms and antonyms, but hyponymy and meronymy are limited to nouns, troponymy to verbs.

When lexical semanticists assume that these relations can be verified by interchanging words in sentences or by the acceptability of sentences like *x is a kind of y*, or *x-ing is a manner of y-ing*, or *x is a part of y*, they are assuming that these semantic relations are part of what every native speaker knows about the words of the language. And if Carnap were right—if the meaning of a word were simply the set of semantic relations it occurred in—then this would be the answer we seek. What a person knows when they know a word would then be simply given by its position in a vast net of words connected by these various syntactic and semantic relations (Quillian 1968, Miller 1978).

Psychologists, of course, want a cognitive theory of this vast semantic network, so exploring the network soon became a topic for psychological experimentation. (But for reasons never made clear, the initial investigations tended to concentrate on nominal concepts and to ignore words in other syntactic categories.) In 1969, Collins & Quillian published a seminal paper claiming that distances in the net could be inferred from the times people took to verify various test sentences. For example, "A canary is a bird" can be verified faster than can "A canary is an animal." Smith (1978) summarized the outburst of experimentation stimulated by this proposal. In short, many exceptions were quickly discovered, and no single theory seemed to explain all the diverse verification times that were observed. One possible conclusion might have been that measuring verification times and eliciting judgments of semantic similarity are not appropriate methods for exploring semantic relations, but instead most psychologists rejected the idea that lexical memory contains a hierarchy of lexicalized nominal concepts.

Even if verification times had proved to be reliable indicators of semantic relations, the result would have been far short of a satisfactory cognitive theory of lexical knowledge. A person who knows a word knows far more than its semantic relations to other words. But a semantic account is not an unreasonable place to begin a search for a cognitive theory.

WordNet

The basic structure of any lexicon is a mapping between word forms and word meanings. If the word forms are alphabetized, it is usually called a dictionary. A modern dictionary, however, provides far more information than would a simple enumeration of word meanings: spelling, pronunciation, etymology, part of speech, inflectional forms, derivational forms, sentences or phrases illustrating the use of the word to express different meanings, occasional pictures and occasional usage notes. Great patience and enormous scholarship are required for such work. Nevertheless, much of the information in a dictionary is familiar to native speakers of the language and so should probably be included in what a person who knows a word knows. But the semantic relations that are so important in lexical semantics are largely implicit in a conventional dictionary; they must be inferred from the definitional glosses.

It is hardly surprising that an alphabetical organization of lexical information should be totally unlike a cognitive organization. But the same information can, of course, be organized in many different ways. Beginning in 1985, a group of cognitive scientists at Princeton University undertook to build a lexicon for a computer wherein the semantic relations between open-class words that are implicit in a dictionary could be made explicit in the computer (Fellbaum 1998). The result is an on-line lexical database called WordNet (Miller 1985). WordNet does not include pronunciations or etymologies or pictures or usage notes, but the basic form-meaning pairs are there.

WordNet is really four lexical databases, one each for nouns, verbs, adjectives, and adverbs. The basic building block of WordNet is a synset (a set of synonyms along with a standard dictionary-type definitional gloss); a synset is WordNet's representation of a lexicalized concept. If a word form appears in more than one synset, it is polysemous (WordNet treats homonymy as kind of polysemy).

Words and synsets are associated with one another by the familiar semantic relations. Synonymy and antonymy are lexical semantic relations between word forms in WordNet; hyponymy, troponymy, meronymy, and various verbal entailments are conceptual semantic relations between synsets. As this is written, WordNet contains 122,000 word forms in 100,000 synsets that are organized by 139,000 pointers representing semantic relations. Thus, the vast net of words that Quillian (1968) imagined has now actually been constructed in a computer.

WordNet has certain advantages over a machine-readable dictionary for the purposes of computational linguistics. For example, synonym sets can be used in information retrieval to expand a user's query and so retrieve relevant items that might otherwise have been missed. Again, many of the so-called semantic extensions of word meanings can be understood hyponymically; e.g. "board" can be used in different contexts to refer to a bulletin board or a drawing board or a surf board because hyponyms can be replaced by their superordinates. More interesting, it is possible with WordNet to retrieve lists of hyponyms; e.g. from the word "food" it is possible to retrieve the names of many different kinds of food. Thus, it is possible to go from, say, "eat food" to "eat x," where "x" is any of the different kinds of food, i.e. any hyponym of food. If x is a hyponym of food, "eat x" is semantically acceptable (Resnik 1993). Other applications of WordNet are described in Fellbaum (1998).

WordNet was constructed as an instantiation of hypotheses proposed in the 1980s. Its relevance to this discussion is to demonstrate what a lexical semantic system designed on those principles does not do. For example, one thing that WordNet does not do is to provide a topical organization of the lexicon. If someone were to ask for all the words used to discuss baseball, the bat and ball would be kinds of artifacts, the players would be kinds of people, the field would be a kind of location, and the game itself would be a kind of activity. Baseball words are scattered throughout WordNet, not clustered together by semantic relations. In short, a topical organization of a lexicon is very different from a semantic organization. (And both, of course, are different from an alphabetical organization.)

Another thing WordNet does not do is provide a way to recognize the alternative meanings of a polysemous word. The alternative meanings of a polysemous word are distinguished, of course, as they are in conventional dictionaries, by synonyms and definitional glosses and, sometimes, by illustrative phrases or sentences. But nothing is said about using that information to decide whether an occurrence of the polysemous word in a particular context conforms to one meaning or another. WordNet is not unique in this neglect of contextual information. Dictionary definitions are deliberately decontextualized.

Lexicographers do not need to specify contexts of use in any detail because the people who use dictionaries seldom need such help. Native speakers are extremely good at recognizing the intended meaning of a polysemous word on the basis of the context in which it is used. But students learning English as a second language are familiar with this lexicographic deficiency; they look up an unfamiliar word in a dictionary where they may find half a dozen different definitions, but little help in determining which of those definitions is appropriate in the context of their reading.

It seems obvious, therefore, that native speakers must know something that is missing from dictionaries and thesauruses and lexical databases. Because the question at hand is what native speakers know when they know a word, this omission from theories of lexical semantics seems sufficiently serious to merit further discussion.

CONTEXTUALIZATION

Although context of use is neglected in WordNet, it has played a major role in theories of many psycholinguistic phenomena. For example, the interactive social context in which children acquire their first language is so obviously important that it is normally taken for granted. Theories of early vocabulary development differ primarily in what kinds of constraints are proposed on children's appreciation of their interactive linguistic context.

Beyond the early years, reading begins to provide an alternative context for vocabulary growth. The rate at which school children learn new words has been estimated at around 20 words per day (Anglin 1993), which is far more than anyone could teach them. The usual explanation is that children learn words while reading, by observing the linguistic contexts in which they are used (Gray & Holmes 1938, Werner & Kaplan 1950, Sternberg & Powell 1983, Jenkins et al 1984, Nagy et al 1987). Unfortunately, learning words from context is a slow process. Many contexts of use must be encountered before a new word is mastered, so extensive reading is required for a large vocabulary.

Not only is context important for acquisition, it is critically important for comprehension. The dramatic example is deixis (Bühler 1934). If someone says, "I need you here now," the referents of "I" and "you" are the speaker and a listener, who can only be identified from the actual context of use; that is deixis of person. Similarly, the referents of "here" and "now" depend on where and when the utterance occurred; those are deixis of place and time. These deictic words presuppose knowledge of the context in which they are used; they are meaningful, but they have no reference outside their context of use. Deixis illustrates how skillfully people use context.

Collocations also illustrate the importance of context. For example, "pen" has several meanings and so does "fountain," but when they occur together in "fountain pen" all the possible combinations of meanings are ignored; the collocation has a single noncompositional meaning and can be treated as if it were a single word. The contribution of adjacent words is especially important for adjectives, whose meaning is strongly influenced by the nouns they modify: A long car and a long train are very different in length. "Long" and "short" express values of the attribute length, "wide" and "narrow" express values of the attribute width, and so forth, but the absolute values depend on the noun that is modified. "Good" and "bad" express values of the function that the head noun is normally expected to serve (Katz 1964): a good meal is nourishing, a good knife cuts well, a good friend is loyal, and other similar examples. The implication is that knowing the meaning of a noun entails knowing the attributes and functions of its referent.

Pustejovsky (1995) emphasized the generality of this phenomenon. One of his examples is the verb "enjoy," where a missing predicate is inferred from information about the complement. In "She enjoyed the book" it is understood that she enjoyed reading the book because that is what one does with books; in "He enjoyed his coffee" it is understood that he enjoyed drinking his coffee because that is what one does with coffee, and so on. It must be part of the meaning of "book," therefore, that one reads it, and part of the meaning of "coffee" that one drinks it. Thus, Pustejovsky would add information about attributes and composition and function and agency to the definitions of some words, plus rules to infer the meaning of other words whose definitions were underspecified. Such an approach has many attractions, but until it has been fully worked out it will be difficult to evaluate.

Another example of the importance of context for comprehension is its use to avoid the potential ambiguities of polysemy.

Polysemy

In developing scientific terminology, a deliberate attempt is made to avoid using the same symbol to mean two different things, but multiplicity of meaning abounds under the less restrictive conditions of everyday discourse. It is a perverse feature of natural languages that the more frequently a word is used, the more polysemous it tends to be (Zipf 1945, Jastrezembski 1981).

It is useful to maintain a distinction between polysemy and ambiguity. Although polysemous open-class words are commonly assumed to be ambiguous, they are only potentially ambiguous. They are ambiguous in isolation, but open-class words are seldom used in isolation. In everyday usage, polysemous words are rarely ambiguous. People navigate daily through a sea of potential ambiguities, resolving them so easily that they seldom notice they are there. Consequently, the ubiquity of multiple meanings is easily overlooked, yet it provides clear proof, if proof is needed, of a remarkable human ability to cope with polysemy.

Psycholinguists have used polysemous words extensively in a variety of experiments attempting to test the hypothesis that components of the language comprehension process are autonomous modules (Fodor 1983). If they were autonomous, then the occurrence of a polysemous word should lead to the simultaneous activation of all of its different meanings, and that information would then be passed as input to a separate module that would select the meaning most appropriate to the given context. If they were not autonomous, the activation of meanings and the evaluation of context could interact, and only the context-appropriate sense would be activated. The issue is complex, however, because any failure to obtain the predicted results could mean either that meaning identification is not modular or that the modules involved have been incorrectly identified. Simpson (1994) gives an excellent review of these studies, which provide strong evidence on both sides of the question; he suggests that the results must be highly dependent on characteristics of the context and characteristics of the tasks required of the subject. He concludes, "Only by taking a broader view of context will we be able to direct our efforts more productively to understanding the nature of lexical ambiguity and its relation to other aspects of language comprehension, rather than focusing on it exclusively as a means to settle a single theoretical debate" (Simpson 1994: 372).

The cognitive processes studied in these experiments occur in a fraction of a second, so fast that in normal listening or reading the alternative meanings, even when they are activated, do not rise above some threshold of conscious awareness. This speed is essential, of course. If polysemy could not be quickly resolved, comprehension would be swamped by a backlog of unprocessed semantic information. Cross-modal priming experiments have established that semantic processing can begin even before a spoken word is recognized (Marslen-Wilson 1987, Moss et al 1997), presumably with contextual facilitation. Thus, the experiments show that the intended sense is identified very quickly, but they say little or nothing about how this trick is performed.

Contextual Representations

Simpson is surely right that a broader view of context is needed (Simpson 1994). A contextual approach to lexical semantics might assume that the meanings of a word form "are fully reflected in appropriate aspects of the relations it contracts with actual and potential contexts" (Cruse 1986:1). The problem is to determine what those "appropriate aspects" are. The lexical semantic relations discussed above must be part of the answer, but it is already clear that something more is required. Miller & Charles (1991) have given it a name: What is needed is a contextual representation—a cognitive representation of the set of contexts in which a given word form can be used to express a given word meaning.

To focus on the context rather than the polysemous word itself requires something of a figure-ground reversal. Charles (1988) introduced a sorting method in which context becomes the object of central interest. He selected two different words, then searched a textual corpus to find a haphazard sample of sentences using those words. Then he printed each context on a separate card, leaving a blank where the target words had been. He shuffled the deck of cards and handed it to subjects with the request to "sort them into piles so that the same word has been deleted from every sentence in the same pile." In other words, Charles asked subjects to discriminate between the contexts of various words; he applied signal detection theory to his results in order to obtain values of d' as a measure of contextual discriminability.

His first discovery was that contextual discriminability seems to be inversely related to the semantic similarity of the deleted words. The larger the d', the smaller the semantic similarity (Miller & Charles 1991). With words like "car" and "automobile" there was considerable confusion of contexts, but when semantically unrelated words like "noon" and "string" were used, their contexts were almost never confused. Miller & Charles proposed that semantic similarity might be assessed in terms of the relative number of contexts in which two words could be interchanged without creating a semantic anomaly.

Miller & Charles (1991) summarized a series of such experiments with the generalization that, associated with each word meaning, there must be a contextual representation. In particular, a polysemous word must have different contextual representations for each of its different senses (Miller & Leacock 1998). A contextual representation is not itself a linguistic context, but is an abstract cognitive structure that accumulates from encounters with a word in various linguistic contexts and that enables the recognition of similar contexts as they occur.

Note that contextual representations are precisely what is missing from most dictionary definitions. But it is not easy to explain to lexicographers what more they should provide. Unfortunately, "contextual representation" is not an explanation; it is merely a name for the thing that needs to be explained.

One thing is clear, however. A lexical representation must contain information limiting the number of alternative meanings that a polysemous word can have. Indeed, a general feature of contextual representations seems to be that they enable people to narrow the range of relevant alternatives they must cope with.

Three sources for the kinds of information embodied in contextual representations (Miller 1978) can be mentioned: situational context, topical context, and local context.

By *situational context* is meant the kind of information required for deixis or, more generally, information about the purposes and goals of the communicative interaction. It is generally assumed that an appreciation of the situational context draws heavily on a person's general knowledge of people and the world they live in. How world knowledge should be characterized is a controversial question that cannot be settled here. But one kind of situational context might be open to observation.

The situational context created by instructions given to participants in psychological experiments should be of particular interest. Giving instructions is an experimenter's way of providing a context that makes an experimental situation meaningful. In the 1950s when information theory (Shannon 1948) was first making psychologists aware of the importance of specifying the number of alternative stimuli and responses in their experiments, it was observed in a variety of experimental situations that instructions could determine what a subject expected, and those expectations could determine performance. That is to say, given instructions to do so, people are very skillful at restricting their attention to a limited range of possible alternatives.

Topical context is another important source of contextual information that can limit the interpretation of polysemous words. For example, the polysemous noun "shot" can have different referents depending on the domain of discourse in which it is used. In a discussion of marksmanship, shot means one thing; to a bartender it is something else; a doctor or nurse gives it with a hypodermic needle; to a photographer it is a snapshot; golfers and basketball players take still different shots. Each different meaning is associated with a different topic. So if the topic could be identified from the linguistic context, it might be possible to tell which meaning was intended.

Looking at topical context is an old idea (Kintsch 1972), although it is not clear exactly what a topic is or how people are able to identify one. The general notion is that each topic is has its own vocabulary, so the problem is to learn what those vocabularies are, and what the meanings of polysemous words are in each different vocabulary. That knowledge is surely part of the contextual representations that help to determine intended meanings.

Local context refers to information provided by words in the immediate neighborhood of a polysemous word. Whereas topical context can disregard word order, local context depends heavily on the order of the words and on their syntactic categories.

Knowing how to use a word implies knowing its syntactic category, so associated with every word form there must be a list of the syntactic roles it can play. Or, to reverse figure and ground again, there is one category of contexts in which nouns can appear, another category of contexts in which verbs can appear, and so forth. Some words can play more than one syntactic role, so to determine their syntactic category in any particular instance it is necessary to examine the context in which they are used. How people do this is an active research question, but one feature is apparent: The syntactic category of nearly every word can be determined immediately by looking at the other words in its local environment, without waiting for a full parse of the sentence.

The notion of a contextual representation, therefore, generalizes an idea already made familiar by syntactic categories. The generalization is that contextual representations are associated with word meanings, not word forms. Semantic as well as syntactic information is involved.

In 1955 Kaplan reported informal experiments in which he asked people to identify the meaning of a polysemous word when they saw only the words in its immediate vicinity. He found that they were almost always able to identify the intended meaning when they saw a string of five words, two to the left and two to the right of the target word. Kaplan's claim was welcomed by those working on machine translation, but those who found it easy to construct counterexamples were not impressed. Yet the result has been replicated (Choueka & Lusignan 1985) and appears to be correct. Local context is an important component of contextual representations.

It is one thing to recognize these sources of contextual information, but something else again to understand how they are used to identify the intended meanings of polysemous words in context. One approach is to simulate sense identification with a computer.

Automatic Word-Sense Identification

Although word-meaning identification is no problem for people, it is a serious problem for computers. It is a major stumbling block for natural language processing by machine.

The difficulty was recognized during the early enthusiasm for machine translation in the 1950s and 1960s. Bar-Hillel (1960) concluded that fully automatic machine translation would be impossible because he believed that automatic word-sense identification is impossible. Word-sense identification is so important, however, that attempts to solve it continued without interruption (Hirst 1987).

An approach that has been popular recently takes advantage of the statistical learning systems and the large machine-readable corpora that are now available. For example, Gale et al (1992) described a statistical approach that took advantage of topical context. They partitioned a sizable number of occurrences of a polysemous word into sets illustrating its different meanings, then, using a statistical classifier based on Bayesian decision theory, searched for co-occurring words that would be diagnostic of the topic and the appropriate sense of the target word. For example, the photographic sense of "shot" should occur with "lens" and "camera," whereas "whiskey" or "brandy" should indicate another sense.

Leacock et al (1996) compared three different statistical learning systems using the noun "line." They collected sentences containing line (or lines or Line or Lines) and sorted them according to meaning until they had a sizable sample of each of six different meanings. Then they divided the resulting sets of instances into training sets and test sets: The statistical sense-classifiers were trained on one set of contexts and tested on the other. For topical context they used a Bayesian classifier, a content vector classifier, and a neural net classifier. Results with the three statistical methods of topical classification were roughly equivalent (71%–76% correct meaning identification), although some meanings were consistently easier to recognize than others.

In order to check that the statistical classifiers were identifying contexts as well as possible on the basis of the information they were given, Princeton undergraduates were given lists of the co-occurring words (in reverse alphabetical order) and asked to guess which sense of "line" was intended. The students did only a little better than the statistical classifiers. The general similarity of their results was striking. Students had little difficulty with contexts that the classifiers got right, and had more trouble with the contexts that the classifiers got wrong. Leacock et al concluded that the statistical systems had reached a ceiling, that 20%–30% of the instances could not be classified on the basis of topical context alone.

Local context might be expected to be more helpful, but it is more difficult to extract and use. One way to exploit the information in local contexts is to use a template classifier (Weiss 1973). A template is a specific string of words (including the target word) that occurs frequently in the training contexts. For example, Leacock et al (1996) found that "a fine line between" correctly selected one meaning of line, whereas "wait in line" selected another, and "telephone lines" selected still a third. The results were excellent when the templates occurred, but all too often they failed to occur. Leacock et al (1998) had better success using a Bayesian method with local context.

There are many instances where the intended sense of a polysemous word can only be inferred by the use of situational context. How computers should be given information about the world and the goals of humans who live in that world is an important issue for artificial intelligence, but the results have not yet been brought to bear on the problem of automatic sense identification.

Automatic sense identification is an active area of research, and considerable ingenuity is apparent, but the results have been discouraging. The reality is that there are still no large-scale, operational systems for identifying the senses of words in connected text, and there probably will not be until nonlinguistic context can be taken into account. Indeed, it was my reluctant recognition of how difficult it is for computers to solve this problem that led me to wonder whether the human capacity to take advantage of context might not be a uniquely important cognitive process.

CONCLUSION

Contextualization has been defined as the use of context to determine meaning and to resolve potential ambiguities. When contextualization is linked so closely to meaning, of course, it inherits all the uncertainties associated with the concept of meaning. But it also inherits the broad scope of meaningfulness. Wherever experience is meaningful, context must be considered. And language provides one of the best avenues to approach a study of the remarkable human capacity to use context.

Word-sense identification is a problem that must challenge anyone interested in how people use language to understand one another—how so much lexical polysemy can result in so little ambiguity. It is argued here that associated with every distinct meaning of a polysemous word there must be some cognitive representation of the contexts in which that word form can be used to express that meaning. But much remains to be done before the precise nature of these contextual representations will be understood.

> **Visit the *Annual Reviews* home page at**
> **http://www.AnnualReviews.org.**

Literature Cited

Anglin JM. 1993. Vocabulary development: a morphological analysis. *Monogr. Soc. Res. Child Dev.* 58 (10), Ser. 238:1–166

Atkins BTS. 1992/1993. Theoretical lexicography and its relation to dictionary-making. *Dictionaries: J. Dict. Soc. North Am.* 14:4–39

Bar-Hillel Y. 1960. A demonstration of the nonfeasibility of fully automatic high quality translation. In *Advances in Computers*, ed. FL Alt, 1:158–63. New York: Academic

Beck I, McKeown M. 1991. Conditions of vo-cabulary acquisition. In *Handbook of Reading Research*, ed. R Barr, LM Kamil, PB Mosenthal, PD Pearson, 2:789–814. New York: Longman

Binet A, Simon T. 1911. *The Development of Intelligence in Children*. Transl. ES Kite, 1916. Baltimore, MD: Williams & Wilkins

Bühler K. 1934. *Sprachtheorie: die Darstellungsfunktion der Sprache*. Jena: Gustav Fischer

Carnap R. 1956. *Meaning and Necessity*. Chicago: Univ. Chicago Press. 2nd ed.

Charles WG. 1988. The categorization of sentential contexts. *J. Psycholinguist. Res.* 17: 403–11

Choueka Y, Lusignan S. 1985. Disambiguation by short contexts. *Comput. Humanit.* 19:147–57

Collins AM, Quillian MR. 1969. Retrieval time from semantic memory. *J. Verbal Learn. Verbal Behav.* 8:240–47

Cronbach LJ. 1942. An analysis of techniques for systematic vocabulary testing. *J. Educ. Res.* 36:206–17

Cruse DA. 1986. *Lexical Semantics.* New York: Cambridge Univ. Press

de Saussure F. 1916. *Cours de Linguistique Générale.* Transl. W. Baskin, 1959, in *Course in General Linguistics.* New York: Philosophical Library

Fellbaum C, ed. 1998. *WordNet: An Electronic Lexical Database.* Cambridge, MA: MIT Press

Fodor JA. 1983. *Modularity of Mind.* Cambridge, MA: MIT Press

Gale W, Church KW, Yarowsky D. 1992. A method for disambiguating word senses in a large corpus. *AT&T Bell Labs. Stat. Res. Rep. 104*

Galton F. 1879. Psychometric experiments. *Brain* 2:149–62

Gray W, Holmes E. 1938. *The Development of Meaning Vocabularies in Reading.* Chicago: Univ. Chicago Press

Hirst G. 1987. *Semantic Interpretation and the Resolution of Ambiguity.* Cambridge: Cambridge Univ. Press

Jackendoff RS. 1972. *Semantic Interpretation in Generative Grammar.* Cambridge, MA: MIT Press

Jastrezembski JE. 1981. Multiple meanings, number of related meanings, frequency of occurrence, and the lexicon. *Cogn. Psychol.* 13:278–305

Jenkins JR, Stein M, Wysocki K. 1984. Learning vocabulary through reading. *Am. Educ. Res. J.* 21:767–87

Kaplan A. 1955. An experimental study of ambiguity and context. *Mech. Transl.* 2: 39–46

Katz J. 1964. Semantic theory and the meaning of 'good'. *J. Philos.* 61:739–66

Katz J, Fodor JA. 1963. The structure of a semantic theory. *Language* 39:170–210

Kintsch W. 1972. *The Representation of Meaning in Memory.* Hillsdale, NJ: Erlbaum

Landau SI. 1984. *Dictionaries: The Art and Craft of Lexicography.* New York: Scribner's

Leacock C, Chodorow M, Miller GA. 1998. Using corpus statistics and WordNet relations for sense identification. *Comput. Ling.* 24: In press

Leacock C, Towell G, Voorhees EM. 1996. Towards building contextual representations of word senses using statistical models. In *Corpus Processing for Lexical Acquisition,* ed. B Boguraev, J Pustejovsky, pp. 97–113. Cambridge, MA: MIT Press

Lyons J. 1977. *Semantics.* Cambridge, UK: Cambridge Univ. Press

Marconi D. 1997. *Lexical Competence.* Cambridge, MA: The MIT Press

Marslen-Wilson WD. 1987. Functional parallelism in spoken word-recognition. *Cognition* 25:71–102

Mel'cuk I, Zholkovsky A. 1988. The explanatory combinatorial dictionary. In *Relational Models of the Lexicon; Representing Knowledge in Semantic Networks,* ed. MW Evens, pp. 41–74. Cambridge, UK: Cambridge Univ. Press

Miller GA. 1978. Semantic relations among words. In *Linguistic Theory and Psychological Reality,* ed. M Halle, J Bresnan, GA Miller, pp. 61–118. Cambridge, MA: MIT Press

Miller GA. 1985. WordNet: A dictionary browser. *Information in Data, Proc. Conf. Univ. Waterloo Cent. New Oxf. Engl. Dict., 1st,* pp. 25–28, Waterloo, Ont., Can: Univ. Waterloo Cent. New Oxf. Engl. Dict.

Miller GA. 1996. Contextuality. In *Mental Models in Cognitive Science: Essays in Honour of Phil Johnson-Laird,* ed. J Oakhill, A Garnham, pp.1–18. East Sussex, England: Psychology Press

Miller GA, Charles WG. 1991. Contextual correlates of semantic similarity. *Lang. Cogn. Proc.* 6:1–28

Miller GA, Johnson-Laird PN. 1976. *Language and Perception.* Cambridge, MA: Harvard Univ. Press

Miller GA, Leacock C. 1998. Lexical representations for sentence processing. In *Polysemy: Theoretical and Computational Approaches,* ed. Y Ravin, C Leacock. New York: Oxford Univ. Press. In press

Montague R. 1974. *Formal Philosophy: Selected Papers.* New Haven, CT: Yale Univ. Press

Moss HE, McCormick SF, Tyler LK. 1997. The time course of activation of semantic information during spoken word recognition. *Lang. Cogn. Proc.* 12:695–731

Nagy WE, Anderson RC, Herman PA. 1987. Learning word meanings from context during normal reading. *Am. Educ. Res. J.* 24:237–70

Ogden CK. 1934. *The System of Basic English.* New York: Harcourt Brace

Pustejovsky J. 1995. *The Generative Lexicon.* Cambridge, MA: MIT Press

Quillian MR. 1968. Semantic memory. In *Semantic Information Processing*, ed. M Minsky, pp. 216–70. Cambridge, MA: MIT Press

Resnik PS. 1993. *Selection and information: a class-based approach to lexical relationships*. PhD thesis. Univ. Penn., Phila.

Seashore RH, Eckerson LD. 1940. The measurement of individual differences in general English vocabularies. *J. Educ. Psychol.* 31:14–37

Shannon CE. 1948. A mathematical theory of communication. *Bell Syst. Tech. J.* 27: 379–423

Simpson GB. 1994. Context and the processing of ambiguous words. In *Handbook of Psycholinguistics*, ed. MA Gernsbacher, pp. 359–74. San Diego, CA: Academic

Smith EE. 1978. Theories of semantic memory. In *Handbook of Learning and Cognitive Processes: Linguistic Functions in Cognitive Theory*, ed. WK Estes. 6:1–56. Hillsdale, NJ: Erlbaum

Sternberg RJ, Powell JS. 1983. Comprehending verbal comprehension. *Am. Psychol.* 38:878–93

Thorndike EL. 1921. *The Teacher's Word Book*. New York: Teachers Coll., Columbia Univ.

Weiss S. 1973. Learning to disambiguate. *Inform. Stor. Retr.* 9:33–41

Werner H, Kaplan E. 1950. Development of word meaning through verbal context: an experimental study. *J. Psychol.* 29:251–57

Zipf GK. 1945. The meaning-frequency relationship of words. *J. Gen. Psychol.* 33: 251–56

Annu. Rev. Psychol. 1999. 50:21–45

COGNITIVE DEVELOPMENT:
Children's Knowledge About the Mind

John H. Flavell

Department of Psychology, Stanford University, Stanford, California 94305-2130;
e-mail: lindab@psych.stanford.edu

KEY WORDS: theory of mind, infancy, childhood, metacognition, social cognition

---

ABSTRACT

This chapter reviews theory and research on the development of children's
knowledge about the mental world, focusing especially on work done during
the past 15 years under the rubric of theory-of-mind development. The three
principal approaches to explaining this development—theory theory, modular theory, and simulation theory—are described first. Next comes a description of infant precursors or protoforms of theory-of-mind knowledge in infancy, including a beginning awareness of the intentionality and goal-
directedness of human actions. This discussion is followed by a summary of
the postinfancy development of children's understanding of visual perception, attention, desires, emotions, intentions, beliefs, knowledge, pretense,
and thinking. Briefly considered next are intracultural, intercultural, and interspecies differences in theory-of-mind development. The chapter then concludes with some guesses about the future of the field.

CONTENTS

21

INTRODUCTION

Historically, there have been three main waves of research on the development of children's knowledge about the mind (Flavell & Miller 1998). The earliest stemmed directly or indirectly from Piaget's theory and research. Piaget believed that children begin development by being cognitively egocentric. That is, initially, they do not know that there exist such things as conceptual, perceptual, and affective perspectives. As a result, they naturally cannot know that they themselves have such perspectives, or that other people do, or that their own perspective may differ from those of others, or that they may be unwittingly reporting their own perspective when asked to report another person's. Even after children become aware of the existence of perspectives and perspective differences, they only gradually acquire skill in discriminating their own from other people's. Consistent with the Piagetian view, many studies since the 1950s have documented increases with age in various perspective-taking abilities (Flavell 1992, Shantz 1983).

The second wave comprises theory and research on children's metacognitive development, beginning in the early 1970s (Flavell et al 1993). Metacognition includes knowledge about the nature of people as cognizers, about the nature of different cognitive tasks, and about possible strategies that can be applied to the solution of different tasks. It also includes executive skills for monitoring and regulating one's cognitive activities. The majority of metacognitive studies have dealt with children's metamemory, especially their knowledge and use of memory strategies, but a large number have also investigated children's metacognition regarding language and communication, perception and attention, comprehension, and problem solving.

The third wave—theory-of-mind development—began in the 1980s and currently dominates the area (Astington 1993, Flavell & Miller 1998). Indeed, it could be argued that it almost dominates the whole field of cognitive development: Publications dealing with theory-of-mind development now number in the hundreds, and the flow shows no signs of diminishing. Consequently, virtually all of the theory and research cited in this chapter belong to this third wave. With the exception of one article by Wellman & Gelman (1992), no previous *Annual Review of Psychology* chapter has surveyed developmental theory and research in this area.

Most theory-of-mind studies have investigated children's knowledge about our most basic mental states—desires, percepts, beliefs, knowledge, thoughts, intentions, feelings, and so on. Theory-of-mind researchers try to find out what children know about the existence and behavior of the different types of states that inhabit the mind and also what children know about how mental states are causally linked to perceptual inputs, to behavioral outputs, and to other mental states. For example, do young children know what a false belief is, or do they know that unsatisfied desires typically cause negative feelings and renewed behavioral efforts to satisfy those desires?

The following is a well-known example of a developmental finding from the theory-of-mind research wave. An experimenter shows a 5-year-old a candy box with pictures of candy on it and asks her what she thinks is in it. "Candy," she replies. Then the child gets to look inside and discovers to her surprise that it actually contains crayons, not candy. The experimenter then asks her what another child who had not yet seen inside the box would think it contained. "Candy," the child answers, amused at the deception. The experimenter tries the same procedure with a 3-year-old. The response to the initial question is the expected "candy," but the response to the second is surprising—an unamused "crayons." Even more surprising is that in response to further questioning, the 3-year-old claims that she had initially thought that there were crayons in the box and had even said that there were (e.g. Gopnik & Astington 1988, Perner et al 1987). Similar developmental results are obtained with a different false-belief test. In this unexpected-transfer test, person A puts an object in box X and then departs. Person B moves the object to box Y during A's absence. When A returns, the question to the child subject is: Where will A search for the object—in X or in Y? Older preschoolers say X, younger ones say Y.

A frequent interpretation of this sort of finding has been that young preschoolers do not yet possess a mental representational conception of the mind. That is, they do not yet realize that people think and act in accordance with the way they represent the world mentally rather than the way the world actually is. Consequently, young preschoolers do not understand that people can believe to be true, and act in accordance with, a mental representation that does not correspond to reality—that is, a false belief.

THEORIES OF DEVELOPMENT

Theory Theory

Several types of theories have been proposed to explain the development of children's knowledge about the mind (Carruthers & Smith 1996, Flavell & Miller 1998, Gopnik & Wellman 1994, Moore 1996). One is the so-called theory theory (Gopnik & Meltzoff 1997, Gopnik & Wellman 1994, Perner 1991, Wellman & Gelman 1998). Theory theorists argue that our knowledge about the mind comprises not an actual scientific theory but an everyday "framework" or "foundational" theory. To constitute such an informal theory, they claim, a body of knowledge must have three properties. First, it must specify a set of entities or processes (an ontology, philosophers call it) that are found in its domain of application and not in other domains. Second, it must use causal principles that are likewise unique to the theory's domain. Finally, the body of knowledge must comprise a system of interrelated concepts and beliefs rather than just a collection of unrelated contents.

Theory theorists claim that our informal theory of mind satisfies all three of these conditions. First, entities or processes such as beliefs, desires, and thinking are found only in the domain of the mental and thus satisfy the ontological criterion. Second, psychological causality (she tried to get it because she wanted it and thought she could get it, etc) is also found only in the domain of the psychological; physical objects are not caused to move by such mental states. Finally, our knowledge about the mind is organized and richly interconnected with different mental states conceptualized as being causally linked to one another, to environmental input, and to behavioral output. As examples of these interconnections, we recognize that what we perceive influences what we think about and believe; that what we believe may bias what we perceive; that various mental and physiological states engender our desires; that beliefs and desires may lead to behavioral intentions, which in turn may lead to goal-directed actions; and that the success or failure of these actions will cause emotional reactions, which will in turn engender additional mental and behavioral activity.

Researchers have identified a number of steps or milestones in children's developmental itinerary toward the adult theory of mind. For example, Bartsch & Wellman (1995) presented evidence for the following three-step developmental sequence. First, around age 2, children acquire a *desire psychology*. This psychology includes an elementary conception not only of simple desires but also of simple emotions and simple perceptual experience or attention. The conception is elementary in that although mentalistic, it is nonrepresentational rather than representational. That is, the child understands that people are subjectively connected to things in the sense of having the inner experience of wanting them, fearing them, seeing them, and so on, but the child does not yet understand that people mentally represent these things, accurately or inaccurately, as being a certain way. Second, around age 3, children begin to talk about beliefs and thoughts as well as desires, and they seem to understand that beliefs are mental representations that can be false as well as true and can differ from person to person. However, at this age they continue to explain their own and other people's actions by appeal to desires rather than beliefs. Bartsch & Wellman (1995) refer to this second level of understanding as a *desire-belief psychology*. Finally, at about age 4, children begin to understand that what people think and believe, as well as what they desire, crucially affects how they behave. That is, they acquire our adult *belief-desire psychology,* in which beliefs and desires are thought to determine actions jointly.

Theory theorists argue that experience plays a formative role in children's theory-of-mind development. They believe that experience provides young children with information that cannot be accounted for by their present theory of mind, information that will eventually cause them to revise and improve that theory. For example, desire psychologists will gradually become belief-desire psychologists by repeatedly seeing people behave in ways that require for their explanation a concept of belief as well as a concept of desire. Thus, the role of experience is viewed as similar to that in Piaget's equilibration theory (Piaget 1985): That is, experience engenders disequilibrium and, eventually, a new, higher state of equilibrium (a new theory).

Modularity Theory

Other theorists have different views about what gets acquired in theory-of-mind development and how. Modularity theorists like Leslie (1994, Leslie & Roth 1993) believe that young children are not acquiring a theory about mental representations at all. Rather, Leslie postulates the acquisition through neurological maturation of a succession of three domain-specific and modular mechanisms for dealing with agents versus nonagent objects. Although experience may be necessary to trigger the operation of these mechanisms, it does not determine their nature. The first mechanism, called Theory of Body mechanism (abbreviated ToBY), develops early in the first year. It allows the baby to recognize, among other things, that agents have an internal source of energy that permits them to move on their own. The next two, called Theory of Mind mechanisms (ToMM), deal with the intentionality or "aboutness" of agents rather than with their mechanical properties. ToMM$_1$, which comes into play later in the first year, will allow the infant to construe people and other agents as perceiving the environment and as pursuing goals. Finally, ToMM$_2$ begins to develop during the second year of life. This third mechanism allows children to represent agents as holding attitudes toward the truth of proposition—what philosophers refer to as *propositional attitudes*. Propositional attitudes are mental states such as *pretending that, believing that, imagining that, desiring that,* and the like. Equipped with ToMM$_2$, children are able to compute that Mary is pretending that this empty cup is filled with tea, that John thinks that this candy box contains candy, and other propositional attitudes. Other theorists proposing innate or early maturing modular mechanisms dedicated to mental state computations are Fodor (1992), Mitchell (1994), and especially Baron-Cohen (1995).

Simulation Theory

Harris (1992) and others have proposed yet a third approach. According to their simulation theory, children are introspectively aware of their own mental states and can use this awareness to infer the mental states of other people through a kind of role-taking or simulation process. For example, in the false-belief task, children could predict what a naive other child would think the candy box contained by imagining or mentally simulating what they themselves would think if they were in his or her shoes and had only the appearance of the box to go on. What develops is the ability to make increasingly accurate simulations of this kind. Although not denying that people also resort to theories in predicting and explaining behavior, Harris (1992) stresses the importance of such mental-simulation processes in the acquisition of social-cognitive knowledge and skills. Like theory theorists, simulation theorists (e.g. Harris 1991) also assume that experience plays an important formative role, in that it is through practice in role taking that children improve their simulation skills.

Other Views

A number of investigators have argued that young children's failures on false-belief and other theory-of-mind tasks are due to more domain-general information-processing or "performance" (as contrasted with "competence") problems (Flavell & Miller 1998). Examples are limited memory abilities and the inability to inhibit a dominant, ready-to-go response; an example of the latter would be the tendency to blurt out the cognitively salient real contents of the candy box when asked for the naive child's belief about its contents (e.g. Carlson et al 1998). Other investigators try to explain young children's failures in other ways. For example, they claim that the tasks may be misunderstood by young children or may not be sufficiently engaging to elicit optimal performance (Flavell & Miller 1998).

As would be expected, advocates of these different theoretical positions have not failed to cite arguments and evidence for their own views and against those of their competitors. My judgment is that the theory theorists have been the most persuasive in this regard so far (e.g. Gopnik & Wellman 1994). However, it is also my judgment that an adequate theory will finally have to include elements from each of these perspectives; indeed, some of the theorists explicitly allow for this possibility. That is, the following seem likely: (*a*) that development in this area builds on some innate or early maturing people-reading capacities; (*b*) that we have some introspective ability that we can and do exploit when trying to infer the mental states of other creatures who are like ourselves but in a different psychological situation (e.g. ignorant of the facts, differently motivated); (*c*) that much of our knowledge of the mind can be characterized as an informal theory; (*d*) that improved information-processing and other abilities (e.g. linguistic skills) enable and facilitate theory-of-mind development (and certainly help children show what they know on theory-of-mind tasks); and (*e*) that a variety of experiences serve to engender and change children's conceptions of the mental world and their ability to use these conceptions in predicting and explaining their own and other people's behavior.

DEVELOPMENTS DURING INFANCY

There recently has been a quickening of research interest in the infant beginnings of theory-of-mind development (Flavell & Miller 1998). At least two questions are of interest. First, what behaviors do infants of different ages show that seem relevant to the development of knowledge about people? Second, how should these behaviors be interpreted? That is, exactly how much and what kind of knowledge about the mind (if any) should we attribute to infants who exhibit them?

Basic Discrimination Abilities

It is clear that infants are born with or acquire early a number of abilities and dispositions that will help them learn about people. They find human faces, voices, and movements particularly interesting stimuli to attend and respond to. They also possess and further develop impressive abilities to perceptually analyze and discriminate human stimuli.

In the case of faces, infants develop considerable skill in discriminating different facial expressions over the first 2 years of life, and there is reason to suspect that a component of the ability to recognize facial expressions is unlearned (Nelson 1987). Infants are also very attracted to people's eyes and develop the ability to follow another person's eye gaze (Butterworth & Jarrett 1991). This ability to use eye gaze to detect what another person is looking at makes it possible for the infant to initiate acts of joint visual attention with an adult, acts that will serve to improve the infant's communicative and other social-cognitive abilities.

In the case of voices, infants are highly attentive to voices from the beginning and can distinguish one voice from another. Incredibly, young infants have even been shown capable of distinguishing their mother's voice from another woman's based on prenatal, intrauterine auditory experience with her voice (Cooper & Aslin 1989). Young babies also have an unlearned ability to hear fine differences between consonant sounds and to perceive them categorically (Kuhl 1987).

Regarding motor movements, studies by Meltzoff and others (e.g. Meltzoff & Moore 1994) have shown that, remarkably, even newborns seem able to perceptually represent and imitate another person's movements (though more conservative interpretations of the results are possible, e.g. Anisfeld 1991). For example, the neonate will imitatively stick out its tongue after it has seen an adult do this. Older infants apparently can tell when they are being imitated and prefer to attend to adults who imitate them (Meltzoff 1990). Babies are also capable of other feats of intermodal perceptual representation involving people. For instance, by the middle of the first year of life they can apparently match a happy voice with a happy face, and a parent's voice with that same parent's face.

All this intense and differentiated responsiveness to people must serve the infant's social-cognitive development. If one wanted to design an infant who would learn much about people, one would obviously want to start by making it deeply interested in and attentive to them. One would also want to design it so that its appearance and behavior would cause adults to interact with it, and by doing so provide additional evidence as to what people—both the adults and the infant—are like. Human infants do indeed seem to be built with these two developmentally useful properties. They are impelled to attend to and interact with other people, and they impel other people to attend to and interact with them.

There is evidence that infants respond differently to people than they do to objects and seem to expect people to behave differently than objects do (Golinkoff 1983, Legerstee 1992, Spelke et al 1995). For example, Legerstee (1991) found that 5- to 8-week-old babies would imitate mouth openings and tongue protrusions produced by an adult but would not imitate similar-looking behaviors produced by an object. Likewise, infants try to retrieve a just-disappeared object by reaching toward its place of disappearance but try to retrieve a just-disappeared person merely by vocalizing to the person (Legerstee 1992). They also tend to act more surprised when an inanimate object seems to move entirely on its own, with nothing pushing it, than when a person does (Golinkoff 1983, Poulin-Dubois & Shultz 1988, Spelke et al 1995). In summary, fairly early on, infants come to construe people as "compliant agents" (Flavell et al 1993:184): that is, entities that are self-propelled and capable of independent movement (agents) but also influenceable at a distance by communicative signals (compliant).

Understanding "Aboutness"

As just described, early in the first year, babies begin to learn how people *differ* from objects. Late in the first year, they begin to learn how people *relate* to objects psychologically. Philosophers have noted that people and other animates are related to objects in ways that other objects are not. This special relation is called "aboutness" or "intentionality" (intentionality in a broad sense—not just in the narrow sense of "on purpose"). A person's behavior is "about" an object in this sense if the person perceptually attends to it, labels it, thinks about it, wants it, fears it, intends or tries to get it, or relates to it in any other psychological way.

Infants do a variety of things that reflect a dawning awareness of intentionality or some precursor thereof. They attempt to engender new "aboutnesses" in others through various communicative gestures, and they also check to see whether their attempts have succeeded. For example, they may look at, point to, hold up, or vocalize about an object or event and check to see whether the other person looks at, comments on, or otherwise responds to it (Bates 1976). They also develop skill at reading the aboutnesses the other person already has going. As one example, we have already noted that babies become able to follow another person's direction of gaze and thereby succeed in looking at what the person is looking at. This state of joint attention, in which baby and adult achieve a common cognitive focus, is of course requisite for all communication and communication development. Recent studies by Meltzoff (1995) have also shown that 18-month-olds can infer what action another person is trying to perform (e.g. trying to pull one object away from another object to which it is attached), even though the person is unsuccessful in the attempt (does not succeed in pulling it away) and therefore never actually demonstrates the intended action. This finding suggests that infants of this age may have some beginning understanding that people's actions are intentional and goal-directed.

Research reported by Spelke et al (1995) further suggests that 12-month-olds expect a person to reach for an object that the person is looking at with positive affect rather than for another one to which the person is not attending. By age 18 months, infants even seem to understand that they should give an experimenter a food that the experimenter reacts to with apparent happiness rather than one toward which the experimenter acts disgusted, even when they themselves prefer the latter food; in contrast, 14-month-olds do not show this understanding (Repacholi & Gopnik 1997). This finding appears to be the first empirical evidence that infants of this age have at least some limited ability to reason nonegocentrically about people's desires.

Infants also learn the names for things by noting what object the adult appears to be attending to when the adult says the label (Baldwin & Moses 1994, Tomasello 1995, Woodward & Markman 1998). For example, Baldwin (1991, 1993; Baldwin & Moses 1994) showed that infants of 19–20 months of age sense that the verbal label an adult utters refers to the object the adult shows clear signs of attending to at that moment. They recognize that it does not refer to other perceptually salient objects that the adult is not focused on, such as an object that they rather than the adult is currently attending to. In short, infants of this age seem to recognize that it is the adult's attentional focus rather than their own that gives clues as to the adult's referential intent.

As just noted, infants develop the ability to learn what an object is *called* by reading the adult's attentional focus when the adult labels it. They also develop the ability to learn what an object is *like* by reading the adult's attentional focus when the adult is expressing a positive or negative emotional reaction to it; for example, they may tend to avoid an object toward which their parent shows negative affect. Thus, they can recognize that the adult's emotional display refers to or is "about" a particular object just as they can recognize that the adult's spoken label refers to or is "about" a particular object. Seeking or using information about objects' positive or negative qualities conveyed by adults' emotional reactions to these objects has been called *social referencing.* One question that has arisen in the social referencing literature is whether the baby actually realizes that the adult's expressions of affect are about the object. An alternative possibility is that these expressions just alter the baby's mood, which in turn alters the baby's reactions to all objects, for instance, dampening them when the mood thus induced is negative. However, recent studies suggest that although such mood modification effects also can occur, by 12 months or so infants are capable of understanding that the adult's behavior is about the object the adult is attending to when expressing the positive or negative affect (Baldwin & Moses 1994, Hornik et al 1987, Mumme et al 1994).

Other Competencies

Older infants also do other things suggestive of a beginning understanding of human psychology. They sometimes appear to be trying to manipulate other people's emotional responses rather than, as in social referencing, just reading these responses for the information about reacted-to objects that they may provide. Even toddlers occasionally seem to try to change other people's feelings, or at least change their affective behavior. In the second year of life, they begin to comfort younger siblings in distress by patting, hugging, or kissing them, and they may even bring a security blanket to an adult in pain (Zahn-Waxler et al 1992). Less positively, young children sometimes tease or otherwise annoy siblings, as though hoping to frustrate or anger them (Dunn 1988). Such behaviors, positive or negative, are revealing, for they suggest that young children are beginning to identify the conditions that elicit or change emotions or behaviors.

Around 1.5 to 2 years of age, children may also begin to evince a more explicit understanding of certain mental states by using words that refer to them (Bartsch & Wellman 1995, Bretherton & Beeghly 1982, Wellman 1993). The states most commonly talked about at this early age are seeing ("I see a car"), wanting ("Want juice"), and reacting emotionally ("Those ladies scare me") (Wellman 1993). Older infants likewise show signs of having acquired at least the beginnings of a self concept (Harter 1998).

Problems of Interpretation

It is apparent from the foregoing review that infants show a number of behaviors that seem relevant to the development of knowledge about people. As Baldwin & Moses (1994), Moore & Corkum (1994), and others have pointed out, however, there is considerable disagreement in the field as to how richly or generously these behaviors should be interpreted. Do the available findings indicate that infants actually represent people as having inner mental states or do they merely show that infants represent various regularities in people's overt behaviors? Many investigators are relatively generous in their interpretations here, crediting infants with at least some genuine understanding of some mental states, whereas others are more cautious, preferring leaner, less mentalistic explanations of infants' actions (Flavell & Miller 1998). To illustrate the latter stance, several theorists have argued that social behaviors such as joint visual attention, social referencing, and various communicative acts should not be taken as evidence that 1-year-olds have any sort of theory of mind (Butterworth & Jarrett 1991, Moore & Corkum 1994). For example, they argue that behaviors such as showing objects to people and checking to see if the people's eyes orient toward those objects do not warrant the inference that infants are actually aware that people have seeing experiences and mentally attend to objects (see also Perner 1991). Although such behaviors may constitute developmental stepping stones to an eventual awareness of mental states, according to these authors they do not attest to the present existence of any such awareness in the 1-year-old.

It is easy to be sympathetic with such lean interpretations. They seem scientifically parsimonious, and they appeal to familiar, general-purpose learning mechanisms rather than to mysterious inborn sensitivities to mental states or the like. Moreover, a convincing case can be made that infants would not necessarily need to be aware of people's mental states to do many of the social-cognitive things that they do (Perner 1991). For example, they would not actually have to realize that their mother felt afraid of an object in order for them to learn to avoid it in cases of social referencing. They would only have to read her visible expressions of fear as meaning "this object is dangerous," something they could have learned through some conditioning process. That is, the received message could be all about the object rather than about both the object and her inner subjective feelings regarding it. Likewise, infants could respond appropriately in many situations if they could merely predict people's overt behavior from their gaze direction. They would not actually have to be aware that the people are also having perceptual and cognitive experiences as their eyes move about (Moore & Corkum 1994).

On the other hand, a case could be made that we ought not to be overly stingy in our interpretation of infants' behavior in this domain, even when—as is usually the case—a knock-down argument for a rich interpretation cannot be made. If our pet puppy looks as though it is attributing seeing and other mental states to us, we are right to interpret that look stingily, because it is not clear that even adult dogs make such attributions. A similar argument for parsimony may even be made for more humanlike creatures such as chimpanzees (Povinelli & Eddy 1997). In contrast, older human infants who show a similar look are undeniably going to be making genuine mental state attributions in a few short months. Given that fact, it is not unreasonable to suppose that they might be doing some precursor or early version of the same thing now. Indeed, theory theorists, modularity theorists, and simulation theorists have all made the argument that it would be hard to imagine how infants could learn to make mental state attributions later if *wholly* incapable of anything like it earlier. In the case of older children, developmentalists have often argued correctly that subjects who look as though they lack a certain understanding in task situations (e.g. of false belief, of conservation of quantity) may nevertheless "really" possess that understanding, down deep. Real competence often lurks beneath apparent lack of competence, they say. In the present case, in contrast, the parsimoniously inclined are wont to deny genuine social-cognitive understanding to infants who look as though they *possess* it rather than lack it. The present argument, then, is that if infant members of a mind-reading species give us the strong feeling that they are doing some kind of mind reading, they probably are.

A final argument for some charity in interpretation here is that older infants do not do just one or two things suggestive of a mentalistic conception of others. Rather, they do a variety of things, all of which point to the dawning of some such conception (Baldwin & Moses 1994, Tomasello 1995, Wellman 1993): "For example, around this age important developments take place in areas as diverse as pretence . . . , self-recognition . . . , imitation . . . , empathy . . . , and internal state language . . . , suggesting that infants may have already achieved some general conceptual insight into the minds of others" (Baldwin & Moses 1994:150).

It is worth emphasizing, however, that all of us who labor in this area—rich and lean interpreters alike—would happily trade all our arguments for better empirical evidence on the matter. The truth is that we really do not know what infants actually impute to themselves and others in the way of mental states and subjective experiences.

LATER DEVELOPMENTS

A vast literature has accrued since the early 1980s on postinfancy developments in the theory-of-mind domain. What follows is a brief summary of what seems to get acquired and when, organized by type of mental state. Most specific references are omitted in the interests of saving space; for many of the primary sources, see reviews by Astington (1993), Bennett (1993), Flavell & Miller (1998), Forguson (1989), Lewis & Mitchell (1994), Mitchell (1997), Perner (1991), Taylor (1996), and Wellman & Gelman (1998).

Visual Perception

It is clear that by the end of infancy, if not earlier, children have some understanding that people see things. They start using vision-related words like "see" correctly as early as 1.5 to 2 years of age. During the early preschool period, they understand that a person will see an object if and only if the person's eyes are open and aimed in the general direction of the object and if there are no vision-blocking obstacles interposed between the person and the object (Flavell 1992). With this understanding, they are able to do simple, nonegocentric visual perspective-taking; for example, they can infer that you may see something that they do not and vice versa (referred to as Level 1 knowledge about visual perception). Later in the preschool period, they go on to recognize that the same thing may present different visual appearances to two people if they view it from different positions (called Level 2 knowledge about visual perception).

Attention

As already described, infants come to understand that people show by their gaze direction and other actions that they are psychologically connected to various objects and events in the world. In this sense, infants could be said to have at least a rudimentary understanding of attention. In subsequent years, children go on to acquire, in greater or lesser degree, at least the following four facts about attention (Fabricius & Schwanenflugel 1994, Flavell et al 1995a, Pillow 1995). First, attention is selective; people do not attend to everything that is in their field of vision or within earshot. Second, attention entails constructive processing of what has been attended to; different people may mentally represent the same perceptual input differently. Third, attention is limited; people can attend to only a very limited number of things at the same time. Fourth, stimuli can be responded to at different levels of attention or awareness. For example, when a videotaped sleeping person stirs in response to a light touch but does not wake up, older children and adults are inclined to believe that the sleeper "sort of" felt it but did not consciously think that he or she had been touched; in contrast, kindergartners tend not to make this distinction, usually saying that the person would experience the conscious thought as well as the low-level feeling (Flavell et al 1998).

Desires

Children seem to show some awareness of the mental state of desire by the end of infancy; recall the study by Repacholi & Gopnik (1997) cited in the "Developments During Infancy" section. Children also begin to use some desire terms appropriately by age 1.5 to 2 (Bartsch & Wellman 1995). By age 3 they tend to grasp simple causal relations among desires, outcomes, emotions, and actions—suggestive evidence that they are developing something like an implicit theory. That is, they seem to recognize that people will feel good if they get what they want and feel bad if they do not, and they seem to understand that people will quit searching if they find the desired object they have been looking for but keep searching if they do not.

Emotions

The use of emotion-descriptive language begins late in the second year and increases rapidly during the third year (Bretherton & Beeghly 1982, Wellman et al 1995). Words such as *happy, sad, mad,* and *scared* are among the first to appear. Here is a sample of 2-year-olds' sagacity concerning emotions: "Santa will be happy if I pee in the potty" (Bretherton & Beeghly 1982:913). Although we do not know yet whether infants actually impute inner feelings to people who display emotions (see the work on social referencing cited in the "Developments During Infancy" section), it seems certain that young preschoolers "evidence an understanding of emotions as experiential states of persons, as distinguished from the actions (e.g., hitting) and expressions (e.g., smiling) that emotions cause, and they distinguish between the subjective emotional experiences of different individuals" (Wellman et al 1995:118). In subsequent years children come to understand subtler and more complex things about emotions: for example, that people do not always really feel what they appear to feel, that people's emotional reactions to an event may be influenced by earlier emotional experiences to similar events or by their current mood, and that people can experience two conflicting emotions more or less simultaneously (Flavell & Miller 1998).

Intentions

Developing the concept of an intention is highly significant for at least two reasons. First, it clarifies how people differ from other objects; human behavior, unlike that of other objects, is driven by intentions and goals. Second, children must draw on the intentional-unintentional distinction to understand personal responsibility and morality. As mentioned earlier, there is evidence that infants come to construe people as agents, that is, as animate beings that, unlike inanimate objects, can move and behave under their own steam; in addition, we have seen that older infants seem able to recognize what a person is trying to do even if the person does not succeed in doing it (Meltzoff 1995).

Shultz (1991) argues that children elaborate their early, possibly innate, concept of agent into the concept of intentions. The latter goes beyond notions of agency and animacy by positing an internal mental state that guides behavior. People not only *can* act, they deliberately *plan* to and *try* to act. By age 3, children may have some ability to distinguish intended actions from nonintentional behaviors such as reflexes and mistakes (Shultz 1980). For example, when 3-year-olds in Shultz's study tried to repeat a tongue twister (e.g. "She sells sea shells by the sea shore") but made errors, they reported that they did not mean to say the sentence wrong. By age 4 or 5 they are able to distinguish intentions from desires or preferences and from the outcomes of intentional actions (Astington 1993, Astington & Lee 1991, Moses 1993, Schult 1996). For example, unlike 3-year-olds, they recognize that a person who tried to get object A but chanced to obtain the more desirable object B instead nevertheless originally intended to get A rather than B (K Abbott, PP Lee, JH Flavell, unpublished data). Children also come to appreciate psychological causes of behavior other than intentions: emotions, motives, abilities, percepts, knowledge, beliefs, and personality traits. In addition, research by Schult & Wellman (1997) has shown that even 3- and 4-year-old children distinguish appropriately between psychological states (e.g. beliefs and desires), biological processes (e.g. reflexes), and physical forces (e.g. gravity) as possible causes of human actions and movements.

Beliefs and Related Mental Representations

There have been a great many investigations of children's developing understanding of "serious" mental representations, that is, nonpretense mental states meant by their owners to portray reality accurately (Flavell & Miller 1998). The majority of these have dealt with children's comprehension of representations that differ from person to person or differ from reality. Principal examples are studies dealing with the appearance-reality distinction (perceptual appearance versus reality), Level 2 knowledge of visual perception (perceptual appearance of something from one position versus another), interpretation and constructive processing, deception, and, most studied of all, false belief. Recall from the Introduction that 3-year-olds tend to fail false-belief tests and that 4- and 5-year-olds tend to pass them; the same is true for tests of Level 2 knowledge of visual perception.

Similar developmental trends are usually seen when children's ability to think about the appearance-reality is assessed—another case in which an erroneous mental impression is pitted against a known reality. For example, after pretraining on the appearance-reality distinction and associated terminology, subjects may be presented with a sponge made to look like a rock or a little object that looks big when viewed through a magnifying glass (Flavell et al 1986). After discovering each object's true identity or property, subjects are asked how the object currently appears to their eyes (rock; big) and how or what it really and truly is (sponge; little). The usual finding is that 3-year-olds tend to give the same answer to both questions, reporting either the appearance twice or the reality twice, as though they do not distinguish conceptually between the misleading perceptual appearance and the underlying reality. In contrast, children of age 4 and older typically show some command of the distinction. As just noted, the distinction between perceptual appearance and reality is conceptually very similar both to the distinction between false belief and reality and to the Level 2 distinction between two different perceptual appearances resulting from different observer perspectives. Consistent with this fact, there is some correlational evidence that these distinctions tend to develop together; that is, young children who perform well (or poorly) on appearance-reality tasks also tend to perform well (or poorly) on false-belief tasks, Level 2 visual perspective-taking tasks, and other conceptually related measures (Flavell & Miller 1998, Taylor & Carlson 1997; but see Slaughter & Gopnik 1996). However, exactly what false-belief and appearance-reality tests measure remains the subject of considerable controversy; some researchers (including me) believe they measure the child's developing understanding of mental representation, albeit imperfectly, but others disagree.

Finally, children's knowledge about mental representations clearly continues to increase after the age of 4. In particular, not until middle childhood and later do children appear to gain any appreciable understanding of the mind as an interpretive, constructive processor (Carpendale & Chandler 1996, Fabricius & Schwanenflugel 1994, Pillow 1995, Taylor 1988, Wellman & Hickling 1994). For example, recognizing that the way people interpret an ambiguous event may be influenced by their preexisting biases or expectations seems to be a middle-childhood rather than an early childhood insight (Pillow & Henrichon 1996).

Knowledge

By the end of the preschool period, children appear to have acquired some important truths about the mental state of knowing (Flavell & Miller 1998, Montgomery 1992, Perner 1991, Taylor 1996). They realize that the word *know* expresses more speaker certainty than *think* or *guess* and is a surer guide to the true state of affairs. Unlike young preschoolers, young elementary school children are good at knowing how and when they came to know some recently acquired fact, for example, by witnessing it firsthand rather than by hearing about it from someone else. Although young preschoolers may have some minimal understanding of knowing (O'Neill 1996), in general they seem to have only a hazy conception of what it means for someone to know something and about how knowledge is acquired (Taylor 1996). Surprisingly, even 4- and 5-year-olds will blithely claim that they have always known information that they have just learned during the experimental session (Taylor et al 1994). In the late preschool and middle-childhood periods, children discover that to acquire knowledge through exposure to perceptual information, that information has to be adequate as well as merely present. In contrast to younger children, for example, they realize that one cannot know an object's color merely by feeling the object, that one often cannot be certain of an object's identity when only a little bit of it is visible, and—as mentioned in the previous paragraph—that one's interpretation of an impoverished or ambiguous perceptual input may be influenced by one's biases or expectations.

Pretense

The development of pretend-play skills during early childhood has been studied for many years. Only recently, however, has it been viewed as part of the development of children's knowledge about the mind, thanks largely to an important analysis by Leslie (1987). According to Leslie (1987, 1994), the maturation of a modular theory-of-mind mechanism, $ToMM_2$ (see the "Theories of Development" section), permits the 18- to 24-month-old to engage in pretend play and to understand as pretense the pretend actions of others. This *metarepresentational* capacity, as Leslie calls it, prevents the child from being confused when, for example, someone pretends that a banana is a telephone. It does so by *decoupling,* or quarantining off cognitively, the temporary pretend identity of the banana (telephone) from its permanent real identity (banana). The child can then compute the relation: "This person is pretending that this banana is a telephone." Leslie's idea that the ability to understand pretense and the ability to understand false-belief and other mental states are mediated by a common, early maturing metarepresentational or theory-of-mind mechanism is certainly plausible on its face. "Pretending that" and "believing that" are both propositional attitudes. Moreover, both are understood by adults as being mental representations or construals of something as being a certain way—either for real (belief) or just temporarily, for play purposes (pretense). Nevertheless, Leslie's claim is currently very controversial, and there are arguments and evidence both for it and against it.

One argument against this claim is the roughly two-year age gap between children's comprehension of pretense and their comprehension of false-belief, deception, appearance-reality, and Level 2 perceptual perspectives. If understanding of pretense and understanding of false belief are both mediated by Leslie's ToMM$_2$, then why does the former appear so much earlier in childhood than the latter? Although Leslie and others have argued that performance obstacles explain the late display of false-belief understanding on standard tests, it is hard for most of us to believe that 2-year-olds really do understand false belief.

Another possible problem is that 2-year-olds and even older children may lack a fully mentalistic conception of pretense as well as belief (Harris 1994; Lillard 1996, 1998c; Perner 1991). Lillard has provided some striking experimental support for this possibility. One of her methods (Lillard 1993) was to present children with, for example, a doll named Moe who knows nothing at all about rabbits but chances to be hopping like one. The children were then asked if Moe was or was not pretending to be a rabbit. The majority of the 4-year-olds and even many 5-year-olds claimed that Moe was indeed pretending to be a rabbit, despite their having agreed that he did not know how rabbits hop. She has further demonstrated (Lillard 1996) that many children of this age classify pretense with physical activities, such as clapping one's hands, rather than with mental activities, such as thinking. By the age of 7 or 8 most children responded like adult subjects to such tasks, insisting that pretense actions were necessarily generated by pretense mentation. However, other studies (e.g. Custer 1996, Hickling et al 1997) suggest that preschoolers might have a more mentalistic conception of pretense than Lillard's tasks give them credit for. Perhaps these studies are assessing a more rudimentary understanding of pretense than Lillard has been tapping (Lillard 1998c). Finally, research has been done on the related topic of children's developing understanding of the imagination and dreams (for a review of this interesting work, see Woolley 1995).

Thinking

Evidence indicates that children acquire some important elementary knowledge and skills concerning thinking during the early preschool years (see Flavell et al 1995b for a summary). First, preschoolers seem to know that thinking is an activity that only people and perhaps some other animates engage in. Second, preschoolers also realize that mental entities like thoughts and images are internal, in-the-head affairs, not to be confused with physical actions or other external objects and events, and they regard the mind and the brain as necessary for mental actions. Third, they realize that like desires and other mental entities, thinking has content and makes reference, and that thoughts can take as their objects nonpresent and even nonreal things. Thus, preschoolers understand some of the most basic and important facts about thinking: namely, that it is an internal human activity that refers to or represents real or imaginary things. Finally, they have some ability to infer the presence of thinking in another person provided that the cues are very strong and clear, and they also can differentiate thinking from other activities in such situations.

However, preschoolers clearly lack other important knowledge and skills concerning thinking. They tend to be poor at determining when a person (self or other) is thinking and also what the person is and is not thinking about. As to when, they greatly underestimate the amount of mental activity that goes on in people. They do not realize that people are continually experiencing mental content of one kind or other spontaneously in an ever-flowing stream of consciousness. For example, unlike older subjects, preschoolers do not consistently attribute any mental activity at all to a person who just sits quietly, "waiting." Even more surprising, they do not automatically assume that something must be "going on in a person's mind" or that the person's mind must be "doing something," even when they know that the person is looking at or listening to something, reading, or talking to another person—activities that adults would regard as necessarily involving some cognition. As to what, on those occasions when preschoolers do assert that a person is thinking, they are often surprisingly poor at inferring what the person is and is not thinking about, even when the evidence is very clear.

These same difficulties are equally evident when preschoolers are asked to report their own mental activity rather than another person's. That is, they tend to be very poor at recalling or reconstructing both the fact and the content of their own recent or present thinking, even in situations especially designed to make such introspection extremely easy (Flavell et al 1995b, but see Estes 1998 for an exception). Similarly, they seem largely unaware of their own ongoing inner speech and may not even know that speech *can* be covert (Flavell et al 1997). Finally, there is evidence (Flavell et al 1998) that younger children are more inclined than older children and adults to attribute self-awareness and decision-making abilities to an unconscious person ("sound asleep and not dreaming"). In one study, for instance, the percentage of 5-year-olds, 7-year-olds, 8-year-olds, and adults claiming that people know they are asleep while they are deeply asleep and not dreaming were 61%, 39%, 28%, and 11%, respectively. These and other findings suggest that young children do not have a clear idea of what it is like, experientially, to be conscious as opposed to unconscious. In particular, they tend to attribute too little ongoing ideation to a conscious person (they are unaware of the stream of consciousness in people who are awake) and too much to an unconscious one (they attribute self-awareness to people who are unconscious).

DIFFERENCES IN DEVELOPMENT

Intracultural Differences

Considerable research attention is currently being paid to three kinds of differences in development: intracultural, intercultural, and interspecies (Flavell & Miller 1998). Studies of intracultural differences in development have identified social experiences that appear to foster theory-of-mind development (Bartsch & Estes 1996). For example, Jenkins & Astington (1996) and Perner et al (1994) have shown that preschoolers who have more siblings to interact with perform better on false-belief tasks than those who have fewer or none. Similarly, deaf children whose hearing parents are not fluent in sign language (as most are not) perform much more poorly on a false-belief test than deaf children of fluent-signing deaf parents (Peterson & Siegal 1997; see also deVilliers et al 1997). These studies suggest the importance of social-communicative experiences for theory-of-mind development. The most striking intracultural differences, however, are seen in the pronounced deficits in theory-of-mind development of autistic children and adults (Baron-Cohen et al 1993). The extent to which these tragic deficits can be reduced or compensated for by training is currently under investigation (S Baron-Cohen, H Wellman, JC Gomez, J Swettenham, E Toye, unpublished research).

What about intracultural differences among unimpaired individuals? Dweck and co-workers have identified some intriguing ones (Dweck et al 1995). Needless to say, they do not find some normal adults who have a concept of false belief and others who lack it—nothing akin to normal-autistic differences. However, they do find important individual differences in people's implicit theories about human attributes. For example, some people think of intelligence as a fixed, uncontrollable trait or entity (*entity theory*), and others think of it as a malleable, controllable quality that can be improved with effort and training (*incremental theory*). Moreover, these differences in people's naive theory of intelligence have important consequences for their achievement motivation and intellectual performance. A perusal of textbooks in the fields of personality, social psychology, and social cognition would reveal many other ways that normal adults have been shown to differ from one another in their naive theories and knowledge regarding themselves and other people. And of course psychologists and other scientists have espoused widely different conceptions of human cognition and personality over the years.

Intercultural Differences

The question of intercultural similarities and differences in this area is a fascinating one about which we still have little solid information. How universal are the developments described in this chapter? An important review of the existing evidence—mostly from ethnographic studies—suggests that there are important differences among cultures in adult theories of mind (Lillard 1998a; see also critiques of this review by Gauvain 1998 and Wellman 1998, and Lillard's 1998b reply). Important similarities also appear to exist across cultures and languages in theory-of-mind development (Avis & Harris 1991; T Tardif, H Wellman, unpublished research).

Interspecies Differences

Similarly unsettled is the question of whether, or to what extent, other primates possess theory-of-mind knowledge and abilities. Observations such as the following suggest that chimpanzees may possess some (Byrne & Whiten 1988): Chimp A observed Chimp B acting as though no food were available at a feeding hopper, although there really was food there. Then Chimp A appeared to depart but actually hid behind a nearby tree and watched until Chimp B took the food, whereupon Chimp A emerged from hiding and snatched it from him! Although such observations may seem persuasive, most recent experimental work with chimps suggests that they may actually be less knowledgeable about the mental world than we had thought previously (Povinelli & Eddy 1996, Tomasello 1997). For example, Povinelli & Eddy (1996) have evidence suggesting that chimps may have a behavioristic rather than mentalistic conception of seeing. Although they follow a person's gaze, they do not seem to understand that the person sees and knows about things as a consequence of directing his or her gaze at them.

CONCLUSIONS

We have learned a great deal about the development of children's knowledge about the mental world, especially since the advent of theory-of-mind-development research some 15 years ago. What will the next 15 years bring? The following are some guesses (see also Flavell & Miller 1998:882–87). The present intense study of infant theory-of-mind competencies will continue, with major breakthroughs awaiting the discovery of better methods for peering into the infant mind. At the other end of ontogenesis, researchers will inquire into the limitations as well as the strengths of adult people-reading and will try to explain why seemingly knowledgeable adults sometimes reason so poorly in this domain (Ross & Ward 1996). This inquiry will inform, and be informed by, further study of intracultural and intercultural differences in adult theory-of-mind competencies. And what researchers learn about the determinants of intracultural differences in development should, in turn, suggest ways of helping children who need such help to acquire socially and academically useful competencies in this area (Flavell 1997). Finally, progress will be made in identifying the neural bases of mentalistic thinking, and this finding may lead to a better understanding of normal and abnormal (especially autistic) development in this important area (Fletcher et al 1995).

> **Visit the *Annual Reviews home page* at**
> **http://www.AnnualReviews.org.**

Literature Cited

Anisfeld M. 1991. Neonatal imitation. *Dev. Rev.* 11:60–97

Astington JW. 1993. *The Child's Discovery of the Mind*. Cambridge, MA: Harvard Univ. Press

Astington JW, Lee E. 1991. *What do children know about intentional causation?* Presented at Meet. Soc. Res. Child Dev., Seattle

Avis J, Harris PL. 1991. Belief-desire reasoning among Baka children: evidence for a universal conception of mind. *Child Dev.* 62:460–67

Baldwin DA. 1991. Infants' contribution to the achievement of joint reference. *Child Dev.* 62:875–90

Baldwin DA. 1993. Early referential understanding: Infants' ability to recognize referential acts for what they are. *Dev. Psychol.* 29:832–43

Baldwin DA, Moses LJ. 1994. Early understanding of referential intent and attentional focus: evidence from language and emotion. See Lewis & Mitchell 1994, pp. 133–56

Baron-Cohen S. 1995. *Mindblindness: An Essay on Autism and Theory of Mind*. Cambridge, MA: MIT Press

Baron-Cohen S, Tager-Flusberg H, Cohen DJ. 1993. *Understanding Other Minds: Perspectives from Autism*. Oxford: Oxford Univ. Press

Bartsch K, Estes D. 1996. Individual differences in children's developing theory of mind and implications for metacognition. *Learn. Individ. Differ.* 8:281–304

Bartsch K, Wellman HM. 1995. *Children Talk About the Mind*. New York: Oxford Univ. Press

Bates E. 1976. *Language and Context: The Acquisition of Pragmatics*. New York: Academic

Bennett M, ed. 1993. *The Development of Social Cognition: The Child as Psychologist*. New York: Guilford

Bretherton L, Beeghly M. 1982. Talking about internal states: the acquisition of an explicit theory of mind. *Dev. Psychol.* 18:906–21

Butterworth G, Jarrett N. 1991. What minds have in common is space: spatial mechanisms serving joint visual attention in infancy. *Br. J. Dev. Psychol.* 9:55–72

Byrne RW, Whiten A. 1988. Toward the next generation in data quality: a new survey of primate tactical deception. *Behav. Brain Sci.* 11:267–83

Carlson SM, Moses LJ, Hix HR. 1998. The role of inhibitory processes in young children's difficulties with deception and false belief. *Child Dev.* In press

Carpendale JI, Chandler MJ. 1996. On the distinction between false belief understanding and subscribing to an interpretive theory of mind. *Child Dev.* 67:1686–706

Carruthers P, Smith PK, eds. 1996. *Theories of Theories of Mind*. Cambridge, UK: Cambridge Univ. Press

Cooper RP, Aslin RN. 1989. The language environment of the young infant: implications for early perceptual development. *Can. J. Psychol.* 43:247–65

Custer WL. 1996. A comparison of young children's understanding of contradictory representations in pretense, memory, and belief. *Child Dev.* 67:678–88

deVilliers PA, Hosler B, Miller K, Whalen M, Wong J. 1997. *Language, theory of mind, and reading other people's emotions: a study of oral deaf children*. Presented at Meet. Soc. Res. Child Dev., Washington, DC

Dunn J. 1988. *The Beginnings of Social Understanding*. Oxford: Blackwell

Dweck CS, Chiu CY, Hong YY. 1995. Implicit theories and their role in judgments and reactions: a world from two perspectives. *Psychol. Inq.* 6:267–85

Estes D. 1998. Young children's understanding of their mental activity: the case of mental rotation. *Child Dev.* In press

Fabricius WV, Schwanenflugel PJ. 1994. The older child's theory of mind. In *Intelligence, Mind, and Reasoning: Structure and Development*, ed. A Demetriou, A Efklides, pp. 111–32. Amsterdam: Elsevier

Flavell JH. 1992. Perspectives on perspective taking. In *Piaget's Theory: Prospects and Possibilities*, ed. H Beilin, P Pufall, pp. 107–39. Hillsdale, NJ: Erlbaum

Flavell JH. 1997. *Recent convergences between metacognitive and theory-of-mind research in children.* Presented at Meet. Soc. Res. Child Dev., Washington, DC

Flavell JH, Green FL, Flavell ER. 1986. Development of knowledge about the appearance-reality distinction. *Monogr. Soc. Res. Child Dev.* 51(1, Ser. 212)

Flavell JH, Green FL, Flavell ER. 1995a. The development of children's knowledge about attentional focus. *Dev. Psychol.* 31: 706–12

Flavell JH, Green FL, Flavell ER. 1995b. Young children's knowledge about thinking. *Monogr. Soc. Res. Child Dev.* 60(1, Ser. 243)

Flavell JH, Green FL, Flavell ER, Grossman JB. 1997. The development of children's knowledge about inner speech. *Child Dev.* 68:39–47

Flavell JH, Green FL, Flavell ER, Lin NT. 1998. Development of children's knowledge about unconsciousness. *Child Dev.* In press.

Flavell JH, Miller PH. 1998. Social cognition. See Kuhn & Siegler 1998, pp. 851–98

Flavell JH, Miller PH, Miller SA. 1993. *Cognitive Development.* Englewood Cliffs, NJ: Prentice-Hall. 3rd ed.

Fletcher PC, Happé F, Frith U, Baker SC, Dolan RJ, et al. 1995. Other minds in the brain: a functional imaging study of "theory of mind" in story comprehension. *Cognition* 57:109–28

Fodor J. 1992. A theory of the child's theory of mind. *Cognition* 44:283–96

Forguson L. 1989. *Common Sense.* London: Routledge

Gauvain M. 1998. Culture, development, and theory of mind: comment on Lillard. *Psychol. Bull.* 123:37–42

Golinkoff RM. 1983. Infant social cognition: self, people and objects. In *Piaget and the Foundations of Knowledge*, ed. LS Liben, pp. 179–200. Hillsdale, NJ: Erlbaum

Gopnik A, Astington JW. 1988. Children's understanding of representational change and its relation to the understanding of false belief and the appearance-reality distinction. *Child Dev.* 59:26–37

Gopnik A, Meltzoff AN. 1997. *Words, Thoughts, and Theories.* Cambridge, MA: MIT Press

Gopnik A, Wellman HM. 1994. The 'theory' theory. In *Mapping the Mind: Domain Specificity in Cognition and Culture*, ed. LA Hirschfeld, SA Gelman, pp. 257–93. Cambridge, UK: Cambridge Univ. Press

Harris PL. 1991. The work of the imagination. See Whiten 1991, pp. 283–304

Harris PL. 1992. From simulation to folk psychology: the case for development. *Mind Lang.* 7:120–44

Harris PL. 1994. Understanding pretense. See Lewis & Mitchell 1994, pp. 235–60

Harter S. 1998. The development of self-representations. In *Handbook of Child Psychology*, Vol. 3: *Social, Emotional, and Personality Development*, ed. N Eisenberg (Ser. ed. W Damon), pp. 553–617. New York: Wiley. 5th ed.

Hickling AK, Wellman HM, Gottfried GM. 1997. Preschoolers' understanding of others' mental attitudes toward pretense. *Br. J. Dev. Psychol.* 15:339–54

Hornik R, Risenhoover N, Gunnar M. 1987. The effects of maternal positive, neutral, and negative affective communications on infant responses to new toys. *Child Dev.* 58:937–44

Jenkins JM, Astington JW. 1996. Cognitive factors and family structure associated with theory of mind development in young children. *Dev. Psychol.* 32:70–78

Kuhl PK. 1987. Perception of speech and sound in early infancy. In *Handbook of Infant Perception*, Vol. 2: *From Perception to Cognition*, ed. P Salapatek, L Cohen, pp. 275–382. Orlando, FL: Academic

Kuhn D, Siegler RS, eds. 1998. *Handbook of Child Psychology*, Vol. 2: *Cognition, Perception, and Language* (Ser. ed. W Damon), New York: Wiley. 5th ed.

Legerstee M. 1991. The role of person and object in eliciting early imitation. *J. Exp. Child Psychol.* 51:423–33

Legerstee M. 1992. A review of the animate-inanimate distinction in infancy: implications for models of social and cognitive knowing. *Early Dev. Parent.* 1:59–67

Leslie AM. 1987. Pretense and representation: the origins of "theory of mind." *Psychol. Rev.* 94:412–26

Leslie A. 1994. ToMM, ToBY and agency: core architecture and domain specificity. In *Mapping the Mind: Domain Specificity in Cognition and Culture*, ed. LA Hirschfeld, SA Gelman, pp. 119–48. Cambridge, UK: Cambridge Univ. Press

Leslie A, Roth D. 1993. What autism teaches us about metarepresentation. In *Under-*

standing *Other Minds: Perspectives from Autism*, ed. S Baron-Cohen, H Tager-Flusberg, DJ Cohen, pp. 83–111. Oxford: Oxford Univ. Press

Lewis C, Mitchell P, eds. 1994. *Children's Early Understanding of Mind: Origins and Development.* Hillsdale, NJ: Erlbaum

Lillard AS. 1993. Young children's conceptualization of pretense: action or mental representational state? *Child Dev.* 64: 372–86

Lillard AS. 1996. Body or mind: children's categorization of pretense. *Child Dev.* 67: 1717–34

Lillard AS. 1998a. Ethnopsychologies: cultural variations in theories of mind. *Psychol. Bull.* 123:3–32

Lillard AS. 1998b. Ethnopsychologies: reply to Gauvain and Wellman. *Psychol. Bull.* 123:43–46

Lillard AS. 1998c. Wanting to be it: children's understanding of intentions underlying pretense. *Child Dev.* In press

Meltzoff AN. 1990. Foundations for developing a concept of self: the role of imitation in relating self to other and the value of social mirroring, social modeling, and self-practice in infancy. In *The Self in Transition: Infancy to Childhood*, ed. D Cicchetti, M Beeghly, pp. 139–63. Chicago: Univ. Chicago Press

Meltzoff AN. 1995. Understanding the intentions of others: re-enactment of intended acts by 18-month-old children. *Dev. Psychol.* 31:838–50

Meltzoff AN, Moore MK. 1994. Imitation, memory, and the representation of persons. *Infant Behav. Dev.* 17:83–89

Mitchell P. 1994. Realism and early conception of mind: a synthesis of phylogenetic and ontogenetic issues. See Lewis & Mitchell 1994, pp. 19–45

Mitchell P. 1997. *Introduction to Theory of Mind: Children, Autism and Apes.* London: Arnold

Montgomery DE. 1992. Young children's theory of knowing: the development of a folk epistemology. *Dev. Rev.* 12:410–30

Moore C. 1996. Theories of mind in infancy. *Br. J. Dev. Psychol.* 14:19–40

Moore C, Corkum V. 1994. Social understanding at the end of the first year of life. *Dev. Rev.* 14:349–72

Moses LJ. 1993. Young children's understanding of belief constraints on intention. *Cogn. Dev.* 8:1–25

Mumme DL, Won D, Fernald A. 1994. *Do one-year-old infants show referent specific responding to emotional signals?* Presented at Meet. Int. Conf. Infant Stud., Paris

Nelson CA. 1987. The recognition of facial expressions in the first two years of life: mechanisms of development. *Child Dev.* 58:889–909

O'Neill DK. 1996. Two-year-olds' sensitivity to a parent's knowledge state when making requests. *Child Dev.* 67:659–77

Perner J. 1991. *Understanding the Representational Mind.* Cambridge, MA: MIT Press

Perner J, Leekam SR, Wimmer H. 1987. Three-year-olds' difficulty with false belief: the case for a conceptual deficit. *Br. J. Dev. Psychol.* 5:125–37

Perner J, Ruffman T, Leekam SR. 1994. Theory of mind is contagious: you catch it from your sibs. *Child Dev.* 65:1228–38

Peterson CC, Siegal M. 1997. Psychological, physical, and biological thinking in normal, autistic, and deaf children. In *The Emergence of Core Domains of Thought: Children's Reasoning About Physical, Psychological, and Biological Phenomena* (*New Directions for Child Development*, No. 75), ed. HM Wellman, K Inagaki, pp. 55–70. San Francisco: Jossey-Bass

Piaget J. 1985. *The Equilibration of Cognitive Structure.* Chicago: Univ. Chicago Press

Pillow BH. 1995. Two trends in the development of conceptual perspective-taking: an elaboration of the passive-active hypothesis. *Int. J. Behav. Dev.* 18:649–76

Pillow BH, Henrichon AJ. 1996. There's more to the picture than meets the eye: young children's difficulty understanding biased interpretation. *Child Dev.* 67:802–19

Poulin-Dubois D, Shultz TR. 1988. The development of the understanding of human behavior: from agency to intentionality. In *Developing Theories of Mind*, ed. JW Astington, PL Harris, DR Olson, pp. 109–25. Cambridge, UK: Cambridge Univ. Press

Povinelli DJ, Eddy TJ. 1996. What young chimpanzees know about seeing. *Monogr. Soc. Res. Child Dev.* 61(2, Ser. 247)

Povinelli DJ, Eddy TJ. 1997. Specificity of gaze-following in young chimpanzees. *Br. J. Dev. Psychol.* 15:213–22

Repacholi BM, Gopnik A. 1997. Early reasoning about desires: evidence from 14- and 18-month-olds. *Dev. Psychol.* 33:12–21

Ross L, Ward A. 1996. Naive realism in everyday life: implications for social conflict and misunderstanding. In *Values and Knowledge*, ed. T Brown, E Reed, E Turiel, pp. 103–35. Hillsdale, NJ: Erlbaum

Schult CA. 1996. *Intended actions and intentional states: young children's understanding of the causes of human actions.* PhD thesis. Univ. Mich., Ann Arbor. 142 pp.

Schult CA, Wellman HM. 1997. Explaining human movements and actions: children's understanding of the limits of psychological explanation. *Cognition* 62:291–324

Shantz CU. 1983. Social cognition. In *Handbook of Child Psychology*, Vol. 3: *Cognitive Development*, ed. JH Flavell, EM Markman (Ser. ed. PH Mussen), pp. 495–555. New York: Wiley. 4th ed.

Shultz TR. 1980. Development of the concept of intention. In *Minnesota Symposia on Child Psychology*, Vol. 13: *Development of Cognition, Affect, and Social Relations*, ed. WA Collins, pp. 131–64. Hillsdale, NJ: Erlbaum

Shultz TR. 1991. From agency to intention: a rule-based, computational approach. See Whiten 1991, pp. 79–95

Slaughter V, Gopnik A. 1996. Conceptual coherence in the child's theory of mind: training children to understand belief. *Child Dev.* 67:2967–88

Spelke ES, Phillips A, Woodward AL. 1995. Infant's knowledge of object motion and human action. In *Causal Cognition: A Multidisciplinary Debate*, ed. D Sperber, D Premack, AJ Premack, pp. 44–78. Oxford: Clarendon

Taylor M. 1988. The development of children's ability to distinguish what they know from what they see. *Child Dev.* 59: 703–18

Taylor M. 1996. A theory of mind perspective on social cognitive development. In *Handbook of Perception and Cognition*, Vol. 13: *Perceptual and Cognitive Development*, ed. R Gelman, T Au (Gen. ed. EC Carterette, MP Friedman), pp. 282–329. New York: Academic

Taylor M, Carlson SM. 1997. The relation between individual differences in fantasy and theory of mind. *Child Dev.* 68:436–55

Taylor M, Esbensen BM, Bennett RT. 1994. Children's understanding of knowledge acquisition: the tendency for children to report they have always known what they have just learned. *Child Dev.* 65:1581–604

Tomasello M. 1995. Joint attention as social cognition. In *Joint Attention: Its Origins and Role in Development*, ed. C Moore, P Durham, pp. 103–30. Hillsdale, NJ: Erlbaum

Tomasello M. 1997. *Primate Cognition.* New York: Oxford Univ. Press

Wellman HM. 1993. Early understanding of mind: the normal case. In *Perspectives from Autism*, ed. S Baron-Cohen, H Tager-Flusberg, D Cohen, pp. 10–39. Oxford: Oxford Univ. Press

Wellman HM. 1998. Culture, variation, and levels of analysis in our folk psychologies. *Psychol. Bull.* 123:33–36

Wellman HM, Gelman SA. 1992. Cognitive development: foundational theories of core domains. *Annu. Rev. Psychol.* 43: 337–75

Wellman HM, Gelman SA. 1998. Knowledge acquisition in foundation domains. See Kuhn & Siegler 1998, pp. 523–73

Wellman HM, Harris PL, Banerjee M, Sinclair A. 1995. Early understanding of emotion: evidence from natural language. *Cogn. Emot.* 9:117–49

Wellman HM, Hickling AK. 1994. The mind's "I": Children's conception of the mind as an active agent. *Child Dev.* 65:1564–80

Whiten A, ed. 1991. *Natural Theories of Mind: Evolution, Development, and Simulation of Everyday Mindreading.* Oxford: Blackwell

Woodward AL, Markman EM. 1998. Early word learning. See Kuhn & Siegler 1998, pp. 371–420

Woolley JD. 1995. The fictional mind: young children's understanding of imagination, pretense, and dreams. *Dev. Rev.* 15: 172–211

Zahn-Waxler C, Radke-Yarrow M, Wagner E, Chapman M. 1992. Development of concern for others. *Dev. Psychol.* 28:126–36

Annu. Rev. Psychol. 1999. 50:47–77

CONFLICT IN MARRIAGE:
Implications for Working with Couples

Frank D. Fincham

PO Box 901, Cardiff CF1 3YG, Great Britain; e-mail: fincham@cf.ac.uk

Steven R. H. Beach

Psychology Department, University of Georgia, Athens, Georgia 30602;
e-mail: sbeach@egon.psy.uga.edu

KEY WORDS: marriage, family, divorce, couple therapy, prevention

ABSTRACT

The investigation of marital conflict has reached a crossroads. Over 25 years of research on marital conflict behavior yields a relatively clear picture of its topography, but its relevance for changing the marital relationship remains controversial. We can continue to amass observations in a relatively atheoretical manner and hope that patterns capable of guiding clinical activity will emerge, or we can begin creating a unified theoretical framework to indicate new directions for clinical activity and empirical investigation. Before exploring the latter option, this chapter reviews briefly the impact of marital conflict on mental, physical, and family health and what is known about the nature of conflict in marriage. After highlighting some recent theoretically grounded advances, we illustrate how conceptualizing marital conflict behavior as goal directed provides an integrative theoretical framework for treatment, prevention, and marital conflict research.

CONTENTS

47

0084-6570/99/0201-0047$08.00

STARTING POINT

Systematic research on marriage in psychology emerged largely in response to the desire to better assist couples experiencing marital distress. The investigation of conflictual interaction has a privileged status in this research, as it has been widely accepted that "distress results from couples' aversive and ineffectual response to conflict" (Koerner & Jacobson 1994, p. 208) that is potentially amenable to change. This chapter therefore begins by discussing the importance of conflict for the mental and physical health of spouses and their children. We then briefly examine the nature of conflict in marriage and the impact of negative conflict behavior on change in the marital relationship. This examination emphasizes the need for conceptual development. After highlighting some recent theoretically grounded advances, we re-examine the nature of conflict and identify the study of goal-directed behavior as an important vehicle for advancing an understanding of marriage. We then illustrate how a goal perspective provides a unifying framework for treatment and prevention of, and research on, marital conflict.

WHY IS MARITAL CONFLICT IMPORTANT?

Evidence documenting the importance of marital conflict for understanding mental, physical, and family health continues to accumulate.

Mental Health

Previous *Annual Review* chapters argued that marital conflict has profound implications for individual well-being (Coyne & Downey 1991, O'Leary &

Smith 1991). The link with depression is increasingly well established (see Beach et al 1998), and a link with eating disorders has been documented (see Van den Broucke et al 1997). Similarly, associations have been noted for physical and psychological abuse of partners (e.g. O'Leary et al 1994), male alcoholism (e.g. O'Farrell et al 1991), and early onset drinking, episodic drinking, binge drinking, and out-of-home drinking (see Murphy & O'Farrell 1994). Marital conflict appears less consequential for anxiety disorders (Emmelkamp & Gerlsma 1994), which may reflect a complex association varying according to spouse gender and type of anxiety disorder (McLeod 1994). Increased research on psychopathology and marital functioning has given rise to recent reviews of this area (e.g. Davila & Bradbury 1998, Halford & Bouma 1997).

Physical Health

Although married individuals are healthier on average than the unmarried (House et al 1988), marital conflict is associated with poorer health (Burman & Margolin 1992, Kiecolt-Glaser et al 1988) and with specific illnesses such as cancer, cardiac disease, and chronic pain (see Schmaling & Sher 1997). Marital interaction studies suggest possible mechanisms that may account for these links by showing that hostile behaviors during conflict relate to alterations in immunological (Kiecolt-Glaser et al 1993, 1997), endocrine (Kiecolt-Glaser et al 1997, Malarkey et al 1994), and cardiovascular (Ewarts et al 1991) functioning. Although consequential for both husbands and wives, marital conflict has more pronounced health consequences for wives (Gottman & Levenson 1992; Kiecolt-Glaser et al 1993, 1996, 1997; Malarkey et al 1994). Thus, marital conflict has been linked to several facets of health and remains a vital area of research.

Family Health

Marital conflict is also associated with important family outcomes, including poorer parenting (see Erel & Burman 1995), poorer child adjustment (see Grych & Fincham 1990), problematic attachment to parents (e.g. Owen & Cox 1997), increased likelihood of parent-child conflict (e.g. Margolin et al 1996), and conflict between siblings (e.g. Brody et al 1994). When manipulated experimentally, it increases subsequent parent-son conflict (Jouriles & Farris 1992). Aspects of marital conflict that have a particularly negative influence on children include more frequent, intense, physical, unresolved, child-related conflicts and conflicts attributed to the child's behavior (see Cummings & Davies 1994, Fincham & Osborne 1993). Increasing attention is being given to mechanisms linking marital conflict and child outcomes, the impact of children on the marriage, and viewing the impact of marital conflict within a broader systemic perspective (see Cox & Paley 1997, Fincham 1998).

THE TOPOGRAPHY OF MARITAL CONFLICT: A SYNOPSIS

The presumed role of conflict in generating marital distress led to research on the topography of marital conflict. Identification of conflict responses was assumed to provide guidance for marital intervention. A selective overview of findings highlights the current state of the field.

Are There Observable Patterns in Marital Conflict?

In the first *Annual Review of Psychology* chapter on marital interaction, O'Leary & Smith (1991) noted that distressed couples emit more negative-statements and fewer positive statements and show greater reciprocation of negative behaviors during problem-solving interactions. Indeed, level of negative affect reciprocity is more consistent across different types of situations than is amount of negative or positive affect (Gottman 1979). With regard to behavioral sequences, escalating, negative sequences during conflict are associated with marital distress, and both frequency and sequences of negative behavior are more pronounced in couples where physical aggression is found (e.g. Burman et al 1992, Gottman 1994). In fact, one of the greatest challenges for couples locked into negative exchanges is to find an adaptive way of exiting from such cycles (Weiss & Heyman 1997). This is usually attempted through responses designed to repair the interaction (e.g. metacommunication, "You're not listening to me") that are typically delivered with negative affect (e.g. irritation, sadness). Distressed couples tend to respond to the negative affect, thereby continuing the cycle. This makes their interactions more structured and predictable. In contrast, nondistressed couples appear to be more responsive to the repair attempt and are thereby able to exit from negative exchanges early on. Their interaction sequences appear more random and less predictable (Weiss & Heyman 1997).

An interaction pattern in which the wife raises issues and the husband withdraws has often been noted by clinicians and has received empirical confirmation. For example, Roberts & Krokoff (1990) found dissatisfied couples displayed more husband withdraw–wife hostility sequences, whereas satisfied couples displayed more husband withdraw–wife withdraw sequences. However, it appears that demand-withdraw patterns and the use of other influence tactics vary as a function of whose issue is being discussed during conflict (Heavey et al 1993, Sagrestano et al 1998).

How frequent and stable is marital conflict? McGonagle et al (1992) collected data from a community sample about the frequency of overt disagreements and found a modal response of once or twice a month. A subsample that kept diaries reported similar rates, and when contacted three years later, reported the same rate of disagreement. These findings are consistent with a broader literature indicating that patterns of coping tend to be stable across occasions (Stone & Neale 1984). Noller et al (1994) found that conflict patterns were stable over the first two years of marriage but that couples lower in satisfaction showed somewhat less stability, briefly becoming more positive in their reported response to conflict after the first year of marriage.

In short, there is greater net negativity, reciprocity of negative behavior, more sustained negative interaction, and escalation of negative interactions among distressed couples. Moreover, conflict behavior seems to be relatively stable over time (see Gottman 1994, Weiss & Heyman 1997).

Is Marital Conflict More Likely in Certain Content Areas?

Dating, newlywed, and established married couples complain about sources of conflict ranging from verbal and physical abusiveness to personal characteristics and behaviors (e.g. Buss 1989). Perceived inequity in division of labor is associated with both marital conflict (Kluwer et al 1996) and more male withdrawal in response to conflict (Kluwer et al 1997). Likewise, conflict over power is strongly related to marital dissatisfaction (Kurdek 1994, Vangelisti & Huston 1994). Reporting problems with spousal extramarital sex, problematic drinking, or drug use is predictive of divorce (Amato & Rogers 1997), as are wives' reports of husbands' jealousy and foolish spending of money. Similarly, reporting greater problem severity (Lindahl et al 1998) increases prediction of divorce. Even though it is often not reported to be a problem (Ehrensaft & Vivian 1996), relationship violence among newlyweds predicts divorce, as does the presence of psychological aggression (Rogge & Bradbury, unpublished observations).

Such findings highlight the need to be vigilant with regard to the effects of conflict area (Baucom et al 1996) and perceived problem difficulty. Some types of problems may be associated with both poorer marital outcomes as well as poorer problem-solving behavior, leading to spurious conclusions if problem-solving behavior is examined in isolation. Also, if some problem areas are associated with an elevated divorce rate, samples of intact couples selected later in marriage will underestimate the extent to which such problems occur and create difficulty for married couples (Glenn 1990). Finally, perceived efficacy or utility of problem discussion may vary with problem area, leading to changes in the relationship between problem-solving behavior and satisfaction as a function of problem area. Accordingly, investigations of how marriages succeed and fail may benefit from including assessments of problem content and personal resources (see Leonard & Roberts 1998).

Do Cognitions Influence Conflict Behavior?

Regardless of their potential to inform predictive models of marital outcome, problem content and personal resources may have limited potential for change.

More useful in a clinical context are accounts that describe the processes that link problems and personal resources to conflict behavior. Within the context of the social learning framework that has guided interaction research, cognitive processes have been used to account for patterns in observed behavior. For example, the finding that satisfied spouses are less likely to respond negatively after displaying negative affect as a listener (thereby avoiding negative escalation, Gottman et al 1977, Notarius et al 1989) is attributed to their ability to "edit" their thoughts during conflict. Attempts to investigate directly the relation between cognition and behavior have yielded encouraging results.

There is increasing evidence that explanations or attributions for negative marital events (e.g. partner comes home late from work) can increase the probability of conflict behavior (e.g. "he only thinks about himself and his needs"). Such conflict-promoting attributions are related to (*a*) less effective problem-solving behaviors (Bradbury & Fincham 1992), (*b*) more negative behaviors during problem-solving and support-giving tasks (Bradbury et al 1996, Miller & Bradbury 1995), and (*c*) specific affects (whining and anger) displayed during problem-solving (Fincham & Bradbury 1992). In addition, wives' unrealistic relationship beliefs are related to higher rates of negative behavior and lower rates of avoidant behavior (Bradbury & Fincham 1993). As regards behavioral sequences, wives' conflict-promoting attributions and husbands' unrealistic relationship beliefs correlate with the tendency to reciprocate negative partner behavior (e.g. Bradbury & Fincham 1993, Miller & Bradbury 1995). The removal of marital satisfaction from these relations shows that they do not simply reflect the spouse's sentiment toward the marriage (Bradbury et al 1996). Finally, manipulating spouses' attributions for a negative partner behavior influenced distressed spouses' subsequent behavior toward their partners (Fincham & Bradbury 1988). Thus, both correlational and experimental findings are consistent with the view that spousal cognitions, particularly attributions, influence marital behavior.

What is the Longer-Term Impact of Marital Conflict?

There has been considerable interest in the impact of negative conflict behavior over time, especially in view of "reversal effects" whereby such behavior predicts improved marital satisfaction. Gottman & Krokoff (1989) found that husbands' "global negative behavior" and "conflict engagement" predicted positive change in husbands' and wives' satisfaction. Wives' "conflict engagement," on the other hand, predicted positive changes in satisfaction for wives only. By highlighting the potential value of some "distressed" communication behaviors, reversal effects led to a crisis of confidence in the behavioral model of marital discord.

Partial replication studies have found that (a) "husband-negative" and "husband-demand" behaviors were positively associated with increases in wives' but not husbands' satisfaction over a 12-month period, (b) wives' "negative" behaviors again did not predict change in satisfaction (Heavey et al 1993), (c) husband-demand behavior for an issue raised by wives was predictive of increased satisfaction for wives but decreased satisfaction for husbands, and (d) wife-demand behavior did not predict changes in satisfaction (Heavey et al 1995). In an apparent replication failure, Karney & Bradbury (1997) found, over eight waves of data collected across four years, that negativity of husbands' behavior was significantly or marginally predictive of decreases in wives' satisfaction but was not significantly associated with change in husbands' own satisfaction. Also, in contrast to results reported by Heavey et al (1993, 1995), negative wife behavior was associated with positive change (or less deterioration) in marital satisfaction for both spouses.

In addition to inconsistency in reported reversal effects, other studies have found negative behaviors predict decreased marital satisfaction (e.g. Julien et al 1989, Noller et al 1994), and similar inconsistencies emerge for the effects of withdrawal/disengagement or positive behavior (cf for withdrawal, Smith et al 1990 vs Heavey et al 1993; for positive behavior, Julien et al 1989 vs Gottman & Krokoff 1989). Finally, overt conflict behavior can predict divorce (Gottman 1994, pp. 379, 384; Lindahl et al 1998; but see Gottman 1994, p. 289, for an apparent nonreplication). Karney & Bradbury (1997) suggest that conflict behavior is related to slope of deterioration in marital satisfaction, which is in turn related to divorce and separation.

ARE REVERSAL EFFECTS AN ARTIFACT?   Are reversal effects an artifact arising from the use of difference scores (Woody & Costanzo 1990)? This does not appear to be the case, as they have now emerged with both partial correlations and hierarchical linear models (HLM). Indeed, results with partial correlations and difference scores appear more similar than different (Heavey et al 1995). Difference scores and slopes obtained using HLM may produce more markedly divergent results (Karney & Bradbury 1997), but this is due to both intact and divorcing/separating couples being included in HLM analyses. The differences are likely to be much smaller when samples are limited to intact marriages. However, reversal effects are not sample specific but have emerged across a number of different types of samples.

Are reversals an artifact of different coding systems or approaches to coding? Reversals have been found using categorical and continuous coding systems, but attempts at replication, even within the same laboratory, have proved disappointing. However, some results may be incommensurate rather than inconsistent. When different observational systems are used or the same system is used, but specific behaviors are combined into different summary codes, the meaning of the resulting categories can be quite different (e.g. at least 15 different operationalizations of negativity have been used within one coding system, see Heyman et al 1995). Accordingly, it is important to use theoretically grounded coding systems so that functional categories of behavior can be identified and results reliably replicated.

WHAT CAN WE CONCLUDE FROM THE LITERATURE ON REVERSAL EFFECTS? Reversal effects suggest that some negative behavior may be useful and perhaps even necessary for long-term marital health. However, to conclude that negative conflict behavior leads to better marital outcomes appears to be as overly simplistic as the previous conclusion that negative conflict behavior leads to poorer outcomes.

Negative conflict behavior may have a curvilinear relationship to outcomes with both too little and too much being associated with poorer outcomes. If so, characterizing discrete conflict behaviors in terms of level of negativity or likelihood of engendering threat may help reconcile differences across studies. Alternatively, it is possible that willingness to engage with problems is sometimes useful, and also incidently sometimes results in the expression of negative affect, suggesting that reversal effects are more spurious than substantive (Holmes & Murray 1996). It may therefore be useful to examine separately ratings of problem engagement and affective display.

Similarly, the meaning and function of conflict behavior can vary: It may reflect either engagement with the problem or withdrawal from the problem (Christensen & Pasch 1993), and it may be in the service of maintaining the relationship or reflect having given up on the relationship (Holmes & Murray 1996). If so, characterizing conflict in terms of participants' goals may be useful. Likewise, the literature on reversal effects has been silent with regard to the effect of contextual variables and the way they may modify conflict behaviors and outcomes (see Cohan & Bradbury 1997).

It seems clear that we have to identify the circumstances in which conflict behaviors are likely to result in enhancement rather than deterioration of marital relationships. Exploring the processes driving conflict and preventing distressed couples from breaking the grip of repetitive negative cycles is likely to prove far more fruitful. These conclusions point to the importance of theory for understanding conflict behavior, a topic to which we now turn.

Conclusion: Being Practical Means Being Theoretical

Kurt Lewin's (1951, p. 169) observation "that there is nothing as practical as a good theory" should have particular appeal to marital researchers, because marital conflict research emerged in response to practical problems. Yet the literature on marital conflict contains very little explicit theory. This lack may appear all the more surprising as social learning and social exchange theories are widely viewed as frameworks informing marital research. When explicit, the association between such theories and research tends to be loose and imprecise and, in some cases, constitutes only a metaphorical connection.

The relative absence of theoretical development most likely reflects attempts of early researchers to avoid theory, believing instead that "a solid data base is a prerequisite to theory development [and] can best be accomplished by descriptive studies which focus on observable behavior" (Markman et al 1981, p. 236). With over 25 years of accumulated observational data, one might expect theory development to be well under way. However, it remains rudimentary. For example, in many coding systems we still need to know what the codes actually measure, how they relate to each other and are best combined, how they relate to other relevant variables (their nomological network), and so on. Also fundamental to further progress is the need to make explicit and critically analyze the assumptions that informed the choice of what to observe in the first place.

Increased awareness of the limits of a purely behavioral account has also prompted greater recognition of the need to expand the study of marital conflict and so find new frameworks capable of guiding clinical intervention. Research on marital conflict in psychology tends to be relatively independent of developments in the parent discipline. However, some recent advances link the study of marital conflict to broader developments in the psychological literature.

ENTERING THE MAINSTREAM: EXPANDING THE STUDY OF MARITAL CONFLICT

Three broad areas of development have the potential to advance understanding of marital conflict and facilitate the development of a broader theoretical framework to guide its investigation.

Contextualizing the Study of Marital Conflict

As noted, the isolated manner in which conflict has been studied yields an incomplete picture of its role in marriage. To illustrate this viewpoint, examples from both nonmarital and marital contexts are highlighted.

NEGATIVE LIFE EVENTS   In the absence of external stressors, problem-solving skills may have little impact on a marriage (Bradbury et al 1998, Karney & Bradbury 1995). External stressors may also influence marital processes directly. In particular, nonmarital stressors may lead to more negative patterns of communication (e.g. Repetti 1989), lower relationship satisfaction (e.g. Cohan & Bradbury 1997), and poor parenting behaviors (e.g. Repetti & Wood 1997). In addition, moderate levels of negative life events provide a context in which positive and negative partner behavior can become more consequential (Tesser & Beach 1998). Level of negative life events may therefore moderate the effect of conflict behavior on subsequent marital satisfaction (see Cohan & Bradbury 1997). Accordingly, incorporation of life-events assessments into examinations of marital conflict will help enhance prediction of outcomes.

SOCIAL SUPPORT   Because marital interaction research has used tasks that maximize the likelihood of conflict and minimize the likelihood of supportive spouse behavior, it may have overestimated the importance of conflict and underestimated the role of spousal support in marriage (Cutrona 1996). Consistent with this possibility, Melby et al (1995) found that a discussion task designed to enable a range of emotions to be displayed elicited both higher levels of observed warmth and more valid assessment of observed warmth than did a standard problem-solving task.

Pasch & Bradbury (1998) showed that behavior exhibited during conflict and support tasks shared little variance (<20%), wives' support behaviors predicted marital deterioration 24 months later independently of either partners' conflict behaviors, and that support behaviors moderated the association between conflict behavior and later marital deterioration, with poor support and conflict skills leading to greater risk of marital deterioration. Supportive spouse behavior is also related to marital satisfaction is more important than negative behavior in determining perceived supportiveness, and among newlyweds, wives' lack of supportive behavior predicts marital stress 12 months later (Cutrona 1996, Cutrona & Suhr 1994, Davila et al 1997). At the same time, social support outside the marriage may also influence the course and outcome of marital conflict. For example, Julien et al (1994) found that when extra-marital confidants were more supportive, wives were less distressed and closer to their husbands after the confiding interaction.

Increasing Importance of Social Psychological Research

Although initially dominated by the concerns of clinical psychologists, social psychologists are increasingly investigating marriage and bring new perspectives to the study of marital processes. Three examples are illustrative.

ATTACHMENT   Social psychological research on adult attachment has provided fertile ground for new hypotheses about couple interactions. In particular, spouses' mental models of attachment may influence their communications and reactions to negative partner behavior. For example, chronically activated mental models can influence both evaluations and interpretations of ambiguous relational events (Pietromonoco & Carnelly 1994) and lead to the display of proceduralized knowledge (i.e. specific action patterns, strategies, or skills, Baldwin 1992, Kihlstrom 1987). Proceduralized knowledge may be particularly important for understanding marital conflict in that it is often not available to conscious introspection, leading to spouses' failure to understand or be able to adequately explain their own reactions and behavior.

Such results make more interesting the findings that persons reporting insecure attachment styles are more likely to be married to others with an insecure attachment style (Feeney 1994, Senchak & Leonard 1992) and to be less satisfied in their relationships. Similarly, those with a preoccupied attachment style may be particularly likely to show an elevated level of marital conflict after an involuntary separation from the partner (Cafferty et al 1994). In addition, persons with secure attachment styles show a greater tendency to compromise and to take into account both their own and their partners' interests during problem-solving interactions, whereas those with anxious-ambivalent styles display a greater tendency to oblige their partners and to focus on relationship maintenance than do those with an avoidant style (Pistole 1989, Scharfe & Bartholomew 1995).

COMMITMENT   A rich, social psychological literature on commitment has also influenced the study of marriage (e.g. Rusbult 1993). Of particular interest here is the finding that greater commitment is associated with more constructive, accommodative responses to negative partner behavior (Rusbult et al 1991, Rusbult et al 1998).

Recent work on commitment highlights additional growth points for marital conflict research. First, even relatively satisfied partners consider nonconstructive responses to a negative partner behavior before engaging in more constructive behavior, and the constructiveness of responses is greater when there is no time pressure (Yovetich & Rusbult 1994). It therefore appears that distressed couples do what comes naturally and that nondistressed couples engage in more effortful processing. Second, spouses who lack evidence of partner commitment (e.g. when structural factors maintaining commitment are greatly diminished) may adopt a shorter-term perspective and preference for a quid pro quo or exchange orientation in which immediate reciprocation of positive behavior is expected and feelings of exploitation are experienced when help is not reciprocated. Conversely, evidence of partner commitment may facilitate a communal orientation that results in more positive attributions for a partner's performance (McCall 1995).

SELF-PROCESSES   Pointing to the potential importance of individual differences and self-processes for marital outcomes, neuroticism was found to predict poorer marital outcomes over an extended time frame (e.g. Kelly & Conley 1987), apparently by influencing the starting point (or level) of marital satisfaction rather than the slope of change over time (Karney & Bradbury 1997). Self-processes are also important for understanding the effects of social support (e.g. Nadler 1997), affective reactions to comparisons with the partner (e.g. Beach et al 1998), and feelings of love (e.g. Aron & Aron 1996).

The application of self-processes to the investigation of marital conflict is illustrated by recent work on self-evaluation maintenance in marriage. Beach et al (1998) found that spouses and partners in romantic relationships had different affective reactions to being outperformed by their partner depending on both the importance of the area to them and the importance of the area to their partner. Beach & Tesser (1993) showed that decision-making power could be conceptualized as a performance dimension: Relative to happy couples, less-satisfied couples reported less decision-making power in areas important to the self and more decision-making power in areas seen as important to the partner. It therefore appears that self-evaluation maintenance processes can influence both feelings toward the partner and satisfaction with the relationship.

Positive self-image appears to influence positive illusions about the partner (Murray et al 1996a), and illusions may positively influence the course of the relationship over time (Murray et al 1996b). Conversely, partner's verification of one's self-view (positive or negative) also appears to influence relationship satisfaction (Katz et al 1996, Swann et al 1992). Thus, self-processes appear to influence marital interaction and conflict in several ways.

Clarifying the Construct of Marital Quality

A problem with marital research is that the construct of marital satisfaction, adjustment, or some other synonym reflective of the quality of the marriage is poorly understood and assessed using omnibus measures consisting of non-equivalent item types. Because indices of marital satisfaction include reported conflict, it can be argued that linking observed conflict to satisfaction simply shows that spouses behave in the way they say they do. For some applications, the use of omnibus satisfaction measures appears relatively nonproblematic. However, increased conceptual clarity may offer empirical advantages. One proposal is to limit marital quality to evaluative judgments (see Fincham & Bradbury 1987). This approach has opened two new avenues of research, as described below.

ATTITUDES, ACCESSIBILITY, AND SENTIMENT OVERRIDE   Conceptualizing marital quality in terms of evaluative judgments links it to a broader field of attitude research in which an attitude is viewed as an association between the cognitive representation of an object and a summary evaluation of the object. The strength of this association indexes the degree to which the attitude is accessible and therefore influences information processing about the attitude object, behavior toward it, and so on. Using response latency as a measure of the accessibility of marital quality (evaluative judgments of the partner), Fincham et al (1995) showed that accessibility moderates the relation between marital quality and attributions and expectations of partner behavior; significantly larger correlations occur when accessibility is relatively high vs low. Because spouses whose marital quality is highly accessible are more likely to process information about their partners in terms of their marital quality, accessibility should also moderate the stability of marital quality. This has been demonstrated over 6-, 12-, and 18-month intervals (Fincham et al 1997). An implication of this research is that the correlates of marital quality need to be reexamined.

THE BI-DIMENSIONAL NATURE OF MARITAL SATISFACTION   Marital conflict research typically uses bipolar measures of marital satisfaction. However, such measures assume rather than demonstrate a bipolar structure for evaluative experience. When this assumption was examined directly, Fincham & Linfield (1997) documented across two assessment procedures a moderate, negative correlation between positive and negative evaluations consistent with that reported in the attitude literature (see Thompson et al 1995). The two dimensions accounted for variance in reported spouse behavior and attributions for spouse behavior over and beyond that which could be attributed to a traditional measure of marital quality or to each spouse's general affectivity. Finally, ambivalent (high positive and negative) and indifferent (low positive and negative) spouses were indistinguishable on an omnibus marital quality measure, but ambivalent wives, compared to their indifferent counterparts, reported a higher ratio of negative to positive behavior and made more conflict-promoting attributions.

Such findings have potentially far-reaching implications. For example, longitudinal change in marital satisfaction may need to be reexamined. It would be theoretically important if happily married spouses first increased only negative evaluations (became ambivalent) before then decreasing positive evaluations and becoming distressed, as compared to a progression in which negative evaluations increased and positive evaluations decreased at the same time. Such progressions may, in turn, differ in important ways from one where there is simply a decline in positive evaluations over time. Documenting the conflict behaviors associated with different avenues of change may illuminate previously undetected aspects of relationships and so advance our understanding of how marriages succeed and fail. In addition, disaggregating positive and negative evaluations may highlight new possibilities for marital intervention.

Conclusion: Being Theoretically Grounded Is Not Enough

Each of the developments outlined is theoretically grounded and can be traced to rich theories in the broader psychological literature. However, they are isolated from each other and none has yet given rise to a broad theoretical framework in the marital domain. Does this mean that the expansion of marital conflict research will lead inevitably to its balkanization? Not necessarily. Attempts to develop integrative frameworks can be found in the marital literature (e.g. Bradbury & Fincham 1991, Karney & Bradbury 1995, Gottman 1994). These researchers have been quite successful in organizing findings and in identifying new lines of inquiry. Nonetheless, there remains a need for broad, integrative models, and we believe that such models are critical to the future vitality of the field.

TOWARD A THEORETICAL FRAMEWORK FOR INTERVENTION, PREVENTION, AND MARITAL CONFLICT RESEARCH

How might we complement recent attempts at theoretical development? In addressing this question we return to basics and ask, "What is marital conflict?"

Back to Basics: What Is Marital Conflict?

What constitutes marital conflict has often been assumed to be self-evident (but see Fincham & Bradbury 1991, Margolin 1988), a circumstance that can be explained by reliance on observed spouse behavior during problem solving as the primary source of data for understanding marital conflict and by a movement away from the idiographic approach characteristic of early behavioral interventions. Two important problems that have resulted are complacency in identifying mechanisms of change, and a presumption that behavioral differences between the "average" conflictual and nonconflictual couple reflect the destructive characteristics of conflict.

The literature reviewed above, particularly that on reversal effects, has been useful in disabusing the field of these misconceptions. However, the atheoretical bias inherent in the purely behavioral approach to conflict persists. Indeed, the absence of strong links with a broader interdisciplinary literature on conflict is striking (for an introduction, see Hocker & Wilmot 1995), but there are suggestions that this might change. Indeed, several excellent, integrative analyses of conflict have appeared in recent years (e.g. Christensen & Pasch 1993, Weiss & Dehle 1994, discussing marital conflict; Holmes & Murray 1996, discussing conflict in close relationships; Emery 1992, Pruitt & Olczak 1995, offering a systems model of conflict; Rubin & Levinger 1995, comparing interpersonal and international conflict; Pruitt 1997, discussing social conflict more generally). Although they differ in foci and definitions of conflict, these analyses share several points of agreement.

First, not all conflicts are overt. Marital conflict can go undetected by one of the partners and have minimal impact on them. Indeed, early in marriage and premaritally, self-reported conflict is unrelated to satisfaction (Kelly et al 1985), and partners may often make virtues out of faults (Holmes & Murray

1996), rendering potential sources of conflict moot. This observation is critical because it highlights (*a*) the need to define conflict without a requirement of overt hostility, (*b*) the importance of assessing cognitive events to obtain a more complete portrait of the conflict process, and (*c*) the inadequacy of behavior during problem solving as the sole measure of conflict behavior.

Second, perceived conflict of interest, incompatible goals, wishes and expectations, and perceived interference with goal-directed behavior all provide starting points for the analysis of conflict. However, not all conflicts of interest result in conflict but are instead successfully transformed into opportunities for cooperative interaction (see Kelley & Thibaut 1978). This observation is important in that it highlights (*a*) the potential for spouses to inhibit or modify initial reactions, thereby transforming hostile impulses in a variety of ways, and (*b*) the potential for partners to approach conflict with a variety of goals and strategies, potentially influencing the course of a conflict episode.

Third, conflict episodes change over time. Salient properties of the conflict process shift depending on when one looks. For example, effortful attributional activity is likely to be most pronounced after overt negative exchanges have stopped, whereas effortful inhibition of negative reactions may be most obvious among satisfied couples in response to negative partner behavior (Yovetich & Rusbult 1994), and much accommodative behavior may occur prior to any conflictual interaction (Rusbult et al 1998). Likewise, many conflicts do not involve overt disagreement and may be handled in ways that do not depend on verbal exchange (e.g. behaving solicitously, Rusbult 1993). Finally, overt marital conflict involves some level of negatively valenced behavior, whether this is directed toward engaging in the conflict or avoiding it. These considerations suggest the relevance of many different approaches to the study of marital conflict, ranging from interactional studies to diary methods and indirect assessments of cognition.

This brief examination of commonalities across analyses of conflict already identifies overlooked issues that need to be considered in developing a theoretical framework. For example, covert conflict is relatively understudied in marriage, and we know nothing about the relation between what happens during and between conflict episodes. Likewise, little is known about the way in which reactions to negative spouse behavior interact with recently or chronically primed attitudes or constructs. Nor is there information about emergent characteristics of conflict, such as the way spouses' intentions for the interaction and view of the partner change after the conflict has begun. However, the primary lesson of this exercise is simple: Conflict is invariably conceptualized in relation to goals.

It is, therefore, surprising that research on marital conflict has paid little attention to the goal construct (but see Fincham & Bradbury 1991). Moreover, the study of goals is both longstanding and ubiquitous in psychology and may even serve as a vehicle to transcend traditional, subdisciplinary boundaries (Austin & Vancouver 1996). Recent work on goal-directed behavior provides insights into the nature and organization of goals, the important characteristics of goals, and the impact of goal orientation on behavior (see Austin & Vancouver 1996, Gollwitzer & Bargh 1996). In the remainder of this section, we argue that a goal theoretic perspective has the potential to provide an overarching framework for understanding marriage. We begin by considering whether such a perspective adds anything new to the marital literature.

Stating the Obvious to Make a Difference

It could be argued that our position is hardly new, as a goal perspective is already pervasive in marital theorizing. There is merit to this view. For example, some spouse behavior is labeled as defensive or is described as an attempt at meta-communication. Other spouses are labeled as engaging in "tit-for-tat" or negative reciprocity. In each case, there is an implication that the behavior is serving one or another goal and that it is the goal that makes the description sensible to us.

The problem is that use of the goal construct remains largely unacknowledged in work on marriage and interpersonal relationships (see Berscheid 1994). Thus, despite frequent, indirect references to goals (as illustrated above), there is substantially less in the way of direct guidance on goals and the effect of goals on marital interaction. This is unfortunate, as a number of heuristic and conceptual advantages follow from making explicit our implicit reliance on the goal construct. We turn now to consider some of these advantages for intervention, prevention, and research on marital conflict phenomena.

Marital Intervention from a Goal Perspective

Four key advantages for intervention follow from adopting a goal perspective: (a) We gain an intuitively simple approach to talking about conflict, (b) we gain the ability to be idiographic in our assessment and interventions while drawing upon a strong experimental research tradition, (c) a large literature documenting the advantages of goal setting can be used in helping couples plan for change, and (d) a rapidly expanding network of research on goals across several subdisciplines creates the potential for new insights and intervention technologies to emerge. We briefly illustrate these advantages by showing how a conflictual interaction can be conceptualized in terms of goals.

Consider a relatively common conflict: a couple arguing over directions while traveling. Like many garden-variety situations in which conflicts occur, there is little obvious basis for conflict. Both partners want to get to the destination, and neither seems to benefit from arguing about directions. Yet, as it becomes clear that they are not on the correct road, here they go again. He becomes angry and asks why she can not read a simple map. She retorts that there is nothing wrong with her map reading, that he must have missed a turn. They progress through several increasingly hostile reproach-denial cycles until she suggests they stop and ask someone for directions. He drives on in stony silence, even angrier than he was prior to her suggestion. Everything happens quickly. Upon later inquiry, neither partner reports planning what they did, but both report a considerable number of very negative thoughts about the other in the silence that followed the brief eruption.

How does a goal analysis help us understand the conflict and discuss it with the couple? We begin with three premises: (a) All behavior is goal directed (discrepancies between current and desired states drive behavior to reduce the difference through such processes as test-operate-test-exit cycles, Miller et al 1960), (b) spouses don't always know what the goal is, even for their own behavior (goals can be latent as well as consciously experienced), and (c) goals vary widely (from internal set points, e.g. for body temperature, to complex, cognitively represented outcomes, e.g. for marital success) and cannot be understood in isolation from each other or from the dynamics of goal system functioning (establishing, planning, striving toward and revising goals, see Austin & Vancouver 1996).

Upon accepting these premises, we can begin to talk with the couple about their argument in an intuitively clear way. We may explain that we can identify goals and changing goals on the basis of what is holding their attention and consuming their energy. For example, we can ask the husband at what point he thinks he switched from focusing on finding his way to focusing on whose fault it was for being lost. This is an important moment, because it is the point at which his goals began to shift without his necessarily realizing it. Such a shift in attentional focus is a good indication that an emergent goal displaced his prospective goal of working jointly with his wife to find their way (see Hocker & Wilmot 1995).

Attempting to find out more about his goal shift is likely to illuminate aspects of their interaction that characteristically precede a negative shift in his conflict behavior. Likewise, we might ask the wife about the point at which she began to shift from her focus on helping her husband to defending herself or even counter-attacking. In both cases, spouses are likely to find such questions rather easy to contemplate and discuss, and the therapist can then undertake an idiographic assessment of each couple's particular pattern of conflict. What triggers the shift to the emergent goal for *this* husband and *this* wife? Are there similarities in the triggers that elicit this shift across conflict episodes? A goal perspective is likely to be understandable to both the therapist and the client couple, while preserving many useful characteristics of a functional analysis.

Does a goal perspective help in any other ways? Yes, we can discuss with our clients the value of setting goals for themselves, examining the relation of the new goals to existing ones (e.g. are they consistent?), and being aware of when their prospective goals are displaced by emergent ones during an interaction. In particular, therapists can highlight the possibility that emergent goals are often self-identity goals (frequently activated automatically and outside of awareness) and that responses often reflect attempts to avoid loss of face (usually manifest in overlearned conflict behavior, see Hocker & Wilmot 1995). In such circumstances, conflict is most likely to escalate, become more global, and generate more rigid conflict behavior as the original content issues that provoked conflict are subsumed by issues of face saving. It can be emphasized that captives of this process are usually quite unaware of it and often express puzzlement about why so much conflict can be generated by trivial issues (e.g. navigation/driving).

In addition, a large literature suggests that goal-setting can facilitate accomplishment in a variety of therapies (see Kanfer & Schefft 1988), and that concrete, small goals are especially useful in this regard. Setting concrete goals allows couples to think about opportunities to implement their goals, further facilitating accomplishment (Gollwitzer & Brandstatter 1997). One resultant approach to helping couples find more adaptive ways to manage conflict is to think through overarching goals (e.g. I want to show I care and also get to the party), and then help the couple break the general goals into smaller, more concrete ones. Accordingly, a goal perspective helps preserve an idiographic approach to intervention.

But what about the danger of emergent goals that may throw all other planning into disarray? If both partners tend to find themselves struggling with identity issues and so responding with self-defensive behavior, they need to satisfy their identity goals in some other way (Tesser et al 1996). In particular, to the extent that a more benign behavior that preserves self identity can substitute for the defensive behavior, the couple may be better able to stay on task and solve their problem.

Once positive goals for the interaction are identified, they can be examined in terms of goal dimensions known to influence a goal's ability to control behavior. Specifically, the couple can explore issues related to perceived goal difficulty, ability to implement goal-relevant behaviors, goal specificity, goal commitment, and perceived rewards of goal attainment. A wide range of interventions may be relevant to helping couples form, make a commitment to, carry out, and maintain behavior related to their positive goals (see Kanfer 1996). By becoming aware of these considerations, spouses can more easily persevere in patterns designed to convey, for example, warmth and regard for the partner. As with the initial assessment of the couple's interaction, the content of each of these goal dimensions is entirely idiographic; however, the importance of the dimensions themselves is tied to a broader experimental literature in which goals have been found to vary along a number of dimensions (e.g. level of consciousness, importance-commitment, difficulty, specificity, temporal range, and connectedness, see Austin & Vancouver 1996).

GOALS AND DEFENSIVE BEHAVIOR   As noted earlier, an important challenge for a goal perspective is its ability to deal with defensive behavior. Why is defensive behavior so challenging for couples and therapists alike? Perhaps it is because the emergent goal structure that guides defensive behavior is particularly stable both within each partner and within the dyadic system, rendering it difficult for couples to exit on their own and difficult for therapists to preempt. To elaborate this hypothesis, we need to distinguish approach, avoidance, and combination goal structures. After doing so, we hypothesize that defensive goals are combination goal structures, that the activation of defensive goals leads spouses to view partner negative behavior as diagnostic, and that each person's defensive behavior has strong potential to activate a symmetrical goal structure in the partner.

Three types of goals   Three types of goals can be distinguished (Carver & Scheier 1998). Approach goals are prototypic positive goals. They are associated with pressure to move toward a given state and with internal feedback designed to encourage discrepancy reduction. Avoidance goals, on the other hand, are also quite familiar in clinical settings. They are associated with pressure to move away from a given state and with internal feedback designed to enlarge discrepancy. A typical example would be a feared state or object. Carver & Scheier (1998) note, however, that avoidance goals are quite commonly connected with an associated approach goal. The resulting combination goal has both an avoidance pole that the individual moves away from in any direction that is possible, and an approach pole that attracts the person as they move further from the avoidance goal. Such combination goals are presumed to be more stable.

Three other general observations are relevant here (Carver & Scheier 1998). First, successful movement away from an avoidance goal most likely produces a different type of affect (relief) than movement toward an approach goal (elation), allowing one to distinguish their effect if one uses a two-dimensional affect system. Second, the approach and avoidance systems are likely to be physiologically distinct, perhaps with approach goals reflecting activity in the behavioral approach system and avoidance reflecting activity in the behavioral inhibition system (Gray 1987). Because underlying activity in these two systems appears to influence tendencies to learn avoidance and approach goals (Corr et al 1997), some individual difference variables may influence spouses' weighting of different goal types. Third, avoidance goals appear to have an inherent primacy, perhaps reflected in the common tendency for negative behavior to be relatively more salient than positive behavior in dyadic interaction.

Defensive goal systems   Our hypothesis is that defensive marital behavior typically reflects a combination goal. Such goal combinations may exert a stronger influence on the course of a conflictual interaction and perhaps on the course of a relationship than does either goal taken alone. An example of a (defensive) combination goal might be the goal of avoiding feeling stupid or small joined to the approach goal of evening the score with one's partner. When the partner's behavior is seen as threatening, this activates the goal of reducing the threat. However, through long association, as the avoidance goal is met, the approach goal is activated. Thus, in this example, a powerful motive to attack and belittle the partner could be set in motion by a relatively minor criticism. One could easily, however, substitute stone-walling, negative mind-reading, or physical violence for the approach goal and retain the same basic goal structure.

One may also wonder about the constellation of factors that predispose some individuals to view partner behavior as attacking or requiring a defensive reaction. There are powerful individual differences in the extent to which particular outcomes are viewed as being diagnostic of something about the self, or simply reflecting a need to create some incremental change. Early attachment experiences most likely contribute to the development of such individual differences in reactivity (Mikulincer 1998), and other factors, such as neuroticism, might also play a role. However, if an individual is vulnerable to reacting to partner criticisms as if they were diagnostic of a feared self-view, that should lead to greater avoidance of partner criticism and less persistence in trying to make things work when the partner is critical (see Dweck 1996).

A more complete understanding of defensive goal systems must incorporate the systemic relationship that exists between spouses. Defensive spouse behavior is both a response to prior events and a stimulus for the partner's next behavior. When a husband or wife responds to defensive partner behavior in kind, this sets the stage for re-energizing the partner's original avoidance goal. That is, the feared goal is moved closer to the partner, energizing their avoidance behavior.

To the extent that couples proceed through many iterations of re-energizing each other's defensive behavior, an important change might also be occurring in perceived self-efficacy to attain positive goals such as closeness and intimacy. Goals related to relationship maintenance or showing concern for the partner are likely to seem ever more unattainable. This combination of outcomes becomes a prescription for viewing the relationship as secondary, decreasing the salience of communal relationship norms, decreasing perceived self-efficacy for positive goals, and so further decreasing constructive accommodation to the partner.

In sum, a goal framework suggests that defensive behavior should be discernable early in the sequence of events leading to marital deterioration. Negative (agitation) affect should increase and then lead to a decrease in positive affect over time. Couples in which both partners are vulnerable to defensiveness should have a poorer prognosis than those in which only one partner is prone to defensive reactions. In addition, it should be possible to assess vulnerability to defensive reactions in a variety of ways, including direct observation and indirect assessment (e.g. via assessment of material activated by the presentation of conflict). Thus, our analysis suggests a theoretically informed cascade beginning with changes in high-level goals and exerting effects throughout the cognitive, behavioral, and affective system. Examining the structure of goals activated during conflict therefore may reveal important differences between couples headed for poorer vs better outcomes.

Prevention of Marital Problems from a Goal Perspective

Some types of marital problems (e.g. violence, infidelity), particularly in the context of reduced personal resources (e.g. poverty, ongoing illness), may be powerful elicitors of defensiveness. It may be useful to acknowledge the possibility that most spouses would respond defensively if placed in the same circumstances. Our analysis suggests, however, that defensiveness may have a special role to play in the subsequent development of marital dysfunction. Once activated, certain types of combination defensive goals may increase negative aspects of the relationship and then, over time, come to erode the positive in the relationship as well. Also, before the activation of these defensive goals, many couples may feel they are doing fine even if they are engaging in considerable overt conflict. Once defensive goals are activated, however, they should heighten the perception of negative partner behavior, intensify its impact, and lead to changes in interpretation of negative partner behavior and to more negative behavioral reactions. This, in turn, should increase the likelihood that the partner will also have defensive goals activated.

The need to provide couples with ways to interrupt this pattern early and return to nondefensive interaction is acute. Recent investigations of premarital prevention programs report modest effects (e.g. Markman et al 1993). It also appears that the couples in greatest need of prevention programs may be the least likely to seek them out, and that premarital prevention programs in the community provide relatively little benefit (Sullivan & Bradbury 1997). Even in the context of research volunteers, more than half declined the opportunity to participate in a prevention program (Markman et al 1993). These findings suggest that widespread prevention programs remain more promise than reality and that there is a need for improvements in both substance (i.e. efficacy) and delivery (i.e. effectiveness).

In the context of such findings, it is perhaps not surprising that we see proposals for "minimal" programs of preventative intervention (Gottman 1994). If brief, effective programs were available, it might be possible to better meet the needs of couples most at risk. Our goal analysis highlights three potential foci for such programs.

First, if avoidance goals are the source of defensive behavior, it is important to give couples a way to recognize when they are getting defensive and provide them with an alternative to attacking, belittling, becoming belligerent, or stonewalling. Recent work suggests that self-protective mechanisms may be interchangeable (e.g. Tesser et al 1996), and so rather than focus on over-learning basic relationship skills (see Gottman 1994), it may be more efficient to provide new methods of self-protection. For example, we might focus on helping partners substitute workable self-enhancement strategies for partner-attacking reactions and thereby reduce a spouse's felt need to attack, demean, or stonewall. If the "attack" goal can be separated from the defensive pattern in this way, the couple has a better chance to emerge from a self-perpetuating pattern of mutual recrimination.

A second component for a minimal intervention is to address directly sensitivity to threat. A goal perspective suggests that there are particular "feared selves" (e.g. Markus & Nurius 1986) that motivate defensive behavior. If so, the areas represented by feared selves represent areas of vulnerability for destructive marital interaction. To the extent that such feared selves can be reliably assessed, it should be possible to design exposure-based interventions that reduce their power to disrupt interaction. Alternatively, awareness of points of vulnerability might allow couples to successfully deal with such issues when they arise.

The third component of a minimal intervention would help couples learn that relationships are always changing and developing so that they develop an incremental theory of marriage and marital happiness rather than an entity theory where marital satisfaction is viewed in finite terms (see Dweck 1996, Knee 1998). An incremental orientation is linked to learning goals and allows for failure and disappointments, whereas an entity orientation is linked to performance goals leading to an ongoing focus on marital behavior as diagnostic of relationship well-being. Inappropriate negative attributions for partner behavior and very low efficacy expectations might indicate such entity-oriented thinking. Once detected, an entity orientation could be addressed didactically, as it is when couples are encouraged to adopt a problem-solving attitude. Alternatively, it might be addressed indirectly through metaphor or humor designed to activate alternative frameworks for interpreting spouse behavior. However, because it is important that couples be able to self-regulate the tendency to reach entity-oriented conclusions, indirect interventions would need to be sufficiently memorable that they could be called upon in later conflict situations.

The suggestions highlighted by a goal perspective do not focus on skills training or on "calming down." Rather, they may be characterized as focusing on taking care of one's self first, facing what one is potentially afraid of finding in the relationship, and refusing to rectify problems. This perspective therefore provides belated recognition of the insight provided by an early study by Birchler et al (1975). These investigators showed that distressed spouses are not characterized by skill deficits so much as by failure to use with the partner those skills that are apparent in conversation with strangers. Indeed, skills in the context of marital discord may contribute to more rather than less dissatisfaction (Burleson & Denton 1997). Such considerations provide grounds for suspecting that it is aims and objectives (goals) that most often differentiate distressed and nondistressed partners rather than skills and capabilities.

Of course, these suggestions are quite rudimentary, lack direct empirical validation, and are not yet associated with a viable assessment technology. Still, they provide a glimpse of the integrative alternative offered by a goal perspective, and as goal theory continues to develop and be applied in the marital domain, increasingly novel implications for intervention and prevention may be forthcoming. A goal perspective can also help make research more clinically relevant in that it has the potential to integrate and direct disparate lines of research on marital conflict phenomena.

Marital Conflict Phenomena from a Goal Perspective

A goal perspective generates new insights regarding conflict patterns, reversal effects, conflict context, and cognitive processes in marital conflict and has potential to integrate theoretical developments in attachment, commitment, and self-processes.

CONFLICT PATTERNS   Goal differences may account for the differing conflict patterns found in distressed and nondistressed couples. Self-protective (e.g. re-establishing equity) and avoidance (e.g. of harm) goals most likely give rise to conflict behavior (e.g. defensiveness) in distressed couples. In contrast, problem-resolution and relationship-enhancement goals appear to underlie the conflict behavior of nondistressed couples. This difference in goals most likely manifests itself in the choice of different "transformations of motivation rules" (Kelley & Thibaut 1978). Whereas distressed couples should be biased to defeat (e.g. maximize the relative difference between partners' outcomes) or not be fooled by the partner (e.g. maximize own outcomes), nondistressed partners should find it easier to focus on trying to find the best outcome for both partners (e.g. maximize joint outcomes), the most equitable outcome (e.g. minimize the difference between partners' outcomes), or the best outcome for the partner (e.g. maximize partner's outcomes). By considering the goals associated with different conflict patterns, our analysis creates the potential for integrating observational approaches to both conflict and support with insights from interdependence theory and the assessment of cognitive processes.

REVERSAL EFFECTS   How does a goal perspective facilitate understanding of reversal effects? Reversal effects should be mediated by the association of certain negative conflict behaviors to the presence of pro-relationship goals by the actor (or the elicitation of pro-relationship goals in the partner). Already discussed in the marital literature is the possibility that reversal effects result when negative conflict behavior represents genuine attempts at engagement of the other rather than simple avoidance of problems. Our analysis helps elaborate and broaden the discussion.

A goal perspective also provides a coherent framework for discussing the circumstances under which conflict engagement and avoidance may work to enhance couple satisfaction. Negative conflict behavior should have positive effects to the extent that it prompts the other to better understand one's reaction and activates prorelationship motives in the other (i.e. "I need to quit thinking just of myself"). At the same time, goal theory suggests the hypothesis that reversal effects should be less likely for behaviors that are associated with retaliation goals or defensive goals or for those behaviors that tend to evoke such goals in the other.

CONFLICT CONTEXT   Unlike current research, a goal perspective can easily incorporate context effects. For example, stressful life events as well as certain personal characteristics and family history variables may lower the threshold for defensive and retaliatory goals. Similarly, stressful life events may activate approach and avoidance motives differently for persons with differing attachment styles (Mikulincer et al 1993), and negative partner behavior results in different explanations depending on attachment style (Collins 1996). At the same time, negative life events may stimulate a felt need for partner support, and may do so differently depending on personal characteristics such as attachment style (Simpson et al 1992).

Thus, both current life events and personal characteristics have the potential to shape the goals activated by marital interaction. This points to possible theoretical continuity between observational literatures on support and conflict and suggests that both literatures may benefit from assessment of goals activated during interaction. Similarly, attempts to assess "entity" interpretations of negative conflict partner behavior or "entity" interpretations of failures to provide supportive behavior might prove to be powerful predictors of emotional and defensive reactions.

COGNITION   A goal perspective can also ground marital research on cognition in a useful way. For example, within a goal framework, attributional effects are of interest both as part of the process leading to emergent defensive goals and as a continuation of the defensive pattern that may remain long after the overt conflict episode is over (e.g. Martin & Tesser 1996). Similarly, our analysis easily incorporates the prediction that high self-efficacy should be associated with more successful implementation of constructive problem-solving efforts (Doherty 1981). Finally, recent work on goals is compatible with both a two-dimensional structure of marital affect (Carver 1996) and the greater impact of more accessible marital evaluations (Kruglanski 1996).

ATTACHMENT, COMMITMENT, AND SELF PROCESSES   Perhaps most importantly, a goal perspective is compatible with, and potentially integrates, areas of current theoretical growth. As regards attachment, secure vs insecure attachment may be thought of as reflecting different patterns of goal organization as well as differences in the goals that are most chronically activated. Likewise, relationship commitment has considerable conceptual overlap with a goal perspective, and the literature on self-processes is often couched in terms of goal systems. Accordingly, our goal analysis is a natural extension of these perspectives and so lends itself to their integration into a single, coherent framework.

Conclusion: Being Goal Oriented Facilitates Being Integrative

Being goal oriented points us toward a broad, integrative framework for development of new intervention and prevention programs as well as future research on marital conflict. This framework is idiographic in its implications for understanding a specific couple, yet provides connections with a nomothetic, experimental research base that has proved to be remarkably generative. In particular, it provides critical insights with regard to both the function of problematic conflict behavior as well as the key process parameters likely to make such behavior more or less difficult to change. Our analysis highlights the utility of verbal prompts to create specific interaction goals, to envision such goals and how they might be implemented, and to clarify the level of commitment to the goals and any lack of perceived ability to realize them. Intervention, prevention, and research efforts might fruitfully and easily incorporate the goal construct at this level.

SUMMARY AND CONCLUSION

Research on marital conflict has reached a crossroads. We can continue amassing observations in an atheoretical manner and hope that patterns will emerge after we attain some critical mass, or we can begin now the hard work of creating a unified theoretical framework for the study of marriage. We chose the latter option and offered a goal perspective as one such potential integrative framework. Our analysis offers suggestions for reconciling anomalies in research findings, is compatible with areas of current theoretical growth, offers suggestions for both clinical and preventative intervention, and suggests opportunities for ties with a thriving area of experimental research. Our analysis is merely a starting point. Whether the marital literature realizes the potential of a goal theoretic framework will depend on our collective efforts.

Visit the *Annual Reviews home page* at
http://www.AnnualReviews.org.

Literature Cited

Amato PR, Rogers SJ. 1997. A longitudinal study of marital problems and subsequent divorce. *J. Marriage Fam.* 59:612–24

Aron EN, Aron A. 1996. Love and the expansion of the self: the state of the model. *Pers. Relat.* 24:45–58

Austin JT, Vancouver JB. 1996. Goal constructs in psychology: structure, process, and content. *Psychol. Bull.* 120:338–75

Baldwin MW. 1992. Relational schemas and the processing of social information. *Psychol. Bull.* 112:461–84

Baucom DH, Epstein N, Rankin LA, Burnett CK. 1996. Understanding marital distress from a cognitive-behavioral orientation. In *Advances in Cognitive Therapy*, ed. KS Dobson, KD Craig, pp. 210–36. Thousand Oaks, CA: Sage

Beach SRH, Fincham FD, Katz J. 1998. Marital therapy in the treatment of depression: toward a third generation of outcome research. *Clin. Psychol. Rev.* In press

Beach SRH, Tesser A. 1993. Decision making power and marital satisfaction: a self evaluation maintenance perspective. *J. Soc. Clin. Psychol.* 12:471–94

Beach SRH, Tesser A, Fincham FD, Jones DJ, Johnson D, Whitaker DJ. 1998. Pleasure and pain in doing well, together: an investigation of peformance-related affect in close relationships. *J. Pers. Soc. Psychol.* 74:923–38

Berscheid E. 1994. Interpersonal relationships. *Annu. Rev. Psychol.* 45:79–129

Birchler GR, Weiss RL, Vincent JP. 1975. Multimethod analysis of social reinforcement exchange between maritally distressed and nondistressed spouse and stranger dyads. *J. Pers. Soc. Psychol.* 31: 349–60

Bradbury TN, ed. 1998. *The Developmental Course of Marital Dysfunction.* New York: Cambridge Univ. Press

Bradbury TN, Beach SRH, Fincham FD, Nelson GM. 1996. Attributions and behavior in functional and dysfunctional marriages. *J. Consult. Clin. Psychol.* 64:569–76

Bradbury TN, Cohan K, Karney BR. 1998. Optimizing longitudinal research for understanding and preventing marital dysfunction. See Bradbury 1998, pp. 279–311

Bradbury TN, Fincham FD. 1991. A contextual model for advancing the study of marital interaction. In *Cognition in Close Relationships*, ed. GJO Fletcher, FD Fincham, pp. 127–47. Hillsdale, NJ: Erlbaum

Bradbury TN, Fincham FD. 1992. Attributions and behavior in marital interaction. *J. Pers. Soc. Psychol.* 63:613–28

Bradbury TN, Fincham FD. 1993. Assessing dysfunctional cognition in marriage: a reconsideration of the Relationship Belief Inventory. *Psychol. Assess.* 5:92–101

Brody GH, Stoneman Z, McCoy JK. 1994. Forecasting sibling relationships in early adolescence from child temperaments and family processes in middle childhood. *Child Dev.* 65:771–84

Bunker B, Rubin JZ, eds. 1995. *Conflict, Cooperation and Justice.* San Francisco: Jossey-Bass

Burleson BR, Denton WH. 1997. The relationship between communication skill and marital satisfaction: some moderating effects. *J. Marriage Fam.* 59:884–902

Burman B, John RS, Margolin G. 1992. Observed patterns of conflict in violent, non-violent, and non-distressed couples. *Behav. Assess.* 14:15–37

Burman B, Margolin G. 1992. Analysis of the association between marital relationships and health problems: an interactional perspective. *Psychol. Bull.* 112:39–63

Buss DM. 1989. Conflict between the sexes: strategic interference and the evocation of anger and upset. *J. Pers. Soc. Psychol.* 56: 735–47

Cafferty TP, Davis KE, Medway FJ, O'Jearn RE, Chappell KD. 1994. Reunion dynamics among couples separated during Operation Desert Storm: an attachment theory analysis. In *Advances in Personal Relationships*, ed. D Perlman, K Bartholomew, 5:309–30. London: Kingsley

Carver CS. 1996. Some ways in which goals differ and some implications of those differences. See Gollwitzer & Bargh 1996, pp. 645–72

Carver CS, Scheier MF. 1998. Theme and issues in the self-regulation of behavior. In *On the Self-Regulation of Behavior*, ed. CS Carver, MF Scheier. New York: Cambridge Univ. Press. In press

Christensen A, Pasch L. 1993. The sequence of marital conflict: an analysis of seven phases of marital conflict in distressed and nondistressed couples. *Clin. Psychol. Rev.* 13:3–14

Cohan CL, Bradbury TN. 1997. Negative life events, marital interaction, and the longitudinal course of newlywed marriage. *J. Pers. Soc. Psychol.* 73:114–28

Collins NL. 1996. Working models of attachment: implications for explanation, emotion, and behavior. *J. Pers. Soc. Psychol.* 71:810–32

Corr PJ, Pickering AD, Gray JA. 1997. Personality, punishment, and procedural learning: a test of J.A. Gray's anxiety theory. *J. Pers. Soc. Pyschol.* 73:337–44

Cox MJ, Paley B. 1997. Families as systems. *Annu. Rev. Psychol.* 48:243–67

Coyne JC, Downey G. 1991. Social factors and psychopathology: stress, social support, and coping processes. *Annu. Rev. Psychol.* 42:401–25

Cummings EM, Davies P. 1994. *Children and Marital Conflict*. New York: Guilford

Cutrona CE. 1996. *Social Support in Couples*. New York: Sage

Cutrona CE, Suhr JA. 1994. Social support communication in the context of marriage: an analysis of couples' supportive interactions. In *Communication of Social Support: Messages, Relationships, and Community*, ed. BB Burleson, TL Albrecht, IG Sarason, pp. 113–35. Thousand Oaks, CA: Sage

Davila J, Bradbury TN. 1998. Psychopathology and the marital dyad. In *Handbook of Family Psychopathology*, ed. L L'Abate. New York: Guilford. In press

Davila J, Bradbury TN, Cohan CL, Tolchluk S. 1997. Marital functioning and depressive symptoms: evidence for a stress generation model. *J. Pers. Soc. Psychol.* 73: 849–61

Doherty WJ. 1981. Cognitive processes in intimate conflict: II. Efficacy and learned helplessness. *Am. J. Fam. Ther.* 9:35–44

Dweck CS. 1996. Implicit theories as organiz-

ers of goals and behavior. See Gollwitzer & Bargh 1996, pp. 69–90

Ehrensaft MK, Vivian D. 1996. Spouses' reasons for not reporting existing marital aggression as a marital problem. *J. Fam. Psychol.* 10:443–54

Emery RE. 1992. Family conflicts and their developmental implications. In *Conflict in Child and Adolescent Development*, ed. CU Shantz, WW Hartup, pp. 270–98. Cambridge, UK: Cambridge Univ. Press

Emmelkamp PMG, Gerlsma C. 1994. Marital functioning and the anxiety disorders. *Behav. Ther.* 25:407–30

Erel O, Burman B. 1995. Interrelatedness of marital relations and parent-child relations: a meta-analytic review. *Psychol. Bull.* 118:108–32

Ewart CK, Taylor CB, Kraemer HC, Agras WS. 1991. High blood pressure and marital discord: not being nasty matters more than being nice. *Health Psychol.* 103: 155–63

Feeney JA. 1994. Attachment style, communication patterns and satisfaction across the life cycle of marriage. *Pers. Relat.* 1: 333–48

Fincham FD. 1998. Child development and marital relations. *Child Dev.* 69:543–74

Fincham FD, Beach SRH, Kemp-Fincham SI. 1997. Marital quality: a new theoretical perspective. In *Satisfaction in Close Relationships*, ed. RJ Sternberg, M Hojjat, pp. 275–304. New York: Guilford

Fincham FD, Bradbury TN. 1987. The assessment of marital quality: a reevaluation. *J. Marriage Fam.* 49:797–809

Fincham FD, Bradbury TN. 1988. The impact of attributions in marriage: an experimental analysis. *J. Soc. Clin. Psychol.* 7: 147–62

Fincham FD, Bradbury TN. 1991. Marital conflict: towards a more complete integration of research and treatment. In *Advances in Family Intervention, Assessment and Theory*, ed. JP Vincent, 5:1–24. Greenwich, CT: JAI

Fincham FD, Bradbury TN. 1992. Assessing attributions in marriage: the Relationship Attribution Measure. *J. Pers. Soc. Psychol.* 62:457–68

Fincham FD, Garnier PC, Gano-Phillips S, Osborne LN. 1995. Pre-interaction expectations, marital satisfaction and accessibility: a new look at sentiment override. *J. Fam. Psychol.* 9:3–14

Fincham FD, Linfield K. 1997. A new look at marital quality: Can spouses be positive and negative about their marriage? *J. Fam. Psychol.* 11:489–502

Fincham FD, Osborne LN. 1993. Marital conflict and children: retrospect and prospect. *Clin. Psychol. Rev.* 13:75–88

Glenn ND. 1990. Quantitative research on marital quality in the 1980s: a critical review. *J. Marriage Fam.* 52:818–31

Gollwitzer PM, Bargh JA, eds. 1996. *The Psychology of Action.* New York: Guilford

Gollwitzer PM, Brandstatter V. 1997. Implementation intentions and effective goal pursuit. *J. Pers. Soc. Psychol.* 73:186–99

Gottman JM. 1979. *Marital Interaction: Experimental Investigations.* New York: Academic

Gottman JM. 1994. *What Predicts Divorce?* Hillsdale, NJ: Erlbaum

Gottman JM, Krokoff LJ. 1989. Marital interaction and satisfaction: a longitudinal view. *J. Consult. Clin. Psychol.* 57:47–52

Gottman JM, Levenson RW. 1992. Marital processes predictive of later dissolution: behavior, physiology, and health. *J. Pers. Soc. Psychol.* 63:221–33

Gottman JM, Markman HJ, Notarius CI. 1977. The topograpy of marital conflict: a sequential analysis of verbal and non-verbal behavior. *J. Marriage Fam.* 39:461–77

Gray JA. 1987. *The Psychology of Fear and Stress.* Cambridge, UK: Cambridge Univ. Press

Grych JH, Fincham FD. 1990. Marital conflict and children's adjustment: a cognitive-contextual framework. *Psychol. Bull.* 108:267–90

Halford WK, Bouma R. 1997. Individual psychopathology and marital distress. See Halford & Markman 1997, pp. 291–321

Halford WK, Markman HJ, eds. 1997. *Clinical Handbook of Marriage and Couples Intervention.* London: Wiley

Heavey CL, Christensen A, Malamuth NM. 1995. The longitudinal impact of demand and withdrawal during marital conflict. *J. Consult. Clin. Psychol.* 63:797–801

Heavey CL, Layne C, Christensen A. 1993. Gender and conflict structure in marital interaction: a replication and extension. *J. Consult. Clin. Psychol.* 61:16–27

Heyman RE, Eddy JM, Weiss RL, Vivian D. 1995. Factor analysis of the marital interaction coding system MICS. *J. Fam. Psychol.* 9:209–15

Hocker JL, Wilmot WW. 1995. *Interpersonal Conflict.* Madison, WI: Brown & Benchmark. 4th ed.

Holmes JG, Murray SL. 1996. Conflict in close relationships. In *Social Psychology: Handbook of Basic Principles*, ed. ET Higgins, A Kruglanski, pp. 622–54. New York: Guilford

House JS, Landis KR, Umberson D. 1988. So-

cial relationships and health. *Science* 241: 540–45

Jouriles EN, Farris AM. 1992. Effects of marital conflict on subsequent parent-son interactions. *Behav. Ther.* 23:355–74

Julien D, Markman HJ, Leveille S, Chartrand E, Begin J. 1994. Networks' support and interference with regard to marriage: disclosures of marital problems to confidants. *J. Fam. Psychol.* 8:16–31

Julien D, Markman HJ, Lindahl KM. 1989. A comparison of a global and a microanalytic coding system: implications for future trends in studying interactions. *Behav. Assess.* 11:81–100

Kanfer FH. 1996. Motivation and emotion in behavior therapy. In *Advances in Cognitive-Behavioral Therapy*, ed. KS Dobson, KD Craig, pp. 1–30. Thousand Oaks, CA: Sage

Kanfer FH, Schefft BK. 1988. *Guiding the Process of Therapeutic Change.* Champaign, IL: Research Press

Karney BR, Bradbury TN. 1995. The longitudinal course of marital quality and stability: a review of theory, method, and research. *Psychol. Bull.* 118:3–34

Karney BR, Bradbury TN. 1997. Neuroticism, marital interaction, and the trajectory of marital satisfaction. *J. Pers. Soc. Psychol.* 72:1075–92

Katz JA, Beach SRH, Anderson P. 1996. Self-enhancement versus self-verification: Does spousal support always help? *Cogn. Ther. Res.* 20:345–60

Kelley HH, Thibaut JW. 1978. *Interpersonal Relations: A Theory of Interdependence.* New York: Wiley

Kelly C, Huston TL, Cate RM. 1985. Premarital relationship correlates of the erosion of satisfaction in marriage. *J. Soc. Pers. Relat.* 2:167–78

Kelly EL, Conley JJ. 1987. Personality and compatibility: a prospective analysis of marital stability and marital satisfaction. *J. Pers. Soc. Psychol.* 52:27–40

Kiecolt-Glaser JK, Glaser R, Cacioppo JT, MacCullum RC, Snydersmith M, et al. 1997. Marital conflict in older adults: endocrine and immunological correlates. *Psychosom. Med.* 59:339–49

Kiecolt-Glaser JK, Kennedy S, Malkoff S, Fisher L, Speicher CE, et al. 1988. Marital discord and immunity in males. *Psychosom. Med.* 50:213–29

Kiecolt-Glaser JK, Malarkey WB, Chee M, Newton T, Cacioppo JT, et al. 1993. Negative behavior during marital conflict is associated with immunological down-regulation. *Psychosom. Med.* 55: 395–409

Kiecolt-Glaser JK, Newton T, Cacioppo JT, MacCallum RC, Glaser R, et al. 1996. Marital conflict and endocrine function: Are men really more physiologically affected than women? *J. Consult. Clin. Psychol.* 64:324–32

Kihlstrom JF. 1987. The cognitive unconscious. *Science* 237:1445–52

Kluwer ES, Heesink JAM, Van de Vliert E. 1996. Marital conflict about the division of household labor and paid work. *J. Marriage Fam.* 58:958–69

Kluwer ES, Heesink JAM, Van de Vliert E. 1997. The marital dynamics of conflict over the division of labor. *J. Marriage Fam.* 59:635–53

Knee CR. 1998. Implicit theories of relationships: assessment and prediction of romantic relationship initiation, coping, and longevity. *J. Pers. Soc. Psychol.* 74:360–70

Koerner K, Jacobson NJ. 1994. Emotion and behavior in couple therapy. In *The Heart of the Matter: Perspectives on Emotion in Marital Therapy*, ed. SM Johnson, LS Greenberg, pp. 207–26. New York: Brunner/Mazel

Kruglanski AW. 1996. Goals as knowledge structures. See Gollwitzer & Bargh 1996, pp. 599–618

Kurdek LA. 1994. Areas of conflict of gay, lesbian, and heterosexual couples: What couples argue about influences relationship satisfaction. *J. Marriage Fam.* 56:923–34

Leonard KE, Roberts LJ. 1998. Marital aggression, quality, and stability in the first year of marriage: findings from the Buffalo newlywed study. See Bradbury 1998, pp. 44–73

Lewin K. 1951. *Field Theory in Social Science: Selected Theoretical Papers by Kurt Lewin*. New York: Academic

Lindahl K, Clements M, Markman H. 1998. The development of marriage: a nine-year perspective. See Bradbury 1998, pp. 205–36

Malarkey WB, Kiecolt-Glaser JK, Pearl D, Glaser R. 1994. Hostile behavior during conflict alters pituitary and adrenal hormones. *Psychosom. Med.* 56:41–51

Margolin G. 1988. Marital conflict is not marital conflict is not marital conflict. In *Social Learning and Systems Approaches to Marriage and the Family*, ed. R Peters, RJ McMahon, pp. 193–216. New York: Brunner/Mazel

Margolin G, Christensen A, John RS. 1996. The continuance and spillover of everyday tensions in distressed and nondistressed families. *J. Fam. Psychol.* 10:304–21

Markman HJ, Notarius CI, Stephen T, Smith T. 1981. Behavioral observation systems for couples: the current status. In *Assessing Marriage: New Behavioral Approaches*, ed. E Filsinger, R Lewis, pp. 234–62. Beverly Hills, CA: Sage

Markman HJ, Renick MJ, Floyd FJ, Stanley SM, Clements M. 1993. Preventing marital distress through communication and conflict management training: a 4- and 5-year follow-up. *J. Consult. Clin. Psychol.* 61:70–77

Markus H, Nurius P. 1986. Possible selves. *Am.. Psychol.* 41:954–69

Martin L, Tesser A. 1996. Some ruminative thoughts. In *Advances in Social Cognition*, ed. RS Wyer, 9:1–48. Hillsdale, NJ: Erlbaum

McCall M. 1995. Orientation, outcome, and other-serving attributions. *Basic Appl. Soc. Psychol.* 17:49–64

McGonagle KA, Kessler RC, Schiling EA. 1992. The frequency and determinants of marital disagreements in a community sample. *J. Soc. Pers. Relat.* 9:507–24

McLeod JD. 1994. Anxiety disorders and marital quality. *J. Abnorm. Psychol.* 103:767–76

Melby JN, Ge X, Conger RD, Warner TD. 1995. The importance of task in evaluating positive marital interactions. *J. Marriage Fam.* 57:981–94

Mikulincer M. 1998. Adult attachment style and individual differences in functional versus dysfunctional experiences of anger. *J. Pers. Soc. Psychol.* 74:513–24

Mikulincer M, Florian V, Weller A. 1993. Attachment styles, coping strategies, and post-traumatic psychological distress: the impact of the Gulf War in Israel. *J. Pers. Soc. Psychol.* 64:817–26

Miller GA, Galanter E, Pribram KH. 1960. *Plans and the Structure of Behavior*. New York: Holt

Miller GE, Bradbury TN. 1995. Refining the association between attributions and behavior in marital interaction. *J. Fam. Psychol.* 9:196–208

Murphy CM, O'Farrell TJ. 1994. Factors associated with marital aggression in male alcoholics. *J. Fam. Psychol.* 8:321–35

Murray SL, Holmes JG, Griffin DW. 1996a. The benefits of positive illusions: idealization and the construction of satisfaction in close relationships. *J. Pers. Soc. Psychol.* 70:79–98

Murray SL, Holmes JG, Griffin DW. 1996b. The self-fulfilling nature of positive illusions in romantic relationships: Love is not blind, but prescient. *J. Pers. Soc. Psychol.* 71:1155–80

Nadler A. 1997. Personality and help seeking:

autonomous versus dependent seeking of help. In *Sourcebook of Social Support and Personality*, ed. GR Pierce, B Lakey, IG Sarason, BR Sarason, pp. 379–407. New York: Plenum

Noller P, Feeney JA, Bonnell D, Callan VJ. 1994. A longitudinal study of conflict in early marriage. *J. Soc. Pers. Relat.* 11: 233–52

Notarius CI, Benson PR, Sloane D, Vanzetti NA, Hornyak LM. 1989. Exploring the interface between perception and behavior. *Behav. Assess.* 11:39–64

O'Farrell TJ, Choquette KA, Birchler GR. 1991. Sexual satisfaction and dissatisfaction in the marital relationships of male alcoholics seeking marital therapy. *J. Stud. Alcohol.* 52:441–47

O'Leary KD, Malone J, Tyree A. 1994. Physical aggression in early marriage: prerelationship and relationship effects. *J. Consult. Clin. Psychol.* 62:594–602

O'Leary KD, Smith DA. 1991. Marital interactions. *Annu. Rev. Psychol.* 42:191–212

Owen MT, Cox MJ. 1997. Marital conflict and the development of infant-parent attachment relationships. *J. Fam. Psychol.* 11: 152–64

Pasch LA, Bradbury TN. 1998. Social support, conflict, and the development of marital dysfunction. *J. Consult. Clin. Psychol.* 66: 219–30

Pietromonoco PR, Carnelly KB. 1994. Gender and working models of attachment: consequences for perceptions of self and romantic relationships. *Pers. Relat.* 1:63–82

Pistole MC. 1989. Attachment in adult romantic relationships: style of conflict resolution and relationship satisfaction. *J. Soc. Pers. Relat.* 6:505–10

Pruitt DG. 1997. Social conflict. In *Handbook of Social Psychology*, ed. DT Gilbert, ST Fiske, G Lindsay, pp. 470–503. New York: Oxford Univ. Press. 4th ed.

Pruitt DG, Olczak PV. 1995. Beyond hope: approaches to resolving seemingly intractable conflict. See Bunker & Rubin 1995, pp. 59–92

Repetti RL. 1989. Effects of daily workload on subsequent behavior during marital interaction: the roles of social withdrawal and spousal support. *J. Pers. Soc. Psychol.* 57: 651–59

Repetti RL, Wood J. 1997. Effects of daily stress at work on mothers' interactions with preschoolers. *J. Fam. Psychol.* 11: 90–108

Roberts LJ, Krokoff LJ. 1990. A time series analysis of withdrawal, hostility, and displeasure in satisfied and dissatisfied marriages. *J. Marriage Fam.* 52:95–105

Rubin JZ, Levinger G. 1995. Levels of analysis: in search of generalizable knowledge. See Bunker & Rubin 1995, pp. 13–38

Rusbult CE. 1993. Understanding responses to dissatisfaction in close relationships: the exit-voice-loyalty-neglect model. In *Conflict between People and Groups: Causes, Processes, and Resolutions*, ed. S Worchel, JA Simpson, pp. 30–59. Chicago: Nelson-Hall

Rusbult CE, Bissonnette VI, Arriaga XB, Cox CL. 1998. Accommodation processes across the early years of marriage. See Bradbury 1998, pp. 74–113

Rusbult CE, Verette J, Whitney GA, Slovik LF, Lipkus I. 1991. Accommodation processes in close relationships: theory and preliminary empirical evidence. *J. Pers. Soc. Psychol.* 60:53–78

Sagrestano LM, Christensen A, Heavey CL. 1998. Social influence techniques during marital conflict. *Pers. Relat.* 5:75–90

Scharfe E, Bartholomew K. 1995. Accommodation and attachment representations in young couples. *J. Soc. Pers. Relat.* 12: 389–401

Schmaling KB, Sher TG. 1997. Physical health and relationships. See Halford & Markman 1997, pp. 323–45

Senchak M, Leonard KE. 1992. Attachment style and marital adjustment among newlywed couples. *J. Soc. Pers. Relat.* 9:51–64

Simpson JA, Rholes WS, Nelligan J. 1992. Support-seeking and support giving within couples in an anxiety provoking situation: the role of attachment styles. *J. Pers. Soc. Pschol.* 62:434–46

Smith DA, Vivian D, O'Leary KD. 1990. Longitudinal predictors of marital discord from premarital expressions of affect. *J. Consult. Clin. Psychol.* 58:790–98

Stone AA, Neale JM. 1984. New measure of daily coping: development and preliminary results. *J. Pers. Soc. Psychol.* 46: 892–906

Sullivan KT, Bradbury TN. 1997. Are premarital prevention programs reaching couples at risk for marital discord? *J. Consult. Clin. Psychol.* 65:24–30

Swann WB, Hixon JG, De LaRonde C. 1992. Embracing the bitter truth: negative self-concepts and marital commitment. *Psychol. Sci.* 3:118–21

Tesser A, Beach SRH. 1998. Life events, relationship quality, and depression: an investigation of judgement discontinuity in vivo. *J. Pers. Soc. Psychol.* 74:36–52

Tesser A, Martin LL, Cornell DP. 1996. On the substitutability of self-protective mechanisms. See Gollwitzer & Bargh 1996, pp. 48–68

Thompson MM, Zanna MP, Griffin DW. 1995. Let's not be indifferent about attitudinal ambivalence. In *Attitude Strength: Antecedents and Consequences*, ed. RE Petty, JA Drosnick, pp. 361–86. Hillsdale, NJ: Erlbaum

Van den Broucke S, Vandereycken W, Norre J. 1997. *Eating Disorders and Marital Relationships.* London: Routledge

Vangelisti AL, Huston TL. 1994. Maintaining marital satisfaction and love. In *Communication and Relational Maintenance*, ed. DJ Canary, L Stafford, pp. 165–86. New York: Academic

Weiss RL, Dehle C. 1994. Cognitive behavioral perspectives on marital conflict. In *Conflict in Intimate Relationships*, ed. DD Cahn, pp. 95–115. Mahwah, NJ: Erlbaum

Weiss RL, Heyman RE. 1997. A clinical-research overview of couple interactions. See Halford & Markman 1997, pp. 13–41

Woody EZ, Costanzo PR. 1990. Does marital agony precede marital ecstasy? A comment on Gottman and Krokoff's "Marital interaction and satisfaction: a longitudinal

Annu. Rev. Psychol. 1999. 50:79–107
Copyright © 1999 by Annual Reviews. All rights reserved

PSYCHOPATHOLOGY: Description and Classification

P. E. Nathan

Department of Psychology, University of Iowa, Iowa City, Iowa 52242;
e-mail: peter-nathan@uiowa.edu

J. W. Langenbucher

Center of Alcohol Studies, Rutgers University, New Brunswick, New Jersey 08854;
e-mail: lngnbchr@rci.rutgers.edu

KEY WORDS: syndromal diagnosis, diagnostic reliability, diagnostic validity, diagnostic nomenclature

ABSTRACT

DSM-IV's strong empirical base has yielded an instrument with good to excellent reliability and improved validity. *Diagnostic reliability* depends on both the clarity and validity of diagnostic criteria and the changeability of disorders over time: The reliability of schizophrenic spectrum disorders, personality disorders, and some childhood and adolescent disorders remains problematic. Findings on *diagnostic validity* appear paradoxical: Attempts to validate schizophrenic spectrum disorders with neurobiological and genetic-familial validators have been only modestly successful, whereas the tripartite personality trait model has differentiated a range of depressive and anxiety disorders. Research on *comorbidity* has identified several highly comorbid disorders (substance-related disorders, personality disorders, depression, and anxiety) as well as some adverse consequences of comorbidity. The advantages of *dimensional approaches* to diagnosis have largely been demonstrated conceptually; ultimate conclusions about the strengths and weaknesses of dimensional and syndromal methods await substantial additional empirical research.

CONTENTS

79

INTRODUCTION

Four *Annual Review of Psychology* chapters published in the 1990s (Clark et al 1995, Mineka et al 1998, Sher & Trull 1996, Widiger & Trull 1991) have considered many of the issues also considered in this chapter. Along with its desirable overlap in coverage with what has gone before, however, this chapter also has a unique identity. It is the first *Annual Review of Psychology* chapter on this topic written following publication of the fourth edition of the *Diagnostic and Statistical Manual of Mental Disorders* (*DSM-IV*) (APA 1994) and its voluminous accompaniments; thus it weighs the advances of this new edition and takes note of criticisms that have been leveled against it. Preparation of this chapter coincided with several efforts by psychologists to develop alternatives to syndromal diagnosis; these efforts are reviewed, and their potential for meaningful improvement in diagnostic reliability and validity is evaluated.

DSM-IV

The DSM-IV Process

The principal goal of the *DSM-IV* process (Frances et al 1989, Nathan 1998, Widiger & Trull 1993, Widiger et al 1994a) was to create an empirically based nomenclature. For this purpose, a three-stage process was used. Thirteen Work Groups were formed that began their efforts with systematic literature reviews designed to address unresolved diagnostic questions. When literature reviews failed to resolve questions, the Work Groups sought to locate clinical data sets to do so; 40 analyses of existing patient data sets were ultimately carried out. The Work Groups also designed and carried out field trials to generate new clinical data; 12 large-scale field trials at more than 70 sites worldwide, involving more than 7,000 participants, were completed.

The DSM-IV Sourcebooks

The results of the three-stage process are or will be chronicled in four *Sourcebooks* that archive Work Group literature reviews and summarize findings from data reanalyses and field trials. Three (Widiger et al 1994b, 1996a, 1997) have been published thus far. They include 155 detailed literature reviews commissioned by the *DSM-IV* Work Groups. The remaining *Sourcebook* will present results of the data reanalyses and field trials.

Reviewing the first *Sourcebook* volume (Widiger et al 1994b), Skodal (1996:432) terms *DSM-IV* "the most ambitious undertaking in the history of American psychiatric nosology" and describes the literature reviews included in the volume as "comprehensive, objective, and dispassionate." Thompson (1997), reviewing the second volume, likens the efforts of Robert Spitzer, who led development of *DSM-III* (APA 1980) and *DSM-III-R* (APA 1987), and Alan Frances, leader of the development of *DSM-IV*, to those of American explorers Lewis and Clark.

The DSM-IV Field Trials

Although summaries of the field trials will be published in the fourth volume of the *Sourcebooks*, nine *DSM-IV* field trial reports have already been published in journals. Field trial reports on mixed anxiety-depression (Zinbarg et al 1994) and oppositional defiant disorder and conduct disorder in children and adolescents (Lahey et al 1994) appeared in August 1994, followed later the same year by field trial reports on sleep disorders (Buysse et al 1994) and autistic disorder (Volkmar et al 1994). In 1995, field trial reports appeared for obsessive-compulsive disorder (Foa & Kozak 1995), somatization disorder (Yutzy et al 1995), mood disorders (Keller et al 1995), and substance-related disorders (Cottler et al 1995). The field trial report for antisocial personality disorder was published in 1996 (Widiger et al 1996b). Most of the field trials contrasted the diagnostic sensitivity and specificity of alternative sets of diagnostic criteria, including those of the *International Classification of Diseases (ICD)-10, DSM-III-R,* and *DSM-III,* and one or more sets of new criteria. Many explored the impact on diagnostic reliability of changes in the wording of criteria. Some field trials also considered the diagnostic consequences of differing criterion thresholds and assessed the need for additional diagnostic categories.

Symptom data from the field trial for schizophrenia and related psychotic disorders were recently factor-analyzed (Ratakonda et al 1998) to determine whether the three common schizophrenic symptom domains, labeled positive, negative, and disorganized, also encompass the symptoms of psychotic disorders other than schizophrenia. These domains were not found to be exclusive to schizophrenia in that they also described the behavior of patients with schizoaffective and primary mood disorder.

DSM-IV Aids

A number of *DSM-IV* learning and training aids have also appeared. These include two volumes of *Clinical Interview Using DSM-IV* (Othmer & Othmer 1994a,b); *DSM-IV Training Guide* (Reid & Wise 1995); *DSM-IV Guidebook* (Frances et al 1995); *DSM-IV Handbook of Differential Diagnosis* (First et al 1995); *DSM-IV Training Guide for Diagnosis of Childhood Disorders* (Rapoport & Ismond 1996); and *DSM-IV Case Studies: A Clinical Guide to Differential Diagnosis* (Frances & Ross 1996). While several of the reviewers of these books (Fenton 1996, Sadock 1995, Thompson 1997, Volkmar 1997) admit to initial skepticism about the utility of these volumes, most go on to say good things about the degree to which they enhance the usefulness of *DSM-IV*.

Reliability and Validity of DSM-IV Diagnoses

Most data reported on the reliability and validity of *DSM-IV* categories have come from field trials. They suggest modest increments in the reliability of a few diagnostic categories (e.g. oppositional defiant disorder and conduct disorder in children and adolescents, substance abuse and dependence) and validity (e.g. autistic disorder, oppositional defiant disorder in childhood and adolescence) but no real progress in addressing the substantial reliability problems of personality disorders, sleep disorders, disorders of childhood and adolescence, and some disorders within the schizophrenic spectrum.

The Research Diagnostic Project (RDP) at Rutgers University has studied diagnostic issues in substance abuse for several years. Initial RDP studies found the reliability of lifetime *DSM-IV* diagnoses of alcohol, cannabis, cocaine, and opiate abuse and dependence to be high (Langenbucher et al 1994a) and the diagnostic concordance of *DSM-III*, *DSM-IV,* and *ICD-10* for alcohol, amphetamines, cannabis, cocaine, hallucinogens, opiates, PCP, and sedative/hypnotics to be high for severe disorders and less so for disorders barely reaching diagnostic threshold (Langenbucher et al 1994b). More recently, Langenbucher and his colleagues (1997) compared the predictive power of four sets of dependence criteria and found the *DSM-IV* criteria for tolerance and dependence to be less discriminating than alternative criteria. Langenbucher & Chung (1995) traced the onset and staging of symptoms of alcohol abuse and dependence and identified three discrete stages—alcohol abuse, alcohol dependence, and accommodation to the illness—thereby supporting the construct validity of alcohol abuse as a discrete first illness phase and alcohol dependence as distinct from and succeeding abuse.

Three additional studies of *DSM-IV* reliability and validity have also appeared. The first (Eaton et al 1997) reported a one-year incidence rate of 3.0 per 1,000 per year for major depression in Baltimore, a rate comparable to earlier estimates using *DSM-III* criteria (Eaton et al 1981). Two other studies explored diagnostic issues raised by personality disorders. Ball and his colleagues (1997) examined relationships between alcohol, cocaine, and opiate abusers' personality disorders and their scores on five-factor and seven-factor models of personality [respectively, the *NEO Personality Inventory* (*NEO-PI*) (Costa & McCrae 1989, 1990) and the *Temperament and Character Inventory* (*TCI*) (Cloninger et al 1993)]. *NEO* scales were strongly linked with specific personality disorders, *TCI* scales somewhat less so, thereby adding to the growing literature attesting to the power of personality trait dimensions to portray personality disorder. Westen (1997) explored differences in how clinicians use Axis I and Axis II. His results point to an additional source of the diagnostic unreliability of personality disorders: While clinicians tend to use questions taken directly from the operational criteria to diagnose Axis I disorders, Axis II diagnoses are more often made by "listening to patients describe interpersonal interactions and observing their behavior with the interviewer" (p. 895), a practice that may further reduce the reliability of personality disorder assessment.

Gender and Cultural Bias in DSM-IV

Corbitt & Widiger (1995) suggest that a paucity of empirical findings on gender prevalence rates in personality disorders (PDs) helped heighten the controversy surrounding *DSM-III-R*'s estimates that more women than men merit the diagnoses of histrionic PD and dependent PD. The *DSM-IV* text now fails to specify a difference in gender prevalence rates for these disorders. *DSM-IV* has also added three PDs (schizoid, schizotypal, and narcissistic) to the three (paranoid, antisocial, and obsessive-compulsive) that *DSM-III-R* indicated were diagnosed more often in males than in females. Corbitt & Widiger ask whether *DSM-IV* has unintentionally introduced diagnostic bias, in the effort to combat it, by going beyond the modest empirical data on gender prevalence rates for histrionic and dependent PDs. Hartung & Widiger (1998) consider the question of gender prevalence rates in *DSM-IV* diagnoses more generally. Although conclusions about these rates were informed by data from the field trials, analyses of existing data sets, and systematic literature reviews, these data sources could possibly have been compromised by sampling biases (e.g. disproportionate numbers of one or the other genders in sample populations) or biases within the diagnostic criteria themselves (e.g. lack of gender neutrality in criteria sets). As a result, *DSM-IV* may retain vestiges of the gender-based bias that characterized its predecessors.

Responding to the addition of material on cultural factors of potential diagnostic significance at a number of points in the *DSM-IV* text, Malgady et al (1996) examined idiomatic expressions of psychological distress among a group of first- and second-generation Puerto Ricans in the New York metropolitan area. They hypothesized that conceptualizing psychiatric symptomatology from the cultural group's perspective would yield better diagnostic case-finding within this minority group. As predicted, an anger idioms scale correlated significantly with both depressive and anxious symptomatology, thereby showing that using the meaning of the forms of anger by which these subjects expressed anger for diagnostic purposes heightened diagnostic sensitivity in this minority group.

Criticisms of DSM-IV

There is general agreement on the strong empirical base that underlies DSM-IV. Yet even persons most involved in the development of the instrument acknowledge limitations on full utilization of the extensive empirical database because of unavoidable biased or misleading interpretations of the data (e.g. Kendler 1990, Widiger & Trull 1993). For example, responding to criticisms that professional issues overshadowed scientific ones in the creation of *DSM-IV* (e.g. Caplan 1991, Carson 1991), Widiger & Trull (1993) defend attention to issues of utility that sometimes preempted issues of validity, as when a valid diagnosis is de-emphasized because so few patients meet its criteria. Nonetheless, even though these authors admit that the *DSM-IV* Task Force had to be sensitive to a variety of forensic, social, international, and public health issues, they see the result as a largely empirically driven instrument. They also expect many of the decisions made during development of the instrument to continue to be debated, in part because the database for these decisions was often ambiguous or inadequate.

The lead review of *DSM-IV* in the *American Journal of Psychiatry* was written by Samuel Guze (1995), a key figure in the development of *DSM-III*. While largely positive, Guze's review (1995) expresses concern that many *DSM-IV* diagnostic conditions continue to fail to meet Robins & Guze's (1970) criteria for diagnostic validity. He criticizes the apparent proliferation of less than fully validated diagnostic entities, a theme others (e.g. Grumet 1995; Kirk & Kutchins 1992, 1994) have also sounded. To this concern, Pincus and colleagues (1996) note that while *DSM-IV* contains 13 diagnoses not in *DSM-III-R*, it has eliminated eight *DSM-III-R* diagnoses, for a net gain of only five.

Sarbin (1997), a long-standing critic of syndromal diagnosis, laments the continuing unreliability and questionable validity of syndromal diagnosis, epitomized by *DSM-IV*, and deplores "the increasing medicalization of distress," which forces clinicians to "search for causes of unwanted behaviors in biomedical anomalies" (p. 233). Sarbin advocates instead the contextualist approach to understanding psychopathology, in which "the person is treated as an agent who employs strategic actions to maintain a self-narrative" (p. 233). Sarbin's rejection of the disease model harkens back to Szasz's portrayal (1960) of mental illness as a myth imposed on society by acquisitive mental health professionals, as well as to Laing's view (1967) that schizophrenic symptoms are a strategy adopted to enable some persons to survive in impossible environments.

Conclusions About DSM-IV

The *DSM-IV* Task Force succeeded in making the instrument's development strongly empirical. Few studies of *DSM-IV* diagnostic reliability and validity have been reported to date. There is no reason to believe that reliability will be less than that of its predecessors, and there is reason to believe that validity will be greater.

RELIABILITY AND VALIDITY OF *DSM-III*, *DSM-III-R*, AND *ICD-10* DIAGNOSES

Diagnostic Reliability

ICD-10 FIELD TRIALS   The international clinical field trials conducted to evaluate draft clinical descriptions and diagnostic guidelines for *ICD-10* also permitted comparison of the interrater reliability of Canadian and US clinicians with that of clinicians worldwide (Regier et al 1994). Interrater reliability of *ICD-10* in Canada and the United States was similar to that of clinicians using *ICD-10* worldwide, as well as to that from the *DSM-III* field trials. Even greater concordance between Canadian and US clinicians and clinicians in other parts of the world is anticipated when *DSM-IV* has been in general use for a longer period because *ICD-10* and *DSM-IV* are substantially more similar than were previous editions of both of these instruments. Field trials of the research version of the *ICD-10* (Sartorius et al 1995) were also undertaken. Most clinician researchers judged the research diagnostic criteria to be explicit and easy to use. Interrater reliability was high for most categories, with two-character kappa coefficients for major disorders such as schizophrenia and substance abuse excellent (with the exception of adult personality disorders, for which it was only good). At the three-character, subtype level, reliability was lower; only half the categories showed excellent agreement.

DIAGNOSTIC STABILITY   Diagnostic stability for a variety of disorders has been studied for periods ranging from 6 months to 8 years. Fennig et al (1994) investigated the 6-month stability of *DSM-III-R* diagnoses in a large group of first-admission patients with psychosis, a notably diagnostically unstable group. Affective psychosis and schizophrenic disorders showed substantial diagnostic stability, with 87–89% of patients remaining in the same broad category. Subtypes of these conditions were less stable; only 62–86% of patients remained in the same subcategory. Forty-three percent of these diagnostic changes could be attributed to clinical course, while the rest were assumed to reflect the imperfect reliability of the diagnostic process. Nelson & Rice (1997) tested the one-year stability of *DSM-III* lifetime diagnoses of obsessive-compulsive disorder (OCD) in data from the Epidemiologic Catchment Area (ECA) study (Eaton et al 1981). The temporal stability of OCD diagnoses over the course of a year turned out to be surprisingly poor: A year later, of subjects in the ECA sample who met criteria for OCD, only 19% reported symptoms that met the OCD criteria. These findings are seen to reflect an excess of false positives for OCD on initial diagnostic examination, raising concern about the validity of diagnoses of other conditions reported in the ECA study.

Mattanah and his colleagues (1995) investigated the stability of a range of *DSM-III-R* disorders in a group of adolescent inpatients followed up to two years after hospitalization. Predictably, diagnostic stability for these subjects was lower than for the same diagnoses given adults. Internalizing disorders (e.g. affective disorders) turned out to be more stable but of uncertain reliability because of more new cases at follow-up, while externalizing disorders [e.g. attention-deficit hyperactivity disorder (ADHD)] were less stable but more reliable because of fewer new cases at follow-up. Surprisingly, personality disorder clusters and substance use disorders were both stable (53%) and reliable. Chen et al (1996) undertook a longitudinal study of changes from schizophrenia diagnoses to those of other disorders and from those of other disorders to schizophrenia in inpatients hospitalized at an urban acute care hospital at least four times over a 7-year period. Only 22% of patients with a schizophrenia diagnosis at the beginning of the study received a different diagnosis during a subsequent hospitalization. Females and patients of Hispanic origin were more likely than others to experience a diagnostic change from schizophrenia. However, 33% of patients with an initial diagnosis other than schizophrenia were later diagnosed with schizophrenia. Males and African Americans were more likely to change to a diagnosis of schizophrenia. These authors conclude that contrary to general consensus, the diagnosis of schizophrenia in current practice is not static. Factors specific to particular groups of patients, interacting with clinical course, produce this surprising degree of diagnostic instability.

Coryell et al (1994) followed a large group of patients initially diagnosed with major depressive disorder according to the Research Diagnostic Criteria (Spitzer et al 1975) at 6-month intervals for 5 years, then annually for another 3 years. During this time, most patients had at least two recurrences of the disorder; some had three or four. The kappa statistic quantified the likelihood that patients with psychotic, agitated/retarded, or endogeneous subtypes of the disorder in a given episode would manifest the same subtype in subsequent episodes. The psychotic subtype showed the greatest diagnostic stability across multiple subsequent episodes; for all three subtypes, diagnostic stability was greater for contiguous episodes than for noncontiguous episodes.

Conclusions about diagnostic stability   These diagnostic stability studies emphasize the extent to which diagnostic reliability depends on both the clarity and validity of diagnostic criteria and the inherent changeability of particular disorders over time, as influenced by alterations in environmental and individual circumstance. These findings also suggest that the stability component attributable to *DSM-III* and *DSM-III-R* diagnostic criteria caused problems for a number of diagnoses.

DEVELOPMENT OF MORE RELIABLE DIAGNOSTIC INSTRUMENTS AND PROCEDURES   The research reviewed here extends a 30-year effort to develop more sensitive and reliable diagnostic instruments and procedures that can be traced to Spitzer's pioneering efforts in the late 1960s (e.g. Spitzer et al 1967, 1970).

Pilkonis and his colleagues (1995) explored the reliability and validity of two structured diagnostic interviews for personality disorders, the *Personality Disorder Examination* (*PDE*) and the *Structured Interview for DSM-III-R* (*SIDP-R*), in an attempt to enhance the diagnostic reliability of personality disorders. While interrater reliabilities were excellent for continuous data, they were substantially lower for categorical diagnoses (e.g. any PD versus no PD), suggesting continued need both to clarify further and/or to reconceptualize the diagnostic criteria for personality disorders.

Hasin and her colleagues (1996) explored the reliability of the *Psychiatric Research Interview for Substance and Mental Disorders* (*PRISM*), a semi-structured diagnostic interview based on *DSM-IV* diagnostic criteria. A test-retest study of patients in dual diagnosis or substance abuse settings revealed good to excellent reliability for many diagnoses in patients for whom the reliability of psychiatric diagnoses has often been problematic in the past.

The diagnosis of childhood disorders, like that of personality disorders and psychiatric disorders comorbid with substance abuse, has also been problematic. Schwab-Stone and her colleagues (1994) examined the reliability of symptom reports by children and their parents on the *Diagnostic Interview Schedule for Children—Revised* (*DISC-R*). The reliability of test-retest interviews of parents of children aged 6–11 showing evidence of five common childhood psychiatric diagnoses was good to excellent for ADHD and separation anxiety disorder but only fair for overanxious disorder, oppositional defiant disorder, and conduct disorder. By contrast, the reliability of children's symptom reports was fair to poor.

Roy et al (1997) assessed the reliability and accuracy of a best-estimate diagnostic procedure to determine the factors associated with its reliability. Subjects were members of large multigenerational pedigrees densely affected by bipolar disorders or schizophrenia. The most problematic diagnostic distinctions involved schizoaffective disorder, which was confused with schizophrenia, bipolar I disorder, and schizophreniform disorder. Diagnostic disagreements were associated with mixed affective and psychotic symptoms, less diagnostic certainty, and shorter duration of illness. McGorry et al (1995) had similar aims—to test the procedural validity of four independent methods of assigning *DSM-III-R* diagnoses of psychotic disorders. First-episode psychotic patients were assessed by independent raters who compared three different diagnostic instruments with one another and with a consensus diagnosis assigned by an expert diagnostic team. Concordance between pairs of diagnostic procedures was only moderate; misclassification rates ranged from 24% to 36%.

Conclusions about the development of more reliable instruments and procedures   While the new instruments and procedures reported here show promise, they nonetheless yielded reliability estimates for certain disorders—those within the schizophrenic spectrum, personality disorders, and some childhood and adolescent disorders—that give continuing cause for concern.

Diagnostic Validity

MODELS OF VALIDITY   *DSM-III* generated a great deal of research that documented the heightened reliability of its operational criteria over its predecessors. With the publication of *DSM-IV*, and especially in the face of criticism that insufficient attention has been paid to diagnostic validity and utility, attention by nosologists has shifted somewhat to that issue.

An editorial in *The American Journal of Psychiatry* by Andreasen (1995) recalls Robins & Guze's (1970) proposal for a gold standard for validation that would include existing validators such as clinical description and family studies but add a new validator, laboratory tests. While acknowledging that laboratory tests have not yet emerged as prime sources of validation information, Andreasen nonetheless believes that psychiatry's neuroscience base is key to the continuing evolution of validation. Specifically, she proposes "an additional group of validators . . . to link symptoms and diagnoses to their neural substrates [which] include molecular genetics and molecular biology, neurochemistry, neuroanatomy, neurophysiology, and cognitive neuroscience . . . (linking) psychiatric diagnosis to its underlying abnormalities in DNA" (Andreasen 1995:162). As what follows indicates, an emphasis on the search for neuronal, neurobiological, and genetic-familial validators characterizes contemporary validation attempts.

SCHIZOPHRENIC SPECTRUM DISORDERS   Four of the five reports published during this period on efforts to validate schizophrenic spectrum disorders explored Andreasen's (1995) "additional group of validators."

Gur and her coworkers (1994) sought to relate whole-brain volume in men and women to clinical subtypes of schizophrenia. Magnetic resonance imaging (MRI) measures of cranial, brain, and ventricular and sulcal cerebrospinal fluid (CSF) volume were examined in schizophrenic men and women and healthy comparison subjects. The MRI measures differentiated males from females, including male patients from female patients, patients from comparison subjects, and subgroups of patients based on symptom profiles. The research revealed two patterns of neuroanatomic whole-brain abnormalities that differ in severity according to symptom differences and may reflect differential involvement of dysgenic and atrophic pathophysiological processes.

In an attempt to determine whether the diagnostic accuracy of the schizophrenic spectrum phenotypes of nonschizophrenic relatives of schizophrenic patients warrants their use in genetic linkage studies of schizophrenia, Faraone et al (1995) reviewed 30 studies of putative indicators of schizophrenic genotype. Although 42 measures of these indicators were found to discriminate the relatives of schizophrenic patients from normal comparison subjects, only six of the indicators actually improved the informational value of genetic linkage data, suggesting the need for further refinement of phenotypes for linkage analysis.

Two studies with related goals reported data from the epidemiologically based Roscommon Family Study. Kendler et al (1995b) separately examined the familial aggregation and coaggregation of five hierarchically defined disorders—schizophrenia, schizoaffective disorder, schizotypal/paranoid personality disorder, other nonaffective psychoses, and psychotic affective illness—in siblings, parents, and relatives of index and comparison probands. The aim was to determine whether these patterns can be explained by a single underlying continuum of liability to the schizophrenic spectrum. While schizophrenia and psychotic affective illness could be clearly assigned to the two extremes of the schizophrenia spectrum, the proper placement of schizoaffective disorder, schizotypal/paranoid personality disorder, and other nonaffective psychoses could not be clearly made. Nonetheless, these results support the existence of a schizophrenic spectrum in which these five disorders manifest, with varying severity, an underlying vulnerability that is strongly transmitted within families. In a companion report, Kendler et al (1995b) found that probands with schizoaffective disorder differed significantly from those with schizophrenia or affective illness in lifetime psychotic symptoms as well as outcome and negative symptoms assessed at follow-up. Relatives of probands with schizoaffective disorder had significantly higher rates of schizophrenia than relatives of probands with affective illness. These data are consistent with the hypotheses that schizoaffective disorder results from the co-occurrence of a high liability to both schizophrenia and affective illness and that *DSM-III-R* criteria for schizoaffective disorder define a syndrome that differs meaningfully from either schizophrenia or affective illness.

Strakowski (1994) reviewed research on antecedent, concurrent, and predictive validators of the *DSM-III/DSM-III-R* schizophreniform disorder diagnosis. Consistent data to support the validity of the diagnosis as either a distinct diagnostic entity or a subtype of schizophrenia or affective illness could not be found. Instead, these patients appear to constitute a heterogenous group with new-onset schizophrenia, schizoaffective disorder, and atypical affective disorder and a small subgroup with a remitting nonaffective psychosis.

Conclusions about the schizophrenic spectrum disorders   Research on schizophrenic spectrum disorders has succeeded in validating the disorders at either end of the spectrum, but it has generally failed to identify distinct validators, either clinical or neurobiological, for those disorders between the extremes. Nonetheless, because the heuristic value of the concept of the schizophrenic spectrum has been high, efforts to validate these disorders will likely continue.

DEPRESSIVE DISORDERS   Kendler & Roy (1995) explored links between two common diagnostic sources of lifetime major depression—family history and personal history—and three independent validators. Although data from personal interviews and family histories agreed diagnostically at only a modest level, controlling for presence or absence of a personal interview diagnosis of major depression permitted family history diagnosis of the same disorder to predict future episodes of major depression, neuroticism, and familial aggregation of major depression. Kendler et al (1996a) applied latent class analysis to 14 disaggregated *DSM-III-R* symptoms for major depression reported over the course of a year by members of more than a thousand female-female twin pairs. Three of the seven identified classes represented clinically significant depressive syndromes: mild typical depression, atypical depression, and severe typical depression. Depression was not etiologically homogeneous in this sample of twins but was, instead, composed of several syndromes at least partially distinct from clinical, longitudinal, and familial/genetic perspectives. Both studies by this group, then, showed a convergence of validators of major depression of both the "new" and "old" varieties. In contrast with Kendler et al's research on schizophrenic spectrum disorders, however, the validity of the major depression diagnostic syndrome was consistently supported.

Haslam & Beck (1994) tested claims for the content and latent structure of five proposed subtypes of major depression. Analysis of self-reported symptom and personality profiles of more than 500 consecutively admitted outpatients with a primary major depressive diagnosis yielded clear evidence for discreteness only for the endogenous subtype; the other proposed forms lacked internal cohesion or were more consistent with a continuous or dimensional account of major depression.

THE INTERFACE OF DEPRESSION AND ANXIETY   One of the most productive efforts to validate co-occurring depression and anxiety has been that of Clark and Watson. Their tripartite model groups symptoms of these conditions into three subtypes: (*a*) largely nonspecific symptoms of general distress; (*b*) the manifestations of somatic tension and arousal that are relatively unique to anxiety; and (*c*) the symptoms of anhedonia specific to depression. These researchers tested the validity of this model in five samples—three student, one adult, and one patient—in two studies reported in 1995 [students were studied even though Coyne (1994) suggests that because the distress of college students is conceptually and empirically different from *DSM-III-R* depression, it cannot serve as an analog for depression].

Watson et al (1995b) used the *Mood and Anxiety Symptom Questionnaire (MASQ)*, along with other symptom and cognition measures, to validate these hypothesized symptom groups. Consistent with the tripartite model, *MASQ* Anxious Arousal and Anhedonic Depression scales differentiated anxiety and depression well and also showed excellent convergent validity. Watson et al (1995a) conducted separate factor analyses of the 90 items on the *MASQ*. The same three factors (general distress, anhedonia versus positive affect, somatic anxiety) emerged in each of the five data sets, suggesting that the symptom structure in this domain is highly convergent across diverse samples. Moreover, the factors broadly corresponded to the symptom groups proposed by the tripartite model.

Joiner and his colleagues provided additional support for the validity of the tripartite model's portrayal of anxiety and depression. The model did the following: (*a*) distinguished among pure forms of depression and anxiety, comorbid depression and anxiety, and mixed anxiety-depression in a group of college students (Joiner & Blalock 1995), (*b*) provided a good fit for data from self-report measures of depression, anxiety, self-esteem, and positive and negative affect completed by another group of undergraduates (Joiner 1996), and (*c*) validly described the psychopathologic behavior of a group of child and adolescent psychiatric inpatients (Joiner et al 1996).

In an attempt to validate Beck's cognitive model of depression and anxiety (Beck 1976, 1987), which shares important features with the tripartite model, Clark et al (1994b) explored the common and specific symptom dimensions of anxiety and depression proposed by both models in groups of psychiatric out-patients and undergraduates. Principal-factor analyses with oblique rotations performed on the items of both the *Beck Depression Inventory* and the *Beck Anxiety Inventory* for both samples revealed two correlated factors, depression and anxiety. Second-order factor analyses yielded a large general distress or negative affect factor underlying the relationship between the two first-order factors. These results are consistent with both the tripartite and cognitive models, with cognitive and motivational symptoms specific to depression, and physiological symptoms unique to anxiety.

Clark et al (1994a) compared symptom features of four *DSM-III* subtypes of depressive and anxiety disorders in a group of outpatients with five standard measures of anxiety and depression. Depression was distinguished by anhedonia, cognitions of personal loss and failure, and dysphoric mood, while anxiety was characterized by specific autonomic arousal symptoms, threat-related cognitions, and subjective anxiety and tension. Major depression and panic disorder were better differentiated by specific symptom markers than were dysthymia and generalized anxiety disorder.

Conclusions about the depression-anxiety interface   The tripartite model has repeatedly shown itself capable of characterizing the common and specific components of depressive and anxiety disorders.

ANXIETY DISORDERS   Zinbarg & Barlow (1996) used a semistructured clinical interview and a self-report battery of questionnaires to identify central features of the anxiety disorders in a large group of patients seeking outpatient treatment. Their results were consistent with both the *DSM-III-R* and *DSM-IV* hierarchical models of anxiety and anxiety disorders as well as with Beck's and Clark and Watson's trait models.

OTHER DISORDERS   Trull & Sher (1994) reported that scores on the *NEO Five-Factor Inventory* (Costa & McCrae 1989) distinguished young adults in a nonclinical sample with and without a variety of *DSM-III-R* Axis I diagnoses. The diagnoses responsive to these basic personality dimensions included lifetime history of any substance use disorder, alcohol abuse or dependence, drug abuse or dependence, nicotine dependence, any anxiety disorder, and major depression. Leckman et al (1997) explored relationships among the symptoms of obsessive-compulsive disorder (OCD) in two large independent groups of patients with OCD. Four factors in each data set that accounted for more than 60% of the variance and were largely congruent with those identified in earlier reports were identified.

Conclusions about diagnostic validity   The diagnostic validation findings for this period cannot be generalized across either syndromes or methods. Thus, efforts to validate the schizophrenic spectrum disorders by means of neurobiological and genetic-familial validators were only modestly successful while, by contrast, validation efforts in which the tripartite personality trait model was used succeeded in consistently differentiating among a range of depressive and anxiety disorders.

COMORBIDITY

In an overview of the comorbidity question, Klein & Riso (1993) considered two fundamental issues: (*a*) whether disorders are discrete, "natural" classes or artificial categories created by the establishment of arbitrary cutoffs on a continuum and (*b*) whether categorical or dimensional models of psychopathology better capture the essence of psychopathology. (We review research on the first of these issues in this section and research on the second in a later section.) These authors outlined six conceptual and statistical approaches to the demanding task of demonstrating the existence of discrete boundaries between psychiatric disorders, and they provided 11 possible explanations for co-occurrences among psychiatric disorders. They ultimately concluded that even these sophisticated methods may not properly account for all instances of comorbidity.

Evaluating the impact of high rates of comorbidity on clinical practice and research design in a large sample of young adults, Newman and her colleagues (1998) concluded that groups that underrepresent comorbidity (e.g. student samples) likely also underestimate effect sizes for relationships between a disorder and its correlates (e.g. physical health problems, interference with daily living, use of treatments), while groups that overrepresent comorbidity (e.g. clinical samples) overestimate effect sizes. Because comorbidity tends to complicate treatment planning, compliance with treatment, and coordination of service delivery, these observations have significance for clinicians as well as researchers.

Similar concerns led to the development of the National Comorbidity Survey (NCS), a nationwide stratified multistage survey of the US population from 15 through 54 years of age. In an initial NCS report, Blazer and his colleagues (1994) reported higher 30-day and lifetime prevalence estimates of major depression than those reported in the Epidemiologic Catchment Area (ECA) study, and they confirmed the high rates of co-occurrence between major depression and a range of other psychiatric disorders. When pure major depression and major depression co-occurring with other psychiatric disorders were compared, risk factor profiles exhibited predictable differences. Kessler et al (1995) examined the prevalence and comorbidity of *DSM-III-R* posttraumatic stress disorder (PTSD) in a second NCS article. An estimated lifetime prevalence of PTSD of 7.8%, higher than previously reported, was found. Traumas most often associated with PTSD included combat exposure among men and rape and sexual molestation among women. PTSD is strongly comorbid with other lifetime *DSM-III-R* disorders in both men and women, especially affective disorders, anxiety disorders, and substance use disorders. Magee and his colleagues (1996) reported general population prevalences, correlates, comorbidities, and impairments associated with *DSM-III-R* phobias in another NCS report. Lifetime prevalences were estimated to be 6.7% for agoraphobia, 11.3% for simple phobia, and 13.3% for social phobia; increasing lifetime prevalences have been found in more recent cohorts. Lifetime phobias are highly comorbid with one another, with other anxiety disorders, and with affective disorders; they are more weakly comorbid with alcohol and drug dependence. As with major depression, comorbid phobias are generally more severe than pure phobias. In an NCS report on the comorbidity of nonaffective psychosis, Kendler et al (1996b) found that one or more psychosis screening questions were endorsed by 28.4% of a nonclinical sample. Lifetime prevalences of narrowly defined psychotic illness (schizophrenia or schizophreniform disorder) and broadly defined psychotic illness (all nonaffective psychoses) were estimated to be 1.3% and 2.2% by a computer algorithm. However, when respondents who had been assigned a narrow diagnosis by computer algorithm were diagnosed by a senior clinician using *DSM-III-R* diagnostic criteria, only 10% and 37% of them actually received narrow and broad diagnoses. Kendler and his colleagues concluded (*a*) that lifetime prevalence estimates of psychosis in community samples are strongly influenced by methods of assessment and diagnosis and (*b*) that even though results from computer algorithms were similar in the NCS and ECA studies, diagnoses so obtained agreed poorly with clinical diagnoses.

Four other comorbidity studies investigated the frequent co-occurrence of substance-related disorders and other psychiatric disorders. Two (Hudziak et al 1996, Morgenstern et al 1997) explored links between personality disorders (PDs) and substance abuse; a third (Brown et al 1995) traced the clinical course of depression in alcoholics; and the fourth (Fletcher et al 1996) investigated cognitive deficits associated with long-term cannabis use. They confirmed that substance abuse and PDs, especially borderline and antisocial PDs, co-occur at high frequency, as does substance abuse and mood disorder, and long-term substance abuse and cognitive dysfunction.

Reflecting growing clinical interest in comorbid psychiatric and physical disorders, Sherbourne et al (1996) reported that patients with anxiety disorder who were in treatment for hypertension, diabetes, heart disease, or current depression functioned at lower levels than medical patients without comorbid anxiety. These differences were most pronounced in mental health–related quality-of-life measures and when anxiety was comorbid with chronic medical conditions rather than depression. A study with related aims (Johnson et al 1995) reported that many primary care patients in the large group they studied also suffered from alcohol abuse or dependence; nearly half also had co-occurring psychiatric disorders. Although substance abusers reported poorer health and greater functional impairment than primary care patients without any psychiatric disorders, they were less impaired than patients who were diagnosed with mood, anxiety, eating, or somatoform disorders.

O'Connor et al (1998) attempted to fit adolescent and parent reports and observational measures of depressive symptoms and antisocial behavior from a national sample of 720 same-sex adolescents to behavioral genetic models to determine the respective genetic and environmental influences on individual differences in and co-occurrence of the two psychopathological behaviors. Approximately half the variability in the depressive symptoms and antisocial behaviors could be attributed to genetic factors; shared and nonshared environmental influences were also significant.

Reflecting another major societal concern, the co-occurrence of violence and mental illness, a 1996 issue of *Archives of General Psychiatry* featured five reports (Eronen et al 1996, Hodgins et al 1996, Jordan et al 1996, Teplin et al 1996, Virkkunen et al 1996) that provide impressive empirical evidence of the link between violence and crime and mental illness. In an accompanying commentary, Marzuk (1996) notes that this relationship "appears strongest for the severe mental illnesses, particularly those involving psychosis, and it is increased by the use of alcohol and other psychoactive substances" (pp. 484–85). Supporting this conclusion are recent findings from a 26-year prospective study of a 1966 Finnish birth cohort (Tiihonen et al 1997), which confirms that risk for criminal behavior is significantly higher among persons with psychotic disorders, especially persons suffering from alcohol-induced psychoses or schizophrenia and coexisting substance abuse.

Conclusions about comorbidity   The extensive research on comorbidity reported during this period has confirmed both the identity of the disorders most highly associated with comorbidity (e.g. substance-related disorders, personality disorders, depression, and anxiety) and comorbidity's substantial adverse social, physical, psychological, and psychiatric consequences.

DIAGNOSTIC BIAS

A recent review explored diagnostic biases in *DSM-III* and *DSM-III-R* based on race, gender, and social class (Garb 1997); the problem was considered sufficiently troubling that the *DSM-IV* Task Force explicitly addressed it in its revision efforts (Frances et al 1989). Findings identified in the 1997 review indicate that African-American and Hispanic patients are less likely than Caucasians to be diagnosed with psychotic mood disorder and more likely to be diagnosed with schizophrenia, despite comparable symptoms (Garb 1996). Females are more likely than males to be diagnosed with histrionic personality disorder, and males are more likely than females to be diagnosed with antisocial personality disorder despite equivalent symptoms (Becker & Lamb 1994). Both male and female clinicians have shown these biases (Adler et al 1990). Furthermore, depression is diagnosed more often in women than in men even when symptoms of mood disorder are equivalent (Potts et al 1991); gender also influences the differential diagnosis of major depression and organic mental disorder (Wrobel 1993).

CONTINUING DIAGNOSTIC CONTROVERSIES

The Categorical-Dimensional Debate

The issue of categorical versus dimensional classification first became a matter of concern when *DSM-III* added many diagnoses to those included in its predecessors, thereby raising the question of boundaries between old and new diagnostic entities. As diagnoses proliferated, the frequency of comorbidity increased, causing clinicians to ask whether comorbidity represents the co-occurrence of two or more mental disorders or a single disorder that has simply been labeled in different ways. As a consequence, the advantages and disadvantages of dimensional and categorical approaches to personality and diagnosis are now being explored extensively (e.g. Clark et al 1995, 1997, Klein & Riso 1993, Widiger 1997a). The focus of these efforts is on personality disorders, where symptom overlap is greatest.

According to Clark (1998a), dimensional approaches to personality disorder "are theoretically consistent with the complexity of symptom patterns that are observed clinically, increase reliability, are theoretically consistent with the observed lack of discrete boundaries between different types of psychopathology and between normality and psychopathology, and provide a basis for understanding symptom heterogeneity within diagnoses by retaining information about component trait levels."

Clark (1998a) distinguishes between two-dimensional approaches to personality disorders. The first, rooted in the traditional categorical system, conceptualizes each separate disorder as a continuum, so that any given patient could exhibit different levels of traits of several personality disorders. The alternative is the trait dimensional approach, in which assessment aims to create a profile of the personality traits that underlie the disorder. Although several instruments that reflect the higher-order factors describing normal personality (e.g. Watson et al 1994, Widiger 1998) have proven useful for studying relations between personality and personality disorders, only recently have instruments been developed that tap into the lower-order traits relevant to personality disorders. These include the 15-dimension *Schedule for Nonadaptive and Adaptive Personality (SNAP)* (Clark 1993) and the 18-dimension *Dimensional Assessment of Personality Pathology—Basic Questionnaire (DAPP-BQ)* (Livesley, unpublished manuscript).

In unpublished research by Clark and her colleagues relating diagnostic and trait dimensional approaches to personality disorder (Clark 1998a), two patient samples were interviewed with the *Structured Interview for DSM-III-R Personality Disorders (SIDP-R)* (Pfohl et al 1989) and completed the *SNAP*. Multiple correlations between *SNAP* scales and diagnostic interview scores revealed a great deal of common variance: The information in a *SNAP* profile enabled prediction of between one quarter and three quarters of the variance in the interview-based diagnostic ratings, suggesting that the trait dimensions assessed by the *SNAP* underlie clinical ratings of personality pathology.

These findings are especially impressive in view of data reviewed by Clark et al (1997) to the effect that obtaining convergent validity for measures of personality disorder assessment has been extremely difficult. Clark et al (1997) also make the following point: "It is widely believed that categorical and dimensional models are inherently incompatible, and that one must choose between them. In actuality, however, it is more accurate to describe these models as existing in a hierarchical relation to one another, with dimensions being the blocks from which categories may be built" (p. 206).

O'Connor & Dyce (1998) recently reviewed the clinical data supporting the several models of personality disorder configuration. They found moderate support for the *DSM-IV* dimensions and Cloninger's (1987) tridimensional theory, and stronger support for the five-factor model (Widiger et al 1994) and Cloninger & Svrakic's (1994) empirically derived seven-factor model. On balance, they conclude that a four-factor model explains the bulk of the variance associated with personality disorder. Unfortunately, these authors failed to include in their comparisons either the tripartite model or the trait dimensional approaches characterized by the *SNAP* and the *DAPP-BQ*.

Watson & Clark (1995) and Watson et al (1995a,b) have also explored the personality trait dimensions that underlie depression and anxiety. Some of that research is considered above, in our review of efforts to validate *DSM-III* and *DSM-III-R* diagnoses. The research is also reviewed extensively by Mineka et al (1998), as well as by Clark (1998b), who traces interest in this topic from its earliest roots in the writings of Hippocrates to the present and identifies links between research on personality trait dimensions underlying depression and anxiety and those underlying personality disorders.

Conclusions about the dimensional-categorical debate   Impressive progress has been made in relatively few years in garnering conceptual and historical support for the advantages of dimensional over syndromal approaches to personality disorders and other overlapping psychopathological conditions. Nonetheless, the ultimate worth and significance of the trait dimensional approach will not be known until substantially more research data have been gathered that demonstrate empirically the advantages of this approach to these disorders.

"Theoretically Coherent" Alternatives to DSM-IV

The *Journal of Consulting and Clinical Psychology* published a special section, entitled "Development of Theoretically Coherent Alternatives to the *DSM-IV*," in 1996. Follette (1996) introduced the section by criticizing the *DSM* system as "a taxonomy based on inadequately explicated theory [which] cannot be a successful basis for a scientific research program" (p. 1117). For that reason, "the *DSM* does not fit well with a great deal of empirical research that psychology has generated in understanding human behavior" (p. 1118). What follows in the journal is a set of "theoretically coherent alternatives" to *DSM-IV*; they are theoretically coherent because all were developed from the behavioral perspective.

Follette & Houts (1996) believe that the proliferation of categories in recent editions of the *DSM* exemplifies the inadequacy of the *DSM* system of classification and its likely inability to facilitate scientific progress. They consider this increase in new diagnoses to be symptomatic of the problem, because every adequate nosological system eventually reduces its categories by reference to its organizing theory. Moreover, the atheoretical stance of the 1980, 1987, and 1994 versions of the *DSM* has produced a topographic rather than theoretically driven system that does not permit evaluation of scientific progress. As a consequence, Follette & Houts indicated, the authors of these articles have adopted a consistently behavioral perspective, which they believe "should be allowed to compete on the basis of how successful they are at achieving their specified goals that might include illuminating etiology, course, and response to treatment" (Follette & Houts 1996:1120). Carson (1996) then contrasts the Aristotelian approach to psychopathological taxonomy, epitomized by *DSM-IV,* with the Galileian mode of thought that emphasizes "the dynamic causal matrix in which behavior occurs," acknowledging at the same time that "it is much easier to be a critic in this area than it is to suggest compelling and pragmatically realistic solutions" (p. 1137).

Illustrating the behavioral alternative to syndromal diagnosis, Wulfert et al (1996) link alcoholism and pedophilia as "reinforcement-based disorders." "Logical functional analyses" of these disorders identify their behavioral topography and detail their antecedents and consequences, which leads logically to specification of treatment operations. These authors justify retaining the syndromal categories to maintain the communication link with the dominant diagnostic system; by also completing a functional analysis of each disorder, they provide the behavioral perspective on each, which, unlike syndromal diagnosis, explicitly links assessment to treatment. The remaining articles in the section propose behavioral classification systems that also largely eschew syndromal classification for such disorders as substance abuse/dependence, obsessive-compulsive disorder, panic disorder with agoraphobia, borderline personality disorder (Hayes et al 1996), personality disorder, (Koerner et al 1996), disorders of childhood and adolescence (Scotti et al 1996), and marital discord (Fruzzetti 1996).

Conclusions about a "theoretically coherent" alternative to DSM-IV   A nonsyndromal approach to psychopathology is attractive to psychologists, both because it will presumably ease the reliability and validity problems of syndromal diagnosis and because it is shaped by psychological theory and research rather than psychiatric tradition. Nonetheless, those who propose a *DSM* alternative must still demonstrate empirically that their new system is at least as reliable, valid, and useful as the *DSM*—hopefully, more so—and that it has equal or greater appeal in the marketplace of ideas.

Making Diagnosis Meaningful: New Psychological Perspectives

The authors of many of the chapters in *Making Diagnosis Meaningful: New Psychological Perspectives* (Barron 1998) ask whether—and how—diagnosis might be made more useful for psychodynamic clinical practice. A number of the chapters (e.g. Jenuwine & Cohler 1998, Jones 1998, Lerner 1998, McWilliams 1998, Vaillant & Vaillant 1998) conclude both that syndromal diagnoses are of only marginal relevance to psychodynamic therapists and that understanding unconscious mental mechanisms—in particular, ego and other mechanisms of defense—is of far greater utility to them. Vaillant & Vaillant (1998) summarize this position in the following words: "There are four serious limitations to a *solely* atheoretical approach as in Axis I and II in *DSM-IV*. *DSM-IV* is reductionistic; it does not emphasize the distinction between state and trait; it is adynamic in that it pays little attention to conflict, adaptation, longitudinal course, and development; and finally, it has consistently sacrificed diagnostic validity on the altar of diagnostic reliability" (Vaillant & Vaillant 1998).

On the other hand, everyone knows that the reliability of assessments of psychodynamic defenses is low: "Too often, different frames of reference or different nosologies are contrasted by studying them in different groups of individuals. This technique makes real comparison of vantage points impossible" (Vaillant & Vaillant 1998). However, Vaillant & Vaillant are able to cite encouraging reliability data on psychodynamic assessments that derive from George Vaillant's long involvement (e.g. Vaillant 1983) in a 35-year longitudinal study of a group of adolescent boys originally chosen as a control group in a well-known study of juvenile delinquency (Gluek & Gluek 1950). When the maturity and nature of each man's predominant defense mechanisms were evaluated toward the end of this lengthy survey, both the reliability of the judgment of predominant defense and its predictive validity vis-à-vis Axis II personality disorders were found to be quite high. Given these encouraging findings, Vaillant & Vaillant (1998) propose an integration of syndromal and psychodynamic assessments: "Thus, as we move closer to the possibility of developing a reliable and valid psychodynamic formulation, it can, and should become, a companion to the more biologically determined Axis I and II *DSM-IV* diagnoses. The dynamic formulation describes the patient's learned response pattern to conflict. The *DSM* symptom diagnosis describes the biological component of the response, and permits the patient to be classified for insurance purposes, and for pharmacological and biological research."

Conclusions about a psychodynamic supplement to DSM-IV   As with the behavioral alternative to syndromal diagnosis described above, the burden of proof of the superiority of psychodynamic formulations over syndromal diagnoses requires psychodynamic clinicians who espouse this perspective to gather more reliability data like Vaillant's (1983).

Reactions to Wakefield's "Harmful Dysfunction" Definition of Mental Disorder

Wakefield defined mental disorder as "harmful dysfunction" in 1992. In this definition, whether a condition is harmful requires a value judgment as to its desirability or undesirability, while "dysfunction" refers to a system's failure to function as shaped by processes of natural selection. As indicated below, Bergner more recently proposed a new definition of mental disorder (1997) after concluding that Wakefield's harmful dysfunction conceptualization requires clinicians to make judgments about patients' mental mechanisms that cannot reliably be made. Disagreeing, Spitzer (1997) calls Wakefield's construct a "brilliant breakthrough" because it emphasizes that what is not working in the organism is the function that we expect to be present and in operation by virtue of evolution and selection. Richters & Hinshaw (1997) also laud Wakefield's construct, even though they are aware that it requires thorough knowledge of internal, neurobiological operations and value judgments about external, social data, both of which are difficult to make reliably. By contrast, Lilienfeld & Marino (1995) are critical of Wakefield's definition. Reasons include that (*a*) many mental functions are not direct evolutionary adaptations but are, instead, neutral by-products of adaptations; (*b*) the concept of the evolutionarily designed response neglects the fact that natural selection often produces extreme behavioral variability across individuals; and (*c*) many disorders that have achieved consensus are best portrayed as evolutionarily adaptive responses to danger, threat, or loss.

Bergner and Ossorio's "Significant Restriction" Definition of Psychopathology and Reactions to It

Bergner (1997) recently published a provocative article whose major thesis was that consensus on a definition of psychopathology has not been achieved despite years of trying. Claiming that this situation has seriously affected efforts to study and treat psychopathology, and to deal with its social consequences, Bergner endorses the definition of psychopathology previously put forth by Ossorio (1985): Psychopathology is best defined as "significant restriction in the ability of an individual to engage in deliberate action and, equivalently, to participate in available social practices" (Bergner 1997:246). This definition "meets the intellectual criteria that an adequate definition represent a non-empirical articulation of the necessary and sufficient conditions for correct application of a concept, and that it successfully discriminate instances of a concept from non-instances."

Comparing the Bergner/Ossorio definition to his own, Wakefield (1997) concludes that conditions are neither necessary nor sufficient to define a disorder. The most serious problem with the definition is its overinclusiveness: Many restrictions on deliberate action are imposed in normal mental functioning. By contrast, Wakefield understandably believes that his own "harmful dysfunction" analysis, criticized by Bergner (1997), adequately discriminates between disorder and nondisorder. Spitzer (1997), whose own attempt to define mental disorder is represented by *DSM-III* (American Psychiatric Association 1980) and its successors, admits to fatigue at efforts to define psychopathology and uncertainty over the value of a consensus definition. He thinks the Bergner/Ossorio definition simply "muddles the issues," while he regards Wakefield's harmful dysfunction conceptualization as a "brilliant breakthrough" because it clarifies important underlying issues. Widiger (1997b) lauds Bergner for addressing the fundamental issues and principal difficulties in defining mental illness, but he agrees with others that the Bergner/Ossorio definition of mental disorder ultimately will not be more successful than earlier efforts. A major reason is the absence of distinct boundaries between either physical disorders or normality for the construct proposed, an attraction for a scientist like Widiger who has espoused dimensional approaches to some forms of psychopathology. Finally, Nathan (1997) takes issue with Bergner's statement that a consensus on a definition of mental disorder does not exist, in view of the widespread acceptance of the value of *DSM-IV* and its predecessors by mental health professionals. Moreover, Nathan (1997) notes, however attractive Bergner's construct may be, in the final analysis data on utility will be the ultimate arbiter of the construct's worth.

Visit the *Annual Reviews home page* at
http://www.AnnualReviews.org.

Literature Cited

Adler DA, Drake RE, Teague GB. 1990. Clinicians' practices in personality assessment: Does gender influence the use of *DSM-III* Axis II? *Compr. Psychiatry* 31: 125–33

American Psychiatric Association. 1980. *Diagnostic and Statistical Manual of Mental Disorders.* Washington, DC: Am. Psychiatr. Assoc. 3rd ed.

American Psychiatric Association. 1987. *Diagnostic and Statistical Manual of Mental Disorders.* Washington, DC: Am. Psychiatr. Assoc. 3rd ed., rev.

American Psychiatric Association. 1994. *Diagnostic and Statistical Manual of Mental Disorders.* Washington, DC: Am. Psychiatr. Assoc. 4th ed.

Andreasen NC. 1995. The validation of psychiatric diagnosis: new models and approaches. *Am. J. Psychiatry* 152:161–62

Ball SA, Tennen H, Poling JC, Kranzler HR, Rounsaville BJ. 1997. Personality, temperament, and character dimensions and the *DSM-IV* personality disorders in substance abusers. *J. Abnorm. Psychol.* 106: 545–53

Barron JW, ed. 1998. *Making Diagnosis Meaningful: New Psychological Perspectives.* Washington, DC: APA Books. In press

Beck AT. 1976. *Cognitive Therapy of the Emotional Disorders.* New York: New Am. Libr.

Beck AT. 1987. Cognitive models of depression. *J. Cogn. Psychother.* 1:2–27

Becker D, Lamb S. 1994. Sex bias in the diagnosis of borderline personality disorder and post traumatic stress disorder. *Prof. Psychol. Res. Pract.* 25:55–61

Bergner RM. 1997. What is psychopathology? And so what? *Clin. Psychol. Sci. Pract.* 4:235–48

Blazer DG, Kessler RC, McGonagle KA, Swartz MS. 1994. The prevalence and distribution of major depression in a national community sample: the National Comorbidity Survey. *Am. J. Psychiatry* 151: 979–86

Brown SA, Inaba RK, Gillin MD, Schuckit MA, Stewart MA, Irwin MR. 1995. Alcoholism and affective disorder: clinical course of depressive symptoms. *Am. J. Psychiatry* 152:435–452

Buysse DJ, Reynolds CF, Hauri PJ, Roth T, Stepanski EJ, et al. 1994. Diagnostic concordance for *DSM-IV* sleep disorders: a report from the APA/NIMH *DSM-IV* field trial. *Am. J. Psychiatry* 151:1351–60

Caplan PJ. 1991. How do they decide who is normal? The bizarre, but true, tale of the *DSM* process. *Can. Psychol.* 32:162–70

Carson RC. 1991. Dilemmas in the pathway of the *DSM-IV. J. Abnorm. Psychol.* 100: 302–7

Carson RC. 1996. Aristotle, Galileo, and the *DSM* taxonomy: the case of schizophrenia. *J. Consult. Clin. Psychol.* 64:1133–39

Chen YR, Swann AC, Burt DB. 1996. Stability of diagnosis in schizophrenia. *Am. J. Psychiatry* 153:682–86

Clark LA. 1993. *Manual for the Schedule for Nonadaptive and Adaptive Personality.* Minneapolis, MN: Univ. Minn. Press

Clark LA. 1998a. Dimensional approaches to personality disorder assessment and diagnosis. In *Personality and Psychopathology,* ed. CR Cloninger. Washington, DC: Am. Psychiatr. Press. In press

Clark LA. 1998b. Mood, personality, and personality disorder. In *Wisconsin Symposium on Emotion: Emotion and Psychopathology.* New York: Oxford Univ. Press. In press

Clark LA, Beck AT, Beck JS. 1994a. Symptom differences in major depression, dysthymia, panic disorder, and generalized anxiety disorder. *Am. J. Psychiatry* 151: 205–9

Clark LA, Livesley WJ, Morey L. 1997. Special feature: Personality disorder assessment: the challenge of contruct validity. *J. Pers. Assess.* 11:205–31

Clark LA, Steer RA, Beck AT. 1994b. Common and specific dimensions of self-reported anxiety and depression: implications for the cognitive and tripartite models. *J. Abnorm. Psychol.* 103:645–54

Clark LA, Watson D, Reynolds S. 1995. Diagnosis and classification of psychopathology: challenges to the current system and future directions. *Annu. Rev. Psychol.* 46: 121–53

Cloninger CR. 1987. A systematic method for clinical description and classification of personality variants. *Arch. Gen. Psychiatry* 44:573–88

Cloninger CR, Svrakic DM. 1994. Differentiating normal and deviant personality by the seven-factor personality model. In *Differentiating Normal and Abnormal Personality,* ed. S Strack, M Lorr, pp. 40–64. New York: Springer

Cloninger CR, Svrakic DM, Przybeck TR. 1993. A psychobiological model of temperament and character. *Arch. Gen. Psychiatry* 50:975–90

Corbitt EM, Widiger TA. 1995. Sex differences among the personality disorders: an exploration of the data. *Clin. Psychol. Sci. Pract.* 2:225–38

Coryell W, Winokur G, Shea T, Maser JD, Endicott J, Akiskal HS. 1994. The long-term stability of depressive subtypes. *Am. J. Psychiatry* 151:199–204

Costa PT, McCrae RR. 1989. *The NEO-PI/NEO-FFI Manual Supplement.* Odessa, FL: Psychol. Assess. Resour.

Costa PT, McCrae RR. 1990. Personality disorders and the five-factor model of personality. *J. Pers. Disord.* 4:362–71

Cottler LB, Schuckit MA, Helzer JE, Crowley T, Woody G, et al. 1995. The *DSM-IV* field trial for substance use disorders: major results. *Drug Alcohol Depend.* 38:59–69

Coyne JC. 1994. Self-reported distress: analog or ersatz depression? *Psychol. Bull.* 116:29–45

Eaton WW, Anthony JC, Gallo J, Cai G, Tien A, et al. 1997. Natural history of *Diagnostic Interview Schedule/DSM-IV* major depression. *Arch. Gen. Psychiatry* 54:993–99

Eaton WW, Regier DA, Locke BZ, Taube CA. 1981. The Epidemiologic Catchment Area Program of the National Institute of Mental Health. *Public Health Rep.* 96:319–25

Eronen M, Hakola P, Tiihonen J. 1996. Mental disorders and homicidal behavior in Finland. *Arch. Gen. Psychiatry* 53:497–501

Faraone SV, Kremen WS, Lyons MJ, Pepple JR, Seidman LJ, Tsuang MT. 1995. Diagnostic accuracy and linkage analysis: How useful are schizophrenia spectrum phenotypes? *Am. J. Psychiatry* 152:1286–90

Fennig S, Kovasznay B, Rich C, Ram R, Pato C, et al. 1994. Six-month stability of psychiatric diagnoses in first-admission patients with psychosis. *Am. J. Psychiatry* 151:1200–8

Fenton WS. 1996. Review of *DSM-IV Training Guide; DSM-IV Guidebook; DSM-IV Handbook of Differential Diagnosis; Diagnostic and Statistical Manual of Mental Disorders, 4th ed.: Primary Care Version. Am. J. Psychiatry* 153:960–61

First MB, Frances AJ, Pincus HA. 1995. *DSM-IV Handbook of Differential Diagnosis.* Washington, DC: Am. Psychiatr. Press

Fletcher JM, Page JB, Francis DJ, Copeland K, Naus MJ, et al. 1996. Cognitive correlates of long-term cannabis use in Costa Rican men. *Arch. Gen. Psychiatry* 53:1051–57

Foa EB, Kozak MJ. 1995. *DSM-IV* field trial: obsessive-compulsive disorder. *Am. J. Psychiatry* 152:90–96

Follette WC. 1996. Introduction to the special section on the development of theoretically coherent alternatives to the *DSM* system. *J. Consult. Clin. Psychol.* 64:1117–19

Follette WC, Houts AC. 1996. Models of scientific progress and the role of theory in taxonomy development: a case study of the *DSM. J. Consult. Clin. Psychol.* 64:1120–32

Frances AJ, First MB, Pincus HA. 1995. *DSM-IV Guidebook.* Washington, DC: Am. Psychiatr. Press

Frances AJ, Ross R, eds. 1996. *DSM-IV Case Studies: A Clinical Guide to Differential Diagnosis.* Washington, DC: Am. Psychiatr. Press

Frances AJ, Widiger TA, Pincus HA. 1989. The development of *DSM-IV. Arch. Gen. Psychiatry* 46:373–75

Fruzzetti AE. 1996. Causes and consequences: individual distress in the context of couple interactions. *J. Consult. Clin. Psychol.* 64:1192–202

Garb HN. 1996. The representativeness and past-behavior heuristics in clinical judgment. *Prof. Psychol. Res. Pract.* 27:272–77

Garb HN. 1997. Race bias, social class bias, and gender bias in clinical judgment. *Clin. Psychol. Sci. Pract.* 4:99–120

Gluek S, Gluek E. 1950. *Unraveling Juvenile Delinquency.* New York: The Commonw. Fund

Grumet GW. 1995. What hath APA wrought? *Am. J. Psychiatry* 152:651–52

Gur RE, Mozley PD, Shtasel DL, Cannon TD, Gallacher F, et al. 1994. Clinical subtypes of schizophrenia: differences in brain and CSF volume. *Am. J. Psychiatry* 151:343–50

Guze SB. 1995. Review of *American Psychiatric Association Diagnostic and Statistical Manual of Mental Disorders, 4th ed. Am. J. Psychiatry* 152:1228

Hartung CM, Widiger TA. 1998. Gender differences in the diagnosis of mental disorders: conclusions and controversies of *DSM-IV. Psychol. Bull.* In press

Hasin DS, Trautman KD, Miele GM, Samet S, Smith M, Endicott J. 1996. *Psychiatric Research Interview for Substance and Mental Disorders (PRISM)*: reliability for substance abusers. *Am. J. Psychiatry* 153: 1195–201

Haslam N, Beck AT. 1994. Subtyping major depression: a taxometric analysis. *J. Abnorm. Psychol.* 103:686–92

Hayes SC, Wilson KG, Gifford EV, Follette VM, Strosahl K. 1996. Experiential avoidance and behavioral disorders: a functional dimensional approach to diagnosis and treatment. *J. Consult. Clin. Psychol.* 64: 1152–69

Hodgins S, Mednick SA, Brennan PA, Schulsinger F, Engberg M. 1996. Mental disorder and crime: evidence from a Danish birth cohort. *Arch. Gen. Psychiatry* 53:489–96

Hudziak JJ, Boffeli TJ, Kriesman JJ, Battaglia MM, Stanger C, Guze SB. 1996. Clinical study of the relation of borderline personality disorder to Briquet's syndrome (hysteria), somatization disorder, antisocial personality disorder, and substance abuse disorders. *Am. J. Psychiatry* 153: 1598–606

Jenuwine M, Cohler BJ. 1998. Treating the very troubled child: conduct disorders, aggression, and the problem of *DSM-IV.* See Barron 1998, In press

Johnson JG, Spitzer RL, Williams JBW, Kroenke K, Linzer M, et al. 1995. Psychiatric comorbidity, health status, and functional impairment associated with alcohol abuse and dependence in primary care patients: findings of the PRIME MD–1000 study. *J. Consult. Clin. Psychol.* 63: 133–40

Joiner TE. 1996. A confirmatory factor-analytic investigation of the tripartite model of depression and anxiety in college students. *Cogn. Ther. Res.* 20:521–39

Joiner TE, Blalock JA. 1995. Gender differences in depression: the role of anxiety and generalized negative affect. *Sex Roles* 33: 91–108

Joiner TE, Catanzaro SJ, Laurent J. 1996. Tripartite structure of positive and negative affect, depression, and anxiety in child and adolescent psychiatric inpatients. *J. Abnorm. Psychol.* 105:401–9

Jones EE. 1998. Depression: intervention as assessment. See Barron 1998

Jordan BK, Schlenger WE, Fairbank JA, Caddell JM. 1996. Prevalence of psychiatric disorders among incarcerated women: II. Convicted felons entering prison. *Arch. Gen. Psychiatry* 53:513–19

Keller MB, Klein DN, Hirschfeld RMA, Kocsis JH, McCullough JP, et al. 1995. Results of the *DSM-IV* mood disorders field trial. *Am. J. Psychiatry* 152:843–49

Kendler KS. 1990. Toward a scientific psychiatric nosology: strengths and limitations. *Arch. Gen. Psychiatry* 47:969–73

Kendler KS, Eaves LJ, Walters EE, Neale MC, Heath AC, Kessler RC. 1996a. The identification and validation of distinct depressive syndromes in a population-based sample of female twins. *Arch. Gen. Psychiatry* 53: 391–99

Kendler KS, Gallagher TJ, Abelson JM, Kessler RC. 1996b. Lifetime prevalence, demographic risk factors, and diagnostic validity of nonaffective psychosis as assessed in a US community sample. *Arch. Gen. Psychiatry* 53:1022–31

Kendler KS, McGuire M, Gruenberg AM, Walsh D. 1995a. Examining the validity of *DSM-III-R* schizoaffective disorder and its putative subtypes in the Roscommon Family Study. *Am. J. Psychiatry* 152:755–64

Kendler KS, Neale MC, Walsh D. 1995b. Evaluating the spectrum concept of schizophrenia in the Roscommon Family Study. *Am. J. Psychiatry* 152:749–54

Kendler KS, Roy M-A. 1995. Validity of a diagnosis of lifetime major depression obtained by personal interview versus family history. *Am. J. Psychiatry* 152:1608–14

Kessler RC, Sonnega A, Bromet E, Hughes M, Nelson CB. 1995. Posttraumatic stress disorder in the National Comorbidity Survey. *Arch. Gen. Psychiatry* 52:1048–60

Kirk SA, Kutchins H. 1992. *The Selling of DSM: The Rhetoric of Science in Psychiatry.* Hawthorne, NY: deGruyter

Kirk SA, Kutchins H. 1994. Is bad writing a mental disorder? *New York Times,* May 28, p. A12

Klein DN, Riso LP. 1993. Psychiatric disorders: problems of boundaries and comorbidity. In *Basic Issues in Psychopathology,* ed. CG Costello, pp. 19–66. New York: Guilford

Koerner K, Kohlenberg RJ, Parker CR. 1996. Diagnosis of personality disorder: a radical behavioral alternative. *J. Consult. Clin. Psychol.* 64:1169–76

Lahey BB, Applegate B, Barkley RA, Garfinkel B, McBurnett K, et al. 1994. *DSM-IV* field trials for oppositional defiant disorder and conduct disorder in children and adolescents. *Am. J. Psychiatry* 151:1163–71

Laing RD. 1967. *The Politics of Experience.* New York: Pantheon Books

Langenbucher JW, Chung T. 1995. Onset and staging of *DSM-IV* alcohol dependence using mean age and survival/hazard methods. *J. Abnorm. Psychol.* 104:346–54

Langenbucher JW, Chung T, Morgenstern J, Labouvie E, Nathan PE, Bavly L. 1997. Physiological alcohol dependence as a "specifier" of risk for medical problems and relapse liability in *DSM-IV. J. Stud. Alcohol.* 58:341–50

Langenbucher JW, Morgenstern J, Labouvie E, Nathan PE. 1994a. Lifetime *DSM-IV* diagnosis of alcohol, cannabis, cocaine and opiate dependence: six-month reliability in a multi-site clinical sample. *Addiction* 89:1115–27

Langenbucher JW, Morgenstern J, Labouvie E, Nathan PE. 1994b. Diagnostic concordance of substance use disorders in *DSM-III, DSM-IV* and *ICD-10. Drug Alcohol Depend.* 36:193–203

Leckman JF, Grice DE, Boardman J, Zhang H, Vitale A, et al. 1997. Symptoms of obsessive-compulsive disorder. *Am. J. Psychiatry* 154:911–17

Lerner PM. 1998. An experiential psychoanalytic approach to the assessment process. See Barron 1998, In press

Lilienfeld SO, Marino L. 1995. Mental disorder as a Roschian concept: a critique of Wakefield's "harmful dysfunction" analysis. *J. Abnorm. Psychol.* 104:411–20

Magee WJ, Eaton WW, Wittchen H-U, McGonagle KA, Kessler RC. 1996. Agoraphobia, simply phobia, and social phobia in the National Comorbidity Survey. *Arch. Gen. Psychiatry* 53:159–68

Malgady RG, Rogler LH, Cortes DE. 1996. Cultural expression of psychiatric symptoms: idioms of anger among Puerto Ricans. *Psychol. Assess.* 8:265–68

Marzuk PM. 1996. Violence, crime, and mental illness: how strong a link? *Arch. Gen. Psychiatry* 53:481–86

Mattanah JK, Becker DF, Levy KN, Edell WS, McGlashan TH. 1995. Diagnostic stability in adolescents followed up 2 years after hospitalization. *Am. J. Psychiatry* 152: 889–94

McGorry PD, Mihalopoulos C, Henry L, Dakis J, Jackson HJ, et al. 1995. Spurious precision: procedural validity of diagnostic assessment in psychotic disorders. *Am. J. Psychiatry* 152:220–23

McWilliams N. 1998. Relationship, subjectivity, and inference in diagnosis. See Barron 1998, In press

Mineka S, Watson D, Clark LA. 1998. Comorbidity of anxiety and unipolar mood disorders. *Annu. Rev. Psychol.* 49: 377–412

Morgenstern J, Langenbucher J, Labouvie E, Miller KJ. 1997. The comorbidity of alcoholism and personality disorders in a clinical population: prevalence rates and rela-

tion to alcohol typology variables. *J. Abnorm. Psychol.* 106:74–84

Nathan PE. 1997. In the final analysis, it's the data that count. *Clin. Psychol. Sci. Pract.* 4:281–84

Nathan PE. 1998. DSM-IV and its antecedents: enhancing syndromal diagnosis. See Barron 1998, In press

Nelson E, Rice J. 1997. Stability of diagnosis of obsessive-compulsive disorder in the Epidemiologic Catchment Area study. *Am. J. Psychiatry* 154:826–31

Newman DL, Moffitt TE, Caspi A, Silva PA. 1998. Comorbid mental disorders: implications for clinical practice and psychopathology research. *J. Abnorm. Psychol.* In press

O'Connor BP, Dyce JA. 1998. A test of models of personality disorder configuration. *J. Abnorm. Psychol.* 107:3–16

O'Connor TG, McGuire S, Reiss D, Hetherington EM, Plomin R. 1998. Co-occurrence of depressive symptoms and antisocial behavior in adolescence: a common genetic liability. *J. Abnorm. Psychol.* 107:27–37

Ossorio P. 1985. Pathology. In *Advances in Descriptive Psychology*, ed. K. Davis, T Mitchell, 4:151–202. Greenwich, CT: JAI

Othmer E, Othmer SC. 1994a. *The Clinical Interview Using DSM-IV: Fundamentals.* Washington, DC: Am. Psychiatr. Press

Othmer E, Othmer SC. 1994b. *The Clinical Interview Using DSM-IV: The Difficult Patient.* Washington, DC: Am. Psychiatr. Press

Pfohl B, Blum N, Zimmerman M, Stangl D. 1989. *Structured Interview for DSM-III-R Personality.* Iowa City, IA: Dep. Psychiatry, Univ. Iowa

Pilkonis PA, Heape CL, Proietti JM, Clark SW, McDavid JD, Pitts TE. 1995. Reliability and validity of two structured diagnostic instruments for personality disorders. *Arch. Gen. Psychiatry* 52:1025–33

Pincus HA, First M, Frances AJ, McQueen L. 1996. Reviewing *DSM-IV. Am. J. Psychiatry* 153:850

Potts MK, Burnam MA, Wells KB. 1991. Gender differences in depression detection: a comparison of clinician diagnosis and standardized assessment. *Psychol. Assess.* 3:609–15

Rapoport JL, Ismond DR. 1996. *DSM-IV Training Guide for Diagnosis of Childhood Disorders.* New York: Brunner/Mazel

Ratakonda S, Gorman JM, Yale SA, Amador XF. 1998. Characterization of psychotic conditions. *Arch. Gen. Psychiatry* 55: 75–81

Regier DA, Kaelber CT, Roper MT, Rae DS, Sartorius N. 1994. The ICD–10 clinical field trial for mental and behavioral disorders: results in Canada and the United States. *Am. J. Psychiatry* 151:1340–50

Reid WH, Wise MG. 1995. *DSM-IV Training Guide.* New York: Brunner/Mazel

Richters JE, Hinshaw S. 1997. Psychiatry's turbid solution. *Clin. Psychol. Sci. Pract.* 4:276–80

Robins E, Guze SB. 1970. Establishment of diagnostic validity in psychiatric illness: its application to schizophrenia. *Am. J. Psychiatry* 126:983–87

Roy M-A, Lanctot G, Merette C, Cliche D, Fournier J-P, et al. 1997. Clinical and methodological factors related to reliability of the best-estimate diagnostic procedure. *Am. J. Psychiatry* 154:1726–33

Sadock BJ. 1995. Review of *The Clinical Interview Using DSM-IV*, Vol. 1 & Vol. 2. *Am. J. Psychiatr.* 152:1526–27

Sarbin TR. 1997. On the futility of psychiatric diagnostic manuals (DSMs) and the return of personal agency. *Appl. Prev. Psychol.* 6:233–43

Sartorius N, Ustun TB, Korten A, Cooper JE, van Drimmelen J. 1995. Progress toward achieving a common language in psychiatry, II: results from the international field trial of the *ICD–10* diagnostic criteria for research for mental and behavioral disorders. *Am. J. Psychiatry* 152:1427–37

Schwab-Stone M, Fallon T, Briggs M, Crowther B. 1994. Reliability of diagnostic reporting for children aged 6–11 years: a test-retest study of the *Diagnostic Interview Schedule for Children—Revised. Am. J. Psychiatry* 151:1048–54

Scotti JR, Morris TL, McNeil CB, Hawkins RP. 1996. *DSM-IV* and disorders of childhood and adolescence: Can structural criteria be functional? *J. Consult. Clin. Psychol.* 64:1177–91

Sher KJ, Trull TJ. 1996. Methodological issues in psychopathology research. *Annu. Rev. Psychol.* 47:371–400

Sherbourne CD, Wells KB, Meredith LS, Jackson CA, Camp P. 1996. Comorbid anxiety disorder and the functioning and well-being of chronically ill patients of general medical providers. *Arch. Gen. Psychiatry* 53:889–95

Skodal AE. 1996. Review of *DSM-IV Sourcebook*, Vol. 1. *Am. J. Psychiatry* 153:432–33

Spitzer RL. 1997. Brief comments from a psychiatric nosologist weary from his own attempts to define mental disorder: Why Ossorio's definition muddles and Wakefield's "harmful dysfunction" illuminates the issues. *Clin. Psychol. Sci. Pract.* 4:259–66

Spitzer RL, Endicott J, Fleiss JL, Cohen J. 1970. *The Psychiatric Status Schedule*: a technique for evaluating psychopathology and impairment of role functioning. *Arch. Gen. Psychiatry* 23:41–55

Spitzer RL, Endicott J, Robins E. 1975. *Research Diagnostic Criteria (RDC) for a Selected Group of Functional Disorders.* New York: NY State Psychiatr. Inst.

Spitzer RL, Fleiss JL, Endicott J, Cohen J. 1967. *Mental Status Schedule*: properties of a factor-analytically derived scale. *Arch. Gen. Psychiatry* 16:479–93

Strakowski SM. 1994. Diagnostic validity of schizophreniform disorder. *Am. J. Psychiatry* 151:815–24

Szasz TS. 1960. The myth of mental illness. *Am. Psychol.* 15:113–18

Teplin LA, Abram KM, McClelland GM. 1996. Prevalence of psychiatric disorders among incarcerated women: 1. pretrial jail detainees. *Arch. Gen. Psychiatry* 53:505–12

Thompson TL. 1997. Review of *DSM-IV Sourcebook*, Vol. 2. *Am. J. Psychiatry* 154:1467–69

Tiihonen J, Isohanni M, Rasanen P, Koiranen M, Moring J. 1997. Specific major mental disorders and criminality: a 26-year prospective study of the 1966 Northern Finland birth cohort. *Am. J. Psychiatry* 154:840–45

Trull TJ, Sher KJ. 1994. Relationship between the five-factor model of personality and axis I disorders in a nonclinical sample. *J. Abnorm. Psychol.* 103:350–60

Vaillant GE. 1983. *The Natural History of Alcoholism.* Cambridge, MA: Harvard Univ. Press

Vaillant GE, Vaillant LM. 1998. The role of ego mechanisms of defense in the diagnosis of personality disorders. See Barron 1998, In press

Virkkunen M, Eggert M, Rawlings R, Linnoila M. 1996. A prospective follow-up study of alcoholic violent offenders and fire setters. *Arch. Gen. Psychiatry* 53:523–29

Volkmar FR. 1997. Review of *DSM-IV Training Guide for Diagnosis of Childhood Disorders. Am. J. Psychiatry* 154:878

Volkmar FR, Klin A, Siegel B, Szatmari P, Lord C, et al. 1994. Field trial for autistic disorder in *DSM-IV. Am. J. Psychiatry* 151:1361–67

Wakefield JC. 1997. Normal inability versus pathological disability: Why Ossorio's definition of mental disorder is not sufficient. *Clin. Psychol. Sci. Pract.* 4:249–58

Watson D, Clark LA. 1995. Depression and

the melancholic temperament. *Eur. J. Pers.* 9:351–66

Watson D, Clark LA, Harkness A. 1994. Structures of personality and their relevance to the study of psychopathology. *J. Abnorm. Psychol.* 103:18–31

Watson D, Clark LA, Weber K, Assenheimer JS, Strauss ME, McCormick RA. 1995a. Testing a tripartite model: II. exploring the symptom structure of anxiety and depression in student, adult, and patient samples. *J. Abnorm. Psychol.* 104:15–25

Watson D, Weber K, Assenheimer JS, Clark LA, Strauss ME, McCormick RA. 1995b. Testing a tripartite model: I. evaluating the convergent and discriminant validity of anxiety and depression symptom scales. *J. Abnorm. Psychol.* 104:3–14

Westen D. 1997. Divergences between clinical and research methods for assessing personality disorders: implications for research and the evolution of Axis II. *Am. J. Psychiatry* 154:895–903

Widiger TA. 1997a. Mental disorders as discrete clinical conditions: dimensional versus categorical classification. In *Adult Psychopathology and Diagnosis,* ed. SM Turner, M Hersen, 3:3–23. New York: Wiley

Widiger TA. 1997b. The construct of mental disorder. *Clin. Psychol. Sci. Pract.* 4: 262–66

Widiger TA. 1998. The *DSM-III-R* categorical personality disorder diagnoses: a critique and an alternative. *Psychol. Inquiry.* In press

Widiger TA, Frances AJ, Pincus HA, First MB, Ross R, Davis W. 1994a. Preface. In *DSM-IV Sourcebook,* ed. TA Widiger, AJ Frances, HA Pincus, MB First, R Ross, W Davis, 1:xvii–xxi. Washington, DC: Am. Psychiatr. Assoc.

Widiger TA, Frances AJ, Pincus HA, First MB, Ross R, Davis W, eds. 1994b. *DSM-IV Sourcebook,* Vol. 1. Washington, DC: Am. Psychiatr. Assoc.

Widiger TA, Frances AJ, Pincus HA, Ross R,
First MB, Davis WW, eds. 1996a. *DSM-IV Sourcebook,* Vol. 2. Washington, DC: Am. Psychiatr. Assoc.

Widiger TA, Frances AJ, Pincus HA, Ross R, First MB, Davis W, eds. 1997. *DSM-IV Sourcebook,* Vol. 3. Washington, DC: Am. Psychiatr. Assoc.

Widiger TA, Hare R, Rutherford M, Corbitt E, Hart S, et al. 1996b. *DSM-IV* antisocial personality disorder field trial. *J. Abnorm. Psychol.* 105:3–16

Widiger TA, Trull TJ. 1991. Diagnosis and clinical assessment. *Annu. Rev. Psychol.* 42:109–33

Widiger TA, Trull TJ. 1993. The scholarly development of *DSM-IV.* In *International Review of Psychiatry,* ed. JAC e Silva, CC Nadelson, 1:59–78. Washington, DC: Am. Psychiatr. Press

Widiger TA, Trull TJ, Clarkin JF, Sanderson C, Costa PT. 1994c. A description of the *DSM-III* and *DSM-IV* personality disorders with the five-factor model of personality. In *Personality Disorders and the Five-Factor Model of Personality,* ed. PT Costa, TA Widiger, pp. 41–57. Washington, DC: Am. Psychol. Assoc.

Wrobel NH. 1993. Effect of patient age and gender on clinical decisions. *Prof. Psychol. Res. Pract.* 24:206–12

Wulfert E, Greenway DE, Dougher MJ. 1996. A logical functional analysis of reinforcement-based disorders: alcoholism and pedophilia. *J. Consult. Clin. Psychol.* 64: 1140–51

Yutzy SH, Cloninger CR, Guze SB, Pribor EF, Martin RL, et al. 1995. *DSM-IV* field trial: testing a new proposal for somatization disorder. *Am. J. Psychiatry* 152:97–101

Zinbarg RE, Barlow DH. 1996. Structure of anxiety and the anxiety disorders. *J. Abnorm. Psychol.* 105:181–93

Zinbarg RE, Barlow DH, Liebowitz M, Street L, Broadhead E, Katon W, et al. 1994. The *DSM-IV* field trial for mixed anxiety-depression. *Am. J. Psychiatry* 151: 1153–62

Annu. Rev. Psychol. 1999. 50:109–35

DEDUCTIVE REASONING

P. N. Johnson-Laird

Department of Psychology, Princeton University, Princeton, New Jersey 08544;
e-mail: phil@clarity.princeton.edu

KEY WORDS: deduction, logic, rules of inference, mental models, thinking

---

ABSTRACT

This chapter describes the main accounts of deductive competence, which explain *what* is computed in carrying out deductions. It argues that people have a modicum of competence, which is useful in daily life and a prerequisite for acquiring logical expertise. It outlines the three main sorts of theory of deductive performance, which explain *how* people make deductions: They rely on factual knowledge, formal rules, or mental models. It reviews recent experimental studies of deductive reasoning in order to help readers to assess these theories of performance.

CONTENTS

109

0084-6570/99/0201-0109$08.00

INTRODUCTION

Reasoning is a process of thought that yields a conclusion from percepts, thoughts, or assertions. The process may be one of which reasoners are painfully aware or of which they are almost unconscious. But it is a systematic process if it is reasoning, as opposed to, say, daydreaming.

This chapter is concerned with one sort of reasoning, deduction. By definition, deduction yields *valid* conclusions, which must be true given that their premises are true, e.g.:

> If the test is to continue, then the turbine must be rotating fast enough.
> The turbine is not rotating fast enough.
> Therefore the test is *not* to continue.

Some deductions are difficult, and the failure to draw this particular valid conclusion probably contributed to the Chernobyl disaster. Despite such mistakes, the business of life depends on the ability to make deductions. Individuals differ in this ability, and those who are better at it—at least as measured by intelligence tests—appear to be more successful. If so, it is not surprising. A person who is poor at reasoning is liable to blunder in daily life. Conversely, without deduction, there would be no logic, no mathematics, and no Annual Review articles.

Psychologists have studied reasoning for a century. Not until Piaget, however, did anyone purport to explain how people were able to make deductions. In his account of the genesis of knowledge, he argued that children spontaneously recapitulate the history of mathematics and arrive at formal reasoning in early adolescence (e.g. Beth & Piaget 1966). By the mid-1970s, researchers assumed that even though Piaget's theory might not be viable in detail, it was right on the grand scale. People were equipped with a mental logic. The task for psychologists—so they thought—was to delineate its principles. This approach ignored an unsettling discovery made by Wason (1966). Intelligent adults in his "selection" task regularly committed a logical error. He laid out four cards in front of them:

A   B   2   3

They knew that each card had a letter on one side and a number on the other side. He showed them a conditional rule: If a card has the letter A on one side, then it has the number 2 on the other side. He then asked them to select those cards that had to be turned over to discover whether the rule was true or false about the four cards. Most people selected the A card alone, or the A and 2 cards. What was puzzling was their failure to select the 3 card: If it has an A on its other side, the rule is false. Indeed, nearly everyone judges it to be false in that case. Yet when Wason changed the content to a sensible everyday generalization, many people made the correct selections (Wason & Johnson-Laird 1972). Insofar as the task is deductive, mental logic is stymied by these effects of content, which have no bearing on its logic.

So much for the historical introduction to the present review. Its plan is simple. It begins with accounts of what the mind is computing when it makes deductions, that is, accounts of *deductive competence*. It then describes theories of how the mind carries out these computations, that is, theories of *deductive performance*. The controversy among these theories is hot, so the chapter reviews recent experiments to enable readers to make up their own minds about deduction.

RATIONALITY AND DEDUCTIVE COMPETENCE

Naive individuals, who have no training in logic, may err in tests of deductive reasoning yet achieve their goals in daily life. This discrepancy is the fundamental paradox of rationality. Psychologists react to it in several different ways, each of which yields a different account of logical competence (for a philosophical analysis, see Engel 1991). This section reviews these accounts, which are couched at the "computational" level—they characterize *what* is computed but not *how* the process is carried out.

One reaction to the paradox is that people are wholly rational but the psychological tests do not reflect their competence. "I have never found errors," Henle (1978) wrote, "which could unambiguously be attributed to faulty reasoning." The philosopher LJ Cohen (1981) has concurred that in such cases there is a glitch in an information-processing mechanism. The strength of this view is that it explains how it was possible for humans to invent logic. Its weakness is that it makes little sense of genuine inferential blunders (for catalogs of the irrational, see Sutherland 1992, Piattelli-Palmarini 1994). Deduction is not tractable: As the number of premises increases, any system of reasoning will eventually run out of time and memory before it reaches a conclusion (Cook 1971). Unless the brain somehow bypasses computational constraints, reasoning is bounded (Simon 1982). Perfect rationality is for the angels.

A different reaction to the paradox is that logic is the wrong normative theory (pace Piaget, Devlin 1997). It permits inferences that no sane individual (other than a logician) is liable to draw, e.g.:

> Ann is here
> Therefore Ann is here or Ben is here, or both.

Inferences of this sort are valid, but naive individuals balk at them, presumably because their conclusions are less informative than their premises (Johnson-Laird & Byrne 1991). Likewise, in logic, if a conclusion follows from premises, then no subsequent premise can invalidate it. But in human reasoning, subsequent information can undermine a deduction. Philosophers and artificial intelligencers formulate such systems of "defeasible" or "nonmonotonic" reasoning (e.g. Harman 1986, Brewka et al 1997), but psychologists do not know how people reason in this way (Chater & Oaksford 1993).

If logic is the wrong normative theory, what should replace it? One strategy, advocated by Anderson (1990), is to make a "rational analysis" of the domain. The analysis calls for a model of the environment in which the cognitive system operates, because, for Anderson, rationality *is* an optimal adaptation to the environment. Evolutionary psychologists assume that natural selection is the main engine of mental adaptation. They abandon general deductive competence in favor of specialized inferential modules, such as a module for "checking for cheaters," which are supposed to have evolved because they conferred a selective advantage on our hunter-gatherer ancestors (Cosmides 1989). But psychologists cannot go back to the Stone Age to test natural selection at work on shaping the mind. The best they can do is to use ethological and paleontological evidence to speculate about what was adaptive for our ancestors (Cummins 1996, Mithen 1996). The strength of the approach is that it explains success in the laboratory where a task taps into a hypothesized module and failure where it does not (Gigerenzer & Hug 1992). But what do evolutionary theorists do if a test fails to corroborate a module (cf Girotto et al 1989, Pollard 1990)? They can allow, like Pinker (1997), that not all modules are adaptations, or they can rewrite their "just so" story to fit the facts (Simon 1991). No result can jeopardize evolutionary psychology. It may be a useful heuristic for generating hypotheses, but it is irrefutable.

Another reaction to the paradox is that people have two sorts of rationality (Evans & Over 1996): rationality$_1$ is a tacit competence for coping with life's problems, and rationality$_2$ is a conscious mechanism for normative reasoning. The commentaries on Evans & Over (1997) are a cross section of the views of leading researchers. Some accept the dichotomy (e.g. Ball et al 1997, Santamaria 1997), and some reject it and argue for a unitary competence based to a first approximation either on rationality$_1$ (e.g. Cummins 1997, Hertwig et al 1997) or on rationality$_2$ (e.g. Noveck 1997, Ormerod 1997). There is a history of similar dichotomies, particularly between tacit and conscious reasoning, and "gut reactions" and deliberation. Sloman (1996) links the two sorts of reasoning to associative and rule-based thinking. The strong point of the dichotomy is that it makes sense of both competence and incompetence in life and the laboratory. Its weakness is that it may accommodate too much.

The various approaches to competence each have their strengths and weaknesses. Perhaps the following conception distills only their strong points. Naive individuals have a modicum of deductive competence (Johnson-Laird & Byrne 1991). The persuasiveness of an inference depends on the credibility of its premises and on the proportion of situations that satisfy both them and the conclusion. The process of reasoning can lead reasoners to abandon a premise or assumption or to abandon an inference as invalid. Conclusions, however, do not throw semantic information away by adding disjunctive alternatives to the premises. They are more parsimonious than their premises, do not repeat those premises that can be taken for granted, and assert a relevant proposition that was not stated explicitly in the premises. When no conclusion meets these constraints, then naive individuals tend to respond, "nothing follows." Logically, the response is wrong, because infinitely many valid conclusions follow from any premises.

The modicum of rationality is important to achieving the goals of everyday life and crucial for technical expertise in logic. But it is only a modicum, so it explains why people make mistakes in reasoning, particularly in the laboratory, but sometimes in life. And it explains why tests of reasoning predict academic success, and how it was possible for humanity to invent logic. The challenge to theories of performance is accordingly to accommodate a modicum of competence.

THEORIES OF DEDUCTIVE PERFORMANCE

This section outlines the three main schools of thought about deductive performance. The first school bases performance on factual knowledge. The second school bases it on a system of formal rules of inference akin to those of a logical calculus. The third school bases it on mental models akin to those of the semantic theory of a logical calculus. In short, deduction is controversial: It may rely on knowledge, formal rules, or mental models, or on some mixture of them (Falmagne & Gonsalves 1995).

Deduction as a Process Based on Factual Knowledge

Psychologists propose that the mind uses content-specific conditional rules to make inferences from general knowledge. The proposal is part of two seminal theories of cognitive architecture: Anderson's (1993) ACT theory and Newell's (1990) SOAR theory, in which the rules, or productions, as they are known, are triggered by the current contents of working memory and then carry out various actions. These actions may, in turn, add new information to working memory and in this way yield a chain of inferences.

Knowledge plays its most specific role in the theory that reasoning is based on memories of previous inferences (e.g. Riesbeck & Schank 1989, Kolodner 1993). Indeed, according to this theory of "case-based" reasoning, human thinking has nothing to do with logic. What happens is that one inference calls to mind another—a procedure that is useful in artificial intelligence (Smyth & Keane 1995). When an activity has been repeated often enough, however, it begins to function like a content-specific rule (cf Eisenstadt & Simon 1997).

Knowledge certainly enters into everyday deductions, but whether it is represented by rules or specific cases is an open question. It might, after all, be represented by *assertions* in a mental language rather than by rules. It might even have a distributed representation that has no explicit structure (Shastri & Ajjanagadde 1993), though it is not known whether distributed systems can acquire the full compositional semantics needed for the representation of assertions.

One drawback with all knowledge-based theories is that they offer no immediate explanation of the ability to reason about the unknown. Even if you know nothing about atonality, you can make the following deduction:

> If it's atonal then it's nondeterministic.
> It's atonal.
> Therefore it's nondeterministic.

This abstract deductive competence is necessary for logic and mathematics. Knowledge-based theories do not explain it, so we turn to alternative accounts.

Deduction as a Formal, Syntactic Process

The idea that deductive performance depends on formal rules of inference is remarkably pervasive. It goes back to the ancient doctrine that the laws of logic are the laws of thought. It was championed by Piaget (e.g. Beth & Piaget 1966), and it underlies several current psychological theories (Nisbett 1993). Rips (1994) and the late Martin Braine (1998) and his colleagues (e.g. Braine & O'Brien 1991) proposed that reasoners extract the logical forms of premises and use rules to derive conclusions. Rips's theory is implemented in a computer program (known as PSYCOP). Both theories have rules for sentential connectives, such as "if" and "or," and for quantifiers, such as "all" and "some." Both are based on a method in logic known as natural deduction, so they have rules for introducing, and for eliminating, sentential connectives. The following rule of *modus ponens*, for instance, eliminates "if":

> If A then B
> A
> Therefore B.

A key feature of natural deduction is the use of suppositions, which are assumptions made for the sake of argument. One way to use a supposition is to show that together with the premises it leads to a contradiction and must therefore be false (*reductio ad absurdum*). Thus, consider the following proof:

> 1. If the test is to continue then the turbine is rotating.
> 2. The turbine isn't rotating.
> 3. The test is to continue. (*A supposition*)
> 4. The turbine is rotating. (*Modus ponens* applied to 1 and 3)

There is a contradiction between a premise (The turbine isn't rotating) and a conclusion derived from the supposition (The turbine is rotating). The rule of *reductio ad absurdum* negates the supposition:

5. Therefore the test is *not* to continue.

Theorists could adopt a single rule for this *modus tollens* inference, but it is more difficult than *modus ponens*, so they assume instead that it depends on the chain of inferential steps. The choice of rules in a theory is thus an empirical matter.

The two main problems in developing a formal rule theory are to ensure that it is computationally viable and that it fits the empirical data. An example of a computational difficulty is that the rule for introducing "and" can run wild, e.g.

A
B
Therefore A and B
Therefore A and (A and B)
Therefore A and [A and (A and B)]

and so on ad infinitum. Two sorts of rules are dangerous: those that introduce a connective and those that make suppositions. One way to curb a rule is to build its effects into another rule that is safe to use (Braine 1994). Alternatively, the dangerous rule can be restricted to chains of inference working backward from a given conclusion to the premises. Rips embodies this idea in PSYCOP, which has forward rules, backward rules, and rules used in either direction.

Rips (1994) advances a Deduction-System hypothesis: Formal rules of inference underlie not just deduction but also the cognitive architecture of the mind. His rules can be used as a programming language in which to implement, for example, a production system. The problem with the Deduction-System hypothesis is illustrated by Eisenstadt & Simon's (1997) counterarguments that a production system underlies cognitive architecture (see also Newell 1990) and that formal rules can be derived from them. The critical question is, What do formal rules contribute to cognitive architecture, as opposed to, say, productions? This issue must be distinguished from the predictions made from the particular use of the rules in "programming" thinking, because what can be programmed by using rules can also be programmed by using productions, the lambda calculus, or any other universal basis for computation. Until this question is answered, it is difficult to test different theories of cognitive architecture.

Deduction as a Semantic Process Based on Mental Models

Human beings can understand the meaning of assertions, envisage the corresponding situations, and ascertain whether a conclusion holds in them. The theory of mental models accordingly postulates that reasoning is based not on syntactic derivations from logical forms but on manipulations of mental models representing situations (Johnson-Laird & Byrne 1991, Polk & Newell 1995). Models can represent the world (e.g. Glasgow 1993), simulate a process (e.g. Hegarty 1992), and yield inductive or deductive inferences (for reviews, see Rogers et al 1992, Oakhill & Garnham 1996).

If deduction depends on models, then the process is semantic because their construction from discourse depends on meaning and knowledge (Glenberg & Langston 1992, Stevenson 1993, Garnham & Oakhill 1996). Each mental model represents a *possibility*, and its structure and content capture what is common to the different ways in which the possibility might occur. For example, when individuals understand a conjunction such as "There is triangle and there is circle," they represent its meaning, from which they can construct a mental model of the situation to which it refers:

o   Δ,

in which o represents a circle, and Δ represents a triangle. The model captures what is common to any situation in which a triangle and a circle are present. Such a model may, or may not, give rise to an image, but models are distinct from images. They can contain abstract elements, such as negation, that cannot be visualized (Johnson-Laird & Byrne 1991).

The theory gives a unified account of deductions about what is possible, probable, and necessary. Given the truth of the premises, a conclusion is *possible* if it holds in at least one model of the premises; its *probability* depends on the proportion of models in which it holds; and it is *necessary* if it holds in all the models of the premises. The model theory gives an account of connectives and quantifiers, including such quantifiers as "most" and "few," and a variety of other sorts of constructions, such as spatial, temporal, and causal relations, and counterfactual conditionals (Johnson-Laird & Byrne 1991, Byrne 1997).

A fundamental assumption of the theory is *the principle of truth*:

> Individuals minimize the load on working memory by tending to construct mental models that represent explicitly only what is true, and not what is false.

The principle applies at two levels. First, individuals represent only true possibilities. Second, for each true possibility, they represent only those literal propositions in the premises—affirmative or negative—that are true (Barres & Johnson-Laird 1997). For example, an inclusive disjunction, such as "There is a circle and/or there is *not* a triangle," elicits three alternative models to represent the three true possibilities:

o

    ¬Δ

o   ¬Δ,

where each row denotes a model of a separate possibility and ¬ represents negation (see Newell 1990, for a defense of such representations). Each model represents only what is true in a particular possibility. Hence, the model in the first row represents that there is a circle, but it does not represent explicitly that it is false that there is not a triangle in this case. Similarly, the second model does not represent explicitly that it is false that there is a circle in this case. Reasoners have only a modicum of competence—they try to remember what is false, but these "mental footnotes" on models are soon forgotten.

In contrast to mental models, *fully explicit* models represent the false components in each possibility. The fully explicit models of the inclusive disjunction above are as follows:

    o   Δ

   ¬o   ¬Δ

    o   ¬Δ

In fully explicit models, false affirmatives are represented by true negations, and false negatives are represented by true affirmatives. The three fully explicit models match the three rows that are true in the truth table of the inclusive disjunction.

The mental models for a conditional

    If there is a circle then there is a triangle

include a model of the salient case (the presence of a circle and a triangle). People realize that there are possibilities in which the antecedent of the conditional (there is a circle) is false. They do not normally represent them explicitly; instead they represent them in a single implicit model that has no content, symbolized here by an ellipsis:

    o   Δ

    . . .

Readers will notice the similarity to the model of the conjunction. The difference is that the conditional has an implicit model allowing for possibilities in which its antecedent is false. A biconditional

    If, and only if, there is a circle, then there is a triangle

has the same mental models as a conditional, but its implicit model corresponds to the possibility in which both the antecedent and the consequent of the conditional are false. If reasoners remember the "mental footnotes" about what is false in the implicit model, then they can construct a set of fully explicit models for a conditional or biconditional. But they soon forget these mental footnotes, especially with assertions that contain more than one connective.

THE PHENOMENA OF DEDUCTIVE REASONING

The previous section reviewed the three principal approaches to deductive performance—the use of knowledge, formal rules, and mental models. The present section turns to the evidence bearing on these theories. The study of deductive performance has burgeoned in recent years (see Evans et al 1993, Garnham & Oakhill 1994, and the new journal *Thinking & Reasoning*). To help readers make sense of the plethora of studies, and to reach their own judgments about the theories of performance, the review is organized in terms of the different branches of deduction.

Reasoning with Sentential Connectives

Most evidence in favor of formal rule theories comes from studies of sentential connectives. According to these theories, the greater the number of steps in a derivation, the harder the inference should be, though other factors cause difficulty, such as the accessibility and complexity of rules. Braine et al (1984) asked naive reasoners to rate the difficulty of each inference in a large set. They used the data to estimate the accessibility of each of their postulated rules and then combined these estimated parameters to predict the ratings for each inference in the set. The fit was satisfactory. Johnson-Laird et al (1992a) used a program to count the overall number of mental models required for each inference, and these parameter-free predictions correlated with the ratings just as well as the post hoc estimates of Braine et al. Bonatti (1994) argued that counting models was inconsistent with the normal use of models. In fact, the theory is not usually used in correlational studies, and it is not clear how else it could yield predictions about the data.

Rips (1994) reported several experiments with sentential connectives, including a study of a sample of inferences in which the participants evaluated given conclusions. His theory fitted the results satisfactorily. It also accounted for the times that the participants took to understand explicit proofs and for their memory of proofs: They remember sentences in the same domain as the premises better than those in a subdomain based on a supposition. Other studies show that individuals automatically make logical inferences in interpreting text (Lea et al 1990, Lea 1995).

There are robust differences in the difficulty of reasoning with the various connectives. Conjunctions are easier than conditionals, which in turn are easier than disjunctions (Johnson-Laird et al 1992a, Schaeken et al 1995). Likewise, exclusive disjunctions (two mental models) are easier than inclusive disjunctions (three mental models; Johnson-Laird et al 1992a). Certain diagrams—those that make alternative possibilities more explicit—both speed up and improve reasoning with disjunctions, but exclusive disjunctions remain easier than inclusive disjunctions (Bauer & Johnson-Laird 1993). These results are predicted by the model theory from the number of mental models required for the respective connectives (for a global experimental confirmation, see Klauer & Oberauer 1995). Formal rule theories contain no machinery for *predicting* differences from one connective to another.

One result at first sight refutes the model theory. Rips (1994) found that an inference of the following form based on a conjunction,

> A and B
> If A then C
> If B then C
> Therefore C,

was no easier to evaluate than one based on a disjunction,

> A or B
> If A then C
> If B then C
> Therefore C.

Contrary to the model theory, PSYCOP predicts that the conjunctive inference should be more difficult than the disjunctive inference, but Rips (1994:368) claims that the disjunctive rule may be "harder for subjects to apply." Madruga et al (1998) argue that Rips's null result is a ceiling effect. They corroborated the model theory's predictions when reasoners drew their own conclusions from these premises. They also showed that when the premises are presented with the conditionals first, or one at a time on a computer screen, the results corroborate the model theory even in the evaluation task. Reasoners' strategies may differ among the different tasks. They develop various high-level strategies in tackling inferential problems, and these strategic principles are just as important as the underlying reasoning mechanisms (Byrne & Handley 1997; M Bucciarelli & PN Johnson-Laird, submitted). The model theory allows for a variety of strategies (Byrne et al 1995), but rule theories rely on a single deterministic strategy.

Conditional Reasoning

Studies of conditionals continue to focus on their four main inferences (e.g. Dugan & Revlin 1990, Evans et al 1995):

If A then B, A,   therefore B.   (*modus ponens*)
If A then B, not B,   therefore not A.   (*modus tollens*)
If A then B, B,   therefore A.   (*affirming the consequent premise*)
If A then B, not A,   therefore not B.   (*denying the antecedent premise*)

Affirming the consequent and denying the antecedent are valid only if the conditional premise is interpreted as a biconditional; otherwise, they are fallacies. Formal rule theorists argue that there are no rules for the fallacies, because they can be suppressed by a second conditional premise, e.g. the premises

If he went fishing then he had fish for supper.
If he bought some fish then he had fish for supper.
He had fish for supper.

suppress the tendency to infer "He went fishing." Byrne (1989), however, showed that an additional conditional premise can also suppress *valid* inferences, e.g. the premises

If he went fishing then he had fish for supper.
If he caught some fish then he had fish for supper.
He went fishing.

suppress the tendency to infer "He had fish for supper." By parity of argument, Byrne claimed, there is no mental rule for *modus ponens*. Politzer & Braine (1991) replied that the additional conditional falsifies the first conditional. But Byrne (1991) demonstrated suppression without affecting its believability (see also RMJ Byrne, O Espino, and C Santamaria, submitted). The tendency to make conditional inferences is influenced by knowledge undermining the sufficiency, or the necessity, of the antecedent to bring about the consequent (Thompson 1994, 1995). Markovits and his colleagues demonstrated subtle effects of this sort, asking the reasoners themselves to generate their own instances of these conditions (Markovits & Vachon 1990; see also Cummins et al 1991). Stevenson & Over (1995) showed that lowering the credibility of a conditional suppresses inferences from it, and they argued that the sufficiency of an antecedent to bring about a consequence is represented by the proportion of models in which the antecedent holds but the consequent does not.

Modus ponens is easier than *modus tollens* (cf the Chernobyl inference in the Introduction). Formal rules and mental models both account for the difference. But Girotto et al (1997) used the model theory to predict a surprising result. *Modus tollens* is easier when the categorical premise is presented first than when it is presented second. Presented first, it provides an initial negative model

$\neg$ B

so that reasoners should be more likely to flesh out their models of the conditional, If A then B, to include the cases where the antecedent is false. RMJ

Byrne & A Tasso (submitted) used the model theory to predict another surprising result. *Modus tollens* is drawn more often from counterfactual than from factual conditionals. A counterfactual of the form "If A had happened then B would have happened" calls for models of both the counterfactual situation (A B) and the factual situation ($\neg$A $\neg$B) that the conditional presupposes. Formal rule theories predict neither phenomena.

Evans et al (1996; see also Evans 1993) proposed a useful correction to the model theory. It had postulated that a negative assertion was likely to elicit models of both the assertion and its corresponding unnegated proposition (Johnson-Laird & Byrne 1991). Thus, a conditional of the form "If not A then B" was supposed to elicit the models

$\neg$A   B
A

The assumption was made to account for "matching" bias, which is the tendency to ignore negatives in conditionals in matching them to categorical premises or situations (Evans 1998; cf Oaksford & Stenning 1992). Evans and his colleagues discovered that the key to the phenomenon is the ease of grasping that one proposition refutes another. The task is easier if one proposition explicitly negates the other than if the relation is merely implicit, e.g. "The number is 4" refutes "The number is 9." Hence, a conditional of the form, If not A then B, should elicit the models,

$\neg$A   B
. . .

The model theory can thus revert to the general principle of truth (cf Evans et al 1998).

One intriguing developmental trend is that very young children treat conditionals as conjunctions; slightly older children treat them as biconditionals, and adolescents and adults are able to treat them as one-way conditionals (see e.g. Taplin et al 1974). If this result is reliable (cf Russell 1987, Markovits 1993), it is a nice confirmation of the model theory: Conjunctions have one fully explicit model, biconditionals have two, and one-way conditionals have three. VM Sloutsky & BJ Morris (submitted) observed that children tend to ignore the second clause of a compound premise, so the premise calls for exactly one model. They are most likely to ignore the second clause of a tautology or contradiction, less likely to ignore it in a disjunction, and least likely to ignore it in a conjunction. Even adults treat conditionals as conjunctions in complex premises. They consider an assertion such as "If A then 2 or if B then 3" to be true in just those cases that they consider the assertion "A and 2, or B and 3" to be true (Johnson-Laird & Barres 1994). The mental models for the two sorts of assertion are identical.

Ormerod and his colleagues have pioneered the study of immediate inferences from one sort of conditional to another, and from conditionals to disjunctions, and vice versa (Ormerod et al 1993, Richardson & Ormerod 1997). They argue that their results can best be explained in terms of a revised model theory. Reasoners construct a minimal set of models of a premise to infer the required paraphrase. Minimal sets of models reduce the load on working memory, and they may underlie reasoning in general.

Reasoning About Relations

Some simple deductions depend on relations, e.g.:

> Ann is better than Beth.
> Cath is worse than Beth.
> Who is worst?

Early studies of these inferences suggested that reasoners construct mental models (De Soto et al 1965, Huttenlocher 1968), though they are also affected by linguistic variables (Clark 1969). Recent studies show that deductions depending on one model are easier than those depending on multiple models. Consider the following spatial problem (from Byrne & Johnson-Laird 1989), which in the original concerned common objects such as knives, forks, and spoons:

> A is on the right of B.
> C is on the left of B.
> D is in front of C.
> E is in front of B.
> What is the relation between D and E?

The model theory predicts that reasoners should construct a single two-dimensional model of the premises:

> C   B   A
> D   E

The model supports the conclusion that D is on the left of E, which no model of the premises refutes. In contrast, the problem

> B is on the right of A.
> C is on the left of B.
> D is in front of C.
> E is in front of B.
> What is the relation between D and E?

calls for two distinct models because the premises do not relate A and C:

```
C   A   B        A   C   B
D       E            D   E
```

Both models yield the same answer: D is on the left of E, so it is valid. But the inference depends on more than one model, so it should be harder than the first one. Formal rule theories predict that there will be no difference between the two problems: Their first premise is irrelevant, and the derivations depend solely on the remaining premises, which are identical in the two problems. In fact, reasoners drew a greater percentage of correct conclusions to the one-model problems than to the multiple-model problems. Rips (1994:415) counters that the instructions may bias people to use images and that the irrelevant premises may sidetrack them. Why they should be sidetracked more by the second problem than the first is unclear. Braine (1994:245) concedes that "much reasoning does use mental models."

Schaeken et al (1996a) replicated the difference between one-model and multiple-model problems in inferences about temporal relations, such as "John takes a shower before he drinks coffee." The difference also occurred when temporal order was implicit only in the use of tense and aspect (Schaeken et al 1996b) and when neither sort of problem contained an irrelevant premise (Schaeken et al 1998). Vandierendonck & De Vooght (1996) confirmed the difference in temporal and spatial problems. They also showed that a task that preoccupies visuo-spatial memory interferes with these inferences (Vandierendonck & De Vooght 1997). This finding contrasts with earlier results (Gilhooly et al 1993, Toms et al 1993) but corroborates an investigation of sentential and spatial reasoning (Klauer et al 1997).

Syllogisms and Reasoning with Quantifiers

Quantifiers underlie many deductions, including syllogisms, such as

> Some actuaries are businessmen.
> All businessmen are conformists.
> Therefore some actuaries are conformists.

One controversy about syllogisms is whether individuals reason or merely select a conclusion that matches the superficial form (or "mood") of a premise (Wetherick & Gilhooly 1990; N Chater & M Oaksford, submitted). Another controversy is whether, if they reason, they use formal rules, Euler circles, or mental models. Stenning & Yule (1997) framed equivalent normative theories of the three sorts, so the real issue is to account for errors.

Rips (1994) fitted his rules to experimental data. He also showed how the theory might account for the results of a study in which the participants drew their own conclusions (Johnson-Laird & Bara 1984): PSYCOP implies that they guessed tentative conclusions to work backward from them. Yang (1997) and Yang et al (1998) fitted Braine's (1998) rules to the rated difficulty of inferences depending on quantifiers and connectives. Yang (personal communication), however, showed that the numbers of tokens in the mental models for these inferences give just as good a fit, even though they do not require the estimate of parameters from the data.

Euler circles represent a premise of the form "All A are B" with two separate diagrams: In one diagram, a circle A lies wholly within a circle B to represent that set A is properly included within set B; in the other diagram, the two circles coincide to represent that the two sets are coextensive. Analogous topological relations between the two circles represent the other sorts of premises. The traditional method calls for the construction of all the different diagrams for each premise and all their different combinations for a pair of premises—a demand that leads to a combinatorial explosion. Stenning and his colleagues, however, devised a way to use Euler circles that obviates the explosion (e.g. Stenning & Yule 1997). Ford (1995) postulates a similar procedure: Reasoners use the verbal premises as reminders of which areas within the circles cannot be empty. Individuals who use Euler circles can thus avoid the traditional method in favor of one resembling the use of mental models (cf Cardaci et al 1996). One puzzle is whether people who have never seen circles used to represent sets spontaneously invent Euler circles. The main disadvantage of the method is that it does not generalize to relational inferences, such as

All horses are animals.
Therefore all horses' heads are animals' heads.

The model theory of quantified reasoning accommodates relations. It postulates that individuals build an initial model from the premises, formulate a conclusion from this model, and, if they are prudent, search for counterexamples to the conclusion (Johnson-Laird & Byrne 1991). The theory predicts the majority of erroneous conclusions, which correspond to the initial models of multiple-model syllogisms (Bara et al 1995). It therefore provides an alternative explanation for the so-called atmosphere effects (Shaw & Johnson-Laird 1998), i.e. the alleged tendency to draw conclusions that merely match the superficial form of a premise.

The model theory has been criticized on several grounds. Ford (1995) has argued vigorously that some reasoners use formal rules, others use Euler circles, but no one uses mental models (for different results, see M Bucciarelli & PN Johnson-Laird, submitted). Ford formulated a set of formal rules for verbal substitutions, but they are equivalent to a model-based procedure proposed by Johnson-Laird & Bara (1984). The outward signs of substitutions are silent on whether their inward occurrence is in sentences or models.

Polk & Newell (1995) claimed that the search for counterexamples appeared to underlie few predictions: Their own model theory gave a better account of individual differences when it dropped this component. With hind-sight, syllogisms are not ideal for demonstrating a search for counterexamples. *Modal* reasoning is better, because the model theory predicts a key interaction hinging on a search for counterexamples: It should be easier to determine that a situation is possible (one model of the premises suffices as an example) than not possible (all the models of the premises must be tested), whereas it should be easier to determine that a situation is not necessary (one model serving as a counterexample suffices) than that it is necessary (all models must be tested). The interaction has been corroborated in reasoning with sentential connectives (Bell & Johnson-Laird 1998) and with quantifiers (JStBT Evans, SE Handley, CNJ Harper & PN Johnson-Laird, submitted). Hence, in tasks where counter-examples are useful, reasoners appear to search for them. Indeed, Barwise (1993) emphasized that the only way to *know* that a conclusion is invalid is by constructing a model of the premises that is a counterexample to it.

Another criticism is that the model theory fails to specify how reasoners search for counterexamples (Martín-Cordero & González-Labra 1994). Vari-ous computer programs implementing the theory contain a search procedure (cf Hardman 1996, for a critique of an earlier program), so the problem was to obtain relevant evidence. M Bucciarelli & PN Johnson-Laird (submitted) therefore devised a technique to externalize thinking: The participants had to construct *external* models using cut-out shapes. They were able to construct counterexamples, that is, models of the premises that refuted invalid conclu-sions. In drawing their own valid conclusions, they constructed more models for multiple-model syllogisms than for one-model syllogisms. In both tasks, they used the same search operations as the program, but it seriously underesti-mated the variety of different reasoning strategies and the variety of different interpretations of the premises (see also Langford & Hunting 1994). The con-struction of external models—let alone counterexamples—is beyond the scope of current formal rule theories.

Inferences can depend on relations and multiple quantifiers, e.g.:

> Some of the Avon letters are in the same place as all the Bury letters.
> All the Bury letters are in the same place as all the Caton letters.
> Therefore some of the Avon letters are in the same place as all the Caton letters.

Johnson-Laird et al (1989) showed that one-model problems of this sort yield a greater proportion of correct conclusions than multiple-model problems. Greene (1992) pointed out a possible confounding: The multiple-model problems called for conclusions of the form "None of the Avon letters are in the same place as *some* of the Caton letters," which are difficult for people to formulate. He argued that there was therefore no need to postulate the use of mental models. However, the multiple-model problems also support straightforward conclusions, such as "Some of the Caton letters are not in the same place as any of the Avon letters." The model theory also predicted the participants' erroneous conclusions: They mainly corresponded to the initial models of the premises (Johnson-Laird et al 1992b).

The Effects of Content on Deduction

If deduction depends on formal rules, the content of inferences cannot affect the *process* of reasoning, which is purely syntactic. But if deduction depends on models, then content can affect the process, because reasoners can stop searching for alternative models of the premises if their initial models yield believable conclusions. Most investigations of the effects of believability concern syllogisms, such as

> All of the Frenchmen are wine drinkers.
>
> Some of the wine drinkers are gourmets.
>
> Therefore some of the Frenchmen are gourmets.

Many early studies were methodologically flawed, but recent research has established three main phenomena (Evans 1989, Newstead & Evans 1993). First, reasoners accept more valid conclusions than invalid conclusions. Second, they accept more believable than unbelievable conclusions. Many people, for example, draw the conclusion in the syllogism above (Oakhill et al 1990). It is invalid, but highly believable. Third, the effects of believability are greater on invalid inferences than on valid ones. But when invalid conclusions are not consistent with the premises, then the interaction disappears (Newstead et al 1992).

There are several possible accounts for the phenomena. Reasoners may rely on mental models. They may not realize that a conclusion that is merely consistent with the premises does not thereby follow from them (the *misinterpreted necessity* hypothesis). They may accept believable conclusions and only assess the validity of unbelievable ones (the *selective scrutiny* hypothesis). As Quayle & Ball (1997) showed, however, the model theory can be reconciled with misinterpreted necessity. Necessary conclusions are supported by models, and impossible conclusions are refuted by them. But if a conclusion is merely possible, then reasoners may be uncertain and so be more likely to accept believable conclusions and to reject unbelievable conclusions (cf Hardman & Payne 1995). This account is supported by reasoners' confidence ratings: They are highly confident in valid conclusions, which is a good index of syllogistic competence.

One study has examined the effects of believability on conditional reasoning (Santamaria et al 1998). A pair of believable conditionals can yield a believable or an unbelievable conclusion, as in

If Marta is hungry, then she takes an afternoon snack.
If Marta takes an afternoon snack, then she has a light dinner.
Therefore if Marta is hungry, then she has a light dinner.

The conclusion lacks the causal link (eating the snack), so it violates the normal relation between hunger and dinner. Reasoners were more likely, and quicker, to draw a valid conclusion when it was believable than when it was unbelievable. Hence, there may be a process of "filtering out" valid conclusions that are not believable (Oakhill et al 1990).

The Selection Task

The selection task (see the Introduction) has launched a thousand studies, but the literature has grown faster than knowledge. Selections are sensitive to the probability of encountering a falsifying instance, and the introduction of such Bayesian considerations has revitalized research (Oaksford & Chater 1994, 1996; Kirby 1994; Nickerson 1996). This normative approach—inspired by Anderson's (1990) "rational analysis"—accounts for many phenomena, but there is, as yet, no corresponding theory of the mental processes underlying performance. Naive individuals are unlikely to be explicitly calculating, say, the expected gain in information from selecting a card.

A change in the content of the selection task can yield a striking improvement in performance, particularly with *deontic* conditionals concerning what is permissible (Cheng & Holyoak 1985, Kroger et al 1993). Manktelow & Over (1991) used the deontic conditional, "If you tidy your room then you may go out to play," and the participants' selections depended on whose point of view they were asked to take. The mother's concern is that her child does not cheat, and those with her point of view tended to select the cards did-not-tidy and played. Her son's concern is that his mother does not renege on the deal, and those with his point of view tended to select the cards tidied and did-not-play. Even children are sensitive to point of view (Light et al 1990), and adults with a neutral point of view tend to select all four cards (Politzer & Nguyen-Xuan 1992).

Theorists debate the causes of these effects (see e.g. Holyoak & Cheng 1995 and the commentaries thereon). Cheng & Holyoak (1985) argued that a deontic conditional maps onto a "pragmatic reasoning schema" such as

If the action (e.g. playing) is to be taken, then the precondition must be satisfied (e.g. tidying the room).

Cosmides (1989) proposed that there is an innate module for "checking for cheaters" (see also Gigerenzer & Hug 1992). But Manktelow & Over (1995) argued against both of these positions and in favor of mental models. However, the model theory, they say, underestimates the importance of probabilities, preferences, and pragmatics.

Because the selection task is sensitive to Bayesian considerations, one might conclude that it does not depend on deductive reasoning. The claim is premature. On the one hand, individuals of higher cognitive ability tend to make deductively correct selections in versions of the task with an abstract content (Stanovich 1998). On the other hand, deductions can yield probabilistic conclusions, and such deductions can be accounted for by the model theory: The probability of an event depends on the proportion of models in which it occurs (Johnson-Laird & Savary 1996, Johnson-Laird et al 1998). The model theory predicts that any manipulation that emphasizes what would falsify the rule should improve performance in the selection task. Such effects do occur, even in tasks that are neither deontic nor concern checking for cheaters. Instructions to check for *violations* improved performance in the abstract task (Platt & Griggs 1993, Griggs 1995, Dominowski 1995). Green (1995) showed that instructions to envisage counterexamples also improved performance (see also Green & Larking 1995). In work that brings together the model theory and Bayesian considerations, Green et al (1997) showed that reasoners' assessments of how likely they were to encounter a counterexample (in four stacks of cards) predicted their selections (see also Green 1997). Sperber et al (1995) used a more indirect procedure to render counterexamples more *relevant*—in the sense of Sperber & Wilson (1995)—and thereby improved performance. Love & Kessler (1995) used a context that suggested the possibility of counterexamples, and Liberman & Klar (1996) demonstrated that apparent effects of "checking for cheaters" are better explained in terms of the participants' grasp of appropriate counterexamples and of the relevance of looking for them.

Systematic Fallacies in Reasoning

The controversy between rules and models has been going on for a long time. Roberts (1993) suggested that it was neither fruitful nor resolvable. Yet most criticisms of formal rules concern their power to explain empirical results, whereas most criticisms of mental models concern alleged shortcomings in the formulation of the theory—it is unfalsifiable, or it is obviously false; it relies on images too much, or it does not rely on images enough; it relies on formal rules or it needs to rely on formal rules. These mutually inconsistent criticisms are strange, especially for a theory systematically implemented in computer programs. They may reflect the difficulty of grasping a different and nondeterministic paradigm.

Evidence in favor of rules and against models is hard to find. The best case rests on studies of hemispherical differences. The lack of right-hemisphere involvement in reasoning about easily visualized content has been taken to jeopardize the model theory (see Wharton & Grafman 1998 for a review). But as these authors point out, the studies are preliminary, and the results count more against the claim that models are images—a claim that Johnson-Laird & Byrne (1991) repudiate—rather than the theory that reasoning depends on models.

Is there any evidence in favor of models and against rules? Preceding sections discussed several cases, but we turn now to a phenomenon that may be decisive. The principle of truth, which underlies the model theory, has a surprising consequence. It implies that human beings reason in a systematically fallacious way. Consider the following problem:

> Only one of the following premises is true about a particular hand of cards:
> There is a king in the hand or there is an ace, or both.
> There is a queen in the hand or there is an ace, or both.
> There is a jack in the hand or there is a 10, or both.
> Is it possible that there is an ace in the hand?

The mental models of the first premise are

> King
>
>   Ace
>
> King   Ace

They support the conclusion that an ace is possible, and most people draw this conclusion (Johnson-Laird & Goldvarg 1997). They fail to take into account that when one premise is true, the others are false. Hence, if the first premise is true, the second premise is false, so there cannot be an ace. Indeed, if there were an ace in the hand, then *two* of the premises would be true, contrary to the rubric that only one of them is true.

Reasoners are vulnerable to a variety of fallacies in modal and probabilistic reasoning (Johnson-Laird & Savary 1996). The rubric "Only one of the premises is true" is equivalent to an exclusive disjunction, and a compelling illusion occurs in the following inference about a particular hand of cards:

> If there is a king in the hand then there is an ace in the hand, or else if there isn't a king in the hand then there is an ace in the hand.
> There is a king in the hand.
> What, if anything, follows?

Nearly everyone, expert and novice alike, infers that there is an ace in the hand. It follows from the mental models of the premises. Yet it is a fallacy granted a disjunction, exclusive or inclusive, between the two conditionals. Hence, one or other of the conditionals could be false. If, say, the first conditional is false, then there is no guarantee that there is an ace in the hand even though there is a king. Granted that the fallacies arise from a failure to reason about what is false, any manipulation that emphasizes falsity should alleviate them. An experiment that used the rubric "Only one of the following two premises is false" did reliably reduce their occurrence (Tabossi et al 1998).

No current formal rule theory predicts the fallacies: These theories rely solely on valid inferential procedures (see e.g. Rips 1997). Perhaps a simple procedural assumption can at least accommodate the fallacies post hoc. If not, then they may resolve the controversy. They do not imply, however, that all possible formal rule theories are wrong. No result could do so. As the Deductive-System hypothesis shows, formal rules can be used to program any computable theory, including the mental model theory itself.

CONCLUSIONS

Deduction is under intense investigation. The two dominant accounts of its underlying mechanisms are based on rules and on models—a distinction that echoes the contrast in logic between "proof" theory and "model" theory. Rule theorists are impressed by the automatic ease with which we make certain inferences. They formulate rules that correspond to these elementary deductions, and they assume that more difficult inferences call for chains of elementary deductions. In contrast, what strikes model theorists is that reasoning is just the continuation of comprehension by other means. They notice that arguments are seldom laid out as proofs and that public reasoning is often dialectical. We are all better critics of other people's inferences than of our own. We recognize the force of counterexamples, but we more readily construct models that reflect our own views than find refutations of them (Baron 1990, Legrenzi et al 1993).

Both theoretical approaches have a penumbra of protective stratagems. Yet both have testable consequences. Psychology is difficult, but it is not impossible. The evidence suggests that naive reasoners have a modicum of deductive competence based on mental models. In principle, rules and models are not incompatible. Indeed, advanced reasoners may learn to construct formal rules for themselves—a process that ultimately leads to the discipline of logic.

Literature Cited

Anderson JR. 1990. *The Adaptive Character of Thought*. Hillsdale, NJ: Erlbaum
Anderson JR. 1993. *Rules of the Mind*. Hillsdale, NJ: Erlbaum
Ball LJ, Sutherland EJ, Quayle JD. 1997. Situating deductive competence within a models framework: some further considerations. *Curr. Psychol. Cogn.* 16:52–62

Bara B, Bucciarelli M, Johnson-Laird PN. 1995. The development of syllogistic reasoning. *Am. J. Psychol.* 108:157–93

Baron J. 1990. *Thinking and Deciding.* New York: Cambridge Univ. Press. 2nd ed.

Barres PE, Johnson-Laird PN. 1997. Why is it hard to imagine what is false? In *Proc. 19th Annu. Conf. Cogn. Sci. Soc.,* pp. 475–78. Mahwah, NJ: Erlbaum

Barwise J. 1993. Everyday reasoning and logical inference. *Behav. Brain Sci.* 16:337–38

Bauer MI, Johnson-Laird PN. 1993. How diagrams can improve reasoning. *Psychol. Sci.* 4:372–78

Bell V, Johnson-Laird PN. 1998. A model theory of modal reasoning. *Cogn. Sci.* In press

Beth EW, Piaget J. 1966. *Mathematical Epistemology and Psychology.* Dordrecht: Reidel

Bonatti L. 1994. Propositional reasoning by model? *Psychol. Rev.* 101:725–33

Braine MDS. 1994. Mental logic and how to discover it. In *The Logical Foundations of Cognition,* ed. J Macnamara, GE Reyes, pp. 241–63. New York: Oxford Univ. Press

Braine MDS. 1998. Steps towards a mental predicate logic. See Braine & O'Brien 1998, pp. 273–331

Braine MDS, O'Brien DP. 1991. A theory of If: a lexical entry, reasoning program and pragmatic principles. *Psychol. Rev.* 98:182–203

Braine MDS, O'Brien DP, eds. 1998. *Mental Logic.* Mahwah, NJ: Erlbaum

Braine MDS, Reiser BJ, Rumain B. 1984. Some empirical justification for a theory of natural propositional logic. In *The Psychology of Learning and Motivation,* 18:313–71. New York: Academic

Brewka G, Dix J, Konolige K. 1997. *Nonmonotonic Reasoning: An Overview.* Stanford, CA: CLSI Publ., Stanford Univ.

Byrne RMJ. 1989. Suppressing valid inferences with conditionals. *Cognition* 31:61–83

Byrne RMJ. 1991. Can valid inferences be suppressed? *Cognition* 39:71–78

Byrne RMJ. 1997. Cognitive processes in counterfactual thinking about what might have been. In *The Psychology of Learning and Motivation, Advances in Research and Theory,* ed. DL Medin, 37:105–54. San Diego, CA: Academic

Byrne RMJ, Handley SJ. 1997. Reasoning strategies for suppositional deductions. *Cognition* 62:1–49

Byrne RMJ, Handley SJ, Johnson-Laird PN. 1995. Reasoning from suppositions. *Q. J. Exp. Psychol.* 48A:915–44

Byrne RMJ, Johnson-Laird PN. 1989. Spatial reasoning. *J. Mem. Lang.* 28:564–75

Cardaci M, Gangemi A, Pendolino G, Di Nuovo S. 1996. Mental models vs. integrated models: explanations of syllogistic reasoning. *Percept. Mot. Skills* 82:1377–78

Chater N, Oaksford M. 1993. Logicism, mental models and everyday reasoning. *Mind Lang.* 8:72–89

Cheng PN, Holyoak KJ. 1985. Pragmatic reasoning schemas. *Cogn. Psychol.* 17:391–416

Clark HH. 1969. Linguistic processes in deductive reasoning. *Psychol. Rev.* 76:387–404

Cohen LJ. 1981. Can human irrationality be experimentally demonstrated? *Behav. Brain Sci.* 4:317–70

Cook SA. 1971. The complexity of theorem proving procedures. In *Proc. 3rd Annu. ACM Symp. Theory Computing,* pp. 151–58. Arlington, VA: Assoc. Comput. Mach.

Cosmides L. 1989. The logic of social exchange: Has natural selection shaped how humans reason? Studies with the Wason selection task. *Cognition* 31:187–276

Cummins DD. 1996. Evidence for the innateness of deontic reasoning. *Mind Lang.* 11:160–90

Cummins DD. 1997. Rationality: biological, psychological, and normative theories. *Curr. Psychol. Cogn.* 16:78–86

Cummins DD, Lubart T, Alksnis O, Rist R. 1991. Conditional reasoning and causation. *Mem. Cogn.* 19:274–82

De Soto LB, London M, Handel LS. 1965. Social reasoning and spatial paralogic. *J. Pers. Soc. Psychol.* 2:513–21

Devlin K. 1997. *Goodbye Descartes: The End of Logic and the Search for a New Cosmology of the Mind.* New York: Wiley

Dominowski RL. 1995. Content effects in Wason's selection task. See Newstead & Evans 1995, pp. 41–65

Dugan CM, Revlin R. 1990. Response options and presentation format as contributors to conditional reasoning. *Q. J. Exp. Psychol.* 42A:829–48

Eisenstadt SA, Simon HA. 1997. Logic and thought. *Minds Mach.* 7:365–85

Engel P. 1991 (1989). *The Norm of Truth: An Introduction to the Philosophy of Logic.* Toronto: Univ. Toronto Press

Evans JStBT. 1989. *Bias in Human Reasoning: Causes and Consequences.* Hillsdale, NJ: Erlbaum

Evans JStBT. 1993. The mental model theory of conditional reasoning: critical appraisal and revision. *Cognition* 48:1–20

Evans JStBT. 1998. Matching bias in conditional reasoning: Do we understand it after 25 years? *Think. Reasoning* 4:45–82

Evans JStBT, Clibbens J, Rood B. 1995. Bias in conditional inference: implications for mental models and mental logic. *Q. J. Exp. Psychol.* 48A:644–70

Evans JStBT, Clibbens J, Rood B. 1996. The role of implicit and explicit negation in conditional reasoning bias. *J. Mem. Lang.* 35:392–404

Evans JStBT, Legrenzi P, Girotto V. 1998. The influence of linguistic form on reasoning: the case of matching bias. *Q. J. Exp. Psychol.* In press

Evans JStBT, Newstead SE, Byrne RMJ. 1993. *Human Reasoning: The Psychology of Deduction.* Mahwah, NJ: Erlbaum

Evans JStBT, Over DE. 1996. *Rationality and Reasoning.* Hove, East Sussex, UK: Psychology Press

Evans JStBT, Over DE. 1997. Rationality in reasoning: the problem of deductive competence. *Curr. Psychol. Cogn.* 16:3–38

Falmagne RJ, Gonsalves J. 1995. Deductive inference. *Annu. Rev. Psychol.* 46:525–59

Ford M. 1995. Two modes of mental representation and problem solution in syllogistic reasoning. *Cognition* 54:1–71

Garnham A, Oakhill JV. 1994. *Thinking and Reasoning.* Oxford: Blackwell

Garnham A, Oakhill JV. 1996. The mental models theory of language comprehension. In *Models of Understanding Text,* ed. BK Britton, AC Graesser, pp. 313–39. Hillsdale, NJ: Erlbaum

Gigerenzer G, Hug K. 1992. Domain specific reasoning: social contracts, cheating, and perspective change. *Cognition* 43:127–71

Gilhooly KJ, Keane MTG, Logie RH, Erdos G, eds. 1990. *Lines of Thinking,* Vol. 1. New York: Wiley

Gilhooly KJ, Logie RH, Wetherick NE, Wynn V. 1993. Working memory and strategies in syllogistic reasoning tasks. *Mem. Cogn.* 21:115–24

Girotto V, Blaye A, Farioli F. 1989. A reason to reason: pragmatic basis of children's search for counterexamples. *Eur. Bull. Cogn. Psychol.* 9:297–321

Girotto V, Mazzocco A, Tasso A. 1997. The effect of premise order in conditional reasoning: a test of the mental model theory. *Cognition* 63:1–28

Glasgow JI. 1993. Representation of spatial models for geographic information systems. In *Proc. ACM Workshop on Advances in Geographic Information Systems,* ed. N Pissinou, pp. 112–17. Arlington, VA: Assoc. Comput. Mach.

Glenberg AM, Langston WE. 1992. Comprehension of text: pictures help to build mental models. *J. Mem. Lang.* 31:129–51

Green DW. 1995. Externalization, counterexamples and the abstract selection task. *Q. J. Exp. Psychol.* 48A:424–46

Green DW. 1997. Hypothetical thinking in the selection task: amplifying a model-based approach. *Curr. Psychol. Cogn.* 16:93–102

Green DW, Larking R. 1995. The locus of facilitation in the abstract selection task. *Think. Reasoning* 1:183–99

Green DW, Over D, Pyne R. 1997. Probability and choice in the selection task. *Think. Reasoning* 3:209–35

Greene S. 1992. Multiple explanations for multiply quantified sentences: Are multiple models necessary? *Psychol. Rev.* 99:184–87

Griggs RA. 1995. The effects of rule clarification, decision justification, and selection instruction on Wason's abstract selection task. See Newstead & Evans 1995, pp. 17–39

Hardman DK. 1996. Mental models: The revised theory brings new problems. *Behav. Brain Sci.* 19:542–43

Hardman DK, Payne SJ. 1995. Problem difficulty and response format in syllogistic reasoning. *Q. J. Exp. Psychol.* 48A: 945–75

Harman G. 1986. *Change in View: Principles of Reasoning.* Cambridge, MA: Bradford Books/MIT Press

Hegarty M. 1992. Mental animation: inferring motion from static displays of mechanical systems. *J. Exp. Psychol.: Learn. Mem. Cogn.* 18:1084–102

Henle M. 1978. Foreword to *Human Reasoning,* ed. R Revlin, RE Mayer. Washington, DC: Winston

Hertwig R, Ortmann A, Gigerenzer G. 1997. Deductive competence: a desert devoid of content and context. *Curr. Psychol. Cogn.* 16:102–7

Holyoak KJ, Cheng PW. 1995. Pragmatic reasoning with a point of view. *Think. Reasoning* 1:289–313

Huttenlocher J. 1968. Constructing spatial images: a strategy in reasoning. *Psychol. Rev.* 75:286–98

Johnson-Laird PN, Bara B. 1984. Syllogistic inference. *Cognition* 16:1–61

Johnson-Laird PN, Barres PE. 1994. When 'or' means 'and': a study in mental models. *Proc. 16th Annu. Conf. Cogn. Sci. Soc.,* pp. 475–78. Hillsdale, NJ: Erlbaum

Johnson-Laird PN, Byrne RMJ. 1991. *Deduction.* Hillsdale, NJ: Erlbaum

Johnson-Laird PN, Byrne RMJ, Schaeken WS. 1992a. Propositional reasoning by model. *Psychol. Rev.* 99:418–39

Johnson-Laird PN, Byrne RMJ, Tabossi P. 1989. Reasoning by model: the case of multiple quantification. *Psychol. Rev.* 96: 658–73

Johnson-Laird PN, Byrne RMJ, Tabossi P. 1992b. In defense of reasoning: a reply to Greene. *Psychol. Rev.* 99:188–90

Johnson-Laird PN, Goldvarg Y. 1997. How to make the impossible seem possible. In *Proc. 19th Annu. Conf. Cogn. Sci. Soc.,* pp. 354–57. Mahwah, NJ: Erlbaum

Johnson-Laird PN, Legrenzi P, Girotto V, Legrenzi MS, Caverni J-P. 1998. Naive probability: a mental model theory of extensional reasoning. *Psychol. Rev.* In press

Johnson-Laird PN, Savary F. 1996. Illusory inferences about probabilities. *Acta Psychol.* 93:69–90

Kirby KN. 1994. Probabilities and utilities of fictional outcomes in Wason's four-card selection task. *Cognition* 51:1–28

Klauer KC, Oberauer K. 1995. Testing the mental model theory of propositional reasoning. *Q. J. Exp. Psychol.* 48A:671–87

Klauer KC, Stegmaier R, Meiser T. 1997. Working memory involvement in propositional and spatial reasoning. *Think. Reasoning* 3:9–47

Kolodner J. 1993. *Case-Based Reasoning.* San Mateo, CA: Morgan Kaufman

Kroger K, Cheng PW, Holyoak KJ. 1993. Evoking the permission schema: the impact of explicit negation and a violation-checking context. *Q. J. Exp. Psychol.* 46A: 615–35

Langford PE, Hunting R. 1994. A representational communication approach to the development of inductive and deductive logic. In *Intelligence, Mind, and Reasoning,* ed. A Demetriou, A Efklides, pp. 191–209. New York: Elsevier

Lea RB. 1995. On-line evidence for elaborative inferences in text. *J. Exp. Psychol. Learn. Mem. Cogn.* 21:1469–82

Lea RB, O'Brien DP, Fisch SM, Noveck IA, Braine MDS. 1990. Predicting propositional-like inferences in text-comprehension. *J. Mem. Lang.* 29:361–87

Legrenzi P, Girotto V, Johnson-Laird PN. 1993. Focussing in reasoning and decision making. *Cognition* 49:37–66

Liberman N, Klar Y. 1996. Hypothesis testing in Wason's selection task: social exchange cheating detection or task understanding. *Cognition* 58:127–56

Light PH, Girotto V, Legrenzi P. 1990. Children's reasoning on conditional promises and permissions. *Cogn. Dev.* 5:369–83

Love R, Kessler C. 1995. Focussing in Wason's selection task: content and instruction effects. *Think. Reasoning* 1:153–82

Madruga JAG, Moreno S, Carriedo N, Gutiérrez F. 1998. Task, premise order and strategies in Rips's conjunction-disjunction and conditionals problems. In *Deductive Reasoning and Strategies,* ed. W Schaeken. In press

Manktelow KI, Over DE. 1991. Social rules and utilities in reasoning with deontic conditionals. *Cognition* 39:85–105

Manktelow KI, Over DE. 1995. Deontic reasoning. See Newstead & Evans 1995, pp. 91–114

Markovits H. 1993. The development of conditional reasoning: a Piagetian reformulation of mental models theory. *Merrill-Palmer Q.* 39:133–60

Markovits H, Vachon R. 1990. Conditional reasoning, representation, and level of abstraction. *Dev. Psychol.* 26:942–51

Martín-Cordero J, González-Labra MJ. 1994. Amnesic mental models do not completely spill the beans of deductive reasoning. *Behav. Brain Sci.* 17:773–74

Mithen S. 1996. *The Prehistory of Mind: The Cognitive Origins of Art, Religion and Science.* London: Thames & Hudson

Newell A. 1990. *Unified Theories of Cognition.* Cambridge. MA: Harvard Univ. Press

Newstead SE, Evans JStBT. 1993. Mental models as an explanation of belief bias effects in syllogistic reasoning. *Cognition* 46:93–97

Newstead SE, Evans JStBT, eds. 1995. *Perspectives on Thinking and Reasoning: Essays in Honour of Peter Wason.* Hillsdale, NJ: Erlbaum

Newstead SE, Pollard P, Evans JStBT, Allen J. 1992. The source of belief bias in syllogistic reasoning. *Cognition* 45:257–84

Nickerson R. 1996. Hempel's paradox and Wason's selection task: logical and psychological puzzles of confirmation. *Think. Reasoning* 2:1–31

Nisbett RE, ed. 1993. *Rules for Reasoning.* Hillsdale, NJ: Erlbaum

Noveck IA. 1997. Deductive competence need not be problematic: some comments on Evans and Over's proposal concerning human rationality. *Curr. Psychol. Cogn.* 16: 162–70

Oakhill J, Garnham A, eds. 1996. *Mental Models in Cognitive Science.* Hove, East Sussex, UK: Psychology Press

Oakhill J, Garnham A, Johnson-Laird PN. 1990. Belief bias effects in syllogistic reasoning. See Gilhooly et al 1990, pp. 125–38

Oaksford M, Chater N. 1994. A rational analysis of the selection task as optimal data selection. *Psychol. Rev.* 101:608–31

Oaksford M, Chater N. 1996. Rational explanation of the selection task. *Psychol. Rev.* 103:381–91

Oaksford M, Stenning K. 1992. Reasoning with conditionals containing negated constituents. *J. Exp. Psychol. Learn. Mem. Cogn.* 18:835–54

Ormerod TC. 1997. Rationalities 1 and 2: dual processes or different task demands? *Curr. Psychol. Cogn.* 16:181–89

Ormerod TC, Manktelow KI, Jones GV. 1993. Reasoning with three types of conditional: biases and mental models. *Q. J. Exp. Psychol.* 46A:653–78

Piattelli-Palmarini M. 1994. *Inevitable Illusions: How Mistakes of Reason Rule Our Minds.* New York: Wiley

Pinker S. 1997. *How the Mind Works.* New York: Norton

Platt RD, Griggs RA. 1993. Facilitation in the abstract selection task: the effects of attentional and instructional factors. *Q. J. Exp. Psychol.* 46A:591–613

Politzer G, Braine MDS. 1991. Responses to inconsistent premises cannot count as suppression of valid inferences. *Cognition* 38: 103–8

Politzer G, Nguyen-Xuan A. 1992. Reasoning about conditional promises and warnings: Darwinian algorithms, mental models, relevance judgements or pragmatic schemas? *Q. J. Exp. Psychol.* 44:401–12

Polk TA, Newell A. 1995. Deduction as verbal reasoning. *Psychol. Rev.* 102:533–66

Pollard P. 1990. Natural selection for the selection task: limits to social exchange theory. *Cognition* 36:195–204

Quayle JD, Ball LJ. 1997. Subjective confidence and the belief bias effect in syllogistic reasoning. In *Proc. 19th Annu. Conf. Cogn. Sci. Soc.*, pp. 626–31. Mahwah, NJ: Erlbaum

Richardson J, Ormerod TC. 1997. Rephrasing between disjunctives and conditionals: mental models and the effects of thematic content. *Q. J. Exp. Psychol.* 50A:358–85

Riesbeck CK, Schank RC. 1989. *Inside Case-Based Reasoning.* Hillsdale, NJ: Erlbaum

Rips LJ. 1994. *The Psychology of Proof.* Cambridge, MA: MIT Press

Rips LJ. 1997. Goals for a theory of deduction: reply to Johnson-Laird. *Minds Mach.* 7: 409–24

Roberts MJ. 1993. Human reasoning: deduction rules or mental models? *Q. J. Exp. Psychol.* 46A:569–89

Rogers Y, Rutherford A, Bibby PA, eds. 1992. *Models in the Mind: Theory, Perspective and Application.* London: Academic

Russell J. 1987. Rule-following, mental models, and the developmental view. In *Meaning and the Growth of Understanding,* ed.

M Chapman, RA Dixon, pp. 23–48. New York: Springer-Verlag

Santamaria C. 1997. On implicit reasoning and mental models. *Curr. Psychol. Cogn.* 16:205–10

Santamaria C, Madruga JAG, Johnson-Laird PN. 1998. Reasoning from double conditionals: the effects of logical structure and believability. *Think. Reasoning.* In press

Schaeken W, Girotto V, Johnson-Laird PN. 1998. The effect of an irrelevant premise on temporal and spatial reasoning. *Kognitionswissenschaft.* In press

Schaeken W, Johnson-Laird PN, Byrne RMJ, d'Ydewalle G. 1995. A comparison of conditional and disjunctive inferences: a case study of the mental model theory of reasoning. *Psychol. Belg.* 35:57–70

Schaeken WS, Johnson-Laird PN, d'Ydewalle G. 1996a. Mental models and temporal reasoning. *Cognition* 60:205–34

Schaeken WS, Johnson-Laird PN, d'Ydewalle G. 1996b. Tense, aspect, and temporal reasoning. *Think. Reasoning* 2:309–27

Shastri L, Ajjanagadde V. 1993. From simple associations to systematic reasoning: a connectionist representation of rules, variables and dynamic bindings using temporal synchrony. *Behav. Brain Sci.* 16: 417–94

Shaw VF, Johnson-Laird PN. 1998. Dispelling the 'atmosphere' effect in reasoning. *Anal. Psychol.* In press

Simon HA. 1982. *Models of Bounded Rationality,* Vols. 1, 2. Cambridge, MA: MIT Press

Simon HA. 1991. Cognitive architectures and rational analysis: comment. In *Architectures for Intelligence: The 22nd Carnegie Mellon Symposium on Cognition,* ed. K VanLehn. Hillsdale, NJ: Erlbaum

Sloman SA. 1996. The empirical case for two systems of reasoning. *Psychol. Bull.* 119: 3–22

Smyth B, Keane MT. 1995. Remembering to forget: a competence- preserving deletion policy for CBR systems. In *14th Int. Jt. Conf. Artificial Intelligence.* Los Altos, CA: Morgan Kaufman

Sperber D, Cara F, Girotto V. 1995. Relevance theory explains the selection task. *Cognition* 52:3–39

Sperber D, Wilson D. 1995. *Relevance: Communication and Cognition.* Oxford: Blackwell. Rev. ed.

Stanovich KE. 1998. *Who Is Rational? Studies of Individual Differences in Reasoning.* Mahwah, NJ: Erlbaum. In press

Stenning K, Yule P. 1997. Image and language in human reasoning: a syllogistic illustration. *Cogn. Psychol.* 34:109–59

Stevenson RJ. 1993. *Language, Thought and Representation.* New York: Wiley

Stevenson RJ, Over DE. 1995. Deduction from uncertain premises *Q. J. Exp. Psychol.* 48A:613–43

Sutherland S. 1992. *Irrationality: The Enemy Within.* London: Constable

Tabossi P, Bell VA, Johnson-Laird PN. 1998. Mental models in deductive, modal, and probabilistic reasoning. In *Mental Models in Discourse Processing and Reasoning,* ed. C Habel, G Rickheit. Berlin: Benjamins. In press

Taplin JE, Staudenmayer H, Taddonio JL. 1974. Developmental changes in conditional reasoning: linguistic or logical? *J. Exp. Child Psychol.* 17:360–73

Thompson VA. 1994. Interpretational factors in conditional reasoning. *Mem. Cogn.* 22: 742–58

Thompson VA. 1995. Conditional reasoning: the necessary and sufficient conditions. *Can. J. Exp. Psychol.* 49:1–60

Toms M, Morris N, Ward D. 1993. Working memory and conditional reasoning *Q. J. Exp. Psychol.* 46A:679–99

Vandierendonck A, De Vooght G. 1996. Evidence for mental-model-based reasoning: a comparison of reasoning with time and space concepts. *Think. Reasoning* 2: 249–72

Vandierendonck A, De Vooght G. 1997. Working memory constraints on linear reasoning with spatial and temporal contents. *Q. J. Exp. Psychol.* 50A:803–20

Wason PC. 1966. Reasoning. In *New Horizons in Psychology,* ed. BM Foss, pp. 135–51. Harmondsworth, Middx, UK: Penguin

Wason PC, Johnson-Laird PN. 1972. *The Psychology of Deduction: Structure and Content.* Cambridge, MA: Harvard Univ. Press/London: Batsford

Wetherick NE, Gilhooly KJ. 1990. Syllogistic reasoning: effects of premise order. See Gilhooly et al 1990, pp. 99–108

Wharton CM, Grafman J. 1998. Deductive reasoning and the brain. *Trends Cogn. Sci.* 2:54–59

Yang Y. 1997. *Predicting the difficulty of predicate-logic inference problems: an empirical examination of a predicate-logic model.* PhD thesis. New York Univ., New York

Yang Y, Braine MDS, O'Brien DP. 1998. Some empirical justifications of the mental-predicate-logic model. See Braine & O'Brien 1998, pp. 333–65

Annu. Rev. Psychol. 1999. 50:137–163

HEALTH PSYCHOLOGY: Mapping Biobehavioral Contributions to Health and Illness

Andrew Baum and Donna M. Posluszny

Behavioral Medicine and Oncology, University of Pittsburgh Cancer Institute,
Pittsburgh, Pennsylvania 15213; e-mail: baum@pcicirs.pci.pitt.edu

KEY WORDS: stress, health behavior, coping, emotion, disease

ABSTRACT

Our evolving understanding of how psychosocial and behavioral factors affect health and disease processes has been marked by investigation of specific relationships and mechanisms underlying them. Stress and other emotional responses are components of complex interactions of genetic, physiological, behavioral, and environmental factors that affect the body's ability to remain or become healthy or to resist or overcome disease. Regulated by nervous, endocrine, and immune systems, and exerting powerful influence on other bodily systems and key health-relevant behaviors, stress and emotion appear to have important implications for the initiation or progression of cancer, HIV, cardiovascular disease, and other illnesses. Health-enhancing and health-impairing behaviors, including diet, exercise, tobacco use, and protection from the sun, can compromise or benefit health and are directed by a number of influences as well. Finally, health behaviors related to being ill or trying to avoid disease or its severest consequences are important. Seeking care and adhering to medical regimens and recommendations for disease surveillance allow for earlier identification of health threats and more effective treatment. Evidence that biobehavioral factors are linked to health in integrated, complex ways continues to mount, and knowledge of these influences has implications for medical outcomes and health care practice.

0084-6570/99/0201-0137$08.00

CONTENTS

INTRODUCTION

Thoughts, feelings, and behaviors affect our health and well-being. Recognition of the importance of these influences on health and disease is consistent with evolving conceptions of mind and body and represents a significant change in medicine and the life sciences. This history of medicine is marked by the rise and fall of misconceptions and ineffective therapies and by ill-conceived notions of how the body works were dominant for hundreds of years. The development of modern theories of atherosclerosis, for example, explained heart disease in ways that prompted effective medical interventions just as germ theories and models of immunity revolutionized the treatment and prevention of infectious illnesses. More recent developments include the idea that emotional processes such as stress moderate activity in nearly all systems of the body and can directly influence the pathophysiology of disease. Discovery of these and other relationships between behavior and health has changed the way health and disease are portrayed.

Interest in health and behavior is expanding at the National Institutes of Health, in the media, at work and school, and increasingly in medical schools and medical practice. This interest is also reflected in the rapid development of health psychology and its more multidisciplinary cousin, behavioral medicine. These fields grew rapidly in the 1980s and now constitute major endeavors in most university and medical center settings. The research upon which these activities is based embraces a broad agenda, including studies of prevention, screening, and early detection, etiology of disease, predictors of prognosis to treatment of disease, rehabilitation, and post-illness adjustment and quality of life. Basic research on the mechanisms and outcomes of bodily changes associated with stress, tobacco, diet, exercise, or other psychosocial variables and clinical studies of intervention and/or treatment outcomes provide compelling evidence of the extent and importance of psychosocial or behavioral variables.

BEHAVIOR AND HEALTH

Although experimental evidence is still inconsistent in some cases, the weight of data from studies of health and behavior strongly suggests that psychological processes and emotional states influence the etiology and progression of disease and contribute to overall host resistance or vulnerability to illness. In general, psychosocial or behavioral factors exert their influence on health or illness in three basic ways (e.g. Krantz et al 1985). First, some of these influences involve direct biological changes that parallel, precede, are induced by, or occur as part of an emotional reaction or behavior pattern. Research has shown, for example, that stress involves increases in blood pressure, heart rate, and sympathetic arousal and is associated with hematological changes that can contribute directly to heart disease, hypertension, or cardiac events (e.g. Manuck & Krantz 1984; Patterson et al 1994, 1995; Schneiderman 1983). Similarly, stress appears to affect the immune system through a complex array of neural and hormonal pathways (Besedovsky & DelRey 1991, Maier & Watkins 1998). Whether these immune system changes are strong or prolonged enough to enhance vulnerability to infection or illness is not clear, but they have been implicated in the etiology and progression of viral infections, wound healing, cancer, and HIV disease (e.g. Andersen et al 1994, Baum & Nesselhof 1988, Cohen & Williamson 1991, Kiecolt-Glaser et al 1985).

A second way in which health and disease are influenced is by behaviors that convey risks or protect against them. *Health-enhancing* behaviors are activities that convey health benefits or otherwise protect people from disease. *Health-impairing* behaviors are activities that have harmful effects on health. Diet and exercise are often cited as protective behaviors, and tobacco use and alcohol abuse as health-impairing behaviors. Diet and exercise can help minimize the conditions underlying cardiovascular disease and cancer. Tobacco use is associated with biological changes in the lungs, heart, and other bodily systems that appear to predispose disease. Similarly, drug use, high-risk sexual activity, and other potentially harmful behaviors are important mediators of disease processes.

A third general pathway for behavioral influences on health and illness is through behaviors associated with illness or the possibility that one is ill. Beginning with early detection, these influences include secondary prevention, surveillance, detection and interpretation of symptoms, and the decision to seek care. Adherence with medical advice or prescription can also affect diagnosis and treatment and affect health outcomes. Interference with any of these can disrupt the process of interpreting and presenting symptoms, obtaining prompt and effective medical care, and complying with treatment, surveillance, or prevention regimens.

Elaborations of this basic model of health and behavior have been developed to help explain the comorbidity of physical and mental health problems and the etiology and progression of cancer and stress-related diseases (e.g. Andersen et al 1994, Cohen & Rodriguez 1996). Evidence linking key pieces of these models has been reported, and although it is far from complete in many instances, it supports the notion that behavioral variables affect health and illness at these three different levels. This review considers evidence for this psychosocial perspective, focusing on major life-threatening illnesses such as cardiovascular disease, cancer, and HIV disease. Because of its complex role in health and illness, stress will be considered briefly before turning to evidence of direct biological effects on health and illness, of indirect and direct effects of health-impairing behaviors, and of the counter-influence of health-enhancing behaviors. Health behaviors, particularly adherence and early detection behavior, are also considered.

Stress

Stress is a particularly important mediator of health-behavior relationships because it is a common and seemingly inevitable aspect of life and because its broad effects can influence a range of bodily systems and behaviors. Its pervasiveness belies the controversy that surrounds its definition, and its breadth has led to debates over measurement and the utility of stress as a singular construct. Stress generally refers to the nonspecific aspects of dealing with environmental change, demand, and/or threat, though some models characterize it as a stimulus and others describe it solely in terms of responses (Cannon 1929, Selye 1976, Mason 1975). Depiction of stress as nonspecific mobilization was consistent with evolutionary theory, suggesting that stress evolved because nonspecific arousal strengthens and supports efforts to adapt to environmental threats. Some have argued that stress is best viewed as a process, with a signature psychological state and associated physiological changes (Lazarus 1966). Similar to emotions, stress consists of characteristic physiological, affective, cognitive, and behavioral changes that can have costs for well-being whether or not successful adaptation is achieved. Integrated biobehavioral patterns of activation such as stress appear to exert fundamental effects on health.

STRESS AND EMOTION   Stress appears to involve more or less simultaneous activation of psychological and biological systems. Recognition of a threat or challenge is accompanied by immediate systemic arousal produced by the sympathetic nervous system (SNS) and the hypothalamic-pituitary-adrenocortical (HPA) axis. At the same time, stress is associated with changes in mood, alertness, attention, memory, problem-solving, task performance, and well being. This cascade of changes is initiated by detection of a stressor and/or appraisal of the extent to which threat, danger, or challenge are likely (Lazarus 1966). This appraisal also includes evaluation of the resources one can bring to bear on a stressor, and appears to affect subsequent response (Tomaka et al 1997). Once threat or demand is recognized, ensuing responses may all occur simultaneously and changes in arousal and discomfort are rapid. It is not clear whether one or another aspect of the stress response triggers the others or whether these changes emerge more or less as a single integrated pattern. Regardless, stress is typically characterized by the same kind of central and peripheral activation as are emotions such as anger or fear.

EFFECTS OF STRESS   Another implication of the foregoing discussion is that the arousal associated with stress may be a primary mechanism by which stress affects health. Nonspecific biological and behavioral changes that accompany appraisal and/or emotional arousal can be thought of as the *stress response*, including heightened cardiovascular and respiratory function, and changes in blood flow, digestion, and skeletal muscle tone. Behavioral changes in attention and alertness are also part of this basic stress response and help focus and support coping activity. Endocrine, immune, and neural changes also occur, and stress responses reflect those that are related to supporting maximal strength and vigilance.

All these changes have negative side-effects or byproducts or can cause harm if stress is prolonged or very intense. Persistent, sustained physiological arousal or frequent, rapid increases in arousal have a range of consequences, including wear and tear on arteries and coronary vessels, formation of thrombi, suppression of host resistance, and other direct biological effects. Changes in alertness, narrowed attention, and irritability could produce consequences such as poorer problem-solving and task performance, disrupted social relationships, and poorer quality of life, which could affect decisions involving health risks and affect health indirectly. The emotional, cognitive, behavioral, and physiological changes that occur as part of the stress response are the mechanisms by which stress conveys consequences for health and well-being.

Coping

Coping constitutes an important aspect of stress, one of the principal routes that behavioral and cognitive responses can take during stress. Ultimately, coping is the main focus of stress responses that support strong, rapid reactions. Stress appears to have two basic functions: to motivate people to manipulate or accommodate stressors and to support activity directed at reduction or elimination of them. Although stress can be generated by positive as well as negative events, it is generally experienced as discomfort, tension, or negative affect. Harm, loss, anger, threat, and uncertainty are all associated with negative emotions, and the arousal experienced as a function of stress is also considered unpleasant or uncomfortable. This discomfort or tension produced during stress motivates the individual experiencing stress to do something about it. This suggests that the changes associated with stress support coping, the primary product of stress. We have suggested, for example, that stress involves arousal designed to support rapid, strong response to danger. Coping is that response to danger consisting of behavior or other activities that are intended to resolve the stressor or minimize its effects.

Coping is the most specific of stress responses. Unlike the readying response described above, coping is thought to be selected by individuals because it is well-suited to the stressor or situation (Lazarus & Folkman 1984). Application of particular kinds of coping is also affected by the resources one brings to the situation and by person variables that influence one's choices or predispositions to act (e.g. Scheier & Carver 1992, Lester et al 1994). The effectiveness of coping aimed at manipulating the stressor or attacking the problem posing the threat can usually be readily assessed. However, coping directed at minimizing, deflecting, or managing distress are more difficult to evaluate and may become more persistent, generalized responses to threat or demand. In this regard, well-learned responses like social withdrawal or helplessness may become predominant coping devices and potentially harmful behaviors such as smoking, drinking, and drug use may be used routinely to reduce distress or self-medicate discomfort.

The arousal that motivates and supports these actions is thought to be one mechanism by which stress affects health, increasing wear and tear on bodily systems and damage to arteries, neural systems, and organ systems, and reducing resistance to pathogenesis. Coping that conveys specific effects on physiological systems (e.g. drug use) can add to the potential for calamity by further suppressing immune system function, taxing the heart and circulatory system, damaging the lungs, or depriving the body of the nutrients it needs during sustained or repeated activation.

If coping is the product of stress response, its potential health consequences are a byproduct of this activity and reflect nonspecific costs of coping. Alternatively, stress-related disease may reflect breakdown in compensatory systems designed to relieve the arousal built up during stress or otherwise protect the body from its harmful effects. Exercise, for example, may help reduce arousal or manage its negative impact. The complex balance that defines good health and the many ways in which stress can disrupt it are among the factors that explain why stress exerts such pervasive effects on health and disease.

BIOBEHAVIORAL INFLUENCES IN DISEASE PROCESSES

At a neural or molecular level, the similarities and interconnectedness of behaviors and biological events are unmistakable, and at higher levels of functioning it appears increasingly certain that psychological or behavioral variables affect and are affected by their biological context. At some levels, behavior is produced by a complex series of neural, hormonal, and effector systems and these systems are regulated by bodily milieu. The biological correlates and consequences of emotional reactions, stress, and many thoughts and behaviors also contribute directly to host defense, health, and illness.

Emotional events are processed in the CNS by several partially redundant structures, including the limbic system and reward centers in the brain. They can be viewed as neural events that have been selected through evolution and that have helped assure our species' survival (LeDoux 1996). Emotional patterns such as stress responses are hardwired in the CNS, but one's experience also defines the content and conditions that give rise to particular responses (LeDoux 1996). In a sense, the emotional system "learns" about the external correlates of internal responses. This "learning" about the external correlates of internal responses may also be characteristic of stress. Factors that affect the magnitude and duration of stress responses are learned but the responses themselves are highly integrated and automated. These response patterns appear to involve nonspecific changes in most bodily systems and more specific reactions associated with the situation and sources of stress affecting the organism.

Stress and Disease Processes

Many biological changes accompanying stress or emotional arousal are extended and intensified by a cascade of endocrine and immunological changes that help to modulate bodily response. These regulatory systems induce circulatory changes, increase heart rate and respiration, and otherwise prepare the organism for action or attention. Research suggests that acute stress is accompanied by increased blood pressure, heart rate, and SNS arousal (e.g. Santagostino et al 1996, Krantz & Manuck 1984, McFetridge & Yarandi 1997). Most systemic arousal associated with stress and emotions such as anger, fear, and sadness reflects catabolic activation in which stored energy is converted into a usable resource and in which growth and repair functions are inhibited (Baum 1990, Mason 1975).

STRESS AND CARDIOVASCULAR RISK   Research on the effects of stress and emotional arousal on the cardiovascular system suggests that these states affect pathophysiology as well as trigger disease-related events (e.g. Johnston

1997). For example, anger is associated with responses that promote ischemia or arterial occlusion, heart attacks, and arrhythmias (R Verrier & Mittelman 1996). Anxiety and bereavement are also associated with cardiac events, and stress appears to predispose cardiovascular disease or precipitate ischemic episodes, heart attacks, or other pathological states (Niedhammer et al 1998, Carney et al 1998). Presumably this occurs through a series of interrelated effects of stress or emotional arousal, including direct effects on the heart, on the vasculature, on blood flow and shear stress, and on the constituents of blood such as platelets (Ku 1997; Niebauer & Cooke 1996; Patterson et al 1994, 1995). Hostility has also been linked to sodium consumption and to cardiovascular hyperactivity and risk for high blood pressure (e.g. Miller et al 1998).

Cardiovascular reactivity reflects the magnitude and duration of response to acute stress or challenge and may reflect mediators of cardiovascular risk (Krantz & Manuck 1984, Matthews et al 1990). The magnitude and elasticity of stress responses vary; larger increases in blood pressure or heart rate that follow introduction of a stressor may predict a range of intermediate and more distal outcomes. Blood pressure reactivity appears to be related to future blood pressure and hypertension (e.g. Matthews et al 1993, Pickering & Gerin 1990). Exaggerated blood pressure reactivity is associated with atherosclerosis, although these relationships appear to be modest and most evident among young men (Manuck et al 1989, Jennings et al 1997). Effects of behavior and stress on cholesterol, lipids, neurohormonal regulatory systems, silent ischemia, and oxidative damage have been observed (e.g. E Verrier & Boyle 1996, Howes et al 1997, Pool 1997, Mosca et al 1997). These effects are also related to age, behaviors like smoking, and psychological variables or personality styles such as defensiveness and repressive coping (e.g. Jennings et al 1997, Girdler et al 1997, Helmers & Krantz 1996).

STRESS AND IMMUNE STATUS   Research on psychosocial mediation of the immune system suggests it is responsive to changing moods and behaviors. Research in human and animal models is consistent in suggesting that immune system activity is regulated by the CNS (Moynihan & Ader 1996). Further, evidence indicates that stress affects activity in the immune system. Research has been complicated by the fact that responses among different components of the immune system are variable (e.g. Zakowski 1995). Some cells, like natural killer cells, appear to respond differently depending on the chronicity of the stressor (Delahanty et al 1996). Some immune cells also appear to respond to stress differently at different times of day and to follow clear circadian rhythms (Wang et al 1998). Direct effects of stress include acute activation and chronic suppression of natural killer cells, increased latent viral activity, decreased lymphocyte proliferation, and cytokine production (Andersen et al 1998, Pariante et al 1997, Schedlowski et al 1995, Kiecolt-Glaser et al 1994).

These influences are thought to be caused by neural and hormonal regulation, principally through arousal of the SNS, the HPA axis, and opioid peptide systems (e.g. Webster et al 1997). Nerve growth factor and cytokine influences are also possible and suggest a broad interface between the nervous and immune systems (e.g. Jenkins & Baum 1995, Aloe et al 1997). The importance of the SNS in observed stress-immune relationships is suggested by studies reporting correlations between SNS indices and immune system change or by studies of the effects of adrenergic blockade (Bachen et al 1995, Manuck et al 1991, Zakowski et al 1992a,b). Exercise and exertion also affect the immune system, often in ways that resemble the impact of stress or emotional arousal (e.g. Perna et al 1997, Nieman 1997).

The immune system communicates directly with the CNS and appears to have a regulatory function in much the same way that the endocrine system supplements and extends neural activation (Maier & Watkins 1998). In addition, some mental health problems are associated with abnormal immune system function (Weisse 1992, Herbert & Cohen 1993). Some of these effects are mediated by cytokines that are activated by neural stimulation (Muller & Ackenheil 1998). Pro-inflammatory cytokines in turn activate the HPA axis and induce fever and illness symptoms, but these effects may also be influenced by glucocorticoids and other stress-related agents (Goujon et al 1997). Interleukin-6 (IL-6) appears to activate the HPA axis as well and may be a component of CNS integration of the stress response (Path et al 1997).

We do not yet know whether observed patterns of change in the immune system reflect alterations that have implications for vulnerability to disease (e.g. Cohen & Rabin 1998). However, there is considerable evidence of changes within the immune system associated with social support, negative affect, stress, and other behavioral or psychological factors, and evidence that these factors affect infectious disease, progression of cancer and HIV disease, and other health outcomes (e.g. Leserman et al 1997, Antoni 1997, Andersen et al 1994, Cohen et al 1991).

Stress, Behavior, and Cancer

Cancer is a generic name for a number of genetic diseases in which normal cells mutate and begin to grow uncontrollably. Cancer typically requires considerable time to develop or to be detected, and there are currently few good markers of disease or disease progression for most forms of cancer. With the lack of good biomarkers for disease processes, surveillance efforts seek to quantify people's risk for cancer and maximize the likelihood of detecting it early in more readily treatable stages.

These limits on our ability to detect very early stage disease or to follow its slow early development make it difficult to study the role of emotions and behavior in the etiology of cancer. Most relevant studies are limited by one or another methodological problem. However, it appears likely that emotional states like stress affect primary cellular functions, such as DNA repair, that could contribute to cancer (e.g. Kiecolt-Glaser et al 1985). It also appears that emotional reactions and adjustment to having cancer or to its treatment can affect progression of disease, survival, quality of life, and other important outcomes of cancer (e.g. Andersen et al 1994, Ramirez et al 1989, Levy et al 1991, Helgeson & Cohen 1996). Some of the strongest evidence of stress or psychosocial mediation of cancer-related outcomes is drawn from intervention programs that provide supportive and/or psychoeducational interventions for cancer patients (e.g. Spiegel et al 1989, Fawzy & Fawzy 1994, V Helgeson et al 1998). Several reviews have concluded that stress management, coping skills training, support, and other aspects of these interventions affect progression of disease, but mechanisms governing these effects are not known (Meyer & Mark 1995, Baum et al 1995, Posluszny et al 1998).

Stress, HIV, and AIDS

HIV disease and AIDS are unusually important as examples of behavior-influenced outcomes. They reflect both direct effects on bodily functioning and on behaviors that may affect disease risk and prognosis. They also affect caregivers in powerful ways that can harm their health as well (e.g. Catalan et al 1996, Folkman et al 1997, Folkman 1997, Park & Folkman 1997). The transmission of the virus that causes HIV disease is typically accomplished through behaviors (sexual activity, IV drug use), and because HIV attacks the immune system directly, behaviors or states that affect the immune system should affect HIV. Mental health problems appear to be associated with an increased risk for HIV infection (Hoff et al 1997, O'Leary & Jemmott 1996), presumably because of distress-related increases in risky behavior. High-risk behaviors such as unprotected sexual activity or IV drug use can be minimized, but stress can trigger impulsive behavior, reduce countervailing constraints against high-risk behaviors, or temporarily inhibit or interfere with intentions to avoid them (e.g. Fishbein et al 1998, O'Keefe et al 1990). These impulsive behaviors may occur because of stress-related drug and alcohol use (e.g. Testa & Collins 1997, Robins et al 1997). The implications of increased drug or alcohol abuse include reduced motivation, a false sense of invulnerability, and lack of attention to details or sanctions leading to increased risk and infection (Dingle & Oei 1997, Chandra et al 1996). As a result, people who are intoxicated by drugs or alcohol may not use good judgement, may be more likely to end up in compromising situations, or may simply not care about risks to their health at that moment.

Emotional arousal, stress, and behaviors such as smoking or drug use may affect resistance to the disease or disease progression. Evidence of this possibility is scant and is largely limited to early outcomes related to testing (Evans et al 1997, Antoni et al 1994). However, stress and related states or behaviors are associated with changes in immune system activity that could affect the body's ability to resist or combat the virus. A study of 104 HIV+ individuals enrolled in the Oslo HIV Cohort Study suggested that negative affect was related to somatic symptoms associated with progression, but there was no evidence of mediation of these effects by the immune system (Vassend et al 1997). Distress associated with concealment of sexual identity was positively related to cancer morbidity and incidence of pneumonia and other infectious illnesses (Cole et al 1996). Stress management interventions that enhance or buffer immune system activity have proven useful in treatment of HIV+ individuals (Littrell 1996, Goodkin et al 1997, Pomeroy et al 1997, Schneiderman et al 1992). Aerobic exercise interventions that also reduced distress have had similar effects (LaPerriere et al 1994).

HEALTH-PROTECTIVE AND HEALTH-IMPAIRING BEHAVIORS

Direct effects of stress and emotions are supplemented or modified by behaviors that affect health and disease processes. Behaviors such as diet or exercise can affect health independently but may mitigate, enhance, or modify the effects of stress. Conversely, stress may suppress these behaviors or their benefits. Diet, exercise, sleep, and relaxation are considered to be protective factors that can exert direct effects on physiological sources of risk and indirect effects by reducing the effects of stress and enhancing mood. In addition, stress can affect the likelihood of maintaining these behaviors. A healthy diet appears to directly reduce risk of disease, but maintenance of good nutrition is based on complex motivation and reward systems, and stress can affect the likelihood that one will maintain healthy dietary behavior. Poor diet, conversely, appears to contribute to pathophysiology of disease. In addition, smoking, alcohol consumption, drug use, and other health-impairing behaviors also have direct effects on disease processes and indirect effects on bodily systems and mood or behavior. Together these behaviors reflect insufficiently studied elements in the etiology of disease and keys to health promotion efforts that seek to minimize risk. Maximum sustained reduction of modifiable risk is an important implication of this reasoning and research.

Diet, Obesity, and Health

What people eat and how much they weigh are inherently behavioral processes. The fact that some people are able to maintain a normal or healthy weight while others become obese is almost certainly a result of behavioral and psychological factors working in concert with genetic and metabolic characteristics. Increasingly, one's diet and weight have been implicated in a number of health problems or adult onset diseases, and weight management and nutritional risk management programs have become a standard part of wellness or health promotion campaigns (e.g. Wing 1995a, Weiss et al 1991). Use of vitamin supplements, increasing consumption of fruits, vegetables, and fiber, and moderation of consumption of animal fat are widely believed to predispose better health. Healthier diets and proper nutritional balance may also facilitate weight management and help to prevent obesity. However, dietary change often requires substantial lifestyle change, and weight control has proven difficult for many people to maintain (Wing 1995b).

OBESITY AND CARDIOVASCULAR RISK   Perhaps the clearest links between diet and health or disease outcomes are for cardiovascular disease, where fat and cholesterol intake as well as salt consumption, obesity, and weight gain have been implicated as major contributors to coronary artery disease, hypertension, and stroke. Many of the dietary characteristics that affect weight gain and obesity are also risk factors for cardiovascular disease, and some programs seek to intervene to address both issues simultaneously. For example, high-fat meals are less satiating than are high-carbohydrate meals (Golay & Bobbioni 1997), and high-fat diets may be associated with greater overall food consumption and weight gain than are high-carbohydrate diets. In addition, people who are or have been obese do not appear to adapt appropriately to dietary fat and respond to it with increased fat storage (Golay & Bobbioni 1997). Consumption of fat affects eating behaviors as well as metabolism of food, weight gain, and cardiovascular risk in several different ways.

Interventions to prevent obesity and help people to lose weight are successful in achieving short-term benefits, but show more complex and poorer outcomes over longer periods (Wing 1995b). Some are very successful as long as the intervention is maintained and participants comply (Metz et al 1997). Interventions targeting specific ethnic or socioeconomic groups and recognizing cross-group differences in diet and disease risk have also had some success in changing dietary behaviors (e.g. Barry & Wassenaar 1996, Fitzgibbon et al 1996, Stolley & Fitzgibbon 1997).

DIET AND CANCER   The literature on the impact of diet and overall weight on the etiology and progression of cancer is more speculative and difficult to evaluate than is research on diet and heart or vascular disease. Nonetheless, research suggests that careful dietary management may help to prevent or control cancers. The literature on the impact of vitamins, foods, and natural products on cancer is growing rapidly.

Data provide some support for the possibility that what people eat affects their risk of developing cancer, but findings are mixed. For example, high-fat/low-fiber diets are associated with mammography results indicating high risk of breast cancer, while lower-fat/high-fiber diets are associated with much lower risk mammography profiles (Nordevang et al 1993). However, research has also failed to find associations between fat or fiber intake and cancer-relevant outcomes (Negri et al 1996). Estrogen levels are associated with fat consumption, and dietary fat has been associated with recurrence of breast cancer among women with estrogen-receptor–positive tumors (Longcope et al 1987, Holm et al 1993). These findings are provocative, but more definitive evidence of these relationships must await the results of several ongoing trials.

As with interventions to reduce risk of cardiovascular disease, efforts to manage cancer risk through diet have achieved significant changes in diet. Randomized trials seeking to decrease the percentage of caloric intake from fat have shown that people can modify their diet and achieve recommended or target levels of fat intake or weight loss (e.g. Heber et al 1992, Meyskens et al 1985, Schapira et al 1991). Similar efforts have been linked to increased consumption of healthy foods and fiber (Domel et al 1993, Atwood et al 1992). Attitudes, knowledge, or beliefs about associations between diet and disease can also be manipulated to help alter patterns of food consumption. People who believe that diet and cancer are linked, who know what recommendations to follow, and who believe that others support modification of diet to reduce cancer risk are more likely to make healthy changes in diet than people who do not (Patterson et al 1996). Among people considering their risk of cancer, it appears that many adults are willing and able to modify diet when there is clear evidence for it.

STRESS AND DIET   Stress is thought to affect diet and weight at several different levels. Negative mood may lead people to eat more and may result in their seeking "comfort foods" or foods that make them feel better. Most of these foods are relatively high in fat and salt or sugar, meaning that stress may increase consumption of less healthy fatty, salty, or sweet foods. These effects can be traced at any of a number of levels, as in stress-related enhancement of metabolic rate, stress-related increases in physical activity or in time pressures and busy schedules that can increase consumption of fast or convenience foods. Enhanced metabolic demand during stress may increase consumption of food without necessarily affecting weight.

The literature on stress and eating behavior, weight gain, and obesity is complicated and focused most intently on acute stress-eating relationships (e.g. Greeno & Wing 1994). The relationship between stress and eating is complicated by personality or behavioral factors that qualify stress-related changes in food consumption, and thoughtful analysis of chronic stress and weight or diet changes have not been evaluated. Systematic examination of these and other possibilities will clarify the relationship between stress and diet and should help to design programs that more effectively manage weight and risk of disease.

Exercise

Exercise appears to be important as a means of managing weight, managing stress, and modifying the impact of stress- or other-induced disequilibrium. Regular exercise alters endocrine activity, circulatory function, muscle tone, and a number of other aspects of physical functioning. As a result, some risks for disease may be altered. Its influence on cardiovascular risk is well established and is not discussed here. Exercise is also very important in weight control and prevention of obesity. Some of the mechanisms linking exercise to these health outcomes have been identified, but many are not well characterized.

EXERCISE AND CANCER   Results of several large population studies of cancer risk indicate that exercise decreases the relative risk of developing cancer (e.g. Francis 1996, Shepard 1993, Thune et al 1997). Sedentary activities appear to increase the risk for colon cancer (Shephard 1993), and evidence suggests that breast cancer and some reproductive cancers in women are negatively correlated with exercise history, although these findings are mixed (Bernstein et al 1994, Friedenreich & Rohan 1995, Kramer & Wells 1996, Mink et al 1996, Paffenbarger et al 1987, Thune et al 1997, Vena et al 1987). Adult weight gain also appears to contribute to risk for breast cancer (e.g. Huang et al 1997). Systematic evidence of links between exercise and cancer will await determination of the extent to which exercise suppresses risk factors, reduces stress, and/or increases the elasticity and adaptability of the organism.

STRESS AND EXERCISE   Exercise has also received attention as a coping strategy or means of dealing with stress (e.g. Rostad & Long 1996, Perna et al 1997). Evidence of psychological benefits of exercise would suggest another layer of influence on health; in addition to fitness benefits, exercise may be related to mood and to perceived stress. Some studies support these possibilities, and many suggest that regular exercise has psychological and emotional benefits (Leith & Taylor 1990, Plante & Rodin 1990). For example, regular exercise appears to attenuate physiological reactivity to stressors in the laboratory (Anshel 1996, Holmes & Roth 1988). Mood effects and perceived control may also be associated with exercise and may help buffer stress. Ironically, this form of coping may be one of the first casualties of stress; although regular exercise may convey benefits, research suggests that stress reduces physical activity (Steptoe et al 1996).

Cigarette Smoking and Tobacco Use

Tobacco use is a primary cause of premature mortality and a modifiable risk for many debilitating or fatal diseases. Smoking tobacco, using snuff, and ingesting other smokeless tobacco have become pervasive around the world.

The primary active ingredient in tobacco is nicotine, which has stimulant properties that appear to increase SNS arousal and alertness and to reduce appetite. Once tobacco use is established as a habit, it is highly resistant to change. Among tobacco users, the relief from withdrawal, appetite suppression, arousal, and sensation of well being associated with tobacco make it a very desirable behavior (Kassel 1997, Parrott et al 1996).

Smoking and other forms of tobacco use are major contributors to heart disease, hypertension, stroke, cancer, and several serious diseases of the lungs and airways. These effects are generated by a combination of constituents and smoke associated with smoking tobacco as well as by tobacco itself. Tobacco use also affects endocrine and immune system activity (e.g. Canals et al 1997, Mol et al 1993). Direct effects of tobacco use underlie its broad negative impact on health (e.g. Lykkesfeldt et al 1997). Passive exposure to tobacco smoke is also a problem, and research suggests that it has many effects consistent with exposure to nicotine (Hausberg et al 1997).

Because of the difficulty in getting people to stop using tobacco once they have started, considerable attention has been paid to prevention, particularly with children and adolescents (e.g. Chassin et al 1997). Risk factors for smoking vary by culture, but in the United States, adolescent cigarette smoking has been associated with perceived availability of cigarettes, cost, social models, social pressures, and mental health (Robinson et al 1997, Milberger et al 1997, Wang & Chou 1996, Unger et al 1997). The combination of social pressures and immediate reinforcers may induce people to try smoking when they do not intend to smoke (Engels et al 1997). Prevention efforts are most effective when continued for long periods (Eckhardt et al 1997), but a recent meta-analysis suggests that the average effect of social programs is small (Rooney & Murray 1996). Stress is one cause of tobacco use. Smoking and tobacco use appear to reduce stress or ameliorate its aversive effects (e.g. Viinamaki et al 1997, Todd et al 1996, Naquin & Gilbert 1996, Ogden & Mitandabari 1997). Smoking also alters acute stress responses. Smokers exhibit greater increases in peripheral resistence than nonsmokers during challenge (Girdler et al 1997). The synergistic effects of stress and smoking may heighten the negative effects of smoking and increase the incidence of tobacco-related illnesses (Maser 1997). Stress increases the amount and frequency of tobacco use (e.g. Steptoe et al 1996, Acierno et al 1996, Beckham et al 1996).

Stress also appears to be a major cause of relapse after cessation and often leads to resumption of smoking (Shiffman et al 1996, Matheny & Weatherman 1998). Newer approaches to cessation and relapse prevention hold some promise for success, appropriate motivation, and pharmacological adjuncts, while addressing individual level of addiction and recognition of barriers and supports (Lichtenstein & Glasgow 1997). Consideration of openness to change may also increase the efficacy of interventions by matching people to all appropriate intervention and fashioning changes in pre-contemplation behavior (e.g. Parrott et al 1996).

Sun Protection and Skin Cancer Prevention

Another behavior associated with serious health consequences is sun exposure. The majority of skin cancers are caused by exposure to ultraviolet (UV) radiation in sunlight. Cumulative lifetime exposure to sun is associated with basal-cell and squamous-cell cancers. More serious melanomas are more likely to be associated with intermittent but intense exposure (infrequent or periodic sunburn) (Albino et al 1997, Balch et al 1997). Use of sunscreens that block UV radiation or more prudent exposure (e.g. sitting in the shade, covering more of the body with clothing) should reduce or eliminate most skin cancers. Estimates range up to 78% of lifetime basal-cell and squamous-cell skin cancers that could be prevented by regular use of sunscreens rated at SPF 15 or greater during childhood and adolescence (Stern et al 1986).

Efforts have been made to increase knowledge about the risks of sun exposure and skin cancer, but the results have not been encouraging. Surveys suggest that fewer than half of sunbathers use sunscreen, and that of those who do, fewer than half use sunscreens that convey adequate protection (Bak et al 1992, Banks et al 1992). Educational interventions have increased awareness and knowledge of skin cancers, but there is little evidence of associated behavior change (Katz & Jernigan 1991, Mermelstein & Riesenberg 1992, Hughes et al 1993). Beliefs persist that tanning makes people look healthy and more attractive, that exposure to the sun is good for health, and that the risks of skin cancer are outweighed by these more immediate factors (e.g. Baum & Cohen 1998, Grob et al 1993, Maducdoc et al 1992, Miller et al 1990, Keesling & Friedman 1987). Some intensive intervention programs have produced evidence of short-term behavior change (Girgis et al 1993, Lombard et al 1991). However, long-term behavior change is usually not evaluated and there is little evidence that these programs achieve measurable reductions in skin cancer morbidity (Baum & Cohen 1998).

HEALTH BEHAVIOR

A third general mechanism linking behavior and health is the behavior that characterizes how people behave when they are ill, suspect they are ill, or learn they are at risk for serious illness. Early detection of disease is a critical element of health care because identification and treatment of early disease is usually more effective. Even more basic are prevention behaviors that help people manage modifiable risk for disease. Prevention behaviors include proper diet and exercise, cessation of smoking, and elimination of other health-impairing behaviors. Genetic risk testing programs for an increasing number of diseases reflect important public health advances and suggest immediate implications for health psychology (C Lerman 1998). Increasingly precise risk estimates of disease are attractive from a number of perspectives but also may have far-reaching psychological, social, and economic consequences that need to be studied (Baum et al 1997). Screening and surveillance have received a great deal of attention as means of early detection, and success in achieving good screening rates varies considerably. In general, there are a number of barriers to such behavior, including stress, social or support-related factors, and the perceived risk and emotional reaction to this perception (Rimer et al 1998).

Screening and Surveillance

Research has addressed screening and surveillance for many diseases and disease risks and has had some success in reducing cholesterol and blood pressure in people at risk for heart disease or hypertension (Heath et al 1995, Hoffmeister et al 1996). One of the most extensively studied diseases for which screening is important is breast cancer. Women are encouraged to have regular mammography and to perform monthly breast self-examination (American Cancer Society 1997), but many do not follow this recommendation. Socioeconomic factors, lack of physician support, perceptions of risk, and emotional reactions to the knowledge of being at risk appear to affect appropriate surveillance (e.g. Calle et al 1993, Fox et al 1991, Costanza et al 1992, Aiken et al 1994). Health beliefs are also associated with surveillance (e.g. Aiken et al 1994), but the focus of research has shifted from health beliefs to the emotional reaction that perceptions of risk may bring, including distress and worry about disease. Several studies suggest that women at higher risk for breast cancer experience heightened distress (e.g. Lerman et al 1994, Valdimarsdottir et al 1995, Gilbar 1997, Kash et al 1992). Women also report elevated anxiety about developing breast cancer and experience intrusive thoughts about their worries (e.g. Lerman et al 1993). Intrusive thoughts about breast cancer were also reported by women undergoing genetic counseling for breast cancer (Lloyd et al 1996). Some studies suggest that distress increases surveillance (e.g. McCaul et al 1996). Studies also suggest the opposite, that distress decreases surveillance activities (e.g. Kash et al 1992). Risk and distress have also been associated with overadherence to surveillance activities (e.g. Epstein et al 1997), but in some studies, distress is not related to surveillance at all (e.g. Sutton et al 1995).

A different kind of surveillance is testing for the human immunodeficiency virus (HIV). Testing for HIV indicates the presence of antibodies to the virus that can ultimately result in AIDS. The decision to undergo HIV screening is not universal, and many patients receive their first test near end-stage disease

(Wortley et al 1995). In one study, almost half of the HIV patients indicated that they waited to be tested for a year or more after first suspecting that they were HIV-positive (Wenger et al 1994). Again, emotional responses may be implicated. Studies have linked AIDS-related anxiety to not getting screened (e.g. Wilson et al 1996), undergoing screening (Stehlow & Kampmann 1993), and failure to return for test results (Bell et al 1997). Other factors also affect decisions regarding HIV testing (Myers et al 1993), but stress and emotional responses may be major factors in this decision.

There have been several interventions to increase knowledge about HIV risk reduction and adoption of less risky behaviors. Some have been encouraging, achieving population-level reductions in rates of risky behavior (Kelly et al 1997). However, results are not always consistent; one study with women at risk has shown some success initially and at three-month follow-up (e.g. Carey et al 1997). Another intervention in men at risk failed to show maintenance of these changes (Kalichman et al 1997). Culturally targeted interventions were also successful (Kalichman et al 1993). Past behavior was often a better predictor of future behavior than was the counseling and negative test result (Ickovics et al 1994).

Adherence

Adherence refers to the extent to which people comply with medical advice or prescription for treatment or surveillance (Haynes et al 1979). Nonadherence is a major problem when treating patients or seeking to prevent or detect disease states early, in part because care providers rarely know whether patients are being compliant.

Nonadherence also complicates treatment by affecting outcomes and may lead to errors in subsequent diagnoses (Becker & Maiman 1980). Successful adherence involves remembering to do something, doing it properly, and being motivated to continue. Unintentional noncompliance reflects adherence problems that result from patients' inadequate understanding of the condition, treatment, or prevention regimen prescribed (e.g. Hussey & Gilliland 1989). Forgetting or misunderstanding instructions or explanations are major sources of adherence problems. Other kinds of noncompliance are more intentional and often indicate attempts to find an alternative treatment (Cameron 1996). Satisfaction, health beliefs, naive theories of illness, preferences for health care, and other factors influence adherence as well (Claydon & Efron 1994, Brownell & Cohen 1995, Morris & Schulz 1993). The costs and consequences of misdiagnosis or failure to detect readily treatable disease associated with noncompliance underscore the importance of this aspect of health behavior.

Research has sought to identify personality or demographic predictors of adherence. Identification of likely noncompliers, for example, would facilitate selective intervention and increase adherence. However, this effort has not produced robust predictors of compliance or of an "adherent style." The quality of provider-patient interaction and behavior of health care providers in these interactions is related to adherence (Cameron 1996). High-quality interactions, sensitivity to patient concerns, and other aspects of care provision predict better adherence (DiMatteo & DiNicola 1981). Supervision is related to better adherence as well, and increasing supervision of health behaviors or outcomes or reminders to comply are effective means of increasing competence (Haynes et al 1976, Schapira et al 1992). Social support and health beliefs also affect willingness to comply and may influence the extent and accuracy of the understanding of a recommendation, health threat, or health communication (Cameron 1996). Stress interferes with adherence by increasing memory problems, decreasing satisfaction, or altering receptiveness and capacity to adjust to treatment demands (e.g. Brickman et al 1996).

CONCLUSIONS

Research increasingly suggests a strong link between how people think, feel, and behave and how well they withstand illness and poor health. Stress provides one model for understanding and predicting the impact of more specific emotional arousal and distress. The unique interactions of nonspecific stress responses and more specific emotional changes associated with anger, sadness, uncertainty, or other psychological states are not known. However, the behavioral implications of mood are well recognized and behaviors tied to these states, including self-medication with food, alcohol, or drugs, are important aspects of health. Interest has gradually shifted from confirmation of links between psychosocial or behavioral factors and health outcomes to investigation of mechanisms by which health benefits or harm are conveyed. Whether the negative influences of emotional arousal, health-impairing behaviors, and ineffective or disrupted illness behaviors can be managed or minimized is a major question that will be addressed next, and the continued integration of this knowledge into health care practice and prevention/treatment of disease should contribute to better medical outcomes. Stress management, enhanced coping, and reduction of modifiable risk for disease associated with harmful behaviors have already been targeted. A broad approach—one that considers these factors in the context of genetic variables, environmental constraints, and health-protective resources and behaviors— seems most likely to succeed.

Literature Cited

Acierno R, Kilpatrick DG, Resnick HS, Saunders BE. 1996. Violent assault, posttraumatic stress disorder, and depression: risk factors for cigarette use among adult women. *Behav. Modif.* 20(4): 363–84

Aiken LS, West SG, Woodward CK, Reno RR. 1994. Health beliefs and compliance with mammography-screening recommendations in asymptomatic women. *Health Psychol.* 12:122–29

Albino A, Reed JA, McNutt NS. 1997. Molecular biology of cutaneous malignant melanoma. Malignant melanoma. In *Cancer Principles and Practice of Oncology,* ed. V DeVita, S Hellman, SA Rosenberg, pp. 1935–46. New York: Lippincott-Raven. 5th ed.

Aloe L, Bracci-Laudiero L, Bonini S, Manni L. 1997. The expanding role of nerve growth factor: from neurotrophic activity to immunologic diseases. *Allergy* 52(9): 883–94

American Cancer Society. 1997. *Cancer Facts and Figures.* New York: Am. Cancer Soc.

Andersen BL, Farrar WB, Golden-Kreutz D, Kutz LA, MacCallum R, et al. 1998. Stress and immune responses after surgical treatment for regional breast cancer. *J. Natl. Cancer Inst.* 90(1):30–36

Andersen BL, Kiecolt-Glaser JK, Glaser R. 1994. A biobehavioral model of cancer stress and disease course. *Am. Psychol.* 49(5):389–404

Anshel M. 1996. Coping styles among adolescent competitive athletes. *J. Soc. Psychol.* 136(3):311–23

Antoni MH. 1997. Cognitive-behavioral intervention for persons with HIV. In *Group Therapy for Medically Ill Patients,* ed. JL Spira, pp. 55–91. New York: Guilford

Antoni MH, Schneiderman N, Esterling B, Ironson G. 1994. Stress management and adjustment to HIV-1 infection. *Homeost. Health Dis.* 35(3):149–60

Atwood JR, Aickin M, Giordana L, Benedict J, Bell M, et al. 1992. The effectiveness of adherence intervention in a colon cancer prevention field trial. *Prev. Med.* 21(5): 637–53

Bachen EA, Manuck SB, Cohen S, Muldoon MF. 1995. Adrenergic blockade ameliorates cellular immune responses to mental stress in humans. *Psychosom. Med.* 57(4): 366–72

Bak S, Koh HK, Howland J, Mangiove T, Hingson R, Levenson S. 1992. Sunbathing habits and sunscreen use in 2485 Caucasian adults: results of a national survey. In

Progr. Abstr. Am. Public Health Assoc. Meet., Washington, DC, Session 2052, pp. XX—XXX

Balch CM, Reintgen DS, Kirkwood JM, Houghton A, Peters L, Ango KK. 1997. Cutaneous melanoma. Malignant melanoma. In *Cancer Principles and Practice of Oncology,* ed. V DeVita, S Hellman, SA Rosenberg, pp. 1947–94. New York: Lippincott-Raven. 5th ed.

Banks BA, Silverman RA, Schwartz RH, Tunnessen WW. 1992. Attitudes of teenagers toward sun exposure and sunscreen use. *Pediatrics* 89:40–42

Barry TA, Wassenaar DR. 1996. An investigation into the relationship between coronary risk factors and coronary heart disease among the Pietermaritzburg Asian population. *South Afr. J. Psychol.* 26(1):29–34

Baum A. 1990. Stress, intrusive imagery, and chronic distress. *Health Psychol.* 9(6): 653–75

Baum A, Cohen L. 1998. Successful behavioral interventions to prevent cancer: the example of skin cancer. *Annu. Rev. Publ. Health* 19:319–33

Baum A, Friedman AL, Zakowski SG. 1997. Stress and genetic testing for disease risk. *Health Psychol.* 16 (1):8–19

Baum A, Herberman H, Cohen L. 1995. Managing stress and managing illness: survival and quality of life in chronic disease. *J. Clin. Psychol. Med. Settings* 2(4):309–33

Baum A, Nesselhof SE. 1988. Psychological research and the prevention, etiology, and treatment of AIDS. *Am. Psychol.* 43(11): 900–6

Becker MH, Maiman LA. 1980. Strategies for enhancing patient compliance. *J. Commun. Health* 6(2):113–35

Beckham JC, Lytle BL, Vrana SR, Hertzberg MA, Feldman ME, Shipley RH. 1996. Smoking withdrawal symptoms in response to a trauma-related stressor among Vietnam combat veterans with posttraumatic stress disorder. *Addict. Behav.* 21(1):93–101

Bell R, Molitor F, Flynn N. 1997. On returning for one's HIV testing result: demographic, behavioral and psychological predictors. *AIDS* 11:263–64

Bernstein L, Henderson BE, Hanisch R, Sullivan-Halley J, Ross RK. 1994. Physical exercise and reduced risk of breast cancer in young women. *J. Natl. Cancer Inst.* 86(18):1403–8

Besedovsky HO, DelRey A. 1991. Feed-back interactions between immunological cells and the hypothalamus-pituitary-adrenal axis. *Neth. J. Med.* 39(3–4):274–80

Brickman AL, Yount SE, Blaney NT, Rothberg ST, De-Nour AK. 1996. Personality traits and long-term health status. The influence of neuroticism and conscientiousness on renal deterioration in type-I diabetes. *Psychosomatics* 37(5):459–68

Brownell KD, Cohen LR. 1995. Adherence to dietary regimens. 2: Components of effective interventions. *Behav. Med.* 20(4): 155–64

Calle EE, Flanders WD, Thun MJ, Martin LM. 1993. Demographic predictors of mammography and pap smear screening in US women. *Am. J. Public Health* 83:53–60

Cameron C. 1996. Patient compliance: recognition of factors involved and suggestions for promoting compliance with therapeutic regimens. *J. Adv. Nurs.* 24(2):244–50

Canals J, Colomina MT, Domingo JL, Domenech E. 1997. Influence of smoking and drinking habits on salivary cortisol levels. *Pers. Indiv. Differ.* 23(4):593–99

Cannon WB. 1929. *Bodily Changes in Pain, Hunger, Fear, and Rage.* Boston: Branford

Carey MP, Kalichman SC, Forsyth AD, Wright EM. 1997. Enhancing motivation to reduce the risk of HIV infection for economically disadvantaged urban women. *J. Consult. Clin. Psychol.* 65(4):531–41

Carney RM, Mcmahon P, Freedland KE, Becker L, Krantz DS, et al. 1998. Reproducibility of mental stress-induced myocardial ischemia in the psychophysiological investigations of myocardial ischemia (PIMI). *Psychosom. Med.* 60(1):64–70

Catalan J, Burgess A, Pergami A, Hulme N, Gazzard B, Phillips R. 1996. The psychological impact on staff of caring for people with serious diseases: the case of HIV infection and oncology. *J. Psychosom. Res.* 40(4):425–35

Chandra PS, Ravi V, Puttaram S, Desai A. 1996. HIV and mental illness. *Br. J. Psychiatry* 168(5):654

Chassin L, Barrera M Jr, Montgomery H. 1997. Parental alcoholism as a risk factor. In *Handbook of Children's Coping: Linking Theory and Intervention. Issues in Clinical Child Psychology,* ed. SA Wolchik, IN Sandler, pp. 101–29. New York: Plenum

Claydon BE, Efron M. 1994. Non-compliance in general health care. *Ophthalmic Physiol. Opt.* 14(3):257–64

Cohen S, Rabin BS. 1998. Psychological stress, immunity, and cancer. *J. Natl. Cancer Inst.* 90(1):3–4

Cohen S, Rodriguez MS. 1996. Pathways linking affective disturbances and physical disorders. *Health Psychol.* 14(5):374–80

Cohen S. Tyrrell DAJ, Smith AP. 1991. Psychological stress and susceptibility to the common cold. *N. Engl. J. Med.* 325: 606–12

Cohen S, Williamson GM. 1991. Stress and infectious disease in humans. *Psychol. Bull.* 109(1):5–24

Cole SW, Kemeny ME, Taylor SE, Visscher BR. 1996. Elevated physical health risk among gay men who conceal their homosexual identify. *Health Psychol.* 15(4): 243–51

Costanza M, Stoddard A, Gaw V, Zapka J. 1992. *J. Am. Geriatr. Soc.* 40:774–78

Delahanty DL, Dougall AL, Hawken L, Trakowski JH, Schmitz JB. 1996. Time course of natural killer cell activity and lymphocyte proliferation in response to two acute stressors in healthy men. *Health Psychol.* 15(1): 48–55

DiMatteo MR, DiNicola DD. 1981. Sources of assessment of physician performance: a study of comparative reliability and patterns of intercorrelation. *Med. Care* 19(8): 829–42

Dingle GA, Oei TPS. 1997. Is alcohol a cofactor of HIV and AIDS? Evidence from immunological and behavioral studies. *Psychol. Bull.* 122(1):56–71

Domel SB, Baranowski T, Davis H, Leonard SB, Riley P, et al. 1993. Measuring fruit and vegetable preferences among 4th–5th grade students. *Prev. Med.* 22(6):866–79

Eckhardt L, Woodruff SI, Elder JP. 1997. Relative effectiveness of continued, lapsed, and delayed smoking prevention intervention in senior high school students. *Am. J. Health Promot.* 11(6):418–21

Engels R, Knibbe RA, Drop MJ, Dehaan YT. 1997. Homogeneity of cigarette smoking within peer groups—influence or selection? *Health Educ. Behav.* 256:801–11

Epstein SA, Lin TH, Audrain J, Stefanek M, Rimer B, et al. 1997. Excessive breast self-examination among first-degree relatives of newly diagnosed breast cancer patients. High-risk breast cancer consortium. *Psychosomatics* 38(3):253–61

Evans DL, Leserman J, Perkins DO, Stern RA, Murphy C. 1997. Severe life stress as a predictor of early disease progression in HIV infection. *Am. J. Psychiatry* 154(5): 630–34

Fawzy FI, Fawzy NW. 1994. A structured psychoeducational intervention for cancer patients. *Gen. Hosp. Psychiatry* 16(3): 149–92

Fishbein M, Triandis HC, Kanfer FH, Becker M, Middlestadt SE, Eichler A. 1998. Factors influencing behavior and behavior change. *Handb. Health Psychol.* In press

Fitzgibbon ML, Stolley MR, Avellone ME, Sugerman S, Chavez N. 1996. Involving parents in cancer risk reduction: a program for Hispanic American families. *Health Psychol.* 15(6):413–22

Folkman S. 1997. Introduction to the special section: use of bereavement narratives to predict well-being in gay men whose partner died of AIDS—four theoretical perspectives. *J. Pers. Soc. Psychol.* 72(4): 851–54

Folkman S, Moskowitz JT, Oer EM, Park CL. 1997. Positive meaningful events and coping in the context of HIV/AIDS. In *Coping with Chronic Stress. The Plenum Series on Stress and Coping*, ed. BH Gottlieb, pp. 293–314. New York: Plenum

Fox SA, Murata PJ, Stein JA. 1991. The impact of physician compliance on screening mammography for older women. *Arch. Intern. Med.* 151(1):50–56

Francis K. 1996. Physical activity: breast and reproductive cancer. *Compr. Ther.* 22(2): 94–99

Friedenreich CM, Rohan TE. 1995. A review of physical activity and breast cancer. *Epidemiology* 6(3):333–17

Gilbar O. 1997. Women with high risk for breast cancer: psychological symptoms. *Psychol. Rep.* 80:800–2

Girdler SS, Jamner LD, Jarvik M, Soles JR, Shapiro D. 1997. Smoking status and nicotine administration differentially modify hemodynamic stress reactivity in men and women. *Psychosom. Med.* 59(3): 294–306

Girgis A, Sanson-Fisher RW, Tripodi DA, Golding T. 1993. Evaluation of interventions to improve protection in primary schools. *Health Educ. Q.* 20:275–87

Golay A, Bobbioni E. 1997. The role of dietary fat in obesity. *Int. J. Obes. Rel. Metab. Disord.* 21(Suppl. 3):S2–11

Goodkin K, Burkhalter JE, Blaney NT, Leeds B, Tuttle R, Feaster D. 1997. A research derived bereavement support group technique for the HIV-1 infected. *Omega J. Death Dying* 34(4): 279–300

Goujon E, Laye S, Parnet P, Dantzer R. 1997. Regulation of cytokine gene expression in the central nervous system by glucocorticoids: mechanisms and functional consequences. *Psychoneuroendocrinology* 22 (Suppl. 1):S75–80

Greeno CG, Wing RR. 1994. Stress-induced eating. *Psychol. Bull.* 115(3):444–64

Grob JJ, Guglielmena C, Gouvernet J, Zarour H, Noe C, Bonerandi JJ. 1993. Study of sunbathing habits in children and adolescents: application to the prevention of melanoma. *Dermatology* 186:94–98

Hausberg M, Mark AL, Winniford MD, Brown RE, Somers VK. 1997. Sympathetic and vascular effects of short-term passive smoke exposure in healthy nonsmokers. *Circulation* 96(1):282–87

Haynes RB, Sackett DL, Gobson ES, Taylor DW, Hackett BC, et al. 1976. Improvement of medication compliance in uncontrolled hypertension. *Lancet* 1:1265–68

Haynes RB, Taylor DW, Sackett DL. 1979. *Compliance In Health Care*. Baltimore, MD: Johns Hopkins Univ. Press

Heath GW, Fuchs R, Croft JB, Temple SP, Wheller FC. 1995. Changes in blood cholesterol awareness: final results from the South Carolina Cardiovascular Disease Prevention Project. *Am. J. Prev. Med.* 11(3):190–96

Heber D, Ashley JM, McCarthy WJ, Solares ME, Leaf DA, et al. 1992. Assessment of adherence to a low-fat diet for breast cancer prevention. *Prev. Med.* 21(2):218–27

Helgeson VS, Cohen S. 1996. Social support and adjustment to cancer: reconciling descriptive, correlation, and intervention research. *Health Psychol.* 15(2):135–48

Helgeson VS, Cohen S, Fritz H. 1998. Social ties and the onset and progression of cancer. In *Psycho-oncology*, ed. J Holland. New York: Oxford Univ. Press. In press

Helmers KF, Krantz DS. 1996. Defensive hostility, gender and cardiovascular levels and responses to stress. *Ann. Behav. Med.* 18(4):246–54

Herbert TB, Cohen S. 1993. Stress and immunity in humans: a meta-analytic review. *Psychosom. Med.* 55(4):364–79

Hoff RA, Beam-Goulet J, Rosenheck RA. 1997. Mental disorder as a risk factor for human immunodeficiency virus infection in a sample of veterans. *J. Nerv. Mental Dis.* 185(9):556–60

Hoffmeister H, Mensink GBM, Stolzenberg H, Hoeltz J, Kreuter H, et al. 1996. Reduction of coronary heart disease risk factors in the German Cardiovascular Prevention study. *Prev. Med.* 25(2):135–45

Holm LE, Nordevang E, Hjalmar ML, Lidbrink E, Callmer E, et al. 1993. Treatment failure and dietary habits in women with breast cancer. *J. Natl. Cancer Inst.* 85(1): 32–36

Holmes DS, Roth DL. 1988. Effects of aerobic exercise training and relaxation training on cardiovascular activity during psychological stress. *J. Psychosom. Res.* 32(4–5): 469–74

Howes JB, Ryan J, Fairbrother G, O'Neill K, Howes LG. 1997. Alcohol consumption and blood pressure in recently hospitalized patients. *Blood Press.* 6(2):109–11

Huang Z, Hankinson SE, Colditz GA, Stampfer MJ, Hunter DJ, et al. 1997. Dual effects of weight and weight gain on breast cancer risk. *J. Am. Med. Soc.* 278(17): 1407–11

Hughes BR, Altman DG, Newton JA. 1993. Melanoma and skin cancer: evaluation of a health education program for secondary schools. *Br. J. Dermatol.* 128:412–17

Hussey LC, Gilliland K. 1989. Compliance: low literacy, and locus of control. *Nurs. Clin. N. Am.* 24(3):605–11

Ickovics JR, Morrill AC, Beren SE, Walsh U, Rodin J. 1994. Limited effects of HIV counseling and testing for women: a prospective study of behavioral and psychological consequences. *J. Am. Med. Assoc.* 272(6): 443–48

Jenkins FJ, Baum A. 1995. Stress and reactivation of latent herpes simplx virus: a fusion of behavioral medicine and molecular biology. *Ann. Behav. Med.* 17(2): 116–23

Jennings JR, Kamarck T, Manuck S, Everson SA, Kaplan GA, Salonen JF. 1997. Aging or disease? Cardiovascular reactivity in Finnish men over the middle years. *Psychol. Aging* 12(2): 225–38

Johnston DW. 1997. Cardiovascular disease. In *Science and Practice of Cognitive Behavior Therapy,* ed. D Clark, C Fairburn, pp. 341–58. Oxford, UK: Oxford Univ. Press

Kalichman SC, Kelly JA, Hunter TL, Murphy DA, Tyler R. 1993. Culturally tailored HIV- AIDS risk-reduction messages targeted to African American urban women: impact on risk sensitization and risk reduction. *J. Consult. Clin. Psychol.* 61(2): 291–95

Kalichman SC, Kelly JA, Rompa D. 1997. Continued high-risk sex among HIV seropositive gay and bisexual men seeking HIV prevention services. *Health Psychol.* 16(4):369–73

Kash KM, Holland JC, Halper MS, Miller DG. 1992. Psychological distress and surveillance behaviors of women with a family history of breast cancer. *J. Natl. Cancer Inst.* 84:24–30

Kassel JD. 1997. Smoking and attention: a review and reformulation of the stimulus-filter hypothesis. *Clin. Psychol. Rev.* 17(5):451–78

Katz RC, Jernigan S. 1991. Brief report: an empirically derived educational program for detecting and preventing skin cancer. *J. Behav. Med.* 14:421–27

Keesling B, Friedman HS. 1987. Psychosocial factors in sunbathing and sunscreen use. *Health Psychol.* 6:477–93

Kelly JA, Murphy DA, Sikkema KJ, McAuliffe TL, Roffman RA, et al. 1997. Randomized, controlled, community-level HIV-prevention intervention for sexual-risk behavior among homosexual men in US cities. *Lancet* 350:1500–5

Kiecolt-Glaser JK, Malarkey WB, Cacioppo JT, Glaser R. 1994. Stressful personal relationships: immune and endocrine factors. In *Handbook of Human Stress and Immunity,* ed. R Glaser, JK Kiecolt-Glaser, pp. 321–40. San Diego, CA: Academic

Kiecolt-Glaser JK, Stephens RE, Lipetz PD, Speicher CE, Glaser R. 1985. Distress and DNA repair in human lymphocytes. *J. Behav. Med.* 8(4):311–20

Kramer MM, Wells CL. 1996. Does physical activity reduce risk of estrogen-dependent cancer in women? *Med. Sci. Sports Exercise* 28(3):322–34

Krantz DS, Grunberg NE, Baum A. 1985. Health psychology. *Annu. Rev. Psychol.* 36:349–83

Krantz DS, Manuck SB. 1984. Acute psychophysiologic reactivity and risk of cardiovascular disease: a review and methodologic critique. *Psychol. Bull.* 96(3): 435–64

Ku DN. 1997. Blood flow in arteries. *Annu. Rev. Fluid Mech.* 29:399–434

LaPerriere A, Ironson G, Antoni MH, Schneiderman N. 1994. Exercise and psychoneuroimmunology. *Med. Sci. Sports Exercise* 26(2):182–90

Lazarus RS. 1966. *Psychological Stress and the Coping Process.* New York: McGraw-Hill

Lazarus RS, Folkman S. 1984. *Stress, Appraisal, and Coping.* New York: Springer

LeDoux JE. 1996. The emotional brain: the mysterious underpinnings of emotional life. In *The Emotional Brain: The Mysterious Underpinnings of Emotional Life.* New York: Simon & Schuster

Leith LM, Taylor AH. 1990. Psychological aspects of exercise: a decade literature review. *J. Sport Behav.* 13(4):219–39

Lerman C. 1998. Psychological aspects of genetic testing for cancer susceptibility. In *Technology and Methodology in Behavioral Medicine,* ed. DS Krantz, A Baum. In press

Lerman C, Daly M, Sands C, Balshem A, Lustbader E, et al. 1993. Mammography adherence and psychological distress among women at risk for breast cancer. *J. Natl. Cancer Inst.* 85:1074–80

Lerman C, Kash K, Stefanek M. 1994. Younger women at increased risk for breast cancer: perceived risk, psychological well-being, and surveillance behavior. *J. Natl. Cancer Inst. Monogr.* 16:171–76

Leserman J, Petitto JM, Perkins DO, Folds JD, Golden RN, et al. 1997. Severe stress, depressive symptoms, and changes in lymphocyte subsets in human immunodeficiency virus-infected men. A 2-year follow-up study. *Arch. Gen. Psychiatry* 54(3):279–85

Lester N, Smart L, Baum A. 1994. Measuring coping flexibility. *Psychol. Health* 9(6):409–24

Levy SM, Herberman RB, Lippman M, D'Angelo T, Lee J. 1991. Immunological and psychosocial predictors of disease recurrence in patients with early-stage breast cancer. *Behav. Med.* 17(2):67–75

Lichtenstein E, Glasgow RE. 1997. A pragmatic framework for smoking cessation: implications for clinical and public health programs. *Psychol. Addict. Behav.* 11(2):142–51

Littrell J. 1996. How psychological states affect the immune system: implications for interventions in the context of HIV. *Health Soc. Work* 21(4):287–95

Lloyd S, Watson M, Waites B, Meyer L, Eeles R, et al. 1996. Familial breast cancer: a controlled study of risk perception, psychological morbidity and health beliefs in women attending for genetic counseling. *Br. J. Cancer* 74:482–87

Lombard D, Neubauer TE, Canfield D, Winett RA. 1991. Behavioral community intervention to reduce the risk of skin cancer. *J. Appl. Behav. Anal.* 24:677–87

Longcope C, Gorbach S, Goldin B, Woods M, Dwyer J, et al. 1987. The effect of a low fat diet on estrogen metabolism. *J. Clin. Endocrinol. Metab.* 64(6):1246–50

Lykkesfeldt J, Loft S, Nielsen JB, Poulsen HE. 1997. Ascorbic acid and dehydroascorbic acid as biomarkers of oxidative stress caused by smoking. *Am. J. Clin. Nutr.* 64(4):959–63

Maducdoc JR, Wagner RF, Wagner KD. 1992. Parents use of sunscreen on beach going children. *Arch. Dermatol.* 128:628–29

Maier SF, Watkins LR. 1998. Cytokines for psychologists-implications of bidirectional immune-to-brain communication for understanding behavior, mood, and cognition. *Psychol. Rev.* 105(1):83–107

Manuck SB, Cohen S, Rabin BS, Muldoon MF, Bachen EA. 1991. Individual differences in cellular immune response to stress. *Psychol. Sci.* 2(2):111–15

Manuck SB, Kaplan JR, Adams MR, Clarkson TB. 1989. Behaviorally elicited heart rate reactivity and atherosclerosis in female cynomolgus monkeys. *Psychosom. Med.* 51(3):306–18

Manuck SB, Krantz DS. 1984. Psychophysiologic reactivity in coronary heart disease. *Behav. Med. Upd.* 6(3):11–15

Maser E. 1997. Stress, hormonal changes, alcohol, food constituents and drugs-factors that advance the incidence of tobacco smoke-related cancer. *Trends Pharmacol. Sci.* 18(8):270–75

Mason JW. 1975. A historical view of the stress field. *J. Hum. Stress* 1:22–36

Matheny KB, Weatherman KE. 1998. Predictors of smoking cessation and maintenance. *J. Clin. Psychol.* 54(2):223–35

Matthews KA, Woodall KL, Allen MT. 1993. Cardiovascualr reactivity to stress predits future blood pressure status. *Hypertension* 22(4):479–85

Matthews KA, Woodall KL, Stoney CM. 1990. Changes in and stability of cardiovascular responses to behavioral stress: results from a four-year longitudinal study of children. *Child Dev.* 61(4):1134–44

McCaul K, Schroeder D, Reid P. 1996. Breast cancer worry and screening: some prospective data. *Health Psychol.* 15:430–33

McFetridge JA, Yarandi HN. 1997. Cardiovascular function during cognitive stress in men before and after coronary artery bypass grafts. *Nurs. Res.* 46(4):188–94

Mermelstein RJ, Riesenberg LA. 1992. Changing knowledge and attitudes about skin cancer risk factors in adolescents. *Health Psychol.* 11:371–76

Metz JA, Kris-Etherton PM, Morris CD, Mustad VA, Stern JS, et al. 1997. Dietary compliance and cardiovascular risk reduction with a prepared meal plan compared with a self-selected diet. *Am. J. Clin. Nutr.* 66(2):373–85

Meyer TJ, Mark MM. 1995. Effects of psychological interventions with adult cancer patients: a meta-analysis of randomized experiments. *Health Psychol.* 14(2):101–8

Meyskens FL Jr, Thomson SP, Moon TE. 1985. Similar self-renewal properties for different sizes of human primary melanoma colonies replated in agar. *Cancer Res.* 45(3):1101–7

Milberger S, Biederman J, Faraone SV, Chen L, Jones J. 1997. Further evidence of an association between attention-deficit/hyperactivity disorder and cigarette smoking: findings from a high-risk sample of siblings. *Am. J. Addict.* 6(3):205–17

Miller AG, Ashton WA, McHoskey JW, Gimbel J. 1990. What price attractiveness? Stereotypes and risk factors in suntanning behavior. *J. Appl. Soc. Psychol.* 20:1272–300

Miller SB, Freise M, Dolgoy L, Sita A, Lavoie K, et al. 1998. Hostility, sodium consumption, and cardiovascular response to interpersonal stress. *Psychosom. Med.* 60(1): 71–77

Mink PJ, Folsom AR, Sellers TA, Kushi LH. 1996. Physical activity, waist-to-hip ratio, and other risk factors for ovarian cancer: a follow-up study of older women. *Epidemiology* 7(1):38–45

Mol MJ, Demacker PN, Stalenhof AF. 1993. The role of modification of lipoproteins and of the immune system in early atherogenesis. *Neth. J. Med.* 43(1–2):83–90

Morris LS, Schulz RM. 1993. Medication compliance: the patient's perspective. *Clin. Therapeut.* 15(3):593–606

Mosca L, Rubenfire M, Mandel C, Rock C, Tarshis T, et al. 1997. Antioxidant nutrient supplementation reduces the susceptibility of low density lipoprotein to oxidation in patients with coronary artery disease. *J. Am. Coll. Cardiol.* 30(2):392–99

Moynihan JA, Ader R. 1996. Psychoneuroimmunology: animal models of disease. *Psychosom. Med.* 58(6):546–58

Muller N, Ackenheil M. 1998. Psychoneuroimmunology and the cytokine action in the CNS-implications for psychiatric disorders. *Progr. Neuro-Psychopharmacol. Biol. Psychiatry* 22(1):1–33

Myers T, Orr K, Locker D, Jackson E. 1993. Factors affecting gay and bisexual men's decisions and intentions to seek HIV testing. *Am. J. Public Health* 83:701–4

Naquin MR, Gilbert GG. 1996. College students' smoking behavior, perceived stress, and coping styles. *J. Drug Educ.* 26(4): 367–76

Negri E, LaVecchia C, Franceschi S, D'Avanzo B, Talamini R, et al. 1996. Intake of selected micronutrients and the risk of breast cancer. *Int. J. Cancer* 65(2):140–44

Niebauer J, Cooke JP. 1996. Cardiovascular effects of exercise: role of endothelial shear stress. *J. Am. Coll. Cardiol.* 28(7): 1652–60

Niedhammer I, Goldberg M, Leclerc A, David S, Landre MF. 1998. Psychosocial work environment and cardiovascular risk factors in an occupational cohort in France. *J. Epidemiol. Commun. Health* 52(2): 93–100

Nieman DC. 1997. Immune response to heavy exertion. *J. Appl. Physiol.* 82(5):1385–94

Nordevang E, Azavedo E, Svane G, Nilsson B, Holm LE. 1993. Dietary habits and mammographic patterns in patients with breast cancer. *Breast Cancer Res. Treat.* 26(3): 207–15

Ogden J, Mitandabari T. 1997. Examination stress and changes in mood and health related behaviors. *Psychol. Health* 12(2): 288–99

O'Keeffe MK, Nesselhof-Kendall S, Baum A. 1990. Behavior and prevention of AIDS: bases of research and intervention. *Pers. Soc. Psychol. Bull.* 16(1):166–80 (Spec. issue)

O'Leary A, Jemmott LS. 1996. Women and AIDS: coping and care. In *AIDS Prevention and Mental Health*, ed. A O'Leary, LS Jemmott. New York: Plenum

Paffenbarger RS Jr, Hyde RT, Wing AL. 1987. Physical activity and incidence of cancer in diverse populations: a preliminary report. *Am. J. Clin. Nutr.* 45(1):312–17 (Suppl.)

Pariante CM, Carpiniello B, Orru MG, Sitzia R, Piras A, et al. 1997. Chronic caregiving stress alters peripheral blood immune parameters—the role of age and severity of stress. *Psychother. Psychosom.* 66(4): 199–207

Park CL, Folkman S. 1997. Stability and change in psychosocial resources during caregiving and bereavement in partners of men with AIDS. *J. Pers.* 65(2):421–47

Parrott AC, Garnham NJ, Wesnes K, Pincock C. 1996. Cigarette smoking and abstinence: comparative effects upon cognitive task performance and mood state over 24 hours. *Hum. Psychopharmacol.* 11(5): 391–400

Path G, Bornstein SR, Ehrhart-Bornstein M, Scherbaum WA. 1997. Interleukin-6 and the interleukin-6 receptor in the human adrenal gland: expression and effects on steroidogenesis. *J. Clin. Endocrinol. Metabol.* 82(7):2343–49

Patterson RE, Kristal AR, White E. 1996. Do beliefs, knowledge, and perceived norms about diet and cancer predict dietary change? *Am. J. Public Health* 86(10): 1394–400

Patterson SM, Matthews KA, Allen MT, Owens JF. 1995. Stress-induced hemoconcentration of blood cells and lipids in healthy women during acute psychological stress. *Health Psychol.* 14(4):319–24

Patterson SM, Zakowski SG, Hall M, Cohen L, Wollman K, Baum A. 1994. Psychological stress and platelet activation: differences in platelet reactivity in healthy men during active and passive stressors. *Health Psychol.* 13(1):34–38

Perna FM, Schneiderman N, LaPerriere A. 1997. Psychological stress, exercise and immunity. *Int. J. Sports Med.* 18(1): S78–83 (Suppl.)

Pickering TG, Gerin W. 1990. Cardiovascular reactivity in the laboratory and the role of behavioral factors in hypertension. *Ann. Behav. Med.* 12:3–16

Plante TG, Rodin J. 1990. Physical fitness and enhanced psychological health. *Curr. Psychol. Res. Rev.* 9(1):3–24

Pomeroy EC, Rubin A, Van Laningham L, Walker RJ. 1997. "Straight talk": the effectiveness of a psychoeducational group intervention for heterosexuals with HIV/AIDS. *Res. Soc. Work Pract.* 7(2):149–64

Pool PE. 1997. The clinical significance of neurohormonal activation. *Clin. Ther.* 19(Suppl. A):53–73

Posluszny DM, Hyman KB, Baum A. 1998. Group intervention in cancer: the benefits of social support and education on patient adjustment. In *Theory and Research on Small Groups,* ed. RS Tindaleat. New York: Plenum

Ramirez AJ, Craig TKJ, Watson JP, Fentiman IS, North WR, et al. 1989. Stress and relapse of breast cancer. *Br. Med. J.* 298: 291–93

Rimer BK, McBride CM, Crump C. 1998. Women's health promotion. *Handb. Health Psychol.* In press

Robins AG, Dew MA, Kingsley LA, Becker JT. 1997. Do homosexual and bisexual men who place others at potential risk for HIV have unique psychosocial profiles? *AIDS Educ. Prev.* 9(3):239–51

Robinson LA, Klesges RC, Zbikowski SM, Glaser R. 1997. Predictors of risk for different stages of adolescent smoking in a biracial sample. *J. Consult. Clin. Psychol.* 65(4):653–62

Rooney BL, Murray DM. 1996. A meta-analysis of smoking prevention programs after adjustment for errors in the unit of analysis. *Health Educ. Q.* 23(1):48–64

Rostad FG, Long BC. 1996. Exercise as a coping strategy for stress: a review. *Int. J. Sport Psychol.* 27(2):197–222

Santagostino G, Amoretti G, Frattini P, Zerbi F, Cucchi ML, et al. 1996. Catecholaminergic, neuroendocrine and anxiety responses to acute psychological stress in healthy subjects: influence of alprazolam administration. *Neuropsychobiology* 34(1):36–43

Schapira DV, Kumar NB, Clark RA, Yag C. 1992. Mammography screening credit card and compliance. *Cancer* 70(2): 509–12

Schapira DV, Kumar NB, Lyman GH, Baile WF. 1991. The effect of duration of intervention and locus of control on dietary change. *Am. J. Prev. Med.* 7(6):341–47

Schedlowski M, Fluge T, Richter S, Tewes U, Schmidt RE, et al. 1995. Beta-endorphin,

but not substance-P, is increased by acute stress in humans. *Psychoneuroendocrinology* 20(1):103–10

Scheier MF, Carver CS. 1992. Effects of optimism on psycholoigcal and physical well-being: theoretical overview and empirical update. *Cogn. Ther. Res.* 16:201–28

Schneiderman N. 1983. Animal behavior models of coronary heart disease. In *Handbook of Psychology and Health,* Vol. 3 *Cardiovascular Disorders and Behavior,* ed. DS Krantz, A Baum, JE Singer. Hillsdale, NJ: Erlbaum

Schneiderman N, Antoni MH, Ironson G, LaPerriere A. 1992. Applied psychological science and HIV-1 spectrum disease. *Appl. Prev. Psychol.* 1(2):67–82

Selye H. 1976. *The Stress of Life.* New York: McGraw-Hill

Shephard RJ. 1993. Exercise in the prevention and treatment of cancer: an update. *Sports Med.* 15(4):258–80

Shiffman S, Hickcox M, Paty JA, Gnys M, Kassel JD, Richards T. 1996. Progression from a smoking lapse to relapse: prediction from abstinence violation effects, nicotine dependence, and lapse characteristics. *J. Consult. Clin. Psychol.* 64(5):993–1002

Spiegel D, Bloom J, Kraemer H, Gottheil E. 1989. Effect of psychosocial treatment on survival of patients with metastatic breast cancer. *Lancet* 2:888–91

Stehlow U, Kampmann G. 1993. AIDS anxieties of adolescents: determinants of "state" and "trait" anxiety. *J. Adolesc. Health* 14: 475–84

Steptoe A, Wardle J, Pollard TM, Canaan L. 1996. Stress, social support and health-related behavior: a study of smoking, alcohol consumption and physical exercise. *J. Psychosom. Res.* 41(2):171–80

Stern RS, Weinstein MD, Baker SG. 1986. Risk reduction for nonmelanoma skin cancer with childhood sunscreen use. *Arch. Dermatol.* 122(5):537–45

Stolley MR, Fitzgibbon ML. 1997. Effects of an obesity prevention program on the eating behavior of African American mothers and daughters. *Health Educ. Behav.* 24(2): 152–64

Sutton S, Saidi G, Bickler G, Hunter J. 1995. *J. Epidemiol. Commun. Health* 49:413–18

Testa M, Collins RL. 1997. Alcohol and risky sexual behavior: event-based analyses among a sample of high-risk women. *Psychol. Addict. Behav.* 11(3):190–201

Thune I, Brenn T, Lund E, Gaard M. 1997. Physicial activity and the risk of breast cancer. *N. Engl. J. Med.* 336(18):1269–75

Todd M, Chassin L, Presson CC, Sherman SJ.

1996. Role stress, role socialization, and cigarette smoking: examining multiple roles and moderating variables. *Psychol. Addict. Behav.* 10(4):211–21

Tomaka J, Blascovich J, Kibler J, Ernst JM. 1997. Cognitive and physiological antecedents of threat and challenge appraisal. *J. Pers. Soc. Psychol.* 73(1):63–72

Unger JB, Johnson CA, Stoddard JL, Nezami E, Chou CP. 1997. Identification of adolescents at risk for smoking initiation: validation of a measure of susceptibility. *Addict. Behav.* 22(1):81–91

Valdimarsdottir H, Bovbjerg D, Kash K, Holland J, Osborne M, et al. 1995. Psychological distress in women with a familial risk of breast cancer. *Psycho-oncology* 4:133–41

Vassend O, Eskild A, Halvorsen R. 1997. Negative affectivity, coping, immune status, and disease progression in HIV infected individuals. *Psychol. Health* 12(3):375–88

Vena JE, Graham S, Zielezny M, Brasure J, Swanson MK. 1987. Occupational exercise and risk of cancer. *Am. J. Clin. Nutr.* 45(1):318–27 (Suppl.)

Verrier E, Boyle EM Jr. 1996. Endothelial cell injury in cardiovascular surgery. *Ann. Thorac. Surg.* 62(3):915–22

Verrier RL, Mittelman MA. 1996. Life-threatening cardiovascular consequences of anger in patients with coronary heart disease. *Cardiol. Clin.* 14(2):289–307

Viinamaki H, Niskanen L, Koskela K. 1997. Factors predicting health behavior. *Nord. J. Psychiatry* 51(6):431–38

Wang CS, Chou P. 1996. The prevalence and motivating factors of adolescent smoking at a rural middle school in Taiwan. *Subst. Use Misuse* 31(10):1447–58

Wang T, Delahanty DL, Dougall AL, Baum A. 1998. Responses of natural killer cell activity to acute laboratory stressors at different times of the day. *Health Psychol.* In press

Webster EL, Elenkov IJ, Chrousos GP. 1997. The role of corticotropin-releasing hormone in neuroendocrine-immune interactions. *Mol. Psychiatry* 2(5):368

Weiss SM, Fielding JE, Baum A, eds. 1991. *Perspectives in Behavioral Medicine: Health at Work.* Hillsdale, NJ: Erlbaum

Weisse C. 1992. Depression and immunocompetence: a review of the literature. *Psychol. Bull.* 111(3):475–89

Wenger NS, Kusseling FS, Beck K, Shapiro MF. 1994. When patients first suspect and find out they are infected with the human immunodeficiency virus: implications for prevention. *AIDS Care* 6(4):339–405

Wilson T, Jaccard J, Minkoff H. 1996. HIV-antibody testing: beliefs affecting the consistency between women's behavioral intentions and behavior. *J. Appl. Soc. Psychol.* 26:1734–48

Wing RR. 1995a. Changing diet and exercise behaviors in individuals at risk for weight gain. *Obesity Res.* 3(Suppl. 2):S277-82

Wing RR. 1995b. What are our psychotherapeutic options? In *Obesity Treatment: Establishing Goals, Improving Outcomes, and Reviewing the Research Agenda,* ed. DB Allison, FX Pi-Sunyer, pp. 163–65. New York: Plenum

Wortley P, Chu S, Diaz T, Ward J, Doyle B, et al. 1995. HIV testing patterns: where, why and when were persons with AIDS tested for HIV? *AIDS* 9:487–92

Zakowski SG. 1995. The effects of stressor predictability on lymphocyte proliferation in humans. *Psychol. Health* 10(5):409–25

Zakowski SG, Hall MH, Baum A. 1992a. Stress, stress management, and the immune system. *Appl. Prev. Psychol.* 1(1):1–13

Zakowski SG, McAllister CG, Deal M, Baum A. 1992b. Stress, reactivity, and immune function in healthy men. *Health Psychol.* 11(4):223–32

Annu. Rev. Psychol. 1999. 50:165–90

INTERVENTIONS FOR COUPLES

A. Christensen[1] and C. L. Heavey[2]

[1]Department of Psychology, University of California, Los Angeles, California 90095;
e-mail: Christensen@psych.ucla.edu; [2]Department of Psychology, University of
Nevada, Las Vegas, Nevada 89154; e-mail: Heavey@Nevada.edu

KEY WORDS: couple therapy, marital therapy, enrichment, prevention, premarital counseling

ABSTRACT

A substantial body of empirical research has documented both the promise
and the shortcomings of psychological interventions for preventing or ameliorating marital distress. Couple therapy reduces relationship distress and
may affect individual psychopathology, such as depression. However, some
couples are unresponsive and others improve but relapse later. Interventions
to prevent marital distress usually produce short-term changes in behavior
and relationship satisfaction, but little evidence exists demonstrating a
longer-term prevention effect. Furthermore, these interventions have yet to
be examined on a diverse population of couples or with a diverse set of outcome criteria (e.g. effects on children). Concern about the negative impact of
marital discord and divorce will continue to provide the impetus for research
on more effective means of intervening with couples. Future research could
benefit from a focus on a more diverse population of couples, treatment in
natural settings, the development of more powerful interventions, and the examination of those interventions over longer periods of time and with more
comprehensive outcome measures.

CONTENTS

INTRODUCTION

Marital distress and divorce are not psychiatric disorders per se, but they take a heavy toll on human welfare. Marital discord is a risk factor for psychiatric disorders such as depression (Gotlib & Beach 1995), bipolar disorder (Miklowitz et al 1988), and alcohol abuse (Jacob & Krahn 1988), and it has even been associated with depressed immune-system functioning (Kielcolt-Glaser et al 1987). Moreover, parental discord increases risk for a myriad of children's problems, such as conduct disorders and depression (Cherlin et al 1991). Divorce, usually the result of marital discord, is one of life's most stressful events and is associated with a variety of physical and psychological disorders (Bloom et al 1978). These data clearly indicate the importance of efforts to prevent and remediate relationship distress.

Our review focuses first on couple therapy—interventions for couples who are clearly in distress. Next we focus on prevention programs for couples— interventions for couples prior to the development of marital discord. We organize our review of the literature in both of these areas by focusing on particular applied questions of interest to researchers and clinicians alike. Finally, we review some methodological and conceptual issues common to both efforts.

Consistent with recent developments in the field, we use the more inclusive term couple therapy rather than marital therapy (Jacobson & Christensen 1996). Although the majority of research has been conducted on married couples, most of the therapeutic procedures that have been developed should be applicable to other adult romantic relationships, such as heterosexual cohabiting relationships and gay and lesbian relationships.

THERAPY FOR COUPLES

Does Couple Therapy Work?

The most basic question that can be asked about couple therapy is whether it helps. The scientific literature has addressed this question by comparing couple therapy with no treatment at all. The result of dozens of these comparisons indicates unequivocally that couple therapy increases satisfaction more than does no treatment. For example, Jacobson & Addis (1993:85) write that "...in no published study has a tested model failed to outperform a control group. In virtually every instance in which a bona fide treatment has been tested against a control group, the treatment has shown reliable change."

This research assumes that positive outcomes occur only when relationship satisfaction improves. However, it is easy to imagine (and clinicians sometimes report) that some couples are so ill-suited for each other that for them separation and divorce are positive outcomes. The research literature has not yet dealt with this conundrum. In our discussion of methodological issues below, we offer some possibilities for a broader definition of outcomes from couple therapy.

How Powerful Is Couple Therapy?

The question of whether a therapy works cannot be answered with a simple yes or no. The mere fact that a treatment group produces outcomes significantly greater in a statistical sense than those of a control condition does not mean all members of the treatment group have done well or even that any of them have done well. Couples in the treatment group could still be seriously dissatisfied but have merely scored a few points higher than their counterparts in the control group. In fact, couples in control groups typically show minimal change or even deterioration, so establishing a statistically significant effect of treatment is easy (Jacobson et al 1984).

A common way to quantify the power of treatment is with an effect-size statistic. In the Shadish et al (1993) meta-analysis, the average effect size, measured by Cohen's (1988) d but corrected for small sample bias (Hedges & Olkin 1985) was 0.60 (standard error = 0.09) for 27 studies of couple therapies. This level of effect implies that a therapy couple at the mean was better off than approximately 70% of the control subjects. With this effect size, the probability that a randomly chosen treatment couple will have a better outcome than will a randomly chosen control couple is approximately 65%. This effect size converts to a correlation coefficient of about 0.28, which suggests that treatment accounted for approximately 8% of the variance in outcome. Based on Rosenthal & Rubin's (1982) criteria of success rate $(0.50 + r/2)$, that means approximately 65% of couples in marital therapy improved versus approximately 35% in control conditions.

Although the effect-size statistic is used widely to measure the power of a treatment, it is a measure of comparative effects rather than absolute effects. Therefore, it is possible for a treatment to have a large effect size but fail to leave its clients in a "normal" state. For example, a treatment for severely dissatisfied couples might attain a large effect size because most of the control group couples remained severely dissatisfied whereas treatment moved couples from severe to moderate dissatisfaction.

The notion of clinically significant change invokes an absolute standard rather than a comparative standard to judge the strength of a treatment. Clinically significant change can be defined in terms of a specifiable condition, such as a couple remaining together versus getting separated, or in terms of two statistical criteria: a reliable change index and a clinically significant change index (Jacobson & Truax 1991). The reliable change index, based on the standard error of measurement, simply assesses whether an individual or couple has improved more than would be expected by chance. Clinically significant change, however, occurs when an individual's or couple's score changes from being more like scores in a dysfunctional population prior to treatment to being more like scores in a functional population after treatment. Based on normative data on the measure under consideration, one can calculate a cutoff point, such that scores above the point are more indicative of a functional or "normal" population and scores below the point are indicative of a dysfunctional or "abnormal" population.

Jacobson et al (1984) reexamined four studies of behavioral couples therapy, involving a total of 148 couples, using the two criteria above. They found that 54.7% of couples showed reliable improvement. However, only 36.1% of couples showed reliable improvement for both spouses. Using the more rigorous criteria of reliable change and clinically significant change, they found that the three clinical studies in their sample showed an averaged success rate of 35.3% when results were weighted by sample size; an analogue study showed only a 16.7% success rate.

To provide an indication of clinical significance in their meta-analysis of the literature, Shadish and associates (1993) located 19 studies that reported pretreatment and posttreatment means on either of two commonly used measures of marital satisfaction, the Marital Adjustment Test (Locke & Wallace 1959) and the Dyadic Adjustment Scale (Spanier 1976). Both of the these measures have a commonly accepted cutoff for dissatisfaction versus satisfaction, 100 on the Marital Adjustment Test and 97 on the Dyadic Adjustment Scale, which is about one standard deviation below the mean for nondistressed couples. These 19 studies included 39 treatment and 11 control conditions. All 11 of the control conditions and 34 of the 39 treatments started with pretreatment means in the distressed range. At posttreatment, 14 of the 34 treatments had means in the nondistressed range; none of the control conditions had means in the nondistressed range. Therefore, Shadish et al (1993) calculated that 41% (14/34) of the treatment conditions were successful in bringing couples from a nondistressed to a distressed status. This calculation, though based on average performance rather than individual couple performance, is similar to Jacobson's figure of a 35% success rate for couples. Therefore, based on these two reviews, we can say with some confidence that fewer than half of couples treated in therapy will move from distressed to nondistressed status.

How Durable Are the Effects of Couple Therapy?

Most studies have no or short follow-up assessments. In the Shadish et al (1993) meta-analysis of 163 marital and family treatment studies, nine studies reported treatment control comparisons at posttest and at follow-up. Shadish et al found no differences between effect sizes at posttest and at follow-up. However, only one follow-up assessment was conducted longer than 9 months after treatment; the remaining studies had a median follow-up period of 5 months. In the Hahlweg & Markman (1988) meta-analysis of behavioral couple therapy, eight studies had follow-ups between 3 and 6 months after treatment; five studies had follow-ups between 9 and 12 months after treatment. Their analysis suggested that treatment effects were maintained over these periods. Finally, the Jacobson et al (1984) review of three clinical trials also found evidence for the maintenance of treatment gains for the 6-month follow-up in each of these studies. Based on these analyses of follow-up, we can say that treatment effects are largely maintained over at least the first 6 months after treatment termination.

Two outcome studies have looked at functioning more than a year after treatment termination. In the first study (Jacobson et al 1985,1987), couples receiving a full course of behavioral couple therapy fared well through their first 6-month follow-up, improving their outcome since posttest, but by the 1- and 2-year follow-ups, some couples had relapsed. Of the 12 couples available at year 2, 25% had deteriorated below their pretest functioning and 9% had separated or divorced. The second study, a comparison between behavioral versus insight-oriented couple therapy (Snyder & Wills 1989, Snyder et al 1991), provided the most lengthy follow-up in the history of intervention research with couples. Both treatments performed better than a control condition at the posttreatment assessment and generally maintained their improvement at a 6-month follow-up (Snyder & Wills 1989). However, at a 4-year follow-up assessment, only 50% of 29 couples in behavior therapy were classified as happy whereas 70% of 30 couples in insight-oriented therapy were classified as happy. A full 38% of the behavior therapy couples were divorced whereas only 3% of the insight-oriented couples were divorced.

These two studies of long-term follow-up warn us that couples in behavior therapy may do well at posttreatment and through a 6-month follow-up but may relapse some 1 to 4 years posttreatment. The latter study also suggests some possible differences between types of treatment, a topic to which we now turn.

What Effects Do Different Types of Couple Therapy Have?

There are a number of different interventions for couples but only three have more than one published study supporting their effectiveness: behavioral couple therapy, cognitive behavioral couple therapy, and emotion-focused couple therapy.

BEHAVIORAL COUPLE THERAPY   Based on a social learning theory of human behavior, behavioral couple therapy (BCT) views marital satisfaction and distress in reinforcement terms. Couples are satisfied to the extent that their ratio of reinforcement to punishment in the relationship is positive; they are dissatisfied to the extent that this ratio is negative. Couples get together because of the mutual reinforcement they generate for each other. However, over time this mutual reinforcement decreases through processes such as habituation and satiation. More important, as couples face the inevitable differences between them, they get into arguments that increase the mutual punishment and decrease the reinforcement they experience (Jacobson & Margolin 1979).

To remedy this situation, BCT attempts to increase the level of reinforcing exchange and to teach communication and problem solving skills that will enable couples to cope with their differences in a constructive manner that minimizes punishment and maximizes reinforcement. The three major interventions of BCT are behavior exchange, communication training, and problem solving training. In behavior exchange, BCT therapists help couples identify positive acts that each can do for the other, encourage couples to engage in these behaviors, and train them to show appropriate acknowledgment for them. In communication training, BCT therapists teach couples to express themselves without blame and accusation and to employ active listening skills (Jacobson & Margolin 1979). Finally, in problem solving training, BCT therapists teach couples how to define problems explicitly, how to generate potential solutions to those problems, how to negotiate and compromise on possible solutions, and how to implement and evaluate solutions.

BCT is by far the most thoroughly investigated of the treatments for couples; more than two dozen clinical trials support its efficacy. Hahlweg & Markman (1988) conducted a meta-analysis on 17 studies of BCT and found an overall effect size of 0.95. As reported earlier, they found that results were generally maintained over follow-up periods lasting up to 1 year. In a more recent analysis, Dunn & Schwebel (1995) examined 11 studies published between 1980 and 1993 that contained 13 BCT treatment groups. On measures of marital behavior, they found a weighted mean effect size of 0.79 at posttreatment and 0.52 at follow-up. On measures of relationship quality, they found a weighted mean effect size of 0.78 at posttreatment and 0.54 at follow-up. The average follow-up time in their study was 8.75 months.

COGNITIVE BEHAVIORAL COUPLE THERAPY   A number of researchers (e.g. Baucom & Epstein 1990) argue that it is not just behavior that matters in relationships, but partners' interpretation of that behavior. These investigators further suggest that strategies of cognitive restructuring, similar to those used in cognitive therapy for individuals (e.g. Beck et al 1979), can be used to alter partners' interpretations of each other's behavior. The goals of cognitive restructuring as applied to couple therapy are to facilitate partners' ability "to identify their cognitions that are associated with marital discord, to test the validity or appropriateness of those cognitions, and to modify dysfunctional cognitions" (Baucom et al 1995:80).

Cognitive behavioral couple therapy (CBCT) therapists utilize a number of cognitive restructuring strategies to modify different types of dysfunctional cognitions. If partners use terms like "always" and "never" to describe negative characteristics of their partner, the therapist may engage the couple in a search for identifiable exceptions that might alter their selective attention to negatives. To modify attributions and expectancies, therapists may employ logical analysis (Beck et al 1979), in which a client is asked to examine the evidence for an explanation about the partner. To alter assumptions and standards, therapists may engage partners in a Socratic approach where they are asked to evaluate the consequences of living according to their standards and assumptions, such as a standard that "one should never be angry at your partner."

In their meta-analysis of couples therapy, Dunn & Schwebel (1995) report on three outcome studies involving a total of 74 couples, which examined the effectiveness of cognitive procedures in combination with behavioral procedures. On measures of marital behavior, they found a weighted mean effect size of 0.54 at posttreatment and 0.75 at follow-up for these treatments. On measures of relationship quality, they found a weighted mean effect size of 0.71 at posttreatment and 0.54 at follow-up. Only two of the three studies included follow-up assessments; average follow-up time was 6.0 months.

There are also studies that have shown the effectiveness of cognitive strategies alone, not in combination with behavioral strategies. For example, Emmelkamp et al (1988) showed that cognitive restructuring alone was an effective treatment for marital distress.

EMOTIONALLY FOCUSED COUPLE THERAPY   Developed by Greenberg & Johnson (1988, Johnson & Greenberg 1995), emotionally focused couple therapy (EFCT) conceptualizes distress in close, romantic adult relationships in terms of attachment theory (Bowlby 1969). Relationship distress represents "the failure of an attachment relationship to provide a secure base for one or both partners" (Bowlby 1969:124). The disruption of attachment bonds that leads to relationship distress stimulates strong primary emotions within partners, such as a fear of abandonment by the other. In addition, there are secondary emotions and reactions, such as angry withdrawal in response to one's fear. In EFCT, a focus on primary emotions is used to reestablish attachment bonds.

The two main tasks of EFCT are "(1) to access and reprocess the emotional experience of partners and (2) to restructure interaction patterns" (Johnson & Greenberg 1995:127). EFCT therapists try to expose and highlight the primary emotions that partners experience in their interaction with each other. "Secondary or instrumental expression is expanded or bypassed in order to expose an underlying experience" (Johnson & Greenberg 1995:127). As partners experience their primary emotions and voice them in the session, they encounter new aspects of themselves and each other. They are then able to develop more functional interaction patterns that satisfy their attachment needs. For example, an EFCT therapist might help a pursuer, angry at the lack of contact with a withdrawn partner, to access his or her fear of abandonment and express this fear, rather than the secondary anger. The partner in term may respond to the expressed fear with support rather than withdrawal and the beginnings of a new, more functional interaction pattern is generated.

In their meta-analysis of marital therapy outcome research, Dunn & Schwebel (1995) examined five studies of what they called insight-oriented marital therapy; four of these studies specifically examined EFCT and one examined Snyder and Wills' insight-oriented marital therapy (Snyder et al 1991). Dunn & Schwebel (1995) argue that the two approaches are similar. On measures of marital behavior, they found a weighted mean effect size of 0.87 at posttreatment and 0.69 at follow-up. On measures of relationship quality, they found a weighted mean effect size of 1.37 at posttreatment and 1.04 at follow-up. The average follow-up time in the four studies that included follow-up was 12.4 months.

Which Couple Therapy Is Most Effective?

Given that there are several different treatments for relationship distress, one naturally wonders: Which treatment is more effective? In their meta-analysis, Dunn & Schwebel (1995) did a statistical comparison of the weighted mean effect sizes of the three major types of couple therapy discussed above. On measures of couple behavior, they found no statistically significant differences at either posttreatment or follow-up. On measures of relationship quality, there were significant differences at posttreatment favoring the studies they grouped together as insight-oriented couple therapy but no significant differences at follow-up.

What is more impressive than a meta-analytic comparison—which groups together studies with diverse couples, treatments, and measures—is when two treatments are compared in a clinical trial. Couples are randomly assigned to treatment conditions, so that differences in outcome can be attributed to the treatments rather than to differences in the couples being treated. A number of studies have shown no significant differences between active treatments. For example, studies have shown that CBCT is as effective as BCT in improving relationship satisfaction but is not more effective (e.g. Halford et al 1993). Occasionally, studies have demonstrated the superiority of one treatment over another, such as the superiority of insight-oriented couple therapy over BCT at 4 year follow-up, alluded to earlier (Snyder et al 1991). But this study and others showing the superiority of one treatment over another have favored the investigator's treatment and have not been replicated. Furthermore, there is sometimes controversy over the definition or implementation of the comparison treatment [e.g. see Jacobson's (1991) concerns about BCT in the Snyder et al 1991 study]. In short, there is no convincing evidence at this point that any one couple therapy is better than another. The more interesting question of which therapies might be best for which couples remains to be addressed.

What Is New and Important in Couple Therapy?

Arguably the most important findings about couples in the last decade concerns violence. We now know that (a) violence occurs in the relationships of a majority of couples who self-refer for generic marital therapy and (b) few of these couples report aggression as one of their primary problems (Cascardi et al 1992, O'Leary et al 1992, Ehrensaft & Vivian 1996). Therefore, violence may not come to the attention of the therapist unless he or she asks about it directly. We believe the field has been negligent because few treatment programs have routinely screened for violence or incorporated strategies for dealing with violence. It is our guess that most couples' therapists have been similarly negligent.

Gender-specific treatments have been the primary interventions for violence in relationships. Severe violence in couples (battering) is almost always perpetrated by men (Jacobson & Gottman 1998). As a result, shelters were established for women; battering men were often mandated to treatment by the courts. However, most of the violence that occurs in relationships is not as severe as battering and does not come to the attention of the legal system. Recently, two clinical trials have compared conjoint treatment with gender-specific treatment for couples in which there is male-to-female violence (Brannen & Rubin 1996; KD O'Leary, RE Heyman, PH Neidig, submitted for publication). Both used a similar form of conjoint treatment that is unlike typical couple therapy in that it focuses specifically on violence. The study by Brannen & Rubin (1996) used a court-referred sample of couples, some of whom had incidents of severe abuse; another study (KD O'Leary, RE Heyman, PH Neidig, submitted for publication) used a less-abusive, recruited sample (the wife never had injuries requiring medical attention and she indicated her comfort with a conjoint format) but had a serious dropout problem (only 49% completed treatment). Both treatments were successful in reducing violence at posttreatment and at 6 month (Brannen & Rubin) or 1 year follow-up (O'Leary et al), but neither eliminated violence in all couples. Contrary to the concerns of many feminists, women in the conjoint treatment were not at greater risk than those in gender-specific treatment. Furthermore, on some measures the conjoint treatment was superior (greater marital satisfaction in husbands in the study by O'Leary et al; greater reduction in violence for those with a history of alcohol problems in the study by Brannen & Rubin). These controversial findings need replication.

Another recent treatment development is integrative couple therapy (ICT) (Christensen et al 1995, Jacobson & Christensen 1996), which focuses on promoting acceptance in couples but also incorporates the change strategies of BCT. Independent reviewers have praised the approach (Hendrick 1997); three small, unpublished studies have provided empirical support for the treatment. Wimberly (1997) showed that eight couples randomly assigned to a group format of ICT were superior to nine wait-listed couples. In a clinical trial of 21 couples, Jacobson & Christensen (1996) demonstrated the superiority of ICT over BCT. Finally, in a study of 29 depressed women who were maritally distressed, it was shown that ICT was as effective as cognitive behavior therapy (MC Trapp, TM Pace, CD Stoltenberg, submitted for publication). Currently a major, multi-site clinical trial, supported by NIMH, is under way comparing ICT with BCT (A. Christensen, NS Jacobson, personal communication).

Is Couple Therapy an Effective Treatment for Individual Disorders?

Because couple and family relationships are the most important social context for most adults, several therapies specifically include spouses or romantic partners in the treatment of an individual disorder. Baucom et al (1998) classify these therapies into three different categories: (*a*) Partner-assisted intervention refers to treatments that include the partner as a helper or coach in conducting treatment assignments at home but that do not focus on the couple relationship per se; (*b*) disorder-specific couple intervention focuses on the couple's relationship only in so far as it affects the individual disorder; and (*c*) general couples therapy uses treatments like those described above to improve the functioning of the individual and the relationship. Our discussion below is based in large part on Baucom et al (1998).

DEPRESSION   Because of the documented high comorbidity between depression and marital discord and the common assumption that marital distress may generate, promote, or maintain depression (Gotlib & Beach 1995), the use of marital therapy to treat depression was a natural development for the field. Two important clinical trials (O'Leary & Beach 1990, Jacobson et al 1991) have used standard BCT to treat depression in married women and compared it with cognitive therapy, a well-researched individual treatment for depression. Although there are important differences between the two studies, they converge in their findings that BCT is (*a*) as effective as cognitive therapy in alleviating depression among maritally distressed couples and (*b*) more effective than cognitive therapy in improving the marital relationship. However, the study by Jacobson et al (1991) indicates that cognitive therapy is more effective than BCT in alleviating depression among women who are not maritally distressed. Furthermore, a small study by O'Leary and Associates (as reported in Gotlib & Beach 1995) suggests that BCT may not be as useful as cognitive therapy when treatment patients are actively suicidal.

ANXIETY DISORDERS   Several researchers have examined the effectiveness of partner-assisted exposure in the treatment of obsessive-compulsive disorder (e.g. Emmelkamp et al 1990) and in the treatment of agoraphobia (e.g. Cobb et al 1984). In these treatments, partners are instructed to encourage and praise the patients for exposing themselves to feared situations. Generally these treatments have performed at least as well as exposure treatments that don't incorporate the partner. If, however, the partner-assisted exposure is enhanced with communication training (Arnow et al 1985) or with cognitive therapy (Barlow et al 1984), the treatment may be more powerful.

SEXUAL DISORDERS   The most influential treatment for sexual dysfunction was developed by Masters & Johnson (1970). This short-term, directed treatment typically begins with education about sex and a ban on intercourse or other genital stimulation. Then, through assignments discussed in session but completed at home, the treatment guides couples through a gradual progression of mutual pleasuring, called sensate focus. The sensate focus begins with nongenital pleasuring such as back rubs but eventually leads to genital pleasuring and finally intercourse. Given the great impact this treatment had on the field and its publication more than a quarter century ago, one might think that numerous clinical trials would have been conducted to evaluate its efficacy. In fact, few clinical trials have been conducted on this approach or on any psychological treatment. Most research consists of reports of improvement rates from treated cases (e.g. Hawton 1995, Rosen & Leiblum 1995). However, randomized clinical trials do support the efficacy of the treatment, in one case supplemented by BCT, for female orgasmic disorder (e.g. Zimmer 1987).

For primary or lifelong orgasmic disorder in women, sexual-skills training through directed masturbation is considered the treatment of choice. This approach, developed by LoPiccolo & Lobitz (1972), consists of a series of steps such as education and self-exploration, sensual exercises, directed individual masturbation, and partner-assisted masturbation. There are clinical trials that support the efficacy of this treatment (e.g. Ersner-Hershfield & Kopel 1979).

For treating hypoactive sexual desire disorder in women, Hurlbert and associates (1993) evaluated a treatment that combined BCT, sexual-skills training, and orgasm-consistency training, which involves a series of couple exercises such as training in sexual positions that offer the greatest possibility for orgasm. At both posttreatment and 6-month follow-up, this combined treatment for couples was superior to a woman-only treatment and a wait-list control.

Although there are case reports supporting the efficacy of psychological treatments for male sexual disorders (Hawton 1995), there is little in the way of randomized clinical trials. In fact, the focus has shifted to medical treatments for male sexual disorders, particularly for erectile problems (Rosen & Leiblum 1995). The recent introduction of viagra for erectile problems is a dramatic example.

ALCOHOL ABUSE AND DEPENDENCE   There are two approaches to the treatment of alcohol abuse and dependence that involve the couple and that have received empirical support: the community reinforcement approach (CRA) of Azrin (1976) and Project CALM (counseling for alcoholic marriages) by O'Farrell and his colleagues (1993). Designed from an operant behavioral perspective, CRA is an intense, multifaceted treatment that tries to remove social reinforcement for drinking and institute adaptive behaviors that are incompatible with drinking. Spouses and significant others are trained in how to engage the drinker in treatment and how to respond during drinking episodes. Sometimes partners get involved in making contracts with the patient for using disulfiram (antabuse) and are trained in how to handle situations when the patient wants to stop taking disulfiram. Several small clinical trials have shown that CRA is more effective than the treatment that was usually provided in the settings where CRA has been tested (e.g. Azrin 1976).

Project CALM (O'Farrell et al 1993) consists of partner-negotiated disulfiram contracts, BCT, and relapse prevention. The treatment begins with couple sessions designed to build commitment to treatment and to establish disulfiram contracts. Then a series of BCT sessions are aimed at increasing positive behavior and teaching communication and problem solving skills. Although each session includes a focus on drinking, the main focus is on increasing relationship skills. Finally, there is a relapse-prevention module where patients are trained, within conjoint sessions, to identify high-risk situations and to deal with relapses. During these sessions, therapists also work to continue the disulfiram contracts and to maintain relationship gains. Two clinical trials by O'Farrell and associates (e.g. 1993) have supported the efficacy of Project Calm.

PREVENTION OF COUPLE PROBLEMS

Although efforts to prevent relationship distress by preparing couples for marriage have been ongoing since at least the 1930s (Mudd et al 1941, Rutledge 1968), the pace of research in this area has gained momentum over the last two decades from two sources. First, the high rates of divorce and marital distress, combined with the realization that these outcomes are generic risk factors for psychiatric and physical illnesses (Coie et al 1993, Markman & Hahlweg 1993), has led to the realization that the reduction of marital distress should be a high priority. Second, the initial optimism about the ability of marital therapy to solve the problems of distressed couples has waned as data have accumulated showing only a moderate success rate for couple therapy. The limited outcome of marital therapy is compounded by the fact that few couples actually seek therapy before separation or divorce (Bradbury & Fincham 1990). Thus, there has been a general call to investigate the ability of prevention programs to improve relationship outcomes (e.g. Markman & Floyd 1980).

The typical prevention program is a semi-structured series of meetings employing some combination of brief lectures, couple exercises, group or couple discussions, and skill practice. Generally programs have the explicit goals of teaching couples some set of skills believed relevant to maintaining a healthy relationship (e.g. communication and conflict resolution skills), modifying attitudes and/or expectations (e.g. commitment), and preparing couples for common relationship problems and transitions (e.g. conflict over money, the transition to parenthood). Given these goals, efficacy is typically measured in the short-term (e.g. posttest) by looking at targeted behaviors and attitudes, and in the longer term by looking for differences in relationship adjustment or stability. The reasoning is that targeted behaviors and attitudes mediate the process of deterioration of relationship adjustment and therefore changes in these targets will affect later relationship adjustment. Because the distinction between programs designed to prevent relationship distress and those designed to enhance relationship functioning (i.e. promote health) is subtle within this domain (see Munoz et al 1996, Van Widenfelt et al 1997), we include both types of programs without distinction and use the terms prevention and enrichment interchangeably.

Do Prevention Programs Work?

Reviews of prevention studies published over the last two decades suggest that prevention programs can change the behavior of couples over relatively brief periods of time and that they may be able to produce moderate-term increases in relationship adjustment and stability (Bagarozzi & Rauen 1981, Giblin et al 1985, Guerney & Maxson 1990, Hahlweg & Markman 1988, Sayers et al 1998). However, due to methodological issues, reviewers have placed different degrees of confidence in this conclusion. For example, Guerney & Maxson concluded "there is no doubt that, on the whole, enrichment programs work and the field is an entirely legitimate one" (1990:1133). Reviewing the same data, Bradbury & Fincham drew the more conservative conclusion that "there is a slight tendency for prevention programs to improve relationships relative to no-treatment or attention-only controls, and prevention programs have not yet been shown to produce lasting changes in relationships" (1990:397).

How Powerful Are Prevention Programs?

Two meta-analyses have examined the ability of prevention programs to improve relationship behavior and outcome. Giblin et al (1985) conducted a meta-analysis of 85 prevention studies completed prior to 1982. They included all studies addressing prevention of distress or relationship enrichment that they could obtain and that included a comparison or control group and sufficient information for the calculation of effect sizes. In contrast, Hahlweg & Markman (1988) reviewed only seven published studies in their meta-analysis. It appears that six of these seven studies were included in the Giblin et al (1985) review.

The average effect size for all studies and measures in the Giblin et al study was 0.44, indicating that the average couple in the experimental group was functioning better than were 67% of the control couples. The review by Hahlweg & Markman (1988) yielded a mean effect size of 0.79, indicating that the average couple in the experimental group was functioning better than were 79% of the control couples.

Both reviews showed differences in effect sizes as a function of the type of measure used to assess change, with observational measures showing substantially larger differences between groups than the self-report measures [0.76 vs 0.35 in Giblin et al (1985), and 1.51 vs 0.52 in Hahlweg & Markman (1988)]. This large difference suggests a number of important possible interpretations. One possible interpretation is that the typical focus of the programs on changing behaviors leads to short-term changes in behaviors but slower or more gradual changes in attitudes or perceptions of behaviors. However, another possible interpretation for this differential is that couples in the experimental groups experience greater demand characteristics when assessed with observational measures than when assessed with self-report measures. In other words, couples trained in a set of skills, such as a structured model of problem solving, may experience considerable internal pressure to demonstrate these skills when asked to attempt to resolve a problem while being videotaped, usually in a lab setting, shortly after completing the enrichment program. Because the differences in effect sizes for observational versus self-report measures are large and there is ambiguity involved in understanding the meaning of these differences, this is an important area for future research. It should be noted that both of these explanations, as well as others, may contribute to the observed differences in effect sizes.

Other noteworthy findings included a small but significant relationship between program length and outcome ($r = 0.16$), the finding in the review by Giblin et al (1985) of greater effect sizes for measures classified as assessing relationship skills (0.63) than for measures classified as assessing relationship satisfaction (0.34), and a larger effect size for studies including more distressed couples (0.51) than for studies with fewer distressed couples (0.27) (Giblin et al 1985). This latter finding suggests that the size of initial gains in prevention studies may be limited by ceiling effects when primarily satisfied couples participate. It also argues against the notion that enrichment programs are not useful for couples already experiencing distress (cf Van Widenfelt et al 1996).

How Durable Are the Effects of Prevention Programs?

The durability of changes produced by prevention programs is obviously of central importance because of the long-term goal of prevention, but few studies have employed even relatively short-term follow-ups. Of the studies reviewed by Giblin et al (1985), only 34% conducted follow-ups and the average length of the follow-ups was only 12 weeks. From posttest to follow-up, the average effect size declined from 0.44 to 0.34 ($p < 0.05$). Four of the seven studies reviewed by Hahlweg & Markman (1988) conducted follow-ups; the three studies with follow-ups between 6 and 18 months had an average effect size of 1.01. One of these studies reported a second, 3-year follow-up with an average effect size of 0.65. Thus, both reviews indicate that the effects of the prevention programs dissipate over time. A critical challenge for future research is to understand this decay and how to effectively use some type of booster regimen to maintain enhancements in functioning.

What Effects Do Different Prevention Programs Have?

There are now numerous programs designed to prevent relationship distress, including popular and long-standing programs such as Marriage and Engaged Encounter and Association for Couples in Marriage Enrichment (ACME) programs (see, for example, Berger & Hannah 1998; see also the Website of the Coalition for Marriage, Family, and Couple Education, www.smartmarriages.com). Three programs, however, stand out because of their widespread use and their substantial body of evaluative research: the Couple Communication Program, Relationship Enhancement, and the Prevention and Relationship Enhancement Program.

The Couple Communication program (CC), developed in the late 1960s (Miller et al 1976), is grounded primarily in systems theory. This structured program has four primary goals: (*a*) to increase awareness of self, other and relationship; (*b*) to teach skills for communicating more effectively; (*c*) to teach couples new ways to enrich their relationship; and (*d*) to increase relationship satisfaction (Miller & Sherrard 1998). The group format for this program typically consists of four 2- to 3-h sessions with up to 12 couples.

Wampler reviewed studies evaluating CC and concluded that "CC has a strong positive effect on couple communication behavior, immediately after the program, but this effect diminishes over time. CC has a very positive impact on relationship quality with evidence that in many cases this positive impact is maintained at follow-up one to several months later" (1990:29). She also notes CC has been found to positively affect individual adjustment and that there have been no documented cases in which CC produced negative effects. A recent meta-analysis of CC studies (MH Butler, KS Wampler, submitted for publication) supported these conclusions, finding large effect sizes for improvements in observer-rated communication for CC versus control couples and medium to small effect sizes for improvements in relationship satisfaction for CC couples versus control couples. There was consistent deterioration of effect sizes from posttest to follow-up. Finally, the authors noted that the large variability of the individual effect sizes produced confidence intervals for all mean effect sizes that included zero.

Relationship Enhancement (RE) (Guerney 1977) is an eclectic model, drawing from many schools of psychotherapy, with an emphasis on the work of Carl Rogers and on learning theory. RE teaches couples a set of nine skills that emphasize communicating effectively, responding empathically, resolving conflicts in a mutually satisfying manner, and ways to break out of negative cycles and implement more constructive behaviors (Cavedo & Guerney 1998). RE can be delivered in a range of formats including weekly sessions of approximately 2 h lasting between 10 and 15 weeks.

Numerous studies have evaluated the impact of RE enrichment programs for couples. These studies have typically found that couples make significant gains in the areas of communication, self-disclosure, empathy, and relationship adjustment (see Cavedo & Guerney 1998, Guerney & Maxon 1990 for reviews). For example, Avery et al (1980) found that RE couples showed significant gains in self-disclosure and empathy compared with pretest levels and compared with couples participating in a lecture/discussion control condition. These gains deteriorated between the posttest and the six-month follow-up.

The Prevention and Relationship Enhancement Program (PREP) was developed in the 1980s (Markman et al 1994, Stanley et al 1998) based primarily on social learning theory, BCT, and cognitive behavioral research on the predictors of relationship outcome. PREP focuses on the central role of poorly handled conflict and negative affect in the erosion of relationship adjustment. Thus, PREP helps couples avoid the potentially corrosive effects of conflict while enhancing positive and protective factors in the relationship. PREP has four primary goals: (*a*) teaching couples effective communication and conflict resolution skills; (*b*) helping couples to clarify and evaluate their expectations for the relationship and each other; (*c*) helping couples to evaluate and renew their commitment to having a successful relationship; and (*d*) enhancing the positive aspects of the relationship including fun, friendship, and sensuality.

A number of studies have been conducted to evaluate PREP (see Stanley et al 1998 for a review). Markman et al (1988, 1993) have conducted a long-term evaluation study that has shown intervention couples fared better than controls in terms of chances of breaking up, constructiveness of communication, level of problem intensity, frequency of physical violence, and relationship satisfaction up to 5 years postintervention. Similarly impressive long-term results were found by others (K Hahlweg, HJ Markman, F Thurmaier, J Engl, V Eckert, submitted for publication). They found that PREP couples showed better communication and conflict management skills and reported higher relationship satisfaction and lower frequency of divorce than control couples through 3 years postintervention. Van Widenfelt et al (1996) found less promising results but the comparability of the control and intervention groups was not clear in this study.

Which Prevention Program Is Most Effective?

Although there are few data to provide a definitive answer to this question, a number of studies have compared programs directly. We focus only on those studies that have investigated the treatments described above (see Hawley & Olson 1995 for a comparison of three other treatments).

PREP was compared with an alternative treatment, Engaged Encounter (see Renick et al 1992); PREP couples showed greater increases in communication constructiveness and a trend toward greater satisfaction than did couples in Engaged Encounter. Russell et al (1984) compared CC with an alternative treatment, the Structured Behavior Exchange program. Both programs led to improvement in relationship quality through the 4-month follow-up, and to a lesser extent in communication quality, but there was no evidence that one treatment was generally superior to the other. Jessee & Guerney (1981) compared RE to an alternative treatment, Gestalt Relationship Facilitation, and found that RE was superior at posttest. In a carefully designed study, Brock & Joanning (1983) found RE to be superior to CC both at posttest and at a 3-month follow-up on measures of quality of communication and relationship satisfaction. These authors also conducted a useful series of analyses in which they identified the number of couples within each condition experiencing declines in relationship quality from pre- to posttest; more CC couples experienced declines in adjustment (30%) than RE couples (15%). Finally, Giblin et al (1985) noted in their meta-analysis that RE programs produced the largest average effect sizes (0.96) of all programs examined, including CC (0.44). Thus, extant data comparing programs currently favors RE, though we should note that PREP is the only program with data showing improvements in functioning beyond 6 months posttest.

What Is New and Important in Prevention Programs?

One important innovation in prevention programs is the development of special prevention programs for groups who are at elevated risk for relationship distress because of developmental transitions and/or known psychosocial stressors. An example of this type of selective prevention (Munoz et al 1996) is the project of Howe & Price (1997). It uses a relationship-based intervention to prevent depression and relationship distress in couples coping with job loss. Another example of selective prevention is the program developed by Jordan and colleagues to help couples make a successful transition to parenthood (P Jordan, personal communication). This Becoming Parents Program is a modified version of PREP, with added components addressing the specific concerns of new parents (e.g. coping with the stress of a new baby, reading infant cues). Another important innovation is the recent addition to the PREP program of a curriculum designed to help couples avoid violence (Holtzworth-Munroe et al 1995).

Efforts to prevent marital distress at a broader level than the couple is another important development. For example, Marriage Savers is an organization that works with religious institutions to support marriages in a variety of ways, such as through premarital counseling and the use of trained mentor couples to provide assistance and guidance to new couples. Some state legislators are proposing legal changes to make both marriage and divorce more difficult. Although these legislators hope that these legal changes will promote healthier relationships, there are a number of important reasons to be wary of and resist such changes (see Stanley & Markman 1997). Other factors, such as levels of unemployment, relevant governmental policies (e.g. family leave), and even cultural values concerning relationships and marriage, have powerful effects on the health of relationships and therefore present possible points at which to intervene to promote relationship health.

METHODOLOGICAL AND CONCEPTUAL ISSUES

Both therapy and prevention research raise some common methodological and conceptual issues such as sampling problems and the outcome criteria used to evaluate intervention success. In this section we discuss what we believe are the most important of these issues.

Outcome Criteria

Both preventive and therapeutic interventions for couples are evaluated by two criteria: measures of relationship quality and stability. If a couple stays together and is satisfied in their relationship, then the intervention is clearly successful. If a couple is dissatisfied, success or failure can be judged by whether they improved from pre- to posttreatment. However, if the relationship dissolves, the intervention is considered a failure. No further assessment is conducted, as there is no longer a relationship to assess.

We are uncomfortable with the unequivocal labeling of relationship dissolution as an intervention failure. In fact, some premarital prevention programs have as an explicit goal helping couples reevaluate their decision to marry (Bagarozzi & Rauen 1981). A divorce, or decision not to marry, may in fact be the best outcome for all parties involved. Thus, it is possible that one marital intervention could lead to fewer divorces than another but at a cost to individual happiness. Even if two interventions lead to an equivalent dissolution rates, one intervention may lead to better individual outcomes for the partners. However, current methods do not provide us with data to make these kinds of conclusions.

We recommend that future intervention research measure individual outcomes, such as individual well-being, social functioning, and psychological symptoms, as well as relationship outcomes. Because of the documented effects of marital discord on children, we recommend that children's individual functioning also be assessed. Finally, we recommend that assessment of individual outcomes continue during follow-up periods even after relationship dissolution. If followed, these recommendations would provide data with which to conduct a more complete evaluation of the positive as well as the negative effects of couple interventions, not just on the relationship itself, but on the individuals directly affected by it.

Long-Term Follow-Up

Researchers clearly need to employ longer-term follow-ups. In prevention research, long-term follow-up is essential to evaluate whether there has been a true prevention effect. Most studies of prevention have been woefully inadequate in that no follow-ups were conducted at all or were extremely short [e.g. an average of 12 weeks in the review by Giblin et al (1985)]. The PREP studies (see Stanley et al 1998) have been unique, with several including follow-ups of 2 years or more posttest. Even with short follow-ups, the effects in prevention research have been found to deteriorate.

Therapy studies have generally done better than prevention studies in assessing follow-up. However, follow-ups are made usually a year or less after treatment, and some provocative studies, reviewed above, have suggested that deterioration may occur a year or more after treatment. We suggest that both prevention and therapy studies should assess outcome for at least 2 years postintervention. Furthermore, we suggest experimentation with booster sessions in both therapy and prevention contexts as a means of maintaining treatment gains over the long term.

Sampling and Selection Effects

Most participants in the research on therapy and prevention programs are white, middle class heterosexual couples recruited through advertisements (Hahlweg & Markman 1988, Baucom et al 1998). Clearly they are not a random sample of the population at large. Even couples who participate in interventions that are not part of a research project may be a highly select group. For example, Sullivan & Bradbury (1997) found that couples who participated in community prevention programs were less at risk for later marital discord than were couples who did not participate. These findings suggest great caution in generalizing our results and point to a pressing need to apply current interventions to a more diverse sample of couples. Along this line, more research on issues related to the marketing of couple interventions would be useful (Roberts & Morris 1998).

Selection is a greater problem for prevention than for therapy research because of the broader reach of prevention. A preventionist may wish to prevent marital problems in the population at large and may envision participation in premarital training as a prerequisite for marriage. In contrast, a therapy researcher is content to ameliorate problems in distressed couples who seek treatment.

Some prevention programs recruit couples for an "enrichment program" (e.g. Brock & Joanning 1983); however, results can then only be generalized to those couples who seek enrichment. Other prevention programs recruit a presumably broader sample of couples for a general study of marriage (e.g. Markman et al 1988), which is then randomly divided into intervention and control conditions. However, some couples assigned to the intervention group choose not to participate in the intervention, raising concerns about the equivalence of control and intervention groups. Moreover, as both types of studies progress, some degree of attrition occurs and often the rate of attrition is greater for the control group than for the intervention group. Couples dropping out of either group may be those who are not functioning well. Because these complex issues have the potential to systematically bias the results of prevention studies, they require greater attention than they have received (see Sayers et al 1998, Stanley 1997). In general, we recommend an intention-to-treat analysis, in which all couples who were assigned to intervention are analyzed, whether they participated, refused treatment, or dropped out (Flick 1988).

Criteria for Empirically Supported Treatments

There is a strong movement within psychology to develop methodological criteria for classifying psychological treatments according to their level of empirical support (Chambless & Hollon 1998). Recently, couple therapies were classified using these criteria (Baucom et al 1998). Although we are strongly supportive of the general effort to base therapy and preventive interventions on a firm empirical foundation, we have a number of concerns about this movement in psychology. First, the criteria as currently set forth say little about the power of treatment. For example, BCT has the highest level of empirical support, but as this review has demonstrated, it is not a particularly powerful treatment for couples. Second, the emphasis in this movement is on type of treatment rather than therapist or couple variables that may account for more of the variance in outcome (Garfield 1998). Third, there may be common factors in all couple therapies, such as the presence of a neutral but involved third party and the provision of a forum for constructive discussion of problems, that outweighs the impact of particular treatment techniques. It would be a sad commentary on this movement toward empirically validated treatments if the emphasis on treatment methods served as a detriment to empirical research on client, therapist, and common factors variables that might be far more influential in outcome than particular treatment methods.

Efficacy Versus Effectiveness Research

There has been considerable discussion and controversy in the clinical literature regarding the distinction between efficacy research, in which treatments are tested under controlled conditions, and effectiveness research, in which treatments are tested under more naturalistic conditions (e.g. Seligman 1995). Efficacy research often involves carefully selected samples, the use of treatment manuals to define procedures, and extensive training and supervision, whereas effectiveness research may involve heterogeneous samples, loosely defined treatments, and no specialized training or supervision. The central issue is the extent to which findings from efficacy research can be generalized to effectiveness contexts.

There are few studies of the effectiveness of couple therapy. In their meta-analysis, Shadish et al (1995) found only one study that compared couples undergoing clinic therapy with couples who went untreated; there were no differences between these conditions. More recently, a *Consumer Reports* survey (Seligman 1995) found that couple therapy was experienced as less effective by their readers than was individual therapy, although in efficacy research, the effect sizes for couple therapy are comparable to those for individual therapy (Hahlweg & Markman 1988). Finally, a recent study of marital counseling agencies in Germany and Austria found lower effect sizes for couple outcomes than are usually found in efficacy studies (Hahlweg & Klann 1997). Clearly, the available research suggests that the findings from efficacy studies cannot be generalized to naturalistic contexts. This should serve as a further caution to prematurely limiting the types of therapies practiced (i.e. empirically validated treatments) based solely on efficacy research.

We do not respond to this situation with a cry for more effectiveness research. From a methodological perspective, effectiveness research is often of poor quality, involving such features as retrospective data, an absence of any randomized comparisons, select samples, or high levels of attrition. We are not certain that more of this kind of data is what the field needs. Rather, along the lines outlined by Jacobson & Christensen (1996), we would like to see clinical trials, with their methodological sophistication, being conducted in more naturalistic settings. As an example, we would point to a study currently being conducted by Markman & Stanley (S Stanley, personal communication). These investigators are undertaking a clinical trial of the PREP program, which has been validated in previous efficacy studies. They are comparing three conditions: (*a*) PREP delivered by the research team, (*b*) PREP delivered by clergy and lay leaders trained by the research team, and (*c*) the church's typical premarital training program. With this design, they will be able to test whether treatment developed in an efficacy context can be transported to the field and is superior to the naturally occurring program. This model of moving from laboratory to field is a useful one for clinical research on couple interventions.

CONCLUSION

There is now a substantial and promising body of evidence that psychological interventions may prevent couple distress or ameliorate it once it occurs. These interventions may also be useful for individual psychopathology, such as depression and alcoholism. Because of the widespread negative impact of relationship conflict and dissolution on both physical and mental health, these interventions could become an important part of health service delivery. Along with the bright promise of couple interventions are its many limitations. Future research needs to address these limitations by reaching a broad, more-diverse sample of couples, by examining interventions in natural settings, by developing more-powerful interventions, and by conducting more-thorough and long-term evaluations of the effects of intervention.

ACKNOWLEDGMENT

This work was supported by NIMH Grant R10 MH56233, which was awarded to the senior author.

Literature Cited

Arnow BA, Taylor CB, Agras WS, Telch MJ. 1985. Enhancing agoraphobia treatment outcome by changing couple communication patterns. *Behav. Ther.* 16:452–67

Avery AW, Ridley CA, Leslie LA, Milholland T. 1980. Relationship enhancement with premarital dyads: a six-month follow-up. *Am. J. Fam. Ther.* 8:23–30

Azrin NH. 1976. Improvements in the community-reinforcement approach to alcoholism. *Behav. Res. Ther.* 14:339–48

Bagarozzi DA, Rauen P. 1981. Premarital counseling: appraisal and status. *Am. J. Fam. Ther.* 9:13–30

Barlow DH, O'Brien GT, Last CG. 1984. Couples treatment of agoraphobia. *Behav. Ther.* 15:41–58

Baucom DH, Epstein N. 1990. *Cognitive Behavioral Marital Therapy.* New York: Brunner/Mazel

Baucom DH, Epstein N, Rankin LA. 1995. Cognitive aspects of cognitive-behavioral marital therapy. See Jacobson & Gurman 1995, pp. 65–90

Baucom DH, Shoham V, Meuser KT, Daiuto AD, Stickle TR. 1998. Empirically supported couple and family interventions for marital distress and adult mental health problems. *J. Consult. Clin. Psychol.* 66:53–88

Beck AT, Rush AJ, Shaw BF, Emery G. 1979. *Cognitive Therapy of Depression.* New York: Guilford

Berger R, Hannah M. 1998. *Handbook of Preventive Approaches in Couple Therapy.* New York: Brunner/Mazel. In press

Bloom BL, Asher SJ, White SW. 1978. Marital disruption as a stressor: a review and analysis. *Psychol. Bull.* 85:867–94

Bowlby J. 1969. *Attachment and Loss,* Vol. 1. *Attachment.* New York: Basic Books

Bradbury TN, Fincham FD. 1990. Preventing marital dysfunction: review and analysis. In *Psychology of Marriage*, ed. FD Fincham, TN Bradbury, pp. 375–401. New York: Guilford. 432 pp.

Brannen SJ, Rubin A. 1996. Comparing the effectiveness of gender-specific and couples groups in a court mandated spouse abuse treatment program. *Res. Soc. Work Pract.* 6:405–24

Brock GW, Joanning H. 1983. A comparison of the Relationship Enhancement Program and the Minnesota Couple Communication Program. *J. Marital Fam. Ther.* 9:413–21

Cascardi M, Langhinrichsen J, Vivian D. 1992. Marital aggression, impact, injury, and health correlates for husbands and wives. *Arch. Intern. Med.* 152:1178–84

Cavedo C, Guerney BG. 1998. Relationship enhancement (RE) enrichment/problem-prevention programs: therapy-derived, powerful, versatile. See Berger & Hannah 1998. In press

Chambless DL, Hollon SD. 1998. Defining empirically supported therapies. *J. Consult. Clin. Psychol.* 66:7–18

Cherlin AJ, Furstenberg FF, Chase-Lansdale PL, Kiernan KE, Robins PK, et al. 1991. Longitudinal studies of effects of divorce on children in Great Britain and the U.S. *Science* 252:1386–89

Christensen A, Jacobson NS, Babcock JC. 1995. Integrative behavioral couple therapy. See Jacobson & Gurman 1995, pp. 31–64

Cobb JP, Mathews AM, Childs-Clarke A, Blowers CM. 1984. The spouse as co-therapist in the treatment of agoraphobia. *Br. J. Psychol.* 144:282–87

Cohen J. 1988. *Statistical Power Analysis for the Behavioral Sciences.* Hillsdale, NJ: Erlbaum

Coie JD, Watt NF, West SG, Hawkins D, Asarnow JR, et al. 1993. The science of prevention: a conceptual framework and some directions for a national research program. *Am. Psychol.* 48:1013–22

Dunn RL, Schwebel AI. 1995. Meta-analytic review of Marital Therapy Outcome Research. *J. Fam. Psychol.* 9:58–68

Ehrensaft MK, Vivian D. 1996. Spouses reasons for not reporting existing marital aggression as a marital problem. *J. Fam. Psychol.* 10:443–53

Emmelkamp PMG, de Hann E, Hoogduin CAL. 1990. Marital adjustment and obsessive-compulsive patients. *Br. J. Psychol.* 156:55–60

Emmelkamp PMG, van Linden van den Heuvell C, Ruphan M, Sanderman R, Scholing

A, Stroink F. 1988. Cognitive and behavioral interventions: a comparative evaluation with cinically distressed couples. *J. Fam. Psychol.* 1:365–77

Ersner-Hershfield R, Kopel S. 1979. Group treatment of preorgasmic women. *J. Consult. Clin. Psychol.* 47:750–59

Flick SN. 1988. Managing attrition in clinical research. *Clin. Psychol. Rev.* 8:499–515

Garfield SL. 1998. Some comments on empirically supported treatments. *J. Consult. Clin. Psychol.* 66:121–25

Giblin P, Sprenkle DH, Sheehan R. 1985. Enrichment outcome research: a meta-analysis of premarital and family interventions. *J. Marital Fam. Ther.* 11:257–71

Gotlib IH, Beach SRH. 1995. A marital/family discord model of depression: implications of therapeutic intervention. See Jacobson & Gurman 1995, pp. 411–10

Greenberg LS, Johnson SM. 1988. Emotionally focused couples therapy. In *Clinical Handbook Marital Therapy,* ed. NS Jacobson, AS Gurman. pp. 253–76. New York: Guilford. 657 pp.

Guerney BG. 1977. *Relationship Enhancement.* San Francisco: Jossey-Bass. 400 pp.

Guerney BG, Maxson P. 1990. Marital and family enrichment: a decade review and look ahead. *J. Marriage Fam.* 52:1127–35

Hahlweg K, Klann N. 1997. The effectiveness of marital counseling in Germany: a contribution to health services research. *J. Fam. Psychol.* 11:410–21

Hahlweg K, Markman HJ. 1988. Effectiveness of behavioral marital therapy: empirical status of behavioral techniques in preventing and alleviating marital distress. *J. Consult. Clin. Psychol.* 56:440–77

Halford KW, Sanders MR, Behrens BC. 1993. A comparision of the genralization of behavioral marital therapy and enhanced behavioral marital therapy. *J. Consult. Clin. Psychol.* 61:51–60

Hawley DR, Olson DH. 1995. Enriching newlyweds: an evaluation of three enrichment programs. *Am. J. Fam. Ther.* 23:129–47

Hawton K. 1995. Treatment of sexual dysfunctions by sex therapy and other approaches. *Br. J. Psychol.* 17:307–14

Hedges LV, Olkin I. 1985. *Statistical Methods for Meta-Analysis.* San Diego, CA: Academic

Hendrick SS. 1997. Dig it, change it, suck it up, or split. *Cont. Psychol.* 43:1097–98

Holtzworth-Munroe A, Markman H, O'Leary KD, Neidig P, Leber D, et al. 1995. The need for marital violence prevention efforts: a behavioral-cognitive secondary prevention program for engaged and newly married couples. *Appl. Prev. Psychol.* 4:77–88

Howe GW, Price RH. 1997. Preventing depression in couples facing job loss. *Multisite NIMH Res. Proj. R10MH52817/ R10MH52913*

Hurlbert DF, White LC, Powell RD, Apt C. 1993. Orgasm consistency training in the treatment of women reporting hypoactive sexual desire: an outcome comparison of women-only groups and couples-only groups. *J. Behav. Ther. Exp. Psychol.* 24: 3–13

Jacob T, Krahn GL. 1988. Marital interactions of alcoholic couples: comparison with depressed and nondistressed couples. *J. Consult. Clin. Psychol.* 56:73–79

Jacobson NS. 1991. Behavioral versus insight-oriented marital therapy: labels can be misleading. *J. Consult. Clin. Psychol.* 59: 142–45

Jacobson NS, Addis ME. 1993. Research on couples and couple therapy: What do we know? *J. Consult. Clin. Psychol.* 61:85–93

Jacobson NS, Christensen A. 1996. *Integrative Couple Therapy.* New York: Norton

Jacobson NS, Dobson K, Fruzzetti AE, Schmaling KB, Salusky S. 1991. Marital therapy as a treatment for depression. *J. Consult. Clin. Psychol.* 59:547–57

Jacobson NS, Follette VM, Follette WC, Holtzworth-Munroe A, Katt JL, Schmaling KB. 1985. A component analysis of behavioral marital therapy: 1 year follow-up. *Behav. Res. Ther.* 23:549–55

Jacobson NS, Follette WC, Revenstorf D, Baucom DH, Hahlweg K, Margolin G. 1984. Variability in outcome and clinical significance of behavioral marital therapy: a reanalysis of outcome data. *J. Consult. Clin. Psychol.* 52:497–504

Jacobson NS, Gottman JM. 1998. *When Men Batter Women.* New York: Simon & Schuster

Jacobson NS, Gurman AS. 1995. *Clinical Handbook of Couple Therapy.* New York: Guilford. 510 pp.

Jacobson NS, Margolin G. 1979. *Marital Therapy: Strategies Based on Social Learning Behavior Exchange Principles.* New York: Brunner/Mazel

Jacobson NS, Schmaling KB, Holtzworth-Munroe A. 1987. Component analysis of behavioral marital therapy: 2-year follow-up and prediction of relapse. *J. Marital Fam. Ther.* 13:187–95

Jacobson NS, Truax P. 1991. Clinical significance: a statistical approach to defining meaningful change in psychotherapy research. *J. Consult. Clin. Psychol.* 58: 12–19

Jessee RE, Guerney BG. 1981. A comparison of gestalt and relationship enhancement treatments with married couples. *Am. J. Fam. Ther.* 9:31–41

Johnson SM, Greenberg LS. 1995. The emotionally focused approach to problems in adult attachment. See Jacobson & Gurman 1995, pp. 121–41

Kiecolt-Glaser JK, Fisher LD, Ogrocki P, Stout JC, Speicher CE, et al. 1987. Marital quality, marital disruptions, and immune function. *Psychosom. Med.* 49:13–34

Locke HJ, Wallace KM. 1959. Short marital adjustment and prediction tests: their reliability and validity. *Marriage Fam. Living* 21:251–55

LoPiccolo J, Lobitz WC. 1972. The role of masturbation in the treatment of orgasmic dysfunction. *Arch. Sex. Behav.* 2:163–71

Markman HJ, Floyd FJ. 1980. Possibilities for the prevention of marital discord: a behavioral perspective. *Am. J. Fam. Ther.* 8:29–48

Markman HJ, Floyd FJ, Stanley SM, Storaasli RD. 1988. Prevention of marital distress: a longitudinal investigation. *J. Consult. Clin. Psychol.* 56:210–17

Markman HJ, Hahlweg K. 1993. The prediction and prevention of marital distress: an international perspective. *Clin. Psychol. Rev.* 13:29–43

Markman HJ, Renick MJ, Floyd FJ, Stanley SM, Clements M. 1993. Preventing marital distress through communication and conflict management training: a 4- and 5-year follow-up. *J. Consult. Clin. Psychol.* 61:70–77

Markman HJ, Stanley SM, Blumber SL. 1994. *Fighting for Your Marriage: Positive Steps for Preventing Divorce and Preserving Lasting Love.* San Francisco: Jossey-Bass

Masters WH, Johnson VE. 1970. *Human Sexual Inadequacy.* Boston: Little Brown

Miklowitz DJ, Goldstein MJ, Neuchterlein KH, Snyder KS, Doane JA. 1988. Family factors and the course of bipolar affective disorder. *Arch. Gen. Psychiatry* 45:225–31

Miller SL, Nunnally EW, Wackman DB. 1976. Minnesota Couples Communication Program: premarital and marital groups. In *Treating Relationships*, ed. DHL Olson, pp. 21–39. Lake Mills, IA: Graphic. 579 pp.

Miller SL, Sherrard PAD. 1998. Couple communication: a system for equipping partners to talk, listen, and resolve conflicts effectively. See Berger & Hannah 1998. In press

Mudd E, Freeman C, Rose E. 1941. Premarital counseling in the Philadelphia Marriage Counsel. *Ment. Hyg.* 10:98–119

Munoz RF, Mrazek PJ, Haggerty RJ. 1996. Institute of medicine report on prevention of mental disorders: summary and commentary. *Am. Psychol.* 51:1116–22

O'Farrell TJ. 1993. A behavioral marital therapy couples' group program for alcoholics and their spouses. In *Treating Alcohol Problems: Marital Family Interventions,* ed. TJ O'Farrell, pp. 170–209. New York: Guilford

O'Leary KD, Beach SRH. 1990. Marital therapy: a viable treatment for depression and marital discord. *Am. J. Psychol.* 147:183–86

O'Leary KD, Vivian D, Malone J. 1992. Assessment of physical aggression in marriage; the need for a multimodal method. *Behav. Assess.* 14:5–14

Renick MJ, Blumberg SL, Markman HJ. 1992. The Prevention and Relationship Enhancement Program (PREP): an empirically based preventive intervention program for couples. *Fam. Relat.* 41:141–47

Roberts LC, Morris ML. 1998. An evaluation of marketing factors in marriage enrichment program promotion. *Fam. Relat.* 47:37–44

Rosen RC, Leiblum SR. 1995. Treatment of sexual disorders in the 1990s: an integrated approach. *J. Consult. Clin. Psychol.* 63:877–90

Rosenthal R, Rubin DB. 1982. A simple, general purpose display of magnitude of experimental effect. *J. Ed. Psychol.* 74:166–69

Russell CS, Bagarozzi DA, Atilano RB, Morris JE. 1984. A comparison of two approaches to marital enrichment and conjugal skills training: Minnesota Couples Communication Program and structured behavior exchange contracting. *Am. J. Fam. Ther.* 12:13–25

Rutledge AL. 1968. An illustrative look at the history of pre-marital counseling. In *Marriage Family Counseling: Perspecitive Prospect,* ed. JA Peterson, pp. 110–29. New York: Association Press. 188 pp.

Sayers SL, Kohn CS, Heavey CL. 1998. Prevention of marital dysfunction: behavioral approaches and beyond. *Clin. Psychol. Rev.* In press

Seligman MEP. 1995. The effectiveness of psychotherapy: the *Consumer Reports* study. *Am. Psychol.* 50:965–74

Shadish WR, Montgomery LM, Wilson P, Wilson MR, Bright I, Okwumabua T. 1993. Effects of family and marital psychotherapies: a meta-analysis. *J. Consult. Clin. Psychol.* 61:992–1002

Shadish WR, Ragsdale R, Glaser RR, Montgomery LM. 1995. The efficacy and effectiveness of marital and family therapy: a persepctive from meta-analysis. *J. Marriage Fam. Ther.* 21:345–60

Snyder DK, Wills RM. 1989. Behavioral versus insight-oriented marital therapy: effects on individual and interspousal functioning. *J. Consult. Clin. Psychol.* 57:39–46

Snyder DK, Wills RM, Grady-Fletcher A. 1991. Long-term effectiveness of behavioral versus insight-oriented marital therapy: a 4-year follow-up study. *J. Consult. Clin. Psychol.* 59:138–41

Spanier GB. 1976. Measuring dyadic adjustment: new scales for assessing the quality of marriage and similar dyads. *J. Marr. Fam.* 38:15–28

Stanley SM. 1997. *Acting on what we know: the hope of prevention*. Presented at Fam. Impact Semin., Washington, DC

Stanley SM, Blumberg SL, Markman HJ. 1998. Helping couples fight for their marriage: the PREP approach. See Berger & Hannah 1998, In press

Stanley SM, Markman HJ. 1997. *Can government rescue marriages?* Univ. Denver, Denver, CO. Unpublished manuscript

Sullivan KT, Bradbury TN. 1997. Are premarital prevention programs reaching couples at risk for marital dysfunction? *J.*

Consult. Clin. Psychol. 65:24–30

Trapp MC, Pace TM, Stoltenberg CD. 1997. Cognitive-behavioral therapy (CBT), integrative couple therapy (ICT), and combined CBT/ICT for the treatment of depression in women who are also maritally distressed. Submitted for publication.

Van Widenfelt B, Hosman C, Schaap C, van der Staak C. 1996. The prevention of relationship distress for couples at risk: a controlled evaluation with nine-month and two-year follow-ups. *Fam. Relat.* 45:156–65

Van Widenfelt B, Markman HJ, Guerney B, Behrens BC, Hosman C. 1997. Prevention of relationship problems. In *Clinical Handbook of Marriage and Couples Interventions*, ed. WK Halford, HJ Markman, pp. 651–75. New York: Wiley

Wampler KS. 1990. An update on research on the Couple Communication Program. *Fam. Sci. Rev.* 3:21–40

Wimberly JD. 1997. *An outcome study of integrative couples therapy delivered in a group format*. PhD thesis. Univ. Montana, Bozeman. 118 pages.

Zimmer D. 1987. Does marital therapy enhance the effectiveness of treatment for sexual dysfunction? *J. Sex Marriage Ther.* 13:193–209

Annu. Rev. Psychol. 1999. 50:191–214

EMOTION

John T. Cacioppo

Department of Psychology, The Ohio State University, Columbus, Ohio 43210-1222;
e-mail: Cacioppo.1@osu.edu

Wendi L. Gardner

Department of Psychology, Northwestern University, Evanston, Illinois 60208-2710;
e-mail: WGardner@nwu.edu

KEY WORDS: affect, evaluation, cognitive appraisal, positivity, negativity

ABSTRACT

We review recent trends and methodological issues in assessing and testing
theories of emotion, and we review evidence that form follows function in
the affect system. Physical limitations constrain behavioral expressions and
incline behavioral predispositions toward a bipolar organization, but these
limiting conditions appear to lose their power at the level of underlying
mechanisms, where a bivalent approach may provide a more comprehensive
account of the affect system.

CONTENTS

INTRODUCTION

Recent research on emotions is almost as vast and diverse as emotional life itself. A literature search limited to the term "emotion" using PsychInfo re-

0084-6570/99/0201-0191$08.00

turned 5064 citations over the past five years, and a comparable search using Medline returned 3542. A *Handbook of Emotions* appeared (Lewis & Haviland 1993) with a second edition already in preparation, journals are now devoted almost exclusively to the topic (e.g. *Cognition and Emotion, Motivation and Emotion*), and numerous textbooks on the topic have surfaced. The swell of interest in emotion continues to ascribe a large role to deliberation and civil discourse. Humans have walked the surface of the earth for about 2,000,000 years, and for all but the last 2000–3000 years humans have been hunter-gatherers. We nevertheless tend to see our distant past "through a reverse telescope that compresses it: a short time as hunter-gatherers, a long time as 'civilized' people" (Ackerman 1990, p. 129). We begin by reviewing recent developments in the study of human emotions. We then consider the general features of an affect system, archaic in some respects, that can be conceived as underlying emotion.

Methodological Developments in the Study of Emotion

The study of emotion has been aided in recent years by the development of standardized stimulus materials and procedures for eliciting emotions, and this continued to be an active area of inquiry in recent years (e.g. see Davidson & Cacioppo 1992, Gerrards-Hesse et al 1994). New developments were seen in stimulus sets consisting of pictures (Lang et al 1995), films (Gross & Levenson 1995, Philippot 1993, Westermann et al 1996), sounds (Bradley et al 1994), words (Bradley et al 1997), and stories, imagery, or social interactions (Westermann et al 1996, Gerrards-Hesse et al 1994).

The measurement of emotions also remained a bustling research area. The interplay among social, cognitive, and biological processes in emotion is becoming increasingly tractable, and emotional phenomena are now fruitfully studied drawing upon theories and methodologies that require collaboration among social, cognitive, developmental, clinical, and neuroscientists. For instance, methods for stereogeometric functional brain imaging and complementary methods for mapping the temporal dynamics of neural processing have become a reality over the past two decades. Positron emission tomography (PET) (e.g. Drevets & Raichle 1995, George et al 1995, Lane et al 1997, Paradiso et al 1997) and functional magnetic resonance imaging (fMRI) (e.g. Grodd et al 1995, Maddock & Buonocore 1997, Lang et al 1998) offer considerable promise in studies of affective processes (cf Fox & Woldorff 1994, Kutas & Federmeier 1998, Sarter et al 1996).

As Kutas & Federmeier note, the temporal resolution of the fMRI is still limited by the fact that the blood flow response typically lags the actual electrical signal by one to two seconds and does not track activity on a millisecond-by-millisecond basis. The temporal resolution of PET is similarly limited. In studies in which higher temporal resolution is required, fMRI or PET studies can be complemented by other measures. Indeed, advances in tracking phasic aspects of emotion were seen in (*a*) event-related brain potential paradigms (Cacioppo et al 1994, Crites et al 1995, Gardner & Cacioppo 1998); (*b*) startle probe methods (Davis 1997, Lang 1995); (*c*) continuous self-report measures (Stayman & Aaker 1993); (*d*) retrospective verbal protocols (Cacioppo et al 1997c, Davison et al 1997, Hurlburt 1997); (*e*) nonverbal pictorial assessment techniques (Bradley & Lang 1994); (*f*) facial electromyography (Tassinary & Cacioppo 1992, Witvliet & Vrana 1995); and (*g*) observational methods of infants (Emde et al 1993) and interactants (Carroll & Russell 1997, Gottman 1993).

Laboratory studies can afford impressive control over relevant variables, an important feature when dissecting phenomena as complex and multiply determined as the emotions. The ecological and external validity of laboratory paradigms and measures can sometimes be uncertain, however. Advances in electronics and statistics have improved the feasibility and methodological sophistication of both ecological momentary assessments (e.g. Diener & Lucas 1998, Larsen 1991, Suls et al 1998) and ambulatory monitoring of affective states (e.g. Guyll & Contrada 1998, Kamarck et al 1998). These assessments introduce their own set of statistical (cf Schwartz & Stone 1998) and methodological problems (e.g. Litt et al 1998) but are noteworthy developments as they should make it possible to identify which laboratory findings generalize to the real world and to improve laboratory models of human emotions. Two additional developments that are needed are: (*a*) programmatic studies of emotion that test specific conceptual hypotheses based on both the internal validity of the laboratory and the external and ecological validity of field sampling methods and ambulatory assessments; and (*b*) greater use of experimental manipulations (e.g. an intervention program) in conjunction with field sampling methods and ambulatory assessments.

There has been no shortage of debates over methods and measures, either. Over the past couple years alone, discussions appeared on topics in a wide range: (*a*) import of linguistic analyses of emotion (e.g. Wierzbicka 1995; cf Forsyth & Eifert 1996); (*b*) the role and limits of self-reports in studies of emotion (Lazarus 1995, Reisenzein 1995, Schwarz & Strack 1998) and moods (Bagozzi 1993, Green et al 1993, Watson & Clark 1997); (*c*) the pancultural agreement in emotion judgments (Ekman 1994, Rosenberg & Ekman 1995, Russell 1994); (*d*) the methodological nuances in research on cerebral asymmetries in emotion (Davidson 1993, Hagemann et al 1998, Reid et al 1998); and (*e*) the nature and existence of basic emotions (Ekman 1992, Izard 1992, Ortony & Turner 1990, Panksepp 1992).

Individual differences in emotional disposition (Davidson 1994, Depue 1996, Gray 1994, Rosenthal 1995, Tangney et al 1995), intensity (e.g. Keltner

& Ekman 1996), and reactivity (e.g. Cacioppo et al 1992, Gilboa & Revelle 1994, Larsen et al 1996) continued to be popular areas of theory and research. Explanations of the origins of the individual differences in emotion have turned in part to studies of socioemotional development, work that now extends across the life span from infancy (e.g. Izard & Ackerman 1997, Nelson & de Haan 1997, Walker-Andrews 1997) through adolescence (Flannery et al 1994) to old age (Carstensen et al 1997, Schulz & Heckhausen 1997). Related reports of the genetic determinants of emotion (e.g. McGuire 1993, Plomin et al 1993) and the universality of emotional expressions (e.g. Averill et al 1994, Ekman & Keltner 1997, Izard 1994) were counterbalanced by studies of cultural determinants (Mesquita et al 1997, Russell 1994). As this work attests, emotion is a short label for a very broad category of experiential, behavioral, sociodevelopmental, and biological phenomena.

The Relation Between Emotion and Cognition

An assumption by rationalists dating back to the ancient Greeks has been that higher forms of human existence—mentation, rationality, foresight, and decision making—can be hijacked by the pirates of emotion. In accordance with the classic assumption that emotion wreaks havoc on human rationality, the emphasis for years in psychology has been on cognition and rationality, and on ways of diminishing the influence of subjectivity and emotion in decision making and behavior. Research with chimpanzees (*Pan troglodytes*) supported the notion that symbolic representations (e.g. arabic numerals) evolved in part to lessen the primal grip of appetitive or aversive stimuli (e.g. candies) on decision making and behavior (Boysen et al 1996). However, emotions are much more than primitive reflexes. The notion that emotions are a disruptive force in rational thought and adaptive action was shown to be a gross oversimplification (e.g. Berntson et al 1993). Although the obstacles of a civilized world still occasionally call forth blind rages, emotions are increasingly recognized for the constructive role they play in higher forms of human experience.

Consider the neurological case of Elliot reported by Damasio (1994). Elliot was a businessman who developed a brain tumor that damaged his prefrontal cortex. Although Elliot began behaving irrationally, testing of Elliot revealed that his intelligence, attention, and memory remained unaffected by his illness. Instead, Elliot had lost the ability to experience emotion; and the lack of emotional guidance rendered decision making a dangerous game of roulette.

The notion that emotion contributes not only to an intelligent but also to a fulfilling life emerged most strikingly in the work on emotional intelligence. The heightened ability to monitor one's own and others' emotions, to discriminate among them, and to use the information to guide one's thinking and action has proven to be as important a determinant of life success as traditional measures of intelligence such as IQ (Goleman 1995, Mayer & Salovey 1993).

Societal changes have also influenced the direction of research on emotions. With rising health costs threatening to ravage families and finances, attention has turned to the role of emotion in cancer progression (Andersen et al 1998, Spiegel 1997), cardiovascular disease (Brezinka & Kittel 1996, Carney et al 1995), respiratory disease (Lehrer et al 1993), infectious illness (Cohen & Rodriguez 1995, Leventhal et al 1997), and immune function (Herbert & Cohen 1993, Kiecolt-Glaser et al 1994, Sternberg 1997). A second societal trend, the dawning of the information age and advances in computer vision, robotics, and telecommunications, has placed a premium on speech and facial recognition and production software. For these programs to be realistic, they must capture the emotion in the message. This need has fueled interest in the acoustic (Murray & Arnott 1993, Pittam & Scherer 1993) and rapid facial signals of emotion (Ekman 1993, Russell & Fernandez-Dols 1997). Although these represent relatively new areas of research, the economic stakes make these likely areas of new developments.

Research over the past two decades on cognition and emotion provides further evidence for the ubiquity of emotion, with the influence of emotion extending to all aspects of cognition and behavior. Perhaps of particular note in recent years are advances in our understanding of the role of emotions in attention and perception (Niedenthal & Kitayama 1994, Zajonc 1998); memory (Bradley et al 1995, Cahill 1996, Phelps & Anderson 1997); psychological defense (Paulhus et al 1997); subjective well-being (e.g. Diener & Suh 1998, Myers 1993); attitudes and persuasion (Cacioppo et al 1992, Chen & Bargh 1998); reasoning and decision making (Forgas 1995, Schwarz & Clore 1996); the meaning of expressive displays (Hess et al 1995, Rosenberg & Ekman 1994); emotional contagion (Hatfield et al 1994, Hietanen et al 1998); interpersonal relationships (Gardner et al 1998, Reis & Patrick 1996); and political information processing (Ottati et al 1992, Way & Masters 1996).

Emotions are also physiological processes and cannot be understood fully without considering the structural and functional aspects of the physical substrates (cf LeDoux 1995). Physiological investigations not only delineate underlying mechanisms but also contribute to better psychological theories by inspiring what is possible (e.g. implicit versus explicit knowledge representations) and by placing constraints on what is plausible (e.g. forward versus backward propagation). The biological (e.g. Boiten et al 1994, Cacioppo et al 1997a, Davidson 1994, Levenson 1996), biochemical (e.g. Rubinow & Schmidt 1996), and neural substrates of emotion (e.g. Damasio 1996, Davis 1997, LeDoux 1995, Neafsey et al 1993), as well as neuropsychological aspects of emotional expressions (Borod et al 1997), continued to be important and active areas of research. For instance, Shizgal (1998), in summarizing research using electrical brain stimulation to probe emotion, stated that in contrast to cognitive (i.e. perceptual and timing) channels, "the evaluative [affective] channel operates without even a pretense of objectivity." He noted that a cool stimulus applied to the skin can be pleasant if one is overheated and unpleasant if one is hypothermic. The affective value of a stimulus, he concluded, depends in part on the prevailing physiological and ecological conditions. Shizgal's (1998) physiological research implies that the brain is organized in part as an affect system, and that the operation of the affect system is not controlled in an absolute fashion by the objective features of a stimulus.

The Relativity of Emotion

The notion that there are absolute features that trigger emotional reactions was further undercut by new evidence that relativity governs the province of emotion. Kahneman and colleagues demonstrated that pain, long a bastion of absolutism, was preferred when its duration was extended while its intensity paled (Kahneman et al 1993). Kahneman and colleagues (e.g. Kahneman 1998) offered the intriguing hypothesis that the affective representation of a complex event varied as a function of the peak experience and the experience at the end of the event (i.e. the peak-end rule).

Schwarz & Strack (1998) noted that most objective life circumstances, even when combined across a dozen domains of life, account for no more than 10% of the variance in measures of subjective well-being. Indeed, they demonstrated that the same event can increase or decrease judgments of subjective well-being depending on its use in construing one's life or its use as a standard. Specifically, Schwarz & Strack (1998) suggested that a contrast effect is likely to occur when an extreme (negative or positive) event is used as a standard against which to compare a stimulus or one's current state, whereas an assimilation effect is more likely when the extreme event is included in the transient representation of the affective event. For example, a moderately negative target stimulus (e.g. an argument with a spouse) is perceived more positively when preceded by the experience of a rare, extremely negative event (e.g. a death in the family) than when not preceded by such an event (Parducci 1995) as long as the preceding event served as a comparison standard rather than as part of the target event.

Yet other ways were discovered in which the determinants of emotion are relative. Brendl & Higgins (1995) reviewed evidence that an incentive is greater when it is compatible with a person's goal (see also Shah et al 1998). Counterfactual thinking, or comparing objective outcomes with imagined outcomes that "might have been," was shown to leave bronze medalists at the 1992 Summer Olympics apparently happier than silver medalists (Medvec et al 1995; see also Roese 1997) even though, by objective standards, an Olympic silver medal is of higher value than a bronze medal. Similarly, stories or confabulations that place an evocative event in a historical context were shown to be as important a determinant of the emotions elicited by the event as the event itself (Harvey et al 1995, Kitayama & Masuda 1995, Traue & Pennebaker 1993). In addition to the perceived valuation of a stimulus or endstate, investigators demonstrated that the rates of movement toward or away from the endstate are important determinants of emotion in and of themselves (Carver & Scheier 1990, Carver et al 1996, Hsee et al 1994).

Research concerning cognitive appraisals represented an especially active area of relativity research, complementing the research that emphasized the features of the emotional eliciting stimulus by focusing upon the relativity of the internal elicitors of the emotional experience. Indeed, more than 100 articles, various books (e.g. Lazarus 1991, Omdahl 1995), and special issues of academic journals (e.g. *Cognition and Emotion, Psychological Inquiry*) were devoted to the topic in recent years. The premise in cognitive appraisal theories is that the appraisal of the significance of a stimulus involves "relational meaning"—the import of an event in conjunction with the conditions present in the environment and personal goals, beliefs, and adaptational resources (Lazarus 1994). Accordingly, universal antecedents are defined in terms of appraisal dimensions rather than stimulus features (e.g. Ellsworth 1994, Frijda 1994). Roseman et al (1996) argued that appraisals of unexpectedness, situational state, motivational state, probability, control potential, problem source, and agency differentiate 17 emotions, whereas in a cross-cultural study Scherer (1997) found that fewer appraisal dimensions of the eliciting event provided a reasonably good account of the major emotion categories (e.g. joy, sadness, fear, anger, disgust, shame, and guilt) (see also Fitness & Fletcher 1993, Frijda 1993, Parkinson & Manstead 1993, Reisenzein & Hofmann 1993, Smith et al 1993). Importantly, suggestive evidence that the unfolding of cognitive appraisals were themselves influenced by subcortical neural structures long associated with emotion emerged from neuropsychological cases such as Scott et al's (1997) report of a patient with lesions of the left and right amygdala (see also Bechara et al 1995, Damasio 1994, Scherer 1993).

Cognitive appraisals may be more important for some types of emotional elicitors than others. In an illustrative line of research summarized by Ohman et al (1998), two types of emotional conditioning were identified. In one type of conditioning, the knowledge that the conditioned stimulus (CS) and unconditioned stimulus (US) are associated in time is explicit (i.e. expectancy-based learning)—that is, autonomic responses occur on the same trials on which subjects develop the expectancy that the CS is followed by the US. This learning does not require an aversive US (Hamm & Vaitl 1996), is accessible to consciousness, and modifies responses related to orienting responses (LeDoux 1995, Ohman et al 1998). In a second type of visceral conditioning, the knowledge that the CS and US are associated in time is implicit (Ohman et al 1998). This learning appears most reliably when an aversive US is combined with a fear-relevant CS (e.g. snake, angry facial display), results in an enhanced startle response and tachycardia, is relatively resistant to extinction, and, although not dependent on conscious awareness of the CS-US contingency, it modifies the perceived valence of the CS as revealed by ratings (Davey 1992, Schell et al 1991, see Ohman 1993). The hippocampus appears to be especially important in the explicit learning of emotional expectancies, whereas the amygdala appears especially important in the implicit emotional conditioning. For instance, Bechara et al (1995) found that two patients with bilateral lesions of the amygdala learned the conditioning contingencies but did not acquire conditioned skin conductance responses in aversive conditioning paradigms. Patients with bilateral hippocampal damage, in contrast, failed to learn the conditioning contingencies but acquired conditioned skin conductance responses. Together, these studies suggest that cognitive appraisals may play a more important causal role in human autonomic conditioning based on explicit than implicit knowledge (LeDoux 1995, Ohman et al 1998).

Classical conditioning has traditionally provided a valuable paradigm for studying behavioral preference in nonvertebrates and nonprimates, and more contemporaneously it has been used to examine the mechanisms underlying the learning and memory of affective associations. The evolutionary advantage is obvious; recognizing the neutral trappings of a predator as a danger signal allows organisms to avoid becoming a meal. Additional evidence for the special status accorded to motivationally significant stimuli can be found in research on orienting responses. Orienting responses to threat-related stimuli are found whether the stimuli are masked or not, whereas orienting responses to neutral stimuli are found for unmasked but not masked stimuli (Dimberg & Ohman 1996, Ohman 1993). According to Ohman's theory of the orienting response, evolution has sculpted perceptual and attentional systems to provide preferential access to those classes of stimuli with adaptive significance for organisms (Ohman et al 1998). Based on comparative data, Hunt & Campbell (1997) have further suggested that orienting responses to neutral stimuli may have evolved from earlier, more motivationally basic responses, answering the questions "Is it dangerous?" or "Is it food?" rather than the "What is it?" response posited by Pavlov.

THE AFFECT SYSTEM UNDERLYING EMOTION

Evolutionary forces do not value knowledge or truth per se but species survival. Hunt & Campbell's provocative proposition underscores the primeval importance of a system that differentiates between hostile and hospitable stimuli (1997). The human brain and body have been shaped by natural selection to perform this affective categorization and to respond accordingly. Affective categorizations and responses are so critical that organisms have rudimentary reflexes for categorizing and approaching or withdrawing from certain classes of stimuli and for providing metabolic support for these actions (Davis 1997, LeDoux 1995). These rudimentary processes are evident in humans as well, but a remarkable feature of humans is the extent to which the affective categorizations are shaped by learning and cognition (Berntson et al 1993, Kahneman et al 1998). As various authors have noted, an additional adaptive advantage is conferred to species whose individual members have the capacity to learn based on the unique environmental contingencies to which they are exposed, to represent and predict events in their environment, to manipulate and plan based on representations, and to exert some control over their attentional and cognitive resources.

Zajonc's influential paper "Preferences Need No Inferences" underscored the utility of the affect system as an object of study (1980). Evidence that the neural circuitry involved in computing the affective significance of a stimulus (i.e. evaluative processing) diverges at least in part from the circuitry involved in identification and discrimination (i.e. nonevaluative processing) was provided by Shizgal (1998) in a series of studies involving brain stimulation in rats and by Cacioppo and colleagues (Cacioppo et al 1996, Crites & Cacioppo 1996) in a series of studies of ERP topographies in humans. For instance, investigations of the spatial distribution of late positive potentials across the scalp have revealed a relatively symmetrical distribution during nonaffective categorizations, whereas the spatial distribution of the late positive potentials associated with affective categorizations were more right lateralized (Cacioppo et al 1996). This asymmetrical activation is consistent with the importance of the right hemisphere in emotion (see Tucker & Frederick 1989). Furthermore, the similarities in ERP topographies indicate that affective and non-affective appraisals are not entirely different but rather rely on a number of common information-processing operations.

In the last chapter on emotion in the *Annual Review of Psychology*, LeDoux covered in detail some of the neural substrates of the affect system (1995). Here, therefore, we focus on the structure and operating characteristics of the affect system.

Operating Characteristics of the Affect System

Stimuli and events in the world are diverse, complex, multidimensional—in short, seemingly incomparable. Yet each perceptual system has evolved to be tuned to specific features, resulting in the expression of these stimuli on a common metric (Tooby & Cosmides 1990). Seemingly incomparable stimuli and events can also be conceived as being expressed on common *motivational* metrics (Cacioppo & Berntson 1994, Lang 1995, Shizgal 1998). As Ohman et al note, "Evolution has primed organisms to be responsive to stimuli that more or less directly are related to the overall task of promoting one's genes to prosper in subsequent generations. . ... Stimuli of these types are embedded within emotional systems that help regulate behavior within critical functional domain" (Ohman et al 1998).

Information is lost in translating a multidimensional representation of a stimulus onto a common motivational metric (i.e. a currency function). However, as Shizgal states, "the information lost due to the collapsing of multiple dimensions is essential for identifying the stimulus and distinguishing it from others. . ..The circuitry that computes instantaneous utility must diverge from the perceptual circuitry subserving identification and discrimination" (Shizgal 1998). As noted above, there is now considerable evidence for differences in the circuitry in affective processing versus the processes of identification and discrimination.

From classical learning theory came the principle that motivational strength increases as the distance from a desired or undesired endstate decreases. Currency functions, in essence, represent the activation function for motivational strength. Perceptual activation functions tend to be negatively accelerating, and this appears to describe the activation function for emotion as well (Boysen et al 1996, Kemp et al 1995). For example, Boysen et al (1996) demonstrated that, for chimpanzees judging the differential incentive values of candy arrays, the relative effectiveness of a given increment in payoff diminished as the base size of the payoff increased. The activation function for affective responses is thus reminiscent of microeconomic marginal utility functions.

Stages and Channels of Evaluative Processing

One distinction Shizgal (1998) made between the evaluative (affective) and perceptual channels is that the former is constructed not to return objective properties of the stimulus but to provide a subjective estimate of the current significance of these properties. How many evaluative channels are there? Most have posited one in which subjective, valent information is derived from the flow of sensation (e.g. Green et al 1993). Studies of the conceptual organization of emotion, for instance, suggest that people's knowledge about emotions is hierarchically organized and that a superordinate division is between positivity and negativity (e.g. Lang et al 1990).

One reason underlying this superordinate division in emotional knowledge may be that physical constraints restrict behavioral manifestations to bivalent actions (approach/withdrawal). Evolution favors the organism that can learn, represent, and access rapidly whether approach or withdrawal is adaptive when confronted by a stimulus. Accordingly, mental guides for one's actions in future encounters with the target stimuli—attitudes (e.g. Cacioppo & Berntson 1994), preferences (e.g. Kahneman 1998), and conceptual organizations of emotion (e.g. Ortony et al 1988)—also tend to be more expected and stable when organized in terms of a bipolar evaluative dimension (ranging from very good and not at all bad to very bad and not at all good).

Physical limitations may constrain behavioral expressions and incline behavioral guides toward bipolar (good/bad; approach/withdraw) dispositions,
but these constraints do not have the same force at the level of underlying
mechanism. That is, the fact that approach and withdrawal tend to be reciprocally activated behavioral manifestations does not mean that they were derived
from a single bipolar evaluative channel; it only means that the outputs of all of
the evaluative processors comprising the affect system are combined in order
to compute preference and organize action. Various theorists have posited
that the module in the affect system that computes attitudes, preferences, and
actions derives input from at least two specialized evaluative channels that
process information in parallel—one in which threat-related (i.e. negative) information is derived from the flow of sensation and a second in which safety
and appetitive (i.e. positive) information is derived (e.g. Cacioppo et al 1998a,
Gilbert 1993, Lang et al 1990, Marcus & Mackuen 1993, Watson & Clark
1992, Zautra et al 1997).

According to the model of evaluative space (Cacioppo & Berntson 1994,
Cacioppo et al 1997b), the common metric governing approach/withdrawal is
a single dimension at response stages but is the consequence of two intervening metrics (i.e. evaluative channels)—the activation function for positivity
and the activation function for negativity—at the inaugural affective processing stages. Further, multiple modes of activation are posited to exist for the two
evaluative channels: (a) reciprocal activation occurs when a stimulus has opposing effects on the activation of positivity and negativity; (b) uncoupled activation occurs when a stimulus affects only positive or only negative evaluative activation; and (c) nonreciprocal activation occurs when a stimulus increases (or decreases) the activation of both positivity and negativity. This
model thus does not reject the reciprocal activation that is assumed in subjective reports of affect, and demanded in behavioral manifestations of affect, but
rather subsumes it as one of the possible modes of activation and explores the
antecedents for each mode of evaluative activation.

Evidence for the existence of multiple modes of evaluative activation has
been observed across all levels of analysis (cf Cacioppo & Berntson 1994). For
instance, Hoebel (1998) reviewed evidence that whereas morphine has reciprocal effects on neurochemical processes underlying approach and withdrawal behavior, food restriction alters neurochemical effects underlying approach behavior in an uncoupled fashion. At the verbal level, Goldstein & Strube (1994)
demonstrated the uncoupled activation of positivity and negativity in affective
reports collected from students at the beginning and end of three consecutive
class periods. The intensity of positive and negative reactions on any particular
day were found to be uncorrelated. Moreover, exam feedback activated positivity and negativity differently. Students who performed well on an exam showed
an increase in positive affect relative to their beginning-of-class level, whereas

their level of negative affect remained unchanged; and students who performed poorly showed an increase in negative affect but no change in positive affect.

Such distinctions between positive and negative affective processes have also been observed in (*a*) uplifts and hassles (Gannon et al 1992, Zautra et al 1990); (*b*) mood states (Lawton et al 1992, Zautra et al 1997); (*c*) organization of self-knowledge (e.g. Showers 1995, Showers & Kling 1996); (*d*) self-regulatory focus (e.g. Higgins 1997); (*e*) self-efficacy (Zautra et al 1997); (*f*) personality processes (Robinson-Whelen et al 1997, Rusting & Larsen 1998, Watson et al 1992); (*g*) achievement motivations (Elliot & Church 1997, Elliot & Harackiewicz 1996); (*h*) attitudes and persuasion (Cacioppo & Berntson 1994); (*i*) emotional expressivity (Gross & John 1997); (*j*) social interactions (Berry & Hansen 1996, Cacioppo et al 1997b); (*k*) affect toward political leaders (Marcus & Mackuen 1993); and (*l*) intergroup discrimination (Blanz et al 1997, Brewer 1996).

However, Green et al (1993) questioned the notion that positive and negative affect were separable on methodological grounds (see also Bagozzi 1993, Marsh 1996). Specifically, they argued that measures of affect typically rely on similarly worded scales with identical endpoints. This feature, they argued, can lead to positively correlated measurement error effectively suppressing the magnitude of the true negative correlation between positive and negative affective states. Thompson et al (1995), in contrast, suggested that methodological artifacts (e.g. carryover between unipolar positive and negative rating scales) could instead inflate the negative correlation between positive and negative rating scales, and they recommended segregating self-report measures of positive and negative affect to avoid self-presentational biases.

A recent investigation by Nelson (1998) addressed these methodological concerns and found evidence for the operation of multiple modes of evaluative activation. Nelson (1998) used a structural modeling approach to examine the structure of affect toward two different social categories—African Americans and the poor—while accounting for correlated measurement error among the observed variables. Nelson's analyses of the structure of the emotional responses toward the poor revealed substantial independence between positive and negative factors. This two-factor model was significantly better than the bipolar model even when the effects of correlated measurement error were extracted. This result is precisely what would be expected if positive and negative affect were separate dimensions at a basic level. Nelson's analyses of the structure of students' emotional responses toward African Americans, however, revealed a bipolar model to be sufficient when the effects of correlated measurement error were considered. This latter result illustrates that affect is not invariably organized in a bipolar *or* a bivariate structure but rather the structure of affective response is influenced by the mode of evaluative activation elicited by the stimulus (Cacioppo & Berntson 1994).

Methodological issues are important to consider, but assuming that the affect system consists only of a single bipolar evaluative channel can also be costly in terms of the fertile avenues of research it precludes. Brain imaging studies, for instance, have tended to contrast positive and negative states, a procedure that impedes the differentiation of the conditions in which positive and negative processes are separable. This may be unwise because, although preliminary at this juncture, some brain imaging studies suggest that different neural structures may be involved in positive and negative hedonic processes. George et al, for instance, used PET during the recall of happy, sad, or neutral memories while viewing congruent happy, sad, or neutral faces (George et al 1995). Comparisons between the sadness-minus-neutral and the happy-minus-neutral conditions revealed that, rather than reciprocal changes in blood flow to the same brain regions, a change from sad to happy affective state produced increased cerebral blood flow to distinguishable brain regions (see also Lane et al 1997).

Research on cortical asymmetry is also consistent with the notion of specialized evaluative channels for the processing of positive and negative information that are subsequently integrated in the production of an affective response (e.g. Davidson 1993, Davidson et al 1990). In a study by Sutton & Davidson, for instance, resting EEG asymmetries were compared with scores on Carver & White's Behavioral Approach System/Behavioral Inhibition System measure, a self-report instrument designed to assess individual differences in the tendency to approach or withdraw and to experience concomitant affective states (Sutton & Davidson 1997, Carver & White 1994). Consistent with the notion that positivity and negativity are separable systems differentially associated with left and right hemispheric activation, respectively, greater relative left asymmetry at midfrontal electrode sites was positively correlated with behavioral activation system scores and negatively correlated with behavioral inhibition system scores. Similarly, studies using computerized tomography to investigate the relationship between the location of stroke-related lesions and affective symptoms showed that the severity of post-stroke depression was positively related to lesion proximity to the left frontal pole but negatively related to lesion proximity to the right frontal pole (Robinson & Downhill 1995). Robinson and colleagues further observed that patients with right lateralized infarctions were more likely than their left-hemisphere–lesioned counterparts to display inappropriate cheerfulness.

The evidence for the separability of positive and negative evaluative processes becomes more controversial when one turns to the literature on the conceptual organization of moods, affect, and emotion. Among the best known research bearing on the centrality of people's net positive and negative feelings is Osgood et al's classic work on the measurement of meaning (1957). In multiple studies and cultures, evaluative bipolar word pairs (e.g. pleasant-unpleasant) were found to comprise a fundamental dimension underlying people's understanding of the world. Conceptually similar results have been found in crosscultural, multidimensional scaling studies of emotional feelings (e.g. Bradley & Lang 1994, Larsen & Diener 1992) and in crosscultural ratings of emotionally evocative pictures (e.g. Lang et al 1995). Thus, the two-dimensional representation that best represents people's conceptual organization of affect and emotion may tend to be positive/negative X active/inactive rather than positive/nonpositive X negative/non-negative. Given that psychological states such as conflict, ambivalence, and inconsistency among beliefs about an attitude object tend to be unexpected, nonharmonious, and unstable, people's conceptual organization of evaluative processes and affective states (e.g. moods) may tend toward a bipolar structure because of the operation of motives to maintain a simple and psychologically consistent representation of the world.

In sum, the common metric governing approach/withdrawal can perhaps be best conceptualized as a single dimension at response stages with the bivalent affective response the consequence of two intervening evaluative channels, one for positivity (appetition) and one for negativity (aversion). Consistent with the notion that input from these evaluative channels is combined with antagonistic effects on action dispositions and behavior, a bivalent organization of affect is more likely to be observed as one moves down the neuraxis (see Berntson et al 1993, Cacioppo et al 1998). For instance, relative to neutral states, negative states tend to potentiate startle eyeblink whereas positive states tend to inhibit it (see reviews by Filion et al 1998, Lang et al 1990) because of the modulating effects of the amygdala (Davis 1997, Lang 1995).

The value of considering the additional complexities introduced by multiple evaluative channels and modes of evaluative activation derives not only from the data it explains but also from the questions it generates and the bridges it builds across data previously thought to be separate. Research in areas of inquiry as distinct as coping in chronic pain patients (Zautra et al 1995), classroom performance and academic motivation (Elliot & Church 1997), frequency and quality of social interactions (Berry & Hansen 1996), blood and organ donation (Cacioppo & Gardner 1993), and racial prejudice (Schofield 1991) all support the wisdom of considering the two motivational systems as functionally separable.

The partial segregation of the positive and negative evaluative channels in the affect system not only confers an additional flexibility of orchestrating appetitive and aversive motivational forces via modes of evaluative activation, but also affords evolution the opportunity to sculpt distinctive activation (i.e. currency) functions for positivity and negativity. Interest in differences in the effects of positive versus negative information has grown substantially in recent years. Not only have numerous articles and several major reviews on the topic appeared (e.g. Cacioppo & Berntson 1994, Levy 1992, Peeters & Czapinski 1990, Skowronski & Carlston 1989, Taylor 1991) but two issues of the *European Journal of Social Psychology* are devoted to the topic. The extant data suggest at least two differences in these currency functions: (*a*) a positivity offset—the output of positivity is higher than the output of negativity at very low levels of affective input; and (*b*) a negativity bias—the increase in output per quantum of input is greater for negativity than positivity (see Cacioppo et al 1998).

POSITIVITY OFFSET   The positivity offset is the tendency for there to be a weak positive (approach) motivational output at zero input, an intercept difference in the affective system. As a consequence of the positivity offset, the motivation to approach is stronger than the motivation to avoid at low levels of evaluative activation (e.g. at distances far from a goal). What might be the possible evolutionary significance of the positivity offset? Without a positivity offset, an organism in a neutral environment may be unmotivated to approach novel objects, stimuli, or contexts. Such organisms would learn little about novel or neutral-appearing environments and their potential value or threat. With a positivity offset, however, an organism facing neutral or unfamiliar stimuli would be weakly motivated to engage in exploratory behavior. Such a tendency may have important survival value, at least at the level of a species.

How might this evolutionarily endowed tendency manifest itself in the present day? One line of evidence may be the prevalence of "unrealistic optimism," the tendency to expect generally positive outcomes for unknown future events (Brinthaupt et al 1991, Hoorens & Buunk 1993, Pulford & Colman 1996, Regan et al 1995). A second line of evidence may be the robust "positivity bias" found in impressions of neutral, unknown, or ambiguous human and nonhuman targets (Klar & Giladi 1997, Sears 1983, Peeters 1991). Finally, research concerning the "mere exposure" effect demonstrates that affectively neutral stimuli may be evaluated positively even when presented outside of conscious awareness (Bornstein 1989, Harmon-Jones & Allan 1998). These lines of research support the existence of a positivity offset in a myriad of domains; when asked to evaluate stimuli or situations that by objective standards should be affectively neutral (e.g. the unknowable future, the "average" person, an unfamiliar Chinese idiogram), people show a consistent tendency to respond in a mildly positive fashion.

NEGATIVITY BIAS   Exploratory behavior can provide useful information about an organism's environment, but exploration can also place an organism in proximity to hostile stimuli. Because it is more difficult to reverse the consequences of an injurious or fatal assault than those of an opportunity unpursued, the process of natural selection may also have resulted in the propensity to react more strongly to negative than to positive stimuli. Termed the negativity bias, this heightened sensitivity to negative information is a robust psychological phenomenon (see reviews by Cacioppo & Berntson 1994, Cacioppo et al 1997b, Peeters & Czapinski 1990, Taylor 1991).

Miller's research on rodent behavior provided some of the earliest evidence for a negativity bias through determining that the slope for the avoidance gradient was steeper than the slope for the approach gradient (Miller 1961). Forty years later, evidence supporting a negativity bias has been found in domains as varied as impression formation (e.g. Skowronski & Carlston 1989), person memory (e.g. Ybarra & Stephan 1996), blood and organ donation (e.g. Cacioppo & Gardner 1993), hiring decisions (e.g. Rowe 1989), personnel evaluations (e.g. Ganzach 1995), and voting behavior (e.g. Klein 1991, 1996). It has been found to characterize the judgments of children as well as adults (e.g. Aloise 1993, Robinson-Whelen et al 1997). Taylor summarized a wide range of evidence showing that negative events in a context evoke stronger and more rapid physiological, cognitive, emotional, and social responses than neutral or positive events (Taylor 1991; see also Westermann et al 1996). As further evidence, Ito et al (1998) have recently uncovered ERP evidence consistent with a negativity bias in the affect system.

In sum, negative emotion has been depicted previously as playing a fundamental role in calibrating psychological systems; it serves as a call for mental or behavioral adjustment. Positive emotion, in contrast, serves as a cue to stay the course or as a cue to explore the environment. This characterization may help account for evolutionary forces sculpting distinctive activation functions for positive and negative affect; the separable activation functions serve as complementary, adaptive motivational organization. Species with a positivity offset *and* a negativity bias enjoy the benefits of exploratory behavior and the self-preservative benefits of a predisposition to avoid or withdraw from threatening events. The features reviewed in this section represent only the rudimentary operations of an affect system, however. Work on the relativity of emotion shows that cognitive factors and physiological states affect the extent to which appetitive or defensive motivations are aroused, and recent work suggests that self-regulatory focus also influences approach and withdrawal gradients (Carver & Scheier 1990, Higgins 1997, Shah et al 1998). The organization of the affect system warrants further study as a reflection of our evolutionary heritage and as a continued force in the shaping of even our most civilized responses.

Literature Cited

Ackerman D. 1990. *A Natural History of the Senses.* New York: Vintage Books

Aloise PA. 1993. Trait confirmation and disconfirmation: the development of attribution biases. *J. Exp. Child Psychol.* 55: 177–93

Andersen BL, Farrar WB, Golden-Kreutz D, Kutz LA, MacCallum R, et al. 1998. Stress and immune responses after surgical treatment for regional breast cancer. *J. Natl. Cancer Inst.* 90:30–36

Averill JR, Ekman P, Ellsworth PC, Frijda NH, Lazarus R, et al. 1994. *How is Evidence of Universals in Antecedents of Emotion Explained?* New York: Oxford Univ. Press

Bagozzi RP. 1993. An examination of the psychometric properties of measures of negative affect in the PANAS-X scales. *J. Pers. Soc. Psychol.* 65:836–51

Bechara A, Tranel D, Damasio H, Adolphs R, Rockland C, Damasio AR. 1995. Double dissociation of conditioning and declarative knowledge relative to the amygdala and hippocampus in humans. *Science* 269: 1115–18

Berntson GG, Boysen ST, Cacioppo JT. 1993. Neurobehavioral organization and the cardinal principle of evaluative bivalence. *Ann. NY Acad. Sci.* 702:75–102

Berry DS, Hansen JS. 1996. Positive affect, negative affect, and social interaction. *J. Pers. Soc. Psychol.* 71:796–809

Blanz M, Mummendey A, Otten S. 1997. Normative evaluations and frequency expectations regarding positive versus negative outcome allocations between groups. *Eur. J. Soc. Psychol.* 27:165–76

Boiten FA, Frijda NH, Wientjes CJE. 1994. Emotions and respiratory patterns: review and critical analysis. *Int. J. Psychophys.* 17:103–28

Bornstein RF. 1989. Exposure and affect: overview and meta-analysis of research, 1968–1987. *Psychol. Bull.* 106:265–89

Borod JC, Haywood CS, Koff E. 1997. Neuropsychological aspects of facial asymmetry during emotional expression: a review of the normal adult literature. *Neuropsychol. Rev.* 7:41–60

Boysen ST, Berntson GG, Hannan MB, Cacioppo JT. 1996. Quantity-based choices: interference and symbolic representations in chimpanzees (*Pan troglodytes*). *J. Exp. Psychol. Anim. Behav. Proc.* 22:76–86

Bradley BP, Mogg K, Williams R. 1995. Implicit and explicit memory for emotion-congruent information in clinical depression and anxiety. *Behav. Res. Ther.* 33: 755–70

Bradley MM, Lang PJ. 1994. Measuring emotion: the self-assessment manikin and the semantic differential. *J. Behav. Ther. Exp. Psychiatry* 25:49–59

Bradley MM, Lang PJ, Cuthbert BN. 1997. *Affective Norms for English Words (ANEW).* NIMH Cent. Stud. Emot. Atten., Univ. FL

Bradley MM, Zack J, Lang PJ. 1994. Cries, screams, and shouts of joy: affective responses to environmental sounds. *Psychophysiology* 31:S29

Brendl CM, Higgins ET. 1995. Principles of judging valence: what makes events positive or negative? *Adv. Exp. Soc. Psychol.* 28:95–160

Brewer MB. 1996. In-group favoritism: the subtle side of intergroup discrimination. In *Codes of Conduct: Behavioral Research Into Business Ethics,* ed. DM Messick, AE Tenbrunsel, pp. 160–70. New York: Russell Sage Found.

Brezinka V, Kittel F. 1996. Psychosocial factors of coronary heart disease in women: a review. *Soc. Sci. Med.* 42:1351–65

Brinthaupt LJ, Moreland RL, Levine JM. 1991. Sources of optimism among prospective group members. *Pers. Soc. Psychol. Bull.* 17:36–43

Cacioppo JT, Berntson GG. 1994. Relationship between attitudes and evaluative space: a critical review, with emphasis on the separability of positive and negative substrates. *Psychol. Bull.* 115:401–23

Cacioppo JT, Berntson GG, Klein DJ, Poehlmann KM. 1997a. The psychophysiology of emotion across the lifespan. *Annu. Rev. Gerontol. Geriatr.* 17:27–74

Cacioppo JT, Crites SL Jr, Gardner WL. 1996. Attitudes to the right: evaluative processing is associated with lateralized late positive event-related brain potentials. *Pers. Soc. Psychol. Bull.* 22:1205–19

Cacioppo JT, Crites SL Jr, Gardner WL, Berntson GG. 1994. Bioelectrical echoes from evaluative categorizations. I. A late positive brain potential that varies as a function of trait negativity and extremity. *J. Pers. Soc. Psychol.* 67:115–25

Cacioppo JT, Gardner WL. 1993. What underlies medical donor attitudes and behavior? *Health Psychol.* 12:269–71

Cacioppo JT, Gardner WL, Berntson GG. 1997b. Beyond bipolar conceptualizations and measures: the case of attitudes and evaluative space. *Pers. Soc. Psychol. Rev.* 1:3–25

Cacioppo JT, Gardner WL, Berntson GG. 1998a. The affect system: form follows function. *J. Pers. Soc. Psychol.* In press

Cacioppo JT, Marshall-Goodell BS, Tassinary LG, Petty RE. 1992. Rudimentary determinants of attitudes: classical conditioning is more effective when prior knowledge about the attitude stimulus is low than high. *J. Exp. Soc. Psychol.* 28:207–33

Cacioppo JT, Tassinary LG, Berntson GG, ed 1998b. *The Handbook of Psychophysiology.* New York: Cambridge Univ. Press. In press

Cacioppo JT, Uchino BN, Crites SL Jr, Snydersmith MA, Smith G, et al. 1992. Relationship between facial expressiveness and sympathetic activation in emotion: a critical review, with emphasis on modeling underlying mechanisms and individual differences. *J. Pers. Soc. Psychol.* 62: 110–28

Cacioppo JT, von Hippel W, Ernst JM. 1997c. Mapping cognitive structures and processes through verbal content: the thought-listing technique. *J. Consult. Clin. Psychol.* 65:928–40

Cahill L. 1996. Neurobiology of memory for emotional events: converging evidence from infra-human and human studies. *Cold Spring Harbor Symp. Quant. Biol.* 61:259–64

Carney RM, Rich MW, Jaffe AS. 1995. Depression as a risk factor for cardiac events in established coronary heart disease: a review of possible mechanisms. *Ann. Behav. Med.* 17:142–49

Carroll JM, Russell JA. 1997. Facial expressions in Hollywood's portrayal of emotion. *J. Pers. Soc. Psychol.* 72:164–76

Carstensen L, Gross J, Fung H. 1997. The social context of emotional experience. *Annu. Rev. Gerontol. Geriatr.* 17:325–52

Carver CS, Scheier MF. 1990. Origins and functions of positive and negative affect: a control-process view. *Psychol. Rev.* 97: 19–35

Carver CS, Lawrence JW, Scheier ME. 1996. A control-process perspective on the origins of affect. In *Striving and Feeling: Interactions Among Goals, Affect, and Self-Regulation,* ed. LL Martin, A Tesser, pp. 11–52. Mahwah, NJ: Erlbaum

Carver CS, White TL. 1994. Behavioral inhibition, behavioral activation, and affective responses to impending reward and punishment: the BIS/BAS scales. *J. Pers. Soc. Psychol.* 67:319–33

Chen M, Bargh JA. 1998. Motivational and emotional consequences of automatic evaluation. *Pers. Soc. Psychol. Bull.* In press

Cohen S, Rodriguez MS. 1995. Pathways link-ing affective disturbances and physical disorders. *Health Psychol.* 14:374–80

Crites SL Jr, Cacioppo JT. 1996. Electrocortical differentiation of evaluative and non-evaluative categorizations. *Psychol. Sci.* 7: 318–21

Crites SL Jr, Cacioppo JT, Gardner WL, Berntson GG. 1995. Bioelectrical echoes from evaluative categorizations. II. A late positive brain potential that varies as a function of attitude registration rather than attitude report. *J. Pers. Soc. Psychol.* 68: 997–1013

Damasio AR. 1994. *Descartes' Error: Emotion, Reason, and the Human Brain.* New York: Grossett/Putnam & Sons

Damasio AR. 1996. The somatic marker hypothesis and the possible functions of the prefrontal cortex. *Philos. Trans. R. Soc. London Ser. B* 351:1413–20

Davey GC. 1992. An expectancy model of laboratory preparedness effects. *J. Exp. Psychol. Gen.* 121:24–40

Davidson RJ. 1993. Parsing affective space: perspectives from neuropsychology and psychophysiology. *Neuropsychology* 7: 464–75

Davidson RJ. 1994. Honoring biology in the study of affective style. See Ekman & Davidson 1994, pp. 321–28

Davidson RJ. 1998. Anterior electrophysiological asymmetries, emotion and depression: conceptual and methodological conundrums. *Psychophysiology.* In press

Davidson RJ, Cacioppo JT. 1992. New developments in the scientific study of emotion. *Psychol. Sci.* 3:21–22

Davidson RJ, Ekman P, Saron CD, Senulis JA, Friesen WV. 1990. Approach-withdrawal and cerebral asymmetry: emotional expression and brain physiology. *J. Pers. Soc. Psychol.* 58:330–41

Davis M. 1997. The neurophysiological basis of acoustic startle modulation: research on fear motivation and sensory gating. In *Attention and Orienting,* ed. PJ Lang, RF Simons, M Balaban, pp. 69–96. Mahwah, NJ: Erlbaum

Davison GC, Vogel RS, Coffman SG. 1997. Think-aloud approaches to cognitive assessment and the articulated thoughts in simulated situations paradigm. *J. Consult. Clin. Psychol.* 65:950–58

Depue RA. 1996. A neurobiological framework for the structure of personality and emotion: implications for personality disorders. In *Major Theories of Personality Disorder,* ed. JF Clarkin, MF Lenzenweger, pp. 347–90. New York: Guilford

Diener E, Lucas RE. 1998. Personality and

subjective well-being. See Kahneman et al 1998. In press

Diener E, Suh E. 1998. National differences in subjective well-being. See Kahneman et al 1998. In press

Dimberg U, Ohman A. 1996. Behold the wrath: psychophysiological responses to facial stimuli. *Motiv. Emot.* 20:149–82

Drevets WC, Raichle ME. 1995. Positron emission tomographic imaging studies of human emotional disorders. In *The Cognitive Neurosciences,* ed. MS Gazzaniga, pp. 1153–64. Cambridge, MA: MIT Press

Ekman P. 1992. Are there basic emotions? *Psychol. Rev.* 99:550–53

Ekman P. 1993. Facial expression and emotion. *Am. Psychol.* 48:384–92

Ekman P. 1994. Strong evidence for universals in facial expressions: a reply to Russell's mistaken critique. *Psychol. Bull.* 115:268–87

Ekman P, Davidson RJ, eds. 1994. *The Nature of Emotion: Fundamental Questions.* New York: Oxford Univ. Press

Ekman P, Keltner D. 1997. Universal facial expressions of emotion: an old controversy and new findings. In *Nonverbal Communication: Where Nature Meets Culture.* ed. UC Segerstrale, P Molnar, pp. 27–46. Mahwah, NJ: Erlbaum

Elliot AJ, Church MA. 1997. A hierarchical model of approach and avoidance achievement motivation. *J. Pers. Soc. Psychol.* 72:218–32

Elliot AJ, Harackiewicz JM. 1996. Approach and avoidance achievement goals and intrinsic motivation: a mediational analysis. *J. Pers. Soc. Psychol.* 70:461–75

Ellsworth PC. 1994. Some reasons to expect universal antecedents of emotion. See Ekman & Davidson 1994, pp. 150–54

Emde RN, Osofsky JD, Butterfield PM. 1993. *The IFEEL Pictures: A New Instrument for Interpreting Emotions.* Madison, CT: International Univ. Press

Filion DL, Dawson ME, Schell AM. 1998. The psychological significance of human startle eyeblink modification: a review. *Biol. Psychol.* 47:1–43

Fitness J, Fletcher G. 1993. Love, hate, anger, and jealousy in close relationships: a prototype and cognitive appraisal analysis. *J. Pers. Soc. Psychol.* 65:942–58

Flannery DJ, Torquati JC, Lindemeier L. 1994. The method and meaning of emotional expression and experience during adolescence. *J. Adoles. Res.* 9:8–27

Forgas JP. 1995. Mood and judgment: the affect intrusion model (AIM). *Psychol. Bull.* 117:39–66

Forsyth JP, Eifert GH. 1996. The language of feeling and the feeling of anxiety: contributions of the behaviorisms toward understanding the function-altering effects of language. *Psychol. Rec.* 46:607–49

Fox PT, Woldorff MG. 1994. Integrating human brain maps. *Curr. Opin. Neurobiol.* 4:151–56

Frijda NH. 1993. The place of appraisal in emotion. *Cogn. Emot.* 7:357–87

Frijda NH. 1994. Universal antecedents exist, and are interesting. See Ekman & Davidson 1994, pp. 155–62

Gannon L, Vaux A, Rhodes K, Luchetta T. 1992. A two-domain model of well-being: everyday events, social support, and gender-related personality factors. *J. Res. Pers.* 26:288–301

Ganzach Y. 1995. Negativity (and positivity) in performance evaluation: three field studies. *J. Appl. Psychol.* 80:491–99

Gardner WL, Cacioppo JT. 1998. A brain based index of evaluative processing: a late positive brain potential reflects individual differences in the extremity of a negative evaluation. *Soc. Cogn.* In press

Gardner WL, Gabriel S, Diekman A. 1998. Interpersonal processes. See Cacioppo et al 1998. In press

George MS, Ketter TA, Parekh PI, Horwitz B, Herscovitch P, Post RM. 1995. Brain activity during transient sadness and happiness in healthy women. *Am. J. Psychiatry* 152:341–51

Gerrards-Hesse A, Spies K, Hesse FW. 1994. Experimental inductions of emotional states and their effectiveness: a review. *Br. J. Psychol.* 85:55–78

Gilbert P. 1993. Defence and safety: their function in social behaviour and psychopathology. *Br. J. Clin. Psychol.* 32:131–53

Gilboa E, Revelle W. 1994. Personality and the structure of affective responses. In *Emotions: Essays on Emotion Theory*, ed. SHM van Goozen, NE Van de Poll, JA Sergeant, pp. 135–59. Hillsdale, NJ: Erlbaum

Goldstein MD, Strube MJ. 1994. Independence revisited: the relation between positive and negative affect in a naturalistic setting. *Pers. Soc. Psychol. Bull.* 20:57–64

Goleman D. 1995. *Emotional Intelligence.* New York: Bantam

Gottman JM. 1993. Studying emotion in social interaction. See Lewis & Haviland 1993, pp. 475–87

Gray JA. 1994. Personality dimensions and emotion systems. See Ekman & Davidson 1994, pp. 329–31

Green DP, Goldman SL, Salovey P. 1993. Measurement error masks bipolarity in affect ratings. *J. Pers. Soc. Psychol.* 64: 1029–41

Grodd W, Scheider F, Klose U, Nagele T. 1995. Functional magnetic resonance tomography of psychological functions exemplified by experimentally induced emotions. *Radiologe* 35:283–89

Gross JJ, John OP. 1997. Revealing feelings: facets of emotional expressivity in self-reports, peer ratings, and behavior. *J. Pers. Soc. Psychol.* 72:435–48

Gross JJ, Levenson RW. 1995. Emotion elicitation using films. *Cogn. Emot.* 9:87–108

Guyll M, Contrada RJ. 1998. Trait hostility and ambulatory cardiovascular activity: responses to social interaction. *Health Psychol.* 17:30–39

Hamm AO, Vaitl D. 1996. Affective learning: awareness and aversion. *Psychophysiology* 33:698–710

Harmon-Jones E, Allan JB. 1998. Probing the mere exposure effect with psychophysiological indices of affect. *Psychol. Sci.* In press

Hagemann D, Naumann E, Becker G, Maier S, Bartussek D. 1998. Frontal brain asymmetry and affective style: a conceptual replication. *Psychophysiology.* In press

Harvey JH, Stein SK, Scott PK. 1995. Fifty years of grief: accounts and reported psychological reactions of Normandy invasion veterans. *J. Narrat. Life Hist.* 5: 315–32

Hatfield E, Cacioppo JT, Rapson RL. 1994. *Emotional Contagion.* New York: Cambridge Univ. Press

Herbert TB, Cohen S. 1993. Depression and immunity: a meta-analytic review. *Psychol. Bull.* 113:472–86

Hess U, Banse R, Kappas A. 1995. The intensity of facial expression is determined by underlying affective state and social situation. *J. Pers. Soc. Psychol.* 69:280–88

Hietanen J, Surakka V, Linnankoski I. 1998. Facial electromyographic responses to vocal affect expressions. *Psychophysiology.* In press

Higgins ET. 1997. Beyond pleasure and pain. *Am. Psychol.* 52:1280–1300

Hoebel BG. 1998. Neural systems for reinforcement and inhibition of behavior: relevance to eating, addiction and depression. See Kahneman et al 1998. In press

Hoorens V, Buunk BP. 1993. Social comparison of health risks: locus of control, the person-positivity bias, and unrealistic optimism. *J. Appl. Soc. Psychol.* 23: 291–302

Hsee CK, Salovey P, Abelson RP. 1994. The quasi-acceleration reaction: satisfaction as a function of the change of velocity of out-come over time. *J. Exp. Soc. Psychol.* 30: 96–111

Hunt PS, Campbell BA. 1997. Autonomic and behavioral correlates of appetitive conditioning in rats. *Behav. Neurosci.* 111: 494–502

Hurlburt RT. 1997. Randomly sampling thinking in the natural environment. *J. Consult. Clin. Psychol.* 65:941–49

Ito TA, Cacioppo JT, Lang PJ. 1998. Eliciting affect using the International Affective Picture System: trajectories through evaluative space. *Pers. Soc. Psychol. Bull.* In press

Ito TA, Larsen JT, Smith NK, Cacioppo JT. 1998. Negative information weighs more heavily on the brain: the negativity bias in evaluative categorizations. *J. Pers. Soc. Psychol.* In press

Izard CE. 1992. Basic emotions, relations among emotions, and emotion-cognition relations. *Psychol. Rev.* 99:561–65

Izard CE. 1994. Innate and universal facial expressions: evidence from developmental and cross-cultural research. *Psychol. Bull.* 115:288–99

Izard CE, Ackerman BP. 1997. Emotions and self-concepts across the life span. *Annu. Rev. Gerontol. Geriatr.* 17:1–26

Kahneman D. 1998. Objective happiness. See Kahneman et al 1998. In press

Kahneman D, Diener E, Schwarz N, eds. 1998. *Hedonic Psychology: Scientific Perspectives on Enjoyment, Suffering, and Well-Being.* New York: Cambridge Univ. Press. In press

Kahneman D, Fredrickson BL, Schreiber CA, Redelmeier DA. 1993. When more pain is preferred to less: adding a better end. *Psychol. Sci.* 4:401–5

Kamarck TW, Shiffman SM, Smithline L, Goodie JL, Paty JA, et al. 1998. Effects of task strain, social conflict, and emotional activation on ambulatory cardiovascular activity: daily life consequences of recurring stress in a multiethnic adult sample. *Health Psychol.* 17:17–29

Keltner D, Ekman P. 1996. Affective intensity and emotional responses. *Cogn. Emot.* 10: 323–28

Kemp S, Lea SEG, Fussell S. 1995. Experiments on rating the utility of consumer goods: evidence supporting microeconomic theory. *J. Econ. Psychol.* 16:543–61

Kiecolt-Glaser JK, Malarkey W, Cacioppo JT, Glaser R. 1994. Stressful personal relationships: endocrine and immune function. In *Handbook of Human Stress and Immunity,* ed. R Glaser, JK Kiecolt-Glaser, pp. 321–39. San Diego: Academic

Kitayama S, Masuda M. 1995. Reappraising

cognitive appraisal from a cultural perspective. *Psychol. Inq.* 6:217–23

Klar Y, Giladi EE. 1997. No one in my group can be below the group's average: a robust positivity bias in favor of anonymous peers. *J. Pers. Soc. Psychol.* 73:885–901

Klein JG. 1991. Negativity effects in impression formation: a test in the political arena. *Pers. Soc. Psychol. Bull.* 17:412–18

Klein JG. 1996. Negativity in impressions of presidential candidates revisited: the 1992 election. *Pers. Soc. Psychol. Bull.* 22: 288–95

Kutas M, Federmeier KD. 1998. Minding the body. *Psychophysiology* 35:135–50

Lane RD, Reiman EM, Ahern GL, Schwartz GE. 1997. Neuroanatomical correlates of happiness, sadness, and disgust. *Am. J. Psychiatry* 154:926–33

Lang PJ. 1995. The emotion probe: studies of motivation and attention. *Am. Psychol.* 50: 372–85

Lang PJ, Bradley MM, Cuthbert BN. 1990. Emotion, attention, and the startle reflex. *Psychol. Rev.* 97:377–95

Lang PJ, Bradley MM, Cuthbert BN. 1995. *International Affective Picture System (IAPS): Technical Manual and Affective Ratings*. NIMH Cent. Study Emot. Atten., Univ. FL

Lang PJ, Bradley M, Fitzsimmons J, Cuthbert B, Scott J, et al. 1998. Emotional arousal and activation of the visual cortex: an fMRI analysis. *Psychophysiology* 35: 199–210

Larsen RJ. 1991. Day-to-day physical symptoms: individual differences in occurrence, duration, and emotional concomitants of minor daily illnesses. *J. Pers.* 59:387–423

Larsen RJ, Billings DW, Cutler SE. 1996. Affect intensity and individual differences in informational style. *J. Pers.* 64:185–207

Larsen RJ, Diener E. 1992. Promises and problems with the circumplex model of emotion. *Rev. Pers. Soc. Psychol.* 13:25–59

Lawton MP, Kleban MH, Dean J, Rajogopal D, Parmelee PA. 1992. The factorial generality of brief positive and negative affect measures. *J. Gerontol.* 47:228–37

Lazarus R. 1991. *Emotions and Adaptation.* New York: Oxford Univ. Press

Lazarus R. 1994. Universal antecedents of the emotions. See Ekman & Davidson 1994, pp. 163–71

Lazarus RS. 1995. Vexing research problems inherent in cognitive-mediational theories of emotion—and some solutions. *Psychol. Inq.* 6:183–96

LeDoux JE. 1995. Emotion: clues from the brain. *Annu. Rev. Psychol.* 46:209–35

Lehrer PM, Isenberg S, Hochron SM. 1993. Asthma and emotion: a review. *J. Asthma* 30:5–21

Levenson RW. 1996. Biological substrates of empathy and facial modulation of emotion: two facets of the scientific legacy of John Lanzetta. *Motiv. Emot.* 20:185–204

Leventhal H, Patrick-Miller L, Leventhal E, Burns E. 1997. Does stress-emotion cause illness in elderly people? *Annu. Rev. Gerontol. Geriatr.* 17:138–84

Levy JS. 1992. An introduction to prospect theory. *Polit. Psychol.* 13:171–86

Lewis M, Haviland JM, eds. 1993. *Handbook of Emotions.* New York: Guilford

Litt MD, Cooney NL, Morse P. 1998. Ecological momentary assessment (EMA) with treated alcoholics: methodological problems and potential solutions. *Health Psychol.* 17:48–52

Maddock RJ, Buonocore MH. 1997. Activation of left posterior cingulate gyrus by the auditory presentation of threat-related words: an fMRI study. *Psychiatry Res.* 75: 1–14

Marcus GE, Mackuen MB. 1993. Anxiety, enthusiasm, and the vote: the emotional underpinnings of learning and involvement during presidential campaigns. *Am. Polit. Sci. Rev.* 87:672–85

Marsh HW. 1996. Positive and negative global self-esteem: a substantively meaningful distinction of artifactors? *J. Pers. Soc. Psychol.* 70:810–19

Mayer JD, Salovey P. 1993. The intelligence of emotional intelligence. *Intelligence* 17: 433–42

McGuire TR. 1993. *Emotion and Behavior Genetics in Vertebrates and Invertebrates.* New York: Guilford

Medvec VH, Madey SF, Gilovich T. 1995. When less is more: counterfactual thinking and satisfaction among Olympic medalists. *J. Pers. Soc. Psychol.* 69:603–10

Mesquita B, Frijda NH, Scherer KR. 1997. *Culture and Emotion.* Boston: Allyn & Bacon

Miller NE. 1961. Some recent studies on conflict behavior and drugs. *Am. Psychol.* 16: 12–24

Murray IR, Arnott JL. 1993. Toward the simulation of emotion in synthetic speech: a review of the literature on human vocal emotion. *J. Acoust. Soc. Am.* 93:1097–108

Myers DG. 1993. *The Pursuit of Happiness.* London: Aquarian

Neafsey EJ, Terreberry RR, Hurley KM, Ruit KG, Frysztak RJ. 1993. *Anterior Cingulate Cortex in Rodents: Connections, Visceral Control Functions, and Implications for Emotion.* Boston: Birkhauser

Nelson CA, de Haan M. 1997. *A Neurobehav-*

ioral Approach to the Recognition of Facial Expressions in Infancy. New York: Cambridge Univ. Press

Nelson TE. 1998. Group affect and attribution in social policy opinion. *J. Politics*. In press

Niedenthal PM, Kitayama S. 1994. *The Heart's Eye: Emotional Influences in Perception and Attention*. San Diego, CA: Academic

Ohman A. 1993. Fear and anxiety as emotional phenomena: clinical phenomenology, evolutionary perspectives, and information-processing mechanisms. See Lewis & Haviland 1993, pp. 511–36

Ohman A, Hamm A, Hugdahl K. 1998. Cognition and the autonomic nervous system: orienting, anticipation, and conditioning. See Cacioppo et al 1998. In press

Omdahl BL. 1995. *Cognitive Appraisal, Emotion, and Empathy*. Mahwah, NJ: Erlbaum

Ortony A, Clore GL, Collins A. 1988. *The Cognitive Structure of Emotions*. Cambridge: Cambridge Univ. Press

Ortony A, Turner TJ. 1990. What's basic about basic emotions? *Psychol. Rev.* 97: 315–31

Osgood CE, Suci GJ, Tannenbaum PH. 1957. *The Measurement of Meaning*. Urbana, IL: Univ. Ill. Press

Ottati VC, Steenbergen MR, Riggle E. 1992. The cognitive and affective components of political attitudes: measuring the determinants of candidate evaluations. *Polit. Behav.* 14:423–42

Panksepp J. 1992. A critical role for "affective neuroscience" in resolving what is basic about basic emotions. *Psychol. Rev.* 99: 554–60

Paradiso S, Robinson RG, Andreasen NC, Downhill JE, Davidson RJ, Kirchner PT, et al. 1997. Emotional activation of limbic circuitry in elderly normal subjects in a PET study. *Am. J. Psychiatry* 154:384–89

Parducci A. 1995. *Happiness, Pleasure, and Judgment: The Contextual Theory and Its Applications*. Hillsdale, NJ: Erlbaum

Parkinson B, Manstead A. 1993. Making sense of emotion in stories and social life. *Cogn. Emot.* 7:295–323

Paulhus DL, Fridhandler B, Hayes S. 1997. *Psychological Defense: Contemporary Theory and Research*. San Diego, CA: Academic

Peeters G. 1991. Evaluative influence in social cognition: the roles of direct versus indirect evaluation and positive-negative asymmetry. *Eur. J. Soc. Psychol.* 21: 131–46

Peeters G, Czapinski J. 1990. Positive-negative asymmetry in evaluations: the distinction between affective and informa-tional negativity effects. In *Eur. Rev. Soc. Psychol.* 1:33–60. New York: Wiley

Phelps EA, Anderson AK. 1997. Emotional memory: what does the amygdala do? *Curr. Biol.* 7:R311–14

Philippot P. 1993. Inducing and assessing differentiated emotion-feeling states in the laboratory. *Cogn. Emot.* 7:171–93

Pittam J, Scherer KR. 1993. Vocal expression and communication of emotion. See Lewis & Haviland 1993, pp. 185–97

Plomin R, Emde RN, Braungart JM, Campos J, Corley R, et al. 1993. Genetic change and continuity from fourteen to twenty months: the MacArthur Longitudinal Twin Study. *Child Dev.* 64: 1354–76

Pulford BD, Colman AM. 1996. Overconfidence, base rates and outcome positivity/negativity of predicted events. *Br. J. Psychol.* 87:431–45

Regan PC, Snyder M, Kassin SM. 1995. Unrealistic optimism: self-enhancement or person positivity? *Pers. Soc. Psychol. Bull.* 21:1073–82

Reid SA, Duke LM, Allen JJB. 1998. Resting frontal electroencephalographic asymmetry in depression: inconsistencies suggest the need to identify mediating factors. *Psychophysiology*. In press

Reis HT, Patrick BC. 1996. Attachment and intimacy: component processes. In *Social Psychology: Handbook of Basic Principles*, ed. ET Higgins, AW Kruglanski, pp. 523–63. New York: Guilford

Reisenzein R. 1995. On appraisals as causes of emotions. *Psychol. Inq.* 6:233–37

Reisenzein R, Hofmann T. 1993. Discriminating emotions from appraisal-relevant situational information: baseline data for structural models of cognitive appraisals. *Cogn. Emot.* 7:271–93

Robinson RG, Downhill JE. 1995. Lateralization of psychopathology in response to focal brain injury. In *Brain Asymmetry*, ed. RJ Davidson, K Hugdahl, pp. 693–711. Cambridge, MA: MIT Press

Robinson-Whelen S, Kim C, MacCallum RC, Kiecolt-Glaser JK. 1997. Distinguishing optimism from pessimism in older adults: is it more important to be optimistic or not to be pessimistic? *J. Pers. Soc. Psychol.* 73:1345–53

Roese NJ. 1997. Counterfactual thinking. *Psychol. Bull.* 121:133–48

Roseman IJ, Antoniou AA, Jose PE. 1996. Appraisal determinants of emotions: constructing a more accurate and comprehensive theory. *Cogn. Emot.* 10:241–77

Rosenberg EL, Ekman P. 1994. Coherence between expressive and experiential systems in emotion. *Cogn. Emot.* 8:201–29

Rosenberg EL, Ekman P. 1995. Conceptual and methodological issues in the judgment of facial expressions of emotion. *Motiv. Emot.* 19:111–38

Rosenthal J. 1995. *Galen's Prophecy: Temperament in Human Nature.* New York: Basic Books

Rowe PM. 1989. Unfavorable information and interview decisions. In *The Employment Interview: Theory, Research, and Practice,* ed. RW Eder, GR Ferris, pp. 77–89. Newbury Park, CA: Sage

Rubinow DR, Schmidt PJ. 1996. Androgens, brain, and behavior. *Am. J. Psychiatry* 153:974–84

Russell JA. 1994. Is there universal recognition of emotion from facial expressions? A review of the cross-cultural studies. *Psychol. Bull.* 115:102–41

Russell JA, Fernandez-Dols JM. 1997. *The Psychology of Facial Expression.* New York: Cambridge Univ. Press

Rusting CL, Larsen RJ. 1998. Personality and cognitive processing of affective information. *Pers. Soc. Psychol. Bull.* 24:200–13

Sarter M, Berntson GG, Cacioppo JT. 1996. Brain imaging and cognitive neuroscience: towards strong inference in attributing function to structure. *Am. Psychol.* 51:13–21

Schell AM, Dawson ME, Marinkovic K. 1991. Effects of potentially phobic conditioned stimuli on retention, reconditioning, and extinction of the conditioned skin conductance response. *Psychophysiology* 28:140–53

Scherer KR. 1993. Neuroscience projections to current debates in emotion psychology. *Cogn. Emot.* 7:1–41

Scherer KR. 1997. Profiles of emotion-antecedent appraisal: testing theoretical predictions across cultures. *Cogn. Emot.* 11:113–50

Schofield JW. 1991. School desegregation and intergroup relations. In *Rev. Res. Educ.,* 17:335–409. Washington, DC: Am. Educ. Res. Assoc.

Schulz R, Heckhausen J. 1997. Emotion and control: a life-span perspective. *Annu. Rev. Gerontol. Geriatr.* 17:185–205

Schwartz JE, Stone AA. 1998. Strategies for analyzing ecological momentary assessment data. *Health Psychol.* 17:6–16

Schwarz N, Clore GL. 1996. *Feelings and Phenomenal Experiences.* New York: Guilford

Schwarz N, Strack F. 1998. Reports of subjective well-being: judgmental processes and their methodological implications. See Kahneman et al 1998. In press

Scott SK, Young AW, Calder AJ, Hellawell DJ, Aggleton JP, Johnson M. 1997. Impaired auditory recognition of fear and anger following bilateral amygdala lesions. *Nature* 385:254–57

Sears DO. 1983. The person positivity bias. *J. Pers. Soc. Psychol.* 44:233–49

Shah J, Higgins ET, Friedman RS. 1998. Performance incentives and means: how regulatory focus influences goal attainment. *J. Pers. Soc. Psychol.* 74:285–93

Shizgal P. 1998. On the neural computation of utility: implications from studies of brain stimulation reward. See Kahneman et al 1998. In press

Showers CJ. 1995. The evaluative organization of self-knowledge: origins, processes, and implications for self-esteem. In *Efficacy, Agency, and Self-Esteem,* ed. M Kernis, pp. 101–20. New York: Plenum

Showers CJ, Kling KC. 1996. Organization of self-knowledge: implications for recovery from sad mood. *J. Pers. Soc. Psychol.* 70:578–90

Skowronski JJ, Carlston DE. 1989. Negativity and extremity biases in impression formation: a review of explanations. *Psychol. Bull.* 105:131–42

Smith CA, Haynes KN, Lazarus RS, Pope LK. 1993. In search of the "hot" cognitions: attributions, appraisals, and their relation to emotion. *J. Pers. Soc. Psychol.* 65:916–29

Spiegel D. 1997. Psychosocial aspects of breast cancer treatment. *Semin. Oncol.* 24:S136–47

Stayman DM, Aaker DA. 1993. Continuous measurement of self-report of emotional response. *Psychol. Mark.* 10:199–214

Sternberg EM. 1997. Emotions and disease: from balance of humors to balance of molecules. *Nat. Med.* 3:264–67

Suls J, Green P, Hillis S. 1998. Emotional reactivity to everyday problems, affective inertia, and neuroticism. *Pers. Soc. Psychol. Bull.* 24:127–36

Sutton SK, Davidson RJ. 1997. Prefrontal brain asymmetry: a biological substrate of the behavioral approach and inhibition systems. *Psychol. Sci.* 8:204–10

Tangney JP, Burggraf SA, Wagner PE. 1995. Shame-proneness, guilt-proneness, and psychological symptoms. In *Self-Conscious Emotions: The Psychology of Shame, Guilt, Embarrassment, and Pride,* ed. JP Tangney, KW Fischer, pp. 343–67. New York: Guilford

Tassinary LG, Cacioppo JT. 1992. Unobservable facial actions and emotion. *Psychol. Sci.* 3:28–34

Taylor SE. 1991. Asymmetrical effects of positive and negative events: the mobilization-minimization hypothesis. *Psychol. Bull.* 110:67–85

Thompson MM, Zanna MP, Griffin DW. 1995. Let's not be indifferent about (attitudinal) ambivalence. In *Attitude Strength: Antecedents and Consequences,* ed. RE Petty, JA Krosnick, pp. 361–86. Hillsdale, NJ: Erlbaum

Tooby J, Cosmides L. 1990. On the universality of human nature and the uniqueness of the individual: the role of genetics and adaptation. *J. Pers.* 58:17–67

Traue HC, Pennebaker JW. 1993. *Emotion Inhibition and Health.* Gottingen, Germany: Hogrefe & Huber

Tucker DM, Frederick SL. 1989. Emotion and brain lateralization. In *Handbook of Social Psychophysiology,* ed. H Wagner, A Manstead, pp. 27–70. Chichester: Wiley

Walker-Andrews AS. 1997. Infants' perception of expressive behaviors: differentiation of multimodal information. *Psychol. Bull.* 121:437–56

Watson D, Clark LA. 1992. Affects separable and inseparable: on the hierarchical arrangement of the negative affects. *J. Pers. Soc. Psychol.* 62:489–505

Watson D, Clark LA. 1997. Measurement and mismeasurement of mood: recurrent and emergent issues. *J. Pers. Assess.* 68: 267–96

Watson D, Clark LA, McIntyre CW, Hamaker S. 1992. Affect, personality and social activity. *J. Pers. Soc. Psychol.* 63:1011–25

Way BM, Masters RD. 1996. Political attitudes: interactions of cognition and affect. *Motiv. Emot.* 20:205–36

Westermann R, Spies K, Stahl G, Hesse FW. 1996. Relative effectiveness and validity of mood induction procedures: a meta-analysis. *Eur. J. Soc. Psychol.* 26:557–80

Wierzbicka A. 1995. The relevance of language to the study of emotions. *Psychol. Inq.* 6:248–52

Witvliet C, Vrana SR. 1995. Psychophysiological responses as indices of affective dimensions. *Psychophysiology* 32:436–43

Ybarra O, Stephan WG. 1996. Misanthropic person memory. *J. Pers. Soc. Psychol.* 70: 691–700

Zajonc RB. 1980. Feeling and thinking: preferences need no inferences. *Am. Psychol.* 35:157–93

Zajonc RB. 1998. Emotions. In *Handbook of Social Psychology,* ed. DT Gilbert, ST Fiske, L Gardner, pp. 591–634. New York: Oxford Univ. Press

Zautra AJ, Burleson MH, Smith CA, Blalock SJ, Wallston KF, et al. 1995. Arthritis and perceptions of quality of life: an examination of positive and negative affect in rheumatoid arthritis patients. *Health Psychol.* 14:399–408

Zautra AJ, Potter PT, Reich JW. 1997. The independence of affects is context-dependent: an integrative model of the relationship between positive and negative affect. *Annu. Rev. Gerontol. Geriatr.* 17: 75–103

Zautra AJ, Reich JW, Gaurnaccia CA. 1990. The everyday consequences of disability and bereavement for older adults. *J. Pers. Soc. Psychol.* 59:550–61

Annu. Rev. Psychol. 1999. 50:215–41

QUANTIFYING THE INFORMATION VALUE OF CLINICAL ASSESSMENTS WITH SIGNAL DETECTION THEORY

Richard M. McFall and Teresa A. Treat

Department of Psychology, Indiana University, Bloomington, Indiana 47405;
e-mail: mcfall@indiana.edu; ttreat@indiana.edu

KEY WORDS: ROC, Bayesian, probability theory, base rates, cutoff value

ABSTRACT

The aim of clinical assessment is to gather data that allow us to reduce uncertainty regarding the probabilities of events. This is a Bayesian view of assessment that is consistent with the well-known concept of incremental validity. Conventional approaches to evaluating the accuracy of assessment methods are confounded by the choice of cutting points, by the base rates of the events, and by the assessment goal (e.g. nomothetic vs idiographic predictions). Clinical assessors need a common metric for quantifying the information value of assessment data, independent of the cutting points, base rates, or particular application. Signal detection theory (SDT) provides such a metric. We review SDT's history, concepts, and methods and provide examples of its application to a variety of assessment problems.

CONTENTS

0084-6570/99/0201-0215$08.00

FUNDAMENTALS REVISITED

Psychologists too often make the mistake of equating clinical assessment with the administration of tests or interviews to clinical patients for purposes of arriving at individual diagnoses, predicting outcomes, planning interventions, or tracking therapeutic changes. These applied activities may be the most visible part of clinical assessment, but they are only the exposed tip of the whole clinical assessment enterprise, which really is much broader, deeper, and more complicated than these surface activities reveal. Beneath every clinical application of a valid psychological test lies an extensive foundation of scientific theory, empirical research, and quantitative modeling. To the extent that psychologists neglect this foundation, construing clinical assessment narrowly as the clinical application of psychological tests, they are impeding scientific advances in clinical assessment.

This review critically examines the current status and future prospects of clinical assessment, broadly defined. The review focuses on the aims, concepts, methods, and evaluative criteria that underlie the clinical assessment enterprise in general. It is not about specific tests; it is about the functions of clinical assessment, the standards by which methods can be evaluated, and the most promising approaches to achieving the broad goals of clinical assessment. Of course, to the extent that the review helps strengthen the foundations of clinical assessment, it also—as a byproduct—should have practical implications for the more applied aspects of clinical assessment.

Let us start by recapping the basics: The purpose of all psychological assessment is to gather data that provide information regarding specific theoretical questions. This seemingly simple sentence is saturated with important implications. First, the sentence highlights the essential link between theory and assessment (McFall 1993). All assessments are driven by questions; these questions, in turn, always reflect the assessor's theoretical preconceptions, hunches, and assumptions, whether formal or informal, explicit or implicit (Popper 1962). To be useful, an assessment must be tailored to the specific questions that gave rise to it in the first place; its value is determined entirely by its ability to illuminate these questions (Meehl 1971).

Second, the ties between theory and assessment are bidirectional. The ability of an assessment to shed light on a theory is constrained by the validity of the underlying assumptions and constructs of the theory it is attempting to illuminate (Popper 1962). No assessment is atheoretical or assumption-free. Just as water cannot rise naturally above its source, no assessment can be more valid than the theoretical conceptions and assumptions from which it springs.

Third, the term information, in this sentence, has a very specific meaning. It is defined as "the reduction of uncertainty," which is a relativistic concept referring to the relative increment in predictive accuracy, or the relative decrease in predictive error, that is yielded by data (Gigerenzer & Murray 1987). Thus, data reduce uncertainty: They have information value or are illuminating to the degree that they allow us to predict or control events with greater accuracy or with less error than we could have done without them (Mischel 1968).

Fourth, this conception of information is fundamentally quantitative (Gigerenzer & Murray 1987, Meehl & Rosen 1955). The information value of assessment data is represented by a scaled numerical value corresponding to the magnitude of the quantitative difference between the predictive accuracy of our prior model (i.e. the accuracy achieved without the data) and the predictive accuracy of our posterior model (i.e. the accuracy achieved after adjusting the model to reflect the new data). This quantitative view of assessment information suggests a Bayesian epistemology both conceptually and computationally. We will elaborate these Bayesian connections below, but for now, the spirit of this epistemology is reflected in the familiar assessment concept of incremental validity.[1]

Probability Theory

Before proceeding to the main level of our review, we must lay one final block in our conceptual foundations. The cornerstone of psychological assessment is probability theory.[2] Contemporary scientific theories increasingly assume that events in nature including human behavior are probabilistic, or stochastic, rather than deterministic (Gigerenzer et al 1989). Events are determined, in part, by the chance confluence of many other events that are, themselves, unpredictable, random, or the result of chance. Thus, not all assessment variability (error, uncertainty) is due to the inadequacies of our theories and measures; some simply is due to the fact that the events we are attempting to assess and predict are inherently probabilistic.

This means that we cannot expect nature to be so well-behaved as to allow us to predict single events with certainty; instead, the best we can hope for is to identify an array of possible outcomes and to estimate the relative likelihood of 1 each. From this probabilistic perspective, the idealized goal of traditional assessment predicting unique, remote events with precision is fanciful, reflecting our naivete and/or hubris. A more realistic assessment goal would be to estimate with incremental accuracy the relative probabilities of the array of possible outcomes for an event. Useful assessments provide data with infor-

---

[1] We have traced the origins of the concept of incremental validity to Meehl (1959).

[2] Probability theory, as discussed in this chapter, is not synonymous with the concept of probability as taught in the usual psychology statistics courses.

mation value, data that improve the relative accuracy of our probability estimates.

The mechanics of empirically generating a normative probability distribution are straightforward. First, we must impose some category structure on nature, segmenting our target event into two or more mutually exclusive and exhaustive classes of outcomes. Our choice of category structures is guided by our theoretical preconceptions, by our assessment questions, and by practical and methodological considerations. It is up to us to decide, for example, whether to employ a dichotomous category structure (e.g. yes-no, success-failure) or a finer-grained structure (e.g. ratings on a 5-point scale, scores on a 100-point scale, age in years). This choice invariably involves trade-offs. On one hand, simple category structures require smaller samples to fill them, and tend to be more reliable, more readily analyzed and interpreted, and easier to work with. On the other hand, finer-grained structures tend to capture and retain more information. Once we have decided on our category structure, we must observe a suitably large and representative sample of actual outcomes, tabulating and summing the frequencies for each of our categories. These raw frequency data then are normalized by transforming them into proportions; each category total is divided by the grand total of observations. The resulting proportions represent the empirically observed relative probabilities of the categorical events.

Thus, empirically derived probability distributions actually are quantitative records of historical events. As clinical assessors, however, we usually are more interested in predicting the future than in recounting the past. So why should we care about historical probabilities? Because we assume that such historical probability distributions provide the best estimates of the future probabilities for maximally similar events assessed under maximally similar circumstances. The assumption that past probabilities are predictive of future probabilities seems to be a huge leap of faith. Fortunately, however, this idea has been studied extensively by probability theorists, actuaries, mathematicians, philosophers, and scientists for more than three centuries, and consistently has shown itself to be a robust and extremely useful basis for predicting all sorts of events—even random or chance events. Although it seldom yields perfect predictions, no other approach does as well. Note that this assumption cannot be proven, so it must remain an assumption. No matter how many times past probabilities provide useful estimates of future probabilities, we never can be certain that they will do so the next time. This uncertainty notwithstanding, probability theory is the cornerstone of all clinical assessment and prediction.

Conditional Probabilities

We have asserted that historical probability distributions provide the best estimates of the future probabilities for maximally similar events assessed under maximally similar circumstances. Imbedded in this assertion is an important caveat: As the variability of the circumstances surrounding our assessment of past and future events increases, the accuracy of our probability estimates is likely to decrease. For example, if we used a sample consisting primarily of men to estimate the probability distribution of body weights for a sample consisting primarily of women, our estimates would be unacceptably inaccurate. Fortunately, we can reduce the threat that varying conditions pose to our probabilistic predictions by identifying the specific conditions that systematically affect the outcomes, and incorporating these variables into our probability models.

Until now, we have described only probability models based on a simple, one-dimensional array of categories. To deal with the added complexity of other factors that systematically affect the variability of our probability estimates, we need multidimensional models, which yield joint probability distributions. The simplest form of a joint distribution is a two-dimensional, two-category model, as represented by a 2 x 2 contingency table.[3] The horizontal axis of such a table, for example, might represent the dimension of body weight with two categories (e.g. light = 150 lbs or below; heavy = more than 150 lbs); the vertical axis might represent the two-category dimension of gender. Each observation in a sample would be tabulated in one of the table's four cells (e.g. heavy-male; light-female). To normalize this two-dimensional table of joint frequencies, the observed frequency for each cell would be divided by the total number of observations.

With multidimensional probability models, we not only can compute joint probabilities, but also can compute conditional probabilities, which are even more useful. In our simple two-dimensional table, for example, we can generate separate estimates—one for men, one for women—of the relative probabilities of the two weight categories (light, heavy). These conditional probabilities are computed by dividing each cell total by the marginal total for each level of the conditional variable (e.g. for each sex separately). Conditional probabilities provide more accurate estimates because, in effect, they yield separate estimates of probability distributions for each level of conditions suspected of systematically affecting the outcome.

Clinical psychologists' interest in conditional probabilities is not unique. Virtually all scientific research and theory involves probabilistic models of conditional relations among variables (along with hypothetical explanations for these relations). The careers of epidemiologists, insurance actuaries, business executives, and casino operators, for example, all hinge on an ability to

---

[3]There may be more than two dimensions, of course, and each dimension may be divided into more than two categories; however, a model's complexity increases rapidly as the number of joint probability cells increases multiplicatively.

estimate conditional probabilities with reasonable accuracy. Laypeople, too, have a vital interest in estimating conditional probabilities; almost every life decision involves a subjective appraisal of the likely outcomes (risks and gains) of different choices. No doubt the popular appeal of astrology and numerology stems from their illusory reduction of uncertainty. The horoscopes in daily newspapers, after all, are nothing but tables of conditional probability statements (e.g. if you are a Leo, you can expect this event; if you are a Capricorn, you can expect that event, and so forth).

The distinguishing characteristics of scientific clinical psychology46s interest in conditional probabilities are (a) its use of a scientific epistemology and quantitative methods to build and test theoretical models of conditional probabilities, and (b) its focus on a specific content area: psychopathology (the assessment, prediction, prevention, amelioration, and explanation of abnormal human behavior). Clinical psychologists and meteorologists employ similar scientific methods, for example, but focus on different content. Clinical psychologists and fortune tellers share some content interests, but employ different methods.

In their scientific pursuit of psychopathology, clinical psychologists engage in a wide variety of tasks, all involving probability theory. They might work, for example, on the development of a classification system for abnormal behaviors, searching for conditional probabilities related to clusters of symptom patterns, common causes, expected course, or treatment response. Once they have settled on a working classification system (e.g. DSM-IV), they might search for diagnostic signs to help them diagnose, differentiate, refine, or explain the categories. In an effort to predict, prevent, or explain disorders, they might search for antecedent characteristics associated with increased risks of specific pathology. Alternatively, they might search within diagnostic groups for client characteristics that predict differential responses to different treatments.

We could go on describing various content questions that might drive the research programs and assessment interests of clinical scientists, but this sample is sufficient to help us make two important points: First, all of these examples—if performed properly—involve the clinical assessment and multidimensional quantitative modeling of conditional probabilities. Second, all of these are nomothetic activities. That is, they all represent attempts to build general models with which to increase the accuracy of predictions for groups of individuals. In general, they all address questions of the following type: $p(S|D)$. That is, what is the probability (p) of a diagnostic sign (S), given membership in a diagnostic category (D)?

To illustrate, imagine a hypothetical study in which the Revised Hamilton Rating Scale for Depression (HRSD-R) (Riskind et al 1987) is administered to two groups, one composed of patients known to be clinically depressed, the

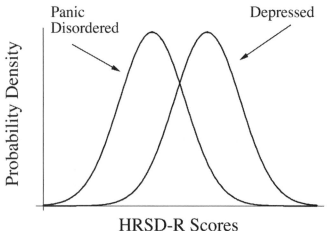

Panic Disordered   Depressed

Probability Density

HRSD-R Scores

Figure 1   Hypothetical distributions of scores on HRSD-R for persons receiving panic disorder and major depression diagnoses. Prevalence of depression is assumed to be 0.5.

other made up of patients known to be suffering from panic disorder. The study's aim is to evaluate how well HRSD-R ratings differentiate depressed patients from panic patients.[4] Fictitious idealized results are displayed in Figure 1. We see a separate (conditional) probability distribution of HRSD-R ratings for each patient group. We also see that the mean of the depressed group's distribution is higher than the mean of the panic group. Now, how might we quantify and evaluate the information value of these data?

If we were to analyze these data using traditional Fisherian statistical methods (Gigerenzer et al 1989), we would test the null hypothesis; that is, we would ask, "Can we reject the hypothesis that the means of these two distributions are not significantly different from one another?" This is an odd, double-negative question. Even before collecting the data, we know that the likelihood of rejecting the null hypothesis for a given absolute difference (no matter how trivially small) between sample means increases as the sample size increases (Cohen 1994, Loftus 1996, Meehl 1978). Besides, rejecting the null hypothesis tells us nothing about which of the many plausible rival hypotheses might be supported by the results. Furthermore, traditional statistical tests shed little light on the question that gave rise to the study in the first place. They don't tell us how useful the HRSD-R is for differentiating between depressed and panic patients. Neither do correlation-based methods, as favored in the Neyman-

---

[4]We're ignoring for the moment another major issue—the criterion problem. That is, how does the investigator "know" for certain the patients' "true" diagnoses. We will return to it later

Pearson tradition (Gigerenzer et al 1989), although they shed some light on our research question by telling us the strength of the association between HRSD-R scores and group membership. Still, we need better methods of quantifying the information value of such data.

Cutting Scores, Base Rates, and Inverse Probabilities

Over 40 years ago, Meehl & Rosen (1955) identified three classical problems that further complicate the task of evaluating the information value of data sets. The first of these was the problem of choosing the optimal cutting score (cut-point) for differentiating between two groups. This problem is illustrated in Figure 2, where three possible cutting scores (A = liberal; B = moderate; C = conservative) have been applied to our fictitious HRSD-R data. Setting the cutting score at point A correctly identifies most of the depressed patients as depressed, but also misidentifies a high percentage of panic patients as depressed. Thus, cut-point A shows what epidemiologists call good sensitivity (i.e. a high true positive rate, or the proportion of depressed patients classified as depressed), but also shows poor specificity (i.e. a low true negative rate, or the proportion of panic patients classified as not depressed). Shifting the cutting score to point C results in the correct identification of most panic patients as not depressed, but also misidentifies a high percentage of depressed patients as not depressed. Thus, cut-point C shows good specificity, but poor sensitivity. This example illustrates the inevitable trade-off between sensitivity and specificity as a function of changes in the cutoff value.

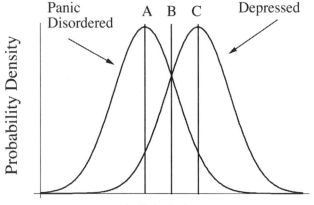

Figure 2 Hypothetical distributions of scores on HRSD-R for persons receiving panic disorder and major depression diagnoses. Prevalence of depression is assumed to be 0.5. Liberal (*A*), moderate (*B*), and conservative (*C*) cutoff values are shown.

The second problem identified by Meehl & Rosen (1955) was the base-rate problem. In short, the discriminatory power of a particular measure will vary as a function of the base rate of the variable being predicted (e.g. depression) in the population being assessed. In our imaginary data set, for example, HRSD-R ratings were obtained from equal numbers of depressed and panic patients, so the relative density of cases under the two curves was equal. Thus, the base rate, or prevalence, of depression in this fictitious study was 0.5. Suppose instead that the base rate, or prevalence, of depression had been 0.1. The hypothetical distributions of HRSD-R scores for depressed and panic patients have been redrawn in Figure 3 to illustrate the effects of these altered base rates. We can see, for example, how the problem of choosing a cutting score is compounded by the base rate problem. For a fixed cut-point (say, point B), the sensitivity and specificity indices will not change (i.e. the proportion of depressed persons classified as depressed will remain constant), but the practical utility of the measure will change as a result of changes in the base rate, or prevalence, of the disorder. The 9:1 ratio of panic patients to depressed patients shown in Figure 3 means that where the two distributions overlap, classification errors are far more frequent for panic patients than for depressed patients.

The third problem identified by Meehl & Rosen (1955) (see also Meehl 1973) was the logical fallacy of using nomothetic, or normative, probability distributions to make idiographic decisions and predictions. This is called the

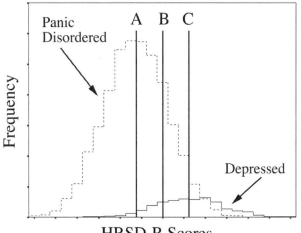

HRSD-R Scores

Figure 3   Hypothetical distributions of scores on HRSD-R for persons receiving panic disorder and major depression diagnoses. Prevalence of depression is assumed to be 0.1. Liberal (*A*), moderate (*B*), and conservative (*C*) cutoff values are shown.

inverse probability problem. The problem arises when clinical assessors confuse two types of probability: $p(S|D)$, the probability of a particular score on a diagnostic test, given membership in a diagnostic group; and $p(D|S)$, the probability of being a member of a diagnostic group, given a particular score on the diagnostic test. The inverse probability problem interacts with the base rate problem. When the base rate, or prevalence, of a disorder in the sample is exactly 0.5, then $p(S|D) = p(D|S)$. When the prevalence is not 0.5, however, these two probabilities are not equal. The more asymmetrical the prevalence rates, the greater the inequality. Meehl and Rosen (1955) showed how Bayes' Theorem (Bayes 1763; see Gigerenzer & Murray 1987) solves the problem by controlling for base rates while using normative probability distributions to estimate inverse probabilities. Bayes' Theorem is as follows:

$$p(\text{Hypothesis} \mid \text{Data}) = \frac{p(\text{Hyp}) * p(\text{Data} \mid \text{Hyp})}{p(\text{Data})}$$

or, using our notation,

$$p(D|S) = \frac{p(D) * p(S|D)}{p(S)}.$$

The Bayesian approach addresses two of Meehl & Rosen's problems (base rates and inverse probabilities), but not the third (cutting scores). Selecting optimal cutting scores always requires subjective judgments regarding how best to resolve the inevitable trade-offs between sensitivity and specificity, or between the relative costs and benefits of different types of classification errors. Because cutoff decisions never can be value free, there is no magic formula for finding an absolute, all-purpose, optimal cutoff. Every formula for optimal cutoffs is based on hidden assumptions and values. Given a data set and population base rate, for example, we might choose a cutting score that maximizes overall percent correct; however, this choice assumes that the optimal solution should assign equal weights to the two types of error (i.e. false positives and false negatives). Often the costs of these two errors are unequal, however. To prevent airplane terrorism, for instance, society tolerates a very high false positive rates and treats everyone at airports as potential terrorists because society places a greater value on ensuring the highest possible true positive rate, i.e. catching the rare terrorist.

The choice of cutting scores also is influenced by the personal biases of the individuals involved. Suppose we asked three psychologists (A, B, and C) to view videotaped HRSD-R interviews of a mixed sample of depressed and panic patients, and to make a dichotomous diagnostic judgment (depressed | not depressed) for each patient. Although the three psychologists view the same interview data, their judgments are likely to differ. Such interjudge differences arise from two sources. The judges may differ in their perception of the diagnostic information contained in the videotapes. But even if they were equally perceptive of the presence of diagnostic cues, their judgments still could differ as a result of the cutting score, or decision criterion, that they selected for calling a patient depressed. Figures 2 and 3 depict our three judges (with 0.5 and 0.1 base rates, respectively). Judge A has been very liberal in setting the criterion for discriminating between normal and abnormal; judge B has employed a moderate criterion; and judge C has drawn the line very conservatively. Here we see how three equally perceptive judges might produce three different diagnostic results as a function of their individual biases in selecting the criterion, or cutting score, for calling a patient depressed.

Wanted: A Common Metric for Information Value

Paradoxically, Meehl & Rosen's (1955) paper on the problems of cutting scores, base rates, and inverse probabilities, with its focus on Bayes' Theorem, has been cited widely for nearly half a century, yet it has had surprisingly little impact on actual practice in clinical assessment. Over the years, major texts on clinical assessment (e.g. Mischel 1968, Wiggins 1973) have reiterated the problems and reemphasized the importance of a Bayesian solution, but with minimal added impact. This is puzzling. Clinical assessors should have been attracted to Bayes' Theorem on epistemological grounds, if not on methodological grounds. As we noted at the outset, the concept of incremental validity is central to clinical assessment and prediction. Bayes' Theorem provides a quantitative method of iteratively incrementing the accuracy of probability estimates by systematically using the information contained in each new batch of data to transform the prior model into a more precise posterior model (Schmitt 1969). In this respect, the Bayesian approach provides a solid foundation for a more rigorously quantitative approach to clinical assessment.

Unfortunately, however, the Bayesian approach provides an incomplete solution to the clinical assessor's needs. It still does not provide a common metric with which to quantify the information value of assessment data that is independent of changes in cutoffs and prevalence rates. Such a standard scale is essential if clinical assessors wish to compare the incremental validity, or relative utility, of different assessment methods. Without such a metric, assessors will have little choice but to continue using current, inadequate strategies, typically evaluating the statistical significance, relative to the null hypothesis, of the difference between group means (disordered vs normal, treated vs control). But if research in clinical assessment is to build cumulative knowledge, assessors must be able to quantify and compare the results of assessment methods across studies, populations, and conditions. Scientific progress in clinical assessment will be stymied until assessors find a way of doing this (e.g. see Meehl 1973, 1978).

A metric for the information value of data yielded by an assessment method should be a property of the method alone, not the prevalence of the disorder in the sample to which the method was applied or the decision biases or criterion choices of the assessors using the method. Although the differential information value provided by various assessment methods may guide our selection of an assessment method, practical application of the method for assessment or prediction purposes hinges in part upon these latter factors, such as prevalence and cutoff scores. For an assessment method with a specific information value, for example, we might ask, "How does the practical utility of this assessment method vary as a function of prevalence rates or selection criteria?" But examination and quantification of the practical utility of an assessment method in a particular context require separate metrics that should be independent of the metric defining the information value of the method.

In sum, future advances in clinical assessment await the development of a common metric for quantifying assessment information. We believe that signal detection theory (SDT) provides such a metric. In the next section, we outline the history, concepts, and methods of SDT. Then we review recent examples of SDT's application to a cross-section of assessment problems. We conclude with a discussion of SDT's possible limitations and its potential contributions to clinical assessment.

SIGNAL DETECTION THEORY: MEASURING MEASURES

Background

SDT's history is not the story of a theory evolving smoothly and continuously over time; rather, it is the story of a conceptual framework being reborn periodically, each incarnation more elaborated and refined than the last, but with little apparent memory of former lives (see Ashby 1992; Gigerenzer & Murray 1987; Gigerenzer et al 1989; Link 1994; Murray 1993). Historians trace the roots of contemporary SDT to Neyman & Pearson's (1933) work on hypothesis testing and statistical inference (e.g. Gigerenzer et al 1989), but the underlying probabilistic concepts can be traced back chronologically, if not genealogically, more than 200 years. The concepts were central, for example, in the prepsychology contributions of Bayes and Gauss. The concepts reappeared at psychology's beginning in the work of Fechner, who extended Gauss's "true score plus error" model to the psychophysics of sensory perception (Link 1994, Murray 1993). The concepts resurfaced again during the first half of this century in Thurstone's (1927) pioneering work on the Law of Comparative Judgment, a unidimensional probabilistic scaling model (Murray 1993). They then played a featured role in the work of Neyman & Pearson, as noted. Around midcentury they reappeared in the guise of information theory, which included the work of engineers and physicists such as Shannon & Weaver (1949), Peterson, Birdsall, and Wiener (see Macmillan & Creelman 1991 and Pierce 1980) , as well as psychologists [e.g. Tanner, Green, and Swets (Swets 1973)]. Today, the concepts are prominent in the work of cognitive scientists such as Luce, Townsend, Ashby, Ennis, MacKay, and Zinnes (see Ashby 1992). SDT's concepts and methods also are being adopted with increasing frequency by scientists in other fields that place a premium on minimizing error through the development of assessment, prediction, and decision systems with high accuracy and discriminatory power—fields such as information retrieval, aptitude testing, psychiatric diagnosis, and medical detection and decision-making (Murphy et al 1987, Swets 1996).

It is beyond the scope of this review to provide a detailed and comprehensive summary of SDT. Our aims here are (a) to provide a clear overview of SDT that is more conceptual than mathematical; (b) to highlight SDT's relevance and potential contributions to clinical assessment in psychology; and (c) to stimulate and entice readers into pursuing the topic further on their own, in greater depth. Throughout, we try to supply readers with linked pointers to key resources. In the end, we hope to convince readers that there no longer is any excuse for continuing to conduct business as usual, now that SDT provides the necessary tools for comparing and evaluating the information value of our clinical assessment methods. SDT-based indices represent a clear and significant advance over traditional accuracy indices such as sensitivity, specificity, and predictive power (Hsiao et al 1989; Metz 1978; Murphy et al 1987). Moreover, the practical application of SDT methods has been enhanced by the development of methods to help determine optimal cutoff scores and to examine the influence of prevalence, or base rates, on both the selection of cutoff scores and the accuracy of estimates (Metz et al 1973, Somoza & Mossman 1991, Somoza et al 1989).

Overview of SDT

The aim of diagnostic assessment systems is to discriminate between two mutually exclusive states, such as the presence or absence of a signal. For instance, a radiologist uses X-rays to help decide whether a tumor is present or absent; a psychologist uses an HRSD-R score to help decide whether to diagnose a patient as suffering from depression or panic disorder. SDT methods partition the variability in the data produced by such diagnostic systems into two independent components: perceptual and decisional. The perceptual index is a measure of diagnostic accuracy; that is, it represents quantitatively how well the system discriminates between the two possible states. The decisional index, in contrast, represents quantitatively the position of the cutoff score, or criterion, employed to arrive at the discriminations, e.g. whether the criterion was liberal or conservative.

By providing separate indices of these perceptual and decisional components, SDT offers a significant improvement over other, more traditional
methods of assessing the accuracy of diagnostic systems (e.g. percent correct;
sensitivity; specificity; positive predictive power; negative predictive power).
All the traditional indices confound the contributions of these two components, thereby yielding estimates of diagnostic accuracy, or discriminatory
power, that are influenced by the diagnostic system's criterion for discrimination. For reasons discussed in the previous section, this is not good.

To illustrate, suppose we wanted to evaluate the accuracy of the Bulimia
Inventory-Revised (BULIT-R) (Thelen et al 1996), a self-report questionnaire
designed to assist in diagnosing bulimia nervosa. The gold standard, or presumably true diagnoses, against which we evaluate the accuracy of the
BULIT-R, will be the diagnostic decisions of experts who conducted extensive
diagnostic interviews.[5] Table 1 summarizes the relevant frequency data in a
two-dimensional contingency table, where one dimension classifies cases (bulimia present or absent) based on a conventional BULIT-R cutting score of 104
or above. The second dimension classifies cases based on the experts' true diagnosis (bulimia present or absent). Displayed in the cells are raw frequencies
and both traditional and SDT cell labels. Hit, false alarm, miss, and correct rejection rates are identical to true positive, false positive, false negative, and
true negative rates; each is equal to the cell frequency divided by the corresponding column marginal frequency. For example, the miss rate (the probability of a true bulimia present case being identified by the BULIT-R as a bulimia absent case) is 2/23, or 0.087.

We could use the data in Table 1 to compute several traditional indices of
the BULIT-R's discriminatory power, or its ability to predict true diagnoses:
(*a*) Percent correct is the sum of hits and correct rejections divided by the overall sample size (140/147 = 0.952); (*b*) Sensitivity is the hit rate (or true positive
rate; 21/23 = 0.913); (*c*) specificity is the correct rejection rate (or true negative
rate; 119/124 = 0.960); (*d*) positive predictive power (PPP) and negative predictive power (NPP) are computed using Bayes' Theorem, as discussed before. The calculation of PPP = 0.808 is illustrated below (NPP = 0.983).

p(bulimia | score of 104+) = p(bulimia)*p(score of 104+ | bulimia)/p(score
of 104+) = 0.1565*0.9130/0.1768 = 0.1429/0.1768 =0.808.

PPP and NPP also may be obtained more easily by dividing the hit or correct rejection cell frequency, respectively, by the corresponding row marginal.

---

[5]Meehl (1959) pointed out the silliness of using tests for the sole purpose of predicting the
opinions of psychological experts. We use this gold standard because we presume that the experts'
opinions represent some true state of nature. Ultimately, the validity of the gold standard must be
demonstrated somehow.

Table 1 Frequencies of hits (true positives), misses (false negatives), false alarms (false positives), and correct rejections (true negatives) using a cutoff score of 104 on bulimia inventory—revised (BULIT-R) to diagnose the presence or absence of bulimia nervosa. [Adapted from Thelen et al (1996).]

Diagnosis based upon BULIT-R	True diagnosis		Row totals
	Bulimia present	Bulimia absent	
Bulimia present (score 104+)	21 hits or true positives	5 false alarms or false positives	26
Bulimia absent (score <104)	2 misses or false negatives	119 correct rejections or true negatives	121
Column totals	23	124	147

It is interesting to note that sensitivity, specificity, PPP, and NPP all are conditional probabilities. Sensitivity and specificity are conditional on the true diagnosis (i.e. they summarize the column data), whereas PPP and NPP are conditional on the diagnostic system's classification (i.e. they summarize the row data).

Each of these indices summarizes the BULIT-R's discriminatory power in this unique situation, as long as the prevalence and cutoff values are fixed. The values of all of these indices will change, however, if different cutoff values are used. In addition, the values of PPP and NPP will change if the prevalence, or base rate, changes. This is because PPP and NPP, unlike the other indices, include prevalence information in their formulas. Because the optimal cutoff value will vary, in part, as a function of prevalence, the other indices also are influenced indirectly by prevalence. Thus, all these common accuracy indices are unsatisfactory; none provides a unique measure of accuracy that is independent of cutoff (criterion, decision bias) and base rate (prevalence). None of these indices can serve as a common metric for comparing the information value and discriminatory power of the data from assessment methods.[6]

In contrast to these conventional indices of accuracy, which are unacceptable because they confound decisional and perceptual contributions to performance, SDT provides an estimate of diagnostic accuracy that is not confounded by changing cutoff values or prevalence rates. SDT estimates accuracy by analyzing the receiver (or relative) operating characteristic (ROC). Engineers originally developed ROC analysis to quantify how well an electronic receiver detects electronic signals in the presence of noise; ROC analysis ac-

---

[6]Other common reliability or concordance indices, such as kappa and the Y and Q statistics, also fluctuate as a function of prevalence, and thus are inadequate indices of information value (see Langenbucher et al 1996; Swets 1996, Ch. 3).

quired its name from its application to radar detection problems during World War II (Pierce 1980).

ROC analysis yields a quantitative index of accuracy corresponding to what we have been calling the information value of the data. The axes of an ROC plot are the hit and false alarm rates, and each point on an ROC curve corresponds to a pair of hit and false alarm rates that result from use of a specific cutoff value.[7] In more traditional language, the ROC curve is a plot of sensitivity against 1–specificity at all possible cutoff values. Figure 4 presents several idealized ROC curves on a single plot. As one moves along a specific ROC curve from the lower left corner (where false alarm and hit rates both are 0.0), to the upper right corner (where false alarm and hit rates both are 1.0), the cutoff changes from maximally conservative to maximally liberal. Traditional accuracy indices would vary widely as a function of such marked variability in cutoff values, but the area under the ROC curve (AUC) quantifies the information value of the assessment method independently of the cutoff value. Alternative indices in the SDT family, such as d' and d'_e, quantify the distance between the means of the two underlying distributions in standard deviation units. Both indices assume that the underlying distributions are normal, and d' also assumes that the variances of the distributions are homogeneous. Presently, AUC is the preferred SDT accuracy index because nonparametric procedures are available for estimating AUC and many users prefer a proportion-based, rather than a distance-based, measure of accuracy (Macmillan & Creelman 1991; Swets 1996).

An ROC curve that lies on the main diagonal indicates that the diagnostic system is operating at the level of chance, because the hit and false alarm rates are equal across the range of possible cutoff values. Chance performance corresponds to an AUC of 0.5. As the information value of the diagnostic system increases, the distance of the observed ROC curve from the chance line increases. Several ROC curves and their corresponding AUC values are depicted in Figure 4. The values for AUC can range from 0.0 (when the ROC curve passes from the lower left corner through the lower right corner to the upper right corner) to 1.0 (when the ROC curve passes from the lower left corner through the upper left corner to the upper right corner). AUC also has a readily interpretable probabilistic meaning: It corresponds to the probability that a randomly selected pair of observations drawn from the two underlying distributions will be ranked (and thus classified) correctly (Green & Swets 1974,

---

[7]In some presentations, the ROC curve is a plot of z-transformed hit and false alarm rate pairs [z(FAR), z(HR)]. In this coordinate system, the ROC curve becomes a straight line with a slope of 1.0 when the underlying distributions are normal and have homogeneous variances, whereas the ROC curve becomes a straight line with a slope other than 1.0 when the underlying distributions are normal but show nonhomogeneous variances (Swets 1996).

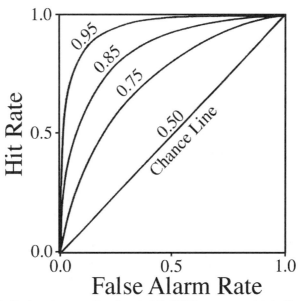

Figure 4   Idealized receiver operating characteristic (ROC) curves associated with various Area Under Curve (AUC) values. [Adapted from Swets (1988).]

Hanley & McNeil 1982). Thus, the value 1-AUC intuitively reflects the degree of overlap between the two distributions.

ROC curves can be generated in a variety of ways. First, multiple pairs of hit and false alarm rates can be calculated from a single data set by varying the cutoff. Second, the assessment method may be used repeatedly with different decision criteria employed on each occasion (i.e. from conservative to liberal). Each occasion provides a unique set of hit and false alarm rates. Third, a rating scale method may be used, in which raters not only classify the stimulus into one of two categories, but also indicate their confidence level for the accuracy of their classification, typically on a five-point scale. In this case, multiple pairs of hit and false alarm rates can be obtained by treating each confidence level as a separate cutoff value (Macmillan & Creelman 1991).

Earlier, we summarized a study by Thelen et al (1996) that examined the discriminatory power of the BULIT-R for the diagnosis of bulimia. Thelen et al presented the hit (0.808) and false alarm (0.017) rates for a BULIT-R cutoff score of 104, thus providing the coordinates for a single point on an ROC curve. However, we cannot compute an ROC curve from a single data point. This is a common limitation of published data, restricting our ability to perform ROC analyses on data from multiple studies to compare the information value of different methods.

To illustrate the benefits of ROC analyses of information value, therefore, we now turn to a study by Somoza et al (1994) that actually used SDT to examine the differential discriminatory power of six self-report measures (three for mood, three for anxiety) for the diagnosis of major depression and panic disorder. (We have been using this study as a model for our hypothetical examples up to now.) Figure 5 presents the ROC curves for the Revised Hamilton Psychiatric Rating Scale for Depression (HRSD-R), the Beck Depression Inventory (BDI) (Beck & Steer 1987), and the Beck Anxiety Inventory (BAI) (Beck et al 1988). To obtain an ROC curve for each self-report measure, Somoza et al calculated the hit and false alarm rates resulting from multiple cutoff values and used ROC programs developed by Metz et al (1973) to fit smoothed curves to these values. For the BAI, for example, they used cutoff values of 7, 13, 17, 24, and 32; these values are indicated by filled circles and are labeled *A* through *E*, respectively. Cutoff value *A* corresponds here to a very liberal criterion, which results in a substantial hit rate, but also a high false alarm rate. In contrast, the conservative cutoff value *E* results in a very low false alarm rate, but also an unimpressive hit rate. The AUC values for the HRSD-R, BDI, and BAI were .0896, 0.816, and 0.696, respectively. Further statistical analyses demonstrated that the HRSD-R does a significantly better job than the remaining five measures of discriminating between persons diagnosed with depression and panic disorder, regardless of whether a liberal, moderate, or conservative cutoff value is used. This example highlights the utility of the AUC index

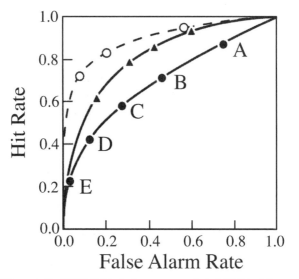

Figure 5   ROC curves for HRSD-R (*dashed curve, open circles*), BDI (*solid curve, solid triangles*), and BAI (*solid curve, solid circles*). [Adapted from Somoza et al (1994).]

as a common metric for quantifying information value independent of prevalence rates and cutoff values.

Of course, ROC models, like any mathematical model, are constrained by assumptions and limited in scope. ROC curves and AUC values typically are estimated using parametric methods only when the underlying distributions are normal and show homogeneous variances. Fortunately, parametric estimation appears to be robust to violations of these assumptions (Hanley 1988), and nonparametric estimation methods also are available when either or both of these assumptions are violated (Hanley & McNeil 1982). Both parametric and nonparametric methods allow the user to compare AUC values either to chance performance values (AUC = 0.5) or to the maximum AUC value attainable, given the prevalence rate of the phenomenon. AUC values for different diagnostic systems also can be compared statistically. Presently, ROC analysis is applicable only to unidimensional classifications into dichotomous categories, although diagnosticians often are called upon to make multidimensional classifications into more than two discrete categories. Fortunately, well-developed multidimensional generalizations of SDT exist (Ashby & Townsend 1986, Kadlec & Townsend 1992) that may be amenable to ROC analysis, and Scurfield (1996) recently generalized ROC analysis to unidimensional classifications into three or more categories.

Selection of Cutoff Values and Effects of Prevalence

Although ROC analysis provides an index of information value independent of cutoff value and prevalence, it neither provides the optimal cutoff value nor illustrates how prevalence affects cutoff selection (Hsiao et al 1989; Mossman & Somoza 1989; Murphy et al 1987; Somoza et al 1994). Selection of an optimal cutoff value necessarily involves specification of a function to be maximized. Thus, there is no true and unique optimal cutoff value. Because the usefulness of a diagnostic test in a practical setting is a function of the hit rate, false alarm rate, and prevalence of the phenomenon, researchers must consider all three factors when choosing a cutoff. The indices of percent correct, hit frequency, sensitivity, and specificity do not reflect all three factors.

There are two common approaches to selecting optimal cutoff values that incorporate these three factors in their criterion function. Meehl & Rosen (1955) and Somoza & Mossman (1991), among others, have advocated the use of an approach that combines an SDT analysis with utility-based decision theory (see also Metz 1978; Somoza et al 1989). This approach allows the user to place a differential value upon (i.e. to specify the differential utility of) hits (H), false alarms (FA), correct rejections (CR), and misses (M). Frequently, the user does not value these four possible outcomes equally because of their differential implications. As summarized in the following equation, the overall utility of a specific cutoff value is a function of the hit and false alarm rates (HR and FAR) that result from a given cutoff value and a prevalence estimate (Pr):

$$U_{overall} = (Pr)(HR)(U_H) + (Pr)(1-HR)(U_M) + (1-Pr)(FAR)(U_{FA}) + (1-Pr)(1-FAR)(U_{CR}). \qquad (2)$$

This utility approach has been criticized because it requires the user to specify quantitatively the utilities of the four outcomes, even though these often are thought of qualitatively. A user may view hits as more important than correct rejections, for example, but struggle to specify precisely how much more important hits are. Fortunately, it is possible for the user to specify a range of utility estimates rather than precise utility estimates (see Somoza & Mossman 1991). It also is important to reiterate that there is no absolute optimal cutoff value, apart from assumptions and criteria specifying the meaning of optimal. Ultimately, users have no option but to pay their money and make their choice.

To finesse the use of subjective utilities, Metz et al (1973) proposed that an information theory (Shannon & Weaver 1949) analysis of the ROC curve provides a natural criterion (information maximum, or I_{max}) for the selection of an optimal cutoff value (see also Mossman & Somoza 1989; Somoza et al 1989, 1994). According to Metz et al's approach, information refers to the reduction of uncertainty about the true classification of a person that results from administering the diagnostic measure (i.e. the difference between the prior and posterior uncertainties).

Inspection of the criterion functions specified by decision theorists and information theorists reveals that both incorporate the false alarm rate, the hit rate, and the prevalence rate, but I_{max} maximizes information, whereas $U_{overall}$ maximizes overall utility. Interestingly, $U_{overall}$ is simply a general case of I_{max}, because I_{max} simply provides an alternative specification of the utilities of the four outcomes; the two formulas are equivalent if U_H is constrained to be $\log_2(HR/B)$, U_M is constrained to be $\log_2[(1-HR)/(1-B)]$, U_{FA} is constrained to be $\log_2(FAR/B)$, and U_{CR} is constrained to be $\log_2[(1-FAR)/(1-B)]$. Thus, whereas METZ et al's (1973) approach to criterion selection sidesteps the necessity of the researcher's explicitly specifying the outcome utilities, the assumptions underlying the information theory formulation of the criterion function nonetheless exert an implicit influence on the criterion selection. There may be advantages to explicit specification of the outcomes' utilities, or at least to weighting the I_{max} terms by the more traditional utility estimates.

Regardless of the approach taken to specification of the criterion function, the user proceeds by calculating the value of the function for a wide range of cutoff values and prevalence rates (as the latter will influence the optimality of varying cutoff values). The maxima in the resulting three-dimensional topography correspond to the optimal cutoff values, given the criterion function specification. Various qualitative characteristics of this topography, such as the number of maxima and the steepness of their surrounding areas, may provide helpful indicators of the measure's robustness under suboptimal conditions. It is important to note here that neither $U_{overall}$ nor I_{max} are indices of information value as we have defined it. Both utility and information vary as a function of prevalence and the cutoff value, so they are not equivalent to the AUC index of information value.

Somoza et al (1994), in their analysis of the relative discriminatory power of mood and anxiety measures for the diagnosis of major depression and panic disorder, used the I_{max} criterion function to select the optimal cutoff values for each of the six measures for varying prevalence rates. To illustrate the impact of the cutoff score and prevalence on I_{max} for each of the six measures, Somoza et al present three two-dimensional figures (I_{max} by cutoff score, I_{max} by prevalence, and prevalence by cutoff score). We discuss only the HRSD-R results below. The steepness of the criterion function around the maximal cutoff score in their I_{max} by cutoff figure indicates that the practical utility of the HRSD-R decreases rapidly as the cutoff deviates from its optimal value. It also is interesting to note in their I_{max} by prevalence figure that minimal values of the criterion function are much more likely when the prevalence rate is extreme, whereas maximal values are more likely when the prevalence rate is nearer 0.5. Thus, these figures illustrate quantitatively what Meehl & Rosen (1955) described long ago. Ideally, of course, we would like to depict I_{max} for the HRSD-R as a function of cutoff score and prevalence simultaneously, in a three-dimensional rendition of their three separate two-dimensional figures, as cutoff values and prevalence exert interactive influences as well as independent influences on the value of the criterion function.

Specific SDT Applications

Swets (1988, 1996) summarized the use of ROC methods to evaluate the diagnostic performance of assessments in various fields outside of clinical psychology. In clinical medicine, for example, ROC methods are used to quantify both the discriminatory power of medical imaging techniques (for the detection of pathology) and the decision criteria used by individual interpreters. In the field of aptitude testing, ROC analyses are used to evaluate the validity of various aptitude indices for predicting dichotomous outcomes, such as satisfactory or unsatisfactory school or work performance, regardless of whether the criterion used to distinguish the two outcomes is conservative, moderate, or liberal. ROC methods also are used to evaluate the performance of various information retrieval methods independent of the criteria used for inclusion of information.

A systematic search of the empirical literature in clinical psychological assessment, however, yielded surprisingly few published examples of SDT's application to real-world clinical problems. Thus, the aim of this section is not to provide a detailed and exhaustive summary of all studies that have used SDT; rather, the aim is simply to give readers a sense of the range or diversity of problems that can be analyzed by SDT methods.

ROC methods have been used most extensively to evaluate the utility of laboratory tests or questionnaires for discriminating between diagnostic classes or between disordered and nondisordered persons. Several studies of this type are noteworthy for their methodological rigor and conceptual clarity. Our explication of SDT's theoretical and methodological foundations has drawn heavily from one leading example from this class of applications—Somoza et al's (1994) use of SDT to quantify and compare the relative ability of three depression measures to differentiate between samples of depressed patients and panic disorder patients. In that same paper, they also describe the use of SDT to quantify and compare the ability of three anxiety measures to differentiate between the same samples of diagnostic groups. In an earlier study, Mossman & Somoza (1989) used ROC methods to evaluate the literature on the utility of the dexamethasone suppression test (DST) for discriminating between depressed and nondepressed persons. Although AUC indices suggested moderate discriminatory power for the DST across studies, the optimal cutoff (as assessed by the I_{max} criterion function) varied widely across studies and as a function of prevalence, demonstrating clearly the nonexistence of a context-free optimal cutoff value. Similarly, Battaglia & Perna (1995) used ROC analyses to contrast the discriminatory power of two laboratory assessments of panic disorder and provided optimal cutoffs (using the I_{max} criterion function) for their particular prevalence rates (although not for others). Finally, Somoza & Mossman (1991) quantified the adequacy of REM latency for discriminating between depressed and nondepressed persons, and illustrated the use of utility-based decision theory for selecting optimal cutoff values as a function of prevalence.

Although diagnostic status has been the primary criterion variable investigated using ROC methods, several researchers have used, or have suggested using, ROC methods to evaluate clinical assessment and prediction across a wide range of criterion variables, including the presence of child maltreatment (Camasso & Jagannathan 1995), the likelihood of suicide attempts (Erdman et al 1987), decisions about whether to remove a child from a home (Dalgleish 1988), risk of future disorder (Olin et al 1995), the presence of violence (Mossman 1994), violence recidivism (Rice & Harris 1995), malingering (Mossman & Hart 1996), treatment relapse (Marder et al 1991), and treatment response (Ackerman et al 1996). In each instance, ROC methods provided an improved estimate of predictive power, relative to traditional methods, that resulted from their independence from cutoff values and their attention to the impact of prevalence on the optimal cutoff values.

Future Directions

SDT is a theory-based method of quantifying the performance of diagnostic systems. We are aware of no competing methods that are as well developed, powerful, promising, or enduring. Indeed, the probabilistic concepts underlying SDT are at least as old as psychology itself. Nevertheless, our review of the assessment literature uncovered surprisingly few empirical reports of clinical psychologists employing SDT. In contrast, we found that the method has been discovered by diagnosticians and decision makers in other fields, such as medicine, aptitude testing, and information retrieval systems. Given SDT's demonstrated value in these other fields, we found it all the more puzzling that clinical psychologists still have not adopted SDT as their primary method for evaluating and comparing competing clinical assessments (and interventions). At this point, we only can speculate about the possible reasons.

Two related factors may be (a) the quantitative demands of SDT, and (b) the conceptual demands of classical probability theory upon which it is based. These features may be intimidating to clinical psychologists whose quantitative training has been limited to psychology courses in traditional statistical methods. Even psychologists who study this approach may find it elusive. Sedlmeier (1997) reported that past efforts to teach Bayesian inference, for example, have achieved disappointing results; this way of thinking does not seem to stick, for some reason. This certainly is consistent with the apparent lack of practical impact that Meehl & Rosen's (1955) widely cited paper has had over the years. To overcome this problem, Sedlmeier (1997) has developed a computerized tutorial (BasicBayes) that has shown promise.

Another factor may be that SDT has not gone without criticism. Like all theories, it is based on assumptions that sometimes may not be appropriate. In its original form, for example, SDT assumed that the variable used to discriminate between two states (e.g. the test score used to distinguish diseased from healthy) was normally distributed within each state; however, this assumption is not always valid. As it turns out, investigators have explored the implications of non-normal distributions, and have found that AUC analyses tend to be robust, even when the normality assumption is violated (Hanley 1988). These same investigators also have introduced nonparametric methods of analyzing AUC that do not require this assumption, but still yield similar results (Hanley & McNeil 1982).

Yet another possible criticism of SDT is that it is limited to diagnostic prob0lems involving dichotomous decisions. This is a lesser concern than it might appear at first. Virtually any diagnostic task—whether dimensional or categorical—can be recast as a dichotomous problem. For analysis of those infrequent diagnostic problems that absolutely require more elaborate structures, more elaborate multidimensional modeling methods that generalize unidimensional SDT have been developed (e.g. general recognition theory) (see Ashby & Townsend 1986; Kadlec & Townsend 1992; see also Macmillan & Creelman 1991 for information on a related method based upon choice theory).

Swets (1988) has identified several other possible threats to the reliability and validity of SDT as a method of quantifying the information value and accuracy of diagnostic tests. One is the so-called gold standard problem. If we cannot determine with certainty for every case in our sample the true state, that is, whether each case is positive or negative, then we cannot possibly expect SDT to provide a valid evaluation of a test's accuracy. For example, how can the discriminatory power of polygraph tests in real-world criminal cases be determined if the true guilt or innocence of each case is uncertain? Another problem arises when the assessment system and the determination of actual truth are not independent. For example, if the gold standard in criminal cases is defined by criminals' confessions, and the polygraph test is used to predict guilt or innocence, then the predictive system may contaminate the truth because confessions may be more likely after the polygraph has indicated guilty. It is also a problem when the procedures for determining the gold standard influence the selection of cases for the test sample. In general, methodological concerns about the representativeness of samples are just as critical to the evaluation of diagnostic test accuracy as they are in any other clinical research. Swets (1988) emphasized, however, that none of these problems is due to weaknesses in SDT; all stem from inadequacies in our tests and in our ability to determine truth.

Clinical psychology's failure to discover SDT over the years cannot be blamed on lack of access to the method. Several authors have made extensive efforts to promote an awareness and understanding of SDT's value as a method of evaluating diagnostic systems [e.g. see Meehl's collected works (1973); the collected papers of Swets (1996); the last in a series of seven papers by Somoza & Mossman in the *Journal of Neuropsychiatry and Clinical Neurosciences* (1992)]. Clinical assessors simply have not responded to these efforts with appropriate enthusiasm.

The time is ripe, however, for clinical psychologists at long last to acquire the requisite knowledge and skills to employ SDT methods (and their multidimensional cousins, when necessary) as the standard benchmark system for evaluating and comparing the incremental validity and accuracy of clinical assessment methods. For example, Langenbucher et al (1996) emphasized the importance of comparing empirically the classification results yielded by competing nosologies (e.g. DSM-IV vs ICD-10). For all the reasons outlined in this review, SDT is the obvious method of choice for such comparisons.

Clinical psychologists should be able to pursue on their own the use of SDT in clinical assessment. A number of excellent resources are available for this.

We recommend the following resources, which we have listed in order from the most accessible and general overviews to the most demanding theoretical and quantitative analyses: (*a*) Somoza and Mossman (1990—first in a series in the same journal); (*b*) Swets (1988); (*c*) Murphy et al (1987); (*d*) Hsiao et al (1989); (*e*) Mossman & Somoza (1989); (*f*) Metz (1978); (*g*) Swets (1996); (*h*) Macmillan & Creelman (1991).

We acknowledge that some clinical psychologists may find daunting the up-front investment required to retool as experts in signal detection theory, and to reconceptualize the clinical assessment enterprise from this new perspective. The long-term benefits of such an investment promise to be well worth these up-front costs. This review began with descriptions of conceptual and methodological problems that have stymied scientific progress in clinical assessment. The review then introduced signal detection theory as a solution to many of those problems, and gave specific examples of SDT's successful application to similar problems across a range of fields. We have given readers a bite of the SDT apple. It is our hope that, having tasted of this knowledge, readers will not find it easy to return to old, inferior ways of evaluating clinical assessment methods. For those willing to make the effort to learn and adopt SDT methods, the future of clinical assessment should look brighter.

Visit the *Annual Reviews home page* at
http://www.AnnualReviews.org.

Literature Cited

Ackerman DL, Greenland S, Bystritsky A. 1996. Use of receiver-operator characteristic (ROC) curve analysis to evaluate predictors of response to clomipramine therapy. *Psychopharmacol. Bull.* 32:157–65

Ashby FG, ed. 1992. *Multidimensional Models of Perception and Cognition.* Hillsdale, NJ: Erlbaum

Ashby FG, Townsend JT. 1986. Varieties of perceptual independence. *Psychol. Rev.* 93:154–79

Battaglia M, Perna G. 1995. The 35% CO_2 challenge in panic disorder: optimization by receiver operating characteristic (ROC) analysis. *J. Psychiatr. Res.* 29:111–19

Bayes T. 1763. An essay towards solving a problem in the doctrine of chances. *Philos. Trans. R. Soc. London* 53:370–418

Beck AT, Epstein N, Brown G, Steer RA. 1988. An inventory for measuring clinical anxiety: psychometric properties. *J. Consult. Clin. Psychol.* 56:893–97

Beck AT, Steer RA. 1987. *Manual for the Revised Beck Depression Inventory.* San Antonio, TX: Psychol. Corp.

Camasso MJ, Jagannathan R. 1995. Prediction accuracy of the Washington and Illinois risk assessment instruments: an application of receiver operating characteristic curve analysis. *Soc. Work Res.* 19:174–83

Cohen J. 1994. The earth is round (*p*<.05). *Am. Psychol.* 49:997–1003

Dalgleish LI. 1988. Decision making in child abuse cases: applications of social judgment theory and signal detection theory. In *Human Judgment: The SJT View*, ed. B Brehmer, CRB Joyce, 54:317–60. Amsterdam: Elsevier

Erdman HP, Greist JH, Gustafson DH, Taves JE, Klein MH. 1987. Suicide risk prediction by computer interview: a prospective study *J. Clin. Psychiatry* 48:464–67

Gigerenzer G, Murray DJ. 1987. *Cognition as Intuitive Statistics.* Hillsdale, NJ: Erlbaum

Gigerenzer G, Swijtink Z, Porter T, Daston L, Beatty J, Krüger L. 1989. *The Empire of Chance: How Probability Changed Science and Everyday Life.* Cambridge, UK: Cambridge Univ. Press

Green DM, Swets JA. 1974. *Signal Detection Theory and Psychophysics.* Huntington, NY: Krieger. 2nd ed. Reprint. New York: Wiley, 1966. 1st ed.

Hanley JA. 1988. The robustness of the "binormal" assumptions in fitting ROC curves. *Med. Decis. Mak.* 8:197–203

Hanley JA, McNeil BJ. 1982. The meaning and use of the area under a receiver operating characteristic (ROC) curve. *Radiology* 143:29–36

Hsiao JK, Bartko JJ, Potter WZ. 1989. Diagnosing diagnoses. *Arch. Gen. Psychiatry* 46:664–67

Kadlec H, Townsend JT. 1992. Signal detection analyses of dimensional interactions. In *Multidimensional Models of Perception and Cognition*, ed. FG Ashby, pp. 181–227. Hillsdale, NJ: Erlbaum

Langenbucher J, Labouvie E, Morgenstern J. 1996. Measuring diagnostic agreement. *J. Consult. Clin. Psychol.* 64:1285–89

Link SW. 1994. Rediscovering the past: Gustav Fechner and signal detection theory. *Psychol. Sci.* 5:335–40

Loftus GR. 1996. Psychology will be a much better science when we change the way we analyze data. *Curr. Dir. Psychol. Sci.* 5: 161–71

Macmillan NA, Creelman CD. 1991. *Detection Theory: A User's Guide.* Cambridge, UK: Cambridge Univ. Press

Marder SR, Mintz J, Van Putten T, Lebell M, Wirshing WC, Johnston-Cronk K. 1991. Early prediction of relapse in schizophrenia: an application of receiver operating characteristic (ROC) methods. *Psychopharmacol. Bull.* 27:79–82

McFall R. 1993. The essential role of theory in psychological assessment. In *Improving Assessment in Rehabilitation and Health*, ed. RL Glueckauf, LB Sechrest, GR Bond, EC McDonel, pp. 11–32. Newbury Park, CA: Sage

Meehl PE. 1959. Some ruminations on the validation of clinical procedures. *Can. J. Psychol.* 13:102–28

Meehl PE. 1971. High school yearbooks: a reply to Schwarz. *J. Abnorm. Psychol.* 77: 143–48

Meehl PE. 1973. *Psychodiagnosis: Selected Papers.* New York: Norton

Meehl PE. 1978. Theoretical risks and tabular asterisks: Sir Karl, Sir Ronald, and the slow progress of soft psychology. *J. Consult. Clin. Psychol.* 46:806–34

Meehl PE, Rosen A. 1955. Antecedent probability and the efficiency of psychometric signs, patterns, or cutting scores. *Psychol. Bull.* 52:194–216

Metz CE. 1978. Basic principles of ROC analysis. *Semin. Nucl. Med.* 8:283–98

Metz CE, Goodenough DJ, Rossmann K. 1973. Evaluation of receiver operating characteristic curve data in terms of information theory, with applications in radiography. *Radiology* 109:297–303

Mischel W. 1968. *Personality and Assessment.* New York: Wiley

Mossman D. 1994. Assessing predictions of violence: being accurate about accuracy. *J. Consult. Clin. Psychol.* 62:783–92

Mossman D, Hart KJ. 1996. Presenting evidence of malingering to courts: insights from decision theory. *Behav. Sci. Law* 14:271–91

Mossman D, Somoza E. 1989. Maximizing diagnostic information from the dexamethasone suppression test: an approach to criterion selection using receiver operating characteristic analysis. *Arch. Gen. Psychiatry* 46:653–60

Murphy JM, Berwick DM, Weinstein MC, Borus JF, Budman SH, Klerman GL. 1987. Performance of screening and diagnostic tests. *Arch. Gen. Psychiatry* 44: 550–55

Murray DJ. 1993. A perspective for viewing the history of psychophysics. *Behav. Brain Sci.* 16:115–86

Neyman J, Pearson ES. 1933. On the problem of the most efficient tests of statistical hypotheses. *Philos. Trans. R. Soc. London Ser. A* 231:289–337

Olin SS, John RS, Mednick SA. 1995. Assessing the predictive value of teacher reports in a high risk sample for schizophrenia: a ROC analysis. *Schizophr. Res.* 16:53–66

Pierce JR. 1980. *An Introduction to Information Theory: Symbols, Signals and Noise.* New York: Dover. 2nd rev. ed.

Popper K. 1962. *Conjectures and Refutations.* New York: Basic Books

Rice ME, Harris GT. 1995. Violent recidivism: assessing predictive validity *J. Consult. Clin. Psychol.* 63:737–48

Riskind JH, Beck AT, Brown G, Steer RA. 1987. Taking the measure of anxiety and depression: validity of the reconstructed Hamilton scales. *J. Nerv. Ment. Dis.* 175: 474–79

Schmitt SA. 1969. *Measuring Uncertainty: An Elementary Introduction to Bayesian Statistics.* Reading, MA: Addison-Wesley

Scurfield BK. 1996. Multiple-event forced-choice tasks in the theory of signal detectability. *J. Math. Psychol.* 40:253–96

Sedlmeier P. 1997. BasicBayes: a tutor system for simple Bayesian inference. *Behav. Res. Methods Instrum.* 29:328–36

Shannon CE, Weaver W. 1949. *The Mathematical Theory of Communication.* Urbana: Univ. Ill. Press

Somoza E, Mossman D. 1990. Introduction to neuropsychiatric decision making: binary diagnostic tests. *J. Neuropsychol. Clin. Neurosci.* 2:297–300

Somoza E, Mossman D. 1991. "Biological markers" and psychiatric diagnosis: risk-benefit balancing using ROC analysis. *Biol. Psychiatry* 29:811–26

Somoza E, Mossman D. 1992. Comparing diagnostic tests using information theory: the INFO-ROC technique. *J. Neuropsychol. Clin. Neurosci.* 4:214–19

Somoza E, Soutullo-Esperon L, Mossman D. 1989. Evaluation and optimization of diagnostic tests using receiver operating characteristic analysis and information theory. *Int. J. Biomed. Comput.* 24:153–89

Somoza E, Steer RA, Beck AT, Clark DA. 1994. Differentiating major depression and panic disorders by self-report and clinical rating scales: ROC analysis and information theory. *Behav. Res. Ther.* 32:771–82

Swets JA. 1988. Measuring the accuracy of diagnostic systems. *Science* 240:1285–93

Swets JA. 1996. *Signal Detection Theory and ROC Analysis in Psychological Diagnostics: Collected Papers.* Mahwah, NJ: Erlbaum

Thelen MH, Mintz LB, Vander Wal JS. 1996. The bulimia test—revised: validation with DSM-IV criteria for bulimia nervosa. *Psychol. Assess.* 8:219–21

Thurstone LL. 1927. A law of comparative judgment. *Psychol. Rev.* 34:273–86

Wiggins JS. 1973. *Personality and Prediction: Principles of Personality Assessment.* Reading, MA: Addison-Wesley

Annu. Rev. Psychol. 1999. 50:243–71
Copyright © 1999 by Annual Reviews. All rights reserved

HIGH-LEVEL SCENE PERCEPTION

John M. Henderson and Andrew Hollingworth

Department of Psychology, Michigan State University, East Lansing, Michigan
48824; e-mail: john@eyelab.msu.edu, andrew@eyelab.msu.edu

KEY WORDS: eye movements, vision, scene identification, object identification, change
             blindness

ABSTRACT

Three areas of high-level scene perception research are reviewed. The first
concerns the role of eye movements in scene perception, focusing on the influence of ongoing cognitive processing on the position and duration of fixations in a scene. The second concerns the nature of the scene representation
that is retained across a saccade and other brief time intervals during ongoing
scene perception. Finally, we review research on the relationship between
scene and object identification, focusing particularly on whether the meaning of a scene influences the identification of constituent objects.

CONTENTS

0084-6570/99/0201-0243$08.00

INTRODUCTION

To a first approximation, research in human vision can be divided into three areas of investigation. Low-level or early vision is concerned with extraction of physical properties such as depth, color, and texture from an image as well as the generation of representations of surfaces and edges (Marr 1982). Intermediate-level vision concerns extraction of shape and spatial relations that can be determined without regard to meaning but that typically require a selective or serial process (Ullman 1996). Finally, high-level vision concerns the mapping from visual representations to meaning and includes the study of processes and representations related to the interaction of cognition and perception, including the active acquisition of information, short-term memory for visual information, and the identification of objects and scenes. In this chapter we review three important areas of investigation in the study of high-level scene perception. First, we examine eye movements in scene perception, focusing on the cognitive control of eye movements and the degree to which meaning and ongoing cognitive processes influence eye movement behavior. Second, we review recent work on the nature of the scene representation that is retained across a saccade and other similarly brief intervals during ongoing scene perception. Finally, we review work on the interaction of cognition and perception, focusing on object and scene identification. Although these topics have a long tradition of empirical investigation, they each have received a flurry of new work in the past few years.

In research on high-level scene perception, the concept of *scene* is typically defined (though often implicitly) as a semantically coherent (and often nameable) view of a real-world environment comprising background elements and multiple discrete objects arranged in a spatially licensed manner. Background elements are taken to be larger-scale, immovable surfaces and structures, such as ground, walls, floors, and mountains, whereas objects are smaller-scale discrete entities that are manipulable (e.g. can be moved) within the scene. Clearly, these definitions are neither exact nor mutually exclusive. For example, the distinction between a scene and an object depends on spatial scale. An office scene may contain a desk as one of its component objects. But in a more focused view, the desktop might become a scene, with its surface forming the background and a stapler, phone, and pen serving as individuated objects. It is difficult to determine precisely when the spatial scale becomes too small or too large to call the resulting view a scene. Is the inside of a desk drawer a scene? Is a box of paperclips a scene? Most research on scene perception has avoided this problem of definition by using views of environments scaled to a human size. So an encompassing view of a kitchen or a playground would be considered a good scene, whereas a view of a box of paperclips or an aerial view of a city would not. For the current purposes we adopt this imprecise, intuitive, and not wholly satisfying definition, holding to the belief that definitions are often best refined as a product of empirical investigation.

EYE MOVEMENT CONTROL IN SCENE PERCEPTION

Because of the optical structure of the eyes, the gradient in cone density in the retina, and the preferential mapping of foveal photoreceptors onto visual cortical tissue, acuity is highest at the point of fixation and drops off precipitously and continuously with increasing visual eccentricity (Anstis 1974, Riggs 1965). The highest-quality visual information is acquired from the region of the scene that projects to the fovea, a region of the retina corresponding to about the central 2° of the viewed scene (about the size of a thumbnail at arm's length). The human visual-cognitive system takes advantage of the high resolving power of the fovea by reorienting the fixation point around the viewed scene an average of three times each second via saccadic eye movements. During a *saccade*, the point of regard sweeps rapidly across the scene at velocities of up to 900°/s as the eyes rotate in their sockets (Carpenter 1988). During a *fixation*, the point of regard is relatively (though not perfectly) still. Pattern information is acquired during the fixations; information useful for ongoing perceptual and cognitive analysis of the scene normally cannot be acquired during a saccade (Matin 1974, Volkmann 1986).

A complete understanding of scene perception requires understanding the processes that control *where* the fixation point tends to be centered during scene viewing and *how long* the fixation position tends to remain centered at a particular location. In this section we review the literature on eye movements during scene perception. The scope of this review is restricted in two important ways. First, we focus on eye movements during the viewing of pictorial representations of static scenes. Eye movements during viewing of dynamic scenes have recently been reviewed by Land & Furneaux (1997). Second, we focus on molar-level eye movement behavior associated with ongoing perceptual and cognitive processing. We ignore, for the purposes of this review, other types of eye movements (e.g. smooth pursuit, vergence, slow drifts, microsaccades, and stabilization reflexes; see Carpenter 1988) as well as stimulus-based oculomotor effects like the global effect (Findlay 1982) and the optimal viewing position effect (O'Regan 1992a). Although these phenomena are important, they represent aspects of eye movement behavior that do not directly reflect ongoing visual-cognitive processing related to high-level scene perception.

Fixation Position During Scene Perception

In a classic study, Buswell (1935) reported the first systematic exploration of the spatial distribution of fixations during scene perception. Two hundred viewers examined 55 pictures of different types of artwork, such as architecture, sculpture, and paintings, under a variety of viewing instructions. Buswell found that fixation positions were highly regular and related to the information in the pictures. For example, viewers tended to concentrate their fixations on the people rather than on background regions when examining the painting *Sunday Afternoon on the Island of La Grande Jatte* by Georges Seurat. These data provided some of the earliest evidence that eye movement patterns during complex scene perception are related to the information in the scene and, by extension, to ongoing perceptual and cognitive processing.

In another classic study, Yarbus (1967) asked viewers to examine color paintings of scenes and other artwork over extended viewing times. Yarbus found that when viewers examined a picture of IE Repin's *An Unexpected Visitor* to determine the ages of the people in the scene, they tended to concentrate their fixations on the people and particularly on the faces of those people. When viewers were instead attempting to estimate the material circumstances of the family in the scene, they distribute their fixations more widely over the scene. Yarbus observed similar systematicity in eye movements for other scenes and for other types of pictures such as faces and drawings of objects and suggested that the eyes tend to land on regions containing information that is either actually or in the viewer's opinion "useful or essential for perception."

The observation by Buswell (1935) and Yarbus (1967) that more informative scene regions receive more fixations has been replicated many times. In the first study to explore this relationship analytically, Mackworth & Morandi (1967) divided each of two color photographs into 64 square regions, and a first group of viewers rated the informativeness of each region based on how easy it would be to recognize on another occasion. A second group of viewers then examined the photographs with the task of deciding which of the two they preferred. *Fixation density* (the total number of discrete fixations in a given region over the course of scene viewing) in each of the 64 regions in each scene was found to be related to the rated informativeness of the region, with regions rated more informative receiving more fixations. In addition, viewers were as likely to fixate an informative region in the first two seconds of scene viewing as in other two second intervals, suggesting that region informativeness could be detected relatively early during scene viewing. Furthermore, regions that received low informativeness ratings were often not fixated at all, suggesting that uninformative regions could be rejected as potential fixation sites based on information acquired from the visual periphery.

The two pictures used by Mackworth & Morandi (1967) were visually and informationally simple: One picture depicted a pair of eyes within a hooded mask and the other a coastal map. In both, large regions were relatively uniform in their visual properties. Using scenes taken predominantly from the Thematic Apperception Test, Antes (1974) provided evidence that region informativeness also affects fixation position in relatively complex scenes. Like Mackworth & Morandi (1967), Antes first asked a group of participants to rate the informativeness of scene regions. A separate group of viewers then examined the scenes while their eye movements were recorded. Antes found that the very first fixation position selected by a viewer (following the experimenter-induced initial fixation position at the center of the scene) was much more likely to be within an informative than an uninformative region of a scene, suggesting rapid control of fixation position by scene characteristics.

The studies reviewed thus far suggest that the positions of individual fixations in scenes, including initial fixations, are determined by the informativeness of specific scene regions. However, because informativeness was defined in these studies on the basis of experimenter intuition (Buswell 1935, Yarbus 1967) or ratings provided by other viewers (Antes 1974, Mackworth & Morandi 1967), and because a subjective assessment of informativeness may be based on either visual or semantic factors (or both), it is not possible to determine from these studies whether the eyes were controlled by perceptual factors, semantic factors, or both. If fixation position reflects ongoing cognitive operations as well as perceptual processes during scene viewing, then semantically informative regions should also be more likely to receive fixations than semantically uninformative regions, holding visual informativeness constant.

Loftus & Mackworth (1978) reported the first study designed to investigate directly the influence of semantic informativeness on fixation position while holding visual informativeness constant. Participants viewed line drawings of scenes in which a manipulated target object was either high or low in semantic informativeness. Semantic informativeness was defined as the degree to which a given object was predictable within the scene, with unpredictable objects taken to be more informative. An attempt was made to control visual informativeness by exchanging objects across scenes. For example, a farm scene and an underwater scene were paired so that either scene could contain an octopus or a tractor. Participants viewed the scenes for 4 s each in preparation for a later memory recognition test. Loftus & Mackworth reported three important results. First, fixation density was greater for semantically informative than uninformative regions, suggesting that fixation position was controlled by the semantic informativeness of a region with respect to the scene. This result accords with the qualitative data available in the figures of Buswell (1935) and Yarbus (1967). Second, viewers also tended to fixate the semantically inconsistent objects earlier than the consistent objects during the course of scene viewing, suggesting that the semantics of the extrafoveal region could control fixation placement. Third, viewers were more likely to fixate the semantically informative objects immediately following the first saccade within the scene. Because the average distance of the saccade to the target object was greater than $7°$ of visual angle, these data suggest that fixation sites could be selected based on a semantic analysis of scene regions relatively distant in the visual periphery.

Two recent studies have called into question the conclusion that fixation placement is initially affected by a semantic analysis of scene regions that have only been viewed peripherally. First, De Graef et al (1990) manipulated semantic informativeness in a visual search task. Participants searched line drawings of scenes for nonobjects, objectlike figures that were meaningless. Using the same manipulation as Loftus & Mackworth (1978), prespecified meaningful target objects were placed in the scenes, and these objects were either semantically inconsistent (informative) or consistent (uninformative) with the rest of the scene. In contrast to Loftus & Mackworth, De Graef et al found no evidence that informative objects were initially fixated first or were fixated earlier than uninformative objects. In fact, viewers were equally likely to fixate the two types of objects for the first eight fixations in each scene. After the first eight fixations, viewers tended to fixate the uninformative objects sooner than the informative objects. These data thus contradict the finding that the eyes are immediately drawn to semantically informative objects in scenes and so call into question the conclusion that a semantic analysis of peripheral scene regions can control fixation placement.

Henderson et al (1999) reported two experiments designed to provide additional evidence concerning the influence of semantic informativeness on eye movements. The first used the Loftus & Mackworth (1978) methodology. Participants viewed line drawings of scenes under the same viewing instructions and with the same manipulation of semantic informativeness as used by Loftus & Mackworth. In contrast to Loftus & Mackworth but similar to De Graef et al (1990), Henderson et al (1999) found that viewers were no more likely to fixate initially the semantically informative target. Three specific results supported this conclusion. First, participants were equally likely to fixate the semantically informative and uninformative targets after the first (or second) saccade in the scene. Second, participants made the same average number of saccades in the scene prior to the initial fixation on the target object regardless of informativeness. Finally, the magnitude of the initial saccade to the target object was the same (about $3°$) regardless of informativeness. These data suggest that the eyes are not initially driven by peripheral semantic analysis of individual objects.

In a second experiment, Henderson et al (1999) used a visual search task to further examine the relationship between semantic informativeness and initial fixation placement. Viewers were given the name of a target object at the beginning of each trial. A line drawing of a scene was then presented, and the participant's task was to determine as quickly as possible whether the target object was present in the scene. The instructions were designed to motivate the participants to find the targets as quickly as possible. If initial eye movements are drawn to semantically informative objects in the periphery, informative objects should be found more quickly than uninformative objects. Instead, uninformative targets were fixated following fewer fixations (by about 0.5 fixations on average) than informative targets. Thus, there was no evidence that the eyes were drawn to semantically informative objects. Henderson et al (1999) suggested that the eyes reached the uninformative objects sooner because their positions were more spatially constrained by the scenes, not because local scene regions were analyzed for their meaning in the periphery. That is, information about the identity of the scene available during the initial fixation, in combination with a perceptual analysis of large-scale scene properties such as locations and orientations of surfaces, allowed participants to limit their search to likely target locations more easily when the target was semantically consistent with the scene (uninformative) than when it was inconsistent (informative) with the scene and so less spatially constrained.

Recent evidence presented by Mannan et al (1995) also suggests that initial fixation placements are controlled by perceptual features alone. In this study, eye movements were measured while viewers examined gray-scale photographs of real-world scenes that were presented for 3 s each. The photographs were high-pass filtered, low-pass filtered, or unfiltered. Fixation positions were found to be similar on the unfiltered and low-pass filtered scenes, particularly during the first 1.5 s of viewing. This result was found even when viewers were unable to describe the semantic content of the low-pass filtered scene. The direction of the initial saccade in a given scene was also similar for the low-pass and unfiltered versions. Mannan et al (1995) concluded that initial fixations are controlled by local visual rather than semantic features. In a subsequent analysis of these data, Mannan et al (1996) attempted to specify the visual features that determined initial fixation placement. They analyzed local regions of their scenes for seven spatial features: luminance maxima, luminance minima, image contrast, maxima of local positive physiological contrast, minima of local negative physiological contrast, edge density, and high spatial frequency. Only edge density predicted fixation position to any reliable degree, and even this feature produced only a relatively weak effect. Thus, the nature of the visual features that control fixation placement in scenes is still unclear.

Assuming that the Loftus & Mackworth result was not due to statistical error, there are at least two possible explanations for the inconsistency across studies. First, semantic informativeness and visual informativeness may have been correlated in the Loftus & Mackworth experiment (De Graef et al 1990, Rayner & Pollatsek 1992) so that effects that seemed to be due to semantic factors were actually due to visual factors. Second, the scenes used in later studies (De Graef et al 1990, Henderson et al 1999, Mannan et al 1995) may have been more visually complex than those used by Loftus & Mackworth (1978), so that peripheral semantic analysis would be more difficult in the former cases. Supporting this view, Loftus & Mackworth (1978) observed an average saccadic amplitude of more than 7° in their study, roughly twice the amplitude of the average saccade observed over a large range of scene-viewing experiments (Henderson & Hollingworth 1998). Taken together, then, the data suggest that initial fixations in a scene are controlled by visual rather than semantic features of local regions.

While semantic informativeness does not appear to influence initial fixation placement, qualitative analysis of the figures presented by Buswell (1935) and Yarbus (1967) suggests that it does influence overall fixation density in a scene region. Loftus & Mackworth (1978) also observed that fixation density was greater for semantically informative regions. Similarly, Henderson et al (1999) found that both the number of fixations viewers made in a region when that region was first fixated, and the number of fixations due to looks back to a region from other regions of the scene, were greater for semantically informative objects. In contrast to these results, Friedman (1979, presented in Friedman & Liebelt 1981) found no effect of semantic informativeness on fixation density. In this study, line drawings of scenes containing objects that had been rated for their a priori likelihood in the scene were presented to viewers who examined them in preparation for a difficult recognition memory test. Fixation density was not found to be correlated with rated likelihood. An explanation for the difference in results across studies rests on the strength of the informativeness manipulation. In Loftus & Mackworth (1978) and Henderson et al (1999), semantically informative regions contained semantically anomalous objects (e.g. a microscope in a bar), whereas in Friedman (1979), the manipulation of informativeness was relatively weak, with objects ranging continuously from very likely to somewhat likely in the scenes. Thus, the effect of semantic informativeness on fixation density was probably easier to detect in the former studies.

Together, the available data suggest that fixation placement in a scene is initially based on a combination of visual characteristics of local scene regions, knowledge of the scene category, and global visual properties (large-scale visual features) of the scene. Fixation placement does not seem to depend initially on semantic analysis of peripheral scene regions. However, once a region has been fixated so that semantic analysis is possible based on foveal vision, immediate refixations within the region and later returns to that region can then be based on the semantic informativeness of the region. The extent to which a region is semantically informative is dependent on the viewer's task as well as the nature of the region, leading to changes in fixation density as a function of task. While this basic framework accounts for the majority of available evidence, a large number of questions are yet to be answered. For example, it is not clear what visual features are used to select fixation sites, how specific sites are weighted during selection, what the selection mechanism is, and how visual and semantic factors trade off over time in controlling fixation placement. It is also not clear how visual features in the scene and cognitive factors related to the goals of the viewer interact in determining fixation sites. These issues are not trivial; while there is some similarity in initial fixation placement across individuals viewing the same scene, this similarity drops rapidly as scene perception unfolds (Mannan et al 1995). Furthermore, the eyes very rarely fixate the same positions in the same order; very few two-fixation sequences are the same across individuals or even within the same individual viewing the same scene a second time (Mannan et al 1997).

Fixation Time During Scene Perception

The *total time* a viewer fixates a given scene region (the sum of the durations of all fixations in a region) varies for different regions in a scene (Buswell 1935, Henderson et al 1999). This finding is not surprising, given that the total time that a region is fixated is correlated with fixation density in that region, and, as discussed above, fixation density tends to be higher for visually and semantically informative regions. At a more fine-grained level of analysis, we can ask whether the durations of individual fixations and temporally contiguous clusters of fixations are also affected by the perceptual and semantic characteristics of particular scene regions. The average fixation duration during scene viewing is about 330 ms, with a significant amount of variability around this mean. Fixation durations range from less than 50 to more than 1000 ms in a skewed distribution with a mode of about 230 ms (Henderson & Hollingworth 1998). The question is whether ongoing perceptual and semantic processing accounts for any of this variability.

There is currently some direct evidence that the visual information available in a fixation affects the duration of that fixation. In the study described above, Mannan et al (1995) found that fixation durations were longest during viewing of low-pass filtered scenes, intermediate for high-pass filtered scenes, and shortest for the unfiltered versions, suggesting that individual fixation durations are affected by the nature of the visual information available in the scene. In this study, however, it was not possible to determine if fixation durations were affected by the nature of the visual information available at fixation, the visual information available in the periphery, or both. To separate these possibilities, van Diepen and colleagues (1998) used a moving mask paradigm and directly manipulated the quality of the visual information available at fixation independently of that available beyond fixation. In this paradigm, a mask or other type of visual degradation can be made to move across the scene in spatial and temporal synchrony with the current fixation position (van Diepen et al 1998). Viewers searched for nonobjects in line drawings of scenes, and the image at fixation was presented normally or was degraded by overlaying a noise mask or by decreasing contrast at the fixated region (van Diepen et al 1995, 1998). When the image was degraded beginning at the onset of a fixation, *first fixation duration* (the duration of the initial fixation in a particular scene region) was longer than in a control condition, suggesting that the duration of the initial fixation was controlled, at least in part, by the acquisition of visual information from the fixated region. This result is similar to that observed when an artificial foveal scotoma is introduced via the moving mask technique during visual analysis of pictures of individual objects (Henderson et al 1997). These studies show that fixation duration is sensitive to the quality of the visual information available during that fixation. However, because stimulus manipulations such as filtering and masking affect both the visual characteristics of the image and the viewer's ability to semantically interpret that image, it is possible that difficulties of semantic analysis rather than visual analysis lead to the longer fixation durations. Contriving manipulations of visual but not semantic characteristics of a given region is a problem that will be difficult to solve with meaningful scene stimuli.

The effect of semantic informativeness on fine-grained measures of fixation time during scene viewing has also been studied. Loftus & Mackworth (1978) found that *first pass gaze duration* (the sum of all fixations from first entry to first exit in a region) was longer for semantically informative objects. Friedman (1979) similarly showed that first pass gaze duration was longer for objects that were less likely to be found in a particular scene. (Loftus & Mackworth and Friedman used the term *duration of the first fixation* to refer to first pass gaze duration.) Using the nonobject counting task, De Graef et al (1990) found that first pass gaze durations were longer for semantically informative objects, though this difference appeared only in the later stages of scene viewing. De Graef et al also found that whereas overall first fixation durations did not differ as a function of the semantic informativeness of the fixated region, first fixation durations on regions that were initially encountered late during scene exploration (following the median number of total fixations) were shorter on semantically uninformative objects. Finally, Henderson et al (1999) found that first pass gaze duration and *second pass gaze duration* (the sum of all fixations from second entry to exit in a region) were longer for semantically informative than uninformative objects. Together, these results show a clear effect of the meaning of a scene region on gaze duration in that region but a less clear effect on first fixation duration.

Conclusions

The results of eye movement studies during scene viewing show that fixation positions are nonrandom, with fixations clustering on both visually and semantically informative regions. The placement of the first few fixations in a scene seems to be controlled by the visual features in the scene and global semantic characteristics of the scene (e.g. the scene concept) but not by semantic characteristics of local scene regions. As viewing progresses and local regions are fixated and semantically analyzed, positions of later fixations come to be controlled by both the visual and semantic properties of those local regions. The length of time the eyes remain in a given region is immediately affected by both the visual and semantic properties of that region. Thus, although the eyes are not initially drawn to a region based on its meaning, they may remain longer in that region upon first encountering it if it is more semantically informative.

Although there is reasonable consistency in the results of the reviewed studies, there are also some notable discrepancies. It is often difficult to determine the cause of these differences because a number of potentially important factors vary from study to study, including image size, viewing time per scene, image content, and image type (Henderson & Hollingworth 1998). Each factor could produce an independent effect and could also interact with the others in complex ways to influence eye movements. Further investigation of these issues is required before eye movement control in high-level scene perception will be completely understood. Also, another potentially important factor that might exert strong effects on eye movement patterns is the viewing task. Very little systematic work has been conducted to examine the degree to which viewing patterns change as a function of task, but to the extent that eye movement patterns are driven by the goals of the cognitive system (Ballard 1991, Land & Furneaux 1997, Rayner 1978, Yarbus 1967), this will be a critical factor to examine in future studies.

SCENE MEMORY ACROSS SACCADES

In this section, we explore the nature of the representation that is generated across saccades as we view a scene over an extended period of time. Phenomenologically, the visual system seems to construct a complete, veridical perceptual representation of the environment, akin to a high-resolution, full-color photograph. Such a representation could not be based on the information contained in any given fixation, however, because of the rapid drop-off from the current fixation point in both acuity (Anstis 1974, Riggs 1965) and color sensitivity (Mullen 1990). Thus, if our phenomenology reflects reality, the visual system must build up a composite perceptual image over consecutive fixations. Historically, this composite image hypothesis has been instantiated by models in which a perceptual image is generated during each fixation and stored in the brain, with images from consecutive fixations overlapped or spatially aligned in a system that maps a retinal reference frame onto a spatiotopic reference frame (e.g. Brietmeyer et al 1982, Davidson et al 1973, Duhamel et al 1992, Feldman 1985, Jonides et al 1982, McConkie & Rayner 1975, Pouget et al 1993). In composite image models, the perceptual image formed during two consecutive fixations could be aligned by tracking the extent of the saccade and/or by comparing the similarity of the images themselves.

Although many different models of transsaccadic visual perception based on this basic scheme have been proposed, psychophysical and behavioral data have almost uniformly provided evidence against them (see reviews by Irwin 1992, 1996; O'Regan 1992b; Pollatsek & Rayner 1992). For example, when two dot patterns forming a matrix of dots are presented in rapid succession at the same spatial position within a fixation, a single fused pattern is perceived and performance (e.g. identification of a missing dot from the matrix) can be based upon this percept (Di Lollo 1977, Eriksen & Collins 1967, Irwin 1991). However, when the two patterns are viewed in rapid succession at the same spatial position across a saccade, no such fused percept is experienced and performance is dramatically reduced (Bridgeman & Mayer 1983; Irwin 1991, Irwin et al 1983, 1990; Rayner & Pollatsek 1983; see also O'Regan & Levy-Schoen 1983). Similarly, spatial displacement of a visual stimulus is very difficult to detect when the displacement takes place during a saccade (Bridgeman et al 1975, Henderson 1997, McConkie & Currie 1996). If internal images were being spatially aligned to form a composite image (based, for example, on the distance of the saccade), spatial displacement should be very obvious to the viewer. Other types of image changes, such as enlargements or reductions in object size and changes to object contours, often go unnoticed when they take place during a saccade (Henderson 1997, Henderson et al 1987). Again, if a composite image were being generated via spatial alignment and image overlap, then these kinds of changes should be quite noticeable.

Change Blindness Across Saccades During Scene Viewing

The studies reviewed above strongly suggest that the visual system does not (and, in fact, cannot) retain a detailed perceptual image of the visual input across saccades. Recent research on scene perception lends additional support to this conclusion and further suggests that even the amount of conceptual information that is carried across a saccade is limited. This conclusion comes from a strikingly counterintuitive result in recent scene perception research: Viewers often fail to notice large and seemingly salient changes to scene regions and objects when those changes take place during a saccade (Grimes 1996, McConkie 1990, McConkie & Currie 1996). In a striking demonstration of this effect, Grimes and McConkie (see Grimes 1996) presented viewers with full-color pictures of scenes over extended viewing times. The participants were instructed to view the scenes in preparation for a relatively difficult memory test and were further told that something in a scene would occasionally change and that they should press a button if and when that happened. Participants' eye movements were monitored, and occasionally one region of a scene was changed during the nth saccade, where n was predetermined. The striking result was that viewers often failed to detect what would seem to be very obvious perceptual and conceptual changes in the scene. For example, 100% of the viewers failed to detect a 25% increase in the size of a prominent building in a city skyline, 100% failed to detect that the hats on the heads of two men who were central in a scene switched one to the other, and 50% failed to notice when the heads were exchanged between two cowboys sitting on a bench (Grimes 1996). Even assuming that only a relatively detailed conceptual representation of a scene (in contrast to a complete perceptual representation) is retained across saccades, these changes should be noticed with relatively high frequency. Thus, these results call into question the idea that a detailed scene representation is carried across saccades in the service of constructing a composite perceptual image.

The study reported by Grimes is important because the results have broad implications for our understanding of perception, cognition, and the nature of consciousness (Dennett 1991). However, it is important to note that the Grimes (1996) report was anecdotal, providing few specific details about the experiment. For example, participants were freely moving their eyes around the scene during the experiment, and the change occurred during a prespecified saccade (i.e. the nth saccade) without respect for the position of the fixation prior to or following that saccade. Thus, it is not known whether the change detection performance was related to fixation position in the scene. This factor could be critical, given the evidence reviewed above that semantic analysis of local regions is at least initially constrained to areas of the scene at or near fixation. Thus, it will be important to replicate these results with fixation position controlled.

Change Blindness and Simulated Saccades

In an attempt to determine whether the change blindness phenomenon is a consequence of the execution of a saccade, Rensink et al (1997) introduced a change detection paradigm in which scene changes were decoupled from saccades. A photograph of a scene (A) was presented for 240 ms, followed by a gray field for 80 ms, followed by a changed version of the initial scene (A′), and so on alternating between A, the gray field, and A′. (In some experiments, each version of the scene was repeated before the change, e.g. A, A, A′, A′, to prevent participants from predicting when a change would happen.) The participant was asked to press a button when the change was detected and then to state what the change was. The result was that scene changes were very difficult to detect in this *flicker paradigm*, often requiring tens of seconds of viewing time. Interestingly, once a change had been detected by an observer, it became obvious thereafter. Rensink et al (1997) suggested that when local motion signals are removed from the visual signal (via the intervening gray field), the detection of what would otherwise be highly salient changes becomes extraordinarily difficult, at least until attention is directed to the changing region and perceptual information is explicitly encoded and compared across images.

Because the scene changes in the Rensink et al (1997) study were not synchronized to the viewer's saccades, the researchers concluded that the change blindness effect reported by Grimes (1996) is not tied to the saccadic system. However, given that participants were allowed to move their eyes as they searched for the changing object in the Rensink et al (1997) study, it is possible that a fortuitous relationship between viewers' saccades and the scene changes might still have accounted for their effect. To test this hypothesis, A Hollingworth & JM Henderson (submitted) modified the flicker paradigm so that the first scene image was displayed briefly and one time only, followed by an intervening gray field, followed by a comparison image of the same scene with or without a change to an object in the scene. Because the initial view of the scene was presented only briefly, there was no time for the viewer to execute a saccade. Although better than in the flicker paradigm, change detection performance in this task was still poor. This result suggests that when local motion signals are removed from the input, changes in a scene are difficult to detect, regardless of whether they take place across a saccade or within a fixation. Additional support for this hypothesis was provided by O'Regan et al (1996), who used multiple gray patches (similar to mud splattering on a windshield) presented on a scene simultaneously with the scene change. Although the splatter never covered the changing region, changes were difficult to detect in the splatter condition compared with a control condition without splatter. Similarly, Levin & Simons (1997) showed that visual changes to objects in an ongoing film are difficult to detect across a film cut, where different viewing angles are used before and after the cut. As in the "splatter" condition, a film cut introduces discontinuities across much of the visual field. Together, these results suggest that when local motion signals are eliminated as a result of an intervening blank period (caused by a saccade or a uniform gray field inserted within a fixation), or overwhelmed because of additional motion signals across the visual field (e.g. a splatter or film cut), change blindness results. Thus, change blindness appears to reflect a general and fundamental characteristic of the way in which information is acquired, represented, and retained from a dynamically viewed scene.

The change blindness effect suggests that little of the information that is latent in the retinal image during a fixation is encoded into an enduring form that can be retained across a saccade or other intervening temporal gap. Thus, it becomes important to understand the processes that control the selection of the information to be encoded into a more enduring form. Rensink et al (1997) proposed that a limited-capacity attentional mechanism must select perceptual information from an iconic store during a fixation and transfer it to a more stable and longer-lasting visual short-term memory (VSTM) representation if it is to be retained. In this hypothesis, scene regions that are more likely to be attended during scene viewing should be more likely to be encoded and stored in a stable format. Supporting this hypothesis, Rensink et al (1997) demonstrated that change detection was facilitated for scene regions that were rated more interesting by a group of viewers who independently judged scene regions in isolation. However, this method is problematic because "interest" was not directly manipulated (see discussion of informativeness ratings in the eye movement section above). Thus, because the interesting and uninteresting regions of the scenes may have differed along many physical dimensions, it is difficult to attribute the change detection differences to interest alone.

In a study designed to direct attention to specific scene regions in a more principled manner, A Hollingworth & JM Henderson (submitted) used semantic consistency to manipulate the semantic informativeness of a scene region. Target objects that were semantically constrained in pairs of scenes were exchanged across scenes to produce images in which a given object was either semantically consistent (e.g. a mixer in a kitchen) or semantically inconsistent (e.g. a live chicken in a kitchen) with the rest of the scene, as described in the eye movement section above. These stimuli were then employed both in the Rensink et al (1997) change detection paradigm and in the simpler version of the paradigm in which a scene was presented only twice rather than alternating back and forth. In both paradigms, the main result was that change detection was better when the changing object was semantically informative. On the assumption that semantic informativeness holds attention (Friedman 1979, Henderson et al 1999, Loftus & Mackworth 1978), these data support the Rensink et al (1997) hypothesis that attention is needed to transfer information to a stable medium (e.g. VSTM; Potter 1976) if that information is to be available to support the detection of changes.

A third set of data supporting the hypothesis that covert attention plays a critical role in the encoding of information from a scene was provided by CB Currie & GW McConkie (submitted), who demonstrated that spatial displacements to objects in scenes that take place during a saccade are much more noticeable when the displaced object is the target of the saccade than when it occupies a position elsewhere in the scene. Given the behavioral and neurophysiological evidence that covert visual-spatial attention tends to be allocated to a saccade target prior to the execution of the saccade (e.g. Deubel & Schneider 1996, Henderson 1992a, Henderson et al 1989; reviewed by Henderson 1996), these data can also be taken to support the view that saccade targets are attended and so are more likely to be retained in memory than other objects in a scene.

Conclusions

The literature reviewed in this section strongly suggests that only a limited amount of information is carried across saccades during complex, natural scene viewing and that this information is coded and stored in a relatively abstract (nonperceptual) format. What, then, accounts for our experience of a complete and integrated visual world? Current evidence suggests that this experience is an illusion or construction based on an abstract conceptual representation coding general information about the scene (e.g. its category) combined with perceptual information derived from the current fixation (e.g. O'Regan 1992b, Grimes 1996; see also Churchland et al 1994, Dennett 1991, but see Deubel et al 1996, for an alternative view).

SCENE CONTEXT AND OBJECT IDENTIFICATION

In this section we review the literature on object identification in scenes. The central question is whether the context established by a scene influences the identification of objects in that scene. In other words, does object identification operate exclusively on bottom-up visual information, as proposed by current theories of object recognition (e.g. Biederman 1987, Bülthoff et al 1995)? Or is object identification sensitive to the meaning of the scene in which an object appears, as proposed by theories of object identification in scenes (e.g. Biederman et al 1982, Friedman 1979, Kosslyn 1994)? First, we review research on scene identification. Second, we review models of the relationship between scene knowledge and object identification. Third, we review the empirical evidence mediating between these models.

Scene Identification

Scene identification research has focused primarily on two issues: (*a*) the time-course of scene identification and (*b*) the types of information used to identify a scene as a particular scene type. Potter (Potter 1975, 1976; Potter & Levy 1969) conducted a series of studies to investigate the time-course of scene identification and memory encoding. These studies presented a series of photographs of scenes in rapid succession. When a verbal description of a target scene was provided prior to presentation of the series, participants were able to detect the target scene quite reliably, even at a presentation rate of 113 ms per scene. Potter (1976) concluded that a scene can be identified in approximately 100 ms. One concern with these studies is that the scene descriptions did not specify the global identity of the scene but instead described individual objects in the scene (e.g. *a baby reaching for a butterfly*). Thus, detection performance may have been based on the identification of individual objects rather than on identification of the scene as a whole. Schyns & Oliva (1994, Oliva & Schyns 1997) have demonstrated that a photograph of a scene can be identified as a particular scene type (e.g. highway or living room) from a masked presentation as short as 45–135 ms. This result demonstrates that the information necessary to identify a scene can be extracted quickly, but it does not indicate the precise amount of time required to achieve identification. Future research will be needed to characterize the time-course of scene identification. In particular, the comparative speed of scene versus object identification is important for theories that propose interactions between scene context and the identification of constituent objects.

A second area of research has investigated the scene information used for identification. First, scene identity could be inferred from the identification of one or more key objects (Friedman 1979) and, perhaps, their spatial relations (De Graef et al 1990). Second, a scene could be identified from scene-level information independent of the identities of individual objects (Biederman 1981, 1988; Schyns & Oliva 1994). Most research has supported the latter idea that early scene processing is based on global scene information rather than local object information (Antes et al 1981, Loftus et al 1983, Metzger & Antes 1983, Schyns & Oliva 1994). Schyns & Oliva (1994) demonstrated that scenes can be identified from low-spatial-frequency images that preserve the spatial relations between large-scale structures in the scene but which lack the visual detail needed to identify local objects. In addition, when identifying a scene from a very brief view (50 ms), participants tend to base their interpretation on low-frequency information rather than on high-frequency information (Schyns & Oliva 1994), though this global-to-local bias does not appear to be a hard constraint (Oliva & Schyns 1997).

A related issue concerns the internal representations functional in scene identification. Biederman (1981, 1988) proposed that an arrangement of volumetric primitives (geons), each representing a prominent object in the scene, may allow rapid scene identification independently of local object identification. According to this view, scenes employ the same representational vocabulary as objects, except on a larger spatial scale. This proposal has not been tested empirically; however, there are a number of reasons to think that scenes may not be represented as large objects. Whereas an object tends to have a highly constrained set of component parts and relations between parts, a scene places far less constraint on objects and spatial relations between objects (Henderson 1992b, Hollingworth & Henderson 1998). Evidence from neuropsychology suggests that within- and between-object spatial relations may be represented differently (Humphreys & Riddoch 1994, 1995). In addition, neural imaging results suggest that there may be separate cortical areas supporting object and scene identification (Epstein & Kanwisher 1998). Future research will need to identify more precisely the internal representations constructed from a scene and the processes by which these representations are compared to stored scene representations.

Models of Object Identification in Scenes

Object identification can be assumed to consist of the following component processes. First, the retinal image is translated into a set of visual primitives (e.g. surfaces and edges). Second, these primitives are used to construct structural descriptions of the object tokens in the scene. Third, these constructed descriptions are matched to stored long-term memory descriptions. When a match is found, identification has occurred, and semantic information stored in memory about that object type becomes available. In this view of object identification, the first two stages can be considered perceptual in that the task is to translate retinal stimulation into a structural description that is compatible with stored memory representations. The matching stage, however, can be seen as an interface between perception and cognition, in which perceptual information must make contact with memory representations. Models of object identification in scenes can be divided into three groups based on the stage of object identification at which scene context is proposed to exert an influence. One group of theories proposes that expectations derived from scene knowledge interact with the perceptual analysis of object tokens (i.e. the first two stages of object identification). A second group proposes that the locus of interaction is at the matching stage, when perceptual descriptions are matched to long-term memory representations. A third group proposes that object identification (including the matching stage) is isolated from scene knowledge.

The *perceptual schema model* proposes that expectations derived from knowledge about the composition of a scene type interact with the perceptual analysis of object tokens in that scene (Biederman 1981; Biederman et al 1982, 1983; Boyce et al 1989; Metzger & Antes 1983; Palmer 1975b). According to this view, the memory representation of a scene type (a *schema* or *frame*) contains information about the objects and spatial relations between objects that form that type. The early activation of a scene schema facilitates the subsequent perceptual analysis of schema-consistent objects and, perhaps, inhibits the perceptual analysis of schema-inconsistent objects (Biederman et al 1982). The mechanisms by which schema activation facilitates the perceptual analysis of consistent objects have not been specified in detail. Some researchers (Boyce et al 1989, Metzger & Antes 1983) have suggested that perceptual facilitation could be explained within an interactive activation model, in which partial activation of nodes at the scene level constrains perceptual analysis at the object level. The perceptual schema model predicts that the identification of objects consistent with a scene will be facilitated compared to inconsistent objects. In addition, the constructed description of a consistent object should be more elaborated than that of an inconsistent object.

At the level of the architecture of the visual system, the perceptual schema model assumes that there is no clear distinction between perceptual processing and cognitive processing. It draws from New Look theories of perception, which propose that cognitively derived hypotheses modulate the encoding of perceptual information (Bruner 1957, 1973; Neisser 1967). In addition, it is consistent with current theories proposing that vision is a constraint-satisfaction problem, in which all available constraints are consulted when interpreting an input pattern (Mumford 1994, Rumelhart et al 1986).

The *priming model* proposes that the locus of the contextual effect is at the stage when a structural description of an object token is matched against long-term memory representations (Bar & Ullman 1996, Friedman 1979, Friedman & Liebelt 1981, Kosslyn 1994, Palmer 1975a, Ullman 1996). According to the priming model, the activation of a scene schema primes the stored representations of schema-consistent object types. This priming can be viewed as a modulation of the criterion amount of perceptual information necessary to select a particular object representation as a match. Relatively less perceptual information will need to be encoded to select a primed object representation compared with an unprimed object representation (Friedman 1979). Similar to the perceptual schema model, the priming model proposes that identification of objects consistent with a scene will be facilitated compared with inconsistent objects. However, the priming model differs from the perceptual schema model because it proposes that scene knowledge influences only the criterion used to determine that a particular object type is present, without directly influencing the perceptual analysis of the object token.

The *functional isolation model* proposes that object identification is isolated from expectations derived from scene knowledge (Hollingworth & Henderson 1998). This model is consistent with current theories of object identification (Biederman 1987, Bülthoff et al 1995; see also Marr & Nishihara 1978) that propose that bottom-up visual analysis is sufficient to discriminate between entry-level object categories. This model is also consistent with theories proposing an architectural division between perceptual processing and cognitive processing (Fodor 1983; Pylyshyn 1980, 1998). The functional isolation model predicts that experiments examining the perceptual analysis of objects should find no effect of the relation between object and scene. However, context effects may arise in experiments that are sensitive to later influences of scene constraint.

Before turning to the literature on object identification in scenes, it is important to establish the boundary conditions under which scene context could plausibly interact with object perception. First, a scene must be identified early enough to influence the identification of constituent objects. As reviewed above, the information necessary to identify a scene can be extracted quite quickly, possibly from an analysis of global rather than local scene features. Second, scenes must place significant constraints on the objects that can appear in them, and stored knowledge about scene types must include these constraints. Supporting this assumption, participants are quite reliable in their judgments about what objects are consistent versus inconsistent with a particular scene (e.g. Friedman 1979, Henderson et al 1999) and exhibit strong response biases as a function of the consistency between object and scene (e.g. Biederman et al 1982, Hollingworth & Henderson 1998, Palmer 1975a). Thus, there seems adequate evidence to suppose that if the architecture of the visual system allows interactions between scene knowledge and object identification, scene-contextual constraint is available early enough and is robust enough to influence the identification of objects.

Studies of Object Identification in Scenes

In this section we review the experimental evidence mediating between these models. The principal difficulty in this literature has been to determine the representational level at which prior scene knowledge interacts with the processing of objects. As an illustrative example, consider a study by Palmer (1975a). Palmer presented a line drawing of a scene for 2 s followed by a brief presentation of an isolated target object that was either semantically consistent with that scene (i.e. likely to appear in the scene) or semantically inconsistent (i.e. unlikely to appear in that scene). In addition, semantically inconsistent target objects could be shaped similarly to the consistent target or not. Palmer found that consistent objects were named more accurately than inconsistent objects and that inconsistent objects shaped similarly to a consistent target were named least accurately. Although this result has been cited as evidence for the influence of scene knowledge on object identification, the effect could arise at a number of different stages of analysis. First, consistent scene context could facilitate the perceptual analysis of consistent objects, as proposed by the perceptual schema model. Second, it could reduce the criterion amount of information needed to reach an identification threshold, as proposed by the priming model and by Palmer. Third, scene context could influence postidentification processing, such as response generation or educated guessing, consistent with the functional isolation model.

Designing experimental paradigms to discriminate between these possibilities has proven difficult. In the remainder of this section, we review experiments that have sought to investigate whether consistent scene context facilitates the identification of objects, with particular focus on the extent to which each experiment is able to discriminate between the models reviewed above. The principal manipulation of object consistency in these studies has been the likelihood of an object appearing in a scene (i.e. the semantic consistency between object and scene), though some studies have manipulated other types of scene relations, including an object's spatial position and size (e.g. Biederman et al 1982, De Graef et al 1990). For further discussion of this literature, see

Boyce & Pollatsek (1992a), De Graef (1992), Henderson (1992b), and Rayner & Pollatsek (1992).

EYE MOVEMENT PARADIGMS   In eye movement paradigms, the duration of the fixation(s) on a target object has been taken as a measure of the speed of object identification. Friedman (1979; see eye movement section for detailed discussion of this experiment) found that first pass gaze duration was shorter for semantically consistent versus inconsistent target objects and interpreted the difference in gaze duration as support for the priming model. This interpretation has been questioned, however, because it is unlikely that the difference in gaze duration (more than 300 ms) was due to identification processes alone (Biederman et al 1982, Henderson 1992b, Rayner & Pollatsek 1992). First, the difference may have been caused by the difficulty of integrating an already identified object into a conceptual representation in which it was incongruous (Henderson 1992b). Second, the instructions to prepare for a difficult memory test may have caused participants to dwell longer on objects that were difficult to encode into memory (Hollingworth & Henderson 1998). Third, once identified, inconsistent objects are likely to be more interesting to participants than consistent objects, leading to the longer gaze durations (Biederman et al 1982).

De Graef et al (1990) found shorter first fixation durations on semantically consistent versus inconsistent objects, but this effect arose only when the target object was initially encountered relatively late in scene viewing. The absence of a context effect early in viewing is consistent with the functional isolation model. The context effect obtained later in scene viewing is more difficult to reconcile with this view. However, it is not at all clear why a context effect would develop only late during viewing. One possibility is that participants initially ignored the larger scene, registering scene meaning only after the accumulation of enough local information (Boyce & Pollatsek 1992a, De Graef et al 1990, Rayner & Pollatsek 1992). This explanation, however, runs counter to strong evidence that scenes are identified within the first fixation on the scene and that identification occurs even when such processing is not necessary to perform the task (e.g. Biederman et al 1982, Boyce & Pollatsek 1992b, Hollingworth & Henderson 1998). A more general problem with drawing strong conclusions from this study is that we have no direct evidence to indicate whether first fixation duration reflects object identification alone or later processing as well (Henderson 1992b, Rayner & Pollatsek 1992). Until we know more about the types of object processing reflected in different fixation duration measures, results from eye movement paradigms are unlikely to be able to resolve the question of whether scene context influences the identification of objects.

Boyce & Pollatsek (1992b) developed a variant of the eye movement paradigm in which the naming latency for a fixated object was used as a measure of object identification performance. In this study, the participant first fixated the center of the screen. A line drawing of a scene then appeared, and 75 ms later, a target object wiggled (shifted about half a degree and then shifted back 50 ms later). The participant's task was to make an eye movement to the wiggled object and, upon completion of the eye movement, to name the object as quickly as possible. Boyce & Pollatsek found that naming latency was shorter for semantically consistent versus inconsistent target objects. As with fixation duration measures, however, we do not know whether differences in naming latency reflect the influence of scene context on object identification or on postidentification processing as well.

OBJECT DETECTION PARADIGMS   In object detection paradigms, the accuracy of detecting a target object in a briefly presented scene has been taken as a measure of object identification performance. Biederman (Biederman 1972; Biederman et al 1973, 1974) sought to assess the influence of coherent scene context on object identification by measuring detection performance for target objects presented in normal versus jumbled scenes. The normal images were photographs of common environments, and the jumbled images were created by cutting the photographs into six rectangles and rearranging them (though the rectangle containing the target object remained in its original position). Scenes were presented briefly (20–700 ms) followed by a mask and a cue marking the position where the target object had appeared. Participants more accurately discriminated the target object from distractors when the scene was normal versus jumbled. Similar results were found in a search paradigm (Biederman et al 1973); participants took less time to find the target object when it appeared in a normal versus in a jumbled scene. These results have been widely cited as support for the perceptual schema model. However, this paradigm has been criticized because the jumbling manipulation introduced new contours to the jumbled scenes and thus did not control the visual complexity of the normal versus jumbled images (Bar & Ullman 1996, Henderson 1992b). In addition, the normal scene advantage may not have reflected differences in the perceptual analysis of objects. Compared to the jumbled condition, participants may have more successfully encoded the spatial relation between the cued region and the rest of the scene when the scene was normal. They could then choose the test object that was likely to have appeared in that position (Biederman 1972).

More recent object detection experiments have tested detection performance for consistent versus inconsistent objects presented in the same scene context (Biederman et al 1982, 1983; Boyce et al 1989; Hollingworth & Henderson 1998; Masson 1991). These experiments employed signal detection measures to discriminate contextual influence at the level of perceptual analysis from influence at later levels of analysis. The logic behind signal detection methodology is that effects of context on perceptual processing will be reflected in measures of sensitivity, whereas later effects of context (e.g. at the matching stage or at postidentification stages) will be reflected in measures of bias (but see Norris 1995).

Biederman et al (1982) asked participants to decide whether a target object had appeared within a briefly presented scene at a particular location. During each trial, a label naming a target object was presented until the participant was ready to continue, followed by a line drawing of a scene for 150 ms, followed by a pattern mask with an embedded location cue. Participants indicated whether the target had appeared in the scene at the cued location. The object appearing at the cued location either could be consistent with the scene or could violate scene expectations along one or more dimensions, including probability (semantic consistency), position, size, support, and interposition (whether the object occluded objects behind it or was transparent). Biederman et al found that detection sensitivity (d') was best when the cued object did not violate any of the constraints imposed by scene meaning. Performance was poorer across all violation dimensions, with compound violations (e.g. semantically inconsistent and unsupported) producing even greater performance decrements. Biederman et al (1982, Biederman 1981) interpreted these results as supporting a perceptual schema model. They argued that because semantic violations were no less disruptive than structural violations, the locus of semantic contextual influence must be during the perceptual analysis of object tokens (but see Henderson 1992b, De Graef et al 1990).

Boyce et al (1989) explored whether the detection advantage observed for semantically consistent versus inconsistent objects was due to the global meaning of the scene or to the presence of other semantically related objects within the scene, as had been suggested by Henderson et al (1987). Boyce et al manipulated the consistency of the cued object with both the global scene and with other cohort objects appearing in the scene. For example, a doll could appear in a bedroom with other bedroom objects, in a bedroom with objects more likely to be found in a refrigerator, in a refrigerator scene with other bedroom objects, or in a refrigerator with other refrigerator objects. Detection sensitivity was facilitated when the cued object was semantically consistent with the global scene in which it appeared compared with when it was inconsistent with the global scene. In contrast, there was no effect of the consistency of the cued object with the cohort objects in the scene. Boyce et al concluded that the global meaning of the scene, rather than the specific objects present in the scene, is functional in facilitating object identification.

The results of Biederman et al (1982) and Boyce et al (1989) provide the strongest evidence to date that consistent scene context facilitates object identification and provide the core support for the perceptual schema model. However, a number of methodological concerns have been raised regarding these paradigms (De Graef et al 1990, De Graef 1992, Henderson 1992b, Hollingworth & Henderson 1998). First, there is reason to believe that the signal detection methodology did not adequately eliminate response bias from sensitivity measures. These object detection studies did not compute sensitivity using the correct detection of a particular signal when it was present and the false detection of the same signal when it was absent, as required by signal detection theory. Catch trials presented the same scene (and cued object) as in target-present trials but merely changed the label appearing before the scene. In addition, the Biederman et al studies (1982, 1983) did not control the semantic consistency between the target label and the scene on catch trials: False alarms were computed in both consistent and inconsistent cued object conditions by averaging across catch trials on which the target label was semantically consistent and semantically inconsistent with the scene. Hollingworth & Henderson (1998) replicated the Biederman et al (1982) study first using the original signal detection design and then using a corrected design in which participants attempted to detect the same object on corresponding target-present and catch trials. The experiment using the original design replicated the consistent object advantage found by Biederman et al and Boyce et al (1989). However, the experiment using the corrected design showed no advantage for the detection of semantically consistent versus semantically inconsistent objects. These results suggest that the consistent object advantage in previous object detection experiments likely arose from the inadequate control of response bias and not from the influence of scene context on the perceptual analysis of objects.

The second concern with previous object detection paradigms (Biederman et al 1982, 1983; Boyce et al 1989) is that participants may have searched areas of the scene where the target object was likely to be found. If the spatial positions of semantically consistent objects were more predictable than those of inconsistent objects, detection of the former would have been facilitated compared to the latter, even if there were no differences in the perceptibility of each type of object (Hollingworth & Henderson 1998). Supporting this idea, Henderson et al (1997) demonstrated that semantically consistent objects are indeed easier to locate in scenes than inconsistent objects (as described in the above section on eye movements in scenes). A similar advantage may have been afforded to consistent objects in object detection paradigms, leading to an apparent advantage for the perceptual processing of these objects. Hollingworth & Henderson (1998) tested whether differences in search efficiency influence performance in the object detection paradigm. They presented the target object label after the scene so that participants could not form a search strategy. Contrary to earlier studies, Hollingworth & Henderson found a reliable advantage for the detection of semantically inconsistent objects (see discussion in above section on change detection, and Hollingworth & Henderson 1998).

To investigate the identification of objects in scenes independently of response bias, Hollingworth & Henderson (1998) introduced a post-scene, forced-choice discrimination procedure. This procedure is a variant of the Reicher-Wheeler paradigm (Reicher 1969), which has proven the best means to assess the identification of letters in words. A scene was presented for a short time (250 ms) and could contain either one of two semantically consistent target objects or one of two semantically inconsistent target objects. For example, a farm scene could contain either a chicken or a pig in the consistent condition, and it could contain either a mixer or a coffee maker in the inconsistent condition. The scene was masked for 30 ms, and the mask was followed immediately by a forced-choice screen displaying two labels either corresponding to the two consistent targets or to the two inconsistent targets. Under these conditions, response bias should be eliminated because contextual information will not assist in discriminating between two consistent object alternatives and it will not assist in discriminating between two inconsistent object alternatives. In addition, this paradigm provides a stronger test of the priming model: Effects of criterion modulation should be reflected in discrimination performance, but such effects may not be reflected in detection sensitivity (Farah 1989, but see Norris 1995). Using this procedure, Hollingworth & Henderson found no advantage for the discrimination of consistent versus inconsistent objects: The nonreliable trend was in the direction of better inconsistent object discrimination. Masson (1991) has reported a similar effect for the discrimination of object tokens using a post-scene, forced-choice procedure.

Conclusions

The majority of studies investigating object identification in scenes have found advantages for consistent versus inconsistent objects. It could be argued that despite the existence of methodological problems in each of these studies, there is sufficient converging evidence to support the general conclusion that consistent scene context facilitates the identification of objects (Rayner & Pollatsek 1992, Boyce & Pollatsek 1992a). Such a conclusion would be plausible if it were not for the fact that the same methodological problem seems to be present in all studies to date that have found advantages for the identification of consistent versus inconsistent objects. Namely, these paradigms do not appear to have adequately discriminated between effects of context on object identification and postidentification effects. Recent experiments indicate that when later effects of context are eliminated from measures of object identification, no consistent object advantage is obtained (Hollingworth & Henderson 1998). Thus, we believe that the functional isolation model currently provides the best explanation of the relation between scene knowledge and object identification. This conclusion must be viewed as preliminary, however, given the relatively small set of studies that have investigated object identification in scenes.

CONCLUSION

The topics discussed in this chapter include some of the most important outstanding questions remaining for high-level vision. How are the eyes controlled during active scene exploration? What types of representations are constructed and retained as scene viewing unfolds over time? How does the stored knowledge that is accessed during ongoing scene perception interact with incoming perceptual information? The ultimate answers to these questions will have important implications for our understanding of the functional and architectural properties of the human visual and cognitive systems, and so for the fundamental nature of the human mind.

ACKNOWLEDGMENTS

Preparation of this chapter was supported by a grant from the National Science Foundation (SBR 9617274) to JMH and by a National Science Foundation graduate fellowship to AH. We would like to thank Fernanda Ferreira for her insightful comments and discussions.

> Visit the *Annual Reviews home page* at
> http://www.AnnualReviews.org.

Literature Cited

Akins K, ed. 1996. *Perception: Vancouver Studies in Cognitive Science,* Vol. 5. Oxford: Oxford Univ. Press

Anstis SM. 1974. A chart demonstrating variations in acuity with retinal position. *Vis. Res.* 14:589–92

Antes JR. 1974. The time course of picture viewing. *J. Exp. Psychol.* 103:62–70

Antes JR, Penland JG, Metzger RL. 1981. Processing global information in briefly presented scenes. *Psychol. Res.* 43:277–92

Ballard DH. 1991. Animate vision. *Artif. Intell.* 48:57–86

Bar M, Ullman S. 1996. Spatial context in recognition. *Perception* 25:343–52

Biederman I. 1972. Perceiving real-world scenes. *Science* 177:77–80

Biederman I. 1981. On the semantics of a glance at a scene. In *Perceptual Organization,* ed. M Kubovy, JR Pomerantz, pp. 213–53. Hillsdale, NJ: Erlbaum

Biederman I. 1987. Recognition-by-components: a theory of human image understanding. *Psychol. Rev.* 94:115–47

Biederman I. 1988. Aspects and extensions of a theory of human image understanding. In *Computational Processes in Human Vision: An Interdisciplinary Perspective,* ed. ZW Pylyshyn, pp. 370–428. Norwood, NJ: Ablex

Biederman I, Glass AL, Stacy EW Jr. 1973. Searching for objects in real-world scenes. *J. Exp. Psychol.* 97:22–27

Biederman I, Mezzanotte RJ, Rabinowitz JC. 1982. Scene perception: detecting and judging objects undergoing relational violations. *Cogn. Psychol.* 14:143–77

Biederman I, Rabinowitz JC, Glass AL, Stacy

EW Jr. 1974. On the information extracted from a glance at a scene. *J. Exp. Psychol.* 103:597–600

Biederman I, Teitelbaum RC, Mezzanotte RJ. 1983. Scene perception: a failure to find a benefit from prior expectancy or familiarity. *J. Exp. Psychol.: Learn. Mem. Cogn.* 9:411–29

Boyce SJ, Pollatsek A. 1992a. An exploration of the effects of scene context on object identification. See Rayner 1992, pp. 227–42

Boyce SJ, Pollatsek A. 1992b. Identification of objects in scenes: the role of scene background in object naming. *J. Exp. Psychol.: Learn. Mem. Cogn.* 18:531–43

Boyce SJ, Pollatsek A, Rayner K. 1989. Effect of background information on object identification. *J. Exp. Psychol.: Hum. Percept. Perform.* 15:556–66

Bridgeman B, Hendry D, Stark L. 1975. Failure to detect displacements of the visual world during saccadic eye movements. *Vis. Res.* 15:719–22

Bridgeman B, Mayer M. 1983. Failure to integrate visual information from successive fixations. *Bull. Psychon. Soc.* 21:285–86

Brietmeyer BG, Kropfl W, Julesz B. 1982. The existence and role of retinotopic and spatiotopic forms of visual persistence. *Acta Psychol.* 52:175–96

Bruner JS. 1957. On perceptual readiness. *Psychol. Rev.* 64:123–52

Bruner JS. 1973. *Beyond the Information Given.* New York: Norton

Bülthoff HH, Edelman SY, Tarr MJ. 1995. How are three-dimensional objects represented in the brain? *Cereb. Cortex* 3: 247–60

Buswell GT. 1935. *How People Look at Pictures.* Chicago: Univ. Chicago Press

Carpenter RHS. 1988. *Movements of the Eyes.* London: Pion

Churchland PS, Ramachandran VS, Sejnowski TJ. 1994. A critique of pure vision. See Koch & Davis 1994, pp. 23–60

Davidson ML, Fox MJ, Dick AO. 1973. Effect of eye movements on backward masking and perceived location. *Percept. Psychophys.* 14:110–16

De Graef P. 1992. Scene-context effects and models of real-world perception. See Rayner 1992, pp. 243–59

De Graef P, Christiaens D, d'Ydewalle G. 1990. Perceptual effects of scene context on object identification. *Psychol. Res.* 52: 317–29

Dennett DC. 1991. *Consciousness Explained.* Boston: Little Brown

Deubel H, Schneider WX. 1996. Saccade target selection and object recognition: evidence for a common attentional mechanism. *Vis. Res.* 36:1827–37

Deubel H, Schneider WX, Bridgeman B. 1996. Postsaccadic target blanking prevents saccadic suppression of image displacement. *Vis. Res.* 36:985–96

Di Lollo V. 1977. Temporal characteristics of iconic memory. *Nature* 267:241–43

Duhamel JR, Colby CL, Goldberg ME. 1992. The updating of the representation of visual space in parietal cortex by intended eye movements. *Science* 255:90–92

Epstein R, Kanwisher N. 1998. A cortical representation of the local visual environment. *Nature* 392:598–601

Eriksen CW, Collins JF. 1967. Some temporal characteristics of visual pattern recognition. *J. Exp. Psychol.* 74:476–84

Farah MJ. 1989. Semantic and perceptual priming: How similar are the underlying mechanisms? *J. Exp. Psychol.: Hum. Percept. Perform.* 15:188–94

Feldman JA. 1985. Four frames suffice: a provisional model of vision and space. *Behav. Brain Sci.* 8:265–89

Findlay JM. 1982. Global processing for saccadic eye movements. *Vis. Res.* 22: 1033–45

Fodor JA. 1983. *Modularity of Mind.* Cambridge, MA: MIT Press

Friedman A. 1979. Framing pictures: the role of knowledge in automatized encoding and memory for gist. *J. Exp. Psychol.: Gen.* 108:316–55

Friedman A, Liebelt LS. 1981. On the time course of viewing pictures with a view towards remembering. In *Eye Movements: Cognition and Visual Perception,* ed. DF Fisher, RA Monty, JW Senders, pp. 137–55. Hillsdale, NJ: Erlbaum

Grimes J. 1996. On the failure to detect changes in scenes across saccades. See Akins 1996, pp. 89–110

Henderson JM. 1992a. Visual attention and eye movement control during reading and picture viewing. See Rayner 1992, pp. 260–83

Henderson JM. 1992b. Object identification in context: the visual processing of natural scenes. *Can. J. Psychol.* 46:319–41

Henderson JM. 1996. Visual attention and the attention-action interface. See Akins 1996, pp. 290–316

Henderson JM. 1997. Transsaccadic memory and integration during real-world object perception. *Psychol. Sci.* 8:51–55

Henderson JM, Hollingworth A. 1998. Eye movements during scene viewing: an overview. See Underwood 1998, pp. 269–95

Henderson JM, McClure KK, Pierce S, Schrock G. 1997. Object identification without foveal vision: evidence from an artificial scotoma paradigm. *Percept. Psychophys.* 59:323–46

Henderson JM, Pollatsek A, Rayner K. 1987. The effects of foveal priming and extrafoveal preview on object identification. *J. Exp. Psychol.: Hum. Percept. Perform.* 13: 449–63

Henderson JM, Pollatsek A, Rayner K. 1989. Covert visual attention and extrafoveal information use during object identification. *Percept. Psychophys.* 45:196–208

Henderson JM, Weeks PA Jr, Hollingworth A. 1999. The effects of semantic consistency on eye movements during scene viewing. *J. Exp. Psychol.: Hum. Percept. Perform.* In press

Hollingworth A, Henderson JM. 1998. Does consistent scene context facilitate object perception? *J. Exp. Psychol.: Gen.* In press

Humphreys GW, Riddoch MJ. 1994. Attention to within-object and between-object spatial representations: multiple sites for visual selection. *Cogn. Neuropsychol.* 11: 207–41

Humphreys GW, Riddoch MJ. 1995. Separate coding of space within and between perceptual objects: evidence from unilateral visual neglect. *Cogn. Neuropsychol.* 12: 283–311

Irwin DE. 1991. Information integration across saccadic eye movements. *Cogn. Psychol.* 23:420–56

Irwin DE. 1992. Perceiving an integrated visual world. In *Attention and Performance XIV: Synergies in Experimental Psychology, Artificial Intelligence, and Cognitive Neuroscience*, ed. DE Meyer, S Kornblum, pp. 121–42. Cambridge, MA: MIT Press

Irwin DE. 1996. Integrating information across saccadic eye movements. *Curr. Dir. Psychol. Sci.* 5:94–100

Irwin DE, Yantis S, Jonides J. 1983. Evidence against visual integration across saccadic eye movements. *Percept. Pychophys.* 34: 35–46

Irwin DE, Zacks JL, Brown JS. 1990. Visual memory and the perception of a stable environment. *Percept. Pychophys.* 47:35–46

Jonides J, Irwin DE, Yantis S. 1982. Integrating visual information from successive fixations. *Science* 215:192–94

Koch C, Davis JL, eds. 1994. *Large-Scale Neuronal Theories of the Brain.* Cambridge, MA: MIT Press

Kosslyn SM. 1994. *Image and Brain.* Cambridge, MA: MIT Press

Land MF, Furneaux S. 1997. The knowledge base of the oculomotor system. *Philos. Trans. R. Soc. London Ser. B* 352:1231–39

Levin DT, Simons DJ. 1997. Failure to detect changes to attended objects in motion pictures. *Pschonom. Bull. Rev.* 4:501–6

Loftus GR, Mackworth NH. 1978. Cognitive determinants of fixation location during picture viewing. *J. Exp. Psychol.: Hum. Percept. Perform.* 4:565–72

Loftus GR, Nelson WW, Kallman HJ. 1983. Differential acquisition rates for different types of information from pictures. *Q. J. Exp. Psychol.* 35A:187–98

Mackworth NH, Morandi AJ. 1967. The gaze selects informative details within pictures. *Percept. Psychophys.* 2:547–52

Mannan S, Ruddock KH, Wooding DS. 1995. Automatic control of saccadic eye movements made in visual inspection of briefly presented 2-D images. *Spat. Vis.* 9:363–86

Mannan SK, Ruddock KH, Wooding DS. 1996. The relationship between the locations of spatial features and those of fixations made during visual examination of briefly presented images. *Spat. Vis.* 10:165–88

Mannan SK, Ruddock KH, Wooding DS. 1997. Fixation sequences made during visual examination of briefly presented 2D images. *Spat. Vis.* 11:157–78

Marr D. 1982. *Vision.* San Francisco: Freeman

Marr D, Nishihara HK. 1978. Representation and recognition of the spatial organization of three-dimensional shapes. *Proc. R. Soc. London Ser. B* 200:269–94

Masson MEJ. 1991. Constraints on the interaction between context and stimulus information. *Proc. Conf. Cogn. Sci. Soc., 13th, Chicago*, ed. KJ Hammond, D Gentner, pp. 540–45. Hillsdale, NJ: Erlbaum

Matin E. 1974. Saccadic suppression: a review and an analysis. *Psychol. Bull.* 81:899–917

McConkie GW. 1990. *Where vision and cognition meet.* Presented at Hum. Front. Sci. Program Workshop Object Scene Percept., Leuven, Belgium

McConkie GW, Currie CB. 1996. Visual stability across saccades while viewing complex pictures. *J. Exp. Psychol.: Hum. Percept. Perform.* 22:563–81

McConkie GW, Rayner K. 1975. The span of the effective stimulus during a fixation in reading. *Percept. Psychophys.* 17:578–86

Metzger RL, Antes JR. 1983. The nature of processing early in picture perception. *Psychol. Res.* 45:267–74

Mullen KT. 1990. The chromatic coding of space. In *Vision: Coding and Efficiency*, ed. C Blakemore, pp. 150–58. Cambridge: Cambridge Univ. Press

Mumford D. 1994. Neuronal architectures for pattern-theoretic problems. See Koch & Davis 1994, pp. 125–52

Neisser U. 1967. *Cognitive Psychology.* Englewood Cliffs, NJ: Prentice Hall

Norris D. 1995. Signal detection theory and modularity: on being sensitive to the power of bias models of semantic priming. *J. Exp. Psychol.: Hum. Percept. Perform.* 21:935–39

Oliva A, Schyns PG. 1997. Coarse blobs or fine edges? Evidence that information diagnosticity changes the perception of complex visual stimuli. *Cogn. Psychol.* 34: 72–107

O'Regan JK. 1992a. Optimal viewing position in words and the strategy-tactics theory of eye movements in reading. See Rayner 1992, pp. 333–54

O'Regan JK. 1992b. Solving the "real" mysteries of visual perception: the world as an outside memory. *Can. J. Psychol.* 46: 461–88

O'Regan JK, Levy-Schoen A. 1983. Integrating visual information from successive fixations: does trans-saccadic fusion exist? *Vis. Res.* 23:765–68

O'Regan JK, Rensink RA, Clark JJ. 1996. "Mud splashes" render picture changes invisible. *Invest. Opthamol. Vis. Sci.* 37:979

Palmer SE. 1975a. The effects of contextual scenes on the identification of objects. *Mem. Cogn.* 3:519–26

Palmer SE. 1975b. Visual perception and world knowledge: notes on a model of sensory-cognitive interaction. In *Explorations in Cognition,* ed. DA Norman, DE Rumelhart, LNR Res. Group, pp. 279–307. San Francisco: Freeman

Pollatsek A, Rayner K. 1992. What is integrated across fixations? See Rayner 1992, pp. 166–91

Potter MC. 1975. Meaning in visual search. *Science* 187:965–66

Potter MC. 1976. Short-term conceptual memory for pictures. *J. Exp. Psychol.: Hum. Learn. Mem.* 2:509–22

Potter MC, Levy EI. 1969. Recognition memory for a rapid sequence of pictures. *J. Exp. Psychol.* 81:10–15

Pouget A, Fisher SA, Sejnowski TJ. 1993. Egocentric spatial representation in early vision. *J. Cogn. Neurosci.* 5:150–61

Pylyshyn Z. 1980. Computation and cognition: issues in the foundations of cognitive science. *Behav. Brain Sci.* 3:111–32

Pylyshyn Z. 1998. Is vision continuous with cognition? The case for cognitive impenetrability of visual perception. *Behav. Brain Sci.* In press

Rayner K. 1978. Eye movements in reading and information processing. *Psychol. Bull.* 85:618–60

Rayner K, ed. 1992. *Eye Movements and Visual Cognition: Scene Perception and Reading.* New York: Springer-Verlag

Rayner K, Pollatsek A. 1983. Is visual information integrated across saccades? *Percept. Psychophys.* 34:39–48

Rayner K, Pollatsek A. 1989. *The Psychology of Reading.* Englewood Cliffs, NJ: Prentice-Hall

Rayner K, Pollatsek A. 1992. Eye movements and scene perception. *Can. J. Psychol.* 46: 342–76

Reicher GM. 1969. Perceptual recognition as a function of meaningfulness of stimulus material. *J. Exp. Psychol.* 81:275–80

Rensink RA, O'Regan JK, Clark JJ. 1997. To see or not to see: the need for attention to perceive changes in scenes. *Psychol. Sci.* 8:368–73

Riggs LA. 1965. Visual acuity. In *Vision and Visual Perception,* ed. CH Graham, pp. 321–49. New York: Wiley

Rumelhart DE, Smolensky P, McClelland JL, Hinton GE. 1986. Schemata and sequential thought processes in PDP models. In *Parallel Distributed Processing: Explorations in the Microstructure of Cognition: Psychological and Biological Models,* ed. JL McClelland, DE Rumelhart, PDP Res. Group, 2:7–57. Cambridge, MA: MIT Press

Schyns PG, Oliva A. 1994. From blobs to boundary edges: evidence for time and spatial scale dependent scene recognition. *Psychol. Sci.* 5:195–200

Ullman S. 1996. *High-Level Vision: Object Recognition and Visual Cognition.* Cambridge, MA: MIT Press

Underwood G, ed. 1998. *Eye Guidance in Reading and Scene Perception.* Oxford: Elsevier

van Diepen PMJ, De Graef P, d'Ydewalle G. 1995. Chronometry of foveal information extraction during scene perception. In *Eye Movement Research: Mechanisms, Processes and Applications,* ed. JM Findlay, R Walker, RW Kentridge, pp. 349–62. Amsterdam: Elsevier. In press

van Diepen PMJ, Wampers M, d'Ydewalle G. 1998. Functional division of the visual field: moving masks and moving windows. See Underwood 1998. In press

Volkmann FC. 1986. Human visual suppression. *Vis. Res.* 26:1401–16

Yarbus AL. 1967. *Eye Movements and Vision.* New York: Plenum

Annu. Rev. Psychol. 1999. 50:273–303

INTERPERSONAL PROCESSES: The Interplay of Cognitive, Motivational, and Behavioral Activities in Social Interaction

Mark Snyder

Department of Psychology, University of Minnesota, Minneapolis, Minnesota 55455;
e-mail: msnyder@tc.umn.edu

Arthur A. Stukas, Jr.

Department of Psychiatry, University of Pittsburgh, Pittsburgh, Pennsylvania 15213;
e-mail: stukas+@pitt.edu

KEY WORDS: expectations, self-fulfilling prophecies, perceptual confirmation, behavioral confirmation, hypothesis-testing

ABSTRACT

This analytic review is concerned with the interpersonal processes, and the characteristics of situations and persons that influence them, that lead to the confirmation and disconfirmation of expectations in the course of social interaction. We examine the steps in the chain of events by which the expectations of one person guide and direct the dynamics of social interaction such that the behavior of the target of those expectations comes to confirm or disconfirm those expectations. We further inquire into the motivational and structural foundations of confirmation and disconfirmation in social interaction, using these inquiries to address frequently asked, but rarely answered, questions about expectations and social interaction. Finally, we argue that investigations of expectations in social interaction provide a paradigm for more general theoretical and empirical considerations of interpersonal processes and social relationships.

0084-6570/99/0201-0273$08.00

CONTENTS

INTRODUCTION

For most of us, many of the moments of our lives are spent in social interactions through which we learn about ourselves, other people, and the world. Theorists have long considered the origin of the self to be within the context of social interactions, with other people's responses to our actions providing some understanding of who we are (Bem 1972, Cooley 1902, Mead 1934, Stryker & Stratham 1985). As well, the social contexts of our interactions can influence our dealings with other people. Many social interactions, especially those that occur between strangers, are ritualized and formal (Goffman 1955, 1959; Grice 1975). At other times, in less formal interactions, the qualities of those with whom we interact (such as gender, age, race) may determine how we act; as social interaction becomes habitualized, many of these factors may affect us so automatically that we may not recognize their influence (Higgins 1989, Bargh 1997).

The combination of interaction rules, the personalities of the people who are interacting, and the settings and the purpose of their interactions affects not only each person's perception of the other and of self but also the outcomes of the interaction, including the likelihood of future interactions. Given the importance of these outcomes, people have learned to make use of cues that may signal the likely course of interaction. Among these cues are the expectations with which people begin their interactions with others, expectations about what will be required of them and expectations about how their interaction partners will act (Olson et al 1996). Indeed, these preconceived expectations, and those formed immediately on beginning interaction, can channel our thought and behavior toward others before they have a chance to provide any behavioral basis for our impressions (Snyder 1984).

Much of the time, expectations are based on personal experience with specific others' behaviors in past interactions; at other times, when people interact with strangers or even with familiar people in strange situations, their behaviors may be guided by overgeneralized and/or erroneous expectations (Fiske & Neuberg 1990). Whatever their origins, these expectations may elicit the very behaviors that are expected—a self-fulfilling prophecy (Merton 1948). Our own behavior, too, may be affected by others' expectations; we may conform to others' visions of who we are rather than to our own, perhaps not even realizing that our own self-presentations have been influenced by the expectations of others (Vorauer & Miller 1997).

This analytic review is concerned with the interpersonal processes, and the characteristics of situations and persons that influence them, that lead to confirmation and disconfirmation of expectations in social interaction. Research has revealed a process that links one person's expectations to another person's actions in response, actions that confirm or disconfirm those expectations. Such research, we argue, provides a paradigm for studying the dynamic processes of social interaction. Our goals are, first, to review and integrate diverse programs of research on the confirmation and disconfirmation of expectations in social interaction, and second, to point out how this integrative review suggests answers to persistent questions about the nature of these processes, as well as how it helps to chart new directions for research on interpersonal processes.

THE PHENOMENA

The self-fulfilling prophecy in social interaction has been demonstrated in empirical investigations in which one person (the perceiver), having adopted beliefs about another person (the target), acts in ways that cause the behavior of the target to appear to confirm these beliefs. The consequences of expectations can be separated into two kinds: (a) *perceptual confirmation* of expectations in the mind of the perceiver (as revealed in perceivers' impressions of targets) and (b) *behavioral confirmation* of expectations by the actions of the target during the interaction (as documented by third-party raters' judgments of targets).

The Prevalence of the Phenomena

Early work on perceptual and behavioral confirmation demonstrated that these phenomena exist and can be documented in diverse domains. Several research traditions can be identified, each with its own characteristic features. One tradition began in the field and is best exemplified by demonstrations that teachers, led to expect particular levels of performance from students in their classrooms, act in ways that elicit performances that confirm initial expectations (Rosenthal 1974, 1993, 1994; Rosenthal & Jacobson 1968). Related studies have demonstrated confirmation in organizational settings (Dougherty et al 1994, Dvir et al 1995, Eden 1993). Another research tradition has used the psychological laboratory to investigate social interaction sequences. One such study demonstrated, in getting-acquainted conversations, perceptual and behavioral confirmation of the stereotyped assumption that physically attractive people have socially appealing personalities (Snyder et al 1977). For previous reviews of laboratory studies of confirmation, see Miller & Turnbull (1986), Neuberg (1996a,b), and Snyder (1984).

In addition, research traditions on confirmation can be characterized by whether survey or experimental methods are used (a characterization partially confounded with the lab/field split). Survey methods allow a glimpse at naturally occurring expectations and how they may be related to perceptual and behavioral confirmation (Hart 1995; Jussim & Eccles 1992, 1995a). Because many such studies concern expectations based on objective and presumably valid information (e.g. records of students' past performance), they may have greater relevance for the effects of accurate, rather than erroneous, expectations. Experimental methods are at their best in the use of random assignment and experimental control to determine causal influences. Experiments are particularly suited to precise control of the perceiver's expectation, which is essential to knowing that the perceiver's expectation, and not some preexisting attributes of the target that happen to be correlated with the perceiver's expectation, is affecting the target's behavior.

Boundary and Delimiting Conditions

At present, the accumulated body of evidence indicates that confirmation effects occur reliably, although they are not the inevitable consequences of expectations (Jussim 1986, 1993; Jussim et al 1996; Miller & Turnbull 1986; Neuberg 1994; Snyder 1984, 1992). Rather, most researchers agree that there are boundary conditions to the effects of expectations (Jones 1986; Jussim 1986, 1991; Snyder 1984, 1992). Just as there are circumstances in which confirmation occurs, other situations produce outcomes that neither validate nor dismiss initial expectations, and others provide opportunities for targets to disconfirm expectations (Hilton & Darley 1991; Jussim et al 1996; Neuberg 1994, 1996a,b; Snyder 1984, 1992; Madon et al 1997). On yet other occasions, behavior that appears to confirm expectations may do so because the expectations are accurate; specifically, research on teachers' expectations suggests that expectations based on earlier achievement scores and reports from other teachers may reflect long-standing behavioral differences (Jussim 1989, 1991, 1993; Jussim & Eccles 1995b; Jussim et al 1994), and more so than expectations based on gender or racial differences (Jussim et al 1996, Madon et al 1997).

THE MECHANISMS

One approach to examining social phenomena is to decompose them into their microlevel constituent elements (Kelley 1992). Following this strategy, researchers have parsed the behavioral confirmation sequence into a series of steps: (*a*) perceivers adopt beliefs about targets; (*b*) perceivers behave toward targets as if these beliefs were true; (*c*) targets fit their behavior to perceivers' overtures; and (*d*) perceivers interpret targets' behavior as confirming their beliefs. Researchers have developed strategies for looking at one or more of these steps (Brophy & Good 1974; Darley & Fazio 1980; Deaux & Major 1987; Harris & Rosenthal 1985; Jones 1986; Jussim 1986; Miller & Turnbull 1986; Rosenthal 1974; Snyder 1984, 1992).

A study by Pelletier & Vallerand (1996) elegantly captures all of the steps in the sequence of events in behavioral confirmation. They led supervisors to believe that their subordinates were intrinsically or extrinsically motivated to complete spatial puzzles. They then observed the instructional strategies of the supervisors, the subordinates' perceptions of the supervisors, and the eventual motivation of the subordinates. With all of the pieces in place, Pelletier & Vallerand (1996) were able to demonstrate how supervisors' expectations were translated into supportive or controlling actions that then produced intrinsically or extrinsically motivated subordinates.

Origin and Activation of Expectations

To understand the expectations that start the behavioral confirmation process, Olson et al (1996) distinguished between *properties* of expectations and *types* of expectations. Properties of expectations include certainty, accessibility, explicitness, and importance. Increases in certainty, accessibility, explicitness, and importance of expectations should lead perceivers to act on expectations in ways that generate confirmation. As an exception to this rule, Olson et al

(1996) note that the relation between expectation-certainty and hypothesis-testing may be curvilinear: No tests are needed for expectations held with absolute certainty.

Although Olson et al (1996) did not offer a categorization of types of expectations, we suggest that the content domains of expectations may be classified as being positive or negative, as about morality or ability, and as having a domain circumscribed to the situation or attributed to general dispositions of personality. Relevant to this system, researchers have asked whether positive and negative expectations result in asymmetrical confirmation effects (Madon et al 1997, Major et al 1988), whether diagnosticity varies according to whether traits concern ability or morality (Reeder & Brewer 1979; Skowronski & Carlston 1987, 1989), and about the role of global and circumscribed accuracy of expectations (Stukas & Snyder 1995, Swann 1984).

But from where do expectations come? Some expectations come from past experiences with targets or from third parties who know the targets (e.g. teachers' expectations derive in part from students' past academic work and the reports of previous teachers). Such detailed, often firsthand, information may provide the most accurate basis on which perceivers can base their expectations, accurate in the sense that such expectations about the dispositions of targets and their likely future behavior are clearly linked to their prior behavioral histories. For such expectations, it may be difficult to disentangle the effects of the perceiver's expectations and the target's actual behavioral dispositions on the target's behavior, since both expectations and dispositions would tend to promote the same actions on the part of the target.

Other expectations may be generalizations based on characteristics associated with group membership; for example, research has demonstrated that perceivers easily generate expectations about others based on such relatively nondiagnostic traits as physical attractiveness (Snyder et al 1977), race (Chen & Bargh 1997, Word et al 1974), and gender (Skrypnek & Snyder 1982). These expectations often involve the application of general stereotypes about the personalities thought to be associated with membership in certain categories to specific individuals who happen to belong to such categories. There appears to be greater inherent potential for "slippage" between such expectations and the actual attributes of individual targets, and hence greater potential for the confirmation of general stereotypes erroneously applied to specific cases.

There are also emerging indications that perceivers' own personalities may be related to the expectations they hold about other people. For example, Downey (Downey et al 1998, Downey & Feldman 1996) and Murray (Murray & Holmes 1997, Murray et al 1996) have suggested that individuals who fear rejection may be likely to form expectations of their relationship partners as rejecters and may even elicit such rejection. Deaux & Major (1987) have suggested that gender serves as a filter for expectations about men and women; Andersen & Bem (1981) have made the same point with regard to sex-typing. Similarly, self-certainty about their own traits may lead perceivers to see those traits in others (Sedikides & Skowronski 1993).

Such personality-based expectations may develop from repeated encounters that lead familiar expectations to become chronically accessible (Higgins & King 1981). Chronically accessible expectations may influence perceivers to interpret target behavior as consistent with expectations (Skowronski et al 1993). Expectations may also be automatically activated by features of situations and persons and thus made more accessible to perceivers (Higgins 1989). In fact, situationally primed and chronically accessible expectations have similar effects on attentional and interpretational activities of perceivers (Bargh 1997). Once activated, both types of expectations can lead perceivers to act in ways that elicit behavioral confirmation from targets (Chen & Bargh 1997).

Ways in Which Perceivers Act on Expectations

Recently, researchers have begun to compare whether automatically activated expectations affect confirmation in different ways than overt expectations. Skowronski et al (1993) have reported that overt expectations lead to greater attention to expectation-incongruent information and that automatically activated expectations lead to greater attention to expectation-congruent information. This finding implies that automatically activated expectations may result in stronger perceptual and behavioral confirmation effects than the overt expectations typically used in research, suggesting that results found using overt expectations may actually be attenuated estimates of the power of expectations to influence behavior.

Bargh (Bargh 1997, Bargh et al 1996, Chen & Bargh 1997) has proposed that automatically activated (and chronically accessible) expectations can induce perceivers to act in line with these expectations through an ideomotor process. As evidence, Bargh et al (1996) demonstrated that students in whom an "elderly" expectation was automatically activated (by subliminal presentation of a photo on a computer screen) walked more slowly down the hall after the study than those for whom the expectation was not activated. Additionally, students for whom an African-American expectation was activated acted in a more hostile fashion than did those without this expectation. Moreover, Chen & Bargh (1997) have extended their research to involve an actual behavioral confirmation sequence and showed that automatically activated expectations can and do lead to behavioral confirmation—both perceivers and targets acted in a more hostile fashion when perceivers were subliminally primed with an

African-American photo than when perceivers were primed with a White photo.

Reliance on expectations, whether automatically activated or controlled, has been theorized to become more pronounced when perceivers are under greater cognitive load (Fiske & Neuberg 1990, Harris & Perkins 1995). Thus, with less attention to devote to individuating targets, perceivers may rely on categorical expectations to dictate their behavior toward the target. Yet the use of expectations may not be entirely the result of a need to preserve diminished cognitive resources. In fact, Leyens and Yzerbyt (Leyens et al 1992, Yzerbyt et al 1994) have demonstrated that when situations justify social judgments, perceivers expend great amounts of energy to seek confirmation of expectations (rather than to seek out individuating information), suggesting the utility of viewing some confirmation processes as products of deliberate and intentional expenditure of effort and resources (Yzerbyt et al 1997).

Much research has focused on how perceivers elicit confirmation of their beliefs in the context of explicit hypothesis-testing paradigms (Snyder & Swann 1978b, Swann & Giuliano 1987). Recent studies provide a new perspective on such hypothesis-testing activities, suggesting that confirmatory strategies may reflect perceivers' social competence and may help to create an appearance of empathy between perceivers and targets (B Dardenne, manuscript in preparation; Dardenne & Leyens 1995; Leyens 1989; Leyens et al 1998). Thus, confirmatory strategies may have social value, increasing the smoothness and pleasantness of interaction; intriguingly, a recent study by Judice & Neuberg (1998) demonstrated that perceivers seeking to explicitly confirm *negative* expectations also created more smooth and pleasing interactions than those seeking accurate impressions. Therefore, confirmatory strategies may occur via two routes: one rather effortless and automatic and one relatively effortful and intentional (SA Goodwin, ST Fiske, VY Yzerbyt, manuscript under review).

Even the very grammar that people use to frame questions to test their hypotheses may have substantial effects on the responses they receive. Semin & De Poot (1997a,b) have demonstrated that questions that use action verbs elicit different answers than questions that use state verbs. What is even more fascinating is that targets appear to be unaware of the differing connotations of their answers; third-party observers, however, judge targets quite differently depending on their responses (Semin & De Poot 1997a). In addition, Semin & De Poot (1997b) have shown that perceivers select questions with verbs that indicate their expectations about the agency of the victim or the accused in a rape investigation, questions that presumably will guide interviewees' responses.

In other approaches to the ways perceivers act on expectations, Rosenthal and Harris (Harris 1993, Harris et al 1994, Harris & Rosenthal 1985, Rosenthal

1993) have examined particular behaviors that mediate self-fulfilling consequences, particularly for teachers' expectations in the classroom, including
the effects of such nonverbal behaviors as smiles, nods, and eye contact. Finally, an additional (but little-studied) mechanism by which confirmation
may be elicited is the guiding influence of the perceiver on the situations in
which they interact with the target, with expectations about the likely behaviors of targets leading perceivers to choose to interact with targets in situations conducive to those very behaviors (Gresham & Snyder 1990, Ickes et al
1997).

Ways in Which Targets Respond to Perceivers' Actions

Research on the effects of perceivers' expectations on targets' behaviors has
often viewed targets as rather passive, reciprocating or matching the actions of
perceivers (Miller & Turnbull 1986). In part, this may be due to the impoverished situation that targets are placed in, without knowledge of the perceivers'
expectation (Miller & Turnbull 1986, Snyder 1992). Still, recent evidence suggests that it may be targets' tendency to fall prey to an "acquiescence orientation" (being more likely to answer positively than negatively to perceivers'
questions) that leads to confirmation as much as their presumed passivity
(Zuckerman et al 1995).

Increasingly, researchers have come to conceptualize an "active target," a
target who uses active strategies of coping with their interactions (Hilton &
Darley 1985, Smith et al 1997, Snyder 1992, Stukas & Snyder 1995). There are
indications that when targets confirm expectations, they do so in an attempt to
facilitate the flow of their interactions with perceivers (Snyder & Haugen
1995). For example, when Smith et al (1997) instructed targets to act in either a
"deferent" or a "nondeferent" manner in an interview, targets who acted defer-
entially were more likely to confirm perceivers' expectations than those who
acted nondeferentially. Thus, targets' active strategies may contribute to the
outcomes of their interactions with perceivers.

Effects on Perception of Self and Other

Perceptual confirmation is a reliable, although not necessarily inevitable, phenomenon (Darley & Gross 1983, Kulik 1983). Perceivers often maintain initial
expectations throughout the course of social interaction (Miller & Turnbull
1986; Snyder 1984, 1992). What is striking is that even when targets have behaviorally disconfirmed their perceivers' expectations, perceivers may still
retain these expectations (Hilton & Darley 1985, Ickes et al 1982, Neuberg
1989, Snyder & Haugen 1995). In part, perceptual confirmation in the face of
behavioral disconfirmation may be due to perceivers' coming to believe in the

truth of their own expectations merely by thinking about them and using congruent language (Fiedler et al 1996).

Researchers have also examined targets' self-conceptions after interactions with perceivers who hold incongruent expectations of them (Fazio et al 1981, Major et al 1988, Swann & Ely 1984). In some studies, targets retained their original self-conceptions even when providing behavioral confirmation (Judice & Neuberg 1998, Major et al 1988, Vorauer & Miller 1997). In other studies, targets changed their self-conceptions in the direction of the expectations they had confirmed (Fazio et al 1981, Harris 1990, Snyder & Swann 1978a).

Characterizing the issue in a different way, some researchers have asked whether it is perceivers' expectations or targets' self-conceptions that are more stable. Many of these studies (Grinder & Swim 1991, Major et al 1988, McNulty & Swann 1994, Miene et al 1991, Swann & Ely 1984, Testa & Major 1988) have sought to pit behavioral confirmation, in which perceivers bring targets to act in line with expectations, against self-verification (Swann 1983, Swann & Hill 1982, Swann & Read 1981), in which targets bring perceivers to change their expectations to be congruent with targets' self-conceptions. One resolution to this "battle of wills" is that both processes work simultaneously (Jussim 1991, Miene et al 1991, Swann 1987); indeed, McNulty & Swann (1994) found that in a longitudinal study of college roommates, perceivers' expectations and targets' self-conceptions both changed in the direction of their roommate's views. Similarly, Miene et al (1991) found that both perceivers' expectations and targets' actual personalities contributed significantly to targets' behavior.

Consequences for Future Behavior and Interaction

The effects of expectations on interpersonal processes may extend beyond the circumstances in which confirmation first occurs. If targets have provided behavioral confirmation for perceivers' expectations, this "evidence" may be used by perceivers to justify further actions toward targets. Among these actions are decisions about further interaction between perceiver and target. Individuals may be more likely to initiate further social contact with the targets of positive rather than negative expectations. Indeed, given the confirmation of a negative expectation, there may only be a first encounter—that is, perceivers may choose to avoid future interactions with targets who have confirmed their negative expectations (Harris 1993).

MOTIVATIONAL FOUNDATIONS

When it comes to understanding the confirmation sequence scenario, the strategy of parsing the sequence into its steps is particularly fruitful because the constituent elements of the behavioral confirmation scenario are themselves key aspects of interpersonal processes—attribution, person perception, belief-behavior relations, self-presentation, reciprocity, and so on. Use of this strategy, however, can entail some loss of the perspective that is provided by seeing the entire sequence unfolding (Kelley 1992); for that reason, studies that articulate all of the steps of an interaction sequence in a single investigation may provide the most clarity.

With the evident success of the parsing strategy in informing us about what is happening in confirmation scenarios, researchers have turned their attentions to the social and psychological processes that underlie interactions between the holders of expectations and the targets of expectations. They have been seeking to understand *why* perceivers act in ways that initiate confirmation and disconfirmation scenarios and *why* targets come to behave in ways that confirm or disconfirm expectations. Conducted from interrelated theoretical perspectives, such research suggests that the motivations of perceivers and targets are those that may be most useful to them and that the interactional strategies that lead to confirmation and disconfirmation are ones that perceivers and targets regard as functional to them in their dealings with each other.

The Interaction Goals Approach

One line of research by Hilton & Darley (Darley et al 1988; Hilton 1995; Hilton & Darley 1985, 1991; Hilton et al 1989) has examined the "interaction goals" that arise for both targets and perceivers in the context of their interaction. They suggest that perceivers may be in an "assessment set," with the goal of forming an accurate impression of the target, or in an "action set," with the goal of working on a specific task in which impression formation is only indirectly involved. Perceivers in an "action set" are thought to elicit behavioral confirmation more readily than perceivers in an "assessment set." Hilton (1995) has expanded the taxonomy of interaction goals to include explicit goals (seeking an accurate impression), nonconscious goals (reducing threats to self-esteem), implicit goals (following unstated conversational norms), and recursive goals (such as second-guessing targets' own interaction goals).

Another line of work on the goals of perceivers and targets has been pursued by Neuberg (Judice & Neuberg 1998; Neuberg 1989, 1994, 1996a,b; Neuberg et al 1993; Smith et al 1997). Neuberg (1989) has demonstrated that perceivers who were motivated to gain an accurate understanding of targets were more likely to elicit disconfirmation than confirmation. Similarly, Neuberg et al (1993) have shown that when perceivers are motivated to get targets to like them, they do not elicit self-fulfilling outcomes. On the target side of the equation, Smith et al (1997) have examined targets' motivations to be either deferent to perceivers or nondeferent, finding confirmation only in the former condition.

The Functional Approach

Another approach to studying motivational foundations takes a "functional" perspective to examine the reasons and purposes, needs and goals, and plans and motives that underlie and generate confirmation and disconfirmation (Copeland 1993, 1994; Copeland & Snyder 1995; Miene et al 1991; Snyder 1992; Snyder & Haugen 1994, 1995). Researchers using this framework seek to identify the psychological functions being served by the activities of perceivers and targets that generate behavioral confirmation. Empirical investigations have indicated that behavioral confirmation occurs most readily when the activities of the perceiver serve the function of *acquiring knowledge* and the activities of the target serve the function of *facilitating interaction* (Copeland & Snyder 1995; Snyder & Haugen 1994, 1995). In a study of perceiver functions, Snyder & Haugen (1994) demonstrated that perceivers, interacting with targets who were depicted as either obese or normal weight, elicited behavioral confirmation only when they were motivated to acquire stable and predictable knowledge and not when they were motivated to facilitate smooth and coordinated interactions. In a study of target functions, Snyder & Haugen (1995) demonstrated that targets, who were believed to be either obese or normal weight, confirmed expectations only when they were motivated to facilitate interaction and not when they were motivated to seek knowledge about perceivers.

An understanding of the motivational foundations of behavioral confirmation may also provide the basis for an understanding of the interpersonal processes of social interaction more generally. The motivation to seek social knowledge and the motivation to facilitate social interaction may capture the orientations of "getting to know" and "getting along," respectively, that are thought to be integral to and intricately intertwined in acquaintance processes and, by extension, social interaction and social relations more generally (Snyder 1992).

Research on the motivational foundations of confirmation is also informative about the origins of disconfirmation. It suggests that interactions in which perceivers are not motivated by considerations known to initiate confirmatory orientations to social interaction and/or ones in which targets are not motivated by the considerations that lead them to adopt their confirmatory orientations will not lead to self-fulfilling consequences of expectations.

STRUCTURAL FOUNDATIONS

That perceivers and targets differ in their motivations has led to inquiry about differing features of the roles of perceiver and target that may be linked to their differing motivational orientation to their interactions with each other. Scrutiny of perceiver-target dyadic relationships has revealed that there are relevant structural features of interactions between perceivers and targets that may set the stage for confirmation to occur. In particular, researchers and theorists have examined power differentials between individuals engaging in social interaction (Copeland 1994; Darley & Fazio 1980; Harris 1993; Harris et al 1998; D Operario & ST Fiske, manuscript in preparation; Snyder 1992, 1995; Virdin & Neuberg 1990).

Power and the Structural Relations Between Perceiver and Target

Typically, the role of the perceiver is defined in terms of the guiding influence of his or her beliefs about the target. It is the perceiver and not the target who holds preconceived beliefs and expectations. It is also the perceiver who has more explicit opportunities than the target to use their interaction as an opportunity to evaluate beliefs. For example, in interview formats for studying behavioral confirmation, the perceiver asks the questions and the target answers them. Similarly, in the getting-acquainted situations used in many behavioral confirmation experiments, it is typically the perceiver who initiates conversation by speaking first and taking a guiding and directing influence in the ensuing interaction (M Snyder & LJ Mobilio, manuscript under review). Moreover, explicitly manipulating the flow of information so that perceivers start by talking about themselves, rather than by getting the targets to talk about themselves, blocks this chain of events and prevents behavioral confirmation (Mobilio & Snyder 1996).

By contrast, the role of the target is defined in relation to behavioral reactions to the perceiver's overtures. The very fact that targets know less about perceivers than perceivers know about them (a direct consequence of the fact that perceivers rather than targets are provided with expectations) indicates that the role of target is one characterized by an informational deficit that may lead targets to turn to perceivers for guidelines for how to construe their interaction and how to behave in the course of it. Thus, in the absence of competing considerations, the role of the target seems to be defined to promote taking cues from, and fitting oneself into, the outlines laid down by one's interaction partner—a role of essentially low power to influence, to determine, and to control the ensuing interaction.

In effect, these considerations point to *power differences* inherent in the roles of perceiver and target (Snyder 1995). Structural differences in information available to them combined with differing potential to direct interaction make the perceiver's role one of greater power and the target's role one of lesser power. In addition, perceivers and targets often interact in circumstances that themselves dictate an imbalance of power. Many demonstrations of the self-fulfilling prophecy have occurred in real or simulated interactions between teachers and students (Harris & Rosenthal 1985), between employers and employees (Pelletier & Vallerand 1996), and between therapists and clients (Copeland & Snyder 1995). In these cases, therapists, employers, and teachers, by virtue of their roles, can be thought of as often functioning as perceivers with the power to influence individuals who depend on them for jobs, education, or solutions to problems (who may be the targets of expectations about their likely job performance, educational attainments, and therapeutic prognosis). These differences in power between perceivers and the dependent targets of their expectations may set the stage for self-fulfilling prophecies.

Research on Power, Status, and Behavioral Confirmation

An empirical examination of power and behavioral confirmation has been conducted by Copeland (1994), who explicitly manipulated the presence of an expectation about the partner and the power to control the partner's outcomes and found that during a getting-acquainted interaction, behavioral confirmation occurred only when the perceiver had the power to control the target's outcomes. When targets had the power to control perceivers' outcomes, behavioral confirmation did not occur. Copeland (1994) also reported that the motivations of perceivers and targets changed with the power they were granted in the interaction. When perceivers had power over targets' outcomes, they were motivated to seek knowledge about targets (the motivation linked to the activities of the perceiver in behavioral confirmation scenarios; Snyder & Haugen 1994), but when they did not have power, perceivers were motivated to facilitate favorable interaction outcomes. Similarly, targets with power were motivated to acquire knowledge about their partners, but those without power were motivated to facilitate pleasant interactions (a target function that contributes to behavioral confirmation; Snyder & Haugen 1995). Thus, the structural effect of power may serve to create the very motivations that underlie the behavioral confirmation sequence.

Also relevant to the dynamics of power and behavioral confirmation, research by Harris et al (1998) suggests that the activities of high-power perceivers may be more influential in determining confirmation than the behaviors of low-power targets. In addition, social power may elicit behavioral confirmation through mechanisms of attentional focus. Power may reduce attentional focus on the individuating characteristics of others, thus leading to greater reliance on existing knowledge structures that may be confirmed when acted on by perceivers (Fiske 1993; Fiske & Morling 1996; Fiske & Neuberg 1990; SA Goodwin, ST Fiske, VY Yzerbyt, manuscript under review). However, JC Georgeson, MJ Harris, and RM Lightner (manuscript under review) found that powerful perceivers who initiated confirmation sequences actually reported paying greater attention to the targets of their expectations.

A consideration of power and behavioral confirmation takes on added meaning when one realizes that the same people who are typically the targets of social and cultural stereotypes are often those who have less power in our society (e.g. members of minority groups). These low-power targets may find themselves dependent on powerful perceivers for their outcomes. Their positions of lesser power may engender a deferent orientation as they seek to get along well with, and to accommodate themselves to the will of, those with power. Because of this outcome dependency, these targets may be more responsive to cues given off by their perceivers (Geis 1993), cues that may be founded on stereotype-based expectations, cues that effectively lead targets onto the path of behavioral confirmation, possibly in hopes of minimizing negative outcomes at the hands of those with power over their fates.

Research on gender differences in behavioral confirmation is potentially relevant to matters of power and the dynamics of social interaction. Some research has suggested that the largest confirmation effects tend to occur in dyads composed of male perceivers and female targets (Christiansen & Rosenthal 1982), a dyadic relationship that may be construed as involving a perceiver relatively higher in status and power than the target (for related points about women and men as perceivers, see Dvir et al 1995, and as targets, see Jussim et al 1996). Other research, however, has indicated that the magnitude of behavioral confirmation may not be so reliably linked to the gender composition of the perceiver-target dyads (Andersen & Bem 1981, Hall & Briton 1993).

SOME ANSWERS TO FREQUENTLY ASKED QUESTIONS

Throughout the course of research on the effects of expectations in social interaction, there have been questions that have been often asked. The accumulated body of theory and research now places us in a position to bring new perspectives to these questions.

Aren't Both Parties to the Interaction Really Perceivers and Targets?

Typically, in experiments on behavioral confirmation, one participant is assigned to be a perceiver, by virtue of being provided with an expectation, and the other participant becomes, de facto, the target. The question can be asked: Is it perhaps artificial to designate one interactant as perceiver and the other as target? After all, it can be argued, it is probably the case that both parties have expectations about each other that they bring to their interaction (Olson et al 1996). To be sure, it is a procedural convenience to have participants function either as perceivers or as targets, a procedural convenience that may facilitate the demonstration of causal linkages between the perceiver's expectations and the target's behavior.

Yet, without denying that both parties to an interaction may bring expectations into their encounter, we wish to assert that there are considerations that will make one of these parties functionally the perceiver and the other party functionally the target. These considerations are precisely the same considerations of status and power that we have already seen to be relevant to understanding why and when perceivers' expectations will influence targets' behavior. As we have already noted, some role relationships are structured in ways that confer more power to one member than to the other—therapists have more power than clients, teachers have more power than students, and employers have more power than employees. In such role relationships, we predict that the flow of influence will be from the expectations of the party with higher structurally conferred power (who will functionally be the perceiver) to the behavior of the party with lower structurally conferred power (who will functionally become the target). Thus, even though therapists and clients, teachers and students, and employers and employees each may harbor expectations about the other, the power differences structured into their roles dictate that it will be the expectations of therapists, teachers, and employers that will likely find behavioral confirmation in the actions of clients, students, and employees.

However, even when there are no explicit role relationships to structurally confer power differentials, there are often differences in the "resources" possessed by the parties to ostensibly "equal" relationships. In getting-acquainted interactions, in friendships, and in romantic relationships, the parties involved may differ in the "resources" of, for example, physical attractiveness, wealth, charm, or alternate choices for companionship that they bring to their dealings with each other. These greater resources may give greater "power" to one party and hence make that party functionally the perceiver, resulting in a flow of influence from that party's expectations to the other party's behavior.

What Are the Consequences of Expectations That Are Not Erroneous?

In many investigations of confirmation processes, particularly those conducted with experimental methods, great care is taken to decouple the perceiver's expectations from actual attributes of the target through the random assignment of perceivers to expectation conditions. This research strategy, of course, facilitates the goal of being able to make causal inferences about the impact of perceivers' expectations on targets' behavior. But it also reflects the particular interests of many researchers in understanding the self-fulfilling consequences of initially *erroneous* expectations, particularly those that derive from global stereotypes of questionable validity, and the possibility that the behavior of targets may be as much, if not more, a reflection of the expectations of perceivers than a reflection of their own personalities. Relevant to this possibility, PK Miene, M Snyder & A Gresham (manuscript in preparation) have demonstrated, in a laboratory investigation of interactions between perceivers and targets, that the behavior of targets reflected not only their perceivers' expectations that they were extraverts or introverts but also their own extraverted or introverted dispositions of personality; moreover, the effects of the perceivers' manipulated expectations remained in evidence even when the effects of the targets' measured personalities had been controlled statistically.

Nevertheless, it is important to recognize that studies of naturally occurring expectations have suggested that such expectations may be at times less erroneous than those often used in laboratory studies (Jussim 1991). Indeed, expectations that are based on presumably valid and/or readily observable information (such as students' test scores and their records of past achievement) may be more accurate for a given target than expectations based on hearsay or social stereotypes. In this regard, Jussim (1991, Jussim et al 1996) has reported that in studies of teachers and students, expectation effects (that is, associations between teachers' expectations and students' performance) are typically smaller than "accuracy" effects (that is, associations between students' prior performance and their current performance). This finding has led to a search for the "powerful" self-fulfilling prophecy (Jussim et al 1996, Madon et al 1997), which has suggested that the effects of teachers' expectations are larger for female students, African-American students, students from lower socioeconomic groups, and students who were lower achievers in the past—groups that may be particularly low in status and power vis-à-vis their teachers. This pattern of results from field studies of teachers and students would seem to be consistent with laboratory studies that link confirmation processes to dyads in which targets have less power and status than perceivers (e.g. Copeland 1994, Virdin & Neuberg 1990).

Still, there are consequences even of the most accurate expectations. For one, whether these expectations are negative or positive will likely determine whether there will be further interaction; future interaction seems more likely to be chosen in the context of positive expectations about one's prospective interaction partners than when expectations are negative. And, given that perceivers will be particularly likely to see evidence that confirms expectations that are accurate (because targets are likely to behave consistently), such accurate expectations may be particularly resistant to change, even if the target's behavior were to change over time (and the expectation thereby became inaccurate). There may be tremendous pressure placed on targets not to change; in other words, even accurate expectations may serve to preserve the status quo. Smith et al (1997) suggest that even expectations based on the most objective information (teachers' expectations based on earlier student performance) may result in self-fulfilling prophecies if previous teachers held erroneous expectations and these expectations were internalized by students after their behavior changed in reaction.

The matter of accuracy is a particularly difficult one, especially when it comes to defining appropriate criteria for assessing the accuracy of expectations. Some guidance is provided by the standards of criterion validity and predictive validity as used in evaluating the accuracy of psychological assessment procedures. For all intents and purposes, if targets come to behave congruently with perceivers' expectations (that is, if objective outside raters judge them to have behaved so, which is the criterion used in research on behavioral confirmation), then, in those particular interactions, perceivers' expectations were accurate—at least by typical standards of criterion validity (Snyder & Gangestad 1980). Of course, such confirmatory behavior may have been elicited by perceivers' behaviors, even behaviors based on initially erroneous expectations. It may also be the case that if perceivers and targets regularly meet in the same situations, perceivers' expectations may also hold predictive validity, another standard for assessing accuracy; of course, this accuracy also may be the result of perceivers eliciting expectation-congruent behavior from targets on repeated occasions (Snyder & Gangestad 1980).

Similarly, and of relevance to considerations of the accuracy of expectations, it may be that, through their treatment of targets, perceivers are able to elicit exaggerated displays of traits that targets actually possess. In such cases, perceivers will have a distorted sample of target behavior, but again one that might be considered accurate since the target possesses the trait, just not to the degree indicated by his or her behavior. As Swann (1984) has argued, perceivers may pragmatically need only circumscribed accuracy of their expectations; thus, it may be functionally important only for them to know targets under the conditions in which they will interact with them. Therefore, even a distorted view of targets may be accurate enough for perceivers to predict behavior in the specific situations in which they interact.

Is There an Asymmetry Between Positive and Negative Expectations?

Often, studies of the consequences of expectations contrast a condition in which perceivers hold a positive expectation (e.g. this attractive person will have a good personality) with one in which perceivers hold a negative expectation (e.g. that unattractive person will have a bad personality). Quite understandably, researchers have asked whether the effects in studies of behavioral confirmation are being carried by the positive or the negative expectations and whether there are differences in size or likelihood of effects for negative and positive expectations (Darley & Oleson 1993). As it happens, points about asymmetry have been difficult to make because most research on behavioral confirmation has not included a no-expectation condition as a baseline. However, it is unclear what kind of a baseline a no-expectation condition would provide. Perceivers in such a condition just might give targets about whom nothing is known the benefit of the doubt; therefore, a no-expectation condition, rather than serving as a neutral (i.e. neither positive nor negative) expectation condition, might be functionally more like a positive expectation condition (making the negative expectation effect look much larger, artifactually).

Nevertheless, the literature on person perception does provide a firm basis for theorizing about positive and negative asymmetries in the effects of expectations (Reeder & Brewer 1979, Rothbart & Park 1986). For many expectations, particularly those that concern morality, negative actions are taken by perceivers as more diagnostic (e.g. one theft makes you dishonest) than positive actions (Martijn et al 1992; Reeder & Brewer 1979; Reeder & Coovert 1986; Skowronski & Carlston 1987, 1992). Thus, a negative expectation concerning moral behavior may be weighted more heavily in a perceiver's mind than a positive one and may lead to an asymmetry favoring the confirmation of negative expectations over positive ones.

However, researchers (Reeder & Brewer 1979) have also suggested that for expectations related to ability, positive behaviors may be more diagnostic than negative ones (e.g. to demonstrate intelligence, you must actually be intelligent). Extending this analysis to the behavioral confirmation arena, it may be that ability-based expectations lead to asymmetrical effects favoring the confirmation of positive judgments of ability over the confirmation of negative judgments of ability. Indeed, Madon et al (1997) recently found a stronger effect for positive teacher expectations of student ability than for negative teacher expectations. However, when Martijn et al (1992) presented behaviors related to morality and ability to perceivers, they found that perceivers weighted moral behaviors, especially negative ones, more strongly than behaviors related to ability when making global judgments about targets.

Considerations of the diagnosticity of behavior suggest that when perceivers encounter behavioral evidence that they regard as particularly diagnostic of the dispositions of the targets of their expectations (e.g. negative expectations about morality and positive expectations about ability), there will be more perceptual confirmation of their expectations. But for behavioral confirmation to follow from such expectations, there should also be asymmetries in perceivers' actual investment in eliciting behavioral evidence from targets. As evidence for such asymmetries, Yzerbyt & Leyens (1991) found that perceivers spent more time gathering information from targets when they had positive expectations than when they had negative ones, which implies that perceivers may believe less evidence is needed to confirm negative than positive expectations. As a result, targets may have fewer opportunities to disconfirm negative expectations and more opportunities to confirm positive ones; in fact, in a study by Major et al (1988), the targets of positive expectations were more likely to change their behavior and their self-concepts in line with perceiver expectations than were targets of negative expectations.

In addition to these sources of asymmetry, positive and negative expectations may function differently in the interpersonal orientations behind the confirmation scenarios associated with them. It is not unreasonable to propose that most people would prefer to interact with others about whom they hold positive expectations than with the targets of negative expectations. And, given the choice, most people would probably choose to seek further contact with those about whom they hold positive expectations and to avoid further contact with the targets of negative expectations. That is, people may harbor *inclusionary* orientations toward the targets of positive expectations (wishing to include them in their patterns of social relations) and *exclusionary* orientations toward targets of negative expectations (wishing to exclude them from their patterns of social relations). When, in the course of social interaction, perceivers create perceptual and behavioral confirmation for their positive expectations, this confirming evidence may appear to support and justify an inclusionary orientation toward the targets of these expectations; by the same logic, when perceivers create perceptual and behavioral confirmation for their negative expectations, this confirming evidence may appear to support and justify an exclusionary orientation toward the targets of those expectations. Even though the end result may be the same, namely confirmation, there may be an asymmetry in the inclusionary and exclusionary interpersonal orientations served by the confirmation of positive and negative expectations.

Is Behavioral Confirmation a Phenomenon of First Encounters Between Strangers?

Much research on behavioral confirmation has been conducted in analogs of first encounters between strangers (Miller & Turnbull 1986, Neuberg 1994, Snyder 1992). To be sure, most (if not all) relationships do begin as first meetings between previously unacquainted parties. And what happens in first encounters may set the stage for what is to come as relationships grow and develop. From this perspective, studies of behavioral confirmation provide opportunities to study the dynamics of relationships in their infancy and to see how the relationships that emerge from initial encounters are structured into the roles of relatively powerful holders of expectations, who set the terms of the relationships, and relatively powerless objects of expectations, who fit themselves into the outlines provided for them. Such roles, laid down early on, may take on lives of their own over the course of the relationships that ensue.

Yet, as much as these considerations underscore the importance of understanding the early stages of relationships, it is surely necessary for research to go beyond beginnings and to look at the effects of expectations in the context of social relationships that go beyond first encounters. One way to do so is to examine the effects of expectations in first interactions that are themselves the preludes to longer-term interaction. Will such interactions attenuate confirmation effects? This attentuation might happen if perceivers become more cautious about relying on expectations and if targets become more wary of accommodating themselves to perceivers when they feel that the course of their future relationship rides on the outcomes of their first interaction. Or, will such interactions enhance confirmation effects? This enhancement might happen if perceivers and targets become more motivated to carry out their respective agendas of acquiring knowledge and facilitating interaction if these motivations become more functionally relevant in the context of interactions that provide more time and more opportunity for them to be useful. In answer to these questions, Haugen & Snyder (1995) demonstrated that when participants believed that there was the definite possibility of future interaction, behavioral confirmation effects were larger than when they were explicitly told that there would be no further meetings. Thus, it may be that behavioral confirmation, when it occurs in first encounters, may be occurring precisely because of the relevance of first encounters for subsequent interaction; moreover, behavioral confirmation may occur in first interactions to the extent that first interactions are steps along the way to future interaction.

Another way to address the effects of expectations over time is, of course, for research to go beyond studies of first interactions and to study those second, third, fourth, and subsequent interactions. One way to do so is to examine multiple interactions, either a succession of interactions between a single perceiver and target or a diversity of interactions involving multiple perceivers, each of whom hold expectations about the same target. Presumably, repeated interactions in which confirmation occurs should result in an accumulated confirmation effect (Jussim et al 1996). In the case of a single perceiver, the extent of accumulation should depend on continued activation of the perceiver's expectation. If repeated contact facilitates the activation of the expectation, accumulation of confirmation should occur, but if repeated interactions lead to habituation and diminished salience of the expectation, accumulation should be attenuated. In the case of multiple perceivers, the extent of accumulation should depend on the consensus of the perceivers' expectations about the target (if they all share the same expectation, confirmation should accumulate) and on the consensus of perceivers' actions based on their expectations (if they all adopt the same strategies of coping with the target, confirmation should accumulate). In a related vein, Darley & Oleson (1993) have suggested that bystanders to an interaction that involves behavioral confirmation of an expectation may learn to treat targets as perceivers did; such bystanders should contribute to an amplified expectation effect.

The next question to ask is whether these repeated encounters, perhaps over a lifetime in the case of individuals with continuing stigmatizing conditions, will have a resultant effect on targets' actual conceptions of self and their personalities. Certainly, self-perception theory (Bem 1972) would suggest that they will. Two recent studies that included more than one interaction are instructive in regard to these hypotheses about encounters between perceivers and targets.

In one study, Smith et al (1997) had targets interact with two different perceivers, holding opposing expectations, in an interview setting. Targets motivated to be deferent to perceivers confirmed the expectations of the perceiver in the first interview and continued to confirm the first perceiver's expectations in a second interview, even though they were interacting with a new interviewer who held the opposite expectation for them.

In another study of successive interactions, Stukas & Snyder (1995) had dyads converse with each other twice. In the interval between the two interactions, targets learned of the perceivers' expectations; targets also learned that perceivers thought that their expectation-congruent behavior was due either to their personalities or to situational constraints. When they learned that they were targets of negative expectations attributed to their personalities, targets acted in a more positive fashion in the second encounter (as did all targets who learned that perceivers held positive expectations); however, when targets learned that they were the objects of negative expectations attributed to situational causes, they continued to behave in a negative and expectation-congruent fashion.

Thus, these two studies suggest that interactions with perceivers who hold erroneous expectations may have lasting effects; however, they also indicate that the continuing effects of these early interactions may be moderated by targets' motivations and perceptions. As Smith et al (1997) point out, targets may be "complicit" in the continued confirmation of expectations, even those of which they have been made explicitly aware (Stukas & Snyder 1995).

Hasn't the Literature Overemphasized the Perceiver and Underestimated the Target?

Typically, the confirmation scenario is characterized as a flow of influence from perceivers' expectations to targets' behavior—a scenario in which the perceiver, having adopted beliefs about the target, acts in ways that cause the behavior of the target to confirm these beliefs. Such a characterization clearly imputes a more active role to the perceiver, who forms and acts on expectations and who guides and directs interaction, than to the target, who may seem by comparison rather passive, reacting and adapting to the overtures of the perceiver. Over time, as we have seen, it has become increasingly apparent that targets take an active role in shaping the dynamics and outcomes of their interactions with perceivers. Their interaction goals (Hilton & Darley 1991) and their motivational functions (Snyder 1992) are essential ingredients in producing behavioral confirmation. And it is very often the active role played by targets, whether using power granted to them (Copeland 1994) or taking a challenging stance toward perceivers (Smith et al 1997), that attenuates or eliminates behavioral confirmation.

Moreover, as the active role of target has been more clearly delineated, it has also become increasingly apparent that targets can and do take actions that generate behavioral *disconfirmation* outcomes. They are particularly likely to do so when they experience others' views of them as threatening to their identities. Thus, targets, made aware of perceivers' negative expectations about them, may actively seek to disconfirm these expectations (Hilton & Darley 1985). Targets, when motivated to do so, can maintain their strategic self-presentations in the face of powerful perceivers who might be expected to hold negative views of them (D Operario & ST Fiske, manuscript in preparation). Similarly, targets of social stigmas may be able to overcome the negative effects of such expectations through their own actions; for example, obese targets act in ways that overcome perceivers' negative expectations, but only when they believe that they are visible to these perceivers (Miller & Myers 1998, Miller et al 1995). Disconfirmatory outcomes of this form can be interpreted as serving an identity-defensive function of protecting targets from accepting potentially unpleasant, unflattering, threatening, or otherwise unwelcome beliefs about the self (Snyder 1992).

These considerations of an "active" target lead to the question: If the target is an active participant in the interaction with the perceiver, why would he or she ever confirm a negative expectation? Of course, targets may never even become aware of negative expectations, as perceivers may be less likely to reveal negative expectations directly to targets than positive ones (Hilton & Darley 1985, Swann et al 1992). If targets are more likely to become aware of positive than negative expectations, they may also find themselves with more opportunities to actively confirm positive expectations and fewer opportunities to actively disconfirm negative expectations. The lack of opportunity to actively disconfirm negative expectations may facilitate perceptual confirmation, in that perceivers with negative expectations may consider the absence of overt disconfirmation to be tantamount to confirmation of their negative expectations (one can almost hear perceivers saying to themselves, "Well, he never actually denied being a bad person, so it must mean that he really is a bad person").

But what happens when people become explicitly aware that they are targets of negative expectations? Will they confirm those expectations? And if so, why? It is, of course, possible that targets might knowingly and willingly confirm negative expectations that they believe to be accurate (Swann 1983). But even with erroneous negative expectations, targets may find it difficult to disconfirm such expectations, motivated as they may be to cast off such labels. As we have suggested, targets are often in low-power roles and therefore they may not be able to take sufficient charge of their interactions to disconfirm the negative expectations held by powerful perceivers. Moreover, targets in positions of low power may fear possible recriminations were they to actively contradict the negative expectations of powerful perceivers (who may use their positions of power to punish those who challenge their preferred views of the social world). For this reason, targets may knowingly, but not happily, confirm the negative expectations of powerful perceivers. In such circumstances, they may use situational pressures not only to allow but also to justify their confirmation of erroneous negative expectations, regarding such confirmation as circumscribed to specific interactions (Swann 1984) and not carrying necessary implications for their own global dispositions (Stukas & Snyder 1995).

Further, targets who are aware of the negative expectations of perceivers may at times choose a strategy of neither actively confirming nor actively disconfirming these expectations. That is, targets may choose to ambiguate their behavior (so that self-presentations, even if not explicitly disconfirming negative expectations, at least do not overtly confirm them either). However, the consequences of this strategy of ambiguation may nevertheless be the perceptual confirmation of negative expectations. In line with research demonstrating that ambiguous behavior is often taken by perceivers as consistent with initial expectations (Darley & Gross 1983, Hamilton et al 1990), low-power targets who ambiguate their behavior in an effort to avoid confirming negative expectations may still be the targets of perceptual confirmation on the part of perceivers who manage to "read" confirmation into these ambiguated self-presentations.

Still, ambiguated behavior may protect targets from the negative ramifications to their self-concepts of enacting behavior that confirms a negative expectation. Ambiguous behavior also has the possibility of being interpreted by third-party observers, who do not hold negative expectations, as being unrelated or even opposed to possible negative expectations (Fleming 1993). Notable here is the possibility that both perceivers and targets may finish their interactions believing that behavior has conformed to their view of reality, with perceivers satisfied that their initial negative expectations remain intact and targets satisfied that they have withheld active confirmation of negative expectations (see Major et al 1988).

CONCLUSION

As we conclude this analytic review, we wish to underscore a recurring and integrative theme in our considerations of the confirmation and disconfirmation of expectations in social interaction. As we have seen, theory and research in this domain have involved a progression from attempts to document the existence of these phenomena and to define their limiting conditions to efforts to parse the scenarios of confirmation and disconfirmation into their constituent elements, to inquiries into the motivational foundations of confirmation and disconfirmation, and to investigations that place confirmation and disconfirmation in their structural contexts. In each case, it has become readily apparent that considerations of the confirmation and disconfirmation of expectations are considerations of the dynamics of social interaction itself. The processes of confirmation and disconfirmation involve a complex intertwining of cognitive, motivational, and behavioral activities in social interaction—a dynamic intertwining in which features of perceivers and targets, of their motivation and their roles, and of their personal characteristics and their situational contexts are all integrated into scenarios of mutual and reciprocal influence on the processes and outcomes of social interaction. Also, the motivational foundations of confirmation and disconfirmation appear to be interaction goals and psychological functions of more generic relevance to social interaction. And the structural contexts that provide opportunities for confirmation and disconfirmation seem to involve features of roles and social position that themselves are of more generic relevance to interpersonal processes. Finally, as we look to the future, we note that emerging attempts to place scenarios of confirmation and disconfirmation in a more extended temporal context of continuing and ongoing interactions can only enhance the potential for investigations of confirmation and disconfirmation in social interaction to serve as paradigmatic opportunities for theoretical and empirical inquiry into interpersonal processes and social relationships.

ACKNOWLEDGMENTS

Over the years, theory and research on behavioral confirmation in social interaction have been supported by grants from the National Science Foundation and the National Institute of Mental Health to Mark Snyder. This chapter was written while Mark Snyder held the Chaire Francqui Interuniversitaire au Titre Étranger at the Université Catholique de Louvain (Louvain-la-Neuve, Belgium) and Art Stukas served as a postdoctoral fellow at the Western Psychiatric Institute and Clinic. We also gratefully acknowledge the advice and counsel of our many colleagues and fellow researchers whose theoretical and empirical work has contributed immensely to this chapter.

> Visit the *Annual Reviews home page* at
> http://www.AnnualReviews.org.

Literature Cited

Andersen SM, Bem SL. 1981. Sex typing and androgyny in dyadic interaction: individual differences in responsiveness to physical attractiveness. *J. Pers. Soc. Psychol.* 41:74–86

Bargh JA. 1997. The automaticity of everyday life. In *Advances in Social Cognition,* ed. RS Wyer Jr, 10:1–61. Mahwah, NJ: Erlbaum

Bargh JA, Chen M, Burrows L. 1996. Automaticity of social behavior: direct effects of trait construct and stereotype activation on action. *J. Pers. Soc. Psychol.* 71:230–44

Bem DJ. 1972. Self-perception theory. In *Advances in Experimental Social Psychology,* ed. L Berkowitz, 6:1–62. New York: Academic

Blanck PD, ed. 1993. *Interpersonal Expectations: Theory, Research, and Applications.* London: Cambridge Univ. Press

Brophy J, Good T. 1974. *Teacher-Student Relationships: Causes and Consequences.* New York: Holt, Rinehart & Winston

Chen M, Bargh JA. 1997. Nonconscious behavioral confirmation processes: the self-fulfilling consequences of automatic stereotype activation. *J. Exp. Soc. Psychol.* 33:541–60

Christiansen D, Rosenthal R. 1982. Gender and nonverbal decoding skill as determinants of interpersonal expectancy effects. *J. Pers. Soc. Psychol.* 42:75–87

Cooley CH. 1902. *Human Nature and the Social Order.* New York: Scribners

Copeland JT. 1993. Motivational approaches to expectancy confirmation. *Curr. Dir. Psychol. Sci.* 2:117–21

Copeland JT. 1994. Prophecies of power: motivational implications of social power for behavioral confirmation. *J. Pers. Soc. Psychol.* 67:264–77

Copeland JT, Snyder M. 1995. When counselors confirm: a functional analysis. *Pers. Soc. Psychol. Bull.* 21:1210–20

Dardenne B, Leyens JP. 1995. Confirmation bias as a social skill. *Pers. Soc. Psychol. Bull.* 21:1229–39

Darley JM, Fazio RH. 1980. Expectancy confirmation processes arising in the social interaction sequence. *Am. Psychol.* 35:867–81

Darley JM, Fleming JH, Hilton JL, Swann WB. 1988. Dispelling negative expectancies: the impact of interaction goals and target characteristics on the expectancy confirmation process. *J. Exp. Soc. Psychol.* 24:19–36

Darley JM, Gross PH. 1983. A hypothesis-confirming bias in labeling effects. *J. Pers. Soc. Psychol.* 44:20–33

Darley JM, Oleson KC. 1993. Introduction to research on interpersonal expectations. See Blanck 1993, pp. 45–63

Deaux K, Major B. 1987. Putting gender into context: an interactive model of gender-related behavior. *Psychol. Rev.* 94:369–89

Dougherty TW, Turban DB, Callender JC. 1994. Confirming first impressions in the employment interview: a field study of interviewer behavior. *J. Appl. Psychol.* 79: 659–65

Downey G, Feldman SI. 1996. Implications of rejection sensitivity for intimate relationships. *J. Pers. Soc. Psychol.* 70:1327–43

Downey G, Freitas AL, Michaelis B, Khouri H. 1998. The self-fulfilling prophecy in close relationships: rejection sensitivity and rejection by romantic partners. *J. Pers. Soc. Psychol.* In press

Dvir T, Eden D, Banjo ML. 1995. Self-fulfilling prophecy and gender: Can women be Pygmalion and Galatea? *J. Appl. Psychol.* 80:253–70

Eden D. 1993. Interpersonal expectations in organizations. See Blanck 1993, pp. 154–78

Fazio RH, Effrein EA, Falender VJ. 1981. Self-perceptions following social interaction. *J. Pers. Soc. Psychol.* 41:232–42

Fiedler K, Armbruster T, Nickel S, Walther E, Asbeck J. 1996. Constructive biases in social judgment: experiments on the self-verification of question contents. *J. Pers. Soc. Psychol.* 71:861–73

Fiske ST. 1993. Controlling other people: the impact of power on stereotyping. *Am. Psychol.* 48:621–28

Fiske ST, Morling B. 1996. Stereotyping as a function of personal control motives and capacity constraints: the odd couple of power and anxiety. In *Handbook of Motivation and Cognition*, ed. RM Sorrentino, ET Higgins, 3:322–46. New York: Guilford

Fiske ST, Neuberg SL. 1990. A continuum of impression formation, from category-based to individuating processes: influences of information and motivation on attention and interpretation. In *Advances in Experimental Social Psychology*, ed. MP Zanna, 23:1–74. New York: Academic

Fleming JH. 1993. Multiple audience problems, tactical communication, and social interaction: a relational-regulation perspective. In *Advances in Experimental Social Psychology*, ed. MP Zanna, 26: 215–92. San Diego: Academic

Geis FL. 1993. Self-fulfilling prophecies: a social psychological view of gender. In *The Psychology of Gender*, ed. AE Beall, RJ Sternberg, pp. 9–54. New York: Guilford

Goffman E. 1955. On face work: an analysis of ritual elements in social interaction. *Psychiatry* 18:213–31

Goffman E. 1959. *The Presentation of Self in Everyday Life*. Garden City, NY: Doubleday Anchor

Gresham AW, Snyder M. 1990. *Situation choice as a mechanism of behavioral confirmation*. Presented at Annu. Meet. Am. Psychol. Soc., Dallas

Grice HP. 1975. Logic and conversation. In *Syntax and Semantics: Speech Acts*, ed. P Cole, J Morgan, 3:41–58. New York: Academic

Grinder EL, Swim JK. 1991. *Am I who you think I am? The role of behavioral confirmation and self-verification in gender identity negotiation*. Presented at Annu. Meet. Am. Psychol. Assoc., San Francisco

Hall JA, Briton NJ. 1993. Gender, nonverbal behavior, and expectations. See Blanck 1993, pp. 276–95

Hamilton DL, Sherman SJ, Ruvolo CM. 1990. Stereotype-based expectancies: effects on information processing and social behavior. *J. Soc. Issues* 46:35–60

Harris MJ. 1990. Effect of interaction goals on expectancy confirmation in a problem-solving context. *Pers. Soc. Psychol. Bull.* 16:521–30

Harris MJ. 1993. Issues in studying the mediation of expectancy effects: a taxonomy of expectancy situations. See Blanck 1993, pp. 350–78

Harris MJ, Lightner RM, Manolis C. 1998. Awareness of power as a moderator of expectancy confirmation: Who's the boss around here? *Basic Appl. Soc. Psychol.* In press

Harris MJ, Moniz AJ, Sowards BA, Krane K. 1994. Mediation of interpersonal expectancy effects: expectancies about the elderly. *Soc. Psychol. Q.* 57:36–48

Harris MJ, Perkins R. 1995. Effects of distraction on interpersonal expectancy effects: a social interaction test of the cognitive busyness hypothesis. *Soc. Cogn.* 13:163–82

Harris MJ, Rosenthal R. 1985. Mediation of interpersonal expectancy effects: 31 meta-analyses. *Psychol. Bull.* 97:363–86

Hart AJ. 1995. Naturally occurring expectation effects. *J. Pers. Soc. Psychol.* 68: 109–15

Haugen JA, Snyder M. 1995. *Effects of perceivers' beliefs about future interactions on the behavioral confirmation process.* Presented at Annu. Meet. Am. Psychol. Soc., New York

Higgins ET. 1989. Knowledge accessibility and activation: subjectivity and suffering from unconscious sources. In *Unintended Thought*, ed. JS Uleman, JA Bargh, pp. 75–123. New York: Guilford

Higgins ET, King GA. 1981. Accessibility of social constructs: information-processing consequences of individual and contextual variability. In *Personality, Cognition, and Social Interaction*, ed. N Cantor, JF Kihlstrom, pp. 69–122. Hillsdale, NJ: Erlbaum

Hilton JL. 1995. *Interaction goals and person perception.* Presented at "Attribution Processes, Person Perception, and Social Interaction: The Legacy of Ned Jones." Princeton, NJ

Hilton JL, Darley JM. 1985. Constructing other persons: a limit on the effect. *J. Exp. Soc. Psychol.* 21:1–18

Hilton JL, Darley JM. 1991. The effects of interaction goals on person perception. In *Advances in Experimental Social Psychology*, ed. MP Zanna, 24:236–67. Orlando, FL: Academic

Hilton JL, Darley JM, Fleming JH. 1989. Self-fulfilling prophecies and self-defeating behavior. In *Self-Defeating Behaviors: Experimental Research, Clinical Impressions, and Practical Implications*, ed. RC Curtis. New York: Plenum

Ickes W, Patterson ML, Rajecki DW, Tanford S. 1982. Behavioral and cognitive consequences of reciprocal versus compensatory responses to pre-interaction expectancies. *Soc. Cogn.* 1:160–90

Ickes W, Snyder M, Garcia S. 1997. Personality influences on the choice of situations. In *Handbook of Personality Psychology*, ed. R Hogan, JA Johnson, SR Briggs, pp. 165–95. San Diego: Academic

Jones EE. 1986. Interpreting interpersonal behavior: the effects of expectancies. *Science* 234:41–46

Judice TN, Neuberg SL. 1998. When perceivers have the explicit desire to confirm negative expectations: self-fulfilling prophecies and inflated target self-perceptions. *Basic Appl. Soc. Psychol.* In press

Jussim L. 1986. Self-fulfilling prophecies: a theoretical and integrative review. *Psychol. Rev.* 93:429–45

Jussim L. 1989. Teacher expectations: self-fulfilling prophecies, perceptual biases, and accuracy. *J. Pers. Soc. Psychol.* 57: 469–80

Jussim L. 1991. Social perception and social reality: a reflection-construction model. *Psychol. Rev.* 98:54–73

Jussim L. 1993. Accuracy in interpersonal expectations: a reflection-construction analysis of current and classic research. *J. Pers.* 61:637–68

Jussim L, Eccles J. 1992. Teacher expectations II: construction and reflection of student achievement. *J. Pers. Soc. Psychol.* 63:947–61

Jussim L, Eccles J. 1995a. Naturally occurring interpersonal expectancies. *Rev. Pers. Soc. Psychol.* 15:74–108

Jussim L, Eccles J. 1995b. Are teacher expectations biased by students' gender, social class, or ethnicity? In *Stereotype Accuracy: Toward Appreciating Group Differences*, ed. YT Yee, L Jussim, CR McCauley, pp. 245–71. Washington, DC: Am. Psychol. Assoc.

Jussim L, Eccles J, Madon S. 1996. Social perception, social stereotypes, and teacher expectations: accuracy and the quest for the powerful self-fulfilling prophecy. In *Advances in Experimental Social Psychology*, ed. MP Zanna, 28:281–388. Orlando, FL: Academic

Jussim L, Madon S, Chatman C. 1994. Teacher expectations and student achievement: self-fulfilling prophecies, biases, and accuracy. In *Applications of Heuristics and Biases to Social Issues*, ed. L Heath, RS Tindale, J Edwards, EJ Posavac, FB Bryant, E Henderson-King, Y Suarez-Balcazar, J Myers, pp. 303–34. New York: Plenum

Kelley HH. 1992. Common-sense psychology and scientific psychology. *Annu. Rev. Psychol.* 43:1–23

Kulik JA. 1983. Confirmatory attribution and the perpetuation of social beliefs. *J. Pers. Soc. Psychol.* 44:1171–81

Leyens JP. 1989. Another look at confirmatory strategies during a real interview. *Eur. J. Soc. Psychol.* 19:255–62

Leyens JP, Dardenne B, Fiske ST. 1998. Why and under what circumstances is a hypothesis-consistent testing preferred in interviews? *Br. J. Soc. Psychol.* In press

Leyens JP, Yzerbyt VY, Schadron G. 1992. Stereotypes and social judgeability. *In European Review of Social Psychology*, ed. W Stroebe, M Hewstone, 3:91–120. Chichester, UK: Wiley

Madon S, Jussim L, Eccles J. 1997. In search of the powerful self-fulfilling prophecy. *J. Pers. Soc. Psychol.* 72:791–809

Major B, Cozzarelli C, Testa M, McFarlin DB. 1988. Self-verification vs. expectancy confirmation in social interaction: the impact of self-focus. *Pers. Soc. Psychol. Bull.* 14:346–59

Martijn C, Spears R, Van der Plight J, Jakobs E. 1992. Negativity and positivity effects in person perception and inference: ability versus morality. *Eur. J. Soc. Psychol.* 22: 453–63

McNulty SE, Swann WB Jr. 1994. Identity negotiation in roommate relationships: the self as architect and consequence of social reality. *J. Pers. Soc. Psychol.* 67:1012–23

Mead GH. 1934. *Mind, Self and Society from the Standpoint of a Social Behaviorist.* Chicago: Univ. Chicago Press

Merton RK. 1948. The self-fulfilling prophecy. *Antioch Rev.* 8:193–210

Miene PK, Gresham AW, Snyder M. 1991. *Motivational functions influence behavioral confirmation.* Presented at Annu. Meet. Am. Psychol. Assoc., Washington, DC

Miller CT, Myers AM. 1998. Compensating for prejudice: how heavyweight people (and others) control outcomes despite prejudice. In *Prejudice: The Target's Perspective,* ed. JK Swim, C Stangor, pp. 191–218. San Diego, CA: Academic

Miller CT, Rothblum ED, Felicio D, Brand P. 1995. Compensating for stigma: obese and nonobese women's reactions to being visible. *Pers. Soc. Psychol. Bull.* 21: 1093–106

Miller DT, Turnbull W. 1986. Expectancies and interpersonal processes. *Annu. Rev. Psychol.* 37:233–56

Mobilio LJ, Snyder M. 1996. *Knowledge is power: a study of behavioral confirmation.* Presented at Annu. Meet. Am. Psychol. Soc., San Francisco

Murray SL, Holmes JG. 1997. A leap of faith? Positive illusions in romantic relationships. *Pers. Soc. Psychol. Bull.* 23: 586–604

Murray SL, Holmes JG, Griffin DW. 1996. The self-fulfilling nature of positive illusions in romantic relationships: Love is not blind, but prescient. *J. Pers. Soc. Psychol.* 71:1155–80

Neuberg SL. 1989. The goal of forming accurate impressions during social interactions: attenuating the impact of negative expectations. *J. Pers. Soc. Psychol.* 56: 374–86

Neuberg SL. 1994. Expectancy-confirmation processes in stereotype-tinged social encounters: the moderating role of social goals. In *The Psychology of Prejudice: The Ontario Symposium,* ed. MP Zanna, JM Olson, 7:103–30. Hillsdale, NJ: Erlbaum

Neuberg SL. 1996a. Social motives and expectancy-tinged social interactions. In *Handbook of Motivation and Cognition: The Interpersonal Context,* ed. RM Sorrentino, ET Higgins, 3:225–61. New York: Guilford

Neuberg SL. 1996b. Expectancy influences in social interaction: the moderating role of social goals. In *The Psychology of Action: Linking Cognition and Motivation to Behavior,* ed. PM Gollwitzer, JA Bargh, pp. 529–52. New York: Guilford

Neuberg SL, Judice TN, Virdin LM, Carrillo MA. 1993. Perceiver self-presentation goals as moderators of expectancy influences: ingratiation and the disconfirmation of negative expectancies. *J. Pers. Soc. Psychol.* 64:409–20

Olson JM, Roese NJ, Zanna MP. 1996. Expectancies. In *Social Psychology: Handbook of Basic Principles,* ed. ET Higgins, AW Kruglanski. New York: Guilford

Pelletier LG, Vallerand RJ. 1996. Supervisors' beliefs and subordinates' intrinsic motivation: a behavioral confirmation analysis. *J. Pers. Soc. Psychol.* 71:331–40

Reeder GD, Brewer MB. 1979. A schematic model of dispositional attribution in interpersonal perception. *Psychol. Rev.* 86: 61–79

Reeder GD, Coovert MD. 1986. Revising an impression of morality. *Soc. Cogn.* 4:1–17

Rosenthal R. 1974. *On the Social Psychology of the Self-fulfilling Prophecy: Further Evidence for Pygmalion Effects and Their Mediating Mechanisms.* New York: MSS. Inf. Corp. Modul. Publ.

Rosenthal R. 1993. Interpersonal expectations: some antecedents and some consequences. See Blanck 1993, pp. 3–24

Rosenthal R. 1994. Interpersonal expectancy effects: a 30-year perspective. *Curr. Dir. Psychol. Sci.* 3:176–79

Rosenthal R, Jacobson L. 1968. *Pygmalion in the Classroom.* New York: Holt, Rinehart & Winston

Rothbart M, Park B. 1986. On the confirmability and disconfirmability of trait concepts. *J. Pers. Soc. Psychol.* 50:131–42

Sedikides C, Skowronski JJ. 1993. The self in impression formation: trait centrality and social perception. *J. Exp. Soc. Psychol.* 29:347–57

Semin GR, De Poot CJ. 1997a. The question-answer paradigm: You might regret not noticing how a question is worded. *J. Pers. Soc. Psychol.* 73:472–80

Semin GR, De Poot CJ. 1997b. Bringing partiality to light: question wording and choice as indicators of bias. *Soc. Cogn.* 15: 91–106

Skowronski JJ, Carlston DE. 1987. Social judgment and social memory: the role of cue diagnosticity in negative, positive, and extremity biases. *J. Pers. Soc. Psychol.* 52:689–99

Skowronski JJ, Carlston DE. 1989. Negativity and extremity biases in impression formation: a review of the explanations. *Psychol. Bull.* 105:131–42

Skowronski JJ, Carlston DE. 1992. Caught in the act: when impressions based on highly diagnostic behaviors are resistant to contradiction. *Eur. J. Soc. Psychol.* 22:435–52

Skowronski JJ, Carlston DE, Isham JT. 1993. Implicit versus explicit impression formation: the differing effects of overt labeling and covert priming on memory and impressions. *J. Exp. Soc. Psychol.* 29: 17–41

Skrypnek BJ, Snyder M. 1982. On the self-perpetuating nature of stereotypes about women and men. *J. Exp. Soc. Psychol.* 18:277–91

Smith DM, Neuberg SL, Judice TN, Biesanz JC. 1997. Target complicity in the confirmation and disconfirmation of erroneous perceiver expectations: immediate and longer term implications. *J. Pers. Soc. Psychol.* 73:974–91

Snyder M. 1984. When belief creates reality. In *Advances in Experimental Social Psychology*, ed. L Berkowitz, 18:248–305. Orlando, FL: Academic

Snyder M. 1992. Motivational foundations of behavioral confirmation. In *Advances in Experimental Social Psychology*, ed. MP Zanna, 25:67–114. Orlando, FL: Academic

Snyder M. 1995. *Power and the dynamics of social interaction*. Presented at the 8th Annu. Conf. Advers., Amherst, MA

Snyder M, Gangestad S. 1980. Hypothesis-testing processes. In *New Directions in Attribution Research*, ed. JH Harvey, W Ickes, RF Kidd, 3:171–96. Hillsdale, NJ: Erlbaum

Snyder M, Haugen JA. 1994. Why does behavioral confirmation occur? A functional perspective on the role of the perceiver. *J. Exp. Soc. Psychol.* 30:218–46

Snyder M, Haugen JA. 1995. Why does behavioral confirmation occur? A functional perspective on the role of the target. *Pers. Soc. Psychol. Bull.* 21:963–74

Snyder M, Swann WB. 1978a. Behavioral confirmation in social interaction: from social perception to social reality. *J. Exp. Soc. Psychol.* 14:148–62

Snyder M, Swann WB. 1978b. Hypothesis-testing processes in social interaction. *J. Pers. Soc. Psychol.* 36:1202–12

Snyder M, Tanke ED, Berscheid E. 1977. Social perception and interpersonal behavior:

on the self-fulfilling nature of social stereotypes. *J. Pers. Soc. Psychol.* 35: 656–66

Stryker S, Statham A. 1985. Symbolic interaction and role theory. In *Handbook of Social Psychology*, ed. G Lindzey, E Aronson, 2:311–78. New York: Random House

Stukas AA, Snyder M. 1995. *Individuals confront negative expectations about their personalities.* Presented at Annu. Meet. Am. Psychol. Soc., New York

Swann WB Jr. 1983. Self-verification: bringing social reality into harmony with the self. In *Psychological Perspectives on the Self*, ed. J Suls, AG Greenwald, 2:33–66. Hillsdale, NJ: Erlbaum

Swann WB Jr. 1984. Quest for accuracy in person perception: a matter of pragmatics. *Psychol. Rev.* 91:457–77

Swann WB Jr. 1987. Identity negotiation: where two roads meet. *J. Pers. Soc. Psychol.* 53:1038–51

Swann WB Jr, Ely RJ. 1984. A battle of wills: self-verification versus behavioral confirmation. *J. Pers. Soc. Psychol.* 46: 1287–1302

Swann WB Jr, Giuliano T. 1987. Confirmatory search strategies in social interaction: how, when, why, and with what consequences. *J. Soc. Clin. Psychol.* 5:511–24

Swann WB Jr, Hill CA. 1982. When our identities are mistaken: reaffirming self-conceptions through social interaction. *J. Pers. Soc. Psychol.* 43:59–66

Swann WB Jr, Read SJ. 1981. Self-verification processes: how we sustain our self-conceptions. *J. Exp. Soc. Psychol.* 17: 351–72

Swann WB Jr, Stein-Seroussi A, McNulty SE. 1992. Outcasts in a white-lie society: the enigmatic worlds of people with negative self-conceptions. *J. Pers. Soc. Psychol.* 62: 618–24

Testa M, Major B. 1988. Self-verification and expectancy confirmation in social interaction: independent or interactive processes? *Represent. Res. Soc. Psychol.* 18:35–48

Virdin LM, Neuberg SL. 1990. *Perceived status: a moderator of expectancy confirmation effects.* Presented at Annu. Meet. Am. Psychol. Assoc., Boston

Vorauer JD, Miller DT. 1997. Failure to recognize the effect of implicit social influence on the presentation of self. *J. Pers. Soc. Psychol.* 73:281–95

Word CO, Zanna MP, Cooper J. 1974. The nonverbal mediation of self-fulfilling prophecies in interracial interaction. *J. Exp. Soc. Psychol.* 10:109–20

Yzerbyt VY, Leyens JP. 1991. Requesting information to form an impression: the influence of valence and confirmatory status. *J. Exp. Soc. Psychol.* 27:337–56

Yzerbyt VY, Rocher S, Schadron G. 1997. Stereotypes as explanations: a subjective essentialistic view of group perception. In *The Social Psychology of Stereotyping and Group Life*, ed. R Spears, PJ Oakes, N Ellemers, SA Haslam, pp. 20–50. Oxford: Blackwell

Yzerbyt VY, Schadron G, Leyens JP, Rocher S. 1994. Social judgeability: the impact of meta-informational cues on the use of stereotyping. *J. Pers. Soc. Psychol.* 66: 48–55

Zuckerman M, Knee CR, Hodgins HS, Miyake K. 1995. Hypothesis confirmation: the joint effect of positive test strategy and acquiescence response set. *J. Pers. Soc. Psychol.* 68:52–60

Annu. Rev. Psychol. 1999. 50:305–31

SOMESTHESIS

James C. Craig

Department of Psychology, Indiana University, Bloomington, Indiana 47405;
e-mail:Craigj@indiana.edu

Gary B. Rollman

Department of Psychology, University of Western Ontario, London, Ontario, N6A
5C2, Canada; e-mail: Rollman@julian.uwo.ca

KEY WORDS: touch, tactile patterns, thermal sensitivity, haptics, pain

ABSTRACT

In this review we focus on the perceptual and psychophysical aspects of somesthesis, although some information on neurophysiological aspects will be
included as well; we look primarily at studies that have appeared since 1988.
In the section on touch, we cover peripheral sensory mechanisms and several
topics related to spatial and temporal pattern perception, specifically measures of spatial sensitivity, texture perception with particular emphasis on
perceived roughness, complex spatial-temporal patterns, and the use of
touch as a possible channel of communication. Other topics under this section include the effects of attention on processing tactile stimuli, cortical
mechanisms, and the effects of aging on sensitivity. We also deal with thermal sensitivity and some aspects of haptics and kinesthesis. In the section on
pain, we review work on the gate-control theory, sensory fibers, and higher
neural organization. In addition, studies on central neurochemical effects
and psychophysics of pain are examined.

CONTENTS

0084-6570/99/0201-0305$08.00

INTRODUCTION

Workers in somesthesis have often complained of the difficulty of conveying to others the importance of the sense of touch and position. For vision and audition, one can imagine being deprived of sight or hearing, and there are, of course, blind and profoundly deaf individuals who can help us understand the nature of their experiences. A head cold lets us know the information derived from olfaction, but what would it be like to be without somesthesis? In May 1971, Ian Waterman lost all sensation of light touch and kinesthesis below his neck. The probable cause was a viral infection that destroyed the functioning of the large-diameter, peripheral fibers. The book *Pride and a Daily Marathon* (Cole 1995), a popular scientific account of Mr. Waterman's experiences, provides a description of what it is like to lose the sense of touch and position. Mr. Waterman must monitor all movements visually. If the lights go out unexpectedly, he falls down. He still has temperature sensitivity and experiences pain (cf large-diameter) consistent with neurophysiological evidence of the involvement of small diameter fibers in these modalities. The book allows readers to appreciate the importance of somesthesis and the extraordinary lengths to which a person must go to cope with its loss. With regard to the personal experience of pain, a compelling account of a battle with spinal cancer by the acclaimed novelist and poet Reynolds Price (1994) provides valuable insights into the many ways in which pain affects the patient and the enormous psychological challenges that accompany physical afflictions.

Studies of the perceptual aspects of somesthesis have benefitted from a long association with parallel neurophysiological experiments. It has been possible to use the same stimuli with both human subjects (psychophysics) and awake monkeys (neurophysiology). The connection between perceptual and neurophysiological responses is even closer in experiments using percutaneous recording techniques (microneurography) wherein human subjects have microelectrodes inserted into their hands and forearms to permit recordings from single, first-order afferents. Subjects report the sensations elicited by stimuli applied to the receptive field of neurons at the same time the activity in these single units is recorded. Human perceptual responses can also be correlated with records of cortical activity obtained using noninvasive electrophysiological or imaging techniques.

TOUCH

Peripheral Afferents and Mechanoreception

Studies on glabrous (hairless) skin of the hand support the view that there are four different types of mechanoreceptive afferents. These afferents are characterized by the size of their receptive fields, large vs small, and by the rate at which they adapt to a sustained indentation, slowly vs rapidly, resulting in a two-by-two classification system. There are afferents that are slowly adapting, with small receptive fields, SAIs; slowly adapting, large receptive fields, SAIIs; rapidly adapting, small receptive fields, RAs [also known as FAIs (fast adapting)]; and rapidly adapting with large receptive fields. These latter fibers are associated with Pacinian corpuscles and are thus known as PCs (or FAIIs). Some areas of the body, such as the perioral region, may lack Pacinian corpuscles (Hollins et al 1991). A four-channel model of mechanoreception has been developed based on correlations with the likely afferents. A summary of much information about these channels can be found in several sources (Table 2.2, Cholewiak & Collins 1991; Table 2, Greenspan & Bolanowski 1996; see also Greenspan & LaMotte 1993). Work on both the psychophysical and the physiological bases of mechanoreception has recently been reviewed (Greenspan & Bolanowski 1996). The four-channel model of mechanoreception maintains that tactile experience results from combined neural activity in the various mechanoreceptive channels (Bolanowski 1996, Bolanowski et al 1988).

There remain psychophysical results that are not easily explained by the properties of the first-order afferents and the four-channel model. For example, accuracy in localizing stimuli that should activate afferents with large receptive fields (Pacinian corpuscles) may be nearly as good as that in localizing stimuli that should activate afferents with small receptive fields (Sherrick et al 1990). Mechanoreceptive afferents have also been examined in hairy skin (Edin et al 1995), where the number and nature of the receptors are less clear (Greenspan & Bolanowski 1996, Vallbo et al 1994), as is the number of channels (Bolanowski et al 1994).

Spatial and Temporal Patterns

SPATIAL SENSITIVITY   Interest continues in developing and evaluating measures of spatial acuity. There has been a long history of criticism of the two-point threshold as a measure of resolution on the skin. Perhaps like bad theories, suspect measures are driven out not by data, but by better measures. Johnson et al (1994) discuss many of the criticisms of the two-point threshold, chief among them the problem of maintaining a stable criterion for responding "one" or "two." They offer support for a different measure, grating orientation.

In this technique, square-wave gratings are presented to the skin in one of two orthogonal spatial orientations. The subject's task is to indicate the orientation. Performance varies as a function of the width of the grooves (Craig & Kisner 1998; Patel et al 1997; Van Boven & Johnson 1994a,b). The measure shows promise in neurological testing (Van Boven & Johnson 1994a). A second promising approach requires subjects to detect the presence of a gap in an otherwise smooth edge (Stevens & Choo 1996, Stevens & Patterson 1995). Both measures benefit from being able to be tested in a forced-choice procedure. Essick (1992) and Greenspan & LaMotte (1993) discuss measures of spatial acuity and other measures of tactile sensitivity that might be used in a clinical setting.

Sensitivity to spatial features such as curvature, local shape, and orientation of small objects has also been examined in psychophysical and neurophysiological studies (Goodwin et al 1996; Goodwin & Wheat 1992; LaMotte & Srinivasan 1993, 1996; LaMotte et al 1996). In general, it appears that the responses of SAIs are important for encoding these spatial features, with a possible contribution of RAs (Greenspan & Bolanowski 1996).

TEXTURE   The perception of surface texture includes attributes such as roughness, hardness-softness, elasticity, and viscosity (Loomis & Lederman 1986). Work on various aspects of texture, including roughness perception, has been summarized in several articles (Johnson & Hsiao 1992, Loomis & Lederman 1986). Hollins et al (1993) used multidimensional scaling techniques to study the perception of the surface texture of objects. The result was a three-dimensional space. One of the dimensions corresponded to roughness-smoothness and a second dimension to hardness-softness. The third dimension appeared to be related to compressional elasticity. In other studies, subjects attempt to identify or classify an object based on its texture (Klatzky & Lederman 1995, Klatzky et al 1989, Reed 1994) or to match surface texture (Van Doren & Menia 1993). Other researchers have had subjects—both human and nonhuman—attempt to discriminate differences in texture (Burton & Sinclair 1994, Kops & Gardner 1996, Sinclair & Burton 1991, Trembly et al 1996).

Although there have been some recent studies of hardness-softness (Srinivasan & La Motte 1995), roughness continues to be the most widely examined textural dimension, and a number of studies have examined judgments of the perceived roughness of surfaces (Connor et al 1990, Connor & Johnson 1992, Sathien et al 1989). Using surfaces that vary in the spacing between elements, it was found that the function relating roughness judgments to dot spacing is an inverted U, with perceived roughness declining as dot spacing increases beyond 3 mm (Johnson & Hsiao 1994). Based on these human judgments and recordings from first-order afferents in monkeys exposed to similar surfaces, Johnson & Hsiao (1992) offer a model of roughness perception. The model involves spatially structured responses from SAIs, a between-fiber as opposed to a within-fiber code (Johnson & Hsiao 1994). The model accounts for the perception of roughness across a spatially extended surface. As the authors indicate, the model does not account for other situations, such as perceiving the roughness of a surface by touching the surface with a tool. Also relevant to the issue of SAIs encoding roughness is a study by Stevens (1990) in which subjects judged the perceived roughness of surfaces presented to various parts of the body. Although there were differences attributable to different sites, an interesting result was that the variations in spatial acuity, and presumably the distribution of receptors sensitive to spatial variations, did not necessarily correlate with judgments of perceived roughness. For example, in comparing three sites such as the fingerpad, forearm, and back, spatial acuity would be highest on the fingerpad and poorest on the back; however, in judging roughness, the same textured surfaces were judged to be slightly rougher on the forearm than on the fingerpad and less rough on the back. The results suggest that central mechanisms responsible for roughness are sensitive to the density of peripheral innervation.

Phillips & Matthews (1993) used a novel technique to alter peripheral afferent discharge and the perception of roughness. They cooled the ulnar nerve at the elbow on one arm and had subjects scan surfaces with their little fingers, which are innervated by that nerve. Subjects matched the roughness of surfaces scanned by the cooled arm and by the unaffected arm (and hand). Surfaces felt significantly smoother on the cooled side, an effect that was correlated with inhibition of high-frequency discharge patterns in the ulnar nerve.

COMPLEX PATTERNS   Several chapters provide good reviews of the perception of complex spatial patterns (Loomis & Lederman 1986, Sherrick 1991), including braille (Foulke 1991), and neural mechanisms associated with such patterns (Johnson & Hsiao 1992). Loomis (1990) presents a model of pattern recognition that is consistent with neurophysiological data and that postulates that tactile spatial patterns are initially subjected to low-pass spatial filtering. He presents results comparing the recognition of raised letters and braille cells to blurred visual representations of the same patterns.

Studies using arrays of tactors have examined some of the interactions that occur when two spatial patterns are presented in close temporal proximity to the same site. Pattern identification may be interfered with because the target pattern is masked by the nontarget pattern (Craig 1995, Mahar & Mackenzie 1993) or because the subject responds with the nontarget pattern (Craig 1996), an effect referred to as "response competition." Moving the nontarget pattern to a separate location reduces masking but still leaves interference due to response competition (Craig & Evans 1995, Evans et al 1992, Evans & Craig 1992), an apparent failure of selective attention.

Accuracy in judging whether two patterns are similar in shape depends on whether they are presented to the same or different locations. Accuracy declines as the distance between the two locations on the same fingerpad increases (Horner 1995). If subjects are asked to judge the direction of movement across the finger, then the orientation of the hand in space affects the perceived similarity (Rinker & Craig 1994). Heller (1992) reports effects of spatial orientation on the identification of braille cells. Other studies of braille have examined scanning strategies (Davidson et al 1992), the effects of braille reading on spatial acuity (Stevens et al 1996), and the representation of braille characters in first-order afferents in humans using microneurographic techniques (Phillips et al 1990).

Investigators have also studied the ability of subjects to identify raised line drawings of objects (Loomis et al 1991, Shimizu et al 1993) and have compared the performance achieved by blind and sighted subjects (Heller et al 1996a,b, Heller & Kennedy 1990). In addition, investigators have examined the identification of raised line drawings of objects as compared to the identification of the actual objects by means of haptic exploration. The relatively poor performance with raised line drawings may be due to a number of factors, such as the lack of 3-D shape and size information about the real object (Klatzky et al 1993).

Sensitivity to the movement per se of objects across the skin has been studied both psychophysically (Essick et al 1991) and neurophysiologically (Essick & Edin 1995, Edin et al 1995). Judgments of the velocity (Essick et al 1996a) and direction of movement (Essick 1991) have been made in response to a brushing stimulus. Directional sensitivity varies as a function of a number of factors such as skin site, velocity of movement, and the length of movement (Essick et al 1991, 1996b). From testing of sites on the fingerpad, hand, and arm, it was found that directional sensitivity was greater at the more distal sites (Essick et al 1991), similar to the results obtained with other measures of spatial sensitivity. Directional sensitivity is related to velocity by an inverted U-shaped function. For example, on the perioral region, sensitivity is better at velocities of 6 cm/sec than at higher or lower velocities (Essick et al 1996b). Generating the movement with a tactile array produced levels of sensitivity similar to those obtained with the brushing stimulus (Essick et al 1996b).

COMMUNICATION   There continues to be interest in using touch as a channel of communication, particularly for blind and deaf individuals. Braille, discussed below, has long been used to communicate written material to the blind. The Tadoma method of speech reception involves a deaf-blind individual placing his or her hand on the face of a talker (Loomis & Lederman 1986, Reed et al 1992). By means of feeling the articulatory gestures, such as lip and jaw movements, individuals can understand speech at low-normal rates. This ability has been cited as evidence for the information-processing capabilities of the hand (Weisenberger 1992). To explore this ability and to gain better control of the stimulus, devices have been built that combine both tactile and kinesthetic stimulation (Eberhardt et al 1994, Tan et al 1989). One such device, which provided large-amplitude finger movements and vibratory stimulation for three fingers, achieved impressive rates of information transmission (Tan 1996).

The book *Tactile Aids for the Hearing Impaired* (Summers 1992) has chapters on the sense of touch, electrotactile stimulation, and the design of tactile stimulators. There are also chapters on communicating acoustic information via touch, the use of single- and multichannel systems, the evaluation of tactile aids, and the necessity of training users. Kaczmarek & Bach-y-Rita (1995), in a book on virtual environments, review many of the systems for presenting information tactually and cover such topics as telepresence, transmitting information through gloves, and electrotactile stimulation, as well as practical considerations in using tactile displays.

Attention

Paralleling results with visual stimuli, a number of studies have found that reaction times were faster when subjects were responding to a site at which a vibratory stimulus was expected (80% validly cued trials) as compared to responding to unexpected sites (20% invalidly cued trials). Bradshaw et al (1992) report a 46-msec advantage for validly cued locations. The advantage for validly cued locations extends to cross-modal conditions in which visual stimuli cue tactile locations and the reverse (Butter et al 1989). Post & Chapman (1991) cued subjects to switch between visual and tactile stimuli. They reported that reaction times to detect a vibrotactile stimulus, when the subject had been invalidly cued to the visual modality, increased by more than 100 msec.

Whang et al (1991) developed a task in which subjects were required to detect either the presence of an amplitude change at one of four fingerpads or the absence of a change. They found that valid cuing did not aid the detection of the presence of an amplitude change but did assist detection of the absence of such change. Similarly, Sathian & Burton (1991) found an abrupt change in texture was unaffected by cuing. The authors suggest that the increase in stimulation may be processed preattentively.

Neurophysiological correlates of intramodal attention are also being examined (Hsiao et al 1996). Hsiao et al (1993) trained monkeys to respond to either visual or tactile stimuli depending upon a cue stimulus. Recording from SI and SII cortex, they found that discharge rates evoked by the tactile patterns (raised letters) were altered as a function of whether the visual task or the tactile task was cued. Importantly, tactile spatial patterns were presented continuously. Only the cuing changed.

Cortical Mechanisms

Many of the types of stimuli that have been used in psychophysical experiments and in single-unit studies of peripheral afferents have also been used in single-unit studies of cortical neurons. There have been examinations of the responses of cortical cells to such stimuli as textured surfaces, vibration, spatial patterns, motion, and so forth. These types of studies are discussed by Burton & Sinclair (1996).

Work with brain-injured patients has helped to establish the nature of tactile agnosia, the inability to recognize objects through touch (Caselli 1991, 1993). A case study was conducted with one such patient who had suffered a left, parietal infarction (Reed & Caselli 1994, Reed et al 1996). The patient showed significantly poorer object recognition with the right as compared to the left hand, even though measures of basic touch sensitivity were normal for both hands. The authors conclude that there can be specific interference in shape perception independent of other tactile or spatial abilities.

Issues concerning altered sensory inputs, cortical reorganization in adult animals, and plasticity and its functional significance have been examined from a number of perspectives; neurophysiological (Garraghty et al 1994), perceptual (Benedetti 1991b, Craig 1993), and clinical (Halligan et al 1993). Changes in peripheral input may alter the representation of tactile stimuli in the somatosensory cortex. For example, cutting the nerves from digit D3 (middle finger) in monkeys silences the corresponding region in SI, but over time, stimulating adjacent fingers D2 (index finger) and D4 (ring finger) may activate cortical cells in the D3 cortical region (Jenkins et al 1990, Merzenich & Jenkins 1993). An impressive example of reorganization was demonstrated in a monkey tested 12 years after undergoing deafferentation of an upper limb. In this monkey, stimulating the face evoked activity in the cortical region that is normally evoked by stimulation of the upper limb (Pons et al 1991). Clinical studies have also been carried out with human amputees. In some cases, stimulation of the facial region has elicited reports of sensations in the missing portion of the arm (Ramachandran et al 1992). Training at a particular site on the skin with intact subjects may result in increased cortical representation, results that have been observed with both human (Elbert et al 1995) and nonhuman subjects (Merzenich et al 1988), and may also result in improved discriminability (Recanzone et al 1992).

Cortical reorganization has also been studied using noninvasive techniques with human subjects (Mogilner et al 1993, Sterr et al 1998, Yang et al 1994). As with microneurography, there is an advantage in having subjects with whom one can correlate perceptual and neural responses. In the Mogilner et al (1993) study, two adult patients were examined. The patients were undergoing surgical treatment for syndactyly (webbed fingers). Magnetoencephalographic images of these patients, prior to surgery, showed a reduced area representing the hand. Following surgery, several effects were observed: The cortical hand area expanded, with a greater distance between the thumb and little finger; the individual digits functioned independently; and one patient reported that the fingers were now perceived as individual entities (Mogilner et al 1993). These results are consistent with data obtained in recording from single units in the cortex of monkeys whose fingers had been surgically joined to produce an artificial syndactyly (Allard et al 1991). Other noninvasive studies have used positron emission tomography (PET) to examine cortical responses to textured surfaces (Burton et al 1997, O'Sullivan et al 1994) and to vibratory stimuli (Burton et al 1993).

Aging

As compared to younger subjects, older subjects have reduced absolute sensitivity to vibratory stimuli (Schmidt & Wahren 1990), particularly high-frequency vibration (Gescheider et al 1994b). They also show greater forward masking (Gescheider et al 1992) and reduced temporal summation (Gescheider et al 1994a). Many of these findings have been reviewed by Verrillo (1993). These effects are more prominent with stimuli that affect Pacinian corpuscles. Difference thresholds for intensity, however, remain relatively unchanged with age, as long as the thresholds are expressed in relative rather than absolute terms (Gescheider et al 1996).

Spatial acuity, as measured by a variety of tasks, also declines with age (Stevens & Cruz 1996, Stevens & Patterson 1995, Stevens et al 1996, Woodward, 1993), although it should be noted that there are large individual differences (Stevens & Patterson 1995, Verrillo 1993). Stevens & Choo (1996) measured spatial acuity at 13 different body sites and found that sensitivity declined with age at some sites much more than at others. The feet and hands showed the greatest drop in sensitivity, a result that may be due to reduced circulation.

THERMAL SENSITIVITY

For many years, textbooks and review chapters (Sherrick & Cholewiak 1986) have been showing a supine figure with vertical lines, the heights of which indicate spatial acuity measured at various locations on the body. A twin, fraternal rather than identical, has now been created showing warm and cold thresholds across the body. Based on the results from 60 subjects, this map shows the facial region to be the most sensitive area of the body and the extremities, particularly the lower ones, to be considerably less sensitive. Subjects were more sensitive to cold stimuli than to warm ones, and as noted for tactile sensitivity, thermal sensitivity declined with age (Stevens & Choo

1998). Thermal testing on the face and in the mouth showed the mouth to be less sensitive to warming than the facial regions. No differences were seen for cooling (Green & Gelhard 1987).

Also widely noted in textbooks is the impressive inaccuracy in localizing warm stimuli unaccompanied by tactile stimulation. Cain (1973) found that subjects were unable to tell whether a radiant heat source was focused on the front or back of the torso on a significant portion of trials (14% error rate). Lee et al (1996) asked subjects to indicate which of two contact thermal stimulators was raised (or lowered) in temperature. Subjects were more accurate in localizing cooling stimuli than warming ones and more accurate when the two thermal probes were positioned to stimulate different dermatomes as compared to the same dermatome.

The heat grill is part of a classic demonstration of thermal interaction. The device consists of alternating warm and cool bars that elicit a sensation of painful heat. A study of this effect combined human and animal work (Craig & Bushnell 1994). The same stimulus conditions that elicited reports of painful heat from human subjects were applied to cats' hindpaws. The analysis of the response of spinal cord neurons to warm, cool, and "grill" stimuli suggested that the illusion may result from a central disinhibition process. More recently, Craig et al (1996) used PET imaging of regional cerebral blood flow in humans to show that the grill produces activation in the anterior cingulate cortex (a region also activated by noxious levels of heat and cold), whereas the component warm and cold stimuli do not. Warm stimuli primarily activated the insula and SI while cool stimuli produced significant activation in the insula and SII, implying differential cortical processing of these submodalities.

Thermal stimulation has also been investigated for the way it interacts with, or the effects that it has on, other types of cutaneous sensitivity such as vibratory (Apkarian et al 1994, Green 1987), chemical (Green 1991, 1992), and spatial (Sherrick & Cholewiak 1986, Stevens 1989).

HAPTICS AND KINESTHESIS

Most of the information that we gain by means of touch comes by way of the hand, which is both a perceptual and manipulative organ. In haptics, which combines tactile and kinesthetic stimulation, there is a long history of distinguishing between active and passive touch and the differences between the two modes of stimulation. In their review, Loomis & Lederman (1986) propose a classification system they refer to as "tactual modes." The five categories of tactual modes incorporate both the idea of subjects' control (active) and no control (passive) over the pickup of information and whether the information is cutaneous, kinesthetic, or both. (Although active touch, which involves efferent control, afferent kinesthetic information, cutaneous stimuli, and an ac-

tive observer, is the most common way of gaining touch information in everyday life, most of the experimental work has involved the presentation of cutaneous stimuli to a passive observer, in large part because that permits greater
stimulus control.)

A traditional issue in haptics is the degree to which active exploration increases the accuracy of the perception of objects. This issue is also important in
studies of neurophysiological responses to spatial patterns. Most of these studies
involve the imposition of a spatial pattern on a passive, nonhuman subject. To
answer the question of whether sensitivity to passively imposed spatial patterns is much less than to patterns actively scanned, human subjects were
tested in a letter-identification task. The subjects were allowed to move their
fingers laterally back and forth a few centimeters over raised letters. This provided no advantage over having the raised letters scanned across the stationary
fingerpad (Vega-Bermudez et al 1991). Srinivasan & LaMotte (1995) examined
how subjects discriminate the softness of objects under a variety of conditions.
For example, reducing tactile sensitivity by anesthetizing the fingertip resulted
in judgments of softness dropping to chance for samples of rubber. They also
tested active vs passive contact and found that pressing the sample of rubber
down onto the passive fingerpad of the subject produced performance nearly
as good as allowing the subject to actively contact the sample. Chapman
(1994) reviewed work on active and passive touch in light of the intriguing
finding of diminished cortical input, referred to as input "gating," that occurs
during active touch. Several explanations are offered for the findings that sensitivity is, in fact, not reduced during active as compared to passive touch.

Klatzky, Lederman, and their coworkers have analyzed hand movements
when subjects are asked to identify objects and properties of objects. Based on
these analyses, they identified a series of relatively stereotyped hand movements
they call "exploratory procedures" (EPs). Particular EPs are associated with the
extraction of certain properties of objects. For example, an EP such as lateral
movement is associated with the extraction of texture, the EP of static contact
is associated with the extraction of thermal properties, that of enclosure (mold-
ing the hand around an object) with extracting global shape and volume, and so
forth (Klatzky & Lederman 1993, Lederman & Klatzky 1993). The use of EPs
has been investigated in a variety of tasks, such as in speed of object classification (Lederman et al 1993), in identifying, matching, or classifying objects on
the basis of particular properties such as surface texture (Klatzky et al 1987,
1989), and in directed exploration (Lederman & Klatzky 1987), in which subjects are required (constrained) to use a particular EP to explore an object.

Haptic exploration is also involved in a different task, the exploration of the
near space around us (Loomis & Lederman 1986). Several studies have investigated distortions of this space such as that produced in the horizontal-vertical
illusion (vertical generally judged greater than horizontal) (Heller et al 1993,

Heller & Joyner 1993), which corresponds to judging lengths of objects oriented tangentially vs radially (Marks & Armstrong 1996) and in judging the length of objects. In this latter case, Hollins & Goble (1988) showed that velocity had a large effect on perceived length. As velocity increased from 0.5 to 50 cm/sec, perceived length declined by a factor of 3.

Textbooks in sensation and perception occasionally mention Aristotle's Illusion. In this illusion, two fingers are crossed over one another, such as D3 over D2, and a pencil is placed between the two crossed fingertips. Typically, subjects report a sensation of two objects. The illusion of double sensation, or "tactile diplopia," can also be produced by bringing together nonadjacent fingers (D2 and D4 or D2 and D5) (Benedetti 1986a) or by squeezing adjacent fingers tightly together and bringing together locations on the adjacent fingers that are normally apart from one another (Benedetti 1986b). Benedetti has quantified the crossed-fingers effect by touching each finger with one of two objects, for example, a sharp point and a small ball. The subjects indicated the relative position of the two stimuli (Benedetti 1991a). Benedetti has also used these effects to examine the adaptation of motor and perceptual responses with altered inputs. In one study relevant to the issue of plasticity, subjects kept their fingers crossed (D3 over D2) for as long as six months. The crossed fingers were maintained in position for several subjects by putting screws through the distal ends of the fingernails. Both motor and perceptual responses showed adaptation over a period of several months (Benedetti 1991a). Readers of Frank Geldard's *The Human Senses* (1972) may be reminded that the days of "somewhat Spartan" experiments in somesthesis are not over.

Clark & Horch's (1986) chapter on kinesthesis provides a valuable review of this topic. Particularly noteworthy from the point of view of understanding the perceptual aspects are the explanations that are offered of both the psychophysical testing procedures and the results of such testing. With regard to kinesthetic receptor mechanisms, the consensus continues to be that receptors in muscles play the major role (Jones 1994, Matthews 1988). The contributions of other receptors, such as cutaneous and joint receptors, may depend on the joint being examined (Clark & Horch 1986, Ferrell & Craske 1992). Studies using nerve block (Ferrell & Smith 1987, 1989), microneurography (Edin 1990), and other techniques (Ferrell 1995) have found evidence that nonmuscle receptors may provide kinesthetic information about the hand. The nature and role of kinesthetic feedback are also discussed in an article by Gandevia & Burke (1992) and in associated commentaries.

PAIN

Books and articles about pain often begin with attempts to find a suitable definition for the topic. Many provide the "official" definition offered by the International Association for the Study of Pain (IASP) (Merskey & Bogduk 1994), "An unpleasant sensory or emotional experience associated with actual or potential tissue damage, or described in terms of such damage." While that may do justice to the subject matter, it fails to capture the extensive scholarly, clinical, public, and commercial interest in the topic. For that purpose, a definition generally given tongue in cheek may be preferable: "Pain is a growth industry."

There are numerous ways to quantify that interest and that growth and numerous reasons to account for it. In 1973, IASP was formed. By 1975, when the Society held its first World Congress on Pain, there were 1200 members. That number increased to 2100 in 1984 and to nearly 4500 by 1996. The numbers attending the triennial pain congresses mushroomed from 760 in 1975 to 4300 in 1996. Clearly, academic interest in pain comes from many disciplines, but psychology figures very prominently among them. About 550 IASP members list psychology as their main discipline, a number second only to anesthesiology.

Bibliographic databases provide another perspective on the current interest in pain research. A search of PsycLIT for the period 1990–1997 reveals that there were 1025 journal articles on the "exploded terms" of "tactual perception" or "somesthetic perception" if articles related to "pain" are not included. Performing the reverse search, looking for articles devoted solely to "pain," comes up with 4343 references. The medical literature, of course, yields a much larger sum: Entering "pain" into Medline and asking for references over the past five years yields an astonishing count of 47,092.

Research on pain touches on every aspect of psychology presented in a typical introductory psychology course: brain and behavior, psychophysics and perception, learning and motivation, memory and cognition, individual differences, development, personality, psychological disorders, and social behavior. Many of the 81 chapters in the encyclopedic *Textbook of Pain* (Wall & Melzack 1994) deal with psychological issues. Psychologists play major roles in the leadership of the International Association for the Study of Pain and the American and Canadian Pain Societies, and on the editorial boards of the major journals *Pain, Pain Forum, Clinical Journal of Pain,* and *Journal of Pain and Symptom Management.*

Gate-Control Theory

While psychology's involvement in the field of pain has long been recognized, Melzack & Wall's (1965) classic paper on the gate-control theory served as a major catalyst by moving the field of pain research away from the Cartesian model of a direct connection between a source of injury and a pain center in the brain. Their model provided instead for a variable link between injury and pain, with descending influences from the central nervous system serving to modulate afferent activity in response to noxious inputs. Suddenly, it seemed, pain research and pain management, both of which had largely been the domain of the medical profession, were open to many other disciplines, and, over the years, psychology's value was established.

The gate-control theory has undergone modifications (Melzack & Wall 1996) since its formulation, but the basic conception remains unchanged. Small-diameter fibers respond to noxious inputs and convey information to the dorsal horn of the spinal cord and then to subcortical and cortical structures subserving three dimensions of pain: sensory-discriminative, motivational-affective, and cognitive-evaluative. In addition, descending influences from higher regions act via the midbrain and medulla to exert an inhibitory influence on the spinal cord and to inhibit the response of transmitting cells to injury.

Clearly, this description is farcically simplistic. Wall & Melzack's *Textbook of Pain* (1994) devotes its first dozen chapters and over 250 pages to an elaboration of the neurophysiological and neurochemical mechanisms that might account for pain transmission and modulation. Theoretical developments regarding pain transmission and encoding continue apace. One such is Melzack's (1990) concept of the "neuromatrix," a genetically determined neural network subserving body sensation that can be modified by experience. It has been applied particularly to phantom-limb phenomena. Magnetic source imaging in phantom-limb patients (Flor et al 1995) has disclosed extensive reorganization of the somatosensory cortex, an example of neuronal plasticity that may be revealed repeatedly in future studies of chronic pain conditions.

Sensory Fibers

Considerable interest among neuroscientists has focused on each of the elements in the complex pain-transmission system. The two sets of highly specialized peripheral sensory fibers, one myelinated (A-delta) and one unmyelinated (C), are characterized by high thresholds but differ in other respects. C-fiber nociceptors that respond to both intense mechanical stimulation and high temperatures ($<38°C$) show a nice monotonic relationship between number of impulses and temperature or pressure, but selective analgesia to heat by the application of capsaicin in humans (Simone & Ochoa 1991) suggests independent transducer mechanisms (Meyer et al 1994).

The neural response of C-fiber nociceptors is intimately linked to the nature of prior stimulation. Presentation of noxious heat 10 sec before a test stimulus reduces the response to the latter by about 65%; even at 5 min there is a measurable suppression. Likewise, response to a heat pulse of, say, 47°C, is markedly less if the previous stimulus was 47° or 49°C than if it was 41° or 43°C (Meyer et al 1994).

Interesting issues about the appropriate neurophysiological measure to use in correlating human and nonhuman data about C-fiber mechano-heat nociceptors arise from the finding by Tillman et al (1995a) that heat pain thresholds decreased as stimulus ramp rate increased, but the threshold for detecting an action potential in the C-fiber of the monkey increased with ramp rate. Tillman et al (1995b) developed a three-layer heat-transfer model to describe temperature distribution after application of heat to the skin, relating threshold to base temperature, ramp rate, and duration of the heat step. Their results suggest that the heat threshold for C-fiber mechano-heat nociceptors is determined by receptor depth.

Schmidt et al (1995) found new classes of C-fiber nociceptors, namely ones responding only to mechanical stimuli, only to heat stimuli, and ones that were unresponsive to pressure or heat. Some of each of these units were sensitized after topical application of the irritants capsaicin or mustard oil, acquiring responsiveness to a stimulus modality to which they were previously nonresponsive. The discovery that previously silent nociceptors can be recruited by local injury suggests that central sensitization may result from spatial summation of a nociceptive barrage, with implications for chronic pain that are discussed below.

A-fiber units have high thresholds to both mechanical pressure and temperature, but since they typically respond to temperatures greater than 50°C, it is more likely that the C-fiber nociceptors signal pain around the human pain threshold (~ 45°C). As temperature rises, particularly for long-duration stimuli, the A-delta nociceptors begin to respond vigorously (Meyer et al 1994). Moreover, the A-fiber nociceptors display an extraordinary response to burn injury, showing both a sharply reduced threshold and a marked increase in response rate to thermal stimuli after a 30-sec burn to the hand (Meyer et al 1994). This pattern closely matches the hyperalgesia seen in human observers following a similar burn.

Single-fiber recordings from A-delta and C-fibers in awake humans have revealed a great deal about the physiological properties of these units (Torebjork 1994). Curiously, although the A-delta fibers are much larger in diameter than the unmyelinated C-afferents, it is exceedingly difficult to record from the former, perhaps because the electrode tip must be close to the node of Ranvier. Lundberg et al (1992) used small electrodes to stimulate groups of A-delta and C-fibers, with trains of electrical pulses varying regularly in frequency from 1 to 15 Hz or mimicking some of the irregular patterns seen in microneurographic recordings. The data indicated that the subjective magnitude of pain increased monotonically as a function of frequency for the regular patterns, but that even greater peak magnitudes of pain were reported for the irregular but natural patterns.

Many phenomena are seen in parallel when examining neurophysiological data and psychophysical ratings. Often, the correlations are evident in peripheral recordings, as in studies of primary hyperalgesia at the site of an injury, but higher-level influences become apparent in studies of secondary hyperalgesia, an enhanced level of pain to mechanical stimuli seen in a large area surrounding a burn. Baumann et al (1991) and Simone et al (1991) concluded that central rather than peripheral sensitization is responsible for these effects.

Higher Neural Organization

The second-order neural organization of the spinal cord reveals both elegance and complexity, since it is at this level that one finds the interplay between nociceptive and non-nociceptive afferents, excitatory and inhibitory neurotransmitters, and both afferent and descending influences. Nociceptive neurons respond maximally to high intensities, project to higher areas known to be involved in processing pain information, generate pain experiences when stimulated electrically, and reduce pain when their activity is inhibited (Fields 1987). About a quarter of the spinal neurons tend to be "high-threshold" or "nociceptive-specific" but they are outnumbered by "wide-dynamic-range" (WDR) neurons that have large receptive fields, respond weakly to brushing, pressure, and mild touch but vigorously to strong pressure, pinch, or high temperature (Price 1988).

Simone et al (1991) injected capsaicin into the skin of human observers. This produced an immediate burning pain that built over about 15 seconds and declined over the next half hour, increased the perceived intensity of noxious stimulation (hyperalgesia), and caused even gentle strokes to be perceived as painful (allodynia). After a similar treatment in monkeys, both the high-threshold and WDR cells showed increased activity whose time course correlated with magnitude estimates from the human observers, although the correlation was greater for the activity of the WDR cells. More recently, Pertovaara (1998) found that secondary hyperalgesia, the altered responsiveness in the region away from the injury, is submodality-specific; neurogenic inflammation induced by the injection of mustard oil in the rat enhanced the response of WDR cells in the dorsal horn to intense mechanical but not thermal stimuli. Even weak mechanical stimuli produced enhanced spinal activity, suggesting that the injury engaged a descending facilitatory feedback loop that may enforce inactivity and thus promote healing.

Submodality specificity was also seen in an elegant study by Torebjork et al (1992), who demonstrated that the secondary hyperalgesia to mechanical stimuli following capsaicin injections is mediated by input from large myelinated fibers. These fibers normally evoke nonpainful tactile sensations, but nerve compression, which selectively blocked their capacity to respond, also abolished the mechanical hypersensitivity in the wide surrounding area. Hyperalgesia to heat in that region was unaffected, however, indicating that afferent signals from other fibers, presumably the C-polymodal nociceptors, must be responsible for that effect. The mechanical hyperalgesia appears to be due to reversible changes in central processing.

Central Neurochemical Effects

The role of higher-order centers in such inflammation-produced hyperalgesia was supported by the findings of Kolhekar et al (1997), who found that blockade of receptors for N-methyl-D-aspartate (NMDA) in the rat thalamus significantly reduced both thermal and mechanical hyperalgesia induced by injection of carrageenin in the contralateral hindpaw of the rat. NMDA is an excitatory amino acid whose receptor, when unmasked, permits previously weak inputs to be expressed and produces much larger than normal responses in postsynaptic cells (McMahon 1994). NMDA is seen to play a role in many chronic pain states, since it markedly influences central excitability [even more in the neonate (Fitzgerald 1994) than the adult].

NMDA antagonists, then, ought to be helpful in blocking and reversing central sensitization (Coderre et al 1997, Dubner & Basbaum 1994) and thus preventing and reducing pain. Stubhaug et al (1997) showed that ketamine, a selective blocker of the NMDA receptor, when administered postoperatively in humans, markedly reduced hyperalgesia in the region surrounding the surgical incision. A recent study used ketamine to enhance the effects of preemptive analgesia. In this procedure, a local anesthetic or an opiate is administered prior to general anesthesia in surgery. It is based on the notion, which has received considerable support, that it is prudent to block nociceptive inputs from the site of the operation, even if the pain they would produce is not consciously experienced. Otherwise, the thinking goes, a strong afferent barrage may alter the activity of central neurons and lead to extended pain. Barbieri et al (1997) divided patients into three groups, all of whom received the potent synthetic opiate, fentanyl, on arrival in the operating room and then a general anesthetic. One group of patients received ketamine 30 min before this preemptive analgesia treatment. Their visual analog scale ratings of postoperative pain were sharply reduced compared to those of patients who had the standard procedure or who received ketamine in the recovery room. Ketamine or fentanyl, given as an adjuvant to general anesthesia, altered electrocutaneous detection and pain thresholds for up to 5 days in patients who underwent abdominal surgery (Wilder-Smith et al 1998).

Psychophysical studies of central sensitization have often focused on the phenomenon of second pain, seeing it as a correlate of the neurophysiological "wind-up effect" that occurs after repeated application of an electrical or thermal stimulus. A single application of an intense pulse can elicit both a localized pricking sensation and, a second or so later, a diffuse throbbing or burning experience. After repeated applications of thermal pulses, each a second or two apart, the perceived intensity of the first pain declines to about one third of its original level while that of the second pain doubles (Price 1994). This differential effect has been linked to suppression of the A-delta heat nociceptive afferents and central summation of activity initiated by C-fiber polymodal nociceptive afferents. Price et al (1994) have shown that the cough suppressant dextromethorphan, which is an NMDA antagonist, attenuated the level of second pain, leaving first pain unaffected. Arendt-Nielsen et al (1995), in a related study, found that ketamine inhibited temporal summation for trains of electrical pulses in human observers, although ratings of a single stimulus were unaffected. These data reinforce the notion that central mechanisms, involving NMDA-receptors, are involved in temporal summation studies in the laboratory and secondary hyperalgesia phenomena in the pain clinic.

Pain Psychophysics

There is a growing interest in combining the elegance of laboratory research with the relevance of clinical studies. While such traditional measures as pain threshold and pain tolerance still provide many useful insights into the pain experience, the tools for studying pain responsiveness have expanded enormously in recent years. The applicability of signal-detection theory methods to studying noxious signals remains contentious, with both adherents (Clark 1994) and critics (Rollman 1977) debating whether the discrimination of two intense stimuli provides insights into possible changes in their painfulness. Irwin & Whitehead (1991), using category scaling and identification tasks with electrocutaneous stimuli, have attempted some resolution of the conflicting views.

Technological advances have strongly influenced pain investigations, at both the stimulus and response end, in recent years. It is comforting to see that good research can still be accomplished on a meager budget. Koltzenburg et al (1993), who wanted to measure localization ability for noxious stimuli as compared to innocuous ones, asked subjects to localize pin pricks, noxious heat (using small copper probes heated to 50°C), and chemical irritants (mustard oil applied to a small cotton ball). The mean mislocalization was about 9 mm, with no difference among the submodalities and no effects of blocking the large fibers. Localization of tactile sensations induced by von Frey hairs, signaled by the large fibers, was only marginally better (a mean error of about 6 mm), suggesting that somatotopic representation in the brain for noxious inputs is similar to that found for tactile ones.

There has been considerable interest in the scaling of both the intensity and unpleasantness of pain, using visual analog scales or scaled verbal descriptors (Gracely 1994), multidimensional scaling (Clark et al 1989), measures of reflex activity (DeBroucker et al 1989), studies of pupil diameter (Chapman et al 1997), somatosensory evoked potentials (Chen & Bromm 1995), and a number of other methods (Chapman & Loeser 1989, Rollman 1992) designed to elicit information about the sensory, affective, and to a much smaller extent, cognitive components of pain experiences. These behavioral and physiological instruments have helped to address fundamental issues such as gender differences in pain responsiveness (Berkley 1997) and the assessment of pediatric pain (McGrath & Unruh 1994). Neuroimaging studies have begun to appear in abundance (Casey et al 1995, Casey & Minoshima 1997), but technical, interpretational, and philosophical issues will remain with us for many years.

Attempts to bridge the laboratory-clinical gap come from studies of pain perception among pain patients. Naliboff et al (1981) contrasted Chapman's (1978) model of hypervigilance with Rollman's (1979) model of adaptation level in examining the threshold for noxious input in pain patients. Chapman's model suggests that pain patients have diminished pain threshold and tolerance levels, hyper-responding to both internal and external stimuli. In contrast, the adaptation-level model suggests that pain patients compare external stimuli to their endogenous pain, rating the stimuli as less intense than they would if they did not have a high level of pain as an internal anchor or comparison point. Both models have received support (Naliboff & Cohen 1989, Rollman 1992), but for different populations of pain patients.

For example, fibromyalgia patients who have exquisite sensitivity at a number of tender points also show much lower pain threshold and pain tolerance to pressure applied at control sites (Scudds et al 1987). Lautenbacher et al (1994) showed that fibromyalgia patients had significantly lower pain thresholds when the noxious stimulus was heat or a train of electrical pulses, and McDermid et al (1996) demonstrated that they have an extremely low discomfort threshold for white noise. At the least, fibromyalgia patients generally show a considerable degree of responsiveness to noxious stimuli, whatever the origin.

More recent studies have employed psychophysical methods to look at possible deficiencies of pain modulation in these patients. Using the diffuse noxious inhibitory control paradigm, in which a tonic noxious stimulus (such as a tourniquet or a long-lasting intense heat stimulus) at one site on the body, such as the arm, suppresses the pain threshold or rated painfulness of a noxious phasic stimulus (such as electrical shock) applied to a distant body part, both Kosek & Hansson (1997) and Lautenbacher & Rollman (1997) found less suppression of pain in patients than in controls. It remains to be determined whether this reflects a dysfunction of physiological inhibition or an attentional disorder in which the fibromyalgia sufferers concentrate on all noxious inputs while pain-free individuals channel their attentional capacity to the more lasting and noxious input.

This examination of recent findings on touch, haptics, and pain indicates that both biological and psychological perspectives are necessary to uncover the phenomena that make up these areas. The future direction of work on somesthesis will be enormously exciting, but it is unlikely that we will see a unified theory emerging that covers the complexities of the separate modalities and their interactions, just as it is unlikely that we will see a unified theory that covers the complexities of vision or hearing. We do expect continued close co-operation between the psychophysical approach and the neurophysiological approach, particularly as the latter continues to put increasing emphasis on central mechanisms. The improved resolution in both the spatial and temporal dimensions of brain imaging, coupled with increased emphasis on multidimensional behavioral assessment, will enable us to better understand the sensory, affective, and cognitive components of normal and abnormal states. Basic scientists and clinicians will seek to integrate their models, investigative tools, and findings in dealing with a wide range of disorders, with behavioral medicine increasing in scope and influence. Finally, we expect to see an increased emphasis on the complex interactions between modalities as investigators capture the richness of somesthetic experience.

AKNOWLEDGMENTS

This review was supported by Grant DC-00095 from the National Institute on Deafness and Other Communication Disorders to JCC and Grant AO392 from the Natural Sciences and Engineering Research Council of Canada and the Agnes Cole Dark Fund, Faculty of Social Science, University of Western Ontario, to GBR.

> Visit the *Annual Reviews home page* at
> http://www.AnnualReviews.org.

Literature Cited

Allard T, Clark SA, Jenkins WM, Merzenich MM. 1991. Reorganization of somatosensory area 3b representations in adult owl monkeys after digital syndactyly. *J. Neurophysiol.* 66:1048–58

Apkarian AV, Stea RA, Bolanowski SJ. 1994. Heat-induced pain diminishes vibrotactile perception: a touch gate. *Somatosens. Mot. Res.* 11:259–67

Arendt-Nielsen L, Petersen-Felix S, Fischer M, Bak P, Bjerring P, Zbinden AM. 1995. The effect of N-methyl-D-aspartate antagonist (ketamine) on single and repeated nociceptive stimuli: a placebo-controlled experimental human study. *Anesth. Analg.* 81:63–68

Barbieri M, Colnaghi S, Tommasino C, Zangrillo A, Galli L, Torri G. 1997. Efficacy of the NMDA antagonist ketamine in preemptive analgesia. See Jensen et al 1997, pp. 343–49

Baumann TK, Simone DA, Shain CN, LaMotte RH. 1991. Neurogenic hyperalgesia: the search for the primary cutaneous afferent fibers that contribute to capsaicin-induced pain and hyperalgesia. *J. Neurophysiol.* 66:212–27

Benedetti F. 1986a. Spatial organization of the

diplesthetic and nondiplesthetic areas of the fingers. *Perception* 15:285–301

Benedetti F. 1986b. Tactile diplopia (diplesthesia) on the human fingers. *Perception* 15:83–91

Benedetti F. 1991a. Perceptual learning following a long-lasting tactile reversal. *J. Exp. Psychol.: Hum. Percept. Perform.* 17: 267–77

Benedetti F. 1991b. Reorganization of tactile perception following the simulated amputation of one finger. *Perception* 20:687–92

Berkley KJ. 1997. Sex differences in pain. *Behav. Brain Sci.* 20:371–80

Boff KR, Kaufman L, Thomas JP, eds. 1986. *Handbook of Perception and Human Performance. Sensory Processes and Perception,* Vol. 1. New York: Wiley & Sons. 2 Vols.

Boivie J, Hansson P, Ludblom U, eds. 1994. *Touch, Temperature, and Pain in Health and Disease: Mechanisms and Assessments,* Vol 3. Seattle, WA: IASP

Bolanowski SJ. 1996. Information processing channels in the sense of touch. See Franzen et al 1996, pp. 49–58

Bolanowski SJ, Gescheider GA, Verrillo RT. 1994. Hairy skin: psychophysical channels and their physiological substrates. *Somatosens. Mot. Res.* 11:279–90

Bolanowski SJ, Gescheider GA, Verrillo RT, Checkosky CM. 1988. Four channels mediate the mechanical aspects of touch. *J. Acoust. Soc. Am.* 84:1680–94

Bradshaw JL, Howard MJ, Pierson JM, Phillips J, Bradshaw JA. 1992. Effects of expectancy and attention in vibrotactile choice reaction time tasks. *Q. J. Exp. Psychol.* 44A:509–28

Bromm B, Desmedt JS, eds. 1995. *Pain and The Brain: From Nociception to Cognition.* New York: Raven

Burton H, MacLeod AK, Videen TO, Raichle ME. 1997. Multiple foci in parietal and frontal cortex activated by rubbing embossed grating patterns across fingerpads: a positron emission tomography study in humans. *Cereb. Cortex* 7:3–17

Burton H, Sinclair R. 1996. Somatosensory cortex and tactile perceptions. See Kruger 1996, pp. 105–77

Burton H, Sinclair RJ. 1994. Representation of tactile roughness in thalamus and somatosensory cortex. *Can. J. Physiol. Pharmacol.* 72:546–57

Burton H, Videen TO, Raichle ME. 1993. Tactile-vibration-activated foci in insular and parietal-opercular cortex studied with positron emission tomography: mapping the second somatosensory area in humans. *Somatosens. Mot. Res.* 10:297–308

Butter CM, Buchtel HA, Santucci R. 1989. Spatial attentional shifts: further evidence for the role of polysensory mechanisms using visual and tactile stimuli. *Neuropsychologia* 27:1231–40

Cain WS. 1973. Spatial discrimination of cutaneous warmth. *Am. J. Psychol.* 86:169–81

Caselli RJ. 1991. Bilateral impairment of somesthetically mediated object recognition in humans. *Mayo Clin. Proc.* 66:357–64

Caselli RJ. 1993. Ventrolateral and dorsomedial somatosensory association cortex damage produces distinct somesthetic syndromes in humans. *Neurology* 43:762–71

Casey KL, Minoshima S. 1997. Can pain be imaged? See Jensen et al 1997, pp. 855–66

Casey KL, Minoshima S, Morrow TJ, Koeppe RA, Frey KA. 1995. Imaging the brain in pain: potentials, limitations, and implications. See Bromm & Desmedt 1995, pp. 201–11

Chapman CE. 1994. Active versus passive touch: factors influencing the transmission of somatosensory signals to primary somatosensory cortex. *Can. J. Physiol. Pharmacol.* 72:558–70

Chapman CR. 1978. The perception of noxious events. In *The Psychology of Pain,* ed. RA Sternbach, pp. 169–203. New York: Raven

Chapman CR, Loeser JD, eds. 1989. *Issues in Pain Measurement. Advances in Pain Research and Therapy,* Vol. 12. New York: Raven

Chapman CR, Oka S, Jackson RC. 1997. Phasic pupil dilation response to noxious stimulation in humans. See Jensen et al 1997, pp. 449–58

Chen ACN, Bromm B. 1995. Pain-related generators of laser-evoked brain potentials: brain mapping and dipole modelling. See Bromm & Desmedt 1995, pp. 245–66

Cholewiak RW, Collins AA. 1991. Sensory and physiological bases of touch. See Heller & Schiff 1991, pp. 23–60

Clark FJ, Horch KW. 1986. Kinesthesia. See Boff et al 1986, pp. 1–62

Clark WC. 1994. The psyche in the psychophysics of pain: an introduction to sensory decision theory. See Boivie et al 1994, pp. 41–62

Clark WC, Janal MN, Carroll JD. 1989. Multidimensional pain requires multidimensional scaling. See Chapman & Loeser 1989, pp. 285–325

Coderre TJ, Fisher K, Fundytus ME. 1997. The role of ionotropic and metabotropic glutamate receptors in persistent nociception. See Jensen et al 1997, pp. 259–75

Cole JD. 1995. *Pride and a Daily Marathon.* Cambridge, MA: MIT Press. 1st ed.

Connor CE, Hsiao SS, Phillips JR, Johnson KO. 1990. Tactile roughness: neural codes that account for psychophysical magnitude estimates. *J. Neurosci.* 10:3823–36

Connor CE, Johnson KO. 1992. Neural coding of tactile texture: comparison of spatial and temporal mechanisms for roughness perception. *J. Neurosci.* 12:3414–26

Craig AD, Bushnell MC. 1994. The thermal grill illusion: unmasking the burn of cold pain. *Science* 265:252–55

Craig AD, Reiman EM, Evans A, Bushnell MC. 1996. Functional imaging of an illusion of pain. *Nature* 384:258–60

Craig JC. 1993. Anomalous sensations following prolonged tactile stimulation. *Neuropsychologia* 31:277–91

Craig JC. 1995. Vibrotactile masking: the role of response competition. *Percept. Psychophys.* 57:1190–200

Craig JC. 1996. Interference in identifying tactile patterns: response competition and temporal integration. *Somatosens. Mot. Res.* 13:199–213

Craig JC, Evans PM. 1995. Tactile selective attention and temporal masking. *Percept. Psychophys.* 57:511–18

Craig JC, Kisner JM. 1998. Factors affecting tactile spatial acuity. *Somatosens. Mot. Res.* 15:29–45

Davidson PW, Appelle S, Haber RN. 1992. Haptic scanning of braille cells by low- and high-proficiency blind readers. *Res. Dev. Disabil.* 13:99–111

DeBroucker T, Willer JC, Bergeret S. 1989. The nociceptive flexion reflex in humans: a specific and objective correlate of experimental pain. See Chapman & Loeser 1989, pp. 337–52

Dubner R, Basbaum AI. 1994. Spinal dorsal horn plasticity following tissue or nerve injury. See Wall & Melzack 1994, pp. 225–41

Eberhardt SP, Bernstein LE, Barac-Cikoja D, Coulter DC, Jordan J. 1994. Inducing dynamic haptic perception by the hand: system description and some results. *Proc. Am. Soc. Mech. Eng.* 55:345–51

Edin BB. 1990. Finger joint movement sensitivity of non-cutaneous mechanoreceptor afferents in the human radial nerve. *Exp. Brain Res.* 82:417–22

Edin BB, Essick GK, Trulsson M, Olsson KA. 1995. Receptor encoding of moving tactile stimuli in humans. 1. Temporal pattern of discharge of individual low-threshold mechanoreceptors. *J. Neurosci.* 15:830–47

Elbert T, Pantev C, Wienbruch C, Rockstroh B, Taub E. 1995. Increased cortical representation of the fingers of the left hand in string players. *Science* 270:305–7

Essick GK. 1991. Human capacity to process directional information provided by tactile stimuli which move across the skin: characterization and potential neural mechanisms. In *Wenner-Gren International Symposium Series: Information Processing in the Somatosensory System*, ed. O Franzen, J Westman, 57:329–39. London: Macmillan

Essick GK. 1992. Comprehensive clinical evaluation of perioral sensory function. *Oral Maxillofac. Surg. Clin. NA* 4:503–26

Essick GK, Bredehoeft KR, McLaughlin DF, Szanislzo JA. 1991. Directional sensitivity along the upper limb in humans. *Somatosens. Mot. Res.* 8:13–22

Essick GK, Edin BB. 1995. Receptor encoding of moving tactile stimuli in humans. II. The mean response of individual low-threshold mechanoreceptors to motion across the receptive field. *J. Neurosci.* 15:848–64

Essick GK, Franzen O, Nguyen TA, Jowers K, Shores JW, et al. 1996a. Experimental assessment of the temporal hypothesis of velocity scaling. See Franzen et al 1996, pp. 83–99

Essick GK, Rath EM, Kelly DG, James A, Murray RA. 1996b. A novel approach for studying direction discrimination. See Franzen et al 1996, pp. 59–72

Evans PM, Craig JC. 1992. Response competition: a major source of interference in a tactile identification task. *Percept. Psychophys.* 51:199–206

Evans PM, Craig JC, Rinker MA. 1992. Perceptual processing of adjacent and nonadjacent tactile nontargets. *Percept. Psychophys.* 52:571–81

Ferrell WR. 1995. Contribution of joint afferents to proprioception and motor control. In *Neural Control of Movement*, ed. WR Ferrell, U Proske, pp. 61–66. New York: Plenum

Ferrell WR, Craske B. 1992. Contribution of joint and muscle afferents to position sense at the human proximal interphalangeal joint. *Exp. Physiol.* 77:331–42

Ferrell WR, Smith A. 1987. The effect of digital nerve block on position sense at the proximal interphalangeal joint of the human index finger. *Brain Res.* 425:369–71

Ferrell WR, Smith A. 1989. The effect of loading on position sense at the proximal interphalangeal joint of the human index finger. *J. Physiol.* 418:145–61

Fields HL, ed. 1987. *Pain*. New York: McGraw-Hill

Fitzgerald M. 1994. Neurobiology of fetal and neonatal pain. See Wall & Melzack 1994, pp. 153–63

Flor H, Elbert T, Knecht S, Wienbruch C, Pantev C, et al. 1995. Phantom-limb pain as a perceptual correlate of cortical reorganization following arm amputation. *Nature* 375:482–84

Foulke E. 1991. Braille. See Heller & Schiff 1991, pp. 219–33

Franzen O, Johansson R, Terenius L, eds. 1996. *Somesthesis and the Neurobiology of the Somatosensory Cortex.* Basel, Switz. Birkhauser

Gandevia SC, Burke D. 1992. Does the nervous-system depend on kinesthetic information to control natural limb movements? *Behav. Brain. Sci.* 15:614–32

Garraghty PE, Kaas JH, Florence SL. 1994. Plasticity of sensory and motor maps in adult and developing mammals. In *Advances in Neural and Behavioral Development*, ed. VA Casagrande, PG Shinkman, 4:1–36. Norwood, NJ: Ablex

Geldard FA. 1972. *The Human Senses.* New York: Wiley & Sons. 2nd ed.

Gescheider GA, Beiles EJ, Checkosky CM, Bolanowski SJ, Verrillo RT. 1994a. The effects of aging on information-processing channels in the sense of touch: II. Temporal summation in the P channel. *Somatosens. Mot. Res.* 11:359–65

Gescheider GA, Bolanowski SJ, Hall KL, Hoffman KE, Verrillo RT. 1994b. The effects of aging on information-processing channels in the sense of touch: I. Absolute sensitivity. *Somatosens. Mot. Res.* 11:345–57

Gescheider GA, Edwards RR, Lackner EA, Bolanowski SJ, Verrillo RT. 1996. The effects of aging on information-processing channels in the sense of touch: III. Differential sensitivity to changes in stimulus intensity. *Somatosens. Mot. Res.* 13:73–80

Gescheider GA, Valetutti AA Jr, Padula MC, Verrillo RT. 1992. Vibrotactile forward masking as a function of age. *J. Acoust. Soc. Am.* 91:1690–96

Goodwin AW, Browning AS, Wheat HE. 1996. Representation of the shape and contact force of handled objects in populations of cutaneous afferents. See Franzen et al 1996, pp. 137–45

Goodwin AW, Wheat HE. 1992. Human tactile discrimination of curvature when contact area with the skin remains constant. *Exp. Brain Res.* 88:447–50

Gracely RH. 1994. Studies of pain in normal man. See Wall & Melzack 1994, pp. 315–36

Green BG. 1987. The effect of cooling on the vibrotactile sensitivity of the tongue. *Percept. Psychophys.* 42:423–30

Green BG. 1991. Interactions between chemical and thermal cutaneous stimuli: inhibition (counterirritation) and integration. *Somatosens. Mot. Res.* 8:301–12

Green BG. 1992. The sensory effects of l-menthol on human skin. *Somatosens. Mot. Res.* 9:235–44

Green BG, Gelhard B. 1987. Perception of temperature on oral and facial skin. *Somatosens. Res.* 4:191–200

Greenspan JD, Bolanowski SJ. 1996. The psychophysics of tactile perception and its peripheral physiological basis. See Kruger 1996, pp. 25–103

Greenspan JD, LaMotte RH. 1993. Cutaneous mechanoreceptors of the hand: experimental studies and their implications for clinical testing of tactile sensation. *J. Hand Ther.* 6:75–82

Halligan PW, Marshall JC, Wade DT, Davey J, Morrison D. 1993. Thumb in cheek? Sensory reorganization and perceptual plasticity after limb amputation. *NeuroReport* 4:233–36

Heller MA. 1992. The effect of orientation on tactual braille recognition: optimal touching positions. *Percept. Psychophys.* 51:549–56

Heller MA, Calcaterra JA, Burson LL, Tyler LA. 1996a. Tactual picture identification by blind and sighted people: effects of providing categorical information. *Percept. Psychophys.* 58:310–23

Heller MA, Calcaterra JA, Tyler LA, Burson LL. 1996b. Production and interpretation of perspective drawings by blind and sighted people. *Perception* 25:321–34

Heller MA, Joyner TD. 1993. Mechanisms in the haptic horizontal-vertical illusion: evidence from sighted and blind subjects. *Percept. Psychophys.* 53:422–28

Heller MA, Joyner TD, Dan-Fodio H. 1993. Laterality effects in the haptic horizontal-vertical illusion. *Bull. Psychon. Soc.* 31:440–42

Heller MA, Kennedy JM. 1990. Perspective taking, pictures, and the blind. *Percept. Psychophys.* 48:459–66

Heller MA, Schiff W, eds. 1991. *The Psychology of Touch.* Hillsdale, NJ: Erlbaum

Hollins M, Delemos KA, Goble AK. 1991. Vibrotactile adaptation on the face. *Percept. Psychophys.* 49:21–30

Hollins M, Faldowski R, Rao S, Young F. 1993. Perceptual dimensions of tactile surface texture: a multidimensional scaling analysis. *Percept. Psychophys.* 54:697–705

Hollins M, Goble AK. 1988. Perception of the length of voluntary movements. *Somatosens. Res.* 5:335–48

Horner DT. 1995. The effect of location on the discrimination of spatial vibrotactile patterns. *Percept. Psychophys.* 57:463–74

Hsiao SS, Johnson KO, Twonbly A, DiCarlo J. 1996. Form processing and attention effects in the somatosensory system. See Franzen et al 1996, pp. 229–47

Hsiao SS, O'Shaughnessy DM, Johnson KO. 1993. Effects of selective attention on spatial form processing in monkey primary and secondary somatosensory cortex. *J. Neurophysiol.* 70:444–47

Irwin RJ, Whitehead PR. 1991. Towards an objective psychophysics of pain. *Psychol. Sci.* 2:230–35

Jenkins WM, Merzenich MM, Ochs MT, Allard T, Guic-Robles E. 1990. Functional reorganization of primary somatosensory cortex in adult owl monkeys after behaviorally controlled tactile stimulation. *J. Neurophysiol.* 63:82–104

Jensen TS, Turner JA, Wiesenfeld-Hallin Z, eds. 1997. *Proc. 8th World Congr. Pain.* Seattle, WA: IASP

Johnson KO, Hsiao SS. 1992. Neural mechanisms of tactual form and texture perception. *Annu. Rev. Neurosci.* 15:227–50

Johnson KO, Hsiao SS. 1994. Evaluation of the relative roles of slowly and rapidly adapting afferent fibers in roughness perception. *Can. J. Physiol. Pharmacol.* 72:488–97

Johnson KO, Van Boven RW, Hsiao SS. 1994. The perception of two points is not the spatial resolution threshold. See Boivie et al 1994, 3:389–404

Jones LA. 1994. Peripheral mechanisms of touch and proprioception. *Can. J. Physiol. Pharmacol.* 72:484–87

Kaczmarek KA, Bach-y-Rita P. 1995. Tactile displays. In *Virtual Environments and Advanced Interface Design*, ed. W Barfield, TA Furness, pp. 349–414. New York: Oxford Univ. Press

Klatzky RL, Lederman SJ. 1993. Toward a computational model of constraint-driven exploration and haptic object identification. *Perception* 22:597–621

Klatzky RL, Lederman SJ. 1995. Identifying objects from a haptic glance. *Percept. Psychophys.* 57:1111–23

Klatzky RL, Lederman SJ, Reed C. 1987. There's more to touch than meets the eye: the salience of object attributes for haptics with and without vision. *J. Exp. Psychol. Gen.* 116:356–69

Klatzky RL, Lederman SJ, Reed C. 1989. Haptic integration of object properties: texture, hardness, and planar contour. *J. Exp. Psychol. Hum. Percept. Perform.* 15:45–57

Klatzky RL, Loomis JM, Lederman S, Wake H, Fujita N. 1993. Haptic identification of objects and their depictions. *Percept. Psychophys.* 54:170–78

Kolhekar R, Murphy S, Gebhart GF. 1997. Thalamic NMDA receptors modulate inflammation-produced hyperalgesia in the rat. *Pain* 71:31–40

Koltzenburg M, Handwerker HO, Torebjork HE. 1993. The ability of humans to localise noxious stimuli. *Neurosci. Lett.* 150:219–22

Kops CE, Gardner EP. 1996. Discrimination of simulated texture patterns on the human hand. *J. Neurophysiol.* 76:1145–65

Kosek E, Hansson P. 1997. Modulatory influence on somatosensory perception from vibration and heterotopic noxious conditioning stimulation (HNCS) in fibromyalgia patients and healthy subjects. *Pain* 70:41–51

Kruger L, ed. 1996. *Pain and Touch.* San Diego, CA: Academic. 2nd ed.

LaMotte RH, Lu C, Srinivasan MA. 1996. Tactile neural codes for the shapes and orientations of objects. See Franzen et al 1996, pp. 113–22

LaMotte RH, Srinivasan MA. 1993. Responses of cutaneous mechanoreceptors to the shape of objects applied to the primate fingerpad. *Acta Psychol.* 84:41–51

LaMotte RH, Srinivasan MA. 1996. Neural encoding of shape: responses of cutaneous mechanoreceptors to a wavy surface stroked across the monkey fingerpad. *J. Neurophysiol.* 76:3787–97

Lautenbacher S, Rollman GB. 1997. Possible deficiencies of pain modulation in fibromyalgia. *Clin. J. Pain* 13:189–96

Lautenbacher S, Rollman GB, McCain GA. 1994. Multi-method assessment of experimental and clinical pain in patients with fibromyalgia. *Pain* 59:45–53

Lederman SJ, Klatzky RL. 1987. Hand movements: a window into haptic object recognition. *Cogn. Psychol.* 19:342–68

Lederman SJ, Klatzky RL. 1993. Extracting object properties through haptic exploration. *Acta Psychol.* 84:29–40

Lederman SJ, Klatzky RL, Reed CL. 1993. Constraints on haptic integration of spatially shared object dimensions. *Perception* 22:723–43

Lee DK, McGillis SLB, Greenspan JD. 1996. Somatotopic localization of thermal stimuli: I. A comparison of within- versus across-dermatomal separation of innocuous thermal stimuli. *Somatosens. Mot. Res.* 13:67–71

Loomis JM. 1990. A model of character recognition and legibility. *J. Exp. Psychol.: Hum. Percept. Perform.* 16:106–20

Loomis JM, Klatzky RL, Lederman SJ. 1991. Similarity of tactual and visual picture recognition with limited field of view. *Perception* 20:167–77

Loomis JM, Lederman SJ. 1986. Tactual perception. In *Handbook of Perception and Human Performance. Cognitive Processes and Performance*, ed. KR Boff, L Kaufman, JP Thomas, pp. 1–41. New York: Wiley & Sons. 2 Vols.

Lundberg LE, Jorum E, Holm E, Torebjork HE. 1992. Intra-neural electrical stimulation of cutaneous nociceptive fibres in humans: effects of different pulse patterns on magnitude of pain. *Acta Physiol. Scand.* 146:41–48

Mahar DP, Mackenzie BD. 1993. Masking, information integration, and tactile pattern perception: a comparison of the isolation and integration hypotheses. *Perception* 22: 483–96

Marks LE, Armstrong L. 1996. Haptic and visual representations of space. In *Attention and Performance*, ed. T Inui, JL McClelland, 16:263–87. Cambridge, MA: MIT Press

Matthews PB. 1988. Proprioceptors and their contribution to somatosensory mapping: complex messages require complex processing. *Can. J. Physiol. Pharmacol.* 66: 430–38

McDermid AJ, Rollman GB, McCain GA. 1996. Generalized hypervigilance in fibromyalgia: evidence of perceptual amplification. *Pain* 66:133–44

McGrath PJ, Unruh AM. 1994. Measurement and assessment of paediatric pain. See Wall & Melzack 1994, pp. 303–13

McMahon SB. 1994. Mechanisms of cutaneous, deep and visceral pain. See Wall & Melzack 1994, pp. 129–51

Melzack R. 1990. Phantom limbs and the concept of a neuromatrix. *Trends Neurosci.* 13:88–92

Melzack R, Wall PD. 1965. Pain mechanisms: a new theory. *Science* 150:971–79

Melzack R, Wall PD. 1996. *The Challenge of Pain*. Harmondworth, UK: Penguin. 2nd ed.

Merskey H, Bodguk N. 1994. *Classification of Chronic Pain: Descriptions of Chronic Pain Syndromes and Definitions of Pain Terms*. Seattle, WA: IASP. 2nd ed.

Merzenich MM, Jenkins WM. 1993. Reorganization of cortical representations of the hand following alterations of skin inputs induced by nerve injury, skin island transfers, and experience. *J. Hand Ther.* 6:89–104

Merzenich MM, Recanzone GH, Jenkins WM, Allard TT, Nudo RJ. 1988. Cortical representational plasticity. In *Neurobiology of Neocortex*, ed. P Rakic, W Singer, pp. 41–67. Chichester, UK: Wiley & Sons

Meyer RA, Campbell JN, Raja SN. 1994. Peripheral neural mechanisms of nociception. See Wall & Melzack 1994, pp. 13–44

Mogilner A, Grossman JAI, Ribary U, Joliot M, Volkmann J, et al. 1993. Somatosensory cortical plasticity in adult humans revealed by magnetoencephalography. *Proc. Natl. Acad. Sci. USA* 90:3593–97

Naliboff BD, Cohen MJ. 1989. Psychophysical laboratory methods applied to clinical pain patients. See Chapman & Loeser 1989, pp. 365–86

Naliboff BD, Cohen MJ, Schandler SL, Heinrich RL. 1981. Signal detection and threshold measures for chronic back pain patients, chronic illness patients, and cohort controls to radiant heat stimuli. *J. Abnorm. Psychol.* 3:271–74

O'Sullivan BT, Roland PE, Kawashima R. 1994. A PET study of somatosensory discrimination in man. Microgeometry versus macrogeometry. *Eur. J. Neurosci.* 6: 137–48

Patel J, Essick GK, Kelly DG. 1997. Utility of square-wave gratings to assess perioral spatial acuity. *J. Oral Maxillofac. Surg.* 55:593–601

Pertovaara A. 1998. A neuronal correlate of secondary hyperalgesia in the rat spinal dorsal horn is submodality selective and facilitated by supraspinal influence. *Exp. Neurol.* 149:193–202

Phillips JR, Johansson RS, Johnson KO. 1990. Representation of braille characters in human nerve fibres. *Exp. Brain Res.* 81: 589–92

Phillips JR, Matthews PBC. 1993. Texture perception and afferent coding distorted by cooling the human ulnar nerve. *J. Neurosci.* 13:2332–41

Pons TP, Garraghty PE, Ommaya AK, Kaas JH, Taub E, Mishkin M. 1991. Massive cortical reorganization after sensory deafferentation in adult macaques. *Science* 252:1857–60

Post LJ, Chapman CE. 1991. The effects of cross-modal manipulations of attention on the detection of vibrotactile stimuli in humans. *Somatosens. Mot. Res.* 8:149–57

Price DD. 1988. *Psychological and Neural Mechanisms of Pain*. New York: Raven

Price DD. 1994. Psychophysical measurement of normal and abnormal pain processing. See Boivie et al 1994, pp. 3–25

Price DD, Mao J, Frenk H, Mayer DJ. 1994. The N-methyl-D-aspartate receptor antagonist dextromethorphan selectively reduces temporal summation of second pain in man. *Pain* 59:165–74

Price R. 1994. *A Whole New Life.* New York: Scribner

Ramachandran VS, Rogers-Ramachandran DC, Stewart M. 1992. Perceptual correlates of massive cortical reorganization. *Science* 258:1159–60

Recanzone GH, Merzenich MM, Jenkins WM. 1992. Frequency discrimination training engaging a restricted skin surface results in an emergence of a cutaneous response zone in cortical area 3a. *J. Neurophysiol.* 67:1057–70

Reed CL. 1994. Perceptual dependence for shape and texture during haptic processing. *Perception* 23:349–66

Reed CL, Caselli RJ. 1994. The nature of tactile agnosia: a case study. *Neuropsychologia* 32:527–39

Reed CL, Caselli RJ, Farah MJ. 1996. Tactile agnosia: underlying impairment and implications for normal tactile object recognition. *Brain* 119:875–88

Reed CM, Durlach NI, Delhorne LA. 1992. Natural methods of tactual communication. See Summers 1992, pp. 218–30

Rinker MA, Craig JC. 1994. The effect of spatial orientation on the perception of moving tactile stimuli. *Percept. Psychophys.* 56:356–62

Rollman GB. 1977. Signal detection theory measurement of pain: a review and critique. *Pain* 3:187–211

Rollman GB. 1979. Signal detection theory pain measures: empirical validation studies and adaptation-level effects. *Pain* 6: 9–21

Rollman GB. 1992. Cognitive variables in pain and pain judgments. In *Psychophysical Approaches to Cognition*, ed. D Algom, pp. 515–74. Amsterdam: North Holland

Sathian K, Burton H. 1991. The role of spatially selective attention in the tactile perception of texture. *Percept. Psychophys.* 50:237–48

Sathian K, Goodwin AW, John KT, Darian-Smith I. 1989. Perceived roughness of a grating: correlation with responses of mechanoreceptive afferents innervating the monkey's fingerpad. *J. Neurosci.* 9: 1273–79

Schmidt R, Schmelz M, Forster C, Ringkamp M, Torebjork E, Handwerker H. 1995. Novel classes of responsive and unresponsive C nociceptors in human skin. *J. Neurosci.* 15:333–41

Schmidt RF, Wahren LK. 1990. Multiunit neural responses to strong finger pulp vibration. II. Comparison with tactile sensory thresholds. *Acta Physiol. Scand.* 140: 11–16

Scudds RA, Rollman GB, Harth M, McCain GA. 1987. Pain perception and personality measures as discriminators in the classification of fibrositis. *J. Rheumatol.* 14: 563–69

Sherrick CE. 1991. Vibrotactile pattern perception: some findings and applications. See Heller & Schiff 1991, pp. 189–217

Sherrick CE, Cholewiak RW. 1986. Cutaneous sensitivity. See Boff et al 1986, pp. 1–58

Sherrick CE, Cholewiak RW, Collins AA. 1990. The localization of low- and high-frequency vibrotactile stimuli. *J. Acoust. Soc. Am.* 88:169–79

Shimizu Y, Saida S, Shimura H. 1993. Tactile pattern recognition by graphic display: importance of 3-D information for haptic perception of familiar objects. *Percept. Psychophys.* 53:43–48

Simone DA, Ochoa J. 1991. Early and late effects of prolonged topical capsaicin on cutaneous sensibility and neurogenic vasodilatation in humans. *Pain* 47:285–94

Simone DA, Sorkin LS, Oh U, Chung JM, Owens C, et al. 1991. Neurogenic hyperalgesia: central neural correlates in responses of spinothalmic tract neurons. *J. Neurophysiol.* 66:228–46

Sinclair RJ, Burton H. 1991. Tactile discrimination of gratings: psychophysical and neural correlates in human and monkey. *Somatosens. Mot. Res.* 8:241–48

Srinivasan MA, LaMotte RH. 1995. Tactual discrimination of softness. *J. Neurophysiol.* 73:88–101

Sterr A, Muller MM, Elbert T, Rockstroh B, Pantev C, Taub E. 1998. Changed perceptions in braille readers. *Nature* 391:134–35

Stevens JC. 1989. Temperature and the two-point threshold. *Somatosens. Mot. Res.* 6: 275–84

Stevens JC. 1990. Perceived roughness as a function of body locus. *Percept. Psychophys.* 47:298–304

Stevens JC, Choo KK. 1996. Spatial acuity of the body surface over the life span. *Somatosens. Mot. Res.* 13:153–66

Stevens JC, Choo KK. 1998. Temperature sensitivity of the body surface over the life span. *Somatosens. Mot. Res.* 15:13–28

Stevens JC, Cruz LA. 1996. Spatial acuity of touch: ubiquitous decline with aging revealed by repeated threshold testing. *Somatosens. Mot. Res.* 13:1–10

Stevens JC, Foulke E, Patterson MQ. 1996. Tactile acuity, aging, and braille reading in long-term blindness. *J. Exp. Psychol.: Appl.* 2:91–106

Stevens JC, Patterson MQ. 1995. Dimensions of spatial acuity in the touch sense: changes over the life span. *Somatosens. Mot. Res.* 12:29–47

Stubhaug A, Breivik H, Eide PK, Kreunen M, Foss A. 1997. Mapping of punctuate hyperalgesia around a surgical incision demonstrates that ketamine is a powerful suppressor of central sensitization to pain following surgery. *Acta Anaesthesiol. Scand.* 41:1124–32

Summers IR, ed. 1992. *Tactile Aids for the Hearing Impaired.* London: Whurr

Tan HZ. 1996. *Information transmission with a multi-finger tactual display.* PhD thesis. MIT, Cambridge, MA

Tan HZ, Rabinowitz WM, Durlach NI. 1989. Analysis of a synthetic Tadoma system as a multidimensional tactile display. *J. Acoust. Soc. Am.* 86:981–88

Tillman DB, Treede RD, Meyer RA, Campbell JN. 1995a. Response of C fibre nociceptors in the anaesthetized monkey to heat stimuli: correlation with pain threshold in humans. *J. Physiol.* 485:767–74

Tillman DB, Treede RD, Meyer RA, Campbell JN. 1995b. Response of C fibre nociceptors in the anaesthetized monkey to heat stimuli: estimates of receptor depth and threshold. *J. Physiol.* 485:753–65

Torebjork E. 1994. Nociceptor dynamics in humans. In *Proc. 7th World Congr. on Pain*, ed. GF Gebhart, DL Hammond, TS Jensen, pp. 277–84. Seattle, WA: IASP

Torebjork HE, Lundberg LE, LaMotte RH. 1992. Central changes in processing of mechanoreceptive input in capsaicin-induced secondary hyperalgesia in humans. *J. Physiol.* 448:765–80

Tremblay F, Ageranioti-Belanger SA, Chapman CE. 1996. Cortical mechanisms underlying tactile discrimination in the monkey. 1. Role of primary somatosensory cortex in passive texture discrimination. *J. Neurophysiol.* 76:3382–403

Vallbo AB, Olausson H, Wessberg J, Kakuda N. 1994. Receptive field characteristics of tactile units with myelinated afferents in hairy skin of human subjects. *J. Physiol.* 483:783–95

Van Boven RW, Johnson KO. 1994a. The limit of tactile spatial resolution in humans: grating orientation discrimination at the lip, tongue, and finger. *Neurology* 44: 2361–66

Van Boven RW, Johnson KO. 1994b. A psychophysical study of the mechanisms of sensory recovery following nerve injury in humans. *Brain* 117:149–67

Van Doren CL, Menia LL. 1993. Representing the surface texture of grooved plates using single-channel, electrocutaneous stimulation. See Verrillo 1993, pp. 177–97

Vega-Bermudez F, Johnson KO, Hsiao SS. 1991. Human tactile pattern recognition: active versus passive touch, velocity effects, and patterns of confusion. *J. Neurophysiol.* 65:531–46

Verrillo RT. 1993. The effects of aging on the sense of touch. In *Sensory Research: Multimodal Perspectives*, ed. RT Verrillo, pp. 285–98. Hillsdale, NJ: Erlbaum

Wall PD, Melzack R. 1994. *Textbook of Pain.* Edinburgh, UK: Churchill Livingstone. 3rd ed.

Weisenberger JM. 1992. Communication of the acoustic environment via tactile stimuli. See Summers 1992, pp. 83–109

Whang KC, Burton H, Shulman GL. 1991. Selective attention in vibrotactile tasks: detecting the presence and absence of amplitude change. *Percept. Psychophys.* 50: 157–65

Wilder-Smith OH, Arendt-Nielsen L, Gaumann D, Tassonyi E, Rifat KR. 1998. Sensory changes and pain after abdominal hysterectomy: a comparison of anesthetic supplementation with fentanyl versus magnesium or ketamine. *Anesth. Analg.* 86:95–101

Woodward KL. 1993. The relationship between skin compliance, age, gender, and tactile discriminative thresholds in humans. *Somatosens. Mot. Res.* 10:63–67

Yang TT, Gallen CC, Ramachandran VS, Cobb S, Schwartz BJ, Bloom FE. 1994. Noninvasive detection of cerebral plasticity in adult human somatosensory cortex. *NeuroReport* 5:701–4

Annu. Rev. Psychol. 1999. 50:333–59

PEER RELATIONSHIPS AND SOCIAL COMPETENCE DURING EARLY AND MIDDLE CHILDHOOD

Gary W. Ladd

Departments of Educational Psychology and Psychology, University of Illinois at Urbana-Champaign, Champaign, Illinois 61820; e-mail: g-ladd@uiuc.edu

KEY WORDS: children, social development, friendship, peer acceptance, peer victimization

ABSTRACT

This review demarcates major periods of empirical activity and accomplishment (i.e. "generations") in research on children's peer relations and social competence during recent decades and identifies the investigative agendas that were dominant or ascendant during these periods. A sampling of studies that were conducted during the most recent generation of peer relations research is organized and reviewed in relation to two types of research objectives: (*a*) enduring agendas—aims from past research generations that have continued to serve as an impetus for empirical investigation during the 1990s—and (*b*) *innovative* agendas—newly emergent objectives that are predicated on novel conceptual issues or ongoing research controversies and deficiencies. This profile of continuity and change in investigators' research agendas provides a platform for delineating and analyzing recent empirical accomplishments in the field of peer relations research.

CONTENTS

INTRODUCTION

Scientific interest in children's peer relations can be traced to an assumption that was inherent in many of the theories that guided the social sciences during the twentieth century. Prominent writers, including George H Mead, Sigmund Freud, Erik Erickson, and Jean Piaget, argued that social groups have a significant impact on the individual's development. Extension of this premise to the period of childhood, along with empirical investigaton of children's peer relations, emerged in the 1930s when social scientists began to study the nature of children's peer groups and the association between children's characteristics and their positions in peer groups. Investigations addressed to these topics constituted the first generation of peer relations research (see Renshaw 1981 for a review), and continued until the outbreak of World War II, after which they fell dormant for more than a decade.

Although interest in children's peer relations began to revive in the 1960s (see Sherif et al 1961), the current prominence of the peer relations field within the social sciences grew out of a flurry of investigation that began in the mid-1970s and intensified during the 1980s. This burst of empirical activity, or second generation of research on children's peer relations, was triggered by a series of discoveries that emerged during the late 1960s and early 1970s. Harlow and colleagues (1969) found that young rhesus monkeys who were reared by their mothers but deprived of peer contact failed to develop essential social skills and traversed abnormal developmental trajectories. However, these investigators also showed that play with younger peers could compensate for some of the deficits that were attributable to maternal deprivation (see also Freud & Dann 1951). Together, this evidence suggested that peers played an essential role in the socialization of interpersonal competence and that skills acquired in this manner affected the individual's long-term adjustment. This premise was further strengthened by findings from a series of follow-up and follow-back longitudinal studies that came into print during the same era (e.g. Cowen et al 1973, Roff & Sells 1967). Intending to elucidate the origins of later-life social problems (e.g. delinquency, psychopathology), these investigators gathered data on a range of potential childhood antecedents, including aspects of children's peer relations. Results converged in the sense that poor peer relations during childhood were consistently implicated in the etiology of later deviance.

The implications of this evidence for both basic research (i.e. understanding how agemates influence social development) and applied concerns (i.e. helping children with poor peer relations) shaped the agendas that were pursued by a new cohort of researchers during the second generation of peer relations research, which spanned the 1970s and 1980s. The accomplishments of this period are considered briefly in the next section because these findings became the foundation for the third generation of research on children's peer relations and the impetus for many new research agendas during the 1990s.

SECOND GENERATION (1970s AND 1980s): OVERVIEW OF MAJOR RESEARCH AGENDAS AND ACCOMPLISHMENTS

Investigators in the 1970s and 1980s initially sought to understand how children developed relationships and worked from the assumption that children's social behaviors influenced relationship formation. Accordingly, investigators in this era first attempted to identify aspects of social competence, or behaviors that correlated with relational constructs, such as peer group acceptance, and later conducted complex play group studies to identify the behavioral antecedents of these outcomes. Evidence from this "competence-correlates" strategy supported the conclusion that whereas antisocial and disruptive behaviors were likely causes of poor peer relations (e.g. peer rejection), prosocial behaviors led to positive outcomes, such as peer acceptance (see review by Coie et al 1990). Researchers also examined the behavioral antecedents of children's friendships and found that specific (conversational) skills increased the likelihood that children would become friends with a peer (see Gottman 1983).

By the early 1980s, these correlational findings were supplemented with experimental evidence. Using coaching paradigms, researchers trained children low in acceptance to interact with peers using skills that had been identified as correlates of peer acceptance and compared them to counterparts in control groups. Most of these studies (see Ladd & Mize 1983) showed that only the trained children made gains in peer acceptance, lending support to the hypothesis that the skills had produced improvements in children's peer relations. Overall, evidence from these correlational and experimental studies was interpreted as support for the social skill hypothesis. Social skills were behaviors that appeared to enhance peer acceptance, friendship, or other positive relational outcomes. Conversely, problematic relationships were explained in terms of the skill-deficit hypothesis, which held that peer rejection and friendlessness developed from an absence of social skills, because they either were absent in the child's repertoire or were supplanted by behaviors that fostered negative relational outcomes, such as aggression (i.e. behavioral excess hypothesis).

As support for the social skill hypothesis increased, investigators pursued a second major agenda, which was to determine why some children exhibited social skills in their interactions with peers and other children manifested skill deficits. Two relatively distinct literatures grew from this objective: The first had its origins in early skill acquisition and information processing models (e.g. see Dodge 1986, Ladd & Mize 1983). These paradigms focused investigators' attention on a number of social-cognitive constructs, including aspects of children's interpersonal cognitions (e.g. goals, strategies, outcome expectations, peer attributions) and children's intrapersonal cognitions (e.g. self-perceptions, perceived competence, self-efficacy). Evidence (see reviews by Dodge & Feldman 1990, Ladd & Crick 1989) indicated that children with high versus low peer acceptance tended to construct different types of goals and strategies for peer interactions. Children with low acceptance were more likely to possess instrumental or self-focused goals; devise atypical, ineffectual, or aggressive strategies; and believe that self-centered goals and aggressive strategies would effect positive peer outcomes. Children who were prone to aggress against peers tended to manifest hostile attribution biases—that is, they construed peers' motives toward them as hostile in ambiguous provocation situations. Links were also found between children's social self-perceptions and their behavioral and relational competence among peers. Higher levels of perceived competence and self-efficacy were found among children who were well liked as opposed to disliked by peers and among gregarious as compared with withdrawn children.

Thus, theories about how children acquire skills and process social information offered not only an explanation for variation in children's social skills but also an avenue for explaining the origins of children's relational difficulties with peers. Peer rejection or friendlessness was attributable not only to deficits in behavioral skills but also to the cognitions that might underlie and maintain such deficits, such as misplaced goals or strategies, biased interpretations of peers' motives, and debilitating self-perceptions.

The second line of inquiry into the origins of social competence emerged in the early 1980s. This research was based on the premise that children acquire social skills or manifest skill deficits within early socialization contexts, such as the family. In the models used to guide this research, conceptual distinctions were drawn between direct family influences (e.g. parents' attempts to influence children's peer relations) and indirect influences (i.e. family processes with no direct bearing on children's peer relations, such as parenting, attachment, or child abuse). Research on direct influences (see Parke & Ladd 1992 for reviews) suggested that parents' involvement in the socialization of children's peer relations varied across families, was characteristic of mothers more than fathers, and was differentially associated with children's competence, depending on the parents' practices and the child's age. Mothers' participation in peer play, for example, was linked with interactive and relational competence in very young children but was associated with skill deficits and peer rejection in older children. Children (especially boys) tended to be adept with kindergarten classmates if their parents had arranged peer-play activities before school entrance or had taught them to initiate their own play dates.

Other findings suggested that parents who gave competent advice about peer interaction, supervised play in supportive and developmentally sensitive ways, and provided regular opportunities for peer interaction (e.g. play groups, pre-school) tended to have children who were skillful and successful in their peer relationships.

Evidence of indirect family influences began to accumulate as well (see Parke & Ladd 1992). Children with secure parent-child relationships, as com-pared with those with insecure attachments, were found to be more engaging, affectively positive, and cooperative in their dealings with peers. Aspects of parents' child-rearing and disciplinary styles, such as warmth, agreeableness, and responsiveness, were linked with children's social competence whereas features such as directiveness, disagreeableness, coercion, and permissiveness correlated with skill deficits and behavior problems. Poor social skills and skill deficits were found to be more common among children who were experienc-ing family disruption (e.g. marital discord, divorce) and dysfunction (e.g. pa-rental depression, child abuse).

Also during this era, theory and investigation expanded beyond the goal of understanding the determinants of peer relationships and social competence to address questions about the nature and functions of peer relationships in children's development (see Berndt & Ladd 1989). As part of this third major objective, researchers attempted to differentiate among the types of relation-ships children formed with peers and among the features or psychological re-sources ("provisions") that were made available to children within each form of relationship. Conceptually, arguments were made for distinguishing be-tween friendship and peer acceptance on both structural and psychological grounds. In general, friendship was defined as a voluntary, dyadic form of rela-tionship that often embodied a positive affective tie, whereas peer acceptance was defined as a child's relational status in a peer group, as indicated by the de-gree to which they were liked or disliked by group members (see Bukowski & Hoza 1989). This distinction also focused attention on other premises that emerged in theory and research on children's peer relations during this period, including the contentions that a child's relationships may differ in quality (e.g. different friendships may offer children more or less of particular provisions, such as support; see Bukowski & Hoza 1989) and that relationships may be both specialized in the types of provisions they offer children (i.e. intimacy may be found primarily in friendships) and multifaceted (i.e. both friendships and peer group acceptance may provide companionship; see Furman & Rob-bins 1985).

Early efforts to define the central features of children's peer relationships were focused largely on friendship, and they were guided by conceptual analy-ses of relationships and their social provisions (see Sullivan 1953, Weiss 1974). Several investigators, notably Furman & Buhrmester (1985) and

Berndt & Perry (1986), developed taxonomies of friendship provisions and measures that were designed to tap these dimensions. Although these schemes contained different provisions, as a result of the diversity of theories on which they were based, most included both positive and negative constructs (e.g. intimacy, loyalty, conflict). Early findings suggested that children sought different provisions from parents, teachers, and peers and viewed friendships with peers as an important source for companionship and intimacy (Furman & Buhrmester 1985). Other studies showed that children saw friends as offering higher levels of positive provisions than nonfriends (e.g. acquaintances)—for example, they viewed friends as offering higher levels of attachment, intimacy, or emotional support (e.g. Berndt et al 1986, Berndt & Perry 1986)—but were less likely to make such discriminations for negative properties such as conflict (Berndt & Perry 1986).

By the close of the 1980s, progress toward distinguishing relationship types and identifying relationship provisions provided a new basis for examining the premise that peer relationships contribute to children's development. In a volume devoted to this topic, Berndt & Ladd (1989) concluded that although this premise had been an impetus for peer relations research for many decades, little evidence had accumulated that could confirm or deny this assumption. Exceptions at this stage of the literature included early studies showing that children adapted better when in the presence of friends or familiar peers (see Ladd & Kochenderfer 1996 for a review) and later research (see Bukowski & Hoza 1989, Ladd 1990) indicating that both the quantity of a child's friendships and the quality of those relationships (e.g. variations in support and closeness) predicted changes in children's social perceptions, competence, and adjustment. As evident in the next section, greater empirical strides were made in addressing this agenda during the third generation of peer relations research and, in particular, the question of whether distinct forms of peer relationships, and the provisions they afford, differentially affect children's development.

Advances in theory and evidence about the role of peer relationships in children's development also led investigators to propose more complex models of the determinants of child maladjustment. Rather than attribute maladjustment primarily to child attributes such as deviant behavior patterns (e.g. aggression, withdrawal), investigators also considered relational experiences with peers as potential causes. Emergent frameworks included causal models, in which experiences such as peer rejection were seen as adding to or exacerbating the vulnerability caused by deviant behavior, and incidental models, in which peer rejection was construed as a marker for deviant behavior rather than an additive or moderating contributor to maladjustment (see Parker & Asher 1987). These contentions also shaped the agenda for the third generation of peer relations research.

THIRD GENERATION (1990s AND BEYOND): ADVANCING OLD AND NEW AGENDAS

Major agendas in the third generation of research on children's peer relations and social competence can be parsed into two categories: (*a*) *enduring* agendas—aims from past research generations that continue to serve as an impetus for empirical investigation during the 1990s and (*b*) *innovative* agendas—emergent objectives predicated on novel conceptual issues or ongoing research controversies and deficiencies. This taxonomy provides a context for mapping continuity (e.g. elaborations, extensions) and change in investigators' research agendas and a platform for analyzing contemporary empirical accomplishments during the third generation of peer relations research.

Enduring Agendas and Areas of Investigation

EFFECTS OF CHILDREN'S BEHAVIOR ON THE FORMATION AND MAINTENANCE OF PEER RELATIONSHIPS   Researchers continued to investigate the determinants of children's peer relationships during the 1990s, and they expanded this domain to include a broader range of antecedents/correlates (e.g. behavioral skills or deficits), relationship types (e.g. peer acceptance, friendship), and relationship stages (i.e. formation, maintenance). True to its heritage, this research was grounded largely in extensions of the social skill (deficit) hypothesis and was conducted with methods introduced during the prior generation (e.g. experiments, play group studies, correlational designs).

Peer acceptance/rejection   Evidence from a second wave of correlational, play group, and experimental studies lent support for the established linkage between prosocial behavior and peer acceptance (Dodge et al 1990, Denham & Holt 1993, Mize & Ladd 1990). However, inferences about the role of aggression were qualified by evidence from play group studies (e.g. Dodge et al 1990, Coie et al 1991) showing that certain forms of aggression (e.g. instrumental aggression) were important antecedents of peer rejection throughout grade school, whereas others became pivotal (e.g. angry-reactive aggression) or remained inconsequential (e.g. rough play) as children grew older. Other findings intimated that the behavioral pathways to peer rejection were more diverse than anticipated and implicated a range of deficits (e.g. poor sociability, communicative unresponsiveness; Rubin 1993, Black & Hazen 1990) as well as behavioral excesses (e.g. hyperactivity; Pope et al 1991). Further, subclassification of rejected children based on concurrent behaviors supported similar conclusions: Included among the ranks of peer-rejected children were subgroups with aggressive as well as withdrawn profiles (see Bierman et al 1993, Cillessen et al 1992).

Such findings tempered the prevailing view that aggression was the principal cause of peer rejection and focused greater attention on other behaviors, such as social withdrawal. Drawing on bio/psycho/social frameworks (see Rubin & Asendorpf 1993), researchers further distinguished among withdrawn behaviors and their potential impact on peer relationships. Passive withdrawal was seen as originating from low-approach or avoidance motives that, in turn, limited children's interactions and opportunities to form peer relationships. In contrast, active isolation was deemed more a consequence than a cause of relational difficulties because it resulted from peers' efforts to exclude children from social activities. Findings corroborated the notion that behavioral withdrawal is a multidimensional construct that maps onto children's psychological, temperamental, and motivational attributes and varies by age and social context (e.g. Asendorpf 1991, Rubin 1993). Passive withdrawal was found to predict peer rejection, but only later in childhood when peers were likely to discern such behaviors and judge them deviant (see Rubin 1993). Attempts to further delineate withdrawn subtypes (i.e, unsociable, passive-anxious, active-isolated, sad-depressed; see Harrist et al 1997) have shown that (a) unsociable children suffer higher levels of peer neglect, (b) active isolates incur higher levels of peer rejection, and (c) sad-depressed children become both neglected and rejected by classmates.

This era was also characterized by theoretical debate about factors that might contribute to the stability of peer acceptance and rejection during childhood. Some researchers (see Hymel et al 1990b) argued that emergent peer reputations were sustained by group-psychological processes (e.g. discounting new information) and were thus likely to endure over long periods of time. Others (see Ladd et al 1988) contended that peers were more empirical in their assessments, utilizing information from ongoing interactions to form and revise their feelings about particular children. Although early evidence supported both contentions (see Cillessen et al 1992; Hymel et al 1990b; Ladd et al 1988, Dodge et al 1990), subsequent studies (e.g. Denham & Holt 1993) suggested that behavioral experience tended to shape reputation formation but that once formed, reputations became self-perpetuating.

Friendship   Significant insights into the behavioral antecedents of friendship were also achieved during this era. Particularly noteworthy was a shift from frameworks focused on friendship formation to models that incorporated subsequent relationship developments, such as friendship maintenance or dissolution. This shift was, in part, motivated by evidence indicating that even young children sustain friendships longer than might have been predicted by conventional wisdom or theory (see Berndt & Perry 1986, Howes 1988, Ladd 1990). One such advance resulted from Parker & Seal's (1996) efforts to identify the behavioral correlates of differing friendship trajectories—that is, temporal patterns in children's tendencies to form or sustain friendships (termed rotation, growth, decline, stasis, friendless). Children who rotated through friendships evidenced a blend of positive and negative behaviors, including some that may have attracted friends (e.g. playful teasing, knowing interesting gossip) and others that may have destabilized their relationships (e.g. bossiness, hitting, disclosing secrets). Children on the decline trajectory gradually lost friends, yet their behaviors were relatively prosocial (e.g. caring, sharing) and nonaggressive. These children, the investigators suggested, appeared to jettison friends so as to decrease conflict and enhance intimacy within their networks. Chronically friendless children manifested a behavioral profile that was likely to discourage interaction and subvert relationships. They were socially inhibited and disengaged (e.g. shy, timid), emotionally undercontrolled (easily angered), or self-centered (i.e. less caring, honest).

ORIGINS OF CHILDREN'S SOCIAL SKILLS AND SKILL DEFICITS *Cognitive underpinnings of children's social skills and deficits* Cognitive models, especially those explicating the processes thorough which children encode, interpret, and apply social-behavioral information [i.e. social information processing (SIP) models], remained at the forefront of research on the origins of social skills/deficits during the 1990s and led to important empirical advances.

Reformulation of the Dodge (1986) SIP model (see Crick & Dodge 1994) not only recast the paradigm's theoretical foundations, but also broadened the types of processes (i.e. steps) and subprocesses (i.e. constructs associated with each step) that were included in the model. As a result, much of the research conducted during this decade (and reviewed in this section) can be interpreted in the context of this model. Coverage here is limited to major empirical extensions and innovations.

Considerable research has been conducted on validity issues, including whether the processes specified in SIP frameworks are distinct from other types of cognitive operations and operate in ways that are consistent with their hypothesized functions. Findings reported by Waldman (1996) suggest that a well-documented aspect of interpretive processing (e.g. the tendency for aggressive boys to infer hostile peer intent in ambiguous situations) generalized across boys with differing aggressive profiles and was partially distinct from broader social-perceptual deficits such as inattention and impulsivity. Courtney & Cohen (1996) employed a behavior segmentation procedure that permitted stronger inferences about the source of information that aggressive boys utilize to construct biased intent attributions (i.e. both "on-line" processing of immediate social cues and latent mental structures are implicated in SIP models). Results suggested that in ambiguous peer situations, aggressive boys utilize perceptual input, or information gleaned from on-line mental processing, as a database for the construction of intent attributions. Similarly, new evidence has been gathered to address a debate about whether children construct behavioral responses automatically (mindlessly) by relying on previously formed (latent) behavioral schemes or engage in more conscious, deliberate, reflective styles of problem solving (see Rubin & Krasnor 1986). Rabiner et al (1990) investigated this issue with samples of peer-rejected boys who were either aggressive or nonaggressive in their social interactions. They found that regardless of the boys' aggressive reputations, maladaptive response tendencies were more common when elicited under conditions designed to promote automatic processing. These findings lent credence to the proposition that maladaptive social responses are constructed from information stored in latent mental structures (e.g. dysfunctional schemas or scripts).

Other investigations during this period were aimed at testing hypothesized linkages between social-cognitive processes and children's behavioral competence (e.g. skills, deficits, excesses) and social adjustment. Associations between SIP constructs and aggression remain at the forefront of this work. Hudley & Graham (1993) experimentally demonstrated that it was possible to induce changes in aggressive boys' intent attributions and that improvements in this aspect of interpretational processing were associated with reductions in aggressive behavior. Evidence gathered by Crick & Dodge (1996) suggested that differences in processing patterns may underlie the form of aggression that children utilize with peers. Interpretational biases were more prevalent among children who relied on aggression as an angry, defensive response to provocation (reactive aggression), whereas deviations in goals and response decision processes were more common among children who used aggression as a means to an end (instrumental aggression). Children in the latter category tended to judge aggression and its consequences more favorably and saw it as an effective means for obtaining social goals.

Similar efforts have been undertaken with children who, in addition to being aggressive, are rejected by peers. Rejected-aggressive children, compared to nonaggressive-rejected counterparts, appear to overestimate their social skills, competence, and self-esteem (Hymel et al 1993, Patterson et al 1990) and underestimate the extent to which peers dislike them (Cillessen et al 1992). Zakriski & Coie (1996) have shown that distortions such as these may be attributable to self-protective errors, or biases in the way aggressive-rejected children process peers' rejection feedback.

SIP constructs have also been investigated as determinants of childhood social withdrawal. Harrist et al (1997) found that active isolates, who were withdrawn as well as aggressive toward peers, exhibited processing patterns that were similar to those found for aggressive children (e.g. attributing hostile intent to peers in ambiguous situations). Passive-anxious children, in contrast, were less likely than nonwithdrawn children (controls) to see peers' motives as hostile.

Comparative studies of aggressive versus withdrawn children's social cognitions are rare but emergent in recent literature. Erdley & Asher (1996) found that children whose responses to peer provocation were typified by aggressive, withdrawn, or problem-solving behaviors tended to have social goals and self-efficacy perceptions that were congruent with their behavioral orientations. Whereas aggressive responders exhibited hostile goals and higher efficacy for attaining these goals, withdrawn and problem-solving responders manifested prosocial goals and greater confidence in producing such outcomes. Only withdrawn responders tended to endorse avoidant goals such as evading confrontations.

Socialization of children's social skills and deficits   The premise that family processes influence children's social competence remained an important force in shaping investigative agendas and empirical inquiry during the 1990s (see Parke & Ladd 1992, Parke & Buriel 1998). Researchers interested in direct influences focused primarily on processes such as parents' initiation and supervision of children's informal peer activities. Building on earlier models, Ladd & Hart (1992) proposed that young children learn interpersonal and relationship-management skills during informal peer-play activities. Results showed that the frequency with which parents arranged such activities predicted greater classroom peer acceptance for boys and a propensity for both girls and boys to engage in prosocial skills with classmates. Additional evidence suggested that many parents teach children how to initiate and negotiate peer interaction by mentoring them during the process of arranging informal play dates. Research on parental supervision proceeded from the proposition that highly involved, intrusive forms of supervision inhibit child competence, whereas more indirect supervisory styles enhance child autonomy and skill mastery. Evidence gathered by Mize et al (1995) clarified this linkage by showing that mothers who were less engaged in supervision tended to see their children as skillful, suggesting that the child's manifest competence affected the mother's supervisory involvement rather than visa versa. However, these data also indicated that children who received low-quality supervision tended to be less competent when their mothers had highly involved supervisory styles, suggesting that low-quality supervision may have negative effects on children's social competence if it is applied frequently. It has also become apparent that the form and functions of direct parental influences may change as children mature. Data gathered during middle childhood, where parental monitoring (e.g. awareness of child's whereabouts) becomes a modal method for supervising peer activities, suggest that parents' reliance on this strategy may discourage the development of antisocial behavior and peer rejection (Dishion 1990).

Investigations undertaken to explicate indirect parental influences were more plentiful during this period, and empirical efforts were focused on processes inherent to social learning perspectives (e.g. harsh discipline, coercive cycles, family violence), ethological/affective perspectives (e.g. insecure attachment, lack of warmth/affection), or dispositional typologies (e.g. parenting, disciplinary styles). Coverage here is limited to several prominent agendas, beginning with research on parent-child interaction patterns and children's behavioral and relational competence with peers.

The contention that harsh discipline leads to aggression by encouraging children to develop maladaptive processing patterns received further support; linkages between harsh discipline and antisocial behavior were found to be independent of confounds such as family socioeconomic status (SES) and child temperament and partially mediated by maladaptive social information processing patterns (e.g. Weiss et al 1992). Also substantiated was the premise that children learn oppositional behaviors that generalize to peer relations from coercive parent-child interactions (see Patterson et al 1992); key elements include both parent's power-assertive tactics (Dishion 1990, Hart et al 1990) and children's aggressiveness toward the parent (MacKinnon-Lewis et al 1994). Similarly, children exposed to conflictual marital relations or child abuse were found to be more oppositional in their interactions with peers and less successful at forming friendships (Katz & Gottman 1993, Parker & Herrera 1996). In contrast, aspects of parenting such as emotional expressiveness, responsiveness, and support have been stipulated in a number of frameworks as mechanisms that enable children to acquire skills essential to peer interaction and the development of friendships or peer acceptance (see Parke & Ladd 1992, Parke & Buriel 1998). Advances in this domain include evidence linking children's peer-relational competence with parents' ability to engage children in reciprocally positive interactions (Pettit & Harrist 1993), parents' inductive reasoning (Hart et al 1992, Herrera & Dunn 1997), and parents' emotional and linguistic responsiveness (Black & Logan 1995, Cassidy et al 1992). Investigators have begun to test more complex models by evaluating the combined or relative contributions of multiple parenting processes. McFadyen-Ketchum et al (1996) found that among boys, the combination of maternal coercion and nonaffection predicted gains in aggressiveness over the early grade school years—a result consistent with recent formulations of coercion training theory (Patterson et al 1992). Among girls, however, only coercion predicted changes in aggressiveness over time, and the direction of this trajectory was negative (declining), suggesting that these parenting processes differentially affected boys' and girls' behavior. Similarly, Mize & Pettit (1997) found that a lack of responsiveness in mother-child relationships was associated with boys' aggressiveness but that unresponsive mothers who provided social coaching (i.e. guidance about how to relate with agemates) tended to have sons who were less aggressive toward peers.

Evidence has also accrued, beyond that compiled in the prior generation, as to the role of early parent-child affective processes or attachment relations in the development of children's peer competence and relationships. There is further support for the assertion that the affective tone of parent-child interactions, especially in play with fathers, affects children's social skills and peer relationships. Children who had more reciprocated negative affect with fathers were found to elicit higher levels of negative reciprocity in peer interactions (Fagot 1997) and tended to be avoidant, aggressive, and less prosocial toward peers (Carson & Parke 1996). In contrast, children with positive father-child relations tended to form higher-quality friendships (Youngblade & Belsky 1992). Research in this domain has also been guided by the proposition that attachment quality influences children's emotional and relational competencies (e.g. responsiveness) and internalized representations (i.e. working models) of relationships (see Fagot 1997, Kerns 1994). Prior findings buttressed the notions that attachment security fosters children's relational competence and that insecure ties cause social difficulties. Recent data gathered in the peer context elaborate these linkages by suggesting that children with secure attachments nurture peer relationships by being more responsive and less critical and form ties that are higher in quality, such as friendships that are less negative, more harmonious, and higher in companionship (Kerns et al 1996, Youngblade & Belsky 1992). In contrast, children with insecure attachments appear less competent with peers (Cohn 1990) and more prone to negative peer responses even when they display positive overtures (Fagot 1997). At older ages, children's styles of coping with insecurity were predictive of behavior problems (Finnegan et al 1996): Whereas avoidant coping was associated with externalizing problems, preoccupied coping was linked with internalizing problems. Investigators have also attempted to elucidate the role of children's representations (working models) of relationships. Evidence supports the premise that children's representations of the parent-child relationship generalize to peers (e.g. Cassidy et al 1996, Rudolph et al 1995). Cassidy et al, for example, found that children who tended to see their parents as rejecting were more likely to ascribe hostile intentions to familiar and unfamiliar peers. Evidence gathered by Rudolph et al (1995) also supports the contention that such representations mediate the quality of children's interactional and relationship competencies in the peer context.

TYPES OF PEER RELATIONSHIPS AND RELATIONSHIP FEATURES   *Expanding the taxonomy of peer relationship Types*   From the late 1980s to the 1990s, researchers began to draw more explicit and precise distinctions among peer relationships. The conceptual distinction between peer group acceptance and friendship (see Bukowski & Hoza 1989) was augmented by the addition of peer victimization as another form of relation—one in which children are exposed to abusive processes that promote cognitive-affective states such as insecurity, mistrust, or fearfulness (see Kochenderfer & Ladd 1996). Some investigators (see Elicker et al 1992) have argued that peer victimization is a relationship rather than a child characteristic because it is marked by a unique patterning of interactions that endure over time. Moreover, unlike the constructs of peer acceptance and friendship, which tend to be defined at the level of the peer group or dyad, respectively, peer victimization appears to involve a "limited minority of the peer group—aggressors and their victims" (Perry et al 1988).

Recent aims include exploring the level of concordance that exists among different peer relationships. Investigators have found that many children low in acceptance have friends and that not all highly accepted children have friends (Parker & Asher 1993, Vandell & Hembree 1994). Similarly, peer rejection and victimization appear to be partially nonoverlapping aspects of peer relationships (Perry et al 1988). Convergence across types of peer relationships appears higher for peer group acceptance and number of mutual friendships and for number of friendships and very best friendship (Ladd et al 1997).

Features of peer relationships and linkages with relationship quality and stability   Beyond these structural distinctions, refinements emerged in theory and research on the psychological properties of children's peer relationships. These refinements were particularly evident in the literature on friendships, where terms such as features and qualities had been used interchangably to describe and distinguish friendships on qualitative grounds. Berndt (1996), for example, proposed more precise definitions for the concepts of friendship features, friendship quality, and friendship effects, suggesting that "features" referred to positive or negative characteristics of a friendship (e.g. intimacy, conflict), "quality" denoted an evaluation of the friendship (e.g. satisfaction with a friendship, presence of more positive than negative features in a friendship), and "effects" connoted the influence of friendship on its participants. Ladd & Kochenderfer (1996) further dismantled the notion of "features" into constructs termed friendship "processes" (i.e. observable forms of interaction or exchange, such as validation or conflict) and friendship "provisions" (i.e. putative benefits or costs derived from friendship processes by one or both partners, such as security or support).

Included among the empirical advances of this era were findings that further illuminated the features of friendship during middle and early childhood. With older children, efforts were made to describe and delineate the processes that operate within friendship and the extent to which these processes varied across friendships (e.g. by child, gender) or other types of associative pairings (e.g. acquaintances, nonfriends). Conflict, a process specified within earlier models of friendship (see Furman & Buhrmester 1985, Berndt & Perry 1986), was investigated by Hartup & colleagues (1993) who found that disagreements between friends were more frequent and longer than those of nonfriends, suggesting that friendships provide provisions (e.g. trust, support) that allow partners greater latitude to express disagreements. Parker & Asher (1993) extended prior models of friendship features by developing a multidimensional self-report measure that tapped grade schoolers' perceptions of six friendship processes: validation, help, companionship, intimate exchange, conflict, and conflict resolution. Children's perceptions of these processes varied by gender such that boys characterized their friendships as having less intimate exchange, validation, and help than did girls.

Research with young children produced similar advances. Ladd et al (1996) found that kindergartners reliably distinguished among five friendship processes (validation, aid, disclosure of negative affect, exclusivity, and conflict) and organized their perceptions in a manner consistent with reward-cost principles (e.g. helpful friends were also seen as validating and exclusive). Unlike older children (cf Parker & Asher 1993), young girls and boys did not differ in their perceptions of these friendship processes. Observational studies (e.g. Park et al 1993) extended evidence indicating that young friends are capable of adapting to their partners (Ross & Lollis 1989) by showing that they are also able to elaborate and sustain processes that enhance friendship development and maintenance. Other findings (e.g. Costin & Jones 1992, Slomkowski & Dunn 1996) suggest that because young friends become attuned to each other's emotional states, they are able to coordinate play and offer emotional support when their friends are distressed.

In addition, more has been learned about how friendship processes are linked with outcomes such as relationship satisfaction and stability. Parker & Asher (1993) found that among grade schoolers, friendship satisfaction was positively associated with processes such as validation, companionship, and help but was negatively related to conflict. A similar pattern was found for young children (Ladd et al 1996): Validation and conflict predicted not only friendship satisfaction but also friendship stability. Consistent with reward-cost models, children appear to sustain and feel satisfied in friendships where the ratio of positive to negative processes is maximized. Other findings corroborate earlier evidence linking friendship stability with processes such as conflict resolution. In a study conducted by Whitesell & Harter (1996), data on children's feelings and reactions were gathered in response to an anger-provoking action that was attributed to either a best friend or a nonfriend classmate. Results showed that children's feelings and reactions to the provocation differed for best friends versus nonfriend classmates. Whereas children felt more violated, hurt, and angry with friends than nonfriends, their coping responses toward friends were less blaming and more focused on preserving the relationship. Similarly, Fonzi et al (1997) found that children who sustained friendships were more sensitive to the needs of their partners when negotiating a structured task than were children who failed to maintain their friendships.

Investigators have also sought to determine whether the friendships of children who deviate from interpersonal norms (for social behaviors or reputations) differ from those formed by children within the social mainstream. Available findings suggest that this is the case: Children who are disparate from social norms often lack friends (Parker & Asher 1993), and when they do possess friendships, these relationships tend to be deficient in supportive processes. For example, Parker & Asher (1993) found that children low in peer acceptance reported lower levels of validation, conflict resolution, and help in their friendships than did children whose acceptance was average or high. Similarly, East & Rook (1992) found that socially isolated children perceived their friendships to be less supportive than did children with average or aggressive peer reputations. Among aggressive children, especially those who hurt others through indirect means, friendships appear to be characterized by higher levels of jealousy, exclusivity, and aggressiveness toward partners (Grotpeter & Crick 1996).

CONTRIBUTIONS OF PEER RELATIONSHIPS TO CHILDREN'S DEVELOPMENT AND ADJUSTMENT   In addition to distinguishing among the forms and features of children's peer relationships, researchers have acquired more information about the potential contributions of peer relationships to children's adjustment and development. These issues have traditionally been addressed with separate lines of research focused on different forms of peer relationship, and a number of studies conducted during this era exemplify this trend. Longitudinal studies conducted in the 1990s corroborated earlier evidence indicating that peer rejection is a relatively stable characteristic that predicts both internalizing and externalizing problems as well as absenteeism during the grade school years (e.g. DeRosier et al 1994; Hymel et al 1990a); rejection also predicts grade retention and adjustment difficulties during the transition to middle school (Coie et al 1992). The DeRosier et al findings also show that the severity of children's internalizing and externalizing problems varies as a function of the proximity and chronicity of peer rejection. Past results linking peer rejection with loneliness in middle childhood were replicated with younger samples (Cassidy & Asher 1992), and neglected peer status was found to be a correlate of adaptive outcomes such as achievement motivation (Wentzel & Asher 1995). Friendship and the quality of children's friendships were found to be important predictors of children's emotional well-being (Parker & Asher 1993) and adjustment trajectories during early and middle grade school (Ladd et al 1996). Considerable attention was focused on the potential effects of peer victimization on children's adjustment, and findings link abusive peer relations with a number of adjustment difficulties during childhood, including anxiety, loneliness, depression, and school maladaptation (Boulton & Underwood 1992, Kochenderfer & Ladd 1996).

Recently, this tendency to study peer relationships in isolation has been supplemented with strategies that allow investigators to assess children's participation in multiple forms of relationship and examine the relative (differential) contributions of each relationship to specific adjustment outcomes. Initial efforts to investigate differential relationship contributions focused on friendship and peer acceptance. Although it had been proposed that the provisions children derive from friendship and peer acceptance are both unique and overlapping (see Furman & Robbins 1985), the weight of initial evidence suggests that these relationships contribute uniquely to children's adjustment. Research with adolescents shows that loneliness is more closely linked with friendship than peer acceptance, and feelings of isolation are more closely tied to peer acceptance than friendship (see Bukowski & Hoza 1989). Among grade school children, friendship and peer acceptance have been found to make separate contributions to the prediction of both socioemotional adjustment and academic competence (Parker & Asher 1993, Vandell & Hembree 1994). With young children, Ladd (1990) found that friendship and peer acceptance uniquely predicted changes in kindergartners' school attitudes, avoidance, and performance. These findings are consistent with the hypothesis that friendship offers children provisions that are unique relative to those conferred by peer acceptance—that is, resources that differ in their adaptive value for specific adjustment outcomes. However, in a recent investigation in which a broader range of peer relationships were examined (i.e. friendship, peer acceptance, and peer victimization; Ladd et al 1997), it was found that multiple relational influences played a role in most of the adjustment outcomes examined and that the adaptive significance of particular forms of relationship (i.e. presence of unique versus shared linkages) varied across adjustment domains. Overall, these findings were consistent with the view that peer relationships are specialized in the types of social provisions they offer children but also diverse in the sense that some provisions may be found in more than one form of relationship.

Innovative Agendas and Areas of Investigation

CHILD BEHAVIORS VERSUS PEER RELATIONSHIPS AS POTENTIAL CAUSES OF DEVELOPMENT AND ADJUSTMENT   Propositions that grew out of child by relational context models in the late 1980s, particularly those pitting child behavior against peer relationships as potential contributors to adjustment (i.e. causal versus incidental models; see Parker & Asher 1987), became the impetus for a number of longitudinal investigations during the 1990s. One prominent objective was to examine the relative importance of childhood aggression and peer group rejection as predictors of subsequent adjustment outcomes. The evidence accumulated thus far supports the causal model, suggesting that in addition to aggression, peer rejection increases children's risk for maladjustment. This includes evidence from a short-term longitudinal study (Panak & Garber 1992) in which aggression's contribution to depression was found to be partially mediated by gains in peer rejection. Findings from longer-term longitudinal studies (e.g. Coie et al 1992, Hymel et al 1990a) suggest that both aggression and peer rejection in grade school make unique contributions to maladjustment in early adolescence. In contrast, however, Kupersmidt & Coie (1990) found that the strength of these linkages varied with the type of adjustment outcome examined: Whereas aggression in middle childhood best predicted delinquency in adolescence, both aggression and peer rejection anteceded other types of externalizing problems. Similar results have emerged in studies where these linkages have been examined concurrently (see Boivin & Hymel 1997).

The question of whether the same model holds for other deviant behavior patterns (e.g. withdrawn behavior) has been examined, although not as extensively. Renshaw & Brown (1993) found that withdrawn behavior and low peer acceptance were additively associated (both concurrently and predictively) with loneliness in grade school children. A similar pattern of concurrent linkages was reported by Boivin & Hymel (1997).

AFFECTIVE AND PHYSIOLOGICAL CORRELATES OF CHILDREN'S PEER COMPETENCE AND RELATIONSHIPS   Research on affective and physiological correlates of children's peer competence and relationships moved from a position of relative obscurity during the 1970s and 1980s to a position of prominence in the 1990s. Much of the research that has been conducted in this domain has been guided by frameworks that focus on the interplay of emotional dispositions or temperament (e.g. intensity with which individuals feel emotion), emotional regulation (e.g. modulating internal affective states and processes), and behavioral regulation (i.e. modulating the expression of emotionally driven behavior). Eisenberg & Fabes (1992), for example, contend that children who have difficulty regulating emotions or emotionally driven behaviors are prone to externalizing problems (e.g. aggression) and that this propensity is exacerbated in children who experience their emotions intensely. Thus far, the constructs represented in these models have been investigated individually or in combination, and the results obtained have been largely consistent with expectations. Fox et al (1995) have uncovered patterns of brain activity (asymmetries in left versus right hemispheric activation) that appear to reflect individual differences in children's affective responsivity that, in turn, correspond to sociable versus inhibited behavior patterns. Among several dimensions of early temperament assessed by Caspi et al (1995), one element of behavioral regulation, the inability to modulate impulsive behavior, emerged as a significant predictor of externalizing problems later in childhood. Similarly, Eisenberg et al (1996) found that children who were low in negative emotionality were less prone to externalizing problems and that children's ability to regulate their emotions reduced the effects of negative emotionality on externalizing behavior. The latter contention—that emotional dispositions (e.g. felt intensity) and their effects on behavior are buffered by children's ability to regulate their emotions—received further support in a subsequent study conducted by Eisenberg et al (1997). Linkages like these have also been shown to account for variation in other aspects of children's social competence and peer relations, including social skills, prosocial behavior, and peer acceptance (e.g. Eisenberg et al 1993). In addition, it would appear that forces outside the child, such as relational circumstances and affiliations, may affect the extent to which children regulate their emotions. Fabes et al (1996) found that during peer provocations, young children appeared to be less angry and exert greater control over anger expressions when the provocateur was a liked rather than a disliked peer.

There has also been increasing interest in the social cognitions, behaviors, and peer relationships of children who have chronic emotional problems such as depression. Recent findings link childhood depression with aggressiveness and peer rejection (e.g. Panak & Garber 1992). Depression has also been linked to internalizing tendencies, such as lower levels of assertiveness, and self-blaming attributional patterns (e.g. Quiggle et al 1992). Harrist et al (1997) have shown that among those children who can be classified as behaviorally withdrawn, some manifest low mood states or are comorbid on sad or depressed affect. These children appear no different from normals on measures of social information processing (however, see Quiggle et al 1992), but assessments of their behavior and peer relations suggest that they are self-isolating, timid, immature, and are often classified as rejected or neglected.

ROLE OF SEX/GENDER IN CHILDREN'S PEER RELATIONSHIPS   As illustrated in prior sections, the constructs of sex/gender have been an enduring consideration in the study of children's peer relations. However, rarely have peer relations researchers developed innovative frameworks and lines of investigation related to gender. In fact, because sizable bodies of evidence have been assembled for males on topics such as aggression and peer rejection, some have argued that the resulting literatures constitute a psychology of boys' peer relations. Beginning in the 1990s, this trend began to shift as researchers placed greater emphasis on sex/gender issues, especially the study of girls' peer relations. The prevailing assumption that boys are more aggressive than girls has been contested (see Cairns & Cairns 1994, Crick & Grotpeter 1995) by evidence indicating that girls and boys may express aggressive behavior differently. Aggression in girls, for example, is more likely to be expressed in nonconfrontive (e.g. attempts to damage a peer's reputations or relationships) rather than confrontive forms (e.g. blows, insults directed at peers). Other findings reveal that both direct and relational forms of aggression predict social maladjustment (Crick & Grotpeter 1995, Crick 1996); therefore, girls who engage in nonconfrontive forms of aggression appear to be as much at risk for maladjustment as are boys who exhibit confrontive forms.

Greater attention has been devoted to sex differences in the study of peer rejection. As with boys, it has been possible to identify behavioral subtypes of rejected girls (see French 1990), but the behaviors that distinguish the subtypes (i.e. withdrawal, anxiety, underachievement) are not the same as those that differentiate rejected boys (i.e. aggression), suggesting that the causes or consequences of peer rejection may be different in boys' and girls' peer groups. There is also evidence to suggest that the proximity and chronicity of peer rejection take a greater toll on boys' than girls' adjustment (DeRosier et al 1994), although research of this type has tended to focus on externalizing outcomes, which are more common among boys.

Gender differences have also received further attention in the study of children's friendships. Longitudinal examination in grade schoolers' friendship networks (Parker & Seal 1996) revealed that boys' friendship networks, in contrast to girls', were more likely to become interconnected over time. The investigators suggested that girls may be more likely than boys to winnow network affiliations as a means of managing conflicts and rivalries among members. Other evidence implies that unskilled children, who may be disliked by peers, are more likely to seek friendships among opposite-sex peers. Kovacs et al (1996) found that although neither grade school boys or girls were more likely to have primarily opposite-sex friends, those who did (as compared with children with primarily same-sex friends or friends of both genders) tended to have weaker social skills. However, it may also be the case that play with same-sex peers is a risk factor for some children; Fabes et al (1997) found that for boys (but not girls) who were highly arousable, play among same-sex peers increased the likelihood of behavior problems. Additionally, there is further support for the premise that boys and girls have different relational priorities that shape their interactions and responses to friends or well-liked peers (see Maccoby 1990). In conflicts with friends, Hartup et al (1993) found that girls were more likely than boys to accompany assertive behaviors with rationales, suggesting that girls have greater concern for relationship issues whereas boys have greater concern for mastery and status. Likewise, Whitesell & Harter (1996) found that girls were more likely than boys to judge a friend's misdeeds from a relationship perspective, and Fabes et al (1996) found that boys were more likely than girls to express anger toward well-liked peers—a response that may be motivated by concerns about dominance and competition.

CULTURAL AND ETHNIC SIMILARITIES AND DIFFERENCES IN CHILDREN'S SOCIAL COMPETENCE AND PEER RELATIONSHIPS   A number of developments during the 1990s encouraged investigators to consider whether the current knowledge base was sufficiently broad to permit inferences about children from different ethnic or cultural backgrounds. This agenda gained momentum as it became apparent that even though the study of children's peer relations has become a worldwide endeavor, systematic efforts to explore ethnic and cultural variations have been rare (see Krappman 1996). Recent initiatives include attempts to investigate ethnic and cultural diversity in children's peer relations both within and across national boundaries.

Within North America, investigators have begun to profile the peer relations of majority (typically Euro-American) and minority (typically African-American) children using descriptive and comparative methodologies. Some of this research suggests that minority status, as a risk factor, interacts in complex ways with children's social environments. Kupersmidt et al (1995), for example, found that middle-SES neighborhoods appeared to operate as a protective factor against aggressive behavior for low-income, single-parent African-American children. Schools that enroll children from diverse backgrounds appear to promote ethnically diverse friendship and peer-interaction patterns (e.g. Howes & Wu 1990). Other studies reveal differences between minority and majority groups. Kovacs et al (1996) found that African-American children tend to have more friendships as well as more opposite-sex friendships than do Euro-American children, and they infer that African-American children may be socialized to develop larger networks or may reside in family systems (e.g. extended families) that nurture broader ties. Other findings suggest that children who are members of minority groups are more likely to engage in self-protective, self-esteem-maintaining behaviors. Zakriski & Coie (1996) found that even though both Euro-American and African-American children were more likely to recast peer feedback about themselves in self-enhancing ways, self-protective distortions were more pronounced among African-American children, especially when the feedback was negative.

Cross-national comparisons of children's peer relations are rare, but increasing in number. Fonzi and colleagues (Fonzi et al 1997; Schneider et al 1997) have argued that variations in cultural values may cause differences in the ways children interact and maintain friendships. In support of this contention, they found that friendships tend to be more stable in Italy than in Canada. Likewise, the role of children's social behaviors in determining relationship and adjustment outcomes may also vary by culture. Chen and colleagues (Chen et al 1992, 1995) found that even though aggressive and leadership behaviors predicted similar adjustment outcomes in Canadian and Chinese samples, shy and sensitive behaviors did not. During childhood (but not adolescence), shy, sensitive behaviors and peer acceptance and competence were positively correlated for Chinese children but inversely related for Canadian children.

CONCLUSIONS

This review has demarcated major periods of empirical activity and accomplishment in research on children's peer relations and competence, identified investigative agendas that were dominant or ascendant during these periods, and illustrated continuity and change in these objectives across recent generations of research. It is apparent from this analysis that the discipline's progress across the last two generations has evolved along patterns that are analogous to the Piagetian metaphor of horizontal and vertical development. Some agendas have spurred relatively enduring and penetrating lines of research that, over time, have produced a deeper and elaborated understanding of specific phenomena. This kind of focused, systematic investigation has tended to isolate key principles and mechanisms and expand our understanding of the conditions and contexts under which they apply. Examples of such agendas are investigators' attempts to explicate the behavioral and social-cognitive determinants of children's peer competence and relationships and recent efforts to gauge the specificity or generalizability of these determinants across factors such as gender and context (e.g. cultures). We have learned, for example, that certain behavioral patterns (e.g. aggression, withdrawal) increase children's risk for peer rejection or loss of friendship but that these patterns may be expressed differently in males and females and have stronger or weaker links with relational outcomes depending on the child's age and social-cultural context. Research on peer relationships has matured in a similar way; progressive empirical advances and associated conceptual refinements have yielded a more precise and elaborated understanding of relationship types, features, and effects. Other agendas, in contrast, have had the effect of opening new domains and integrating existing lines of inquiry and thus have broadened the entire discipline. To illustrate, the premise that children's social competence derives from early family socialization processes brought about an interface between peer relations research and a number of empirical traditions in the parenting and family relations fields. These alliances not only expanded dramatically the purview of peer relations research but also led to an infusion and blending of investigative perspectives (constructs, models) and paradigms (designs, measures). Recent initiatives into domains such as affect, brain neurology, temperament, gender, and culture suggest that such cross-disciplinary connections will proliferate and further broaden the field of children's peer relations. Most likely, these developments will produce more complex frameworks, including greater integration of bio-psycho-social perspectives and new agendas that will shape the progress of future research generations within this discipline.

ACKNOWLEDGMENTS

This review was partially supported by National Institutes of Mental Health grants R01-49233 and R02-49233 and written while the author was a Fellow at the Center for Advanced Study in the Behavioral Sciences at Stanford, California. Support from the Spencer Foundation (grant 199400132) is also gratefully acknowledged. I am grateful to Nancy Eisenberg for her comments on an earlier version of this article.

> **Visit the *Annual Reviews* home page at**
> **http://www.AnnualReviews.org.**

Literature Cited

Asendorpf J. 1991. Development of inhibited children's coping with unfamiliarity. *Child Dev.* 62:1460–74

Asher SR, Coie JD, eds. 1990. *Peer Rejection in Childhood.* New York: Cambridge Univ. Press

Berndt TJ. 1996. Exploring the effects of friendship quality on social development. See Bukowski et al 1996, pp. 346–65

Berndt TJ, Hawkins JA, Hoyle SG. 1986. Changes in friendship during a school year: effects on children's and adolescents' impressions of friendship and sharing with friends. *Child Dev.* 57:1284–97

Berndt TJ, Ladd GW. 1989. *Peer Relationships in Child Development.* New York: Wiley

Berndt TJ, Perry TB. 1986. Children's perceptions of friendships as supportive relationships. *Dev. Psychol.* 22:640–48

Bierman KL, Smoot DL, Aumiller K. 1993. Characteristics of aggressive-rejected, aggressive (nonrejected), and rejected (nonaggressive) boys. *Child Dev.* 64:139–51

Black B, Hazen NL. 1990. Social status and patterns of communication in acquainted and unacquainted preschool children. *Dev. Psychol.* 26:379–87

Black B, Logan A. 1995. Links between communication patterns in mother-child, father-child, and child-peer interactions and children's social status. *Child Dev.* 66: 255–71

Boivin M, Hymel S. 1997. Peer experiences and social self-perceptions: a sequential model. *Dev. Psychol.* 33:135–45

Boulton MJ, Underwood K. 1992. Bully/victim problems among middle school children. *Br. J. Ed. Psychol.* 62:73–87

Bukowski WM, Hoza B. 1989. Popularity and friendship: issues in theory, measurement, and outcome. See Berndt & Ladd 1989, pp. 15–45

Bukowski WM, Newcomb AF, Hartup WW, eds. 1996. *The Company They Keep: Friendship in Childhood and Adolescence.* New York: Cambridge Univ. Press

Cairns RB, Cairns BD. 1994. *Lifelines and Risks: Pathways of Youth in Our Time.* Cambridge, UK: Cambridge Univ. Press

Carson JL, Parke RD. 1996. Reciprocal negative affect in parent-child interactions and children's peer competency. *Child Dev.* 67:2217–26

Caspi A, Henry B, McGee RO, Moffitt TE, Silva PA. 1995. Temperamental origins of child and adolescent behavior problems: from age three to fifteen. *Child Dev.* 66: 55–68

Cassidy J, Asher SR. 1992. Loneliness and peer relations in young children. *Child Dev.* 63:350–65

Cassidy J, Kirsh SJ, Scolton KL, Parke RD. 1996. Attachment and representation of relationships. *Dev. Psychol.* 32:892–904

Cassidy J, Parke RD, Butkovsky L, Braungart

JM. 1992. Family-peer connections: the role of emotional expressiveness within the family and children's understanding of emotions. *Child Dev.* 63:603–18

Chen X, Rubin KH, Li Z. 1995. Social functioning and adjustment in Chinese children: a longitudinal study. *Dev. Psychol.* 31:531–39

Chen X, Rubin KH, Sun Y. 1992. Social reputation and peer relationships in Chinese and Canadian children: a cross-cultural study. *Child Dev.* 63:1336–43

Cillessen AH, van Ijzendoorn HW, van Lieshout FM. 1992. Heterogeneity among peer-rejected boys: subtypes and stabilities. *Child Dev.* 63:893–905

Cohn DA. 1990. Child-mother attachment of six-year-olds and social competence at school. *Child Dev.* 61:152–62

Coie JD, Dodge KA, Kupersmidt JB. 1990. Peer group behavior and social status. See Asher & Coie 1990, pp. 17–59

Coie JD, Dodge KA, Terry R, Wright V. 1991. The role of aggression in peer relations: an analysis of aggression episodes in boys' play groups. *Child Dev.* 62:812–26

Coie JD, Lochman JE, Terry R, Hyman C. 1992. Predicting early adolescent disorder from childhood aggression and peer rejection. *J. Consult. Clin. Psychol.* 60: 783–92

Costin SE, Jones DC. 1992. Friendship as a facilitator of emotional responsiveness and prosocial interventions among young children. *Dev. Psychol.* 28:941–47

Courtney ML, Cohen R. 1996. Behavior segmentation by boys as a function of aggressiveness and prior information. *Child Dev.* 67:1034–47

Cowen EL, Pederson A, Babijian H, Izzo L, Trost MA. 1973. Long-term followup of early detected vulnerable children. *J. Consult. Clin. Psychol.* 41:438–46

Crick NR. 1996. The role of overt aggression, relational aggression, and prosocial behavior in the prediction of children's future social adjustment. *Child Dev.* 7:2317–27

Crick NR, Dodge KA. 1994. A review and reformulation of social information-processing mechanisms in children's social adjustment. *Psychol. Bull.* 115:74–101

Crick NR, Dodge KA. 1996. Social information-processing mechanisms in reactive and proactive aggression. *Child Dev.* 67: 993–1002

Crick NR, Grotpeter JK. 1995. Relational aggression, gender, and social-psychological adjustment. *Child Dev.* 66:710–22

Denham SA, Holt RW. 1993. Preschoolers' likeability as cause or consequence of their social behavior. *Dev. Psychol.* 29:271–75

DeRosier ME, Kupersmidt JB, Patterson CJ. 1994. Children's academic and behavioral adjustment as a function of the chronicity and proximity of peer rejection. *Child Dev.* 65:1799–1813

Dishion TJ. 1990. The family ecology of boys' peer relations in middle childhood. *Child Dev.* 61:874–92

Dodge KA. 1986. A social information processing model of social competence in children. See Perlmutter 1986, pp. 77–125

Dodge KA, Coie JD, Pettit GS, Price JM. 1990. Peer status and aggression in boys' groups: developmental and contextual analyses. *Child Dev.* 61:1289–1309

Dodge KA, Feldman E. 1990. Issues in social cognition and sociometric status. See Asher & Coie 1990, pp. 17–59

East PL, Rook KS. 1992. Compensatory patterns of support among children's peer relationships: a test using school friends, nonschool friends, and siblings. *Dev. Psychol.* 28:163–72

Eisenberg N, Fabes RA. 1992. Emotion, regulation, and the development of social competence. In *Review of Personality and Social Psychology. Emotion and Social Behavior,* ed. MS Clark, 14:119–50. Newbury Park, CA: Sage

Eisenberg N, Fabes RA, Bernzweig J, Karbon M, Poulin R, et al. 1993. The relations of emotionality and regulation to preschoolers' social skills and sociometric status. *Child Dev.* 64:1418–38

Eisenberg N, Fabes RA, Guthrie IK, Murphy BC, Maszk P, et al. 1996. The relations of regulation and emotionality to problem behavior in elementary school children. *Dev. Psychopathol.* 8:141–62

Eisenberg N, Guthrie IK, Fabes RA, Reiser M, Murphy BC, et al. 1997. The relations of regulation and emotionality to resiliency and competent social functioning in elementary school children. *Child Dev.* 68: 295–311

Elicker J, Englund M, Sroufe LA. 1992. Predicting peer competence and peer relationships in childhood from early parent-child relationships. See Parke & Ladd 1992, pp. 77–106

Erdley CA, Asher SR. 1996. Children's social goals and self-efficacy perceptions as influences on their responses to ambiguous provocation. *Child Dev.* 67:1329–44

Fabes RA, Eisenberg NA, Smith MC, Murphy BC. 1996. Getting angry at peers: associations with liking of the provocateur. *Child Dev.* 67:942–56

Fabes RA, Shepard SA, Guthrie IK, Martin CL. 1997. Roles of temperamental arousal and gender-segregated play in young children's social adjustment. *Dev. Psychol.* 33: 693–702

Fagot BI. 1997. Attachment, parenting, and peer interactions of toddler children. *Dev. Psychol.* 33:489–99

Finnegan RA, Hodges VE, Perry DG. 1996. Preoccupied and avoidant coping during middle childhood. *Child Dev.* 67:1318–28

Fonzi A, Schneider BH, Tani F, Tomada G. 1997. Predicting children's friendship status from their dyadic interaction in structured situations of potential conflict. *Child Dev.* 68:496–506

Fox NA, Rubin KH, Calkins SD, Marshall TR, Coplan RJ, et al. 1995. Frontal activation asymmetry and social competence at four years of age. *Child Dev.* 66:1770–84

French D. 1990. Heterogeneity of peer rejected girls. *Child Dev.* 61:2028–31

Freud A, Dann S. 1951. An experiment in group upbringing. In *The Psychoanalytic Study of the Child,* ed. RS Eisler, A Freud, H Hartmann, E Kris, 6:127–68. New York: Int. Univ. Press

Furman W, Buhrmester D. 1985. Children's perceptions of the personal relationships in their social networks. *Dev. Psychol.* 21: 1016–21

Furman W, Robbins P. 1985. What's the point? Issues in the selection of treatment objectives. In *Children's Peer Relations: Issues in Assessment and Intervention,* ed. B Schneider, KH Rubin, JE Ledingham, pp. 41–54. New York: Springer-Verlag

Gottman JM. 1983. How children become friends. *Monogr. Soc. Res. Child Dev.* 48: 1–85

Grotpeter J, Crick NR. 1996. Relational aggression, overt aggression, and friendship. *Child Dev.* 67:2328–38

Harlow HF. 1969. Agemate or peer affectional system. In *Advances in the Study of Behavior,* ed. DS Lehrman, RA Hinde, E Shaw, 2:333–83. New York: Academic

Harrist AW, Zaia AF, Bates JE, Dodge KA, Pettit GS. 1997. Subtypes of social withdrawal in early childhood: sociometric status and social-cognitive differences across four years. *Child Dev.* 68:278–94

Hart CH, DeWolf M, Wozniak P, Burts DC. 1992. Maternal and paternal disciplinary styles: relations with preschoolers' playground behavioral orientations and peer status. *Child Dev.* 63:879–92

Hart CH, Ladd GW, Burleson BR. 1990. Children's expectations of the outcomes of social strategies: relations with sociometric status and maternal disciplinary styles. *Child Dev.* 61:127–37

Hartup WW, French DC, Laursen B, Johnston MK, Ogawa JR. 1993. Conflict and friendship relations in middle childhood: behavior in a closed-field situation. *Child Dev.* 64:445–54

Herrera C, Dunn J. 1997. Early experiences with family conflict: implications for arguments with a close friend. *Dev. Psychol.* 33:869–81

Howes C. 1988. Peer interaction of young children. *Monogr. Soc. Res. Child Dev.* 53:1–92

Howes C, Wu F. 1990. Peer interactions and friendships in an ethnically diverse school setting. *Child Dev.* 61:537–41

Hudley C, Graham S. 1993. An attributional intervention to reduce peer-directed aggression among African-American boys. *Child Dev.* 64:124–38

Hymel S, Bowker A, Woody E. 1993. Aggressive versus withdrawn unpopular children: variations in peer and self perceptions in multiple domains. *Child Dev.* 52:171–78

Hymel S, Rubin KH, Rowden L, LeMare L. 1990a. Children's peer relationships: longitudinal prediction of internalizing and externalizing problems from middle to late childhood. *Child Dev.* 61:2004–21

Hymel S, Wagner E, Butler LJ. 1990b. Reputational bias: the view from the peer group. See Asher & Coie 1990, pp. 156–87

Katz LF, Gottman JM. 1993. Patterns of marital conflict predict children's internalizing and externalizing behaviors. *Dev. Psychol.* 29:940–50

Kerns KA. 1994. A longitudinal examination of the links between mother-child attachments and children's friendships in early childhood. *J. Soc. Pers. Relat.* 11:379–81

Kerns KA, Klepac L, Cole AK. 1996. Peer relationships and preadolescents' perceptions of security in the child-mother relationship. *Dev. Psychol.* 1996:457–66

Kochenderfer B, Ladd GW. 1996. Peer victimization: cause or consequence of school maladjustment? *Child Dev.* 67:1305–17

Kovacs DM, Parker JG, Hoffman LW. 1996. Behavioral, affective, and social correlates of involvement in cross-sex friendship in elementary school. *Child Dev.* 67: 2269–86

Krappman L. 1996. Amicitia, drujba, shin-yu, philia, Freundshaft, friendship: on the cultural diversity of a human relationship. See Bukowski et al 1996, pp. 19–40

Kupersmidt JB, Coie JD. 1990. Preadolescent peer status, aggression, and school adjustment as predictors of externalizing problems in adolescence. *Child Dev.* 61: 1350–62

Kupersmidt JB, Griesler PC, DeRosier ME, Patterson CJ, Davis PW. 1995. Childhood aggression and peer relations in the context of family and neighborhood factors. *Child Dev.* 66:360–75

Ladd GW. 1990. Having friends, keeping friends, making friends, and being liked by peers in the classroom: predictors of children's early school adjustment? *Child Dev.* 61:1081–1100

Ladd GW, Crick NR. 1989. Probing the psychological environment: children's cognitions, perceptions, and feelings in the peer culture. In *Advances in Motivation and Achievement*, ed. C Ames, M Maehr, pp. 1–44. Greenwich, CT: JAI

Ladd GW, Hart CH. 1992. Creating informal play opportunities: Are parents and preschooler's initiations related to children's competence with peers? *Dev. Psychol.* 28: 1179–87

Ladd GW, Kochenderfer BJ. 1996. Linkages between friendship and adjustment during early school transitions. See Bukowski et al 1996, pp. 322–45

Ladd GW, Kochenderfer BJ, Coleman CC. 1996. Friendship quality as a predictor of young children's early school adjustment. *Child Dev.* 67:1103–18

Ladd GW, Kochenderfer BJ, Coleman CC. 1997. Classroom peer acceptance, friendship, and victimization: distinct relational systems that contribute uniquely to children's school adjustment? *Child Dev.* 68: 1181–97

Ladd GW, Mize J. 1983. A cognitive-social learning model of social skill training. *Psychol. Rev.* 90:127–57

Ladd GW, Price JM, Hart CH. 1988. Predicting preschoolers' peer status from their playground behaviors. *Child Dev.* 59: 986–92

Maccoby EE. 1990. Gender and relationships. *Am. Psychol.* 45:513–21

MacKinnon-Lewis C, Volling BL, Lamb ME, Dechman K, Rabiner D, Curtner ME. 1994. A cross-contextual analysis of boys' social competence: from family to school. *Dev. Psychol.* 30:325–33

McFadyen-Ketchum SA, Bates JE, Dodge KA, Pettit GS. 1996. Patterns of change in early childhood aggressive-disruptive behavior: gender differences in predictions from early coercive and affectionate mother-child interactions. *Child Dev.* 67: 2417–33

Mize J, Ladd GW. 1990. Toward the development of successful social skill training with preschool children. See Asher & Coie 1990, pp. 338–61

Mize J, Pettit GS. 1997. Mothers' social coaching, mother-child relationship style, and children's peer competence: Is the medium the message? *Child Dev.* 68:312–32

Mize J, Pettit GS, Brown G. 1995. Mothers' supervision of their children's peer play: relations with beliefs, perceptions, and knowledge. *Dev. Psychol.* 31:311–21

Panak WF, Garber J. 1992. Role of aggression, rejection, and attributions in the prediction of aggression in children. *Dev. Psychopathol.* 4:145–65

Park KA, Lay KL, Ramsay R. 1993. Individual differences and developmental changes in preschoolers' friendships. *Dev. Psychol.* 29:264–70

Parke RD, Buriel R. 1998. Socialization in the family: ethnic and ecological perspectives. In *Handbook of Child Psychology*, ed. W Damon, N Eisenberg, 3:463–552. New York: Wiley

Parke RD, Ladd GW. 1992. *Family-Peer Relations: Modes of Linkage*. Hillsdale, NJ: Erlbaum

Parker JG, Asher SR. 1987. Peer relations and later personal adjustment: Are low-accepted children "at risk"? *Psychol. Bull.* 102:357–89

Parker JG, Asher SR. 1993. Friendship and friendship quality in middle childhood: links with peer group acceptance and feelings of loneliness and social dissatisfaction. *Dev. Psychol.* 29:611–21

Parker JG, Herrera C. 1996. Interpersonal processes in friendship: a comparison of abused and nonabused children's experiences. *Dev. Psychol.* 32:1025–38

Parker JG, Seal J. 1996. Forming, losing, renewing, and replacing friendships: applying temporal parameters to the assessment of children's friendship experiences. *Child Dev.* 67:2248–68

Patterson CJ, Kupersmidt JB, Griesler PC. 1990. Children's perceptions of self and of relationships with others as a function of sociometric status. *Child Dev.* 61: 1335–49

Patterson GR, Reid JB, Dishion TJ. 1992. *A Social Interactional Approach, Vol 4: Antisocial Boys*. Eugene, OR: Castalia

Perlmutter M, ed. 1986. *The Minnesota Symposium on Child Psychology, Vol. 18.* Hillsdale: Erlbaum

Perry DG, Kusel SJ, Perry LC. 1988. Victims of peer aggression. *Dev. Psychol.* 24: 807–14

Pettit GS, Harrist AW. 1993. Children's aggressive and socially unskilled behavior with peers: origins in early family relations. In *Children on Playgrounds*, ed. CH Hart, pp. 240–70. Albany, NY: SUNY Press

Pope AW, Bierman KL, Muma GH. 1991. Aggression, hyperactivity, and inattention-immaturity: behavior dimensions associated with peer rejection. *Dev. Psychol.* 27: 663–71

Quiggle NL, Garber J, Panak WF, Dodge KA. 1992. Social information processing in aggressive and depressed children. *Child Dev.* 63:1305–20

Rabiner DL, Lenhart L, Lochman JE. 1990. Automatic versus reflective social problem solving in relation to children's sociometric status. *Dev. Psychol.* 26: 1010–16

Renshaw PD. 1981. The roots of current peer interaction research. In *The Development of Children's Friendships,* ed. SR Asher, JM Gottman, pp. 1–25. New York: Cambridge Univ. Press

Renshaw PD, Brown PJ. 1993. Loneliness in middle childhood: concurrent and longitudinal predictors. *Child Dev.* 64:1271–84

Roff M, Sells SB. 1967. Juvenile delinquency in relation to peer acceptance-rejection and socioeconomic status. *Psychol. Sch.* 5:3–18

Ross HR, Lollis SP. 1989. A social relations analysis of toddler peer relationships. *Child Dev.* 60:1082–91

Rubin KH. 1993. The Waterloo Longitudinal Project: correlates and consequences of social withdrawal from childhood to adolescence. In *Social Withdrawal, Inhibition, and Shyness in Childhood,* ed. KH Rubin, JB Asendorpf, pp. 291–314. Hillsdale, NJ: Erlbaum

Rubin KH, Asendorpf JB. 1993. *Social Withdrawal, Inhibition, and Shyness in Childhood.* Hillsdale, NJ: Erlbaum

Rubin KH, Krasnor L. 1986. Social-cognitive and social behavioral perspectives on problem solving. See Perlmutter 1986, pp. 1–68

Rudolph KD, Hammen C, Burge D. 1995. Cognitive representations of self, family, and peers in school-age children: links with social competence and sociometric status. *Child Dev.* 66:1385–1402

Schneider BH, Fonzi A, Tani F, Tomada G. 1997. A cross-cultural exploration of the stability of children's friendship and the

predictors of their continuation. *Soc. Dev.* In press

Sherif M, Harvey OJ, White BJ, Hood WR, Sherif CW. 1961. *Intergroup Conflict and Cooperation: The Robbers Cave Experiment.* Norman: Univ. Okla. Press

Slomkowski C, Dunn J. 1996. Young children's understanding of other people's beliefs and feelings and their connected communication with friends. *Dev. Psychol.* 32: 442–47

Sullivan HS. 1953. *The Interpersonal Theory of Psychiatry.* New York: Norton

Vandell DL, Hembree SE. 1994. Peer social status and friendship: independent contributors to children's social and academic adjustment. *Merrill-Palmer Q.* 40:461–77

Waldman ID. 1996. Aggressive boys' hostile perceptual and response biases: the role of attention and impulsivity. *Child Dev.* 67: 1015–33

Weiss B, Dodge K, Bates JE, Pettit GS. 1992. Some consequences of early harsh discipline: child aggression and a maladaptive social information processing style. *Child Dev.* 63:1321–35

Weiss R. 1974. The provisions of social relationships. In *Doing Unto Others,* ed. Z Rubin, pp. 17–26. Englewood Cliffs, NJ: Prentice-Hall

Wentzel KR, Asher SR. 1995. The academic lives of neglected, rejected, popular, and controversial children. *Child Dev.* 66: 754–63

Whitesell NR, Harter S. 1996. The interpersonal context of emotion: anger with close friends and classmates. *Child Dev.* 67: 1345–59

Youngblade LM, Belsky J. 1992. Parent-child antecedents of 5-year olds' close friendships: a longitudinal analysis. *Dev. Psychol.* 28:700–13

Zakriski AL, Coie JD. 1996. A comparison of aggressive-rejected and nonaggressive-rejected children's interpretations of self-directed and other-directed rejection. *Child Dev.* 67:1048–70

Annu. Rev. Psychol. 1999. 50:361–86

ORGANIZATIONAL CHANGE AND DEVELOPMENT

Karl E. Weick and Robert E. Quinn

University of Michigan Business School, University of Michigan, Ann Arbor, Michigan 48109; e-mail: karlw@umich.edu; requinn@umich.edu

KEY WORDS: adaptation, learning, intervention, transformation

ABSTRACT

Recent analyses of organizational change suggest a growing concern with the tempo of change, understood as the characteristic rate, rhythm, or pattern of work or activity. Episodic change is contrasted with continuous change on the basis of implied metaphors of organizing, analytic frameworks, ideal organizations, intervention theories, and roles for change agents. Episodic change follows the sequence unfreeze-transition-refreeze, whereas continuous change follows the sequence freeze-rebalance-unfreeze. Conceptualizations of inertia are seen to underlie the choice to view change as episodic or continuous.

CONTENTS

0084-6570/99/0201-0361$08.00

INTRODUCTION

Analyses of organizational change written since the review by Porras & Silvers (1991) suggest that an important emerging contrast in change research is the distinction between change that is episodic, discontinuous, and intermittent and change that is continuous, evolving, and incremental. This contrast is sufficiently pervasive in recent work and sufficiently central in the conceptualization of change that we use it as the framework that organizes this review.

The contrast between episodic and continuous change reflects differences in the perspective of the observer. From a distance (the macro level of analysis), when observers examine the flow of events that constitute organizing, they see what looks like repetitive action, routine, and inertia dotted with occasional episodes of revolutionary change. But a view from closer in (the micro level of analysis) suggests ongoing adaptation and adjustment. Although these adjustments may be small, they also tend to be frequent and continuous across units, which means they are capable of altering structure and strategy. Some observers (e.g. Orlikowski 1996) treat these ongoing adjustments as the essence of organizational change. Others (e.g. Nadler et al 1995) describe these ongoing adjustments as mere incremental variations on the same theme and lump them together into an epoch of convergence during which interdependencies deepen. Convergence is interrupted sporadically by epochs of divergence described by words like revolution, deep change, and transformation.

We pursue this contrast, first by a brief overview of change as a genre of analysis and then by a more detailed comparison of episodic and continuous change using a framework proposed by Dunphy (1996).

CHANGE AS A GENRE OF ORGANIZATIONAL ANALYSIS

The basic tension that underlies many discussions of organizational change is that it would not be necessary if people had done their jobs right in the first place. Planned change is usually triggered by the failure of people to create continuously adaptive organizations (Dunphy 1996). Thus, organizational change routinely occurs in the context of failure of some sort. A typical storyline is "First there were losses, then there was a plan of change, and then there was an implementation, which led to unexpected results" (Czarniawska & Joerges 1996:20).

Representative descriptions of change vary with the level of analysis. At the most general level, "change is a phenomenon of time. It is the way people talk about the event in which something appears to become, or turn into, something else, where the 'something else' is seen as a result or outcome" (Ford & Ford 1994:759). In reference to organizations, change involves difference "in how an organization functions, who its members and leaders are, what form it takes, or how it allocates its resources" (Huber et al 1993:216). From the perspective of organizational development, change is "a set of behavioral science-based theories, values, strategies, and techniques aimed at the planned change of the organizational work setting for the purpose of enhancing individual development and improving organizational performance, through the alteration of organizational members' on-the-job behaviors" (Porras & Robertson 1992:723).

The concepts used to flesh out these definitions have been surprisingly durable over the years. Lewin's (1951) three stages of change—unfreeze, change, and refreeze—continue to be a generic recipe for organizational development. As Hendry (1996) notes, "Scratch any account of creating and managing change and the idea that change is a three-stage process which necessarily begins with a process of unfreezing will not be far below the surface. Indeed it has been said that the whole theory of change is reducible to this one idea of Kurt Lewin's" (p. 624). Lewin's assertion that "you cannot understand a system until you try to change it" (Schein 1996:34) survives in Colville et al's (1993) irony of change: "one rarely fully appreciates or understands a situation until after it has changed" (p. 550). Lewin's concept of resistance to change survives in O'Toole's (1995:159–66) list of 30 causes of resistance to change and in renewed efforts to answer the question, "Just whose view is it that is resisting change?" (Nord & Jermier 1994). The distinction between incremental and radical change first articulated by Watzlawick et al (1974) and Bateson (1972) as the distinction between first- and second-order change continues to guide theory construction and data collection (Roach & Bednar 1997; Bartunek 1993). The rhythms of change (Greiner 1972) continue to be described as periods of convergence marked off from periods of divergence by external jolts (e.g. Bacharach et al 1996). The continuing centrality of these established ideas may suggest a certain torpor in the intellectual life of scholars of change. We think, instead, that this centrality attests to the difficulty of finding patterns when difference is the object of study.

While work within the past 10 years has become theoretically richer and more descriptive, there is a continuing debate about whether change research is developing as a cumulative and falsifiable body of knowledge. Kahn's (1974:487) assessment of organizational change research in the 1970s is cited by Macy & Izumi (1993:237) as a statement that remains relevant: "A few theoretical propositions are repeated without additional data or development; a few bits of homey advice are reiterated without proof or disproof; and a few sturdy empirical observations are quoted with reverence but without refinement or explication." Similar sentiments are found in Woodman (1989), in Golembiewski & Boss (1992), and in the withering popular books on "the change business" titled *The Witch Doctors* (Micklethwait & Wooldridge 1996) and *Dangerous Company* (O'Shea & Madigan 1997). The tone of these critiques is illustrated by the obvious pleasure the authors of *The Witch Doc-*

tors take in their observation that "the reason American businessmen talk about gurus is because they can't spell the word charlatan" (Micklethwait & Wooldridge 1996:11).

Remedies to the above problems are seen to lie in the direction of the following, all coupled with greater efforts to articulate the situated nature of organizational action (e.g. Laurila 1997): (*a*) cross-organizational meta-analysis (e.g. Macy & Izumi 1993), (*b*) cross-organizational interview-surveys (e.g. Huber & Glick 1993), (*c*) simulations that are cross-organizational by virtue of their generality (e.g. Sastry 1997), (*d*) ethnographies (e.g. Katz 1997) and case studies (e.g. Starbuck 1993) that are treated as prototypes, (*e*) reconceptualization of organizational change as institutional change (e.g. Greenwood & Hinings 1996), and (*f*) cross-disciplinary borrowing (e.g. Cheng & Van de Ven 1996). Coupled with efforts to improve the quality of evidence in change research have been parallel efforts to better understand the limitations of inquiry (e.g. Kilduff & Mehra 1997, McKelvey 1997). When these are combined, there appears to be simultaneous improvement of tools and scaling down of the tasks those tools must accomplish.

The sheer sprawl of the change literature is a continuing challenge to investigators who thrive on frameworks (e.g. Mintzberg & Westley 1992). An important recent attempt to impose order on the topic of organizational change is the typology crafted by Van de Ven & Poole (1995). They induced four basic process theories of change, each characterized by a different event sequence and generative mechanism:

1. Life cycle theories have an event sequence of start-up, grow, harvest, terminate, and start-up. They have a generative mechanism of an immanent program or regulation.
2. Teleological theories have an event sequence of envision/set goals, implement goals, dissatisfaction, search/interact, and envision/set goals. They have a generative mechanism of purposeful enactment and social construction.
3. Dialectical theory has an event sequence of thesis/antithesis, conflict, synthesis, and thesis/antithesis. It has a generative mechanism of pluralism, confrontation, and conflict.
4. Evolutionary theory has an event sequence of variation, selection, retention, and variation. It has a generative mechanism of competitive selection and resource scarcity.

These four motors are classified along two dimensions: (*a*) the unit of change, which depicts whether the process focuses on the development of a single organizational entity (life cycle, teleological) or on interactions between two or more entities (evolution, dialectic) and (*b*) the mode of change, which depicts whether the sequence of change events is prescribed by deterministic laws and produces first-order change (life cycle, evolution) or whether the sequence is constructed, emerges as the process unfolds, and generates novel second-order change (dialectic, teleology).

The language of motors is useful because it alerts investigators to missing motors in change theories that aspire to comprehensiveness, it draws attention to mechanisms of interplay among motors and the necessity for balance (Van de Ven & Poole (1995:534), it tempts people to look for a "fifth motor" and other hybrids, and (because the language of motors is a language of process rather than of outcome) it enables investigators to identify what is happening before it has concluded (p. 524). Because the authors propose a detailed list of conditions that must be met if a motor is to operate (Van de Ven & Poole 1995:525, Figure 2), they imply that when change interventions fail, there is a mismatch between the prevailing conditions and the kind of motor activated by the change intervention.

Van de Ven & Poole's review (1995) suggested that mode of change and unit of change were important partitions of the change literature. Our review suggests that tempo of change, defined as "characteristic rate, rhythm, or pattern of work or activity" (Random House 1987:1954), is also a meaningful partition. We explore the contrast between episodic and continuous change by comparing the two forms on five properties that Dunphy (1996:543) suggests are found in any comprehensive theory of change (Table 1). These properties are (a) a basic metaphor of the nature of organization; (b) an analytical framework to understand the organizational change process; (c) an ideal model of an effectively functioning organization that specifies both a direction for change and values to be used in assessing the success of the change intervention (e.g. survival, growth, integrity); (d) an intervention theory that specifies when, where, and how to move the organization closer to the ideal; and (e) a definition of the role of change agent. Because we are building a composite picture using portions of work that may have been designed to answer other questions, readers should treat our placement of specific studies as evocative rather than definitive.

EPISODIC CHANGE

The phrase "episodic change" is used to group together organizational changes that tend to be infrequent, discontinuous, and intentional. The presumption is that episodic change occurs during periods of divergence when organizations are moving away from their equilibrium conditions. Divergence is the result of a growing misalignment between an inertial deep structure and perceived environmental demands. This form of change is labeled "episodic" because it tends to occur in distinct periods during which shifts are precipitated by external events such as technology change or internal events such as change in key personnel.

Table 1   Comparison of episodic and continuous change

	Episodic change	Continuous change
Metaphor of organization	Organizations are inertial and change is infrequent, discontinuous, intentional.	Organizations are emergent and self-organizing, and change is constant, evolving, cumulative.
Analytic framework	Change is an occasional interruption or divergence from equilibrium. It tends to be dramatic and it is driven externally. It is seen as a failure of the organization to adapt its deep structure to a changing environment.	Change is a pattern of endless modifications in work processes and social practice. It is driven by organizational instability and alert reactions to daily contingencies. Numerous small accommodations cumulate and amplify.
	Perspective: macro, distant, global.	Perspective: micro, close, local.
	Emphasis: short-run adaptation.	Emphasis: long-run adaptability.
	Key concepts: inertia, deep structure of interrelated parts, triggering, replacement and substitution, discontinuity, revolution.	Key concepts: recurrent interactions, shifting task authority, response repertoires, emergent patterns, improvisation, translation, learning.
Ideal organization	The ideal organization is capable of continuous adaptation.	The ideal organization is capable of continuous adaptation.
Intervention theory	The necessary change is created by intention. Change is Lewinian: inertial, linear, progressive, goal seeking, motivated by disequilibrium, and requires outsider intervention.	The change is a redirection of what is already under way. Change is Confucian: cyclical, processional, without an end state, equilibrium seeking, eternal.
	1. Unfreeze: disconfirmation of expectations, learning anxiety, provision of psychological safety.	1. Freeze: make sequences visible and show patterns through maps, schemas, and stories.
	2. Transition: cognitive restructuring, semantic redefinition, conceptual enlargement, new standards of judgment.	2. Rebalance: reinterpret, relabel, resequence the patterns to reduce blocks. Use logic of attraction.
	3. Refreeze: create supportive social norms, make change congruent with personality.	3. Unfreeze: resume improvisation, translation, and learning in ways that are more mindful.
Role of change agent	Role: prime mover who creates change.	Role: Sense maker who redirects change.
	Process: focuses on inertia and seeks points of central leverage.	Process: recognizes, makes salient, and reframes current patterns. Shows how intentional change can be made at the margins. Alters meaning by new language, enriched dialogue, and new identity. Unblocks improvisation, translation, and learning.
	Changes meaning systems: speaks differently, communicates alternative schema, reinterprets revolutionary triggers, influences punctuation, builds coordination and commitment.	

Basic Metaphors: Organizing for Episodic Change

The metaphor of organization implied by conceptualizations of episodic change is of a social entity that combines the following characteristics: dense, tightly coupled interdependencies among subunits; efficiency as a core value; a preoccupation with short-run adaptation rather than long-run adaptability; constraints on action in the form of the invisible hand of institutionalization; powerful norms embedded in strong subcultures; and imitation as a major motivation for change. The importance of interdependencies as a precondition for episodic change is found in discussions of alignment (e.g. Pfeffer 1998:Ch. 4), configurations (e.g. Miller 1990), and cultural inertia (e.g. Tushman & O'Reilly 1996). The importance of imitation is reflected in Sevon's (1996) statement that "every theory of organizational change must take into account the fact that leaders of organizations watch one another and adopt what they perceive as successful strategies for growth and organizational structure" (pp. 60–61).

Images of organization that are compatible with episodic change include those built around the ideas of punctuated equilibria, the edge of chaos, and second-order change. The image of an organization built around the idea of a punctuated equilibrium (Tushman & Romanelli 1985) depicts organizations as sets of interdependencies that converge and tighten during a period of relative equilibrium, often at the expense of continued adaptation to environmental changes. As adaptation lags, effectiveness decreases, pressures for change increase, and a revolutionary period is entered. As these pressures continue to increase, they may result in an episode of fundamental change in activity patterns and personnel, which then becomes the basis for a new equilibrium period. Apple Computer illustrated a series of discontinuous changes in strategy, structure, and culture as it moved from the leadership of Steve Jobs through that of John Sculley, Michael Spindler, Gil Amelio, and back to Jobs (Tushman & O'Reilly 1996). Romanelli & Tushman (1994) found this pattern of discontinuous episodic change when they examined changes in the activity domains of strategy, structure, and power distribution for 25 minicomputer producers founded between 1967 and 1969. Changes in these three domains were clustered, as would be predicted from a punctuated change model, rather than dispersed, as would be predicted from a model of incremental changes that accumulate.

The image of an organization built around the idea of operating at "the edge of chaos" (McDaniel 1997, Stacey 1995) depicts the organization as a set of simple elements tied together by complex relationships involving nonlinear feedback (Arthur 1995). An important property of nonlinear systems is bounded instability or what is referred to as the edge of chaos. Here a system has developed both negative and positive feedback loops and is hence simultaneously capable of stability and instability. Behavior at the edge of chaos is paradoxical because the system moves autonomously back and forth between stability and instability. Applied to organizations, Cheng & Van de Ven (1996), for example, show that biomedical innovation processes are nonlinear systems that move episodically from stages of chaos to greater order within a larger context containing random processes. Browning et al (1995) show how the unprecedented successful alliance called Sematech emerged from a set of small, discrete events that occurred at a point of irreversible disequilibrium when the entire US semiconductor industry was about to collapse.

The image of an organization built around the idea of second-order change in frames of reference depicts the organization as a site where shared beliefs operate in the service of coordinated action (Langfield-Smith 1992, Bougon 1992). These shared frames of reference may be "bent" when first-order changes produce minor alterations in current beliefs or "broken" when second-order changes replace one belief system with another (Dunbar et al 1996). First-order change is illustrated by a shift of culture at British Rail from a production-led bureaucracy to a market-led bureaucracy (the firm remained a top-down bureaucracy). Second-order change is illustrated by the later culture shift at British Rail from a market-led bureaucracy to a network-partnership culture in which power was distributed rather than concentrated (Bate 1990). Second-order change is episodic change and "refers to changes in cognitive frameworks underlying the organization's activities, changes in the deep structure or shared schemata that generate and give meaning to these activities" (Bartunek & Moch 1994:24). Recently, it has been proposed that there exists a third order of change that basically questions the adequacy of schemas themselves and argues for direct exposure to the "ground for conceptual understanding" in the form of music, painting, dance, poetry, or mystical experience. Organizational change thus gains intellectual power through alignment with aesthetics (e.g. Sandelands 1998). Examples of third-order change are found in the work of Torbert (1994), Nielsen & Bartunek (1996), Mirvis (1997), Olson (1990), and Austin (1997).

In each of these three images, organizational action builds toward an episode of change when preexisting interdependencies, patterns of feedback, or mindsets produce inertia.

Analytic Framework: The Episodic Change Process

Episodic change tends to be infrequent, slower because of its wide scope, less complete because it is seldom fully implemented, more strategic in its content, more deliberate and formal than emergent change, more disruptive because programs are replaced rather than altered, and initiated at higher levels in the organization (Mintzberg & Westley 1992). The time interval between episodes of discontinuous change is determined by the amount of time organizations expend in other stages of organizational development. If, for example, the stages of organizational change are labeled development, stability, adaptation, struggle, and revolution (Mintzberg & Westley 1992), then episodic change is contemplated when adaptation begins to lag. It takes provisional form as organizations struggle to confront problems and experiment with solutions, and it produces actual shifts in systems during the stage of revolution. The frequency of revolutions and episodic change depends on the time spent in the four prior stages, which varies enormously. This temporal variation in processes building up to revolution is the reason why this form of change is best described as episodic, aperiodic, infrequent.

Three important processes in this depiction of episodes are inertia, the triggering of change, and replacement. Inertia, defined as an "inability for organizations to change as rapidly as the environment" (Pfeffer 1997:163), takes a variety of forms. Whether the inability is attributed to deep structure (Gersick 1991), first-order change (Bartunek 1993), routines (Gioia 1992), success-induced blind spots (Miller 1993), top management tenure (Virany et al 1992), identity maintenance (Sevon 1996), culture (Harrison & Carroll 1991), complacency (Kotter 1996), or technology (Tushman & Rosenkopf 1992), inertia is a central feature of the analytic framework associated with episodic change. Romanelli & Tushman (1994) are representative when they argue that it takes a revolution to alter "a system of interrelated organizational parts that is maintained by mutual dependencies among the parts and with competitive, regulatory, and technological systems outside the organization that reinforce the legitimacy of managerial choices that produced the parts" (p. 1144). Because interrelations are dense and tight, it takes larger interventions to realign them. An example of processes of inertia is Miller's research (1993, 1994) demonstrating that inertia is often the unintended consequence of successful performance. Successful organizations discard practices, people, and structures regarded as peripheral to success and grow more inattentive to signals that suggest the need for change, more insular and sluggish in adaptation, and more immoderate in their processes, tending toward extremes of risk-taking or conservatism. These changes simplify the organization, sacrifice adaptability, and increase inertia.

Although inertia creates the tension that precedes episodic change, the actual triggers of change come from at least five sources: the environment, performance, characteristics of top managers, structure, and strategy (Huber et al 1993). Huber et al found that all five were associated with internal and external changes, but in ways specific to the kind of change being examined (ten specific changes were measured; see Huber et al 1993:223). For example, consistent with Romanelli & Tushman's data, Huber et al found that downturns in growth (a potential revolutionary period) were positively related to externally focused changes and to changes in organizational form. Interestingly, upturns in growth were also positively related to externally focused changes, a finding interpreted to suggest that "desirable but risky changes might be held in abeyance until performance improves" (Huber et al 1993:230).

A final property of the analytic framework associated with episodic change is that it often assumes that change occurs through replacement (Ford & Backoff 1988, Ford & Ford 1994). The idea of replacement is that "one entity sequentially takes the place of or substitutes for a second. The first identity does not *become* the second but is substituted for it. . . . [T]he change process becomes a sequence of events in which a person (a) determines or defines what currently exists (what is A), (b) determines or defines its replacement (Not-A), (c) engages in action to remove what is currently there, and (d) implants its replacement" (Ford & Ford 1994:773, 775). Beer et al (1990) demonstrate that replacement of one program with another seldom works. The problem with such a logic is that it restricts change to either-or thinking. The only way to prevent A is to apply its reciprocal or a counterbalance or its opposite, which precludes the possible diagnosis that both A and not-A may be the problem. For example, authoritarian decision making may be counterbalanced by mandating that decisions be made at lower levels (Roach & Bednar 1997). However, this change is simply authoritarian decision-abdication, which means that authoritarian control from the top persists. As lower-level managers try harder to guess what the right decisions are (i.e. those decisions top management would have made) and err in doing so, the mandate is reaffirmed more forcefully, which worsens performance even more and creates a vicious circle. What was really intended was the creation of expectations of individual autonomy that allowed decisions to be made at the level where the expertise and information are lodged.

In conclusion, the basic analytical framework involving episodic change assumes in part that inertia is a force to contend with. When inertia builds, some trigger usually precipitates an episode of replacement. To understand episodic change is to think carefully about inertia, triggers, and replacements.

Ideal Episodic Organizations

There is no one "ideal model of an effectively functioning organization" that suggests directions for episodic change and values to be used in judging the success of an episodic change intervention (e.g. survival, growth). This is so for the simple reason that episodic change is a generic description applicable across diverse organizational forms and values. There is no direct parallel in the case of episodic change for Dunphy's (1996) assertion that the ideal model of an effectively functioning sociotechnical system is "a representative democratic community composed of semi-autonomous work groups with the ability to learn continuously through participative action research" (p. 543). If organizational change generally occurs in the context of failures to adapt, then the ideal organization is one that continuously adapts. And this holds true whether the focus is episodic or continuous change. The ideal in both cases would resemble the successful self-organizing firms that Brown & Eisenhardt (1997) found in the computer industry. Successful firms did not rely on either a purely mechanistic or purely organic process and structure. Instead, successful firms had well-defined managerial responsibilities and clear project priorities while also allowing the design processes to be highly flexible, improvisational, and continuously changing. Successful firms also had richly connected communication systems, including informal and electronic grapevines, and a very high value on cross-project communication. Two important features that encouraged both episodic and continuous change were (*a*) semistructures poised between order and disorder with only some features being prescribed and (*b*) intentional links in time between present projects and future probes to reduce discontinuity and preserve direction. The authors interpret this pattern as an instance of bounded instability and argue that it may be more motivating, more attuned to sense-making in a fast-changing environment, and more flexible (as a result of capabilities for improvisation) than patterns that are pure instances of either mechanistic or organic systems.

A more generic ideal, suited for both episodic and continuous-change interventions, is found in Burgelman's (1991) attempt to show how organizations adapt by a mixture of continuous strategic initiatives that are within the scope of the current strategy (induced processes) and additional episodic initiatives that are outside the current strategy (autonomous processes). An ideal model framed more in terms of management practices is Pfeffer's (1998) description of seven "high performance management practices" that produce innovation and productivity, are difficult to copy, and lead to sustained profitability. These practices are employment security, selective hiring, self-managed teams and decentralization, extensive training, reduction of status differences, sharing of information, and high and contingent compensation.

Intervention Theory in Episodic Change

Episodic change tends to be dramatic change, as Lewin made clear: "To break open the shell of complacency and self-righteousness it is sometimes necessary to bring about deliberately an emotional stir-up" (Lewin 1951, quoted in Marshak 1993:400). While strong emotions may provide "major sources of energy for revolutionary change" (Gersick 1991), they may also constrain cognition and performance in ways analogous to those of stress (Barr & Huff 1997, Driskell & Salas 1996).

Because episodic change requires both equilibrium breaking and transitioning to a newly created equilibrium, it is most closely associated with planned, intentional change. Intentional change occurs when "a change agent deliberately and consciously sets out to establish conditions and circumstances that are different from what they are now and then accomplishes that through some set or series of actions and interventions either singularly or in collaboration with other people" (Ford & Ford 1995:543). And this is where Lewin comes into his own.

Lewin's ideas remain central to episodic change because they assume that inertia in the form of a quasi-stationary equilibrium is the main impediment to change (Schein 1996). Lewin's insight was that an equilibrium would change more easily if restraining forces such as personal defenses, group norms, or organizational culture were unfrozen. Schein's (1996) work suggests that unfreezing basically involves three processes: (a) disconfirmation of expectations, (b) induction of learning anxiety if the disconfirming data are accepted as valid and relevant (we fear that "if we admit to ourselves and others that something is wrong or imperfect, we will lose our effectiveness, our self-esteem, and maybe even our identity," p. 29), and (c) provision of psychological safety that converts anxiety into motivation to change.

Schein's (1996) work also suggests an updated understanding of what happens after unfreezing. Change occurs through cognitive restructuring in which words are redefined to mean something other than had been assumed, concepts are interpreted more broadly, or new standards of judgment and evaluation are learned. Thus, when Lewin persuaded housewives during World War II to serve kidneys and liver, he cognitively redefined their standards of what was acceptable meat by means of a process that mixed together identification with positive role models, insight, and trial-and-error learning. When unfreezing occurs and people are motivated to learn something, they tend to be especially attentive to ideas that are in circulation, a mechanism discussed later as "translation." Refreezing that embeds the new behavior and forestalls relapse is most likely to occur when the behavior fits both the personality of the target and the relational expectations of the target's social network.

Lewin also remains relevant to episodic change because his other five assumptions about change are compatible with its analytical framework. These five assumptions (Marshak 1993) are (a) linear assumption (movement is from one state to another in a forward direction through time); (b) progressive assumption (movement is from a lesser state to a better state); (c) goal assumption (movement is toward a specific end state); (d) disequilibrium assumption (movement requires disequilibrium); and (e) separateness assumption (movement is planned and managed by people apart from the system). Summarized in this form, Lewin's change model resembles "Newtonian physics where movement results from the application of a set of forces on an object" (Marshak 1993:412). Complexity theory is the least "Newtonian" of the several formulations associated with episodic change, and its continued development may broaden our understanding of episodic interventions. For example, complexity theory implies that improved performance may at times be linked to the surrender of control, which is a very different image from one of attacking inertia through coercive means (e.g. Dunphy & Stace 1988).

Newer analyses relevant to episodic change suggest how difficult it is to unfreeze patterns but also that attempts at unfreezing start earlier than was previously thought. Both conclusions are the result of microlevel research on smoking cessation and weight loss by Prochaska and his colleagues (Grimley et al 1994, Prochaska et al 1992). They propose that when people are exposed to change interventions, they are at one of four stages: precontemplation, contemplation, action, and maintenance. Precontemplators are unaware of any need to change, whereas contemplators are aware that there is a problem and they are thinking about change but have not yet made a commitment. People can remain in the contemplation stage for long periods, up to two years in the case of smokers. Action, the stage most change agents equate with change, is the stage in which people actually alter their behaviors. In any change intervention, few people are in the action stage. In smoking cessation programs, for example, empirical findings suggest that only 15% of the smokers in any given worksite are ready for action.

The important result, in the context of episodic change, is the finding that most people who reach the action stage relapse and change back to previous habits three or four times before they maintain the newer sequence. Beer et al (1990:50) found several false starts in renewal efforts at General Products. This suggests that change is not a linear movement through the four stages but a spiral pattern of contemplation, action, and relapse and then successive returns to contemplation, action, and relapse before entering the maintenance and then termination stages. Relapse should be more common in discrete episodic change than in cumulative continuous change because larger changes are involved. What is interesting is that 85% of the relapsers return to the stage of contemplation, not to the stage of precontemplation. This means that they are closer to taking action again following relapse than change agents suspected. The fact that change passes through a contemplation stage also means that people are changing before we can observe any alterations in their behavior. This suggests that interventions may have value even when no action is observed.

Role of Change Agent in Episodic Change

The role of the change agent in episodic change is that of prime mover who creates change. Macy & Izumi (1993:245–50) list 60 work design changes made by prime movers in North American interventions. The steps by which people enact the role of prime mover (e.g. Kotter 1996, Nadler 1998) look pretty much the same. What is different in newer work is the demonstration that one can be a prime mover on a larger scale than in the past (Weisbord 1987). Many practitioners are focusing on larger gatherings (Axelrod 1992,

Dannemiller & Jacobs 1992) with more issues on the table for immediate action (e.g. Ashkenas & Jick 1992), concentrated in shorter periods of time (Torbert 1994). Large-scale change in very large groups is counterintuitive, since size and participation tend to be negatively related (e.g. Pasmore & Fagans 1992, Gilmore & Barnett 1992). Normally, large group settings induce stereotyping, decreased ownership of ideas, increased abstraction, and less willingness to express unique thoughts. The challenge for prime movers is to neutralize these tendencies. To do so requires that they abandon several traditional organizational development (OD) assumptions. Large-scale interventions rely less on action theory and discrepancy theory and more on systems theory; less on closely held, internal data generation and more on gathering data from the environment and sharing it widely; less on slow downward cascades and more on real-time analysis and decision making; less on individual unit learning and more on learning about the whole organization; less on being senior management driven and more on a mixed model of being driven by both senior management and the organization; less consultant centered and more participant centered; less incremental and more fundamental in terms of the depth of change (Bunker & Alban 1992).

There has also been an increasingly refined understanding of specific ways in which change agents can be effective prime movers. As Rorty (1989) observed, "a talent for speaking differently rather than for arguing well, is the chief instrument of cultural change" (p. 7). Language interventions are becoming a crucial means for agents to create change (e.g. Bate 1990, O'Connor 1995). Bartunek (1993) argues that to produce second-order change in a preexisting shared schema requires a strong alternative schema, presented clearly and persistently. Barrett et al (1995) demonstrate that changes symbolizing a successful revolution are basically interpretations that point to a new alignment of the triggers that initiated the revolutionary period.

Wilkof et al (1995) report on their attempt to intervene in the relationships between two companies in a difficult partnership. Their initial attempts to improve cooperation focused on feeding back problems from a traditional data collection. This failed and led to the discovery that although there were technical or structural solutions available, the actors could not agree because of a vast difference in cultural lenses and diametrically opposed interpretations of meaning. The consultant, therefore, changed her strategy. She began meeting independently with the actors from each organization. In the meetings she would meet each condemnation not with data or argument but with an alternative interpretation from the cultural lens of the other company. She calls the process "cultural consciousness raising." The authors underscore the importance of working with actors to interpret the actions of others not as technical incompetence but as behaviors that are consistent with a particular cultural purpose, meaning, and history.

CONTINUOUS CHANGE

The phrase "continuous change" is used to group together organizational changes that tend to be ongoing, evolving, and cumulative. A common presumption is that change is emergent, meaning that it is "the realization of a new pattern of organizing in the absence of explicit a priori intentions" (Orlikowski 1996:65). Change is described as situated and grounded in continuing updates of work processes (Brown & Duguid 1991) and social practices (Tsoukas 1996). Researchers focus on "accommodations to and experiments with the everyday contingencies, breakdowns, exceptions, opportunities, and unintended consequences" (Orlikowski 1996:65). As these accommodations "are repeated, shared, amplified, and sustained, they can, over time, produce perceptible and striking organizational changes" (p. 89). The distinctive quality of continuous change is the idea that small continuous adjustments, created simultaneously across units, can cumulate and create substantial change. That scenario presumes tightly coupled interdependencies. When interdependencies loosen, these same continuous adjustments, now confined to smaller units, remain important as pockets of innovation that may prove appropriate in future environments.

Basic Metaphors: Organizing for Continuous Change

The metaphor of organization that is implicit in conceptualizations of continuous change is not the reciprocal of metaphors associated with episodic change. The dynamics are different, as would be expected from a shift to a more micro perspective and to the assumption that everything changes all the time (Ford & Ford 1994). From closer in, the view of organization associated with continuous change is built around recurrent interactions as the feedstock of organizing, authority tied to tasks rather than positions, shifts in authority as tasks shift, continuing development of response repertoires, systems that are self-organizing rather than fixed, ongoing redefinition of job descriptions, mindful construction of responses in the moment rather than mindless application of past responses embedded in routines (Wheatley 1992:90), and acceptance of change as a constant. Although these properties may seem prescriptive rather than descriptive and better suited to describe the "ideal organization" than the "basic metaphor," they are straightforward outcomes when people act as if change is continuous, organizing constitutes organization, and stability is an accomplishment.

Images of organization that are compatible with continuous change include those built around the ideas of improvisation, translation, and learning. The image of organization built around improvisation is one in which variable inputs to self-organizing groups of actors induce continuing modification of work practices and ways of relating. This image is represented by the statement that change "is often realized through the ongoing variations which emerge frequently, even imperceptibly, in the slippages and improvisations of everyday activity" (Orlikowski 1996:88–89). Improvisation is said to occur when "the time gap between these events [of planning and implementation] narrows so that in the limit, composition converges with execution. The more improvisational an act, the narrower the time gap between composing and performing, designing and producing, or planning and implementing" (Moorman & Miner 1998a). Empirically, Moorman & Miner (1998b) found that improvisation often replaced the use of standard procedures in new product development and, in the presence of developed organizational memory, had positive effects on design effectiveness and on cost savings. Orlikowski (1996), in her study of changes in an incident tracking system, found repeated improvisation in work practices that then led to restructuring. Similar descriptions are found in Crossan et al (1996), Brown & Eisenhardt (1997), and Weick (1993).

The image of organization built around the idea of translation is one of a setting where there is continuous adoption and editing (Sahlin-Andersson 1996) of ideas that bypass the apparatus of planned change and have their impact through a combination of fit with purposes at hand, institutional salience, and chance. The idea that change is a continuous process of translation derives from an extended gloss (Czarniawska & Sevon 1996) of Latour's observation that "the spread in time and place of anything—claims, orders, artefacts, goods—is in the hands of people; each of these people may act in many different ways, letting the token drop, or modifying it, or deflecting it, or betraying it or adding to it, or appropriating it" (Latour 1986:267). The controlling image is the travel of ideas and what happens when ideas are turned into new actions in new localities (Czarniawska & Joerges 1996). Translation is not a synonym for diffusion. The differences are crucial. The impetus for the spread of ideas does not lie with the persuasiveness of the originator of the idea. Instead, the impetus comes from imitators and from their conception of the situation, their self-identity and others' identity, and their analogical reasoning (Sevon 1996). The first actor in the chain is no more important than the last; ideas do not move from more saturated to less saturated environments; it is impossible to know when the process concludes, since all ideas are in the air all the time and are implemented depending on the purpose at hand (Czarniawska & Joerges 1996). A match between a purpose and an idea does not depend on inherent properties of the idea. Instead, it is assumed that "most ideas can be proven to fit most problems, assuming good will, creativity, and a tendency to consensus" (p. 25). Thus, the act of translation creates the match.

The image of organization built around the idea of learning is one of a setting where work and activity are defined by repertoires of actions and knowledge and where learning itself is defined as "a change in an organization's response repertoire" (Sitkin et al 1998). What this adds to the understanding of continuous change is the idea that it is a range of skills and knowledge that is altered rather than a specific action, as well as the idea that a change is not just substitution but could also include strengthening existing skills. A change in repertoire is also a change in the potential for action, which means action may not be manifest at the time of learning (Pye 1994). To specify learning in terms of a response repertoire is also to specify a mechanism by which change is retained (Moorman & Miner 1997). Other retention-learning mechanisms discussed in the literature include organizational routines (March 1994), know-how embedded in communities of practice (Brown & Duguid 1991), distributed memory (Wegner 1987), distributed information processing systems (Tsoukas 1996), structures of collective mind (Weick & Roberts 1993), and organizational memory (Walsh & Ungson 1991). Summaries of recent work on organizational learning can be found in Huber (1991), Miller (1996), Easterby-Smith (1997), Mirvis (1996), and Lundberg (1989).

In each of these three images, organizations produce continuous change by means of repeated acts of improvisation involving simultaneous composition and execution, repeated acts of translation that convert ideas into useful artifacts that fit purposes at hand, or repeated acts of learning that enlarge, strengthen, or shrink the repertoire of responses.

Analytic Framework: The Continuous Change Process

The following description summarizes the analytic framework of continuous change:

> Each variation of a given form is not an abrupt or discrete event, neither is it, by itself discontinuous. Rather, through a series of ongoing and situated accommodations, adaptations, and alterations (that draw on previous variations and mediate future ones), sufficient modifications may be enacted over time that fundamental changes are achieved. There is no deliberate orchestration of change here, no technological inevitability, no dramatic discontinuity, just recurrent and reciprocal variations in practice over time. Each shift in practice creates the conditions for further breakdowns, unanticipated outcomes, and innovations, which in turn are met with more variations. Such variations are ongoing; there is no beginning or end point in this change process. (Orlikowski 1996:66)

Implicit in that description are several important processes, including change through ongoing variations in practice, cumulation of variations, continuity in place of dramatic discontinuity, continuous disequilibrium as variations beget variations, and no beginning or end point. What is less prominent in this description are key properties of episodic change, such as inertia, triggers, and replacement. Continuous change could be viewed as a series of fast mini-episodes of change, in which case inertia might take the form of tendencies to normalization (Vaughan 1996) or competency traps (Levinthal & March

1993). Triggers to change might take the form of temporal milestones (Gersick 1989, 1994) or dissonance between beliefs and actions (Inkpen & Crossan 1995). Replacements might take the form of substituting expert practices for practices of novices (Klein 1998). But the more central issues in the case of continuous change are those of continuity and scale.

Issues of continuity are associated with the concept of organizational culture (Trice & Beyer 1993). Culture is important in continuous change because it holds the multiple changes together, gives legitimacy to nonconforming actions that improve adaptation and adaptability (Kotter & Heskett 1992), and embeds the know-how of adaptation into norms and values (O'Reilly & Chatman 1996). Culture as the vehicle that preserves the know-how of adaptation is implied in this description: "If we understand culture to be a stock of knowledge that has been codified into a pattern of recipes for handling situations, then very often with time and routine they become tacit and taken for granted and form the schemas which drive action" (Colville et al 1993:559). Culture, viewed as a stock of knowledge, serves as a scheme of expression that constrains what people do and a scheme of interpretation that constrains how the doing is evaluated. To change culture is to change climate (e.g. Schneider et al 1996), uncover the tacit stock of knowledge by means of experiments that surface the particulars (Colville et al 1993), or deconstruct organizational language paradigms (Bate 1990). Although culture has been a useful vocabulary to understand stability and change, there are growing suggestions that as one moves away from treating it as a social control system, the concept may become less meaningful (Jordan 1995).

The separate issue of scale arises because continuous changes in the form of "situated micro-level changes that actors enact over time as they make sense of and act in the world" (Orlikowski 1996:91) are often judged to be too small, too much a follower strategy (Huber & Glick 1993:385), and even too "unAmerican" (Hammond & Morrison 1996:Ch. 3) to be of much importance when hyperturbulence and quantum change confront organizations (Meyer et al 1993).

The analytical framework associated with continuous change interprets scale in a different way. The fact that the changes are micro does not mean that they are trivial (Staw & Sutton 1993, Staw 1991). Representative of this view is Ford & Ford's (1995) observation, "The macrocomplexity of organizations is generated, and changes emerge through the diversity and interconnectedness of many microconversations, each of which follows relatively simple rules" (p. 560). Small changes do not stay small, as complexity theory and the second cybernetics (Maruyama 1963) make clear. Small changes can be decisive if they occur at the edge of chaos. Furthermore, in interconnected systems, there is no such thing as a marginal change, as Colville et al (1993) demonstrated in their study of small experiments with culture change at British Customs. Microlevel changes also provide the platform for transformational change and the means to institutionalize it. Depictions of successful revolutions, however, tend to downplay the degree to which earlier sequences of incremental changes made them possible. This oversight is serious because people tend to attribute the success of revolution to its break with the past and its vision of the future, whereas that success may actually lie in its connection with the past and its retrospective rewriting of what earlier micro-changes meant.

In conclusion, the basic analytical framework for continuous change assumes that revolutions are not necessary to shatter what basically does not exist. Episodic change is driven by inertia and the inability of organizations to keep up, while continuous change is driven by alertness and the inability of organizations to remain stable. The analytic framework for continuous change specifies that contingencies, breakdowns, opportunities, and contexts make a difference. Change is an ongoing mixture of reactive and proactive modifications, guided by purposes at hand, rather than an intermittent interruption of periods of convergence.

Ideal Continuous Organizations

The "ideal organizations" described above in the context of episodic change serve just as well as ideals for continuous change, since those ideals incorporate capabilities for both forms of change. Thus, that discussion is compatible with the metaphors and analytical framework for continuous change.

Intervention Theory in Continuous Change

Lewin's change model, with its assumptions of inertia, linearity, progressive development, goal seeking, disequilibrium as motivator, and outsider intervention, is relevant when it is necessary to create change. However, when change is continuous, the problem is not one of unfreezing. The problem is one of redirecting what is already under way. A different mindset is necessary, and Marshak (1993) has suggested that one possibility derives from Confucian thought. The relevant assumptions are (a) cyclical assumption (patterns of ebb and flow repeat themselves), (b) processional assumption (movement involves an orderly sequence through a cycle and departures cause disequilibrium), (c) journey assumption (there is no end state), (d) equilibrium assumption (interventions are to restore equilibrium and balance), (e) appropriateness assumption (correct action maintains harmony), and (f) change assumption (nothing remains the same forever).

In the face of inertia, it makes sense to view a change intervention as a sequence of unfreeze, transition, refreeze. But in the face of continuous change, a more plausible change sequence would be freeze, rebalance, unfreeze. To freeze continuous change is to make a sequence visible and to show patterns in what is happening (e.g. Argyris 1990). To freeze is to capture sequences by means of cognitive maps (Fiol & Huff 1992, Eden et al 1992, Cossette &

Audet 1992), schemas (Bartunek 1993, Tenkasi & Boland 1993), or war stories (Boje 1991, O'Connor 1996). To rebalance is to reinterpret, relabel, and resequence the patterns so that they unfold with fewer blockages. To rebalance is to reframe issues as opportunities (Dutton 1993), reinterpret history using appreciative inquiry (e.g. Cooperrider & Srivasta 1987, Hammond 1996), to differentiate more boldly among "the external world, the social world, and the world of inner subjectivity" (Thachankary 1992:198), or to be responsive to concerns about justice (Novelli et al 1995). Thus, a story of intense but unproductive meetings is rewritten as a story affirming the value of "corporateness" in an international nonprofit organization (Thachankary 1992:221). Finally, to unfreeze after rebalancing is to resume improvisation, translation, and learning in ways that are now more mindful of sequences, more resilient to anomalies, and more flexible in their execution.

An important new means of rebalancing continuous change is the use of a logic of attraction, which is the counterpart of the logic of replacement in episodic change. As the name implies, people change to a new position because they are attracted to it, drawn to it, inspired by it. There is a focus on moral power, the attractiveness or being state of the change agent, the freedom of the change target, and the role of choice in the transformational process. Kotter (1996) asks the question, is change something one manages or something one leads? To manage change is to tell people what to do (a logic of replacement), but to lead change is to show people how to be (a logic of attraction). RE Quinn (1996) argues that most top managers assume that change is something that someone with authority does to someone who does not have authority (e.g. Boss & Golembiewski 1995). They overlook the logic of attraction and its power to pull change.

To engage this logic of attraction, leaders must first make deep changes in themselves, including self-empowerment (Spreitzer & Quinn 1996). When deep personal change occurs, leaders then behave differently toward their direct reports, and the new behaviors in the leader attract new behaviors from followers. When leaders model personal change, organizational change is more likely to take place. A similar logic is implicit in Cohen & Tichy's (1997) recent emphasis on top managers developing a teachable point of view. Leaders who first consolidate their stories and ideas about what matters undergo personal change before organizational change is attempted. Subsequent organizational change is often more effective because it is led by more attractive leaders. Beer et al (1990:194–95) raise the interesting subtlety, based on their data, that inconsistency between word and action at the corporate level does not affect change effectiveness, but it does have a negative effect for leaders at the unit level. Their explanation is that inconsistency at the top is seen as necessary to cope with diverse pressures from stockholders and the board but is seen as insincerity and hypocrisy at other levels.

Role of Change Agent in Continuous Change

If continuous change is altered by freezing and rebalancing, then the role of the change agent becomes one of managing language, dialogue, and identity, as we saw above. Change agents become important for their ability to make sense (Weick 1995) of change dynamics already under way. They recognize adaptive emergent changes, make them more salient, and reframe them (Bate 1990). They explain current upheavals, where they are heading, what they will have produced by way of a redesign, and how further intentional changes can be made at the margins.

To redirect continuous change is to be sensitive to discourse. Schein (1993) argues that dialogue, which he defines as interaction focused on thinking processes and how they are preformed by past experience, enables groups to create a shared set of meanings and a common thinking process. "The most basic mechanism of acquiring new information that leads to cognitive restructuring is to discover in a conversational process that the interpretation that someone else puts on a concept is different from one's own" (Schein 1996:31). Barrett et al (1995) and Dixon (1997) also argue that the most powerful change interventions occur at the level of everyday conversation. J Quinn (1996) demonstrates in the context of strategic change that good conversation is vocal, reciprocating, issues-oriented, rational, imaginative, and honest. And Ford & Ford (1995) argue that change agents produce change through various combinations of five kinds of speech acts: assertives or claims, directives or requests, commissives or promises, expressives that convey affective state, and declarations that announce a new operational reality. These speech acts occur in different combinations to constitute four different conversations: conversations of change, understanding, performance, and closure.

CONCLUSION

Our review suggests both that change starts with failures to adapt and that change never starts because it never stops. Reconciliation of these disparate themes is a source of ongoing tension and energy in recent change research. Classic machine bureaucracies, with their reporting structures too rigid to adapt to faster-paced change, have to be unfrozen to be improved. Yet with differentiation of bureaucratic tasks comes more internal variation, more diverse views of distinctive competence, and more diverse initiatives. Thus, while some things may appear not to change, other things do. Most organizations have pockets of people somewhere who are already adjusting to the new environment. The challenge is to gain acceptance of continuous change throughout the organization so that these isolated innovations will travel and be seen as relevant to a wider range of purposes at hand.

Recent work suggests, ironically, that to understand organizational change one must first understand organizational inertia, its content, its tenacity, its interdependencies. Recent work also suggests that change is not an on-off phenomenon nor is its effectiveness contingent on the degree to which it is planned. Furthermore, the trajectory of change is more often spiral or open-ended than linear. All of these insights are more likely to be kept in play if researchers focus on "changing" rather than "change." A shift in vocabulary from "change" to "changing" directs attention to actions of substituting one thing for another, of making one thing into another thing, or of attracting one thing to become other than it was. A concern with "changing" means greater appreciation that change is never off, that its chains of causality are longer and less determinate than we anticipated, and that whether one's viewpoint is global or local makes a difference in the rate of change that will be observed, the inertias that will be discovered, and the size of accomplishments that will have been celebrated.

ACKNOWLEDGMENTS

We acknowledge with appreciation fruitful discussions of key points with Dave Schwandt, Lance Sandelands, Jane Dutton, Wayne Baker, Anjali Sastry, and Matt Brown, with special thanks to Kathleen Sutcliffe for thoughtful commentary on various drafts of the complete argument.

> Visit the *Annual Reviews* home page at
> http://www.AnnualReviews.org.

Literature Cited

Argyris C. 1990. *Overcoming Organizational Defenses: Facilitating Organizational Learning.* Boston: Allyn & Bacon

Arthur WB. 1995. Positive feedbacks in the economy. In *Increasing Returns and Path Dependence in the Economy,* ed. T Kuran, pp. 1–32. Ann Arbor: Univ. Mich. Press

Ashkenas RN, Jick TD. 1992. From dialogue to action in GE work-out: developmental learning in a change process. *Res. Organ. Change Dev.* 6:267–87

Austin JR. 1997. A method for facilitating controversial social change in organizations: Branch Rickey and the Brooklyn Dodgers. *J. Appl. Behav. Sci.* 33:101–18

Axelrod D. 1992. Getting everyone involved: how one organization involved its employees, supervisors, and managers in redesigning the organization. *J. Appl. Behav. Sci.* 28:499–509

Bacharach SB, Bamberger P, Sonnenstuhl WJ. 1996. The organizational transformation process: the micropolitics of dissonance reduction and the alignment of logics of action. *Admin. Sci. Q.* 41:477–506

Barr PS, Huff AS. 1997. Seeing isn't believing: understanding diversity in the timing of strategic response. *J. Manage. Stud.* 34: 337–70

Barrett FJ, Thomas GF, Hocevar SP. 1995. The central role of discourse in large-scale change: a social construction perspective. *J. Appl. Behav. Sci.* 31:352–72

Bartunek JM. 1993. The multiple cognitions and conflicts associated with second order organizational change. In *Social Psychology in Organizations: Advances in Theory and Research,* ed. JK Murnighan, pp. 322–49. Englewood Cliffs, NJ: Prentice Hall

Bartunek JM, Moch MK. 1994. Third-order

organizational change and the western mystical tradition. *J. Organ. Change Manage.* 7: 24–41

Bate P. 1990. Using the culture concept in an organization development setting. *J. Appl. Behav. Sci.* 26:83–106

Bateson G. 1972. *Steps to An Ecology of Mind.* New York: Ballantine

Beer M, Eisenstat RA, Spector B. 1990. *The Critical Path to Corporate Renewal.* Boston, MA: Harv. Bus. Sch.

Boje D. 1991. The storytelling organization: a study of story performances in an office-supply firm. *Admin. Sci. Q.* 36:106–26

Boss RW, Golembiewski RT. 1995. Do you have to start at the top? The chief executive officer's role in successful organization development efforts. *J. Appl. Behav. Sci.* 31:259–77

Bougon MG. 1992. Congregate cognitive maps: a unified dynamic theory of organization and strategy. *J. Manage. Stud.* 29: 369–89

Brown JS, Duguid P. 1991. Organizational learning and communities-of-practice: toward a unified view of working, learning, and innovation. *Organ. Sci.* 2:40–57

Brown SL, Eisenhardt KM. 1997. The art of continuous change: linking complexity theory and time-paced evolution in relentlessly shifting organizations. *Admin. Sci. Q.* 42:1–34

Browning LD, Beyer JM, Shetler JC. 1995. Building cooperation in a competitive industry: Sematech and the semiconductor industry. *Acad. Manage. J.* 38:113–51

Bunker BB, Alban BT. 1992. Conclusion: what makes large group interventions effective? *Appl. Behav. Sci.* 28:579–91

Burgelman RA. 1991. Intraorganizational ecology of strategy making and organizational adaptation: theory and field research. *Organ. Sci.* 2:239–62

Cheng YT, Van de Ven AH. 1996. Learning the innovation journey: order out of chaos? *Organ. Sci.* 7:593–614

Cohen E, Tichy N. 1997. How leaders develop leaders. *Train Dev.* 51:58–74

Colville I, Dalton K, Tomkins C. 1993. Developing and understanding cultural change in HM customs and excise: there is more to dancing than knowing the next steps. *Public Admin.* 71:549–66

Cooperrider DL, Srivasta S. 1987. Appreciative inquiry in organizational life. In *Research in Organizational Change and Development,* ed. RW Woodman, WA Pasmore, 1:129–69. Greenwich, CT: JAI

Cossette P, Audet M. 1992. Mapping of an idiosyncratic schema. *J. Manage. Stud.* 29: 325–47

Crossan MM, Lane HW, White RE, Klus L. 1996. The improvising organization; where planning meets opportunity. *Organ. Dyn.* 24:20–35

Czarniawska B, Joerges B. 1996. Travels of ideas. See Czarniawska & Sevon 1996, pp. 13–48

Czarniawska B, Sevon G, eds. 1996. *Translating Organizational Change.* New York: Walter de Gruyter

Dannemiller KD, Jacobs RW. 1992. Changing the way organizations change: a revolution of common sense. *J. Appl. Behav. Sci.* 28: 480–98

Dixon NM. 1997. The hallways of learning. *Organ. Dyn.* 25:23–34

Driskell JE, Salas E, eds. 1996. *Stress and Human Performance.* Mahwah, NJ: Erlbaum

Dunbar RLM, Garud R, Raghuram S. 1996. A frame for deframing in strategic analysis. *J. Manage. Inq.* 5:23–34

Dunphy D. 1996. Organizational change in corporate setting. *Hum. Relat.* 49(5): 541–52

Dunphy DC, Stace DA. 1988. Transformational and coercive strategies for planned organizational change: beyond the OD model. *Organ. Stud.* 9(3):317–34

Dutton JE. 1993. The making of organizational opportunities: an interpretive pathway to organizational change. *Res. Organ. Behav.* 15:195–226

Easterby-Smith M. 1997. Disciplines of organizational learning: contributions and critiques. *Hum. Relat.* 50:1085–113

Eden C, Ackerman F, Cropper S. 1992. The analysis of cause maps. *J. Manage. Stud.* 29:309–23

Fiol CM, Huff AS. 1992. Maps for managers: where are we? Where do we go from here? *J. Manage. Stud.* 29:267–85

Ford J, Backoff R. 1988. Organizational change in and out of dualities and paradox. In *Paradox and Transformation,* ed. R Quinn, K Cameron, pp. 81–121. Cambridge, MA: Ballinger

Ford JD, Ford LW. 1994. Logics of identity, contradiction, and attraction in change. *Acad. Manage. Rev.* 19:756–85

Ford JD, Ford LW. 1995. The role of conversations in producing intentional change in organizations. *Acad. Manage. Rev.* 20(3): 541–70

Gersick CJG. 1989. Marking time: predictable transitions in task groups. *Acad. Manage. J.* 32:274–309

Gersick CJG. 1991. Revolutionary change theories: a multilevel exploration of the punctuated equilibrium paradigm. *Acad. Manage. Rev.* 16:10–36

Gersick CJG. 1994. Pacing strategic change: the case of a new venture. *Acad. Manage. J.* 37:9–45

Gilmore TN, Barnett C. 1992. Designing the social architecture of participation in large groups to effect organizational change. *J. Appl. Behav. Sci.* 28:534–48

Gioia DA. 1992. Pinto fires and personal ethics: a script analysis of missed opportunities. *J. Bus. Ethics* 11:379–89

Golembiewski RT, Boss RW. 1992. Phases of burnout in diagnosis and intervention: individual level of analysis in organization development and change. *Res. Organ. Change Dev.* 6:115–52

Greenwood R, Hinings CR. 1996. Understanding radical organizational change: bringing together the old and the new institutionalism. *Acad. Manage. Rev.* 21: 1022–54

Greiner L. 1972. Evolution and revolution as organizations grow. *Harv. Bus. Rev.* 50(4): 37–46

Grimley D, Prochaska JO, Velicer WF, Blais LM, DiClemente CC. 1994. The transtheoretical model of change. In *Changing the Self: Philosophies, Techniques, and Experiences*, ed. M Brinthaupt, pp. 201–27. New York: State Univ. NY Press

Hammond J, Morrison J. 1996. *The Stuff Americans Are Made Of.* New York: Macmillan

Hammond SA. 1996. *The Thin Book of Appreciative Inquiry.* Plano, TX: Kodiak Consult.

Harrison JR, Carroll G. 1991. Keeping the faith: a model of cultural transmission in formal organization. *Admin. Sci. Q.* 36: 552–82

Hendry C. 1996. Understanding and creating whole organizational change through learning theory. *Hum. Relat.* 49:621–41

Huber GP. 1991. Organizational learning: an examination of the contributing processes and a review of the literatures. *Organ. Sci.* 2:88–115

Huber GP, Glick WH, eds. 1993. *Organizational Change and Redesign.* New York: Oxford Univ. Press

Huber GP, Sutcliffe KM, Miller CC, Glick WH. 1993. Understanding and predicting organizational change. See Huber & Glick 1993, pp. 215–65

Inkpen AC, Crossan MM. 1995. Believing is seeing: joint ventures and organization learning. *J. Manage. Stud.* 32:595–618

Jordan AT. 1995. Managing diversity: translating anthropological insight for organization studies. *J. Appl. Behav. Sci.* 31: 124–40

Kahn RL. 1974. Organizational development:

some problems and proposals. *J. Appl. Behav. Sci.* 10:485–502

Katz J. 1997. Ethnography's warrants. *Sociol. Methods Res.* 25:391–423

Kilduff M, Mehra A. 1997. Postmodernism and organizational research. *Acad. Manage. J.* 22:453–81

Klein G. 1998. *Sources of Power.* Cambridge, MA: MIT Press

Kotter JP. 1996. *Leading Change.* Boston, MA: Harv. Bus. Sch.

Kotter JP, Heskett JL. 1992. *Corporate Culture and Performance.* New York: Free Press

Langfield-Smith K. 1992. Exploring the need for a shared cognitive map. *J. Manage. Stud.* 29:349–68

Latour B. 1986. The powers of association. In *Power, Action, and Belief,* ed. J Law, pp. 264–80. London: Routledge & Kegan

Laurila J. 1997. The thin line between advanced and conventional new technology: a case study on paper industry management. *J. Manage. Stud.* 34:219–39

Levinthal DA, March JG. 1993. The myopia of learning. *Strateg. Manage. J.* 14:95–112

Lewin K. 1951. *Field Theory in Social Science.* New York: Harper & Row

Lundberg CC. 1989. On organizational learning: implications and opportunities for expanding organizational development. *Res. Organ. Change Dev.* 3:61–82

Macy BA, Izumi H. 1993. Organizational change, design, and work innovation: a meta-analysis of 131 North American field studies—1961–1991. *Res. Organ. Change Dev.* 7:235–313

March JG. 1994. *A Primer on Decision Making.* New York: Free Press

Marshak RJ. 1993. Lewin meets Confucius: a review of the OD model of change. *J. Appl. Behav. Sci.* 29:393–415

Maruyama M. 1963. The second cybernetics: deviation-amplifying mutual causal processes. *Am. Sci.* 51:164–79

McDaniel RR Jr. 1997. Strategic leadership: a view from quantum and chaos theories. *Health Care Manage. Rev.* Winter:21–37

McKelvey B. 1997. Quasi-natural organization science. *Organ. Sci.* 8:352–80

Meyer AD, Goes JB, Brooks GR. 1993. Organizations reacting to hyperturbulence. See Huber & Glick 1993, pp. 66–111

Micklethwait J, Wooldridge A. 1996. *The Witch Doctors.* New York: Times Books

Miller D. 1990. Organizational configurations: cohesion, changes, and prediction. *Hum. Relat.* 43:771–89

Miller D. 1993. The architecture of simplicity. *Acad. Manage. Rev.* 18:116–38

Miller D. 1994. What happens after success:

the perils of excellence. *J. Manage. Stud.* 31:325–58

Miller D. 1996. A preliminary typology of organizational learning: synthesizing the literature. *J. Manage.* 22:485–505

Mintzberg H, Westley F. 1992. Cycles of organizational change. *Strateg. Manage. J.* 13:39–59

Mirvis PH. 1996. Historical foundations of organization learning. *J. Organ. Change Manage.* 9:13–31

Mirvis PH. 1997. Crossroads: "social work" in organizations. *Organ. Sci.* 8:192–206

Moorman C, Miner AS. 1997. The impact of organizational memory on new product performance and creativity. *J. Mark. Res.* 34:91–106

Moorman C, Miner AS. 1998a. Organizational improvisation and organizational memory. *Acad. Manage. Rev.* In press

Moorman C, Miner AS. 1998b. The convergence of planning and execution: improvisation in new product development. *J. Mark.* In press

Nadler DA. 1998. *Champions of Change.* San Francisco: Jossey-Bass

Nadler DA, Shaw RB, Walton AE. 1995. *Discontinuous Change.* San Francisco: Jossey-Bass

Nielsen RP, Bartunek JM. 1996. Opening narrow routinized schemata to ethical stakeholder consciousness and action. *Bus. Soc.* 35:483–519

Nord WR, Jermier JM. 1994. Overcoming resistance to resistance: insights from a study of the shadows. *Public Admin. Q.* 17:396–409

Novelli L, Bradley LK, Shapiro DL. 1995. Effective implementation of organizational change: an organizational justice perspective. In *Trends in Organizational Behavior,* ed. CL Cooper, 2:15–37. London: Wiley & Sons

O'Connor ES. 1995. Paradoxes of participation: textural analysis and organizational changes. *Organ. Stud.* 16(5):769–803

O'Connor ES. 1996. Telling decisions: the role of narrative in decision making. In *Organizational Decision Making,* ed. Z Shapiro, pp. 304–23. New York: Cambridge Univ. Press

Olson EE. 1990. The transcendent function in organizational change. *J. Appl. Behav. Sci.* 26:69–81

O'Reilly CA, Chatman JA. 1996. Culture as social control: corporations, cults and commitment. *Res. Organ. Behav.* 18:157–200

Orlikowski WJ. 1996. Improvising organizational transformation overtime: a situated change perspective. *Inf. Syst. Res.* 7(1): 63–92

O'Shea J, Madigan C. 1997. *Dangerous Company.* New York: Times Books

O'Toole J. 1995. *Leading Change.* San Francisco: Jossey-Bass

Pasmore WA, Fagans MR. 1992. Participation, individual development, and organizational change: a preview and synthesis. *J. Manage.* 18:375–97

Pfeffer J. 1997. *New Directions For Organization Theory.* New York: Oxford Univ. Press

Pfeffer J. 1998. *The Human Equation.* Boston: Harv. Bus. Sch.

Porras JI, Robertson PJ. 1992. Organizational development: theory, practice, research. *Handbook of Organizational Psychology,* ed. MD Dunnette, LM Hough, 3:719–822. Palo Alto, CA: Consult. Psychol. Press. 2nd ed.

Porras JI, Silvers RC. 1991. Organization development and transformation. *Annu. Rev. Psychol.* 42:51–78

Prochaska JO, DiClemente CC, Norcross JC. 1992. In search of how people change: applications to addictive behaviors. *Am. Psychol.* 47:1102–14

Prochaska JO, DiClemente CC, Norcross JC. 1997. In search of how people change: applications to addictive behaviors. In *Addictive Behaviors: Readings on Etiology, Prevention, and Treatment,* ed. G Marlatt, pp. 671–96. Washington, DC: Am. Psychol. Assoc.

Pye A. 1994. Past, present and possibility: an integrative appreciation of learning from experience. *Manage. Learn.* 25:155–73

Quinn JJ. 1996. The role of 'good conversation' in strategic control. *J. Manage. Stud.* 33:381–94

Quinn RE. 1996. *Deep Change: Discovering the Leader Within.* San Francisco: Jossey-Bass

Random House Dictionary of The English Language. 1987. New York: Random House. 2nd ed. unabridged

Roach DW, Bednar DA. 1997. The theory of logical types: a tool for understanding levels and types of change in organizations. *Hum. Relat.* 50:671–99

Romanelli E, Tushman ML. 1994. Organizational transformation as punctuated equilibrium: an empirical test. *Acad. Manage. J.* 37:1141–66

Rorty R. 1989. *Contingency, Irony, and Solidarity.* New York: Cambridge Univ. Press

Sahlin-Andersson K. 1996. Imitating by editing success: the construction of organizational fields. See Czarniawska & Sevon 1996, pp. 69–92

Sandelands L. 1998. *Feeling and Form In Social Life.* Lanham, MD: Rowman & Littlefield

Sastry MA. 1997. Problems and paradoxes in a model of punctuated organizational change. *Admin. Sci. Q.* 42:237–75

Schein EH. 1993. On dialogue, culture, and organizational learning. *Organ. Dyn.* 21: 40–51

Schein EH. 1996. Kurt Lewin's change theory in the field and in the classroom: notes toward a model of managed learning. *Syst. Pract.* 9:27–47

Schneider B, Brief AP, Guzzo RA. 1996. Creating a climate and culture for sustainable organizational change. *Organ. Dyn.* 24: 7–19

Sevon G. 1996. Organizational imitation in identity transformation. See Czarniawska & Sevon 1996, pp. 49–68

Sitkin SB, Sutcliffe KM, Weick KE. 1998. Organizational learning. In *The Technology Management Handbook,* ed. R Dorf. Boca Raton, FL: CRC Press. In press

Spreitzer GM, Quinn RE. 1996. Empowering middle managers to be transformational leaders. *J. Appl. Behav. Sci.* 32(3):237–61

Stacey RD. 1995. The science of complexity: an alternative perspective for strategic change processes. *Strateg. Manage. J.* 16: 477–95

Starbuck WH. 1993. Keeping a butterfly and an elephant in a house of cards: the elements of exceptional success. *J. Manage. Stud.* 30:885–921

Staw BM. 1991. Dressing up like an organization: when psychological theories can explain organizational action. *J. Manage.* 17: 805–19

Staw BM, Sutton RI. 1993. Macro organizational psychology. In *Social Psychology in Organizations: Advances in Theory and Research,* ed. JK Murnighan, pp. 350–84. Englewood Cliffs, NJ: Prentice Hall

Tenkasi RV, Boland RJ. 1993. Locating meaning making in organizational learning: the narrative basis of cognition. *Res. Organ. Change Dev.* 7:77–103

Thachankary T. 1992. Organizations as "texts": hermeneutics as a model for understanding organizational change. *Res. Organ. Change Dev.* 6:197–233

Torbert WR. 1994. Managerial learning, organizational learning: a potentially powerful redundancy. *Manage. Learn.* 25:57–70

Trice HM, Beyer JM. 1993. *The Culture of Work Organizations.* Englewood Cliffs, NJ: Prentice Hall

Tsoukas H. 1996. The firm as a distributed knowledge system: a constructionist approach. *Strateg. Manage. J.* 17:11–26

Tushman ML, O'Reilly CA III. 1996. The ambidextrous organization: managing evolutionary and revolutionary change. *Calif. Manage. Rev.* 38:1–23

Tushman ML, Romanelli E. 1985. Organizational revolution: a metamorphosis model of convergence and reorientation. *Res. Organ. Behav.* 7:171–222

Tushman ML, Rosenkopf L. 1992. Organizational determinants of technological change: toward a sociology of technological evolution. *Res. Organ. Behav.* 14: 311–47

Van de Ven AH, Poole MS. 1995. Explaining development and change in organizations. *Acad. Manage. Rev.* 20(3):510–40

Vaughan D. 1996. *The Challenger Launch Decision.* Chicago: Univ. Chicago Press

Virany B, Tushman ML, Romanelli E. 1992. Executive succession and organization outcomes in turbulent environments: an organization learning approach. *Organ. Sci.* 3:72–91

Walsh JP, Ungson GR. 1991. Organizational memory. *Acad. Manage. Rev.* 16:57–91

Watzlawick P, Weakland J, Fisch R. 1974. *Change.* New York: Norton

Wegner DM. 1987. Transactive memory: a contemporary analysis of the group mind. In *Theories of Group Behavior,* ed. B Mullen, GR Goethals, pp. 185–208. New York: Springer-Verlag

Weick KE. 1993. Organizational redesign as improvisation. In *Organizational Change and Redesign,* ed. GP Huber, WH Glick, pp. 346–79. New York: Oxford Univ. Press

Weick KE. 1995. *Sensemaking in Organizations.* Thousand Oaks, CA: Sage

Weick KE, Roberts KH. 1993. Collective mind in organizations: heedful interrelating on flight decks. *Admin. Sci. Q.* 38: 357–81

Weisbord MR. 1987. *Productive Workplaces.* San Francisco: Jossey-Bass

Wheatley MJ. 1992. *Leadership and the New Science.* San Francisco: Berrett-Koehler

Wilkof MV, Brown DW, Selsky JW. 1995. When the stories are different: the influence of corporate culture mismatches on interorganizational relations. *J. Appl. Behav. Sci.* 31:373–88

Woodman RW. 1989. Organizational change and development: new arenas for inquiry and action. *J. Manage.* 15:205–28

Annu. Rev. Psychol. 1999. 50:387–418

SOCIAL, COMMUNITY, AND PREVENTIVE INTERVENTIONS

N. D. Reppucci,[1] J. L. Woolard,[2] and C. S. Fried[1]

[1]Psychology Department, University of Virginia, Charlottesville, Virginia 22903, and [2]Center for Studies in Criminology and Law, University of Florida, PO Box 115950, Gainesville, Florida 32611-5950; e-mail: ndr@virginia.edu; jwoolard@crim.ufl.edu; csf7n@virginia.edu

KEY WORDS: prevention, violence, health promotion, diversity

ABSTRACT

Psychology can and should be at the forefront of participation in social, community, and preventive interventions. This chapter focuses on selective topics under two general areas: violence as a public health problem and health promotion/competence promotion across the life span. Under violence prevention, discussion of violence against women, youth violence, and child maltreatment are the focal points. Under health and competence promotion, attention is paid to the prevention of substance abuse and HIV/AIDS. We highlight a few significant theoretical and empirical contributions, especially from the field of community/prevention psychology. The chapter includes a brief overview of diversity issues, which are integral to a comprehensive discussion of these prevention efforts. We argue that the field should extend its role in social action while emphasizing the critical importance of rigorous research as a component of future interventions.

CONTENTS

0084-6570/99/0201-0387$08.00

INTRODUCTION

The efficacy of prevention has been the impetus for the development of a national research agenda on preventive interventions. With the publication of the National Institute of Mental Health (NIMH) report *The Prevention of Mental Disorders: A National Research Agenda* (NIMH Prevention Research Steering Committee 1994) and the Institute of Medicine (IOM) report *Reducing Risks for Mental Disorders: Frontiers for Preventive Intervention Research* (Mrazek & Haggerty 1994), a theoretical and practical debate concerning the definition of preventive interventions emerged. Both reports define a preventive intervention as one that aims to reduce the incidence of diagnoses of mental illnesses in the population as defined by the *Diagnostic and Statistical Manual of Mental Disorders* (*DSM*)-*IV*. This agenda, which is supported by Reiss & Price (1996) and Muñoz et al (1996), includes the following controversial elements: (*a*) the use of risk reduction of psychiatric disorders as the criteria for acceptable research, (*b*) rejection of studies of general competence promotion, and (*c*) the rejection of prevention studies that advocate social and political change to achieve social equality for disadvantaged groups (Albee 1996). Some believe that the agenda put forth by NIMH and IOM is too narrow. Albee (1996) argues that by focusing exclusively on *DSM-IV* diagnoses, the emphasis becomes a search for individual-level, or at best micro-level, causes for the disorder. An additional concern is that competence building and mental health promotion efforts—which are excluded from the definition—may be the most promising strategies for preventing mental illness, as evidenced by the effectiveness of comprehensive, competence-oriented programs in preventing delinquency (Cowen 1994) and by Durlak & Wells's (1997) meta-analysis of 177 primary prevention programs designed to prevent behavioral and social problems in children and adolescents. Most types of programs were found to reduce adjustment problems and increase competencies significantly. (For a summary of the reports see Muñoz et al 1996, Reiss & Price 1996.)

Both reports and related commentaries have implications for the dissemination and implementation of interventions in communities. One positive outcome is national recognition that the past decade has been productive and promising for the field of prevention. Significant gains include improvements in methodology (Mrazek & Haggerty 1994), a move from unidimensional programs to more sophisticated, theory-driven programs, and an increase in the number and effectiveness of prevention efforts (Cowen 1994). The issues of diversity and cultural sensitivity have also gained prominent attention and a recognized importance in the delivery of mental health services. This chapter highlights the strides that psychology has made in prevention in the past 6 years by reviewing some types of programs covered in the reports (e.g. programs aimed at reducing substance abuse) as well as wellness promotion programs that were intentionally left out of the reports.

Psychology can and should be at the forefront of participation in social, community, and preventive interventions. Since the first *Annual Review of Psychology* chapter on this topic (Kessler & Albee 1975), the ensuing 23 years have, in fact, seen a vastly increased participation rate by psychologists into the problems of society. Six subsequent *Annual Review of Psychology* chapters have documented this ever increasing involvement (Levine et al 1993, Heller 1990, Gesten & Jason 1987, Iscoe & Harris 1984, Bloom 1980, Kelly et al 1977). Since the 1993 chapter, numerous public policies regarding social services have been adopted amid much controversy as to what is in the best interests of society. Four of these policies have been at the center of changes in the delivery of human services:

1. Health care policy, especially in the form of managed care, has been drastically altering the form and number of services that are being delivered by mental health practitioners and others (Chisholm et al 1997, Iglehart 1996, Boyle & Callahan 1995).
2. Welfare reforms have been adopted by federal and state legislatures that promise to change the system as we have known it. Some have suggested that the reforms amount to an abandonment of the poor, while proponents suggest that an enhancement of the human spirit and work ethic will result.
3. A "get tough" approach to violent and other crime is exemplified by (*a*) the vast increase in prison populations and expansion of correctional facilities over the past decade and (*b*) the abandonment of a treatment focus for juveniles to one of punishment, as indicated by the lowering of the age of transfer to adult court by most states so that youth can be tried as adults.
4. An increased interest in preventive interventions to alleviate mental health problems, violence, teen pregnancy, school dropout, child abuse, substance abuse, and other societal woes.

The first three of these policies have received much public attention; a review of their implications and the contributions of psychology is beyond the scope of this chapter. However, the fourth policy—prevention—has occurred with much less public attention, and psychology has been one of the disciplines at the forefront of this movement. Therefore, this chapter focuses on selective topics under two general areas: violence as a public health problem and health promotion/competence promotion across the life span. Under violence prevention, discussion of violence against women, youth violence, and child maltreatment are the focal points. Under health and competence promotion, attention is paid to the prevention of substance abuse and HIV/AIDS. Obviously, an exhaustive review of all relevant research during the past 6 years is not possible; rather, we highlight a few significant theoretical and empirical contributions, especially from the field of community/prevention psychology. Before moving to these two focal areas, we give a brief overview of diversity issues, which are integral to a comprehensive discussion of these prevention efforts.

Diversity

The development of theory, research, and interventions that account for the interactions among and between individuals, settings, and communities in a sociocultural context has been a critical tenet of community psychology since its inception. However, only recently has the concept taken center stage, as exemplified by the creation of culturally sensitive interventions (e.g. Catalano et al 1993) and the development of multicultural training practices in community psychology programs (see Weinstein 1994, Suarez-Balcazar et al 1994). Trickett and associates (1993) propose an ecological framework for incorporating the concept of culture as an essential element of individual and institutional life. Some of the challenges to the inclusion of culture and context into community/prevention psychology include (a) increased use of qualitative methods to understand culture and context, (b) sampling from difficult-to-reach groups or settings, (c) the development of cross-level strategies of data analysis, (d) more detailed examinations of the relationships between cultural groups and their ecological environments, and (e) the need for conceptual clarifications about the development of empowering relationships (Trickett 1996).

Interventions should be designed to reflect human diversity and cultural sensitivity. Many interventions have failed because the frame of reference for most researchers reflects middle-class Anglo cultural norms, causing the researchers to make inappropriate cultural assumptions (Vega 1992). Culturally appropriate interventions, as defined by Marín (1993), are those that meet the following criteria: (a) The intervention is based on the cultural values of the group; (b) the strategies that make up the intervention reflect the subjective culture of the group; and (c) the components that make up the strategies reflect the behavioral preferences and expectations of the group's members.

Recently Trickett and associates (1994) delineated the general issues involved in incorporating human diversity into the field of prevention and included chapters that offer multiple perspectives on diversity. The dual minority status of women of color was featured in a special issue of the *American Journal of Community Psychology* (April 1997). Such publications emphasize the central importance of embracing human diversity as a salient component of all social interventions. Culturally appropriate interventions are highlighted throughout this chapter.

VIOLENCE AS A PUBLIC HEALTH PROBLEM

Both psychology and law have focused much effort on responding to crime and violence. In particular, violence against women and violence committed by and against youth have shared the national spotlight. Federal and state legislation, funding initiatives, and grassroots organizing have coalesced to create substantial social change. At a policy level, the federal Violence Against Women Act (1994) represented the first comprehensive legislative agenda focusing on a national response to violence against women. In this section, we examine research with implications for community-level interventions to prevent violence and ameliorate the effects of violence for victims. We also briefly review national trends in juvenile justice law and their implications for the justice system's treatment and rehabilitation of young offenders. We discuss the effects of context on the widespread dissemination and implementation of violence prevention efforts as well as the developmental implications of intervention strategies. Finally, we examine the problem of child abuse and the proliferation of prevention programs, with specific emphasis on parent education and community-based family support programs.

Violence Against Women

The 1990s have been an extraordinary decade for highlighting the problem of violence against women. Grassroots efforts of victims and women's advocates in both family violence and sexual assault in the 1960s sparked the rest of the community, including researchers and policy makers, to examine the causes, correlates, and responses to violence against women. Since that time, an extensive amount of research has investigated the incidence and prevalence of violence, the costs of victimization to the individual as well as society, the criminal justice system's response, and treatment services (for reviews, see Crowell & Burgess 1996, Goodman et al 1993). Despite the significant gains in understanding the nature and impact of violence, only recently has research examined interventions for the prevention of sexual assault and family violence (Browne 1993). Sexual assault interventions have focused primarily on risk reduction in women, although recent efforts target males as well. Family violence interventions include changes in criminal justice processing and treatment efforts that affect both victims and offenders. A consistent theme highlights the promise of innovative techniques and approaches that have not yet been systematically documented or evaluated.

EDUCATION AS PRIMARY PREVENTION   Like other social problems, violence against women is a complex, multidetermined phenomenon that is difficult to prevent through single or isolated strategies. In part because many studies have documented the existence of "rape myths" or rape-supportive beliefs and a correlation between such attitudes/beliefs and aggression (or proclivity for aggression), many prevention programs for men and women focus on debunking such myths and changing attitudes. Although some argue that interventions for women do not "prevent" rape (which is usually perpetrated by males), a number of intervention programs tailored for women focus on identifying and ameliorating risk factors associated with increased likelihood of sexual assault. Several reviews of rape prevention document that some rape education programs do show postintervention changes in rape-supportive beliefs and attitudes (Hanson & Gidycz 1993, Lonsway et al 1998), but the field generally lacks a consistent, theoretical approach to preventive intervention (McCall 1993). Common intervention techniques include addressing rape mythology, interactive participation, sex education and feminist orientation, empathy induction, and confrontation for women-only and mixed-sex groups (Lonsway 1996). Reviews of primary rape education programs (Schewe & O'Donohue 1993), acquaintance rape education programs (Lonsway 1996), and the prevention of violence against women generally (Crowell & Burgess 1996) all identify common goals for the field. Perhaps most important, prevention programs need better measures of process and outcome, with replications to substantiate the findings of individual and pilot programs. The current research on attitudes and behaviors provides an important step in understanding the short-term impact of educational interventions, but as with other types of social interventions, the connection between attitude change and behavior change is critical.

ADVOCACY AND SOCIAL SUPPORT INTERVENTIONS   Although victim advocates have been providing shelter and advocacy services to victims of family violence for more than two decades, researchers have been somewhat slower to devise theory-based methods of systematic evaluation. A number of programs have developed to provide support services to battered women and their children, and treatment services to male offenders. In the past several years, a few studies have begun to evaluate the efficacy of these services (see Gordon 1996).

Recent studies have extended the intervention evaluation research with short- and long-term follow-up of service efficacy (Campbell et al 1995, Sullivan & Rumptz 1994, Sullivan et al 1994). Sullivan and colleagues (1994) have conducted an experimental evaluation of post-shelter advocacy services provided to domestic violence shelter residents. Their 2-year longitudinal study follows women from shelter exit through a 10-week intervention to 24 months of post-shelter stay. The 10-week intervention includes a trained undergraduate providing advocacy services that focus on accessing community resources (including facilitating system change to meet women's needs) and providing social support. The intervention is based on an ecological approach addressing several barriers that women face to leaving their abusers, including a lack of community resources, ineffective community response to needs, and social isolation/lack of social support. The study takes the important methodological step of randomly assigning participants to experimental (advocacy services) and control (no advocacy services) conditions. Sullivan et al (1994) tested the hypotheses that (*a*) battered women need a number of resources when leaving a shelter; (*b*) advocacy intervention would improve women's effectiveness in obtaining needed resources and social support; and (*c*) gains in these areas would improve quality of life and decrease risk of further abuse.

Self-report data gathered immediately following the 10-week intervention documented that the women needed a variety of resources when leaving the shelter. Women in the experimental condition were more likely to have worked on, and been successful at, obtaining needed resources than the control group. Women in the experimental condition also reported higher levels of satisfaction with their social support and better quality of life. No group differences in experiences of further abuse were found, however; approximately 46% of the entire group reported abuse experiences, including 29% of the women not involved with their assailants.

At 6 months postintervention, women in both groups reported more positive lives, including less depression, fear, anxiety, and attachment to the abuser, and increased feelings of control, quality of life, and satisfaction with social support. The experimental group reported small but significantly higher ratings of quality of life than the control group. Analysis of income data confirmed that more women who were financially independent before coming to the shelter were no longer with their assailant (79%) than those women who relied on their abuser for more than half of their income (57% were no longer with the assailant). Again, no group differences in abuse experience were found.

This ongoing study underscores the importance of tracking intervention effects longitudinally. Several of the group differences found immediately postintervention had disappeared or diminished at the 6-month follow-up. It is clear that long-term change may require a more extended advocacy intervention, a more comprehensive intervention, or more likely a combination of both. Even so, the study documents the strengths of shelter clients in overcoming significant obstacles once they leave the shelter and suggests there are still gains to be made in providing community-based support and systemwide change. This study also demonstrates the viability of experimental designs for interventions targeting violence against women. Future research can continue the important effects of documenting the impact of victimization, the process of accessing resources, and the barriers to negotiating systems successfully. However, research must also move forward to include multiple methods and information sources to evaluate the impact of interventions and to place interventions within the larger community context of advocacy, service delivery, and justice system processing.

Youth Violence and Antisocial Behavior

Weaving together the strands of literature on youth violence interventions is difficult in part because of a lack of clarity in the definition of "youth violence." Target behaviors or screening criteria for interventions range on psychological diagnoses (e.g. conduct disorder, antisocial behavior) to aggressive behavior (e.g. fighting) to delinquency and crime (e.g. court involvement, convictions) to institutional placement (e.g. correctional centers, mental hospitals, schools) (Mulvey et al 1993, Tate et al 1995). The criteria are identified through different information sources (e.g. justice records, self-report, observation), each with its own limitations. Regardless of the definitional elements, however, it is clear that youth violence is affecting a substantial number of youths and a significant proportion of society.

Despite overall decreases in violent crime in the United States, Federal Bureau of Investigation (FBI) crime statistics have documented increasing rates of juvenile crime in every major offense category between 1988 and 1992, suggesting that given the size of the juvenile population in the United States, juveniles are committing disproportionately more violent crime than are adults (Snyder & Sickmund 1995). Increases in the juvenile homicide rate (51%) have surpassed those of adults (20%), as have the increases in rates of juvenile aggravated assault (49% versus 23% among adults) and juvenile robbery (50% versus 13% for adults). Firearm violence in particular takes a heavy toll, especially for African-American males (Hammond & Yung 1993). Adolescents disproportionately suffer the consequences of violent victimization as well. Reviewing data from the Centers for Disease Control, Bureau of Justice Statistics (BJS), and the FBI over the past 29 years, Lowry and colleagues (1995) document stable offending rates for the population as a whole but increasing rates of offending and victimization for persons under 18. According to the FBI (1996), 12% of homicide victims in 1996 were under 18. In 1995, 30% of those arrested for Crime Index offenses were under 18, including 12% under the age of 15 (FBI 1995). Beyond criminal justice statistics, studies of delinquency and self-report offending indicate that some form of offending is a common component of adolescence for most juveniles, particularly males (e.g. Elliott 1994, Moffitt 1993).

Although systematic research on youth violence is under way (see following section), it is clear that social policy on violence prevention has frequently outpaced its empirical foundation. Understandably, the pressure to respond immediately has often resulted in well-intentioned programs that lack a clear theoretical base or evaluative component. Although recent justice system responses emphasize punishment and deterrence over rehabilitation, the goals of prevention remain strong in other sectors of society. Since the 1980s, the Centers for Disease Control and Prevention highlighted a public health approach to violence prevention, funding a number of demonstration intervention projects (e.g. Powell & Hawkins 1996) and publications designed to help communities develop prevention efforts (National Center for Injury Prevention and Control 1993). The Department of Justice continues to sponsor delinquency prevention projects and has developed the Partnerships Against Violence Network (PAVNET), an electronic resource for community violence prevention initiatives. The National Institutes of Health has developed programs on youth violence, including specific foci on minority youth health behavior and violence (Hammond & Yung 1993). Other organizations such as the American Psychological Association (e.g. Eron et al 1994) and various foundations have also focused on youth violence prevention in recent years.

Research on youth violence has benefited from integrating the paradigms of several disciplines and subspecialties, including public health and developmental, community, and clinical psychology. In particular, recent intervention research has identified important risk and protective factors, adopted an epidemiological and developmental framework, and targeted multiple forms of intervention.

RISK AND PROTECTIVE FACTORS   Clinical and developmental research has identified a number of factors that place youth at risk for violent behavior (Tolan et al 1995). Most factors focus either on the individual youth or the youth's family. Important individual factors include social cognitive components, such as attitudes and beliefs favorable toward aggression, poor problem-solving skills, and disruptive behavior patterns during the early years (e.g. Guerra & Slaby 1990, Tremblay et al 1995). Risk factors at the family level have focused primarily on parental characteristics such as ineffective parenting (reviewed in Tremblay et al 1995), lack of adequate supervision, skills deficits, and violent behavior in the household (e.g. Widom 1991).

Researchers have begun to identify community or contextual factors that place youths at risk for violent behavior (Lowry et al 1995). These include media portrayals and sanctioning of violence, availability of alcohol and drugs, access to weapons, and poor economic conditions (e.g. low socioeconomic status, poverty, lack of opportunity). Guerra and colleagues (1997) identify the chronic stress and violent environment that is characteristic of inner-city communities as critical factors that increase the risk of youth violence as well as have an impact on the effectiveness of preventive interventions.

CONNECTING RISK, PROTECTION, AND ECOLOGY TO INTERVENTION STRATEGIES   Hammond & Yung (1993) use a public health framework to identify intervention opportunities in host-related factors (the person and their behavior), agent-related factors (the weapon or other instrument), and environment-related factors (social, economic, and cultural influences). They argue that most of psychology has focused on host-related interventions, in part because of psychology's history of focusing on the individual. In a review of 15 violence prevention projects, Powell et al (1996) document the consistent, primary focus on the individual, partly as a function of the relative practical and financial ease of targeting individual youth. A number of the projects also included other components, but they usually centered on parents/peer groups or, in some situations, the local school or neighborhood.

Intervention strategies can be classified in many ways, but most of the individual/family-oriented interventions are biological or cognitive behavioral in orientation and focus on enhancing social skills and problem-solving skills in juveniles (Tate et al 1995) and parenting and discipline strategies used by their parents (Dishion & Andrews 1995). However, the field is moving in the direction of influencing community-level factors in tandem with individually oriented interventions (Reid & Eddy 1997). Hawkins and colleagues (1997) review promising community mobilization, media, and policy interventions aimed at reducing antisocial behavior. The numerous reviews of intervention programs identify several key characteristics of successful programs: They use a broad-based approach, target multiple issues in multiple domains, and address behavior in its social context, including coordinating strategies across social domains (Mulvey et al 1993, Tolan et al 1995, Slaby 1998).

DEVELOPMENTAL APPROACH   Identification of risk and protective factors is not a sufficient basis for a preventive intervention, however; researchers and practitioners struggle with the developmental implications for the timing and process of intervention (Coie et al 1993). Risk factors must be mapped to the appropriate developmental periods (Reid & Eddy 1997). Although the general maxim of "earlier is better" holds for violence and antisocial behavior, research has begun to specify the hypothesized process by which risk factors relate to the target condition and what role they play at particular developmental periods (Cicchetti & Toth 1992, Kazdin 1993). Recent reviews of early parent-child education programs have documented clear reductions in delinquency into late adolescence (Yoshikawa 1994, Zigler et al 1992). Although significant progress has been made in the development of preventive interventions for younger children, few primary prevention programs exist for adolescents; most programs focus on treatment of identified adolescent offenders (Guerra et al 1997).

The FAST Track (Families and Schools Together) program provides a good example of a preventive intervention that specifies the connection between short-term changes and long-term prevention goals within a theoretical framework of the developmental psychopathology of conduct disorder in young children (Conduct Problems Prevention Research Group 1992). Based on theories of multiple influences on the development of antisocial behavior, the intervention targets kindergarten-age children scoring in the top 10% of conduct problems through a two-stage screening process. Intervention components include parent training, home visiting/case management, social skills training, academic tutoring, and classroom intervention. Analyses of this longitudinal multisite study are under way, but preliminary results indicate improvements after 1 year of intervention (Bierman, Conduct Probl. Prev. Res. Group. 1996). The FAST Track program represents an excellent example of a theory-based approach to preventive intervention that operates in multiple domains of a child's life.

REMAINING ISSUES   The development of violence prevention programming has traditionally followed the prevention-intervention research cycle method of moving from research-based demonstration programs to community implementation. Although a significant amount of work has been accomplished in the substance of interventions, critical issues of implementation and evaluation remain understudied.

Part of the difficulty in evaluation occurs when moving demonstration projects into the field. Kendall & Southam-Gerow (1995) describe three types of factors that may explain the differences in research-based and community-based intervention outcomes in the context of clinical treatment for anxiety disorders. Client factors include the nature of the client problems and the clients' expectations for outcome. The therapist or "interventionist" factors can include the differences in the training and worldview of those implementing the research project versus community-based professionals. Theoretical as well as very practical differences, such as caseload, can be responsible for outcome differences. Studies of effective programs often point to the "dynamic leader" or key individual who makes the program prosper; those critical characteristics may not be available for multisite implementation of a program that may experience a higher staff turnover rate than the original program staffed by the design team.

Finally, the research factors that can affect transportability include the isolation of research from community input (Henggeler et al 1995). More important, researchers have often failed to identify, operationalize, and assess key characteristics of the community context that affect program process and outcome (Mulvey & Woolard 1997). The difficulty lies in balancing the core components of a violence prevention program with the flexibility necessary for implementation in a wide variety of settings. Organization and implementation issues are key in considering the factors that influence a community's selection and implementation of strategies as well as the community's readiness for implementation (Hammond & Yung 1993, Hawkins et al 1997).

Child Maltreatment

Physical, sexual, and emotional abuse and neglect affect astounding numbers of children in the United States. Statistics from the National Committee to Prevent Child Abuse indicate that in 1997 there were over 3 million reported cases of child maltreatment and that 969,000 were substantiated. The magnitude and severity of the problem explain the proliferation of prevention programs in the 1980s and 1990s. Unfortunately, few programs are based on sound theory, and even fewer are evaluated in a methodologically rigorous fashion, using experimental controls and collecting sufficient multilevel data. Program efficacy in reducing child maltreatment is often difficult to assess because many studies measure only variables associated with abuse (e.g. parental attitudes toward corporal punishment, paternal stress, social support) instead of abuse statistics (Whipple & Wilson 1996, Wekerle & Wolfe 1993). This section reviews current research on the two types of programs that appear most frequently in child maltreatment literature focused on physical abuse and neglect: parent training programs and community-based family support programs. A brief comment is also made regarding child sexual abuse programs that focus on children.

Parent training programs attempt to change maternal attitudes, improve parenting skills, and reduce the use of corporal punishment by concentrating on parent and child characteristics (McInnis-Dittrich 1996, Wurtele 1993). Recent reviews indicate that parent training programs improve maternal global adjustment and child-rearing skills and enhance parenting knowledge and attitudes (Reppucci et al 1997, Wekerle & Wolfe 1993, Whipple & Wilson 1996). However, the direct effects of these programs on child maltreatment are not well documented. Because improving the context in which the family lives is increasingly being considered an essential element in the prevention of child abuse and neglect, parent training is often only one service offered as part of broader-based family support programs.

Effects of community-level and societal-level factors are now accepted as integral parts of the etiology of child maltreatment. The ecological model posits that poverty, unemployment, access to health care, fragmented social services, social isolation, and neighborhood violence are factors that have an impact on individuals and families in ways that affect rates of child maltreatment (Belsky 1980, Limber & Nation 1998). Community-based family support programs are prevention efforts that aim to alter some of these community- and societal-level risk factors (Hay & Jones 1994). Typically, support programs offer one or more of the following: parent education, support groups, drop-in centers, home visits, child health screening, and child care relief (Reppucci et al 1997, Whipple & Wilson 1996, Wekerle & Wolfe 1993). Several excellent reviews offer support for the use of home visiting services and the necessity of long-term interventions to produce lasting effects (Reppucci et al 1997, Daro & McCurdy 1994, Wekerle & Wolfe 1993, Olsen & Widom 1993). Evaluation results from the Hampton Family Resource Project, which offers home visiting services for 2 years, indicate that in addition to improving multiple other maternal and child health variables, participating first-time mothers

to be used with success in medical care, especially in the care of patients with chronic diseases (Steckler et al 1995). However, recent preventive interventions are often based on an ecological model that redirects the focus beyond the individual to include community- and policy-level factors (Steckler et al 1995, Winett 1995).

COMMUNITY REVITALIZATION IN HEALTH PROMOTION   The role of poverty in the rates of numerous health problems makes overall community revitalization a goal of many health educators and health specialists (Eisen 1994). In the 1990s principles of community mobilization and development have increasingly been used in health and wellness promotion efforts. Wellness promotion campaigns have emphasized broad-based education and competency enhancement of citizens about issues related to physical and mental health. In these programs, the concentration of effort on at-risk populations has been de-emphasized, in favor of promoting healthy behaviors in all people within a community. Community development relies on citizen involvement in identifying health needs and implementing initiatives to improve the health of neighborhood residents. (See Fawcett et al 1993 and Eisen 1994 for reviews of health promotion, community development, and community empowerment initiatives.)

THE USE OF MULTIPLE SETTINGS   One dimension of the expanding focus of health promotion and prevention efforts is the use of multiple settings for health care and health education, including the community, the workplace, schools, churches, and traditional health care settings. By increasing the number of settings available for information about health care, the chances of reaching alienated individuals increase (Mullen et al 1995). Mediating social structures, which are institutions like churches and neighborhoods that connect individuals to large public institutions, such as the health care system, play an important role in linking individuals to health care and health education, especially by increasing social support, advocating for health programs, and supplying financial resources (Eng & Hatch 1991, Sutherland et al 1995). Linking agents, who connect community residents to health care and health education, are important in enlisting community participation and increasing social support, especially among isolated and disenfranchised groups (Eng & Young 1992).

REACHING UNDERSERVED POPULATIONS   Populations that have been largely ignored in health education and prevention efforts have recently been the focus of considerable research attention. Historically underserved populations, including members of ethnic minority groups, women, elderly persons, and children, have diverse health problems and require special attention from educators, policy makers, and program developers (Pasick et al 1996, Marín et al 1995). The importance of targeting underserved populations is underscored by the fact that programs found to be effective with one group are not necessarily effective with another group. In the 1990s, remarkable progress has been made in initiating culturally sensitive preventive interventions with multiple underserved groups, e.g. elderly members of ethnic minority groups (Maynard 1996), elderly African-American women (LaVeist et al 1997), elderly adults (Levkoff et al 1996, Schweitzer 1994), elderly adults in rural communities (Lave et al 1995), Native Americans (LeMaster & Connell 1994), and homosexual Hispanic males (Zimmerman et al 1997). These programs clearly suggest that interventions must deal with diversity. (For extensive reviews of diversity issues in health psychology, effective programs, and health education approaches with underserved populations, see Kato & Mann 1996 and Marín et al 1995.)

The following sections review multilevel prevention and health promotion efforts in two specific areas: substance abuse and HIV/AIDS. Within each section we highlight recent work with underserved and culturally diverse populations. The importance of community empowerment and settings in health education and promotion programs and research in these areas is also reviewed. In addition, we examine the role of social support mobilization as a coping strategy.

Alcohol and Drug Abuse

Empowering community involvement in issue identification and problem solving has been a core component of substance abuse interventions yet is rarely studied systematically. Certainly community organization has led to social change in a variety of arenas, including patients' rights, victim advocacy and social justice, and drunk driving. Organizational efforts such as these have emerged from the bottom up, through grassroots efforts as well as from the top down through legislative and professional efforts. Efforts such as the Prevention Plus program through the federal Office of Substance Abuse Prevention (Linney & Wandersman 1991) and the Community Partnership Program (Kaftarian & Hansen 1994) highlight the importance of community involvement from defining the substance abuse issues in a community to developing appropriate interventions. Paralleling the recognition that many social problems are widespread, complex, multidetermined, and often "targeted" by multiple efforts and initiatives, community coalitions have emerged as potentially powerful vehicles for creating community change (Mitchell et al 1996).

COMMUNITY READINESS   Until recently, little systematic research examined community coalition development and implementation (Florin et al 1993, Francisco et al 1993, McMillan et al 1995). Goodman et al (1996) argue that coalitions and their associated interventions can be conceptualized across the two dimensions of targeted social levels and community readiness. Literature using the case-study approach to describe and evaluate community coalitions has incorporated descriptive dimensions of readiness, sometimes indirectly, e.g. in discussions of turf issues, coalition-building processes, and coalition impact (e.g. Nelson 1994).

Moving beyond the descriptive phase, Goodman & Wandersman (1994) use triangulation, or multiple assessment methods, to evaluate the effectiveness of a community coalition to prevent substance abuse [ATOD (alcohol, tobacco, and other drugs)]. Quantitative and qualitative approaches are used to evaluate the coalition at each developmental stage. For example, during the formation stage, the FORECAST system (Goodman & Wandersman 1994) structures the problem identification and goal-setting functions of early coalition development, analyzing the coalition's progress in achieving the identified "markers" of the development process. Butterfoss and colleagues (1996) evaluated the efficacy of several coalition characteristics, including leadership, decision making, interorganizational links, and social climate, in predicting the quality of prevention planning as well as member satisfaction and participation in coalition activities. The coalition was composed of approximately 224 members organized into 20 committees, the majority of which developed prevention plans on a specific topic. Coalition member surveys and independent ratings of plan quality indicated that coalition effectiveness was associated with higher participation by the coalition's committees and that increased committee participation was associated with higher levels of satisfaction with the committee's work. However, no relationship was found between plan quality and coalition effectiveness or committee satisfaction, a finding that was attributed to a lack of variance in scores of plan quality among the committees. These results provide important clues to the process of coalition organization and maintenance.

EMPOWERMENT THEORY   Coalitions are presumed to promote positive outcomes for participating members as well as the community that receives the coalition's change efforts. McMillan et al (1995) use empowerment theory to examine empirically what factors and characteristics of coalitions are associated with variations in individual psychological empowerment, the collective empowering of members (an empowering organization), and the degree of community change (organizational empowerment). In a study of 35 coalitions to prevent substance abuse, McMillan et al found significant variation in the organizational climate and the degree to which coalitions empowered their members. Organizational variables such as climate were important unique contributors to levels of individual psychological empowerment, reinforcing the importance of context in improving empowerment levels. These organizational variables also related to the task forces empowering their members and being empowered as an entity in effecting community change. Although this study has several limitations, it provides an important step toward using a multilevel approach to understand the relationship between individuals, an organized group process, and social change outcomes. This and other studies demonstrate the use of advanced statistical techniques to partial out individual and group effects in a multilevel intervention design (e.g. Hedeker et al 1994).

RISK-FOCUSED PREVENTION   Reducing risk and promoting positive social development is the two-pronged approach to community action facilitated by the Communities That Care (CTC) strategy for preventing adolescent problem behavior (Hawkins & Catalano 1992). The CTC approach can be applied to a variety of problem behaviors, including substance abuse, delinquency, teen pregnancy, and violence. Using a community approach, this strategy is intended to involve key community leaders in identifying and prioritizing risks and resources, developing a plan, and monitoring the ongoing action and implementation. The driving force behind program development and implementation is a community board, similar to a coalition, that should include representatives from different professional, citizen, and advocacy constituencies. A 4-year demonstration project, TOGETHER! Communities for Drug-free Youth, involved 35 communities using the CTC strategy to develop and implement comprehensive prevention plans to reduce the prevalence of adolescent substance abuse. Harachi and colleagues (1996) used a variety of data sources, including surveys, documentation of community/advisory board activities, and prevention plans to evaluate the implementation of the CTC program across communities. Thirty-five of 40 communities initially involved in the program completed all of the necessary training, and 31 boards remained active 4 years after project initiation. Twenty-seven boards had begun implementing prevention plan strategies during the first part of the planning and implementation phase (1 year). Ongoing evaluation of these initiatives should provide clues as to how effective such a strategy can be, as well as critical variables in the intervention.

Each of these community approaches to substance use prevention contributes to a key component of preventive intervention research—they have moved beyond the anecdotal information on community mobilization to delineate the key processes and outcomes involved in community mobilization and coalition interventions, identified quantitative and qualitative methods of measuring the internal development and external impact of such coalitions, and in some cases, evaluated the outcome of the intervention strategies. These efforts take advantage of theoretical and methodological advances to evaluate effects at the individual, group, and community levels.

Smoking and Tobacco Use

Over the past several years, the costs and consequences of smoking, particularly among youth, have captured national media and policy attention. In 1994 the Food and Drug Administration (FDA) began to consider whether it could establish jurisdiction over nicotine-containing tobacco products. During the subsequent 2 years, Congress and the FDA investigated the tobacco industry and the manipulation of nicotine. In the summer of 1995, President Clinton announced the proposed FDA rule to reduce tobacco use by children and adolescents. After extensive public comment, the final legislation included language to reduce young people's access to tobacco products through sales restrictions, to reduce the appeal of tobacco products to children and adolescents through restrictions on advertising and promotional materials, and to educate youth about the harmful effects of tobacco. These and other efforts at the state and local levels define a changing community landscape for smoking prevention efforts. A substantial body of research has examined the risk factors for smoking initiation, persistence, and cessation, particularly among adolescents. Community efforts to reduce adolescent tobacco use have historically focused on changing adolescents' attitudes about tobacco, although the connection between attitude and behavior change is not always strong.

In light of the changing legal landscape regarding adolescent tobacco use, one set of interventions focuses on reducing illegal sales of tobacco to youth within the community system. Although cigarette sales to minors have been illegal for some time, several research studies and media exposés have documented the relative ease with which adolescents can purchase tobacco products from local merchants (Biglan et al 1995, DiFranza et al 1992, Feighery et al 1991, Forster et al 1992, Hinds 1992, Jason et al 1991). Hypothesizing that reducing the availability of cigarettes will reduce the initiation and continuation of teen smoking, one increasingly common intervention strategy focuses on reducing merchant sales to youth. These interventions usually use minors (or legal adults who look under 18) to attempt to purchase tobacco products from merchants, documenting such variables as whether age identification was requested and the purchase was successful. After a baseline assessment, some type of intervention or enforcement is implemented and minor purchases are assessed during the intervention period.

Using this general approach, Jason and colleagues (1996a) evaluated the effect of enforcement on purchase rates in three of Chicago's ethnic geographic areas (Latino, African-American, Caucasian), indexed by employing minors (with parental and personal consent). After a baseline measurement period, a warning condition was implemented for 1 month in which merchants who sold cigarettes to minors were issued a warning packet that included information about the new law, training tips, and information about a program of unannounced inspections by the city. Merchants who refused to sell to minors were congratulated and received the same packet of materials. During the 12-month enforcement phase, merchants were randomly assigned to a control condition (no enforcement) or 2-, 4-, and 6-month conditions of enforcement that en-

tailed an administrative ticket and $200 fine for illegal sales to minors partici-
pating in the study. During the non-enforcement months, minors' purchase attempts without enforcement continued monthly to track compliance with the
law. During the baseline period, over 80% of merchants sold cigarettes to minors. During the enforcement phase, all enforcement conditions demonstrated
significant decreases in sales to minors, but the control condition remained
high. Moreover, reductions in illegal sales increased under conditions of more
frequent enforcement. No significant differences across ethnic neighborhoods
in the enforcement conditions were found. Jason and colleagues (1996a) suggest that active enforcement of sales laws are a critical component to reducing
youth access to tobacco products and that frequency of enforcement can have
an important impact. They recommend that enforcement schedules occur at
least every 4 months.

Using the same paradigm, Biglan and colleagues (1996) evaluated a community intervention to mobilize positive reinforcement for not selling tobacco
products to minors. The intervention contained five components: mobilizing
community support through public information campaigns and proclamations;
educating merchants about the law and the proposed rewards for compliance;
changing the consequences of law compliance by rewarding with gift certifi-
cates those clerks who refused sales to minors; publicity about those clerks
who complied with the law; and monthly feedback to store managers about the
extent of illegal sales in their establishment. Across four communities, illegal
sales dropped an average of 38%, which suggests that positive reinforcement
can be effective in creating change even in the absence of penalties or punish-
ments. The effects of individual intervention components could not be distinguished.

This line of research demonstrates the utility of system- or community-
focused interventions that create changes in the larger context of adolescent tobacco use. Although further work must make explicit the link between reduced
availability of tobacco and reduced prevalence of adolescent tobacco use,
these studies demonstrate community policies that may work in concert with
individual-based interventions to reduce smoking.

HIV/AIDS

> Slogans that teach young people to "Say no" to drugs and sex have a nice ring
> to them. But . . . they are as effective in preventing adolescent pregnancy and
> drug abuse as the saying "Have a nice day" is in preventing clinical depres-
> sion...
>
> Michael Carrera, Ed.D., at the hearings of the Presidential
> Commissions on AIDS

In 1996, the XI International Conference on AIDS in Vancouver emphasized
the necessity of recognizing the complex social, cultural, and political forces

shaping both the spread of HIV and the issues confronting prevention efforts. Over the past decade, AIDS prevention projects have moved from models focused on changes in individual risk behavior to models emphasizing community mobilization (Parker 1996). Perceived risk of infection is one individual-level factor that has received considerable attention. However, based on the mixed results of 60 studies of HIV-related risk perceptions (Kowalewski et al 1997), the role that perceived risk of HIV infection plays in determining behavior changes is inconclusive. The limited success of interventions based solely on the provision of information to changed behavior has led to the increased use of collective empowerment strategies, which require the recognition that even though the transmission of HIV takes place through the behavioral practices of individuals, some individuals and groups are particularly vulnerable to infection (Parker 1996).

HIV prevention efforts differ from those of other health problems because the consequences of other high-risk behaviors, like smoking, develop over time and are often reversible, thus offering multiple opportunities for intervention. For many health problems, failure at one point of intervention can be overcome by later success, but the consequences of failure of AIDS interventions can be HIV infection, and in the absence of a cure, almost certain premature death (Chesney 1994).

A review of HIV prevention programs indicates that three approaches have shown some promise in reducing high-risk behaviors: (*a*) cognitive-behavioral interventions that teach self-management skills for risk reduction to at-risk individuals or small groups, (*b*) community-based interventions that aim to change social norms, and (*c*) multifaceted community mobilization approaches that target specific segments of the population through media, opinion leaders, and community volunteers (Kelly et al 1993). Regardless of the type of intervention, effective planning and implementation of programs require rigorous process and outcome evaluations; these evaluations have been largely lacking in the field (Kelly et al 1993, Booth & Koester 1996).

One of the major challenges to HIV prevention interventionists is reaching diverse target groups including, but not limited to, gay males, intravenous drug users, adolescents, and heterosexual adults. All of these groups have different intervention needs based on disparate motivations, environments, cognitions, and behavior patterns (Fisher & Fisher 1996, Rhodes & Malotte 1996, Fishbein et al 1996). Sexual behavior and drug use are complex, personal issues that need to be addressed in their social and cultural contexts, which differ for each target group. In the remainder of this section we briefly review the central issues and interventions related to four target groups: adolescents, intravenous drug users (IDUs), homosexual men, and ethnic minority populations. Obviously, some intervention efforts target overlapping groups, e.g. Latino drug users or homosexual adolescents.

ADOLESCENT PROGRAMS   Numerous HIV prevention efforts have been targeted at reducing high-risk behaviors among adolescents. While the prevalence of AIDS cases among adolescents is relatively low, the length of time
between HIV infection and the development of AIDS-related symptoms may
mask the extent of the health threat that HIV poses to adolescents (Chesney
1994, DiClemente 1996). Yet even within the adolescent population there are
multiple subgroups in need of diverse interventions. For example, in planning
programs, researchers should consider the difference in male and female exposure risks and adjust interventions accordingly. An examination of the differences between adolescent and adult exposure categories indicates that adolescent females are at a much higher risk of contracting HIV through heterosexual
intercourse (52%) than either adult (7%) or adolescent males (2%). The hemo-
phelia category is the largest risk factor for adolescent males (44%), followed
by homosexual contact (32%) (DiClemente 1996). Kim and associates (1997)
reviewed 40 adolescent HIV risk-reduction interventions, evaluating the interventions for changes in knowledge, attitudes, intentions, and behaviors. The
most effective interventions were theory-based, included training in coping
skills, employed community input or culturally relevant materials, and were
longer in duration. These same elements are endorsed in a behavioralecological model of adolescent sexual development (Hovell et al 1994), which
emphasizes the importance of multiple interventions focusing on change in social networks to control the AIDS epidemic. One example of a well-
documented and -evaluated intervention effort with adolescents is the Focus
on Kids program, which emphasizes the importance of community involvement
(Galbraith et al 1996). Other researchers have targeted specific populations,
like Slonim-Nevo and associates' (1996) study of HIV preventive interventions for delinquent and abused adolescents. Still others have concentrated on
examining particular aspects of prevention efforts, such as Ozer and colleagues' (1997) study of the impact of peer educator qualities on intervention
efficacy.

INTRAVENOUS DRUG USER (IDU) PROGRAMS   A substantial body of literature
has accumulated on HIV preventive interventions for IDUs. Like interventions
targeted toward other groups, programs for IDUs are most effective when they
include an individual behavior modification component and a social or physical environment modification component (Rhodes & Malotte 1996). For
IDUs, particularly effective community-level approaches are needle exchange,
bleach distribution, and outreach programs (Watters 1996). The most commonly reported behavior changes in response to interventions are (*a*) increased
use of sterile needles, (*b*) use of needle exchange programs, (*c*) bleaching needles to kill the virus, and (*d*) reduction in the number of partners with whom an
individual shares needles (Singer & Needle 1996). Excellent work has docu-

mented the efficacy of syringe exchange programs (Kochems et al 1996), personal network interventions using social influence process (Latkin et al 1996), and distribution of intervention kits that included condoms, bleach bottles, and role model stories (Rietmeijer et al 1996). Unfortunately, controversy currently surrounds needle exchange programs because some members of the general public, politicians, and government officials think they might encourage illegal drug use, even though many more individuals may become infected with the HIV virus.

The Stop AIDS for Everyone (SAFE) project demonstrates how personal networks can be used to reduce carrying the risk of HIV behaviors among drug users. Latkin and associates (1996) undertook a unique approach to HIV prevention among inner-city, low-income drug users by focusing on the injection behaviors of drug sharing networks. Based on findings indicating that perceived normative expectations and peer pressure are determinants of risky injection practices (Des Jarlais et al 1985, Friedman et al 1987, Magura et al 1989), the researchers explored the role of personal networks on the adoption and maintenance of HIV-related behaviors. They employed a true experimental design and used pre- and postintervention self-reports of behaviors to evaluate effectiveness of the intervention. Rates of sharing unhygienic injection equipment were measured at 18 months after the initial interview.

Participants in the experimental condition brought in at least 3 other members of their drug network for a series of 6 group intervention sessions. Facilitators were former heroin users who employed role playing and group exercises to demonstrate the power of social norms and their influence on behaviors. Network members engaged in group decision making, including planning how to monitor and reinforce safer behaviors of each member. Throughout the sessions, participants practiced effective assertiveness skills, specifically rejection of high-risk settings and negotiation of risk reduction with other members.

Of the 189 potential participants, 66 completed at least 4 sessions with their drug network and 47 of them completed the 18-month follow-up interview. Analyses were separated for HIV-positive and HIV-negative experimental participants and controls. For the HIV-negative participants, group assignment predicted HIV-related behaviors: Those in the control group were 2.8 times more likely to report sharing needles and 2.7 times more likely to report sharing cookers than those in the experimental group. However, for the HIV-positive participants, group membership was not associated with either needle or cooker sharing.

These findings underscore the importance of examining personal network processes as a point of intervention with injection drug users. The researchers also emphasize exploration of the interactions between personal networks and relationships to larger social networks and how these social networks might be used in promoting community-based HIV preventive interventions. (See Watters 1996 for a review of several exemplary efforts to reduce the incidence of HIV infection.)

PROGRAMS FOR HOMOSEXUAL AND BISEXUAL MALES   The first group targeted for interventions to halt the spread of HIV was composed of homosexual and bisexual males. Most of the original prevention programs were grassroots efforts organized by gay communities in urban areas. Kalichman et al's (1997) review of 12 community-based HIV risk-reduction programs targeting gay and bisexual men clearly suggested the importance of peer behavior and social norms as the key issues in planning interventions with these populations. For example, the Mpowerment Project reduced rates of unprotected sex by 27% among young gay men in one community by using social activities to connect men with peers who support and encourage safe sex practices (Kegeles et al 1996).

PROGRAMS TARGETING SPECIFIC ETHNIC GROUPS   Rates of HIV infection are disproportionately high in Latino and African-American populations, so it is essential that interventions include ethnic and cultural components. Traditional gender roles and pervasive cultural messages may have an important effect on sexual behavior among Latinos, which needs to be considered in planning interventions with this population (Marín 1996). Kalichman and associates (1993) demonstrated the importance of framing AIDS information in a culturally relevant context in a study of public service videotapes. African-American women who viewed culturally sensitive prevention messages delivered by other African-American women were more likely to request condoms and be tested for HIV than were women who viewed standard public health messages. Another study produced significant decreases in high-risk behavior for African-Americans and Latinos who participated in culturally targeted, enhanced interventions (Weeks et al 1996). Empowerment strategies can be effectively used with minority populations to give participants responsibility for the design and implementation of HIV interventions, as demonstrated in the Zimmerman et al (1997) prevention project for Mexican homosexual men. (For excellent reviews of HIV prevention programs, see Oskamp & Thompson 1996; for an empirical review of the use of HIV prevention videotapes, see Kalichman 1996.)

CONCLUSION

The 1990s have ushered in an ever-increasing number of preventive/community and policy/social interventions. The publication of the IOM and NIMH prevention reports, although narrowly focused on *DSM-IV* mental illnesses, suggests the embracing of prevention as a legitimate governmental social policy.

Our review has been selective in scope, but it clearly suggests several goals for the future. In all areas, there is a major need for rigorous process and outcome evaluations of preventive interventions and social policies. The social climate and political landscape of our communities and of the larger society clearly influence the problems that have been tackled. For example, many vocal advocates have called for service programs to decrease violence and the spread of AIDS. The needs are immediate, but programs without systematic evaluation of both implementation and efficacy (as most of them are) may lead to a sense of accomplishment without really solving the problem. Our suggestion is not to slow down the interventions but rather to emphasize meaningful evaluation so that what works and what does not can actually be determined.

Programs focused solely on the individual seem destined to failure if they do not take into account community context. Thus the suggestions of researchers focused on decreasing cigarette smoking among teens to target seller behavior and media advertising may hold more likelihood of success than interventions with the teens themselves. Programs designed to alleviate large social problems must become multilevel in nature, e.g. focusing on individuals, families, community settings (such as churches, schools, neighborhoods), and societal norms (e.g. smoking is hazardous to your health rather than smoking is a positive adult activity). We know from past successes in public health that environmental modification is often more effective than pursuing individual change alone. All of the interventions that we have reviewed reinforce this conception.

As our society has become more pluralistic in its ethnic composition and in its focus on gender equality, the importance of embracing diversity has taken center stage. Increased attention to feminist and minority perspectives strongly indicates that the roots of some behaviors, e.g. violence against women and children, may be at least a partial result of socialization. If so, more responsibility for prevention should be directed at socialization agents, such as parents, schools, churches, and service providers, in an effort to heighten society's awareness of problems that could potentially be alleviated if future generations grow up with a different set of attitudes. However, such attitude change usually is accomplished only as social policies implemented by legislation and legal rulings come into being to provide an ongoing framework in which such changes can occur. For example, the desegregation of schools in the 1950s and 1960s clearly contributed to younger generations developing less prejudicial attitudes than existed in the past. By this example, we are not suggesting that all prejudice has been eliminated—far from it! Nevertheless, those who have lived through the past half century have witnessed substantial change. Such changes take a long time to accomplish, and the end result is seldom complete alleviation of the problems. Rather, such social problem solving must be conceived as never being solved in a once-and-for-all fashion (Sarason 1978).

Focusing on diversity also suggests that alleviating a particular problem (e.g. preventing HIV transmission) may require multiple interventions targeted in ways that can be utilized by different groups. In other words, identical packaging of an intervention may be inappropriate and therefore ineffective for all groups. By being alert to diversity, interventions on the same problem can be tailored for various age, gender, ethnic, and other groups, as was summarized in the section on HIV preventive interventions.

In sum, psychology in the 1990s has played an ever-increasing role in developing and implementing effective social, community, and preventive interventions for some of society's most pressing social problems. The field should look forward to extending its role in social action while at the same time emphasizing the critical importance of rigorous research as a component of future interventions.

> **Visit the *Annual Reviews home page* at http://www.AnnualReviews.org.**

Literature Cited

Albee GW. 1996. Revolutions and counter-revolutions in prevention. *Am. Psychol.* 51:1130–33

Auslander WF, Haire-Joshu D, Houston CA, Fisher EB. 1992. Community organization to reduce the risk of non-insulin-dependent diabetes among low-income African-American women. *Ethn. Dis.* 2: 176–84

Battle EK, Brownell KD. 1996. Confronting a rising tide of eating disorders and obesity: treatment vs. prevention and policy. *Addict. Behav.* 21:755–65

Belsky J. 1980. Child maltreatment: an ecological integration. *Am. Psychol.* 35: 320–35

Bierman K, Conduct Probl. Prev. Res. Group. 1996. Integrating social-skills training interventions with parent training and family-focused support to prevent conduct disorder in high-risk populations: the Fast Track Multisite Demonstration Project. In *Understanding Aggressive Behavior in Children,* ed. CF Ferris, T Grisso, 794:256–64. New York: NY Acad. Sci. 426 pp.

Biglan A, Ary D, Yudelson H, Duncan TE, Hood D, et al. 1996. Experimental evaluation of a modular approach to mobilizing antitobacco influences of peers and par-ents. *Am. J. Community Psychol.* 24: 311–39

Biglan A, Henderson J, Humphrey D, Yasui M, Whisman R, et al. 1995. Mobilising positive reinforcement to reduce youth access to tobacco. *Tob. Control* 4:42–48

Bloom BL. 1980. Social and community interventions. *Annu. Rev. Psychol.* 31:111–42

Booth RE, Koester SK. 1996. Issues and approaches to evaluating HIV outreach interventions. *J. Drug Issues* 26:525–39

Boyle PJ, Callahan D. 1995. Managed care in mental health: the ethical issues. *Health Aff.* 14:7–22

Britner PA, Reppucci ND. 1997. Prevention of child maltreatment: evaluation of a parent education program for teen mothers. *J. Child Family Stud.* 6:165–75

Brownson RC, Mayer JP, Dusseault PM, Dabney S, Wright KS, et al. 1997. Developing and evaluating a cardiovascular risk reduction project. *Am. J. Health Behav.* 21: 333–44

Browne A. 1993. Violence against women by male partners: prevalence, outcomes, and policy implications. *Am. Psychol.* 48: 1077–87

Butterfoss FD, Goodman RM, Wandersman A. 1996. Community coalitions for prevention and health promotion: factors predicting satisfaction, participation, and planning. *Health Educ. Q.* 23:65–79

Campbell R, Sullivan CM, Davidson WS. 1995. Women who use domestic violence shelters: changes in depression over time. *Psychol. Women Q.* 19:237–55

Catalano RF, Hawkins JD, Krenz C, Gillmore M, et al. 1993. Using research to guide culturally appropriate drug abuse prevention. *J. Consult. Clin. Psychol.* 61:804–11

Chesney MA. 1994. Prevention of HIV and STD infections. *Prev. Med.* 23:655–60

Chisholm M, Howard PB, Boyd MA, Clement JA, Hendrix MJ, Reiss-Brennan B. 1997. Quality indicators for primary mental health within managed care: a public health focus. *Arch. Psychiatr. Nurs.* 11: 167–81

Cicchetti D, Lynch M. 1993. Toward an ecological/transactional model of community violence and child maltreatment: consequences for children's development. *Psychiatry* 56:96–118

Cicchetti D, Toth SL. 1992. The role of developmental theory in prevention and intervention. *Dev. Psychopathol.* 4:489–94

Coie JD, Watt NF, West SG, Hawkins JD, Asarnow JR, et al. 1993. The science of prevention: a conceptual framework and some directions for a national research program. *Am. Psychol.* 48:1013–22

Conduct Problems Prevention Research Group. 1992. A developmental and clinical model for the prevention of conduct disorder: the FAST Track Program. *Dev. Psycholpathol.* 4:509–28

Cowen EL. 1994. The enhancement of psychological wellness: challenges and opportunities. *Am. J. Community Psychol.* 22:149–79

Crowell NA, Burgess AW, eds. 1996. *Understanding Violence Against Women.* Washington, DC: Natl. Acad. Press. 225 pp.

Darmstadt GL. 1990. Community-based child abuse prevention. *Soc. Work* 35:487–89

Daro D, McCurdy K. 1994. Preventing child abuse and neglect: programmatic interventions. *Child Welf.* 73:405–30

Des Jarlais DC, Friedman SR, Hopkins W. 1985. Risk reduction for AIDS among intravenous drug users. *Annu. Rev. Intern. Med.* 103:755–59

DiClemente R. 1996. Adolescents at risk for AIDS: AIDS epidemiology, and prevalence and incidence of HIV. See Oskamp & Thompson 1996, pp. 13–30

DiFranza JR, Carlson RP, Caisse X. 1992. Reducing youth access to tobacco. *Tob. Control* 1:58

Dishion TJ, Andrews DW. 1995. Preventing escalation in problem behaviors with high risk young adolescents: immediate and one-year outcomes. *J. Consult. Clin. Psychol.* 63:538–48

Durlak JA, Wells AM. 1997. Primary prevention programs for children and adolescents: a meta-analytic review. *Am. J. Community Psychol.* 25:115–52

Earls F, McGuire J, Shay S. 1994. Evaluating a community intervention to reduce the risk of child abuse: methodological strategies in conducting neighborhood surveys. *Child Abuse Negl.* 18:473–85

Eisen A. 1994. Survey of neighborhood-based, comprehensive community empowerment initiatives. *Health Educ. Q.* 21: 235–52

Elliott DS. 1994. Serious violent offenders: onset, developmental course, and termination. *Criminology* 32:1–21

Eng E, Hatch JW. 1991. Networking between agencies and Black churches: the lay health advisor model. *Prev. Hum. Serv.* 10:123–46

Eng E, Young R. 1992. Lay health advisors as community change agents. *Fam. Community Health* 15:24–40

Eron LD, Gentry JH, Schlegel P. 1994. *Reason to Hope: A Psychosocial Perspective on Violence and Youth.* Washington, DC: Am. Psychol. Assoc. 492 pp.

Fawcett SB, Paine AL, Francisco VT, Vliet M. 1993. Promoting health through community development. See Glenwick & Jason 1993, pp. 233–55

Federal Bureau of Investigation. 1995. Uniform Crime Reports. Washington, DC: FBI

Federal Bureau of Investigation. 1996. Uniform Crime Reports. Washington, DC: FBI

Feighery E, Altman DG, Shaffer G. 1991. The effects of combining education and enforcement to reduce tobacco sales to minors: a study of four Northern California communities. *JAMA* 266:3168–71

Ferrari JR. 1994. Systematic approaches to reducing a national health problem: infrequent blood donations. *Community Psychol.* 26:16–18

Ferrari JR, Leippe MR. 1992. Noncompliance with persuasive appeals for a prosocial, altruistic act: blood donating. *J. Appl. Soc. Psychol.* 22:83–101

Fishbein M, Guenther-Grey C, Johnson WD, Wolitski RJ, McAlister A, et al. 1996. Using a theory-based community intervention to reduce AIDS risk behaviors: the CDC's AIDS community demonstration projects. See Oskamp & Thompson 1996, pp. 177–206

Fisher JD, Fisher WA. 1996. The information-

414 REPPUCCI, WOOLARD & FRIED

motivation-behavioral skills model in
AIDS risk behavior change: empirical support and application. See Oskamp &
Thompson 1996, pp. 100–27

Florin P, Mitchell R, Stevenson J. 1993. Identifying training and technical assistance
needs in community coalitions: a developmental approach. *Health Educ. Res.* 8:
417–32

Foreyt JP, Carlos Poston WS II, Goodrick GK.
1996. Future directions in obesity and eating disorders. *Addict. Behav.* 21:767–78

Forster JL, Hourigan M, McGovern P. 1992.
Availability of cigarettes to underage
youth in three communities. *Prev. Med.*
21:320–28

Francisco VT, Paine AL, Fawcett SB. 1993. A
methodology for monitoring and evaluating community health coalitions. *Health
Educ. Res.* 8:403–16

Friedman SR, Des Jarlais DC, Sotheran JL,
Garber J, Cohen H, Smith D. 1987. AIDS
and self-organization among intravenous
drug users. *Int. J. Addict.* 23:201–19

Frost JJ, Forrest JD. 1995. Understanding the
impact of effective teenage pregnancy prevention programs. *Family Plan. Perspect.*
27:188–95

Galbraith J, Ricardo I, Stanton B, Black M,
Feigelman S, Kaljee L. 1996. Challenges
and rewards of involving community in research: an overview of the "Focus on
Kids" HIV risk reduction program. *Health
Educ. Q.* 23:383–94

Gesten EL, Jason LA. 1987. Social and community interventions. *Annu. Rev. Psychol.*
38:427–60

Glenwick DS, Jason LA, eds. 1993. *Promoting Health and Mental Health in Children,
Youth, and Families.* New York: Springer

Goodman LA, Koss MP, Fitzgerald LF, Russo
NF, Keita GP. 1993. Male violence against
women: current research and future directions. *Am. Psychol.* 48(10):1054–58

Goodman RM, Wandersman A. 1994. FORECAST: a formative approach to evaluating
community coalitions and communitybased initiatives. See Kaftarian & Hansen
1994, pp. 6–26

Goodman RM, Wandersman A, Chinman M,
Imm P, Morrissey E. 1996. An ecological
assessment of community-based interventions for prevention and health promotion:
approaches to measuring community coalitions. *Am. J. Community Psychol.* 24:
33–61

Gordon JS. 1996. Community services for
abused women: a review of perceived usefulness and efficacy. *J. Fam. Viol.* 11:
315–29

Guerra NG, Attar B, Weissberg RP. 1997. Prevention of aggression and violence among
inner-city youths. *Handbook of Antisocial
Behavior,* ed. DM Stoff, J Breiling, JD Maser, pp. 375–83. New York: Wiley. 600 pp.

Guerra NG, Slaby RG. 1990. Cognitive mediators of aggression in adolescent offenders: II. Intervention. *Dev. Psychol.* 26:
269–77

Hammond WR, Yung B. 1993. Psychology's
role in the public health response to assaultive violence among young AfricanAmerican men. *Am. Psychol.* 48:142–54

Hanson KA, Gidycz CA. 1993. Evaluation of a
sexual assault prevention program. *J. Consult. Clin. Psychol.* 61(6):1046–52

Harachi TW, Ayers CD, Hawkins JD,
Catalano RF. 1996. Empowering communities to prevent adolescent substance
abuse: process evaluation results from a
risk- and protection-focused community
mobilization effort. *J. Prim. Prev.* 16:
233–54

Hawkins JD, Arthur MW, Olson JJ. 1997.
Community intervention to reduce risks
and enhance protection against antisocial
behavior. In *Handbook of Antisocial Behavior,* ed. DM Stoff, J Breiling, JD Maser, pp. 365–74. New York: Wiley. 600 pp.

Hawkins JD, Catalano RF. 1992. *Communities
That Care: Action for Drug Abuse Prevention.* San Francisco: Jossey-Bass. 247 pp.

Hay T, Jones L. 1994. Societal interventions to
prevent child abuse and neglect. *Child
Welf.* 73:379–403

Healthy Families Partnership. 1996. *The Impact of the Healthy Families Partnership:
Summary Evaluation.* Hampton, VA:
Healthy Fam. Partnersh.

Hedeker D, McMahon SD, Jason LA, Salina
D. 1994. Analysis of clustered data in community psychology: with an example from
a worksite smoking cessation project. *Am.
J. Community Psychol.* 22:595–615

Heller K. 1990. Social and community intervention. *Annu. Rev. Psychol.* 41:141–68

Henggeler SW, Schoenwald SK, Pickrel SG.
1995. Multisystemic therapy: bridging the
gap between university- and communitybased treatment. Special Section: efficacy
and effectiveness in studies of child and
adolescent psychotherapy. *J. Consult.
Clin. Psychol.* 63:709–17

Hinds MW. 1992. Impact of a local ordinance
banning tobacco sales to minors. *Public
Health Rep.* 107:355–58

Hovell MF, Hillman ER, Blumberg E, Sipan
C, Atkins C, et al. 1994. A behavioralecological model of adolescent sexual development: a template for AIDS prevention. *J. Sex Res.* 31:267–81

Iglehart JK. 1996. Health policy report: managed care and mental health. *N. Engl. J. Med.* 334:131–35

Iscoe I, Harris LC. 1984. Social and community interventions. *Annu. Rev. Psychol.* 35: 333–60

Jason LA, Billows W, Schnopp-Wyatt D, King C. 1996a. Reducing the illegal sales of cigarettes to minors: analysis of alternative enforcement schedules. *J. Appl. Behav. Anal.* 29:333–44

Jason LA, Ferrari JR, Taylor RR, Slavich SP, Stenzel CL. 1996b. A national assessment of the service, support, and housing preferences by persons with chronic fatigue syndrome: toward a comprehensive rehabilitation program. *Eval. Health Prof.* 19: 194–207

Jason LA, Ji PY, Anes MD, Birkhead SH. 1991. Active enforcement of cigarette control laws in the prevention of cigarette sales to minors. *JAMA* 266:3159–61

Jason LA, Taylor R, Wagner L, Holden J, Ferrari JR, et al. 1995. Estimating rates of chronic fatigue syndrome from a community-based sample: a pilot study. *Am. J. Community Psychol.* 23:557–68

Kaftarian SJ, Hansen WB, eds. 1994. *Community Partnership Program. J. Community Psychol. Monogr. Ser.,* CSAP Special Issue. Cent. Subst. Abuse Prev. 205 pp.

Kalichman SC. 1996. HIV-AIDS prevention videotapes: a review of empirical findings. *J. Prim. Prev.* 17:259–79

Kalichman SC, Belcher L, Cherry C, Williams EA. 1997. Primary prevention of sexually transmitted HIV infections: transferring behavioral research technology to community programs. *J. Prim. Prev.* 18: 149–72

Kalichman SC, Kelly JA, Hunter TL, Murphy DA, Tyler R. 1993. Culturally tailored HIV-AIDS risk-reduction messages targeted to African-American urban women: impact on risk sensitization and risk reduction. *J. Consult. Clin. Psychol.* 16: 291–95

Kato PM, Mann T, eds. 1996. *Handbook of Diversity Issues in Health Psychology.* New York: Plenum

Kazdin AE. 1993. Adolescent mental health: prevention and treatment programs. *Am. Psychol.* 48:127–41

Kegeles SM, Hays RB, Coates TJ. 1996. The Mpowerment project: a community-level HIV prevention intervention for young gay men. *Am. J. Public Health* 86:1129–36

Kelly JA, Murphy DA, Sikkema KJ, Kalichman SC. 1993. Psychological interventions to prevent HIV infection are urgently needed. *Am. Psychol.* 48:1023–34

Kelly JG, Snowden LR, Muñoz RF. 1977. Social and community interventions. *Annu. Rev. Psychol.* 28:323–61

Kendall PC, Southam-Gerow MA. 1995. Issues in the transportability of treatment: the case of anxiety disorders in youths. Special Section: efficacy and effectiveness in studies of child and adolescent psychotherapy. *J. Consult. Clin. Psychol.* 63: 702–8

Kessler M, Albee GW. 1975. Primary prevention. *Annu. Rev. Psychol.* 26:557–91

Kim N, Stanton B, Li X, Dickersin K, Galbraith J. 1997. Effectiveness of the 40 adolescent AIDS-risk reduction interventions: a quantitative review. *J. Adol. Health* 20: 204–15

Kochems LM, Paone D, Des Jarlais DC, Ness I, Clark J, Friedman SR. 1996. The transition from underground to legal syringe exchange: the New York city experience. *AIDS Educ. Prev.* 8:471–89

Korbin JE, Coulton CJ. 1996. The role of neighbors and the government in neighborhood-based child protection. *J. Soc. Issues* 52:163–76

Kowalewski MR, Henson KD, Longshore D. 1997. Rethinking perceived risk and health behavior: a critical review of HIV prevention research. *Health Educ. Behav.* 24: 313–25

Latkin CA, Wallace M, Vlahov D, Oziemkowska M, Celentano DD. 1996. The long-term outcome of a personal network-oriented HIV prevention intervention for injection drug users: the SAFE study. *Am. J. Community Psychol.* 24:341–63

Lave JR, Ives DG, Traven ND, Kuller LH. 1995. Participation in health promotion programs by the rural elderly. *Am. J. Prev. Med.* 11:46–53

LaVeist TA, Sellers RM, Elliott Brown KA, Nickerson KJ. 1997. Extreme social isolation, use of community-based senior support services, and mortality among African American elderly women. *Am. J. Community Psychol.* 25:721–32

LeMaster PL, Connell CM. 1994. Health education interventions among Native Americans: a review and analysis. *Health Educ. Q.* 21:521–38

Levine M, Toro PA, Perkins DV. 1993. Social and community interventions. *Annu. Rev. Psychol.* 44:525–58

Levkoff S, Berkman B, Balsam A, Minaker K. 1996. Health promotion/disease prevention: new directions for geriatric education. *Educ. Gerontol.* 22:93–104

Limber S, Nation M. 1998. Violence within the neighborhood and community. In *Violence Against Children in the Family and the Community,* ed. P Trickett, C Schellenbach, pp. 171–93. Washington, DC: Am. Psychol. Assoc. 511 pp.

Linney JA, Wandersman A. 1991. *Prevention Plus III: Assessing Alcohol and Other Drug Prevention Programs at the School and Community Level.* Washington, DC: US Dep. Health Hum. Serv., Off. Substance Abuse Prevent. 461 pp.

Lonsway KA. 1996. Preventing acquaintance rape through education: What do we know? *Psychol. Women Q.* 20:229–65

Lonsway KA, Klaw EL, Berg DR, Waldo CR, Kothari C, et al. 1998. Beyond "No means no": outcomes of an intensive program to train peer facilitators for campus acquaintance rape education. *J. Interpers. Viol.* 13(1):73–92

Lowry R, Sleet D, Duncan C, Powell K, Kolbe L. 1995. Adolescents at risk for violence. *Educ. Psychol. Rev.* 7:7–39

Magura S, Grossman JI, Lipton DS, Siddiqi Q, Shapiro J, et al. 1989. Determinants of needle sharing among intravenous drug users. *Am. J. Public Health* 79:459–62

Marín BV. 1996. Cultural issues in HIV prevention for Latinos: Should we try to change gender roles? See Oskamp & Thompson 1996, pp. 157–76

Marín G. 1993. Defining culturally appropriate community interventions: Hispanics as a case study. *J. Community Psychol.* 21: 149–61

Marín G, Burhansstipanov L, Connell CM, Gielen AC, Helitzer-Allen D, et al. 1995. A research agenda for health education among underserved populations. *Health Educ. Q.* 22:346–63

Maynard M. 1996. Promoting older ethnic minorities health behaviors: primary and secondary prevention considerations. *J. Prim. Prev.* 17:219–29

McCall GJ. 1993. Risk factors and sexual assault prevention. *J. Interpers. Viol.* 8: 277–95

McCormick LK, Ureda J. 1995. Who's driving? College students' choices of transportation home after drinking. *J. Prim. Prev.* 16:103–15

McInnis-Dittrich K. 1996. Violence prevention: an ecological adaptation of systematic training for effective parenting. *Fam. Soc.* 77:414–22

McMillan B, Florin P, Stevenson J, Kerman B, Mitchell RE. 1995. Empowerment praxis in community coalitions. *Am. J. Community Psychol.* 23:699–728

Mitchell RE, Stevenson JF, Florin P. 1996. A typology of prevention activities: applications to community coalitions. *J. Prim. Prev.* 16:413–36

Moffitt TE. 1993. Adolescence-limited and life-course persistent antisocial behavior: a developmental taxonomy. *Psychol. Rev.* 100:674–701

Mrazek PJ, Haggerty RJ. 1994. *Reducing Risks for Mental Disorders: Frontiers for Preventive Intervention.* Washington, DC: Natl. Acad.

Mullen PD, Evans D, Forster J, Gottlieb NH, Kreuter M, et al. 1995. Settings as an important dimension in health education/promotion policy, programs, and research. *Health Educ. Q.* 22:329–45

Mulvey EP, Arthur MW, Reppucci ND. 1993. The prevention and treatment of juvenile delinquency: a review of the research. *Clin. Psychol. Rev.* 13:133–67

Mulvey EP, Woolard JL. 1997. Themes for consideration in future research on prevention and intervention with antisocial behaviors. In *Handbook of Antisocial Behavior*, ed. DM Stoff, J Breiling, JD Maser, pp. 554–62. New York: Wiley. 600 pp.

Muñoz RF, Mrazek PJ, Haggerty RJ. 1996. Institute of Medicine report on prevention of mental disorders: summary and commentary. *Am. Psychol.* 51:1116–22

National Center for Injury Prevention and Control. 1993. *The Prevention of Youth Violence: A Framework for Community Action.* Atlanta, GA: CDC. 96 pp.

Nelson G. 1994. The development of a mental health coalition: a case study. *Am. J. Community Psychol.* 22:229–55

NIMH Prevention Research Steering Committee. 1994. *The Prevention of Mental Disorders: A National Research Agenda.* Washington, DC: NIMH

Olsen JL, Widom CS. 1993. Prevention of child abuse and neglect. *Appl. Prev. Psychol.* 2:217–29

Oskamp S, Thompson SC, eds. 1996. *Understanding and Preventing HIV Risk Behavior: Safer Sex and Drug Use.* Thousand Oaks, CA: Sage

Ozer EJ, Weinstein RS, Maslach C, Siegel D. 1997. Adolescent AIDS prevention in context: the impact of peer educator qualities and classroom environments on intervention efficacy. *Am. J. Community Psychol.* 25:289–323

Parker RG. 1996. Empowerment, community mobilization and social change in the face of HIV/AIDS. *AIDS* 10(Suppl. 3):27–31

Pasick RJ, D'Onofrio CN, Otero-Sabogal R. 1996. Similarities and differences across cultures: questions to inform a third generation for health promotion research. *Health Educ. Q.* 23(Suppl.):142–61

Powell KE, Dahlberg LL, Friday J, Mercy JA, Thornton T, Crawford S. 1996. Prevention of youth violence: rationale and characteristics of 15 evaluation projects. *Am. J. Prev. Med.* 12(Suppl.5):3–12

Powell KE, Hawkins DF, eds. 1996. Youth violence prevention: descriptions and baseline data from 13 evaluation projects. *Am. J. Prev. Med.* 12(Suppl. 5):1—134

Reid JB, Eddy JM. 1997. The prevention of antisocial behavior: some considerations in the search for effective interventions. In *Handbook of Antisocial Behavior*, ed. DM Stoff, J Breiling, JD Maser, pp. 343–56. New York: Wiley. 600 pp.

Reiss D, Price RH. 1996. National research agenda for prevention research: the National Institute of Mental Health report. *Am. Psychol.* 51:1109–15

Reppucci ND, Britner PA, Woolard JL. 1997. *Preventing Child Abuse and Neglect Through Parent Education.* Baltimore, MD: Brookes. 233 pp.

Reppucci ND, Land DJ, Haugaard JJ. 1998. Child sexual abuse programs that target young children. In *Violence Against Children in the Family and the Community*, ed. P Trickett, C Schellenback, pp. 317–37. Washington, DC: Am. Psychol. Assoc.

Rhodes F, Malotte CK. 1996. HIV risk interventions for active drug users: experience and prospects. See Oskamp & Thompson 1996, pp. 207–36

Rietmeijer CA, Kane MS, Simons PZ, Corby NH, Wolitski RJ, et al. 1996. Increasing the use of bleach and condoms among injecting drug-users in Denver. Outcomes of a targeted, community level HIV prevention program. *AIDS* 10:291–98

Sarason SB. 1978. The nature of problem solving in social action. *Am. Psychol.* 33: 370–80

Schewe P, O'Donohue W. 1993. Rape prevention: methodological problems and new directions. *Clin. Psychol. Rev.* 13:667–82

Schweitzer SO, Atchison KA, Lubben JE, Mayer-Oakes SA, De Jong FJ, Matthias RE. 1994. Health promotion and disease prevention for older adults: opportunity for change or preaching to the converted? *Am. J. Prev. Med.* 10:223–29

Silverman MM, Felner RD. 1995. Suicide prevention programs: issues of design, implementation, feasibility, and developmental appropriateness. *Suicide Life-Threat. Behav.* 25:92–104

Silverman MM, Maris RW. 1995. The prevention of suicidal behaviors: an overview. *Suicide Life-Threat. Behav.* 25:10–21

Singer M, Needle R. 1996. Preventing AIDS among drug users: evaluating efficacy. *J. Drug Issues* 26:521–23

Slaby RG. 1998. Preventing youth violence through research-guided intervention. In *Violence Against Children in the Family and the Community*, ed. P Trickett, C Schellenbach, pp. 371–99. Washington, DC: Am. Psychol. Assoc. 511 pp.

Slonim-Nevo V, Auslander WF, Ozawa MN, Jung KG. 1996. The long-term impact of AIDS-preventive interventions for delinquent and abused adolescents. *Adolescence* 31:409–21

Snyder HN, Sickmund M. 1995. *Juvenile Offenders and Victims: A National Report.* Washington, DC: Off. Juv. Justice Delinq. Prev. 188 pp.

Steckler A, Allegrante JP, Altman D, Brown R, Burdine JN, et al. 1995. Health education intervention strategies: recommendation for future research. *Health Educ. Q.* 22:307–28

Suarez-Balcazar Y, Durlak JA, Smith C. 1994. Multicultural training practices in community psychology programs. *Am. J. Community Psychol.* 22:785–98

Sullivan CM, Campbell R, Angelique H, Eby KK, et al. 1994. An advocacy intervention program for women with abusive partners: six-month follow-up. *Am. J. Community Psychol.* 22:101–22

Sullivan CM, Rumptz MH. 1994. Adjustment and needs of African-American women who utilized a domestic violence shelter. Special Issue: violence against women of color. *Viol. Vict.* 9:275–86

Sutherland M, Hale CD, Harris GJ. 1995. Community health promotion: the church as partner. *J. Prim. Prev.* 16:201–16

Tate DC, Reppucci ND, Mulvey EP. 1995. Violent juvenile delinquents: treatment effectiveness and implications for future action. *Am. Psychol.* 50:777–81

Tolan PH, Guerra NG, Kendall PC. 1995. A developmental-ecological perspective on antisocial behavior in children and adolescents: towards a unified risk and intervention framework. *J. Consult. Clin. Psychol.* 63:579–84

Tremblay RE, Pagani-Kurtz L, Masse LC, Vitaro F, Pihl RO. 1995. A bimodal preventive intervention for disruptive kindergarten boys: its impact through mid-adolescence. *J. Consult. Clin. Psychol.* 63:560–68

Trickett EJ. 1996. A future for community psychology: the contexts of diversity and the diversity of contexts. *Am. J. Community Psychol.* 24:209–34

Trickett EJ, Watts R, Birman D, eds. 1994. *Human Diversity: Perspectives on People in Context.* San Francisco: Jossey-Bass

Trickett EJ, Watts R, Birman D. 1993. Human diversity and community psychology: still hazy after all these years. *J. Community Psychol.* 21:264–79

Vega WA. 1992. Theoretical and pragmatic implications of cultural diversity for community research. *Am. J. Community Psychol.* 20:375–91

Violence Against Women Act, Title IV of the Violent Crime Control and Law Enforcement Act of 1994 (P.L. 103–322)

Watters JK. 1996. Impact of HIV risk and infection and the role of prevention services. *J. Subst. Abuse Treat.* 13:375–85

Weeks MR, Himmelgreen DA, Singer M, Woolley S, Romero-Daza N, Grier M. 1996. Community-based AIDS prevention: preliminary outcomes of a program for African American and Latino injection drug users. *J. Drug Issues* 26:561–90

Weinstein RS. 1994. Pushing the frontiers of multicultural training in community psychology. *Am. J. Community Psychol.* 22: 811–20

Weissberg RP, Greenberg MT. 1997. School and community competence-enhancement and prevention programs. In *Handbook of Child Psychology: Child Psychology in Practice,* ed. IE Sigel, KA Renninger, Ser. ed. W Damon, 4:877–954. New York: Wiley & Sons

Wekerle C, Wolfe DA. 1993. Prevention of child physical abuse and neglect: promising new directions. *Clin. Psychol. Rev.* 13: 501–40

Whipple EE, Wilson SR. 1996. Evaluation of a parent education and support program for families at risk of physical child abuse. *Fam. Soc.* 77:227–39

Widom CS. 1991. Childhood victimization: risk factor for delinquency. In *Adolescent Stress: Causes and Consequences,* ed. ME Colton, S Gore, pp. 201–21. New York: Aldine de Gruyter. 330 pp.

Winett RA. 1995. A framework for health promotion and disease prevention programs. *Am. Psychol.* 50:341–50

Wolfe DA, Reppucci ND, Hart S. 1995. Child abuse prevention: knowledge and priorities. *J. Clin. Child Psychol.* 24(Suppl.): 5–22

Wurtele S. 1993. Prevention of child physical and sexual abuse. See Glenwick & Jason 1993, pp. 33–49

Yoshikawa H. 1994. Prevention as cumulative protection: effects of early family support and education on chronic delinquency and its risks. *Psychol. Bull.* 115:28–54

Zigler E, Taussig C, Black K. 1992. Early childhood intervention: a promising preventive for juvenile delinquency. *Am. Psychol.* 47:997–1006

Zimmerman MA, Ramirez-Valles J, Suarez E, de la Rosa G, Castro MA. 1997. An HIV/AIDS prevention project for Mexican homosexual men: an empowerment approach. *Health Educ. Behav.* 24: 177–90

Annu. Rev. Psychol. 1999. 50:419–39

THE SUGGESTIBILITY OF CHILDREN'S MEMORY

Maggie Bruck

Department of Psychology, McGill University, Montreal, Quebec H31 1B1;
e-mail: bruck@hebb.psych.mcgill.ca

Stephen J. Ceci

Human Development and Family Studies, Cornell University, Ithaca, New York
14853; e-mail: sjc9@cornell.edu

KEY WORDS: interviewer bias, eyewitness testimony, development

ABSTRACT

In this review, we describe a shift that has taken place in the area of developmental suggestibility. Formerly, studies in this area indicated that there were
pronounced age-related differences in suggestibility, with preschool children being particularly susceptible to misleading suggestions. The studies on
which this conclusion was based were criticized on several grounds (e.g. unrealistic scenarios, truncated age range). Newer studies that have addressed
these criticisms, however, have largely confirmed the earlier conclusions.
These studies indicate that preschool children are disproportionately vulnerable to a variety of suggestive influences. There do not appear to any strict
boundary conditions to this conclusion, and preschool children will sometimes succumb to suggestions about bodily touching, emotional events, and
participatory events. The evidence for this assertion is presented in this review.

CONTENTS

419

0084-6570/99/0201-0419$08.00

INTRODUCTION

In the 1980s, there was an enormous change in society's sensitivity to and recognition of the problems of violence and abuse that were suffered by children. Spurred by an increased awareness of the pervasiveness of child sexual abuse, state after state revised its criminal procedures to enable prosecutors to deal more effectively with victims and defendants. This led to important changes in the legal system, not only in the United States but also in other countries in the western world. These changes included allowing children to provide uncorroborated testimony in cases concerning sexual abuse—a crime that by its very nature often does not involve an eyewitness other than the perpetrator and the victim—and the elimination of the competency requirement for child witnesses. (For a description of these changes, see Bottoms & Goodman 1996; Davies et al 1995; Goodman et al 1992b; McGough 1994.) With a relaxation of standards, there has come an increase in the number of children who provide statements in legal cases. At the beginning of this decade, we estimated that over 13,000 children testified each year in sexual abuse cases (Ceci & Bruck 1993), and many thousands more gave depositions and unsworn statements to judges, law enforcement officials, and social workers. Additionally, a large number of civil and family court cases entailed allegations of sexual impropriety involving a child. Hence, the question of whether children's reports are reliable has taken on added significance in recent years.

Although we have previously stated that most of the cases that end up in the legal system probably involve true claims of sexual abuse, a number of sensational cases during the 1980s and 1990s raised fundamental concerns about the reliability of children's statements. In these cases (for some descriptions see Ceci & Bruck 1995; Nathan & Snedeker 1995), young children claimed that their parents or other adults had sexually abused them. The claims were often fantastic, involving reports of ritualistic abuse, pornography, multiple perpetrators, and multiple victims . There was little medical evidence of sexual abuse in these cases, nor were there any adult eyewitnesses. Nonetheless, children's often fantastic and uncorroborated claims (e.g. of being forced to eat live babies) were believed by mental health professionals, by police officers, by prosecutors, and by parents. In the ensuing legal proceedings, the major issue before the jury was whether to believe the children. Prosecutors argued that children do not lie about sexual abuse, that the child witnesses' reports were authentic, and that their bizarre and chilling accounts of events—which were well beyond the realm of most preschoolers' knowledge and experience—substantiated the fact that the children had actually been brutally victimized. The defense tried to argue that the children's reports were the product of repeated suggestive interviews by parents, law enforcement officials, social workers, and therapists. However, because there was no direct scientific evidence to support the defense's arguments, and in light of the common belief of that time that children do not lie about sexual abuse, many of these cases eventuated in convictions.

Today, 10 to 15 years later, social scientists have developed a sociological and psychological understanding of the possible factors that might influence children's testimonies in such cases. This research has been primarily driven by the issues raised in these legal cases, issues that experts were heretofore not able to address. Specifically, in the decade of the 1990s there has been an exponential increase in research on the accuracy of young children's memories. Although some studies document strengths of young children's memories, increasing numbers of studies highlight their weaknesses, demonstrating how children's memories and reports can be molded by suggestions implanted by adult interviewers.

In this chapter, we review the research on children's suggestibility with a particular focus on studies that have been conducted in the decade of the 1990s. Our focus is on the contextual factors that influence the accuracy of children's statements. Although our focus throughout this review is predominantly on those techniques that have deleterious effects on children's memory, we also review research that demonstrates children's mnemonic strengths. This emphasis on weaknesses is not because young children are lacking mnemonic strength, but rather to illustrate what can happen if interviewers employ various suggestive techniques with young children. Another reason for our focus on weaknesses rather than strengths is that while children's memory strength is intuitively obvious to many social scientists and nonexperts, their weaknesses are not. At least, not the ones we review here.

Earlier Studies of Children's Suggestibility

Before the 1980s most studies of suggestibility involved asking children a misleading question (i.e. a question that contains a false supposition) about some experienced or observed event (a story, a school demonstration). A consistent finding of this literature was that younger children were more suggestible than older children (see Ceci & Bruck 1993, for a review). However, for the following reasons, this literature was of little value in assessing issues of reliability or suggestibility of children who make allegations of sexual abuse or other potentially criminal acts. First, the age of the children studied was problematic. Despite the fact that a disproportionate number of sexually abused children are preschoolers [39% of all victims are age seven and under, according to the latest national data (US Department of Health and Human Services 1998)], and a disproportionate number of court cases involve preschool witnesses (see Ceci & Bruck 1995), only a handful of suggestibility studies included preschool children (e.g. Dale et al 1978; Lipmann & Wendriner 1906; Marin et al 1979). It was unclear whether the available studies that used older children could be extrapolated downward. Second, the children in the older studies were questioned about neutral events that had little personal salience (e.g. the color of a man's beard). It was unclear whether child victims of highly personal events would behave similarly. And third, the questioning of the children in the earlier studies seemed to bear little, if any, similarity to the conditions under which children are questioned in actual cases.

In actual forensic investigations, because children are rarely questioned about benign events and under such neutral conditions, it became clear to scientists that there would have to be major revisions to existing paradigms to provide pertinent information to the court about whether a child's testimony could be the product of interviewing methods.

There have been three important changes in the direction of the newer research. First, preschool children are frequently included in many of the newer studies. Second, studies increasingly are designed to examine children's suggestibility about events that are personally salient, that involve bodily touching, and/or insinuations of sexual abuse. Third, the concept of suggestive techniques has been expanded from the traditional view of asking misleading questions or planting misinformation to using a larger range of interviewing devices that were adapted from actual forensic and therapeutic interviews where children made allegations of sexual abuse.

A recurring theme of these newer studies is the attempt to question children about the main actions that occurred during the experienced event rather than only about the peripheral details, such as the color of an actor's beard. The ultimate challenge has been to ask questions in an ethically permissible manner about whether potentially sexual actions occurred during these events.

Children's Responses to Misleading Questions about Salient Events

Some researchers have designed studies to examine children's responses to misleading questions about bodily touching and other events suggestive of sexual abuse. These studies represent significant departures from the traditional studies of children's suggestibility that were described above.

In one study that is typical of this new genre, researchers examined children's report accuracy after they had been participants, as opposed to mere bystanders, in an event that was reminiscent of some types of sexual abuse (Rudy & Goodman 1991). Pairs of four-year-old and seven-year-old children were left in a trailer with a stranger. One child played a game with the stranger, who dressed the child in a clown's costume and lifted and photographed him/her. As this child participated in the activity, the paired child was instructed to observe this event as a bystander. Ten days later, children were interviewed, first with open-ended questions, and then with 58 questions that were either direct or misleading. Although it might be expected that children who actually participated in the event would be more than accurate than those who were mere bystanders, there were few differences. Seven-year-olds were more accurate than four-year-olds, as predicted, for all types of questions except misleading questions that implied abuse (e.g. "He took off your clothes, didn't he?"). In fact, these researchers found only a single false report of abuse-related questions: A four-year-old bystander falsely claimed that he and the participant had been spanked. The major conclusion that has been drawn from this study and others with similar designs (see Goodman et al 1991a,b; Saywitz et al 1991) is that although there may be age differences in suggestibility for noncentral features of an event, there are no age differences when children are asked misleading questions about central salient events; in fact children are mainly accurate when asked about such details.

Although these studies represented an advance in the understanding of the nature of children's suggestibility, there were limitations to the generalizability of the results. Specifically, studies such as those conducted by Goodman and her colleagues reflect children's responses to single misleading questions when they are asked in a disconnected fashion. That is, a neutral interviewer asks the child a list of unrelated questions. If the child provides a negative response to the question, then the next question is asked. This approach is quite unlike many investigative interviews. Generally, the types of situations that have caused the most concern are those where the child denies that he has been abused when first asked by a concerned adult. It is only with repeated questions and interviews centered on the theme of abuse, conducted by an interviewer who often believes the child was abused, that a child comes to make an allegation. In some interviews, children are asked to talk about abuse through the use of anatomically detailed dolls, puppets, or role playing. Sometimes when children do not disclose abuse, they are asked to "pretend." Because of the mismatch of this situation to the earlier laboratory studies, another paradigm, one that goes beyond simply asking children misleading questions, has been developed. This approach is described in the next section.

Children's Responses in Suggestive Interviews

INTERVIEWER BIAS   To capture a central feature of many formal and informal interviews, we have emphasized the importance of interviewer bias (Ceci & Bruck 1995). Interviewer bias characterizes those interviewers who hold a priori beliefs about the occurrence of certain events and, as a result, mold the interview to maximize disclosures from the interviewee that are consistent with the interviewer's prior beliefs. One hallmark of interviewer bias is the single-minded attempt to gather only confirmatory evidence and to avoid all avenues that may produce disconfirmatory evidence (e.g. testing incompatible hypotheses). Thus, biased interviewers do not ask questions that might provide alternate explanations for the allegations (e.g. "Did your mommy tell you to say this or did you see it with your own eyes?"). Nor do biased interviewers ask about events that are inconsistent with their hypothesis (e.g. "Who else beside your teacher touched your private parts? Did your brother touch them, too?"). And biased interviewers do not challenge the authenticity of the child's report when it is consistent with their hypothesis (e.g. "It's important to tell me only about those things that really happened. Did this really happen?"). When children provide inconsistent or bizarre evidence, it is either ignored or else interpreted within the framework of the biased interviewer's initial hypothesis (e.g. "His claim that he karate-chopped the chains off his wrists was his attempt to regain control over his victimization.").

A number of studies highlight the effects of interviewer bias on the accuracy of children's reports (reviewed in Ceci & Bruck 1995). In some studies, children are engaged in a staged event. Later, naive interviewers, who did not witness the event, are either given accurate or false information about the events and then told to question the children. Interviewers who are given false information are unaware of this deliberate deception, which is carried out to "bias" their hypotheses. In other studies, children are asked to recall a staged event by an experimenter who intentionally conveys a bias that is either consistent or inconsistent with the staged event. In both types of studies, when questioned by interviewers with false beliefs, children often make inaccurate reports that are consistent with the biased interviewers' scripts.

For example, Thompson et al (1997) conducted a study in which five- and six-year-olds viewed a staged event that could be construed as either abusive or innocent. Some children interacted with a confederate named Chester as he cleaned some dolls and other toys in a playroom. Other children interacted with Chester as he handled the dolls roughly and in a mildly abusive manner. The children were then questioned by two different interviewers about this event. The interviewers were consistently either (a) "accusatory" in tone (suggesting that the janitor had been inappropriately playing with the toys instead of working); (b) "exculpatory" in tone (suggesting that the janitor was just cleaning the toys and not playing); or (c) "neutral" and nonsuggestive in tone. In the first two types of interviews, the questions changed from mildly to strongly suggestive as the interview progressed. At the end of each interview, the children were then asked questions about the event. Immediately after the interview and two weeks later, the children were asked by their parents to recount what the janitor had done.

When questioned by a neutral interviewer or by an interviewer whose interpretation was consistent with the activity viewed by the child, children's accounts were both factually correct and consistent with the janitor's script. However, when the interviewer was biased in a direction that contradicted the activity viewed by the child, those children's stories conformed to the suggestions or beliefs of the interviewer. Also, children's answers to interpretive questions (e.g. "Was he doing his job or just being bad?") were in agreement with the interviewer's point of view, as opposed to what actually happened. When asked neutral questions by their parents, the children's answers remained consistent with the interviewers' biases.

This study and earlier ones reviewed by Ceci & Bruck (1995) provide important evidence that interviewers' beliefs about an event can influence the accuracy of children's answers. The data highlight the dangers of having only one hypothesis about an event, particularly an event involving an ambiguous act such as touching.

According to our model, interviewer bias influences the entire architecture of interviews, and it is revealed through a number of different component features that are suggestive. We briefly describe some of these below.

SPECIFIC VERSUS OPEN-ENDED QUESTIONS   To obtain confirmation of their suspicions, biased interviewers often do not ask children open-ended questions such as "What happened?," but instead resort to a barrage of specific questions, many of which are repeated, and many of which are "leading." This strategy is problematic because children's responses to open-ended questions are more accurate than their responses to specific questions. This finding has been consistently reported since the beginning of the century (e.g. see Ceci & Bruck 1995) and is highlighted in a recent study by Peterson & Bell (1996) who interviewed children after an emergency room visit for a traumatic injury. Children were first asked open-ended questions ("Tell me what happened."), and then more specific questions (e.g. "Where did you hurt yourself?" or "Did you hurt your knee?"). The children were most likely to accurately report the important details in free recall (91% accuracy); errors increased when children were asked specific questions (45% accuracy).

Forced choice questions (e.g. "Was it black or white?") also compromise the reliability of children's reports because children commonly do not provide "I don't know" responses (e.g. see Walker et al 1996) even when the question is nonsensical (Hughes & Grieve 1980). One of the reasons that children so willingly provide answers to specific yes/no or to forced-choice questions even though they may not know the answer is that young children are cooperative: They perceive their adult interviewer as truthful, not deceptive. To comply with a respected adult, children sometimes attempt to make their answers consistent with what they see as the intent of the questioner rather than consistent with their knowledge of the event [see Ceci & Bruck (1993) for a review].

REPEATING SPECIFIC QUESTIONS   Not only does accuracy decrease when children are asked specific questions, but there is increased risk of inaccurate reports when young children are repeatedly asked the same specific questions, either within the same interview or across different interviews (e.g. Poole & White 1991). Young children tend to change their answers, perhaps to provide the interviewer with the information that the child perceives he wants.

The results of a study by Poole & White best illustrates this phenomenon. These investigators examined the effects of repeated questioning within and across sessions. Four-, six-, and eight-year-olds witnessed an ambiguous event. Half the children were interviewed immediately after the event as well as one week later. The remaining children were interviewed only one week after the event. Within each session, all questions were asked three times. Repeated open-ended questions (e.g. "What did the man look like?") had little effect, positive or negative, on children's responses. However, on repeated yes/no questions (e.g. "Did the man hurt Melanie?"), the younger children were most likely to change their responses, both within and across sessions. Also, when children were asked a specific question about a detail for which they had no information (i.e. "What did the man do for a living?"), many answered with sheer speculations. Furthermore, with repeated questions, they used fewer qualifiers, omitting phrases such as "it might have been," and consequently they sounded increasingly confident about their statements. In other words, children will often cooperate by guessing, but after several repetitions, their uncertainty is no longer apparent.

REPEATING MISINFORMATION   Some interviewers convey their bias through leading questions and information about the alleged target events. When these techniques are repeated across multiple interviews, children's reports may become unreliable. For example, in one study (Bruck et al 1995a), five-year old children received an inoculation from a pediatrician. One year later, they were interviewed four times about salient details of that visit. Children who were repeatedly interviewed in a neutral, nonleading manner provided accurate reports about the original medical visit. In contrast, children who were repeatedly given misinformation about some of the salient details incorporated the misleading suggestions into their reports (e.g. falsely claiming that a female research assistant inoculated them rather than the male pediatrician), they also reported nonsuggested but inaccurate events (e.g. falsely reporting that the female research assistant had checked their ears and nose).

Other studies (e.g. Bruck et al 1997a; Ceci et al 1994a) show that when children are repeatedly and suggestively interviewed about false events, assent rates rise for each interview. For example, children are more likely to assent to a false event in a third interview than in a second interview.

When children provide new information in repeated suggestive interviews (that involve the repetition of misinformation or misleading questions), it raises the issue of whether the new reports are accurate memories that were not remembered in previous interviews or whether the new reports are false and the result of previous suggestive interviews. The scientific evidence provides support for the second hypothesis, especially when there is a delay between some alleged event and the interviews. This is because children's memory of the original event (e.g. what happened at day-care) fades with time, allowing the misinformation (e.g. "The teacher did bad things to kids.") to become more easily planted. For example, in the pediatrician study just described, the children were given suggestions immediately after they had received their inoculation about how much the inoculation had hurt (e.g. some children were told that it did not hurt very much when in fact it did). This suggestive interview had no effect on children's reports taken one week after the inoculation, presumably because the episode was still fresh in their mind. However, one year later, when the same children were given similar suggestions (e.g. "You were so brave that day; it seemed like the shot hardly hurt you."), these children now routinely underestimated their level of pain and crying as a result of suggestions about how brave and courageous they had been.

Another set of recent studies provides important new evidence to dispute the common claim that children need to be reinterviewed because it helps them to remember new and important details. These studies show that reports that emerge in a child's first interview with a neutral interviewer are the most accurate. When children are later interviewed about the same event and report new details not mentioned in the first interview, these have a high probability of being inaccurate (Bruck et al 1997a; Salmon & Pipe 1997).

EMOTIONAL ATMOSPHERICS   Interviewers can also use subtle verbal and nonverbal cues to communicate bias. At times, these cues can set the emotional tone of the interview, and they can also convey implicit or explicit threats, bribes, and rewards for the desired answer. Children are attuned to these emotional tones and act accordingly. For example, children were asked to recall the details of a visit to a university laboratory that had occurred four years previously (Goodman et al 1989). At the four-year followup interview, researchers deliberately created an atmosphere of accusation by telling the children that they were to be questioned about an important event and saying, "Are you afraid to tell? You'll feel better once you've told." Few children remembered the original event from four years earlier, but their performance on suggestive questions was mixed; some children falsely reported that they had been hugged or kissed, or that they had their picture taken in the bathroom, or that they had been given a bath. Thus, children may give incorrect information to misleading questions about events for which they have no memory if the interviewer creates an emotional tone of accusation.

STEREOTYPE INDUCTION   Stereotype induction is another component of a suggestive interview. For example, if a child is repeatedly told that a person "does bad things," then the child may begin to incorporate this belief into his or her reports. In one study, Leichtman & Ceci (1995) provided animated descriptions of their "clumsy" friend Sam Stone to preschool children. On a number of occasions, these children were told of Sam's exploits, which included accidently breaking Barbie dolls or ripping sweaters. Later, the children met Sam Stone, who came to their classroom for a short, accident-free visit. The next day, the teacher showed the children a torn book and a soiled teddy bear. Several weeks later, a number of three- and four-year-old children reported that Sam Stone had been responsible, with some even claiming that they had seen him do this. Children who had not received the stereotype induction rarely made this type of error (see Lepore & Sesco 1994 for similar findings).

ANATOMICALLY DETAILED DOLLS   Techniques that have been especially designed for interviewing children about sexual abuse may be potentially suggestive. For example, anatomically detailed dolls are commonly used by professionals when interviewing children about suspected sexual abuse. It is thought that the use of the dolls overcomes language, memory, and motivational (e.g. embarrassment) problems. However, the existing data indicate that the dolls do not facilitate accurate reporting (e.g. Goodman & Aman 1990). It also appears that the use of dolls increases errors for younger children (three and four-year- olds) when they are asked to use the dolls to act out an experienced medical procedure (Goodman et al 1997) or when asked to demonstrate certain events that never happened (e.g. Gordon et al 1993) .

Thus, dolls may be suggestive if children have not made any allegations but are asked by an interviewer, who suspects abuse, to demonstrate abuse with the dolls. Our recent studies provide evidence for this hypothesis (Bruck et al 1995b,c). Three- and four-year-old children had a medical examination where some of the children had received a routine genital examination. The children were then interviewed about the examination. They were then given an anatomical doll and told, "Show me on the doll how the doctor touched your genitals." A significant proportion of the children (particularly the girls) showed touching on the doll even though they had not been touched. Furthermore, when children who had received a genital examination were asked the same question, a number of children (particularly the girls) incorrectly showed that the doctor had inserted a finger into their genitals or anus; the pediatrician never did this. Next, when the children were given a stethoscope and a spoon and asked to show what the doctor did or might do with these instruments, some children incorrectly showed that he used the stethoscope to examine their genitals and some children inserted the spoon into the genital or anal openings or hit the doll's genitals. None of these actions occurred. We concluded that these false actions were the result of implicit suggestions that it is permissible to show sexualized behaviors. These suggestions were communicated through enjoinders to use the dolls to show and talk about touching of the genitals and buttocks. Also, because of the novelty of the dolls, children were drawn to insert fingers and other objects into their cavities.

THINKING ABOUT AND IMAGINING   Guided imagery is another interviewing technique that is potentially suggestive. Interviewers sometimes ask children to try to remember or pretend if a certain event occurred, and then to create a mental picture of the event and to think about its details. Because young children sometimes have difficulty distinguishing between memories of actual events and memories of imagined events (e.g. Parker 1995; Welch-Ross 1995), when asked to pretend about or imagine certain events, children may later come to report and believe these imagined activities. This hypothesis is supported by studies conducted by Ceci and colleagues (1994a,b). Here, young children were repeatedly asked to think about real as well as imaginary events, creating mental images each time they did. In one study (Ceci et al 1994b), children increasingly assented to false events with each interview. When after 11 sessions these children were told that some of the imagined events had not happened, most of the children who had previously assented to false events continued to cling to their false statements. These data may suggest that a number of the children had actually come to believe that they had experienced the false events.

SUBTLE SUGGESTIVE INFLUENCES   Many of the techniques that have been described seem quite explicit and when used repeatedly can appear to be coercive. There are other techniques whereby suggestions can be subtly introduced to children who subsequently incorporate them into their reports. In a series of studies, Poole & Lindsay (1995, 1996) have shown how parents can subtly suggest false events to their children. In their initial study (Poole & Lindsay 1995), preschoolers played with "Mr. Science" in a university laboratory. During this time, the child participated in four demonstrations (e.g. lifting cans with pulleys). Four months later, the children's parents were mailed a storybook that contained a biographical description of their child's visit to Mr. Science. Although the story described two of the experiments that the child had seen, it also described two that the child had not seen. Furthermore, each story finished with the following fabricated account of what had happened when it was time to leave the laboratory: "Mr. Science wiped (child's name) hands and face with a wet-wipe. The cloth got close to (child's name) mouth and tasted really yucky."

Parents read the story to their children three times. Later, the children told the experimenters that they had participated in demonstrations that, in actuality, had only been mentioned in the stories read by their parents. For example, when asked whether Mr. Science put anything "yucky" in their mouths, more than half the children inaccurately replied "yes," and many of these children elaborated their "yes" answers. When asked, "Did Mr. Science put something yucky in your mouth, or did your Mom just read you this in a story?," 71% of the children said that it really happened.

This study demonstrates that subtle suggestions can influence children's inaccurate reporting of nonevents that, if pursued in followup questioning by an interviewer who suspected something sexual had occurred, could lead to a sexual interpretation. The study, along with several others, also illustrates preschoolers' difficulty in identifying the source of a suggestion (these are called source-monitoring errors); children in this study confused their parent reading them the suggestion with their experience of the suggestion.

Poole & Lindsay (1996) recently replicated these findings with children from a wider age range (three- to eight-year-olds). The findings were similar across ages, with one exception: The source-monitoring procedures enabled the older but not the younger children to reduce the rate at which they reported having experienced the suggested events. That is, when asked, "Did Mr. Science really put something yucky in your mouth, or did your Mom just read you this in a story?," the older children recanted their previous claims and said that their Mom had told them.

MULTIPLE SUGGESTIVE TECHNIQUES   The studies discussed above have predominantly examined the effect of using a single suggestive technique on the accuracy of children's reports. According to our model, the number of suggestive techniques used in an actual interview is a function of the degree of the interviewer's bias. Interviewers who have strong a priori beliefs and who view their role as one of obtaining information to confirm these beliefs will include the most suggestive elements in their interviews. However, when a number of techniques are combined in one interview, these procedures have detrimental effects much larger than seen in studies where only one suggestive technique is used (e.g. Leichtman & Ceci 1995). Two recent studies support this conclusion.

The first study (Bruck et al 1997a) examined the impact of repeatedly interviewing children with a combination of suggestive procedures. Preschool children were asked to tell about two true events (a recent punishment and helping a visitor who had hurt her ankle) and about two false events (helping a lady find her monkey in the park and witnessing a thief steal food from the day-care facility).

Children were interviewed on five different occasions about the four events. In the first interview, the children were asked if the event had happened and if so to provide as many details as possible about its occurrence. The next three interviews included a combination of suggestive interviewing techniques that have been shown to increase children's assents to false events. These techniques included (a) the use of peer pressure ("Megan and Shonda were there and they told me you were there, too."); (b) guided imagery techniques ("Try to think about what might have happened."); and (c) repeating (mis)information and providing selective reinforcement ("It's so wonderful that there are such nice kids like yourself to help people out when they need it."). The same interviewer questioned the children for the first four interviews. In the fifth interview, a new interviewer questioned each child about each event in a nonsuggestive manner.

Across the five interviews, all the children consistently assented to the true-helping event. However, children were at first reluctant to talk about the true--punishment event, many denying that it had occurred. With repeated suggestive interviews, however, the children agreed that the punishment had occurred. Similar patterns of disclosure occurred for the false events; that is, children initially denied the false events, but with repeated suggestive interviews they began to assent to these events. By the third interview, almost all the children had assented to all true and false events, which included witnessing a thief take food from the day-care. This pattern continued to the end of the experiment. Thus, the combination of suggestive techniques produced high assent rates for true and false events, one of which was a criminal act.

This study illustrates both the beneficial as well as detrimental consequences of using suggestive techniques to elicit reports from young children. For children who may not want to talk about true-unpleasant (the punishment), the use of repeated interviews with suggestive components did prompt them to correctly assent to previously denied events. However, the use of these very same techniques prompted children to assent to events that never occurred.

Garven et al (1998) showed how a combination of suggestive interviewing techniques that were used in the McMartin case can compromise the accuracy of children's reports in one 10-minute interview. In this study, a stranger visited children at their day care and read them a story. One week later, children were interviewed about the visit. Half the children were asked leading questions (e.g. "Did Manny break a toy?"). The other children were also asked leading questions, but in addition, other suggestive techniques were used, including (a) peer pressure ("The other kids said that . . . "); (b) positive consequences (giving the child praise for certain answers and telling him that he is a good helper); (c) negative consequences (telling the child that this was not the appropriate answer, and repeating the question); (d) enjoinders to think about it (children were asked to think hard about questions they said "no" to); and (e) enjoinders to speculate (asking children to pretend or to tell what might have happened). Children in the combined technique condition accurately answered 42% of the questions, compared with an accuracy rate of 83% of children who were just asked leading questions. The children in the combined suggestion group misreported that Manny said a bad word, that he threw a crayon, that he broke a toy, that he tore a book, and that he bumped the teacher. Another important result of this study is that children in the combined suggestion condition came to make more false claims as the interview progressed: That is, within a short (5- to 10-minute interview), children made more false claims in the second half than in the first half of the interview. Thus, the children had learned what types of answers the interviewer wanted to hear.

The Effect of Suggestive Interviews on Children's Credibility

It has often been stated that it is easy to detect false reports that are the result of suggestion, because it was thought that children were merely "parroting" the words of their interrogators. However, evidence from the past decade provides no support for this assertion. First, we have found that when children are suggestively interviewed, their subsequent narratives include false reports that were not suggested to them, but that are consistent with the suggestions (e.g. Bruck et al 1995a, 1997a). Second, subjective ratings of children's reports after suggestive interviewing reveal that these children appear highly credible to trained professionals in the fields of child development, mental health, and forensics (e.g. Leichtman & Ceci 1995, Ceci et al 1994a,b); these professionals cannot reliably discriminate between children whose reports are accurate from those whose reports are inaccurate as the result of suggestive interviewing techniques.

Third, results of our most recent study revealed that linguistic markers do not consistently differentiate true from false narratives that emerge as a result of repeated suggestive interviews (Bruck et al 1997a). In the Bruck et al study (1997a), wherein children were repeatedly and suggestively interviewed about true and false events (described above), the children's narratives of the false events became more embellished and detailed, so that by the third interview, it was impossible to differentiate the true from the false narratives on a number of factors that are generally considered to be markers of good narratives and of autobiographical recall. That is, by the third interview, the false narratives contained the same number of spontaneous statements, details, adjectives, emotional terms, and dialogue statements as did the true narratives. Two measures differentiated the true and false stories. First, children were more likely to repeat the same details across interviews for true than for false narratives. Thus, the true narratives were more consistent than the false narratives. One reason for this difference was the fact that with each retelling, children included more new details in their false than in their true narratives (i.e. the false stories expanded and sometimes changed). Second, for some of the children, with repeated suggestive interviews, the number of aggressive, exaggerated, and fantastical details increased for false narratives, but not for true narratives.

Children's False Reports: Compliance or False Belief?

We have had little to say in the foregoing description about the mechanisms underlying the children's suggestibility. Because the field is only beginning to develop in this area, we focus on one major area of concern: Do children's assents to suggestive interviewing procedures reflect social compliance to the perceived wishes of their interviewer, or do they reflect fundamental changes in their cognitive system such that they come to believe their false statements (false beliefs)? To preview our conclusion, this either/or dichotomy is probably too simplistic to account for all reports that result from suggestive interviews.

A number of arguments supports the view that children's suggestibility is socially motivated. One of the most salient characteristics of young children, and one that is required for socialization, involves their compliance, their willingness to please adults, and their inherent trust of adults (see Ceci & Bruck 1993, for a review). Thus, it has been argued that children may be especially prone to suggestive influences because of their natural tendency to trust the honesty and cooperation of their adult interviewers. It has been argued that young children trust that adults are asking them well-intentioned and reasonable questions, and as a result they provide a response regardless of their comprehension or knowledge about the questioned event. For example, when asked nonsensical questions such as "Is milk bigger than water?" or "Is red heavier than yellow?", most five- and seven-year-olds replied "yes" or "no"; they only rarely responded "I don't know" (Hughes & Grieve 1980). It also seems that when asked the same question twice, young children change their answers to please the adult who is questioning them; they reason that the "adult must not have liked the first answer I gave so I will give another answer" (e.g. Siegal et al 1988).

The strong claim of this position is that children's inaccurate responses in suggestive interviews always reflect compliance, and that if later questioned about what really happened, children will be able to throw off the suggestive veil and report events accurately. The results of at least two studies support this position (Cassel et al 1996; Cohen & Harnick 1980). In these studies, it was found that compared with older children and adults, younger children were more prone to inaccurately answer misleading questions about a film. When subjects were later tested, however, there was no differential effect of the misleading questions on the accuracy of the younger children's recall. In general, at the later testing, subjects accurately recalled the original events. These results suggest that younger children were more likely to consciously submit to suggestions than older subjects, but that the suggestions did not differentially affect their memory for the event.

The opposite strong claim is that children's false reports that result from suggestive interviews reflect basic changes in memory; that is to say, children believe their reports. One basic assumption that motivates this claim is that there are developmental differences in memory that contribute to suggestibility. Thus, there are developmental differences in the degree to which children accurately encode, store and retrieve memories (Brainerd & Ornstein 1991). There are also developmental differences in forgetting, retention, and relearning curves (Brainerd et al 1985). Furthermore, young children are especially prone to making source misattributions (Ackil & Zaragoza 1995; Parker 1995; Poole & Lindsay 1996).

Direct evidence for the position that false reports reflect basic changes in memory is provided by several studies, all of which involve asking children to substantiate the basis of their false claims made in suggestive interviews. In these studies, children are asked if the misreported event really happened, and if they remember where they heard about the event. If children misreport an event and then claim that they actually saw it (and don't necessarily remember being told about it), then this is evidence for a false belief. In other studies, children are warned that the experimenter may have made a mistake and are given an another opportunity to provide a report in response to a suggestive interviewing technique. If children continue to provide false reports, then this is another indication that the child has lost the source of the suggestion and has come to believe that the event actually happened. When these procedures are included in suggestibility studies, a significant number of preschoolers maintain that that the suggested event really happened, and a significant number cannot remember the source of the suggestion (e.g. Ceci et al 1994b; Leichtman & Ceci 1995; Poole & Lindsay 1995, 1996). However, some recent evidence suggests that if these suggested interviews cease for a time, children's previous false memories fade (e.g. Huffman et al 1996; Poole & Lindsay 1996); they accurately claim that the false events that were previously assented to never occurred.

We hypothesize that a more detailed inspection of children's responses over time will reflect a more complex condition with a comingling of social (compliance) and cognitive (memory) factors in the emergence of false reports. For example, children may start out knowingly complying to suggestions, but with repeated suggestive interviews, they may come to believe and incorporate the suggestions into their memories. However, depending upon the strength of the false belief, children may eventually come to forget their misreports and thus recant their previous allegations, especially if suggestive interviewing has ceased for a long period.

SUMMARY AND CONCLUSIONS

A considerable body of research now exists to indicate that numerous suggestive techniques can compromise the accuracy of young children's reports. These techniques are especially powerful when used by biased interviewers and when used in combination. A review of the literature reveals that (*a*) there are age differences in children's susceptibility to suggestion; (*b*) there are individual differences in susceptibility; and (c) the techniques we have reviewed can produce major distortions in children's reports about highly salient events. Each of these topics is now discussed.

First. although we have not placed much emphasis on age differences in children's suggestibility, when studies include developmental comparisons there are often age differences, with preschoolers being the most suggestible age group. This conclusion is based on our previous literature review (Ceci & Bruck 1993), wherein we reported that approximately 88% of the studies (14 out of 16) that involved comparisons of preschoolers with older children or adults, preschool children were the most suggestible group. Since that publication, new studies on children's suggestibility are being published regularly; these newer data continue the trend that we reported in 1993. In the most recent analysis of this literature, McAuliff et al (1998) also concluded that indeed, preschoolers do differ from older children and adults in their susceptibility to misleading or incorrect post-event information, although these authors estimated a smaller effect size than heretofore assumed.

Despite these significant age differences, it is nonetheless important to point out that concern remains about the reliability of older children's testimony when they are subjected to suggestive interviews. Ample evidence may be cited that children older than six years of age are suggestible about a wide range of events (e.g. Goodman et al 1989; Poole & Lindsay 1996; Warren & Lane 1995) and that adults' recollections also are impaired by suggestive interviewing techniques (e.g. Hyman & Pentland, 1996; Loftus & Pickrell 1995; Malinowski & Lynn 1995, 1996). Clearly, it is important to extend the research to develop newer paradigms for middle childhood and adolescence in order to examine the magnitude, boundary conditions, and factors (as discussed below) involved in suggestibility of these ages—factors that have been as neglected today as the preschoolers were during the first half of this century.

Second, although consistent findings of age differences across studies exist, there are nevertheless individual differences. Some preschoolers are very resistant to interviewers' suggestions, whereas some older children immediately fall sway to the slightest suggestion. We are a long way from understanding the source of these individual differences, although researchers are beginning to assess the association between suggestibility and a number of cognitive (e.g. knowledge base, trace strength, source monitoring); psychosocial (e.g. compliance, self-esteem); demographic (gender, social class); and physiological (salivary and blood cortisol levels) factors that might contribute to these differences (see Bruck et al 1997b for a review).

Third, children are not merely suggestible about peripheral details but also about central details that sometimes involve their bodies. Children can be suggestible about positive as well as negative events (for a review, see Bruck et al 1997a). At times, children's false reports can be tinged with sexual connotations. In laboratory studies, young children have made false claims about "silly events" that involved body contact (e.g. "Did the nurse lick your knee? Did she blow in your ear?"), and these false claims persisted in repeated interviewing over a three-month period (Ornstein et al 1992). A significant number of pre-schoolers assented to suggestions that a doctor had cut out some bone in the center of the child's nose to stop the child from bleeding (JA Quas et al 1998). Young children falsely reported that a man put something "yucky in their mouth" (Poole & Lindsay 1995, 1996). Preschoolers falsely alleged that their pediatrician had inserted a finger or a stick into their genitals (Bruck et al 1995a) or that some man touched their friends, kissed their friends on the lips, and removed some of the children's clothes (Lepore & Sesco 1994). A signifi-cant number of preschool children falsely reported that someone touched their private parts, kissed them, and hugged them (Goodman et al 1991a; Rawls 1996; Melnyk et al 1997). When suggestively interviewed, children will make false allegations about nonsexual events that have serious legal consequences, were they to have actually occurred. For example, preschoolers claimed to have seen a thief in their day-care. (Bruck et al 1997a). The suggestive tech-niques described in this paper have powerful effects on children's reporting in laboratory controlled conditions.

Notwithstanding the above conclusion, it is clear that children—even pre-schoolers— are capable of accurately recalling much that is forensically rele-vant. For example, in many of our own studies, children in the control group conditions recalled events flawlessly. This indicates that the absence of sug-gestive techniques allows even very young preschoolers to provide highly accurate reports, although they may be sparse in the number of details. Numer-ous other studies also highlight the strengths of young children's memories (e.g. see Fivush 1993; Goodman et al 1992a). What characterizes many such studies is the neutral tone of the interviewer, the limited use of misleading questions (for the most part, if suggestions are used, they are limited to a single occasion), and the absence of the induction of any motive for the child to make a false report. When such conditions are present, it is a common (although not universal) finding that children are much more immune to suggestive influ-ences, particularly about sexual details.

Thus, the question of whether a young child's report is accurate can be an-swered tentatively, "maybe, maybe not," depending on the type, number, and severity of suggestive techniques they have been exposed to. In a very real sense, the reliability of young children's reports has more to do with the skills of the interviewer than to any natural limitations on their memory. Research on this topic has been fast finding its way into courts of law, used by one side or the other to bolster or discredit child witnesses' testimony. As we tried to dem-onstrate in this review, a need exists for practitioners to sift through this re-search carefully, making certain that the studies they call upon resemble the case at bar in terms of the type of acts, the severity of suggestions, and so on. Failure to do this could lead to miscarriages of justice.

ACKNOWLEDGMENT

Portions of this research were supported by a grant from the National Science Foundation to SJ Ceci (SBR9312202) and from the Natural Sciences and Engneering Research Council of Canada to M Bruck.

> **Visit the *Annual Reviews home page* at**
> **http://www.AnnualReviews.org.**

Literature Cited

Ackil JK, Zaragoza MS. 1995. Developmental differences in eyewitness suggestibility and memory for source. *J. Exp. Child Psychol.* 60:57–83

Bottoms B, Goodman G, eds. 1996. *International Perspectives on Child Abuse and Children's Testimony.* Thousand Oaks, CA: Sage

Brainerd CJ, Kingma J, Howe ML. 1985. On the development of forgetting. *Child Dev.* 56:1103–19

Brainerd CJ, Ornstein PA. 1991. Children's memory for witnessed events: the developmental backdrop. In *The Suggestibility of Children's Recollections,* ed. JL Doris, pp. 10–20. Washington, DC: Am. Psychol. Assoc.

Bruck M, Ceci SJ, Francoeur E, Barr RJ. 1995a. "I hardly cried when I got my shot!": influencing children's reports about a visit to their pediatrician. *Child Dev.* 66:193–208

Bruck M, Ceci SJ, Francoeur E, Renick A. 1995b. Anatomically detailed dolls do not facilitate preschoolers' reports of a pediatric examination involving genital touching. *J. Exp. Psychol. Appl.* 1:95–109

Bruck M, Ceci SJ, Francoeur E. 1995c. *Anatomically detailed dolls do not facilitate preschoolers' reports of touching.* Presented at Annu. Meet. Soc. Res. Child Dev., Indianapolis, IN

Bruck M, Ceci SJ, Hembrooke H. 1997a. Children's reports of pleasant and unpleasant events. In *Recollections of Trauma: Scientific Research and Clinical Practice,* ed. D Read, S Lindsay, pp. 199–219. New York: Plenum

Bruck M, Melnyk L, Ceci S. 1997b. External and internal sources of variation in the creation of false reports in children. *Indiv. Diff.* 9:289–316

Cassel W, Roebers C, Bjorklund D. 1996. Developmental patterns of eyewitness responses to repeated and increasingly suggestive questions. *J. Exp. Child Psychol.* 61:116–33

Ceci SJ, Bruck M. 1993. The suggestibility of the child witness: a historical review and synthesis. *Psychol. Bull.* 113:403–39

Ceci SJ, Bruck M. 1995. *Jeopardy in the Courtroom: A Scientific Analysis of Children's Testimony.* Washington, DC: Am. Psychol. Assoc.

Ceci SJ, Crotteau-Huffman M, Smith E, Loftus EF. 1994a. Repeatedly thinking about non-events. *Conscious. Cogn.* 3: 388–407

Ceci SJ, Loftus EF, Leichtman M, Bruck M. 1994b. The role of source misattributions in the creation of false beliefs among preschoolers. *Int. J. Clin. Exp. Hypn.* 62: 304–20

Cohen RL, Harnick MA. 1980. The susceptibility of child witnesses to suggestion. *Law Hum. Behav.* 4:201–10

Dale PS, Loftus EF, Rathbun L. 1978. The influence of the form of the question on the eyewitness testimony of preschool children. *J. Psycholinguist. Res.* 7:269–77

Davies G, Lloyd-Bostock S, McMurran M, Wilson C, eds. 1995. *Psychology, Law, and Criminal Justice: International Developments in Research and Practice.* Berlin: de Gruyter

Fivush R. 1993. Developmental perspectives

on autobiographical recall. In *Child Victims and Child Witnesses: Understanding and Improving Testimony*, ed. GS Goodman, B Bottoms, pp. 1–24. New York: Guilford

Garven S, Wood JM, Shaw JS, Malpass R. 1998. More than suggestion: consequences of the interviewing techniques from the McMartin preschool case. *J. Appl. Psychol.* In press

Goodman G, Aman C. 1990. Children's use of anatomically detailed dolls to recount an event. *Child Dev.* 61:1859–71

Goodman GS, Batterman-Faunce JM, Kenney R. 1992a. Optimizing children's testimony: research and social policy issues concerning allegations of child sexual abuse. In *Child Abuse, Child Development, and Social Policy*, ed. D Cicchetti, S Toth. Norwood, NJ: Ablex

Goodman GS, Bottoms BL, Schwartz-Kenney B, Rudy L. 1991a. Children's testimony about a stressful event: improving children's reports. *J. Narrat. Life Hist.* 1:69–99

Goodman GS, Hirschman JE, Hepps D, Rudy L. 1991b. Children's memory for stressful events. *Merrill Palmer Q.* 37:109–58

Goodman GS, Quas JA, Batterman-Faunce JM, Riddlesberger MM, Kuhn J. 1997. Children's reactions to a stressful event: influences of age, anatomical dolls, knowledge, and parental attachment. *Appl. Dev. Sci.* 1:54–75

Goodman GS, Taub EP, Jones DP, England P, Port L, et al. 1992b. Testifying in criminal court. *Monogr. Soc. Res. Child Dev.* 57(5):229

Goodman GS, Wilson ME, Hazan C, Reed RS. 1989. *Children's testimony nearly four years after an event*. Presented at Annu. Meet. East. Psychol. Assoc., 63rd, Boston

Gordon B, Ornstein PA, Nida R, Follmer A, Creshaw C, Albert G. 1993. Does the use of dolls facilitate children's memory of visits to the doctor? *Appl. Cogn. Psychol.* 7:459–74

Huffman ML, Crossman A, Ceci S. 1996. *An investigation of the long-term effects of source misattribution error: Are false memories permanent?* Poster presented at Meet. Am. Psychol. Law Soc., 15th, Hilton Head, SC

Hughes M, Grieve R. 1980. On asking children bizarre questions. *First Lang.* 1:149–60

Hyman I, Pentland J. 1996. The role of mental imagery in the creation of false childhood memories. *J. Mem. Lang.* 35:101–17

Leichtman MD, Ceci SJ. 1995. The effects of stereotypes and suggestions on preschoolers' reports. *Dev. Psychol.* 31:568–78

Lepore SJ, Sesco B. 1994. Distorting children's reports and interpretations of events through suggestion. *Appl. Psychol.* 79:108–20

Lipmann O, Wendriner E. 1906. Aussageexperimente im Kindergarten. *Beitr. Psycol. Aussage. (Stern)* 2(Suppl.):418–23

Loftus EF, Pickrell J. 1995. The formation of false memories. *Psychiatr. Ann.* 25:720–25

Malinoski P, Lynn SJ. 1995. *The pliability of early memory reports*. Presented at Annu. Conv. Am. Psychol. Assoc., 103rd, Washington, DC

Malinoski P, Lynn SJ. 1996. *The temporal stability of early memory reports*. Presented at Annu. Conv. Soc. Clin. Exp. Hypn., Tampa, FL

Marin BV, Holmes DL, Guth M, Kovac P. 1979. The potential of children as eyewitnesses. *Law Hum. Behav.* 3:295–304

McAuliff B, Kovera M, Viswesvaran C. 1998. *Methodological issues in child suggestibility research: a meta-analysis*. Presented at Meet. Am. Psychol.-Law Soc., Redondo Beach, CA

McGough L. 1994. *Fragile Voices: The Child Witness in American Courts*. New Haven, CT: Yale Univ. Press

Melnyk L, Bruck M, Ceci SJ. 1997. *The effects of drawing of children's reports of past events*. Presented at Meet. Am. Psychol. Assoc., Chicago

Nathan D, Snedeker M. 1995. *Satan's Silence: Ritual Abuse and the Making of a Modern American Witch Hunt*. New York: Basic Books

Ornstein P, Gordon BN, Larus D. 1992. Children's memory for a personally experienced event: implications for testimony. *Appl. Cogn. Psychol.* 6:49–60

Parker J. 1995. Age differences in source monitoring of performed and imagined actions. *J. Exp. Child Psychol.* 60:84–101

Peterson C, Bell M. 1996. Children's memory for traumatic injury. *Child Dev.* 67:3045–70

Poole DA, Lindsay DS. 1995. Interviewing preschoolers: effects of nonsuggestive techniques, parental coaching and leading questions on reports of nonexperienced events. *J. Exp. Child Psychol.* 60:129–54

Poole DA, Lindsay DS. 1996. *Effects of parents' suggestions, interviewing techniques, and age on young children's event reports*. Presented at NATO Adv. Study Inst. Recollect. Trauma: Sci. Res. Clin. Practice. Port de Bourgenay, France

Poole D, White L. 1991. Effects of question repetition on the eyewitness testimony of children and adults. *Dev. Psychol.* 27:975–86

Quas JA, Goodman GS, Bidrose S, Pipe ME, Craw S, Abline DS. 1998. Emotion and memory: children's long-term remembering, forgetting, and suggestibility. *J. Exp. Child Psychol.* In press

Rawls J. 1996. *How question form and body-parts diagrams can affect the content of young children's disclosures.* Presented at NATO Adv. Study Inst. Recollect. Trauma: Sci. Res. Clin. Practice. Port de Bourgenay, France

Rudy L, Goodman GS. 1991. Effects of participation on children's reports: implications for children's testimony. *Dev. Psychol.* 27:527–38

Salmon K, Pipe M-E. 1997. Providing props to facilitate young children's event recall: the impact of a one year delay. *J. Exp. Child Psychol.* 65:261–92

Saywitz K, Goodman G, Nicholas G, Moan S. 1991. Children's memory of a physical examination involving genital touch: implications for reports of child sexual abuse. *J. Consult. Clin. Psychol.* 5:682–91

Siegal M, Waters L, Dinwiddy L. 1988. Misleading children: causal attributions for inconsistency under repeated questioning. *J. Exp. Child Psychol.* 45:438–56

Thompson WC, Clarke-Stewart KA, Lepore S. 1997. What did the janitor do? Suggestive interviewing and the accuracy of children's accounts. *Law Hum. Behav.* 21:405–26

US Department of Health and Human Services. 1998. *Reports from the States to the National Child Abuse and Neglect Data System, 1998. Children's Bureau, Child Maltreatment, 1996.* Washington, DC: US Gov. Print. Off

Walker N, Lunning S, Eilts J. 1996. *Do children respond accurately to force choice questions?* Presented at NATO Adv. Study Inst. Recollect. Trauma: Sci. Res. Clin. Practice. Talmont Saint Hilaire, France

Warren AR, Lane P. 1995. The effects of timing and type of questioning on eyewitness accuracy and suggestibility. In *Memory and Testimony in the Child Witness*, ed. M Zaragoza, pp. 44–60. Thousand Oaks, CA: Sage

Welch-Ross M. 1995. Developmental changes in preschoolers' ability to distinguish memories of performed, pretended, and imagined actions. *Cogn. Dev.* 10:421–41

Annu. Rev. Psychol. 1999. 50:441–69

INDIVIDUAL PSYCHOTHERAPY OUTCOME AND PROCESS RESEARCH: Challenges Leading to Greater Turmoil or a Positive Transition?

S. Mark Kopta

Department of Psychology, University of Evansville, Evansville, Indiana 47722;
e-mail: mk35@evansville.edu

Robert J. Lueger and Stephen M. Saunders

Department of Psychology, Marquette University, Milwaukee, Wisconsin 53201;
e-mail: 6282LUEGERR@marquette.edu and saunderss@vms.csd.mu.edu

Kenneth I. Howard

Department of Psychology, Northwestern University, Evanston, Illinois 60208;
e-mail: k-howard@nwu.edu

KEY WORDS: psychological treatments, outcomes, managed mental health care, mental disorder, empirically supported psychotherapies

ABSTRACT

Psychotherapy is facing challenges that relate to the emergence of managed health care, the possibility of a national health care system, and advances in biological psychiatry. These situations have created pressure to achieve a more accurate assessment of psychotherapeutic effectiveness. Psychotherapy has been proven to be generally effective; however, there is uncertainty as to why. The field is currently experiencing apparent turmoil in three areas: (*a*) theory development for psychotherapeutic effectiveness, (*b*) research design, and (*c*) treatment technique. This chapter reviews the dynamics within each of the areas and highlights the progress made in treating mental disorders. We conclude that recent advances in research design may provide a transition that will bring psychotherapy closer to becoming a unified paradigm with an acceptable theory of effectiveness.

0084-6570/99/0201-0441$08.00

CONTENTS

INTRODUCTION

The field of psychotherapy research has faced many new challenges during its brief life. The first challenge was the publication of Eysenck's (1952) review of 24 studies which concluded that psychotherapy is no more effective with neurotics than is spontaneous remission. His article stimulated years of controversy among academics and clinicians about the effectiveness of psychotherapy. It also inspired a successful, directed effort by researchers to confirm empirically that psychotherapy generally produces beneficial effects (e.g. Elkin et al 1989, Lambert & Bergin 1994, Lipsey & Wilson 1993, McNeilly & Howard 1991, Smith & Glass 1977).

The emergence of managed health care, the looming possibility of a national health care system, and recent advances in biological psychiatry pose new challenges for the field of psychotherapy. These events have created pressure for more accurate assessment of psychotherapeutic effectiveness. For example, many (e.g. Barlow 1994, Broskowski 1995) believe that the effectiveness of specific psychological treatments must be empirically validated to justify reimbursement by insurance and managed care companies and by government agencies that are demanding more accountability.

In this chapter we review the progress made from 1989 through early 1998 in improving the assessment of psychotherapy research. In preparing this review we were motivated by a realization that the psychotherapy research field is beginning to be in a position to advance (or rescue?) the professional and economic interests of psychotherapy practice. In the past, the gap between psychotherapy research and clinical practice has been wide (e.g. Goldfried & Wolfe 1996, Morrow-Bradley & Elliott 1986), with clinicians seeing little value in research which was perhaps too often performed for scholarly interest rather than for clinical application. At present, however, the focus of research is increasingly on justifying psychotherapy as a legitimate treatment and explaining how psychotherapy alleviates psychological suffering. Within this movement, an awareness exists that research findings must become more generalizable to clinical practice (e.g. Beutler et al 1996, Campbell 1996, Fensterheim & Raw 1997, Goldfried & Wolfe 1996, Strupp 1997).

Hundreds of studies have shown that psychotherapy works better than nothing. What is not so clear is whether psychotherapy works for reasons specified by theory.

Unfortunately, instead of giving the appearance of developing a more unified paradigm, psychotherapy is experiencing a period of conceptual-theoretical turmoil. More than ever, cherished "truths" as well as traditional research methodologies are being questioned. Three areas of apparent turmoil are (a) theory development for psychotherapeutic effectiveness, (b) research design, and (c) treatment techniques. This chapter reviews the dynamics within each of these areas and highlights the progress made in treatments for specific clinical disorders.

Contemporary developments in the psychotherapy research field have been well summarized by Bergin & Garfield (1994a). Also, *Psychotherapy Research,* the official quarterly journal of the Society for Psychotherapy Research (SPR), was introduced in 1991 as a response to the dramatic interest in and expansion of psychotherapy research over the past few years. This growth has greatly increased membership in SPR as well as the quantity and quality of research presented at its meetings and in the literature.

THREE AREAS UNDER STRESS: THEORY DEVELOPMENT FOR EFFECTIVENESS

Outcome Research

UNIQUE INGREDIENTS VERSUS COMMON INGREDIENTS AND THE DODO BIRD CONTROVERSY   A primary issue for outcome researchers has been whether the different psychotherapies each contain unique active ingredients, as medications are purported to do, or whether a set of common factors accounts for psychotherapy's benefits. The traditionally accepted unique-ingredients theory implies that different psychotherapies produce different specific effects for different types of patients.

However, researchers have repeatedly failed to find convincing evidence that different psychotherapies are differentially effective. Meta-analyses—which statistically combine and compare the effect sizes of treatment, placebo, and control groups—continually report no differences among different types of therapies (e.g. Smith & Glass 1977, Grissom 1996, Wampold et al 1997). Occasionally, when differences are found, they disappear after methodological confounds are taken into account; for example, Robinson et al (1990) discovered that researcher allegiance influenced the superiority of some treatment classes over others for depressed patients.

The aforementioned dilemma (that the different psychotherapies produce equivalent outcomes) has been labeled the "dodo bird verdict" (Luborsky et al 1975) after the dodo bird in *Alice in Wonderland* who proclaimed, "Everybody has won and all must have prizes." Exactly what the dodo effect means has been open to a variety of explanations. It seems clear though that no one believes all psychotherapies are equally effective for all disorders. Giles' edited book, *Handbook of Effective Psychotherapy* (1993), presents several experts' attempts to solve the equivalence paradox and concludes with a critique of their positions by Elliott et al (1993), who assert that researchers should focus on the specific effects of specific psychotherapies on specific types of patients.

Among those who expect treatment differences, the consensus is that the lack of evidence is caused by faulty design strategies. The most frequent design criticism of comparative studies is that they are not built to detect interaction effects with variables other than type of treatment; instead, they focus on outcomes among treatments alone, omitting the investigation of such moderating variables as setting, patient characteristics, and therapist skill. As one example of the influence of moderating variables, variance attributable to therapist differences has been found to be greater than variance attributed to treatment differences (e.g. Crits-Christoph et al 1991, Crits-Christoph & Mintz 1991). Wampold's analogy (1997) cleverly summarizes the issue of comparing different psychotherapies without considering the moderating influence of therapist skill and other factors:

> We suspect that a great deal of the variance in success of (basketball) teams is due to the players' ability, institutional support, and motivation and very little is due to whether the teams play man-to-man defense or zone defense. If the goal is to identify the most important factors related to winning records so coaches could build the best teams possible, it would make little sense to arrange studies that examine the type of defense used by homogenizing players' abilities, institutional support, and so forth. Why then are we trying to homogenize therapy and therapists, when we know that these very variables contribute to much variance in outcomes, so that we can examine differences between treatments, when treatment differences historically have accounted for so little variance? (p. 34)

Still the task of empirically assessing the specific psychotherapies to cover all the possible influential interactions is a daunting one. Beutler (1991) presents a schema indicating that, to evaluate all relevant differences among treatment types, about 1.5 million interactions between potentially important patient, therapist, and therapy variables would have to be studied.

Some authors assert that, even if the different psychotherapies are generally equivalent in effectiveness, they still have value as legitimate treatments for psychological disorders. Concluding from one of the most sophisticated meta-analyses to date, Wampold et al (1997) argue that psychotherapy equivalence is a reality and that the active-ingredients model borrowed from medicine is not a useful analogy. Howard et al (1997) also do not rule out the possibility of treatment equivalence. However, they accept the medication analogy. They note that equivalent psychotherapies can be viewed like equivalent drugs such as antibiotics, which affect patients differently depending on the clinical characteristics and responsiveness of the patient.

Psychotherapy equivalence also suggests that common beneficial ingredients among the different treatments are mostly or completely responsible for the similar outcomes. Providing a list of 30 (e.g. catharsis, therapeutic alliance, rationale, and cognitive learning), Lambert & Bergin (1994) mention that these common factors are active ingredients shared by a variety of psychotherapies. Some writers consider factors common to different forms of psychotherapy to be sufficient and necessary (e.g. Frank & Frank 1991, Patterson 1984), whereas others (e.g. Crits-Christoph 1997, Garfield 1991) view them as playing a substantial role in patient improvement but often in conjunction with unique ingredients. Explaining psychotherapeutic effects on the basis of common ingredients begs the question of how we then distinguish psychotherapy from other interventions, such as pastoral counseling or psychic advising. Furthermore, accepting the common-ingredients theory in its entirety would discourage theory development that could lead to new, more effective treatments. Still, the search for unique effective ingredients has thus far been unsuccessful. For instance, although attempts have been made, no one has yet validated the hypothesized unique active ingredients of cognitive therapy for depression (Jacobson et al 1996).

IDENTIFYING EMPIRICALLY SUPPORTED THERAPIES   The increased momentum to empirically validate the different psychotherapeutic approaches is a response to political and economic forces as well as to the growth of biological psychiatry. This momentum has resulted in the establishment of the American Psychological Association Task Force on Promotion and Dissemination of Psychological Procedures (American Psychological Association Task Force, 1995). Its mission has been to identify a set of criteria that characterize effective treatments and to determine which of 400-plus therapies satisfy these criteria. Beutler (1998) has reviewed the circumstances leading to the focus on identifying empirically supported therapies as well as the creation of the task force. Briefly, he listed the following events as influential: (*a*) courts and legislative bodies are moving in the direction of defining without reference to empirical findings the types of psychotherapies that can be practiced and reimbursed; (*b*) managed health care programs are shifting from cost to empirical validation as the criterion for reimbursement; (*c*) medical and primary-care organizations have already established treatment guidelines that give priority to drug treatments over psychotherapy, e.g. the practice guidelines of the American Psychiatric Association (1993) and the Agency for Health Care Policy and Research publication *Depression in Primary Care Guidelines* (1993).

The task force's efficacy criteria were adapted from those used by the US Food and Drug Administration. Three categories of treatment efficacy were used to identify treatments as follows: 22 "well-established" treatments, 7 "probably efficacious" treatments, and the remainder "experimental" treatments (those not qualifying for at least "probably efficacious" rating); efficacious and probably efficacious treatments were identified for 21 syndromes listed in the *Diagnostic and Statistical Manual of Mental Disorders IV* (DSM-IV) of the American Psychiatric Association (1994). Behavioral treatments dominated the two efficacious categories. An update in 1996 added 27 more treatments to the two categories with all but 5 being behavioral. The committee producing these lists has asserted that the lists are incomplete, should not be used by third-party payers to make reimbursement decisions, and are not meant to replace clinical judgment in recommending the best treatment for patients.

Not surprisingly, reactions to the guidelines and to the general concept of empirically supported treatments have been mixed. Criticisms include the following: (*a*) empirical validation strategies reinforce the inappropriate "medicalization" of psychotherapy (Goldfried & Wolfe 1998, Wampold et al 1997); (*b*) omitting quasi-experimental studies, the task force criteria require only randomized clinical trials, which do not represent psychotherapy as practiced in the field or require a large number of single case design studies (Beutler 1998, Goldfried & Wolfe 1998); (*c*) the DSM-IV standard for categorizing patient types has problems with reliability as well as validity and provides patient categories that are too heterogeneous (Garfield 1996, Goldfried & Wolfe 1998); and (*d*) most psychotherapies used in real clinical settings are not on the validation list (e.g. eclectic, long-term psychodynamic therapies; Seligman 1995).

Supporters of the effort to identify empirically validated therapies often make their case by asking hypothetically, "What if we don't move in this direction?" For example, Beutler (1998) asserts that psychotherapy's scientific base would be abandoned, likely resulting in a loss of credibility with policymakers, other health care professionals, and the public. Barlow (1996) warns that if the profession does not promote evidence of psychotherapeutic effectiveness, the existence of psychotherapy in the health care system will be threatened. Emphasizing that practice guidelines that identify empirically supported treatments "are here to stay" (p. 290), Nathan (1998) notes their potential to enhance psychotherapeutic effectiveness as well as strengthen treatment accountability. In a special volume of *Clinical Psychology: Science and Practice*, a majority of contributors (e.g. Barlow 1996, Chambless 1996, Crits-Christoph 1996, Nathan 1996, Wilson 1996) agreed that despite the current limitations on identifying empirically supported therapies, the endeavor—including the task force's efforts—is worthwhile and in the best interests of the psychotherapy profession. In his article in that volume, Kazdin (1996) provides an accurate perspective on this issue: "By and large, there is general agreement that validated treatments are worthwhile and important, but agreement breaks down after that in deciding how to go about identifying and selecting these treatments" (p. 16).

Process Research

Process research attempts to identify the active ingredients of psychotherapy and the mechanisms of change. The rationale of this process research is that by increasing the understanding of human change processes, greater control can be obtained in the effective design and delivery of therapeutic interventions. The study of process variables and process-outcome relationships has recently been overshadowed by the much stronger focus on outcomes assessment.

The fourth edition of the *Handbook of Psychotherapy and Behavior Change* (Bergin & Garfield 1994a) features the third (Orlinsky et al 1994) in a series of comprehensive chapters that have reviewed psychotherapy process-outcome studies. In their chapter, Orlinsky et al cite five process variables that have consistently demonstrated robust relationships with outcome in the research literature: (*a*) overall quality of the therapeutic relationship, (*b*) therapist skill, (*c*) patient cooperation versus resistance, (*d*) patient openness versus defensiveness, and (*e*) treatment duration.

Other compilations of research findings have challenged traditionally accepted assumptions and models about process-outcome relationships. One of the most comprehensive of these is the volume by Russell (1994), which covers recent research and future directions of process research. Several of the book's chapters are referenced later in the review.

LINKING PROCESS TO OUTCOME: THE DRUG METAPHOR AND ALTERNATIVES
Despite the wealth of data on process-outcome relationships, several authors have noted that the number of conclusions that can be drawn from process-outcome studies is disappointing (cf Shapiro et al 1994b). In reviewing meth-

ods of linking processes and outcomes, Lambert & Hill (1994) identified three approaches: (*a*) correlating the frequency or proportion of an occurrence of a process variable with an outcome measure, (*b*) using sequential analyses to study the immediate effects (minioutcomes) of process variables, and (*c*) considering longer patterns of process variables.

Stiles & Shapiro (1994) argued that the reason for the poor yield of process-outcome studies is that the primary research design is based on the drug metaphor, with its correlational approach to linking process and outcome at the end of therapy. Specifically, the drug metaphor operates from the "more-is-better" assumption that process variables represent the active ingredients of psychotherapy. In their criticism of the drug metaphor, Stiles & Shapiro (1994) asserted that therapists vary their intervention techniques based on feedback from and about the client, giving more of an ingredient when they perceive greater need on the part of the client. However, these variations can result in near-zero correlations when greater amounts are given to clients with poorer as well as to clients with better outcomes. Stiles (1996) concluded that the more-is-better assumption is appropriate only when the clients are not already getting enough of a critical ingredient; he also suggested that process research adopt developmental models or empirical approaches that do not rely on the correlational model to assess process-outcome relationships.

Greenberg & Newman (1996) edited a special section of the *Journal of Consulting and Clinical Psychology* devoted to new directions in the psychotherapy change process. Most of the studies that were included in this special section used the sequential approach to studying process-outcome relationships; they consisted of statistical analyses of various complexities, such as log-linear, path, and hierarchical linear modeling. The topics of the studies included the resolution of unfinished business, the resolution of ruptured therapeutic alliances, the contributions of generic model components to session outcomes, and the processes of cognitive therapy.

THE THERAPEUTIC ALLIANCE   Advances in understanding the therapeutic alliance (the working relationship between patient and therapist) and its relationship to psychotherapy outcome have continued during the last decade of research. Horvath & Greenberg (1994) edited a book in which researchers from programs investigating the alliance presented a review and synthesis of their work. The contributors indicated that major advances include the following: (*a*) recognition of the central role of the alliance in successful therapies, (*b*) more complete and precise explication and operationalization of the construct, (*c*) increased attention to pretreatment and process variables that promote a positive alliance, and (*d*) greater understanding of the changing nature and purpose of the alliance over the course of treatment, as well as of alliance ruptures.

Randomized clinical trials repeatedly find that a positive alliance is one of the best predictors of outcome. For example, Krupnick and associates (1996) analyzed data from the large-scale National Institute of Mental Health Treatment of Depression Collaborative Research Program that compared treatments for depression; their analysis indicated that the therapeutic alliance was predictive of treatment success for all conditions. In another large study of diverse therapies for alcoholism, the alliance was also significantly predictive of success (Connors et al 1997).

The positive association between scores on measures of early treatment alliance and outcome is found repeatedly (Horvath & Symonds 1991), despite the variety of alliance conceptualizations and instruments used to measure it (Horvath & Greenberg 1994). Different programs of research have emphasized different aspects of the alliance. For example, Luborsky (1994) conceptualized the alliance from the psychoanalytic perspective and measured it as two parts: the patient experiencing the therapist as helpful and the patient sensing that therapy is a collaborative effort. In contrast, Bordin (1994) emphasized the pan-theoretical nature of the alliance, arguing that—regardless of the modality—the alliance always involves agreement on tasks and goals as well as a sense of compatibility or bonding. This latter viewpoint has been confirmed in the Working Alliance Inventory (Horvath 1994). Both Luborsky's and Bordin's programs have consistently found a predictive association between alliance and outcome.

Studies of the predictors of the development of a positive alliance have emphasized both pretreatment and in-treatment process variables. The research suggests that clients with healthy object relations (Piper et al 1991), generally satisfying social relationships, and lack of hostility or dominance in their interpersonal attitudes (e.g. Muran et al 1994) are prone to develop positive alliances. As noted earlier, in a study comparing the effectiveness of different therapies for depression (i.e. cognitive, interpersonal, and medication), the presence of a therapeutic alliance was a predictor of a favorable outcome for each treatment (Krupnick et al 1996).

THREE AREAS UNDER STRESS: RESEARCH DESIGN

Traditionally held in the highest esteem, the randomized clinical trial (RCT) randomly assigns members of a relatively homogeneous group of patients to different treatment conditions to control for potentially confounding independent variables. The RCT is concerned with empirical validation and thus focuses on internal validity. However, several investigators argue that this approach should be replaced by naturalistic designs, which can provide results more applicable to real clinical practice, therefore strengthening external validity.

Consumer Reports Survey

Consumer Reports magazine (*CR*; 1995) reported that most of the 2900 treated readers responding to its survey about whether psychotherapy helps received benefits from psychotherapy and were satisfied with the treatment they received. Among the other findings were the following: (*a*) there were no differences in effectiveness between the different psychotherapy types, again confirming the dodo effect; (*b*) long-term psychotherapy produced more improvement than short-term therapy; and (*c*) medication plus psychotherapy contributed no more benefits than psychotherapy alone.

In his praise of the *CR* survey, Seligman (1995) asserted that the findings provide crucial public confirmation of psychotherapy's general effectiveness and value. Seligman's article triggered considerable criticism and debate in the professional community. The *American Psychologist* (October 1996) devoted an entire issue to the controversy. Some of the criticism was directed toward the *CR* design, including for example that no control group was used to rule out factors such as regression toward the mean (Mintz et al 1996), spontaneous remission, or the influences of simply talking to a friend (Hollon 1996, Jacobson & Christensen 1996); that only a small percentage (4%) of the original sample responded to the mental health survey (Brock et al 1996, Jacobson & Christensen 1996); and that outcome was assessed only from the patient's perspective (Strupp 1996). Seligman noted and defended many of the survey's flaws in his original article and later rebutted critics in the *American Psychologist* special issue (1996a,b). Seligman's (1996b) defense of the *CR* survey was perhaps best summarized by Seligman himself:

> ...none of the criticism I have seen is about what *CR* did but what they *might* have done with a great deal more money and time: a longitudinal study, using blind diagnosis, with a more representative sample of Americans, for example. But in the limits imposed by a cross-sectional survey of *CR*'s readership, this was first-rate journalism and creditable science as well. (p. 1086)

In his concluding comments, Seligman (1995) proposed an ideal survey design that includes a sufficiently large sample, pre- and postassessment methodology, and multidimensional outcome measures.

Randomized Clinical Trials

Additional controversy over Seligman's (1995) article relates to his comments that the RCT—or, as he calls it, the efficacy study—is inadequate for empirically validating psychotherapy as practiced in real clinical settings. His argument, as well as those by others (e.g. Hollon 1996, Howard et al 1996), is that the efficacy study does not represent what happens in routine clinical practice. For example, unlike in the RCT, in actual clinical practice, manuals are not used, patients rarely suffer from a singular disorder, numbers of sessions are not limited and predetermined, and patients are not randomly assigned to treatments. Howard et al (1995) add that, because of attrition, randomization seldom equates groups and rarely controls for patient-treatment interactions. Consequently, the randomized experiment usually becomes an inadequately designed quasi-experiment.

Some authors disagree. Jacobson & Christensen (1996) propose that despite their limitations, RCTs can provide clinically relevant effectiveness information by varying such factors as treatment length, therapist experience, whether a manual is used, and whether the therapy has a specific theoretical orientation or is eclectic. There is also disagreement about the value of information from RCTs for practicing psychotherapists (Persons & Silberschatz 1998). The consensus (e.g. Crits-Christoph 1997, Hollon 1996, Howard et al 1996, Seligman 1996a) is that RCTs provide valuable information about psychotherapeutic efficacy—for example, whether a type of psychotherapy can possibly work under certain conditions or the identification of a specific active ingredient—but that the degree to which such findings have value for actual clinical application is questionable.

Effectiveness Studies

Seligman and others (e.g. Howard et al 1996, Wampold 1997) recommend effectiveness studies for understanding how psychotherapy works in actual clinical settings; in this case, uncontrolled treatments are applied in self-correcting fashion to patients who typically suffer from multiple problems. Most effectiveness designs have emanated from the dosage model (Howard et al 1986). Dose-effect studies have confirmed a positive rate of effect (i.e. percentage of patients improved or normalized probability of improvement for one patient) across dose (i.e. number of sessions), with diminishing returns at higher dosage levels. Information obtained from these studies includes the following: (a) Psychological symptoms demonstrate different improvement rates across sessions that can be categorized into three response classes—acute distress (fastest), chronic distress (intermediate), and characterological (slowest) (Barkham et al 1996b, Kopta et al 1994); (b) for most clinical syndromes, 16 sessions provide at least a 50% chance for recovery to normal functioning (Barkham et al 1996b, Kadera et al 1996, Kopta et al 1994) and 26 (Kadera et al 1996) to 58 sessions (Kopta et al 1994) provide a 75% chance.

Dose-effect designs as well as RCT designs use grouped data to provide information about an "average" patient; however, patterns of improvement across sessions for specific patients have been shown to vary substantially from the general linear trend (Kadera et al 1996, Barkham et al 1993). At the clinical practive level, the therapist needs to know, "Is this patient's condition responding to the treatment that is being applied now?" Two groups of researchers (Howard et al 1995, Tingey et al 1996) have presented a single case application of the dosage model, the dose-outcome design. Here, the patient's progress toward reaching clinically significant improvement on some outcome measure is tracked across sessions. Going further, Howard et al (1996) developed patient profiling, which models the patient's expected course of improvement based on pretreatment clinical characteristics by using a hierarchical linear modeling strategy. The patient's progress (as indicated by the dose-outcome method) can now be compared with his/her expected progress, which serves as the outcome criterion for decision making. With these strategies, treatment can be adjusted if the patient's response to therapy moves in an undesirable direction.

Advances in Establishing Outcome Criteria

Clinical significance (Jacobson et al 1984)—that is, when a patient's functioning moves into the range of functioning for a sample of nonpatients or normals—is one of the most frequently used outcome criteria. Methodological extensions concerning the concept were proposed and discussed in a special section of *Psychotherapy Research* (Summer 1996). As one example, Tingey et al (1996) proposed a social validation method that included distinguishing different normative samples for clinically significant improvement: mildly symptomatic ("normal") and asymptomatic ("healthy").

Influenced by dosage model findings, Howard and his colleagues (1993) validated a phase model of improvement. They found that psychotherapeutic improvement occurs in three sequentially dependent phases: first, greater well-being is experienced, then symptoms remit, and finally life functioning improves.

The two dimensions for outcome—amount of benefit and phase—allow for the selection of specific outcome goals emanating from an empirical foundation. These goals can range from a return to normal well-being, requiring fewer treatment sessions, to the achievement of healthy life functioning, requiring considerably more sessions.

A Positive Transition

At first look, outcome research design appears to be experiencing turmoil similar to that of theory development and the empirical validation of treatments. However, even though some things appear to be declining (e.g. the universal acceptance for the RCT design and the importance of meta-analyses), something else may be emerging. More specifically, since the last *Annual Review of Psychology* chapter on psychotherapy (Goldfried et al 1990), designs are now available that can address the current vital issues of outcome research:

(*a*) which psychotherapies can work as specified by theory under controlled conditions; (*b*) which psychotherapies work as practiced in actual clinical settings; (*c*) to use Paul's (1967) famous question, "Which treatments are most effective for which patients under which conditions?" and (*d*) which psychotherapies work most efficiently.

For (*a*), creative RCTs have been used (e.g. Jacobson et al 1996) and proposed (Jacobson & Christensen 1996, Crits-Christoph 1997) that are able to distinguish unique active ingredients if indeed they exist. To answer (*b*), dose-effect studies can discover lawful outcome relationships across sessions for patients treated by different therapies as practiced in real clinical settings. Concurrently tracking control groups over time in these studies would allow for clinically relevant treatment effectiveness to be validated. More advanced survey methods such as those proposed by Seligman (1995) can also provide valuable information. Using dose-outcome designs to group individual patients by treatment type and similar dose-response patterns, researchers can answer Paul's patient-focused question in (*c*). These methods best address the complexity of the unique individual clinical situation.

Regarding (*d*)—with cost containment a concern for managed health care and biological psychiatry asserting that medication is faster, cheaper, and more effective than psychotherapy (e.g. Klein 1996)—outcome studies now need to distinguish which psychotherapies are more efficient in addition to which ones are simply effective. The best designs to do that are in the form of dose-effect strategies that provide an index of the rate of improvement for groups of patients and the use of growth curves rather than change scores.

In moving from demonstrating efficacy to proving effectiveness, Shadish and associates (1997) describe the technology transfer model, which can guide the dissemination of scientific findings into clinical practice. The model includes five phases that feature efficacy and effectiveness strategies: (*a*) pilot testing of a therapy for feasibility and risk; (*b*) evaluation in randomized clinical trials to see whether the therapy is efficacious under ideal conditions; (*c*) treatment of specific populations to measure the impact of the therapy with distinct, well-defined patients; (*d*) demonstration studies of the therapy being implemented and assessed in public health contexts; and (*e*) evaluation of the therapy as it is used in clinical practice.

THREE AREAS UNDER STRESS: TREATMENT TECHNIQUE

The need to clarify and improve treatment technique exists along two lines: (*a*) the relationship between psychotherapy and pharmacotherapy and (*b*) the conceptualization of psychotherapy integrationism and its role as a recognized type of psychological treatment.

Psychotherapy and Pharmacotherapy

Modern psychopharmacology continues to grow and evolve as evidenced by the increasing number of psychotropic medications that reach the marketplace, the expanding range of medications that are demonstrating efficacy in the treatment of mental disorder, and the increasing interest in psychopharmacological agents by the public. Today, a significant proportion of patients receive a combination of medication and psychotherapy. Consequently, an understanding of the comparative and interactive effects of pharmacotherapy and psychotherapy is necessary to maximize effectiveness in mental health care.

Comparative studies of psychotherapy versus pharmacotherapy have most aggressively investigated the treatments' effects on depression and panic disorder; usually psychotherapy is represented by cognitive behavior therapy. With regard to depression, the most cited results were reported by the National Institute of Mental Health Treatment of Depression Collaborative Research Program (TDCRP; Elkin et al 1989). Two hundred fifty unipolar depressed patients at three sites were randomly assigned to one of four conditions: cognitive-behavior therapy (CBT), interpersonal therapy (IPT), imipramine (a tricyclic antidepressant) plus clinical management (IMI-CM), and pill placebo with clinical management (PLA-CM). Results (Elkin et al 1989, Gibbons et al 1993) were generally as follows: (a) all four conditions resulted in significant improvement; (b) neither form of psychotherapy was superior to the other; (c) the only significant treatment difference for all patients occurred between IMI-CM and PLA-CM; (d) for the more severe cases, IMI-CM and IPT produced more improvement than PLA-CM whereas CBT did not; and (e) IMI-CM generally produced more rapid effects than the other conditions.

A lively debate about the meaning and general applicability of the findings was featured in a special section of the *Journal of Consulting and Clinical Psychology* (February 1996). The authors, in reviewing additional research studies as well as TDCRP, provided a spectrum of conclusions regarding CBT. Jacobson & Hollon (1996) asserted, "We still consider CBT to be a viable alternative to pharmacotherapy in the treatment of even severe outpatient depression (the TDCRP notwithstanding)...." (p. 79). Elkin et al (1996) stated that a conclusion cannot be reached yet, whereas Klein (1996) argued that CBT is not an effective treatment.

In contrast to the situation for depression, there is evidence that panic disorder's response to psychotherapy is greater than its response to some medications. Clark et al (1994) found that CBT (cognitive therapy plus in vivo self-exposure) produced significantly greater remission rates (90%) than imipramine (55%), applied relaxation (50%), and a wait-list control experience (7%). Likewise, Klosko and his colleagues (1990) reported that there was more panic remission for CBT (87%) than either pill placebo (36%) or wait-list (30%) conditions; however, the same differences were not found when re-mission with Alprazolam (50%), a benzodiazepine, was compared with the placebo and wait-list conditions. In a review of research studying the com-bined effects of benzodiazepines and exposure-based cognitive therapy, Spiegel & Bruce (1997) concluded that there was no convincing evidence that this treatment combination improves outcomes. Whereas CBT has been shown as successful in preventing relapse (e.g. Ballenger 1993, Chambless & Gillis 1993), many patients relapse after drug discontinuation (Gorman 1994). How-ever, methodological concerns regarding the validity of CBT's success have been raised, for example, investigator allegiance biasing results (Jacobson & Hollon 1996), panic remission as an insufficient measure of outcome (Shear & Maser 1994), and exclusion of a pill placebo condition (Klein 1996).

Specific Theoretical Orientations Versus Integration

There are three distinct threads that focus on the issue of treatment selection. First, specific theories of psychotherapy delineate unique active ingredients working through particular, sequenced interventions. This thread is tied to the desire to identify effective treatments and to the development of practice guidelines to be used in treatment selection. The second thread is the move-ment toward integration, in which the putative active ingredients for each theory are delineated and an attempt is made to bring these processes under a single, more generic, theoretical umbrella. The final thread is eclecticism, the use of theoretically different interventions with selection based on the needs of a particular patient.

An increasingly popular view is that the long-term dominance of the major psychotherapies has ended and that integrationism and eclecticism is now the direction for technical advances in treatment. Indeed, more therapists identify themselves as eclectic than any other individual orientation. At least five hand-books on psychotherapy integration have been published in the 1990s (e.g. Norcross & Goldfried 1992, Stricker & Gold 1993). There is also a national so-ciety (Society for the Exploration of Psychotherapy Integration) as well as as-sociated journals (e.g. *Journal of Psychotherapy Integration*). Some attempts have been made to provide guidelines for the selection of interventions (e.g. Beutler & Clarkin 1990, Gaw & Beutler 1995). Still, many authors assert that the effectiveness of integrative approaches has not been proven (e.g. Lambert 1992, Norcross 1993), that there is little consensus about what integrationism is, and that progress in this area has stalled (Norcross 1997).

PROGRESS IN TREATING SPECIFIC DISORDERS

The efficacy of psychotherapy for adult disorders has been the topic of special sections of journals over the past 10 years. Several compendia of treatments have been presented in book format, including edited volumes by Barlow (1993) and Mavissakalian & Prien (1996) and Roth & Fonagy's (1996) book. The latter book was commissioned by England's Department of Health in response to the growing influence of the evidence-based medicine movement. A special section of the *Journal of Consulting and Clinical Psychology* (February 1998) included 13 articles on empirically supported therapies. Several of these articles focused on therapies for specific disorders and are reviewed below. Our review summarizes evidence for efficacy, effectiveness, and efficiency of treatments for the variety of psychological disorders.

Depression

Knowledge about the most effective way to treat depression is advancing (see reviews by Dobson 1989, Docherty & Streeter 1993, Hollon et al 1993, Robinson et al 1990). This knowledge is aided by increasingly sophisticated statistical analyses, including growth curve and random regression modeling (e.g. Gibbons et al 1993). Also relatively new are the studies of the process of outcome or the shape of change of outcome in treatments of depression (e.g. Barkham et al 1996a,b).

COGNITIVE THERAPY   Cognitive therapy (CT) focuses on altering the maladaptive, depression-causing thoughts, beliefs, attitudes, and behaviors of patients. CT is the most widely studied psychotherapy for depression, and its efficacy has been established by a number of research programs (e.g. DeRubeis et al 1990, Whisman et al 1991). There is also evidence that CT offers relapse prevention benefits not found with pharmacotherapy (e.g. Evans et al 1992), which would be predicted by the hypothesized mechanism of change (i.e. that patients change long-standing maladaptive attitudes and perceptions).

Uncertainty remains about the mechanism of effect of CT and about its relative effectiveness when compared with other treatments; however, and more specifically, conclusions (beyond "it works well") are still being pursued (cf DeRubeis & Crits-Christoph 1998). Jacobson and colleagues (1996) conducted a component analysis of CT, comparing behavioral activation (BA) alone, BA and cognitive restructuring to modify automatic thoughts, and the complete CT treatment package. They found that BA and BA plus cognitive restructuring were as effective as CT. It is also uncertain whether CT is more effective than other psychotherapies. For example, the TDCRP research team (i.e. Elkin et al 1989) found that interpersonal therapy (IPT) was equally effective, and the Sheffield group reported that psychodynamic-interpersonal therapy (IP) was generally as effective (e.g. Barkham et al 1996a, Shapiro et al 1994a).

OTHER THERAPIES   Researchers have also evaluated a variety of alternative psychotherapies and modes of treatment. IPT (Shapiro et al 1994) has been investigated, although not as extensively as CT. IPT emphasizes interpersonal problems as the root of depressive disorders; treatment focuses on improving the interpersonal deficits. In large-scale, controlled, experimentally rigorous studies, IPT has been found to be as efficacious as other treatments, including CT (e.g. Barkham 1996a, Elkin et al 1989).

Behavior therapy for depression emphasizes behavioral activation and increasing pleasant event experiences (e.g. Lewinsohn et al 1980). Although it has received relatively little attention as a stand-alone intervention, behavior therapy is a major emphasis of the cognitive-behavioral treatment program used in the TDCRP and numerous other studies. As a singular treatment, however, there is evidence of its efficacy. As noted above, in their component analysis of CBT, Jacobson et al (1996) found that behavior therapy was as effective as CT in alleviating depression.

PREDICTING RESPONSIVENESS TO TREATMENT   Studies examining predictors of treatment response or failure have proliferated, as have prospective studies examining the matching of patients to treatments (e.g. Beach & O'Leary 1992, Beutler et al 1991). Researchers have attempted to delineate the relevant aspects of effective therapy for depression. Burns & Nolen-Hoeksema (1991, 1992) found that while patient motivation and compliance with the requirements of CT are predictive of success, the quality of the therapeutic relationship is also predictive. Castonguay and colleagues (1996) found that improvement was predicted by level of therapeutic alliance and the patient's emotional involvement, but not by process variables unique to CT. Blatt and colleagues (1995, 1996) reanalyzed the TDCRP data set to investigate potential predictors of patient responsiveness to treatment. They found that patients' pretreatment level of perfectionism was negatively correlated with clinical improvement and that perfectionism interacted with the quality of the therapeutic alliance. Mohr and colleagues (1990) examined the relationship between pretherapy patient variables (interpersonal problems and level of distress) and outcome, defined as either negative change, no change (nonresponse), or positive change. While negative change was predicted by high levels of interpersonal difficulty and low levels of distress, nonresponders displayed moderate levels of both, and positive responders displayed high levels of both.

LIMITATION   The primary limitation of concluding that CT and other therapies for depression have clinical utility is the lack of evidence that these treatments—with proven clinical trial efficacy—are effective in actual clinical settings (see also Hollon et al 1993).

Anxiety Disorders

EFFICACY   Efforts to identify efficacious treatments have achieved greater success for anxiety disorders than for any other major class of diagnosis (cf Roth & Fonagy 1996). In a review of psychosocial treatments for the variety of anxiety disorders, Barlow & Lehman (1996) declared, "Evidence now exists on the effectiveness (i.e. efficacy) of psychosocial treatment approaches for every anxiety disorder when compared with no treatment or credible psychosocial placebos" (p. 727). DeRubeis & Crits-Christoph (1998) provided a similar review of anxiety disorder treatments. They classified the well-specified treatments for 10 disorders, including 6 anxiety disorders, into 3 categories of empirical support for treatment efficacy: (a) efficacious and specific, (b) efficacious, and (c) possibly efficacious.

For panic disorder, CT and panic control therapy (PCT) have been shown to be efficacious and specific (cf Arntz & van den Hout 1996, Beck et al 1994, Clark et al 1994). Two other treatments, exposure (Williams & Falbo 1996) and applied relaxation (Barlow et al 1989, Ost 1988), are supported by evidence indicating that they are efficacious with panic patients. Barlow & Lehman (1996) note that 80% of patients who receive CT or PCT are panic free at the end of treatment. In September 1991, the National Institute of Mental Health convened a panel of experts who reviewed the treatment outcome literature comparing CBT, other psychosocial treatments, drug treatments, and control conditions; they concluded that CBT is an effective treatment for panic disorder (Wolfe & Maser 1994).

For agoraphobia, only exposure therapy has been shown to be efficacious and specific; unfortunately, only a few efficacy studies have been recently reported for this disorder (cf DeRubeis & Crits-Christoph 1998). For generalized anxiety disorder (GAD), one efficacious and specific treatment has been identified, CT. A review (Chambless & Gillis 1993) of CT for GAD included nine studies. Two more recent studies (Barlow et al 1992, Durham et al 1994) supported the summary conclusion that CT is superior to wait-list control conditions and to other more active treatments such as pill placebos and nondirective therapy. One treatment, applied relaxation (Borkovec & Costello 1993), has been shown to be efficacious with GAD. This is a difficult disorder and these findings represent considerable progress in recent years.

Epidemiological studies indicate that social phobia is the most prevalent diagnosable disorder. Two treatments have been shown to be efficacious for social phobia, exposure alone (Turner et al 1994) and exposure plus cognitive restructuring (Feske & Chambless 1995, Heimberg et al 1995). Barlow & Lehman (1996) note that there is a developing consensus that a combination of exposure to social situations and cognitive therapy may be the most powerful treatment for social phobia.

Obsessive-compulsive disorder (OCD)—a difficult-to-treat disorder with very low spontaneous remission rates—has one efficacious and specific treatment, exposure plus response prevention (ERP; Fals-Stewert et al 1993, Foa et al 1992). Cognitive therapy (Emmelkamp & Beens 1991, Van Oppen et al 1995) is the only possibly efficacious treatment for OCD.

For post-traumatic stress disorder (PTSD), only exposure (Foa et al 1991) has been shown to be efficacious. Two other treatments, stress inoculation therapy (Foa et al 1991) and eye movement desensitization and reprocessing (EMDR; Wilson et al 1995) have been shown to be better than wait-list control groups in the treatment of patients who have experienced trauma. Inclusion of EMDR in a list of possibly efficacious treatments has been controversial (see Renfry & Spates 1994).

EFFECTIVENESS AND EFFICIENCY   Despite the impressive evidence for the efficacy of treatments for anxiety disorders, there is very little evidence for their effectiveness in real clinical settings. Furthermore, little is known about the efficiency of treating anxiety disorders (see Gould et al 1995 for a review of the cost-efficiency of treating panic disorders).

Eating Disorders

The eating disorders include bulimia nervosa (BN), anorexia nervosa (AN), and binge-eating disorder (BED), a newly-proposed DSM category. They are characterized by severely impaired cognitions centered on weight and severely maladaptive eating behavior. As a consequence, most of the research involving these disorders has focused on cognitive and behavioral interventions, which have recently been examined in a number of large-scale, controlled studies (e.g. Fairburn et al 1991, 1993, 1995).

BULIMIA NERVOSA   Most of the psychotherapy research on eating disorders has been conducted on BN. Originally thought to be resistant to treatment (Russell 1979), research indicates that BN does respond to psychotherapy (Garfinkel & Goldbloom 1993, Hartman et al 1992). The most widely researched treatment is cognitive behavior therapy (CBT), which has repeatedly proven superior to other therapy modalities (e.g. Fairburn et al 1989, 1991, 1993) and has emerged as the treatment of choice (cf Walsh et al 1997).

Other treatments for BN have been less researched but have demonstrated promise for being effective. Similar to findings in the depression literature, interpersonal psychotherapy (IPT) has been shown to be as effective as CBT. Fairburn and colleagues (1991, 1993) compared CBT with IPT, which focuses on the interpersonal problems surrounding bulimic behavior. At the end of treatment, CBT was clearly superior, but the treatments were equally effective over the course of long-term follow-up.

ANOREXIA NERVOSA AND BINGE EATING DISORDER   Anorexia nervosa is usually treated on an inpatient basis because of the medical necessity of restoring healthy weight (Beumont et al 1993). However, with recent restrictions on length of inpatient care (Baran et al 1995), the small pool of outpatient care research (e.g. Gowers et al 1994) needs to be expanded.

BED might be considered a sub-category of BN, wherein the patient engages in excessive, seemingly uncontrolled eating but not in the purging behaviors. Research suggests that both CBT and IPT are effective treatments of BED (Smith et al 1992, Wilfley et al 1993).

Substance Abuse

A previous *Annual Review of Psychology* chapter on individual psychotherapy (Goldfried et al 1990) did not include a section on treatment of substance use disorders, perhaps because the field was dominated by uncontrolled comparisons of poorly specified treatments (Floyd et al 1996). We review the increasing number of studies that have used stringent experimental design procedures.

PSYCHOLOGICAL INTERVENTIONS FOR SUBSTANCE ABUSE DISORDERS   There is considerable evidence that alcohol-abusing patients who undergo treatment drink less frequently and consume less when they do drink. Inpatient treatment does not appear to be superior to outpatient treatment (e.g. McKay & Maisto 1993), although length of treatment is positively associated with better outcomes (Moos et al 1990). The treatments that have been most systematically investigated are twelve-step-based counseling, psychodynamic therapy, and CBT. Holder et al (1991) reviewed the extant studies and concluded that CBT was slightly more efficacious, but other studies suggest an equivalency of treatments (e.g. Cooney et al 1991). Similarly, in a recent large-scale study, both supportive-expressive psychodynamic psychotherapy and CT were found to be efficacious with opiate dependence (Woody et al 1990, 1995).

TREATMENT MATCHING STUDIES   The alcohol and drug use literature is growing rapidly with studies examining the effects of trying to match patient characteristics to the most efficacious treatment. Mattson et al (1994) reviewed 30 experimental studies and found evidence supporting this practice.

A larger-scale matching study (Project MATCH 1997) was recently completed and is generating numerous reports. This study was a clinical trial wherein two groups of patients (one receiving outpatient therapy and the other receiving care after either inpatient or day treatment) were randomly assigned to one of three individualized treatments lasting 12 weeks: cognitive behavioral coping skills treatment (CBCST), motivational enhancement therapy, or twelve-step facilitation therapy (TSF). Significant and sustained improvements in drinking outcomes were observed for all three groups. Only one pretreatment patient attribute, psychiatric severity, interacted with treatment, as clients low in severity did better in TSF than CBCST; high-severity clients did equally well in all treatments.

Personality Disorders

The use of psychotherapy to treat personality disorders is largely in the discovery phase of research, with a few exceptions. To be sure, theoretical approaches to treatment have been presented from cognitive (Beck & Freeman 1990), interpersonal (Benjamin 1993), psychodynamic (Clarkin et al 1992), and behavioral (Linehan 1993) perspectives. One of these treatments, dialectical behavior therapy for borderline personality disorder (Linehan et al 1991), has met the criteria for a probably efficacious therapy. Other outcome studies of psychotherapy with personality-disordered patients have been reported (e.g. Hull et al 1993, Stevenson & Meares 1992). However, the greatest attention has been directed to the assessment of personality as part of psychological therapies (e.g. Pilkonis 1997, Shea 1997), the identification of interpersonal and intrapersonal styles as risk factors or vulnerabilities receiving attention in psychotherapy (cf Ouimette et al 1994), and the influence of personality disorders as comorbid conditions that influence treatment outcomes (e.g. Shea et al 1990).

Serious Mental Illness

The term "serious mental illness" has developed favor as a rubric to include disorders such as the schizophrenias, schizo-affective disorders, and bipolar disorders that formerly were termed chronic mental illnesses (Coursey et al 1997). Psychological therapies have more typically been offered as adjuncts to the psychopharmacological management of primary symptoms in these disorders. Many if not most of the psychotherapies involve modalities other than individual psychotherapy, such as couples, group, or family interventions (Bedell et al 1997). Although the results of psychodynamic psychotherapy continue to be reported, this treatment has generally been found to be ineffective with persons having serious mental illness (Scott & Dixon 1995). Supportive therapies that strengthen the therapeutic alliance, educate, strengthen adaptive defenses, and offer praise for successes have fared better (Rockland 1993). Social skills training (Benton & Schroeder 1990) is the only treatment that meets the efficacy criteria used by the empirically supported therapy advocates; it has been judged to be probably efficacious for the treatment of persons with schizophrenia (DeRubeis & Crits-Christoph 1998).

CLOSING COMMENTS

We now know that psychotherapy is generally effective but we are uncertain as to why. Researchers are currently trying to validate psychotherapy's specific effectiveness and hypothesized operations for change; at the same time, the search for an acceptable guiding theory continues.

The traditional view that the different psychotherapies—similar to medication treatments—contain unique active ingredients resulting in specific effects has not been validated. The nature of the relationship between psychotherapy and pharmacotherapy continues to be uncertain. The most frequently practiced and most rapidly growing brand of treatment, eclectic therapy, is still poorly defined as well as inadequately researched; yet, this movement in clinical practice may be the phenomenon that best defines psychotherapy's maturation process.

Although the aforementioned situations are evidence of a profession in turmoil, there is the possibility for a positive transition here. New research designs are emerging that can uncover needed knowledge, and established ones (RCT) are becoming more sophisticated in their application. The order of events described in this review (from unexpected findings to critical debate to new methodologies) has led in some cases to paradigm shifts. It is premature to declare that a paradigm shift is beginning to take place because presently there is little clue as to its form. However, some have implied that psychotherapy may be in a "pre-paradigm-shift phase" (Bergin & Garfield 1994b). The picture should become clearer as researchers apply the newer methodologies to psychotherapy as practiced in actual clinical settings.

ACKNOWLEDGMENT

We are grateful to Wolfgang Lutz for his helpful and insightful comments.

Visit the *Annual Reviews home page* at
http://www.AnnualReviews.org.

Literature Cited

Agency Health Care Policy Res. Depression Guideline Panel. 1993. *Depression in Primary Care,* Vol. 2. *Treatment of Major Depression* (Clin. Pract. Guideline No. 5, AHCPR Publ. No. 93-0551). Rockville, MD: US DHHS, US Public Health Serv., Agency Health Care Policy Res.

Am. Psychiatric Assoc. 1993. Practice guidelines for the treatment of major depressive disorder in adults. *Am. J. Psychiatry* 150: 1–26

Am. Psychiatric Assoc. 1994. *Diagnostic and Statistical Manual of Mental Disorders.* Washington, DC: Am. Psychiatr. Assoc. 4th ed.

Am. Psychol. Assoc. Task Force Promotion Dissemination Psychol. Procedures, Div. Clin. Psychol. 1995. Training in and dissemination of empirically-validated psychological treatments: report and recommendations. *Clin. Psychol.* 48:3–23

Arntz A, van den Hout MA. 1996. Psychological treatment of panic disorder without agoraphobia: cognitive therapy versus applied relaxation. *Behav. Res. Ther.* 34: 113–21

Ballenger JC. 1993. Panic disorder: efficacy of current treatments. *Psychopharm. Bull.* 29:477–86

Baran SA, Weltzin TE, Kaye WH. 1995. Low discharge weight and outcome in anorexia nervosa. *Am. J. Psychiatry* 152:1070–72

Barkham M, Rees A, Shapiro DA, Stiles WB, Agnew RM, et al. 1996a. Outcomes of time-limited psychotherapy in applied settings: replicating the Second Sheffield Psychotherapy Project. *J. Consult. Clin. Psychol.* 64:1079–85

Barkham M, Rees A, Stiles WB, Shapiro DA, Hardy GE, Reynolds S. 1996b. Dose-effect relations in time-limited psychotherapy for depression. *J. Consult. Clin. Psychol.* 64:927–35

Barkham M, Stiles WB, Shapiro DA. 1993. The shape of change in psychotherapy: longitudinal assessment of personal problems. *J. Consult. Clin. Psychol.* 61: 667–77

Barlow DH, ed. 1993. *Clinical Handbook of Psychological Disorders.* New York: Gifford. 2nd ed.

Barlow DH. 1994. Psychological intervention in the area of managed competition. *Clin. Psychol.: Sci. Pract.* 1:109–22

Barlow DH. 1996. The effectiveness of psychotherapy: science and policy. *Clin. Psychol.: Sci. Pract.* 3:236–40

Barlow DH, Lehman CL. 1996. Advances in the pyschosocial treatment of anxiety disorders. *Arch. Gen. Psychiatry* 53:727–35

Barlow DH, Rapee RM, Brown TA. 1992. Behavioral treatment of generalized anxiety disorder. *Behav. Ther.* 23:551–70

Barlow DH, Raske MG, Cerny JA, Klosko JS. 1989. Behavioral treatment of panic disorder. *Behav. Ther.* 20:261–82

Beach S, O'Leary KD. 1992. Treating depression in the context of marital discord: outcome and predictors of response of marital therapy versus cognitive therapy. *Behav. Ther.* 23:507–28

Beck AT, Freeman AA. 1990. *Cognitive Therapy of Personality Disorders.* New York: Guilford

Beck JG, Stanley MA, Baldwin LE, Deagle EA III, Averill PM. 1994. Comparison of cognitive therapy and relaxation training for panic disorder. *J. Consult. Clin. Psychol.* 62:818–26

Bedell JR, Hunter RH, Corrigan PW. 1997. Current approaches to assessment and treatment of persons with serious mental illness. *Prof. Psychol.* 28:217–28

Benjamin LS. 1993. *Interpersonal Diagnosis and Treatment of Personality Disorders.* New York: Guilford

Benton MK, Schroeder HE. 1990. Social skills training with schizophrenics: a meta-analytic evaluation. *J. Consult. Clin. Psychol.* 54:741–47

Bergin AE, Garfield SL. 1994a. *Handbook of Psychotherapy and Behavior Change.* New York: Wiley. 4th ed.

Bergin AE, Garfield SL. 1994b. Overview, trends, and future issues. In *Handbook of Psychotherapy and Behavior Change,* ed. AE Bergin, SL Garfield, pp. 821–30. New York: Wiley. 4th ed.

Beumont PJV, Russell JD, Touyz SW. 1993. Treatment of anorexia nervosa. *Lancet* 341:1635–40

Beutler LE. 1991. Have all won and must all have prizes: revisiting Luborsky et al.'s verdict. *J. Consult. Clin. Psychol.* 59: 226–32

Beutler LE. 1998. Identifying empirically supported treatments: what if we didn't? *J. Consult. Clin. Psychol.* 66:113–20

Beutler LE, Clarkin J. 1990. *Systematic Treatment Selection: Toward Targeted Therapeutic Interventions.* New York: Brunner/Mazel

Beutler LE, Engle D, Mohr D, Daldrup RJ, Bergan J, et al. 1991. Predictors of differential response to cognitive, experiential, and self-directed psychotherapeutic procedures. *J. Consult. Clin. Psychol.* 59:333–40

Beutler LE, Kim EJ, Davison E, Karno M, Fisher D. 1996. Research contributions to improving managed health care outcomes. *Psychotherapy* 33:197–206

Blatt SJ, Quinlan DM, Pilkonis PA, Shea MT. 1995. Impact of perfectionism and need for approval on the brief treatment of depression: the National Institute of Mental Health Treatment of Depression Collaborative Research Program revisited. *J. Consult. Clin. Psychol.* 63:125–32

Blatt SJ, Quinlan DM, Zuroff DC, Pilkonis PA. 1996. Interpersonal factors in brief treatment of depression: further analyses of the National Institute of Mental Health Treatment of Depression Collaborative Research Program. *J. Consult. Clin. Psychol.* 64:162–71

Bordin ES. 1994. Theory and research on the therapeutic working alliance: new directions. See Horvath & Greenberg 1994, pp. 13–37

Borkovec TD, Costello E. 1993. Efficacy of applied relaxation and cognitive behavioral therapy in the treatment of generalized anxiety disorder. *J. Consult. Clin. Psychol.* 61:611–19

Brock T, Green M, Reich D, Evans L. 1996. The *Consumer Reports* study of psychotherapy: invalid is invalid. *Am. Psychol.* 51:1083–84

Broskowski AT. 1995. The evolution of health care: implications for the training and careers of psychologists. *Prof. Psychol.: Res. Pract.* 26:156–62

Burns D, Nolen-Hoeksema S. 1992. Therapeutic empathy and recovery from depression in cognitive-behavioral therapy: a structural equation model. *J. Consult. Clin. Psychol.* 60:441–49

Burns DD, Nolen-Hoeksema S. 1991. Coping styles, homework compliance, and the effectiveness of cognitive-behavioral therapy. *J. Consult. Clin. Psychol.* 59:305–11

Campbell LF. 1996. The treatment outcome pursuit: a mandate for the clinical and researcher working alliance. *Psychotherapy* 33:190–96

Castonguay LG, Goldfried MR, Wiser S, Raue PJ, Hayes AM. 1996. Predicting the effect of cognitive therapy for depression: a study of unique and common factors. *J. Consult. Clin. Psychol.* 64:497–504

Chambless DL. 1996. In defense of dissemination of empirically supported psychological interventions. *Clin. Psychol. Sci. Pract.* 3:230–35

Chambless DL, Gillis MM. 1993. Cognitive therapy of anxiety disorders. *J. Consult. Clin. Psychol.* 66:248–60

Clark DM, Salkovskis PM, Hackmann A, Middleton H, Anastasiades P, Gelder M. 1994. A comparison of cognitive therapy, applied relaxation and imipramine in the treatment of panic disorder. *Br. J. Psychiatry* 164:759–69

Clarkin JF, Koenigsberg H, Yoemans F, Selzer M, Kernberg P, Kernberg OF. 1992. Psychodynamic psychotherapy of the borderline patients. In *Borderline Personality Disorder: Clinical and Empirical Perspectives*, ed. JF Clarkin, E Marziali, H Munroe-Blum, pp. 268–87. New York: Guilford

Connors GJ, Carroll KM, DiClemente CC, Longabaugh R, Donovan DM. 1997. The therapeutic alliance and its relationship to alcoholism treatment participation and outcome. *J. Consult. Clin. Psychol.* 65:588–98

Consumer Reports. 1995. Mental health: does therapy help? Nov.: 734–39

Cooney NL, Kadden RM, Litt MD, Getter H. 1991. Matching alcoholics to coping skills or interactional therapies: two-year follow-up results. *J. Consult. Clin. Psychol.* 59:598–601

Coursey RD, Alford J, Safarjan B. 1997. Significant advances in understanding and treating serious mental illness. *Prof. Psychol.* 28:205–16

Crits-Christoph P. 1996. The dissemination of efficacious psychological treatments. *Clin. Psychol.: Sci. Pract.* 3:260–63

Crits-Christoph P. 1997. Limitations of the "dodo bird" verdict and the role of clinical trials in psychotherapy research: comment on Wampold et al. (1997). *Psychol. Bull.* 122:216–20

Crits-Christoph P, Baranackie K, Kurcias JS, Carroll K, Luborsky L, et al. 1991. Meta-analysis of therapist effects in psychotherapy outcome studies. *Psychother. Res.* 1: 81–91

Crits-Christoph P, Mintz J. 1991. Implications of therapist effects for the design and analysis of comparative studies of psychotherapies. *J. Consult. Clin. Psychol.* 59: 20–26

DeRubeis RJ, Crits-Christoph P. 1998. Empirically supported individual and group psychological treatments for adult mental disorders. *J. Consult. Clin. Psychol.* 66: 37–52

DeRubeis RJ, Evans MD, Hollon SD, Garvey MJ, Grove WM, Tuason VB. 1990. How does cognitive therapy work? Cognitive change and symptom change in cognitive therapy and pharmacotherapy for depression. *J. Consult. Clin. Psychol.* 58: 862–69

Dobson KS. 1989. A meta-analysis of the efficacy of cognitive therapy for depression. *J. Consult. Clin. Psychol.* 57:414–19

Docherty JP, Streeter MJ. 1993. Progress and limitations in psychotherapy research: a focus on depression. *J. Psychother. Pract. Res.* 2:100–18

Durham RC, Murphy T, Allan T, Richard K, Treliving LR, Fenton GW. 1994. Cognitive therapy, analytic psychotherapy, and anxiety management training for generalized anxiety disorder. *Br. J. Psychiatry* 165:315–23

Elkin I, Gibbons RD, Shea TM, Shaw BF. 1996. Science is not a trial (but it can sometimes be a tribulation). *J. Consult. Clin. Psychol.* 64:92–103

Elkin I, Shea MT, Watkins JT, Imber SD, Sotsky SM, et al. 1989. NIMH treatment of depression collaborative research program: general effectiveness of treatments. *Arch. Gen. Psychiatry* 46:971–82

Elliott R, Stiles WB, Shapiro DA. 1993. Are some psychotherapies more equivalent than others? See Giles 1993, pp. 455–79

Emmelkamp PMG, Beens H. 1991. Cognitive therapy with obsessive-compulsive disorder: a comparative evaluation. *Behav. Res. Ther.* 29:293–300

Evans MD, Hollon SD, DeRubeis RJ, Piasecki JM, Grove WM, et al. 1992. Deferential relapse following cognitive therapy and pharmacotherapy for depression. *Arch. Gen. Psychiatry* 49:802–8

Eysenck HJ. 1952. The effects of psychotherapy: an evaluation. *J. Consult. Psychol.* 16:319–24

Fairburn CG, Jones R, Peveler RC, Carr SJ, Solomon RA, et al. 1991. Three psychological treatments for bulimia nervosa. *Arch. Gen. Psych.* 48:463–69

Fairburn CG, Jones R, Peveler RC, Hope RA, O'Connor M. 1993. Psychotherapy and bulimia nervosa: longer-term effects of interpersonal psychotherapy, behavior therapy, and cognitive behavior therapy. *Arch. Gen. Psych.* 50:419–28

Fairburn CG, Marcus MD, Wilson GT. 1993. Cognitive-behavioral therapy for binge eating and bulimia nervosa: a comprehensive treatment manual. In *Cognitive Behaviour Therapy for Psychiatric Problems*, ed. K Hawton, PM Salkovskis, J Kirk, DM Clark, pp. 361–404. New York: Oxford Univ. Press

Fairburn CG, Norman PA, Welch SL, O'Connor ME, Doll HA, Peveler RC. 1995. A prospective study of outcome in bulimia nervosa and the long-term effects of three psychological treatments. *Arch. Gen. Psychiatry* 52:304–12

Fals-Stewart W, Marks A, Schafer B. 1993. A comparison of behavioral group therapy and individual behavior therapy in treating obsessive-compulsive disorder. *J. Nerv. Ment. Dis.* 181:189–93

Fensterheim H, Raw SD. 1996. Psychotherapy research is not psychotherapy practice. *Clin. Psychol.: Sci. Pract.* 4:168–71

Feske U, Chambless DL. 1995. Cognitive behavioral versus exposure only treatment for social phobia: a meta-analysis. *Behav. Ther.* 26:695–720

Floyd AS, Monahan SC, Finney JW, Morley JA. 1996. Alcoholism treatment outcome studies, 1980-1992: the nature of the research. *Addict. Behav.* 21:413–28

Foa EB, Kozak MJ, Steketee GS, McCarty PR. 1992. Treatment of depressive and obsessive-compulsive symptoms in OCD by imipramine and behavior therapy. *Br. J. Psychiatry* 31:279–92

Foa EB, Rothbaum BO, Riggs DS, Murdock TB. 1991. Treatment of post-traumatic stress disorder in rape victims: a comparison between cognitive-behavioral procedures and counseling. *J. Consult. Clin. Psychol.* 59:715–23

Frank JD, Frank JB. 1991. *Persuasion and Healing: A Comparative Study of Psychotherapy.* Baltimore, MD: Johns Hopkins Univ. Press

Garfield SL. 1991. Common and specific factors in psychotherapy. *J. Integr. Eclect. Psychother.* 10:5–13

Garfield SL. 1996. Some problems associated with "validated" forms of psychotherapy. *Clin. Psychol.: Sci. Pract.* 3:218–29

Garfinkel PE, Goldbloom DS. 1993. Bulimia nervosa: a review of therapy research. *J. Psychother. Pract. Res.* 2:38–50

Gaw KF, Beutler LE. 1995. Integrating treatment recommendations. In *Integrative Assessment of Adult Personality*, ed. LE Beutler, M Berren, pp. 280–319. New York: Guilford

Gibbons RD, Hedeker D, Elkin I, Waternaux C, Kraemer HC, et al. 1993. Some conceptual and statistical issues in the analysis of longitudinal psychiatric data: application to the NIMH TDCRP dataset. *Arch. Gen. Psychiatry* 50:739–50

Giles TR, ed. 1993. *Handbook of Effective Psychotherapy.* New York: Plenum

Goldfried MR, Greenberg LS, Marmar C. 1990. Individual psychotherapy: process and outcome. *Annu. Rev. Psychol.* 41: 659–88

Goldfried MR, Wolfe BE. 1996. Psychotherapy practice and research: repairing a strained alliance. *Am. Psychol.* 51: 1007–16

Goldfried MR, Wolfe BE. 1998. Toward a more clinically valid approach to therapy research. *J. Consult. Clin. Psychol.* 66: 143–50

Gorman JM. 1994. New and experimental pharmacological treatments for panic disorder. See Wolfe & Maser 1994, pp. 83–90

Gould RA, Otto MW, Pollack MH. 1995. A meta-analysis of treatment outcome for panic disorder. *Clin. Psychol. Rev.* 15: 819–44

Gowers S, Norton K, Halek C, Crisp AH. 1994. Outcome of outpatient psychotherapy in a random allocation treatment study of anorexia nervosa. *Int. J. Eating Disord.* 15:165–77

Greenberg LS, Newman FL. 1996. An approach to psychotherapy change process research: introduction to the special section. *J. Consult. Clin. Psychol.* 64:435–38

Grissom RJ. 1996. The magical number .7 plus or minus .2: meta-analysis of the probability of superior outcome in comparisons involving therapy, placebo, and control. *J. Consult. Clin. Psychol.* 64:973–82

Hartmann A, Herzog T, Drinkmann A. 1992. Psychotherapy of bulimia nervosa: what is effective? A meta analysis. *J. Psychosom.* 36:159–67

Heimberg RG, Liebowitz MR, Hope DA, Schneier FR, eds. 1995. *Social Phobia:*

Diagnosis, Assessment, and Treatment. New York: Guilford

Holder HD, Longabaugh R, Miller WR, Rubonis AV. 1991. The cost effectiveness of treatment for alcohol problems: a first approximation. *J. Stud. Alcohol* 52:517–40

Hollon S. 1996. The efficacy and effectiveness of psychotherapy relative to medications. *Am. Psychol.* 51:1025–30

Hollon SD, Shelton RC, Davis DD. 1993. Cognitive therapy for depression: conceptual issues and clinical efficacy. *J. Consult. Clin. Psychol.* 61:270–75

Horvath AO. 1994. Empirical validation of Bordin's pantheoretical model of the alliance: the Working Alliance Inventory perspective. See Horvath & Greenberg 1994, pp. 109–28

Horvath AO, Greenberg LS, eds. 1994. *The Working Alliance: Theory, Research, and Practice.* New York: Wiley & Sons

Horvath AO, Symonds BD. 1991. Relation between working alliance and outcome in psychotherapy: a meta-analysis. *J. Couns. Psychol.* 38:139–49

Howard KI, Kopta SM, Krause MS, Orlinsky DE. 1986. The dose-effect relationship in psychotherapy. *Am. Psychol.* 41:159–64

Howard KI, Krause MS, Saunders SM, Kopta SM. 1997. Trials and tribulations in the meta-analysis of treatment differences: comment on Wampold et al. (1997). *Psychol. Bull.* 122:221–25

Howard KI, Lueger RJ, Kolden GG. 1997. Measuring progress and outcome in the treatment of affective disorders. See Strupp et al 1997, pp. 263–82

Howard KI, Lueger RJ, Maling MS, Martinovich Z. 1993. A phase model of psychotherapy: causal mediation of outcome. *J. Consult. Clin. Psychol.* 61:678–85

Howard KI, Moras K, Brill PL, Martinovich Z, Lutz W. 1996. Evaluation of psychotherapy: efficacy, effectiveness, and patient progress. *Am. Psychol.* 51:1059–64

Howard KI, Orlinsky DE, Lueger RJ. 1995. The design of clinically relevant outcome research: some considerations and an example. In *Research Foundations for Psychotherapy Practice,* ed. M Aveline, DA Shapiro, pp. 3–47. Sussex, UK: Wiley

Hull JW, Clarkin JF, Kakuma T. 1993. Treatment response of borderline inpatients: a growth curve analysis. *J. Nerv. Ment. Dis.* 181:503–8

Jacobson N, Christensen A. 1996. Studying the effectiveness of psychotherapy: how well can clinical trials do the job? *Am. Psychol.* 51:1031–39

Jacobson NE, Hollon SD. 1996. Cognitive-behavior therapy versus pharmacother-

apy: now that the jury has returned its verdict, it's time to present the rest of the evidence. *J. Consult. Clin. Psychol.* 64:74–80

Jacobson NS, Dobson KS, Truax PA, Addis ME, Koerner K, et al. 1996. A component analysis of cognitive-behavioral treatment for depression. *J. Consult. Clin. Psychol.* 64:295–304

Jacobson NS, Follette WC, Revenstorf D. 1984. Psychotherapy outcome research: methods for reporting variability and evaluating clinical significance. *Behav. Ther.* 15:336–52

Kadera SW, Lambert MJ, Andrews AA. 1996. How much therapy is really enough? A session-by-session analysis of the psychotherapy dose-effect relationship. *J. Psychother. Pract. Res.* 5:132–51

Kazdin AE. 1996. Validated treatments: multiple perspectives and issues—introduction to the series. *Clin. Psychol.: Sci. Pract.* 3:216–17

Klein DF. 1996. Preventing hung juries about therapy studies. *J. Consult. Clin. Psychol.* 64:81–87

Klosko JS, Barlow DH, Tassinari R, Cerny JA. 1990. A comparison of alprazolam and behavior therapy in treatment of panic disorder. *J. Consult. Clin. Psychol.* 58:77–84

Kopta SM, Howard KI, Lowry JL, Beutler LE. 1994. Patterns of symptomatic recovery in psychotherapy. *J. Consult. Clin. Psychol.* 62:1009–16

Krupnick JL, Sotsky SM, Simmens S, Moyer J, Elkin I, et al. 1996. The role of the therapeutic alliance in psychotherapy and pharmacotherapy outcome: findings in the National Institute of Mental Health Treatment of Depression Collaborative Research Program. *J. Consult. Clin. Psychol.* 64:532–39

Lambert MJ. 1992. Psychotherapy outcome research: implications for integrative and eclectic therapies. See Norcross & Goldfried 1992, pp. 94–129

Lambert MJ, Bergin AE. 1994a. The effectiveness of psychotherapy. See Bergin & Garfield 1994a, pp. 143–89

Lambert MJ, Hill CE. 1994. Assessing psychotherapy outcomes and processes. See Bergin & Garfield 1994a, pp. 72–113

Lewinsohn PM, Sullivan JM, Grosscup SJ. 1980. Changing reinforcing events: an approach to the treatment of depression. *Psychother. Theory Res. Pract.* 17:322–34

Linehan MM. 1993. *Cognitive-Behavioral Treatment of Borderline Personality Disorder.* New York: Guilford

Linehan MM, Armstrong HE, Suarez A, Allmon D, Heard HL. 1991. Cognitive-behavioral treatment of chronically parasuicidal borderline patients. *Arch. Gen. Psychiatry* 48:1060–64

Lipsey MW, Wilson DB. 1993. The efficacy of psychological, educational, and behavioral treatment: confirmation from meta-analysis. *Am. Psychol.* 48:1181–1209

Luborsky L. 1994. Therapeutic alliances as predictors of psychotherapy outcomes: factors explaining the predictive success. See Horvath & Greenberg 1994, pp. 38–50

Luborsky L, Singer B, Luborsky L. 1975. Comparative studies of psychotherapy. *Arch. Gen. Psychiatry* 32:995–1008

Mattson ME, Allen JP, Longabaugh R, Nickless CJ, Connors G, et al. 1994. A chronological review of empirical studies matching alcoholic clients to treatment. *J. Stud. Alcohol* 55:16–29

Mavissakalian M, Prien R, eds. 1996. *Long-Term Treatments of Anxiety Disorders*. Washington, DC: Am. Psychiatr. Assoc.

McKay JR, Maisto SA. 1993. An overview and critique of advances in the treatment of alcohol use disorders. *Drugs Soc.* 8:1–29

McNeilly CL, Howard KI. 1991. The effects of psychotherapy: a reevaluation based on dosage. *Psychother. Res.* 1:74–78

Mintz J, Drake R, Crits-Christoph P. 1996. The efficacy and effectiveness of psychotherapy: two paradigms, one science. *Am. Psychol.* 51:1084–85

Mohr DC, Beutler LE, Engle D, Shoham-Soloman V, Bergan J, et al. 1990. Identification of patients at risk for nonresponse and negative outcome in psychotherapy. *J. Consult. Clin. Psychol.* 58:622–28

Moos RH, Finney JW, Cronkite RC. 1990. *Alcoholism Treatment: Context, Process, and Outcome*. New York: Oxford Univ. Press

Morrow-Bradley C, Elliott R. 1986. The utilization of psychotherapy research by practicing psychotherapists. *Am. Psychol.* 41:188–97

Muran JC, Segal ZV, Wallner Samstag L, Crawford CE. 1994. Patient pretreatment interpersonal problems and therapeutic alliance in short-term cognitive therapy. *J. Consult. Clin. Psychol.* 62:185–90

Nathan PE. 1996. Validated forms of psychotherapy may lead to better-validated psychotherapy. *Clin. Psychol.: Sci. Pract.* 3:251–55

Nathan PE. 1998. Practice guidelines: not yet ideal. *Am. Psychol.* 53:290–99

Norcross JC. 1997. Emerging breakthroughs in psychotherapy integration: three predictions and one fantasy. *Psychotherapy* 34:86–90

Norcross JC, ed. 1993. Research directions for psychotherapy integration: a roundtable. *J. Psychother. Integr.* 3:91–131

Norcross JC, Goldfried MR, eds. 1992. *Handbook of Psychotherapy Integration*. New York: Basic Books

Orlinsky DE, Grawe K, Parks BK. 1994. Process and outcome in psychotherapy—noch einmal. See Bergin & Garfield 1994a, pp. 270–378

Ost L. 1988. Applied relaxation vs progressive relaxation in the treatment of panic disorder. *Behav. Ther. Res.* 26:13–22

Ouimette PC, Klein DN, Anderson R, Riso LP, Lizardi H. 1994. Relationship of sociotropy/autonomy and dependency/self criticism to DSM-III-R personality disorders. *Am. J. Psychiatry* 149:1645–53

Patterson CH. 1984. Empathy, warmth, and genuineness in psychotherapy: a review of reviews. *Psychotherapy* 21:431–38

Paul GL. 1967. Outcome research in psychotherapy. *J. Consult. Psychol.* 31:109–18

Persons JB, Silberschatz G. 1998. Are results of randomized controlled trials useful to psychotherapists? *J. Consult. Clin. Psychol.* 66:126-\35

Pilkonis PA. 1997. Measurement issues relevant to personality disorders. See Strupp et al 1997, pp. 371–88

Piper WE, Azim HFA, Joyce AS, McCallum M, Nixon GWH, et al. 1991. Quality of object relations versus interpersonal functioning as predictors of therapeutic alliance and psychotherapy outcome. *J. Nerv. Ment. Dis.* 179:432–38

Project MATCH Research Group. 1997. Matching alcoholism treatments to client heterogeneity: project MATCH posttreatment drinking outcomes. *J. Stud. Alcohol* 58:7–29

Renfry G, Spates CR. 1994. Eye movement desensitization: a partial dismantling study. *J. Behav. Exp.* 25:231–39

Robinson LA, Berman JS, Neimeyer RA. 1990. Psychotherapy for the treatment of depression: a comprehensive review of controlled outcome research. *Psychol. Bull.* 108:30–49

Rockland LH. 1993. A review of supportive psychotherapy, 1986-1982. *Hosp. Community Psychol.* 44:1053–60

Roth A, Fonagy P. 1996. *What Works for Whom? A Critical Review of Psychotherapy*. New York: Guilford

Russell GFM. 1979. Bulimia nervosa: an ominous variant of anorexia nervosa. *Psychol. Med.* 9:429–48

Russell RL, ed. 1994. *Reassessing Psychotherapy Research*. New York: Guilford

Scott JE, Dixon LB. 1995. Psychological interventions for schizophrenia. *Schizophr. Bull.* 21:621–30

Seligman MEP. 1995. The effectiveness of psychotherapy: the *Consumer Reports* study. *Am. Psychol.* 50:965–74

Seligman MEP. 1996a. Science as an ally of practice. *Am. Psychol.* 51:1072–79

Seligman MEP. 1996b. A creditable beginning. *Am. Psychol.* 51:1086–88

Shadish WR, Matt GE, Navarro AM, Siegle G, Crits-Christoph P, et al. 1997. Evidence that therapy works in clinically representative conditions. *J. Consult. Clin. Psychol.* 65:355–65

Shapiro DA, Barkham M, Rees A, Hardy GE, Reynolds S, et al. 1994a. Effects of treatment duration and severity of depression on the effectiveness of cognitive-behavioral and psychodynamic-interpersonal psychotherapy. *J. Consult. Clin. Psychol.* 62:522–34

Shapiro DA, Harper H, Startup MJ, Reynolds S, Bird D, Suokas A. 1994b. The high watermark of the drug metaphor: a meta-analytic critique of process-outcome research. See Russell 1994, pp. 1–35

Shea MT. 1997. Core Battery Conference: assessment of change in personality disorders. See Strupp et al 1997, pp. 389–400

Shea MT, Pilkonis PA, Beckham E, Collins JF, Elkin I, et al. 1990. Personality disorders and treatment outcome in the NIMH Treatment of Depression Collaborative Research Program. *Am. J. Psychiatry* 147: 711–18

Shear MK, Maser JD. 1994. Standardized assessment for panic disorder research: a conference report. *Arch. Gen. Psychiatry* 51: 346–54

Smith D, Marcus, MD, Kaye W. 1992. Cognitive-behavioral treatment of obese binge-eaters. *Int. J. Eating Disord.* 12: 257–62

Smith ML, Glass GV. 1977. Meta-analysis of psychotherapy outcome studies. *Am. Psychol.* 32:752–60

Spiegel DA, Bruce BJ. 1997. Benzodiazepines and exposure-based cognitive behavior therapies for panic disorder: conclusions from combined treatment trials. *Arch. Gen. Psychiatry* 154:773–80

Stevenson J, Meares R. 1992. An outcome study of psychotherapy for patients with borderline personality disorder. *Am. J. Psychiatry* 149:358–62

Stiles WB. 1996. When more of a good thing is better: reply to Hayes et al. 1996. *J. Consult. Clin. Psychol.* 64:915–18

Stiles WB, Shapiro DA. 1994. Abuse of the drug metaphor: psychotherapy process-outcome research. *Clin. Psychol. Rev.* 9: 521–43

Stricker G, Gold JR, eds. 1993. *Comprehensive Handbook of Psychotherapy Integration.* New York: Plenum

Strupp H. 1996. The tripartite model and the *Consumer Reports* study. *Am. Psychol.* 51: 1017–24

Strupp H. 1997. Research, practice, and managed care. *Psychotherapy* 34:91–94

Strupp HH, Horowitz LM, Lambert MJ, eds. 1997. *Measuring Patient Changes in Mood, Anxiety, and Personality Disorders: Toward a Core Battery.* Washington, DC: Am. Psychol. Assoc.

Tingey RC, Lambert MJ, Burlingame GM, Hansen NB. 1996. Assessing clinical significance: proposed extensions to method. *Psychother. Res.* 6:109–23

Turner SM, Beidel DC, Jacob RG. 1994. Social phobia: a comparison of behavior therapy and atenolol. *J. Consult. Clin. Psychol.* 62:350–58

Van Oppen P, De Haan E, Van Balkom AJLM, Spinhoven P, Hoogduin K, Van Dyck R. 1995. Cognitive therapy and exposure in vivo in the treatment of obsessive compulsive disorder. *Behav. Res. Ther.* 33:379–90

Walsh BT, Wilson GT, Loeb KL, Devlin MJ, Pike KM, et al. 1997. Medication and psychotherapy in the treatment of bulimia nervosa. *Am. J. Psychiatry* 154:523–31

Wampold BE. 1997. Methodological problems in identifying efficacious psychotherapies. *Psychother. Res.* 7:21–43

Wampold BE, Mondin GW, Moody M, Stich F, Benson K, et al. 1997. A meta-analysis of outcome studies comparing bona fide psychotherapies: empirically "all must have prizes." *Psychol. Bull.* 203–15

Whisman MA, Miller IW, Norman WH, Keitner GI. 1991. Cognitive therapy with depressed inpatients: specific effects on dysfunctional cognitions. *J. Consult. Clin. Psychol.* 59:282–88

Wilfley DE, Agras WS, Telch CF, Rossiter EM, Schneider JA, et al. 1993. Group cognitive-behavioral therapy and group interpersonal psychotherapy for the nonpurging bulimic individual: a controlled comparison. *J. Consult. Clin. Psychol.* 61: 296–305

Williams SL, Falbo J. 1996. Cognitive and performance-based treatments for panic attack in people with varying degrees of agoraphobic disability. *Behav. Res. Ther.* 34:253–64

Wilson GT. 1996. Empirically validated treatments: reality and resistance. *Clin. Psychol. Sci. Pract.* 3:241–44

Wilson SA, Becker LA, Tinker RH. 1995. Eye movement desensitization and reprocessing (EMDR) treatment for psychologically traumatized individuals. *J. Consult. Clin. Psychol.* 63:928–37

Wolfe BE, Maser JD, eds. 1994. *Treatment of Panic Disorder: A Consensus Development Conference.* Washington, DC: Am. Psychiatr. Assoc.

Woody GE, Luborsky L, McLellan AT, O'Brien CP. 1990. Corrections and revised analyses for psychotherapy in methadone maintenance programs. *Arch. Gen. Psychiatry* 47:788–89

Woody GE, McLellan AT, Luborsky L, O'Brien CP. 1995. Psychotherapy in community methadone programs: a validation study. *Am. J. Psychiatry* 192:1302–8

Annu. Rev. Psychol. 1999. 50:471–507

LIFESPAN PSYCHOLOGY: Theory and Application to Intellectual Functioning

Paul B. Baltes, Ursula M. Staudinger, and Ulman Lindenberger

Max Planck Institute for Human Development, Berlin, Germany;
e-mail: sekbaltes@mpib-berlin.mpg.de; staudinger@mpib-berlin.mpg.de;
lindenberger@mpib-berlin.mpg.de

KEY WORDS: aging, cognitive development, co-evolution, child development, developmental theory, intelligence, lifespan development, lifespan psychology

ABSTRACT

The focus of this review is on theory and research of lifespan (lifespan developmental) psychology. The theoretical analysis integrates evolutionary and ontogenetic perspectives on cultural and human development across several levels of analysis. Specific predictions are advanced dealing with the general architecture of lifespan ontogeny, including its directionality and age-differential allocation of developmental resources into the three major goals of developmental adaptation: growth, maintenance, and regulation of loss. Consistent with this general lifespan architecture, a meta-theory of development is outlined that is based on the orchestrated and adaptive interplay between three processes of behavioral regulation: selection, optimization, and compensation. Finally, these propositions and predictions about the general nature of lifespan development are examined and supported by empirical evidence on the development of cognition and intelligence across the life span.

CONTENTS

471

INTRODUCTION

Lifespan developmental psychology or lifespan psychology (LP) deals with the study of individual development (ontogenesis) from conception into old age (PB Baltes et al 1980, Dixon & Lerner 1988, Neugarten 1996, Thomae 1979). A core assumption of LP is that development is not completed at adulthood but that it extends across the entire life course and that from conception onward lifelong adaptive processes of acquisition, maintenance, transformation, and attrition in psychological structures and functions are involved. The simultaneous concern for acquisition, maintenance, transformation, and attrition exemplifies the view of lifespan psychologists that the overall ontogenesis of mind and behavior is dynamic, multidimensional, multifunctional, and nonlinear (PB Baltes 1997).

Lifespan research and theory is intended to generate knowledge about three components of individual development: (*a*) interindividual commonalities (regularities) in development; (*b*) interindividual differences in development; and (*c*) intraindividual plasticity (malleability) in development. Joint attention to each of these components and the specification of their age-related interplays are the conceptual and methodological foundations of the developmental enterprise (PB Baltes et al 1988, Nesselroade 1991, Weinert & Perner 1996).

On a strategic level, there are two ways to construct lifespan theory: person-centered (holistic) and function-centered. The holistic approach (Magnusson 1996, Smith & Baltes 1997) proceeds from consideration of the person as a system and attempts to generate a knowledge base about lifespan development by describing and connecting age periods or states of development into one overall pattern of lifetime individual development. An example would be Erikson's (1959) theory of eight lifespan stages. Often, this holistic approach to the life span is identified with life-course psychology (Bühler 1933; see also Elder 1998). The function-centered way to construct lifespan theory is to focus on a category of behavior or a mechanism (such as perception, information processing, action control, attachment, identity, personality traits, etc.) and to describe the lifespan changes in the mechanisms and processes associated with the category selected. To incorporate both approaches to lifespan ontogenesis in one conceptual framework, the concept of lifespan developmental psychology (PB Baltes & Goulet 1970) was advanced.

Contrary to the American tradition (Parke et al 1991), in Germany Johann Nikolaus Tetens (1777) is considered the founder of the field of developmental psychology (PB Baltes 1983, Müller-Brettel & Dixon 1990, Reinert 1979). From the beginning, the German conception of developmental psychology covered the entire life span and, in its emergence, was closely tied to the role of philosophy, humanism, and education (Bildung). In contrast, the Zeitgeist in North America and some European countries, such as England, was different when developmental psychology emerged as a specialty, around the turn of the twentieth century. At that time, the newly developed fields of genetics and biological evolution were at the forefront of ontogenetic thinking. From biology, with its maturation-based concept of growth, may have sprung the dominant American emphasis in developmental psychology on child psychology and child development. As a consequence, in American psychology a strong bifurcation evolved between child developmentalists, adult developmentalists, and gerontologists.

In recent decades, however, a lifespan approach has become more prominent in North America because of several factors. First was a concern with lifespan development in neighboring social-science disciplines, especially sociology. Life-course sociology took hold as a powerful intellectual force (Elder 1998, Featherman 1983, Mayer 1990, Riley 1987). A second factor was the emergence of gerontology as a field of specialization, with its search for the life-long precursors of aging (Birren & Schaie 1996, Neugarten 1996). A third factor, and a source of rapprochement between child developmentalists and adult developmentalists, was the aging of several classic longitudinal studies on child development begun in the 1920s and 1930s. In the wake of these developments, the need for better collaboration among all age specialties of developmental scholarship has become an imperative of current-day research in developmental psychology (Cairns 1998, Hetherington et al 1988, Rutter & Rutter 1993). But for good lifespan theory to evolve, it takes more than courtship and mutual recognition. It takes a new effort and serious exploration of theory that—in the tradition of Tetens (1777)—has as its primary substantive focus the structure, sequence, and dynamics of the entire life course in a changing society.

THE OVERALL ARCHITECTURE OF LIFESPAN DEVELOPMENT

We approach psychological theories of LP proceeding from the distal and general to the more proximal and specific. The first level of analysis is the overall biological and cultural architecture of lifespan development (PB Baltes 1997, PB Baltes et al 1998). As shown in Figure 1, the benefits of evolutionary selection decrease with age, the need for culture increases with age, and the efficacy of culture decreases with age. The specific form (level, shape) of the functions showing the overall dynamics between biology and culture across the life span is not critical. What is critical is the overall direction and the reciprocal relationship between these functions.

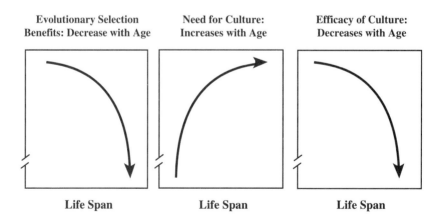

Evolutionary Selection Benefits: Decrease with Age   **Need for Culture: Increases with Age**   **Efficacy of Culture: Decreases with Age**

Life Span   **Life Span**   **Life Span**

Figure 1   Schematic representation of the average dynamics between biology and culture across the life span (after PB Baltes 1997). There can be much debate about the specific forms of the functions, but less about their direction.

Evolutionary Selection Benefits for the Human Genome Decrease Across the Lifespan

The first component of the tri-partite argument derives from an evolutionary perspective on the nature of the genome and its age-correlated changes in expressivity and biological potential (Finch 1996, Jazwinski 1996, Martin et al 1996): During evolution, the older the organism, the less the genome benefited from the genetic advantages associated with evolutionary selection. In other words, the benefits resulting from evolutionary selection display a negative age correlation. Certainly after maturity, and with age, the expressions and mechanisms of the genome lose in functional quality.

This assertion is in line with the idea that evolutionary selection was tied to the process of reproductive fitness and its location in the first half of the life course. This general statement holds true even though indirect positive evolutionary selection benefits are carried into old age, for instance, through grandparenting (Mergler & Goldstein 1983), coupling, or exaptation (Gould 1984).

This age-associated diminution of evolutionary selection benefits and its implied association with an age-related loss of biological potential was further affected by the fact that in earlier times few people reached old age. Thus, in addition to the negative correlation between age and selection pressure, most people died before possible negative genetic attributes were activated or possible negative biological effects of earlier developmental events became manifest. The relative neglect during evolution of the second half of life is amplified further by other aspects of the biology of aging. For all living systems, there are costs involved in creating and maintaining life (Finch 1996, Jazwinski 1996, Martin et al 1996, Yates & Benton 1995). For instance, biological aging involves wear-and-tear as well as the cumulation of errors in genetic replication and repair.

Age-Related Increase in Need for Culture

The middle part of Figure 1 summarizes the overall perspective on lifespan development associated with culture and culture-based processes. By culture, we mean all the psychological, social, material, and symbolic (knowledge-based) resources that humans have produced over the millennia. These, as they are transmitted across generations in increasing quantity and quality, make possible human development as we know it (Cole 1996, Durham 1991, Valsiner & Lawrence 1997). Among these cultural resources are cognitive skills, motivational dispositions, socialization strategies, literacy, written documents, physical structures, and the world of economics as well that of medical and physical technology.

The argument for an age-related increase in the "need" for culture has two parts. First, for human ontogenesis to have reached higher and higher levels of functioning, whether in physical or psychological domains, there had to be a conjoint evolutionary increase in the richness and dissemination of the resources and "opportunities" of culture (Durham 1991, Valsiner & Lawrence 1997). The farther we expect human ontogenesis to extend itself into adult life and old age, the more necessary it will be for particular cultural factors and resources to emerge to make this possible. Consider, for instance, what happened to average life expectancy and educational status (such as reading and writing skills) in industrialized countries during the twentieth century. The genetic make-up of the population did not change during this time. It is primarily through the medium of more advanced levels of culture including technology that people have had the opportunity to continue to develop throughout longer spans of life.

The second argument for the proposition relates to the biological weakening associated with age. That is, the older we are, the more we need culture-based resources (material, social, economic, psychological) to generate and maintain high levels of functioning. A case in point is that for cognitive efficacy to continue into old age at comparable levels of performance, more cognitive support and training are necessary (PB Baltes & Kliegl 1992, Dixon & Bäckman 1995, Hoyer & Rybash 1994, Salthouse 1991).

Age-Related Decrease in Efficacy of Culture

The third cornerstone of the overall nature of lifespan development is the lifespan script of a decreasing efficacy of cultural factors and resources. During the second half of life, and despite the advantages associated with the developmental acquisition of knowledge-based mental representations (Klix 1993), there is an age-associated reduction in the efficiency of cultural factors, even though large interindividual and interdomain differences exist in onset and rate of these losses in efficiency (Hoyer & Rybash 1994, Lindenberger & Baltes 1997, Nelson & Dannefer 1992, Salthouse 1991, Schaie 1996). The older the adult, the more time and practice it takes to attain the same learning gains. Moreover, at least in some domains of information processing, and when it comes to high levels of performance, older adults may not be able to reach the same levels of functioning as younger adults, even after extensive training and under positive life circumstances (PB Baltes 1997, PB Baltes & Smith 1997, Kliegl et al 1989).

There are two causes for this age-related reduction in cultural efficacy or efficiency. The first is age-related loss in biological potential. The second can be seen by viewing the life course in analogy to a learning curve and the acquisition of expertise (Ericsson & Lehmann 1996). Similar to reduced gains in later phases of learning, more and more effort and better technology are necessary to produce further advances as during development we reach higher levels of functioning. Moreover, there is the possibility of age-related increases in negative transfer and costs of specialized knowledge.

The age-related reduction in cultural efficacy argument is likely to raise objection in some social-science circles (PB Baltes et al 1998, Cole 1996, Lerner 1998a). One objection would be that the specifics of cultural systems, namely its symbolic-representational form, may follow different mechanisms of efficiency. For instance, the lifespan developmental entropy costs of symbolic systems may be less than those observed for basic biological processes. A second objection would be that the concept of efficiency contains assumptions about human functioning which are inherently opposed to phenomena such as meaning of life, a sense of religion, or an understanding of one's finitude. However, such perspectives, important and critical as they are to understanding human development, do not alter the general direction of the lifespan function outlined.

Together, the three conditions and trajectories outlined in Figure 1 form a robust and interrelated fabric (architecture) of the lifespan dynamics between biology and culture. This fabric represents a first tier of lifespan theory (PB Baltes 1997). For evolutionary and historical reasons, the ontogenetic structure of the life course displays a kind of unfinished architecture. Whatever the specific content and form of a given psychological theory of lifespan development, it needs to be consistent with the framework outlined.

LIFESPAN CHANGES IN THE RELATIVE ALLOCATION OF RESOURCES TO VARIOUS GOALS OF DEVELOPMENT

To what degree does the overall architecture of age-related dynamics between biology and culture outlined here prefigure pathways of development and the kind of adaptive challenges that we face as we move through life? One way to understand some of the consequences is to distinguish between three goals of ontogenetic development: growth, maintenance (including resilience), and the regulation of loss. The allocation of available resources for growth, the first of these major adaptive tasks, decreases with age, whereas investments into the latter, maintenance and regulation of loss, increase with age (PB Baltes et al 1998, Staudinger et al 1995).

By growth, we mean behaviors aimed at reaching higher levels of functioning or adaptive capacity. Under the heading of maintenance, we group behaviors aimed either at maintaining levels of functioning in the face of a new challenge or at returning to previous levels after a loss. With the adaptive task of regulation of loss, we identify behaviors that organize adequate functioning at lower levels when maintenance or recovery—for instance because of external or internal losses in resources—is no longer possible.

In our view, the lifespan shift in the relative allocation of resources, away from growth towards the goals of maintenance and the regulation of loss, is a critical issue for any theory of lifespan development (for related arguments, see also Brandtstädter & Greve 1994, Brim 1992, Uttal & Perlmutter 1989). This is true even for those theories that, on the surface, seem to focus only on growth or positive aging (e.g. Erikson 1959, Labouvie-Vief 1995, McAdams & de St. Aubin 1998, Perlmutter 1988, Staudinger 1996). In Erikson's theory, for instance, acquiring generativity and wisdom is the positive developmental goal of adulthood. Despite the growth orientation of these constructs, their attainment is inherently tied to recognizing and managing generational turnover as well as managing or becoming reconciled to one's functional losses, finitude, and impending death.

The dynamics between the lifespan trajectories of growth, maintenance, and regulation should also be emphasized. The mastery of life often involves conflicts and competition among the three goals of human development. Consider, for example, the interplay between autonomy and dependence in children and older adults (MM Baltes 1996, MM Baltes & Silverberg 1994). Whereas the primary focus of the first half of life is the maximization of independence and autonomy, the goal-profile changes in old age. The productive and creative use of dependence rather than independence becomes critical. By invoking dependence and support, older people free up resources for use in other domains involving personal efficacy and growth.

The age-related weakening of the biological foundation and the change in the overall lifespan script associated with growth, maintenance, and regulation of loss does not imply that there is no opportunity for growth at all in the second half of life in some domains. Deficits in biological status can also be the foundation for progress, that is, antecedents for positive changes in adaptive capacity. The most radical view of this proposition is contained in the notion of "culture as compensation." Under the influence of cultural-anthropological as well as evolutionary biological arguments, researchers have recognized that suboptimal biological states or imperfections are catalysts for the evolution of culture and for advanced states achieved in human ontogeny (PB Baltes 1997, Klix 1993, Magnusson 1996, Uttal & Perlmutter 1989). In this line of thinking, the human organism is by nature (Gehlen 1956) a "being of deficits" (Mängelwesen) and social culture has developed or emerged in part to deal specifically with biological deficits.

This "deficits-breed-growth" mechanism may not only account for cultural-biological evolution, it may also affect ontogenesis. Thus it is possible that when people reach states of increased vulnerability in old age, social forces and individuals invest more and more heavily in efforts that are explicitly oriented toward regulating and compensating for age-associated biological deficits, thereby generating a broad range of novel behaviors, new bodies of knowledge and values, new environmental features, and, as a result, a higher level of adaptive capacity. Emerging research on psychological compensation is a powerful illustration of the idea that deficits can be catalysts for positive changes in adaptive capacity (MM Baltes 1996, PB Baltes & Baltes 1990, Brandtstädter 1998, Dixon & Bäckman 1995, Marsiske et al 1995)

METATHEORETICAL AND METHODOLOGICAL PROPOSITIONS WITHIN LIFESPAN PSYCHOLOGY

Development as Change in Adaptive Capacity

From a lifespan theory point of view, it is important to articulate concepts of development that go beyond linear, unidimensional, unidirectional, and unifunctional models, which had flourished in conjunction with the traditional biological conceptions of growth or physical maturation. In these traditional conceptions of development, attributes such as qualitative change, ordered sequentiality, irreversibility, and the definition of an end state were critical.

DEVELOPMENT AS SELECTION AND SELECTIVE ADAPTATION   In their conceptual work, lifespan developmentalists attempted either to modulate the traditional definitional approach to development or to offer alternative conceptions of ontogenetic development that departed from the notion of holistic and unidirectional growth, according to which all aspects of the developing system were geared toward a higher level of integration and functioning. Labouvie-Vief (1982, 1992), for instance, introduced new forms (stages) of systemic functioning for the period of adulthood, based on conceptions of development as adaptive transformation and structural reorganization, thereby opening a new vista on neo-Piagetian constructivism.

Baltes and his colleagues (e.g. PB Baltes 1997, PB Baltes et al 1980, 1998) were more radical in their departure from extant theoretical models of development. Considering evolutionary perspectives (PB Baltes 1987, Magnusson 1996), neofunctionalism (Dixon & Baltes 1986), and lifespan contextualism (Lerner 1991), they opted for a more flexible construction of development. One such model was to define development as selective age-related change in adaptive capacity. With the focus on selection and selective adaptation, lifespan researchers were able to be more open about the pathways of life-long ontogenesis. For instance, with this neofunctionalist approach, it becomes possible to treat the developing system as multidimensional, multifunctional, and dynamic, in which differing domains and functions develop in a less than fully integrated manner, and where trade-offs between functional advances and discontinuities between age levels are the rule rather than the exception (see also Brim & Kagan 1980, Labouvie-Vief 1982, Siegler 1997, Thelen & Smith 1998).

DEVELOPMENT AS A GAIN-LOSS DYNAMIC   A related change in emphasis advanced in lifespan theory and research was to view development as always being constituted by gains and losses (PB Baltes 1987, PB Baltes et al 1980, 1998, Brandtstädter 1998, Labouvie-Vief 1982). Aside from functionalist arguments, several empirical findings gave rise to this focus.

One example important to lifespan researchers was the differing lifespan trajectories proposed and observed for various components of intelligence (Cattell 1971, Horn & Hofer 1992, Schaie 1994, 1996). For intelligence, throughout the life span gains and losses co-exist. In addition, the open systems view of the incomplete biological and cultural architecture of lifespan development and the multiple ecologies of life made it obvious that postulating a single end state to development was inappropriate. Moreover, when considering the complex and changing nature of the criteria involved in everyday adaptation (which, for instance, across ages differ widely in the characteristics of task demands and outcome criteria; e.g. Berg 1996), the capacity to move between levels of knowledge and skills rather than to operate at one specific developmental level of functioning appeared crucial for effective individual development. Furthermore, the dynamics between gains and losses were highlighted by the phenomenon of negative transfer associated with the evolution of any form of specialization or expertise (Ericsson & Lehmann 1996). As a result, a monolithic view of development as universal growth was rejected as theoretically false and empirically inappropriate.

Recently, one additional concept has been advanced to characterize the nature of lifespan changes in adaptive capacity. This concept is equifinality: As a special case of multifunctionality, the same developmental outcome can be reached by different means and combination of means (Kruglanski 1996, Ribaupierre 1995). The role of equifinality is perhaps most evident in the different ways by which individuals reach an identical level of subjective well-being (Brandtstädter & Greve 1994, Heckhausen & Brim 1997, Smith & Baltes 1997, Staudinger et al 1995). The potential for developmental impact is larger if the resources acquired during ontogenesis carry, in the sense of equifinality and multifunctionality, much potential for generalization and adaptive use in rather different contexts.

Plasticity and Age-Associated Changes

The strong concern of lifespan researchers with intraindividual plasticity (malleability) highlights the search for the potentialities of development, including its upper and lower boundary conditions. Implied in the idea of plasticity is that any given developmental outcome is but one of numerous possible outcomes, and that the search for the conditions and range of ontogenetic plasticity, including its age-associated changes, is fundamental to the study of development.

As lifespan psychologists initiated systematic work on the concept of plasticity, further differentiation of it was introduced. One involved the differentiation between baseline reserve capacity and developmental reserve capacity (PB Baltes 1987, Kliegl et al 1989). Baseline reserve capacity identifies the current level of plasticity available to individuals. Developmental reserve capacity is aimed at specifying what is possible in principle over developmental time if optimizing interventions are employed to estimate future ontogenetic potential. Furthermore, major efforts were made to specify the kind of methodologies that lend themselves to a full exploration of age-related changes in plasticity and its limits (Kruse et al 1993, Lindenberger & Baltes 1995).

Methodological Developments

Metatheory and methodology have been closely intertwined since the very early origins of LP (e.g. Quetelet 1842). Not surprisingly, therefore, the search for methods adequate for the study of developmental processes is a continuing part of the agenda of lifespan researchers (Cohen & Reese 1994, Hertzog 1996, Lindenberger & Baltes 1995, Lindenberger & Pötter 1998, Magnusson 1996, Nesselroade & Thompson 1995).

LIFE EVENTS AND EVENT-HISTORY ANALYSIS   One methodological development concerns methods to organize and study the temporal flow, correlates, and consequences of life events. Life-course sociologists, in particular, have made major contributions to the advancement of this methodology. Among the relevant methods, models of event-history analysis and associated methods such as hazard rate and survival analysis are especially important (Blossfeld & Rohwer 1995, Willett & Singer 1991).

One of the critical events for lifespan researchers is mortality or death. As life unfolds from birth into old age, the population itself changes in composition as a result of migration and especially mortality. In advanced old age, for instance, the surviving age cohort becomes smaller and smaller until it reaches zero. Understanding the intricacies of selective survival and its impact on the nature of ontogenetic functions is a serious methodological challenge (for instance, Lindenberger et al 1998).

TESTING THE LIMITS OF PLASTICITY   The second example of methodological innovations involves a strategy to examine the scope and limits of plasticity (Kliegl et al 1989, Lindenberger & Baltes 1995). This method is similar to efforts in child development to study the zone of proximal development, for instance, through methods of microgenetic analysis or cognitive engineering (Kuhn 1995, Siegler & Crowley 1991).

Again, because of the long time frame of lifespan ontogenesis, it is difficult to identify the sources and scope of plasticity and its age-related changes. At the same time, the inquiry into what is possible in principle in human development across the life span is important. One example is the perennial question of cognitive-aging researchers about whether aging losses in functions reflect experiential practice deficits rather than effects of biological aging. In testing-the-limits research (Kliegl et al 1989, Lindenberger & Baltes 1995), the goal is to compress time by providing for high-density developmental experiences; and, by doing so, to identify asymptotes of performance potential (plasticity). These asymptotes, obtained under putatively optimal conditions of support, are expected to estimate the upper range of the age-specific developmental potentiality, comparable to the traditional notion of the upper limit of the "norm of reaction."

Testing-the-limits research and related strategies of developmental simulation, however, are relevant not only for the study of long-term ontogenetic processes, but also for other important aspects of developmental research and theory, for example the question of inherited differences in cognitive functioning (Lerner 1995, Plomin 1994). Much of the work on behavior genetics is essentially descriptive and based on ex post analysis. Based on the premise that knowledge about differences in asymptotic levels of functioning is crucial, we need to depart from simple, noninterventive comparative research and to invest scientific resources into testing-the-limits work: to expose smaller samples of participants to time-compressed experiential interventions and to search for interindividual differences between identical and fraternal twins at the upper or lower levels of functioning (see also PB Baltes 1998a, Fox et al 1996, Kruse et al 1993).

A SYSTEMIC THEORY OF LIFESPAN DEVELOPMENT: SELECTIVE OPTIMIZATION WITH COMPENSATION

During the recent decade, several efforts at theoretical development in lifespan psychology have emanated from both child-adolescent researchers (e.g. Hetherington et al 1988, Lerner 1998a, Rutter & Rutter 1993) and the community of researchers on aging (e.g. Schroots 1996). For the present purpose, with its emphasis on exploring consistency and fertility between levels of analysis, we focus on a theory of development, selective optimization with compensation, that Margret Baltes, Paul Baltes and their colleagues have developed (MM Baltes & Carstensen 1996, PB Baltes 1997, PB Baltes & Baltes 1990, PB Baltes et al 1984, Freund & Baltes 1998, Marsiske et al 1995; see also Carstensen 1995, Featherman et al 1990, Heckhausen & Schulz 1995, Schulz & Heckhausen 1996).

Successful development is defined in this theoretical approach as the conjoint maximization of gains (desirable goals or outcomes) and the minimization of losses (undesirable goals or outcomes). The nature of what constitutes gains and losses, and of the dynamic between gains and losses, is conditioned by cultural and personal factors as well as by the position in the lifetime of an individual. Thus an achieved developmental outcome can at a later ontogenetic time or in a different context be judged as dysfunctional. Moreover, what constitutes a gain and what a loss also depends on whether the methods used to define it are subjective or objective (MM Baltes & Carstensen 1996, Heckhausen & Schulz 1995).

The theory SOC is both universal and relativistic. In its metatheoretical universality, it postulates that any process of human development involves an orchestration of selection, optimization, and compensation (Figure 2). In its concrete theoretical specification, however, processes of SOC are person-specific and contextually bound. Thus, as the theoretical model is applied to specific domains and contexts of psychological functioning (such as control, autonomy, and professional expertise, or to different cultural contexts), it requires further specification to be derived from the knowledge base of the domain of functioning selected for application and for the context in which this phenomenon is embedded (e.g. Abraham & Hansson 1995, MM Baltes & Lang 1997, Freund & Baltes 1998, Heckhausen & Schulz 1995, Marsiske et al 1995).

Definition of Selection, Optimization, and Compensation

An everyday example may help to clarify the meaning of SOC (PB Baltes & Baltes 1990). When the concert pianist Arthur Rubinstein, as an 80-year-old, was asked in a television interview how he managed to maintain such a high level of expert piano playing, he hinted at the coordination of three strategies.

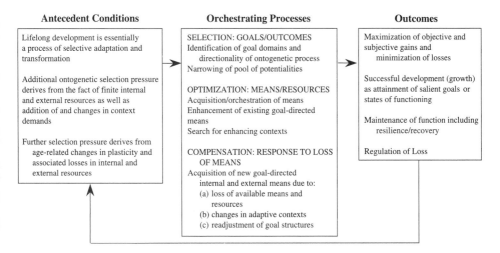

Figure 2 The lifespan model of selective optimization with compensation. The essentials of the model are proposed to be universal, but specific phenotypic manifestations will vary by domain, individual, sociocultural context, and theoretical perspective (adapted from PB Baltes 1987, 1997, PB Baltes &Baltes 1990, Marsiske et al 1995).

First, he played fewer pieces (selection); he practiced these pieces more often (optimization); and to counteract his loss in mechanical speed he now used a kind of impression management, such as playing more slowly before fast segments to make the latter appear faster (compensation).

The specific definitions of selection, optimization, and compensation are conditioned by the theoretical framework chosen. Within an action-theoretical framework, for instance, the following characterizations hold: Selection involves goals or outcomes; optimization involves goal-related means to achieve success (desired outcomes); and compensation involves a response to loss in goal-relevant means in order to maintain success or desired levels of functioning (outcomes). Each of the processes can be active or passive, conscious or subconscious, internal or external.

SELECTION   Selection involves directionality, goals, and outcomes. Strictly speaking, selection already begins in embryonic development. For instance, neurophysiological processing of information represents a fundamental example of selection and selection-based specialization (Edelman & Tononi 1996, Siegler 1997).

During ontogeny, there are several additional sources for selection. First is the goal and outcome orientation of development. Individuals and societies sample from a population of possibilities or opportunities and evolve specific articulations and differentiations of goal structures. A second source is limited individual capacity in time and resources. The third source is the incompatibility of goals and outcomes. A fourth source is age-related changes in plasticity or basic potential. Because of the different conditions of selection, it is also useful to distinguish between two kinds of selection: Elective and loss-based selection (Freund & Baltes 1998). Elective selection is assumed to be primarily the result of a prepared module-driven and motivation-driven selection from a number of possible pathways. Loss-based selection results from the unavailability of outcome-relevant means or resources.

OPTIMIZATION   The focus of optimization is on the acquisition, refinement, and maintenance of means or resources that are effective in achieving desirable outcomes and avoiding undesirable ones. In general, and at a systemic level, optimization requires a mutually enhancing coalition of factors, including health, environmental, and psychological conditions such as goal investment and goal pursuit (Brandtstädter 1998, Gollwitzer & Bargh 1996, Marsiske et al 1995, Staudinger et al 1995). The most domain-general notion of optimization is the generation of developmental reserve capacity in the sense of a set of general-purpose mechanisms (PB Baltes et al 1998, Staudinger et al 1995). The development of a certain personality profile can also be considered a case of optimization (Staudinger & Pasupathi 1998).

COMPENSATION   Compensation involves a functional response to the loss of an outcome-relevant means (see also Brandtstädter & Wentura 1995, Dixon & Bäckman 1995). There are two major functional categories of compensation. The first is to enlist new means as strategies of compensation to reach the same goal. The second compensatory strategy concerns means to change goals of development in response to loss of goal-relevant means (PB Baltes & Baltes 1990, Brandtstädter & Wentura 1995, Heckhausen & Schulz 1995).

Three main causes give rise to a compensatory situation (Marsiske et al 1995). A first is conditioned by the very fact of selection and optimization. Because time and effort have limits, selection of and optimization toward a given goal can imply the loss of means relevant for the pursuit of other goals. Negative transfer from the acquisition of one expert skill system to another is another possible result of selection and optimization (Ericsson & Lehmann 1996).

A second category of causes of compensation stems from environment-associated changes in resources. Changing from one environment to another may involve a loss in environment-based resources (means) or may make some acquired personal means dysfunctional. The third category of causes resulting in a situation of compensation are losses in means due to age-associated declines in plasticity associated with the biology of aging and the lifespan structure of societal opportunities that, for instance, is less developed for later life. Such normative age-associated decline in biology-based plasticity and environment-based opportunity can be accelerated further by nonnormative events such as accidents or illnesses. In each of these instances, the central issue is a loss in outcome-relevant means.

Distinguishing between these categories of causes for compensation is not always easy (Dixon & Bäckman 1995, Freund & Baltes 1998, Marsiske et al 1995). The principles of multicausality, equifinality, and multifunctionality suggest that multiple antecedent and outcome criteria can be involved. Moreover, the categorical status of a given event is likely to change. For instance, as compensatory responses become automatic they can then be used for other purposes such as optimization. Indeed, it is central to the temporal and sequential dynamics of ontogenetic development that the logical status of selection, optimization, and compensation varies. Nevertheless, their collaborative function is always to achieve "successful development" as defined above.

Selective Optimization with Compensation: Orchestration and Dynamics in Development

Without specifying the substantive goals and outcomes of development, then, the SOC model is intended to characterize the processes that in their coordinated orchestration result in desired outcomes of development while minimizing undesirable ones. One recent illustration (Freund & Baltes 1998) is research showing that individuals who report using SOC strategies also report higher levels in subjective indicators of successful aging.

Depending on which level of analysis is chosen (societal, individual, microbehavioral, etc.), SOC requires the use of a different lens for different levels of measurement and specification. For instance, at a biographical level of analysis and everyday competence (MM Baltes & Lang 1997), the lens might focus on the interplay among cognitive, physical, sensory, and motor functioning. But when studying cognitive reserve capacity, for instance by means of dual-task or parallel-task processing, the lens might focus on the SOC-related interplay between components of working memory and other attentional resources (U Lindenberger, M Marsiske, PB Baltes, submitted manuscript).

The model of selective optimization with compensation is but one of the theoretical efforts that lifespan research and theory have spawned. However, the SOC model displays much consistency across levels of analysis and can be usefully linked to other current theoretical streams in developmental psychology, such as dynamic systems theory (Magnusson 1996, Thelen & Smith 1998). Moreover, the study of the orchestration of the processes of selection, optimization, and compensation is a promising strategy toward understanding how effective human development emerges, and how lifespan developmental changes in resources, contexts, and challenges require an adaptive reorganization and transformation of means and ends (MM Baltes & Carstensen 1996, PB Baltes et al 1998, Heckhausen & Brim 1997, Schulz & Heckhausen 1996).

THE TWO–COMPONENT MODEL OF LIFESPAN INTELLECTUAL DEVELOPMENT

The usefulness of LP depends critically on examining the degree of convergence between the theoretical propositions regarding the macroscopic overall landscape of the entire course of ontogeny and more microscopic research on developmental functions, processes, and age periods. Currently, perhaps no other field within developmental psychology is better suited to test this correspondence than the field of intellectual development.

The lifespan concepts of multidimensionality and multidirectionality permit the charting of differing trajectories of intellectual functioning across the life span (cf. Cattell 1971, Horn & Hofer 1992). In this vein, a lifespan theory of intellectual development has been proposed that distinguishes between two main categories or components of intellectual functioning: The mechanics and the pragmatics of cognition (PB Baltes 1987, 1997, PB Baltes et al 1984). As illustrated in Figure 3, the mechanics of cognition are construed as an expression of the neurophysiological architecture of the mind (McClelland 1996, Singer 1995) as it evolved during biological evolution (cf. Tooby & Cosmides

1995) and unfolds during ontogenesis (Rakic 1995). In contrast, the pragmatics of cognition are associated with acquired bodies of knowledge available from and mediated through culture. Thus, in accordance with our view of the overall architecture of human development, the two-component model locates intellectual development within biological and cultural systems of inheritance or "co-evolution" (Durham 1991).

Empirical evidence in support of the two–component model comes from a great variety of research traditions (PB Baltes et al 1998). Probably the most longstanding supportive evidence is the difference between maintained and vulnerable intellectual abilities (Jones & Conrad 1933, PB Baltes & Lindenberger 1997, Salthouse 1991, Schaie 1994, 1996). Abilities that critically involve mechanics, such as reasoning, spatial orientation, or perceptual speed, generally show monotonic and roughly linear decline during adulthood, with some further acceleration of decline in very old age. In contrast, more pragmatic abilities, such as verbal knowledge (e.g. semantic memory) and certain facets of numerical ability, have weak, and sometimes positive, age relations up to the sixth or seventh decade of life, and start to decline only in very old age. Figure 4 illustrates for the case of old age the fact that, as suggested by the overall architecture of the life course and the two-component model, the cognitive mechanics and the cognitive pragmatics are regulated differentially by cultural and biological factors, and that in late life the role of biological factors becomes stronger.

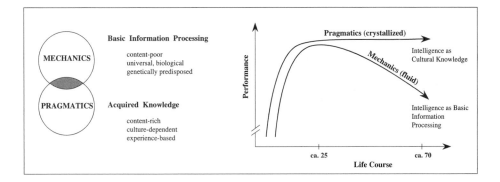

Figure 3   Lifespan research on two components of cognition, the fluid mechanics and the crystallized pragmatics. The *left panel* defines the categories; the *right panel* illustrates postulated lifespan trajectories (after PB Baltes et al 1998; cf. Cattell 1971, Hebb 1949, Horn & Hofer 1992).

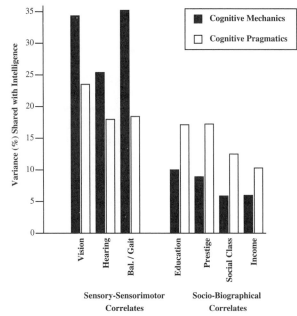

Figure 4   Explanatory sources of intellectual functioning in very old age provide support for the two-component model of lifespan intellectual development and lifespan changes in the relative importance of cultural vs. biological determinants of individual differences. The figure displays differential correlational links of perceptual speed, a marker of the cognitive mechanics, and verbal knowledge, a marker of the cognitive pragmatics, to indicators of socio-biographical life history and biological (e.g. sensory-motor) status. Perceptual speed is more highly correlated with biological indicators than verbal knowledge, and verbal knowledge is more highly correlated with socio-biographical indicators than perceptual speed. At the same time, both are more strongly related to biological than to socio-biographical indicators, reflecting aging-induced changes in the functional integrity of the brain. Data are taken from the Berlin Aging Study (N = 516, age range = 70–103 years). Lindenberger & Baltes 1997.

THE TWO–COMPONENT MODEL: RELATIONS TO OTHER THEORIES   The closest relative, both conceptually and historically, to the two-component model of lifespan intellectual development is the psychometric theory of fluid (Gf) and crystallized (Gc) abilities (Cattell 1971, Horn & Hofer 1992). Other approaches related to the two-component model include Hebb's (1949) distinction between intelligence A (intellectual power) and intelligence B (intellectual products), Ackerman's (1996) PPIK (process, personality, interests, and knowledge) theory, and the encapsulation model of adult intelligence (Hoyer & Rybash 1994). In addition, Hunt (1993) offered an information-processing reinterpretation of the Gf-Gc theory that resonates well with the two–component model (see also Welford 1993).

The Mechanics of Cognition

In cognitive-intellectual operations, we assume that the cognitive mechanics are indexed by the speed, accuracy, and coordination of elementary processing operations. In these mechanics of cognition, biological (e.g. brain-related) conditions reign supreme, and the predominant lifespan pattern shows maturation, stability, and aging-induced decline.

Early in ontogeny (i.e. during embryogenesis, infancy, and early childhood), age changes in the mechanics are assumed to reflect, for the most part, the unfolding and active construction of more or less domain-specific and predisposed processing capabilities (Karmiloff-Smith 1995, Wellman & Gelman 1992). In contrast, negative age changes in the mechanics of cognition late in life presumably reflect brain aging as well as the pathological dysfunctions resulting from aging-associated insults to the brain (cf. Martin et al 1996, Morrison & Hof 1997).

THE SEARCH FOR LIFESPAN DETERMINANTS OF THE COGNITIVE MECHANICS Researchers in the fields of both child development (e.g. McCall 1994) and aging (e.g. Birren & Fisher 1995, Cerella 1990) have been trying to identify developmental determinants or "developables" (Flavell 1992) that regulate the rate of age-based changes in cognitive and intellectual functioning. In addition, some investigators have linked research from both ends of the age spectrum to arrive at lifespan comparisons of the structure and efficiency of information processing (e.g. Dempster 1992, Kail & Salthouse 1994, Mayr et al 1996, Ribaupierre 1995).

So far, three constructs have been studied most extensively as regulators of development in the cognitive mechanics: (a) *Information processing rate* (Salthouse 1996), or the speed with which elementary processing operations can be executed (child development: Fry & Hale 1996, Rose & Feldman 1997; aging: Park et al 1996, Verhaeghen & Salthouse 1997), (b)*Working memory* (Baddeley 1996, Just et al 1996), or the ability to preserve information in one or more short-term stores while simultaneously transforming the same or some other information (child development: Mayr et al 1996, Miller & Vernon 1996, Swanson 1996; aging: Fisk & Warr 1996, Kirasic et al 1996, Mayr et al 1996, Verhaeghen & Salthouse 1997), and (c) *Inhibition* (Bjorklund & Harnishfeger 1995, Zacks & Hasher 1997), or the ability to automatically inhibit or intentionally suppress the processing of goal-irrelevant information (child development: McCall 1994, Ridderinkhof & van der Molen 1995; aging: Zacks & Hasher 1997, Stoltzfus et al 1996).

Currently, the information processing rate, especially if measured with psychometric tests of perceptual speed, seems to be the strongest mediator of age differences in the mechanics of cognition in childhood (Fry & Hale 1996), adulthood (Verhaeghen & Salthouse 1997), and old age (Lindenberger et al 1993). It is however unclear whether perceptual speed represents a "processing primitive" in the sense of information processing rate, or a complex construct with substantial contributions from working memory (Graf & Uttl 1995) and more basic sensory functioning (PB Baltes & Lindenberger 1997, Lindenberger & Baltes 1994). The explanatory power of the working-memory construct, in turn, is also difficult to judge. First, age-based changes in working memory are often described by alluding to changes in processing speed (Case 1985) or inhibition (Brainerd 1995, Stoltzfus et al 1996). Second, an essential function of working memory consists in the goal-directed control of action and thought (Duncan et al 1996, Grafman et al 1995). This complex function puts working memory at the center of intelligent behavior and raises doubts about its status as a "processing primitive" or "basic determinant" of intellectual development. Finally, the curvilinear lifespan age gradients observed with typical measures of interference proneness (e.g. the Stroop color-word test) may reflect age changes in changes in processing rate (Salthouse & Meinz 1995), selective attention (Plude et al 1994), or discrimination learning (Hartman 1995), rather than age changes in inhibitory functioning.

These difficulties in identifying determinants of developmental change in the mechanics of cognition have led to productive discussions at the interface of multivariate-psychometric, cognitive-experimental, and radically reductionist approaches (Cerella 1990, Hertzog 1996, Kliegl et al 1994, Lindenberger & Baltes 1994, Perfect 1994, Rabbitt 1993). Future research on this topic is likely to profit also from closer contact with the neurosciences (Gazzaniga 1995) and the careful examination of the systemic properties of developing brains (Fischer & Rose 1994, Nelson & Bloom 1997, Thatcher 1994) as well as a heightened awareness for interindividual differences in intraindividual change (Fischer et al 1992, Ribaupierre 1995, Schneider & Sodian 1997; cf. Nesselroade 1991).

PURIFICATION OF MEASUREMENT   One problem of age-comparative research of intellectual functioning is that much of our knowledge about the lifespan trajectory of the mechanics of cognition is based on imprecise indicators. Age differences and age changes in measures of the cognitive mechanics are influenced by a wealth of additional but extraneous factors, such as pre-assessment differences in practice, task-relevant knowledge, and person characteristics such as test anxiety or arousal. A likely indication for this admixture of pragmatic variance to supposedly mechanical measures is the secular rise in performance on typical psychometric marker tests of fluid intelligence (cf. Flynn 1987, Schaie 1996). As a consequence of ability-extraneous performance factors, individuals' cognitive performance under standard testing conditions represents just one possible phenotypic manifestation of their range of performance potential. In our view, to separate the possible from the impossible over age, the context of measurement needs to be moved toward the upper limits of performance potential.

Within LP, and as mentioned earlier, testing-the-limits has been introduced as a research strategy to uncover adult age differences in the upper (asymptotic) limits of mechanical functioning. The main focus of this paradigm is to arrange for experimental conditions that produce maximum (i.e. asymptotic) levels of performance. In such research, robust age differences were identified. For instance, after 38 sessions of training in a memory technique, not a single older adult was performing above the mean of the young adults (PB Baltes & Kliegl 1992, Kliegl et al 1989). It appears worthwhile to intensify the use of the testing-the-limits paradigm with lower age groups to obtain genuine lifespan gradients regarding maximum limits of performance potential in different domains. Our prediction is that lifespan peaks are shifted toward younger ages whenever cognitive tasks of the mechanics are freed from pragmatic, that is, knowledge- and experience-based influence. Also, cohort differences in the cognitive mechanics will become smaller if efforts are made to test individuals at their asymptotic limits of performance potential.

The Pragmatics of Cognition

In contrast to the mechanics, the pragmatics of cognition direct the attention of lifespan developmentalists toward the role of culture and the increasing importance of knowledge-based forms of intelligence as human ontogeny evolves (Ackerman 1996, PB Baltes 1997, Ericsson & Lehmann 1996, Marsiske & Willis 1998). Positive developmental changes in the pragmatic component reflect the acquisition and lifelong practice of culturally transmitted bodies of declarative and procedural knowledge that are made available to individuals in the course of socialization and lifetime experiences. Some of the lifetime experiences leading to the acquisition of pragmatic knowledge are normative but specific to certain cultures (e.g. formal schooling), others are more universal (e.g. mentoring), and still others are idiosyncratic or person-specific (e.g. specialized ecological and professional knowledge).

We assume that the pragmatics of cognition build on, extend, and reorganize prestructured core domains (Wellman & Gelman 1992) associated with the cognitive mechanics and their foundation in the biological nature of the human processing system (Saffran et al 1996, Smotherman & Robinson 1996, Spelke et al 1995). For instance, pragmatic knowledge may evolve from or mimic predisposed knowledge in evolutionarily privileged domains, but come with the advantage of being tuned to the idiosyncratic demands of specific cultures, biographies, and contexts (Siegler & Crowley 1994). These processes of extension and transformation eventually give rise to forms of knowledge and behavior that are, in part by virtue of necessity, compatible with the biological architecture of the mind, but that are not the direct consequence of evolutionary selection pressures.

NORMATIVE AND PERSON-SPECIFIC PRAGMATIC KNOWLEDGE   An important, albeit necessarily imperfect, distinction within the pragmatics of cognition concerns normative versus person-specific knowledge. Normative bodies of knowledge are of general value, either across or within cultures. Typical examples include language proficiency as indexed by verbal abilities, number proficiency, and basic knowledge about the world. Individual differences in these domains are closely linked to years of education and other aspects of social stratification, and are well captured by psychometric testing and theorizing (Cattell 1971, Carroll 1993, Horn & Hofer 1992).

Person-specific bodies of knowledge that branch off from the normative knowledge-acquisition path result from specific combinations of experiential settings, personality characteristics, motivational constellations, action-control strategies, and cognitive abilities or talent (Marsiske et al 1995). As a consequence, these idiosyncratic bodies of knowledge often escape psychometric operationalization and are better amenable to study within the expertise paradigm (Ericsson & Lehmann 1996) or other conceptions of everyday cognitive functioning (Marsiske & Willis 1998, Smith 1996, Staudinger & Pasupathi 1998).

Two main conclusions can be drawn from lifespan research within the expertise paradigm. First, expertise effects, or the consequences of specific bodies of declarative and procedural knowledge, rarely transcend the boundaries of the target domain. Specifically, there is little evidence to suggest that the mechanics of cognition are altered in themselves by domain-specific knowledge (Krampe & Ericsson 1996, Salthouse 1991). The second major conclusion concerns the power of pragmatic knowledge to make up for losses in the mechanics within the domain of expertise (Bosman & Charness 1996, Hess & Pullen 1996, Krampe & Ericsson 1996). Here, the results from several studies suggest that acquired knowledge endows aging individuals with a local (e.g. domain-bound) ability to withstand the consequences of aging-induced losses in the mechanics. Negative adult age differences, compared with standard psychometric or cognitive-experimental assessments, tend to be attenuated in knowledge-rich domains of everyday relevance, such as practical problem solving (Berg 1996, Marsiske & Willis 1995), social cognition (Blanchard-Fields & Hess 1996), memory in collaborative contexts (Dixon & Gould 1996, Hess & Pullen 1996), life planning (Smith 1996, Staudinger 1998), wisdom (PB Baltes & Staudinger 1993, Staudinger 1996), interactive-minds cognition (PB Baltes & Staudinger 1996), and card playing (Charness & Bosman 1990, Knopf et al 1995). This finding of attenuated negative age differences is of central importance for successful intellectual aging, and supports the general lifespan theory of selective optimization with compensation (MM Baltes & Carstensen 1996, PB Baltes 1997).

INTELLECTUAL GROWTH DURING ADULTHOOD: STAGE CONCEPTIONS VERSUS FUNCTIONALIST APPROACHES   An important debate within lifespan intellectual development refers to the question of (a) whether adult intellectual development follows a structuralist, stage-like logic, and can be described as a movement toward higher forms of reasoning and thought (Alexander & Langer 1990, Labouvie-Vief 1992, 1995); or (b) whether functionalist approaches (Dixon & Baltes 1986) emphasizing the local nature of developmental adaptations, as they prevail in the study of knowledge acquisition, selective specialization, and transfer, provide a better, or at least more parsimonious description of adult intellectual growth. Much of the search for stage-like development during adulthood has been inspired by Piaget's theory of cognitive development (Chapman 1988, Pascual-Leone 1995), and it has tried to identify one or more "post-formal" or "dialectical" stages of cognitive development after the advent of formal operations. The conceptual description of these stages often connects personality development (e.g. Eriksonian generativity, reflexivity) with logical considerations (e.g. awareness and acceptance of contradiction; see PB Baltes et al 1998, McAdams & de St. Aubin 1998, Staudinger & Pasupathi 1998). Supporting evidence has been scarce, which is not surprising given the general difficulties in obtaining indicators of stage-like cognitive change (cf. van der Maas & Molenaar 1992).

Despite his constructivist and dialectical epistemology, Piaget himself was reluctant to posit any stages beyond formal operations. Instead, he argued, on one occasion at least (Piaget 1972), that late adolescents and adults would exhibit formal-operational reasoning within their areas of expertise but not necessarily across all domains of knowledge. This view seems consistent with the two-component model of cognition, because the potential for adult intellectual growth is linked to factors operating within rather than across domains (e.g. acquisition of pragmatic knowledge). Thus, in our functionalist view, the structuralist search for higher forms of reasoning can be reframed as the search for bodies of factual and procedural knowledge with a high degree of generality and meaning. In full agreement with the intent of structuralist theorizing on adult intellectual development, the acquisition of such bodies of knowledge is assumed to counteract the lifespan tendency toward fragmentation (Stich 1990) and specialization induced by less general bodies of knowledge.

WISDOM AS EXAMPLE   In the context of growth in adulthood involving the cognitive pragmatics, wisdom has been proposed as a prototypical example (PB Baltes et al 1984, Clayton & Birren 1980, Sternberg 1990). In the Neo-Piagetian tradition, wisdom has been related to the postformal stage of thought (e.g. Labouvie-Vief 1992). In the functionalist lifespan tradition, wisdom has been conceived as the optimal expression of knowledge in the fundamental pragmatics of life, that is, expert and integrative knowledge about the meaning and conduct of life and ways to coordinate mind, personality, and emotion (PB Baltes et al 1998, Blanchard-Fields & Hess 1996, Staudinger 1998, Staudinger & Pasupathi 1998). Indeed, the observed absence of negative adult age differences in wisdom-related performance up to about age 75 and the fact that life experiences such as professional specialization (Smith et al 1994) modulate the level and direction of age gradients stand in contrast to the ubiquity of negative and robust adult age gradients in the cognitive mechanics. In addition, of the top performances in wisdom tasks, a large number come from people in late adulthood (PB Baltes et al 1995). Only in very old age do the mechanics seem to delimit wisdom-related performance, probably because they fall below a critical threshold of functional integrity (PB Baltes et al 1995; cf. Pratt et al 1996, Smith & Baltes 1997).

Originally, research on wisdom was motivated primarily by the search for positive aspects of human aging. Meanwhile, this intellectual agenda has been extended to include aspects of clinical psychology (Smith et al 1994), cultural psychology (Staudinger 1996), and the cognitive psychology of heuristics. As to the latter, Baltes (1998) argues that wisdom is a cognitive and motivational metastrategy that orchestrates diverse bodies of knowledge toward human excellence. As such a high-level heuristic about the conduct of life, wisdom (*a*) protects against the fragmentation of knowledge (Stich 1990) and (*b*) enhances the control of one's vices and the optimization of one's virtues. In this sense, wisdom is a lifetime general-purpose heuristic aimed at the well-being of oneself and that of others.

Mechanic/Pragmatic Interdependence

The mechanics and pragmatics of lifespan intellectual development are intertwined to varying degrees and at various levels of analysis (cf. Bosman & Charness 1996). Phylogenetically, they are connected in the sense that members of the human species are biologically predisposed to acquire cultural knowledge in the sense of co-evolution (cf. Durham 1991, Klix 1993). Ontogenetically, the interdependence is bidirectional as well.

On the one hand, the potential to acquire and use pragmatic knowledge is constrained by age-based changes in the potential and status of the mechanical component (Elbert et al 1995). The mechanics of cognition condition not only the acquisition of pragmatic knowledge, but also its expression (Bosman & Charness 1996, Molander & Bäckman 1996). On the other hand, the pragmatics of cognition provide the medium (content) and, at least during the first tier of life, the structure for the phenotypic unfolding of the cognitive mechanics. Furthermore, the pragmatics of cognition serve to optimize levels of performance in content-rich and evolutionarily nonprivileged domains of intellectual functioning, as research on expertise (Ericsson & Lehmann 1996), wisdom, and on other domains involving interactive minds (PB Baltes & Staudinger 1996) has convincingly demonstrated. As a consequence, pragmatic knowledge helps to counteract the limitations of the mechanics (Gobet & Simon 1996), including the negative consequences of age-based losses (Thompson 1995).

Plasticity (Malleability) in Intellectual Functioning Across Historical and Ontogenetic Time: Evidence from Adult Development

As noted before, lifespan changes in intellectual functioning are determined by a large variety of different sources of influence. As a consequence, differences in level of intellectual performance are influenced, within the age-graded boundaries provided by the mechanics, by variations in the physical or socio-cultural aspects of environmental conditions that in turn are associated with differences in life histories of cognitive experience (Schaie 1996, Willis et al 1997). The systematic analysis of environmental-change influences on intellectual development at varying levels of generality and temporal extension has helped to highlight the plasticity (malleability) of intellectual functioning, including its age-associated changes.

COHORT EFFECTS, PERIOD EFFECTS, AND ENVIRONMENTAL CHANGE   Levels and forms of age gradients in intellectual abilities are shaped, to varying degrees, by history-graded systems of influence, such as enduring differences between people born at different points in historical time (cohort effects), specific influences of historical events across chronological age (period effects), or generalized and enduring shifts in the environment affecting individuals of all ages and subsequent cohorts (general environmental change). Discriminating among these varieties of environmental change is not easy (PB Baltes et al 1988, Magnusson et al 1991, Schaie 1996).

A first step to discern effects of large-scale environmental change is to compare the performance of same-aged individuals across historical time (i.e. time-lag comparisons). With some exceptions (e.g. number ability; cf. Schaie 1996), the general picture resulting from such comparisons is that higher test scores have been obtained in more recent times (Flynn 1987, Schaie 1996). Probably this increase in test scores across time reflects improvements in health-related, education-related, and work-related conditions. Such culturally based cohort effects were instrumental in pointing to the substantial malleability (plasticity) of intellectual performance during all periods of the adult life span.

Studies with cohort-sequential designs allow three kinds of comparisons across age: cross-sectional, longitudinal, and independent-sample same-cohort comparisons (e.g. age comparisons based on independent samples from the same birth cohort). In the case of the Seattle Longitudinal Study (Schaie 1994, 1996), independent-sample same-cohort and cross-sectional comparisons yielded highly similar estimates of a seven-year change after the analysts controlled for the general increase in performance over historical time revealed by time-lag comparisons (Salthouse 1991). In contrast, longitudinal age changes, also corrected for historical change, showed a somewhat smaller decrement with age. Given the convergence between cross-sectional and independent-sample same-cohort comparisons, the more positive age gradients found with longitudinal samples may be partly due to practice effects and selective attrition.

COGNITIVE INTERVENTION WORK: ACTIVATION OF LEARNING POTENTIAL AMONG OLDER ADULTS   Experimentally controlled interventions explore the degree of plasticity in intellectual functioning more directly than does cohort-comparative research (PB Baltes 1993, Willis & Schaie 1994). The evidence of the powerful role of experience and practice in the acquisition, refinement, and maintenance of the cognitive pragmatics is overwhelming (PB Baltes et al 1998, Ericsson & Lehmann 1996, Hoyer & Rybash 1994). Here the review focuses on cognitive intervention work with older adults associated with the study of psychometric intelligence and related tasks that are closer to the cognitive mechanics, such as tests of fluid intelligence. The main results can be summarized in seven points: (*a*) Training gains in the practiced tests among healthy older adults are substantial (e.g. they roughly correspond to the amount of average "natural" longitudinal decline between 50 and 70 years of age); (*b*) transfer, however, is limited to similar tests of the same ability; (*c*) gains observed as a function of self-guided practice are of similar magnitude as gains resulting from tutor-guided practice; (*d*) training gains are maintained over lengthy periods of time up to several years (Stigsdotter Neely & Bäckman 1993, Willis & Schaie 1994); (*e*) the factor structure of the ability space is not altered substantially through training (Schaie et al 1987); (*f*) the amount of training gain is substantially reduced as people reach advanced old age (Lindenberger & Baltes 1997); and (*g*) in persons at risk for Alzheimer's disease or afflicted by other forms of brain pathology, learning gains are substantially reduced (Grober & Kawas 1997) or nonexistent (MM Baltes et al 1995). At limits of functioning and in advanced old age, older adults definitely display less potential for gains from training (PB Baltes & Kliegl 1992, Lindenberger & Baltes 1997).

These results indicate that cognitive plasticity in the mechanics of cognition is preserved among healthy older adults and is easily activated through experiential manipulations (cf. Woodruff-Pak 1993, for relevant neurophysiological evidence). Nevertheless, the general lack of transfer of training to related abilities or to everyday functioning suggests the hypothesis that performance improvements in tests of fluid intelligence primarily reflect changes in pragmatic components of performance potential, rather than improvements in the cognitive mechanics themselves.

Relative Stability of Intellectual Functioning Across the Lifespan

Most of the evidence on relative stability after infancy, that is, stability across age in interindividual differences, is based on undifferentiated measures of intelligence (e.g. IQ tests). Such measures can be seen as mixtures of mechanical and normative–pragmatic components of intellectual functioning that approximate, to varying degrees, the centroid of the intellectual ability factor space (i.e. Spearman's g; see also Horn 1989). With this qualification in mind, we restrict the following discussion, with the exception of infant development, to undifferentiated (e.g. IQ-like) measures of intellectual functioning.

PREDICTING CHILDHOOD INTELLIGENCE ON THE BASIS OF INFANT BEHAVIOR In contrast to earlier findings using standard tests of infant development, research using habituation and recognition-memory paradigms (Bornstein 1989, McCall & Carriger 1993) has revealed a sizable degree of stability in interindividual differences between infant behavior and childhood intelligence. On average, individual differences in habituation and recognition memory performance in infants between the ages of 2 and 8 months are moderately correlated with standard tests of intelligence such as the Wechsler, Bayley, or Binet, administered between 1 and 8 years of age (median correlation, $r = .45$; after attenuation for unreliability, $r = .70$; cf. Bornstein 1989, McCall & Carriger 1993). Thus, both change in and stability of individual differences are important aspects of lifespan intellectual development from its very beginning.

RELATIVE INTERINDIVIDUAL STABILITY AFTER INFANCY For reasons not yet well understood (McCall & Carriger 1993), the magnitude of the correlation between infant measures of habituation (i.e. 2 to 8 months) and childhood measures of intelligence (i.e. 1 to 12 years) is temporally stable or even increasing (Cardon & Fulker 1991, DiLalla et al 1990), rather than decreasing over time. In contrast, relative stability after infancy is rather well described on the basis of quasi-simplex assumptions (Humphreys & Davey 1988, Molenaar et al 1991). Thus, adjacent time points in ontogeny tend to be more highly correlated than more distant time points. In addition, stability coefficients computed over identical lapses of time show a considerable increase in magnitude from childhood to adolescence into middle adulthood and early old age (Gold et al 1995, Hertzog & Schaie 1986, Humphreys & Davey 1988). For instance, Humphreys and Davey (1988) reported a continuous increase in one-year stability coefficients of general intelligence, with a value of .76 between the ages of four and five, and a value of .90 for the ages of eight and nine. With respect to later ages, Hertzog and Schaie (1986) found that seven-year stability coefficients for a general ability composite ranged from .89 to .96 in samples with mean ages between 25 and 67 years at first test. These are extraordinarily high levels of interindividual long-term stability.

Lifespan Changes in Heritability

A detailed coverage of behavior genetics and its role in the study of developmental pathologies (Rutter 1997) is beyond the scope of this article. Instead, the following synopsis is restricted to broad estimates of heritability in normal samples. To avoid misunderstandings, we emphasize that heritability coefficients refer to interindividual differences and therefore do not provide direct information about mechanisms of genetic expression. Specifically, the degree of heritability does not speak to the level (plasticity, malleability) of developmental outcomes (expression) that is available to all members of the population (PB Baltes 1998, PB Baltes et al 1998, Fox et al 1996).

Similar to lifespan changes in stability, heritability of interindividual differences increases from about 40% to 50% during childhood and adolescence to about 80% in early and middle adulthood (Carmelli et al 1995, McGue et al 1993, Saudino et al 1994). In contrast, shared environmental influences on interindividual differences generally do not persist beyond the period of common rearing (McGue et al 1993). The observed lifespan increase in the heritability of interindividual differences in intelligence is consistent with the notion that adolescents and adults have more of a chance to actively select environments that match their genes than infants and children do (Scarr & McCartney 1983). With respect to late-life heritability, recent data from the Swedish Adoption Twin Study of Aging (SATSA) suggest that heritability of interindividual differences in general intelligence may drop to values around 60% in old age (McClearn et al 1997).

Structural Changes in Intellectual Abilities: The Differentiation/Dedifferentiation Hypothesis

A major issue in lifespan intelligence is the question of structure and development-associated changes in structure. The best-known model involves a change in the structure of intellectual abilities toward differentiation in early life followed in late adulthood by the reverse process of dedifferentiation. According to the differentiation/dedifferentiation hypothesis, the amount of positive covariation among intellectual abilities, or the prominence of the general factor of intelligence (Carroll 1993, Reinert 1970), is inversely related to general (common) conditions of performance such as age or ability level. In part, this hypothesis is based on the assumption that low levels of intellectual functioning reflect limitations imposed by a set of common (system-general) biological (Spearman 1927) and/or environmental constraints. When applied to lifespan intellectual development, the differentiation/dedifferentiation hypothesis predicts that the prominence of the general factor decreases during childhood as a function of brain maturation and domain-specific knowledge acquisition, remains relatively stable throughout adolescence, adulthood, and early old age, but increases again late in life when system-general constraints such as biological brain aging regain importance.

Because of methodological difficulties in testing this hypothesis (Nesselroade & Thompson 1995), the relevant evidence is not conclusive, but generally seems to support this conjecture (Babcock et al 1997, PB Baltes & Lindenberger 1997, Deary et al 1996). For instance, recent findings suggest that ability intercorrelations both between and within fluid-mechanic and normative-pragmatic domains are of much higher magnitude in old age than the corresponding ability intercorrelations during middle and early adulthood (PB Baltes & Lindenberger 1997, Lindenberger & Baltes 1997). In addition, the covariance dedifferentiation observed in very old age appears to transcend the cognitive domain, affecting sensory functioning (e.g. vision and hearing) and sensorimotor functioning (e.g. balance/gait) as well (PB Baltes & Lindenberger 1997). One likely possibility for the high degree of ability homogeneity (dedifferentiation) in old age is the common causes of brain aging that affect all cognitive functions similarly.

CONCLUSIONS

During the recent decade, we have witnessed rigorous and varied efforts to understand human development from a lifespan point of view. One major goal of this chapter was to examine the degree of convergence between several levels of theoretical and empirical analysis.

We conclude that the work on lifespan development conducted at different levels of analysis evinces much convergence, and this represents theoretical progress in LP. In developing and refining its multi-level framework, LP has benefited much from transdisciplinary dialogue, especially with modern developmental biologists but also with cultural psychologists. Biologists, for instance, have led the way in moving research away from unilinear, unifunctional, and deterministic models of ontogenesis to a theoretical framework that highlights the contextual, adaptive, probabilistic, and self-organizational dynamic aspects of ontogenesis (Lerner 1998a, Magnusson 1996, Thelen & Smith 1998). In a similar vein, cultural psychologists and development-oriented social scientists (e.g. Cole 1996, Durham 1991, Elder 1998, Mayer 1990, Valsiner & Lawrence 1997) have succeeded equally in demonstrating not only that human ontogenesis is strongly conditioned by culture, but that the architecture of human development is essentially incomplete, not only for reasons of biological incompleteness but also regarding the culturally engineered pathways and possible endpoints (PB Baltes 1997).

The future of lifespan developmental theory will depend significantly on the extent to which the metatheoretical and empirical perspectives it has advanced turn out to be useful not only in the conduct of developmental research, but also in demonstrating the usefulness of the lifespan approach for other psychological specialties such as clinical (MM Baltes et al 1995, Smith et al 1994, Staudinger et al 1995), social (MM Baltes & Carstensen 1998, Carstensen 1995), personality (Heckhausen & Schulz 1995, Lachman & James 1997), and applied psychology (Abraham & Hansson 1995; Sterns & Dorsett 1994). In fact, these intersections of the lifespan approach with other psychological specialties need to be identified and nurtured. In the long run, it is these interconnections that will be the final testing ground of what lifespan theory and research has to offer to psychology, as a science and as a profession.

ACKNOWLEDGMENT

The writing of this chapter was facilitated by a fellowship (1997-1998) of the first author at the Center for Advanced Study in the Behavioral Sciences, Stanford, California.

> **Visit the *Annual Reviews home page* at**
> **http://www.AnnualReviews.org.**

Literature Cited

Abraham JD, Hansson RO. 1995. Successful aging at work: An applied study of selection, optimization, and compensation through impression management. *J. Gerontol. Psychol. Sci.* 50B:P94–103

Ackerman PL. 1996. A theory of adult intellectual development: process, personality, interests, and knowledge. *Intelligence* 22: 227–57

Alexander C, Langer EJ, eds. 1990. *Beyond Formal Operations: Alternative Endpoints to Human Development.* New York: Oxford Univ. Press

Babcock RL, Laguna KD, Roesch SC. 1997. A comparison of the factor structure of processing speed for younger and older adults: Testing the assumption of measurement equivalence across age groups. *Psychol. Aging* 12:268–76

Baddeley A. 1996. Exploring the central executive. *Q. J. Exp. Psychol.* 49A:5–28

Baltes MM. 1996. *The Many Faces of Dependency in Old Age.* New York: Cambridge Univ. Press

Baltes MM, Carstensen LL. 1996. The process of successful ageing. *Aging Soc.* 16: 397–422

Baltes MM, Carstensen LL. 1998. Social psychological theories and their applications to aging: From individual to collective social psychology. In *Handbook of Theories of Aging*, ed. VL Bengston, KW Schaie. New York: Springer. In press

Baltes MM, Kühl K-P, Gutzmann H, Sowarka D. 1995. Potential of cognitive plasticity as a diagnostic instrument: a cross-validation and extension. *Psychol. Aging* 10:167–72

Baltes MM, Lang FR. 1997. Differences in everyday functioning between successfully and unsuccessfully aging adults. *Psychol. Aging* 12:433–43

Baltes MM, Silverberg SB. 1994. The dynamics between dependency and autonomy: illustrations across the life span. In *Life-Span Development and Behavior*, ed. DL Featherman, RM Lerner, M Perlmutter, 12:41–90. Hillsdale, NJ: Erlbaum

Baltes PB. 1983. Life-span developmental psychology: observations on history and theory revisited. In *Developmental Psychology: Historical and Philosophical Perspectives*, ed. RM Lerner, pp. 79–111. Hillsdale, NJ: Erlbaum

Baltes PB. 1987. Theoretical propositions of life-span developmental psychology: on the dynamics between growth and decline. *Dev. Psychol.* 23:611–26

Baltes PB. 1993. The aging mind: potential and limits. *Gerontologist* 33:580–94

Baltes PB. 1997. On the incomplete architecture of human ontogeny: selection, optimization, and compensation as foundation of developmental theory. *Am. Psychol.* 52:366–80

Baltes PB. 1998. Testing-the-limits of the ontogenetic sources of talent. *Behav. Brain Sci.* In press

Baltes PB, Baltes MM. 1990. Psychological perspectives on successful aging: the model of selective optimization with compensation. In *Successful Aging: Perspectives from the Behavioral Sciences*, ed. PB Baltes, MM Baltes, pp. 1–34. New York: Cambridge Univ. Press

Baltes PB, Brim OG Jr, eds. 1979. *Life-Span Development and Behavior*, vol. 2, New York: Academic

Baltes PB, Dittmann-Kohli F, Dixon RA. 1984. New perspectives on the development of intelligence in adulthood: toward a dual-process conception and a model of selective optimization with compensation. In *Life-Span Development and Behavior*, ed. PB Baltes, OG Brim Jr, 6:33–76. New York: Academic

Baltes PB, Goulet LR. 1970. Status and issues of a life-span developmental psychology. In *Life-Span Developmental Psychology: Research and Theory*, ed. LR Goulet, PB Baltes, pp. 4–21. New York: Academic

Baltes PB, Kliegl R. 1992. Further testing of limits of cognitive plasticity: negative age differences in a mnemonic skill are robust. *Dev. Psychol.* 28:121–25

Baltes PB, Lindenberger U. 1997. Emergence of a powerful connection between sensory and cognitive functions across the adult life span: a new window at the study of cognitive aging? *Psychol. Aging* 12:12–21

Baltes PB, Lindenberger U, Staudinger UM. 1998. Life-span theory in developmental psychology. See Lerner 1998b, pp. 1029–143

Baltes PB, Reese HW, Lipsitt LP. 1980. Life-span developmental psychology. *Annu. Rev. Psychol.* 31:65–110

Baltes PB, Reese HW, Nesselroade JR. 1988. (1977). *Life-Span Developmental Psychology: Introduction to Research Methods*. Hillsdale, NJ: Erlbaum

Baltes PB, Smith J. 1997. A systemic-wholistic view of psychological functioning in very old age: introduction to a collection of articles from the Berlin Aging Study. *Psychol. Aging* 12:395–409

Baltes PB, Staudinger UM. 1993. The search for a psychology of wisdom. *Curr. Dir. Psychol. Sci.* 2:75–80

Baltes PB, Staudinger UM, eds. 1996. *Interactive Minds: Life-Span Perspectives on the Social Foundation of Cognition*. New York: Cambridge Univ. Press

Baltes PB, Staudinger UM, Maercker A, Smith J. 1995. People nominated as wise: a comparative study of wisdom-related knowledge. *Psychol. Aging* 10:155–66

Berg CA. 1996. Practical intelligence and problem solving: searching for perspectives. See Blanchard-Fields & Hess 1996, pp. 323–57

Birren JE, Fisher LM. 1995. Aging and speed of behavior: possible consequences for psychological functioning. *Annu. Rev. Psychol.* 46:329–53

Birren JE, Schaie KW, eds. 1996. *Handbook of the Psychology of Aging*. San Diego: CA: Academic. 4th ed.

Bjorklund DF, Harnishfeger KK. 1995. The evolution of inhibition mechanisms and their role in human cognition and behavior. See Dempster & Brainerd 1995, pp. 141–73

Blanchard-Fields F, Hess TM, eds. 1996. *Perspectives on Cognitive Change in Adulthood and Aging*. New York: McGraw-Hill

Blossfeld H-P, Rohwer G. 1995. *Techniques of Event History Modeling. New Approaches to Causal Analysis*. Mahwah, NJ: Erlbaum

Bornstein MH. 1989. Stability in early mental development: from attention and information processing in infancy to language and cognition in childhood. In *Stability and Continuity in Mental Development*, ed. MH Bornstein, NA Krasnegor, pp. 147–70. Hillsdale, NJ: Erlbaum

Bosman EA, Charness N. 1996. Age-related differences in skilled performance and skill acquisition. See Blanchard-Fields & Hess 1996, pp. 428–53

Brainerd CJ. 1995. Interference processes in memory development: the case of cognitive triage. See Dempster & Brainerd 1995, pp. 428–53

Brandtstädter J. 1998. Action perspectives on

human development. See Lerner 1998b, pp. 807–66

Brandtstädter J, Greve W. 1994. The aging self: stabilizing and protective processes. *Dev. Rev.* 14:52–80

Brandtstädter J, Wentura D. 1995. Adjustment to shifting possibility frontiers in later life: complementary adaptive modes. See Dixon & Bäckman 1995, pp. 83–106

Brim OG Jr. 1992. *Ambition: How We Manage Success and Failure Throughout Our Lives.* New York: Basic Books

Brim OG Jr, Kagan J. 1980. Constancy and change: a view of the issues. In *Constancy and Change in Human Development*, ed. OG. Brim Jr, J Kagan, pp. 1–25. Cambridge, MA: Harvard Univ. Press

Bühler C. 1933. *Der menschliche Lebenslauf als psychologisches Problem.* Leipzig: Hirzel.

Cairns RB. 1998. The making of developmental psychology. See Lerner 1998b, pp. 25–105

Cardon LR, Fulker DW. 1991. Sources of continuity in infant predictors of later IQ. *Intelligence* 15:279–93

Carmelli D, Swan GE, Cardon LR. 1995. Genetic mediation in the relationship of education to cognitive function in older people. *Psychol. Aging* 10:48–53

Carroll JB. 1993. *Human Cognitive Abilities.* Cambridge: Cambridge Univ. Press

Carstensen LL. 1995. Evidence for a life–span theory of socioemotional selectivity. *Curr. Dir. Psychol. Sci.* 4:151–56

Case R. 1985. *Intellectual Development: From Birth to Adulthood.* New York: Academic

Cattell RB. 1971. *Abilities: Their Structure, Growth, and Action.* Boston, MA: Houghton Mifflin

Cerella J. 1990. Aging and information-processing rate. In *Handbook of the Psychology of Aging*, ed. JE Birren, KW Schaie, pp. 201–21. San Diego, CA: Academic

Chapman M. 1988. *Constructive Evolution: Origins and Development of Piaget's Thought.* New York: Cambridge Univ. Press

Charness N, Bosman EA. 1990. Expertise and aging: life in the lab. In *Aging and Cognition: Knowledge Organization and Utilization*, ed. TH Hess, pp. 343–85. Amsterdam: Elsevier

Clayton VP, Birren JE. 1980. The development of wisdom across the life span: a reexamination of an ancient topic. In *Life-Span Development and Behavior*, ed. PB Baltes JOG. Brim, 3:103–35. New York: Academic

Cohen SH, Reese HW, eds. 1994. *Life-span Developmental Psychology: Methodological Contributions.* Hillsdale, NJ: Erlbaum

Cole M. 1996. Interacting minds in a life–span perspective: a cultural/historical approach to culture and cognitive development. See Baltes & Staudinger 1996, pp. 59–87

Dawson G, Fischer KW, eds. 1994. *Human Behavior and the Developing Brain.* New York: Guilford

Deary IJ, Egan V, Gibson GJ, Austin EJ, Brand C, Kellaghan T. 1996. Intelligence and the differentiation hypothesis. *Intelligence* 23:105–32

Dempster FN. 1992. The rise and fall of the inhibitory mechanism: toward a unified theory of cognitive development and aging. *Dev. Rev.* 12:45–75

DiLalla LF, Thompson LA, Plomin R, Phillips K, Fagan JF, et al. 1990. Infant predictors of preschool and adult IQ: a study of infant twins and their parents. *Dev. Psychol.* 26:759–69

Dixon RA, Bäckman L, eds. 1995. *Compensating for Psychological Deficits and Declines: Managing Losses and Promoting Gains.* Mahwah, NJ: Erlbaum

Dixon RA, Baltes PB. 1986. Toward life-span research on the functions and pragmatics of intelligence. In *Practical Intelligence: Nature and Origins of Competence in the Everyday World*, ed. RJ Sternberg, RK Wagner, pp. 203–34. New York: Cambridge Univ. Press

Dixon RA, Gould ON. 1996. Adults telling and retelling stories collaboratively. See Baltes & Staudinger 1996, pp. 221–41

Dixon RA, Lerner RM. 1988. A history of systems in developmental psychology. In *Developmental Psychology: An Advanced Textbook*, ed. MH Bornstein, ME Lamb, pp. 3–50. Hillsdale, NJ: Erlbaum. 2nd ed

Duncan J, Emslie H, Williams P, Johnson R, Freer C. 1996. Intelligence and the frontal lobe: the organization of goal-directed behavior. *Cogn. Psychol.* 30:257–303

Durham WH. 1991. *Coevolution: Genes, Culture and Human Diversity.* Stanford, CA: Stanford Univ. Press

Edelman GM, Tononi G. 1996. Selection and development: the brain as a complex system. In *The Life-span Development of Individuals: Behavioral, Neurobiological, and Psychosocial Perspectives,* ed. D Magnusson, pp. 179–204. Cambridge, UK: Cambridge Univ. Press

Elbert T, Pantev C, Wienbruch C, Rockstroh B, Taub E. 1995. Increased cortical representation of the fingers of the left hand in string players. *Science* 270:305–7

Elder GH Jr. 1998. The life course and human development. See Lerner 1998b, pp. 939–92

Ericsson KA, Lehmann AC. 1996. Expert and exceptional performance: evidence of maximal adaption to task constraints. *Annu. Rev. Psychol.* 47:273–305

Erikson EH. 1959. *Identity and the Life Cycle, Psychological Issues Monograph 1.* New York: Int. Univ. Press

Featherman DL. 1983. The life-span perspective in social science research. In *Life-Span Development and Behavior*, ed. PB Baltes, OG Brim Jr, 5:1–59. New York: Academic

Featherman DL, Smith J, Peterson JG. 1990. Successful aging in a "post-retired" society. See Baltes & Baltes 1990, pp. 50–93

Finch CE. 1996. Biological bases for plasticity during aging of individual life histories. In *The Life-Span Development of Individuals: Behavioral, Neurobiological and Psychosocial Perspective*, ed. D Magnusson, pp. 488–511. Cambridge, UK: Cambridge Univ. Press

Fischer KW, Knight CC, Van-Parys M. 1992. Analyzing diversity in developmental pathways: methods and concepts. In *The New Structuralism in Cognitive Development: Theory and Research on Individual Pathways*, ed. R Case, W Edelstein, pp. 33–56. Basel, Switzerland: Karger

Fischer KW, Rose SP. 1994. Dynamic development of coordination of components in brain and behavior: A framework for theory and research. See Dawson & Fischer 1994, pp. 3–66. New York: Guilford

Fisk JE, Warr P. 1996. Age and working memory: the role of perceptual speed, the central executive, and the phonological loop. *Psychol. Aging* 11:316–23

Flavell JH. 1992. Cognitive development: past, present, and future. *Dev. Psychol.* 28: 998–1005

Flynn JR. 1987. Massive IQ gains in 14 nations: what IQ tests really measure. *Psychol. Bull.* 101:171–91

Fox PW, Hershberger SL, Bouchard TJ. 1996. Genetic and environmental contributions to the acquisition of a motor skill. *Nature* 384:356–58

Freund AM, Baltes PB. 1998. Selection, optimization, and compensation as strategies of life-management: correlations with subjective indicators of successful aging. *Psychol. Aging.* In press

Fry AF, Hale S. 1996. Processing speed, working memory, and fluid intelligence: evidence for a developmental cascade. *Psychol. Sci.* 7:237–41

Gazzaniga MS, ed. 1995. *The Cognitive Neurosciences.* Cambridge, MA: MIT

Gehlen A. 1956. *Urmensch und Spätkultur.* Bonn: Athenäum

Gobet F, Simon HA. 1996. The roles of recognition processes and look-ahead search in time-constrained expert problem solving: Evidence from grand-master-level chess. *Psychol. Sci.* 7:52–55

Gold DP, Andres D, Etezadi J, Arbuckle T, Schwartzman A, Chaikelson J. 1995. Structural equation model of intellectual change and continuity and predictors of intelligence in older men. *Psychol. Aging* 10:294–303

Gollwitzer PM, Bargh JA, eds. 1996. *The Psychology of Action: Linking Cognition and Motivation to Action.* New York: Guilford

Gould SJ. 1984. Relationship of individual and group change: Ontogeny and phylogeny in biology. *Hum. Dev.* 27:233–39

Graf P, Uttl B. 1995. Component processes of memory: changes across the adult life span. *Swiss J. Psychol.* 54:113–30

Grafman J, Partiot A, Hollnagel C. 1995. Fables of the prefrontal cortex. *Behav. Brain Sci.* 18:349–58

Grober E, Kawas C. 1997. Learning and retention in preclinical and early Alzheimer's disease. *Psychol. Aging* 12:183–88

Hartman M. 1995. Aging and interference: evidence from indirect memory tests. *Psychol. Aging* 10:659–69

Hebb DO. 1949. *The Organization of Behavior.* New York: Wiley

Heckhausen J, Brim OG. 1997. Perceived problems of self and other: self-protection by social downgrading throughout adulthood. *Psychol. Aging* 12:610–19

Heckhausen J, Schulz R. 1995. A life-span theory of control. *Psychol. Rev.* 102: 284–304

Hertzog C. 1996. Research design in studies of aging and cognition. See Birren & Schaie 1996, pp. 24–37

Hertzog C, Schaie KW. 1986. Stability and change in adult intelligence: 1. Analysis of longitudinal covariance structures. *Psychol. Aging* 1:159–71

Hess TM, Pullen SM. 1996. Memory in context. See Blanchard-Fields & Hess 1996, pp. 387–427

Hetherington EM, Lerner RM, Perlmutter M, eds. 1988. *Child Development in Life-Span Perspective.* Hillsdale, NJ: Erlbaum

Horn JL. 1989. Models of intelligence. In *Intelligence: Measurement, Theory, and Public Policy*, ed. RL Linn, pp. 29–73. Urbana, IL: Univ. Ill. Press

Horn JL, Hofer SM. 1992. Major abilities and

development in the adult period. See Sternberg & Berg 1992, pp. 44–49

Hoyer WJ, Rybash JM. 1994. Characterizing adult development. *J. Adult Dev.* 1:7–12

Humphreys LG, Davey TC. 1988. Continuity in intellectual growth from 12 months to 9 years. *Intelligence* 12:183–97

Hunt E. 1993. What do we need to know about aging? See Cerella et al 1993, pp. 587–98

Jazwinski SM. 1996. Longevity, genes, and aging. *Science* 273:54–59

Jones HE, Conrad H. 1933. The growth and decline of intelligence: a study of a homogeneous group between the ages of ten and sixty. *Genet. Psychol. Monogr.* 13: 223–98

Just MA, Carpenter PA, Keller TA. 1996. The capacity theory of comprehension: new frontiers of evidence and arguments. *Psychol. Rev.* 103:773–80

Kail R, Salthouse TA. 1994. Processing speed as a mental capacity. *Acta Psychol.* 86: 199–225

Karmiloff-Smith A. 1995. The extraordinary cognitive journey from foetus through infancy. *J. Child Psychol. Psychiatry Allied Discipl.* 36:1293–313

Kirasic KC, Allen GL, Dobson SH, Binder KS. 1996. Aging, cognitive resources, and declarative learning. *Psychol. Aging* 11: 658–70

Kliegl R, Mayr U, Krampe RT. 1994. Time-accuracy functions for determining process and person differences: an application to cognitive aging. *Cogn. Psychol.* 26: 134–64

Kliegl R, Smith J, Baltes PB. 1989. Testing-the-limits and the study of age differences in cognitive plasticity of a mnemonic skill. *Dev. Psychol.* 25:247–56

Klix F. 1993. *Erwachendes Denken: Geistige Leistungen aus evolutionspsychologischer Sicht.* Heidelberg: Spektrum Akademischer Verlag

Knopf M, Preussler W, Stefanek J. 1995. "18, 20, 2..." - Kann Expertise im Skatspiel Defizite des Arbeitsgedächtnisses älterer Menschen kompensieren? *Swiss J. Psychol.* 54:225–36

Krampe RT, Ericsson KA. 1996. Maintaining excellence: deliberate practice and elite performance in young and old pianists. *J. Exp. Psychol. Genet.* 125:331–59

Kruglanski AW. 1996. Goals as knowledge structures. See Gollwitzer & Bargh 1996, pp. 599–618

Kruse A, Lindenberger U, Baltes PB. 1993. Longitudinal research on human aging: the power of combining real-time, microgenetic, and simulation approaches. In *Longitudinal Research on Individual Develop-*

ment: Present Status and Future Perspectives, ed. D Magnusson, pp. 153–93. Cambridge, UK: Cambridge Univ. Press

Kuhn D. 1995. Microgenetic study of change: What has it told us? *Psychol. Sci.* 6:133–39

Labouvie-Vief G. 1982. Dynamic development and mature autonomy: a theoretical prologue. *Hum. Dev.* 25:161–91

Labouvie-Vief G. 1992. Neo-Piagetian perspective on adult cognitive development. See Sternberg & Berg 1992, pp. 197–228

Labouvie-Vief G. 1995. *Psyche and Eros: Mind and Gender in the Life Course.* New York: Cambridge Univ. Press

Lachman ME, James JB, eds. 1997. *Multiple Paths of Midlife Development.* Chicago: Univ.Chicago Press

Lerner RM. 1991. Changing organism-context relations as the basic process of development: a developmental contextual perspective. *Dev. Psychol.* 27:27–32

Lerner RM. 1995. The limits of biological influence: behavioral genetics as the emperor's new clothes. *Psychol. Inq.* 6:145–56

Lerner RM. 1998a. Theories of human development: contemporary perspectives. See Lerner 1998b, pp. 1–24

Lerner RM, ed. 1998b. *Handbook of Child Psychology:* Vol. 1. *Theoretical Models of Human Development.* New York: Wiley. 5th ed

Lindenberger U, Baltes PB. 1994. Sensory functioning and intelligence in old age: a powerful connection. *Psychol. Aging* 9: 339–55

Lindenberger U, Baltes PB. 1995. Testing-the-limits and experimental simulation: two methods to explicate the role of learning in development. *Hum. Dev.* 38:349–60

Lindenberger U, Baltes PB. 1997. Intellectual functioning in old and very old age: cross-sectional results from the Berlin Aging Study. *Psychol. Aging* 12:410–32

Lindenberger U, Gilberg R, Little TD, Nuthmann R, Pötter U, Baltes PB. 1998. Sample selectivity and generalizability of the results of the Berlin Aging Study. In *The Berlin Aging Study: From 70 to 100*, ed. PB Baltes, KU Mayer. New York: Cambridge Univ. In press

Lindenberger U, Mayr U, Kliegl R. 1993. Speed and intelligence in old age. *Psychol. Aging* 8:207–20

Lindenberger U, Pötter U. 1998. The complex nature of unique and shared effects in hierarchical linear regression: consequences for cross-sectional developmental research. *Psychol. Methods.* 3:218–30

Magnusson D, ed. 1996. *The Life-Span Development of Individuals: Behavioural, Neurobiological and Psychosocial Perspec-*

tives. Cambridge, UK: Cambridge Univ. Press

Magnusson D, Bergman LR, Rudinger G, Törestad B, eds. 1991. *Problems and Methods in Longitudinal Research: Stability and Change.* Cambridge, UK: Cambridge Univ. Press

Marsiske M, Lang FR, Baltes MM, Baltes PB. 1995. Selective optimization with compensation: life-span perspectives on successful human development. In *Compensation for Psychological Defects and Declines: Managing Losses and Promoting Gains*, ed. RA Dixon, L Bäckman, pp. 35–79. Hillsdale, NJ: Erlbaum

Marsiske M, Willis SL. 1995. Dimensionality of everyday problem solving in older adults. *Psychol Aging* 10:269–83

Marsiske M, Willis SL. 1998. Practical creativity in older adults' everyday problem solving: life-span perspectives. In *Creativity and Successful Aging: Theoretical and Empirical Approaches*, ed. CE Adams-Price, pp. 73–113. New York: Springer

Martin GM, Austad SN, Johnson TE. 1996. Genetic analysis of ageing: role of oxidative damage and environmental stresses. *Nat. Genet.* 13:25–34

Mayer KU. 1990. Lebensverläufe und sozialer Wandel: Anmerkungen zu einem Forschungsprogramm. *Kölner Z. Soziol. Sozialpsychol.* 42(Sonderheft 31):7–21

Mayr U, Kliegl R, Krampe RT. 1996. Sequential and coordinative processing dynamics in figural transformations across the life span. *Cognition* 59:61–90

McAdams DP, de St. Aubin E, eds. 1998. *Generativity and Adult Development.* Washington, DC: Am. Psychol. Assoc.

McCall RB. 1994. What process mediates predictions of childhood IQ from infant habituation and recognition memory? Speculations on the roles of inhibition and rate of information processing. *Intelligence* 18:107–25

McCall RB, Carriger MS. 1993. A meta-analysis of infant habituation and recognition memory performance as predictors of later IQ. *Child. Dev.* 64:57–79

McClearn GE, Johansson B, Berg S, Pedersen NL, Ahern F, et al. 1997. Substantial genetic influence on cognitive abilities in twins 80 or more years old. *Science* 276:1560–63

McClelland JL. 1996. Integration of information: reflections on the theme of attention and performance XVI. In *Attention and Performance XVI*, ed. I Toshui, JL McClelland, pp. 633–56. Cambridge, MA: MIT Press

McGue M, Bouchard TJ Jr, Iacono WG, Lyk-

ken DT. 1993. Behavioral genetics of cognitive ability: a life-span perspective. In *Nature, Nurture, and Psychology*, ed. R Plomin, GE McClearn, pp. 59–76. Washington, DC: Am. Psychol. Assoc.

Mergler NL, Goldstein MD. 1983. Why are there old people? Senescence as biological and cultural preparedness for the transmission of information. *Hum. Dev.* 26:72–90

Miller LT, Vernon PA. 1996. Intelligence, reaction time, and working memory in 4- to 6-year-old children. *Intelligence* 22:155–90

Molander B, Bäckman L. 1996. Cognitive aging in a precision sport context. *Eur. Psychol.* 1:166–79

Molenaar PCM, Boomsma DI, Dolan CV. 1991. Genetic and environmental factors in a developmental perspective. See Magnusson et al 1991, pp. 250–73

Morrison JH, Hof PR. 1997. Life and death of neurons in the aging brain. *Science* 278:412–18

Müller-Brettel M, Dixon RA. 1990. Johann Nicolas Tetens: a forgotten father of developmental psychology? *Int. J. Behav. Dev.* 13:215–30

Nelson AE, Dannefer D. 1992. Aged heterogeneity: fact or fiction? The fate of diversity in gerontological research. *Gerontologist* 32:17–23

Nelson CA, Bloom FE. 1997. Child development and neuroscience. *Child Dev.* 68:970–87

Nesselroade JR. 1991. Interindividual differences in intraindividual change. In *Best Methods for the Analysis of Change*, ed. LM Collins, JL Horn, pp. 92–105. Washington, DC: Am. Psychol. Assoc.

Nesselroade JR, Thompson WW. 1995. Selection and related threats to group comparisons: an example comparing factorial structures of higher and lower ability groups of adult twins. *Psychol. Bull.* 117:271–84

Neugarten DA, ed. 1996. *The Meanings of Age: Selected Papers of Bernice L. Neugarten.* Chicago: Univ. Chicago Press

Park DC, Lautenschlager G, Smith AD, Earles JL. 1996. Mediators of long-term memory performance across the life span. *Psychol. Aging* 11:621–37

Parke RD, Ornstein PA, Rieser JJ, Zahn-Waxler C. 1991. Editors' introduction to the APA Centennial Series. *Dev. Psychol.* 28:3–4

Pascual-Leone J. 1995. Learning and development as dialectical factors in cognitive growth. *Hum. Dev.* 38:338–48

Perfect TJ. 1994. What can Brinley Plots tell us about cognitive aging? *J. Gerontol. Psychol. Sci.* 49:P60–64

Perlmutter M. 1988. Cognitive potential throughout life. In *Emergent Theories of Aging*, ed. JE Birren, VL Bengtson, pp. 247–68. New York: Springer

Piaget J. 1972. Intellectual evolution from adolescence to adulthood. *Hum. Dev.* 15: 1–12

Plomin R. 1994. *Genetics and Experience. The Interplay Between Nature and Nurture*. Thousand Oaks, CA: Sage

Plude DJ, Enns JT, Brodeur D. 1994. The development of selective attention: a lifespan overview. Special Issue: Life span changes in human performance. *Acta Psychol.* 86:227–72

Pratt MW, Diessner R, Pratt A, Hunsberger B, Pancer SM. 1996. Moral and social reasoning and perspective taking in later life: a longitudinal study. *Psychol. Aging* 11: 66–73

Quetelet A. 1842. *A Treatise on Man and the Development of his Faculties*. Edinburgh: Chambers

Rabbitt PMA. 1993. Does it all go together when it goes? The Nineteenth Bartlett Memorial Lecture. *Q. J. Exp. Psychol.* 46A: 385–434

Rakic P. 1995. Corticogenesis. See Gazzaniga 1995, pp. 127–45

Reinert G. 1970. Comparative factor analytic studies of intelligence throughout the human life span. See Goulet & Baltes 1970, pp. 476–84

Reinert G. 1979. Prolegomena to a history of life-span developmental psychology. See Baltes & Brim 1979, pp. 205–54

Ribaupierre Ad. 1995. Working memory and individual differences: a review. *Swiss J. Psychol.* 54:152–68

Ridderinkhof KR, van der Molen MW. 1995. A psychophysiological analysis of developmental differences in the ability to resist interference. *Child. Dev.* 66:1040–56

Riley MW. 1987. On the significance of age in sociology. *Am. Sociol. Rev.* 52:1–14

Rose SA, Feldman JF. 1997. Memory and speed: their role in the relation of information processing to later IQ. *Child. Dev.* 68:630–41

Rutter M, Rutter M. 1993. *Developing Minds: Challenge and Continuity Across the Life Span*. New York: Basic Books

Rutter ML. 1997. Nature-nurture integration: The example of anti-social behavior. *Am. Psychol.* 52:390–98

Saffran J, Aslin RN, Newport EL. 1996. Statistical learning by 8-month-old infants. *Science* 274:1926–28

Salthouse TA. 1991. *Theoretical Perspectives on Cognitive Aging*. Hillsdale, NJ: Erlbaum

Salthouse TA. 1996. The processing-speed theory of adult age differences in cognition. *Psychol. Rev.* 103:403–28

Salthouse TA, Meinz EJ. 1995. Aging, inhibition, working memory, and speed. *J. Gerontol. Psychol. Sci.* 50B:297–306

Saudino KJ, Plomin R, Pedersen N, McClearn GE. 1994. The etiology of high and low cognitive ability during the second half of the life-span. *Intelligence* 19:359–71

Scarr S, McCartney K. 1983. How people make their own environment: a theory of genotype environment effects. *Child. Dev.* 54:424–35

Schaie KW. 1994. The course of adult intellectual development. *Am. Psychol.* 49: 304–13

Schaie KW. 1996. *Adult Intellectual Development: The Seattle Longitudinal Study.* New York: Cambridge Univ. Press

Schaie KW, Willis SL, Hertzog C, Schulenberg JE. 1987. Effects of cognitive training on primary mental ability structure. *Psychol. Aging* 2:233–42

Schneider W, Sodian B. 1997. Memory strategy development: lessons from longitudinal research. *Dev.Rev.* 17:442–61

Schroots JJF. 1996. Theoretical developments in the psychology of aging. *Gerontologist* 36:742–48

Schulz R, Heckhausen J. 1996. A life span model of successful aging. *Am. Psychol.* 51:702–14

Siegler RS. 1997. Beyond competence-toward development. *Cogn. Dev.* 12: 232–332

Siegler RS, Crowley K. 1991. The microgenetic method: a direct means for studying cognitive development. *Am. Psychol.* 46: 606–20

Siegler RS, Crowley K. 1994. Constraints on learning in nonprivileged domains. *Cogn. Psychol.* 27:194–226

Singer JL. 1995. Development and plasticity of cortical processing architectures. *Science* 270:758–64

Smith J, Baltes PB. 1997. Profiles of psychological functioning in the old and oldest old. *Psychol. Aging* 12:458–72

Smith J, Staudinger UM, Baltes PB. 1994. Occupational settings facilitating wisdom-related knowledge: The sample case of clinical psychologists. *J. Consult. Clin. Psychol.* 62:989–99

Smith MB. 1996. Psychology and truth: human science and the post-modern challenge. *Interam. J. Psychol.* 30:145–58

Smotherman WP, Robinson SR. 1996. The development of behavior before birth. *Dev. Psychol.* 32:425–34

Spearman CE. 1927. *The Abilities of Man*. New York: Macmillan

Spelke E, Vishton P, von Hofsten C. 1995. Object perception, object-directed action, and physical knowledge in infancy. See Gazzaniga 1995, pp. 165–79

Staudinger UM. 1996. Wisdom and the social-interactive foundation of the mind. See Baltes & Staudinger 1996, pp. 276–318

Staudinger UM. 1998. Social cognition and a psychological approach to an art of life. In *Social Cognition, Adult Development, and Aging*, ed. F Blanchard-Fields, BT Hess. New York: Academic. In press

Staudinger UM, Marsiske M, Baltes PB. 1995. Resilience and reserve capacity in later adulthood: potentials and limits of development across the life span. In *Developmental Psychopathology* Vol. 2: *Risk, Disorder, and Adaptation*, ed. D Cicchetti, D Cohen, pp. 801–47. New York: Wiley

Staudinger UM, Pasupathi M. 1998. Life-span perspectives on self, personality, and social cognition. In *Handbook of Cognition and Aging*, ed. T Salthouse, FIM Craik. Hillsdale: Erlbaum. In press

Sternberg RJ. 1990. Wisdom and its relations to intelligence and creativity. In *Wisdom: Its Nature, Origins, and Development*, ed. RJ Sternberg, pp. 142–49. New York: Cambridge Univ. Press

Sterns HL, Dorsett JG. 1994. Career development: a life span issue. *Exp. Aging Res.* 20:257–64

Stich SP, ed. 1990. *The Fragmentation of Reason: Preface to a Pragmatic Theory of Cognitive Evaluation.* Cambridge, MA: MIT Press

Stigsdotter Neely A, Bäckman L. 1993. Long-term maintenance of gains from memory training in older adults: two 3 1/2 years follow-up studies. *Gerontol. Psychol. Sci.* 48:P233–37

Stoltzfus ER, Hasher L, Zacks RT. 1996. Working memory and aging: current status of the inhibitory view. In *Working Memory and Human Cognition*, ed. JTE Richardson, pp. 66–88. Cambridge, UK: Oxford Univ. Press

Swanson HL. 1996. Individual and age-related differences in children's working memory. *Mem. Cogn.* 24:70–82

Tetens JN. 1777. *Philosophische Versuche über die menschliche Natur und ihre Entwicklung.* Leipzig, Germany: Weidmanns Erben & Reich

Thatcher RW. 1994. Cyclic cortical reorganization: origins of human cognitive development. See Dawson & Fischer 1994, pp. 232–66

Thelen E, Smith LB. 1998. Dynamic systems theories. See Lerner 1998b, pp. 563–635

Thomae H. 1979. The concept of development and life-span developmental psychology.

See Baltes & Brim 1979, pp. 282–312

Thompson LA. 1995. Encoding and memory for visible speech and gestures: a comparison between young and older adults. *Psychol. Aging* 10:215–28

Tooby J, Cosmides L. 1995. Mapping the evolved functional organization of mind and brain. See Gazzaniga 1995, pp. 1185–97

Uttal DH, Perlmutter M. 1989. Toward a broader conceptualization of development: the role of gains and losses across the life span. *Dev. Rev.* 9:101–32

Valsiner J, Lawrence JA. 1997. Human development in culture across the life-span. In *Handbook of Cross–Cultural Psychology*, ed. JW Berry, PR Dasen, TS Saraswathi, 2:69–106. Boston, MA: Allyn & Bacon

van der Maas HL, Molenaar PCM. 1992. Stagewise cognitive development: an application of catastrophe theory. *Psychol. Rev.* 99:395–417

Verhaeghen P, Salthouse TA. 1997. Meta-analyses of age-cognition relations in adulthood: estimates of linear and non-linear age effects and structural models. *Psychol. Bull.* 122:231–50

Weinert FE, Perner J. 1996. Cognitive development. See Magnusson 1996, pp. 207–22

Welford AT. 1993. The gerontological balance sheet. See Cerella et al 1993, pp. 3–10

Wellman HM, Gelman SA. 1992. Cognitive development: foundational theories of core domains. *Annu. Rev. Psychol.* 43:337–75

Willett JB, Singer JD. 1991. Applications of survival analysis to aging research. *Exp. Aging Res.* 17:243–50

Willis SL, Schaie KW. 1994. Cognitive training in the normal elderly. In *Plasticité cérébrale et stimulation cognitive [Cerebral plasticity and cognitive stimulation]*, ed. F Forette, Y Christen, F Boller, pp. 91–113. Paris, France: Fond. Nat. Gérontol.

Willis SL, Schaie KW, Hayward M, eds. 1997. *Societal Mechanisms for Maintaining Competence in Old Age.* New York: Springer

Woodruff-Pak DS. 1993. Neural plasticity as a substrate for cognitive adaptation in adulthood and aging. See Cerella et al 1993, pp. 13–35

Yates E, Benton LA. 1995. Biological senescence: loss of integration and resilience. *Can. J. Aging* 14:106–20

Zacks R, Hasher L. 1997. Cognitive gerontology and attentional inhibition. A reply to Burke and McDowd. *J. Gerontol. Psychol. Sci.* 52B:P274–83

Annu. Rev. Psychol. 1999. 50:509–35

INFLUENCES ON INFANT SPEECH PROCESSING: Toward a New Synthesis

Janet F. Werker and Richard C. Tees

Department of Psychology, University of British Columbia, Vancouver, British Columbia, V6T 1Z4, Canada; e-mail: Jwerker@cortex.psych.ubc.ca

KEY WORDS: cross-language, perception, development, models, word-learning

ABSTRACT

To comprehend and produce language, we must be able to recognize the sound patterns of our language and the rules for how these sounds "map on" to meaning. Human infants are born with a remarkable array of perceptual sensitivities that allow them to detect the basic properties that are common to the world's languages. During the first year of life, these sensitivities undergo modification reflecting an exquisite tuning to just that phonological information that is needed to map sound to meaning in the native language. We review this transition from language-general to language-specific perceptual sensitivity that occurs during the first year of life and consider whether the changes propel the child into word learning. To account for the broad-based initial sensitivities and subsequent reorganizations, we offer an integrated transactional framework based on the notion of a specialized perceptual-motor system that has evolved to serve human speech, but which functions in concert with other developing abilities. In so doing, we highlight the links between infant speech perception, babbling, and word learning.

CONTENTS

0084-6570/99/0201-0509$08.00

INTRODUCTION

What is remarkable about an infant's ability to successfully process the sounds of speech? The act of perceiving auditory speech represents a difficult and complex computational task. In written speech, each individual letter has its own form; there are spaces between words, and punctuation marks are used to indicate divisions into phrases, sentences, and paragraphs. Although we also think of spoken speech as linear and composed of discrete elements, the acoustic wave form shows no clear boundaries between individual phonemes (a basic sound unit, or phone, used in a language to distinguish one word from another) or between individual syllables, or even words. Moreover, the acoustic cues that signal the beginning of a new phrase or sentence are only probabilistic at best. Yet to perceive (and eventually produce) one's native language, it is essential that an infant not only successfully isolate and segment the individual units in the stream of speech, but that she also represent in some way the information that specifies the regularities among various productions of the same phoneme or word and ignore irrelevant variations.

During the past 30 years, researchers have focused on trying to understand how infants begin to solve the complex computational task of speech processing (for a review of common methods used to test infant speech perception, see Werker et al 1998a). We know that infants begin life with a number of perceptual-motor biases that allow them to "break into" the stream of speech, pull out and represent its units, and eventually map sound to meaning. As well, it is apparent that acoustic and phonological cues in spoken speech provide probabilistic information as to the boundaries of linguistic units, and that infants are well designed to detect and utilize this probabilistic information. Finally, researchers are beginning to identify the developmental achievements that allow infants to use the different kinds of information in the stream of speech in their elaboration of language-specific sensitivities.

WHAT LINGUISTIC SENSITIVITIES DOES THE YOUNG INFANT BRING TO SPEECH PROCESSING?

Sensitivity to Consonants and Vowels

Newborns begin life with a remarkable sensitivity to the acoustic cues that signify different basic elements of speech. For example, they are able to discriminate fine phonetic differences between consonants in syllables such as /ba/ versus /da/ or /ba/ versus /pa/ (Eimas et al 1971). The phonetic differences infants can discriminate most easily in consonants are those that actually occur in one or more of the world's languages. When presented with a series of 8–12 stimuli, with "anchors" synthesized to incorporate the critical acoustic information representing a consonant-vowel sound pair, and with intermediate stimuli to represent equal-step changes in the acoustical differences that differentiate the two consonants , 2- to 3-month-old infants show evidence of discrimination at the same places along the continuum as do adult speakers. For instance, they show evidence of discrimination at precisely those places on the continuum where adults shift their labeling from, for example, /ba/ to /da/ to /ga/ (Eimas 1974) (Figure 1). That young infants detect some equal-sized acoustic changes more readily than others, and that the changes they are able to discriminate "map on" to those used in the world's languages, reveals an initial set of perceptual sensitivities that enables the infant to begin to process the most fundamental information in human speech.

The ability to discriminate one vowel sound from another is also evident in young infants (Trehub 1973). Moreover, early on, infants show a cohesive internal structure to their vowel categories. For example, infants aged 2–4 months are able to perceive vowel identity across a variety of contexts, treating as equivalent the vowel /i/ as spoken by a man, woman, or child in either a rising or falling intonation contour, and distinguish it from the vowel /a/ spoken in these varying contexts (Kuhl 1979). This perception of isolated steady state vowels also seems to involve what Kuhl (1993) labeled a "magnet effect." Presented initially with "good" exemplars of a vowel category and then required to detect occurrences of "poor" instances, both 6-month-old infants and adults showed poorer vowel discrimination than when tested with "poor" exemplars prior to "good" ones (Grieser & Kuhl 1989).

Infants also show a sensitivity to visual information in speech. As adults, our speech percepts represent a combination of what we see and hear and under some circumstances are actually influenced more by what we see (Green

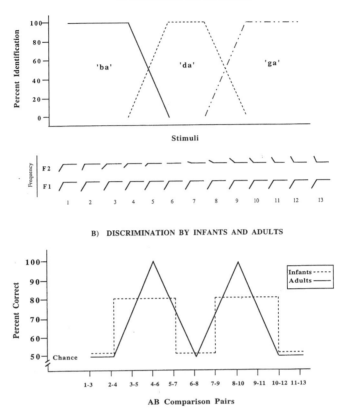

Figure 1   An illustration of adult and infant categorical perception of consonants using 13 syllables taken from the synthetic (and schematically represented) consonant-vowel continuum from
/ba/ to /da/ to /ga/, signaled by differences in the starting frequency of the second format transition. (*A*) Idealized identification by adults. (*B*) Idealized discrimination by infants and adults.
(Adapted from Eimas 1974, Strange & Jenkins 1978.)

1998). In illustration, McGurk & MacDonald (1976) presented subjects with
"talking heads" accompanied by either matching or nonmatching speech
sounds. When presented with an auditory /ba/ and a visible /ga/, adults consistently reported perceiving a /da/, a syllable intermediate between the "seen"
and the "heard" syllables. Furthermore, when presented with an auditory /ba/
and a visible /va/, adults perceived only what they saw, i.e. /va/. What is remarkable is that although in both cases these percepts are different from the
veridical information presented, adults perceive a strong, immediate, and unambiguous syllable.

By 4 months of age, infants can detect the match between heard and seen vowel information, looking preferentially to a talking head producing the matching vowel (Kuhl & Meltzoff 1982, Patterson & Werker 1998). However, the combined percept does not appear to be compelling and unambiguous at this young age . Instead, it appears that infants this young can attend to both the heard and seen sources of information (Rosenblum et al 1997), but that their integration is not yet mandatory or absolute (Desjardins & Werker 1996).

Sensitivity to Syntactic Information in Speech

Infants may be sensitive to the prosodic information that signals the overall grammatical structure of the language. Languages differ in the basic word order allowed. In English, commonly, sentences tend to obey a subject/verb/object structure, wherein complementizing information follows the verb (such languages are called right-branching languages). In left-branching subject/object/verb languages (such as Turkish), the complementizing information precedes the verb (Chomsky 1975). The overall prosodic structure of subject/verb/object languages is different from that of subject/object/verb languages (Nespor & Vogel 1986), yielding perceptible acoustic correlates. Recently, researchers have hypothesized that newborn infants might be sensitive to this prosodic information (Christophe et al 1997, Mazuka 1996). Although there have not yet been studies with newborns, infants 9 months old are able to perceive phonological phrase boundaries (Gerken et al 1994).

Moreover, newborn infants are sensitive to the acoustic information that differentiates broad grammatical classes of words. Acoustic cues to such categories occur in adult speech (Kelly 1992). Across languages, the most fundamental distinction among grammatical classes is the bifurcation into lexical and grammatical words. Lexical words are content words, such as nouns, verb, adjectives, etc, which carry meaning. Grammatical words are function words such as prepositions, articles, etc, which primarily carry structure. Shi et al (1998a) showed that there are acoustic and phonological cues in speech directed to infants that distinguish content and function words. For example, content words tend to be longer and they tend to be spoken more loudly and to have their vowels more fully enunciated than function words. Recently, Shi et al (1998b) tested newborn infants on their ability to distinguish words on the basis of grammatical category. Infants were familiarized first to a list of content (or a list of function) words and then tested on a new list of words either from the same category or from the contrasting category. Infants showed evidence of detecting a switch to the new category but not a switch to a new words from the same category. Thus, one of the perceptual sensitivities infants bring to the task of perceiving speech is a sensitivity to the acoustic and phonological cues that distinguish the two fundamental grammatical categories.

Summary of Initial Infant Sensitivities

Taken together, the findings reviewed above reveal a remarkable level of sophistication in infants' speech processing capabilities. Undoubtedly, these initial biases and capabilities allow the infant to begin to gather the kind of information necessary to move one step closer to the eventual task of language acquisition.

THE EFFECTS OF EXPERIENCE ON INFANT SPEECH PERCEPTION

Languages differ in their inventory of consonants and vowels in both auditory (phonemes) and visible (visemes) speech. They differ as well (a) in the frequencies with which their particular consonants and vowels occur, (b) in the precise acoustic-phonetic characteristics of the consonants and vowels in different positions in words, i.e. allophonic variations, and (c) in the allowable combinations of consonants and vowels (phonotactics) that can occur within words. Also, as noted earlier, the precise set of grammatical categories used (over and above the fundamental lexical versus grammatical word distinction) differs between languages, and the branching parameter is set differently in different languages families. By studying perception in infants raised in different language environments, we can begin to describe how and when infants become attuned to the properties of their native language.

Recognizing One's Native Language

One intriguing finding is that some adaptation to the properties of one's native language occurs either in utero or immediately following birth. English- and Spanish-learning infants as young as 2 days show a preference for listening to their native language (Moon et al 1993). Moreover, within the first few hours and days of life, infants are able to discriminate excerpts from distinct language families. In an early demonstration of this, Mehler and colleagues (Mehler et al 1988, Mehler & Christophe 1994) tested neonates in Paris and infants aged 2 months from Oregon on French versus Russian and English versus Italian. They found that neonates from both environments were able to discriminate between the familiar and the unfamiliar language or between two different unfamiliar languages. More recently, this finding has been qualified. The two unfamiliar languages must be from relatively distinct language families to be discriminable to a newborn. For example, Nazzi et al (1998) reported that although newborn French infants can discriminate English from Japanese, they cannot discriminate English from the rhythmically more similar German. By 4 months of age, however, infants raised in a monolingual environment may be able to distinguish their native language from a very similar unfamiliar language. The evidence for this comes from work of Nazzi et al (1998), showing that English-learning infants aged 4–5 months can distinguish English from the highly similar Dutch, and from the very recent study in which Bosch & Sebastian-Galles (1997) showed that monolingual 4-month-old Spanish- or Catalan-learning infants are able to discriminate Spanish from Catalan. However, 4-month-old infants being raised in bilingual Spanish/Catalan environments failed to provide evidence of discriminating between these two languages. This first study with bilingual infants raises a number of interesting questions regarding the nature of language representations in early bilingualism.

Cross-Language Consonant and Vowel Perception

A research focus over the past 15 years has been on understanding the effects of experience on perception of consonants. Infants younger than 6–8 months of age can not only discriminate categorically native phonetic contrasts (e.g. /ba/ versus /da/, or /ra/ versus /la/), they can also discriminate phonetic contrasts involving syllables that are not used to distinguish meaning in their native language (Aslin et al 1981, Best et al 1988, Polka & Werker 1994, Streeter 1976, Trehub 1976, Werker et al 1981, Werker & Tees 1984a).

In contrast to the language-general sensitivities shown by young infants, adults often have difficulty discriminating between syllables that differ by only a single phoneme, if that particular phonemic contrast is not used in their native language: Japanese adults have difficulty discriminating the difference between /ra/ and /la/ (Strange & Jenkins 1978), and English adults have difficulty discriminating certain Hindi (Werker et al 1981), Nthlakampx (Werker & Tees 1984a), and Czech (Trehub 1976) contrasts. Adults may need short familiarization periods even to discriminate acoustically quite salient non-native distinctions (Pisoni et al 1982, Werker & Tees 1984b). Thus, although the sensitivities of infants allow language-universal phonetic discrimination, their subsequent experience functions to narrow, or "prune," their perceptual sensitivities to enable "mapping on" to the phonology of their native language.

To examine the effects of early experience, we conducted a series of studies comparing infants of different ages, children, and adults on their ability to discriminate non-native phonetic contrasts. The comparison of either Hindi-speaking or English-speaking adults with English-learning infants showed results consistent with the prediction of language-universal infant sensitivities and their subsequent decline. Virtually all subjects in all groups could discriminate the /ba/-/da/ contrast—a distinction common in the world's languages and one that is used in both English and Hindi. The 6- to 8-month-old English-learning infants and the Hindi-speaking adults could easily discriminate both Hindi contrasts. However, the English-speaking adults had trouble discriminating the Hindi contrasts, showing particular trouble with the more difficult retroflex/dental place-of-articulation distinction (Werker et al 1981).

In follow-up studies, we found that this change in ability is evident by 4 years of age (Werker & Tees 1983) and, in fact, occurs within the first year of life. English-learning infants of 6–8, 8–10, and 10–12 months of age were tested on their ability to discriminate the Hindi /Ta/-/ta/ contrast and a Nthlakampx /k'i/-/q'i/ contrast. Although most of the infants 6–8 months old were able to discriminate between both non-English contrasts, few of the infants 10–12 months old were able to discriminate either the Hindi or the Nthlakampx contrast (Werker & Tees 1984a). The pattern of results revealed for infants is shown in Figure 2.

This pattern of change between 6 and 12 months of age has been reported (*a*) for a different retroflex/dental distinction (/Da/-/da/) (Werker & Lalonde 1988); (*b*) for three Zulu contrasts: a bilabial plosive/implosive distinction, a lateral fricative voiced/voiceless contrast, and a velar voiceless/ejective stop distinction (Best 1995); and (*c*) among Japanese infants for the (non-Japanese) English /ra/-lla/ (Kuhl 1998). The change for the Nthlakampx contrast has also been replicated by Best (1995). Importantly, however, the decline in cross-language consonant perception is not always evident at 10–12 months of age. Best and colleagues (see Best 1995) have shown that the decline only occurs for contrasts that involve sounds similar to sounds used in the native language. For example, infants 10–12 months old, and even adults, continue to discriminate the apical/lateral Zulu click contrast <xa>-<ca>, but this contrast sounds to all but the Zulu more like someone clucking to a horse or making a "tsk tsk" sound

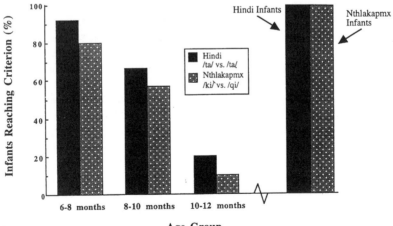

Figure 2   The proportion of infants at each age reaching discrimination criterion on the Hindi and Nthlakampx contrasts. (*Far right*) The performance of infants 11 months old raised in either a Hindi or a Nthlakampx environment. (Adapted from Werker & Tees 1984a.)

than like a linguistic sound. Best suggests that it is experience-dependent assimilability to the phonology of the native language rather than linguistic experience per se that accounts for the maintenance of discriminative abilities.

To further examine what kind of experience is important, Pegg & Werker (1997) conducted a study assessing infants and adults on their ability to recognize a phonetic difference that occurs but is not used to distinguish meaning in the native language. They investigated the ability of English-speaking infants and adults to discriminate the syllable /da/ from the syllable created by removing the [s] in a /sta/ syllable. /Sta/ without the [s] was perceived to be /da/ by the adults, who although labeling all these stimuli as equally good instances of the English phoneme /da/ were nevertheless able to discriminate the two sets of stimuli (the /da/ set from the [s]/ta/ set). Importantly, approximately half of the English-learning infants 6–8 months of age were also able to discriminate the two sets of stimuli, whereas nearly all the English infants 10–12 months of age failed this discrimination task.

One interpretation of the above data is that by 10–12 months of age, infants selectively listen to only that phonetic variation in the native language that conveys meaningful distinctions. A simpler explanation, and the one we prefer, is that by 10–12 months of age, infants are sensitive not only to the phonetic characteristics of the native language, but also to the syllabic context in which that phonetic variation occurs. Thus, when presented with the [s]/ta/ phonetic variate in syllable initial position, infants treated it as an instance of the closest context-appropriate form, which is /da/. This kind of sensitivity would allow infants to represent and attend to acceptable syllable forms in their native language.

The language-specific influences on vowel perception may be evident at an earlier age than those seen for the perception of consonants. For example, Kuhl and colleagues (1992) found that at 6 months of age, Swedish-learning infants showed the magnet effect (described above) when tested on variates of Swedish vowels but not of English vowels, whereas English-learning 6-month-olds showed the magnet effect only for the English vowels.

Polka & Werker (1994) extended the Kuhl work to assess not just possible language-specific influences on the internal structure of vowel categories but also age-related changes in between-category discrimination of non-native vowels. Their work revealed an effect of experience between 4 and 6 months of age, but the full impact of experience was not evident until approximately 10–12 months of age, the same age at which it is found for consonants (but see Polka & Bohn 1996).

Experiential Influences on Bimodal Speech Perception

Although no one has been able to assess experiential influences on bimodal speech perception in infants, postnatal experience does influence bimodal speech perception in children and adults. In an early study, Werker et al (1992) examined bimodal speech perception in five groups of French-speaking Canadians who were studying English in a summer program. Of interest was the perception of the interdental fricative /tha/, which occurs in English but not in French. Canadian French speakers tend to substitute /tha/ with /ta/ or /da/ when speaking English. Perhaps not surprisingly, when tested on their perception of the visible information in /tha/, Canadian French speakers tended to perceive /ta/ or /da/ rather than /tha/. The strength of this effect was inversely proportional to their fluency in English. A similar effect of experience on perception of visible speech was shown by Massaro et al (1993).

Several researchers have presented data indicating that the overall amount of visible influence increases with age (e.g. McGurk & MacDonald 1976). This suggests a role for experience in the perception of visible speech. Recent research is beginning to reveal the kinds of experience that might be important. To illustrate, Desjardin et al (1997) tested children aged 3 and 4 who were either still making or not making typical substitution errors in their production of any one of the consonants /b/, /v/, /th/, or /d/. The children were tested in an engaging bimodal speech perception task, an auditory speech perception task, and a lip-reading task. Although both the substitutors and the nonsubstitutors performed equally well in the auditory speech perception task, the substitutors showed much less influence from the visible speech in their performance in both the bimodal speech perception and the lip-reading tasks. Similarly, Siva et al (1995) showed that the audible and visible information did not appear to be as well integrated in the percepts of adults with cerebral palsy. Taken together, these two studies provide strong evidence that experience producing speech correctly is at least one source of influence on the effective use of visible information.

Prosodic, Phonotactic, and Syntactic Information Processing

In a series of studies, Jusczyk and colleagues have shown that by 6 months of age, infants show a preference for listening to words that correspond to the prosodic (rhythm and intonation) patterns of their native language, but it is not until 9 months of age that they show a preference for listening to words that correspond to the phonetic and phonotactic rules of their native language (Jusczyk 1997). Moreover, by 10 months of age, but not before, infants show a preference for listening to lists of words that conform to the predominant native language strong-weak (SW) stress pattern (Juscyk et al 1993).

Only recently, researchers have begun to assess experiential influences on perception of grammatical information. The question being asked is whether infants can use phonological and acoustic cues to bootstrap into the grammatical structure of the native language. In the first demonstration, Hirsh-Pasek and colleagues (1987) showed that by 7 months of age, infants show a preference for listening to infant-directed speech samples with pauses inserted at phrase boundaries over similar samples wherein the pauses are inserted within a phrase. Jusczyk (1997) extended this work to a cross-language sample. He found that at 4 months, English-learning infants listened equally long to both Polish and English speech samples with pauses inserted at clause boundaries over speech samples with pauses inserted within clauses, but by 6 months of age they only showed this preference for correctly inserted pauses with their native language (English). Thus, between 4 and 6 months of age, infants apparently lose their prior ability to detect the acoustic and phonological cues demarking major grammatical constituents in an unfamiliar language and retain a sensitivity to only those cues that are important in their language.

As noted earlier, Shi et al (1998a) found that newborn infants can discriminate between sets of grammatical and lexical words and that they show detection of a change irrespective of the direction of the change. By 6 months of age, however, infants show a detection of the change in syntactic category only if they are initially familiarized/habituated to grammatical words and then tested on lexical words, i.e. they dishabituate only under those circumstances. Shi and colleagues interpret these findings as showing an emerging preference for lexical words between birth and 6 months of age.

Do These Age-Related Changes Represent Losses in Linguistic/Perceptual Competence?

The language-general perceptual sensitivities in newborns undergo a change and become more language-specific during the first year of life. When first reported, the research community viewed the data as indicating a loss of perceptual capacity due to lack of experience. However, the interpretation has since become more precise. First, as we cited earlier, infants continue discriminating between some non-native phonetic contrasts even though they have never heard them, (e.g. Best et al 1988) and lose the ability to discriminate between others even though they are part of heard speech (Pegg & Werker 1997). Second, even though adults perform poorly on many non-native phoneme contrasts in the testing circumstances we have described, there are other conditions under which continuing adult sensitivity can be demonstrated. Adults can discriminate even difficult non-native contrasts if the critical acoustic information in the speech contrast is presented alone so that the now-truncated syllables no longer sound like speech (Werker & Tees 1984b). Furthermore, adults can be taught to distinguish full syllables if given enough training trials (Tees & Werker 1984), or if tested in sensitive procedures with low memory demands (e.g. Pisoni et al 1982, Werker & Tees 1984b), or if given extensive language instruction (MacKain et al 1981). For these reasons, we have referred to the changes that occur, at least in consonant discriminative ability, as a functional reorganization (Werker 1995) and to the early influences of linguistic experiences as reflective of a sensitive, not critical (i.e. invariant), period (Tees 1986, Werker & Tees 1992). Its nature is further considered at the end of this review.

Summary of Experiential Influences on Infant Speech Processing

In summary, the evidence establishes convincingly that by the end of the first year of life, an infant's phonetic perceptual sensitivities reflect considerable influence from the native language. This influence is reflected both in a preference for highly frequent phonetic patterns and in a narrowing of initial discriminatory abilities to match the contextual distribution of phonetic information from auditory (linguistic) input. As well, by one year of age, infants also show preferential processing for many other aspects of the native language. These changes, which occur during the first year of life, appear to prepare the child for the next functional task—beginning to acquire the ability to understand and speak her native language.

LISTENING FOR WORDS

What Do Infants Know About Words?

Few studies to date have assessed the relationship between the speech perceptual competencies of developing infants and their emerging word-learning. In this section, we briefly review recent work on word-learning in infancy and examine whether or not there is a direct link between changing sensitivity to the native language and the onset of word-learning.

During their first 14–15 months, infants learn to extract words from the speech stream, to recognize word forms they have previously heard, to associate words with objects, to understand the meaning of some words, and even to produce some words. Importantly, although infants are learning a lot about words, none of the kinds of word-learning they show in the first year of life necessarily indicates they have a full referential understanding of words. Indeed, evoked responses show that in 15-month-olds, known words and unknown words are processed differently, but not until 20 months of age (by which time they do have a referential understanding of word meaning) is the recognition of familiar words strongly lateralized to the left hemisphere and to the speech processing areas over the planum temporale (Mills et al 1994). Researchers who study early language acquisition have suggested for some time that children may not attend to fine phonetic detail when they are first learning what words mean, even though they displayed such attention to fine phonetic detail in their perception of speech at a younger age. Indeed, early work suggested that young children either confuse similar-sounding words or tolerate single feature phonetic substitutions in known words (e.g. Eilers & Oller 1976). One proposal to account for this argued that infants initially represent only the vocalic nucleus of the word (Ferguson & Farwell 1975). However, the findings with young children are unconvincing because the methods used to test their perception of words differed greatly in task demands and sensitivity compared with those used to collect evidence about the infant's speech perception. Thus, it remains a matter of conjecture whether children do in fact represent words as meaningful entities with less detail than they do non-meaningful word forms. Recently, investigators have revisited the issue of whether or not infants use fine phonetic detail when they first start learning to understand words. This evidence is discussed below with respect to the various stages of word-learning from recognition and segmentation of word forms, through associative and referential understanding (for a full discussion of various stages of word learning, see Werker & Stager 1998).

Recognizing Word Forms

Even neonates show some sensitivity to the acoustic cues that specify word boundaries. Infants 1–4 days old are able to distinguish two-syllable stimuli in which the two syllables either were excised from a single word (e.g. [mati] from "cinematique") or from two different words (e.g. [mati] from "panorama typique") (Christophe et al 1994). By 4.5 months of age, infants show a preference for listening to their own names, which suggests that even at this early age, infants are beginning to recognize something about word forms (Mandel et al 1995). By 7.5 months of age, when presented with passages containing familiar words, such as "cup," "bike," etc, infants (Jusczyk & Aslin 1995) show a preference for listening to those over unfamiliar words and can remember heard words for up to two weeks (Jusczyk & Hohne 1997). Furthermore, infants of this age can segment and remember bisyllable words that conform to the dominant, SW stress pattern in English (e.g. "doctor"), but fail to pull out the first syllable when familiarized to weak-strong (WS) words. For example, if familiarized to the word "belief," infants of 7.5 months show a preference for listening to "lief" rather than "belief." By 10 months of age, infants successfully pull out words irrespective of whether the SW or WS form is used and successfully recognize even WS forms (Jusczyk 1997).

The question of whether infants detect and represent fine phonetic detail in word-priming tasks has also been addressed. In one study, Jusczyk & Aslin (1995) familiarized infants to a set of words, then tested them on "foils," words that are phonetically similar (e.g. "tup" rather than "cup"). Although infants 7.5 months old once again showed a preference for listening to the words they had been presented with during the familiarization phase, that preference did not extend to the phonetically similar foils. Thus, this suggests that infants are able to detect, access, and use fine phonetic detail to distinguish familiar from unfamiliar items.

Different results were obtained by Halle & de Boysson-Bardies (1996) for slightly older infants. They reported that by 11.5 months of age, infants were able to recognize frequently heard words and showed a preference for listening to such words over the infrequently heard foils, but only if the foils were phonetically quite dissimilar. When tested with phonetically similar foils, infants 11–12 months old treated them as equally familiar. To explain the difference between their findings and those of Jusczyk & Aslin (1995), Hallé & de Boysson-Bardies (1996) proposed that in contrast to 7.5-month-old infants, 11-month-old infants listen to words as potential sources of semantic content, and that such a listening strategy may predispose them to adopt a more holistic, less analytic processing strategy than their younger counterparts.

Word-Object Associative Learning

To test the hypothesis that infants access or store less phonetic detail when they are listening to words as potential sources of meaning than when they are just listening to words as sounds, we decided to test infants on their ability to discriminate among fine phonetic features in more-explicit word-learning tasks. Using a "habituation switch" procedure, infants were familiarized to one or two word-object pairings (Werker et al 1998b). Following the familiarization phase, infants were then tested on their ability to detect a change in either the word, the object, or the pairing of the word with the object. Werker and colleagues (1998a) found that infants 14 months old, but not younger, could learn the association between two words and two moving objects with only minimal exposure when the objects used were physically dissimilar and the words used were phonetically dissimilar (e.g. "lif" and "neem"). In a follow-up series of studies, Stager & Werker (1997) tested infants on their ability to learn the association between phonetically similar words (e.g. "bih" versus "dih") and objects. Surprisingly, when the words were phonetically similar, infants of 14 months failed.

This kind of associative task can be regarded as more demanding than a task that simply requires children to recognize a familiar word form, but less demanding than one that requires referential comprehension. It does not require that the infant adopt or grasp the concept "stands for," but it does require the infant to use the word form in a minimally semantic way. That is, the successful child at least must perceive and remember the "goes with" association between the word and object, whereas no such "goes with" understanding is required in the recognition task used by Jusczyk and colleagues.

The apparent discrepancy between the results obtained when speech perception of infants is assessed and those obtained when word-learning is tested in the same infants is a reflection, we argue, of the real discontinuity in the nature of processing strategies in operation in the two circumstances. It is for this reason that we refer to the inattention to phonetic detail in early word-learning tasks as a second functional reorganization. Further research is required to determine when infants again recover access to fine phonetic detail in word forms. However, we suspect it may not be evident until after the onset of full referential understanding. This referential understanding is thought to allow the rapid spurt in vocabulary growth that occurs at approximately 18–20 months of age. The resulting increased vocabulary could result in sufficient pressure to fill in finer phonetic detail in the lexical representations in order to avoid confusion between similar-sounding, known words. Although we have not yet successfully tested infants 18–20 months old, in the switch procedure, we would predict that at, or shortly after, this age, access to such fine phonetic detail would be evident. The known and proposed relationships between onset of different kinds of word-learning and changes in sensitivity to the amount of phonetic detail is shown in Figure 3.

VOCAL PRODUCTION

Babbling

Although infants begin life with a broad-based, high level of speech perceptual ability, their ability to produce speech is clearly limited by the immaturity of

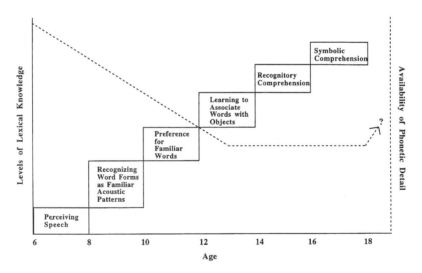

Figure 3 A pictoral representation of the amount of phonetic detail represented or accessed by the infant (*dotted line*) as a function of level of complexity in speech perception and word processing tasks (*boxes*).

both the vocal tract and the related neuromusculature (see Kent & Murray 1982). It is not until approximately 6 months of age that infants first display coordination of the gestures involved in closing the vocal tract for a consonant and the release of a steady state vowel in the form of a consonant-vowel (CV) syllable (Oller 1980). These early canonical forms involve reduplicated productions of the same CV syllable (e.g. /bababa/). By 8–9 months of age, infants begin to be able to combine varying CV syllables in a single production (e.g. /babeedo/). Early appearing syllable forms are those that are the easiest to produce (see Locke 1983). Thus, in the initial stages of development, there do appear to be universals in vocal production.

The question of whether (and when) babbling begins to reflect an influence from the native language has been the subject of great controversy. In the past 15 years, convincing evidence has been collected that infant vocalizations do reflect the properties of the native language and that they begin to do so by 9–10 months of age. By this age, the formant structure of vowels produced by infants is closer to that of their native language than to that of comparison languages (de Boysson-Bardies et al 1989). More convincingly, in a longitudinal study of French, Swedish, English, and Japanese infants, de Boysson-Bardies & Vihman (1991) found that in babbling, the distribution of manner class (e.g. stop consonants such as /b, d, t, k/ versus fricatives such as /sh, th, f, v/ versus nasals such as /m, n/) and of place-of articulation becomes more language-specific by 10 months of age. By that age, both the timing of syllable productions (Levitt et al 1992) and the intonational patterns in infant babbling (Whalen et al 1991) begin to match those of the native language. Thus, we see in babbling the emerging language-specificity we observed in perception.

The Production of Words

What is the relationship between babbling and speech? In his early writings, Jakobson (1941/1968) proposed that there is a discontinuity between babbling and speech. He argued that the sounds produced prior to meaning had no relation at all to those used once an infant attempted to produce words. Indeed, he even suggested that there was a period of silence between the babbling period and the onset of true word production in many children, and that this underlined the fact that one vocal production system was being supplanted by another. At the onset of word production, infants were believed to add sounds in a regular and systematic way, in essence filling out the structure of a formal phonological system.

More recently, it has been shown that infants do not stop babbling prior to beginning to speak. Furthermore, although the phoneme inventories used in babbling and speech may not be identical, careful transcriptions of children's production make clear that those sounds they can articulate well in babbling influence those they attempt to make when first producing words (e.g. Vihman & Miller 1988).

Although infants select sounds they are capable of articulating when attempting to produce words, there are differences between babbling and speech. First, in the initial stages of word learning children do not always produce correctly or consistently even sounds they have mastered in babbling. Indeed, children often eliminate, substitute, or mix the order of segments (e.g. Ferguson & Farwell 1975). Moreover, a child might substitute for one word a sound that she seemed unable to produce in a different setting, for example calling "dog" "gog" but calling "truck" "duck" (Gerken 1994). This variability suggests that when first learning words, infants may not "represent" all the detail found in adult speech. Indeed, it has been suggested that they may only represent sufficient information to contrast the words in their own lexicon (Menyuk et al 1979).

The obvious parallel between production and comprehension is striking, and as reported above, Stager & Werker (1997) showed that infants aged 14 months do confuse similar-sounding words in a word-object association task, which suggests that either not all the phonetic detail of the words is represented by the infant, or that the infant does not use it. Thus, both in the increasing specificity of their babbling toward the end of the first year of life and in the inconsistency of phonetic detail in early word production, we see parallels to the functional reorganizations involved in speech perception and word comprehension.

TOWARD AN EXPLANATION

Several models have been proposed to explain the data detailed above. Any complete explanation must account for the initial sensitivities shown in early infancy, the age-related changes in speech processing which occur during the first year of life, and the inattention to phonetic detail in the initial stages of word-learning. The explanations proposed to date span the spectrum from strong nativist models to extreme empiricist approaches. In this section, we review some of these models and attempt to provide a new synthesis.

Nativist and Ecological Models

According to "strong" nativist models, the initial speech perception capabilities of infants reflect a special-purpose speech-processing module, evolved to detect and analyze the essential properties of human language, available "online" early in ontogeny. The most well-known of these models is the motor theory of speech perception (Liberman & Mattingly 1985), in which specialized computational routines analyze phonetic input in terms of the potential mode of production. Research on the automatic and early coordination of heard-and-seen speech (bimodal speech perception) is seen as support for this explanation, as is evidence that the same areas of brain are activated in both the production and perception of speech (Ojemann 1991, Sams et al 1991).

To account for age-related changes in perceptual performance that reveal increased discriminability of the properties of the native language and decreased sensitivity to non-native phonemes, phonotactics, or rhythmical patterns, proponents of such approaches turn to learnability theories (e.g. Wexler & Culicover 1980). In such models, all possible parameters for language-universal rules (of the proposed device) are "given" at birth, and the contribution of specific experiences is to select some settings for the parameters and effectively "turn off" others. Thus, at birth, infants would be sensitive to both native and non-native phonetic contrasts, and experiential influence would cause those settings that correspond to the consonants and vowels used in the native language to remain activated and allow to be deactivated those that correspond to non-native phones.

Any similarity between production and perception could be easily and logically dealt with. The setting of parameters in such a module could simultaneously affect both perception and production. It is not clear what explanation would be offered to account for the inattention to phonetic detail in the early stages of word-learning, but whatever was proposed would not necessarily need to be tied to that offered to explain age related changes in perception.

Another approach, suggested by advocates of the Gibsonian ecological perspective, explains perception as direct access to the generating properties of the distal object. In the case of speech perception, information in the proximal acoustic wave form is thought to provide direct access to the articulators that produced the sounds. Thus, as in the motor theory, it is believed that perception of at least phonetic information can be explained by reference to production (Fowler & Rosenblum 1991). Furthermore, as in the motor theory, much of the bimodal speech perception research is seen as support for the viability of this approach. However, in the ecological approach, no special-purpose, built-in module need exist: The information is in the world to be "picked up directly." The experiential changes in speech perception that occur during infancy are explained by increasing attention to the specific acoustic information in the wave-form that reflects language-specific properties of vocal production (see Best 1995) for a model in this genre.

No attempt by those adopting this approach has been made to account for the dropping of phonetic detail in the initial stages of word-learning. However, as with the strong nativist approaches, the ecological model need not explain word-learning within the same framework used to explain changes in speech perception.

Evolution and Induction

According to non-nativist models, initial speech perception capabilities reflect the operation of a general auditory perceptual system, a product of mammalian evolution, and age-related changes in speech processing reflect experientially "induced " or "self-organized" systems (e.g. Kuhl 1988, Lindblom 1992). There is no exclusive specialized module or computational device built-in for the perception of speech. Instead, general-purpose auditory sensitivities are seen as contributing to speech perception, and language is said to have evolved either through phylogeny or ontogeny to take advantage of these auditory sensitivities. It is in discussions about the ways experience might induce language-specific linguistic perception that these approaches have made the most exciting advances.

One popular descriptive model of this genre is the "perceptual magnet" approach offered by Kuhl and colleagues (e.g. Kuhl 1993). The basic findings showing the existence of a native language perceptual magnet by 6 months of age were reviewed earlier. The developmental explanation Kuhl offers assumes that, even early in life, some regions in the vowel space are more stable and discriminable than others (see Lindblom 1992), yielding some initial rudimentary neural/perceptual organization to the vowel space. Repeated experience hearing certain acoustic forms (instances of vowels) more often than others remodel the perceptual space by rendering the frequently heard vowels more effective attractors.

The results from the studies of early word-learning, in which infants have been shown to ignore phonetic detail (Halle & de Boysson-Bardies 1996, Stager & Werker 1997), fit into the perceptual magnet model (PK Kuhl, personal communication). Basically, as words are established in the lexicon, the existing words act as a magnet, attracting similar-sounding words to them. Only with the establishment of additional words (following repeated exposure) would new magnets of sufficient strength to establish discrete spheres be created. Although this is an interesting descriptive model, no precise mechanism has been posited.

An approach that is attracting increasing attention is prosodic or phonological bootstrapping. This refers to the possibile existence in input speech of acoustic cues to linguistic structure, and that infants might be able to use this information to help "bootstrap" themselves into knowledge of language (Gleitman et al 1988; for a recent discussion of such phonological bootstrapping, see Morgan & Demuth 1996). A major problem to the prosodic or phonological bootstrapping theory is the lack of consistency in the information. For example, strong syllables provide good cues to word onsets in English, but only approximately 65% of English words start with strong syllables (Cutler & Carter 1987). Nevertheless, adult English speakers have learned to take advantage of this cue in word processing (e.g. Cutler & Norris 1988). Similarly, prosodic cues signaling phonological phrases correspond roughly to syntactic boundaries in English (Demuth 1996), but again, the match is far from perfect. Thus, if infants are to be able to use acoustic and phonological cues to "bootstrap" into a knowledge of language, they need to be able to take advantage of (i.e. learn from) imperfect, probabilistic information.

Recent research shows that even very young infants are indeed able to use frequency, density, and probabilistic information in input speech to establish significant linguistic knowledge (Aslin 1993). For example, in a recent study, Saffran et al (1996) showed that infants 8 months old were able to "learn" acceptable sequences of words in an artificial language when the only information they were given was probabilistic. By 10 months of age, infants learn about phonotactic acceptability on the basis of frequency of occurrence (Jusczyk et al 1993), and by 9 months of age they can use probabilistic cues in input speech to detect phonological phrase boundaries (Gerken et al (1994). In their recent work, Shi and colleagues (1998a) showed that even infants as young as 2–3 days can use probabilistic acoustic and phonological cues to distinguish between the fundamental categories of grammatical and lexical words.

These are but a few of the many demonstrations from the past few years showing an infant's ability to apply general learning techniques to use frequency and probabilistic cues to learn about the structure of his native language (Aslin 1993, Jusczyk 1997). We argue below, however, that although it is undeniable that probabilistic accounts can explain many of the important findings reviewed above, we believe there are limitations. As well, we have difficulty accepting nativist accounts without some mechanism proposed to account for the biases present in the initial state. Thus, we suggest an alternative explanation, neither fully nativist nor fully empiricist, that is more epigenetic in nature.

A Probabilistic Epigenetic Model

We propose a more epigenetic model to account for both the initial state of infant speech perception and the subsequent changes with age. To account for the sensitivities in newborn infants, we suggest there is already a history of interaction between a genetically initiated, overelaborated neural substrate and the normally invariantly occurring critical, species-specific experience (in this case, human speech). Building on Hebb's original idea (1949) about the importance of ubiquitous early experiential factors, Greenough (1986) has characterized this type of influence as involving "experience expectant" brain development. Briefly, decades of research in developmental biology have shown that genes are not deterministic, rather they express themselves in different ways depending on environmental influences (cf Gottlieb 1991). One process that appears common in early neural development is an overproduction of synapses followed by selective retention of a subset. This mechanism appears to have evolved to allow incorporation of expected experiences to re-model, or sculpt, the genetically initiated developing mechanisms that underlie a variety of perceptual and other systems (Cowan et al 1984). The experience-expectant modifications can be relied on because appropriate input is virtually always going to be present for members of the species. Furthermore, although experience-dependent changes occur throughout the life span and thus can often be redone, experience-expectant processes are time-locked, tending to occur in very early development and to result in a stable, and relatively perma-nent, platform of neural architecture (for further discussion, see Werker & Tees 1992) Psychologists would characterize the result as reflecting "innately guided learning" (e.g. Jusczyk & Bertoncini 1988).

We argue that these experience-expectant, interactive changes account for the speech-specific biases shown by the human neonate. By the sixth month of gestation in humans, the peripheral auditory system is fully functioning. However, connections between areas of the brain, and even between the sense organs and neural structures, have yet to be fully established (Kolb & Fantie 1989), and this creates a situation whereby genetic instructions for the estab-lishment of brain connections can be influenced by information arriving from the (newly functioning) peripheral auditory system. With the human voice be-ing a regular and reliable source of input to the fetus through both air and bone conduction (Moon et al 1993), the neural substrate can become organized to respond preferentially to sounds that could be produced by a human vocal tract, and to process both seen and heard speech from an early age (for a full elaboration, see Werker & Tees 1992). Similarly, preferential sensitivity to linguistic information of other kinds could result from such experience-expectant brain modifications. This resembles nativist theory, but it provides a developmental stimulation history to explain the emergence of language-general sensitivities.

To explain the tuning to the properties of the native language during the first year of life, we also suggest an epigenetic process involving changing brain structures and experiential influences. There is no question that the brain (e.g. frontal cortex) continues to mature during the first year of life (Kolb & Fantie 1989), and the organization of language and cognitive-related neural sub-strates are remodeled through both additive (i.e. experience-dependent) and subtractive (experience-expectant) processes. Experientially, the child is hear-ing speech and language and is beginning to vocalize with greater and greater control. Undoubtedly, the input from both heard speech and self-vocalizations has an impact on the emerging neural organization that may lead to a prefer-ential perceptual sensitivity to language-specific phonetic information, and perhaps to the emerging native language specificity in production. And finally, it is apparent that general experience-dependent information storage capabilities of infants are employed to detect, remember, and use both frequency and probabilistic information to learn about the phonetic, rhythmical, and syntactic properties of the native language. We would argue, however, that there are points of discontinuity, leading to the emergence of significant advances in the way infants process their native language. We suggest that epigenetic processes—the continuing transaction between developing brain and experience—are the developmental mechanism that allows the emergence of these discontinuities in perceptual processing.

As noted earlier, there is considerable evidence that infants can use probabilistic information to learn about the characteristics of their native language. However, there are many functionally important tasks to be mastered for the learning of which sensitivity to probabilistic information is insufficient. For example, in order to properly segment words from ongoing speech, infants need not only to be sensitive to language-specific phonetic detail, phonotactics, and stress patterns, they must also be able to coordinate the simultaneous use of these different sources of information. The ability to coordinate two or more sources of information emerges for the first time at approximately 9 or 10 months of age (Diamond et al 1994, Lalonde & Werker 1995). This ability is manifest in speech processing in the ability to coordinate both rhythmical and segmental information simultaneously in the detection and establishment of a "unit" (Morgan & Saffran 1995). Prior to 9 months of age, infants can use a regular SW stress pattern to pull out bisyllabic units, or they can use a regular ordering of the same two syllables to pull out such a unit (Goodsit et al 1993), but it is not until 9 or 10 months of age that they can combine both sources of information and learn to listen for a particular sequence of syllables following a particular stress pattern

With a newly found general coordinative ability, one would expect many language-specific effects to appear simultaneously. And they do. They appear in phonetic perception, in use of phonotactic detail, in preference for native-language stress patterns, and in emerging language-specificity in babbling. The emergence of such an ability can also help explain many other findings in infant speech perception. For example, the full decline in non-native consonant and vowel discrimination seen by the end of the first year of life may rest on the ability to coordinate two sources of information (Lalonde & Werker 1995). In this case, we suggest that the coordination involves information about phonetic detail with position in a word (see Pegg & Werker 1997; see also Jusczyk 1997).

What is left unexplained is which mechanism allows for the appearance of this coordinative ability by 9 to 10 months of age. It is possible, as has been shown by some computational modeling studies (MacWhinney 1998), that self-organizing systems can "jump" to new levels of analysis by the simple accumulation of probabilistic and frequency information. Although we acknowledge this is possible, we find it unlikely. Our skepticism stems primarily from the fact that so many different abilities—both within and outside the domain of speech perception— show the sudden emergence of a coordinative ability at 9 or 10 months of age. For this reason we suggest that the emergence of the ability to coordinate two sources of information rests on some common underlying change in use of information. Specifically, we propose an epigenetic advance in brain development that, once present, allows for coordinative use of information in many different domains. In earlier work, we explored the possibility that the development of prefrontal cortex and its connections might be the advance that allows the functional reorganization in phonetic perception (Diamond et al 1994).

We are not yet able to account for the decline in phonetic detail seen in the initial stages of mapping words to meaning. Yet, in the spirit of the discussion above, we propose another functional reorganization that rests on another discontinuity in development. In the initial stages of constructing a lexicon based on full referential understanding, the child may establish a new level of representation. There may be limits to the amount of information initially encoded in this new level of representation because of additional computational demands of linking sound to objects, or the limits may come from the very act of building a new representation. Although further work is needed to understand this new process, we are confident that there is a discontinuity at this point in development that requires explanation.

SUMMARY

We briefly reviewed a number of existing models that attempt to account for the initial state and age-related changes in speech perception performance during infancy. We have shown that although each explains some aspects of development, none is comprehensive. As well, although different mechanisms are proposed by each, in some ways the differences are potentially complimentary rather than contradictory. We sketched an outline of an integrated, epigenetic model to explain both the language-general sensitivities present in the newborn and the age-related changes that occur during infancy. We, like the others, have been less successful in explaining the relationship between age-related changes in speech processing and the decline in phonetic detail used in the early stages of word-learning. At one level, we can describe each as a functional reorganization in which the child drops detail as she moves on to an increasingly complex task. But at another level, it may be necessary to begin anew when one moves from processing of speech as an acoustic form to processing speech as a unit of meaning. We argue that with the establishment of a new level of representation, a discontinuity is introduced. But we predict that the language-specific processing evident by the end of the first year of life provides the child with a repertoire of sensitivities—perhaps at a different level of representation—to draw on as he fills in that representation required to map sound to communicative intent (Hockett 1954).

Together, the findings reviewed in this chapter show a remarkable preparedness for speech perception and production in the human neonate. This boost from nature enables the infant to attend selectively and efficiently to information in the speech stream and to proceed on to the rapid elaboration of perceptual and productive knowledge of the phonological and syntactic properties of the native language. By, or shortly after, a child's first birthday, the knowledge of acceptable sound and grammatical patterning in the native language is present. The task for the next year of life is to construct a second-order system to effortlessly and efficiently use the medium of speech to map on to meaning.

ACKNOWLEDGMENTS

This work was supported by the Natural Sciences and Engineering Research Council of Canada (OGP0001103 to JF Werker and OGP000179 to RC Tees). We also thank M Bhatnagar, J Pegg, and C Stager for their assistance and comment on the text and figures.

> Visit the *Annual Reviews home page* at
> http://www.AnnualReviews.org.

Literature Cited

Aslin RN 1993. Segmentation of fluent speech into words: learning models and the role of maternal input. See de Boysson-Bardies et al 1993, pp. 305–16

Aslin RN, Pisoni DB, Hennessy BL, Perey AJ. 1981. Discrimination of voice onset time by human infants: new findings and implications for the effects of early experience. *Child Dev.* 52:1135–45

Best CT. 1995. Learning to perceive the sound patterns of English. In *Advances in Infancy Research*, ed. C Rovee-Collier, LP Lipsitt, pp. 217–304. Norwood, NJ: Ablex

Best CT, McRoberts GW, Sithole NM. 1988. Examination of the perceptual re-organization for speech contrasts: Zulu click discrimination by English-speaking adults and infants. *J. Exp. Psychol. Hum. Percept. Perform.* 14:345–60

Bosch L, Sebastian-Galles N. 1997. Native-language recognition abilities in 4-month-old infants from monolingual and bilingual environments. *Cognition* 65:33–69

Chomsky N. 1975. *Reflections on Language.* New York: Random House

Christophe A, Dupoux E, Bertoncini J, Mehler J. 1994. Do infants perceive word boundaries? An empirical approach to the bootstrapping problem for lexical acquisition. *J. Acoust. Soc. Am.* 95:1570–80

Christophe A, Guasti T, Nespor M, Dupoux E, Van Ooyen B. 1997. Reflections on phonological bootstrapping: its role for lexical and syntactic acquisition. *Lang. Cogn. Proc.* 12:585–612

Cowan WM, Fawcett JW, O'Leary DDM, Stanfield BB. 1984. Regressive events in neurogenesis. *Science* 225:1258–65

Cutler A, Carter DM. 1987. The predominance of strong initial syllables in the English vocabulary. *Comput. Speech Lang.* 2:133–42

Cutler A, Norris D. 1988. The role of strong syllables in segmentation for lexical access. *J. Exp. Psychol. Hum. Percept. Perform.* 14:113–21

de Boysson-Bardies B, Halle P, Sagart L, Durand C. 1989. A cross-linguistic investigation of vowel formants in babbling. *J. Child Lang.* 16:1–17

de Boysson-Bardies B, Jusczyk P, McNeilage

P, Morton J, eds. 1993. *Developmental Neurocognition: Speech and Face Processing in the First Year of Life.* Norwell, MA: Kluwer

de Boysson-Bardies B, Vihman MM. 1991. Adaptation to language: Evidence from babbling and first words in four languages. *Language* 67:297–319

Demuth K. 1996. The prosodic structure of early words. See Morgan & Demuth 1996, pp. 171–84

Desjardins R, Werker JF. 1996. Four month old infants are influenced by visible speech. *Infant Behav. Dev.* 19:762

Desjardins RN, Rogers J, Werker JF. 1997. An exploration of why preschoolers perform differently than do adults in audiovisual speech perception tasks. *J. Exp. Child Psychol.* 66:85–110

Diamond A, Werker JF, Lalonde CE. 1994. Toward understanding commonalties in the development of object search, detour navigation, categorization, and speech perception. See Fischer & Dawson 1994, pp. 380–426

Eilers R, Oller DK. 1976. The role of speech discriminations in developmental sound substitutions. *J. Child Lang.* 3:319–29

Eimas PD. 1974. Auditory and linguistic processing of cues for place of articulation by infants. *Percept. Psychophysiol.* 16:513–21

Eimas PD, Siqueland ER, Jusczyk PW, Vigorito J. 1971. Speech perception in infants. *Science* 171:303–6

Ferguson CA, Farwell CB. 1975. Words and sounds in early language acquisition. *Language* 51:419–39

Fischer KW, Dawson G, eds. 1994. *Human Behavior and the Developing Brain.* New York: Guilford

Fowler CA, Rosenblum LD. 1991. Perception of the phonetic gesture. In *Modularity and the Motor Theory,* ed. IG Mattingly, M Studdert-Kennedy, pp. 33–59. Hillsdale, NJ: Erlbaum

Gerken LA. 1994. Child phonology: past research, present questions, future directions. In *Handbook of Psycholinguistics,* ed. MA Gernsbacher, pp. 781–820. New York: Academic

Gerken LA, Jusczyk PW, Mandel DR. 1994. When prosody fails to cue syntactic structure: nine-month-olds' sensitivity to phonological vs. syntactic phrases. *Cognition* 51:237–65

Gleitman L, Gleitman H, Landau B, Wanner E. 1988. Where the learning begins: initial representations for language learning. In *The Cambridge Linguistic Survey,* ed. F Newmeyer, 3:150–93. Cambridge, MA: Harvard Univ. Press

Goodsit JV, Morgan JL, Kuhl PK. 1993. Perceptual strategies in prelingual speech segmentation. *J. Child Lang.* 20:229–52

Gottlieb G. 1991. Experiential canalization of behavioral development: theory. *Dev. Psychol.* 27:4–13

Green KP. 1998. The use of auditory and visual information in phonetic perception. In *Speech Reading by Humans and Machines,* ed. D Stork, ME Henneck. Berlin: Springer-Verlag. In press

Greenough WT. 1986. What's special about development? Thoughts on the bases of experience-sensitive plasticity. See Greenough & Juraska 1986, pp. 387–407

Greenough WT, Juraska JM. 1986. *Developmental Neuropsychobiology.* Orlando, FL: Academic

Grieser D, Kuhl PK. 1989. Categorization of speech by infants: support for speech-sound prototypes. *Dev. Psychol.* 25:577–88

Halle PA, de Boysson-Bardies B. 1996. The format of representation of recognized words in infants' early receptive lexicon. *Infant Behav. Dev.* 19:463–81

Hebb DO. 1949. *The Organization of Behavior.* New York: Wiley

Hirsh-Pasek K, Kemler Nelson DG, Jusczyk PW, Cassidy KW, Druss B, Kennedy L. 1987. Clauses are perceptual for young infants. *Cognition* 26:269–86

Hockett, CA. 1954. Two models of grammatical description. *Word* 10:210–31

Jakobson R. 1941. *Child Language, Aphasia and Phonological Universals.* Transl. A Keller, 1968. The Hague, Netherlands: Mouton

Jusczyk PW. 1997. *The Discovery of Spoken Language.* Cambridge MA: MIT Press

Jusczyk PW, Aslin RN. 1995. Infants' detection of the sound patterns of words in fluent speech. *Cogn. Psychol.* 29:1–23

Jusczyk PW, Bertoncini J. 1988. Viewing the development of speech perception as an innately guided learning process. *Lang. Speech* 31:217–35

Jusczyk PW, Cutler A, Redanz N. 1993. Preference for the predominant stress patterns of English words. *Child Dev.* 64:675–87

Jusczyk PW, Hohne EA. 1997. Infants' memory for spoken words. *Science* 277:1984–86

Kelly M. 1992. Using sound to solve syntactic problems: the role of phonology in grammatical category assignments. *Psychol. Rev.* 9:349

Kent RD, Murray AD. 1982. Acoustic features of infant vocalic utterances at 3, 6, and 9 months. *J. Acoust. Soc. Am.* 72:353–65

Kolb B, Fantie B. 1989. Development of

child's brain and behavior. In *Handbook of Clinical Child Neuropsychology*, ed. CR Reynolds, E Fletcher-Janzen, pp. 17–39. New York: Plenum

Kuhl PK. 1979. Speech perception in early infancy: perceptual constancy for spectrally dissimilar vowel categories. *J. Acoust. Soc. Am.* 66:1168–79

Kuhl PK. 1988. Auditory perception and the evolution of speech. *Hum. Evol.* 3(1–2): 19–43

Kuhl PK. 1993. Innate predispositions and the effects of experience in speech perception: the native language magnet theory. See de Boysson-Bardies et al 1993, pp. 259–74

Kuhl PK. 1998. Effects of language experience on speech perception. *J. Acoust. Soc. Am.* 103(5):2931

Kuhl PK, Meltzoff AN. 1982. The bimodal perception of speech in infancy. *Science* 218:1138–41

Kuhl PK, Williams KA, Lacerda F, Stevens KN, Lindblom B. 1992. Linguistic experiences alters phonetic perception in infants by 6 months of age. *Science* 255:606–8

Lalonde C, Werker JF. 1995. Cognitive influences on cross-language speech perception in infancy. *Infant Behav. Dev.* 18:459–76

Levitt AG, Utman J, Aydelott J. 1992. From babbling towards the systems of English and French: a longitudinal two-case study. *J. Child Lang.* 19:19–49

Liberman AM, Mattingly IG. 1985. The motor theory of speech perception revised. *Cognition* 21:1–36

Lindblom B. 1992. Phonological units as adaptive emergents of lexical development. In *Phonological Development: Models, Research, Implications*, ed. CA Ferguson, L Menn, C Stoel Gammon, pp. 131–63. Timonium, MD: York

Locke JL. 1983. *Phonological Acquisition and Change*. New York: Academic

MacKain KS, Best CT, Strange W. 1981. Categorical perception of English /r/ and /l/ by Japanese bilinguals. *Appl. Psycholinguist.* 2:369–90

MacWhinney B. 1998. Models of the emergence of language. *Annu. Rev. Psychol.* 49: 199–227

Mandel DR, Jusczyk PW, Pisoni DB. 1995. Infants' recognition of the sound patterns of their own names. *Psychol. Sci.* 6:315–18

Massaro DW, Cohen MM, Gesi A, Heredia R, Tsuzaki M. 1993. Bimodal speech perception: an examination across languages. *J. Phon.* 21:445–78

Mazuka R. 1996. Can a grammatical parameter be set before the first word? Prosodic contributions to early setting of a grammatical parameter. See Morgan & Demuth 1996, pp. 313–30

McGurk H, MacDonald J. 1976. Hearing lips and seeing voices. *Nature* 264:746–48

Mehler J, Christophe A. 1994. Language in the infant's mind. *Philos. Trans. R. Soc. London Ser. B* 346:13–20

Mehler J, Juczyk PW, Lambertz G, Halsted N, Bertoncini J, et al. 1988. A precursor of language acquisition in young infants. *Cognition* 29:144–78

Menyuk P, Menn L, Silber R. 1979. Early strategies for the perception and production of words and sounds. In *Studies in Language "Acquisition,"* ed. P Fletcher, M Garman, pp. 198–222. Cambridge, MA: Cambridge Univ. Press

Mills DL, Coffey-Corina SA, Neville HJ. 1994. Variability in cerebral organization during primary language acquisition. See Fischer & Dawson 1994, pp. 427–55

Moon C, Cooper RP, Fifer WP. 1993. Two-day old infants prefer native language. *Infant Behav. Dev.* 16:495–500

Morgan JL, Demuth K, eds. 1996. *Signal to Syntax: Bootstrapping from Speech to Grammer in Early Acquisition*. Mahwah, NJ: Erlbaum

Morgan JL, Saffran JR. 1995. Emerging integration of sequential and suprasegmental information in prelingual speech segmentation. *Child Dev.* 66:911–36

Nazzi T, Bertoncini J, Mehler J. 1998. Language discrimination by newborns: towards an understanding of the role of rhythm. *J. Exp. Psychol. Hum. Percept. Perform.* In press

Nespor M, Vogel I. 1986. *Prosodic Phonology*. Dordrecht, Netherlands: Foris

Ojemann GA. 1991. Cortical organization of language. *J. Neurosci.* 11:2281–87

Oller DK. 1980. The emergence of speech sounds in infancy. In *Child Phonology*, ed. GH Yeni-Komshian, JF Kavanagh, CA Ferguson, pp. 92–112. New York: Academic

Patterson ML, Werker JF. 1998. Matching phonetic information in lips and voice by 40-month-old infants. Poster presented at 11th Bienn. Int. Conf. Infant Stud., Atlanta, GA

Pegg JE, Werker JF. 1997. Adult and infant perception of two English phones. *J. Acoust. Soc. Am.* 102:3742–53

Pisoni DB, Aslin RN, Perey AJ, Hennessy BL. 1982. Some effects of laboratory training on identification and discrimination of voicing contrasts in stop consonants. *J. Exp. Psychol. Hum. Percept. Perform.* 8: 297–314

Polka L, Bohn O-S. 1996. A cross-language

comparison of vowel perception in English-learning and German-learning infants. *J. Acoust. Soc. Am.* 100:577–92

Polka L, Werker JF. 1994. Developmental changes in perception of non-native vowel contrasts. *J. Exp. Psychol. Hum. Percept. Perform.* 20:421–35

Rosenblum LD, Schmuckler MA, Johnson JA. 1997. The McGurk effect in infants. *Percept. Psychophysiol.* 59:347–57

Saffran JR, Aslin RN, Newport EL. 1996. Statistical learning by 8-month old infants. *Science* 274:1926–28

Sams M, Aulanko R, Hamalainen M, Mari R, Lounsamaa OV. 1991. Seeing speech: visual information from lip movements modifies activity in the human auditory cortex. *Neurosci. Lett.* 127:141–45

Shi R, Morgan JL, Allopenna P. 1998a. Phonological and acoustic bases for earliest grammatical category assignment. A cross-linguistic persepctive. *J. Child Lang.* 25:169–201

Shi R, Werker JF, Morgan JL. 1998b. Young infants' perception of lexical and functional categories. Poster presented at 11th Bienn. Int. Conf. Infant Stud., Atlanta, GA

Siva N, Stevens EB, Kuhl PK, Meltzoff AN. 1995. A comparison between cerebralpalsied and normal adults in the perceptions of auditory-visual illusions. *J. Acoust. Soc. Am.* 98:2983

Stager CL, Werker JF. 1997. Infants listen for more phonetic detail in speech perception than in word learning tasks. *Nature* 388: 381–82

Strange W, Jenkins JJ. 1978. Role of linguistic experience in the perception of speech. In *Perception and Experience*, ed. RD Walk, HL Pick, pp. 125–69. New York: Plenum

Streeter LA. 1976. Language perception of 2-month old infants shows effects of both innate mechanisms and experience. *Nature* 259:39–41

Tees RC. 1986. Experience and visual development: behavioral evidence. See Greenough & Juraska 1986, pp. 317–61

Tees RC, Werker JF. 1984. Perceptual flexibility: maintenance or recovery of the ability to discriminate non-native speech sounds. *Can. J. Psychol.* 38:579–90

Trehub SE. 1973. Infants' sensitivity to vowel and tonal contrasts. *Dev. Psychol.* 9:91–96

Trehub SE. 1976. The discrimination of foreign speech contrasts by infants and adults. *Child Dev.* 47:466–72

Vihman MM, Miller R. 1988. *Word*s and babble at the threshold of language acquisition. In *The Emergent Lexicon*, ed. MD

Smith, JL Locke, pp. 151–83. New York: Academic

Werker JF. 1995. Exploring developmental changes in cross-language speech perception. In *An Invitation to Cognitive Science.* Part I: *Language*, ed. L Gleitman, M Liberman, pp. 87–106. Cambridge, MA: MIT Press

Werker JF, Cohen LB, Lloyd V, Stager C, Cassosola M. 1998a. Acquisition of word-object associations by 14-month-old infants. *Dev. Psychol.* In press

Werker JF, Gilbert JHV, Humphrey K, Tees RC. 1981. Developmental aspects of cross-language speech perception. *Child Dev.* 52:349–55

Werker JF, Lalonde CE. 1988. Cross-language speech perception: initial capabilities and developmental change. *Dev. Psychol.* 24: 672–83

Werker JF, McGurk HE, Frost P. 1992. La langue et les lévres: cross-language influences on bimodal speech perception. *Can. J. Psychol.* 46:551–68

Werker JF, Shi R, Desjardins R, Pegg JE, Polka L, et al. 1998b. Three methods for testing infant speech perception. In *Perceptual Development: Visual, Auditory, and Speech Perception in Infancy*, ed. AM Slater. London: Univ. Coll. London Press. In press

Werker JF, Stager C. 1998. Developmental changes in infant speech perception and early word learning. Is there a link? In *Papers in Laboratory Phonology*, ed. M Broe, J Peirre-Humbert. Cambridge, UK: Cambridge Univ. Press. In press

Werker JF, Tees RC. 1983. Developmental changes across childhood in the perception of non-native speech sounds. *Can. J. Psychol.* 37(2):278–86

Werker JF, Tees RC. 1984a. Cross-language speech perception: evidence for perceptual reorganization during the first year of life. *Infant Behav. Dev.* 7:49–63

Werker JF, Tees RC. 1984b. Phonemic and phonetic factors in adult cross-language speech perception. *J. Acoust. Soc. Am.* 75: 1866–78

Werker JF, Tees RC. 1992. The organization and reorganization of human speech perception. *Annu. Rev. Neurosci.* 15:377–402

Wexler K, Culicover P. 1980. *Formal Principles of Language Acquisition.* Cambridge, MA: MIT Press

Whalen DH, Levitt A, Wang Q. 1991. International differences the reduplicative babbling of French- and English-learning infants. *J. Child Lang.* 18:501–6

Annu. Rev. Psychol. 1999. 50:537–67

SURVEY RESEARCH

Jon A. Krosnick

Department of Psychology, Ohio State University, Columbus, Ohio 43210;
e-mail: krosnick@osu.edu

KEY WORDS: surveys, interviewing, polls, questionnaires, pretesting

ABSTRACT

For the first time in decades, conventional wisdom about survey methodology is being challenged on many fronts. The insights gained can not only help psychologists do their research better but also provide useful insights into the basics of social interaction and cognition. This chapter reviews some of the many recent advances in the literature, including the following: New findings challenge a long-standing prejudice against studies with low response rates; innovative techniques for pretesting questionnaires offer opportunities for improving measurement validity; surprising effects of the verbal labels put on rating scale points have been identified, suggesting optimal approaches to scale labeling; respondents interpret questions on the basis of the norms of everyday conversation, so violations of those conventions introduce error; some measurement error thought to have been attributable to social desirability response bias now appears to be due to other factors instead, thus encouraging different approaches to fixing such problems; and a new theory of satisficing in questionnaire responding offers parsimonious explanations for a range of response patterns long recognized by psychologists and survey researchers but previously not well understood.

CONTENTS

0084-6570/99/0201-0537$08.00

INTRODUCTION

These are exciting times for survey research. The literature is bursting with new insights that demand dramatic revisions in the conventional wisdom that has guided this research method for decades. Such dramatic revisions are nothing new for survey researchers, who are quite experienced with being startled by an unexpected turn of events that required changing their standard practice. Perhaps the best known such instance involved surveys predicting US election outcomes, which had done reasonably well at the start of the twentieth century (Robinson 1932). But in 1948 the polls predicted a Dewey victory in the race for the American presidency, whereas Truman actually won easily (Mosteller et al 1949). At fault were the nonsystematic methods used to generate samples of respondents, so we learned that representative sampling methods are essential to permit confident generalization of results.

Such sampling methods soon came into widespread use, and survey researchers settled into a "standard practice" that has stood relatively unchallenged until recently (for lengthy discussions of the method, see Babbie 1990; Lavrakas 1993; Weisberg et al 1996). This standard practice included not only the notion that systematic, representative sampling methods must be used, but also that high response rates must be obtained and statistical weighting procedures must be imposed to maximize representativeness. Furthermore, although face-to-face interviewing was thought to be the optimal method, the practicalities of telephone interviewing made it the dominant mode since the mid-1980s. Self-administered mail surveys were clearly undesirable, because they typically obtained low response rates. And although a few general rules guided questionnaire design (e.g. Parten 1950), most researchers viewed it as more of an art than a science. There is no best way to design a question, said proponents of this view; although different phrasings or formats might yield different results, all are equally informative in providing insights into the minds of respondents.

Today, this conventional wisdom is facing challenges from many directions. We have a refreshing opportunity to rethink how best to implement surveys and enhance the value of research findings generated using this method. This movement has three valuable implications for psychology. First, researchers who use the survey method to study psychological phenomena stand to benefit, because they can enhance the validity of their substantive results by using new methodologies, informed by recent lessons learned. Second, these insights provide opportunities to reconsider past studies, possibly leading to recognize that some apparent findings were illusions. Third, many recent lessons provide insights into the workings of the human mind and the unfolding of social interaction. Thus, these insights contribute directly to the building of basic psychological theory.

Because recent insights are so voluminous, this chapter can describe only a few, leaving many important ones to be described in future *Annual Review of Psychology* chapters. One significant innovation has been the incorporation of experiments within surveys, thus permitting strong causal inference with data from representative samples. Readers may learn about this development from a chapter in the *Annual Review of Sociology* (Sniderman & Grob 1996). The other revelations, insights, and innovations discussed here are interesting because they involve the overturning of long-standing ideas or the resolution of mysteries that have stumped researchers for decades. They involve sampling and response rates, questionnaire pretesting, interviewing, and questionnaire design.

SAMPLING AND RESPONSE RATES

One hallmark of survey research is a concern with representative sampling. Scholars have, for many years, explored various methods for generating samples representative of populations, and the family of techniques referred to as probability sampling methods do so quite well (e.g. Henry 1990, Kish 1965). Many notable inaccuracies of survey findings were attributable to the failure to employ such techniques (e.g. Laumann et al 1994, Mosteller et al 1949). Consequently, the survey research community believes that representative sampling is essential to permit generalization from a sample to a population.

Survey researchers have also believed that, for a sample to be representative, the survey's response rate must be high. However, most telephone surveys have difficulty achieving response rates higher than 60%, and most face-to-face surveys have difficulty achieving response rates higher than 70% (Brehm 1993). Response rates for most major American national surveys have been falling during the last four decades (Brehm 1993, Steeh 1981), so surveys often stop short of the goal of a perfect response rate.

In even the best academic surveys, there are significant biases in the demographic and attitudinal composition of samples obtained. Brehm (1993) showed that, in the two leading, academic national public-opinion surveys (the National Election Studies and the General Social Surveys), certain demographic groups have been routinely represented in misleading numbers. Young and old adults, males, and people with the highest income levels are underrepresented, whereas people with the lowest education levels are overrepresented. Likewise, Smith (1983) found that people who do not participate in surveys are likely to live in big cities and work long hours. And Cialdini et al (unpublished manuscript) found that people who agreed to be interviewed were likely to believe it is their social responsibility to participate in surveys, to believe that they could influence government and the world around them, and to be happy with their lives. They were also unlikely to have been contacted frequently to participate in surveys, to feel resentful about being asked a personal question by a stranger, and to feel that the next survey in which they will be asked to participate will be a disguised sales pitch. According to conventional wisdom, the higher the response rate, the less these and other sorts of biases should be manifest in the obtained data.

In the extreme, a sample will be nearly perfectly representative of a population if a probability sampling method is used and if the response rate is 100%. But it is not necessarily true that representativeness increases monotonically with increasing response rate. Remarkably, recent research has shown that surveys with very low response rates can be more accurate than surveys with much higher response rates. For example, Visser et al (1996) compared the accuracy of self-administered mail surveys and telephone surveys forecasting the outcomes of Ohio statewide elections over a 15-year period. Although the mail surveys had response rates of about 20% and the telephone surveys had response rates of about 60%, the mail surveys predicted election outcomes much more accurately (average error = 1.6%) than did the telephone surveys (average error = 5.2%). The mail surveys also documented voter demographic characteristics more accurately. Therefore, having a low response rate does not necessarily mean that a survey suffers from a large amount of nonresponse error.

Greenwald et al (AG Greenwald, unpublished manuscript) suggested one possible explanation for this finding. They conducted telephone surveys of general public samples just before elections and later checked official records to determine whether each respondent voted. The more difficult it was to contact a person to be interviewed, the less likely he or she was to have voted. Therefore, the more researchers work at boosting the response rate, the less representative the sample becomes. Thus, telephone surveys would forecast election outcomes more accurately by accepting lower response rates, rather than aggressively pursuing high response rates.

Studies of phenomena other than voting have shown that achieving higher response rates or correcting for sample composition bias do not necessarily translate into more accurate results. In an extensive set of analyses, Brehm (1993) found that statistically correcting for demographic biases in sample composition had little impact on the substantive implications of correlational analyses. Furthermore, the substantive conclusions of a study have often remained unaltered by an improved response rate (e.g. Pew Research Center 1998, Traugott et al 1987). When substantive findings did change, no evidence allowed researchers to assess whether findings were more accurate with the higher response rate or the lower one (e.g. Traugott et al 1987). In light of Visser et al's (1996) evidence, we should not presume the latter findings were less valid than the former.

Clearly, the prevailing wisdom that high response rates are necessary for sample representativeness is being challenged. It is important to recognize the inherent limitations of nonprobability sampling methods and to draw conclusions about populations or differences between populations tentatively when nonprobability sampling methods are used. But when probability sampling methods are used, it is no longer sensible to presume that lower response rates necessarily signal lower representativeness.

PRETESTING

Questionnaire pretesting identifies questions that respondents have difficulty understanding or interpret differently than the researcher intended. Until recently, conventional pretesting procedures were relatively simplistic. Interviewers conducted a small number of interviews (usually 15–25), then discussed their experiences in a debriefing session (e.g. Bischoping 1989, Nelson 1985). They described problems they encountered (e.g. identifying questions requiring further explanation or wording that was confusing or difficult to read) and their impressions of the respondents' experiences in answering the questions. Researchers also looked for questions that many people declined to answer, which might suggest the questions were badly written. Researchers then modified the survey instrument to increase the likelihood that the meaning of each item was clear and that the interviews proceeded smoothly.

Conventional pretesting clearly has limitations. What constitutes a "problem" in the survey interview is often defined rather loosely, so there is potential for considerable variance across interviewers in terms of what is reported during debriefing sessions. Debriefings are relatively unstructured, which might further contribute to variance in interviewers' reports. And most important, researchers want to know about what went on in respondents' minds when answering questions, and interviewers are not well positioned to characterize such processes.

Recent years have seen a surge of interest in alternative pretesting methods, one of which is *behavior coding* (Cannell et al 1981, Fowler & Cannell 1996), in which an observer monitors pretest interviews (either live or taped) and notes events that occur during interactions between interviewers and respondents that constitute deviations from the script (e.g. the interviewer misreads the questionnaire, or the respondent asks for more information or provides an unclear or incomplete initial response). Questions that elicit frequent deviations are presumed to require modification.

Another new method is *cognitive pretesting*, which involves asking respondents to "think aloud" while answering questions, verbalizing whatever comes to mind as they formulate responses (e.g. Bickart & Felcher 1996, DeMaio & Rothgeb 1996, Forsyth & Lessler 1991). This procedure is designed to assess the cognitive processes by which respondents answer questions, thus providing insight into the way each item is comprehended and the strategies used to devise answers. Respondent confusion and misunderstandings can readily be identified in this way.

These three pretesting methods focus on different aspects of the survey data collection process and differ in terms of the kinds of problems they detect, as well as in the reliability with which they detect these problems. Presser & Blair (1994) demonstrated that behavior coding is quite consistent in detecting apparent respondent difficulties and interviewer problems. Conventional pretesting also detects both sorts of problems, but less reliably. In fact, the correlation between the apparent problems diagnosed in independent conventional pretesting trials of the same questionnaire can be remarkably low. Cognitive interviews also tend to exhibit low reliability across trials and to detect respondent difficulties almost exclusively. But low reliability might reflect the capacity of a particular method to continue to reveal additional, equally valid problems across pretesting iterations, a point that future research must address.

RIGID INTERVIEWING VERSUS CONVERSATIONAL INTERVIEWING

One prevailing principle of the survey method is that the same questionnaire should be administered identically to all respondents (e.g. Fowler & Mangione 1990). If questions are worded or delivered differently to different people, then researchers cannot be certain about whether differences between the answers are due to real differences between the respondents or are due to the differential measurement techniques employed. Since the beginning of survey research this century, interviewers have been expected to read questions exactly as researchers wrote them, identically for all respondents. If respondents expressed uncertainty and asked for help, interviewers avoided interference by saying something like "it means whatever it means to you."

Some critics have charged that this approach compromises data quality instead of enhancing it (Briggs 1986, Mishler 1986, Suchman & Jordan 1990, 1992). In particular, they have argued that the meanings of many questions are inherently ambiguous and are negotiated in everyday conversation through back-and-forth exchanges between questioners and answerers. To prohibit such exchanges is to straight-jacket them, preventing precisely what is needed to maximize response validity. Schober & Conrad (1997) recently reported the first convincing data on this point, demonstrating that when interviewers were free to clarify the meanings of questions and response choices, the validity of reports increased substantially.

This finding has important implications for technological innovations in questionnaire administration. Whereas survey questionnaires were traditionally printed on paper, most large-scale survey organizations have been using computer-assisted telephone interviewing (CATI) for the last decade. Interviewers read questions displayed on a computer screen; responses are entered immediately into the computer; and the computer determines the sequence of questions to be asked. This system can reduce some types of interviewer error and permits researchers to vary the specific questions each participant is asked on the basis of previous responses.

All this has taken another step forward recently: Interviewers conducting surveys in people's homes are equipped with laptop computers (for computer-assisted personal interviewing, or CAPI), and the entire data collection process is regulated by computer programs. In audio computer-assisted self-administered interviewing (audio CASAI), a computer reads questions aloud to respondents who listen on headphones and type their answers on computer keyboards. Thus, computers have replaced interviewers. Although these innovations have clear advantages for improving the quality and efficiency of questionnaire administration, this last shift may be problematic in light of Schober & Conrad's (1997) evidence that conversational interviewing can significantly improve data quality. Perhaps technological innovation has gone one step too far, because without a live interviewer, conversational questioning is impossible.

QUESTIONNAIRE DESIGN

Open versus Closed Questions

During the 1940s, a major dispute erupted between two survey research divisions of the US Bureau of Intelligence, the Division of Polls and the Division of Program Surveys. The former was firmly committed to asking closed-ended questions, which required people to choose among a set of provided response alternatives. The latter believed in the use of open-ended questions, which respondents answered in their own words (see Converse 1987). Paul Lazarsfeld mediated the dispute and concluded that the quality of data collected by each method seemed equivalent, so the greater cost of administering open-ended questions did not seem worthwhile (see Converse 1987). Over time, closed-ended questions have become increasingly popular, whereas open-ended questions have been asked less frequently (Smith 1987).

Recent research has shown that there are distinct disadvantages to closed-ended questions, and open-ended questions are not as problematic as they seemed. For example, respondents tend to confine their answers to the choices offered, even if the researcher does not wish them to do so (Bishop et al 1988, Presser 1990). That is, people generally ignore the opportunity to volunteer a response and simply select among those listed, even if the best answer is not included. Therefore, a closed-ended question can only be used effectively if its answer choices are comprehensive, and this is difficult to assure.

Some people feared that open-ended questions would not work well for respondents who are not especially articulate, because they might have difficulty explaining their feelings. However, this seems not to be a problem (Geer 1988). Some people feared that respondents would be likely to answer open-ended questions by mentioning the most salient possible responses, not those that are truly most appropriate. But this, too, turns out not to be the case (Schuman et al 1986). Finally, a number of recently rediscovered studies found that the reliability and validity of open-ended questions exceeded that of closed-ended questions (e.g. Hurd 1932, Remmers et al 1923). Thus, open-ended questions seem to be more viable research tools than had seemed to be the case.

Labeling of Rating-Scale Points

Questionnaires have routinely offered rating scales with only the endpoints labeled with words and the points in between either represented graphically or labeled with numbers and not words. However, reliability and validity can be significantly improved if all points on the scale are labeled with words, because they clarify the meanings of the scale points (Krosnick & Berent 1993, Peters & McCormick 1966). Respondents report being more satisfied when more rating-scale points are verbally labeled (e.g. Dickinson & Zellinger 1980), and validity is maximized when the verbal labels have meanings that divide the continuum into approximately equal-sized perceived units (e.g. Klockars & Yamagishi 1988). On some rating dimensions, respondents presume that a "normal" or "typical" person falls in the middle of the scale, and some people are biased toward placing themselves near that point, regardless of the labels used to define it (Schwarz et al 1985).

Another recent surprise is that the numbers used by researchers to label rating-scale points can have unanticipated effects. Although such numbers are usually selected arbitrarily (e.g. an 11-point scale is labeled from 0 to 10, rather than from -5 to +5), respondents sometimes presume that these numbers were selected to communicate intended meanings of the scale points (e.g. a unipolar rating for the 0 to 10 scale and a bipolar rating for the -5 to +5 scale; Schwarz et al 1991). Consequently, a change in the numbering scheme can produce a systematic shift in responses. This suggests either that rating-scale points should be labeled only with words or that numbers should reinforce the meanings of the words, rather than communicate conflicting meanings.

Conversational Conventions

Survey researchers have come to recognize that respondents infer the meanings of questions and response choices partly from norms and expectations concerning how everyday conversations are normally conducted (Schwarz 1996). Speakers conform to a set of conventions regarding what to say, how to say it, and what not to say; these conventions make conversation efficient by allowing speakers to convey unspoken ideas underlying their utterances (e.g. Clark 1996, Grice 1975). Furthermore, listeners presume that speakers are conforming to these norms when interpreting utterances. Respondents bring these same conventions to bear when they interpret survey questions, as well as when they formulate answers (see Schwarz 1996).

Krosnick et al (1990) showed that the order in which information is provided in the stem of a question is sometimes viewed as providing information about the importance or value the researcher attaches to each piece of information. Specifically, respondents presume that researchers provide less important "background" information first and then present more significant "foreground" information later. Consequently, respondents place more weight on more recently presented information because they wish to conform to the researcher's beliefs. From these studies and various others (see Schwarz 1996), we now know that we must guard against the possibility of unwittingly communicating information to respondents by violating conversational conventions, thus biasing answers.

Social Desirability Bias

One well-known phenomenon in survey research is overreporting of admirable attitudes and behaviors and underreporting those that are not socially respected. For example, the percentage of survey respondents who say they voted in the last election is usually greater than the percentage of the population that actually voted (Clausen 1968, Granberg & Holmberg 1991, Traugott & Katosh 1979). Furthermore, claims by significant numbers of people that they voted are not corroborated by official records. These patterns have been interpreted as evidence that respondents intentionally reported voting when they did not, because voting is more admirable than not doing so.

In fact, these two empirical patterns are not fully attributable to intentional misrepresentation. The first of the discrepancies is partly due to inappropriate calculations of population turnout rates, and the second discrepancy is partly caused by errors in assessments of the official records (Clausen 1968, Presser et al 1990). The first discrepancy also occurs partly because people who refuse to be interviewed for surveys are disproportionately unlikely to vote (Greenwald et al, unpublished manuscript) and pre-election interviews increase interest in politics and elicit commitments to vote, which become self-fulfilling prophecies (Greenwald et al 1987, Yalch 1976). But even after controlling for all these factors, some people still claim to have voted when they did not.

Surprisingly, recent research suggests that the widely believed explanation for this fact may be wrong. Attempts to make people comfortable admitting that they did not vote have been unsuccessful in reducing overreporting (e.g. Abelson et al 1992, Presser 1990). People who typically overreport also have the characteristics of habitual voters and indeed have histories of voting in the past, even though not in the most recent election (Abelson et al 1992, Sigelman 1982, Silver et al 1986). And the accuracy of turnout reports decreases as time passes between an election and a postelection interview, suggesting that the inaccuracy occurs because memory traces of the behavior or lack thereof fade (Abelson et al 1992).

Most recently, Belli et al (unpublished manuscript) significantly reduced overreporting by explicitly alerting respondents to potential memory confusion and encouraging them to think carefully to avoid such confusion. These instructions had increasingly beneficial effects on report accuracy as more time passed between election day and an interview. This suggests that what researchers have assumed is intentional misrepresentation by respondents may be at least partly attributable instead to accidental mistakes in recall. This encourages us to pause before presuming that measurement error is due to intentional misrepresentation, even when it is easy to imagine why respondents might intentionally lie. More generally, social desirability bias in questionnaire measurement may be less prevalent than has been assumed.

Optimizing versus Satisficing

Another area of innovation involves new insights into the cognitive processes by which respondents generate answers. These insights have been publicized in a series of recent publications (e.g. Krosnick & Fabrigar 1998, Sudman et al 1996, Tourangeau et al 1998), and some of them have provided parsimonious explanations for long-standing puzzles in the questionnaire design literature. The next section reviews developments in one segment of this literature, focusing on the distinction between optimizing and satisficing.

OPTIMIZING   There is wide agreement about the cognitive processes involved when respondents answer questions optimally (e.g. Cannell et al 1981, Schwarz & Strack 1985, Tourangeau & Rasinski 1988). First, respondents must interpret the question and deduce its intent. Next, they must search their memories for relevant information and then integrate that information into a single judgment (if more than one consideration is recalled). Finally, they must translate the judgment into a response by selecting one of the alternatives offered.

Each of these four steps can be quite complex, involving a great deal of cognitive work (e.g. Krosnick & Fabrigar 1998). For example, question interpretation can be decomposed into four cognitive steps, guided by a complex and extensive set of rules (e.g. Clark & Clark 1977). First, respondents bring the sounds of the words into their "working memories." Second, they break the words down into groups, each one representing a single concept, settling on the meaning of each. If multiple interpretations exist, listeners apparently select one interpretation and proceed ahead with it, revising later only if it leads to implausible or incomprehensible conclusions. Third, respondents build the meaning of the entire question by establishing the relations among the concepts. Finally, respondents discard the original words of the question and retain their interpretations as they begin to formulate an answer.

A great deal of cognitive work is required to generate an optimal answer to even a single question, so the cumulative effort required to answer a long series of questions on a wide range of topics seems particularly substantial. A wide variety of motives may encourage expending considerable cognitive effort to do so, including desires for self-expression, interpersonal response, intellectual challenge, self-understanding, feelings of altruism, or emotional catharsis (see Warwick & Lininger 1975). Expenditure of great effort can also be motivated by desires for gratification from successful performance, to help employers improve working conditions, to help manufacturers produce better quality products, or to help governments make better informed policy decisions. To the extent that these sorts of motives inspire a person to perform the necessary cognitive tasks in a thorough and unbiased manner, a person may be said to be optimizing.

Although we hope all respondents will optimize throughout a questionnaire, this seems to be unrealistic. In fact, some people may agree to complete a questionnaire through a relatively automatic compliance process (e.g. Cialdini 1993) or because they need to fulfill a course requirement. Thus, they may agree merely to provide answers, with no intrinsic motivation toward high quality. Other respondents may satisfy their desires to provide high-quality data after answering a few questions, and become increasingly fatigued and distracted as a questionnaire progresses. Respondents then face a dilemma: They are not motivated to work hard, and the cognitive costs of hard work are burdensome. Nonetheless, the questionnaire continues to pose a seemingly unending stream of questions, suggesting that respondents are expected to expend the effort necessary to generate high-quality responses.

SATISFICING   Respondents sometimes deal with this situation by shifting their response strategy (Krosnick 1991). Rather than expending the effort to generate optimal answers, respondents may compromise their standards and expend less energy. When done subtly, respondents may simply be less thorough in comprehension, retrieval, judgment, and response selection. They may be less thoughtful about a question's meaning; they may search their memories less comprehensively; they may integrate retrieved information carelessly; and they may select a response imprecisely. All four steps are executed, but each one less diligently than when optimizing occurs. Instead of generating the most accurate answers, respondents settle for merely satisfactory ones. This response behavior might be termed "weak satisficing" (borrowing the term from Simon 1957).

A more dramatic approach is to skip the retrieval and judgment steps altogether. That is, respondents may interpret each question superficially and select what they believe will be a reasonable answer to the interviewer and researcher. Yet this answer is selected without referring to any internal psychological cues relevant to the attitude, belief, or event of interest. Instead, the respondent may look to the wording of the question for a cue, pointing to a response that can be easily selected and defended if necessary. If no such cue is present, the respondent may arbitrarily select an answer. This process might be termed "strong satisficing."

Respondents can use a number of possible decision heuristics to arrive at a satisfactory answer without expending substantial effort. A person might select the first reasonable response he or she encounters in a list rather than carefully processing all possible alternatives. Respondents could be inclined to accept assertions made in the questions regardless of content, rather than performing the cognitive work required to evaluate those assertions. Respondents might offer "safe" answers, such as the neutral point of a rating scale, endorsement of the status quo, or saying "don't know" so as to avoid expending the effort necessary to consider and possibly take more risky stands. In the extreme, respondents could randomly select a response from those offered by a closed-ended question.

Optimizing and strong satisficing can be thought of as anchoring the ends of a continuum indicating the degrees of thoroughness of the four response process steps. The optimizing end involves complete and effortful execution of all four steps. The strong satisficing end involves little effort in the interpretation and answer-reporting steps and no retrieval or integration at all. In between are intermediate levels of satisficing.

CONDITIONS THAT FOSTER SATISFICING   The likelihood that a respondent will satisfice when answering a question may be a function of three factors (Krosnick 1991). Satisficing is more likely to occur (a) the greater the task difficulty, (b) the lower the respondent's ability, and (c) the lower the respondent's motivation to optimize. Task difficulty is a function of the difficulty of interpreting the meaning of a question and response choices, the difficulty of retrieving and manipulating information in memory, the pace at which an interviewer reads, the occurence of distracting events, and more. Ability is presumably greater among respondents adept at performing complex mental operations, practiced at thinking about the topic of a question, and equipped with preformulated judgments on the issue. Factors influencing a respondent's motivation to optimize include need for cognition (Cacioppo et al 1996), the personal importance of the question's topic to the respondent, beliefs about whether the questionnaire will have useful consequences, the behavior of the interviewer, and fatigue.

EXPLAINING RESPONSE ORDER EFFECTS   The notion of satisficing casts new light on many past studies of questionnaire design effects, because it provides a novel and parsimonious explanation for these effects. One such effect is the order in which response alternatives are presented on people's selection among them, called response order effects. Studies have shown that presentation order does have effects, but it has not been clear when such effects occur and what their direction might be. Some studies identified primacy effects (in which response choices presented early were most likely to be selected); other studies found recency effects (in which response choices presented last were more likely to be selected), and still other studies found no order effects at all. The satisficing perspective brought order to this evidence.

To understand the satisficing explanation here, one must distinguish categorical questions from rating-scale questions. Rating-scale questions ask people to choose a descriptor from a set that represents a dimension or continuum (e.g. from "strongly agree" to "strongly disagree"). In contrast, categorical questions ask people to choose among a set that does not represent a continuum (e.g. What is the most important problem facing the country today, unemployment or inflation?).

Response order effects in categorical questions seem to be attributable to weak satisficing (see Krosnick 1991, Krosnick & Alwin 1987). When confronted with such questions, a respondent who is optimizing would carefully assess the appropriateness of each response before selecting one. In contrast, a respondent who is a weak satisficer could simply choose the first reasonable response. Exactly which alternative is most likely to be chosen depends on whether the response choices are presented visually or orally.

When choices are presented visually, either on a show card in a face-to-face interview or in a self-administered questionnaire, weak satisficing is likely to bias respondents toward selecting choices displayed early in a list. Respondents begin at the top of the list and consider each alternative individually, and their thoughts are likely to be biased in a confirmatory direction (Klayman & Ha 1987, Koriat et al 1980, Yzerbyt & Leyens 1991). Because researchers typically include response choices that are reasonable, this confirmation-biased thinking is likely to generate at least a reason or two in favor of selecting almost any alternative a respondent considers.

After considering one or two alternatives, the potential for fatigue becomes significant, as respondents' minds become cluttered with thoughts about initial alternatives. Also, fatigue may result from proactive interference, whereby thoughts about the initial alternatives interfere with and confuse thinking about later, competing alternatives (Miller & Campbell 1959). Weak satisficers can cope by thinking only superficially about later response alternatives; the confirmatory bias would thereby give the earlier items an advantage. Alternatively, weak satisficers can terminate their evaluation process altogether once they come upon a seemingly reasonable response. Again, because most answers are likely to seem reasonable, these respondents are likely to choose alternatives near the beginning of a list. Thus, weak satisficing seems likely to produce primacy effects under conditions of visual presentation.

When response alternatives are presented orally, as in face-to-face or telephone interviews, the effects of weak satisficing are more difficult to anticipate because response order effects reflect not only evaluations of each option but also the limits of memory. When alternatives are read aloud, respondents cannot process the first one extensively. Presentation of the second alternative terminates processing of the first one, usually relatively quickly. Therefore, respondents are able to devote the most processing time to the final items read; these items remain in short-term memory after interviewers pause to let respondents answer. Thus, the last options are likely to receive deeper processing dominated by generation of reasons supporting selection.

Some respondents may listen to a short list of response alternatives without evaluating any of them. Once the list is completed, they may recall the first alternative, think about it, and then progress through the list from beginning to end. Because fatigue should instigate weak satisficing relatively quickly, a primacy effect would be expected. However, because this process requires more effort than simply considering the final items in the list first, weak satisficers are unlikely to do this very often. Considering only the allocation of processing, we would anticipate both primacy and recency effects, although the latter should be more common.

These effects are likely to be reinforced by the effects of memory. Items presented early in a list are most likely to enter long-term memory (e.g. Atkinson & Shiffrin 1968), and items presented at the end are most likely to be in short-term memory immediately after the list is heard (e.g. Atkinson & Shiffrin 1968). So items presented at the beginning and end of a list are more likely to be recalled after the question is read, particularly if the list is long. Because a response alternative must be remembered to be selected, both early and late items should be more available for selection, especially among weak satisficers. Typically, short-term memory dominates long-term memory immediately after acquiring a list of information (Baddeley & Hitch 1977), so memory factors should promote recency effects more than primacy effects. Thus, in response to orally presented questions, mostly recency effects would be expected, though some primacy effects might occur as well.

Two additional factors may govern response order effects: the plausibility of the alternatives presented and perceptual contrast effects (Schwarz & Hippler 1991, Schwarz et al 1992). If deep processing is accorded to an alternative that seems highly implausible, even respondents with a confirmatory bias in reasoning may not generate any reasons to select it. Thus, deeper processing of some alternatives may make them especially unlikely to be selected. Also, perceptual contrast may cause a moderately plausible alternative to seem less plausible if considered after a highly plausible one or more plausible if considered after a highly implausible one.

Although the results of past studies seem to offer a mishmash of results when considered as a group, systematic patterns appear when studies are separated into ones involving visual and oral presentation. Whenever a visual presentation study has uncovered a response order effect, it has always been a primacy effect (Ayidiya & McClendon 1990, Becker 1954, Bishop et al 1988, Campbell & Mohr 1950, Israel & Taylor 1990, Krosnick & Alwin 1987, Schwarz et al 1992). And in studies involving oral presentation, nearly all response order effects documented were recency effects (Berg & Rapaport 1954, Bishop 1987, Bishop et al 1988, Cronbach 1950, Krosnick 1992, Krosnick & Schuman 1988, Mathews 1927, McClendon 1986a, 1991, Schuman & Presser 1981, Schwarz et al 1992, Visser et al 1999).

If the response order effects demonstrated in these studies are caused by weak satisficing, then they should be stronger when satisficing is most likely. Indeed, these effects were stronger among respondents with relatively limited cognitive skills (Krosnick 1991; Krosnick & Alwin 1987; Krosnick et al 1996; McClendon 1986a, 1991; Narayan & Krosnick 1996). Mathews (1927) also found stronger response order effects as questions became more difficult and respondents became fatigued. Although McClendon (1986a) found no relation between the number of words in a question and the magnitude of response order effects, Payne (1949/1950) found more response order effects in questions involving more words and words that were difficult to comprehend. Also, Schwarz et al (1992) showed that a strong recency effect was eliminated when prior questions on the same topic were asked, which presumably made respondents' knowledge of the topic more accessible and thereby made optimizing easier. The only surprise was reported by Krosnick & Schuman (1988), who found that response order effects were not stronger among respondents less certain of their opinions, who considered a question's topic to be less important, or who had weaker feelings on the issue. In general, though, this evidence is consistent with the notion that response order effects are attributable to satisficing, and evidence reported by Narayan & Krosnick (1996) and Krosnick et al (1996) ties these effects to weak satisficing in particular.

Much of the logic regarding categorical questions seems applicable to ratings scales, but in a different way. Many people's dimensional attitudes and beliefs are probably not precise points, but rather are ranges or "latitudes of acceptance" (Sherif & Hovland 1961, Sherif et al 1965). If the options on a rating scale are considered sequentially, then the respondent may select the first one that falls in his or her latitude of acceptance. This would yield a primacy effect under both visual and oral presentation, because people probably quickly consider each response alternative in the order in which they are read.

Nearly all studies of response order effects in rating scales involved visual presentation, and when order effects appeared, they were nearly uniformly primacy effects (Carp 1974, Chan 1991, Holmes 1974, Johnson 1981, Payne 1971, Quinn & Belson 1969). Two oral-presentation studies of rating scales found primacy effects as well (Kalton et al 1978, Mingay & Greenwell 1989). Consistent with the satisficing notion, Mingay & Greenwell (1989) found that a primacy effect was stronger for people with more limited cognitive skills. However, they found no relation of the magnitude of the primacy effect to the speed at which interviewers read questions, despite the fact that a fast pace presumably increased task difficulty. Also, response order effects were no stronger when questions were placed later in a questionnaire (Carp 1974). Thus, the moderators of rating-scale response order effects may be different from those for categorical questions, although more research is needed to fully address this matter.

EXPLAINING ACQUIESCENCE   Agree/disagree, true/false, and yes/no questions are very popular, appearing in numerous batteries developed for attitude and personality measurement (e.g. Davis & Smith 1996, Hathaway & McKinley 1940, Robinson et al 1991, Shaw & Wright 1967). They are appealing from a practical standpoint, because they are easy to write and administer. These formats are also seriously problematic, because they are susceptible to bias due to acquiescence—the tendency to endorse any assertion made in a question, regardless of its content.

Evidence of acquiescence is voluminous and consistently compelling, based on a range of different demonstration methods (for a review, see Krosnick & Fabrigar 1998). Consider agree/disagree questions. When people are given such response choices, are not asked any questions, and are told to guess what answers an experimenter is imagining, people guess "agree" much more often than "disagree." When people are asked to agree or disagree with pairs of statements stating mutually exclusive views (e.g. "I enjoy socializing" versus "I don't enjoy socializing"), answers should be strongly negatively correlated. But across more than 40 studies, the average correlation was only -.22. Across 10 studies, an average of 52% of people agreed with an assertion, whereas only 42% disagreed with its opposite. In another eight studies, an average of 14% more people agreed with an assertion than expressed the same view in a corresponding forced-choice question. And averaging across seven studies, 22% agreed with both a statement and its reversal, whereas only 10% disagreed with both.

All of these methods suggest an average acquiescence effect of about 10%, and the same sort of evidence documents comparable acquiescence in true/false and yes/no questions. There is other evidence regarding these latter question formats as well (see Krosnick & Fabrigar 1998). For example, people answer yes/no and true/false factual questions correctly more often when the correct answer is yes or true. Similarly, reports of factual matters are more likely to disagree with reports of informants when the initial reports are yes answers. And when people say they are guessing at true/false questions, they say "true" more often than "false".

Among psychologists, the prevailing explanation for acquiescence is the notion that some people may be predisposed to be agreeable in all domains of social interaction, which is consistent with the literature on the "Big Five" personality traits (Costa & McCrae 1988, Goldberg 1990). Although childhood socialization experiences probably influence an adult's level of agreeableness, this trait may have genetic roots as well (Costa & McCrae 1995). And people who are high in agreeableness are presumably inclined to acquiesce in answering all questionnaires.

Sociologists have offered a different explanation, focusing on the relationship between the respondent and the interviewer, researcher, or both. When researchers and interviewers are perceived as being of higher social status, respondents may defer to them out of courtesy and respect, yielding a tendency to endorse assertions apparently made by the researchers and/or interviewers (Carr 1971, Lenski & Leggett 1960).

Acquiescence can also be explained by the notion of satisficing (Krosnick 1991). When presented with an assertion and asked to agree or disagree, some respondents may attempt to search their memories for reasons to do each. Because of the confirmatory bias in hypothesis testing, most people typically begin by seeking reasons to agree rather than disagree. If a person's cognitive skills or motivation are relatively low, he or she may become fatigued before getting to the task of generating reasons to disagree with the assertion. The person would thus be inclined to agree. This would constitute a form of weak satisficing, because respondents would compromise their effort during the retrieval and integration stages of information processing, not during question interpretation or response expression. This is consistent with the notion that people initially believe assertions, and only upon later reflection do they come to discredit some assertions that appear insufficiently justified (Clark & Chase 1972, 1974; Gilbert et al 1990).

Acquiescence might also be a result of strong satisficing. When respondents are not able or motivated to interpret questions carefully and search their memories for relevant information, agree/disagree, true/false, and yes/no questions offer readily available opportunities for effortless selection of a plausible response. The social convention to be polite is quite powerful, and agreeing with others is more polite than disagreeing (Brown & Levinson 1987, Leech 1983). Therefore, under conditions likely to foster strong satisficing, acquiescence may occur with no evaluation of the question's assertion at all. People may simply choose to agree because it seems like the commanded and polite action to take.

These explanations of acquiescence suggest that some people should be more likely to manifest it than others, because of personalities, social status, or abilities and motivations to optimize. Indeed, some evidence suggests that individual differences in the tendency to acquiesce are quite uniform across questions and over time (see Krosnick & Fabrigar 1998). For example, the cross-sectional reliability of the tendency to agree with a large set of assertions on diverse topics is .65, averaging across dozens of studies. Over time, the tendency to acquiesce is about .75 over one month and .67 over four months. However, consistency over time is only about .35 over four years, suggesting that the relevant disposition is not as firmly fixed as some other aspects of personality.

Evidence suggesting that multiple factors cause acquiescence comes from dozens of studies correlating the tendency across different batteries of items (see Krosnick & Fabrigar 1998). Correlations between the tendency to acquiesce on different sets of items measuring different constructs on the same occasion average .34 for agree/disagree questions, .16 for yes/no questions, and .37 for true/false questions. Correlations between acquiescence on agree/disagree batteries and yes/no batteries average .24, between acquiescence on agree/disagree and true/false item sets average .36, and between yes/no and true/false acquiescence average .21. These numbers are consistent with the conclusions that (*a*) a general disposition to acquiesce explains only some of variance in the acquiescence a person manifests on any particular set of items, and (*b*) yes/no questions may manifest this tendency less than agree/disagree or true/false items. Even more striking is that acquiescence appears to result partly from a transient, moodlike state within a single questionnaire, because the closer in time two items are presented, the more likely people are to answer them with the same degree of acquiescence (Hui & Triandis 1985, Roberts et al 1976).

In line with the status differential explanation, some studies found acquiescence to be more common among respondents of lower social status (e.g. Gove & Geerken 1977, Lenski & Leggett 1960, McClendon 1991, Ross & Mirowsky 1984), but just as many other studies failed to find this relation (e.g. Calsyn et al 1992, Falthzik & Jolson 1974, Gruber & Lehmann 1983, Ross et al 1995). In line with the personality disposition explanation, people who acquiesce are unusually extraverted and sociable (Bass 1956, Webster 1958), cooperative (Heaven 1983, Husek 1961), interpersonally sensitive (Mazmanian et al 1987), and tend to have an external locus of control (Mirowsky & Ross 1991); however, none of these relations is especially strong. And although some studies found that people who acquiesce in answering questionnaires were likely to conform to others' views and comply with others' requests (e.g. Bass 1958, Kuethe 1959), more studies failed to uncover these relations (e.g. Foster 1961, Foster & Grigg 1963, Small & Campbell 1960).

In contrast, a great deal of evidence is consistent with satisficing and cannot be accounted for by these other explanations. For example, acquiescence is more common among people with more limited cognitive skills (e.g. Bachman & O'Malley 1984, Clare & Gudjonsson 1993, Forehand 1962, Gudjonsson 1990, Hanley 1959, Krosnick et al 1996, Narayan & Krosnick 1996) and with less cognitive energy (Jackson 1959), and among those who do not like to think (Jackson 1959, Messick & Frederiksen 1958). Acquiescence is more common when a question is difficult to answer (Gage et al 1957, Hanley 1962, Trott & Jackson 1967), when respondents have been encouraged to guess (Cronbach 1941), after they have become fatigued (e.g. Clancy & Wachsler 1971), and during telephone interviews than during face-to-face interviews (e.g. Calsyn et al 1992, Jordan et al 1980), presumably because people feel more accountable under the latter conditions. People who acquiesce are likely to manifest other forms of satisficing (discussed below), such as nondifferentiation (Goldstein & Blackman 1976, Schutz & Foster 1963) and selecting a no-opinion option (Silk 1971). Finally, studies of thought-listings and response latencies document a confirmatory bias in reasoning when people answer agree/disagree, true/false, and yes/no questions, which is at the heart of the satisficing explanation (Carpenter & Just 1975, Kunda et al 1993). The only evidence inconsistent with the satisficing perspective is that acquiescence is not more common among people for whom the topic of a question is less personally important, who have weaker feelings on the issue, or who hold their opinions with less confidence (Husek 1961, Krosnick & Schuman 1988).

EXPLAINING THE DISCREPANCY BETWEEN RATINGS AND RANKINGS   The satisficing perspective proves useful in explaining the discrepancy between ratings and rankings. An important goal of survey research is to understand the choices people make between alternative courses of action or objects. One way to do so is to explicitly ask respondents to make choices by rank ordering a set of alternatives. Another approach is to ask people to rate each object individually, allowing the researcher to derive the rank order implied by the ratings. Ratings are much less time consuming than rankings (McIntyre & Ryans 1977, Reynolds & Jolly 1980, Taylor & Kinnear 1971), and people enjoy doing ratings more and are more satisfied with their validity (Elig & Frieze 1979, McIntyre & Ryans 1977). Perhaps partly as a result, researchers have typically preferred to use rating questions rather than ranking questions.

However, a number of studies indicate that rankings yield higher-quality data than ratings. Respondents are more likely to make mistakes when answering rating questions, failing to answer an item more often than when ranking (Brady 1990, Neidell 1972). Rankings are more reliable (Elig & Frieze 1979, Miethe 1985, Munson & McIntyre 1979, Rankin & Grube 1980, Reynolds & Jolly 1980) and manifest higher discriminant validity than ratings (Bass & Avolio 1989, Elig & Frieze 1979, Miethe 1985, Zuckerman et al 1989). When manifesting different correlations with criterion measures, rankings evidence greater validity than ratings (Nathan & Alexander 1985, Schriesheim et al 1991, Zuckerman et al 1989).

No explanation for this discrepancy had existed before the satisficing perspective was proposed. When confronted with a battery of ratings asking that a series of objects be evaluated on a single response scale, respondents who are inclined to implement strong satisficing can simply select a reasonable point on the scale and place all the objects at that point. For example, when asked to rate the importance of a series of values (e.g. equality, freedom, and happiness) on a scale from extremely important to not at all important, a satisficing respondent can easily say they are all very important. In the satisficing rubric, this is called nondifferentiation.

Nondifferentiation is most likely to occur under the conditions thought to foster satisficing. Nondifferentiation is more common among less educated respondents (Krosnick & Alwin 1988, Krosnick et al 1996; L Rogers & AR Herzog, unpublished manuscript) and is more prevalent toward the end of a questionnaire (Coker & Knowles 1987, Herzog & Bachman 1981, Knowles 1988, Kraut et al 1975; L Rogers & AR Herzog, unpublished manuscript). Nondifferentiation is particularly pronounced among respondents low in verbal ability, for whom fatigue is presumably most taxing (Knowles et al 1989a,b). Placing rating questions later in a questionnaire makes correlations between ratings on the same scale more positive or less negative (Andrews 1984, Herzog & Bachman 1981; L Rogers & AR Herzog, unpublished manuscript), which are the expected results of nondifferentiation (see Krosnick & Alwin 1988). Not surprisingly, removing nondifferentiators makes the validity of rating data equivalent to that of ranking data (Krosnick & Alwin 1988).

EXPLAINING SELECTION OF NO-OPINION RESPONSE OPTIONS   Another application of satisficing is in explaining the effect of a no-opinion (NO) option. When researchers ask questions about subjective phenomena, they usually presume that respondents' answers reflect information or opinions that they previously had stored in memory. If a person does not have a preexisting opinion, a question presumably prompts him or her to draw on relevant beliefs or attitudes in order to concoct a reasonable, albeit new, belief or evaluation (e.g. Zaller & Feldman 1992). Consequently, whether based on a preexisting judgment or a newly formulated one, responses presumably reflect the individual's belief or orientation.

When people are asked about an object about which they have no knowledge, researchers hope that respondents will say that they have no opinion, are not familiar with the object, or do not know how they feel about it. But if a question's wording suggests that respondents should have opinions, they may not wish to appear uninformed and may therefore give an arbitrary answer (Converse 1964, Schwarz 1996). Indeed, respondents have been willing to offer opinions about obscure or purely fictitious objects (Bishop et al 1986, Ehrlich & Rinehart 1965, Gill 1947, Hartley 1946, Hawkins & Coney 1981, Schuman & Presser 1981). To reduce such behavior, some survey experts have recommended that NO options routinely be offered (e.g. Bogart 1972, Converse & Presser 1986, Payne 1950, Vaillancourt 1973).

Many more respondents say they have no opinion on an issue when this option is explicitly offered than when they must volunteer it on their own (Ayidiya & McClendon 1990; Bishop et al 1980; Kalton et al 1978; McClendon 1986b, 1991; McClendon & Alwin 1993; Presser 1990; Schuman & Presser 1981). And the propensity to offer opinions about obscure or fictitious objects is significantly reduced by explicitly offering a NO option (Schuman & Presser 1981).

People who select NO responses have characteristics suggesting that they are least likely to have formed real opinions. For example, such responses are offered more often by people with relatively limited cognitive skills (Bishop et al 1980, Gergen & Back 1965, Narayan & Krosnick 1996, Sigelman 1981). People who are more knowledgeable about a topic are presumably better equipped to form relevant opinions and are less likely to offer NO responses (Faulkenberry & Mason 1978; Krosnick & Milburn 1990; Leigh & Martin 1987; Rapoport 1981, 1982). The more interested a person is in a topic, the more likely he or she is to form opinions on it, and the less likely he or she is to offer NO responses (Francis & Busch 1975; Krosnick & Milburn 1990; Norpoth & Buchanan 1992; Rapoport 1979, 1982; Wright & Niemi 1983). Opinion formation is presumably facilitated by exposure to information about a topic, and, in fact, greater exposure to the news media is associated with decreased NO answers to political opinion questions (Faulkenberry & Mason 1978, Krosnick & Milburn 1990, Wright & Niemi 1983). The more often a person performs behaviors that can be informed or shaped by an attitude, the more motivated that person is to form such an attitude, and the less likely that person is to say he or she has no opinion on an issue (Durand & Lambert 1988, Krosnick & Milburn 1990). The stronger a person's attitudes are, the less likely he or she is to say "don't know" when asked about their attitudes toward other objects in the domain (Wright & Niemi 1983). The greater an individual's perception of his or her ability to process and understand information relevant to an attitude object, the less likely he or she is to say "don't know" when asked about it (Krosnick & Milburn 1990). The more practical use a person believes there is in possessing attitudes toward an object, the less likely he or she is to say "don't know" when asked to report such attitudes (Francis & Busch 1975; Krosnick & Milburn 1990). And people who consider a particular issue to be of less personal importance are more attracted to NO filters (Bishop et al 1980, Schuman & Presser 1981).

This suggests that NO options should increase the quality of data obtained by a questionnaire. By offering a NO option, respondents would be discouraged from offering meaningless opinions. Remarkably, this is not the case: offering a NO option does not increase the reliability of data obtained (Krosnick & Berent 1990, McClendon & Alwin 1993, Poe et al 1988). Associations between variables generally do not increase in strength when NO options are offered (Presser 1977, Sanchez & Morchio 1992, Schuman & Presser 1981), nor do answers become less susceptible to systematic measurement error caused by nonsubstantive aspects of question design (McClendon 1991). Asking people who offer NO responses to express an opinion anyhow leads to the expression of valid and predictive views (Gilljam & Granberg 1993, Visser et al 1999).

More evidence raises questions about the reliability of NO responses. The frequency of NO responses to a set of items is fairly consistent across different question sets in the same questionnaire (e.g. Cronbach 1950, Durand et al 1983, Durand & Lambert 1988, Fonda 1951, Leigh & Martin 1987, Lorge 1937) and over time (Krosnick & Milburn 1990, Rapoport 1982, Rosenberg et al 1955, Sigelman et al 1982). But there is a fair amount of random variation in whether a person expresses no opinion when answering any particular item (Butler & Stokes 1969, DuBois & Burns 1975, Durand et al 1983, Eisenberg & Wesman 1941, Lentz 1934). This random variation casts further doubt on the notion that NO responses genuinely, precisely, and comprehensively reflect lack of opinions.

Although NO responses sometimes occur because people have no information about an object, they occur more often for a variety of other reasons. People sometimes offer such responses because they feel ambivalent about the issue (e.g. Coombs & Coombs 1976, Klopfer & Madden 1980) or because they do not understand the meaning of a question or the answer choices (e.g. Converse 1976, Faulkenberry & Mason 1978, Fonda 1951, Klare 1950). Some NO responses occur because respondents think that they must know a lot about a topic to legitimately express an opinion (Berger & Sullivan 1970, Hippler & Schwarz 1989, McClendon 1986b), and some occur because people are avoiding honestly answering a question in a way that would be unflattering (Cronbach 1950, Fonda 1951, Johanson et al 1993, Kahn & Hadley 1949, Rosenberg et al 1955). Some NO responses occur because interviewers expect that it will be difficult to administer items, and this expectation becomes a self-fulfilling prophecy (Singer et al 1983).

NO responses appear to result from satisficing as well (Krosnick 1991). According to this perspective, offering a NO option may discourage respondents from providing thoughtful answers. That is, respondents who are disposed to satisfice because of low ability to optimize, low motivation, or high task difficulty may be likely to select NO options as a way of avoiding the cognitive work necessary to generate an optimal answer. If a NO option is not offered, these respondents would be less likely to satisfice and might optimize instead.

Some of the evidence reviewed earlier is consistent with this reasoning. For example, NO filters attract respondents with limited cognitive skills. This is consistent with the notion that NO responses reflect satisficing caused by low cognitive skills. Also, NO responses are common among people for whom an issue is low in personal importance, of little interest, and arouses little affective involvement, and this may be because of lowered motivation to optimize under these conditions. Furthermore, people are likely to say they have no opinion when they feel they lack the ability to formulate informed opinions and when they feel there is little value in formulating such opinions. These associations may arise at the time of attitude measurement: Low motivation may inhibit a person from drawing on available knowledge to formulate and carefully report a substantive opinion on an issue. Also consistent with this perspective are demonstrations that NO responses become more common as questions become more difficult. Although all of this evidence is consistent with the notion that these responses reflect optimizing, it is also consistent with the satisficing view of NO responses.

Stronger support for the satisficing perspective comes from evidence that NO responses are more likely when questions appear later in a questionnaire, at which point motivation is waning (Culpepper et al 1992, Dickinson & Kirzner 1985, Ferber 1966, Ying 1989) and when respondents' intrinsic motivation to optimize has been undermined (Hansen 1980). NO responses are less common when the sponsor of a study is described as prestigious (Houston & Nevin 1977). Furthermore, inducements to optimize decrease NO responses (McDaniel & Rao 1980, Wotruba 1966).

SUMMARY   The satisficing perspective offers new explanations for longstanding response patterns in questionnaire responses. The development of basic psychological theory in this fashion is a hallmark of the blossoming contemporary literature on survey methods.

CONCLUSION

The turn of the century provides an opportunity to reflect on the last 100 years and plot future courses of action in an informed way. Survey researchers are plotting their future with new visions of possibilities, because research is leading them to question old assumptions and to contemplate ways to improve their craft. The benefits of such efforts will be substantial both for psychologists who use survey methods as tools and for psychologists interested in understanding the workings of the human mind and the dynamics of social interaction.

ACKNOWLEDGMENT

The author thanks Catherine Heaney and Allyson Holbrook for helpful comments and Michael Tichy for heroic assistance in the manuscript preparation.

Visit the *Annual Reviews home page* at
http://www.AnnualReviews.org.

Literature Cited

Abelson RP, Loftus EF, Greenwald AG. 1992. Attempts to improve the accuracy of self-reports of voting. In *Questions About Questions*, ed. JM Tanur, pp. 138–53. New York: Russell Sage

Andrews FM. 1984. Construct validity and error components of survey measures: A structural modeling approach. *Public Opin. Q.* 48:409–42

Atkinson RC, Shiffrin RM. 1968. Human memory: a proposed system and its control processes. In *The Psychology of Learning and Motivation: Advances in Research and Theory*, ed. KW Spence, JT Spence, 2:89–195. New York: Academic

Ayidiya SA, McClendon M J. 1990. Response effects in mail surveys. *Public Opin. Q.* 54:229–47

Babbie ER. 1990. *Survey Research Methods.* Belmont, CA: Wadsworth. 395 pp.

Bachman JG, O'Malley PM. 1984. Yea-saying, nay-saying, and going to extremes: black-white differences in response styles. *Public Opin. Q.* 48:491–509

Baddeley AD, Hitch GJ. 1977. Recency re-examined. In *Attention and Performance,* ed. S Dornic. Hillsdale, NJ: Erlbaum. Vol. 6.

Bass BM. 1956. Development and evaluation of a scale for measuring social acquies-cence. *J. Abnorm. Soc. Psychol.* 52: 296–99

Bass BM. 1958. Famous sayings test: general manual. *Psychol. Rep.* 4:479–97

Bass BM, Avolio BJ. 1989. Potential biases in leadership measures: How prototypes, leniency, and general satisfaction relate to ratings and rankings of transformational and transactional leadership constructs. *Educ. Psychol. Meas.* 49:509–27

Becker SL. 1954. Why an order effect. *Public Opin. Q.* 18:271–78

Berg IA, Rapaport GM. 1954. Response bias in an unstructured questionnaire. *J. Psychol.* 38:475–81

Berger PK, Sullivan JE. 1970. Instructional set, interview context, and the incidence of "don't know" responses. *J. Appl. Psychol.* 54:414–16

Bickart B, Felcher EM. 1996. Expanding and enhancing the use of verbal protocols in survey research. In *Answering Questions*, ed. N Schwarz, S Sudman. San Francisco, CA: Jossey-Bass

Bischoping K. 1989. An evaluation of interviewer debriefing in survey pretests. In *New Techniques for Pretesting Survey Questions*, ed. CF Cannell, L Oskenberg, FJ Fowler, G Kalton, K Bischoping. Ann Arbor, MI: Survey Res. Cent.

Bishop GF. 1987. Experiments with the middle response alternative in survey questions. *Public Opin. Q.* 51:220–32

Bishop GF, Hippler HJ, Schwarz N, Strack F. 1988. A comparison of response effects in self-administered and telephone surveys. In *Telephone Survey Methodology,* ed. RM Groves, PP Biemer, LE Lyberg, JT Massey, WL Nicholls II, J Waksberg, pp. 321–34. New York: Wiley

Bishop GF, Oldendick RW, Tuchfarber AJ. 1980. Experiments in filtering political opinions. *Polit. Behav.* 2:339–69

Bishop GF, Oldendick RW, Tuchfarber AJ. 1986. Opinions on fictitious issues: the pressure to answer survey questions. *Public Opin. Q.* 50:240–50

Bogart L. 1972. *Silent Politics: Polls and the Awareness of Public Opinion.* New York: Wiley-Interscience

Brady HE. 1990. Dimension analysis of ranking data. *Am. J. Polit. Sci.* 34:1017–48

Brehm J. 1993. *The Phantom Respondents* Ann Arbor: Univ. Mich. Press

Briggs CL. 1986. *Learning How To Ask: A Sociolinguistic Appraisal of the Role of the Interview in Social Science Research.* Cambridge: Cambridge Univ. Press. 155 pp.

Brown P, Levinson SC. 1987. *Politeness: Some Universals in Language Use.* New York: Cambridge Univ. Press. 345 pp.

Butler D, Stokes D. 1969. *Political Change in Britain: Forces Shaping Electoral Choice.* New York: St. Martin's. 516 pp.

Cacioppo JT, Petty RE, Feinstein JA, Jarvis WBG. 1996. Dispositional differences in cognitive motivation: the life and times of individuals varying in need for cognition. *Psychol. Bull.* 119:197–253

Calsyn RJ, Roades LA, Calsyn DS. 1992. Acquiescence in needs assessment studies of the elderly. *The Gerontol.* 32: 246–52

Campbell DT, Mohr PJ. 1950. The effect of ordinal position upon responses to items in a checklist. *J. Appl. Psychol.* 34:62–67

Cannell CF, Miller PV, Oksenberg L. 1981. Research on interviewing techniques. In *Sociological Methodology,* ed. S Leinhardt, pp. 389–437. San Francisco, CA: Jossey-Bass

Carp FM. 1974. Position effects on interview responses. *J. Gerontol.* 29:581–87

Carpenter PA, Just MA. 1975. Sentence comprehension: a psycholinguistic processing model of verification. *Psychol. Rev.* 82: 45–73

Carr LG. 1971. The srole items and acquiescence. *Am. Sociol. Rev.* 36:287–93

Chan JC. 1991. Response-order effects in Likert-type scales. *Educ. Psychol. Meas.* 51:531–40

Cialdini RB. 1993. *Influence: Science and Practice.* New York: Harper Collins. 253 pp. 3rd ed.

Clancy KJ, Wachsler RA. 1971. Positional effects in shared-cost surveys. *Public Opin. Q.* 35:258–65

Clare ICH, Gudjonsson GH. 1993. Interrogative suggestibility, confabulation, and acquiescence in people with mild learning disabilities (mental handicap): implications for reliability during police interrogations. *Br. J. Clin. Psychol.* 32:295–301

Clark HH. 1996. *Using Language.* New York: Cambridge Univ. Press. 432 pp.

Clark HH, Chase WG. 1972. On the process of comparing sentences against pictures. *Cogn. Psychol.* 3:472–517

Clark HH, Chase WG. 1974. Perceptual coding strategies in the formation and verification of descriptions. *Mem. Cogn.* 2: 101–11

Clark HH, Clark EV. 1977. *Psychology and Language.* New York: Harcourt Brace Jovanovich. 608 pp.

Clausen A. 1968. Response validity: vote report. *Public Opin. Q.* 32:588–606

Coker MC, Knowles ES. 1987. *Testing alters the test scores: Test–retest improvements in anxiety also occur within a test.* Presented at the Midwest. Psychol. Assoc. Annu. Meet., Chicago

Converse JM. 1976. Predicting no opinion in the polls. *Public Opin. Q.* 40:515–30

Converse JM. 1987. *Survey Research in the United States: Roots and Emergence 1890–1960.* Berkeley, Los Angeles: Univ. Calif. Press

Converse JM, Presser S. 1986. *Survey Questions: Handcrafting the Standardized Questionnaire.* Beverly Hills, CA: Sage. 80 pp.

Converse PE. 1964. The nature of belief systems in the mass public. In *Ideology and Discontent,* ed. DE Apter, pp. 206–61. New York: Free Press

Coombs CH, Coombs LC. 1976. "Don't know": item ambiguity or respondent uncertainty? *Public Opin. Q.* 40:497–514

Costa PT, McCrae RR. 1988. From catalog to classification: Murray's needs and the five–factor model. *J. Pers. Soc. Psychol.* 55:258–65

Costa PT, McCrae RR. 1995. Solid ground in the wetlands: a reply to Block. *J. Pers. Soc. Psychol.* 117:216–20

Cronbach LJ. 1941. An experimental comparison of the multiple true-false and multiple-choice tests. *J. Educ. Psychol.* 32:533–43

Cronbach LJ. 1950. Further evidence on response sets and test design. *Educ. Psychol. Meas.* 10:3–31

Culpepper IJ, Smith WR, Krosnick JA. 1992. The impact of question order on satisficing in surveys. Presented at Midwest. Psychol. Assoc. Annu. Meet., Chicago

Davis JA, Smith TW. 1996. *General Social Surveys, 1972–1996: Cumulative Codebook.* Chicago: Natl. Opin. Res. Cent.

DeMaio TJ, Rothgeb JM. 1996. Cognitive interviewing techniques: in the lab and in the field. In *Answering Questions,* ed. N Schwarz, S Sudman, pp. 177–96. San Francisco, CA: Jossey-Bass

Dickinson JR, Kirzner E. 1985. Questionnaire item omission as a function of within-group question position. *J. Bus. Res.* 13: 71–75

Dickinson TL, Zellinger PM. 1980. A comparison of the behaviorally anchored rating mixed standard scale formats. *J. Appl. Psychol.* 65:147–54

DuBois B, Burns JA. 1975. An analysis of the meaning of the question mark response category in attitude scales. *Educ. Psychol. Meas.* 35:869–84

Durand RM, Guffey HJ, Planchon JM. 1983. An examination of the random versus non-random nature of item omission. *J. Mark. Res.* 20:305–13

Durand RM, Lambert ZV. 1988. Don't know responses in surveys: analyses and interpretational consequences. *J. Bus. Res.* 16: 169–88

Ehrlich HL, Rinehart JW. 1965. A brief report on the methodology of stereotype research. *Soc. Forces* 43:564–75

Eisenberg P, Wesman AG. 1941. Consistency in response and logical interpretation of psychoneurotic inventory items. *J. Educ. Psychol.* 32:321–38

Elig TW, Frieze IH. 1979. Measuring causal attributions for success and failure. *J. Pers. Soc. Psychol.* 37:621–34

Falthzik AM, Jolson MA. 1974. Statement polarity in attitude studies. *J. Mark. Res.* 11:102–5

Faulkenberry GD, Mason R. 1978. Characteristics of nonopinion and no opinion response groups. *Public Opin. Q.* 42:533–43

Ferber R. 1966. Item nonresponse in a consumer survey. *Public Opin. Q.* 30:399–415

Fonda CP. 1951. The nature and meaning of the Rorschach white space response. *J. Abnorm. Soc. Psychol.* 46:367–77

Forehand GA. 1962. Relationships among response sets and cognitive behaviors. *Educ. Psychol. Meas.* 22:287–302

Forsyth BH, Lessler JT. 1991. Cognitive laboratory methods: a taxonomy. In *Measurement Error in Surveys,* ed. P Biemer, R

Groves, L Lyberg, N Mathiowetz, S Sudman, pp. 393–418. New York: Wiley

Foster RJ. 1961. Acquiescent response set as a measure of acquiescence. *J. Abnorm. Soc. Psychol.* 63:155–60

Foster RJ, Grigg AE. 1963. Acquiescent response set as a measure of acquiescence: further evidence. *J. Abnorm. Soc. Psychol.* 67:304–6

Fowler FJ, Cannell CF. 1996. Using behavioral coding to identify cognitive problems with survey questions. In *Answering Questions,* ed. N Schwarz, S Sudman. San Francisco, CA: Jossey-Bass

Fowler FJ Jr, Mangione TW. 1990. *Standardized Survey Interviewing.* Newbury Park, CA: Sage. 151 pp.

Francis JD, Busch L. 1975. What we don't know about "I don't knows." *Public Opin. Q.* 34:207–18

Gage NL, Leavitt GS, Stone GC. 1957. The psychological meaning of acquiescence set for authoritarianism. *J. Abnorm. Soc. Psychol.* 55:98–103

Geer JG. 1988. What do open-ended questions measure? *Public Opin. Q.* 52:365–71

Gergen KJ, Back KW. 1965. Communication in the interview and the disengaged respondent. *Public Opin. Q.* 30:385–98

Gilbert DT, Krull DS, Malone PS. 1990. Unbelieving the unbelievable: some problems in the rejection of false information. *J. Pers. Soc. Psychol.* 59:601–13

Gill SN. 1947. How do you stand on sin? *Tide* 14:72

Gilljam M, Granberg D. 1993. Should we take don't know for an answer? *Public Opin. Q.* 57:348–57

Goldberg LR. 1990. An alternative "description of personality": the big-five factor structure. *J. Pers. Soc. Psychol.* 59: 1216–29

Goldstein KM, Blackman S. 1976. Cognitive complexity, maternal child rearing, and acquiescence. *Soc. Behav. Pers.* 4:97–103

Gove WR, Geerken MR. 1977. Response bias in surveys of mental health: an empirical investigation. *Am. J. Sociol.* 82:1289–317

Granberg G, Holmberg S. 1991. Self-reported turnout and voter validation. *Am. J. Polit. Sci.* 35:448–59

Greenwald AG, Carnot CG, Beach R, Young B. 1987. Increasing voting behavior by asking people if they expect to vote. *J. Appl. Psychol.* 72:315–18

Grice HP. 1975. Logic and conversation. In *Syntax and Semantics 3: Speech Acts,* ed. P Cole, JL Morgan, pp. 41–58. New York: Academic

Gruber RE, Lehmann DR. 1983. The effect of omitting response tendency variables from regression models. In *1983 AMA Winter Educators Conference: Research Methods Causal Models in Marketing*, ed. WR Darden, KB Monroe, WR Dillon, pp. 131–36. Chicago: Am. Mark. Assoc.

Gudjonsson GH. 1990. The relationship of intellectual skills to suggestibility, compliance and acquiescence. *Pers. Individ. Differ.* 11:227–31

Hanley C. 1959. Responses to the wording of personality test items. *J. Consult. Psychol.* 23:261–65

Hanley C. 1962. The "difficulty" of a personality inventory item. *Educ. Psychol. Meas.* 22:577–84

Hansen RA. 1980. A self-perception interpretation of the effect of monetary and nonmonetary incentives on mail survey respondent behavior. *J. Mark. Res.* 17: 77–83

Hartley EL. 1946. *Problems in Prejudice.* New York: Kings' Crown. 124 pp.

Hathaway SR, McKinley JC. 1940. A multiphasic personality schedule (Minnesota): I. Construction of the schedule. *J. Psychol.* 10:249–54

Hawkins DI, Coney KA. 1981. Uninformed response error in survey research. *J. Mark. Res.* 18:370–74

Heaven PCL. 1983. Authoritarianism or acquiescence? South African findings. *J. Soc. Psychol.* 119:11–15

Henry GT. 1990. *Practical Sampling.* Newbury Park, CA: Sage

Herzog AR, Bachman JG. 1981. Effects of questionnaire length on response quality. *Public Opin. Q.* 45:549–59

Hippler HJ, Schwarz N. 1989. "No-opinion" filters: a cognitive perspective. *Int. J. Public Opin. Res.* 1:77–87

Holmes C. 1974. A statistical evaluation of rating scales. *J. Mark. Res. Soc.* 16:86–108

Houston MJ, Nevin JR. 1977. The effects of source and appeal on mail survey response patterns. *J. Mark. Res.* 14:374–78

Hui CH, Triandis HC. 1985. The instability of response sets. *Public Opin. Q.* 49: 253–60

Hurd AW. 1932. Comparisons of short answer and multiple choice tests covering identical subject content. *J. Educ. Psychol.* 26: 28–30

Husek TR. 1961. Acquiescence as a response set and as a personality characteristic. *Educ. Psychol. Meas.* 21:295–307

Israel GD, Taylor CL. 1990. Can response order bias evaluations? *Eval. Program. Plan.* 13: 365–71

Jackson DN. 1959. Cognitive energy level, acquiescence, and authoritarianism. *J. Soc. Psychol.* 49:65–69

Johanson GA, Gips CJ, Rich CE. 1993. If you can't say something nice: a variation on the social desirability response set. *Eval. Rev.* 17:116–22

Johnson JD. 1981. Effects of the order of presentation of evaluative dimensions for bipolar scales in four societies. *J. Soc. Psychol.* 113:21–27

Jordan LA, Marcus AC, Reeder LG. 1980. Response styles in telephone and household interviewing: a field experiment. *Public Opin. Q.* 44:210–22

Kahn DF, Hadley JM. 1949. Factors related to life insurance selling. *J. Appl. Psychol.* 33: 132–40

Kalton G, Collins M, Brook L. 1978. Experiments in wording opinion questions. *Appl. Stat.* 27:149–61

Kish L. 1965. *Survey Sampling.* New York: Wiley. 634 pp.

Klare GR. 1950. Understandability and indefinite answers to public opinion questions. *Int. J. Opin. Attitude Res.* 4:91–96

Klayman J, Ha Y. 1987. Confirmation, disconfirmation, and information in hypothesis-testing. *Psychol. Rev.* 94:211–28

Klockars AJ, Yamagishi M. 1988. The influence of labels and positions in rating scales. *J. Educ. Meas.* 25:85–96

Klopfer FJ, Madden TM. 1980. The middlemost choice on attitude items: ambivalence, neutrality, or uncertainty. *Pers. Soc. Psychol. Bull.* 6:97–101

Knowles ES. 1988. Item context effects on personality scales: measuring changes the measure. *J. Pers. Soc. Psychol.* 55: 312–20

Knowles ES, Cook DA, Neville JW. 1989a. *Assessing adjustment improves subsequent adjustment scores.* Presented at the Annu. Meet. Am. Psychol. Assoc., New Orleans, LA

Knowles ES, Cook DA, Neville JW. 1989b. *Modifiers of context effects on personality tests: Verbal ability and need for cognition.* Presented at the Annu. Meet. Midwest. Psychol. Assoc., Chicago

Koriat A, Lichtenstein S, Fischhoff B. 1980. Reasons for confidence. *J. Exp. Psychol.: Hum. Learn. Mem.* 6:107–18

Kraut AI, Wolfson AD, Rothenberg A. 1975. Some effects of position on opinion survey items. *J. Appl. Psychol.* 60:774–76

Krosnick JA. 1991. Response strategies for coping with the cognitive demands of attitude measures in surveys. *Appl. Cogn. Psychol.* 5:213–36

Krosnick JA. 1992. The impact of cognitive sophistication and attitude importance on response order effects and question order effects. In *Order Effects in Social and Psy-*

chological Research, ed. N Schwarz, S Sudman, pp. 203–18. New York: Springer

Krosnick JA, Alwin DF. 1987. An evaluation of a cognitive theory of response–order effects in survey measurement. *Public Opin. Q.* 51:201–19

Krosnick JA, Alwin DF. 1988. A test of the form–resistant correlation hypothesis: ratings, rankings, and the measurement of values. *Public Opin. Q.* 52:526–38

Krosnick JA, Berent MK. 1990. *The impact of verbal labeling of response alternatives and branching on attitude measurement reliability in surveys.* Presented at the Annu. Meet. Am. Assoc. Public Opin. Res., Lancaster, PA

Krosnick JA, Berent MK. 1993. Comparisons of party identification and policy preferences: the impact of survey question format. *Am. J. Polit. Sci.* 37:941–64

Krosnick JA, Fabrigar LR. 1998. *Designing Good Questionnaires: Insights from Psychology.* New York: Oxford Univ. Press. In press

Krosnick JA, Li F, Lehman DR. 1990. Conversational conventions, order of information acquisition, and the effect of base rates and individuating information on social judgments. *J. Pers. Soc. Psychol.* 59:1140–52

Krosnick JA, Milburn MA. 1990. Psychological determinants of political opinionation. *Soc. Cogn.* 8:49–72

Krosnick JA, Narayan S, Smith WR. 1996. Satisficing in surveys: initial evidence. *New Direct. Eval.* 70:29–44

Krosnick JA, Schuman H. 1988. Attitude intensity, importance, and certainty and susceptibility to response effects. *J. Pers. Soc. Psychol.* 54:940–52

Kuethe JL. 1959. The positive response set as related to task performance. *J. Pers.* 27:87–95

Kunda Z, Fong GT, Sanitioso R, Reber E. 1993. Directional questions direct self–conceptions. *J. Exp. Soc. Psychol.* 29:63–86

Laumann EO, Michael RT, Gagnon JH, Michaels S. 1994. *The Social Organization of Sexuality: Sexual Practices in the United States.* Chicago: Univ. Chicago Press. 718 pp.

Lavrakas PJ. 1993. *Telephone Survey Methods: Sampling, Selection, and Supervision.* Newbury Park, CA: Sage, 157 pp. 2nd ed.

Leech GN. 1983. *Principles of Pragmatics.* London/New York: Longman. 250 pp.

Leigh JH, Martin CR Jr. 1987. "Don't know" item nonresponse in a telephone survey: effects of question form and respondent characteristics. *J. Mark. Res.* 24:418–24

Lenski GE, Leggett JC. 1960. Caste, class, and deference in the research interview. *Am. J. Sociol.* 65:463–67

Lentz TF. 1934. Reliability of the opinionaire technique studies intensively by the retest method. *J. Soc. Psychol.* 5:338–64

Lorge I. 1937. Gen-like: Halo or reality. *Psychol. Bull.* 34:545–46

Mathews CO. 1927. The effect of position of printed response words upon children's answers to questions in two-response types of tests. *J. Educ. Psychol.* 18:445–57

Mazmanian D, Mendonca JD, Holden RR, Dufton B. 1987. Psychopathology and response styles in the SCL-90 responses of acutely distressed persons. *J. Psychopathol. Behav. Assess.* 9:135–48

McClendon MJ. 1986a. Response-order effects for dichotomous questions. *Soc. Sci. Q.* 67:205–11

McClendon MJ. 1986b. Unanticipated effects of no opinion filters on attitudes and attitude strength. *Soc. Perspect.* 29:379–95

McClendon MJ. 1991. Acquiescence and recency response–order effects in interview surveys. *Soc. Methods Res.* 20:60–103

McClendon MJ, Alwin DF. 1993. No-opinion filters and attitude measurement reliability. *Soc. Methods Res.* 21:438–64

McDaniel SW, Rao CP. 1980. The effect of monetary inducement on mailed questionnaire response quality. *J. Mark. Res.* 17:265–68

McIntyre SH, Ryans AB. 1977. Time and accuracy measures for alternative multidimensional scaling data collection methods: some additional results. *J. Mark. Res.* 14:607–10

Messick S, Frederiksen N. 1958. Ability, acquiescence, and "authoritarianism." *Psychol. Rep.* 4:687–97

Miethe TD. 1985. The validity and reliability of value measurements. *J. Pers.* 119:441–53

Miller N, Campbell DT. 1959. Recency and primacy in persuasion as a function of the timing of speeches and measurement. *J. Abnorm. Soc. Psychol.* 59:1–9

Mingay DJ, Greenwell MT. 1989. Memory bias and response-order effects. *J. Off. Stat.* 5:253–63

Mirowsky J, Ross CE. 1991. Eliminating defense and agreement bias from measures of the sense of control: a 2 × 2 index. *Soc. Psychol. Q.* 54:127–45

Mishler EG. 1986. *Research Interviewing.* Cambridge, MA: Harvard Univ. Press. 189 pp.

Mosteller F, Hyman H, McCarthy PJ, Marks ES, Truman DB. 1949. *The Pre-Election Polls of 1948: Report to the Committee on*

Analysis of Pre-Election Polls and Forecasts. New York: Soc. Sci. Res. Counc.

Munson JM, McIntyre SH. 1979. Developing practical procedures for the measurement of personal values in cross-cultural marketing. *J. Mark. Res.* 16:48–52

Narayan S, Krosnick JA. 1996. Education moderates some response effects in attitude measurement. *Public Opin. Q.* 60: 58–88

Nathan BR, Alexander RA. 1985. The role of inferential accuracy in performance rating. *Acad. Manage. Rev.* 10:109–15

Neidell LA. 1972. Procedures for obtaining similarities data. *J. Mark. Res.* 9:335–37

Nelson D. 1985. Informal testing as a means of questionnaire development. *J. Off. Stat.* 1: 79–88

Norpoth H, Buchanan B. 1992. Wanted: the education president: issue trespassing by political candidates. *Public Opin. Q.* 56: 87–99

Parten M. 1950. *Surveys, Polls, and Samples: Practical Procedures.* New York: Harper. 624 pp.

Payne JD. 1971. The effects of reversing the order of verbal rating scales in a postal survey. *J. Mark. Res. Soc.* 14:30–44

Payne SL. 1949/1950. Case study in question complexity. *Public Opin. Q.* 13:653–58

Payne SL. 1950. Thoughts about meaningless questions. *Public Opin. Q.* 14:687–96

Peters DL, McCormick EJ. 1966. Comparative reliability of numerically anchored versus job-task anchored rating scales. *J. Appl. Psychol.* 50:92–96

Pew Research Center. 1998. *Opinion poll experiment reveals conservative opinions not underestimated, but racial hostility missed.* Internet posting, http://www.people–press.org/resprpt.htm, March 27

Poe GS, Seeman I, McLaughlin J, Mehl E, Dietz M. 1988. Don't know boxes in factual questions in a mail questionnaire. *Public Opin. Q.* 52:212–22

Presser S. 1977. *Survey question wording and attitudes in the general public.* PhD thesis. Univ. Mich, Ann Arbor. 370 pp.

Presser S. 1990. Measurement issues in the study of social change. *Soc. Forces* 68: 856–68

Presser S, Blair J. 1994. Do different methods produce different results? In *Sociological Methodology*, ed. PV Marsden, pp. 73–104. Cambridge, MA: Blackwell

Presser S, Traugott MW, Traugott S. 1990. Vote "over" reporting in surveys: the records or the respondents? Presented at Int. Conf. Measure. Errors, Tucson, AZ

Quinn SB, Belson WA. 1969. *The Effects of Reversing the Order of Presentation of*

Verbal Rating Scales in Survey Interviews. London: Survey Res. Cent.

Rankin WL, Grube JW. 1980. A comparison of ranking and rating procedures for value system measurement. *Eur. J. Soc. Psychol.* 10:233–46

Rapoport RB. 1979. What they don't know can hurt you. *Am. J. Polit. Sci.* 23:805–15

Rapoport RB. 1981. The sex gap in political persuading: Where the "structuring principle" works. *Am. J. Polit. Sci.* 25:32–48

Rapoport RB. 1982. Sex differences in attitude expression: a generational explanation. *Public Opin. Q.* 46:86–96

Remmers HH, Marschat LE, Brown A, Chapman I. 1923. An experimental study of the relative difficulty of true-false, multiple-choice, and incomplete-sentence types of examination questions. *J. Educ. Psychol.* 14:367–72

Reynolds TJ, Jolly JP. 1980. Measuring personal values: an evaluation of alternative methods. *J. Mark. Res.* 17:531–36

Roberts RT, Forthofer RN, Fabrega H. 1976. The Langer items and acquiescence. *Soc. Sci. Med.* 10:69–75

Robinson CE. 1932. *Straw Votes.* New York: Columbia Univ. Press. 203 pp.

Robinson JP, Shaver PR, Wrightsman LS. 1991. *Measures of Personality and Social Psychological Attitudes.* San Diego, CA: Academic. 735 pp.

Rosenberg N, Izard CE, Hollander EP. 1955. Middle category response: reliability and relationship to personality and intelligence variables. *Educ. Psychol. Meas.* 15:281–90

Ross CE, Mirowsky J. 1984. Socially–desirable response and acquiescence in a cross–cultural survey of mental health. *J. Health Soc. Behav.* 25:189–97

Ross CK, Steward CA, Sinacore JM. 1995. A comparative study of seven measures of patient satisfaction. *Med. Care* 33: 392–406

Sanchez ME, Morchio G. 1992. Probing "don't know" answers. *Public Opin. Q.* 56:454–74

Schober MF, Conrad FG. 1997. Does conversational interviewing reduce survey measurement error? *Public Opin. Q.* 61: 576–602

Schriesheim CA, Hinkin TR, Podsakoff PM. 1991. Can ipsative and single-item measures produce erroneous results in field studies of French and Raven's 1959 five bases of power? An empirical investigation. *J. Appl. Psychol.* 76:106–14

Schuman H, Ludwig J, Krosnick JA. 1986. The perceived threat of nuclear war, salience, and open questions. *Public Opin. Q.* 50:519–36

Schuman H, Presser S. 1981. *Questions and Answers in Attitude Surveys: Experiments on Question Form, Wording, and Context.* New York: Academic. 370 pp.

Schutz RE, Foster RJ. 1963. A factor analytic study of acquiescent and extreme response set. *Educ. Psychol. Meas.* 23: 435–47

Schwarz N. 1996. *Cognition and Communication: Judgmental Biases, Research Methods, and the Logic of Conversation.* Mahwah, NJ: Erlbaum

Schwarz N, Hippler HJ. 1991. Response alternatives: the impact of their choice and presentation order. In *Measurement Error in Surveys*, ed. P Biemer, RM Groves, LE Lyberg, NA Mathiowetz, S Sudman, pp. 41–56. New York: Wiley

Schwarz N, Hippler HJ, Deutsch B, Strack F. 1985. Response scales: effects of category range on reported behavior and subsequent judgments. *Public Opin. Q.* 49: 388–95

Schwarz N, Hippler HJ, Noelle-Neumann E. 1992. A cognitive model of response–order effects in survey measurement. In *Context Effects in Social and Psychological Research*, ed. N Schwarz, S Sudman, New York: Springer-Verlag

Schwarz N, Knauper B, Hippler HJ, Noelle–Neumann E, Clark LF. 1991. Rating scales: Numeric values may change the meaning of scale labels. *Public Opin. Q.* 55:570–82

Schwarz N, Strack F. 1985. Cognitive and affective processes in judgments of subjective well-being: a preliminary model. In *Economic Psychology*, ed. H Brandstatter, E Kirchler, pp. 439–47. Linz, Austria: R. Tauner

Shaw ME, Wright JM. 1967. *Scales for the Measurement of Attitudes.* New York: McGraw-Hill. 604 pp.

Sherif CW, Sherif M, Nebergall RE. 1965. *Attitude and Attitude Change.* Philadelphia: Saunders. 264 pp.

Sherif M, Hovland CI. 1961. *Social Judgment: Assimilation and Contrast Effects in Communication and Attitude Change.* New Haven, CT: Yale Univ. Press

Sigelman CK, Winer JL, Schoenrock CJ. 1982. The responsiveness of mentally retarded persons to questions. *Educ. Train. Mental. Retard.* 17:120–24

Sigelman L. 1981. Question-order effects on presidential popularity. *Public Opin. Q.* 45:199–207

Sigelman L. 1982. The nonvoting voter in voting research. *Am. J. Polit. Sci.* 26: 47–56

Silk AJ. 1971. Response set and the measurement of self-designated opinion leadership. *Public Opin. Q.* 35:383–97

Silver BD, Anderson BA, Abramson RP. 1986. Who overreports voting? *Am. Polit. Sci. Rev.* 80:613–24

Simon HA. 1957. *Models of Man.* New York: Wiley. 287 pp.

Singer E, Frankel MR, Glassman MB. 1983. The effect of interviewer characteristics and expectations on response. *Public Opin. Q.* 47:68–83

Small DO, Campbell DT. 1960. The effect of acquiescence response-set upon the relationship of the F scale and conformity. *Sociometry* 23:69–71

Smith TW. 1983. The hidden 25 percent: an analysis of nonresponse in the 1980 General Social Survey. *Public Opin. Q.* 47: 386–404

Smith TW. 1987. That which we call welfare by any other name would smell sweeter: an analysis of the impact of question wording on response patterns. *Public Opin. Q.* 51:75–83

Sniderman P, Grob DB. 1996. Innovations in experimental design in attitude surveys. *Annu. Rev. Sociol.* 22:377–400

Steeh C. 1981. Trends in nonresponse rates. *Public Opin. Q.* 45:40–57

Suchman L, Jordan B. 1990. Interactional troubles in face-to-face survey interviews. *J. Am. Stat. Assoc.* 85:232–53

Suchman L, Jordan B. 1992. Validity and the collaborative construction of meaning in face-to-face surveys. In *Questions About Questions*, ed. J Tanur, pp. 241–67. New York: Russell Sage Found.

Sudman S, Bradburn NM, Schwarz N. 1996. *Thinking about Answers: The Application of Cognitive Processes to Survey Methodology.* San Francisco, CA: Jossey-Bass. 304 pp.

Taylor JR, Kinnear TC. 1971. Empirical comparison of alternative methods for collecting proximity judgments. *Am. Market. Assoc. Proc. Fall Conf.*, pp. 547–50

Tourangeau R, Rasinski KA. 1988. Cognitive processes underlying context effects in attitude measurement. *Psychol. Bull.* 103: 299–314

Tourangeau R, Rips L, Rasinski K. 1998. *The Psychology of Survey Response.* New York: Cambridge Univ. Press. In press

Traugott MW, Groves RM, Lepkowski JM. 1987. Using dual frame designs to reduce nonresponse in telephone surveys. *Public Opin. Q.* 51:522–39

Traugott MW, Katosh JP. 1979. Response validity in surveys of voting behavior. *Public Opin. Q.* 43:359–77

Trott DM, Jackson DN. 1967. An experimental analysis of acquiescence. *J. Exp. Res. Pers.* 2:278–88

Vaillancourt PM. 1973. Stability of children's survey responses. *Public Opin. Q.* 37: 373–87

Visser PS, Krosnick JA, Marquette J, Curtin M. 1996. Mail surveys for election forecasting? An evaluation of the Columbus Dispatch poll. *Public Opin. Q.* 60:181–227

Visser PS, Krosnick JA, Marquette J, Curtin M. 1999. Improving election forecasting: allocation of undecided respondents, identification of likely voters, and response order effects. In *Election Polls, the News Media, and Democracy*, ed. P Lavrakas, M Traugott. In press

Warwick DP, Lininger CA. 1975. *The Sample Survey: Theory and Practice.* New York: McGraw-Hill. 344 pp.

Webster H. 1958. Correcting personality scales for response sets or suppression effects. *Psychol. Bull.* 55:62–64

Weisberg HF, Krosnick JA, Bowen BD. 1996. *An Introduction to Survey Research, Polling, and Data Analysis.* Newbury Park, CA: Sage. 394 pp. 3rd ed.

Wotruba TR. 1966. Monetary inducements and mail questionnaire response. *J. Mark. Res.* 3:398–400

Wright JR, Niemi RG. 1983. Perceptions of issue positions. *Polit. Behav.* 5:209–23

Yalch RF. 1976. Pre-election interview effects on voter turnout. *Public Opin. Q.* 40: 331–36

Ying Y. 1989. Nonresponse on the center for epidemiological studies–depression scale in Chinese Americans. *Int. J. Soc. Psychol.* 35:156–63

Yzerbyt VY, Leyens J. 1991. Requesting information to form an impression: the influence of valence and confirmatory status. *J. Exp. Soc. Psychol.* 27:337–56

Zaller J, Feldman S. 1992. A simple theory of the survey response: answering questions versus revealing preferences. *Am. J. Polit. Sci.* 36:579–616

Zuckerman M, Bernieri F, Koestner R, Rosenthal R. 1989. To predict some of the people some of the time: in search of moderators. *J. Pers. Soc. Psychol.* 57:279–93

Annu. Rev. Psychol. 1999. 50:569–98

TRUST AND DISTRUST IN ORGANIZATIONS: Emerging Perspectives, Enduring Questions

Roderick M. Kramer

Graduate School of Business, Stanford University, Stanford, California 94305;
e-mail:kramer_roderick@gsb.stanford.edu

KEY WORDS: cooperation, conspiracy, social capital, surveillance, suspicion

---

ABSTRACT

Scholarly interest in the study of trust and distrust in organizations has grown dramatically over the past five years. This interest has been fueled, at least in part, by accumulating evidence that trust has a number of important benefits for organizations and their members. A primary aim of this review is to assess the state of this rapidly growing literature. The review examines recent progress in conceptualizing trust and distrust in organizational theory, and also summarizes evidence regarding the myriad benefits of trust within organizational systems. The review also describes different forms of trust found in organizations, and the antecedent conditions that produce them. Although the benefits of trust are well-documented, creating and sustaining trust is often difficult. Accordingly, the chapter concludes by examining some of the psychological, social, and institutional barriers to the production of trust.

CONTENTS

0084-6570/99/0201-0569$08.00

INTRODUCTION

Broadly construed, the field of organizational behavior is concerned with the study of organizations as complex social systems (Pfeffer 1997, Scott 1997). From a psychological perspective, organizational behavior theory and research examine the antecedents and consequences of human behavior—both individual and collective—within organizational settings (Katz & Kahn 1978, Murnighan 1993, Weick 1979). From its inception, a central concern of the field has been identifying the determinants of intraorganizational cooperation, coordination, and control (Arrow 1974, March & Simon 1958). Within the past few years, there has been a dramatic resurgence of interest among social scientists in exploring the role that trust plays in such processes (Coleman 1990, Fukuyama 1995, Kramer & Tyler 1996, Mayer et al 1995, McAlister 1995, Putnam 1993, Misztal 1996, Seligman 1997, Sitkin & Roth 1993). This burst of scholarly activity has been paralleled by equally earnest efforts to apply emerging trust theory to a variety of important organizational problems (Brown 1994, Carnevale 1995, Shaw 1997, Whitney 1994, Zand 1997).

Despite this intense interest and activity, few attempts have been made to assess the state of this rapidly growing literature or to draw out its links to the psychological literature on trust. A primary aim of this review, accordingly, is to survey some of the prominent themes and emerging perspectives on the nature and functions of trust within organizations. In particular, I summarize progress in conceptualizing trust, noting some of the more influential images of trust found in contemporary organizational research. Second, I describe recent research on the antecedents and consequences of trust in organizations. Finally, I discuss some of the barriers to trust that arise within organizations.

IMAGES OF TRUST IN ORGANIZATIONAL THEORY

Although social scientists have afforded considerable attention to the problem of defining trust (e.g. Barber 1983, Luhmann 1988, Mayer et al 1995), a concise and universally accepted definition has remained elusive. As a consequence, the term trust is used in a variety of distinct, and not always compatible, ways within organizational research. At one end of the spectrum are formulations that highlight social and ethical facets of trust. For example, Hosmer (1995) characterized trust as "the expectation... of ethically justifiable behavior—that is, morally correct decisions and actions based upon ethical principles of analysis" (p. 399). Other conceptions emphasize the strategic and calculative dimensions of trust in organizational settings. Thus, Burt & Knez (1996) defined trust simply as "anticipated cooperation" (p. 70), arguing that the "issue isn't moral... It is office politics" (p. 70).

Despite divergence in such particulars, most trust theorists agree that, whatever else its essential features, trust is fundamentally a psychological state.

Trust as a Psychological State

When conceptualized as a psychological state, trust has been defined in terms of several interrelated cognitive processes and orientations. First and foremost, trust entails a state of perceived vulnerability or risk that is derived from individuals' uncertainty regarding the motives, intentions, and prospective actions of others on whom they depend. For example, Lewis & Weigert (1985) characterized trust as the "undertaking of a risky course of action on the confident expectation that all persons involved in the action will act competently and dutifully" (p. 971). Similarly, Robinson (1996) defined trust as a person's "expectations, assumptions, or beliefs about the likelihood that another's future actions will be beneficial, favorable, or at least not deterimental to one's interests" (p. 576).

Other influential definitions construe trust as a more general attitude or expectancy about other people and the social systems in which they are embedded (Garfinkel 1963, Luhmann 1988). For example, Barber (1983) characterized trust as a set of "socially learned and socially confirmed expectations that people have of each other, of the organizations and institutions in which they live, and of the natural and moral social orders that set the fundamental understandings for their lives" (p. 164–65).

Although acknowledging the importance of these cognitive correlates of trust, other researchers have argued that trust needs to be conceptualized as a more complex, multidimensional psychological state that includes affective and motivational components (Bromiley & Cummings 1996, Kramer et al 1996, Lewis & Weigert 1985, McAlister 1995, Tyler & Degoey 1996b). As

Fine and Holyfield (1996) noted along these lines, cognitive models of trust provide a necessary but not sufficient understanding of trust phenomena. They suggest that trust embodies also, aspects of the "world of cultural meanings, emotional responses, and social relations… one not only thinks trust, but feels trust" (p. 25).

Trust as Choice Behavior

Several organizational researchers have argued the usefulness of conceptualizing trust in terms of individuals' choice behavior in various kinds of trust dilemma situations (Arrow 1974, Kreps 1990, Miller 1992). One advantage of conceptualizing trust in terms of choice is that decisions are observable behaviors. Another is that organizational theorists possess a well-developed conceptual armamentarium for pursuing the theoretical and empirical implications of trust-as-choice (March 1994).

Within this literature, two contrasting images of choice have gained particular prominence, one that construes choice in relatively rational, calculative terms and another that affords more weight to the social and relational underpinnings of choice in trust dilemma situations.

TRUST AS RATIONAL CHOICE   The rational choice perspective, imported largely from sociological (Coleman 1990), economic (Williamson 1993), and political (Hardin 1992) theory, remains arguably the most influential image of trust within organizational science. From the perspective of rational choice theory, decisions about trust are similar to other forms of risky choice; individuals are presumed to be motivated to make rational, efficient choices (i.e. to maximize expected gains or minimize expected losses from their transactions). Such models posit further, as Schelling (1960) noted, that choice is motivated by a "conscious calculation of advantages, a calculation that in turn is based on an explicit and internally consistent value system" (p. 4).

Hardin's (1992) conception of encapsulated trust articulates many of the essential features of this view. A rational account of trust, he notes, includes two central elements. The first is the knowledge that enables a person to trust another. The second is the incentives of the person who is trusted (the trustee) to honor or fulfill that trust. Individuals can trust someone, Hardin proposes, if they have adequate grounds for believing it will be in that person's interest to be trustworthy "in the relevant way at the relevant time" (p. 153). This notion of trust, he observes, is not predicated on individuals' narrow contemplation of their own interests but is enfolded instead in a sophisticated understanding of the other party's interests. "You can more confidently trust me," Hardin (1991) posits, "if you know that my own interest will induce me to live up to your expectations. Your trust then encapsulates my interests" (p. 189).

CRITIQUES OF RATIONAL CHOICE CONCEPTIONS   Given its prominence as a conceptual platform from which much recent organizational theory and research proceeds, it is appropriate to note some of the concerns that have been raised about rational choice perspectives on trust. First, although the approach has proven enormously useful in terms of clarifying how individuals should, from a normative or prescriptive standpoint, make decisions about trust, it's adequacy as a descriptive account of how people actually do make such decisions has been questioned on several grounds. Most notably, a large and robust literature on behavioral decision making suggests that many of the assumptions of rational choice models are empirically untenable. Specifically, the extent to which decisions about trust, or any other risky decision for that matter, are products of conscious calculation and internally consistent value systems is suspect. As March (1994) cogently noted in summarizing such research, rational choice models overstate decision makers' cognitive capacities, the degree to which they engage in conscious calculation, and the extent to which they possess stable values and orderly preferences.

From a psychological perspective, another limitation of conceptions of trust grounded in presumptions regarding the rationality of choice is that they are too narrowly cognitive. Such conceptions afford too little role to emotional and social influences on trust decisions. As Granovetter (1985) aptly noted in this regard, such conceptions provide, at best, an undersocialized conception of trust. At a more fundamental level, March & Olsen (1989) take exception to the idea that notions of rational expectation and calculation are even central to the phenomenon of trust. The core idea of trust, they propose, is that it is not based on an expectation of its justification. "When trust is justified by expectations of positive reciprocal consequences, it is simply another version of economic exchange, as is clear from treatments of trust as reputation in repeated games" (p. 27).

RELATIONAL MODELS OF TRUST   In response to these limitations and concerns, a number of scholars have suggested that an adequate theory of organizational trust must incorporate more systematically the social and relational underpinnings of trust-related choices (Mayer et al 1995, McAlister 1995, Tyler & Kramer 1996). According to these arguments, trust needs to be conceptualized not only as a calculative orientation toward risk, but also a social orientation toward other people and toward society as a whole.

The initial impetus for these relational models, it should be noted, was sociological theory and research on the impact of social embeddedness on economic transactions (Granovetter 1985). The development of relational conceptions of trust was further fueled by research implicating a variety of "macro-level" structures, including networks and governance systems, in the emergence and diffusion of trust within and between organizations (Burt & Knez 1995, Coleman 1990, Kollock 1994, Powell 1996).

Recent psychological research has extended this initial work by elaborating on the cognitive, motivational, and affective underpinnings of relational trust (Shapiro et al 1992, Sheppard & Tuckinsky 1996). Within social psychology, attempts to develop systematic frameworks for conceptualizing the nature, determinants, and consequences of relational trust have taken as a point of departure either social identity theory (Brewer 1981, Kramer et al 1996) or the group-value model (Tyler & Degoey 1996b, Tyler & Lind 1992). A common feature of these models is their broader emphasis on social rather than purely instrumental (resource-based) motives driving trust behavior, including consideration of how actors' self-presentational concerns and identity-related needs and motives influence trust-related cognition and choice.

Unresolved Questions and Enduring Tensions

Rational choice and relational perspectives on trust project fundamentally different images of trust and have pushed empirical research in quite different directions. To a large extent, however, the ongoing tensions between these perspectives owe more to their distinct disciplinary origins, than to inherent features of the organizational phenomena they seek to explain.

To reconcile these diverse views of trust, it is helpful to avoid thinking of the disparity between them as reflecting conflict between mutually incompatible models of choice (i.e. that trust is either instrumental and calculative or social and relational). Rather, a more useful approach is to move in the direction of developing a contextualist account that acknowledges the role of both calculative considerations and social inputs in trust judgments and decisions. In other words, what is needed is a conception of organizational trust that incorporates calculative processes as part of the fundamental "arithmetic" of trust, but that also articulates how social and situational factors influence the salience and relative weight afforded to various instrumental and noninstrumental concerns in such calculations.

Hardin (1992) provides one promising way of moving beyond this conceptual impasse. It is useful, he argues, to conceptualize trust as a three-part relation involving properties of a truster, attributes of a trustee, and a specific context or domain over which trust is conferred. From this perspective, strategic, calculative and instrumental considerations would be expected to exert a dominant influence in some organizational contexts (e.g. transactions involving comparative strangers). However, in other contexts (such as those involving members of one's own group), relational considerations might be more salient and exert more influence over how trust is construed. Fully elaborated, a three-part theory of trust would thus afford adequate attention to both the calculative and relational underpinnings of trust.

BASES OF TRUST WITHIN ORGANIZATIONS

Considerable theory and research has focused on identifying the bases of trust within organizations (Creed & Miles 1996, Lewicki & Bunker 1995, Sheppard & Tuckinsky 1996, Mayer et al 1995, Zucker 1986). Research on this question attempts to explicate antecedent conditions that promote the emergence of trust, including psychological, social, and organizational factors that influence individuals' expectations about others' trustworthiness and their willingness to engage in trusting behavior when interacting with them.

Dispositional Trust

Ample evidence exists from both laboratory experiments and field-based re-search that individuals differ considerably in their general predisposition to trust other people (Gurtman 1992, Sorrentino et al 1995). Research suggests further that the predisposition to trust or distrust others tends to be correlated with other dispositional orientations, including people's beliefs about human nature (PEW 1996, Wrightsman 1991). To explain the origins of such disposi-tional trust, Rotter (1971, 1980) proposed that people extrapolate from their early trust-related experiences to build up general beliefs about other people. As expectancies are generalized from one social agent to another, he argued, people acquire a kind of diffuse expectancy for trust of others that eventually assumes the form of a relatively stable personality characteristic.

While acknowledging their existence, organizational theorists generally have not evinced much interest in such individual differences, except in so far as they might be reliably measured and used as a basis for screening and selec-tion of more trustworthy employees (Kipnis 1996).

History-Based Trust

Research on trust development has shown that individuals' perceptions of oth-ers' trustworthiness and their willingness to engage in trusting behavior when interacting with them are largely history-dependent processes (Boon & Hol-mes 1991, Deutsch 1958, Lindskold 1978, Pilisuk & Skolnick 1968, Solomon 1960). According to such models, trust between two or more interdependent actors thickens or thins as a function of their cumulative interaction. Interac-tional histories give decision makers information that is useful in assessing others' dispositions, intentions, and motives. This information, in turn, pro-vides a basis for drawing inferences regarding their trustworthiness and for making predictions about their future behavior.

Evidence of the importance of interactional histories in judgments about trust comes from a substantial body of experimental research linking specific patterns of behavioral interaction with changes in trust. For example, a number of studies have demonstrated that reciprocity in exchange relations enhances trust, while the absence or violation of reciprocity erodes it (Deutsch 1958, Lindskold 1978, Pilisuk et al 1971, Pilisuk & Skolnick 1968).

In noting the formative role that interactional histories play in the emergence of trust, these models draw attention to two psychological facets of trust judgments. First, individuals' judgments about others' trustworthiness are anchored, at least in part, on their *a priori* expectations about others' behavior. Second, and relatedly, those expectations change in response to the extent to which subsequent experience either validates or discredits them. Boyle and Bonacich's (1970) analysis of trust development is representative of such arguments. Individuals' expectations about trustworthy behavior, they posit, tend to change "in the direction of experience and to a degree proportional to the difference between this experience and the initial expectations applied to it" (p. 130). According to such models, therefore, interactional histories become a basis for initially calibrating and then updating trust-related expectations. In this regard, history-based trust can be construed as an important form of knowledge-based or personalized trust in organizations (Lewicki & Bunker 1995, Shapiro et al 1992).

While personalized knowledge about other organizational members represents one possible foundation for trust, such knowledge is often hard to obtain. Within most organizations, it is difficult for decision makers to accumulate sufficient knowledge about all of the persons with whom they interact or on whom they depend. The size and degree of social and structural differentiation found within most organizations precludes the sort of repeated interactions and dense social relations required for the development of such personalized trust. As a consequence, "proxies" or substitutes for direct, personalized knowledge are often sought or utilized (Creed & Miles 1996, Zucker 1986). Recent research suggests there are several bases for such presumptive trust in others.

Third Parties as Conduits of Trust

Appreciating both the importance of information regarding others' trustworthiness and the difficulty in obtaining such information, Burt & Knez (1995) argued that third parties in organizations are important conduits of trust because of their ability to diffuse trust-relevant information via gossip. As they demonstrated in a study of trust among managers in a high-tech firm, gossip constitutes a valuable source of "second-hand" knowledge about others. However, the effects of gossip on trust judgments are complex and not always in the service of rational assessment of others' trustworthiness. Part of the problem, Burt & Knez theorized, is that third parties tend to make only partial disclosures about others. In particular, third parties often communicate incomplete and skewed accounts regarding the trustworthiness of a prospective trustee because people prefer to communicate information consistent with what they believe the other party wants to hear. Consequently, when a person has a strong relation to a prospective trustee, third parties tend to convey stories and information that corroborate and strengthen the tie, thereby increasing certainty about the person's trustworthiness. Thus, third parties tend to amplify such trust.

Uzzi's (1997) more recent study of exchange relations among firms in the New York apparel industry provides further evidence of the crucial role third parties play in the development and diffusion of trust. He found that third parties acted as important "go-betweens" in new relationships enabling individuals to "roll over" their expectations from well-established relationships to others in which adequate knowledge or history was not yet available. In explaining how this worked, Uzzi argued that go-betweens transfer expectations and opportunities of existing embedded relationships to newly formed ones, thereby "furnishing a basis for trust and subsequent commitments to be offered and discharged" (p. 48).

Category-Based Trust

Category-based trust refers to trust predicated on information regarding a trustee's membership in a social or organizational category—information which, when salient, often unknowingly influences others' judgments about their trustworthiness. As Brewer (1981) noted, there are a number of reasons why membership in a salient category can provide a basis for presumptive trust. First, shared membership in a given category can serve as a "rule for defining the boundaries of low-risk interpersonal trust that bypasses the need for personal knowledge and the costs of negotiating reciprocity" when interacting with other members of that category (p. 356). Further, because of the cognitive consequences of categorization and ingroup bias, individuals tend to attribute positive characteristics such as honesty, cooperativeness, and trustworthiness to other ingroup members (Brewer 1996). As a consequence, individuals may confer a sort of depersonalized trust on other ingroup members that is predicated simply on awareness of their shared category membership.

Orbell et al (1994) investigated the effects of category-based trust on expectations and choice in a trust dilemma situation, using gender as a social category. Consistent with the notion that social perceivers possess category-based expectancies, they found that both male and female judges expected females to cooperate in prisoner's dilemma games more than males. However, females did not actually differ in their cooperation rates. Thus, this expectation was based more on gender categories than on actual gender differences between individual targets. Moreover, Orbell et al found that neither male nor female judges used gender to predict cooperation from particular individuals, or as a criterion for choosing whether to play the game with them. Based on these findings, Orbell et al argued that strong categoric expectations do not necessarily carry over to expectations about particular individuals in particular circumstances, suggesting how readily category-based expectancies are sometimes overridden by target-based expectancies.

Role-Based Trust

Role-based trust represents another important form of presumptive trust found within organizations. As with category-based trust, role-based trust constitutes a form of depersonalized trust because it is predicated on knowledge that a person occupies a particular role in the organization rather than specific knowledge about the person's capabilities, dispositions, motives, and intentions.

Roles can serve as proxies for personalized knowledge about other organizational members in several ways. First, as Barber (1983) noted, strong expectations regarding technically competent role performance are typically aligned with roles in organizations, as well as expectations that role occupants will fulfill the fiduciary responsibilities and obligations associated with the roles they occupy. Thus, to the extent that people within an organization have confidence in the fact that role occupancy signals both an intent to fulfill such obligations and competence in carrying them out, individuals can adopt a sort of presumptive trust based upon knowledge of role relations, even in the absence of personalized knowledge or history of prior interaction.

Such trust develops from and is sustained by people's common knowledge regarding the barriers to entry into organizational roles, their presumptions of the training and socialization processes that role occupants undergo, and their perceptions of various accountability mechanisms intended to ensure role compliance. As numerous scholars (Barber 1983, Dawes 1994, Meyerson et al 1996) have noted, it is not the person in the role that is trusted so much as the system of expertise that produces and maintains role-appropriate behavior of role occupants. As Dawes (1994) suggested in this regard, "We trust engineers because we trust engineering and believe that engineers are trained to apply valid principles of engineering, moreover, we have evidence every day that these principles are valid when we observe airplanes flying" (p. 24).

As with other bases of presumptive trust, roles function to reduce uncertainty regarding role occupant's trust-related intentions and capabilities. Roles thus lessen the perceived need for and costs of negotiating trust when interacting with others. Relatedly, they facilitate unilateral acts of cooperation and coordination, even when other psychological correlates usually associated with trust are missing (Meyerson et al 1996, Weick & Roberts 1993). However, role-based trust also can be quite fragile and produce catastrophic failures of cooperation and coordination, especially during organizational crises or when novel situations arise which blur roles or break down role-based interaction scripts (Mishra 1996, Webb 1996, Weick 1993).

Rule-Based Trust

If trust within organizations is largely about individuals' diffuse expectations and depersonalized beliefs regarding other organizational members, then both explicit and tacit understandings regarding transaction norms, interactional routines, and exchange practices provide an important basis for inferring that others in the organization are likely to behave in a trustworthy fashion, even in the absence of individuating knowledge about them. Rules, both formal and informal, capture much of the knowledge members have about such tacit understandings (March 1994). Rule-based trust is predicated not on a conscious calculation of consequences, but rather on shared understandings regarding the system of rules regarding appropriate behavior. As March & Olson (1989) put it, rule-based trust is sustained within an organization "not [by] an explicit contract... [but] by socialization into the structure of rules" (p. 27). When reciprocal confidence in members' socialization into and continued adherence to a normative system is high, mutual trust can acquire a taken-for-granted quality.

Fine & Holyfield (1996) provide a nice illustration of how explicit rules and tacit understandings function to create and sustain high levels of mutual trust within an organization. Their study examined the bases of trust in the Minnesota Mycological Society, an organization that consists of amateur mushroom afficionados. This organization provides a rich setting in which to study the bases of trust for several reasons. First, the costs of misplaced trust in this organization can be quite severe: eating a mushroom that someone else in the organization has mistakenly declared safe for consumption can lead to serious illness and even, in rare instances, death. Given such risks, Fine & Holyfield note, credibility is lost only once unless a mistake is reasonable. Consequently, members are likely to be vigilant about assessing and maintaining mutual trust and trustworthiness. Second, because membership in the organization is voluntary, exit is comparatively costless. If doubts about others' trustworthiness become too great, therefore, members will take their trust elsewhere and the organization will die. Thus, the organization's survival depends upon its ability to successfully instill and sustain perceptions of mutual trustworthiness among its members.

Fine & Holyfield identified three important bases of trust within this organization, which they termed awarding trust, managing risk, and transforming trust. One way trust is created, they observed, is to award trust to others even when confidence in them may be lacking. For example, considerable social pressure is exerted on novices to consume dishes prepared by other members at banquets. As Fine & Holyfield put it, there is an insistence on trust. Thus, even if members remain privately anxious, their public behavior connotes high levels of trust. Collectively, these displays constitute a potent form of social proof to members that their individual acts of trust are sensible.

This insistence on trust is adaptive, of course, only if collective trustworthiness is actually in place. Accordingly, a second crucial element in the management of trust within this organization occurs through practices and arrangements that ensure competence and due diligence. This result is achieved partially through meticulous socialization of newcomers to the organization. Novices participate in these socialization processes with appropriate levels of commitment because it helps them manage the risks of mushroom eating and secure a place in the social order of the group. In turn, more seasoned organizational members teach novices out of a sense of obligation, having themselves benefitted from instruction from those who came before them. This repaying of their own instruction constitutes an interesting temporal (transgenerational) variant of depersonalized trust.

Over time, Fine and Holyfield argue, as members acquire knowledge about the organization, the nature of trust is transformed. Early on, the organization is simply a "validator" of trust for new members. Subsequently, however, it becomes an "arena in which trusting relations are enacted and organizational interaction serves as its own reward" (p. 29). As with trust in engineers, this form of trust is not simply trust in the expertise of specific individuals, but more importantly, trust in a system of expertise.

Another way in which rules foster trust is through their effects on individuals' self-perceptions and their shaping of expectations about other organizational members. As March (1994) observed in this regard, organizations function much like "stage managers" by providing "prompts that evoke particular identities in particular situations" (p. 72). Miller (1992) offers an excellent example of this kind of socially constructed and ultimately self-reinforcing dynamic. In discussing the underpinnings of cooperation at Hewlett-Packard, he noted that, "The reality of cooperation is suggested by the open lab stock policy, which not only allows engineers access to all equipment, but encourages them to take it home for personal use" (p. 197).

From a strictly economic perspective, this policy simply reduces monitoring and transaction costs. However, from the standpoint of a rule-based conception of trust-related interactions, its consequences are more subtle and far-reaching. As Miller (1992) observes, "the open door symbolizes and demonstrates management's trust in the cooperativeness of the employees" (p. 197). Because such acts are so manifestly predicated on trust in others, they tend to breed trust in turn.

Rule-based practices of this sort can also exert subtle influences, not only on individuals' perceptions of their own honesty and trustworthiness, but also their expectations and beliefs about other organizational members' honesty and trustworthiness. As Miller notes in this regard, by eliminating time clocks and locks on equipment room doors at Hewlett-Packard, the organization builds a "shared expectation among all the players that cooperation will most likely be reciprocated" creating "a shared 'common knowledge' in the ability of the players to reach cooperative outcomes" (p. 197). By institutionalizing trust through practices at the macro-organizational (collective) level, trust becomes internalized at the micro-organizational (individual) level. Thus, rule-based trust becomes a potent form of expectational asset (Knez & Camerer 1994) that facilitates spontaneous coordination and cooperation among organizational members.

Cross-cultural studies on trust provide further insights into the complexity and variety of these subtle links between rule-based understandings and expectational assets. Yamagishi & Yamagishi (1994) reviewed survey evidence that Japanese citizens often report lower levels of trust compared with their American counterparts. At first glance, this result is quite surprising. From the perspective of the widely-held view that Japanese society is characterized by close, stable, long-term social relations, one might expect that trust should be stronger within Japanese society. To resolve this anomaly, Yamagishi & Yamagishi proposed an important distinction between generalized trust and assurance. What characterizes Japanese society, they argue, is not generalized trust but rather mutual assurance. This mutual assurance is predicated on the stability of interpersonal and interorganizational relationships within the society. Because of this high degree of perceived stability, social uncertainty in transactions is greatly reduced. As Yamagishi & Yamagishi observe, individuals within such a society can count more strongly on ingroup bias for preferential treatment!

In American society, in contrast, no comparable sense of stability or assurance is readily available. As a result, social uncertainty in transactions tends to be greater. Thus, trust concerns among Americans revolve around reducing such uncertainty, and this is manifested in terms of greater reliance on personalized knowledge, reputational information about others, or both. The results of this study by Yamagishi & Yamagishi provide strong support for this argument.

BENEFITS OF TRUST

The ascension of trust as a major focus of recent organizational research reflects, in no small measure, accumulating evidence of the substantial and varied benefits, both individual and collective, that accrue when trust is in place. Perhaps most influential in this regard have been Putnam's (1993) provocative findings implicating trust as a critical factor in understanding the origins of civic engagment and its role in the development of democratic regimes in Italian communities. Fukuyama's (1995) more recent, panoramic characterization of the role trust plays in societal functioning has provided further impetus for arguments that trust constitutes an important source of social capital within social systems.

Although strictly speaking, Putnam's and Fukuyama's findings pertain to social systems writ large, their organizational implications have not gone unnoticed. Within organizational settings, trust as a form of social capital has been discussed primarily on three levels, including its constructive effects on 1. reducing transaction costs within organizations, 2. increasing spontaneous sociability among organizational members, and 3. facilitating appropriate (i.e. adaptive) forms of deference to organizational authorities.

Trust and Transaction Costs

In the absence of personalized knowledge about others, or adequate grounds for conferring trust on them presumptively, trust within organizations must be either individually negotiated or substitutes for trust located (Barber 1983, Kollock 1994, Sabel 1993, Shapiro 1987, Sitkin 1995, Sitken & Roth 1993). Even when effective, such remedies are often inefficient and costly. Recognition of this problem has led a number of theorists to focus on the role of trust in reducing the costs of both intra- and interorganizational transactions (Bromiley & Cummings 1996, Chiles & McMackin 1996, Creed & Miles 1996, Granovetter 1985, Uzzi 1997, Williamson 1993).

From a psychological perspective, one way in which trust can function to reduce transaction costs is by operating as a social decision heuristic. Social decision heuristics represent behavioral rules of thumb actors use when making decisions about how to respond to various kinds of choice dilemma situations they encounter (Allison & Messick 1990). The utility of such heuristics in trust dilemma situations is suggested by Uzzi's (1997) study, described earlier, of exchange relations among firms in the New York apparel industry. Uzzi found that trust in this setting operated not like the calculated risk of economic models, but more like a heuristic assumption that decision makers adopted "...a predilection to assume the best when interpreting another's motives and actions" (p. 43). As evidence of the heuristic quality of judgment and action in this setting, he noted an absence of formal monitoring or measuring devices for gauging and enforcing reciprocity. Instead, individuals spontaneously and unilaterally engaged in a variety of actions that helped solve others' problems as they arose. In interpreting these findings, Uzzi reasoned that "The heuristic character of trust permits actors to be responsive to stimuli" (p. 44). In this fashion, he noted, trust heuristics facilitate the exchange of a variety of assets that are difficult to put a price on but that mutually enrich and benefit each organization's ability to compete and overcome unexpected problems.

Recent research on the evolution of cooperation within complex social systems provides further evidence of the substantial benefits that accrue, at both the individual and collective level, from heuristic forms of trust behavior (Bendor et al 1991 Kollock 1993, Messick & Liebrand 1995, Parks & Komorita 1997). Viewed in aggregate, the findings from these studies suggest that heuristics that predicate presumptive trust (i.e. that are generous with respect to giving others the "benefit of the doubt" when "noise" or uncertainty regarding their trustworthiness is present) can produce substantial increases in both individual and joint payoffs—at least within the context of ecologies in which reasonable numbers of other trustworthy actors are present.

Trust and Spontaneous Sociability

Fukuyama (1995) argued that one of the most important manifestations of trust as a form of social capital is the spontaneous sociability such trust engenders. When operationalized in behavioral terms, spontaneous sociability refers to the myriad forms of cooperative, altruistic, and extra-role behavior in which members of a social community engage, that enhance collective well-being and further the attainment of collective goals (PEW 1996). Within organizational contexts, spontaneous sociability assumes many forms. Organizational members are expected, for example, to contribute their time and attention towards the achievement of collective goals (Murnighan et al 1994, Olson 1965), they are expected to share useful information with other organizational members (Bonacich & Schneider 1992), and they are expected to exercise responsible restraint when using valuable but limited organizational resources (Messick et al 1983, Tyler & Degoey 1996a).

Several empirical studies document the important role trust plays in people's willingness to engage in such behaviors. In an early study, Messick et al (1983) investigated the hypothesis that trust, operationalized in terms of individuals' expectations of reciprocity (i.e. their belief that if they cooperated, others would do so as well), would influence individuals' willingness to voluntarily reduce their consumption of a rapidly depleting common resource pool. In support of this prediction, they found that as individuals received feedback that collective resources were becoming more scarce, those who expected reciprocal restraint from others were much more likely to exercise restraint themselves. In contrast, those whose expectations of reciprocity were low displayed little self-restraint. Significantly, the behavior of low and high trusters did not diverge when resources were plentiful.

In a subsequent study, Brann and Foddy (1988) investigated the effects of interpersonal trust on individuals' cooperative response in a simulated social dilemma. They varied the rate at which a shared resource pool was declining, so that some study participants received feedback that the pool was experiencing only minimal decline, whereas others were led to believe it was facing depletion. Before participating in this task, participants' levels of interpersonal trust were measured by using Rotter's Interpersonal Trust Scale (Rotter 1980). Based on their responses, they were classified as either high or low trusters. Brann & Foddy found that, although low trusters' consumption behavior was unaffected by feedback about the state of the collective resource, high trusters showed differential response, consuming more when resource deterioration was minimal but less under conditions of increasing scarcity.

Parks, Henager, & Scamahorn (1996) examined how low- and high-trust individuals respond to messages of intent from other participants in a social dilemma. They found that low trusters reacted to a competitive message by decreasing cooperation, but were unaffected by a cooperative message. In contrast, high trusters reacted to the cooperative message by increasing cooperation but were unaffected by the competitive message. In a second study, they assessed differences in low- and high-trusters' response to inconsistent messages from others about cooperative intent. They found that a period of unconditional, message-consistent behavior immediately after stated intent can make low and high trusters responsive to cooperative and competitive messages, respectively. They also found, interestingly, that low trusters reacted particularly strongly to inconsistent messages about cooperative intent, rating an inconsistent person as less trustworthy compared with high-trusters' ratings of the same person.

In another study, Parks & Hulbert (1995) investigated the effects of trust on decision makers' responses to fear in social dilemma situations. Specficially, they compared individuals' choices in two different forms of social dilemma—a resource contribution (public goods) version of the dilemma and a resource restraint (commons dilemma) version. They used individuals' responses to Yamagishi's Trust Scale to separate study participants into groups of low and high trusters. They found that high trusters cooperated more than low trusters when fear was present, but cooperated at the same rate when fear was absent. However, the effects of fear within each dilemma were complex. Removing fear from the public goods version, they found, decreased high trusters' cooperation, while removing fear from the commons dilemma version increased low truster's cooperation. In discussing these findings, Parks & Hulbert used prospect theory to argue that low trusters may tend to frame zero payoffs in terms of negative reference points ("I didn't gain anything"), whereas high trusters frame comparable outcomes in terms of positive anchors ("I didn't lose anything").

In sum, the results from these studies demonstrate that trust enhances individuals' willingness to engage in various forms of spontaneous sociability, but in complex and often unexpected ways. In assessing the generalizability of this finding, it should be noted that there also exists evidence that the efficacy of trust for solving large-scale collective-action dilemmas of this sort may be limited. Survey results from a study of citizen community involvement (PEW

1996) show that, although trust is important in predicting civic engagement, trust alone is not always enough. Instead, people's level of participation in their communities depends also on perceptions regarding the efficacy of their actions. Additional evidence of possible limitations of trust comes from laboratory research by Sato (1988). Using a simulated social dilemma, she demonstrated that the effects of trust weaken as group size increases. To explain this finding, Sato argued that strategic considerations, including diminished perceptions of the impact of one's own actions on others, as well as diminished expectations about others' cooperativeness, reduce the perceived efficacy of trust as a collective becomes larger.

Trust and Voluntary Deference

Another important stream of organizational research has examined the relationship between trust and various forms of voluntary deference within hierarchical relationships in organizations. Although hierarchical relationships assume varied forms (e.g. leader-follower, manager-subordinate, and employer-employee), the centrality of trust within such relationships has long been recognized (Arrow 1974, Miller 1992).

From the standpoint of those in positions of authority, trust is crucial for a variety of reasons. First, as Tyler & Degoey (1996b) noted, if organizational authorities have to continually explain and justify their actions, their ability to effectively manage would be greatly diminished. Second, because of the costs and impracticality of monitoring performance, authorities cannot detect and punish every failure to cooperate, nor can they recognize and reward every cooperative act. As a result, efficient organizational performance depends on individuals' feelings of obligation toward the organization, their willingness to comply with its directives and regulations, and their willingness to voluntarily defer to organizational authorities. In addition, when conflict arises, trust is important because it influences acceptance of dispute resolution procedures and outcomes. Research has shown that individuals are more likely to accept outcomes, even if unfavorable, when individuals trust an authority's motives and intentions (Tyler 1994).

Recognizing its importance, researchers have investigated the conditions under which people are likely to attribute trustworthiness to those in positions of authority. Early research on this topic sought to identify specific attributes associated with perceived trustworthiness. For example, Gabarro (1978) found that perceived integrity, motives, consistency, openness, discreteness, functional competence, interpersonal competence, and decision making judgment contributed to attributions of trustworthiness between vice-presidents and presidents. Along similar lines, Butler (1991) found that perceived availability, competence, consistency, fairness, integrity, loyalty, openness, overall trust, promise fulfillment, and receptivity influenced subordinates' judgments of an authority's trustworthiness.

More recent social psychological research has refined and extended our understanding of the factors that influence trustworthiness attributions. The most systematic research on this topic has been conducted by Tyler and his associates (reviewed in Tyler & Degoey 1996b and Tyler & Lind 1992). This research identifies several important components of trustworthiness attributions. These include status recognition, which reflects the extent to which authorities recognize and validate individuals' sense of full-fledged membership in their organization, as well as trust in benevolence, which refers to individuals' beliefs that authorities with whom they deal are well intentioned and honest in their decisions. A third important factor is neutrality, which implies perceived fairness and impartiality in decisions. Another finding from this stream of research is that trust matters more in relationships when some sort of common bond exists between authorities and their subordinates.

Other research by Brockner and his associates has investigated the influence of procedural variables on attributions regarding authorities' trustworthiness. Brockner and Siegel (1996) noted that procedures are important because they communicate information not only about authorities' motivation and intention to behave in a trustworthy fashion, but also their ability to do so, a factor they characterize as procedural competence. In support of this general argument, they report evidence that procedures that are structurally and interactionally fair tend to increase trust, whereas lack of perceived structural and procedural fairness tends to elicit low levels of trust.

More recently, Brockner et al (1997) explored some of the conditions under which trust matters more or less. They argued that, all else being equal, trust matters more to individuals when outcomes are unfavorable. In explaining why, they note that receipt of favorable outcomes does not raise issues of authorities' trustworthiness, because the outcomes themselves constitute evidence that the authorities can be counted on to perform behaviors desired by the trustor. Under these circumstances, "...trust is neither threatened nor critical in determining support for authorities" (p. 560). In contrast, when outcomes are unfavorable, trust becomes more critical and authorities are unlikely to receive much support. Brockner et al tested this general prediction in three different studies and found, consistent with it, that trust was more strongly related to support for an authority when outcomes were relatively unfavorable.

BARRIERS TO TRUST

Although recognizing the importance of trust, and the diverse benefits that flow from it, organizational theorists have been cognizant also of the difficulties that attend the creation and maintenance of trust within organizations (Fox 1974, Sitkin & Roth 1993, Sitkin & Stickel 1996). However desirable trust may be, its purchase—to paraphrase Arrow (1974)—is neither easy nor assured. In trying to understand why trust remains such an elusive and ephemeral resource within many organizations, researchers have focused attention on identifying psychological and social factors that impede the development of trust and that contribute to the fragility of ongoing trust relations.

Dynamics of Distrust and Suspicion

There has been widespread recognition among organizational theorists that distrust and suspicion are common and recurring problems within many organizations (Fox 1974, PEW 1998, Sitkin & Roth 1993). Distrust has been defined as a "lack of confidence in the other, a concern that the other may act so as to harm one, that he does not care about one's welfare or intends to act harmfully, or is hostile" (Grovier 1994, p. 240). Suspicion has been viewed as one of the central cognitive components of distrust (Deustch 1958) and has been characterized as a psychological state in which perceivers "actively entertain multiple, possibly rival, hypotheses about the motives or genuineness of a person's behavior" (Fein & Hilton 1994, p. 168).

Fein (1996) argued that suspicion can be triggered by a variety of circumstances, including situations where perceivers have forewarnings that another might be insincere or untrustworthy, in which their expectations have been violated, and when they recognize situational cues or possess contextual information that suggests another might have ulterior motives. Experiments by Fein and his associates (Fein 1996, Hilton et al 1993) have explored two competing predictions about the effects of suspicion on judgment. One possibility, they noted, is that information that makes perceivers suspicious might lead to a state of attributional conservatism, elevating their threshold for accepting behavioral information. In other words, once alerted to the possibility of deception, individuals may be predisposed to avoid a rush to judgment, remaining open to the prospect that there is more to a situation than meets the eye. A second and contrasting possibility is that suspicion triggers more sophisticated attributional analyses "characterized by active, careful consideration of the potential motives and causes that may influence people's behaviors" (Fein 1996, p. 1167). In general, the results of their studies demonstrate that suspicion evokes relatively active, mindful processing of attribution-relevant information, thereby supporting the attributional sophistication argument.

Taken together, the results of Fein et al's studies lend support to an image of social perceivers as "intuitive scientists" attempting to draw reasonable inferences about others' trustworthiness from available social data. Other recent research has highlighted the origins and antecedents of less rational forms of distrust and suspicion that may arise within organizations (Kramer 1998). A number of recent studies, for example, have identified a variety of factors that increase individuals' distrust and suspicion of others, including dispositional and situational factors that influence individuals' self-consciousness and perceptions of being under evaluative scrutiny in organizations (Fenigstein & Vanable 1992, Kramer 1994, Zimbardo et al 1981). As Fein and Hilton (1994) noted along these lines, contextual factors that elevate suspicion regarding an actor's motives can have negative consequences for both the perceiver and the suspected social actor. "Often through no fault of their own," they note, "actors may be the targets of others' suspicions because of the context in which their behavior occurred" (p. 171).

Related psychological research suggests that basic cognitive processes such as social categorization may heighten distrust and suspicion between individuals from different groups within an organization. Evidence for the existence of such category-based distrust was provided initially by ethnographic research and laboratory studies on ingroup bias (reviewed in Brewer 1981, 1996). These studies demonstrated that categorization of individuals into distinct groups often resulted in individuals' evaluating outgroup members as less honest, reliable, open, and trustworthy than members of their own group. These effects were observed, moreover, even when those group boundaries were based on arbitrary, minimal and transient criteria. Recent research by Insko, Schopler, and their associates on the discontinuity effect (reviewed in Insko & Schopler 1997) points to a similar conclusion. Viewed in aggregate, these studies suggest that mere categorization and perceived differentiation may create a climate of presumptive distrust between groups within an organization.

In addition to exploring the antecedents and consequences of distrust and suspicion within organizations, other research has examined the more general problem of distrust in organizations, including both public and private institutions (Brown 1994, Carnevale 1995, Nye et al 1997). As Pfeffer (1997) noted, from the moment we are born and until we die, such institutions exert a profound impact on the quality of our lives. Their ability to do so, however, depends in no small measure upon public trust in them, including trust in both their competence and their integrity (Barber 1983, Brown 1994).

Unfortunately, however important it may be, there is substantial evidence that trust in both public and private institutions has been declining for several decades (Carnevale 1995, Coleman 1990, Nye et al 1997, PEW 1996, 1998). For example, although 75% of Americans said they trusted the federal government in 1964, only 25% expressed comparable levels of trust in 1997. Similarly, trust in universities has fallen from 61 to 30%, medical institutions from 73 to 29%, and journalism from 29 to 14% (Nye 1997). Major private companies fare no better, trust in them having fallen from 55% to 21% over this same period (Nye 1997). Another indicator of the pervasiveness of institutional distrust and suspicion is provided by data regarding the frequency with which many Americans endorse various conspiracy theories and abuses of trust involving public institutions (Butler et al 1995, Goertzel 1994, Harrison & Thomas 1997, Pipes 1997).

Although data regarding their prevalence seem unequivocal, the sources of institutional distrust and suspicion remain much less clear. Researchers have advanced many different explanations for the decline in institutional trust, ranging from historical, economic, organizational, psychological, and sociological factors (for overviews, see Harrison & Thomas 1997, Nye et al 1997). A number of studies highlight the importance of unmet or violated expectancies in explaining why public trust in institutions has eroded. Nye (1997), for example, has noted that the decline of public trust in government can be attributed, at least in part, to its perceived failure to solve a variety of social ills. According to this hypothesis, government promises to remedy urgent social problems (e.g. to eradicate poverty, racial injustice, and catastrophic illnesses) led to heightened expectations that government would solve these problems. As these expectations have gone unfillfulled, so has trust diminished.

Pursuing the effects of violated expectancies on people's trust in intstitutions, Zimmer (1972) argued that individuals, when making judgments regarding institutional trustworthiness, tend to overgeneralize from vivid, highly salient events involving institutions and their leaders. To investigate this hypothesis, he examined the impact of Watergate on public perceptions of trust in government. He noted that, before Watergate, public trust in Richard Nixon had been generally quite high (in fact, voters in one survey had rated Nixon as more trustworthy than either George McGovern or Edward Kennedy!). Zimmer theorized that subsequent revelations during the Watergate hearings demonstrated to people that their trust in Nixon had been misplaced. Such revelations would lead, he predicted, to a decrease in public trust, especially among those who had originally voted for Nixon. After all, he reasoned, the sense of violated trust should be especially acute among such individuals, resulting in greater generalized distrust of government. Zimmer found support for this hypothesis: People who had voted for Nixon showed the highest levels of subsequent distrust in government.

In interpreting these results, Zimmer speculated that people may use the behaviors of institutional leaders as reference points for gauging their basic beliefs about the state of society and as reality-testing mechanisms when appraising the trustworthiness of its institutions in general. In other words, people may draw general inferences about institutional trust from the behavior of highly visible role models. As a consequence, he reasoned, the behavior of public leaders while in office "may unknowingly or indirectly define reality in more ways and for more of the public than has been appreciated" (p. 749).

If unmet expectations and general beliefs about institutions do contribute to the erosion of trust, it is instructive to consider the sources of such expectations and beliefs. Cappella and Jamieson (1997) recently reviewed evidence implicating the media in the growing distrust and cynicism of the public towards its institutions. The framing of news, they argue, directly affects the public's mistrust of institutions. In particular, news stories that adopt strategic frames [i.e. frames that emphasize themes of "winning and losing and the self-interest implied by that orientation" and that activate negative actor traits such as those indicative of "artifice, pandering, deceit, staging, and positioning for advantage" (p. 85)] tend to promote greater mistrust and cynicism than more neutral, issue-oriented frames. To investigate this hypothesis, they conducted a series of carefully controlled experiments in which news involving public leaders and institutions was systematically framed in either strategic terms or in more neutral, issue-pertinent terms. The results from these studies support their argument that strategic frames produce greater mistrust and cynicism.

Although there is little doubt that trust in public institutions has declined substantially over the past several decades and remains disquietingly low today, it is important to note that the implications of this trend are far less evident than sometimes assumed. First, as Cappella and Jamieson (1997) have cogently noted, it is not clear whether observed levels of distrust and suspicion reflect unwarranted cynicism about the state of contemporary institutions or just realism. Second, even if real, the tangible (behavioral) implications of such distrust and suspicion are far from clear. As the PEW Report (1996) concluded, based on its survey results, although a "general distrust of others is an obvious social ill . . . its direct relevance to the way people act is unclear" (p. 7). Finally, although often portrayed in the popular press and social science literature largely in negative terms, distrust and suspicion may constitute appropriate and even highly adaptive stances toward institutions. Vigilance and wariness about institutions, some have argued, constitute essential components of healthy and resilient organizations and societies (Barber 1983, March & Olsen 1994, Shapiro 1987). From this perspective, distrust and suspicion may, in a very fundamental sense, constitute potent and important forms of social capital.

Technologies That Undermine Trust

An emerging area of organizational research, and one that is almost certain to become increasingly important over the next few years, concerns the relationship between technology and trust. Enthusiasm over technological remedies to trust-related problems has been considerable, as evidenced by the rapid infusion into the workplace of surveillance systems and other forms of electronic monitoring of employee performance. For example, according to Aiello

(1993), over 70,000 U.S. companies purchased surveillance software between 1990 and 1992, at an cost of more than $500 million dollars.

Organizations typically adopt such technological remedies in the hope of enhancing employee trustworthiness (e.g. assuring compliance with regulations and deterring misbehavior). Ironically, there is increasing evidence that such systems can actually undermine trust and may even elicit the very behaviors they are intended to suppress or eliminate. In a recent discussion of this evidence, Cialdini (1996) identified several reasons why monitoring and surveillance can diminish trust within an organization. First, there is evidence that when people think their behavior is under the control of extrinsic motivators, intrinsic motivation may be reduced (Enzle & Anderson 1993). Thus, surveillance may undermine individuals' motivation to engage in the very behaviors such monitoring is intended to induce or ensure. For example, innocent employees who are subjected to compulsory polygraphs, drug testing, and other forms of mass screening designed to deter misbehavior may become less committed to internal standards of honesty and intregity in the workplace.

Monitoring systems can produce other unintended and ironic consequences with respect to trust. Hochschild (1983) described how fear of monitoring adversely impacted organizational trust and customer service among flight attendants at Delta Airlines. Flight attendants came to fear and distrust their passengers because of a policy allowing passengers to write letters of complaint about inflight service. No matter how justified or unjustified the complaint from the flight attendant's perspective, such letters would automatically end up in the attendant's file. The resultant climate of suspicion created by this policy was further intensified because flight attendants feared that "passengers" they were serving might not even really be passengers at all. Instead, they might be supervisors working undercover to monitor their performance. Thus, a system intended to produce more trustworthy (reliable) and friendly service encounters unintendedly produced fearful, suspicious ones.

As Cialdini (1996) also notes, monitoring and surveillance systems communicate to employees that they are not trusted, potentially breeding mistrust and resentment in return. When people feel coerced into complying with a behavior, they may resist the behavior when they think monitoring is imperfect and they can get away with it. Because of psychological reactance, even honest employees may try to cheat or sabotage monitoring systems.

Well-intentioned and highly committed organizational members may also feel impelled to cheat when regulations designed to increase trustworthy performance enforce perverse behaviors. Moore-Ede (1993), for example, described the unintended effects of a regulation requiring long-distance truckers to keep detailed logs of their driving time. This policy was implemented to increase driver and public safety by promoting compliance with laws mandating prudent limits on driving hours. Unfortunately, drivers who tried to adhere to these regulations often found themselves trying to sleep when wide awake and, worse, driving when tired. To circumvent these regulations, therefore, some drivers began keeping two sets of books—one for inspection purposes and one that tracked hours actually worked.

Other evidence suggests that the corrosive effects of surveillance extend to those doing the surveillance. Several studies have shown, for example, that the act of surveillance may increase distrust of surveillants over those they monitor (Kruglanski 1970, Strickland 1958). This result has been explained in terms of self-perception theory. Less obvious, but no less insidious in terms of their consequences, are the behaviors that surveillants don't engage in when surveillance and other substitutes for trust are utilized in organizations. As one executive who had implemented a computer monitoring system called Overview mused, "If I didn't have the Overview, I would walk around and talk to people more . . . I would be more interested in what people are thinking about" (Zuboff 1988, quoted in Kipnis 1996, p. 331). Thus, systems intended to guarantee trust may, ironically, not only make it more difficult for employees to demonstrate their trustworthiness, but also for authorities to learn about the distribution of trust within their organizations.

Breach of the Psychological Contract

Another promising stream of recent organizational research has examined the conditions under which initial trust in organizations unravels. Robinson (1996) examined the relationship between employees' trust in an organization and their perceptions of the extent to which the organization had either fulfilled or breached its psychological contract with them. She defined psychological contracts in terms of employees' beliefs regarding the terms and conditions of their reciprocal exchange relation with their employer (i.e. what they owed the employer and what the employer owed them). Psychological contract breach was characterized, in turn, as a subjective experience based on employes' perceptions that the organization had failed to fulfill its perceived obligations.

To investigate the relationship between trust and psychological contract breach, Robinson conducted a longitudinal study of newly hired managers, measuring their initial trust in the organization, as well as their trust levels at 18 and 30 months on the job. She found that initial trust in an employer was negatively related to subsequent perceptions of psychological contract breach. Specifically, individuals with high initial trust were less likely to perceive the psychological contract had been breached compared with those with low initial trust. She also found that prior trust moderated the relationship between psychological contract breach and subsequent trust, such that employees with low initial trust in their employer reported a greater decline in trust after perceived breach than employees with high initial trust. Finally, Robinson found a negative correlation between psychological contract breach and several important forms of employee contributions to the organization, including job performance, civic virtue (extra-role) behaviors, and intentions to remain with the organization.

The Fragility of Trust

Numerous scholars have noted that trust is easier to destroy than create (Barber 1983, Janoff-Bulman 1992, Meyerson et al 1996). To explain the fragility of trust, Slovic (1993) argued that there are a variety of cognitive factors that contribute to asymmetries in the trust-building versus trust-destroying process. First, negative (trust-destroying) events are more visible and noticeable than positive (trust-building) events. Second, trust-destroying events carry more weight in judgment than trust-building events of comparable magnitude. To provide evidence for this asymmetry principle, Slovic evaluated the impact of hypothetical news events on people's trust judgments. In support of his general thesis, he found that negative events had more impact on trust judgments than positive events. Slovic noted further that asymmetries between trust and distrust may be reinforced by the fact that sources of bad (trust-destroying) news tend to be perceived as more credible than sources of good news.

In addition to these purely cognitive factors, researchers have been interested in how organizational factors, such as structural position in an organization, contribute to asymmetries in judgments regarding trust and distrust. Burt and Knez (1995) examined how network structures and the social dynamics they create differentially affect trust and distrust judgments. In the same study described earlier of managers in a high tech firm, they investigated the influence of third parties on the diffusion of distrust within managers' networks. They found that, although both trust and distrust were amplified by third-party disclosures, distrust was amplified to a greater extent than trust. As a result, judgments about distrust had, as Burt and Knez put it, a "catastrophic" quality to them. In explaining these findings, Burt and Knez posited that third parties are more attentive to negative information and often prefer negative gossip to positive information and gossip. Consequently, indirect connections amplify the distrust associated with weak relations much more than they amplify trust among strong relations.

Another study (Kramer 1996) investigated asymmetries in the construal of trust-enhancing versus trust-decreasing behaviors as a function of individuals' location within a hierarchical relationship. Specifically, this study examined how graduate students and their faculty advisors judged the level of trust in their relationship and the evidence they used in making those judgments. Using an autobiographical narrative methodology, students and faculty described the history of their interactions, recalling those behaviors that enhanced or undermined trust in the relationship. Content analysis of these narratives showed that individuals in low status positions (graduate students) tended to code more of their advisors' behaviors as diagnostic of trustworthiness compared with those in positions of high status (faculty advisors). To explain these findings, Kramer argued that, because of their greater dependence and vulnerability, trust concerns are more salient to individuals in low-status positions. As a consequence, they tend to be more viligant and ruminative about trust-relevant transactions. They also code more transactions as diagnostic of trustworthiness and can more easily recall instances of trust violation.

The empirical patterns observed in these studies are consistent with arguments by other theorists, such as Hardin (1992) and Gambetta (1988), that asymmetries in the accumulation of relevant experience by low and high trusters may differentially impact their opportunities to sample and learn from trust-building versus trust-eroding experiences. As Gambetta (1988) noted in this regard, distrust is very difficult to invalidate through experience, because it either "prevents people from engaging in the appropriate kind of social experiment, or, worse, it leads to behavior which bolsters the validity of distrust itself" (p. 234). Consequently, presumptive distrust tends to become perpetual distrust.

CONCLUDING COMMENTS

In assessing the state of social psychological theory at the end of the 1970s, Kelley (1980) once observed that the field read "more like a Sears Roebuck catalogue than like a novel" (p. 8). Athough social psychology contained an impressive listing of items of possible interest, he noted, there was still "no story with a plot, development of characters, and so on" (p. 8). Kelley's quip can be applied just as aptly to contemporary research on trust in organizations. Although there has been an impressive proliferation of middle-range theories about trust, an integrative theory of organizational trust continues to elude researchers. Relatedly, while empirical evidence continues to accumulate at a rapid rate, there been a dearth of studies using overarching concepts and multiple-level measures that might help bridge the increasingly diverse conceptions of trust represented by economic, sociological, and social psychological perspectives.

If the glass remains half empty with respect to trust research, however, it is also half full. Not long ago, Luhmann (1988) was able to lament the existence of "a regretably sparse literature with trust as its main theme" (p. 8). Happily, that lament can no longer be uttered with the same force. Trust has rightly moved from bit player to center stage in contemporary organizational theory and research. Nor does Williamson's (1993) more recent assessment that trust remains a "diffuse and disappointing" (p. 485) concept in the social sciences seem as true today as it did only a few years ago. Recent research has sharpened our understanding of the complexity of trust in organizations and enhanced our appreciation of the myriad and often subtle benefits such trust confers. Future theory and research on trust will undoubtedly add to its stock in the organizational sciences.

> **Visit the *Annual Reviews home page* at http://www.AnnualReviews.org.**

Literature Cited

Aiello JR. 1993. Computer-based monitoring: electronic surveillance and its effects. *J. Appl. Soc. Psychol.* 23:499–507

Allison ST, Messick DM. 1990. Social decision heuristics in the use of shared resources. *J. Behav. Decis. Mak.* 3:195–204

Arrow K. 1974. *The Limits of Organization.* New York: Norton. 173 pp.

Barber B. 1983. *The Logic and Limits of Trust.* New Brunswick, NJ: Rutgers Univ. Press. 310 pp.

Bendor J, Kramer RM, Stout S. 1991. When in doubt: cooperation in the noisy prisoner's dilemma. *J. Confl. Resolut.* 35:691–719

Bonacich P, Schneider S. 1992. Communication networks and collective action. In *A Social Psychological Approach to Social Dilemmas*, ed. WG Liebrand, DM Messick, HAM Wilke, pp. 128–41. Oxford, Engl: Pergammon. 278 pp.

Boon SD, Holmes JG. 1991. The dynamics of interpersonal trust: Resolving uncertainty in the face of risk. In *Cooperation and Prosocial Behavior*, ed. RA Hinde, J Groebel, pp. 167–82. New York: Cambridge Univ. Press. 411 pp.

Boyle R, Bonacich P. 1970. The development of trust and mistrust in mixed-motives games. *Sociometry* 33:123–39

Brann P, Foddy M. 1988. Trust and the consumption of a deteriorating resource. *J. Confl. Resolut.* 31:615–30

Brewer MB. 1981. Ethnocentrism and its role in interpersonal trust. In *Scientific Inquiry and the Social Sciences*, ed. MB Brewer, BE Collins, pp. 345–59. New York: Jossey-Bass. 523 pp.

Brewer MB. 1996. In-group favoritism: the subtle side of intergroup discrimination. In *Codes of Conduct: Behavioral Research and Business Ethics*, ed. DM Messick, A Tenbrunsel, pp. 160–71. New York: Russell Sage Found. 407 pp.

Brockner J, Seigel PA. 1996. Understanding the interaction between procedural and distributive justice: the role of trust. See Kramer & Tyler 1996, pp. 390–413

Brockner J, Siegel PA, Daly JP, Tyler T. 1997. When trust matters: the moderating effects of outcome favorability. *Admin. Sci. Q.* 43:558–83

Bromiley P, Cummings LL. 1996. Transaction costs in organizations with trust. In *Research on Negotiation in Organizations*, ed. R Bies, R Lewicki, B Sheppard, 5: 219–47. Greenwich, CT: JAI

Brown PG. 1994. *Restoring the Public Trust.* Boston: Beacon. 176 pp.

Burt R, Knez M. 1995. Kinds of third-party effects on trust. *J. Ration. Soc.* 7:255–92

Burt R, Knez M. 1996. Third-party gossip and trust. See Kramer & Tyler 1996, pp. 68–69

Butler J. 1991. Toward understanding and measuring conditions of trust: evolution of a condition of trust inventory. *J. Manage.* 17:643–63.

Butler LD, Koopman C, Zimbardo PG. 1995. The psychological impact of viewing the film JFK: emotions, beliefs, and political behavioral intentions. *Polit. Psychol.* 16: 237–57

Cappella JN, Jamieson KH. 1997. *Spiral of Cynicism: The Press and the Public Good.* New York: Oxford Univ. Press. 325 pp.

Carnevale DG. 1995. *Trustworthy Government: Leadership and Management Strategies for Building Trust and High Performance.* San Francisco: Jossey-Bass. 233 pp.

Chiles TH, McMackin JF. 1996. Integrating variable risk preferences, trust, and transaction cost economics. *Acad. Manage. Rev.* 21:73–99

Cialdini R. 1996. The triple tumor structure of organizational behavior. In *Codes of Conduct*, ed. DM Messick, AE Tenbrunsel, pp. 44–58. New York: Russell Sage Found.

Coleman J. 1990. *Foundations of Social Theory.* Cambridge, MA: Harvard Univ. Press. 993 pp.

Creed WD, Miles RE. 1996. Trust in organizations: a conceptual framework linking organizational forms, managerial philosophies, and the opportunity costs of controls. See Kramer & Tyler 1996, pp. 16–38

Dawes RM. 1994. *House of Cards: Psychology and Psychotherapy Built on Myth.* New York: Free Press

Deutsch M. 1958. Trust and suspicion. *J. Confl. Resolut.* 2:265–79

Enzle ME, Anderson SC. 1993. Surveillant intentions and intrinsic motivation. *J. Per. Soc. Psychol.* 64:257–66

Fein S, Hilton JL. 1994. Judging others in the shadow of suspicion. *Motiv. Emot.* 18:167–98

Fenigstein A, Vanable PA. 1992. Paranoia and self-consciousness. *J. Per. Soc. Psychol.* 62:129–38

Fine G, Holyfield L. 1996. Secrecy, trust and dangerous leisure: generating group cohesion in voluntary organizations. *Soc. Psychol. Q.* 59:22–38

Fox A. 1974. *Beyond Contract: Power and Trust Relations.* London: Faber & Faber. 371 pp.

Fukuyama F. 1995. *Trust: The Social Virtues and the Creation of Prosperity.* New York: Free Press. 457 pp.

Gabarro JJ. 1978. The development of trust and expectations. In *Interpersonal Behavior: Communication and Understanding in Relationships*, ed. AG Athos, JJ Gabarro, pp. 290–303. Englewood Cliffs, NJ: Prentice Hall. 398 pp.

Gambetta D. 1988. Can we trust trust? In *Trust: Making and Breaking Cooperative Relationships*, ed. D Gambetta, pp. 213–37. Cambridge: Blackwell

Garfinkel H. 1963. A conception of, and experiments with, trust as a condition of stable concerted actions. In *Motivation and Social Interaction: Cognitive Determinants*, ed. OJ Harvey, pp. 81–93. New York: Ronald. 323 pp.

Goertzel G. 1994. Belief in conspiracy theories. *Polit. Psychol.* 15:731–42.

Granovetter M. 1985. Economic action and social structure: the problem of embeddedness. *Am. J. Sociol.* 91:481–510

Grovier T. 1994. An epistemology of trust. *Int. J. Moral Soc. Stud.* 8:155–74

Gurtman MB. 1992. Trust, distrust, and interpersonal problems: a circumplex analysis. *J. Pers. Soc. Psychol.* 62:989–1002

Hardin R. 1991. Trusting persons, trusting institutions. In *Strategy and Choice*, ed. RJ Zeckahuser, Cambridge, MA: MIT. 487 pp.

Hardin R. 1992. The street-level epistemology of trust. *Anal. Krit.* 14:152–76

Hardin R. 1998. *Trust.* New York: Russell Sage. In press

Harrison AA, Thomas JM. 1997. The Kennedy assassination, unidentified flying objects, and other conspiracies: psychological and organizational factors in the perception of 'cover-up.' *Syst. Res. Behav. Sci.* 14:113–28

Hilton JL, Fein S, Miller DT. 1993. Suspicion and dispositional inference. *Pers. Soc. Psychol. Bull.* 19:501–12

Hochschild AR. 1983. *The Managed Heart: Commercialization of Human Feeling.* Berkeley: Univ. Calif. Press. 307 pp.

Hosmer LT. 1995. Trust: the connecting link between organizational theory and ethics. *Acad. Manage. Rev.* 20:379–400

Insko CA, Schopler J. 1997. Differential distrust of groups and individuals. In *Intergroup Cognition and Intergroup Behavior*, ed. C Sedikides, J Schopler, C Insko. Hillsdale, NJ: Erlbaum. 469 pp.

Janoff-Bulman R. 1992. *Shattered Assumptions.* New York: Free. 256 pp.

Katz D, Kahn R. 1978. *The Social Psychology of Organizations.* New York: Wiley. 531 pp.

Kelley HH. 1980. On the situational origins of human response tendencies. *Pers. Soc. Psychol. Bull.* 9:8–30

Kipnis D. 1996. Trust and technology. See Kramer & Tyler 1996, pp. 39–50

Knez M, Camerer C. 1994. Creating expectational assets in the laboratory: coordination in 'weakest link' games. *Strat. Manage. J.* 15:101–19

Kollock P. 1993. An eye for an eye leaves everyone blind: cooperation and accounting systems. *Am. Sociol. Rev.* 58:768–86

Kollock P. 1994. The emergence of exchange structures: an experimental study of uncertainty, commitment and trust. *Am. J. Sociol.* 100:313–45

Kramer RM. 1994. The sinister attribution error. *Motiv. Emot.* 18:199–231

Kramer RM. 1996. Divergent realities and convergent disappointments in the hierarchic relation: the intuitive auditor at work. See Kramer & Tyler 1996, pp. 216–45

Kramer RM. 1998. Paranoid cognition in social systems: thinking and acting in the shadow of doubt. *Pers. Soc. Psychol. Rev.* 2:251–75

Kramer RM, Brewer MB, Hanna B. 1996. Collective trust and collective action in organizations: the decision to trust as a social decision. See Kramer & Tyler 1996, pp. 357–89

Kramer RM, Tyler TR, eds. 1996 *Trust in Organizations.* Thousand Oaks, CA: Sage. 429 pp.

Kreps DM. 1990. Corporate culture and economic theory. In *Perspectives on Positive Political Economy*, ed. J Alt, K Shepsle. New York: Cambridge Univ. Press

Kruglanski AW. 1970. Attributing trustworthiness in supervisor-worker relations. *J. Exp. Soc. Psychol.* 6:214–32

Lewicki RJ, Bunker BB. 1995. Trust in relationships: a model of trust development and decline. In *Conflict, Cooperation, and Justice*, ed. BB Bunker, JZ Rubin. San Francisco: Jossey-Bass

Lewis JD, Weigert A. 1985. Trust as a social reality. *Soc. Forces* 63:967–85

Lindskold S. 1978. Trust development, the GRIT proposal, and the effects of conciliatory acts on conflict and cooperation. *Psychol. Bull.* 85:772–93

Luhmann N. 1988. Familiarity, confidence, trust: problems and alternatives. In *Trust: Making and Breaking Cooperative Relations*, ed. D Gambetta, pp. 94–108. Cambridge, MA: Oxford Univ. Press

March JG. 1994. *A Primer on Decision Making.* New York: Free Press. 289 pp.

March JG, Olsen JP. 1989. *Rediscovering institutions: The Organizational Basis of Politics.* New York: Free Press. 227 pp.

March JG, Olsen JP. 1994. *Democratic Governance.* New York: Free Press

March JG, Simon HA. 1958. *Organizations.* New York: Wiley

Mayer RC, Davis JH, Schoorman FD. 1995. An integrative model of organizational trust. *Acad. Manage. Rev.* 20:709–34

McAlister DJ. 1995. Affect- and cognition-based trust as foundations for interpersonal cooperation in organizations. *Acad. Manage. J.* 38:24–59

Messick DM, Liebrand WG. 1995. Individual heuristics and the dynamics of cooperation in large groups. *Psychol. Rev.* 102:131–45

Messick DM, Wilke H, Brewer MB, Kramer RM, Zemke PE, Lui L. 1983. Individual adaptations and structural change as solutions to social dilemmas. *J. Pers. Soc. Psychol.* 44:294–309

Meyerson D, Weick K, Kramer RM. 1996. Swift trust and temporary groups. See Kramer & Tyler 1996, pp. 166–195

Miller GJ. 1992. *Managerial Dilemmas: The Political Economy of Hierarchies.* New York: Cambridge Univ. Press. 254 pp.

Mishra N. 1996. Organizational responses to crisis: the centrality of trust. See Kramer & Tyler 1996, pp. 261–87

Misztal BA. 1996. *Trust in Modern Societies.* Cambridge, MA: Blackwell. 296 pp.

Moore-Ede M. 1993. *The Twenty-Four Hour Society: Understanding Human Limita-*tions *in a World That Never Stops.* New York: Addison-Wesley. 230 pp.

Murnighan JK. 1993. *Social Psychology in Organizations.* Englewood Cliffs, NJ: Prentice Hall. 409 pp.

Murnighan JK, Kim JW, Metzger AR. 1994. The volunteer dilemma. *Admin. Sci. Q.* 38:515–38

Nye JS. 1997. The decline of confidence in government. See Nye et al 1997, pp. 1–18

Nye JS, Zelikow PD, King DC. 1997. *Why People Don't Trust Government.* Cambridge, MA: Harvard Univ. Press. 339 pp.

Olson M. 1965. *The Logic of Collective Action.* New Haven, CT: Yale Univ. Press. 271 pp.

Orbell J, Dawes R, Schwartz-Shea P. 1994. Trust, social categories, and individuals: the case of gender. *Motiv. Emot.* 18:109–28

Parks CD, Henager RF, Scamahorn SD. 1996. Trust and reactions to messages of intent in social dilemmas. *J. Confl. Resolut.* 40:134–51

Parks CD, Hulbert LG. 1995. High and low trusters' responses to fear in a payoff matrix. *J. Confl. Resolut.* 39:718–30

Parks CD, Komorita SS. 1997. Reciprocal strategies for large groups. *Pers. Soc. Psychol. Rev.* 1:314–22

PEW Research Center for the People and the Press. 1996. *Trust and Citizen Engagement in Metropolitan Philadelphia: A Case Study.* Washington, DC: PEW. 131 pp.

PEW Research Center for the People and the Press. 1998. *Deconstructing Distrust: How Americans View Government.* Washington, DC: PEW. 264 pp.

Pfeffer J. 1997. *New Directions in Organizational Theory: Problems and Prospects.* New York: Oxford Univ. Press. 264 pp.

Pilisuk M, Kiritz S, Clampitt S. 1971. Undoing deadlocks of distrust: hip Berkeley students and the ROTC. *J. Confl. Resolut.* 15:81–95

Pilisuk M, Skolnick P. 1968. Inducing trust: A test of the Osgood Proposal. *J. Pers. Soc. Psychol.* 8, 121–33

Pipes D. 1997. *Conspiracy.* New York: Free Press. 257 pp.

Powell W. 1996. Trust in governance structures. See Kramer & Tyler 1996, pp. 51–67

Putnam RD. 1993. *Making Democracy Work: Civic Traditions in Modern Italy.* Princeton, NJ: Princeton Univ. Press. 258 pp.

Robinson SL. 1996. Trust and breach of the psychological contract. *Admin. Sci. Q.* 41:574–99

Rotter JB. 1971. Generalized expectancies for interpersonal trust. *Am. Psychol.* 26:443–52

Rotter JB. 1980. Interpersonal trust, trust-worthiness, and gullibility. *Am. Psychol.* 35:1–7

Sabel CF. 1993. Studied trust: building new forms of cooperation in a volatile economy. *Hum. Relat.* 46:1133–70

Sato K. 1988. Trust and group size in a social dilemma. *Jpn. Psychol. Res.* 30:88–93

Schelling TC. 1960. *The Strategy of Conflict.* New Haven, CT: Yale Univ. Press. 269 pp.

Scott WR. 1997. *Institutions and Organizations.* Thousand Oaks, CA: Sage. 178 pp.

Seligman AB. 1997. *The Problem of Trust.* Princeton, NJ: Princeton Univ. Press. 231 pp.

Shapiro DL, Sheppard BH, Cheraskin L. 1992. Business on a handshake. *Negot. J.* 8: 365–77

Shapiro S. 1987. Policing trust. In *Private Policing,* ed. CD Shearing, PC Stenning. Thousand Oaks, CA: Sage. 401 pp.

Shaw RB. 1997. *Trust in the Balance.* San Francisco: Jossey-Bass. 242 pp.

Sheppard BH, Tuchinsky M. 1996. Micro-OB and the network organization. See Kramer & Tyler 1996, pp. 140–65

Sitkin SB. 1995. On the positive effects of legalization on trust. *Res. Negot. Org.* 5: 185–217

Sitkin SB, Roth NL. 1993. Explaining the limited effectiveness of legalistic 'remedies' for trust/distrust. *Organ. Sci.* 4:367–92

Sitkin SB, Stickel D. 1996. The road to hell: the dynamics of distrust in an era of quality. See Kramer & Tyler 1996, pp. 196–215

Slovic P. 1993. Perceived risk, trust, and democracy. *Risk Anal.* 13:675–82

Solomon L. 1960. The influence of some types of power relationships and game strategies upon the development of interpersonal trust. *J. Abnorm. Soc. Psychol.* 61:223–30

Sorrentino RM, Holmes JG, Hanna SE, Sharp A. 1995. Uncertainty orientation and trust in close relationships: individual differences in cognitive styles. *J. Pers. Soc. Psychol.* 68:314–27

Strickland LH. 1958. Surveillance and trust. *J. Pers.* 26:200–15

Tyler TR. 1994. Psychological models of the justice motive. *J. Pers. Soc. Psychol.* 57:830–38

Tyler TR, Degoey P. 1996a. Collective restraint in social dilemmas: procedural justice and social identification effects on support for authorities. *J. Pers. Soc. Psychol.* 69:482–97

Tyler TR, Degoey P. 1996b. Trust in organizational authorities: the influence of motive attributions on willingness to accept decisions. See Kramer & Tyler 1996, pp. 331–57

Tyler TR, Kramer RM. 1996. Whither trust? See Kramer & Tyler 1996, pp. 1–15

Tyler TR, Lind EA. 1992. A relational model of authority in groups. In *Advances in Experimental Social Psychology,* ed. M Snyder, 25:115–92. New York: Academic

Uzzi B. 1997. Social structure and competition in interfirm networks: the paradox of embeddedness. *Admin. Sci. Q.* 42:35–67

Webb G. 1996. Trust and crises. See Kramer & Tyler 1996, pp. 288–302

Weick KE. 1979. *The Social Psychology of Organizing.* 314 pp. 2nd ed.

Weick KE. 1993. The collapse of sensemaking in organizations: the Mann Gulch disaster. *Admin. Sci. Q.* 38:628–52

Weick KE, Roberts K. 1993. Collective mind in organizations: heedful interrelating on flight decks. *Admin. Sci. Q.* 38:357–81

Whitney J. 1994. *The Trust Factor.* New York: McGraw-Hill. 235 pp.

Williamson O. 1993. Calculativeness, trust, and economic organization. *J. Law Econ.* 34:453–502

Wrightsman LS. 1991. Interpersonal trust and attitudes toward human nature. In *Measures of Personality and Psychological Attitudes,* ed. J Robinson, P Shaver, L Wrightsman, pp. 373–412. San Diego, CA: Academic

Yamagishi T, Yamagishi M. 1994. Trust and commitment in the United States and Japan. *Motiv. Emot.* 18:129–66

Zand DE. 1997. *The Leadership Triad: Knowledge, Trust, and Power.* New York: Oxford Univ. Press. 221 pp.

Zimbardo PG, Andersen SM, Kabat LG. 1981. Induced hearing deficit generates experimental paranoia. *Science* 212:1529–31

Zimmer T. 1972. The impact of Watergate on the public's trust in people and confidence in the mass media. *Soc. Sci. Q.* 59:743–51

Zuboff S. 1988. *In the Age of the Smart Machine.* New York: Basic Books. 178 pp.

Zucker LG. 1986. Production of trust: institutional sources of economic structure, 1840–1920. *Res. Organ. Behav.* 8:53–111

Annu. Rev. Psychol. 1999. 50:599–624

SINGLE-GENE INFLUENCES ON BRAIN AND BEHAVIOR

D. Wahlsten

Department of Psychology, University of Alberta, Edmonton, Alberta, Canada T6G 2E9; e-mail: wahlsten@psych.ualberta.ca

KEY WORDS: Human Genome Project, quantitative trait locus, reductionism, World Wide Web, targeted mutation

---

ABSTRACT

As traditional behavioral genetics analysis merges with neurogenetics, the field of neurobehavioral genetics, focusing on single-gene effects, comes into being. New biotechnology has greatly accelerated gene discovery and the study of gene function in relation to brain and behavior. More than 7,000 genes in mice and 10,000 in humans have now been documented, and extensive information about the genetics of several species is readily available on the World Wide Web. Based on knowledge of the DNA sequence of a gene, a targeted mutation with the capacity to disable it can be created. These knock-outs— also called null mutants— are employed in the study of a wide range of phenotypes, including learning and memory, appetite and obesity, and circadian rhythms. The era of examining single-gene effects from a reductionistic perspective is waning, and research with interacting arrays of genes in various environmental contexts is demonstrating a need for systems-oriented theory.

CONTENTS

INTRODUCTION

Unlike previous behavioral genetics reviews in this series, which divided the field by species (human and nonhuman) (Wimer & Wimer 1985, Rose 1995), this review divides the field according to single-gene and biometrical methodologies. It focuses on remarkable progress and prospects in the discovery and understanding of specific gene effects in several species, including humans. Many neurological mutations exhibiting large effects have had their DNA sequences decoded and their protein products identified, and much has been learned about how gene expression is regulated by the environment. Behavioral genetics researchers have advanced to a new stage, and have now begun to examine interacting pairs of genes and to identify viable genetic variants that exert more subtle effects on behavior. As the field of neurobehavioral genetics emerges, genetic tools are becoming central to research in physiological psychology.

Typically, the biometrical or quantitative genetic approach is applied when many unknown genes, each with presumably small effect, are believed to be involved. Instead of identifying specific genes, this methodology seeks to partition variance among several components attributable to genetic and environmental variation. There has been a tension between the two approaches since the early days of genetics, as reflected in Johannsen's (1911:138) opinion of the correlational methods employed by Francis Galton and Karl Pearson: "They have nothing at all to do with genetics—or general biology! Their premises are inadequate for insight into the nature of heredity." This tension continues. Although the mathematical models of biometrics have undoubtedly become more sophisticated and are being applied to both nervous system and behavioral analysis (Rijsdijk & Boomsma 1997), fundamental disagreements abound concerning the basic formulation and assumptions of the quantitative models (Devlin et al 1997, Schönemann 1997, Wahlsten 1990, 1994), and many practitioners of quantitative genetics are being drawn to the study of single-gene effects (Boomsma et al 1997, McClearn et al 1991). In the view of Plomin and associates (1994), "additional quantitative genetic studies are no longer needed to document the importance of genetic influence" (i.e. heritability) on intelligence, and researchers should instead attempt to identify specific genes.

GENE DISCOVERY

The ultimate goal of behavioral and neural genetics is a comprehensive understanding of the identities, functions, and multifarious relations of genes relevant to the behavior of organisms. In this regard, it is important to know how many distinct genes a species possesses, how many of these have already been identified, and how many are likely to be important for behavior.

The Compleat Genome

The Human Genome Project seeks to determine the entire sequence of the nucleotide bases (A, C, G, T, or adenine, cytosine, guanine, thymine) in the DNA of the chromosomes of several species. The overall size of the genome in terms of millions of bases (Mb) is listed for several species in Table 1. Once the entire DNA sequence is known, molecular biologists can identify every unique gene by noting the telltale signatures of base sequences that indicate where to start and stop the transcription of DNA into messenger RNA (mRNA). Each mRNA molecule is translated into a protein molecule. If one knows the DNA sequence of a gene, the structure of its corresponding protein can be readily deduced from the genetic code. This has been accomplished in several unicellular organisms, including a yeast with 6297 genes.

The task of sequencing is immensely more tedious in vertebrates because the segments of DNA (exons) that are transcribed into mRNA and translated

Table 1   Size of the genome in relation to the number of genes, proteins, and neurons in several species that are intensively studied in behavior genetics[a]

Species	Genome (Mb)	Genes	Known proteins	Nerve cells	Web sites
Yeast (*Saccharomyces cerevisiae*)	13.5	6,297	6,297	1 cell	genome-www. stanford.edu
Nematode worm (*Caenorhabditis elegans*)	100	14,000	11,274	302	elegans.swmed.edu
Fruit fly (*Drosophila melanogaster*)	165	12,000	1,566	250,000	flybase.bio.indiana.edu
House mouse (*Mus domesticus*)	3,300	70,000	7,161	40 million	www.informatics.jax.org; biomednet.com
Human being (*Homo sapiens*)	3,300	70,000	11,060	85 billion	bioinfo.weizmann.ac.il/ cards; gdbwww.gdb.org; www3.ncbi.nlm.nih.gov/ Omim

[a]Sources: Miklos & Rubin (1996), Henikoff et al (1997), Gottlieb (1998).

into protein are interspersed by numerous and large segments (introns) that do not code for protein. It is estimated that in humans and mice the informative exons comprise a paltry 2% of the total DNA; a fabulously expensive effort to date has completed the sequencing for only 2% of the human and 0.2% of the mouse genomes (Rowen et al 1997). Once the numbers of genes in DNA that has already been sequenced are known, the total number can be estimated (Table 1). The process of gene identification in vertebrates can be greatly accelerated by studying the mRNA expressed in a variety of tissues from different age groups. This mRNA can be reverse-transcribed into complementary DNA (cDNA), which consists entirely of exons that can be analyzed to yield expressed sequence tags (ESTs). This has been accomplished on a large scale for the human genome, and ESTs exist for one or more exons of some 40,000 of the expected total of 70,000 human genes (Rowen et al 1997). Progress toward a relatively complete accounting of expressed genes can be assessed by the number of protein structures known in a species (Table 1).

Sequencing the genome of convenient, nonhuman species has major benefits for gene discovery in humans because many genes and proteins are homologous owing to descent from a common but remote ancestor. For example, at least 1914 of the 6297 proteins of the yeast *S. cerevisiae* have homologs in mammals (Botstein et al 1997), and homology is substantially greater in more closely related species such as mice and humans (see www.informatics.jax.org/reports.html for an extensive list of homologies).

Targeted Mutations

Of the tens of thousands of genes in a mammal, how many might be relevant for understanding nervous system development and behavior? This question can be approached directly. Once the DNA sequence of an exon of a gene is known, a custom DNA probe can be constructed and then inserted into that specific gene (Joyner 1993). This procedure creates a targeted mutation that usually prevents synthesis of the corresponding protein (called a knockout, or null mutation), but it is also possible to change only one specific amino acid in a protein (Giese et al 1998). The mouse is the preferred subject for this technique, and the 129 inbred strain is commonly the source of cells that are genetically altered. Because one common substrain (129/SvJ) has been genetically contaminated (Simpson et al 1997, Threadgill et al 1997) and the 129 strain, like all inbred strains, has a number of neural and behavioral abnormalities, interpretation of results is sometimes clouded (Crawley et al 1997, Gerlai 1996, Wahlsten & Sparks 1995, Wolfer et al 1997). Nevertheless, the knockout technique is invaluable and can be refined to address earlier shortcomings. Hundreds of kinds of mice have been created that lack a specific protein (such as the estrogen receptor from the *Estra* gene), and numerous mouse models of human genetic diseases have been created by altering the relevant gene (e.g. the *Fmr1* knockout model of Fragile X mental retardation). The null mutation is a relatively blunt instrument, but in many instances researchers have been surprised to obtain viable animals that experienced only minor damaging effects or showed no perceptible effects at all. For example, mice with a disabled dopamine β-hydroxylase gene (*Dbh*) are unable to synthesize norepinephrine and have motor difficulties, but are otherwise able to learn reasonably well (Thomas & Palmiter 1997). Because the use of small sample sizes is common in work with knockout mice, most such experiments lack statistical power to detect small or moderate effects and make it risky to proclaim the genesis of a completely normal mouse. Furthermore, researchers usually focus on one phenotype and target genes of particular interest, implying that the extant sample of mutations is not at all representative of the mouse genome. A functional scan of the entire genome by knocking out one gene at a time is now feasible for yeast; in the near future the scan may also be applicable to nematode worms, but not to more complex animals.

Another approach is to create random mutations (many of which will occur in unknown genes) and record how many of these then impair development of an organ. Although a precise number cannot be ascertained at present, available data suggest that thousands of genes—perhaps as many as 70% of all genes—are required for the normal development of a complex organ such as the eye (Miklos & Rubin 1996).

Linkage and Chromosome Mapping

DNA-based technology can reveal all genes, whether or not they have alternate forms (alleles) that create protein polymorphism, or individual differences in behavior in a population. Consequently, much of this genetic information is of less interest to psychologists for whom the relatively few genes pertinent to behavioral disorders provide more relevant information. The classical approach to genetics begins with a noteworthy difference in phenotype and then asks whether inheritance follows Mendelian rules and whether the hypothetical gene is linked to a marker at a known location on a chromosome. The search for linkage has been greatly facilitated by the discovery of thousands of phenotypically neutral and highly polymorphic DNA markers scattered widely across the genome of mammals (Dietrich et al 1995). If a mutation in an unknown gene with major effects on brain or behavior occurs, it is now possible to detect it quickly and locate it accurately on a chromosome map.

A good example is provided in mice by the *barrelless* (*brl*) mutation that obliterates the normal barrel-shaped pattern of neuron assemblies in somatosensory cortex. The first description of the phenotype was published recently (Welker et al 1996), and fewer than 2 years later it was mapped to a narrow zone on chromosome 11 (Abdel-Majid et al 1998) that was already known to contain six other genes. These six became plausible candidates for *brl*, and the search quickly narrowed to focus on the gene *Adcy1*, which codes for the enzyme adenylyl cyclase type I, an important part of an intracellular signalling pathway involving cyclic AMP (cAMP) in neurons. As it turned out, that enzyme had reduced activity in the mutant mice, and an unrelated knockout strain that lacked a functional *Adcy1* gene was found to lack the brain barrels. The mutant mice also suffered memory deficits. The causes of the barrel structures were also clarified. This distinct pattern is impressed on the cerebral cortex by neural input from the vibrissae in the animal's snout, and alteration of the cAMP pathway by a mutation prevents the anatomical imprint of sensory experience. Now that the gene is better understood, it is properly referred to as the adenylyl cyclase type I gene, and the mutation becomes the loss of function allele $Adcy1^{brl}$.

Genetic mapping with neutral markers also works well in human subjects and has recently been used to detect genes pertinent to many rare neurological disorders. Most cases of unequivocally successful mapping of disease genes have involved dichotomous phenotypes that differ distinctly between normal and abnormal individuals, and where the mutation has a large effect. Tremendous efforts have been made to detect linkage with hypothetical genes pertaining to some of the more common psychiatric disorders that fall into rather arbitrary diagnostic categories, such as manic depression and schizophrenia. Several published claims of linkage have proven to be false positives, and the most recent evidence for linkage of schizophrenia with markers on chromosomes 6 and 8 remains only weakly suggestive (Kidd 1997, Moldin 1997, Moldin & Gottesman 1997). Given the many studies done on this topic, it is reasonable to conclude that no single gene contributes in a major way to the etiology of schizophrenia. Any genetic influence most likely involves the "nonlinear interaction of multiple genetic and environmental factors" (Cloninger 1997), and these effects will be very difficult to identify with conventional linkage analysis that assumes all effects to be independent (Kidd 1997).

Quantitative Trait Loci

Most behavioral variation is continuous and most genetic effects are probably not very large in the normal range of variation. A moderate effect size of a quantitative trait locus (QTL) can be detected by its linkage with neutral DNA markers (Belknap et al 1997, Lander & Schork 1994, McClearn et al 1991). The results are most readily interpreted when the experiment begins with two inbred strains because there can only be two alleles, and the marker alleles will be known in both strains. In an F_2 hybrid cross, genotype frequencies will have Mendelian ratios at the marker. The closer the marker locus is to the hypothesized gene, the lower will be their recombination probability. Thus, if the QTL has an appreciable effect on behavior, there should be a statistically significant difference in mean behavioral test scores of individuals with different marker genotypes. By examining several markers on the same chromosome and using the MAPMAKER computer program, the QTL can be localized within a confidence interval.

Two major difficulties challenge the users of QTL methodology. (*a*) A scan of the whole genome typically involves several markers on each of 20 independent chromosomes in mice, and in humans, 23. Thus, there is an appreciable risk of a false positive association when the conventional Type I error probability $\alpha = 0.05$ is used for each test, so most of the QTL harvest will probably be spurious. Lander & Krugylak (1995) argued persuasively that researchers should use $\alpha = 0.0001$ for each test to keep Type I error at 5% for the entire linkage study. (*b*) Even if the evidence for existence of a QTL is compelling, the width of the confidence interval along the chromosome may still be too great to allow for rapid gene identification and sequencing. A 1% recombination frequency corresponds to a distance along the chromosome of about 1 centiMorgan (cM), that in mice contains about 2 Mb of DNA and about 65 genes. A review of 22 QTLs believed to be important for alcohol and drug sensitivity (Crabbe et al 1998) found that the interval in most cases was more than 15 cm. If the QTL can be localized only within a 15 cM interval, it could be any one of about 1000 genes (Belknap et al 1997).

Many claims of QTLs assigned to map locations have now been published in the behavioral genetics literature, and in some cases provisional gene symbols have been proposed. In many cases, the validity of these claims is suspect and the field would benefit from greater circumspection and rigor. Crusio (1998) remarks that "on closer examination, as yet the promise of the QTL method has not been fulfilled at all." It makes good sense to reduce Type II errors by casting a wide net in the first phase of a study, but it seems unwise to claim something has been mapped or provisionally mapped merely because there is statistically significant evidence of linkage. Further confirmatory testing should be mandatory to cull the false positives and substantially narrow the confidence interval (Darvasi 1998). Real success should be recognized not in long lists of weakly substantiated QTLs but in one or two conclusive discoveries of genetic variants with moderate effects.

Several fruitful strategies for confirming hypothetical QTLs are available (see Crabbe et al 1998, Darvasi 1998). Buck and coworkers (1997) studied severity of alcohol withdrawal symptoms in mice derived from the strains C57BL/6J and DBA/2J. An initial screening against 1522 genetic markers in 21 recombinant inbred (RI) strains yielded seven chromosomal regions appropriately designated as showing "potential linkage" with a "putative QTL." In a sample of 451 F_2 hybrid mice evaluated only at regions implicated in the first phase, three of these were clearly supported and another weakly supported (see Belknap et al 1996). The researchers then selectively bred two lines of mice for high and low withdrawal severity, and the allele frequencies at three marker loci diverged rapidly and significantly, thereby confirming the existence of three QTLs with independent evidence in the predicted direction. Although map locations suggested plausible candidate genes—including several GABA receptor subunits on chromosome 11—95% confidence intervals were more than 10 cM wide.

A similar approach has been employed to study the acute response (loss of righting reflex) to a high dose of ethanol. When 124 markers were tested in 27 RI strains derived from the long sleep (LS) and short sleep (SS) lines, 11 "provisional QTLs" were located with a very lenient ($\alpha = 0.05$) criterion (Markel et al 1996). A study of the mice with the most extreme scores in a sample of 1072 F_2 hybrids supported only two of these QTLs, which were tentatively localized within intervals of about 16 cM (Markel et al 1997). As a further test, F_2 hybrid mice of known genotype at the marker loci flanking the hypothetical QTL were then mated and their offspring tested for ethanol-induced sleeping (Bennett et al 1997). Although the sample sizes were too small to yield conclusive results, this application of marker-assisted selection (Ruane & Colleau 1995) holds great promise for confirming the presence of a QTL, localizing it to a narrower interval, and studying interlocus interactions.

Once the presence of a QTL has been adequately confirmed, its precise identity must be demonstrated. This is probably feasible only for a gene already documented at the biochemical level. From a chromosome map, researchers can locate plausible candidate genes in the confidence interval for their QTL. For example, Buck and colleagues (1997) noted that a QTL on chromosome 11 was near genes for three subunits of the GABA receptor (Gabra1, Gabra6, Gabrg2). The full DNA sequences of the exons of a gene in the two strains might reveal a polymorphism that gives rise to different forms of the protein. If only one of several candidate genes differs between the strains, it will become the object of intense scrutiny, whereas the presence of several polymorphic genes in the interval will confound progress. Further evidence could be obtained by knocking out the gene in question, but this evidence could also be misleading. The QTL itself might involve a rather minor difference in viable alleles, whereas a total knockout of another nearby gene might very well have major pleiotropic effects on that behavior. Thus, the knockout could implicate one gene without proving that gene to be the source of the QTL.

The task of identifying genes of moderate effect will benefit from a comprehensive effort in a wide variety of common mouse strains to determine the DNA sequence of exons for genes known to code for many nervous system proteins. Genes already proven with the knockout method to be relevant for brain development or behavior would provide a good starting place. To date, the knockout method has taught us much about development but not about individual differences. The classical era of mouse behavioral genetics documented large variations among common inbred strains for a wide range of behavioral phenotypes. We need to know whether the genes targeted by molecular biologists are indeed the genes that gave rise to these ubiquitous strain differences. If researchers would assess the possible relevance for behavior of definite protein polymorphisms rather than search for the proverbial needle in the haystack using the QTL method, answers would come more easily and be less prone to error.

Allele Association Studies

The allele association approach is being used to assess the relevance of well-known nervous system proteins to behavioral variation in humans. In the first step, several alleles of a gene that lead to altered forms of a protein are identified. For example, a 48-base sequence coding for a string of 16 amino acids in the dopamine type 4 receptor (the *DRD4* gene) is often repeated, and a world wide survey identified 9 alleles with 2 to 10 repeats (Chang et al 1996). Many relatively common alleles in the dopamine D_2 receptor (*DRD2*) gene are also well documented (Kidd et al 1996). Of critical importance is the observation that allele frequencies generally differ markedly from one geographic population to another (Kidd 1996).

The second step is to establish a correlation between specific alleles and behavioral differences. Claims have been made—but doubts persist—that the A1 allele of the *DRD2* gene leads to higher risk of alcoholism. If the study sample is ethnically diverse, an allele that is more common in a group which has a higher rate of alcoholism could result in a spurious correlation. The best recourse is to examine allele associations within a more homogeneous population. For example, in three populations in Taiwan, there is no association of alcoholism with alleles in either the *DRD2* or *DRD4* gene (Chang et al 1997, Lu et al 1996). In surveying the literature, Kidd (1996) concluded that "the better designed studies have been consistently negative on association" with alcoholism.

Genetic polymorphisms also speak to the chronically vexatious issue of race in behavioral genetics. A comprehensive assessment of allele frequencies around the world by Cavalli-Sforza and colleagues (1994) found little support for racial categories. More recent data prompted Kidd (1996) to comment: "It is my belief that racial classifications of humans are scientifically indefensible since there are essentially no boundaries of qualitative genetic difference and the vast majority of genetic variation shows a continuous pattern around the world."

Considerable publicity has been given to two studies published in 1996 that claimed an association between the personality trait of novelty seeking and the long 7 repeat allele of the *DRD4* gene. As revealed in Figure 1, eight subsequent studies from several countries have obtained mixed results. A meta-analysis of these data suggests that scores on the novelty seeking questionnaire have a standard deviation roughly $d = 0.06$ higher in people with longer repeat alleles (95% confidence interval from -0.03 to 0.16). Because there is significant heterogeneity among the samples ($Q = 32.9$, $df = 9$, $P = 0.0001$), it is possible that epistatic interaction with the genetic background or interaction with test situations or local environments could yield a significant association in certain populations but not others.

This exercise with meta-analysis and the history of false positive linkage results for schizophrenia teach important lessons. When a new claim is made of weak allele association or linkage with some other measure (such as IQ), experience should caution us against premature enthusiasm until the result is replicated adequately and survives meta-analysis. Otherwise, there arises a serious risk that false claims will mislead public discourse, as allegations of sex-based differences in the human brain (Bishop & Wahlsten 1997) and an alleged relation between serotonin metabolism and impulsive violence (Balaban et al 1996) have already done.

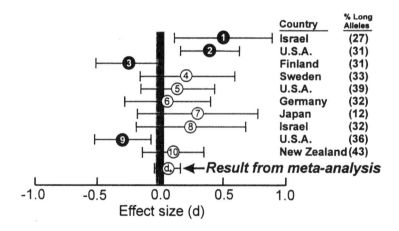

Figure 1   Meta-analysis of 10 studies of novelty seeking in people with different alleles of the dopamine type 4 receptor (*DRD4*) gene. Study number is plotted at the point estimate of effect size (*d*). (*Brackets*) The 95% confidence interval for the true effect size; (*white numerals in black circles*) an effect significant at $\alpha = 0.05$ with a two-tailed test. The studies differed somewhat in the personality test employed, and in the definition of a long allele. In studies that involved more than one sample, a combined estimate was derived. The meta-analysis was done as outlined by Bishop & Wahlsten (1997). Sources of study numbers: 1, Ebstein et al (1996); 2, Benjamin et al (1996); 3, Malhotra et al (1996); 4, Jönsson et al (1997); 5, Vandenbergh et al (1997); 6, Sander et al (1997); 7, Ono et al (1997); 8, Ebstein et al (1997); 9, Gelernter et al (1997); 10, Sullivan et al (1998).

Presuming the allele association method does eventually point to a genetic variant with reliable behavioral correlates, proof that the connection is causal does not follow automatically. The one gene might be linked to another locus that is actually responsible for the observed difference, and hence it would be wise to assess several nearby genes rather than to restrict the scope of the search too early on. The knockout method will not, of course, be available for confirmatory studies in humans, but highly specific DNA-based drugs might be used to substantiate an effect on behavior for the locus in question.

Linkage and allele association methods are entirely adequate for detecting genes with large phenotypic effects, but these kinds of genetic variants tend to be uncommon in the human population. Nevertheless, the work can be justified because of the potential benefit new knowledge may provide for the prevention or alleviation of suffering. Meanwhile, the hunt for ubiquitous polygenes pursues an elusive quarry. Detecting small effects requires extraordinarily large samples, even if the best available research designs are employed (Risch & Merikangas 1996). There is a profound conflict inherent in this enterprise. In terms of a social calculus of the cost-benefit ratio, the smaller the potential good that might result from a new discovery, the more expensive the purchase of that knowledge will be.

Databases of Genetic Information

Despite my reservations about research on genes of small effect, impressive progress has been made in the detection of genes affecting the nervous system and behavior; and even a cursory account of the present state of knowledge exceeds the scope of this review. Fortunately, a vast reservoir of current genetic information is now readily available on the World Wide Web at species-specific sites (Table 1). Investigators can search these databases for long lists of genes residing on a specific chromosome, detailed information about a specific gene, or lists of genes with possible relevance to a specified phenotype or syndrome. A formal course on skills for the Web would be a very useful addition to the neurobehavioral genetics curriculum.

The Mouse Genome Database (MGD) can be reached via the Jackson Laboratory (jax) site. In February of 1998, a search for the phenotype "obesity" yielded 13 relevant genes. The gene symbol *Lep*, or its name, *leptin* (formerly *obese*), yielded the precise map location on chromosome 6, a lengthy abstract, a current bibliography, and other useful information. It also provided links to the homologous gene *LEP* in humans and the DNA sequence of several ESTs. If one does not know the official gene symbol, it is best to start with a search for a closely related keyword. For example, the calmodulin kinase II α subunit gene symbol is *Camk2a*. If the protein symbol CaMKII(often cited in the neuroscience literature) is entered in a search of the MGD, nothing is found, whereas a search using the keyword "calmodulin" successfully calls up information on the gene in question and several others. The MGD currently lists 20,080 genetic markers that have been placed on the mouse chromosome map and 8911 genes, of which 6171 have been mapped and 6396 have at least partial DNA sequences available. One must exercise caution when searching for genes affecting phenotypes, because many in the database are poorly validated and may be ancient apparitions. One such is the gene *absent corpus callosum* (*ac*), originally reported by Keeler (1933) but not seen by anyone in the past 60 years. Once a gene is listed in the catalog—no matter how flimsy the case for its existence—it tends to remain there. Any mouse gene for which an accurate map position is lacking should not be taken seriously.

After completing a brief registration procedure on the BioMedNet Web site, one can access the Mouse Knockout Database, which provides extensive data on targeted mutations. A search detected over 300 articles on over 100 single-gene knockouts that yield viable animals with alterations in the nervous system and/or behavior.

The Weizmann Institute of Science Gene Cards facility is especially recommended for accessing human genetics information. It allows searches for gene symbols or keywords involving phenotypes, yields chromosome map locations, protein characteristics, and homologies with mice, and offers convenient connections to the Genome Database (GDB) or Medline literature search. The GDB is presently the most authoritative source on human genetics, but it may soon cease operations because funding by the US Department of Energy is being discontinued (Letovsky 1998). Online Mendelian Inheritance in Man (OMIM) provides a lengthy abstract and bibliography for each gene and can also be accessed by entering phenotypic keywords. Searching OMIM for "dyslexia" in February 1998 yielded three gene symbols (*DYX1*, *DYX2*, *THRB*). The GDB listing for *DYX1* is based on a single entry from July 19, 1996, and the existence of this gene is far from certain; no information is cited on chromosome map location, and the fine print reveals that it is merely a "reserved symbol," meaning that this will be its official designation if the gene is ever confirmed. *DYX2* yields a map location on chromosome 6 that has been supported by an independent group of researchers (Grigorenko et al 1997) but only for one of five reading-related phenotypes (phonological awareness) and only with nonparametric (rather than parametric) methods. The confidence interval for gene location is more than 10 cM wide, and no protein or DNA sequence information is known. A search on "schizophrenia" yielded 40 entries, including the gene symbol *SCZD1* assigned on April 12, 1989, to a region on chromosome 5 that is now recognized as not harboring a gene influencing schizophrenia (Moldin & Gottesman 1997). Any gene name returned by a search of OMIM should be carefully checked against more authoritative sources, especially the GDB, where a history of the *SCZD1* symbol reveals it was "unassigned" on October 16, 1991. If a protein, DNA sequence, or homology with a mouse gene is listed, one can be confident that the gene is real, but a map location by itself provides no guarantee. Several symbols included in the catalog represent false positives that have not been culled.

The only unequivocal evidence for a gene is elucidation of its DNA sequence and associated protein structure. The quality control for this kind of biochemical information on the Web is good, in part because of facilities provided by the Human Genome Project. Unfortunately, quality control for weaker claims about genes relevant to phenotypes is inadequate, and speculative assertions in the mass media about genetic determination of socially significant behaviors (Colt & Hollister 1998) all too often are based on hasty proclamations from behavioral geneticists who should know better.

GENE FUNCTION

A cornucopia of genes relevant to the nervous system and behavior is now available for research on function. The question of how genes influence behavior and how the activities of genes are themselves regulated is of prime concern for psychology. Function can be understood at different levels.

Natural Polymorphisms

A mutation that seriously impairs the function of an important gene typically is rare in a breeding population, but not all major gene effects on behavior are grossly aberrant misfits. Two remarkable behavioral polymorphisms found in wild fruit flies seem to persist because they aid a species to exploit a wider variety of environments. The *foraging* locus influences activity of larvae in the presence of food; the dominant rover allele (for^R) leads to longer forays into the environment, whereas the recessive sitter allele (for^s) results in more localized feeding. Both alleles are common in wild fruit flies living in an urban habitat (Toronto). An exemplary series of studies demonstrated that the sitter

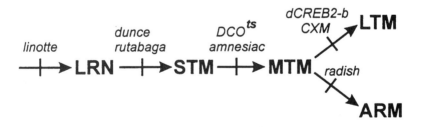

Figure 2   Genes that influence different components of memory formation in fruit flies. The components are LRN, learning; STM, short-term memory; MTM, medium-term memory; LTM, long-term memory; ARM, anesthesia-resistant memory. Adapted with permission from Tully et al (1996).

mutation occurs in a previously documented gene, *dg2,* that codes for a cyclic GMP-dependent protein kinase and causes a small change in activity of the enzyme that is sufficient to alter foraging behavior (Osborne et al 1997). The rover phenotype predominates in crowded living conditions, whereas the sitter allele increases in lower population densities where the food supply is not so readily exhausted (Sokolowski et al 1997). A more subtle polymorphism occurs in the circadian clock gene *period*, where the allele which is more common in northern Europe leads to more efficient adaptation of the 24-h activity rhythm to temperature changes than the allele more common near the Mediterranean (Sawyer et al 1997). By combining carefully controlled genetic analysis in the laboratory with studies further afield, the science of individual differences thus advances our understanding of behavioral ecology and evolution.

Genetic Dissection

Most psychologically interesting behaviors are multifactorial, involving numerous genes whose actions are influenced by diverse features of the environment. Although individual studies usually concentrate attention on one specific gene, it is generally understood that many genes are relevant. As emphasized by Tully (1997), "Single-gene mutant analysis can be informative only when

Table 2   Mouse genes on specified chromosomes that are important for psychological processes[a]

Chromosome	Learning and memory			Appetite and obesity			
1	*Creb1*	*Sele*					
2	*dbh*	*Grin1*		A^Y	*anx*	*Mc3r*	
3	*Gria2*	*Il2*		*Ap2*			
4	*Pde4b*			*Lepr^{db}*			
5	*Ache*	*En2*	*Hdh*				
6	*Kcna1*			*Lep^{ob}*			
7	*Pkcc*			*Ad*	*Gys1*	*tub*	
8	*Pkaca*			*Cpe^{fat}*	*Insr*	*Mclr*	*Mt1*
9	*Ncam*	*Rasgrf1*		*Cck*			
10	*Fyn*			*Adn*			
11	*Adcy1*	*Cbx2*		*Slc2a4*			
12	*Fos*			*Pomc1*			
16	*App*						
18	*Camk2a*						
X	*Fmr1*			*Htr2c*			

[a]Genes included in the table must have an accurate map location in the Mouse Genome Database and be implicated by at least one study in the process. Most were demonstrated by the targeted mutation method, although a few were spontaneous mutations. Superscript symbols refer to the neurological mutations known prior to the discovery of the specific protein for which the gene codes. Human homologues have been verified for all but four genes in the table.

pursued within the framework of interacting polygenes." Powerful techniques to create mutations have spawned new possibilities for genetic dissection of complex processes. No satisfying account of genetic involvement in any complex behavior has yet been achieved, but significant progress has been made in several domains. Olfactory learning and memory in fruit flies is a process in which certain mutations exert their effects primarily on a specific component (see Figure 2), but the famous flow diagram does not imply that one or two genes provide a sufficient explanation for a biologically distinct component of memory; yet the diagram is a useful device for integrating a large corpus of experimental data. The fact that different mutations result in flies with different temporal profiles of memory loss and different interactions with drugs that block protein synthesis proves the multifactorial nature of the memory process. By examining flies affected simultaneously by two different mutations, a scheme for parts arranged in series or in parallel may be perceived. Numerous other genes are undoubtedly involved, and pleiotropy, the occurrence of multiple phenotypic effects of one gene, is to be expected. For example, the *turnip* mutation reduces motor activity and sensitivity to shock while also impairing learning (Mihalek et al 1997). To some readers, this may render it less inter-

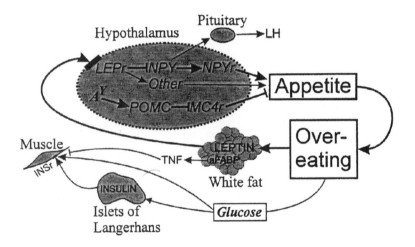

Figure 3 Major components of a system that regulates appetite and leads to obesity in mutant mice. Only the protein products of genes are shown. (*Arrow*) One component stimulates another; (*vertical bar*) a component inhibits or antagonizes another. Abbreviations: A^Y, the mutant agouti peptide; aFABP, α–fatty acid binding protein; INSr, insulin receptor; LEPr, leptin receptor; MC4-R, melanocortin-4 receptor; NPY, neuropeptide Y; NPYr, NPY receptor; POMC, proopiomelanocortin-α; TNF, tumor necrosis factor. The genes corresponding to these proteins are *AY, Ap2, Insr, Lepr, Mc4r, Npy, Npy1r, Pomc1,* and *Tnf,* respectively. LH is lutenizing hormone. See section on Genetic Dissection for explanation.

esting because its effects are not restricted to the memory process, but genetic dissection clearly reveals it to be an integral part of the process.

Targeted mutations have led to a resurgence of interest in learning and memory in mice, and the list of genes known to be important is rapidly growing (see Table 2). Although admirable efforts have been made to comprehend the interconnections of gene-derived proteins involved in memory formation within a synapse (e.g. Abel et al 1998), the horizons of this metabolic landscape are rapidly expanding, with no limit in sight. Many of these genes have pleiotropic effects as well, such as *Camk2a,* which is important in spatial memory but also impinges on numerous other behaviors (Chen et al 1994), and *Creb,* which also reduces symptoms of morphine withdrawal (Maldonado et al 1996).

The organism's genes are of course present from conception, and many participate in formative processes as well as in dynamic adult functions. Embryonic effects can be notably different from involvement in the mature brain, and to distinguish between developmental and current effects of a gene knockout is challenging indeed. Several clever techniques have been employed to overcome this problem. Tsien and coworkers (1996) deleted the NMDA receptor (*Grin1* gene) selectively from the CA1 region of the hippocampus and obtained memory deficits similar to those from a nonspecific gene knockout; Mayford and colleagues (1996) were able to limit the expression of a *Camk2a* mutation to the forebrain of adult mice and still obtained memory deficits. Guzowski & McGaugh (1997) altered spatial memory by injecting synthetic DNA directly into the hippocampus of adult rats to specifically modify the action of the *Creb* gene. These sophisticated methods confer unprecedented clarity on results for psychopharmacology. Molecular genetics is thus becoming a tool in the kit of physiological psychology.

Appetite and obesity in mice are proving to be physiologically and genetically complex (Table 2), and conceptual schemes for synthesizing this knowledge are still lagging behind the burgeoning data. This is happening with regard to circadian rhythms as well, where newly discovered genes are revealing previously unimagined elements of a larger picture (Albrecht et al 1997).

Investigations of obesity provide an emerging portrait of diverse organs connected in feedback loops involving the environment (Figure 3). Under normal conditions, overeating leads to growth of white fat cells (adipocytes) which in turn synthesize the protein leptin and secrete it into the bloodstream. One of leptin's effects occurs in the hypothalamus, where it binds to the leptin receptor and decreases appetite by inhibiting the synthesis of neuropeptide Y (*Npy* gene)—a neurotransmitter that tends to increase appetite. The *obese* mutation ($Lep^{ob/ob}$) prevents the synthesis of leptin in white fat, thereby increasing appetite when NPY levels rise unchecked, and gene therapy to restore leptin in the $Lep^{ob/ob}$ mice prevents both obesity and diabetes (Muzzin et al

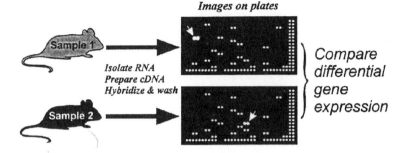

Figure 4   A comparison of profiles of gene expression in tissue from two mice. Complementary cDNA is made from RNA expressed in the tissue, and it binds or hybridizes to a DNA sample from the gene that gave rise to the specific RNA molecule. Each pair of *dots* on the plate represents a different gene that is expressed in the tissue. The *large dots* pointed out by *small arrows* symbolize genes expressed in only one of the samples. The full Atlas[TM] Mouse cDNA Expression Array from CLONTECH Laboratories, Inc., can detect expression of 588 different genes in one tissue sample. Adapted with permission of CLONTECH Laboratories, Inc., from *CLONTECHniques*, January 1998, p. 2.

1996). The *diabetes* mutation ($Lepr^{db/db}$) disables the leptin receptor and renders mice insensitive to high levels of leptin in the blood, which again leads to overeating (Caro et al 1996). By using a double mutant combining $Lep^{ob/ob}$ with the gene knockout $Npy^{-/-}$, it was shown that there are parallel pathways for leptin-related appetite control in the hypothalamus (Erickson et al 1996). The $Lep^{ob/ob}$ plus *lethal yellow* (A^Y/a) double mutant revealed another parallel pathway that acts via the melanocortin-4 receptor (*Mc4r* gene) where normal stimulation of MC4-R decreases appetite but the A^Y gene product antagonizes it (Boston et al 1997). Not all obesity is mediated by the leptin loop (Schonfeld-Warden & Warden 1997), not all leptin effects are mediated by appetite changes (Yu et al 1997), and diabetic symptoms are not joined inexorably with obesity (Hotamisligil et al 1996). Although Table 2 suggests that separate sets of genes impact learning and appetite, this inference may not be warranted because those working with obesity typically do not assess a wide range of behavioral phenotypes. It seems highly likely that variations in appetite would indeed influence the acquisition of certain kinds of tasks, but little recent work with obesity mutations has been done by psychologists interested in motivation.

Genetic dissection thus proceeds through several stages. (*a*) Research projects in the early stages seek to discover a single mutation and explore its phenotypic effects. (*b*) After several genes are known to be important parts of the system, work begins with double mutants and factorial gene-environment or gene-drug interaction studies to elucidate serial and parallel processes, each study focusing on a limited sector of the larger system. (*c*) Eventually, attempts are made to integrate this knowledge into comprehensive models that can be tested with multifactorial experiments. Most research in neurobehavioral genetics is presently entering the second stage, and none has yet reached the third.

Systems of Genes

The question remains of how many genes are involved in memory, appetite, or circadian rhythm. A first approximation can be achieved by examining the array of genes expressed in mRNA under specified conditions. A sensitive and rapid method is now available to assess simultaneously the expression of hundreds of genes in mice (Figure 4) and over 1000 in humans, and customized arrays for screening any desired subset of genes may be anticipated (see Web sites www.resgen.com and atlas.clontech.com). One might contrast brains of trained and untrained mice to assess memory, or brains at midnight and at high noon under a normal light cycle or constant darkness to reveal circadian mechanisms. Furthermore, tissue from mutants and normal siblings tested under the same circumstances could be used to assess pleiotropic effects.

An extraordinary glimpse of complex gene action has been obtained recently for yeast, an organism best known to psychologists for its vital role in synthesizing ethanol from sugar. As the sugar in the yeast's environment is consumed, its metabolism shifts from anerobic fermentation to aerobic respiration. Researchers were able to attach DNA sequences of almost all the 6297 yeast genes to a single glass plate 18 mm by 18 mm and record the abundance of all mRNAs at different stages of the metabolic process (DeRisi et al 1997). During the transition from anerobic to aerobic metabolism, the expression of 1740 genes increased or decreased at least twofold. About half of these genes were new to science, had not yet been named, and had no recognized functions. A mutation in a single gene (*tup1*) altered the expression of 355 other genes. In a remarkable understatement, the authors observed: "The large number of genes whose expression is altered and the diversity of temporal expression profiles highlighted the challenge of understanding the underlying regulatory mechanisms."

The one-celled yeast, of course, is a relatively simple creature that has been thoroughly studied since the time of Pasteur. It seems likely that the complete picture of gene activity during mammalian learning and memory will be even more complex. The molecular tools are close at hand but the prevailing conceptual framework in biological psychology may not be equal to the task of integrating so vast an array of data.

DNA analysis and gene discovery have been dominated by a very successful reductionistic perspective (Beckwith 1996), but research on gene function reveals the necessity of systems-oriented thinking (Gottlieb et al 1998, Strohman 1997). The idea that a gene determines a specific component of a behavioral phenotype is losing scientific credibility. Chenchik and coworkers (1998) forsee that new methods "will lead researchers away from reductionistic approaches which focus on single genes, and towards more systemic approaches that involve the simultaneous, parallel analysis of hundreds or thousands of genes." It must be acknowledged that almost every gene has widespread pleiotropic effects (Miklos & Rubin 1996), that actions of genes are commonly altered by the organism's environment (Gottlieb 1998), and that the consequences of a specific mutation often depend on genotypes at other loci (Varnam et al 1996) and the genetic background (de Belle & Heisenberg 1996, Kelly et al 1998, Miklos & Rubin 1996) as well as on epigenetic effects (Wolf 1997). Strohman (1997) concludes that the origins of complex systems "are not to be found in the matter itself, but in its interactions."

BEHAVIORAL TESTING

Spectacular advances in genetic analysis have captured the imagination of the public and drawn legions of students into molecular biology. The effect has not been to impoverish psychology but to renew interest in the psychology of behavioral testing—especially regarding lab mice—as testified to by the 1996 Society for Neuroscience short course entitled "What's wrong with my mouse?" (Takahashi 1996). Specialists in behavioral genetics have been both impressed by the enthusiasm and appalled at the naïveté of molecular geneticists who believe psychology can provide an off-the-shelf device to measure a specific construct in mice and model its human counterpart. The new molecular genetics has created a need for a wider variety of behavioral testing and for improved test construction and standardization. The skills of psychologists are uniquely suited to this task.

Interactions with Test Situation and Environment

There is a rich variety of tests available for use with mice (Crawley et al 1997, Crawley & Paylor 1997), and it is important to know whether these are likely to yield the same results in the hands of most investigators working with the same strain or mutation. The test situation and the pretest environment are virtually never the same in different laboratories. The central issue is therefore whether genetic and environmental effects are additive or interactive. If additive, then differences among labs will merely change the overall average score but will not alter the pattern of results or rank orders of genotypes, and most tests should yield valid results even in the hands of amateurs.

A clear answer can be provided to this question. Seemingly minor task-specific factors interact strongly with genotype, and reversals of rank orders of strains are commonplace when comparing results across labs. Recent work has emphasized the importance of relatively subtle variations in protocols. Poderycki and coworkers (1998) evaluated hybrid crosses of mice for seizures induced by 5–15 repetitions of gentle tossing. Genetic analysis revealed strong evidence of linkage with a marker on chromosome 9 after 6 tests but not after 15 tests, whereas another gene on chromosome 2 was not apparent after 6 tests but showed clear signs of linkage after 15 tests. Maxson (1992) reported that the effects of the Y chromosome on agonistic behavior in his congenic strains disappeared when the colony was moved to a cleaner environment where the drinking water was acidified to suppress bacteria. Certain Y chromosome effects were most pronounced when males were reared in isolation and tested against males of the same genotype, rather than reared with a sister and tested against a standard opponent strain (Guillot et al 1995). Peeler (1995) conducted avoidance training at different times of day, all during the light phase of the cycle, and found substantial effects on some strains but not others.

Apparatus design and testing protocol are crucially important. Roullet and colleagues (1993) found that BALB/c mice used odor cues and C57BL/6 mice used spatial cues to learn a radial maze, whereas F1 hybrids could utilize either cue. Crusio and coworkers (1993) found large changes in strain rank orders on spatial versus nonspatial versions of a radial maze; only the spatial version revealed genetic correlations with hippocampal mossy fiber anatomy. Peeler (1995) noted differences in strain rank order depending on whether the mice had to run through a hole or slot or jump a barrier to avoid shock. These and other findings show clearly that a single test configuration and procedure cannot define a single psychological construct, although two tests differing in a specific element may indicate a change in a specific construct.

Growing Need for Test Standardization

In view of these findings, there are grounds for concern about the almost universal lack of standardized apparatuses, protocols, and lab environments in psychological testing of animals. In contrast, test construction and standardization are taken more seriously in evaluation of humans. Reviews among labs of the plus-maze, a popular means for assessing anxiety, reveal numerous idiosyncratic variations that are potentially important (Hogg 1996; Rodgers & Dalvi 1997). Tests known to be valid for rats are often used inappropriately with mice. The Morris swimming pool is particularly problematic when used with mice (Whishaw & Tomie 1996). Some common inbred strains (BALB/c, 129) respond quite badly in this device (Francis et al 1995) and often resort to floating after becoming exhausted (Wolfer et al 1997). When mice can locate a submerged platform, they must be using spatial cues, but failure to learn does not necessarily signal a lack of spatial memory (unless only the cues are manipulated in different versions of the task, and a strain can learn one cue but not the other). Additional difficulties are present when investigators submit an individual animal to a battery of tests, each of which was designed and validated for use by itself: Order of testing can markedly alter results when such tests are combined.

Validity of Animal Models

Whereas homology among flies, mice, and humans at the molecular genetic level is undeniable, homology—and even analogy—at the level of the behaving organism is not so clear. Certain genes important for memory in flies (Figure 2) are involved in memory in mammals (e.g. the fly gene *rutabaga*, the mouse gene *barrelless,* and the human gene *ADCY1* all encode an adenylate cyclase), yet the complex nature of metabolic and developmental systems (characterized by pleiotropic and epistatic gene actions plus gene-environment interactions) implies that the function of a particular gene depends on its context. Homology of behaviors must be demonstrated, not assumed. In the domain of agonistic behavior, for example, mice engage in offensive and defensive attacks that appear to be adaptive under appropriate circumstances, but do these provide good models of human violence? According to Maxson (1998), offensive behavior of male mice is not a good model of impulsive aggression in humans, although several recent publications assume uncritically that the two are essentially the same. Balaban and colleagues (1996) also stress the importance of careful definition of behaviors and contexts when seeking to establish the relevance to humans of animal models, and they question the similarity of rodent attack behavior to human crime. A good case can be made for valid mouse models of several severe medical disorders caused by single-gene mutations, but the validity of mouse or fly models for the normal range of variation in human social behavior requires convincing evidence that is generally lacking.

CONCLUSIONS

In his review of human behavioral genetics, Rose (1995) foresaw that "Future reviews of the field are likely to read very differently than this one." The field has indeed changed direction and is advancing like a sailboat with spinnaker unfurled, rather than tacking and making little headway. Many outstanding contributions to neurobehavioral genetics are now published in leading scientific journals with a broad readership rather than in specialty journals. Not long ago, the field was trammeled by crude techniques for detecting the presence and activities of single genes, whereas today we have a panoply of molecular methods and a rich factual base of knowledge about specific genes in relation to brain and behavior. Long lists of human attributes, each accompanied by a terse summary of the latest findings from twin or adoption studies, have become passé. The challenge of keeping aware of current developments in this field is now quite formidable, even with the aid of marvelous Internet and bibliographic search programs. As the individual research project probes ever more deeply into an ever-narrower domain of knowledge, there is a growing need to synthesize existing knowledge and make connections among the isolated parts of an expanding discipline. The next major advance must come in the domain of theory.

ACKNOWLEDGMENTS

I am grateful to John Crabbe, Gilbert Gottlieb, and Pierre Roubertoux for their critical comments on this article and to Sharon Doerksen for assistance with Web searches. Supported by a grant from the Natural Sciences and Engineering Research Council of Canada.

> Visit the *Annual Reviews home page* at
> http://www.AnnualReviews.org.

Literature Cited

Abdel-Majid RM, Leong WL, Schalkwyk LC, Smallman DS, Wong ST, et al. 1998. Loss of adenylyl cyclase type I activity disrupts patterning of mouse somatosensory cortex. *Nat. Genet.* 19:289–91

Abel T, Martin KC, Bartsch D, Kandel ER. 1998. Memory suppressor genes: inhibitory constraints on the storage of long-term memory. *Science* 279:338–41

Albrecht U, Sun ZS, Eichele G, Lee CC. 1997. A differential response of two putative mammalian circadian regulators, *mper1* and *mper2*, to light. *Cell* 91:1055–64

Balaban E, Alper JS, Kasamon YL. 1996. Mean genes and the biology of aggression: a critical review of recent animal and human research. *J. Neurogenet.* 11:1–43

Beckwith J. 1996. The hegemony of the gene: reductionism in molecular biology. In *The Philosophy and History of Molecular Biology: New Perspectives*, ed. S Sarkar, pp. 171–83. Netherlands: Kluwer Acad.

Belknap JK, Dubay C, Crabbe JC, Buck KJ. 1997. Mapping quantitative trait loci for behavioral traits in the mouse. In *Handbook of Psychiatric Genetics*, ed. K Blum, EP Noble, RS Sparkes, THJ Chen, JG Cull, pp. 435–53. New York: CRC Press

Belknap JK, Mitchell SR, O'Toole LA, Helms ML, Crabbe JC. 1996. Type I and type II

error rates for quantitative trait loci (QTL) mapping studies using recombinant inbred mouse strains. *Behav. Genet.* 26:149–60

Benjamin J, Li L, Patterson C, Greenberg BD, Murphy DL, Hamer DH. 1996. Population and familial association between the D4 dopamine receptor gene and measures of novelty seeking. *Nat. Genet.* 12:81–84

Bennett B, Beeson M, Gordon L, Johnson TE. 1997. Quick method for confirmation of quantitative trait loci. *Alcohol Clin. Exp. Res.* 21:1–6

Bishop K, Wahlsten D. 1997. Sex differences in the human corpus callosum: myth or reality? *Neurosci. Biobehav. Rev.* 21: 581–601

Boomsma D, Anokhin A, de Geus E. 1997. Genetics of electrophysiology: linking genes, brain, and behavior. *Curr. Dir. Psychol. Sci.* 6:106–10

Boston BA, Blaydon KM, Varnerin J, Cone RD. 1997. Independent and additive effects of central POMC and leptin pathways on murine obesity. *Science* 278:1641–44

Botstein D, Chervitz SA, Cherry JM. 1997. Yeast as a model organism. *Science* 277: 1259–60

Buck KJ, Metten P, Belknap JK, Crabbe JC. 1997. Quantitative trait loci involved in genetic predisposition to acute alcohol withdrawal in mice. *J. Neurosci.* 17: 3946–55

Caro JF, Sinha MK, Kolaczynski JW, Zhang PL, Considine RV. 1996. Leptin: the tale of an obesity gene. *Diabetes* 45:1455–62

Cavalli-Sforza LL, Menozzi P, Piazza A. 1994. *The History and Geography of Human Genes.* Princeton, NJ: Princeton Univ. Press

Chang F, Kidd JR, Livak KJ, Pakstis AJ, Kidd KK. 1996. The world-wide distribution of allele frequencies at the human dopamine D4 receptor locus. *Hum. Genet.* 98:91–101

Chang F, Ko H, Lu R, Pakstis AJ, Kidd KK. 1997. The dopamine D4 receptor gene (DRD4) is not associated with alcoholism in three Taiwanese populations: six polymorphisms tested separately and as haplotypes. *Biol. Psychiatry* 41:394–405

Chen C, Rainnie DG, Greene RW, Tonegawa S. 1994. Abnormal fear response and aggressive behavior in mutant mice deficient for alpha-calcium-calmodulin kinase II. *Science* 266:291–94

Chenchik A, Chen S, Makhanov M, Siebert P. 1998. Profiling of gene expression in a human glioblastoma cell line using the Atlas Human cDNA Expression Array I. *CLONTECHniques* 13:16–17

Cloninger CR. 1997. Multilocus genetics of schizophrenia. *Curr. Opin. Psychiatry* 10: 5–10

Colt GH, Hollister A. 1998. Were you born that way? *Life* Apr:39–50

Crabbe JC, Phillips TJ, Buck KJ, Cunningham CL, Belknap JK. 1998. Identifying genes for alcohol and drug sensitivity: recent progress and future direction. *Trends Neurosci.* In press

Crawley JN, Belknap JK, Collins A, Crabbe JC, Frankel W, et al. 1997. Behavioral phenotypes of inbred mouse strains: implications and recommmendations for molecular studies. *Psychopharmacology* 132: 107–24

Crawley JN, Paylor R. 1997. A proposed test battery and constellations of specific behavioral paradigms to investigate the behavioral phenotypes of transgenic and knockout mice. *Horm. Behav.* 27:201–10

Crusio WE. 1998. The genetic dissection of brain-behaviour relationships: an introduction to neurobehavioral genetics. *Behav. Brain Res.* 95:1–2

Crusio WE, Schwegler H, Brust I. 1993. Covariations between hippocampal mossy fibres and working and reference memory in spatial and non-spatial radial maze tasks in mice. *Eur. J. Neurosci.* 5:1413–20

Darvasi A. 1998. Experimental strategies for the genetic disssection of complex traits in animal models. *Nat. Genet.* 18:19–24

de Belle JS, Heisenberg M. 1996. Expression of *Drosophila* mushroom body mutations in alternative genetic backgrounds: a case study of the mushroom body miniature gene (*mbm*). *Proc. Natl. Acad. Sci. USA* 93:9875–80

DeRisi JL, Iyer VR, Brown PO. 1997. Exploring the metabolic and genetic control of gene expression on a genomic scale. *Science* 278:680–86

Devlin B, Daniels M, Roeder K. 1997. The heritability of IQ. *Nature* 388:468–71

Dietrich WF, Copeland NG, Gilbert DJ, Miller JC, Jenkins NA. 1995. Mapping the mouse genome: current status and future prospects. *Proc. Natl. Acad. Sci. USA* 92: 10849–53

Ebstein RP, Nemanov L, Klotz I, Gritsenko I, Belmaker RH. 1997. Additional evidence for an association between the dopamine D4 receptor (D4DR) exon III repeat polymorphism and the human personality trait of Novelty Seeking. *Mol. Psychiatry* 2: 472–74

Ebstein RP, Novick O, Umansky R, Priel B, Osher Y, et al. 1996. Dopamine D4 receptor (D4DR) exon III polymorphism associated with the human personality trait of novelty seeking. *Nat. Genet.* 12:78–80

Erickson JC, Hollopeter G, Palmiter RD. 1996. Attenuation of the obesity syndrome of *ob/ob* mice by the loss of neuropeptide Y. *Science* 274:1704–7

Francis DD, Zaharia MD, Shanks N, Anisman H. 1995. Stress-induced distrubances in Morris water-maze performance: interstrain variability. *Physiol. Behav.* 58: 57–65

Gelernter J, Kranzler H, Coccaro E, Siever L, New A, Mulgrew CL. 1997. D4 dopamine-receptor (DRD4) alleles and novelty seeking in substance-dependent, personality-disorder, and control subjects. *Am. J. Hum. Genet.* 61:1144–52

Gerlai R. 1996. Gene-targeting studies of mammalian behavior: Is it the mutation or the background genotype? *Trends Neurosci.* 19:177–81

Giese KP, Fedorov NB, Filipkowski RK, Silva AJ. 1998. Autophosphorylation at Thr[286] of the alpha calcium-calmodulin kinase II in LTP and learning. *Science* 279:870–73

Gottlieb G. 1998. Normally occurring environmental and behavioral influences on gene activity: from central dogma to probabilistic epigenesis. *Psychol. Rev.* In press

Gottlieb G, Wahlsten D, Lickliter R. 1998. The significance of biology for human development: a developmental psychobiological systems view. In *Handbook of Child Psychology. Theoretical Models of Human Development,* ed. RM Lerner, 1:233–73. New York: Wiley. 5th ed.

Grigorenko EL, Wood FB, Meyer MS, Hart LA, Speed WC, et al. 1997. Susceptibility loci for distinct components of developmental dyslexia on chromosomes 6 and 15. *Am. J. Hum. Genet.* 60:27–39

Guillot P, Carlier M, Maxson SC, Roubertoux PL. 1995. Intermale aggression tested in two procedures, using four inbred strains of mice and their reciprocal congenics: Y chromosomal implications. *Behav. Genet.* 25:357–60

Guzowski JF, McGaugh JL. 1997. Antisense oligodeoxynucleotide-mediated disruption of hippocampal cAMP response element binding protein levels impairs consolidation of memory for water maze training. *Proc. Natl. Acad. Sci. USA* 94: 2693–98

Henikoff S, Greene EA, Pietrokovski S, Bork P, Attwood TK, Hood L. 1997. Gene families: the taxonomy of protein paralogs and chimeras. *Science* 278:609–14

Hogg S. 1996. A review of the validity and variability of the elevated plus-maze as an animal model of anxiety. *Pharmacol. Biochem. Behav.* 54:21–30

Hotamisligil GS, Johnson RS, Distel RJ, Ellis R, Papaioannou VE, Spiegelman BM. 1996. Uncoupling of obesity from insulin resistance through a targeted mutation in aP2, the adipocyte fatty acid binding protein. *Science* 274:1377–79

Johannsen W. 1911. The genotype conception of heredity. *Am. Nat.* 45:129–59

Jönsson EG, Nothen MM, Gustavsson JP, Neidt H, Brene S, et al. 1997. Lack of evidence for allelic association between personality traits and the dopamine D4 receptor gene polymorphisms. *Am. J. Psychiatry* 154:697–99

Joyner AL. 1993. *Gene Targeting: A Practical Approach.* New York: Oxford Univ. Press

Keeler CE. 1933. Absence of the corpus callosum as a Mendelizing character in the house mouse. *Proc. Natl. Acad. Sci. USA* 19:609–11

Kelly MA, Rubinstein M, Phillips TJ, Lessov CN, Burkhart-Kasch S, et al. 1998. Locomoter activity in D2 dopamine receptor-deficient mice is determined by gene dosage, genetic background, and developmental adaptations. *J. Neurosci.* 18:3470–79

Kidd KK. 1996. *Human genetic diversity and neuropsychiatric disorders.* Presented at Wenner-Gren Cent. Int. Symp. Genet. Psychiatr. Disord., Stockholm

Kidd KK. 1997. Can we find genes for schizophrenia? *Am. J. Med. Genet.* 74: 104–11

Kidd KK, Pakstis AJ, Castiglione CM, Kidd JR, Speed WC, et al. 1996. DRD2 halotypes containing the TaqI A1 allele: implications for alcoholism research. *Alcohol Clin. Exp. Res.* 20:697–705

Lander E, Kruglyak L. 1995. Genetic dissection of complex traits: guidelines for interpreting and reporting linkage results. *Nat. Genet.* 11:241–47

Lander ES, Schork NJ. 1994. Genetic dissection of complex traits. *Science* 265: 2037–48

Letovsky S. 1998. Termination of GDB project. *http://www.gdb.org/shutdown/notice.html*

Lu R, Ko H, Chang F, Castiglione CM, Schoolfield G, et al. 1996. No association between alcoholism and multiple polymorphisms at the dopamine D2 receptor gene (DRD2) in three distinct Taiwanese populations. *Biol. Psychiatry* 39:419–29

Maldonado R, Blendy JA, Tzavara E, Gass P, Roques BP, et al. 1996. Reduction of morphine abstinence in mice with a mutation in the gene encoding CREB. *Science* 273: 657–59

Malhotra AK, Virkkunen M, Rooney W, Eggert M, Linnoila M, Goldman D. 1996. The association between the dopamine D-4 receptor (D4DR) 16 amino acid repeat polymorphism and Novelty Seeking. *Mol. Psychiatry* 1:388–91

Markel PD, Bennett B, Beeson M, Gordon L, Johnson TE. 1997. Confirmation of quantitative trait loci for ethanol sensitivity in long-sleep and short-sleep mice. *Genome Res.* 7:92–99

Markel PD, Fulker DW, Bennett B, Corley RP, DeFries JC, et al 1996. Quantitative trait loci for ethanol sensitivity in the LS × SS recombinant inbred strains: interval mapping. *Behav. Genet.* 26:447–58

Maxson SC. 1992. Methodological issues in genetic analysis of an agonistic behavior (offense) in male mice. In *Techniques for the Genetic Analysis of Brain and Behavior: Focus on the Mouse,* ed. D Goldowitz, D Wahlsten, RE Wimer, 8:349–73. Amsterdam: Elsevier

Maxson SC. 1998. Homologous genes, aggression, and animal models. *Dev. Neuropsychol.* 14:143–56

Mayford M, Bach ME, Huang Y, Wang L, Hawkins RD, Kandel ER. 1996. Control of memory formation through regulated expression of a CaMKII transgene. *Science* 274:1678–83

McClearn GE, Plomin R, Gora-Maslak G,

Crabbe JC. 1991. The gene chase in behavioral science. *Psychol. Sci.* 2:222–29

Mihalek RM, Jones CJ, Tully T. 1997. The *Drosophila* mutation *turnip* has pleiotropic effects and does not specifically affect learning. *Neurobiol. Learn. Mem.* 3: 425–44

Miklos GL, Rubin GM. 1996. The role of the genome project in determining gene function: insights from model organisms. *Cell* 86:521–29

Moldin SO. 1997. The maddening hunt for madness genes. *Nat. Genet.* 17:127–29

Moldin SO, Gottesman II. 1997. At issue: genes, experience, and chance in schizophrenia—positioning for the 21st century. *Schizophr. Bull.* 23:547–61

Muzzin P, Eisensmith RC, Copeland KC, Woo SLC. 1996. Correction of obesity and diabetes in genetically obese mice by leptin gene therapy. *Proc. Natl. Acad. Sci. USA* 93:14804–8

Ono Y, Manki H, Yoshimura K, Muramatsu T, Mizushima H, et al. 1997. Association between dopamine D4 receptor (D4DR) exon III polymorphism and novelty seeking in Japanese subjects. *Am. J. Med. Genet. Neuropsychiatr. Genet.* 74:501–3

Osborne KA, Robichon A, Burgess E, Butland S, Shaw RA, et al. 1997. Natural behavior polymorphism due to a cGMP-dependent protein kinase of *Drosophila*. *Science* 277: 834–36

Peeler DF. 1995. Shuttlebox performance in BALB/cByJ, C57BL/6ByJ, and CXB recombinant inbred mice: environmental and genetic determinants and constraints. *Psychobiology* 23:161–70

Plomin R, McClearn GE, Smith DL, Vignetti S, Chorney MJ, et al. 1994. DNA markers associated with high versus low IQ: the IQ quantitative trait loci (QTL) project. *Behav. Genet.* 24:107–18

Poderycki MJ, Simoes JM, Todorova MT, Neumann PE, Seyfried TN. 1998. Environmental influences on epilepsy gene mapping in EL mice. *J. Neurogenet.* 12: 67–86

Rijsdijk FV, Boomsma DI. 1997. Genetic mediation of the correlation between peripheral nerve conduction velocity and IQ. *Behav. Genet.* 27:87–98

Risch N, Merikangas K. 1996. The future of genetic studies of complex human diseases. *Science* 273:1516–17

Rodgers RJ, Dalvi A. 1997. Anxiety, defense and the elevated plus-maze. *Neurosci. Biobehav. Rev.* 21:801–10

Rose RJ. 1995. Genes and human behavior. *Annu. Rev. Psychol.* 46:625–54

Roullet P, Lassalle JM, Jegat R. 1993. A study of behavioral and sensorial bases of radial maze learning in mice. *Behav. Neural Biol.* 59:173–79

Rowen L, Mahairas G, Hood L. 1997. Sequencing the human genome. *Science* 278: 605–7

Ruane J, Colleau JJ. 1995. Marker assisted selection for genetic improvement of animal populations when a single QTL is marked. *Genet. Res.* 66:71–83

Sander T, Harms H, Dufeu P, Kuhn S, Rommelspacher H, Schmidt LG. 1997. Dopamine D4 receptor exon III alleles and variation of novelty seeking in alcoholics. *Am. J. Med. Genet. Neuropsychiatr. Genet.* 74:483–87

Sawyer LA, Hennessy JM, Peixoto AA, Rosato E, Parkinson H, et al. 1997. Natural variation in a *Drosophila* clock gene and temperature compensation. *Science* 278: 2117–20

Schönemann PH. 1997. On models and muddles of heritability. *Genetica* 99:97–108

Schonfeld-Warden N, Warden CH. 1997. Pediatric obesity: an overview of etiology and treatment. *Pediatr. Endocrinol.* 44: 339–61

Simpson EM, Linder CC, Sargent EE, Davisson MT, Mobraaten LE, Sharp JJ. 1997. Genetic variation among 129 substrains and its importance for targeted mutagenesis in mice. *Nat. Genet.* 16:19–27

Sokolowski MB, Pereira HS, Hughes K. 1997. Evolution of foraging behavior in *Drosophila* by density-dependent selection. *Proc. Natl. Acad. Sci. USA* 94:7373–77

Strohman RC. 1997. The coming Kuhnian revolution in biology. *Nat. Biotechnol.* 15: 194–200

Sullivan PF, Fifield WJ, Kennedy MA, Mulder RT, Sellman JD, Joyce PR. 1998. No association between novelty seeking and the type 4 dopamine receptor gene (DRD4) in two New Zealand samples. *Am. J. Psychiatry* 155:98–101

Takahashi JS. 1996. *What's Wrong with My Mouse? New Interplays between Mouse Genetics and Behavior.* Washington, DC: Soc. Neurosci.

Thomas SA, Palmiter RD. 1997. Disruption of the dopamine B-hydroxylase gene in mice suggests roles for norepinephrine in motor function, learning, and memory. *Behav. Neurosci.* 111:579–89

Threadgill DW, Yee D, Matin A, Nadeau JH, Magnuson T. 1997. Genealogy of the 129 inbred strains: 129/SvJ is a contaminated inbred strain. *Mamm. Genome* 8: 441–42

Tsien JA, Huerta PT, Tonegawa S. 1996. The essential role of hippocampal CA1 NMDA receptor-dependent synaptic plasticity in spatial memory. *Cell* 87:1327–38

Tully T. 1997. Regulation of gene expression and its role in long-term memory and synaptic plasticity. *Proc. Natl. Acad. Sci. USA* 94:4239–41

Tully T, Bolwig G, Christensen J, Connolly J, DelVecchio M, et al. 1996. A return to genetic dissection of memory in *Drosophila*. *Cold Spring Harbor Symp. Quant. Biol.* 61:207–18

Vandenbergh DJ, Zonderman AB, Wang J, Uhl GR, Costa PT Jr. 1997. No association between novelty seeking and dopamine D4 receptor (D4DR) exon III seven repeat alleles in Baltimore longitudinal study of aging participants. *Mol. Psychiatry* 2:417–19

Varnam CJ, Strauss R, De Belle JS, Sokolowski MB. 1996. Larval behavior of *Drosophila* central complex mutants: interactions between *no bridge, foraging,* and *chaser. J. Neurogenet.* 11:99–115

Wahlsten D. 1990. Insensitivity of the analysis of variance to heredity-environment interaction. *Behav. Brain Sci.* 13:109–61

Wahlsten D. 1994. The intelligence of heritability. *Can. Psychol.* 35:244–58

Wahlsten D, Sparks V. 1995. New recombi-

nant inbred strains expressing 100% total absence of the corpus callosum. *Soc. Neurosci. Abstr.* 21, p.796

Welker E, Armstrong-James M, Bronchti G, Ourednik W, Gheorghita-Baechler F, et al. 1996. Altered sensory processing in the somatosensory cortex of the mouse mutant barrelless. *Science* 271:1864–67

Whishaw IQ, Tomie J. 1996. Of mice and mazes: similarities between mice and rats on dry land but not water mazes. *Physiol. Behav.* 60:1191–97

Wimer RE, Wimer CC. 1985. Animal behavior genetics: a search for the biological foundations of behavior. *Annu. Rev. Psychol.* 36:171–218

Wolf U. 1997. Identical mutations and phenotypic variation. *Hum. Genet.* 100:305–21

Wolfer DP, Müller U, Staglier M, Lipp H. 1997. Assessing the effects of the 129/Sv genetic background on swimming navigation learning in transgenic mutants: a study using mice with a modified β-amyloid precursor protein gene. *Brain Res.* 771:1–13

Yu WH, Kimura M, Walczewska A, Karanth S, McCann SM. 1997. Role of leptin in hypothalamic-pituitary function. *Proc. Natl. Acad. Sci. USA* 94:1023–28

Annu. Rev. Psychol. 1999. 50:625–50
Copyright © 1999 by Annual Reviews. All rights reserved

THE PSYCHOLOGICAL UNDERPINNINGS OF DEMOCRACY: A Selective Review of Research on Political Tolerance, Interpersonal Trust, and Social Capital

J.L. Sullivan and J.E. Transue

Department of Political Science, University of Minnesota, 1414 Social Sciences, Minneapolis, Minnesota 55455-0410; e-mail: jsull@polisci.umn.edu, jtransue@polisci.umn.edu

KEY WORDS: political psychology, democracy, political attitudes, political tolerance, threat, interpersonal trust, postmaterialism, social capital, political culture

ABSTRACT

This chapter explores two psychological orientations that support democratic governance. First, robust democracies require citizens to tolerate others' efforts to participate in politics, even if they promote unpopular views. Research shows that citizens' political tolerance is influenced strongly by the depth of their commitment to democratic values, by their personality, and by the degree to which they perceive others as threatening. Cross-national research generalizes many of these findings to other countries. Second, robust democracies need citizens who will participate in politics. Almond and Verba's cross-national research shows that interpersonal trust and other features of political culture enhance citizen involvement in politics. Inglehart expanded the political culture framework in his work on post-materialism, interpersonal trust, life satisfaction, and cognitive mobilization. Recent theories of social capital also emphasize the role of generalized interpersonal trust, membership in voluntary associations, and norms of reciprocity in enhancing political participation and democracy.

0084-6570/99/0201-0625$08.00

CONTENTS

INTRODUCTION

This chapter reviews the literature on the psychological foundations of democracy. The expectations for citizens in a democracy differ from those for citizens living with other forms of government in many ways. This review concentrates on two of these expectations. The first is that citizens must tolerate their fellow citizens' efforts to participate in politics, even if the latter's views diverge sharply from the norm. The second is that citizens can and do participate in their own governance. Thus this review concentrates on the psychological underpinnings of the restraint that creates the opportunity for a wide range of political groups to express their ideas and to participate in public life (political tolerance), and on the attitudes, values, and orientations that lead citizens to participate in politics. The latter involves a review of research that focuses on the psychological underpinnings of what political scientists call the civic culture and social capital.

DEMOCRATIC VALUES AND SUPPORT FOR CIVIL LIBERTIES

In his mid-19th-century analysis of American democracy and American character, *Democracy in America*, Alexis de Tocqueville devoted an entire chapter to what he called "principal causes which tend to maintain the democratic republic in the United States" (de Tocqueville 1945). He discussed three sets of causes, including situation and context, law, and manners and customs of the people. Of these, he considered the last to be the most important. Although de Tocqueville was imprecise in his analysis of the exact nature of the manners and customs so essential to American democracy, he quite explicitly argued that most analysts had considerably overemphasized the importance of situation and law. De Tocqueville also believed that Americans held in common several general principles that constitute this "peculiar" source of democracy.

In the 1950s and 1960s, modern political scientists elaborated on de Tocqueville's claim. They identified conditions that they, too, believed to be "prerequisites" for democracy. For example, in the mid-1950s, the leading political science disciplinary journal, the *American Political Science Review*, published a symposium by some of the most distinguished political theorists of that time. These theorists concluded that, for democracy to exist, certain attitudes must be widespread. In short, there should be a consensus on the procedural norms by which substantive matters are negotiated, as well as on fundamental values such as liberty, equality, and individualism (Griffith et al 1956). A decade or so later, Neubauer (1967) identified this critical psychological prerequisite as socialization into the "rules of the game."

More generally, empirical theorists of the era argued that the development of democratic political institutions depends critically upon the political culture, by which they meant that citizens must have a particular orientation toward political life (e.g. Almond & Verba 1963; Dahl 1971; Huntington 1984). This orientation was often left rather general, and whenever specific, precisely defined elements of that orientation were specified, agreement dissipated. However, in his more recent analysis of democratization in Russia, Gibson (1992, 1995) argues that there has been some agreement that political tolerance and interpersonal trust are necessary elements of the required orientation.[1] In his own analysis, he focuses on support among Russians for basic rights, liberties, and democratic institutions, under the assumption that mass-belief systems constrain structural processes.[2]

In this chapter, we first review empirical research on mass support for civil liberties and then discuss the connection between this and the concept of political tolerance, which plays a central role in the civic orientation that most theorists believe is a necessary condition for a thriving democracy. We then review research on the civic culture that relates cultural attitudes and beliefs to the development of democracy. Finally, we turn our attention to recent empirical research on what has become known as social capital, and examine the role of interpersonal trust and civic virtue in promoting democratic participation.

---

[1]In this chapter, we will incorporate interpersonal trust in the discussion of social capital, when we present research on participation.

[2]Although, as Caspi & Seligson (1983) demonstrate, "political tolerance by itself cannot explain the survival of democratic regimes"(p. 385).

Support for Civil Liberties: Evidence from Early Survey Research

The development of the sample survey allowed empirical political science researchers to "test" the psychological/cultural prerequisite hypothesis. Assuming that the United States of the 1950s and 1960s was indisputably a fully functioning democracy, they set out to identify whether, or the extent to which, a consensus existed with regard to the rules of the game. If no such consensus existed, then perhaps the mass culture and citizens' attitudes were not very important. Perhaps the "correct" laws and institutions were all that were truly required for a democracy to work well.

One of the first such studies was conducted by Samuel Stouffer (1955), who, in the summer of 1954, administered two extensive national surveys of over 2400 cases each. He used national scientific probability sampling methods to study Americans' support for the civil liberties of socialists, atheists, Communists, and fellow travelers. Stouffer studied an additional sample of 1500 local community leaders in cities of 10,000–150,000. In his leadership sample, Stouffer included public officials, county-level party chairs, industrial leaders, and heads of patriotic groups, among others. Stouffer discovered that most Americans—in fact an overwhelming majority—did not support the civil liberties of the left-wing groups he studied. One of the more important factors that Stouffer identified as explaining citizens' willingness to take away the rights of left-wing groups was the perception of threat. Americans felt threatened at a fairly high level by these unpopular groups. This threat and its consequent feelings of fear and anxiety appeared to drive most citizens' attitudes and beliefs. Stouffer also discovered that, among his sample groups, community leaders were far more supportive of these groups' rights than were ordinary citizens.

Stouffer's research called into question two fundamental assumptions of democratic theorists. The first assumption that was undermined was that United States citizens had internalized properly the rules of the game. It was clear that they had not. Stouffer found that overwhelming majorities of citizens were willing to take away rights—particularly those of communists and atheists—to free speech, to participate fully in the political process, and so on. In other words, most citizens were willing to apply double standards, allowing mainstream groups one set of rights while restricting the rights of more extreme or unpopular left-wing political groups.

The second assumption called into question was that a national consensus on how to apply the democratic rules of the game was a prerequisite to having a democracy. Rather than question the extent to which the United States was a democracy—even though Stouffer's study was conducted during the McCarthy era—the more common conclusion from this research was that a democracy could obviously be sustained despite the significant shortcomings of its citizens.

But, if true, how exactly was democracy being sustained? Shortly after Stouffer's watershed analysis, two classic studies offered answers to this question. Prothro & Grigg (1960) studied local samples in Tallahassee, Florida, and Ann Arbor, Michigan. They asked respondents to express their agreement or disagreement with some general principles of democracy, including majority rule and minority rights, and with some specific applications of these principles, such as restricting voting to well-informed citizens, preventing a duly elected "Negro" from holding office, and so on. Prothro & Grigg found that there was a broad consensus endorsing the principles of democracy but that this consensus disappeared when applying it to specific controversial cases. (Recall that Stouffer's study focused not so much on democratic principles as on their application to unpopular left-wing political groups.) Prothro & Grigg did find, however, a much greater level of consensus in the application of democratic principles among more educated and wealthy citizens.

At about the same time (1957–1958), Herbert McClosky (1964) conducted a study of national political party activists (national convention attenders) and political party supporters among the general public. Just as Prothro & Grigg had found, McClosky reported a much higher level of consensus about the democratic rules of the game (free speech, minority rights, and so on) among party activists than among ordinary citizens. The activists not only exhibited a higher level of support for the rules and principles of democracy, they also more consistently applied these principles to specific situations that challenged citizens' commitment to the principles.

These studies offered a possible resolution to the dilemma. There existed "carriers of the creed" who protected the democratic system from the majority of citizens who did not fully understand or support it. Despite the obvious fact that most citizens did not possess the correct underlying attitudes and understandings to sustain a fully functioning democratic system, the educated and the politically active did. Most citizens who failed to internalize the attitudes and habits that undergird democratic practices were generally inactive politically and even apathetic. Since most ordinary citizens did not act politically based upon their (negative) attitudes, at least not in concert, democracy was rather easily sustained by an activist class with the proper psychological attitudes, values, and predispositions.

In the 1970s, Nunn et al (1978) updated Stouffer's classic analysis, using essentially the same questionnaire Stouffer had used some twenty years earlier. They found that the American public had become far more accepting of the civil liberties of the unpopular groups studied by Stouffer. Nunn and his colleagues attributed much of the change to improvements in education, demographic changes in the electorate, cohort changes, and so on. But most importantly for this review, they concluded that ordinary citizens exhibited a substantial increase in support for the application of democratic principles, and that "attempting to approximate democracy may become increasingly feasible" (p. 159). They argued that we need no longer rely on political leaders to be the carriers of the democratic creed. The cultural prerequisites to democracy noted by de Tocqueville may not have been fully functional at the time he noted them, nor even in the 1950s when political scientists specified them more fully, but by the mid 1970s, political sociologists were beginning to conclude that they were on the brink of fulfillment.

Support for Civil Liberties vs Political Tolerance

In the early 1980s, Sullivan et al (1982) reviewed the conceptual underpinnings of research on civil liberties and public opinion. They argued that, historically, the concept of tolerance evolved from efforts to moderate the harmful and often violent effects of religious conflict. The idea of religious tolerance was promoted as a mechanism to allow religions to "put up with," or tolerate, other religions that they disliked or even hated vehemently. So too did the concept of political tolerance evolve as a way to live with one's ideological and political enemies. Political opponents need not be eliminated physically or even politically. One need not like or support one's opponents and their ideas, but one ought at least to put up with, or tolerate, them. We were urged to learn to agree about how to disagree.

Sullivan et al adopted this understanding of political tolerance and evaluated previous empirical research on public opinion toward civil liberties. Since previous researchers—Stouffer included—had studied support primarily for the civil liberties of unpopular left-wing groups, in a strict sense they had not studied political tolerance. For example, in his studies during the 1950s, Stouffer had asked respondents about whether and to what extent they supported the civil liberties of communists, atheists, socialists, fellow travelers, and so on. This was indeed a test of tolerance for citizens who feared and disliked left-wing groups in American politics, or who were deeply religious and believed that atheists were out to destroy religion. But it was not a test of the tolerance of those who were themselves left-wingers and/or identified themselves as atheists. The latter respondents were in effect being asked whether they supported the rights of groups with whom they identified in a positive manner. That provided absolutely no challenge to them. Answering in the affirmative did not mean these individuals were in fact politically tolerant. They may merely have been indifferent, or they may actually have been supportive of the target groups in question. In order to test whether such individuals and groups were tolerant, we would have to ask them to support the rights of groups and ideologies they actively opposed and disliked. That alone would provide a significant test of their political tolerance.

As a consequence of this conceptualization of political tolerance, Sullivan et al realized that measuring tolerance required a two-step measurement procedure. First, researchers must establish that an individual has political objections and/or negative feelings about a political group. Then they need to measure the extent to which the individual supports or opposes the political rights of that group. As a result, Sullivan et al created a methodology that attempted to provide individualized target groups for each respondent. In one variation of that method, they asked respondents to identify the group or groups in politics that they "like the least" and then asked respondents how far they would support the civil liberties (right to free speech, right to run for office, and so on) of their least-liked group. Another variation asked respondents to provide like-dislike evaluations for a series of extremist political groups. After this, respondents were asked about their degree of support for the civil liberties of these groups, and their levels of political tolerance were assessed only for those groups which they actively disliked or objected to.

Using this methodology, Sullivan et al (1982) found that the American public was far less tolerant than had been indicated by the Nunn et al (1978) update of Stouffer. It appears that the primary change identified by Nunn and his colleagues was not in actual levels of political tolerance, but rather in the level of objection to these left-wing groups. Communists, socialists, and atheists were no longer as salient as they had been, and citizens did not object nearly so strenuously to them as they had in the 1950s. However, that did not mean that other unpopular groups—often racist or right-wing—were tolerated. In fact, these other groups evoked high levels of intolerance beginning in the 1970s and continuing into the 1990s.[3]

THE DETERMINANTS OF POLITICAL INTOLERANCE

Later studies have confirmed and elaborated many of the empirical findings identified by Stouffer, McClosky, and Prothro & Grigg. For example, several studies continue to confirm that political "elites" variously defined are more supportive of civil liberties—and even more generally tolerant—than are ordinary citizens (Nunn et al 1978; McClosky & Brill 1983; McClosky & Zaller 1984; Sullivan et al 1993; but see Sniderman et al 1996 for exceptions). Thus one obvious "cause" of differing levels of tolerance and intolerance is political

[3]By this we mean that many citizens do not support the rights of racist groups to demonstrate, run for office, give political speeches, and so on. Under this understanding of political tolerance, one may strongly oppose racist groups' violent actions or hatred and still be tolerant as long as one is willing to accord racists the same rights of political action as one accords other, more mainstream political groups.

expertise and participation (Sullivan et al 1993). But other important factors have been identified, and they are discussed below.

Political Intolerance and Perceptions of Threat

Many studies find that one of the factors with the strongest direct relationship to levels of political tolerance is threat perception, confirming Stouffer's work which was based on less sophisticated methods and was conducted during a time period that was unique with regard to civil liberties issues (Sullivan et al 1982, 1985; Gibson 1987; Marcus et al 1995). More recent work has confirmed both a chronic, dispositional role for threat perceptions, and a short-term effect due to the current information environment. Some people have a predisposition to be easily threatened and thus are very sensitive and responsive to potential threats in the political environment. They are less tolerant than individuals who are more calm and more easily reassured.[4]

For many citizens, information that describes the nature and activities of potentially unpopular groups has a profound impact on their level of tolerance toward these groups and their ideas and activities. If the information environment portrays such groups as violating normative expectations with regard to orderly behavior and proper procedures, many citizens—even those not particularly predisposed toward intolerance—will refuse to tolerate the group and its activities. If the information environment portrays them as behaving properly and in an orderly fashion, then far more people—often a majority—will tolerate the group and its activities, despite the group's unpopular and/or extremist image (Marcus et al 1995).

Nelson et al (1997) tested for framing effects on tolerance judgments. One frame highlighted free-speech concerns and the other highlighted public order and safety. Using news reports of a KKK rally in Ohio, they experimentally manipulated the frame placed around the same set of facts (that the rally would have implications for both free speech and public order). In two studies they found that the frame placed around the information affected tolerance judgments. The effects were highly mediated by the manipulations' influence on the importance of different values. In the public-order condition, attitudes toward public order significantly predicted tolerance for the KKK's activities, but attitudes toward civil liberties were insignificant. Conversely, in the free-speech condition, attitudes toward public order were insignificant, whereas attitudes toward civil liberties were highly predictive of tolerance of the KKK. In both studies, Nelson et al found that the frame affected the importance attached

---

[4]Altemeyer (1988, 1996) has shown that right-wing authoritarians are highly threatened and highly reactive to threat. He views this as one of the major sources of their authoritarian attitudes, beliefs, and actions. Staub (1989) also identifies threat perceptions as one of the primary contributing factors in mass genocides and malignant political aggression in general

to specific values. The importance attached to these competing values significantly predicted tolerance. For example, the public-order frame significantly increased the importance that subjects attribute to public order in making tolerance judgments. Variation in the importance of public order showed a significant negative relationship to tolerance. For those in the freedom-of-speech condition, the importance attached to freedom of speech shows a significant positive relationship with tolerance. Nelson et al (1997) concluded that these results show how framing by the mass media affects how people think about tolerance and thus their final opinions on tolerance.[5]

Thus aggregate levels of intolerance are somewhat malleable, depending on how political elites and the media portray those with less popular ideas. Threat perceptions—both dispositional and environmental—play a central role in determining whether a set of citizens will internalize and apply the democratic principles of restraint and tolerance, or whether they will set them aside in particularly difficult situations (See Marcus et al 1995).

Political Tolerance and the Internalization of Democratic Values

More recent research has also elaborated on one of the early findings identified by Prothro & Grigg and by McClosky. These earlier scholars not only noted the lack of consensus on fundamental democratic values, but they also emphasized the finding that most ordinary citizens were inconsistent and perhaps even hypocritical. Most citizens expressed a strong belief in democratic values but coupled that belief with an unwillingness to apply these values to groups and ideologies they found most objectionable. Based on these early analyses, it would be easy and even logical to conclude that the ideas and ideals of democracy operate at a level disconnected from actual practices. In other words, ideas did not guide behavior in this very important instance. More recent research, however, does demonstrate that the internalization of democratic norms can make a considerable difference in determining how tolerant an individual will be when her or his tolerance is sorely tested (Lawrence 1976; Sullivan et al 1982; Gibson & Bingham 1983; McClosky & Brill 1983; Gibson 1987, 1992; Marcus et al 1995).

---

[5]Golebiowska's (1996) research examines the connection between the political tolerance literature and the stereotyping literature. She explores the effects of stereotyping and the difference between reactions to a stereotype-congruent target and a target who does not fit the group stereotype. She ran experiments that varied the personal characteristics (stereotypically gay or straight traits and habits) of a target individual. Subjects then answered questions about whether they would tolerate a variety of actions by the individual in question. She hypothesized that a gay man who has characteristics that match the stereotype of gay men will be tolerated less than a gay man with the opposite characteristics (e.g. emotional vs not emotional). The experimental data showed the hypothesized results.

The early studies reviewed above simply noted the aggregate disjunction between abstract beliefs and their concrete application. (They also noted mass-elite differences in this disjunction.) Later studies measured individuals' degree of support for the norms of minority rights, freedom of speech, and so on. They then related individuals' scores on these scales to their scale scores on items designed to measure applications of these norms to unpopular groups. The findings are clear and rather strong—the more completely an individual has internalized and believes strongly in democratic norms, the more likely the individual is to tolerate groups and ideas that he or she finds to be obnoxious. Although there is significant slippage in the aggregate percentage who endorse the abstract norms compared to the percentage who are tolerant in concrete situations, one can predict with fair accuracy which individuals will remain consistent and which will defect (Lawrence 1976; Sullivan et al 1982; Gibson & Bingham 1983; McClosky & Brill 1983; Gibson 1987, 1992; Marcus et al 1995). It turns out, then, that threat perceptions and strength of belief in the more abstract norms of democracy are both very strong predictors of applied tolerance judgments.

Political Tolerance and Personality

In addition to threat perceptions and democratic norms, one additional potent set of variables that explains citizens' beliefs in democratic values and their levels of applied political tolerance is personality. In his mid-1950s study, Stouffer (1955) found that certain types of individuals—those who believed in stern child-rearing techniques and those who tended to be pessimistic—were much less tolerant of ideological nonconformity than were others, whose child-rearing views were more permissive and who were very optimistic. McClosky & Brill (1983) found that several personality characteristics predicted applied tolerance scores quite well, including measures of misanthropy, anomie, self-esteem, flexibility, and so on. Sullivan et al (1982) evaluated the impact on political tolerance of a number of personality factors and found that the strongest relationship was for a factor they labeled "psychological insecurity," measured with the greatest reliability by Rokeach's dogmatism scale. Gibson (1987) also found that measures of dogmatism and trust predicted levels of political tolerance. Finally, Marcus et al (1995) used Costa & McCrae's (1985, 1992) measures and found that neuroticism, extroversion, and openness to experience all predict levels of political tolerance fairly accurately. Those individuals higher on neuroticism and extroversion are less tolerant, while those high on openness to experience are more tolerant. Openness to experience appears to be the most powerful predictor (a zero-order correlation of about .5). Their analysis went on to show that certain types of individuals are more responsive to contemporary information about how threatening unpopular groups are. Individuals high in neuroticism are most responsive, apparently because of their high level of anxiety, which makes them more sensitive and responsive to perceptions of threat (Marcus et al 1995, p. 168–172).

In summary, then, empirical research over a more than forty-year span has demonstrated that there are strong psychological underpinnings to what political scientists have called "support for the rules of the political game." At the abstract level, there is consensual support for democratic values. When these values are applied to difficult cases, however, there is far less consensus. There is some evidence that levels of applied tolerance have increased over time (e.g. Nunn et al 1978), but there is also some evidence that these increases are modest at best (Sullivan et al 1982, Gibson 1989). In general, political experts exhibit higher levels of applied tolerance than do political novices, and in all cases, strongly internalized beliefs in democratic values "constrain" citizens to be more tolerant in practical situations. Individual differences in both perceptions of threat and personality predispositions also influence quite considerably applied tolerance judgments.

CROSS-NATIONAL STUDIES OF POLITICAL TOLERANCE

De Tocqueville's observations about the connection between political culture (manners and customs of the people) and institutional democracy were made about mid-nineteenth-century America. American political scientists have elaborated on his emphasis on the democratic underpinnings of the law, manners, and customs of the people. American political sociologists and political psychologists have studied and identified the more precise connections among underlying social customs, psychological attitudes and predispositions, and support for democratic values and their application. It is, however, difficult if not impossible to make broader claims about psychological prerequisites for democratic attitudes and systems without conducting cross-national, comparative studies. Are the underlying relationships between psychological characteristics and institutional democracy sufficiently sensitive to the historical and political context within which they occur that generalization is virtually impossible? Or do certain psychological predispositions and attitudes invariably sustain a democratic political culture and institutions, while other predispositions and attitudes invariably subvert them? Although we cannot answer these questions in this analysis, we can at least shed some modest light on them.

As a prolegomenon to these broad and difficult issues, scholars have conducted a number of surveys about civil liberties and political tolerance in other countries. Sullivan et al (1985) replicated their US study with samples in Israel and New Zealand. Using the least-liked group methodology described above, they found that New Zealanders were much more tolerant than Americans and Israelis, attributing that in part to the more isolated and peaceful political context.[6] Most importantly, using LISREL (Linear Structural Relations) modeling, they tested a theory created to identify the underlying factors influencing tolerance that should be most sensitive to the political context, and those that should be the most context-invariant. In particular, the theory predicted that perceptions of threat should have the same impact on tolerance judgments, regardless of political context. The context may determine the overall level of perceived threat, but not the consequences for tolerance given any particular level of threat. Although levels of perceived threat might be much higher in Israel than in New Zealand, citizens in both countries who perceive a strong threat from their political enemies should be much less tolerant than those who do not. The findings of this study confirm this expectation. The structural parameters between threat perceptions and tolerance are significant and very strong in all three countries.

Similarly, the impact of personality on political tolerance should be independent of context. Highly dogmatic, authoritarian personalities are expected to be intolerant—unsupportive of the civil liberties of groups they dislike—regardless of where they live. The attitudinal consequences of a personality structure created by a combination of genetics and socialization should be manifest in almost any society. The results of this study also strongly confirm this expectation and indicate that there is a strong relationship between psychological insecurity and dogmatism on the one hand, and intolerance on the other hand.

Finally, the impact on civil-liberties judgments of internalizing democratic values and norms should vary by context, depending in large part on the cultural meaning and interpretation given to these values. Unlike threat perceptions and personality characteristics, whose consequences may be almost automatic, the role played by democracy is mediated by how that concept is understood in the political culture of the country. For example, in the United States, the emphasis in the civil liberties arena is placed on individual rights such as the individual's freedom of speech and the rights of the minority to participate

---

[6]Placing the study of attitudes toward civil liberties into a comparative context highlights the advantages of understanding tolerance as requiring a serious objection or dislike. If one attempted to replicate Stouffer's study, or those reported by subsequent authors using his methodology (e.g. Nunn et al 1978), in other countries, one would be stuck with measures that create more problems of comparison than they solve. For example, in democratic countries that had active and viable socialist and communist parties, asking respondents whether they support the rights of communists and socialists to give speeches and run for public office would not provide a coherent test of tolerance for many citizens. After all, large percentages would have been socialists or communists themselves. Instead, the "least-liked political group" measurement strategy allowed researchers to identify "functionally equivalent" (i.e. strongly disliked) groups in different countries.

fully in the political process. Other democratic nations—including Israel, for example—place a much greater emphasis on majority rule and equality. The former interpretation has a more direct connection to and obvious consequences for political tolerance. The latter interpretation might, at times, even promote intolerance of the minority in the name of the majority. Both of these political cultures might emphasize democracy, but they may also emphasize quite different understandings of what that concept means. As a consequence, the impact of a strong internalization of democratic values on tolerance judgments should vary by political context. It should, for example, be much stronger in the United States than in Israel. The findings of this study are consistent with this argument. The internalization of democratic values and norms has a very strong relationship with tolerance in the United States but not in Israel.[7]

Tolerance in an Emerging Democracy

Gibson (1992) and Gibson, Duch, & Tedin (Gibson et al 1992) applied the least-liked group methodology to the study of tolerance in the former Soviet Union. This research expanded upon previous cross-national research by testing for the same relationships in a country without democratic traditions. Gibson (1992) found that—like citizens in long-standing democracies—Russians were quite supportive of the general norms of democracy. However, when asked to apply these norms to disliked groups, they were intolerant—much more so than citizens surveyed in longer-standing democracies. Importantly, however, Gibson found that democratic beliefs and attitudes formed a single, more general attitude cluster that conceivably could form a foundation for the longer-term development of a democratic political culture.

Gibson et al (1992) report findings that tend to confirm—in a quite different political context—many of the findings about the determinants of political tolerance that were reviewed earlier. By far the most significant predictor of intolerance among Russian citizens is, once again, perceived threat. As in previous studies, threat is an extremely potent, and completely exogenous, influence on tolerance. As the theory described above leads one to expect, the influence of personality is also unchanged by this new political context. Gibson & Duch (1993) find that dogmatism increases intolerance in the former Soviet Union. Additionally, commitment to abstract democratic norms decreased intolerance, just as it had in New Zealand and the United States.

This commitment was put to a strong test by the attempted coup in 1991. Gibson (1997) administered a survey that asked respondents whether they had acted in some way to support or oppose the attempted takeover of the Soviet

---

[7]New Zealand is more like the United States than it is like Israel. The relationship between democratic norms and political tolerance is fairly strong.

Union. He found that commitment to democratic institutions and processes, including minority rights and political tolerance, was one of the strongest influences on people's decisions to act against the coup.[8] Additionally, people were much more likely to act in response to the coup if they had been recruited by another person. Gibson (1997) found that these psychological and interpersonal factors were more predictive than a cost-benefit analysis derived from rational-choice theory. Interestingly, he found that commitment to democratic norms and processes mobilized those people who acted against the coup and, although the effect was smaller, it also mobilized those who acted to support the coup.

ATTITUDES AND POLITICAL PARTICIPATION

In addition to the importance of citizens tolerating the efforts of opponents to influence the political system, democracies also need relatively high levels of political participation by citizens. For this reason, the comparative study of democracy has been as concerned with mass participation as with tolerance. The study of the psychological sources of this aspect of democracy has occurred in two main waves. The first wave began and largely ended with Almond & Verba's (1963) *Civic Culture,* a landmark study of political attitudes in five countries. The second wave is the relatively recent renaissance of political-culture studies by Inglehart (1977, 1990, 1997) and Putnam (1993).

The Civic Culture

Almond & Verba (1963) compared national survey data from two stable democracies with high levels of democratic openness (the United States and Great Britain) to national surveys from three countries with shorter continuous democratic rule (West Germany, Italy, and Mexico) and found three main differences. First, citizens of the United States and the United Kingdom reported higher levels of interpersonal trust.[9] Second, they reported more pride in their political institutions. Third, these respondents showed more widespread feelings of political competence. Almond & Verba (1963) named this collection of attitudes "political culture," defined as a "psychological orientation toward so-

---

[8]He measured a wide range of activities including following events in the mass media, trying to persuade others, staying away from work, distributing leaflets and letters, expressing views to political officials, and participating in demonstrations.

[9]A specific type of interpersonal trust is important: generalized interpersonal trust. That is, the survey questions that measure interpersonal trust refer to people in general rather than trust directed toward specific individuals or types of people. The wording of one of the most widely used interpersonal trust items—administered by the General Social Survey for many years and more recently adopted by the American National Election Studies—is: "Some people say that most people can be trusted. Others say you can't be too careful in your dealings with people. How do you feel about it?"

cial objects. When we speak of the political culture of a society, we refer to the political system as internalized in the cognitions, feelings, and evaluations of its population."

Despite its impressive collection of survey data, *The Civic Culture* was widely criticized. Even though the study succeeded in describing the contours of the attitudes of interest in five nations, the impact that these attitudes have on politics was only vaguely specified. *The Civic Culture* did not explain how variation in interpersonal trust, pride in national institutions, and political efficacy can lead to national differences in the actual practice of politics. The authors were not able to show, for example, how different levels of interpersonal trust affect the institutional arrangements of a country or change the way political processes operate. The notion that a set of attitudes supports democracy is plausible, but *The Civic Culture* did not succeed in explaining how these attitudes enter into the practice of democratic politics (Almond & Verba 1989). It is, of course, interesting to ask citizens abstract questions about participating in a democracy, but attitudes measured at that level of generality may not be diagnostic when a citizen is faced with a specific set of candidates and issues. Additionally, some scholars objected to the authors' assumption that the United States and the United Kingdom should be held up as models against which other democracies should be judged. These critics argued that the ethnocentrism of this approach biased Almond & Verba's analysis because it led them to assume that the patterns found in the United States and United Kingdom were essential to democracy in general, rather than specific to the particular forms of democracy found in those two countries (Almond & Verba 1989).

Almond & Verba's research could not conclusively demonstrate the direction of causality between political culture and democratic governance because their data were drawn from a single cross-sectional sample of citizens within each country. They did not specify a single causal direction; rather, they described political culture as both a cause and a consequence of democratic governance and economic development. However, this question of etiology is important for the study of how attitudes affect democratic governance. If the civic culture is purely a consequence of economic development, there is little reason to study directly the attitudes or the psychological attributes of a citizenry; attention should focus instead on economic development issues.[10] Thus, the ensuing debate over the direction of causality is actually a debate about whether the attitudes studied by Almond & Verba offer any unique explanation of the

---

[10]Indeed, Przeworski et al (1996) write, "Lipset was correct to argue that once established in a wealthy country, democracy is more likely to endure. Indeed we have found that once a country is sufficiently wealthy, democracy is more likely to endure. Indeed we have found that once a country is sufficiently wealthy, with per-capita income of more than $6,000 a year, democracy is certain to survive come hell or high water."

development and survival of democratic institutions beyond that provided by economic-development explanations.

Scholars continue to debate whether the attitudes associated with the civic culture cause transitions to democratic regimes, ensure that democratic regimes persist over time, or actually are a result of the pre-existence of democratic regimes. It is difficult to demonstrate that these psychological orientations cause democracy rather than result from democracy, and even with time-series data, the answers are not conclusive. In fact, Muller & Seligson (1994) show that the hypothesis that most of the attitudes of the civic culture are consequences of democracy fits the data fairly well.[11]

In response, Inglehart (1997) argues that it is a mistake to ignore culture completely or to believe that democracy follows directly on economic development. He notes that many countries are wealthy without being democratic, while many countries with democratic constitutions are not robust democracies in practice (notably the former Soviet Union and Weimar Germany). In his own research, he found that there is an association between high aggregate levels of life satisfaction and the stability of democracy. He argues that this measure shows that when there is diffuse support for a regime (one of the properties of the civic culture), democracy will persist. Scholars who doubt the utility of the civic culture say that life satisfaction is a result of democracy. Inglehart (1997) counters that it is well known (and demonstrated by data from the World Values Survey)[12] that politics is not a high priority for most people. Very few people say that politics directly affects their life satisfaction; family, work, friends, and leisure are far more important. Thus it is equally impossible to demonstrate that democratic institutions are the primary cause of observed variation in life satisfaction or its link to democratic stability.

Culture Shift

Ronald Inglehart (1977, 1990, 1997) has pursued the question of the role of political culture for over twenty years. He argues that economic development can lead to changes in peoples' psychological orientations and preferences. This in turn creates attitudes and expectations that favor democracy over other, less participatory forms of government and sustain democracy once it begins to develop in a country. These assertions are supported by aggregate analyses of a large collection of survey data. Instead of a single cross section, Inglehart

---

[11]See also Inglehart (1997) for a point-by-point rebuttal of Muller & Seligson (1994).

[12]The World Values Survey includes public opinion surveys conducted in 1990–1993 on values from citizens in 43 countries representing 70% of the world's population. Twenty-two of these countries were also surveyed in 1981 as part of the European Values Survey. See Inglehart (1997) for a list of the survey organizations, sample sizes, time period, and principal investigators for each of these surveys. Data from the World and European Values Surveys are available from the ICPSR data archive.

(1997) analyzes over twenty years of cross-national survey data from 43 countries (some from the continuing Euro-barometer[13] and some from the more recent World Values Study).

Based on analyses of these extensive data sets, he argues that economic development causes cultural change that is conducive to democracy (Inglehart 1997).[14] The growth of a service sector is particularly critical because careers in this sector of the economy demand skills that are particularly conducive to democracy. According to Inglehart, there are certain key indicators that illustrate the impact of culture and attitudes on democracy. The citizens of countries that have the cultural resources to sustain democracy also exhibit higher levels of interpersonal trust and satisfaction with their lives in general.

INTERPERSONAL TRUST AND LIFE SATISFACTION   Inglehart shows that interpersonal trust and subjective well-being (whether people are satisfied with their lives in general) significantly affect the duration and level of democracy. Interpersonal trust is important because it lends credibility to the concept of a loyal opposition. When people do not trust their fellow citizens, elections and transitions of power appear to be far more dangerous. Citizens may fear that losing an election will mean losing all access to political power. Without trust, it is easy to imagine that one's opponents would not cede power after losing an election and might even resort to force to stay in power. When one believes that this is the political situation, democratic compromise is a dangerous option. Conversely, when people trust their fellow citizens in general, the stakes do not seem to be so high. Losing an election one year does not mean the end of access to political power. Citizens with higher interpersonal trust have reason to believe that their side may be the victor in a later election. Inglehart's data fit this explanation; levels of interpersonal trust consistently predict the existence and stability of democratic regimes.

Inglehart argues that citizens' subjective sense of well-being is a better predictor of legitimacy than direct measures of citizens' satisfaction with political institutions. He advocates using measures of life satisfaction, rather than variables that are more directly relevant to the political system, as barometers of the legitimacy of a political system. There are two reasons for this decision.

---

[13]The Euro-Barometer survey is a cross-national effort sponsored by the European Union (EU). It was first conducted in 1970 and has been run annually since 1976. It includes public opinion surveys conducted in all of the countries of the EU. Euro-Barometer data are available from the ICPSR data archive.

[14]Thus the argument about whether democracy merely evolves somewhat automatically from economic development, or whether it reflects the development of a particular civic culture, is moot. In this view, economic develoment can spur the evolution of the requisite attitudes and beliefs that make sustainable democratic development possible.

First, recent economic successes are likely to be attributed to the politicians who are in office contemporaneously. But, if people's lives have been consistently satisfying over long periods of time, Inglehart argues that resulting positive affect will be attributed to the overall system of governance. Second, he argues that life satisfaction is particularly critical in democracies. Authoritarian regimes can use coercion to remain in power; democracies persist only if citizens are generally contented.

COGNITIVE MOBILIZATION AND POSTMATERIALISM   When there is sufficient economic development to provide for the basic material needs of the population, to create a varied economy with a strong service sector and to educate a high proportion of its population, societies experience several changes that are conducive to democracy (Inglehart 1997). As service sectors and educational opportunities broaden, two psychological changes particularly stand out: cognitive mobilization and a shift from materialist to postmaterialist values.

Basically, cognitive mobilization is an increase in the skills and the motivation required to engage in decision-making, including political decision-making.[15] According to Inglehart, it is a byproduct of economic development because higher levels of education[16] and service-sector employment raise a population's level of cognitive mobilization. Since communication, analytic thinking, and verbal skills are increased through formal education, universal education and increases in the breadth of opportunities for advanced degrees directly contribute to cognitive mobilization. Concomitant changes in the percentage of the population in the service sector affect cognitive mobilization in less obvious ways. Inglehart argues that industrial work centers on routine and changes little from day to day; it does not place demands on people's decision-making skills. On the other hand, service-sector occupations require specialized knowledge. People in these occupations have more autonomy and must exercise their own judgment when making decisions on the job. Thus, when economic changes increase the percentage of a country's population in service occupations and decrease the percentage in industrial occupations, the total cognitive mobilization of the population increases. In Inglehart's words, "they become accustomed to thinking for themselves in their everyday jobs." The importance of cognitive mobilization is one reason why his model places economic development in a causally prior position to a sense of subjective well-

[15]See Verba et al (1995) for a more extensive discussion of the effects of communication and organizational skills (civic skills) on political participation. Their research is confined to the United States, but they provide an extensive analysis of the sources and effects of civic skills.

[16]But also see Nie et al (1996) on the effects of education. In sharp contrast to Inglehart's view that education increases participation across the board, their research shows that education distributes social position and connections in ways that maintain differences in political participation.

being and interpersonal trust.[17] Thus, Inglehart asserts that cognitive mobilization "makes mass publics more likely to *want* democracy and more skillful at *getting* it" (1997, p. 330).

Cognitive mobilization and widespread material and physical security lead, in turn, to a shift from material values to postmaterial values (Inglehart 1990, 1997). Inglehart defines materialist values as emphasizing "economic and physical security" and defines postmaterialist values as emphasizing "individual self-expression and quality of life concerns."[18] When materialists dominate a country's discourse, public opinion will be concerned with inflation, economic growth, and other issues that bear directly on citizens' material well-being. Postmaterialists, on the other hand, are more concerned with personal autonomy, environmental issues, and quality of life concerns besides those directly linked to material possessions.[19] Inglehart argues that the postmaterialist desire for self-expression and autonomy predisposes them toward democratic institutions and practices. Indeed, Inglehart (1997) argues that the same cultural changes that lead to postmaterialism also decrease economic growth.

To summarize, Inglehart's theory and data suggest that the prevalence of a supportive political culture allows democracies to weather the storms of short-term poor economic performance. This political culture is a combination of high levels of life satisfaction and interpersonal trust. Life satisfaction and interpersonal trust sustain democracy, whereas cognitive mobilization creates demand for the open decision-making processes of a democracy (Inglehart 1997).

Making Democracy Work

The quality of democratic decision-making is the heart of Robert Putnam's (1993) landmark book, *Making Democracy Work: Civic Traditions in Modern Italy*. Putnam found substantial variation in the performance of Italian govern-

---

[17]Brehm & Rahn (1997) find that a wide array of economic indicators (household income, national unemployment and inflation, national income inequality and economic expectations) directly and indirectly affect interpersonal trust and participation in voluntary associations (civic engagement).

[18]Inglehart relied on Maslow's need hierarchy (1954) to create survey items to measure materialism and postmaterialism.

[19]Gibson & Duch (1994) included a measure of postmaterialism as a predictor of tolerance. Inglehart (1990, 1997) argued that since postmaterialists are committed to autonomy and expression for themselves, they also believe in tolerance for others. While it did not have strong effects, postmaterialism did lead to higher levels of tolerance. In another study, Gibson & Duch (1994) found that postmaterialism increased support for democracy and unconventional participation in the former Soviet Union. Sullivan et al (1982) also found that level of self-actualization—related to postmaterialism—was strongly related to levels of political tolerance. Thus, postmaterialism and self-actualization appear to promote both political tolerance and democratic political participation.

mental institutions across different regions, both in terms of differences between northern and southern Italy and among regions within the north and
south. His explanation for this variation centered on the concept of social capital. Putnam defines social capital as "features of social organization, such as
trust, norms, and networks, that can improve the efficiency of society by facilitating coordinated actions" (1993, p. 167). When people are embedded in
dense social networks, possess norms of generalized reciprocity,[20] and have
high levels of interpersonal trust, they are more likely to be able to effectively
organize and act collectively.

Putnam reached this conclusion by studying the effects of reforms on the
performance of regional governments. Italy had been a unitary system with
most of its political institutions and decisions located in Rome. In 1970, however, regional governments were given the resources and the mandate to administer several government services. Each of the new regional institutional
arrangements was created with the same constitutional structure, powers, and
goals. This held institutional variables constant. For his dependent variables,
Putnam measured the quality of democratic governance with surveys of voters, surveys of public officials, and measures of institutional performance.[21]
His independent variables included the measures of social capital mentioned
above: interpersonal trust, generalized reciprocity, and dense networks of civic
associations.

CIVIC VIRTUE   Based on these data, Putnam (1993) finds that the regions in
Italy that have higher levels of interpersonal trust and more voluntary associations also have citizens who read newspapers, are interested in public affairs, and believe other citizens will "act fairly and obey the law." Moreover,
public officials in these high social capital regions are more likely to believe in
political equality and mass control of government and to show more willingness to compromise with their opponents than are politicians in regions with
less social capital. In the former regions, public and collective action problems

[20]That is, people will cooperate with others without a clear expectation about when they will be
repaid, but with a belief that they eventually will. Generalized reciprocity can be contrasted to
balanced reciprocity, which is simultaneous exchange. Generalized reciprocity helps people to
solve collective problems because it is not a requirement for people to see how they will personally
benefit from solving a problem. For somebody who holds the norm of generalized reciprocity,
helping to solve a collective problem is worthwhile because they believe that they will benefit at
some point in the future. Putnam (1993) writes, "[f]riendship, for example, almost always involves
generalized reciprocity."

[21]Putnam used twelve different indicators of institutional performance. Some (e.g. cabinet
stability and budget promptness) measured the quality of the regional governments' internal
processes, while others measured the amount and creativity of their legislation. He also measured
the regional governments' capacity to deliver services (e.g. day-care centers) and their bureaucratic
responsiveness to inquiries from citizens (e.g. their response to a request for job training).

are more likely to be communicated to government and also to be solved. The citizens report higher satisfaction with their lives. Putnam's performance measures show that the regional governments are more responsive and deliver services and information more effectively in regions with high social capital. Overall, the citizens in civic communities expect more from their regional governments, and it appears that their governments are more likely to meet citizens' expectations.

In sharp contrast, regions with lower social capital are populated with citizens who are more likely to believe that public affairs are not part of their lives: the 'bosses' or the 'politicians' handle how public institutions are run. To the extent that people seek interaction with political institutions, it is often in pursuit of patronage jobs or narrow self-interest which does not lead to public goods. Corruption is common and expected. In Putnam's words, "Laws, (almost everyone agrees) are made to be broken, but fearing others' lawlessness people demand sterner discipline." There is much less participation in voluntary associations. Finally, public officials fear compromise and are more likely to believe that corruption is neither rare nor surprising. Putnam hypothesizes that since compromise and communication are keys to effective collective action, the collection of attitudes and habits that he finds in the civic regions leads to good government.

ASSOCIATIONS   One of the key features of the more civic-oriented regions is the large number of voluntary associations. Associations include choral societies, model railroad clubs, sports teams, or any group where people assemble face to face to pursue common goals. Putnam asserts, like de Tocqueville (1945), that people acquire trust and the skills required to act collectively through participation in voluntary associations, as well as a sense of public-spiritedness and "shared responsibility for collective endeavors" (Putnam 1993, p 90). The associations need not be political to build interpersonal trust and lead to increased civic engagement. However, this is not to say that all organizations build social capital. Their impact depends upon how they are structured. As long as the members of the association meet with each other as equals, Putnam's evidence suggests that they create social capital.

Horizontally organized (where all members are basically equal) associations build social capital. Vertically organized (where power relations are hierarchical) associations do not build social capital and may, in fact, undermine it. This is a consequence of the form of interactions in each type of organization. In vertically structured organizations, more powerful members can defect from agreements with less powerful members of the group with impunity. There are no sanctions available to enforce norms of reciprocity (Putnam 1993). Horizontal organizations do not accomplish their goals through command and obedience. Instead, the members accomplish their goals through cooperation. Repeated interactions with fellow members build a history of successful collaboration, which in turn builds norms of generalized reciprocity and interpersonal trust. Putnam finds that horizontal associations are more common in areas with good government, whereas vertically organized organizations are more common in regions lacking good government. Putnam's most important findings were mostly supported by aggregate measures that compared regions to each other. His work opened up the puzzle of the individual-level processes and psychological underpinnings of social capital.

Individual-Level Evidence

Brehm & Rahn (1997) explain social capital in the United States with an individual-level analysis. They assert that "the phenomenon of social capital manifests itself in individuals as a tight reciprocal relationship between levels of civic engagement and interpersonal trust." Using structural equation modeling on 22 years of pooled data from the General Social Survey (GSS), they model a three-way causal nexus among interpersonal trust, civic engagement (belonging to voluntary associations), and confidence in American national institutions (the amount of confidence people expressed in the Executive branch, the Supreme Court, and in Congress). They find significant relationships in both directions between interpersonal trust and civic engagement, but the path from civic engagement to interpersonal trust is much stronger than the path from trust to civic engagement. Thus their study finds stronger evidence that engagement builds trust than that interpersonal trust leads people to join voluntary associations. It is also important to note that they have found that individual-level attributes, such as interpersonal trust, predict the other phenomena (civic engagement and confidence in government) found in Putnam's theories. Thus, even though social capital is inherently interpersonal, it manifests in the attitudes and behaviors of individuals.

Trust and Associations

Brehm & Rahn's (1997) research adds to the evidence for an individual-level relationship between generalized interpersonal trust and membership in voluntary associations. However, to date the microprocesses that create this link are poorly understood. Stolle (1998) presents one of the first attempts to directly grapple with this question in a social-capital framework.

Stolle surveyed the members of voluntary associations in Germany and Sweden, concentrating on horizontally structured associations because of Putnam's prediction on the sources of social capital. Her analysis of the variation in members' interpersonal trust generated some surprising results. She finds no evidence of a linear relationship between the time that individuals have spent in an association and their level of interpersonal trust. Instead, in her limited data, it appears that those who have been in an association for one year are more trusting than those who have been members for only a short time (less than a year). Members who have been in the association for long periods of time (more than 5 years) actually show declining levels of interpersonal trust. Thus it appears that joining an association boosts trust, but then the effect subsides for members who stay in the group for long periods. This may be explained by the effect of intragroup trust on generalized interpersonal trust.

Stolle hypothesizes that when members have strong bonds to the other members of their association (measured by their trust toward other members of their association), their trust will not generalize to others in general. As hypothesized, she finds a negative relationship between in-group trust and generalized trust. Thus, it appears that when people are loosely bound to an association, their trust for their fellow members generalizes, but when they are tightly bound, they are more likely to trust only their fellow members.

She also found that diversity, as measured by variation in socio-economic status, does not have significant effects on generalized trust. However, when diversity is measured as the share of "foreigners" in an association, diversity shows a positive relationship with generalized trust.

Putnam (1993) insists that horizontally organized associations increase social capital but that vertical associations do not. To test this hypothesis, Stolle included a variable called engagement in her analyses. The engagement questions asked the respondent whether they had ever done "a responsibility task" for their association and whether they had ever "organized a project." From these questions, she built a mean score for each organization. Higher levels mean that more members have had more organizational experience; more breadth in responsibility and leadership should indicate a horizontal organization. The mean score for each organization was then assigned to each member of the organization; it indicated the breadth of involvement of a given group's members. As expected, she found that engagement is positively related to generalized trust.

Projection of Trust

Orbell & Dawes (1991) ask how trust survives in a society even though it seems that high trusters are setting themselves up to be taken advantage of. In one of the more psychologically informed articles on interpersonal trust, they base their theory of cooperators' advantage on projection. They posit that people project their own trustworthiness onto others; people use information about themselves as a heuristic to form beliefs about what they can expect from others. An individual who honors their agreements expects others to do the same. Orbell & Dawes (1991) expand the normal configuration of the prisoners' dilemma by also giving the players the option of whether to elect to play a game or not. Thus, in their game, a player decides whether to enter into a partnership with another player and also decides whether to cooperate or defect with their partner. Through formal modeling and experimental data, they show that since cooperators (who expect their partners to be trustworthy) will enter into more partnerships than those who do not trust (who expect others to defect from agreements), there is an evolutionary advantage in trusting. Thus, even though expecting people to be trustworthy is riskier than avoiding relationships, the greater gains make it an advantageous strategy.

CONTINUITIES AND RESEARCH OPPORTUNITIES

The importance of interpersonal trust is a recurring theme in the literature's attempt to identify the psychological underpinnings of democracy. In the 19th century, de Tocqueville mentions it as one of the critical ingredients of the young American attempts at democracy. Almond & Verba (1963) also find a strong individual-level relationship between interpersonal trust and democratic participation. Putnam has done the most to advance our understanding of the sources and specific effects of interpersonal trust. If it is true that participating in voluntary associations builds generalized trust, then this insight leads to a host of new research questions. Most importantly, how does the face-to-face trust that one builds with fellow members of a voluntary association generalize? What qualities of the associations lead to generalized trust (besides those identified in Stolle's research)? What qualities of the interactions within and between these associations cause trust to generalize? What kinds of failures of these associations diminish trust and which ones do not influence trust? Are there other sources of generalized interpersonal trust that are independent of civic associations? This is a rich area for psychological inquiry.

Many of the theories of the psychological underpinnings of democracy make the assumption that attitudes generated in one domain will generalize to people in general. Inglehart makes a strong case that making decisions on the job leads to a desire to make (rather than follow) decisions in the public sphere. He also assumes that satisfaction with one's own life leads one to attribute legitimacy to one's system of government. Similarly, Putnam believes that interacting in associations builds citizens' inclination and ability to act collectively. A manifestation of this phenomenon is that citizens who participate in associations are more likely to believe that people in general can be trusted. Psychological studies of perception (e.g. Fiske & Taylor 1991) are rich with examples of how people compartmentalize their attitudes. It is not cognitively demanding for people to hold their evaluations of the trustworthiness of people they know distinct from the trustworthiness of people they have never met. Yet, Putnam's and Inglehart's data do show aggregate relationships between these particular experiences and generalized attitudes. Solving this paradox is an important area for future research.

Literature Cited

Almond GA, Verba S. 1963. *The Civic Culture*. Boston, MA: Little, Brown. 562 pp.
Almond GA, Verba S. 1989. *The Civic Culture Revisited*. Newbury Park, CA: Sage. 421 pp.
Altemeyer B. 1988. *Enemies of Freedom*. San Francisco, CA: Jossey-Bass. 378 pp.
Altemeyer B. 1996. *The Authoritarian Specter*. Cambridge, MA: Harvard Univ. Press. 374 pp.
Brehm J, Rahn W. 1997. Individual-level evidence for the causes and consequences of social capital. *Am. J. Polit. Sci.* 41: 999–1023
Caspi D, Seligson MA. 1983. Toward an empirical theory of tolerance: radical groups in Israel and Costa Rica. *Comp. Polit. Stud.* 15:385–404
Costa PT, McCrae RR. 1985. *The NEO Personality Inventory Manual: Form S and Form R*. Odessa, FL: Psychological Assessment Resources. 44 pp.
Costa PT, McCrae RR. 1992. *Revised NEO Personality Inventory (NEO-PI-R) and NEO Five Factor Inventory (NEO-FFI) Professional Manual*. Odessa, FL: Psychological Assessment Resources. 33 pp.
Dahl RA. 1971. *Polyarchy: Participation and Opposition*. New Haven, CT: Yale Univ. Press. 257 pp.
de Tocqueville A. 1945. *Democracy in America,* Vol. 1, pp. 298–342. New York: Random House. 452 pp.
Fiske ST, Taylor SE. 1991. *Social Cognition*. New York: McGraw-Hill. 718 pp.
Gibson JL. 1987. Homosexuals and the Ku Klux Klan: a contextual analysis of political tolerance. *West. Polit. Q.* 40:427–48
Gibson JL. 1989. The structure of attitudinal tolerance in the United States. *Br. J. Polit. Sci.* 19:562–70
Gibson JL. 1992. The political consequences of intolerance: cultural conformity and political freedom. *Am. Polit. Sci. Rev.* 86: 338–56
Gibson JL. 1995. The resilience of mass support for democratic institutions and processes in nascent Russian and Ukrainian democracies. In *Political Culture and Civil Society in Russia and the United States of Eurasia,* ed. V Tismaneanu. Armonk, NY: Sharpe. 384 pp.

Gibson JL. 1997. Mass opposition to the Soviet Putsch of August 1991: collective action, rational choice, and democratic values in the former Soviet Union. *Am. Polit. Sci. Rev.* 91:671–84
Gibson JL, Bingham RD. 1983. Elite tolerance of Nazi rights. *Am. Polit. Q.* 40:403–12
Gibson JL, Duch RM. 1993. Political intolerance in the USSR: the distribution and etiology of mass opinion. *Comp. Polit. Stud.* 26:286–329
Gibson JL, Duch RM. 1994. Postmaterialism and the emerging Soviet democracy. *Polit. Res. Q.* 47:5–39
Gibson JL, Duch RM, Tedin KL. 1992. Democratic values and the transformation of the Soviet Union. *J. Polit.* 54:329–71
Golebiowska EA. 1996. The "pictures in our heads" and individual-targeted tolerance. *J. Polit.* 58:1010–34
Griffith ES, Plamenatz J, Pennock JR. 1956. Cultural prerequisites to a successfully functioning democracy: a symposium. *Am. Polit. Sci. Rev.* 50:101–37
Huntington S. 1984. Will more countries become democratic? *Polit. Sci. Q.* 99: 193–218
Inglehart R. 1977. *The Silent Revolution: Changing Values and Political Styles*. Princeton, NJ: Princeton Univ. Press. 482 pp.
Inglehart R. 1990. *Culture Shift in Advanced Industrial Society*. Princeton, NJ: Princeton Univ. Press. 484 pp.
Inglehart R. 1997. *Modernization and Postmodernization: Cultural, Economic, and Political Change in 43 Societies*. Princeton, NJ: Princeton Univ. Press. 453 pp.
Lawrence D. 1976. Procedural norms and tolerance: a reassessment. *Am. Polit. Sci. Rev.* 70:70–80
Marcus GE, Sullivan JL, Theis-Morse E, Wood SL. 1995. *With Malice Toward Some: How People Make Civil Liberties Judgments*. Cambridge: Cambridge Univ. Press. 288 pp.
Maslow AK. 1954. *Motivation and Personality*. New York: Harper & Row. 411 pp.
McClosky H. 1964. Consensus and ideology in American politics. *Am. Polit. Sci. Rev.* 58:361–82
McClosky H, Brill A. 1983. *Dimensions of*

Tolerance. New York: Russell Sage Found. 512 pp.

McClosky H, Zaller J. 1984. *The American Ethos*. Cambridge, MA: Harvard Univ. Press. 342 pp.

Muller EN, Seligson MA. 1994. Civic culture and democracy: the question of causal relationships. *Am. Polit. Sci. Rev.* 88:635–52

Nelson T, Clawson RA, Oxley ZM. 1997. Media framing of a civil liberties conflict and its effect on tolerance. *Am. Polit. Sci. Rev.* 91:567–83

Neubauer DE. 1967. Some conditions of democracy. *Am. Polit. Sci. Rev.* 61:1002–9

Nie NH, Junn J, Stehlik-Barry K. 1996. *Education and Democratic Citizenship in America*. Chicago: Univ. Chicago Press. 268 pp.

Nunn CZ, Crockett HJ, Williams JA. 1978. *Tolerance for Nonconformity*. San Francisco, CA: Jossey-Bass. 212 pp.

Orbell J, Dawes RM. 1991. A 'Cognitive Miser' theory of cooperators' advantage. *Am. Polit. Sci. Rev.* 85:515–28

Prothro JW, Grigg CM. 1960. Fundamental principles of democracy: bases of agreement and disagreement. *J. Polit.* 22:276–94

Przeworski A, Alvarez M, Cheibub JA, Limongi F. 1996. What makes democracies endure? *J. Democr.* 7:39–55

Putnam R. 1993. *Making Democracy Work: Civic Traditions in Modern Italy*. Princeton, NJ: Princeton Univ. Press. 258 pp.

Sniderman PM, Fletcher JF, Russell PH, Tetlock PE. 1996. *The Clash of Rights*. New Haven, CT: Yale Univ. Press. 291 pp.

Staub E. 1989. *The Roots of Evil*. New York: Cambridge Univ. Press. 336 pp.

Stolle D. 1998. Bowling together, bowling alone: the development of generalized trust in voluntary associations. *Polit. Psychol.* 19: 497–525

Stouffer SA. 1955. *Communism, Conformity, and Civil Liberties*. New York: Doubleday. 278 pp.

Sullivan JL, Piereson J, Marcus GE. 1982. *Political Tolerance and American Democracy*. Chicago: Univ. Chicago Press. 278 pp.

Sullivan JL, Shamir M, Walsh P, Roberts NS. 1985. *Political Tolerance in Context*. Boulder, CO: Westview. 264 pp.

Sullivan JL, Walsh P, Shamir M, Barnum DG, Gibson JL. 1993. Why politicians are more tolerant: selective recruitment and socialization among political elites in Britain, Israel, New Zealand, and the United States. *Br. J. Polit. Sci.* 23:51–76.

Verba S, Schlozman K, Brady H. 1995. *Voice and Equality: Civic Voluntarism in American Politics*. Cambridge, MA: Harvard Univ. Press. 639 pp.

Annu. Rev. Psychol. 1999. 50:651–82

NEUROETHOLOGY OF SPATIAL LEARNING: The Birds and the Bees

E.A. Capaldi, G.E. Robinson, and S.E. Fahrbach

Department of Entomology, University of Illinois at Urbana-Champaign, Urbana, Illinois 61801; e-mail: capaldi@uiuc.edu

KEY WORDS: animal navigation, *Apis mellifera,* corpora pedunculata, food-storing birds, hippocampus, orientation

ABSTRACT

The discipline of neuroethology integrates perspectives from neuroscience, ethology, and evolutionary biology to investigate the mechanisms underlying the behavior of animals performing ecologically relevant tasks. One goal is to determine if common organizational principles are shared between nervous systems in diverse taxa. This chapter selectively reviews the evidence that particular brain regions subserve behaviors that require spatial learning in nature. Recent evidence suggests that the insect brain regions known as the mushroom bodies may function similarly to the avian and mammalian hippocampus. Volume changes in these brain regions during the life of an individual may reflect both developmental and phylogenetic trends. These patterns may reveal important structure-function relationships in the nervous system.

CONTENTS

651

0084-6570/99/0201-0651$08.00

INTRODUCTION

Legendary feats of animal navigation, such as the seasonal migration of the North American monarch butterfly to its wintering grounds in southern Mexico, have generated not only wonderment but also testable hypotheses about how such long-distance movement is accomplished (Brower 1996). Even the shorter distances traveled by rodents (reviewed by Gallistel 1990) or honeybees (Zhang et al 1996) negotiating laboratory mazes in search of food rewards raise deep questions about how spatial relationships are encoded in the brains of animals.

Studies of spatial learning have played an extremely important role in the development of ideas about the behavioral capacities of animals (Tolman 1948, Tinbergen 1951, von Frisch 1967). This has led to the discovery of unexpected sensory modalities, such as the ability of many insects (Rossel & Wehner 1982, 1984) and birds (Able & Able 1996) to use the polarization of light and the earth's magnetic field as navigational cues. Animal navigation also is dependent upon the formation, storage, and retrieval of spatial memories, which permit repeated visits to fixed points in the environment. Examples include the travel of social insects between a central nest and scattered feeding sites (Wehner 1996), and the return of birds to sites at which they previously stored food (Clayton & Krebs 1995, Sherry & Duff 1996).

In the past 10 years, questions regarding the relationships of animal navigation to learning mechanisms have come into sharp focus (Gallistel 1990, Menzel 1990, Dyer 1994). It is our view, however, that such behaviors remain underexploited as a paradigm for the discovery of the neuroanatomical substrates of naturally occurring, ecologically meaningful learning. Progress made in laboratory-based research linking spatial learning with specific brain structures in mammals, such as the hippocampus, is complemented only by lesion studies on a few species of birds. Given such a restricted phylogenetic view, it is too early to propose, for example, that neural pathways mediating spatial learning will share common organizational principles across the animal phyla.

This review explores aspects of the neuroanatomical correlates of animal spatial learning. We consider what might be referred to as the neuroethology of spatial learning in multiple taxa. We focus on nonmammalian animals, including insects, and on studies that have relied on observations of naturally occurring spatial learning in the field as the starting point for experimental analysis. In particular, we review the literature in light of recent investigations that suggest the mushroom bodies of insects may be comparable to the vertebrate hippocampal formation. We propose that volume plasticity of discrete brain regions related to spatial learning provides an efficient tool with which animal nervous systems can be analyzed, the goal being to identify novel model systems in which the mechanisms linking experience, structure, and function can be investigated. Methods of volume estimation based on sectioned material are straightforward; routine histological methods combined with an appropriate scheme for volume analysis can reveal evidence of novel structural plasticity. The relative simplicity of these methods readily allows studies to be conducted on animals collected in the field. These studies can set the stage for cellular and molecular analyses of spatial learning in selected diverse species.

Neuroethologists seek to investigate the relationship between specific structures of the nervous system and the function of behaviors served by those neural substrates from a comparative point of view. This perspective integrates natural history, phylogeny, and developmental biology (Pirlot 1986, Shettleworth 1996). In this review we adopt the approach of Bullock, a pioneer in this hybrid discipline, who has vigorously argued that careful comparison of diverse animals and behaviors is essential for a complete understanding of structure-function relationships in the nervous system (Bullock 1984a,b). The results of such studies should lead to taxon-independent insights at multiple levels of analysis. The first task in this analysis, the linking of specific brain regions to behaviors dependent upon spatial learning, is under way in mammals and birds but remains to be tackled for most other groups of animals. Recent progress in understanding the structure, chemistry, function, and plasticity of the insect mushroom bodies suggests that this issue can now be profitably addressed in invertebrates.

ANIMAL NAVIGATION

Our general knowledge of spatial behavior and its mechanisms derives from a relatively small number of well-studied animals. In part as a result of conspicuous feats of migration, birds are well known for their navigational abilities. The Arctic tern (*Sterna paradisaea*) spends its summers breeding north of the Arctic Circle, then departs in the fall for the Antarctic to feed in the highly productive waters in the southernmost portion of the Atlantic Ocean (Dingle 1996). A nonmigratory species, a homing pigeon (*Columba livia*) can fly directly to its home loft after displacements of up to several hundred kilometers into unfamiliar areas. Experienced pigeons can return home even when they have been anesthetized during the outbound journey and therefore deprived of information about direction and distance of displacement (Able 1980). A consensus has emerged from this diverse and sometimes controversial literature that birds use a combination of environmental cues to find their way (Berthold 1991). Savannah sparrows (*Passerculus sandwichensis*), for example, complete their seasonal north-south migrations by using a system of interacting senses including magnetic, star, polarized light, and possibly sun compasses (Able & Able 1996). Pigeons can use compass information derived from both the magnetic field and the sun (Wiltschko & Wiltschko 1996), and they also rely upon olfactory cues (Wallraff 1996).

Invertebrates also show seasonal and daily movements over great distances (Collett & Zeil 1998). In the Caribbean Sea around the Bahamas, for example, spiny lobsters (*Panulirus argus*) migrate in grand queues from shallow waters in the summer to deeper waters in the fall (Kanciruk & Herrnkind 1978). Another conspicuous example of long-distance navigation by an invertebrate is the migration of the monarch butterfly (*Danaus plexippus*). Monarchs migrate across the North American continent in the fall, spend the winter in the mountains of Mexico, and return in the spring to southern North America, where they lay eggs and die. The next generation metamorphoses in time to fly to the northernmost part of their range by early summer. Two or more generations are reared throughout the summer; it is these butterflies that begin the cycle anew by flying south at summer's end. The navigational cues used by migrating monarchs remain to be explained (Brower 1996).

The daily movements of animals over shorter distances are, of course, much more common but no less impressive. Animals that forage from a nest face the problem of returning repeatedly to specific places in the environment. Social insects, for example, must be able to move efficiently to and from a nest to forage. Because humans regularly explore, orient, and re-orient within new environments, we tend to overlook the extraordinary challenges of orienting that small, often familiar animals face on a daily basis. The potential foraging range of one well-described social insect, the honeybee (*Apis mellifera*), is approximately 10 km (Visscher & Seeley 1982). Other species of bees have been reported to have foraging ranges of 15–20 km (Wehner 1981). It is an extraordinary feat for animals to find a small nest from such distances.

A related form of spatial learning exhibited by many animals is reflected in their ability to recall the location of objects in the environment. Certain passerine birds store, and then retrieve, numerous items of food in scattered locations (Balda et al 1987, Sherry 1989, Kamil & Balda 1990, Shettleworth 1990, Vander Wall 1990). These feats of memory can be astonishing. A Clark's nutcracker (*Nucifraga columbiana*) may prepare for winter by storing as many as 9000 caches of pine seeds, which may be recovered several months later (Tomback 1982).

What Is Spatial Learning?

Spatial learning encompasses all formation of memories that permit later discrimination of place by reference to the surroundings, and discrimination of position as defined by the relative orientation of the learner (Bitterman 1996). Numerous terms have been used to describe the different movements of animals in their environment (Schöne 1984), many of which involve some form of spatial learning. For example, homing, the regular return to a nest site, is readily distinguished from seasonal migrations. The two widely used terms, orientation and navigation, do not refer to the relative distances over which movements occur; the terms distinguish the moment-to-moment alignment of an animal's body (orientation) from the processes by which an animal uses cues to determine its position relative to a goal as it moves from place to place (navigation). In light of these definitions, it will be seen that effective navigation requires the ability to orient while sensory information changes with movement.

Navigation has been further subdivided into piloting, compass orientation, and true navigation (Griffin 1955). Piloting refers to the ability of animals to find a goal by reference to familiar landmarks. Animals using piloting for homing need to maintain sensory contact with familiar features of the environment (Able 1980). In contrast, compass orientation does not require reference to familiar landmarks; rather, it is the ability to orient in a given compass direction when released in an unfamiliar area. Homing can occur in this form of navigation only if the direction chosen upon release leads toward home or a familiar area. True navigation is more complex. It occurs only in species that can orient toward a familiar place when released in a totally unfamiliar area. Examples of such species include homing pigeons and migratory birds. Animals that use this type of behavior do not maintain any form of sensory contact with the goal or with familiar landmarks (Griffin 1955, Able 1980). Most cases of animal homing do not involve true navigation; instead, they involve some combination of piloting and compass orientation. In other words, animals, like humans, need to be equipped with the equivalent of a map and a compass for navigation.

Historically, one major aim in studying the movements of animals in a landscape was to define the features of the environment that provide directional and positional information and to understand how they are recorded as useful spatial memories. For example, in the case of bees and other insects, olfactory cues may be critical near the nest, but only visual stimuli (landmarks and celestial orientation cues) can provide a basis for rapid and accurate navigation over the hundreds or thousands of meters they travel to forage. This information is in turn useful only if the animal has had prior experience in the area: information for homing is available only if the animal has had the opportunity to learn how these references define the spatial relationship between its current location and its goal. The requirement for familiarity with visual landmarks is not restricted to insects; a similar use of learned visual landmarks permits the return of pigeons to their home loft (Wallraff 1970) and the ability of food-storing birds to recover previously stored items (reviewed by Sherry 1984).

A shared characteristic of the navigational behavior of vertebrates and invertebrates is path integration, sometimes referred to as dead reckoning (Wehner & Wehner 1990; Dyer 1994; Etienne et al 1996, 1998; McNaughton et al 1996; Wehner et al 1996). Path integration allows an animal to use information experienced (learned) on the outward path of a trip to determine its position relative to the starting point. An example of path integration is seen in the behavior of a desert ant, *Cataglyphis bicolor*. These ants roam widely in search of food on vast stretches of featureless desert, but then walk in a straight line back to the nest after food is found (Wehner et al 1983). In insects, this system depends upon a directional reference provided by a celestial compass (Wehner & Müller 1993, Dyer & Dickinson 1994) and distance measured by optic flow cues (Esch & Burns 1995, 1996; Ronacher & Wehner 1995; Srinivasan et al 1996; Wehner et al 1996). Dead reckoning involves integrating all angles turned with the distances covered during the outward course. The process is apparently continuous: At any moment during the trip, the animal can select the direct route between its current location and home.

The general problem of how the brains of animals represent information about objects and events in the outside world has attracted growing interest in the 1990s (Yoerg & Kamil 1991, Ristau 1991, Churchland & Sejnowski 1992, Churchland 1995). A discipline of cognitive ethology has grown as a result of new attempts to understand the mental experiences of nonhuman animals (Griffin 1992). One of the major theoretical constructs employed by a cognitive perspective is the internal representation, which is hypothesized to be an internal model of events or relationships experienced by the animal (Neisser 1967, Roitblat & von Fersen 1992). Once sensory information is formed into an internal representation, computations can act on it (Gallistel 1990). In a cognitive framework, the inputs of information are contained in representations, and processes change them to create the output of behavior (Vauclair 1996). The study of animal spatial memory from a cognitive perspective seeks to understand the spatial relationships that are represented internally, how they are formed, and how they are used. Cognitive ethology can serve as the base for cognitive neuroethology, in which specific neural circuits serving these functions are identified and the relationships between neuroanatomy and function are described. This information can in turn be used to probe the origins of variation in brain structure at both developmental and phylogenetic levels of analysis.

Information on animal spatial learning has been obtained through study of a relatively small number of tasks generally agreed to embody some form of spatial learning. These tasks include navigating mazes, including the radial arm maze and the widely used Morris water maze for rodents in which a rat uses visible landmarks to swim to a hidden platform (Morris 1981); responding to displacement within familiar and unfamiliar environments (Ugolini 1987, Schöne et al 1995, Schöne 1996); and retrieving previously stored food (Krebs et al 1996). Displacement tasks in particular are interesting to the neuroethologist. Artificial displacement from a home base denies an animal the opportunity to use the path integration ability described above. Therefore, depending on the distance of displacement from a familiar area, displaced animals must make use of other mechanisms for homing, including a reliance on memorized landmarks. Learning the location of landmarks is a form of spatial learning that can be relatively easily assayed in an animal's natural environment. Studies on the retrieval of stored food share this feature of strong experimental design derived from a naturally occurring task.

This review focuses primarily on reference to visual landmarks used by animals in their daily foraging movements. We discuss efforts to identify brain regions involved in spatial learning; for most species, such efforts require a combination of laboratory and field studies. Animal navigation and laboratory studies of spatial learning have been the focus of numerous excellent articles and reviews (Gallistel 1990, Krebs 1990, Shettleworth 1990, Dyer 1998). We do not cover this larger literature but instead briefly consider the means by which specific brain regions are associated with spatial learning before presenting case studies focused on the avian hippocampus and the honeybee mushroom bodies.

SPECIFIC BRAIN REGIONS ASSOCIATED WITH SPATIAL LEARNING

Methods

Numerous methods from the neuroscience toolbox have been used to link specific brain regions to spatial learning, in addition to volume measurements. These include studying the effects of reversible lesions (transient disruption of function caused by drugs or cold block, for example) or irreversible lesions (permanent damage caused by ablation of the structure itself or by killing of the neuronal precursor cells for a structure); correlation of patterns of electrical activity with task performance; analysis of mutants or strains that deviate from standard wild type in performance on tasks of spatial learning; and the creation of transgenic animals in which spatial learning can be studied (e.g. Morris et al 1982, de Belle & Heisenberg 1994, Greenspan 1995, Compton et al 1997, Silva et al 1997).

At present, physical lesions and electrophysiological analyses can be used on all animals, but relatively efficient genetic transformation of animals is restricted to mice, fruit flies, and the nematode *Caenorhabditis elegans*. Therefore, in vertebrates our understanding of the association of brain regions to spatial learning is based primarily on electrophysiological, lesion, and pharmacological studies, supplemented more recently with behavioral analyses of mice with altered patterns of gene expression (reviewed by Grant & Silva 1994, Wilson & Tonegawa 1997, Silva et al 1997).

The Hippocampus

A large body of research has implicated the hippocampus as critical for the performance of spatial tasks in vertebrates. This link is best established in rodents but also appears to hold for the avian hippocampus, a structure believed to be homologous with the mammalian hippocampus. Many studies have shown that lesions of the hippocampal formation in mammals cause deficits in spatial learning (reviewed by Jarrard 1995). Neurons in the hippocampus show changes in activity that are correlated with the animal's movements (reviewed by O'Keefe & Nadel 1978, Muller et al 1991, Bures et al 1997, Redish & Touretzky 1997). Blockade of hippocampal N-methyl-D-aspartate (NMDA) receptors for glutamate impairs performance on the Morris water maze (Morris et al 1986), and transgenic mice lacking expression of the gene encoding NMDAR1 gene in the CA1 region of the hippocampus have a similar performance deficit (reviewed by Wilson & Tonegawa 1997). See Leonard & McNaughton (1990), Muller & Stead (1996), Sharp et al (1996), and Thinus-Blanc (1996) among others for excellent additional reviews of the hippocampus and spatial learning in mammals, which is not covered further here. The avian hippocampus has also been experimentally linked to some forms of spatial learning in birds by means of lesion studies (Krushinskaya 1966, Sherry & Vaccarino 1989, Hampton & Shettleworth 1996, Fremouw et al 1997, Patel et al 1997a, Bingman 1998).

The Mushroom Bodies

A small but growing array of evidence links the mushroom bodies (also referred to as the corpora pedunculata) of invertebrates to spatial learning, and the parallels to the vertebrate hippocampus are intriguing. The mushroom bodies are a prominent structure found in the brains of several invertebrate phyla, including the Annelida and Onycophora, but are most highly characteristic of arthropods, with the exception of crustaceans (Strausfeld et al 1995, 1998). The mushroom bodies are identified by their position at the front of the brain; by their intrinsic population of numerous small neurons called Kenyon cells or globuli cells; and by a characteristic organization of neuropil in which calyces are formed from the dendritic processes of the intrinsic neurons and in which distinct lobes are formed by their bifurcating parallel axons (Kenyon 1896; Mobbs 1982, 1984; Strausfeld et al 1995). Although the major inputs to the mushroom bodies of insects arise in olfactory regions, and the mushroom bodies have been convincingly linked with olfactory associative learning (Hammer & Menzel 1995, Menzel & Müller 1996, Hammer 1997), they are also present in anosmic arthropod taxa. This suggests that the mushroom bodies have functions broader than the processing of antennal inputs (Strausfeld et al 1998). Lesion of the mushroom bodies of cockroaches (*Periplaneta americana*) produced deficits in learning in an analog of the Morris water maze, a heated metal plate containing a cooler region that the roach could locate only by reference to visual landmarks (Mizunami et al 1993). The same roaches were still able to associate a visual landmark at the site itself with the cool region, indicating that the deficit was selective for spatial learning rather than associative learning in general. This result is consistent with earlier analyses in which the mushroom bodies were associated with maze-learning ability in *Formica rufa*, the red wood ant. Vowles (1964) showed that bilateral lesions of the mushroom bodies disrupted performance on olfactory discrimination tests in a T-maze, while Bernstein & Bernstein (1969) showed that ants with larger neuropil of the mushroom bodies moved more efficiently on a series of foraging trips through a maze, as indicated by shorter return trips. Electrophysiological studies of the mushroom bodies of the cockroach have demonstrated that the extrinsic neurons associated with the mushroom bodies respond to a variety of stimuli, including mechano-sensory inputs (Li & Strausfeld 1997). Although it may be premature to force the parallels too far, changes in synaptic function comparable to those seen in hippocampal long-term potentiation have also been demonstrated in the mushroom bodies (Oleskevich et al 1997), and both hippocampus and mushroom bodies are characterized by elevated levels of the products of learning-related genes relative to other regions of the brain (Davis 1993, Kandel & Abel 1995).

Comparative Studies of Volume Plasticity

In addition to the methods described above, comparative volume analysis has been used to show that certain brain regions are larger than would be expected on the basis of body size or phylogeny in animals whose daily life imposes demanding tasks of spatial memory. This relationship is particularly clear in some species of food-storing birds; however, as described in subsequent sections, the relationship has also been observed in rodents and insects. Comparative volume analysis is based on a combination of behavioral ecology with standard histological techniques and typically uses species more commonly studied in the field than in the laboratory. Selection of comparison groups for such studies is based both on species differences in behavior and on phylogenetic relationships.

Comparative Volume Analysis and Spatial Learning

Volume changes in specific brain regions during the life of an individual animal may be as informative as interspecific comparisons in revealing the relationship of structure to function. Volume plasticity can reflect experience—as in the case of the larger cortex of rodents reared in a complex and stimulating environment versus those reared in standard laboratory cages (Black & Greenough 1986)—or an experience-independent response to an endocrine signal, as in the case of seasonal volume changes seen in the song nuclei of male song birds (Nottebohm 1981). The hippocampus of food-storing birds and the mushroom bodies of insects have both been associated with developmental and experience-dependent volume plasticity. While the extent to which other brain regions display comparable plasticity may have been underestimated because of lack of study, the potential association of the hippocampus and the mushroom bodies with spatial learning raises several interesting questions. Among these are the benefits to be derived (as an individual or as a species) from having a larger hippocampus (or larger mushroom bodies); the relationship of volume to experience; and the nature of the cellular mechanisms, which, summed over a neuronal population, produce the changes we measure as differences in volume.

The question of whether brain regions that display a relatively high degree of volume plasticity within a species are also those most likely to show phylogenetic plasticity is also important. We might ask, too, whether the differences in volume detected in phylogenetic comparisons are present in naive animals or only arise as a result of performance of a particular spatial learning task. What follows is an integrated account of inter- and intraspecific brain region volume plasticity in two case studies: the avian hippocampus and the mushroom bodies of the honeybee.

CASE STUDIES

Food Storing and the Avian Hippocampus

The link between ecology, behavior, and neuroanatomy has been most thoroughly studied in animals that rely on stored food (for reviews, see Clayton & Krebs 1995, Krebs et al 1996). A wide range of animals actively cache food for later use (Sherry 1985, Vander Wall 1990), but the most detailed investigations of the mechanisms of this behavior have focused on two families of birds, the Corvidae (jays, magpies, jackdaws, and nutcrackers) and the Paridae (chickadees and titmice). Many species of birds in these families dedicate large amounts of time to harvesting food in the late summer and fall. The birds hide the seeds in spots that can be accessed during the winter. Caching behavior most likely evolved as an accommodation to a temporally restricted diet

(Roberts 1979, Vander Wall & Balda 1981, Balda et al 1987). There is considerable variation in the degree to which different species cache food and, among food storers, in their dependence on hidden food stores (Healy & Krebs 1996). Corvids, such as the Clark's nutcracker (*Nucifraga columbiana*), may store thousands of seeds and retrieve them over several months. Chickadees and tits, both members of the parid family, may hide food for only a few days or even hours. The duration of a cache most likely depends on energy requirements, the type of food that is stored, and food availability (Sherry & Duff 1996). Regardless of the interval between storage and retrieval, the birds clearly possess spatial information that allows them to return to different locations to find food. The cache sites for individual food items are often scattered over hundreds of square meters (Shettleworth 1990) and, at least for some parids, the sites are never reused (Krebs 1990). Field studies investigating cache recovery by marsh tits (*Parus palustris*) have demonstrated that the bird that stored the seed is the same individual that retrieves it (Stevens & Krebs 1986). Some birds apparently are able to keep track of hundreds or even thousands of distinct spatial locations (reviewed by Sherry 1985).

There is strong evidence that food-storing birds learn the relationships between landmarks and caches in order to find cached food (Kamil & Balda 1985). For example, in Vander Wall's (1982) study of the Clark's nutcracker, the birds stored pine seeds in the sandy floor of an aviary that contained a variety of landmark arrays. After caching, the birds were removed from the aviary and the objects on one side of the arena were displaced by 20 cm. The birds attempted to retrieve their hidden food by searching at sites that were correct with regard to the general association with a cache site and a particular landmark, but were 20 cm off where the landmark arrays had been shifted. No errors were made near the unmanipulated landmark arrays. Other investigators have also documented that food-storing birds remember the position of caches with respect to prominent features in the environment (Sherry et al 1981, Shettleworth 1990, Herz et al 1994, Bednekoff et al 1997) and demonstrated that the birds rank the relative importance of particular types of information (such as position, color, and pattern) for the recovery of stored foods (Brodbeck 1994, Brodbeck & Shettleworth 1995).

In addition to their noteworthy spatial memory, food-storing birds also have a distinctive brain feature: an enlarged hippocampal formation. The hippocampus, also referred to as the avian dorsomedial forebrain, has been implicated in the neural processing of spatial information by birds in a number of natural settings. Extending over the top of the head along the midline (Karten & Hodos 1967), this brain region of the telencephalon is part of the bird cortex and is thought to be the functional analogue, and possibly the evolutionary homologue, of the mammalian hippocampus (Ariëns Kappers et al 1936, Sherry et al 1993a, Krebs et al 1996, Casini et al 1997).

Krushinskaya (1966, cited in Sherry & Vaccarino 1989) reported that lesions of the hippocampus of the Eurasian nutcracker (*Nucifraga caryocatactes*) rendered the birds incapable of relocating their food stores. The lesioned birds appeared otherwise relatively normal, as they searched (fruitlessly) for their food and continued to make new caches. More recently, bilateral lesions of the hippocampus of black-capped chickadees (*Parus atricapillus*) were also shown to disrupt cache recovery (Sherry & Vaccarino 1989). As in the case of the nutcrackers, the chickadees retained the ability to store new caches and also exhibited normal performance on other tasks, such as color discrimination. Hippocampal lesions also impair the navigation abilities of homing pigeons (reviewed by Bingman 1993). These results provide support for the idea that the formation and processing of spatial memories in birds are dependent upon the hippocampus. Investigations of the effects of hippocampal lesions on memory for location further support the hypothesis that this brain region is involved specifically in spatial cognition, as no effect of hippocampal lesions could be seen on memory for color (Hampton & Shettleworth 1996).

In a typical volume-estimation study, frozen sections of fixed brains (25 to 50 µm thick) are made with a sliding microtome. A subset of sections (typically, one in every four) is collected and stained so that the anatomical boundaries of the hippocampus are visible. Standard Nissl stains are sometimes supplemented by acetylcholinesterase staining, which better demonstrates the rostral and lateral boundaries between the hippocampal complex and other telencephalic regions (e.g. Sherry et al 1993a). Paraffin sections may also be used (e.g. Basil et al 1996). Cross-sectional areas of the hippocampus and telencephalon are determined by tracing enlarged images of the prepared sections, with the volume between the sections calculated using the formula for a truncated cone. Results, often expressed as a ratio of hippocampal volume to telencephalic volume, are subjected to multiple regression analysis to estimate the relative effects of body weight, total brain size, and behavioral variables on hippocampal size. Using these and similar methods, it has been demonstrated that food-storing parids and corvids have hippocampal formations that are significantly larger than those of non-food-storing relatives of comparable body size (Krebs et al 1989; Sherry et al 1989, 1993b). These studies attempted to account for the size relationships using ecological variables such as diet and nesting biology, but no other variables predicted the observed variation in hippocampal size (Healy 1996). Additionally, Old and New World corvid species that store large amounts of food have a bigger hippocampal volume than corvids that store less and store it for a shorter time (Healy & Krebs 1992, Basil et al 1996), a pattern that also holds within the Paridae (Hampton et al 1995, Healy & Krebs 1996).

A particularly interesting study directly compared hippocampal volumes among four species of corvids (Basil et al 1996). The species compared were Clark's nutcracker (*Nucifraga columbiana*), pinyon jays (*Gymnorhinus cya-*

nocephalus), scrub jays (*Aphelocama coerulescens*), and gray-breasted jays (*Aphelocama ultramarina*); the three jay species have a closer phylogenetic relationship to each other than to the nutcracker. Although all of these species store food, the Clark's nutcracker is the most dependent on stored food for survival during the winter and has the most striking anatomical specializations related to food storing, including a long, sharp bill and a unique sublingual pouch (Mewaldt 1956, Bock et al 1973, Vander Wall & Balda 1981). In both field and laboratory tests of spatial memory, the pinyon jay is intermediate in performance between scrub and gray-breasted jays (the least specialized for food storage) and Clark's nutcracker (the most specialized for food storage), although under some test conditions the pinyon jay's performance equaled that of the nutcracker (Balda & Kamil 1989, Bednekoff et al 1997). Volume analysis of the hippocampus, relative to brain and body size, revealed that the pinyon jay resembled the jays that performed relatively poorly on spatial learning tasks (i.e. they had a smaller hippocampal complex than predicted) rather than the Clark's nutcracker (which had a larger hippocampal complex than predicted). These results are interesting because they suggest that the three New World corvids are more similar to each other in terms of hippocampal volume than they are to the Old World Clark's nutcracker (reflecting a closer phylogenetic association), despite the greater similarity of the pinyon jay to the nutcracker on tests of spatial memory. These data can be used in weak support of the hypothesis that hippocampal volume is indeed related to spatial memory and dependence in the wild on stored food (a comparison of the scrub jay and the nutcracker, the behavioral extremes of the species studied, supports this view). But they can also be used to refute the hypothesis, because the behavioral data predicted that the pinyon jay should have had a relatively larger hippocampus than its non-food-storing relatives, which it did not. A third conclusion is that comparative volume analyses conducted on extremely small numbers of wild-caught adult birds of unknown age (two of each jay species and four Clark's nutcrackers) should be interpreted with caution, particularly in light of the following observations.

It is now appreciated that some of the reported interspecific differences among avian brains are at least partly caused by changes in behavioral experience. In one comparison between a storing corvid and a nonstoring related species, the differences in hippocampal volume were detectable only after the birds had left the nest, a relatively late stage of behavioral development (Healy & Krebs 1993). This result suggested that the emergence of the structural difference in brains between the two species is related to the emergence of the behavioral difference in food-storing behavior (Healy & Krebs 1993). Within-species comparisons of parids have similarly revealed that the volume of the hippocampus increases after the initiation of food-storing behaviors, which occurs a few weeks after fledging; age-related changes in the brains of nonstoring birds were not observed (Healy et al 1994). The development of plasticity of these structures means that great care must be taken in interspecific volume comparisons to ensure that individuals compared are equivalent in age and in as many aspects of behavioral experience as possible.

That behavioral development precedes structural development suggests that the experience causes the neuroanatomical changes. This phenomenon was studied in the marsh tit (Clayton & Krebs 1994). The timing of hippocampal enlargement was studied in hand-raised birds in which the age at which they were allowed to store and retrieve food was controlled by the experimenters. Birds deprived of food-storing experience had smaller hippocampal regions than those of similarly aged birds with food-storing experience. If birds were deprived of all experience storing and retrieving food, their hippocampal formations showed attrition and cell loss. Subsequent studies have demonstrated that training on a task that requires spatial memory has an effect on the hippocampus similar to that of food storing (Clayton 1995a,b). These results suggest that a spatial task, whether performed spontaneously as part of a species' normal behavioral repertoire or in response to an artificial environment in the research laboratory, can produce dramatic volume changes within the brain. Experience-dependent enlargement of the hippocampus appears to endure throughout life and may be a one-time, irreversible phenomenon, occurring at whatever age a bird first stores food (Cristol 1996). The connection of food-storing experience and hippocampal development is considered in more detail in two reviews (Clayton 1995c, Clayton & Krebs 1995).

Further indication of the role of the hippocampus in retrieval of stored food caches is the finding that seasonality affects the relationship between brain development and behavior. Smulders et al (1995) found in wild-caught black-capped chickadees (*Parus atricapillus*) that the hippocampus peaks in volume relative to the rest of the brain during October, the month when the most food storing occurs in nature. Association between food-hoarding intensity and the volume of this brain region implies that the anatomical change is caused by the elevated use of spatial memory during this month. Another study found seasonal patterns of neurogenesis in the hippocampus of black-capped chickadees (Barnea & Nottebohm 1994), which, in association with the frequency of food storing and the large volume of this brain area, suggests a mechanism for regulation of hippocampal volume. It is interesting to note that interspecific comparisons have also highlighted the relationship between the volume of the hippocampus and a heavy reliance upon spatial learning in certain rodents. For example, a comparison of hippocampal size relative to brain size showed that the hippocampus is larger in *Dipodyms merriami*, a species of kangaroo rat that stores seeds in scattered locations, than in *Dipodyms spectabilis*, a species that stockpiles seeds at a central site (Jacobs & Spencer 1994). The developmental patterns of these differences in rodent brains have not yet been described.

One poorly described aspect of spatial learning in food-storing birds involves the initial learning of landscape features that permit the recovery of stored food. For example, pigeons denied free-flight experience around their loft prior to their first release from a distant site can navigate homeward from a distant location but are impaired in actually returning to their loft once they are in its vicinity (Wallraff 1970). It is not clear whether an orientation flight is required of food-storing birds, independent of food storing and cache recovery. Parids do not begin to store food until 2–3 weeks after leaving the nest, which would provide them with the opportunity to learn landmarks in their environment. The young birds practice storing and retrieving food; over the course of several days, the birds develop their skills (S Healy, personal communication). The developmental aspects to food-storing behavior are worthy of further exploration.

Homing and the Insect Mushroom Bodies

Age-based division of labor in the insect societies provides the context for studies of behavioral development in the honeybee (*Apis mellifera*). Queens lay eggs, whereas workers (all female) perform all tasks necessary for colony growth and development. Although adult workers do not mature sexually, they do mature behaviorally. Young adult worker honeybees tend the queen, maintain the hive, and rear brood; older workers forage outside of the hive and do not perform "hive" tasks (Winston 1987). Such age polyethism is widespread among other groups of social insects, including social wasps, ants, and termites (Wilson 1971, Robinson 1992, Fahrbach 1997). Foragers, unlike younger bees that work in the dark hive, are notable for their vision-based navigational skills (Dyer 1994, Lehrer 1994, Giurfa & Menzel 1997) and their use of visual landmarks. Evidence that bees use visually acquired information goes far beyond the familiar ability of bees to learn flower color (von Frisch 1967, Chittka & Menzel 1992). Honeybees can learn to follow a path marked by particular visual landmarks (Collett et al 1993), and as would be predicted from such sequence learning, can learn to navigate inside complex mazes (Zhang et al 1996, Collett et al 1997). Experimental evidence indicates that bees use angular orientation cues in order to discriminate between a familiar pattern and an unfamiliar one (Zhang & Srinivasan 1994, Giger & Srinivasan 1995) and can even be trained to distinguish a bilaterally symmetrical pattern from a nonsymmetrical one (Giurfa et al 1996). The ability of organisms to perceive symmetry or other generalized shape information suggests that pattern information is used in the selection of food resources in nature. In addition to these behaviors, we know that bees learn about landmarks surrounding a foraging site when approaching and when departing from that location (Lehrer & Collett 1994).

One prominent form of visual learning is a conspicuous part of adult behavioral development in the bee. This learning occurs during "orientation flights," a behavior performed by many hymenopteran insects before departing from a place to which they will return (von Frisch 1967, Vollbehr 1975, Wehner 1981, Lehrer 1996, Zeil et al 1996, Jander 1997). An orientation flight begins as a departing bee turns and looks back at the hive entrance. She then hovers back and forth while turning in short arcs. The size of the arcs increases until, after a few seconds, she flies in circles while ascending. The flight at the entrance is easily observed by a human observer watching the nest entrance, but the spiraling flight takes the bee out of sight. The bee returns a few minutes later, without nectar or pollen. Human observers differentiate these orientation flights from foraging flights with almost 100 percent accuracy, because foragers fly straight out of the hive entrance without turning and looking and return with nectar or pollen. Foraging flights are also longer in duration than orientation flights (more than five minutes). A role for orientation flights in learning landscape features was established in experiments in which bees were captured when they returned from their first flight and then displaced. Bees that had taken orientation flights returned home, but bees displaced without orientation flight experience did not (Becker 1958).

The neuropil compartment of the mushroom bodies has been shown to exhibit volume plasticity in adult honeybees. An expansion of this neuropil accompanies behavioral maturation in the workers (Withers et al 1993, Durst et al 1994). These volume changes do not simply reflect overall growth of the adult brain but are specific to the mushroom body neuropil. Other brain regions show no volume changes at all during adult life, or display different temporal patterns of growth (Withers et al 1993).

Determination of the volume of the mushroom bodies of the honeybee is typically performed by collecting a complete set of serial sections (10 µm thick) of a brain embedded in paraffin, and then applying the Cavalieri method of sampling to produce a volume estimate for the entire structure based on cross-sectional areas of the sampled section. Sections for cross-sectional area determinations may be drawn with the aid of a camera lucida or traced using simple image analysis software. Using this method, volume estimates can be based upon samples of one-in-four or one-in-six sections. Because honeybees are monomorphic, undergoing no growth during the adult stage of life, the data are presented directly in the form of estimated volumes (Winston 1987). Because of the unique historical relationship between bees and humans, researchers can have access to free-flying bees undergoing natural behavioral development and can also reduce genetic variability in the population sampled through the use of instrumental insemination of honeybee queens (Laidlaw 1989). It is also possible to mark bees on the first day of adult life so that the age of subsequently collected bees can be known. Finally, as in the studies of birds, behavioral development can be manipulated to study the role of intrinsic and extrinsic factors in mushroom body plasticity.

How do the volume changes observed during maturation in bees relate to the cognitive challenges of honeybee life? Worker honeybees typically begin orientation flights in the first week of life and begin to forage at approximately three weeks of age. Neuroanatomical studies compared the volumes of the mushroom body neuropil of one-day-olds, behaviorally defined nurse bees (bees observed tending larval brood) of unknown age, and behaviorally defined foragers of unknown age. The volume of the mushroom body neuropil in foragers was increased 14.8% compared with that of one-day-olds (Withers et al 1993). Unlike the vertebrate nervous system, the invertebrate nervous system has synapses and neuronal somata that are totally segregated: that is, there are no axo-somatic contacts in the insect brain (Burrows 1996). Expansion of the mushroom body neuropil, therefore, likely represents an increase in the brain space devoted to the functions mediated by neural processing by the mushroom bodies. The only other region in which changes were detected was the olfactory glomeruli of the antennal lobes. The volume of this neuropil, however, was larger in nurse bees than in one-day-olds and foragers (Withers et al 1993).

To determine whether this volume increase was associated with chronological age or experience in performing a particular task, Withers et al induced young bees to become precocious foragers by housing them in a small colony lacking older workers and then examined their mushroom bodies. Precocious foragers were only about seven days old; given the six-to-eight-week life span of an adult worker honeybee, this represents a remarkable acceleration of behavioral development. The configuration of the mushroom bodies in precocious foragers resembled that of normal-age foragers rather than that of seven-day-old nurse bees (Withers et al 1993). This important result was independently confirmed using a slightly different anatomical method (Durst et al 1994).

These results suggested two different (but not mutually exclusive) scenarios for the observed increase in mushroom body volume in forager bees. First, it is possible that the experience of orientation flights, a prerequisite for foraging, directly sets in motion patterns of neural activity that lead to an increase in the volume of the mushroom body neuropil. A possible, unproven consequence of this neuropil expansion might be better performance on tasks involving the mushroom bodies. This effect would be similar to that seen in the rodent cerebral and cerebellar cortices as a consequence of being reared in an enriched environment (Bennett et al 1964, Greenough & Chang 1988) or learning a specific motor skill (Black et al 1990); or in the hippocampal formation of food-storing birds given an opportunity to store and retrieve food (see preceding section). The second scenario is based on the well-established correlation between high levels of the insect developmental hormone, juvenile hormone (JH), and foraging (Robinson et al 1989, Robinson 1992, Fahrbach 1997). Exposure to raised levels of JH during adult life might promote expansion of the mushroom body neuropil. This effect would be similar to that observed in steroid-sensitive regions of the vertebrate central nervous system during development of sex differences and as a consequence of seasonal changes in hormone titers (Breedlove 1992).

These hypotheses have been tested by manipulating the bees' experience or their exposure to JH. The experience of orientation flight and foraging was selectively ablated by the creation of "big-back" bees. Plastic disks were glued to the dorsal thorax of one-day-olds, which were then housed in hives with a modified entrance constructed from a small screened enclosure with a plastic grid. Normal bees were able to pass through the modified entrance, but the big-back bees could not, although they were otherwise free to move about the hive. Big-back bees had the same volume of mushroom body neuropil as same-age foragers from the same colony, demonstrating decisively that neither flight outside the hive nor foraging experience was essential for growth of the mushroom body neuropil (Withers et al 1995). Once it occurs, the volume expansion appears to be permanent. Foragers induced to revert to nursing by establishing a colony devoid of younger workers were no different from persistent foragers in the volume of mushroom body neuropil (Farris et al 1995). Bees induced to prolong their tenure as nurses instead of making the transition to foraging also showed expansion of the mushroom body neuropil (Withers et al 1995).

Nor is exposure to JH a primary determinant of mushroom body expansion in bees. Experiments using allatectomized bees (bees with the corpora allata, the glandular source of JH, removed) have shown that expansion of the mushroom body neuropil can occur in bees developing with no adult exposure to JH. (The efficacy of the surgery was verified by radioimmunoassay.) However, such manipulation delays the transition to foraging and may also interfere with spatial learning during orientation flights (Sullivan et al 1996). This may be a consequence of delayed development of the mushroom bodies, a possibility not yet examined.

Additional evidence that changes in mushroom body neuropil volume are not directly responsive to JH comes from studies of the mushroom bodies of queens and drones (males). Queens and drones have different endocrine profiles, but both experience a significant expansion of the mushroom body neuropil early in adult life, as do workers (Fahrbach et al 1995a, Giray & Robinson 1996, Fahrbach et al 1997). The expansion of the mushroom body neuropil is maintained in the oldest queens and drones studied, although at those ages they have extremely low levels of JH (Robinson et al 1992, Fahrbach et al 1995a, Giray & Robinson 1996, Fahrbach et al 1997).

Does the structure of the mushroom bodies reflect a common factor of behavioral development for the queen, drone, and worker bees? All three members of the colony depend on the spatial learning that occurs during orientation flights to return to the hive, regardless of whether they leave for a mating flight (queens and drones) or to forage (workers). In fact, it has been shown that changes occur in the structure of the honeybee mushroom body neurons coincident with the onset of orientation (Coss et al 1980, Brandon & Coss 1982), although the relationship of changes in fine structure to volume has not yet been established. In addition, expansion of the mushroom body neuropil is also first detectable at the time of orientation (SE Fahrbach, SM Farris & GE Robinson, unpublished observations). More experimental work is required to support the hypothesis that the mushroom bodies mediate spatial learning in insects, but strong predictions can be made that any interference with the normal structure or function of the mushroom bodies will produce poorer performance on spatial tasks. Bees with compromised mushroom body function would be more likely to drift into other nearby colonies (i.e. be less able to return reliably to their natal hive); should be unable to "home" with accuracy after displacement in a familiar environment; and may have decreased foraging efficiency because of poor memory for location of food resources. It is now possible for humans to track the flights of free-flying individual bees using harmonic radar (Riley et al 1996), a development that should permit ready assessment of the effects of mushroom body lesions in both pre- and post-orientation–flight bees.

Comparable data on mushroom body volume plasticity during a period of adult behavioral development has been reported for carpenter ants (*Camponotus floridanus*), suggesting that the findings for honeybees will have some generality (Gronenberg et al 1996). It has also been noted that among the insects, the volume of the mushroom bodies is relatively larger in all groups of social insects—the termites (Order Isoptera), and the bees, ants, and wasps (Order Hymenoptera). These insects are characterized not only by social behavior but also by the strategy of foraging from a central nest. The Hymenoptera offer numerous possibilities for comparative studies, representing within a single taxon every possible degree of reliance upon place memory. A particularly interesting comparison is between social Hymenoptera, such as the honeybee, and solitary Hymenoptera, such as the sawfly, which does not have a nest at a fixed location. The volume of the mushroom body neuropil of the social honeybee is, corrected for body size, approximately seven times larger than that of the solitary sawfly (Chapman 1982).

There is currently no reason to suspect that insect spatial abilities are determined by social structure or that the volume of the mushroom bodies is a direct correlate of sociality. Fortunately, many solitary species within the Hymenoptera also rely on learned spatial information to find their way to permanent nest sites or to food sources, which would then provide the right material to avoid confounding the issues of regional brain size, spatial learning, and sociality.

Other insect orders have received less attention from the comparative perspective, with one notable exception. In a study investigating the interspecific variation in mushroom body size among different species of closely related butterflies, Sivinski (1989) documented the sizes of mushroom bodies in seven species of Nymphalid, or passion flower butterflies. The largest mushroom bodies were four times as large as those of other species. The relative size of the mushroom bodies was not related to different amounts of sensory input, as indicated by the relatively uniform size of the olfactory and optic lobes, the sources of mushroom body afferents, across all of the species. It has been suggested, as in the case of food-storing birds and the kangaroo rat, that the size differences among butterfly species in this specific brain structure reflect differential uses of spatial learning in everyday life (Sivinski 1989). Relating the neuropil volume to the natural history of the species provides some preliminary evidence to support this claim. The species of butterfly with the largest mushroom bodies (as a proportion of total brain volume), *Heliconius charitonius*, is a relatively long-lived (six months) pollen feeder that feeds only on passion flowers, learns the position of specific passion flower vines within a home range and returns to them on a regular basis during the day, and then returns regularly to a fixed-site communal roost at night (Gilbert 1975). These behaviors require learning the spatial location of food items and of a central place, the communal roost.

WHAT HAVE WE LEARNED FROM THE BIRDS AND THE BEES?

Comparative volume analyses, both intra- and interspecific, have suggested that two structures linked by laboratory experiments to spatial tasks, particularly place memory—the vertebrate hippocampus and the insect mushroom bodies—are larger in species and in individuals that have a greater demand for spatial learning in their daily lives. While this conclusion must be qualified by the small number of species studied from this perspective, it provides clear predictions for future investigations. Although the available data sets are limited, we can begin the search for general principles by comparing what we know about the birds and the bees.

In the case of the avian hippocampus, interspecific comparisons (some of them based upon a very small number of subjects) show that species dependent upon retrieval of stored food have a larger hippocampal complex than would be predicted on the basis of body size. No other aspect of these birds' lives has been identified to account for this relationship. These interspecific studies led to comparative developmental studies of individuals within a species and revealed that increases in hippocampal volume are a normal part of the life of food-storing birds. Initial studies of the cellular mechanisms underlying this phenomenon suggested that, in at least one species (marsh tit), the experience of storing food reduces the normal rate of attrition of hippocampal neurons. That is, some consequence of performing these spatial learning tasks seemed to act like a trophic factor for hippocampal neurons, because control birds prevented from storing and retrieving food had elevated numbers of dying cells in the hippocampus (Clayton & Krebs 1994). A subsequent study showed that spatial learning also appears to affect neurogenesis in the brains of marsh tits; birds given three trials of food storage and retrieval had a higher rate of cell proliferation in the ventricular zone of the hippocampus than did age-matched, inexperienced controls (Patel et al 1997b). Therefore, the increase in hippocampal volume, previously reported to be part of the normal development of the marsh tit brain, apparently reflects the fact that almost all members of this species share a common experience: the exercise of a specific form of spatial memory.

In the case of the honeybee mushroom bodies, developmental studies were initiated prior to comparative studies, revealing that increases in the volume of the mushroom body neuropil are a normal part of the life of the bee. Interspecific comparisons are just beginning. Initial studies of the underlying cellular mechanisms suggest that the volume changes seen reflect not changes in cell number but changes in the processes of the intrinsic neurons of this structure, because neurogenesis is absent in the brains of adult honeybees (Fahrbach et al 1995b, Malun 1998). In both birds and bees, volume increases develop earlier when behavioral development is accelerated, suggesting that the use of these brain regions is involved in these changes. In contrast to the avian hippocampus, the mushroom bodies of the honeybee exhibit developmental volume increases even in individuals deprived of flight experience (Withers et al 1995) or reared in social isolation in the dark (Fahrbach et al 1998), suggesting that the changes also have an experience-independent component.

Both model systems offer the opportunity to combine field and laboratory analyses of behavior, so that neither relevance to natural history nor the ability to perform well-controlled studies is sacrificed. Examples of field-based studies of learning in honeybees are numerous (Dyer 1991; Collett 1992, 1996; Zhang et al 1990, 1996; Collett et al 1997), but a similar approach can also be applied profitably to birds, as in the case of hummingbirds tested in a "flying" version of a radial arm maze (Healy & Hurly 1995). In bees, it is very easy to distinguish orientation flights (during which learning of visual landmarks around the hive occurs) and foraging flights (during which this information is put to use), because they are temporally separated, often by days or weeks. Although it is clear from studies of homing pigeons that orientation flights taken by birds can serve much the same purpose, studies of food-storing birds have focused on the spatial memories formed in the act of storage itself. Because it is possible to distinguish orientation flights and foraging flights, the relationship of different phases of learning to changes in regional brain volume may be more readily distinguishable in the bee brain than in the bird brain.

In both cases the availability of related species with strikingly contrasting patterns of behavior, and of families of species with graded reliance on spatial learning in the wild, lends itself to phylogenetic as well as developmental analyses. These analyses may yield surprising results. A recent study of hippocampal volume in four species of woodpeckers revealed the predicted volume relationship between the red-bellied woodpecker (*Melanerpes carolinus*), a scatter-hoarding species, and the red-headed woodpecker (*Melanerpes erythrocephalus*), which uses only a single storage site. The red-bellied woodpecker had the larger hippocampal complex of the two (Volman et al 1997). In the same study, however, two non-food-storing woodpeckers were found to have relatively large hippocampal complexes. The limited behavioral data available on these "aberrant" woodpeckers does not permit us to determine whether another aspect of spatial memory is a determinant of hippocampal volume or whether the proposed relationship of hippocampal volume to food storing holds only for the groups in which it was initially investigated.

Another direction for future research involves the exploration of sex differences in hippocampal volume relative to sex differences in the exercise of spatial learning. It has been demonstrated, for example, that female brown-headed cowbirds (*Molothrus ater*) have a larger hippocampus than males (Sherry et al 1993a). This difference is correlated with a striking female-specific behavior: finding host nests in which to lay eggs. Only the female of this brood-parasitic species performs this task, and it has been suggested that selection for spatial ability has been greater in females than in males of this species (reviewed by Jacobs 1996). Sex differences have also been reported for hippocampal volume in some species of voles, in this case favoring the wider-ranging males (Jacobs et al 1990).

Among the social insects, castes provide the functional equivalent of the sexes with regard to the evolution of behavioral differences. Like the sexes, castes in insect societies arise as a result of developmental regulation of gene expression. Sex and caste therefore permit comparable intraspecific analyses in which evolutionary history can be dissociated from the cognitive demands of spatial learning.

In summary, the similarities between birds that use visual learning to store food and insects that use visual landmarks to locate their nest and food plants are that both offer outstanding opportunities to study a naturally occurring, ecologically relevant spatial learning task in both the field and the aviary/apiary. Each has a specific brain region that undergoes volume expansion during normal behavioral development. This brain region has been linked to mediation of spatial learning in both birds and insects, although the evidence is incomplete and largely correlational for both groups, particularly when compared with the much larger experimental literature that describes the function of the rodent and primate hippocampal complexes (Olton et al 1979, Kesner 1990, Squire 1992). Intraspecific, developmental volume plasticity is in both cases also associated with interspecific variation in the size of these structures that correlates with the complexity of the spatial learning tasks an animal performs. In both cases, the underlying (but still unproved) assumption is that this volume difference is interesting because it produces better performance on those spatial learning tasks and because describing the cellular mechanisms responsible will reveal key aspects of the neural basis of learning and provide insight into the evolution of the brain. The present literature suggests a common strategy (despite different cellular mechanisms) for selective volume expansion, namely an increase in the rate of an intrinsic process. In the bird, neurogenesis in the hippocampal ventricular zone is ongoing, but the rate of neurogenesis is sensitive to experience, with an increase coincident with the opportunity to store and retrieve. In the honeybee, the cellular mechanism for the growth of the mushroom body neuropil is not yet known. Growth occurs even in bees prevented from taking orientation flights and foraging (Withers et al 1995) or reared in social isolation in complete darkness (Fahrbach et al 1998), but a precocious onset of foraging accelerates this expansion so that seven-day-old foragers have a volume equivalent to 21-day-old foragers (Withers et al 1993, Durst et al 1994). Our review suggests that developmental volume increases will always contain a mix of experience-expectant and experience-dependent components (following the useful terminology of Black & Greenough 1986) but that the relative proportions will differ from animal to animal, with the bird apparently weighted more heavily to the experience-dependent and the bee to the experience-expectant.

CONCLUSIONS

The brain is a heterogeneous structure with various parts that serve particular behaviors (Harvey & Krebs 1990), and as a result, particular selection pressures are likely to have acted on different brain regions rather than on the brain as a whole. Modern analyses of nervous system evolution use various metrics of cognitive ability, body size, physiology, or allometry to explain regional brain size. By focusing on the size of well-defined regions of the brain, rather than on overall brain size, we divert attention from the sometimes less cognitively relevant constraints on total brain size and instead consider the factors that shape particular regions. In applying this strategy we assume that constraints on total brain size, even if undefined, will operate equally on all brain regions and focus our interests instead on the regions under specific selection pressures. In general, species-specific ecological and behavioral factors appear to affect the size of specific brain components rather than the brain as a whole (Aboitiz 1996). The only assumption required here is the validity of Jerison's principle of proper mass, which states, "The mass of neural tissue controlling a particular function is appropriate to the amount of information processing involved in performing a function" (Jerison 1973, p. 8). Note that this simple assumption is in itself controversial. (See Macphail 1982 and Deacon 1990.)

We have drawn together two literatures that only rarely contact one another—those concerning the brain structures that apparently mediate spatial learning in birds and in bees—to suggest some general principles and some common unresolved issues. The parallels between vertebrates and invertebrates suggest that the divide between these literatures is an artifact of ancient and modern trends in scholarship and research rather than a reflection of fundamental differences in brain structure/function relationships. One question that begs an answer is why is bigger better? That is, exactly how does having a larger hippocampus permit better food storing, or why do forager bees have a larger mushroom body neuropil than nurse bees? The specific advantages conferred remain unknown and worthy of continued investigation.

Another important question is whether brain regions involved with space use have extreme developmental plasticity relative to other brain regions. This correlation is currently unexplained. The importance of spatial cognition in the lives of animals may have selected for exaggerated plasticity. The brain regions that appear to be involved with aspects of spatial behavior, in both vertebrates and invertebrates, mature relatively late in the development of the brain (Ito & Hotta 1992, Gould et al 1998); this extended period of development may make them more accessible for reconfiguration. The follow-up question to these considerations involves the relationship between structural plasticity manifested within the life of the individual and the phylogenetic plasticity of the same brain structures. It is also possible that additional brain regions exhibit volume changes that correlate with particular behaviors, but because they have not been subjected to similar scrutiny, these regions have not been identified.

A critical look at the literature on the hippocampus and the mushroom bodies suggests the question of what other functions brain regions involved in spatial learning might serve, and how these different capacities are integrated. In addition to place memory, experimental evidence reveals that the hippocampus plays a role in various types of declarative memory (Olton et al 1979; Squire 1992, 1993), while the mushroom bodies of insects are clearly associated with olfactory learning (Hammer & Menzel 1995, 1998; Hammer 1997; Rybak & Menzel 1998) and some aspects of sexual behavior (O'Dell et al 1995, Heisenberg et al 1995, Neckameyer 1998). Attribution of a specific form of learning to a specific brain region, such as the mushroom bodies or the hippocampus, does not imply that the brain region has a single function or that those conducting such analyses are unaware that regional brain function is as much, if not more, a product of connectivity as it is of size.

Full understanding of the significance of volume comparisons requires detailed knowledge of the natural history of the species studied and the use of multiple assays of behavior. Developmental and phylogenetic differences in volume revealed by this approach provide an opportunity to explore how cellular and molecular processes of development are related to evolutionary change.

ACKNOWLEDGMENTS

Our research on the honeybee described in this review was conducted with support from the National Science Foundation, the National Institutes of Mental Health, the National Institutes of Health, the US Department of Agriculture, and the University of Illinois Campus Research Board. EAC was supported by a National Research Service Award from the National Institutes of Health. We thank F Dyer, S Healy, and W Wcislo for useful discussions and helpful comments on the manuscript.

Visit the *Annual Reviews home page* at
http://www.AnnualReviews.org.

Literature Cited

Able KP. 1980. Mechanisms of orientation, navigation, and homing. In *Animal Migration, Orientation, and Navigation*, ed. SA Gauthreaux, pp. 283–373. New York: Academic. 387 pp.

Able KP, Able MA. 1996. The flexible migratory orientation system of the Savannah sparrow (*Passerculus sandwichensis*). *J. Exp. Biol.* 199:3–8

Aboitiz F. 1996. Does bigger mean better? Evolutionary determinants of brain size and structure. *Brain Behav. Evol.* 47: 225–45

Ariëns Kappers CU, Huber GC, Crosby EC. 1936. *The Comparative Anatomy of the Nervous System of Vertebrates, Including Man*. New York: Macmillan. 864 pp.

Balda RP, Bunch KG, Kamil AC, Sherry DF, Tomback DF. 1987. Cache site memory in birds. In *Foraging Behavior*, ed. AC Kamil, JR Krebs, HR Pulliam, pp. 645–65. New York: Plenum. 676 pp.

Balda RP, Kamil AC. 1989. A comparative study of cache recovery of three corvid species. *Anim. Behav.* 38:486–95

Barnea A, Nottebohm F. 1994. Seasonal recruitment of hippocampal neurons in adult free-ranging black-capped chickadees. *Proc. Natl. Acad. Sci. USA* 91:11217–21

Basil JA, Kamil AC, Balda RP, Fite KV. 1996. Differences in hippocampal volume among food storing corvids. *Brain Behav. Evol.* 7:156–64

Becker L. 1958. Untersuchungen über das Heimfindevermögen der Bienen. *Z. Vgl. Physiol.* 41:1–25

Bednekoff PA, Balda RP, Kamil AC, Hile AG. 1997. Long-term spatial memory in four seed-caching corvid species. *Anim. Behav.* 53:335–41

Bennett EL, Diamond MC, Krech D, Rosenzweig MR. 1964. Chemical and anatomical plasticity of brain. *Science* 146:610–19

Bernstein S, Bernstein RA. 1969. Relationships between foraging efficiency and the size of the head and component brain and sensory structures in the red wood ant. *Brain Res.* 16:85–104

Berthold P. 1991. Orientation in birds: a final consideration. In *Orientation in Birds,* ed. P Berthold, pp. 322–27. Boston, MA: Birkhäuser. 331 pp.

Bingman VP. 1998. Spatial representation and homing pigeon navigation. See Healy 1998, pp. 68–84

Bingman VP. 1993. Vision, cognition, and the avian hippocampus. In *Vision, Brain and Behavior in Birds,* ed. HP Zeigler, H-J Bischof, pp. 391–407. Cambridge, MA: Bradford/MIT Press. 415 pp.

Bitterman ME. 1996. Comparative analysis of learning in honeybees. *Anim. Learn. Mem.* 24:123–41

Black JE, Greenough WT. 1986. Induction of pattern in neural structure by experience: implications for cognitive development. In *Advances in Developmental Psychology,* ed.. ME Lamb, AL Brown, B Rogoff, 4:1–50. Hillsdale, NJ: Erlbaum. 354 pp.

Black JE, Isaacs KR, Anderson BJ, Alcantara AA, Greenough WT. 1990. Learning causes synaptogenesis, whereas motor activity causes angiogenesis, in cerebellar cortex of adult rats. *Proc. Natl. Acad. Sci. USA* 87:5568–72

Bock WJ, Balda RP, Vander Wall SB. 1973. Morphology of the sublingual pouch and tongue musculature in Clark's nutcracker. *Auk* 90:491–519

Brandon JG, Coss RG. 1982. Rapid dendritic spine stem shortening during one-trial learning: the honeybee's first orientation flight. *Brain Res.* 252:51–61

Breedlove SM. 1992. Sexual dimorphism in the vertebrate nervous system. *J. Neurosci.* 12:4133–42

Brodbeck DR. 1994. Memory for spatial and local cues: a comparison of a storing and a nonstoring species. *Anim. Learn. Behav.* 22:119–33

Brodbeck DR, Shettleworth SJ. 1995. Matching location and color of a compound stimulus: comparison of a food-storing and a non-storing bird species. *J. Exp. Psychol. Anim. Behav. Processes* 22:64–77

Brower LP. 1996. Monarch butterfly orientation: missing pieces of a magnificent puzzle. *J. Exp. Biol.* 199:93–103

Bullock TH. 1984a. Comparative neuroscience holds promise for quiet revolutions. *Science* 225:473–78

Bullock TH. 1984b. Understanding brains by comparing taxa. *Perspect. Biol. Med.* 27: 511–24

Bures J, Fenton AA, Kaminsky Y, Zinyuk L. 1997. Place cells and place navigation. *Proc. Natl. Acad. Sci. USA* 94:343–50

Burrows M. 1996. *The Neurobiology of an Insect Brain.* New York: Oxford Univ. Press. 682 pp.

Casini G, Fontanesi G, Bingman VP, Jones TJ, Gagliardo A, et al. 1997. The neuroethology of cognitive maps: contributions from research on the hippocampus and homing pigeon navigation. *Arch. Ital. Biol.* 135: 73–92

Chapman RF. 1982. *The Insects. Structure and Function.* Cambridge, MA: Harvard Univ. Press. 919 pp.

Chittka L, Menzel R. 1992. The evolutionary adaptation of flower colours and the insect pollinators' colour vision. *J. Comp. Physiol. A* 171:171–81

Churchland PS. 1995. *The Engine of Reason, The Seat of the Soul: A Philosophical Journey into the Brain.* Cambridge, MA: MIT Press. 329 pp.

Churchland PS, Sejnowski TS. 1992. *The Computational Brain.* Cambridge, MA: MIT Press. 544 pp.

Clayton NS. 1995a. Comparative studies of food-storing, memory, and the hippocampal formation in Parids. *Hippocampus* 5:499–510

Clayton NS. 1995b. Development of memory and the hippocampus: comparison of food storing and non-storing birds on a one-trial associative memory task. *J. Neurosci.* 15: 2796–807

Clayton NS. 1995c. The neuroethological development of food-storing memory: a case of use it, or lose it! *Behav. Brain Res.* 7:95–102

Clayton NS, Krebs JR. 1994. Hippocampal growth and attrition in birds affected by experience. *Proc. Natl. Acad. Sci. USA* 91: 7410–14

Clayton NS, Krebs JR. 1995. Memory in food-storing birds: from behaviour to brain. *Curr. Opin. Neurobiol.* 5:149–54

Collett TS. 1992. Landmark learning and guidance in insects. *Philos. Trans. R. Soc. London Ser. B* 337:295–303

Collett TS. 1996. Insect navigation en route to the goal: multiple strategies for the use of landmarks. *J. Exp. Biol.* 199:227–35

Collett TS, Fauria K, Dale K, Baron J. 1997. Places and patterns—a study of context learning in honey bees. *J. Comp. Physiol. A* 181:343–53

Collett TS, Fry SN, Wehner R. 1993. Sequence learning by honeybees. *J. Comp. Physiol. A* 172:693–706

Collett T, Zeil J. 1998. Places and landmarks: an arthropod perspective. See Healy 1998, pp. 54–68

Compton DM, Griffith HR, McDaniel WF, Foster RA, Davis BK. 1997. The flexible use of multiple cue relationships in spatial navigation: a comparison of water maze performance following hippocampal, medial septal, prefrontal cortex, or posterior parietal cortex lesions. *Neurobiol. Learn. Mem.* 68:117–32

Coss RG, Brandon JG, Globus A. 1980. Changes in morphology of dendritic spines on honeybee calycal interneurons associated with cumulative nursing and foraging experiences. *Brain Res.* 192:49–59

Cristol DA. 1996. Food storing does not affect hippocampal volume in experienced adult willow tits. *Behav. Brain Res.* 81: 233–36

Davis RL. 1993. Mushroom bodies and *Drosophila* learning. *Neuron* 11:1–14

Deacon TW. 1990. Fallacies of progression in theories of brain-size evolution. *Int. J. Primatol.* 11:193–235

de Belle JS, Heisenberg M. 1994. Associative odor learning in *Drosophila* abolished by chemical ablation of mushroom bodies. *Science* 263:692–95

Dingle H. 1996. *Migration.* New York: Oxford Univ. Press. 474 pp.

Durst C, Eichmüller S, Menzel R. 1994. Development and experience lead to increased volume of subcompartments of the honeybee mushroom body. *Behav. Neural Biol.* 62:259–63

Dyer FC. 1991. Bees acquire route-based memories but not cognitive maps in a familiar landscape. *Anim. Behav.* 41:239–46

Dyer FC. 1994. Spatial cognition and navigation in insects. In *Behavioral Mechanisms in Evolutionary Ecology*, ed. LA Real, pp. 66–98. Chicago, IL: Univ. Chicago Press. 469 pp.

Dyer FC. 1998. Cognitive ecology of navigation. In *Cognitive Ecology: The Evolutionary Ecology of Information Processing and Decision Making*, ed. R Dukas, pp. 201–60. Chicago: Univ. Chicago Press. 420 pp.

Dyer FC, Dickinson JA. 1994. Development of sun compensation by honeybees: how partially experienced bees estimate the sun's course. *Proc. Natl. Acad. Sci. USA* 91:4471–74

Esch HE, Burns JE. 1995. Honeybees use optic flow to measure the distance of a food source. *Naturwissenschaften* 82:38–40

Esch HE, Burns JE. 1996. Distance estimation by foraging honeybees. *J. Exp. Biol.* 199: 155–62

Etienne AS, Berlie J, Georgakopoulos J, Maurer R. 1998. Role of dead reckoning in navigation. See Healy 1998, pp. 54–68

Etienne AS, Maurer R, Seguinot V. 1996. Path integration in mammals and its interaction with visual landmarks. *J. Exp. Biol.* 199: 201–9

Fahrbach SE. 1997. Regulation of age polyethism in bees and wasps by juvenile hormone. *Adv. Study Behav.* 26:285–316

Fahrbach SE, Giray T, Farris SM, Robinson GE. 1997. Expansion of the neuropil of the mushroom bodies in male honey bees is coincident with initiation of flight. *Neurosci. Lett.* 236:135–38

Fahrbach SE, Giray T, Robinson GE. 1995a. Volume changes in the mushroom bodies of adult honey bee queens. *Neurobiol. Learn. Mem.* 63:181–91

Fahrbach SE, Moore D, Capaldi EA, Farris SM, Robinson GE. 1998. Experience-expectant plasticity in the mushroom bodies of the honey bee. *Learn. Mem.* 5: 115–23

Fahrbach SE, Strande JL, Robinson GE. 1995b. Neurogenesis is absent in the brains of adult honey bees and does not explain behavioral neuroplasticity. *Neurosci. Lett.* 197:145–48

Farris SM, Fahrbach SE, Robinson GE. 1995. Effects of behavioral reversion on brain structural plasticity in the honey bee. *Soc. Neurosci. Abstr.* 21:458

Fremouw T, Jackson-Smith P, Kesner RP. 1997. Impaired place learning and unimpaired cue learning in hippocampal-lesioned pigeons. *Behav. Neurosci.* 111: 963–75

Gallistel CR. 1990. *The Organization of Learning.* Cambridge, MA: Bradford Books/MIT Press. 648 pp.

Giger AD, Srinivasan MV. 1995. Pattern recognition in honeybee: eidetic imagery and orientation discrimination. *J. Comp. Physiol. A* 176:791–96

Gilbert LE. 1975. Ecological consequences of a coevolved mutualism between butterflies and plants. In *Coevolution of Animals and Plants*, ed. LE Gilbert, PR Raven, pp. 100–40. Austin: Univ. Tex. Press. 263 pp.

Giray T, Robinson GE. 1996. Common endocrine and genetic mechanisms of behavioral development in male and worker honey bees and the evolution of division of labor. *Proc. Natl. Acad. Sci. USA* 93: 11718–22

Giurfa M, Eichmann B, Menzel R. 1996. Symmetry perception in honeybee: eidetic imagery and orientation discrimination. *J. Comp. Physiol. A* 176:791–95

Giurfa M, Menzel R. 1997. Insect visual perception: complex abilities of simple nervous systems. *Curr. Opin. Neurobiol.* 7: 505–13

Gould E, Tanapat P, McEwen BS, Flügge G, Fuchs E. 1998. Proliferation of granule cell precursors in the dentate gyrus of adult monkeys is diminished by stress. *Proc. Natl. Acad. Sci. USA* 95:3168–71

Grant SGN, Silva AJ. 1994. Targeting learning. *Trends Neurosci.* 17:71–75

Greenough WT, Chang F-LF. 1988. Plasticity of synapse structure and pattern in the cerebral cortex. In *Cerebral Cortex,* ed. A Peters, EG Jones, 7:391–440. New York: Plenum. 518 pp.

Greenspan RJ. 1995. Flies, genes, learning, and memory. *Neuron* 15:747–50

Griffin DR. 1955. Bird navigation. In *Recent Studies in Avian Biology,* ed. A Wolfson, pp. 154–97. Urbana: Univ. Ill. Press. 479 pp.

Griffin DR. 1992. *Animal Minds.* Chicago: Univ. Chicago Press. 310 pp.

Gronenberg W, Heeren S, Holldöbler B. 1996. Age-dependent and task-related morphological changes in the brain and mushroom bodies of the ant *Camponotus floridanus. J. Exp. Biol.* 199:2011–19

Hammer M. 1997. The neural basis of associative reward learning in honeybees. *Trends Neurosci.* 20:245–52

Hammer M, Menzel R. 1995. Learning and memory in the honeybee. *J. Neurosci.* 15: 1617–30

Hammer M, Menzel R. 1998. Multiple sites of associative odor learning as revealed by local brain microinjections of octopamine in honeybees. *Learn. Mem.* 5:146–56

Hampton RR, Sherry DF, Shettleworth SJ, Khurgel M, Ivy G. 1995. Hippocampal volume and food-storing behavior are related in parids. *Brain Behav. Evol.* 45: 54–61

Hampton RR, Shettleworth SJ. 1996. Hippocampal lesions impair memory for location but not color in passerine birds. *Behav. Neurosci.* 110:831–35

Harvey PH, Krebs JR. 1990. Comparing brains. *Science* 249:140–46

Healy SD. 1996. Ecological specialization in the avian brain. In *Neuroethological Studies of Cognitive and Perceptual Processes,* ed. CF Moss, SJ Shettleworth, pp. 84–110. Boulder, CO: Westview. 329 pp.

Healy S, ed. 1998. *Spatial Representation in Animals.* Oxford, UK: Oxford Univ. Press. 188 pp.

Healy S, Clayton NS, Krebs JR. 1994. Development of hippocampal specialisation in two species of tit (*Parus* spp.). *Behav. Brain Res.* 61:23–28

Healy SD, Hurly TA. 1995. Spatial memory in rufous hummingbirds (*Selasphorus rufus*): a field test. *Anim. Learn. Behav.* 23:63–68

Healy SD, Krebs JR. 1992. Food storing and

the hippocampus in corvids: amount and volume are correlated. *Philos. Trans. R. Soc. London Ser. B* 329:241–45

Healy SD, Krebs JR. 1993. Development of hippocampal specialization in a food-storing bird. *Behav. Brain Res.* 53:127–31

Healy SD, Krebs JR. 1996. Food storing and the hippocampus in Paridae. *Brain Behav. Evol.* 47:195–99

Heisenberg M, Heusipp M, Wanke C. 1995. Structural plasticity in the *Drosophila* brain. *J. Neurosci.* 15:1951–60

Herz RS, Zanette L, Sherry DF. 1994. Spatial cues for cache retrieval by black-capped chickadees. *Anim. Behav.* 48:343–51

Ito K, Hotta Y. 1992. Proliferation pattern of postembryonic neuroblasts in the brain of *Drosophila melanogaster. Dev. Biol.* 149: 134–48

Jacobs LF. 1996. Sexual selection and the brain. *Trends Ecol. Evol.* 11:82–86

Jacobs LF, Gaulin SJC, Sherry DF, Hoffman GE. 1990. Evolution of spatial cognition: sex-specific patterns of spatial behavior predict hippocampal size. *Proc. Natl. Acad. Sci. USA* 87:6349–52

Jacobs LF, Spencer WD. 1994. Natural space-use patterns and hippocampal size in kangaroo rats. *Brain Behav. Evol.* 44: 125–32

Jander R. 1997. Macroevolution of a fixed action pattern for learning. In *Comparative Psychology of Invertebrates,* ed. G Greenberg, E Tobach, pp. 79–99. New York: Garland. 304 pp.

Jarrard LE. 1995. What does the hippocampus really do? *Behav. Brain Res.* 71:1–10

Jerison HJ. 1973. *Evolution of the Brain and Intelligence.* New York: Academic. 482 pp.

Kamil AC, Balda RP. 1985. Cache recovery and spatial memory in Clark's nutcrackers (*Nucifraga columbiana*). *J. Exp. Psych. Anim. Behav. Processes* 11:95–111

Kamil AC, Balda RP. 1990. Spatial memory in seed-caching corvids. *Psychol. Learn. Motiv.* 26:1–25

Kanciruk P, Herrnkind W. 1978. Mass migration of spiny lobster *Panulirus argus* (Crustacea: Palinuridae): behavior and environmental correlates. *Bull. Mar. Sci.* 28: 601–23

Kandel E, Abel T. 1995. Neuropeptides, adenyl cyclase, and memory storage. *Science* 268:8825–26

Karten H, Hodos W. 1967. *A Stereotaxic Atlas of the Brain of the Pigeon (Columbia livia).* Baltimore, MD: Johns Hopkins Press. 193 pp.

Kenyon FC. 1896. The brain of the bee. A preliminary contribution to the morphology of the nervous system of the Arthropoda. *J. Comp. Neurol.* 6:133–210

Kesner RP. 1990. Learning and memory in rats with an emphasis on the role of the hippocampal formation. See Kesner & Olton 1990, pp. 179–204

Kesner RP, Olton DS, eds. 1990. *Neurobiology of Comparative Cognition.* Hillsdale, NJ: Erlbaum. 476 pp.

Krebs JR. 1990. Food-storing birds: adaptive specialization in brain and behaviour? *Philos. Trans. R. Soc. London Ser. B* 329: 153–60

Krebs JR, Clayton NS, Healy SD, Cristol DA, Patel SN, Jolliffe AR. 1996. The ecology of the avian brain: food-storing memory and the hippocampus. *Ibis* 138:343–46

Krebs JR, Sherry DF, Healy SD, Perry VH, Vaccarino AL. 1989. Hippocampal specialization of food-storing birds. *Proc. Natl. Acad. Sci. USA* 86:1388–92

Krushinskaya NL. 1966. Some complex forms of feeding behaviour of nutcracker *Nucifraga caryocatactes*, after removal of old cortex. *Z. Evol. Biokhem. Fisiol.* 11:563–68 [In Russian]

Laidlaw HH. 1989. *Instrumental Insemination of Honey Bee Queens: Pictorial Instruction Manual.* Hamilton, IL: Dadant. 144 pp.

Lehrer M. 1994. Spatial vision in the honeybee: the use of different cues in different tasks. *Vis. Res.* 34:2363–85

Lehrer M. 1996. Small-scale navigation in the honeybee: active acquisition of visual information about the goal. *J. Exp. Biol.* 199: 253–61

Lehrer M, Collett TS. 1994. Approaching and departing bees learn different cues to the distance of a landmark. *J. Comp. Physiol. A* 175:171–77

Leonard B, McNaughton BL. 1990. Spatial representation in the rat: conceptual, behavioral, and neurophysiological perspectives. See Kesner & Olton 1990, pp. 363–422

Li YS, Strausfeld NJ. 1997. Morphology and sensory modality of mushroom body extrinsic neurons in the brain of the cockroach, *Periplaneta americana, J. Comp. Neurol.* 387:631–50

Macphail E. 1982. *Brain and Intelligence in Vertebrates.* Oxford: Clarendon. 423 pp.

Malun D. 1998. Early development of mushroom bodies in the brain of the honeybee *Apis mellifera* and revealed by BrdU incorporation and ablation experiments. *Learn. Mem.* 5:90–101

McNaughton BL, Barnes CL, Gerrard JL, Gothard K, Jung MW, et al. 1996. Deciphering the hippocampal polyglot: the hip-

pocampus as a path integration system. *J. Exp. Biol.* 199:173–85

Menzel R. 1990. Learning, memory and 'cognition' in honey bees. See Kesner & Olton 1990, pp. 237–92

Menzel R, Müller U. 1996. Learning and memory in honeybees: from behavior to neural substrates. *Annu. Rev. Neurosci.* 19: 379–404

Mewaldt LR. 1956. Nesting behavior of the Clark's nutcracker. *Condor* 58:3–23

Mizunami M, Weibrecht JM, Strausfeld NJ. 1993. A new role for the insect mushroom bodies: place memory and motor control. In *Biological Neural Networks in Invertebrate Neuroethology and Robotics,* ed. RD Beer, RE Ritzman, T McKenna, pp. 199–225. New York: Academic. 417 pp.

Mobbs PG. 1982. The brain of the honeybee *Apis mellifera.* I. The connections and spatial organizations of the mushroom bodies. *Philos. Trans. R. Soc. London Ser. B* 298: 309–54

Mobbs PG. 1984. Neural networks in the mushroom bodies of the honeybee. *J. Insect Physiol.* 30:43–58

Morris RGM. 1981. Spatial localization does not require the presence of local cues. *Learn. Motiv.* 12:239–60

Morris RGM, Anderson E, Lynch GS, Baudry M. 1986. Selective impairment of learning and blockade of long-term potentiation by an N-methyl-D-aspartate receptor antagonist. *Nature* 297:774–76

Morris RGM, Garrud P, Rawlins JNP, O'Keefe J. 1982. Place navigation impaired in rats with hippocampal lesions. *Nature* 297:681–83

Muller RU, Kubie JL, Bostock EM, Taube JS, Quirk GJ. 1991. Spatial firing correlates of neurons in the hippocampal formation of freely moving rats. In *Brain and Space,* ed. J Paillard, pp. 296–333. New York: Oxford Univ. Press. 499 pp.

Muller RU, Stead M. 1996. Hippocampal place cells connected by Hebbian synapses can solve spatial problems. *Hippocampus* 6:709–19

Neckameyer WS. 1998. Dopamine and mushroom bodies in *Drosophila*: experience-dependent and -independent aspects of sexual behavior. *Learn. Mem.* 5:157–65

Neisser U. 1967. *Cognitive Psychology.* New York: Appleton-Century-Crofts. 351 pp.

Nottebohm F. 1981. A brain for all seasons: cyclical anatomical changes in song control nuclei of the canary brain. *Science* 214:1368–70

O'Dell KM, Armstrong JD, Yang MY, Kaiser K. 1995. Functional dissection of the *Drosophila* mushroom bodies by selective feminization of genetically defined sub-compartments. *Neuron* 15:55–61

O'Keefe J, Nadel L. 1978. *The Hippocampus as a Cognitive Map.* Oxford: Clarendon. 570 pp.

Oleskevich S, Clements JD, Srinivasan MV. 1997. Long-term synaptic plasticity in the honeybee. *J. Neurophysiol.* 78:528–32

Olton DS, Becker JT, Handelmann GE. 1979. Hippocampus, space, and memory. *Behav. Brain Sci.* 2:313–65

Patel SN, Clayton NS, Krebs JR. 1997a. Hippocampal tissue transplants reverse lesion-induced spatial memory deficits in Zebra finches (*Taeniopygia guttata*). *J. Neurosci.* 17:3861–69

Patel SN, Clayton NS, Krebs JR. 1997b. Spatial learning induces neurogenesis in the avian brain. *Behav. Brain Res.* 89:115–28

Pirlot P. 1986. Understanding taxa by comparing brains. *Perspect. Biol. Med.* 29:499–509

Redish AD, Touretzky DS. 1997. Cognitive maps beyond the hippocampus. *Hippocampus* 7:15–35

Riley JR, Smith AD, Reynolds DR, Edwards AS, Osborne JL, et al. 1996. Tracking bees with harmonic radar. *Nature* 379:29–30

Ristau C, ed. 1991. *Cognitive Ethology.* Hillsdale, NJ: Erlbaum. 332 pp.

Roberts RC. 1979. The evolution of avian food-storing behavior. *Am. Nat.* 114:418–38

Robinson GE. 1992. Regulation of division of labor in insect societies. *Annu. Rev. Entomol.* 37:637–65

Robinson GE, Page RE Jr, Strambi C, Strambi A. 1989. Hormonal and genetic control of behavioral integration in honey bee colonies. *Science* 246:109–12

Robinson GE, Strambi C, Strambi A, Feldlaufer MF. 1992. Comparison of juvenile hormone and ecdysteroid haemolymph titres in adult honeybee workers and queens. *J. Insect Physiol.* 37:929–35

Roitblat HL, von Fersen L. 1992. Comparative cognition: representations and processes in learning and memory. *Annu. Rev. Psychol.* 43:671–710

Ronacher B, Wehner R. 1995. Desert ants *Cataglyphis fortis* use self-induced optic flow to measure distances travelled. *J. Comp. Physiol. A* 177:21–27

Rossel S, Wehner R. 1982. The bee's map of the E-vector pattern in the sky. *Proc. Natl. Acad. Sci. USA* 79:4451–55

Rossel S, Wehner R. 1984. How bees analyse the polarization patterns in the sky. Experiments and model. *J. Comp. Physiol. A* 154:607–15

Rybak J, Menzel R. 1998. Integrative proper-ties of the Pe1 neuron, a unique mushroom body output neuron. *Learn. Mem.* 5:133–45

Schöne H. 1984. *Spatial Orientation.* Princeton, NJ: Princeton Univ. Press. 347 pp.

Schöne H. 1996. Orientation flight behavior in honeybees released from open or covered containers—after or without displacement. *J. Comp. Physiol. A* 179:593–97

Schöne H, Kühme WD, Schöne H. 1995. Take-off behavior and vanishing bearings of honeybees after displacement with open view or in a sight-proof box. *Naturwissenschaften* 82:343–45

Sharp PE, Blair HT, Brown M. 1996. Neural network modeling of the hippocampal formation spatial signals and their possible role in navigation: a modular approach. *Hippocampus* 6:720–34

Sherry DF. 1984. What food-storing birds remember. *Can. J. Psychol.* 38:304–21

Sherry DF. 1985. Food storage by birds and mammals. *Adv. Study Behav.* 15:153–88

Sherry DF. 1989. Food storing in the Paridae. *Wilson Bull.* 101:289–304

Sherry DF, Duff SJ. 1996. Behavioural and neural bases of orientation in food-storing birds. *J. Exp. Biol.* 199:165–72

Sherry DF, Forbes MRL, Khurgel M, Ivy GO. 1993a. Females have a larger hippocampus than males in the brood-parasitic brown-headed cowbird. *Proc. Natl. Acad. Sci. USA* 90:7839–43

Sherry DF, Jacobs LF, Gaulin SJC. 1993b. Spatial memory and adaptive specialization of the hippocampus. *Trends Neurosci.* 15:298–303

Sherry DF, Krebs JR, Cowie RJ. 1981. Memory for the location of stored food in marsh tits (*Parus palustris*). *Anim. Behav.* 29:1260–66

Sherry DF, Vaccarino AL. 1989. Hippocampus and memory for food caches in black-capped chickadees. *Behav. Neurosci.* 103:308–18

Sherry DF, Vaccarino AL, Buckenham K, Herz RS. 1989. The hippocampal complex of food-storing birds. *Brain Behav. Evol.* 34:308–17

Shettleworth SJ. 1990. Spatial memory in food-storing birds. *Philos. Trans. R. Soc. London Ser. B* 329:143–51

Shettleworth SJ. 1996. Introduction: neuroethology, perception, and cognition. In *Neuroethological Studies of Cognitive and Perceptual Processes,* ed. CF Moss, SJ Shettleworth, pp. 1–8. Boulder, CO: Westview. 329 pp.

Silva AJ, Smith AM, Giese KP. 1997. Gene targeting and the biology of learning and memory. *Annu. Rev. Genet.* 31:527–46

Sivinski J. 1989. Mushroom body development in nymphalid butterflies: a correlate of learning? *J. Insect Behav.* 2:277–83

Smulders TV, Sasson AD, DeVoogd TJ. 1995. Seasonal variation in hippocampal volume in a food-storing bird, the black-capped chickadee. *J. Neurobiol.* 27:15–25

Squire LR. 1992. Memory and the hippocampus: a synthesis from findings with rats, monkeys, and humans. *Psychol. Rev.* 99: 195–231

Squire LR. 1993. The hippocampus and spatial memory. *Trends Neurosci.* 16:56–57

Srinivasan MV, Zhang SW, Lehrer M, Collett TS. 1996. Honeybee navigation en route to the goal: visual flight control and odometry. *J. Exp. Biol.* 199:237–44

Stevens TA, Krebs JR. 1986. Retrieval of stored seeds by marsh tits *Parus palustris* in the field. *Ibis* 128:513–25

Strausfeld NJ, Buschbeck EK, Gomez RS. 1995. The arthropod mushroom body: its functional roles, evolutionary enigmas and mistaken identities. In *The Nervous Systems of Invertebrates: An Evolutionary and Comparative Approach*, ed. O Breidbach, W Kutsch, pp. 349–81. Boston, MA: Birkhauser. 448 pp.

Strausfeld NJ, Hansen L, Li Y, Gomez RS, Ito I. 1998. Evolution, discovery, and interpretations of arthropod mushroom bodies. *Learn. Mem.* 5:11–37

Sullivan JP, Robinson GE, Fahrbach SE. 1996. Foraging behavior and mushroom bodies in allatectomized honey bees. *Soc. Neurosci. Abstr.* 22:1144

Thinus-Blanc C. 1996. *Animal Spatial Cognition: Behavioural and Brain Approach.* River Edge, NJ: World Sci. 259 pp.

Tinbergen N. 1951. *The Study of Instinct.* London: Oxford Univ. Press. 228 pp.

Tolman EC. 1948. Cognitive maps in rats and men. *Psychol. Bull.* 55:189–208

Tomback DF. 1982. Dispersal of whitebark pine seeds by Clark's nutcracker: a mutualism hypothesis. *J. Anim. Ecol.* 51: 451–67

Ugolini A. 1987. Visual information acquired during displacement and initial orientation in *Polistes gallicus* (L.) (Hymenoptera, Vespidae). *Anim. Behav.* 35:590–95

Vander Wall SB. 1982. An experimental analysis of cache recovery in Clark's nutcracker. *Anim. Behav.* 30:84–94

Vander Wall SB. 1990. *Food Hoarding in Animals.* Chicago: Univ. Chicago Press. 445 pp.

Vander Wall SB, Balda RP. 1981. Ecology and evolution of food-storage behavior in conifer-seed caching corvids. *Z. Tierpsychol.* 56:217–42

Vauclair J. 1996. *Animal Cognition. An Introduction to Modern Comparative Psychology.* Cambridge, MA: Harvard Univ. Press. 206 pp.

Visscher PK, Seeley TD. 1982. Foraging strategy of honeybee colonies in a temperate deciduous forest. *Ecology* 63:1790–801

Vollbehr J. 1975. Zur Orientierung junger Honigbienen bei ihrem ersten Orientierungsflug. *Zool. Jahrb. Abt. Allg. Zool. Physiol. Tiere* 79:33–69

Volman SF, Grubb TC Jr, Schuett KC. 1997. Relative hippocampal volume in relation to food-storing behavior in four species of woodpeckers. *Brain Behav. Evol.* 49: 110–20

von Frisch K. 1967. *The Dance Language and Orientation of Bees.* London: Oxford Univ. Press. 566 pp.

Vowles DM. 1964. Olfactory learning and brain lesions in the wood ant (*Formica rufa*). *J. Comp. Physiol. Psychol.* 58: 105–11

Wallraff HG. 1970. Über die Flugrichtungen verfrachteter Brieftauben in Abhängigkeit von Heimatort und vom Ort der Freilassung. *Z. Tierpsychol.* 27:303–51

Wallraff HG. 1996. Seven theses on pigeon homing deduced from empirical findings. *J. Exp. Biol.* 199:105–11

Wehner R. 1981. Spatial vision in arthropods. In *Handbook of Sensory Physiology*, ed. H Autrum, VII(6C):287–616. Boston, MA: Springer-Verlag. 663 pp.

Wehner R. 1996. Middle-scale navigation: the insect case. *J. Exp. Biol.* 199:125–27

Wehner R, Harkness RD, Schmid-Hempel P. 1983. Foraging strategies in individually searching ants *Cataglyphis bicolor* (Hymenoptera: Formicidae). In *Information Processing in Animals,* ed. M Lindauer, pp. 1–79. New York: Gustav Fischer Verlag. 79 pp.

Wehner R, Michel B, Antonsen P. 1996. Visual navigation in insects: coupling of egocentric and geocentric information. *J. Exp. Biol.* 199:129–40

Wehner R, Müller M. 1993. How do ants acquire their celestial ephemeris function? *Naturwissenschaften* 80:331–33

Wehner R, Wehner S. 1990. Insect navigation: use of maps or Ariadne's thread? *Ethol. Ecol. Evol.* 2:27–48

Wilson EO. 1971. *The Insect Societies.* Cambridge, MA: Harvard Univ. Press. 548 pp.

Wilson MA, Tonegawa S. 1997. Synaptic plasticity, place cells and spatial memory: study with second generation knockouts. *Trends Neurosci.* 20:102–6

Wiltschko W, Wiltschko R. 1996. Magnetic

682   CAPALDI, ROBINSON & FAHRBACH

orientation in birds. *J. Exp. Biol.* 199: 29–38

Winston ML. 1987. *The Biology of the Honey Bee.* Cambridge, MA: Harvard Univ. Press. 281 pp.

Withers GS, Fahrbach SE, Robinson GE. 1993. Selective neuroanatomical plasticity and division of labour in the honeybee. *Nature* 364:238–40

Withers GS, Fahrbach SE, Robinson GE. 1995. Effects of experience and juvenile hormone on the organization of the mushroom bodies of honey bees. *J. Neurobiol.* 26:130–44

Yoerg SI, Kamil AC. 1991. Integrating cognitive ethology with cognitive psychology. See Ristau 1991, pp. 273–89

Zeil J, Kelber A, Voss R. 1996. Structure and function of learning flights in bees and wasps. *J. Exp. Biol.* 199:245–52

Zhang SW, Bartsch K, Srinivasan MV. 1996. Maze learning by honeybees. *Neurobiol. Learn. Mem.* 66:267–82

Zhang SW, Srinivasan MV. 1994. Pattern recognition in honeybees: analysis of orientation. *Philos. Trans. R. Soc. London Ser. B* 346:399–406

Zhang SW, Xiang W, Zili L, Srinivasan MV. 1990. Visual tracking of moving targets by freely flying honeybees. *Vis. Neurosci.* 4: 379–86

Annu. Rev. Psychol. 1999. 50:683–705

CURRENT ISSUES AND EMERGING THEORIES IN ANIMAL COGNITION

S. T. Boysen and G. T. Himes

Department of Psychology, The Ohio State University, Columbus, Ohio 43210;
e-mail: boysen.1@osu.edu

KEY WORDS: comparative psychology, imitation, tool use, self-recognition, theory of mind, animal behavior

ABSTRACT

Comparative cognition is an emerging interdisciplinary field with contributions from comparative psychology, cognitive/experimental and developmental psychology, animal learning, and ethology, and is poised to move toward greater understanding of animal and human information-processing, reasoning, memory, and the phylogenetic emergence of mind. This chapter highlights some current issues and discusses four areas within comparative cognition that are yielding new approaches and hypotheses for studying basic conceptual capacities in nonhuman species. These include studies of imitation, tool use, mirror self-recognition, and the potential for attribution of mental states by nonhuman animals. Though a very old question in psychology, the study of imitation continues to provide new avenues for examining the complex relationships among and between the levels of imitative behaviors exhibited by many species. Similarly, recent work in animal tool use, mirror self-recognition (with all its contentious issues), and recent attempts to empirically study the potential for attributional capacities in nonhumans, all continue to provide fresh insights and novel paradigms for addressing the defining characteristics of these complex phenomena.

CONTENTS

0084-6570/99/0201-0683$08.00

INTRODUCTION TO CURRENT TOPICS IN
ANIMAL COGNITION

The field of comparative cognition continues to emerge from several intersecting and interdisciplinary fields, including animal learning and behavior, comparative psychology, ethology, primatology, and developmental psychology. These fields have provided both methodological and empirical paradigms, and, along with philosophy, have helped to frame the theoretical issues for comparative cognition. These overlapping areas continue to provoke new directions for research and offer innovative and creative approaches to addressing fundamental questions related to basic psychological processes and their underlying mechanisms. Despite rapidly changing dramatic technological options currently available for assessing complex neural processing through a variety of imaging techniques, such as functional magnetic resonance imaging (fMRI) and positron emission tomography (PET), some perennial questions in psychology remain doggedly difficult to address empirically. From the ethological, biological, and comparative psychological sciences, we know that many species, including humans, have developed complex and dynamic social strategies, likely derived from selective pressures for species survival. How these social pressures may have influenced the cognitive strategies and abilities of species and individual animals is in itself a complex and often controversial component of the field of comparative cognition, and research has barely begun to frame the critical questions with which to address these hypotheses (Boyd & Richerson 1988).

The cognitive abilities necessary for a species to integrate and exploit a fluid social environment remains a broad question with many caveats. Some specified abilities, such as imitation, have a long history of study, whereas others such as "theory of mind" (Premack & Woodruff 1978b, Leslie 1987) are relatively recent. Tangential topics, including self-recognition and tool use in animals, provide additional directions for exploring nonhuman cognitive abilities and capacities, particularly with nonhuman primates, and offer tantalizing glimpses toward precursor capabilities that likely contributed to the evolution of cognition in early hominids.

Although worthy of study in their own right, current issues in animal cognition are invariably viewed in comparison with human intelligence and the array of processes that subserve human memory, attention, and perception, among others, including more ephemeral phenomena like intentionality and consciousness. Nonetheless, there is little question that recent findings have allowed for the emergence of richer and more definitive hypotheses, with broader implications for the ontogeny of cognitive abilities across all phyla. Dealing with these hypotheses will lead to further cross-fertilization between fields, innovation in the questions addressed, and additional methodological advances.

IMITATION

The study of imitation has long been controversial, with serious and continuing debate beginning at the turn of the century over several contentious issues. Three early concepts of imitation were represented in the writings of Romanes (1884), C. Lloyd Morgan (1900), and Thorndike (1898, 1911). Romanes, as an ardent Darwinian, viewed imitation as a capacity that one would expect to find across the psychological continuum, and, indeed, he wrote extensively about imitative processes that he believed could be observed even in bees (Romanes 1884). He defined imitation as requiring the "intelligent perception of the desirability of the modification on the part of certain individuals, who modify their actions accordingly," and he believed that these imitative acts required intentionality as well as high intelligence, representing precursors (to Romanes) of human imitative abilities (Galef 1988).

Morgan (1900), on the other hand, defined imitation as (*a*) instinctive, (*b*) purposeful and intentional, which he called reflective, with reflective behaviors having a defined goal based on observation of another individual engaged in the same behavior, or, finally, (*c*) intelligent imitation, which introduced a conscious component into subsequent occurrences of the behavior. Thus, Morgan proposed that imitationlike behavior observed in other species could be the result of innate, instinctively driven behaviors that could give the appearance of true imitation, but were based on other processes. Reflective imitation, however, was similar in some features to imitative behaviors observed in humans, and intelligent imitation allowed for later demonstrations of the behaviors, based on conscious, intentional reproduction.

Thorndike's (1898) definitions of imitation were ultimately based on empirical efforts to demonstrate the phenomenon with a number of nonhuman species, and failures by chickens, cats, dogs, and monkeys prompted him to cast doubt on the anecdotal instances put forth by his colleagues. He proposed that most instances cited as imitation in animals were likely based more on instinctive acts that were qualitatively different from true imitative learning as observed in humans (Galef 1988).

Nearly 100 years later, Galef (1988) provided a thorough and extensive roster of imitative learning term, which could be applied to behavioral phenomena. These included, in addition to imitation, intelligent imitation, reflective imitation, instinctive imitation, pseudo-imitation, true imitation, allelomimetic behavior, mimesis, protoculture, tradition, contagious behavior, social facilitation, local enhancement, matched dependent behavior, stimulus enhancement, vicarious conditioning, observational conditioning, copying, modeling, social learning, social transmission, and observational learning (Galef 1988). Although the definitions of Galef and others for each of these terms continue to be debated, most agree that imitation is on some level affected by social influences and some aspect of social learning. How then does one separate true imitation from other forms of social learning? This again becomes a debate over definitions and methodologies.

Of all aspects of social learning, three are most commonly associated with imitation: social facilitation, local enhancement, and stimulus enhancement. Local and stimulus enhancements were first introduced by Spence (1937) and later Thorpe (1956) and refer to instances in which an animal's attention is drawn to a particular stimulus or location during (or after) observation of another animal's interest in the same stimulus. Such enhanced attention increases the likelihood that the animal will perform behaviors already present in its repertoire that may, in turn, resemble the behaviors of the observed animal, either in the same physical location or during interaction with the same or a similar object(s). These behaviors, however, would not necessarily be considered imitative of the observed animal's behavior. Social facilitation was first introduced by Clayton (1978), who defined it as the result of increasing the likelihood of an animal performing a behavior already in its repertoire while in the presence of another animal already performing the behavior.

Attempts to define true imitation were made early in the history of comparative psychology by Thorndike (1898): "True imitation is the ability to learn an act solely from seeing the act performed by another individual." In a functional sense, his definition did not allow differentiation of imitation from other types of social learning. More recently, Visalberghi & Fragaszy (1990) elaborated further on Thorndike's original definition and provided additional clarification, as have Nagell et al (1993). The former classify a behavior as imitative if it is sufficiently similar to the behavior of the model, with sufficiency defined a priori, if observation of the model is necessary for its production, and, finally, if the behavior is novel for the observer, with novelty required in a dimension within which it is usually absent (Visalberghi & Fragaszy 1990). Though reference is often made to their definition, it is nevertheless difficult to explicitly define "sufficiently similar," although novel can be more readily defined operationally. Nagell et al (1993) argued that, in true imitation, the observer must not only perform the modeled behavior, but must do so toward the same goal. This distinction helps separate imitation from emulation, in which the observer learns something about the task (Nagell et al 1993).

From her work on imitation in rats, Heyes (1993) originally suggested that the difference between imitation and other forms of social learning was represented by what the animal learned as a result of its observations. Nonimitative social learning involves processes through which an organism learns about a given stimulus or event, whereas imitation involves processes whereby an animal learns about specific responses or behaviors. Imitation therefore implies, according to Heyes, that the animal understands only through observation that a particular behavior or action has a specific relationship with an outcome or is goal-directed. If an individual replicates a behavior without this understanding, both Heyes (1993) and Galef (1988) refer to such a behavioral response as a "copy." There are sufficient implications for these differences in definition, which continue to fuel the debate and encourage additional research on imitation in animals and humans. For example, if an animal "mirrors" another's behavior, what cognitive abilities are necessary? In social facilitation, and local and stimulus enhancement, the mirrored behavior may actually be innate and merely triggered by the presence of a stimulus or conspecific. When imitating a novel behavior, the animal must at least process novel visual input cross-modally into novel kinesthetic output (Zentall 1996). This cross-modal process may be a cognitive process unto itself (Heyes 1993), or it may require the ability to comprehend goal-directed behavior, to form representations, or to role-play and thus be aware of other's perspectives.

There have been several recent experiments designed to explore true imitation in nonhuman species. Zentall et al (1996) attempted to control for several nonimitative aspects of social learning by examining the ability of pigeons to imitate a conspecific's behavior of depressing a treadle in two possible ways. Demonstrator pigeons were trained to either peck or step on a treadle to obtain a food reward. Observer pigeons were then exposed to one type of demonstrator (peck or step). After 15 minutes in an adjacent operant chamber, the demonstrator was removed and the observer placed in the chamber with the available treadle. The behavior of the observer pigeon was recorded over the next 30 minutes. The authors argued that their design controlled for social facilitation as well as local enhancement, because any potential effects for local enhancement would be expected to impact both types of behavior (step or peck) equally. Social facilitation was unlikely because the demonstrator pigeon was removed during the test session and thus was not present to influence the experimental subject during testing. Stimulus enhancement, on the other hand, was more difficult to control. Earlier, Dawson & Foss (1965) proposed using a design in which a task could be completed more than one way. This approach is commonly referred to as the two-action method (Whiten & Ham 1992). Thus, in the Zentall et al study (1996), two different responses, pecking and stepping, could be used to obtain food. Assuming an equivalent likelihood of occurrence, if the pigeon was imitating the demonstrator, then the manner in which the pigeon depressed the treadle could reflect imitation of the demonstrator bird, just as a similar two-action task had been used to demonstrate imitation in rats previously (Heyes & Dawson 1990).

In previous studies, however, local enhancement had been controlled by the use of a duplicate-cage procedure (e.g. Warden & Jackson 1935; Zentall &

Levine 1972). This procedure entailed the use of two identical test chambers, placed side by side. If local enhancement was an influence, then it could be argued that the observer's attention should be drawn to the demonstrator's treadle and away from the treadle in the observer's chamber. In the Zentall et al (1996) study, the duplicate-cage procedure was modified. While the observer subject was in an adjacent chamber, it was subsequently tested in the demonstrator's chamber. One could argue that this change in procedure did not control for local enhancement, since the treadle used in the test was, in fact, the identical treadle used by the demonstrator bird. However, any effect of local enhancement should have impacted both experimental groups similarly, and thus the authors concluded that the birds could copy or imitate the topography of the demonstrator's response (Zentall et al 1996).

It should be no surprise that, among studies addressing imitation, nonhuman primate species would be selected for study as well (e.g. for an extensive discussion, see Visalberghi & Fragaszy 1990). Recently, Bugnyar and Huber (1997) used a similar two-action design during which marmosets (*Callithrix jacchus*), a New World monkey species, were required to either push or pull a pendulum door to get food from inside a box. The investigators exposed an observer monkey to one of two possible behaviors for one daily session over three days. Both behaviors had been previously acquired by the demonstrator animals to obtain food. Immediately after the day-3 demonstration, the observer animal was tested once per day for five days, using the same apparatus. Thus, Bugnyar and Huber's approach was similar to the Zentall et al (1996) paradigm, such that the demonstrator was removed from the original apparatus and the observer monkey was then tested in the same chamber. In this case, however, none of the observer monkeys demonstrated use of the particular strategy exhibited by the demonstrator animals. A control group, which was not a feature of the original Zentall et al (1996) study, included 10 animals not exposed to demonstrators. This group was tested to determine whether one of the two actions (pushing or pulling) was used more often and thus showed a higher baseline occurrence. It is interesting that none of the control animals utilized a "pull" strategy to obtain the food reward. Although some observer animals initially used this demonstrated strategy, it did not persist over the five days of testing, with the animals' responses converging towards the preferred mode seen in the control animals. The authors concluded that, although the observer animals did not persist at using the observed strategies, their results indicated that marmosets were capable of acquiring simple motor skills that were in some respects facilitated by observing conspecifics (Bugnay & Huber 1997).

In addition to studies of imitation in captivity, some innovative field studies have also been reported recently. Russon & Galdikas (1993, 1995) recounted observations of imitation in free-ranging rehabilitant orangutans (*Pongo pyg-*

maeus) at Tanjung Puting, Kalimantan, Borneo, where Galdikas has conducted long-term studies of orangutan behavior for over 25 years (e.g. Galdikas 1978, 1982, 1985, 1988, Galdikas & Vasey 1992). A central distinction in this study was the modified definition of imitation due to field limitations. Russon & Galdikas's operational criteria were that imitative actions were rare, their performance constituted an abrupt change in behavior immediately after the actions were demonstrated, or the imitator had not performed them recently (in the previous 10 minutes), despite the opportunity (Russon & Galdikas 1995). The primary focus of their study was to assess the selectivity of the models and the behavioral responses exhibited by the orangutans.

In general, they noted a preference for models with whom the observer had an established relationship. For human-reared orangutans, this preference was initially for human models and gradually transferred to other orangutans once these relationships had developed. Choice of the model also seemed to follow a dominance structure, with subordinates imitating more dominant animals. They proposed that this type of model specificity might be a possible explanation for the apparent discrepancy in imitative abilities between enculturated and nonenculturated chimpanzees, noted by Tomasello et al (1993). He and his colleagues studied the abilities of mother-reared chimpanzees, enculturated chimpanzees (those raised in close contact with humans, including rich immersion and experience with human cultural artifacts), and children. Three types of imitation tasks were devised, including simple, complex, and delayed imitative learning. For the simple and complex imitative tasks, mother-reared chimpanzees performed more poorly than both enculturated chimpanzees and children whose imitative abilities were comparable. However, the most striking difference was observed in the delayed imitation paradigm, where a 48-hour delay was imposed between the demonstration and an opportunity for a response. Under these conditions, enculturated chimpanzees outperformed mother-reared chimpanzees as well as human children. The enculturated chimpanzees demonstrated imitative behavior, including both the specific means and outcome threefold to fourfold as often as the children they tested (Tomasello et al 1993). Given some of the debate as to whether true imitation has been demonstrated in nonhumans (e.g. Heyes 1993, 1995; Tomasello 1990; Byrne & Tomasello 1995), these findings are clearly of interest.

Under nonsocial conditions, Whiten et al (1996) addressed imitation in a comparative task by using an artificial fruit-processing task. Both chimpanzees and human subjects were tested to determine similarities and differences in their methods for solving the novel task. The authors reasoned that if results from known imitators (humans) were compared with those from subjects whose imitative capacity had not been precisely characterized (chimpanzees), additional insights into the differences between the two species' imitative potential might be elucidated. Previous designs (Tomasello et al 1993, Custance et al 1995) had used arbitrary behaviors to test an animal's ability to imitate. Custance et al (1995) had previously proposed using a more naturalistic behavior such as food processing, which might increase the likelihood of eliciting imitation. The Whiten et al (1996) study was designed to address the latter. Their apparatus consisted of a two-action model that required either poke or twist responses on bolts affixed to a test box, in addition to either pull or turn responses on the handle of the box. Children of ages 2–4 years readily showed imitation of the two actions when tested. The results from young chimpanzees (mean age 4.5 years) were not as impressive, but were nevertheless imitative. Thus, even though "a twist could be done by holding the bolt in a precision grip using a finger and the thumb, a power grip wrapping fingers round it, or a chuck grip using several fingertips and thumb, or both bolts might be twisted simultaneously using two hands," (Whiten et al 1996), the critical actions performed on the bolts by the chimpanzees had the same result, and the authors concluded that they must have arisen through imitation (Whiten et al 1996).

Whiten et al (1996) also re-introduced another distinction in imitation terminology, termed emulation, originally proposed by Wood (1989). Emulation refers to instances in which an animal achieves the same end goal as the demonstrator, but does not follow the exact motor patterns that it has observed. In this sense, the observer may understand the end goal, yet does not replicate the demonstrator's actions as the means to attain the goal. The similarity of the two alternatives (twist/pull) for the barrel on Whiten's apparatus may have confounded their results somewhat, since execution of one alternative could easily facilitate occurrence of the other. However, the authors suggest that, at more primitive levels of cultural evolution, such differences might be easily corrupted by chance slippages, trial-and-error learning, or both within potential nonexclusive responses (as in the case of the barrel manipulation of Whiten's apparatus) and that such fidelity of response(s) will occur only when a species becomes as thoroughly cultural and conventional in their imitative abilities as are humans (Whiten et al 1996).

TOOL USE

Tools offer a natural advantage in imitation studies because they often facilitate the presentation of novel tasks (Whiten et al 1996); conversely, the study of imitation can also lend itself to the study of tool use in nonhuman animals. If an animal is capable of imitating a behavior by visual input only and, by observing the behavior, is able to understand the consequences of that behavior, then it should be able functionally to replicate the behavior in a goal-oriented manner. Because, as Passingham (1982) noted, monkeys are not habitual tool users and because tool use is still fairly rare among nonprimate mammals,

Whiten et al (1996) suggested that the use of tools to test for imitative ability may be inherently biased against the animal. However, such tasks have been often used to examine imitation in nonhuman species, particularly with chimpanzees (Nagell et al 1993; Custance & Whiten et al 1995; Whiten et al 1996), and this approach seems quite appropriate given the wealth of observations and cultural diversity of tool use in wild-chimpanzee populations (e.g. Goodall 1964, 1970, 1986; Kortlandt 1986; Matsuzawa 1994; McGrew 1974, 1992). Tool use has nevertheless been observed in a wide range of animals (Beck 1980, Berthelet & Chavaillon 1993) and is particularly diverse and innovative among wild chimps (Boesch & Boesch 1984a,b, 1990; Inoue-Nakamura & Matsuzawa 1997; Nishida & Haraiwa 1982; Nishida 1987; Sakura & Matsuzawa 1991; Sugiyama 1993, 1994; Sugiyama et al 1988; Yamakoshi & Sugiyama 1995). In fact, it has been recently argued that tool use in chimpanzees appears to have a basis in cultural transmission by imitation, among other potential types of social learning, although this view also has its critics (e.g. see Heyes 1993).

Among other studies of tool use in nonhuman primates, Visalberghi and her colleagues (e.g. Fragaszy & Visalberghi 1989; Visalberghi & Limongelli 1994) have conducted numerous investigations of the abilities of capuchin monkeys to use tools and have also contributed evidence (with chimpanzees) demonstrating understanding of the causal effects of tool use. Their innovative paradigm was similar to the approach of Visalberghi & Trinca (1989) in which a horizontal tube was presented to the subject, and the monkey was then provided a tool (a stick) that could be inserted into the tube to push out small pieces of candy. The capuchins were also able to modify the tool (a stick with a small crosspiece inserted at the end, which had to be removed for the tool to be usable), to obtain the food reward.

In a more recent study, Visalberghi & Limongelli (1994) used the same tool task and then modified the apparatus for a second experiment. In experiment 2, a wide hole was drilled in the center of the clear tube, and a small trap was attached, creating a "t-tube". If the monkeys had understood the causal relationship between using the stick and the new trap, they should have modified their behavior so as not to push the candy into the inaccessible trap. Four female capuchins served as subjects, all of which had successfully completed the plain tube task. With the modified t-tube, only one monkey was able to complete the task without losing the food reward. The other three demonstrated increased attention to the movement of the food reward during pushing, as well as "cautious behavior" (Visalberghi & Limongelli 1994), as the candy edged closer to the location of the trap. Four additional control conditions were completed with the successful animal, in an attempt to determine whether she was solving the task based on a perceptually based learned rule or more cognitively through some form of comprehension of the cause-effect relation between the use of the stick and the trap. In one condition, the tube was inverted so that the trap was now on top, rendering it inconsequential. In a second condition, the monkey was presented with the original clear tube without a trap. During conditions 3 and 4, the subject's performances with both an opaque tube with a trap and one without a trap were compared. Under all four control conditions, the capuchin avoided pushing the reward toward the trap even though the trap either posed no danger in terms of losing the reward or was simply no longer present. These results are consistent with a rule-based solution (e.g. "Insert the stick into the end farthest from the reward") (Visalberghi & Limongelli 1994), and such over-generalization of tool use behaviors that were successfully used in the initial experiment is also consistent with previous findings and may have adaptive importance (Visalberghi 1990, Visalberghi & Limongelli 1994).

The results also suggest that capuchins, although impressive tool users, lacked an understanding of the causal effects of the tools they used; they were able to learn how to use a tool but failed to understand how the tool actually functioned (Visalberghi & Limongelli 1994). Thus Visalberghi & Limongelli (1994) suggest caution when interpreting successful completion of a task by different species, since similar results may be obtained by very different underlying processes.

In a follow-up study, Limongelli et al (1995) conducted a similar experiment with chimpanzees (*Pan troglodytes*). The chimpanzees were first tested with a clear tube as in the previous monkey study and then presented a t-tube containing a trap. All five animals tested were able to solve the initial plain tube task, although the youngest required one instance of modeling by the experimenter. When the t-tube was introduced and the animals allowed a maximum of 150 trials to demonstrate their understanding of the contingency between the use of the stick and the trap, two of the chimps readily solved the task at a performance level significantly above chance. These two chimpanzees continued to a third test, during which the hole to the trap (formerly centrally located in the tube) was relocated closer to one end of the tube. If the chimps were using a rule-based strategy similarly to the capuchins, they should have failed this version of the task, because inserting the stick into the end of the tube farthest from the reward would result in the candy being pushed into the trap. Both chimpanzees, however, were able to correctly solve the task despite the modifications. It is important to note that this change in the design was also repeated with the capuchin from the previous study, and she was unable to solve the task correctly.

Additional analyses were completed to determine whether the successful chimpanzees were using some type of representational or anticipatory strategy. To address these issues, the number of single stick insertions was compared with the number of multiple stick insertions, with the assumption that a greater number of single successful insertions is reflective of a representational strategy, because a correct initial insertion of the stick would suggest that the chimpanzee was covertly determining the correct side from which to insert the stick by using only the visual cues of the location of the candy and its relationship to the trap. One animal always performed single insertions during the initial t-tube task and 27 of 30 times in test 2, suggesting use of a representational strategy (Limongelli et al 1995). Regardless of the strategy used, success indicated some level of understanding of the causal nature of the tool/trap relationship, unlike the results with capuchins, which showed no comprehension of the causality of their actions. However, the performance of the chimpanzees, although sufficient to complete the task, was in contrast to findings with children during which more rapid comprehension of causality was demonstrated (Limongelli et al 1995).

MIRROR SELF-RECOGNITION IN ANIMALS

The flexibility and understanding of causality of tool use behavior in chimpanzees reflects the capacity for complex problem-solving abilities, with questions naturally arising as to the potential adaptive significance of such learning potential in the great apes. Jolly (1966) first proposed the possibility, with similar ideas elaborated on in Humphrey's (1976) classic essay, that pressures associated with complex social living have selected for a set of characteristics that are clearly operative in humans and may also be available in the social cognition domain of all or some of the extant great ape species (Byrne & Whiten 1991, Humphrey 1976, Jolly 1966). Among these characteristics are the ability to appreciate the perspective of another individual, sometimes referred to as theory of mind (Premack & Woodruff 1978b, Byrne & Whiten 1991) or attribution of mental states, as well as the ability to recognize oneself in a mirror, which has been proposed also to reflect a state of self-awareness (e.g. Gallup 1970, 1975, 1982, 1991; Mitchell 1993).

Attributional capacities, which have been suggested as potentially available to the chimpanzee, have far-reaching implications for what we have long considered to be an exclusive domain of human uniqueness. But before one can take the perspective of another, one must understand one's own self-image, as reflected in a mirror for example. Mirror self-recognition or the "mark test" (Gallup 1970), as it has come to be called, has historically been touted as the benchmark technique for assessing self-recognition and, potentially, self-awareness. (Gallup 1982, 1991; Povinelli 1987; Parker et al 1994). Gallup (1970) first demonstrated that chimpanzees were able to recognize themselves in a mirror after being marked with vibrant red dye while asleep, and afterwards, when given access to mirrors, the animals engaged in a variety of self-directed behaviors, including using the mirror to investigate visually inaccessible areas. This differs from other mirror-mediated behaviors such as object discrimination, spatial locating, and mirror-guided reaching, because some animals have been successful with these types of mirror-mediated tasks but have failed to exhibit mirror self-recognition (e.g. Pepperberg et al 1995, with a parrot; Povinelli 1989, testing an elephant). However, a wide range of primate species in particular have been tested with the mark test, and the results include successful performance by at least one member of all four great ape species (chimpanzees, bonobos, orangutans, and gorillas) and failure by the numerous monkey species tested, including rhesus, stumptail, longtail, pigtail, Japanese and Tonkean macaques, mandrills, olive and Hamadryas baboons, and tufted and white-faced capuchins [but see discussion below of recent work by Hauser et al (1995)]. Although the debate continues as to specifically what success on the mark test really measures or reflects in terms of cognitive abilities, the data still overwhelmingly support a division between the great apes and humans versus other species for performance on this task. On one hand, only the great apes and humans have demonstrated the ability to use mirrored information, which is suggestive of self-recognition, and, in contrast, no other species, including virtually all monkeys tested under the original criteria proposed by Gallup (1970), have shown comparable behavioral responses (Anderson & Gallup 1997, Povinelli et al 1993). This includes a lack of definitive self-directed behaviors compared with control baseline measures of spontaneous behavior with or without mirrors.

The most recent debate in the mirror recognition literature revolves around the findings of Hauser et al (1995), who reported self-directed behaviors suggestive of mirror self-recognition in cotton-top tamarins. These authors compared the behavioral responses of this small New World species to their mirror images after the authors had dyed the tufts of hair on top of the animals' heads (which are normally white) either bright pink, blue, purple, green, or some combination of colors. Six tamarins were given 3–4 weeks of mirror exposure before the dye test, two were given short mirror exposure of 20 minutes, and one subject received no mirror exposure before testing. After marking occurred, only individuals with long exposure (3–4 weeks) were observed to touch their dyed hair while looking in the mirror. Individuals with minimal or no mirror exposure were never observed to touch their heads while looking in the mirror, nor were group members ever observed touching their heads after exposure to a single individual whose hair had been dyed. Hauser et al argued that these findings suggested that cotton-top tamarins with extensive mirror exposure show evidence of self-recognition as measured by the mark test. They also proposed that previous failures to show such self-recognition in non-ape species might be a function of a lack of mark salience. In addition, for many primate species, direct eye contact and staring are highly aggressive behaviors, and thus looking into a mirror may cause aversion. Prior methods of marking monkeys also may not have been salient enough to overcome this pre-disposition to avoid looking in the mirror (Hauser et al 1995).

Anderson & Gallup (1997) have raised several issues with the Hauser et al study. They have argued that the crucial control period after marking the animals before the introduction of the mirror was not adequately described or quantified in the study with the cotton-tops. This period of observation, which has traditionally been seen as a necessary procedure in the mark test paradigm (Gallup 1970), provides critical observations of baseline behaviors directed toward the mark, which are later compared with the animals' behavior in the presence of the mirror. In addition, necessary qualitative responses previously reported in mirror studies with chimpanzee subjects were similarly not reported in the Hauser et al report. For example, in numerous other studies, chimpanzees have been observed sniffing their fingers or visually inspecting their fingers after touching the marked areas on their bodies that were visually inaccessible, once they have again been given access to mirrors. Hauser et al (1995) reported that the monkeys touched only their own heads, with no subsequent investigation by any of the other tamarin subjects. Anderson and Gallup (1997) also took issue with Hauser's justification of procedural changes on the basis of mark salience, citing studies by Anderson (1984) and Benhar et al (1975), that have previously investigated the significance of mark salience. For example, Anderson (1984) demonstrated that stumptail macaques responded to visible marks on various parts of their bodies but showed no responses to inaccessible marks on their heads. Therefore, Anderson & Gallup (1997) suggested that the lack of response by the tamarins in the Hauser et al (1995) study to marks on the heads of their subjects' cage mates also provided evidence for the lack of mark salience in this study. Finally, Anderson & Gallup (1997) questioned the reliability and validity of the behaviors termed "mirror-guided," as Hauser et al (1995) reported them. Although interobserver reliability was established for the observations, the tamarins' positions within the cage (relative to the mirror) when these observations were made were not reported. Without such information, questions remain as to whether the monkeys were using the mirror to monitor any responses toward the marks or serendipitously looking toward the mirror while touching their heads.

In response to these criticisms, however, Hauser & Kralik (1997) replied that they believed the controlled version of the mirror dye test that they implemented was sufficient to demonstrate mirror-mediated self-directed behavior and that, in contrast to the specific criticism of Anderson & Gallup (1997) regarding mark salience, the procedural changes they used with the tamarins (marking the prominent white hair tuft, instead of brow ridges and the top of the opposite ear, as in the Gallup (1970) procedure) were instead a direct test of salience and a primary component of their experimental design (Hauser et al 1995). They also proposed that prolonged staring, as demonstrated in their experiment, is related to self-recognition, and that it was unlikely that the observed staring was related to something else in the environment (as suggested by Anderson and Gallup). Finally, Hauser & Kralik (1997) emphasized that it is now appropriate to pursue the question of specifically what cognitive functions might actually be tested with the mirror mark test and that it remains unclear which of these abilities may be the most significant in distinguishing between species. It is possible, as suggested by Heyes (1994) that the mirror test is simply invalid or inappropriate as a metric for self-recognition altogether (Hauser & Kralik 1997). Undoubtedly, additional experiments from several laboratories testing a variety of species will be forthcoming to address these contentious but intriguing issues.

Both methodological issues and the requisite cognitive abilities that may impact on a particular species' capacity for passing the mark test will likely continue to fuel the current debate. Of the great ape species that have demonstrated evidence for mirror self-recognition, chimpanzees' abilities have been investigated in the greatest detail, with numerous studies completed over the past three decades. Until recently, most of the archival literature was based on testing of a fairly limited number of animals and provided evidence of self-recognition at a fixed point of maturity, with the youngest animals described by Gallup (1970) as juveniles.

The first developmental study that focused on the emergence of self-recognition was reported recently by Lin et al (1992), concluding that chimpanzees can, under some conditions, demonstrate self-recognition abilities by about age 2.5 years, at least as measured by the mark test. Using a larger cross-sectional population of captive animals that were housed and raised under different conditions than the population tested by Lin and associates (1992), Povinelli et al (1993) also addressed the possible developmental emergence of self-recognition in chimpanzees and came to a significantly different conclusion about both the age at which chimps were able to definitely pass the mark test and the "loss" of such capacities in some adult animals. Whereas children typically demonstrate mirror self-recognition between 18 and 24 months of age, when tested by methods which are analogous to the mark test (Amsterdam 1972, Bertenthal & Fischer 1978, Lewis & Brook-Gunn 1979, Schulman & Kaplowitz 1977), mirror-naive chimpanzees in the Povinelli study, which included 105 animals ranging in age from 10 months to 40 years, began showing self-directed behaviors within the first 10–20 minutes of mirror exposure. However, self-recognition, with the mark test as the standard, was observed only in chimpanzees between the ages of 4 1/2 and 8 years of age. Within the population tested, the greatest percentage of individuals demonstrating self-recognition was even older, with 75% of the chimps that passed the mark test being between the ages of 8 and 15 years. Interestingly, Povinelli and his colleagues (1993) also found evidence suggesting either a "decline in self-recognition ability between 16 and 20 years of age or a critical-period effect," (Povinelli et al 1993). These findings were supported even after extended exposure of 20 days of mirror presentation for some animals. It is noteworthy that the purported decline in self-recognition ability, although reported as a group or population effect, was not observed in an individual animal. It would be interesting to see whether a longitudinal study of individual chimpanzees demonstrating self-recognition would show a decrease in this ability over time, for a given chimpanzee.

The Povinelli et al (1993) study also found no differences between mother-raised and peer-raised chimpanzees, but, given the observed differences in a small number of enculturated versus mother-reared chimpanzees with other abilities such as imitation (Tomasello et al 1993), it is likely that similar differences in human-raised and chimpanzee-raised (either by mother or peer) chimpanzees would also be exhibited during mirror exposure, the mark test, or both. Similarly, the differences in environmental rearing strategies between the Lin et al (1992) and Povinelli et al (1993) studies could readily account for age-related differences in mirror-related capacities and, thus, the reported differences in the emergence of self-recognition between the two study populations.

In the Povinelli et al (1993) population, with respect to the delayed capacities for passing the mark test and particularly the failure to exhibit such behaviors among the adult population, chimpanzees had been immersed for a longer period of time under housing conditions that likely did not include environmental enrichment and access to manipulable objects, nesting materials, etc. This study also may have included a larger proportion of chimpanzees who were reared under nonsocial conditions, including possible complete social isolation. In contrast, the chimpanzees tested by Lin and his colleagues were socially reared, including constant peer interaction and a program of human social interaction and including environmental enrichment with toys, games and other activities involving joint attention and positive socialization with their human caregivers.

More recently, chimpanzees have been tested for self-recognition by using three unusual types of mirrors, including ones with convex and concave surfaces, as well as triptych mirrors (Kitchen et al 1996). First, each of the six female chimpanzee subjects was tested with a regular mirror, and all successfully passed the mark test. During subsequent tests with the distorting mirrors, the animals' behaviors in response to the different mirror types were observed, but the chimps were not marked as in the Gallup (1970) study. Kitchen et al (1996) found that the animals did not exhibit any type of social behaviors toward the images they observed when the three different types of mirrors were introduced, and these authors also observed a decrease in the chimpanzees' interactions towards the mirror images over time. However, the authors did report evidence for self-referenced behaviors by the subjects with all three mirror types. Although the experimental manipulations used in their study did not allow the animals to have a clearly reflected image of themselves such that self-recognition based on feature cues was possible (because the mirrors distorted these cues), contingent-movement relationships could still be utilized as cues (Kitchen et al 1996; also see Mitchell 1993). If an understanding of these contingencies is accepted as evidence for some level of self-recognition (Mitchell 1993), then from the Kitchen et al (1996) findings, it follows that chimpanzees are able to abstract their self-image on some level to compensate for the distortion.

Although numerous researchers have utilized several different methodologies to assess self-recognition, passing the mark test continues to be most widely accepted as evidence for self-recognition and, in turn, some facet of self-awareness. But as noted previously, precisely what the mark test measures and the resulting implications for self-awareness and, subsequently, theory of mind remain unresolved (Gallup et al 1995; Heyes 1994, 1995, 1996; Mitchell 1993, 1995; Povinelli et al 1997).

ATTRIBUTIONAL CAPACITIES IN NONHUMANS

Premack & Woodruff (1978a), mentioned previously for their studies examining problem solving in apes, were the first to experimentally attempt to address what they termed "theory of mind" (ToM) in a nonhuman species, with the chimpanzee Sarah as their subject. Since their seminal work, studies of attributional capacities have come to represent a burgeoning literature in the human developmental field (e.g. Baron-Cohen et al 1985; Chandler et al 1989; Flavell 1986, 1988; Gopnik & Graf 1988; Leslie 1987; Perner & Wimmer 1985; Wellman 1990; Wimmer et al 1988; Wimmer & Perner 1983), with fewer investigations of these phenomena in primates until more recently (Boysen et al 1997; Cheney & Seyfarth 1990a,, 1992; Povinelli 1993; Povinelli et al 1990, 1992; Povinelli et al 1991; Kummer et al 1996). As noted earlier, Premack & Woodruff (1978a) presented Sarah, an adult female chimpanzee, with a series of videotaped sequences depicting a caregiver experiencing some type of "problem." For example, one scenario showed the caregiver without a coat, shivering violently while standing next to an unplugged portable heater.

As Sarah watched the videotaped sequence, the video recorder was paused just when the actor would have likely come up with a solution. Sarah was then presented with several photographs and was required to choose the one that best depicted a viable solution. In the case described, Sarah chose the photograph that showed the heater plugged in, inferring that, subsequently, heat would be provided, and the caregiver could warm himself. Of the eight problems presented on videotape, Sarah was able to choose correctly for seven problems (Premack & Woodruff 1978a). The authors interpreted these findings as possible evidence for the ability of chimpanzees to attribute mental states to other individuals, including humans and possibly other chimpanzees. To successfully solve the task, Sarah needed to interpret the scenario from the viewpoint of the caregiver, first determining what the caregiver was attempting to accomplish and then choosing a solution that would provide a remedy for the depicted difficulty of the person.

Analogously, role playing in children has also been interpreted as an indicator of theory of mind (Povinelli 1993). Experimental attempts to address role taking in nonverbal animals were originally addressed by Mason & Hollis (1962), using rhesus monkeys. Mason & Hollis designed an apparatus that positioned two monkeys across from each other, separated by a barrier. One monkey, designated as the "operator," could pull one of two handles, which controlled two sets of food trays, each of which would extend identical food dishes towards each of the animals. However, only one set of the food trays was baited on a given trial, and the operator animal did not have visual access to the trays. Therefore, the operator monkey had no means for determining which tray actually contained the food and thus which handle to pull. The observer monkey, on the other hand, had full view of the trays, and thus it was up to the two animals to work cooperatively, through some type of gestural or indicating behaviors from the observer monkey and subsequent understanding of the communicative function of these behaviors by the operator animal. Eventually, the animals were able to work together, with the observer indicating which tray contained food and the operator then able to select the correct handle to pull, which brought a food dish within reach of each monkey. During a second phase of the experiment in which the animals' roles were reversed, their performance dropped to chance, indicating that neither monkey really understood the relative contribution of the other to their previous and successful cooperative efforts.

Povinelli et al (1992) repeated this experiment with two chimpanzees first serving as operators, with the informant role filled by an experimenter and the other two chimpanzees first tested as informants, while the experimenter performed the operator's role. This required the operator chimpanzees to indicate the correct location of the baited food trays to the experimenter by spontaneously learning to point or gesture towards the correct dishes, and it required the operator chimpanzees to pull the correct handle corresponding to the food dishes to which the experimenter was pointing. After successful cooperation between the chimps and the experimenter, the respective social roles were reversed. Three of the four chimpanzees tested showed immediate evidence of their understanding of their new social role, performing above chance levels.

Povinelli et al (1990) modified these procedures slightly to determine whether the chimpanzees were able to comprehend the relationship between the different knowledge states of seeing versus knowing. In this study, two human observers participated, with each chimpanzee tested individually. Both experimenters were initially present, and then one experimenter (the "guesser") left the room while the knowledgeable experimenter (the "knower") hid food under one of four opaque cups that had been placed behind a low barrier in front of the chimp. The subject therefore was able to see that the experimenter was hiding food somewhere among the cups, but was unable to determine, because of the barrier, under precisely which cup. Once the cup was baited, the second experimenter re-entered the room. During each trial, each of the two experimenters pointed to a different cup. Thus, the chimpanzee had to determine which person was providing a "knowledgeable" cue that would allow them to select the correct cup containing the food and which person was simply guessing. The results suggested that, within the first five days of testing, four of the five chimpanzees tested were able to reliably discriminate between which experimenter was guessing and which actually knew the correct location of the food reward, with the fifth subject showing reliable discrimination later in testing. Although one possible explanation for the results was that the animals were able to recognize or comprehend the knowledge state of each experimenter, because the person who had left the room had not witnessed the hiding event and thus did not have visual access to that information, a more parsimonious explanation was also possible. The chimpanzees could have been simply relying on behavioral cues and the subsequent rule, "pick the person who stays in the room," without their necessarily attributing a knowledge state to either of the experimenters. To address this hypothesis, the procedures were modified slightly such that the "guessing" observer remained in the room, but covered his head with a bag to prevent him from seeing where the food was being hidden. Although it can be argued that this change in methodology introduced another confound by merely changing the behavioral cue ("pick the person who does not have a bag on his head"), Povinelli et al (1990) argued that these results suggested that chimpanzees, different from rhesus macaques (Povinelli et al 1991) and long-tailed macaques (Kummer et al 1996), were able to comprehend the perception-knowledge relationship between the two experimenters and that chimpanzees are thus able to model the visual perspectives of others.

Subsequently, Povinelli et al (1993) reported that the ability to comprehend perception-knowledge relationships was a developmental milestone in human children and emerged between 3 and 4 years of age. To assess the validity of this methodology, Povinelli & deBlois (1992) tested 3- and 4-year-old children by using an apparatus similar to that used by the chimpanzees in the earlier studies. In their study with young children, Povinelli & deBlois found evidence to support the validity of the measures used with chimpanzees, with most of the 4-year-olds correct on 7 of 10 discrimination trials between the two experimenters; only one 3-year-old met the same criterion. However, several ambiguities are worth noting in light of the previous discussion on self-recognition as an indicator of self-awareness that may be among a constellation of abilities, which include theory of mind. The ability of children to successfully complete the perception-knowledge paradigm does not emerge until between 3 and 4 years of age, yet infants as young as 18–24 months are capable of demonstrating mirror self-recognition (e.g. Amsterdam 1972, Bertenthal & Fischer 1978). This discrepancy supports the hypothesis that possessing mirror self-recognition or perhaps even self-awareness does not, in turn, indicate attributional capacities. However, these abilities may be viewed as empirical markers, indicative and necessary for the eventual emergence or development of a theory of mind (Povinelli 1993).

SUMMARY

The four areas of study in comparative cognition briefly outlined in this overview represent lively areas of current debate and discussion and should readily bring to mind a variety of directions for future investigations with both humans and nonhuman species. Despite the difficulties associated with implementing more rigorous empirical approaches to the study of topics such as self-awareness, "true" imitation, and, most notably, attributional capacities of other animals, there are methods and paradigms that offer the opportunity to experimentally explore these nonobservable behaviors beyond the anecdote. Psychology as an interdisciplinary field, with greater theoretical depth and a firmer footing than even a decade ago, appears to have developed the requisite philosophical maturity and sophistication to move forward in addressing the same types of elusive phenomena that prompted psychology to emerge as the new science of behavior over a century ago.

> Visit the *Annual Reviews home page* at
> http://www.AnnualReviews.org.

Literature Cited

Amsterdam BK. 1972. Mirror self-image reactions before age two. *Dev. Psychol.* 5:297–305

Anderson JR. 1984. The development of self-recognition: a review. *Dev. Psychobiol.* 17:35–49

Anderson JR, Gallup GG Jr. 1997. Self-recognition in Saguinus? A critical essay. *Anim. Behav.* 54:1563–67

Baron-Cohen S, Leslie AM, Frith U. 1985. Does the autistic child have a "theory of mind"? *Cognition* 21:37–46

Beck BB. 1980. *Animal Tool Behavior.* New York: Garland. 307 pp.

Benhar EE, Carlton PL, Samuel D. 1975. A search for mirror-image reinforcement and self-recognition in the baboon. In *Contemporary Primatology: Proc. 5th Int. Congr. Primatol.*, ed. S Kondo, M Kawai, S Ehara, pp. 202–8. New York: Karger

Bertenthal BI, Fischer KW. 1978. Development of self-recognition in the infant. *Dev. Psychol.* 14:44–50

Berthelet A, Chavaillon J. 1993. *The Use of Tools by Human and Non-Human Primates.* Oxford, UK: Oxford Univ. Press. 424 pp.

Boesch C, Boesch H. 1984a. Possible causes of sex differences in the use of natural hammers by wild chimpanzees. *J. Hum. Evol.* 13:415–40

Boesch C, Boesch H. 1984b. Mental maps in wild chimpanzees: an analysis of hammer transports for nut cracking. *Primates* 25: 160–70

Boesch C, Boesch H. 1990. Tool use and tool making in wild chimpanzees. *Folia Primatol.* 54:86–99

Boyd R, Richerson PJ. 1988. An evolutionary model of social learning: the effects of spatial and temporal variation. In *Social Learning: Psychological and Biological Perspectives*, pp. 29–48. Hillsdale, NJ: Erlbaum

Boysen ST, Kuhlmeier VA, Kuzdak NE. 1997. *Attribution of ignorance by chimpanzees.* Presented at Annu. Meet. Am. Psychol. Assoc., Chicago, IL

Bugnyar T, Huber L. 1997. Push or pull: an experimental study on imitation in marmosets. *Anim. Behav.* 54:817–31

Byrne RW, Tomasello M. 1995. Do rats ape? *Anim. Behav.* 50:1417–20

Byrne RW, Whiten A. 1991. *Machiavellian Intelligence: Social Expertise and the Evolution of Intellect in Monkeys, Apes and Humans.* Oxford, UK: Oxford Univ. Press. 413 pp.

Chandler M, Fritz AS, Hala S. 1989. Small scale deceit: deception marker of 2-, 3- and 4-year-olds' early theories of mind. *Child Dev.* 60:1263–77

Cheney DL, Seyfarth RM. 1990a. Attending to behaviour versus attending to knowledge: examining monkeys' attribution of mental states. *Anim. Behav.* 40:742–53

Cheney DL, Seyfarth RM. 1990b. *How Monkeys See the World.* Chicago: Univ. Chicago Press. 377 pp.

Cheney DL, Seyfarth RM. 1992. Characterizing the mind of another species. *Behav. Brain Sci.* 15:172–79

Clayton DA. 1978. Socially facilitated behavior. *Q. Rev. Biol.* 53:373–91

Custance DM, Whiten A, Bard KA. 1995. Can young chimpanzees imitate arbitrary actions? Hayes and Hayes (1952) revisited. *Behavior* 132:839–58

Dawson BV, Foss BM. 1965. The use of social information in the problem-solving of orangutans and human children. *J. Comp. Psychol.* 109:301–20

Flavell JH. 1986. The development of children's knowledge about the appearance-reality distinction. *Am. Psychol.* 41: 418–25

Flavell JH. 1988. The development of children's knowledge about the mind: from cognition connections to mental representations. In *Developing Theories of Mind*, ed. JW Astington, PL Harris, DR Olson, pp. 244–71. Cambridge, UK: Cambridge Univ. Press

Fragaszy DM, Visalberghi E. 1989. Social influences on the acquisition of tool-using behaviors in tufted capuchin monkeys (Cebus apella). *J. Comp. Psychol.* 103:159–70

Galdikas BMF. 1978. Orangutans and hominid evolution. In *Essays Presented to Sutan Takdir Alisjahbana on his Seventieth Birthday*, ed. S Udin, pp. 287–329. Jakarta: Dian Rakyat

Galdikas BMF. 1982. Orang-utan tool-use in Tanjung Puting Reserve, Central Borneo (Kalimantan Tengah). *J. Hum. Evol.* 10: 19–33

Galdikas BMF. 1985. Orangutan sociality at Tanjung Puting. *Am. J. Primatol.* 9: 101–19

Galdikas BMF. 1988. Orangutan diet, range, and activity at Tanjung Puting, Central Borneo. *Int. J. Primatol.* 9:1–35

Galdikas BMF, Vasey P. 1992. Why are orangutans so smart? Ecological and social hypotheses. In *Social Processes and Mental Abilities in Non-human Primates*, ed. FD Burton, pp. 183–224. Lewiston, NY: Edward Mellon

Galef B. 1988. Imitation in animals: history, definition, and interpretation of data from the psychological laboratory. In *Social Learning, Psychological and Biological Perspectives*, ed. TR Zentall, BG Galef Jr, pp. 3–28. Hillsdale, NJ: Lawrence Erlbaum

Gallup GG Jr. 1970. Chimpanzees: self-recognition. *Science* 167:86–87

Gallup GG Jr. 1975. Towards an operational definition of self-awareness. In *Socioecology and Psychology of Primates*, ed. RH Tuttle, pp. 309–41. The Hague: Mouton

Gallup GG Jr. 1982. Self-awareness and the emergence of mind in primates. *Am. J. Primatol.* 2:237–48

Gallup GG Jr. 1991. Toward a comparative psychology of self-awareness: species limitations and cognitive consequences. In *The Self: an Interdisciplinary Approach,* ed. GR Goethals, J Strauss, pp. 121–35. New York: Springer

Gallup GG Jr, Povinelli DJ, Suarez SD, Anderson JR, Lethmate J, Menzel EW Jr. 1995. Further reflections on self-recognition in primates. *Anim. Behav.* 50: 1525–32

Goodall J. 1964. Tool-using and aimed throwing in a community of free-living chimpanzees. *Nature* 201:1264–66

Goodall J. 1970. Tool using in primates and other vertebrates. In *Advances in the Study of Behavior,* ed. D Lehrman, R Hinde, E Shaw, pp. 195–249. New York: Academic

Goodall J. 1986. *The Chimpanzees of Gombe: Patterns of Behavior.* Cambridge, MA: Harvard Univ. Press. 673 pp.

Gopnik A, Graf P. 1988. Knowing how you know: young children's ability to identify and remember the sources of their beliefs. *Child Dev.* 59:1366–71

Hauser MD, Kralik J. 1997. Life beyond the mirror: a reply to Anderson & Gallup. *Anim. Behav.* 54:1568–71

Hauser MD, Kralik J, Bott-Mahan C, Garrett M, Oser J. 1995. Self-recognition in primates: phylogeny and the salience of species-typical traits. *Proc. Natl. Acad. Sci. USA* 92:10811–14

Heyes CM. 1993. Imitation, culture and cognition. *Anim. Behav.* 46:999–1010

Heyes CM. 1994. Reflections on self-recognition in primates. *Anim. Behav.* 47: 909–19

Heyes CM. 1995. Self-recognition in primates: further reflections create a hall of mirrors. *Anim. Behav.* 50:1533–42

Heyes CM. 1996. Self-recognition in primates: irreverence, irrelevance and irony. *Anim. Behav.* 51:470–73

Heyes CM, Dawson GR. 1990. A demonstration of observational learning using a bidirectional control. *Q. J. Exp. Psychol.* 42: 59–71

Humphrey NK. 1976. The social function of intellect. In *Growing Points in Ethology,* ed. PPG Bateson, RA Hinde, pp. 303–17. Cambridge, UK: Cambridge Univ. Press

Inoue-Nakamura N, Matsuzawa T. 1997. Development of stone tool use by wild chimpanzees (Pan troglodytes). *J. Comp. Psychol.* 111:159–73

Jolly A. 1966. Lemur social behavior and primate intelligence. *Science* 153:501–6

Kitchen A, Denton D, Brent L. 1996. Self-recognition and abstraction abilities in the common chimpanzee studied with distorting mirrors. *Proc. Natl. Acad. Sci. USA* 93:7405–8

Kortlandt A. 1986. The use of tools by wild-living chimpanzees and earliest hominids. *J. Hum. Evol.,* 15:77–132

Kummer H, Anzenberger G, Hemelrijk CK. 1996. Hiding and perspective taking in long-tailed macaques (Macaca fascicularis). *J. Comp. Psychol.* 110:97–102

Leslie AM. 1987. Pretense and representation in infancy: the origins of theory of mind. *Psychol. Rev.* 94:412–26

Lewis M, Brooks-Gunn J. 1979. *Social Cognition and the Acquisition of Self.* New York: Plenum. 296 pp.

Limongelli L, Boysen ST, Visalberghi E. 1995. Comprehension of cause-effect relations in a tool-using task by chimpanzees (Pan troglodytes). *J. Comp. Psychol.* 109: 18–26

Lin AC, Bard KA, Anderson JR. 1992. Development of self-recognition and self-conscious emotions. *Child Dev.* 106: 120–27

Mason WA, Hollis JH. 1962. Communication between young rhesus monkeys. *Anim. Behav.* 10:211–21

Matsuzawa T. 1994. Field experiments on use of stone tools by chimpanzees in the wild. In *Chimpanzee Cultures,* ed. R Wrangham, WC McGrew, F de Waal, P Heltne, pp. 351–70. Cambridge, MA: Harvard Univ. Press

McGrew WC. 1974. Tool use by wild chimpanzees in feeding upon driver ants. *J. Hum. Evol.* 3:501–8

McGrew WC. 1992. *Chimpanzee Material Culture.* Cambridge, MA: Harvard Univ. Press. 277 pp.

Mitchell R. 1993. Mental models of mirror self-recognition: two theories. *New Ideas Psychol.* 11:211–17

Mitchell R. 1995. Self-recognition, methodology and explanation: a comment on Heyes (1994). *Anim. Behav.* 51:467–69

Morgan CL. 1900. *Animal Behavior.* London: Arnold. 344 pp.

Nagell K, Olguin RS, Tomasello M. 1993. Processes of social learning in the tool use of chimpanzees (Pan troglodytes) and human children (Homo sapiens). *J. Comp. Psychol.* 107:174–86

Nishida T. 1987. Local traditions and cultural transmission. In *Primate Societies,* ed. B Smuts, D Cheney, R Seyfarth, R Wrangham, T Struhsaker, pp. 462–74. Chicago: Univ. Chicago Press

Nishida T, Hiraiwa M. 1982. Natural history of tool-using behavior by wild chimpanzees in feeding upon wood-boring ants. *J. Hum. Evol.* 11:73–99

Parker ST, Mitchell RW, Boccia ML. 1994. *Self-awareness in Animals and Humans.*

New York: Cambridge Univ. Press. 442 pp.

Passingham RE. 1982. *The Human Primate.* New York: Freeman. 390 pp.

Pepperberg IM, Garcia SE, Jackson EC, Marconi S. 1995. Mirror use by African Grey parrots (Psittacus erithacus). *J. Comp. Psychol.* 109:182–95

Perner J, Wimmer H. 1985. "John thinks that Mary thinks that...": attribution of second-order beliefs by 5- to 10-year-old children. *J. Exp. Child Psychol.* 39:437–71

Povinelli DJ. 1987. Monkeys, apes, mirrors and minds: the evolution of self-awareness in primates. *J. Hum. Evol.* 2:493–509

Povinelli DJ. 1989. Failure to find self-recognition in Asian elephants (Elephas maximus) in contrast to their use of mirror cues to discover hidden food. *J. Comp. Psychol.* 103:122–31

Povinelli DJ. 1993. Reconstructing the evolution of mind. *Am. Psychol.* 48(5):493–509

Povinelli DJ, deBlois S. 1992. Young children's understanding of knowledge information in themselves and others. *J. Comp. Psychol.* 106:228–38

Povinelli DJ, Gallup GG Jr., Eddy TJ, Bierschwale DT, Engstrom MC, et al. 1997. Chimpanzees recognize themselves in mirrors. *Anim. Behav.* 53:1083–88

Povinelli DJ, Nelson KE, Boysen ST. 1990. Inferences about guessing and knowing in chimpanzees (Pan troglodytes). *J. Comp. Psychol.* 104:203–10

Povinelli DJ, Nelson KE, Boysen ST. 1992. Comprehension of role reversal in chimpanzees: evidence of empathy? *Anim. Behav.* 43:633–40

Povinelli DJ, Parks KA, Novak MA. 1991. Do rhesus monkeys (Macaca mulatta) attribute knowledge and ignorance to others? *J. Comp. Psychol.* 105:318–25

Povinelli DJ, Rulf AB, Landau KR, Bierschwale DT. 1993. Self-recognition in chimpanzees (Pan troglodytes): distribution, ontogeny, and patterns of emergence. *J. Comp. Psychol.* 107:347–72

Premack D, Woodruff G. 1978a. Chimpanzee problem-solving: a test for comprehension. *Science* 202(3):532–35

Premack D, Woodruff G. 1978b. Does the chimpanzee have a theory of mind? *Behav. Brain Sci.* 1:515–26

Romanes GJ. 1884. *Mental Evolution in Animals.* New York: AMS. 357 pp.

Russon AE, Galdikas BMF. 1993. Imitation in free-ranging rehabilitant orangutans (Pongo pygmaeus). *J. Comp. Psychol.* 107:147–61

Russon AE, Galdikas BMF. 1995. Constraints on great apes' imitation: model and action selectivity in rehabilitant orangutan (Pongo pygmaeus) imitation. *J. Comp. Psychol.* 109:5–17

Sakura O, Matsuzawa T. 1991. Flexibility of wild chimpanzees nut-cracking behavior using stone hammers and anvils: an experimental analysis. *Ethology* 87:237–48

Schulman AH, Kaplowitz C. 1977. Mirror image response during the first two years of life. *Dev. Psychobiol.* 10:133–42

Spence KW. 1937. Experimental studies of learning and higher mental processes in infra-human primates. *Psychol. Bull.* 34:806–50

Sugiyama Y. 1993. Local variation of tools and tool use among wild chimpanzee populations. In *The Use of Tools by Human and Non-Human Primates,* ed. A Berthelet, J Chavaillon, pp. 175–87. Oxford, UK: Clarendon

Sugiyama Y. 1994. Tool use by wild chimpanzees. *Nature* 376:327

Sugiyama Y, Koman J, Bhoye Show M. 1988. Ant-catching wands of wild chimpanzees at Bossou, Guinea. *Folia Primatol.* 51:56–60

Thorndike EL. 1898. Animal intelligence: an experimental study of the associative process in animals. *Psychol. Rev. Monogr.* 2(4). 109 pp.

Thorndike EL. 1911. *Animal Intelligence.* New York: Macmillan. 297 pp.

Thorpe WH. 1956. *Learning and Instinct in Animals.* London: Metheun. 493 pp.

Tomasello M. 1990. Cultural transmission in the tool use and communicatory signaling of chimpanzees? In *"Language" and Intelligence in Monkeys and Apes: Comparative Developmental Perspectives,* ed. ST Parker, KR Gibson. Cambridge, UK: Cambridge Univ. Press

Tomasello M, Savage-Rumbaugh S, Kruger AC. 1993. Imitative learning of actions on objects by children, chimpanzees, and enculturated chimpanzees. *Child Dev.* 64:1688–705

Visalberghi E. 1990. Tool use in Cebus. *Folia Primatol.* 54:146–54

Visalberghi E, Fragaszy DM. 1990. Do monkeys ape? In *"Language" and Intelligence in Monkeys and Apes,* ed. ST Parker, KR Gibson, pp. 247–73. Cambridge, UK: Cambridge Univ. Press

Visalberghi E, Limongelli L. 1994. Lack of comprehension of cause-effect relations in tool-using capuchin monkeys (Cebus apella). *J. Comp. Psychol.* 108:15–22

Visalberghi E, Trinca L. 1989. Tool use in capuchin monkeys: distinguishing between performing and understanding. *Primates* 30:511–21

Warden CJ, Jackson TA. 1935. Imitative behaviour in the rhesus monkey. *J. Genet. Psychol.* 46:103–25

Wellman HM. 1990. *The Child's Theory of Mind.* Cambridge, MA: Bradford MIT Press. 358 pp.

Whiten A, Custance DM, Gomez JC, Teixidor P, Bard KA. 1996. Imitative learning of artificial fruit processing in children (Homo sapiens) and chimpanzees (Pan troglodytes). *J. Comp. Psychol.* 110:3–14

Whiten A, Ham R. 1992. On the nature and evolution of imitation in the animal kingdom: reappraisal of a century of research. In *Advances in the Study of Behavior*, ed. PJB Slater, JS Rosenblatt, C Beer, M Milinski, 21:239–83. New York: Academic

Wimmer H, Hogrefe GJ, Perner J. 1988. Children's understanding of informational access as a source of knowledge. *Child Dev.* 59:386–96

Wimmer H, Perner J. 1983. Beliefs about beliefs: representation and constraining function of wrong beliefs in young children's understanding of deception. *Cognition* 13:103–28

Wood D. 1989. Social interactions as tutoring. In *Interactions in Human Development*, ed. PJB Slater, JS Rosenblatt, C Beer, M Milinski, pp. 59–80. Cambridge, MA: Harvard Univ. Press

Yamakoshi G, Sugiyama Y. 1995. Pestle-pounding behavior of wild chimpanzees at Bossou, Guinea: a newly observed tool-using behavior. *Primates* 36:489–500

Zentall TR. 1996. An analysis of imitative learning in animals. In *Social Learning in Animals: the Roots of Culture*, ed. CM Heyes, BG Galef Jr, pp. 221–43. New York: Academic

Zentall TR, Levine JM. 1972. Observational learning and social facilitation in the rat. *Science* 178:1220–21

Zentall TR, Sutton JE, Sherburne LM. 1996. True imitative learning in pigeons. *Psychol. Sci.* 7:343–46

AUTHOR INDEX

A

Aaker DA, 193
Abdel-Majid RM, 603
Abel T, 614, 659
Abelson JM, 94
Abelson RP, 197, 546
Able KP, 652, 654, 655
Able MA, 652, 654
Abline DS, 436
Aboitiz F, 674
Abraham JD, 483, 500
Abram KM, 95
Abramson RP, 546
Acierno R, 151
Ackenheil M, 145
Ackerman BP, 194
Ackerman D, 192
Ackerman DL, 236
Ackerman F, 379
Ackerman PL, 488, 491
Ackil JK, 434
Adams MR, 144
Addis ME, 167, 445, 453, 457
Ader R, 144
Adler DA, 96
Adolphs R, 197, 198
Ageranioti-Belanger SA, 308
Aggleton JP, 197
Agnew RM, 456, 457
Agras WS, 49, 175, 460
Ahern F, 498
Ahern GL, 192, 203
Aickin M, 149
Aiello JR, 590
Aiken LS, 153
Ajjanagadde V, 114
Akiskal HS, 86
Alban BT, 374
Albee GW, 388, 389
Albert G, 428
Albino A, 152
Albrecht U, 614
Alcantara AA, 667
Alexander C, 493
Alexander RA, 556
Alford J, 461
Alksnis O, 120
Allan JB, 205

Allan T, 458
Allard T, 312, 313
Allard TT, 312
Allegrante JP, 400, 401
Allen GL, 489
Allen J, 126
Allen JJB, 193
Allen JP, 460
Allen MT, 139, 144
Allison ST, 582
Allmon D, 461
Allopenna P, 513, 519, 528
Almond GA, 627, 638, 639, 648
Aloe L, 145
Aloise PA, 206
Alper JS, 608, 619
Altemeyer B, 632
Altman DG, 152, 400, 401, 405
Alvarez M, 639
Alwin DF, 549, 551, 556-58
Amador XF, 82
Aman C, 428
Amato PR, 51
Amoretti G, 143
Amsterdam BK, 696, 701
Anastasiades P, 454, 458
Andersen BL, 139, 140, 144-46, 195
Andersen SM, 279, 287, 588
Anderson AK, 195
Anderson BA, 546
Anderson BJ, 667
Anderson E, 658
Anderson JR, 112, 113, 127, 694-98
Anderson P, 58
Anderson RC, 10, 461
Anderson SC, 591
Andreasen NC, 88, 89, 192
Andres D, 497
Andrews AA, 451
Andrews DW, 396
Andrews FM, 556
Anes MD, 405
Angelique H, 392, 393
Anglin JM, 3, 10
Ango KK, 152
Anisfeld M, 28

Anisman H, 618
Anokhin A, 600
Anshel M, 150
Anthony JC, 83
Antoni MH, 145, 147
Antoniou AA, 197
Antonsen P, 656
Anzenberger G, 698, 700
Apkarian AV, 314
Appelle S, 310
Applegate B, 81
Apt C, 176
Arbuckle T, 497
Arendt-Nielsen L, 321, 322
Argyris C, 379
Ariëns Kappers CU, 661
Armbruster T, 282
Armstrong HE, 461
Armstrong JD, 674
Armstrong L, 316
Armstrong-James M, 603
Arnott JL, 195
Arnow BA, 175
Arntz A, 458
Aron A, 58
Aron EN, 58
Arriaga XB, 57, 61
Arrow K, 570, 572, 585, 587
Arthur MW, 394, 396, 397
Arthur WB, 367
Ary D, 406
Asarnow JR, 177, 396
Asbeck J, 282
Asendorpf J, 340
Asendorpf JB, 340
Ashby FG, 226, 227, 233, 238
Asher SJ, 166
Asher SR, 338, 342, 346, 348
Ashkenas RN, 374
Ashley JM, 149
Ashton WA, 152
Aslin RN, 28, 491, 515, 519, 521, 522, 528
Assenheimer JS, 91, 97
Astington JW, 23, 33, 35, 40
Atchison KA, 402
Atilano RB, 181
Atkins BTS, 5
Atkins C, 408

SUBJECT INDEX

A

Abandonment fears
intervention for couples
and, 171
"Aboutness"
understanding
cognitive development
and, 29–30
Abstraction
organizational change and
development, 374
Abuse
intervention for couples
and, 173–74
interventions and, 387,
391–400
marital conflict and, 49, 51,
67–68
preventive interventions
and, 402–6
suggestibility of children's
memory and, 420,
422–24, 428–29, 435–36
Acceptance
peer relationships in childhood and, 333–55
Accessibilty
marital conflict and, 58–59
Acquiescence
survey research and, 552–55
Acquired immunodeficiency
syndrome (AIDS)
health psychology and,
146–47
preventive interventions
and, 387, 406–410, 412
Action
organizational change and
development, 373
Activation
of learning potential
lifespan psychology and,
496–97
Adaptation
lifespan psychology and,
479–80
organizational change and
development, 361–82
single-gene influences on
brain and behavior, 619
trust and distrust in organizations, 580

"Additional group of validators"
psychopathology and, 89
Adherence
health psychology and,
154–55
Adjustment
peer relationships and social competence during
early and middle child-
hood, 348–54
Adolescents
psychopathology and,
79–101
Adoption studies
single-gene influences on
brain and behavior, 619
Advocacy
preventive interventions
and, 392–93
Affect
emotion and, 191–206
peer relationships and social competence during
early and middle child-
hood, 350–51
Age
lifespan psychology and,
471–500
somesthesis and, 305, 313
suggestibility of children's
memory and, 419–37
Age differential allocation
of differential resources
lifespan psychology and,
471–500
Aggression
animal cognition and, 694
single-gene influences on
brain and behavior, 619
Agitation
marital conflict and, 67
Alcohol abuse
intervention for couples
and, 176
marital conflict and, 49
preventive interventions
and, 402–4
single-gene influences on
brain and behavior, 607
Allele association studies
single-gene influences on
brain and behavior, 607–9

Ambiguity
word knowledge and, 12, 17
Analytic frameworks
organizational change and
development, 361, 365–
66, 368–69, 370, 377–79
Anatomically detailed dolls
suggestibility of children's
memory and, 428–29
Animal cognition
attributional capacities,
698–701
imitation, 685–90
introduction, 684–88
mirror self–recognition,
693–98
tool use, 690–93
Animal models
validitiy of
single-gene influences on
brain and behavior, 619
Animal navigation
neuroethology of spatial
learning and, 653–57
Anorexia nervosa
individual psychotherapy
and, 459–60
Antisocial behavior
interventions and, 394–97
Antisocial personality disorder
psychopathology and, 96
Antonymy
word knowledge and, 7
Anxiety disorders
individual psychotherapy
and, 457–59
intervention for couples
and, 175
psychopathology and, 79,
91–92
signal detection theory and,
232, 236
single-gene influences on
brain and behavior, 618
Anxious-ambivalent style
marital conflict and, 57
Aphelocama spp.
neuroethology of spatial
learning and, 663
Apis mellifera
neuroethology of spatial
learning and, 651–75

CUMULATIVE INDEXES

CONTRIBUTING AUTHORS, VOLUMES 40–50

CHAPTER TITLES, VOLUMES 40–50

COMPARATIVE PSYCHOLOGY, ETHOLOGY, AND ANIMAL BEHAVIOR

CONSUMER BEHAVIOR

COUNSELING (See also EDUCATION AND COUNSELING; CLINICAL AND

COUNSELING PSYCHOLOGY)

DEVELOPMENTAL PSYCHOLOGY

VISION